Almut Fries
Pseudo-Euripides, *Rhesus*

Untersuchungen zur
antiken Literatur und Geschichte

Herausgegeben von
Heinz-Günther Nesselrath, Peter Scholz
und Otto Zwierlein

Band 114

De Gruyter

Pseudo-Euripides, *Rhesus*

Edited with
Introduction and Commentary
by

Almut Fries

De Gruyter

ISBN 978-3-11-036501-6
e-ISBN 978-3-11-034225-3
ISSN 1862-1112

Library of Congress Cataloging-in-Publication Data

A CIP catalog record for this book has been applied for at the Library of Congress.

Bibliografische Information der Deutschen Nationalbibliothek

Die Deutsche Nationalbibliothek verzeichnet diese Publikation in der Deutschen Nationalbibliografie; detaillierte bibliografische Daten sind im Internet über http://dnb.dnb.de abrufbar.

© 2017 Walter de Gruyter GmbH, Berlin/Boston
Dieser Band ist text- und seitenidentisch mit der 2014 erschienenen gebundenen Ausgabe.

Satz: Dörlemann Satz GmbH & Co. KG, Lemförde
Druck: Hubert & Co. GmbH & Co. KG, Göttingen
∞ Gedruckt auf säurefreiem Papier

Printed in Germany

www.degruyter.com

For
Martin and Stephanie West

Preface

> 'The curious thing about the *Rhesus* is that, when all this has been said, the play is not nearly so bad as it ought to be' (A. C. Pearson, *CR* 35 [1921], 59)

It is my hope to have shown with this edition that *Rhesus* is not simply a literary curiosity – spurious Euripides based on spurious Homer – but a play that is well worth studying in its own right and deserves attention as a witness to the theatrical expectations of its time (which I assume to be the early fourth century BC). As in the case of papyrus finds, we should consider ourselves fortunate that occasionally a text survives that might have been lost entirely but for the protection afforded by a famous author's name.

The idea for this book was conceived more than thirteen years ago in an Oxford seminar on *Rhesus* conducted by Martin West. A first attempt at a commentary with introduction (on vv. 1–84) was passed for the *Staatsexamen* in Göttingen by Professors Klaus Nickau and Heinz-Günther Nesselrath (2002), but the present version is an extension of my doctoral dissertation ('[Euripides], *Rhesus* 565–996: Introduction and Commentary'), written in Oxford under the supervision of Angus Bowie and examined by Christopher Collard and James Diggle (2004–8). A Junior Research Fellowship at University College, Oxford (2008–11) and the subsequent hospitality of both the Classics Faculty and my graduate college, Corpus Christi, enabled me to complete my work in ideal surroundings.

Many further obligations have been incurred. Above all, my parents never questioned their daughter's pursuit of a distant past and languages no longer in current use, and over the years were ever ready to give practical, moral and indeed financial support. The need for the last was substantially reduced by an Oxford Classics Faculty Graduate Studentship (2006–8), and I also thank Corpus Christi College for electing me to a Senior Scholarship (2006–7) and the Committees who proposed my thesis for, and awarded it a share in, the Hellenic Foundation Prize 2008.

All or significant portions of the typescript were read by Angus Bowie, Christopher Collard, James Diggle, Patrick Finglass, Heinz-Günther Nesselrath, Martin West and Alan Woolley, each of whom improved it in countless ways. My supervisor Angus Bowie, Christopher Collard and Martin West in particular have always been there to discuss textual and other problems, whereas Laetitia Parker and Nigel Wilson provided invaluable help with the lyric metres and questions of palaeography and manuscript transmission respectively. My mother cheerfully assisted in compiling the bibliography and list of abbreviations and took on the gruelling task of checking the cross-references and testimonial apparatus. At a later stage she also helped with the proofs, as did Nigel Wilson, who read them in their entirety with a characteristically sharp eye for detail. Heinz-Günther Nesselrath, Otto Zwierlein and Peter Scholz have my thanks for accepting the book into the series of *Untersuchungen zur antiken Literatur und Geschichte* (*UaLG*).

Throughout my academic life so far I have been spoilt by the excellent library facilities in Göttingen and Oxford. But not everything required is available at all times, and I am grateful to all those who have facilitated my research with the gift or loan of books, photocopies and offprints, by letting me see their own work ahead of publication and by looking up references in distant places: Angus Bowie, Christopher Collard, Marcus Deufert, James Diggle, Patrick Finglass, Michael Griffin, Rolf Heine, Gregory Hutchinson, David Kovacs, Vayos Liapis, Fiachra MacGóraín, Anke Walter, Martin West and Nigel Wilson. Gregory Klyve kindly allowed me to cite his unpublished Oxford dissertation.

Revision of the introduction and commentary was completed at the end of May 2013. I have not included any material published after that date.

This book, and its author, have benefited immeasurably from the advice and friendship of some of the finest classical scholars of our time. I record this with a sense of privilege and gratitude and dedicate the volume to the couple who have believed in the project from beginning to end.

Oxford A. F.
June 2014

Contents

Abbreviations XI

Introduction 1

I. The Play 3

II. Plot and Myth 8
   1. The Greek Tradition 8
      (a) *Iliad* 10 and Homer 8
      (b) Other Sources 11
   2. Rhesus of Thrace 14
   Appendix: The 'Macedonian Theory' 18

III. Authenticity and Date 22
   1. External Evidence 22
   2. Language and Style 28
      (a) Repetition 29
      (b) Vocabulary 30
      (c) Poetic Borrowings 31
      (d) Conclusion and Outlook 38
   3. Dramatic Technique 39
   4. Rhesus and the 'Euripidean Selection' 43
      (a) Literary Reception 44
      (b) Ancient and Medieval Quotations, Lexica 46

IV. Textual Tradition 48
   1. Manuscripts 48
   2. Evidence from Lost Manuscripts 52
   3. Papyri 54
   4. Scholia and Other Indirect Sources 54
   5. The Aldine 55

V. The Edition 56

Text and Critical Apparatus	57
Conspectus Siglorum	59
Ὑπόθεσις Ῥήσου	63
Ῥῆσος	67
Commentary	107
The Hypotheses	109
The Play	114
Select Bibliography	483
Indexes	499

Abbreviations

ANRW	H. Temporini – W. Haase (eds.), *Aufstieg und Niedergang der Römischen Welt*, 89 vols. to date, Berlin – New York 1972–
Arch. Hom.	F. Matz – H. G. Buchholz (eds.), *Archaeologia Homerica. Die Denkmäler und das frühgriechische Epos*, 25 vols. to date, Göttingen 1967–
ARV^2	J. D. Beazley, *Attic Red-Figure Vase-Painters*, Oxford ²1963
BCH	*Bulletin de Correspondance Hellénique*
BK	J. Latacz *et al.* (eds.), *Homers Ilias. Gesamtkommentar, auf der Grundlage der Ausgabe von Ameis–Hentze–Cauer (1868–1913)*, 9 vols. to date, Munich – Leipzig – Berlin – New York 2000– (= *Basler Kommentar*)
Breitenbach	W. Breitenbach, *Untersuchungen zur Sprache der Euripideischen Lyrik*, Stuttgart 1934
Burnett, 'Smiles'	A. P. Burnett, '*Rhesus*. Are Smiles Allowed?', in P. Burian (ed.), *Directions in Euripidean Criticism*, Durham (NC) 1985, 13–51
CA	J. U. Powell (ed.), *Collectanea Alexandrina*, Oxford 1925
CCSL	*Corpus Christianorum. Series Latina*, 194 vols. to date, Turnhout 1954–
CEG	P. A. Hansen (ed.), *Carmina Epigraphica Graeca*, 2 vols., Berlin – New York 1983–9
Chantraine, GH	P. Chantraine, *Grammaire Homérique*. Tome I: *Phonétique et Morphologie*, Paris ⁶1988; Tome II: *Syntaxe*, Paris ²1986
CIG	A. Boeckh *et al.* (eds.), *Corpus Inscriptionum Graecarum*, 4 vols., Berlin 1828–77
Collard, 'Supplement'	C. Collard, 'Colloquial Language in Tragedy: A Supplement to the Work of P. T. Stevens', *CQ* n.s. 55 (2005), 350–86

CPG	E. L. von Leutsch – F. H. Schneidewin (eds.), *Corpus Paroemiographorum Graecorum*, 2 vols., Göttingen 1839–51
Cobet, *VL*²	C. G. Cobet, *Variae Lectiones*, Leiden ²1873
Dale, *LM*¹/²	A. M. Dale, *The Lyric Metres of Greek Drama*, Cambridge ¹1948, ²1968
Dale, *MATC*	A. M. Dale, *Metrical Analyses of Tragic Choruses*, 3 vols. (*BICS* Suppl. 21.1–3, edd. T. B. L. Webster, E. W. Handley), London 1971–83
Daremberg–Saglio	C. Daremberg – E. Saglio, *Dictionnaire des antiquités grecques et romaines: d'après les textes et les monuments*, 5 vols., Paris 1877–1919
Dawe, *STS*	R. D. Dawe, *Studies on the Text of Sophocles*, 3 vols., Leiden 1973–8
DELG	P. Chantraine, *Dictionnaire étymologique de la langue grecque. Histoire des mots* (avec un Supplément sous la direction de A. Blanc, C. de Lamberterie, J.-L. Perpillou), Paris 1999
DK	H. Diels – W. Kranz (eds.), *Die Fragmente der Vorsokratiker*, 3 vols., Berlin ⁶1951–2
EG	G. Kaibel (ed.), *Epigrammata Graeca ex lapidibus conlecta*, Berlin 1878
FD III.1	École Française d'Athènes. *Fouilles de Delphes (1892–1903). Tome III. Épigraphie. Fascicule 1. Inscriptions de l'entrée du sanctuaire au trésor d'Athènes*, Paris 1910
Foed.Delph.Pell.	B. Haussoullier (ed.), *Traité entre Delphes et Pellana. Etude en droit grec*, Paris 1917
FGE	D. L. Page (ed.), *Further Greek Epigrams* (revised and prepared for publication by R. D. Dawe and J. Diggle), Cambridge 1981
FGrHist	F. Jacoby *et al.* (eds.), *Die Fragmente der griechischen Historiker*, Berlin – Leiden – Boston – Cologne 1923–
FHG	K. Müller – T. Müller (eds.), *Fragmenta Historicorum Graecorum*, 5 vols., Paris 1841–72
FJW	H. Friis Johansen – E. W. Whittle, *Aeschylus: The Suppliants*, 3 vols., Copenhagen 1980

Fraenkel, *Rev.*	E. Fraenkel, Review: W. Ritchie, *The Authenticity of the Rhesus of Euripides*, Cambridge 1964, *Gnomon* 37 (1965), 228–41
Furley–Bremer	W. D. Furley – J. M. Bremer, *Greek Hymns. Selected Cult Songs from the Archaic to the Hellenistic Period*, 2 vols., Tübingen 2001
GCS	*Die griechischen christlichen Schriftsteller der ersten Jahrhunderte*, 59 vols., n.s. 18 vols. to date, Leipzig – Berlin 1897–
GE	A. Wilhelm, *Griechische Epigramme* (edd. H. Engelmann, K. Wundsam), Bonn 1980
GEF	M. L. West (ed.), *Greek Epic Fragments*, Cambridge (Mass.) – London 2003[1]
GEW	H. Frisk, *Griechisches etymologisches Wörterbuch*, Heidelberg 1960–70
GGM	C. Müller (ed.), *Geographi Graeci Minores*, 2 vols., Paris 1855–61
GL	G. T. H. Keil (ed.), *Grammatici Latini*, 7 vols. (+ a supplement by H. Hagen), Leipzig 1857–80 (repr. Hildesheim 1961)
Gow–Page *GPh*	A. S. F. Gow – D. L. Page (eds.), *The Greek Anthology. The Garland of Philip and Some Contemporary Epigrams*, 2 vols., Cambridge 1968
Gow–Page *HE*	A. S. F. Gow – D. L. Page (eds.), *The Greek Anthology. Hellenistic Epigrams*, 2 vols., Cambridge 1965
GP	J. D. Denniston, *The Greek Particles* (rev. K. J. Dover), Oxford ²1954
GrGr	G. Uhlig – R. Schneider – A. Hilgard – A. Lentz (eds.), *Grammatici Graeci*, 4 vols. (in 10 parts), Leipzig 1867–1910 (repr. Hildesheim 1965)
H.–Sz.	J. B. Hofmann (rev. A. Szantyr), *Lateinische Syntax und Stilistik. Mit dem allgemeinen Teil der lateinischen Grammatik*, Munich 1965
IEG	M. L. West (ed.), *Iambi et Elegi Graeci ante Alexandrum cantati*, 2 vols., Oxford ²1989–92

---

[1] References to the editions of Davies (*Epicorum Graecorum Fragmenta*, Göttingen 1988) and Bernabé (*Poetae Epici Graeci. Testimonia et Fragmenta* I, Stuttgart – Leipzig ²1996) can be found in his concordance (pp. 299–308).

IG	*Inscriptiones Graecae*
IGRom	R. Cagnat *et al.* (eds.), *Inscriptiones Graecae ad res Romanas pertinentes*, vols. I, III, IV, Paris 1901–27
IG Urb. Rom.	L. Moretti (ed.), *Inscriptiones Graecae Urbis Romae*, 4 vols., Rome 1968–90
Inscr. Cret.	M. Guarducci (ed.), *Inscriptiones Creticae. Opera et consilio Friderici Halbherr collectae*, 4 vols., Rome 1935–50
KB	R. Kühner (rev. F. Blass), *Ausführliche Grammatik der griechischen Sprache. Erster Teil: Elementar- und Formenlehre*, 2 vols., Hanover ³1890–2
KG	R. Kühner (rev. B. Gerth), *Ausführliche Grammatik der griechischen Sprache. Zweiter Teil: Satzlehre*, 2 vols., Hanover – Leipzig ³1898–1904
KS	*Kleine Schriften*
LfgrE	B. Snell *et al.* (eds.), *Lexikon des frühgriechischen Epos*, Göttingen 1955–2010
LGPN	P. M. Fraser *et al.* (eds.), *A Lexicon of Greek Personal Names*, 5 vols. to date, Oxford 1987–
Liapis, 'Notes'	V. Liapis, 'Notes on *Rhesus*', *ExClass* 15 (2011), 47–111
LIMC	*Lexicon Iconographicum Mythologiae Classicae*, 8 vols. (+ Indices), Zurich – Munich – Düsseldorf 1981–1997
Ll-J/W, *Sophoclea*	P. H. J. Lloyd-Jones – N. G. Wilson, *Sophoclea. Studies on the Text of Sophocles*, Oxford 1990
Ll-J/W, *Second Thoughts*	P. H. J. Lloyd-Jones – N. G. Wilson, *Sophocles: Second Thoughts*, Göttingen 1997
LSJ	H. G. Liddell – R. Scott (rev. H. Stuart Jones *et al.*), *A Greek-English Lexicon*, Oxford ⁹1940 (with a revised Supplement, 1996)
Matthiae, *GG* I–III³	A. H. Matthiae, *Ausführliche Griechische Grammatik*, 3 vols., Leipzig ³1835
Mertens–Pack³	*CEDOPAL: Base de données expérimentale Mertens–Pack³ en ligne* (http://promethee.philo.ulg.ac.be/cedopal/index.htm)
M.–W.	R. Merkelbach – M. L. West (eds.), *Fragmenta Hesiodea*, Oxford 1967

NAGP	A. Rijksbaron (ed.), *New Approaches to Greek Particles*, Amsterdam 1997
Nilsson, *GGR* I³	M. P. Nilsson, *Geschichte der griechischen Religion* I. *Die Religion Griechenlands bis auf die griechische Weltherrschaft*, Munich ³1967
OLD	P. G. W. Glare (ed.), *Oxford Latin Dictionary*, Oxford ¹1968–82, ²2012
Pack²	R. A. Pack, *The Greek and Latin Literary Texts from Graeco-Roman Egypt*, Ann Arbor ²1965
PCG	R. Kassel – C. F. L. Austin (eds.), *Poetae Comici Graeci*, 8 vols. to date, Berlin – New York 1983–
Pf.	R. Pfeiffer (ed.), *Callimachus*, 2 vols., Oxford ²1965
Pickard-Cambridge, *DFA*²	A. W. Pickard-Cambridge, *The Dramatic Festivals of Athens* (rev. J. Gould, D. M. Lewis), Oxford ²1968
PMG	D. L. Page (ed.), *Poetae Melici Graeci*, Oxford 1962
PMGF	M. Davies (ed.), *Poetarum Melicorum Graecorum Fragmenta*, 1 vol. to date, Oxford 1991–
Pritchett, *GSW*	W. K. Pritchett, *The Greek State at War*, 5 vols., Berkeley – Los Angeles – London 1971–91
*PSG*¹	W. Dindorf (ed.), *Poetae Scenici Graeci. Accedunt perditarum fabularum fragmenta*, Leipzig – London ¹1830
*PSG*²,⁵	W. Dindorf (ed.), *Poetarum Scenicorum Graecorum: Aeschyli, Sophoclis, Euripidis, et Aristophanis fabulae superstites et perditarum fragmenta*, Oxford ²1851, Leipzig ⁵1869
RE	G. Wissowa *et al.* (eds.), *Paulys Real-Encyclopädie der classischen Altertumswissenschaft*, Stuttgart 1893–
Ritchie	W. Ritchie, *The Authenticity of the Rhesus of Euripides*, Cambridge 1964
Roscher	W. H. Roscher (ed.), *Ausführliches Lexikon der Griechischen und Römischen Mythologie*, 6 vols., Leipzig 1884–1937

Rosivach	V. J. Rosivach, 'Hector in the *Rhesus*', *Hermes* 106 (1978), 54–73
Schroeder²	O. Schroeder, *Euripidis Cantica*, Leipzig ²1928
Schwyzer	E. Schwyzer, *Griechische Grammatik. Erster Band. Allgemeiner Teil: Lautlehre, Wortbildung, Flexion*, Munich 1939
SD	E. Schwyzer – A. Debrunner, *Griechische Grammatik. Zweiter Band. Syntax und Syntaktische Stilistik*, Munich 1950
SEG	J. J. E. Hondius *et al.* (eds.), *Supplementum Epigraphicum Graecum*, 58 vols. to date, Leiden – Boston 1923–
SGO	R. Merkelbach – J. Stauber (eds.), *Steinepigramme aus dem griechischen Osten*, 5 vols., Stuttgart – Munich 1998–2004
SH	P. H. J. Lloyd-Jones – P. J. Parsons (eds.), *Supplementum Hellenisticum*, Berlin – New York 1983
*SIG*³	W. Dittenberger (ed.), *Sylloge Inscriptionum Graecarum*, 4 vols., Leipzig ³1915
SLG	D. L. Page (ed.), *Supplementum Lyricis Graecis. Poetarum Lyricorum Graecorum Fragmenta quae recens innotuerunt*, Oxford 1974
Sn.–M.	B. Snell – H. Maehler (eds.), *Pindari Carmina cum Fragmentis*, 2 vols., Stuttgart – Leipzig ⁸1987–9
	— Bacchylides. *Carmina cum Fragmentis*, Munich – Leipzig ¹¹2003
Stevens, *CEE*	P. T. Stevens, *Colloquial Expressions in Euripides*, Wiesbaden 1976
Strohm	H. Strohm, 'Beobachtungen zum 'Rhesos'', *Hermes* 87 (1959), 257–74
SVF	H. F. A. v. Arnim (ed.), *Stoicorum Veterum Fragmenta*, 4 vols., Leipzig 1903–24
ThGL	H. Stephanus, *Thesaurus Graecae Linguae* (rev. C. B. Hase, W. Dindorf, L. Dindorf *et al.*), 8 vols., Paris 1831–65
Threatte	L. Threatte, *The Grammar of Attic Inscriptions*, 2 vols. to date, Berlin – New York 1980–
TLL	*Thesaurus Linguae Latinae*, Leipzig 1900–

*TRF*³	O. Ribbeck, *Tragicorum Romanorum Fragmenta*, Leipzig 1897
TrGF	B. Snell – R. Kannicht – S. L. Radt (eds.), *Tragicorum Graecorum Fragmenta*, 5 vols., Göttingen ²1986–2004²
TrGFS	J. Diggle (ed.), *Tragicorum Graecorum Fragmenta Selecta*, Oxford 1998
van Thiel	H. van Thiel, (ed.), *Scholia D in* Iliadem (URL: http://kups.ub.uni-koeln.de/volltexte/2006/1810)
West, *GM*	M. L. West, *Greek Metre*, Oxford 1982
West, *EFH*	M. L. West, *The East Face of Helicon. West Asiatic Elements in Greek Poetry and Myth*, Oxford 1997
West, *IEPM*	M. L. West, *Indo-European Poetry and Myth*, Oxford 2007
Wilamowitz, *GV*	U. von Wilamowitz-Moellendorff, *Griechische Verskunst*, Berlin 1921
Willink, 'Cantica'	C. W. Willink, 'Studies in the *cantica* of Euripides' *Rhesus*', *ICS* 27–28 (2002–2003), 21–43 (= *Collected Papers*, 560–82)

The name of the editor alone is given for conjectures proposed in his text and/or critical apparatus. Abbreviations of ancient authors, work titles and modern periodicals largely follow LSJ and the *Année Philologique*. I leave out 'Homer' in citations from the *Iliad* and *Odyssey* and name Aeschylus, Sophocles and Euripides only in case of homonymous plays and where omission may lead to confusion. *Prometheus Bound* is regarded as non-Aeschylean.

---

2 All tragic fragments are quoted from these, unless otherwise indicated.

Introduction

I. The Play

Rhesus occupies a unique and important place in literary history for the following three reasons:
(1) it is the only extant Greek tragedy that takes its plot from an episode in Homer, the spurious *Iliad* 10, also called *Doloneia*.[1]
(2) if we reject Euripidean authorship (as most scholars now do), it is the only Greek tragedy surviving intact from the fourth century BC.
(3) it has influenced several later authors, most notably Virgil in *Aeneid* 9, and found its way into the late-antique 'Selection' of Euripides' ten most popular plays.

The play has been much maligned, especially by critics who wished to prove it spurious, for its episodic structure, extravagant stage-action, wooden characters and the ostensible lack of any intellectual or 'tragic' import.[2] Part of this can hardly be denied. But we have to ask what the poet wanted to achieve and whether some of the play's alleged flaws are not in fact explained by his dramatic intentions.

A delight in spectacle, perhaps in accordance with the theatrical expectations of the day, is obvious (cf. ch. III.3). The shortest of all Greek tragedies, *Rhesus* boasts two messenger scenes (264–341, 728–803), two *agones* (388–526, 804–81) and two divine epiphanies in the middle and at the end of the play (595–674, 882–982). Athena's impersonation of another goddess, Aphrodite, and the Muse's lament from the top of the *skene* have no precedents in classical drama, and the rapid movements of the chorus (1–51, 675–91) far surpass earlier choral prologues and search-scenes. If one further adds Rhesus' 'god-like' splendour in his costume (301–8), the possibility of a chariot entry (380–7) and the rarity of having an entire play set in the darkness of night,[3] it is no wonder that

---

1   That *Iliad* 10 does not belong to to the original poem is 'the almost unanimous (and certainly correct) view of modern scholars' (West, *Making of the Iliad*, 233[-5]; cf. Hainsworth, *The Iliad: A Commentary* III, 151–5). The notion goes back to antiquity: Σ^T *Il.* 10.0 (III 1.4–5 Erbse) φασὶ τὴν ῥαψῳδίαν ὑφ' Ὁμήρου ἰδίᾳ τετάχθαι καὶ μὴ εἶναι μέρος τῆς Ἰλιάδος, ὑπὸ δὲ Πεισιστράτου τετάχθαι εἰς τὴν ποίησιν (~ Eust. 785.42–4).
2   E.g. H. D. F. Kitto, *YCS* 25 (1977), 317–50 and Burnett, 'Smiles' (who regards it as a youthful 'joke' of Euripides). The most recent attack on *Rhesus* is Liapis' commentary (see the reviews by D. Zuckerberg, *CR* n.s. 63 [2013], 29–31 and A. Fries, *Mnemosyne* IV 66 [2013], 814–21 + 'Corrigendum', *Mnemosyne* IV 67 [2014], 179).
3   S. *Lakainai* and Ion *Phrouroi*, which dramatised the Palladion theft and *Ptôcheia* respectively (501–2, 503–7a nn.), may be parallels (Ritchie 136–7), and also A. *Phrygians* =

Rhesus became a success and was revived more than once during the fourth century BC (cf. p. 26).

Yet *Rhesus* is no tale of adventure, in contrast to its model, *Iliad* 10. The poet chose the perspective of the Trojans, who despite their recent victory and some further successes in the future, were destined to be overcome by the Greeks. The audience's knowledge of this will have coloured their perception of Hector's confidence and outspoken reliance on the support of Zeus or 'fate' (cf. 52–84, 319–20nn.), which remains unshaken by Rhesus' death and the Muse's revelation that it was divinely ordained (938–49; cf. 983–96n.).

The Thracian is presented as Troy's greatest asset, a hero not only able to defeat Achilles (cf. 314–16n.), but also resembling him in much of his life and posthumous fate (pp. 10, 13–14). Crucially, however, neither Hector nor the chorus (who are much more enthusiastic about the unexpected ally) ever learn that, far from just boasting about his martial prowess (443–53) and being elevated to near-divine status (342–79, 380–7), he could really have changed the course of the war.[4] This information Athena imparts to Odysseus and Diomedes as the reason why they should direct their assault at him (600–4). Again only the audience can measure the extent to which the Trojans are in danger.

If the Trojans are deluded about their situation, the two Greeks hardly appear in a better light, as they enter the enemy camp, timidly and prepared to retreat when they do not find Hector in the place Dolon indicated (565–94). It is a fine touch, rather than a mark of dramatic incompetence, that in *Rhesus* he leaves before the arrival of the Thracians and so cannot betray them to Odysseus and Diomedes. Instead Athena guides their steps before and after the attack (595–641, 568–74).[5]

More often than the Greeks, who effect a cunning escape in 675–91 (n.), the Trojans and their allies (in the person of Rhesus' charioteer) are seen making false decisions or groping in the dark, literally as well as metaphorically (1–51, 52–84, 65–9, 85–148, 692–727, 728–55nn.). The night, frequently referred to for the sake of maintaining the theatrical illusion,[6] thus becomes both a cause and symbol of human improvi-

---

Ἕκτορος Λύτρα (+ Dionysius' tragedy of that title: *TrGF* 76 F 2a?), if the poet(s) followed *Iliad* 24 strictly. S. *Syndeipnoi* = Ἀχαιῶν Σύλλογος perhaps started in the evening (fr. 143); cf. Sommerstein, in *Shards from Kolonos*, 359–60 (with n. 16) and *Sophocles. Selected Fragmentary Plays* I, 89, 92.

4 T. Thum, *Philologus* 149 (2005), 221.
5 Strohm 260–1.
6 Cf. Ritchie 137 with n. 2 (where add 45, 765, 774, 788, 824 and 852) and Liapis, xxxiv–xxxv.

dence – unlike in *Iliad* 10, where it worries the Achaean leaders, but ultimately helps Odysseus and Diomedes to succeed.⁷

Dramatic meaning, action and structure are closely interrelated in *Rhesus*.⁸ The play falls into two halves. In the first part (1–564) we witness a build-up of Trojan confidence in the characters of Hector, Dolon and Rhesus, whereas the second (565–996) deals with the destruction of the high hopes set in and expressed by Dolon and the Thracian king. The agents of their death – Odysseus and Diomedes (with Athena in the background) – appear suddenly and unannounced, engaged in a conversation that in form and content resembles a second prologue (565–94n.).

The doubling of typical scenes fits into this pattern. Each half of the play contains a messenger speech, the one by the Shepherd (284–316) describing Rhesus' glorious arrival, the one by the Charioteer (756–803) his inglorious death. The two *agones* likewise mirror each other. In the first one (388–526) Hector accuses Rhesus of tardiness in coming to his aid, in the second (804–81) he himself is accused by the Charioteer of having killed his ally (cf. 804–81, 833–81nn.). The scenic reversal, which illustrates the reversal in the Trojans' fortune, is underlined by the distantly separated lyric stanzas 454–66 ~ 820–32 (nn.).⁹

Continuity, on the other hand, is visible in the parodos (1–51) and epiparodos (675–727), where each time the chorus act 'in whirling motion – but with nothing at all as a result'.¹⁰ The epiphanies of Athena (595–674) and the Muse (882–982) are similar in function. Just as the Greeks are unable to achieve their goal without divine assistance, the Trojans need supernatural elucidation to solve the mystery of Rhesus' death.

Regarding the poet's use of leitmotifs, we have already seen how Hector persists in his belief that he is fated to prevail and how Rhesus is elevated by regular juxtaposition with Achilles (and Ajax). In addition, wolf-imagery characterises Dolon and produces an ironic contrast when, rather than taking the head of Odysseus or Diomedes (219–23n.) and getting Achilles' horses as a reward, he himself is killed and robbed of his wolf-skin by the Greeks, whom subsequently the Charioteer in his dream pictures as wolves attacking Rhesus' team of horses (201–23, 780–8nn.). A similar paradox is created by the watchword, 'Phoebus', which (because

---

7   Strohm 257–66, 274, G. Paduano, *Maia* n.s. 25 (1973), 13–15 and, on the ironical interplay of light and darkness in the drama, H. Parry, *Phoenix* 18 (1964), 283–93.
8   B. Fenik, *The Influence of Euripides on Vergil's* Aeneid, diss. Princeton 1960, 84–93 (especially 91–3). He largely depends on Strohm and does not take sides in the authenticity debate (cf. 54–5).
9   For further inversions between scenes see 85–148, 467–526 and 642–74nn.
10 Strohm 261.

of Dolon's betrayal) not only fails to protect the Trojan camp, but actually helps the Achaeans to escape (521–2, 675–91nn.).[11]

Rhesus is simply, but carefully, constructed, with a whole network of visual and thematic correspondences between the scenes.[12] Its unity does not lie in the Aristotelian principle of having one episode follow upon another with probability or necessity (cf. *Poet.* 1450b22–34, 1451b32–5), but in the idea of human fallibility and men's dependence, for good or ill, on the will of the gods. This also constitutes the 'tragedy' of the play, as does the prospect of Hector's death and the fall of Troy. In contrast to what we know of fifth-century drama, the characters on stage remain for the most part unaware of their fate,[13] which also perhaps accounts for the absence of a true 'tragic hero' and the fact that none of the Trojans (as opposed to the Charioteer and the Muse) seems genuinely moved by Rhesus' death. He is but an incident in the much larger tragedy of their war.

What then does *Rhesus* offer and where are its limitations? It is excellent theatre – not only in terms of stagecraft, but also for some impressive set pieces (the two messenger speeches and the Muse's account of Rhesus' past and future) and, it must be added, very competent, even beautiful, lyrics (the 'Dawn-Song', 527–64, stands out). For those who knew their Homer and were not too dazzled by the 'spectacle' it also afforded a deeply pessimistic outlook on the story of Troy and human life in general, which may have suited a period of restoration after the Peloponnesian Wars.[14] That many of the characters (notably Hector, Dolon and Rhesus) are overdrawn, their conflicts pointless or not fully developed[15] and the language and scene composition heavily dependent on earlier sources[16] is equally true, but should not prevent us from taking this poet seriously. His agenda is perhaps best described by the four lines Athenaeus (10.411b) quotes from the satyric *Heracles* of Astydamas II (*TrGF* 60 F 4):

---

11 On both motifs see Fenik (n. 8), 93 n. 1
12 Cf. also Strohm 264–5 and, in comparison with Iliadic patterns, R. S. Bond, *AJPh* 117 (1996), 262–3.
13 The chorus express some scepticism in 332 and particularly 882–4 and 995–6 (nn.).
14 A careful examination of the external evidence suggests a dating in the first quarter or third of the fourth century BC (ch. III.1).
15 Note Hector's censure of the Shepherd (264–77), the speed with which he is persuaded to accept Rhesus as an ally (264–341, 333–41nn.) and the topic of especially the first *agon* (388–526n.).
16 See ch. III.2.

I. The Play

ἀλλ' ὥσπερ δείπνου γλαφυροῦ ποικίλην εὐωχίαν
τὸν ποιητὴν δεῖ παρέχειν τοῖς θεαταῖς τὸν σοφόν,
ἵν' ἀπίῃ τις τοῦτο φαγὼν καὶ πιών, ὅπερ λαβών
χαίρει <τις>, καὶ σκευασία μὴ μί' ᾖ τῆς μουσικῆς ...[17]

A clever poet should supply his audience with
a rich feast that resembles an elegant dinner,
so everyone eats and drinks whatever he likes before
he leaves, and the entertainment doesn't consist of a single course.[18]

---

17 A. Lesky, *Die tragische Dichtung der Hellenen*, Göttingen ³1972, 529. Cf. T. Thum, *Philologus* 149 (2005), 228.
18 Tr. S. D. Olson (ed.), *Athenaeus. The Learned Banqueters* IV, Cambridge (Mass.) – London 2008, 425.

II. Plot And Myth

Rhesus is the only surviving Attic drama, except for Euripides' satyr-play *Cyclops*, where we also possess the epic version and can compare the two in a productive way.[1] As will be seen (and has already been demonstrated by Ritchie), the poet essentially keeps to *Iliad* 10, developing hints from it in many of his more original scenes. At the same time, however, he has enhanced his adaptation by including other motifs from Homer and the Epic Cycle, as well as divergent information about of Dolon and especially Rhesus, taken from Hellenic sources and Thracian cult. The result is an exciting representation of what happened on the Trojan side that night, particularly after the narrative returned to the Greeks at *Il.* 10.526.[2]

1. The Greek Tradition

(a) *Iliad* 10 and Homer

This section analyses the action of *Rhesus* in relation to its epic models. For greater detail the reader is referred to the commentary, especially the scene introductions.

In terms of plot-construction, the parodos (1–51) and first *epeisodion* (52–223) show all the techniques our poet employed. For lack of an adequate precedent among the Trojans in 'Homer', the sequence of 1–148 has been devised as a mirror-image of *Il.* 10.1–179, which describes the anxious commotion in the Greek naval camp. Yet after a closely adapted introductory scene (1–51, 23–51nn.), other Iliadic material comes in. Hector's speech in 52–75 largely follows that of his epic self at *Il.* 8.497–541, with only the occasional nod to *Iliad* 10 there and in the ensuing

---

[1] Among fragmentary plays, enough of Sophocles' satyric *Ichneutae* survives to define its relationship to the *Homeric Hymn to Hermes* (cf. Richardson, *Three Homeric Hymns*, 25–6).

[2] Cf. G. Paduano, *Maia* n.s. 25 (1973), 15. On the sources of the plot see Ritchie 64–81, 83–6, R. S. Bond, *AJPh* 117 (1996), 255–73 and Liapis, xvii–xxvii, xxx–xxxi. To view our poet's habit of modelling scenes and characters on others in the *Iliad* as an attempt to mislead the audience or reader (Fantuzzi, in *I luoghi*, 244–56, *Entretiens Hardt* LII, 148–51) is to credit him with the qualities of a Hellenistic or Roman poet.

dialogue with the coryphaeus (52–84, 56–69, 82–3nn.). Conversely, Aeneas advising Hector to dispatch a scout before attacking the Greeks in the dark (85–148) corresponds to Menelaus in *Il.* 10.37–41, whereas his actual character and words are based on Polydamas in *Iliad* 12, 13 and 18 (85–148, 105–30nn.).

With the two Dolon scenes (149–94 + 201–23) the plot turns to the Trojan assembly in *Il.* 10.299–337. But again the narrative has been expanded from elsewhere in Homer and, for the first time, an external source. The 'guessing-game' by which Dolon elicits the promise of Achilles' horses as a reward for his expedition is informed by the proxy negotiations between Agamemnon and Achilles in *Iliad* 9, and the animals themselves are described after *Il.* 16.149–51 + 23.276–8 (cf. 149–94, 185–8nn.). Dolon's wolf-disguise and four-footed walk (208–13), on the other hand, go back to a parallel tradition attested in vase paintings since the early fifth century BC and were doubtless considered more effective than his semi-military outfit in *Il.* 10.333–5 (cf. 201–23n.).

Even concerning Rhesus, our poet used what was available in *Iliad* 10. The epic Thracian is a nonentity, a sleeping source of booty for Odysseus and Diomedes, but the memorable description of his god-like appearance and snow-white horses (*Il.* 10.435–41) has been incorporated into the Shepherd's report of his approach (301–8) and is further elaborated in the chorus' 'cletic hymn' and entry announcement (342–79, 380–7nn.). Likewise, the position Hector assigns to Rhesus and his men in 518–20 (cf. 613–15) matches that of *Il.* 10.434, a telling detail after different precedents (including the τειχοσκοπία in *Iliad* 3) had to be invoked for the encounter between Hector and the Thracian king (388–526, 388–453, 467–526nn.).

Adaptation of *Iliad* 10 continues with a series of worried remarks about Dolon's absence (523–6, 557–61, 557–8nn.), shortly before Odysseus and Diomedes arrive carrying his spoils (591–3n.). Their entry dialogue (565–94) contains several allusions to the spy's interception and death (*Il.* 10.339–468),[3] which allow the audience to reconstruct his fate. Knowledge of Rhesus, however, has to come from Athena, since Dolon never set eyes on him. The goddess' role in 595–641 (n.) seems closer to Pindar's version of the Rhesus myth (pp. 11–12), but her conversation with Odysseus and Diomedes is replete with echoes of *Iliad* 10, and a new stage in the action is reached when the heroes divide their 'duties' between killing the Thracians and leading away the marvellous steeds (*Rh.* 622–3 ~ *Il.* 10.479–81).

Athena's deception of Paris (642–67) is another invented episode. Yet one may argue that it presents a variation on the typical epic scene

---

3   Including the betrayal of the watchword, which is not in 'Homer' (cf. 572–3n.).

in which a god misleads a human in the guise of a mortal friend and in particular Athena's deluding of Hector in *Il.* 22.222–305 (cf. 642–74n.). After the Trojan's departure the goddess addresses the returning Greeks (668–74), just as in *Il.* 10.509–11 she had warned Diomedes to escape while they could.

The epiparodos (675–91 + 692–727) dramatises a single sentence in the epic source. The commotion caused by the searching chorus parallels that of the Trojans when, alerted by Hippocoon, they discover the massacre in the Thracian camp (*Il.* 10.523–4). Rhesus' cousin has an equivalent in the Charioteer, who comes on stage, first to bewail his master and himself (728–55n.), then to give a highly idiosyncratic account of the attack (756–803n.). The latter adapts the authorial narrative of *Il.* 10.471–97, with two important modifications: (a) the Thracians ineptly rest in complete disorder (762–9n.), and (b) Rhesus' climactic nightmare of Diomedes standing at his head (*Il.* 10.496–7) becomes an uncanny symbolic dream of the Charioteer (780–8n.).

With the circumstances of Rhesus' death ends the straightforward application of *Iliad* 10. The following scene of accusations between Hector, the chorus and the Charioteer (804–81) mentions Odysseus as the presumable killer of both Rhesus and Dolon (861–6), but otherwise springs entirely from our poet's mind. The same is true of the Muse's apparition (882–982). As the mother of Rhesus she has no precedent in the epic, nor probably any earlier version of the myth (p. 13); instead the lament for her son is modelled on that of Thetis for Achilles in *Il.* 18.54–64 (cf. 890–914, 915–49nn.), while Rhesus' background and translation to cultic honours are developed from parallels in the Epic Cycle, Sarpedon's story and Thracian lore (pp. 13–14, 14–18). After a look ahead to Achilles' death and funeral (*Rh.* 974–9 ~ *Od.* 24.58–64, *Aethiopis* Arg. p. 112 (4) *GEF*), she departs, leaving the humans to prepare for battle in a way that recalls both *Il.* 8.497–541 and the beginning of *Iliad* 11 (cf. 983–96n.).

It emerges that *Rhesus* moves through *Iliad* 10 almost in the order of events, making extensive use also of the 'Greek part'.[4] The material is skilfully integrated, and our poet takes care to return to the epic plot after each digression. Allusions to other Iliadic episodes centre on the surrounding books (8–12), with occasional references back and forward. We

---

4 To repeat schematically (and a little more fully): *Rh.* 1–148 ~ *Il.* 10.1–179, *Rh.* 149–223 ~ *Il.* 10.299–337, *Rh.* 264–387 ~ *Il.* 10.436–41, *Rh.* 388–526 (end) ~ *Il.* 10.434, *Rh.* 527–64 ~ *Il.* 10.251–3 (time of night), 428–31 (allies), 561–3 (Dolon's killing), *Rh.* 565–94 ~ *Il.* 10.339–468, *Rh.* 595–641 ~ *Il.* 433–41, 463–4, 474–5, 479–81, *Rh.* 642–74 (end) ~ *Il.* 10.509–11, *Rh.* 675–727 ~ *Il.* 10.523–4, *Rh.* 728–881 ~ *Il.* 10.515–21 (Charioteer ~ Hippocoon), *Rh.* 756–803 ~ *Il.* 10.471–97 (narrated in retrospect).

thus get a comprehensive picture not only of that single night, but also of the entire war, including Hector's death and the fall of Troy.⁵ Some of the 'cyclic' echoes discussed in the next section work in the same direction.

(b) Other Sources

Not surprisingly, non-Homeric accounts have mainly been called upon in scenes that bear no direct relationship to *Iliad* 10. But they do not simply fill mythological gaps or provide pathos and additional dramatic interest; we also note shifts in the interaction between gods and men and an intention to go beyond the legend of Troy.

While our poet may or may not have had a written source for Dolon's wolf-disguise (p. 9), his other models can be traced in the fragments of early epic, lyric and tragedy. The most important ones are two alternative tales about Rhesus, recorded in the scholia to *Il.* 10.435.

According to the first, which is ascribed to Pindar (fr. 262 Sn.–M.), the Thracian wrought havoc among the Greeks for one day until Athena, on Hera's orders, incited Odysseus and Diomedes to kill him:

Σ^(bT) *Il.* 10.435 (III 93.64–8 Erbse) ~ Eust. 817.29
Ῥῆσος Στρυμόνος τοῦ ποταμοῦ τῆς Θρᾴκης υἱὸς καὶ Εὐτέρπης Μούσης. ἱστορεῖ δὲ Πίνδαρος ὅτι καὶ μίαν ἡμέραν πολεμήσας πρὸς Ἕλληνας μέγιστα αὐτοῖς ἐνεδείξατο κακά, κατὰ δὲ πρόνοιαν Ἥρας καὶ Ἀθηνᾶς ἀναστάντες οἱ περὶ Διομήδεα ἀναιροῦσιν αὐτόν.

Σ^(AD) *Il.* 10.435 (pp. 355–6 van Thiel = I 364.3–11 Dindorf)
Ῥῆσος γένει μὲν Θρᾷξ ἦν, υἱὸς δὲ Στρυμόνος, τοῦ αὐτόθι ποταμοῦ, καὶ Εὐτέρπης, μιᾶς τῶν Μουσῶν. διάφορος δὲ τῶν καθ' αὑτὸν γενόμενος ἐν πολεμικοῖς ἔργοις ἐπῆλθε τοῖς Ἕλλησιν, ὅπως Τρωσὶ συμμαχήσῃ, καὶ συμβαλὼν πολλοὺς τῶν Ἑλλήνων ἀπέκτεινεν. δείσασα δὲ Ἥρα περὶ τῶν Ἑλλήνων Ἀθηνᾶν ἐπὶ τὴν τούτου διαφθορὰν πέμπει, κατελθοῦσα δὲ ἡ θεὸς Ὀδυσσέα τε καὶ Διομήδην ἐπὶ τὴν κατασκοπὴν ἐποίησεν προελθεῖν. ἐπιστάντες δὲ ἐκεῖνοι κοιμωμένῳ Ῥήσῳ αὐτόν τε καὶ τοὺς ἑταίρους αὐτοῦ κτείνουσιν, ὡς ἱστορεῖ Πίνδαρος.

From there, it seems, stems Rhesus' extravagant claim of being able to end the Trojan War in one day (447–53n.) and especially the expansion

---

5 Cf. R. S. Bond, *AJPh* 117 (1996), 271–2 (although he probably goes too far in regarding *Rhesus* as an attempt 'to create a dramatic equivalent of the *Iliad*') and ch. I above.

of Athena's role from the benevolent force behind the Achaeans in *Iliad* 10[6] to the coolly manipulative operator who leaves men little freedom to decide or act (565–94, 595–674, 595–641, 642–74nn.).[7]

The mythical pre-existence of Rhesus' earlier campaigns (406–11a, 426–42nn.), on the other hand, is not guaranteed by the extended narrative of Σ^AD *Il.* 10.435.[8] Much of it reads like extrapolations from 'Homer', and it is possible that διάφορος δὲ τῶν καθ' αὑτὸν γενόμενος ἐν πολεμικοῖς ἔργοις also comes from our play rather than from Pindar or an unknown source.

The same note continues to report an oracle that Rhesus would be invincible once he and his horses drank from the Scamander and the animals grazed on the local pastures:

Σ^AD *Il.* 10.435 (p. 356 van Thiel = I 364.11–15 Dindorf) ~ Eust. 817.27–8
ἔνιοι δὲ λέγουσιν νυκτὸς παραγεγονέναι τὸν Ῥῆσον εἰς τὴν Τροίαν, καὶ πρὶν γεύσασθαι αὐτὸν τοῦ ὕδατος τῆς χώρας φονευθῆναι. χρησμὸς γὰρ ἐδέδοτο αὐτῷ φασιν, ὅτι εἰ αὐτός τε γεύσεται τοῦ ὕδατος καὶ οἱ ἵπποι αὐτοῦ τοῦ Σκαμάνδρου πίωσι καὶ τῆς αὐτόθι νομῆς, ἀκαταμάχητος ἔσται εἰς τὸ παντελές.

Virgil used this version for his description of the Tyrian temple of Juno (*Aen.* 1.469–73), but without making Troy's fall dependent on the fulfilment of the prophecy, as Servius and others did.[9] In *Rhesus* there is a trace of the invincibility motif when Athena, somewhat unexpectedly, verifies the hero's boasts by declaring that nobody will be able to stop him from sacking Greek camp if he survives his first night at Troy (600–4n.; cf. 388–526, 595–641nn.).

---

6   *Il.* 10.245, 274–95, 366–8, 460–4, 482, 496–7, 507–12 + 516, 552–3, 570–1, 578–9. Some of these passages are reflected in *Rhesus* (ch. II.1(a)).

7   Thus also the second spurious prologue (Hyp. (b) *Rh.* 65.37–47 = 431.34–44 Diggle = fr. tr. adesp. 81 = *TrGF* V.2 (60) ΡΗΣΟΣ 642.12–22) is a dialogue between Hera and Athena. In the part cited, which betrays itself as just the 'un-Euripidean' pastiche the ancient critics took it for (pp. 26, 38 with n. 61), Hera worries about the hard-pressed Achaeans and would probably have turned to mentioning Rhesus and sending Athena on her 'errand' (Ritchie 110; cf. Fenik, *Iliad X*, 36–7 on the similarities with *Il.* 5.714–18 and 8.352–6).

8   Contrast e.g. Ritchie 63, Fenik, *Iliad X*, 30 and Jouan 54 n. 275. On Rhesus' parentage see below.

9   Serv. on Verg. *Aen.* 1.469 ~ *Myth. Vat.* 1.200 Kulcsár (*CCSL* 91 C) = 203 Mai. Cf. Serv. on *Aen.* 2.13, Serv. auct. on *Aen.* 12.347 *equos fatales*, and the scholia to Ov. *Ib.* 629. On the many conditional oracles relating to the fate of Troy (most notably the fetching of Philoctetes and Neoptolemus) see W. Kullmann, *Die Quellen der Ilias*, Wiesbaden 1960, 221–3 and, in his wake, Fenik, *Iliad X*, 10–12.

Both sets of scholia begin by identifying Rhesus' parents, Strymon and Euterpe, and the assumption that at least the Muse already belonged to Pindar's treatment was essential to Fenik's controversial reconstruction of an epic-cyclic narrative from *Rhesus* and the said variants (*Iliad X*, 5–63). But her very anonymity in the play and the fact that subsequent witnesses disagree about her name suggest that there was no fixed tradition,[10] and our poet either invented the connection (by analogy with Orpheus?) or, less likely, followed some Thracian belief. He would probably have heard of Clio's sanctuary near the μνημεῖον for Rhesus in Amphipolis (Marsyas II *FGrHist* 136 F 7 = Σ^V *Rh*. 346 [II 335.12–13 Schwartz = 94.6–7 Merro]; cf. p. 15).

Still, in other ways, the Epic Cycle has had a defining influence on *Rhesus*. Episodes like the Palladion theft, the 'Ptôcheia' and perhaps the capture of Helenus (all from the *Little Iliad*) were brought forward in time to underline the Trojans' contempt for Odysseus and the threat he poses to them (498b–509, 501–2, 503–7a, 507b–9a, 692–727, 710–21nn.).

In particular, however, we find pertinent overlaps between Rhesus' dramatic personality and fate and those of Achilles, Cycnus, Penthesileia, Memnon, Eurypylus and Sarpedon, as portrayed in the *Iliad*, the Epic Cycle and tragedies based on their accounts.[11] Four of these heroic figures (Cycnus, Penthesileia, Memnon, Eurypylus) form a group of foreign allies to Troy who arrived late or, in the case of Cycnus, at the very beginning of the war only to be killed in battle by Achilles or Neoptolemus. The analogies with Rhesus are obvious,[12] and even if he was not part of that tradition from an early date, as Fenik argued, it is easy to see how his biography and theatrical representation came to share the following further elements with their and related tales:

---

10 W. Leaf, *JHS* 35 (1915), 2 n. 5, J. Rempe, *De Rheso Thracum heroe*, diss. Münster 1927, 38–40 (+ 53). Euterpe features most frequently (Heraclid. Pont. fr. 159 Wehrli + Apollod. *FGrHist* 244 F 146 = Σ^V *Rh*. 346 [II 335.13–25 Schwartz = 94.7–95.20 Merro], Serv. auct. on Verg. *Aen*. 1.469, Eust. 817.27; cf. 'Apollod.' 1.3.4 [1.18]: Euterpe or Calliope, Σ^V *Rh*. 393 [II 336.21–2 Schwartz = 97 Merro]: Clio or Euterpe, Σ^{AD} *Il*. 10.435 [p. 356 van Thiel = I 364.17–18 Dindorf]: Terpsichore or Euterpe). Alone also Clio (Σ^V *Rh*. 346 [II 335.8–13 Schwartz = 94.2–7 Merro] ~ Marsyas II *FGrHist* 136 F 7), Calliope (Hyp. (a) *Rh*. 64.20 = 430.19 Diggle) and Terpsichore (Ar. Byz. Hyp. (c) *Rh*. 65.48, 53 = 431.45, 432.50 Diggle, Σ^{Tz} Lyc. 831 [II 266.10–11 Scheer], Tz. *Carm. Il*. p. 65 Schirach). Strymon (cf. 279n.) became canonical, except for Dict. Cret. 2.45.1 ('Eioneus' as in *Iliad* 10) and Conon's attempt to reconcile the two genealogies by having a mortal king Strymon give his name to the river Eioneus (*FGrHist* 26 F 1 IV; cf. [Plut.] *Fluv*. 11.1).

11 Achilles: *Iliad*, *Aethiopis*, A. *Nereids*, Cycnus: *Cypria*, S. *Poimenes*, Penthesileia: *Aethiopis*, Memnon: *Aethiopis*, A. *Memnon*, *Psychostasia*, S. *Aethiopes* (perhaps identical with his *Memnon*; only two fragments survive), Eurypylus: *Little Iliad*, S. *Eurypylus*, Sarpedon: *Iliad*, A. (?) *Cares = Europa*.

12 Penthesileia, Memnon and presumably Eurypylus also came in the evening to join battle on the following day (West, *Epic Cycle*, 138–9, 143, 190).

(1) a Trojan appeal for military assistance: Eurypylus and, from at least the early fourth-century BC, Memnon (399–403n.).
(2) parental reluctance to let the son go to war, with divine foreknowledge of his death at Troy: (Eurypylus), Achilles (899–901, 934–5a nn.).
(3) grief and lament at his untimely demise: Sarpedon, Achilles, Memnon, Eurypylus (882–9, 908–9, 915–49, 967–9, 974–7nn.).
(4) supernatural intervention for his body: Sarpedon, Memnon, Achilles (882–9, 962–6nn.).
(5) childhood in the care of nymphs: Achilles (926–31n.).
(6) a boastful attitude, splendid armour and perhaps a chariot displayed on stage: Cycnus, Memnon (301b–8, 380–7, 388–526nn. and pp. 1, 41).[13]

The overall pattern of *Rhesus* has been successfully compared to Aeschylus' (?) *Cares = Europa*,[14] which arguably covered, from Europa's perspective, the death of Sarpedon, his miraculous transfer to Caria and the ensuing funeral preparations[15] and so, like our play, supplied the tragic aftermath to a myth 'begun' in Homer. A. *Nereids* would be similar if it indeed stood third after *Myrmidons* and *Phrygians* and dealt with Achilles' last battle and elevation to the Island of the Blessed (882–9, 915–49, 978–9nn.).

2. Rhesus of Thrace

While the Muse's prediction of her son's metamorphosis into a subterranean 'man-god' and Bacchus prophet on Mt. Pangaeus (962–73) remains our only evidence for a possible association of Rhesus with the Satrae's oracle of Thracian Dionysus (cf. 962–82, 970–1, 972–3nn.), there can be no doubt that the hero played a considerable part in north-eastern Mediterranean myth and belief. Unfortunately, however, most sources are late and do not readily admit conclusions about actual religious practice.

One positive case is the Greek-style hero cult which, for a time at least, Rhesus received at Amphipolis. It was installed by the city's founder Hagnon in 437/6 BC after a (probably Delphic) oracle had declared that he could colonise the site of Ennea Hodoi only if Rhesus' bones were returned from Troy (Polyaen. 6.53). Despite the many picturesque details

---

13 At length Ritchie 79–81, who suggests that some of these details were already attached to the Rhesus myth in the fifth century. Pindar certainly could have noted the parallels with Penthesileia, Memnon and Eurypylus and transferred the *aristeia*-motif himself.
14 Fantuzzi, in *Entretiens Hardt* LII, 143–5, *Eikasmos* 18 (2007), 186–7.
15 See M. L. West, *CQ* n.s. 50 (2000), 347–9 = *Hellenica* II, 241–3. The analogy would be reinforced if *Cares = Europa* had also contained an *aition* of Sarpedon's cult at home.

that riddle the story,[16] the event as such is generally accepted as historic and compared to the Spartans' divinely ordained 'theft' of Orestes' relics from Tegea (Hdt. 1.67–8)[17] and that of Theseus when the Athenians seized Scyrus about 475 BC.[18] Moreover, the description by Marsyas of Philippi of a Clio sanctuary in Amphipolis opposite a memorial for Rhesus (p. 13) has been partly confirmed by the excavation of the former, which from its style and the letters of a votive inscription (Εὔμητις | Ἡγησιστράτο | Κλεοῖ | ἀνέθηκεν) was dated to the early fourth century BC.[19] Malkin, among others, indeed believes the herôon might go back to Hagnon 'because the cult seems to have ceased after the citizens of Amphipolis transferred the title of oikist to Brasidas in 422 B.C., and turned against the "Hagnoneia" in anger' (~ Thuc. 5.11.1).[20]

A note in Strabo (7 fr. 16a [II 366.5–7 Radt]) to the effect that Rhesus once ruled among the Odomantes, Edoni and Bisaltae[21] strengthens his claim to being a 'native' of the lower Strymon area. Further east he is linked by Hippon. fr. 72. 5–7 *IEG* ἐπ' ἁρμάτων τε καὶ Θρεϊκίων πώλων / λευκῶν †ὀείους κατεγγὺς† Ἰλίου πύργων / ἀπηναρίσθη Ῥῆσος, Αἰνειῶν πάλμυς to Aenus at the mouth of the Hebrus,[22] but it would be hazardous to infer local worship from that. More likely Hipponax meant

---

16 Contrast Thucydides' secularised account of this expedition (4.102.3) and also Cimon's invasion of Scyrus (1.98.2) below.
17 Cf. Paus. 3.3.5–7, 3.11.10, 8.54.4 and see D. Boedeker, in C. Dougherty – L. Kurke (eds.), *Cultural Poetics in Archaic Greece. Cult, Performance, Politics*, Cambridge 1993, 164–77, I. Malkin, *Myth and Territory in the Spartan Mediterranean*, Cambridge 1994, 26–33 (especially 26–8 and 136–7).
18 Plut. *Thes.* 36 and *Cim.* 8.3–7, who unlike Pausanias (3.3.7) does not specify the causal nexus between the oracle (476/5 BC) and the capture of the island (cf. A. J. Podlecki, *JHS* 91 [1971], 141–3).
19 D. Lazaridis, *Ergon* 6 (1959), 42–3, Ἀμφίπολις καί Ἄργιλος (Ἀρχαίες Ἑλληνικές Πόλεις 13), Athens 1972, 60 (no. 257), *Amphipolis*, Athens 1997, 44–5, 88 (plt. 49), G. Daux, *BCH* 84 (1960), 797–8 (with plts. 8, 9).
20 I. Malkin, *Religion and Colonization in Ancient Greece*, Leiden 1987, 82. Cf. e.g. P. Perdrizet, *Cultes et mythes du Pangée*, Paris 1910, 15 and W. Leaf, *JHS* 35 (1915), 6–7, who by combination with the Muse's prophecy saw in *Rhesus* a *pièce d'occasion* for the re-foundation of the colony. Similarly P. Perdrizet, in *In Memoria lui Vasile Pârvan*, Bucharest 1934, 284–90 and still tentatively Z. H. Archibald, *The Odrysian Kingdom of Thrace. Orpheus Unmasked*, Oxford 1998, 101.
21 The name Ῥῆσος is mostly recognised as Thracian for 'king', from the same IE root *(H)reĝ-* as e.g. Vedic *rāj-* and Latin *rēx*. For an extensive bibliography, including some critical voices, see V. Liapis, *Kernos* 24 (2011), 99 n. 26.
22 Rather than Aenia on the Chalkidike (cf. St. Byz. α 132 Billerbeck Αἴνεια· τόπος Θρᾴκης ... τὸ ἐθνικὸν Αἰνειεύς). Thus Degani, most recently, reads Αἰνίων with ten Brink (*Philologus* 6 [1851], 39), who cites St. Byz. 52.8 Meineke = α 135 Billerbeck Αἶνος· ... τὸ ἐθνικὸν Αἴνιος, ὡς Τήνιος (add e.g. Thuc. 7.57.5, *IG* I³ 261 IV.2, *FD* III.1 497.6, Call. *Iamb.* 7 fr. 197.1 Pf. Ἑρμᾶς ὁ Π]ερφεραῖος, Αἰνίων θεός). Some also made Rhesus a son of Hebrus (Serv. auct. on Verg. *Aen.* 1.469).

Θρῃκῶν βασιλεύς and chose the only Thracian town named in the *Iliad* (4.520) to stand for its entire country.²³

Outside Byzantium, by contrast, the *Suda* (ρ 146 Adler) explicitly mentions a precinct of the naturalised epic hero: Ῥῆσος: ... στρατηγὸς τῶν Βυζαντίων, τὰς οἰκήσεις ἔχων πρὸ τῆς πόλεως ἐν τόπῳ ἐπιλεγομένῳ Ῥησίῳ, ἔνθα νῦν ὁ οἶκος τοῦ μεγάλου μάρτυρος Θεοδώρου γνωρίζεται,²⁴ ἦλθεν εἰς συμμαχίαν τῶν Τρώων ... This could be a mere deduction from the place name,²⁵ were it not the case that churches frequently occupied former pagan sites and Appian (*Mith.* 1.1–2) reported a Greek tradition that part of Rhesus' surviving force made a detour via Byzantium before settling with the rest in what would become Bithynia. And Herodotus (7.75.2) says the Bithynians were originally Thracians from the Strymon.

Philostratus (*Her.* 17.3–6) tells of a Rhesus who haunts Mt. Rhodope – breeding horses, marching in armour, hunting and protecting the mountain villages from pestilence, while groups of wild animals come to his altar for voluntary sacrifice. In the absence of parallel testimonies we cannot be sure how far the story represents true folklore or was re-created by the author from other myths or his own resources.²⁶ It certainly looks as if he thought of the Thracian Hero or Horseman, an indigenous divinity (usually represented as a rider) who was venerated well into the Christian era and whose functions and activities are known from countless plaques and cult reliefs to have coincided with those of Rhesus in the *Heroicus*.²⁷ Yet archaeological evidence for the identifica-

---

23 Cf. B. ten Brink, *Philologus* 6 (1851), 40, E. Degani (ed.), *Hipponax. Testimonia et Fragmenta*, Stuttgart – Leipzig ²1991, 87 and *id.* (ed.), *Ipponatte. Frammenti. Introduzione, traduzione e note* (ed. G. Burzacchini, with additions by A. Nicolosi), Bologna 2007, 116.

24 Cf. *Exc. Salm.*, *An. Par.* II 390.31–2 = [Ioan. Antioch.] fr. 24.6 *FHG* IV 551 Ῥῆσος τὰς οἰκήσεις ἔχων ἐν Βυζαντίῳ ἐν τῷ λεγομένῳ Ῥηάτῳ, ὅπου νῦν ἐστιν ὁ τοῦ μεγαλομάρτυρος ἁγίου Θεοδώρου ναός, Procop. *Aed.* I 4 (26.20–2 Haury-Wirth). One of Byzantium's gates was called πόρτη τοῦ Ῥησίου (Theoph. Conf. *Chronogr.* 229.30–230.3, 231.20 de Boor). In general see V. J. Liapis, *CQ* n.s. 57 (2007), 396–7.

25 A neuter adjective of the IE 'king' root (n. 21). The type has several parallels from Ireland to the east of Europe, including the well-known R(h)egium in Calabria (West, *IEPM* 413).

26 On the often fictional character of Philostratus' works see G. Anderson, *Philostratus. Biography and Belles Lettres in the Third Century AD*, London et al. 1986, 253–4, E. L. Bowie, in J. R. Morgan – R. Stoneman (eds.), *Greek Fiction. The Greek Novel in Context*, London – New York 1994, 181–99 (especially 184). P. Grossardt (*Einführung, Übersetzung und Kommentar zum Heroikos von Flavius Philostrat*, 2 vols., Basel 2006) seems more sceptical in his commentary (II, pp. 435–441) than in the introduction (I, pp. 35 with n. 8, 115 with n. 362) about Rhesus' mountainous existence.

27 Earlier discoveries are listed by G. I. Kazarow, *Die Denkmäler des thrakischen Reitergottes in Bulgarien*, I *Textband*, II *Tafelband*, Budapest – Leipzig 1938. For additions to these and the Hero's place in Thracian religion see e.g. A. Foll et al., *Légendes Thraces*, Sofia 1977, 7–40, V. Velkov – V. Gerassimova-Tomova, *ANRW* II 18.2, 1322–30

tion²⁸ is lacking, despite the frequent syncretism of the Horseman with other deities – notably Apollo, Asclepius and Dionysus (below) – and such non-specific titles as Ἥρως, Κύριος or Δεσπότης, to which Ῥῆσος in the sense 'King' (n. 21) would also have belonged. All we can safely posit therefore is a generic affinity between Rhesus and the Hero as ancestor figures, without ruling out the possibility that Philostratus' narrative was based on more than that. At the gates of Byzantium Rhesus may have had apotropaic qualities (like the Heros Προπύλαιος),²⁹ and in view of his status as a cave-dwelling 'prophet of Bacchus', it is interesting to note the regular association also of the Thracian Horseman with Dionysus and/or the underworld.³⁰ Significantly perhaps, as Perdrizet called to mind, the Pangaean Bacchus oracle was served by Bessi from western Rhodope.³¹

Finally, in a way that appears to be purely literary, and to a large degree dependent on our play (cf. pp. 44–5), Rhesus has been incorporated into the Cian legend of Arganthone. According to Parthenius of Nicaea (*Erot. Path.* 36),³² the hero's earlier campaigns around the Propontis (*Erot. Path.* 36.1 ~ *Rh.* 426–42) also brought him to Mt. Arganthon, in the hope of winning the beautiful, reclusive hunting-maiden who bore its name. Having been successful by stealth, he one day follows a noble embassy to Troy (*Erot. Path.* 36.4 ~ *Rh.* 399–403, 839–40, 935–7, 954–7), although Arganthone, from dire premonitions, desperately tries to hold him back (*Erot. Path.* 36.4 ~ *Rh.* 900–1, 934–5). Like the Muse again, she is consumed by grief upon learning of his death (uniquely in battle with Diomedes, on the banks of the river whose eponym he would become)³³ and, as a mortal woman, eventually passes away through self-starvation.

---

and Hoddinott, *Thracians*, 169–75. *LIMC* VI.1/2 s.v. Heros Equitans (A. Cermanović-Kuzmanović *et al.*) treats the Thracian Horseman in the wider context of mounted heroes.
28 First proposed by G. Seure, *RPh* 54 (1928), 106–39. The issue has recently been revisited (with cautious approval) by V. Liapis, *Kernos* 24 (2011), 95–104.
29 Cf. e.g. *LIMC* VI.1/2 s.v. Heros Equitans 170 (Varna, late II AD), 501 (Nesebăr, late II/early III AD).
30 See V. Liapis, *Kernos* 24 (2011), 102–4.
31 *Cultes et mythes du Pangée*, 19, 27–8, 39. Cf. A. D. Nock, *CR* 40 (1926), 186 and *Rh.* 972–3n.
32 Possibly after Asclepius of Myrlea's *Bithyniaca* (*FGrHist* 697 F 2). But see Lightfoot, *Parthenius*, 249–50, 253 on our inability to prove that those manuscript notices or 'manchettes' name the actual source in any one case.
33 The location of this river Rhesus, which is mentioned already in *Il.* 12.20 (with Hainsworth on 20–2, 20) and Hes. *Th.* 340 (with West), was disputed in classical times. Demetrius of Scepsis (fr. 31 Gaede = Strab. 13.1.44) assumed it was the Rhoeites (cf. Σᵀ *Il.* 12.20 [III 299.35–7 Erbse] ~ Eust. 889.59–61) – εἰ μὴ ἄρα ὁ εἰς τὸν Γρανικὸν ἐμβάλλων * * Ῥησός ἐστιν. The Elder Pliny (*NH* 5.124) could not find it, but gives 'Rhesus' as an

The essence of the story recurs in Stephanus of Byzantium (α 394 Billerbeck Ἀργανθών· ὄρος Μυσίας ἐπὶ τῇ Κίῳ, ἀπὸ Ἀργανθώνης Ῥήσου γυναικός), and Arrian presumably took Rhesus to be the father of Arganthone's sons Thynus and Mysus (*FGrHist* 156 FF 59, 83). From that one can see most easily how the compound myth evolved 'to explain the [ethnic] links between Thrace and Bithynia / Mysia and north-western Asia Minor generally'.[34]

Despite certain reservations, therefore, it is clear that Cicero (*nat. deor.* 3.45) was wrong to claim that Rhesus (and Orpheus), although born of Muses, were not considered deities and hence nowhere worshipped.[35] Our poet seems to have been aware of some genuinely Thracian cultic realities, which he used to dignify an unpromising tragic hero and perhaps to astonish his audience again at the end of the play. An easy connection would have been provided by Amphipolis, the goal of several further Athenian expeditions between 422 and 360/59 BC. Their military and economic aspirations for the lower Strymon valley ended only with the rise of the Macedonian kingdom (921–2a n.).

Appendix: The 'Macedonian Theory'

In this context mention must be made of Liapis' hypothesis that *Rhesus* was first produced in Macedon during the reign of Philip II or Alexander the Great (i.e. between ca. 350 and 330 BC).[36] So late a dating does not seem to fit what little external evidence we possess (cf. pp. 27–8), but above all the theory rests on a series of arguments from the play which do not bear close examination. The Pangaean cult of Rhesus has already been established as of potential interest to the Athenians, and even if this were not the case, we know too little about fourth-century tragedy to tell whether a cult *aition* that bore no relationship to Attica would have been impossible. Six further points are put forward in *JHS* 129 (2009), 71–88 (n. 36):

---

alternative name for the Bithynian Rhebas (*NH* 6.4). Cf. Solin. 43.1 and, further on the Trojan river, D. Detschew, *Die thrakischen Sprachreste*, Vienna 1957, 397.

34 Lightfoot, *Parthenius*, 553. St. Byz. β 97 Billerbeck also declares Bithys, the ancestor of the Thracian Bithyans, to be a son of Ares and Rhesus' sister Sete. The relationship of the anonymous *SH* 939 (II AD) with our tale is unclear.

35 Cf. V. Liapis, *Kernos* 24 (2011), 96. Ustinova (*Kernos* 15 [2002], 283 n. 154) assumes that Cicero ignored the fringes of the known world.

36 The main publications are in Θυμέλη, 159–88 and *JHS* 129 (2009), 71–88. See also *CQ* n.s. 57 (2007), 408–11 (on the non-Greek character of the cult envisaged by the Muse) and his commentary *passim*. He suggests as author the tragic actor Neoptolemus, who spent some time at the court of Philip II.

(1) The *peltai* borne by Rhesus and his people in 305–6, 311–13, 383–4, 409–10 and 485–7 'do not seem to be the small, light, crescent- or round-shaped shields' (p. 74) normally connected with Thracian warriors (who to the Athenians were known as auxiliaries first in the Persian army and later in their own), but rather resemble the larger round Macedonian *peltai* carried by the main infantry troops.

(2) *Rh.* 2 ὑπασπιστῶν ... βασιλέως 'recalls a Macedonian technical term, ὑπασπισταὶ οἱ βασιλικοί, which designated the Foot Guardsmen associated with the Macedonian king' (p. 77). These apparently developed under Philip II.[37]

(3) When in 26–7 πέμπε φίλους ἰέναι ποτὶ σὸν λόχον, / ἁρμόσατε ψαλίοις ἵππους the sentries ask Hector 'to send his 'friends' to his 'own cavalry company' and order that the horses be harnessed' (p. 78), this may refer to the Macedonian heavy cavalry, called ἑταῖροι or φίλοι, and more specifically the king's personal squadron (ἴλη ἡ βασιλική).

(4) The chorus' outspoken manner towards Hector (cf. 23–33, 76–7, 131–2) and his deference to their judgement (137) may reflect Macedonian ἰσηγορία, the traditional right of every soldier to express his own opinion.

(5) The introduction of Aeneas as an adviser to Hector (85–149), without any hint of 'the strained relations' between him and 'the house of Priam' (*Il.* 13.459–61, 20.178–86, 302–8), could have been meant to bring on stage and 'cast in as glorious a light as possible the man who was by some accounts a mythical ancestor of certain Macedonians', having founded 'a number of cities in the region named Aenus and Aenia after him' (p. 81).

(6) The pro-barbarian attitude of *Rhesus*, combined with distinct hostility towards the Greeks and their patron goddess Athena (especially in 938–49) is 'best ... explained by the hypothesis that [the play] was produced before an audience wary of Athens, and of Greece as a whole' (p. 83).

To each of these arguments one or more objections can be raised:

(1) Thracians in drama are regularly equipped with *peltai* (e.g. *Alc.* 498 ~ *Rh.* 370–2, E. fr. 369.4, Ar. *Lys.* 563). At the same time tragedy tends to describe 'mythical' fighting in terms of contemporary hoplite warfare, transferring the appropriate gear and/or vocabulary to the epic heroes. This almost certainly also happened with regard to Rhesus and his men (cf. 305–6a, 311–13, 383–4, 485–7nn.). Note that 370–3 seems to presuppose a crescent-shaped shield (372b–3a n.).

---

37 Cf. R. D. Milns, *Historia* 16 (1967), 509–12.

(2) The lexical similarity, striking as it appears, may be coincidental, especially since the normal interpretation of the phrase as 'the king's squires' (2–3n.) avoids a near-tautology with 3 ἢ τευχοφόρων ('ordinary soldiers').[38] It is possible, however, that ὑπασπισταί had a history of denoting the private retinue of the Macedonian nobility and king (as opposed to the later corps of 3000 (!) men), in which case a 'northern' allusion could exist.[39]

(3) *Rh.* 26 far more probably means 'Send for your friends to join your company', with absolute πέμπω, 'send word', governing an infinitive clause. In that case the allusion is to *Il.* 10.53–179 + 299–302, where the Greek chiefs and Hector respectively call together their most important companions (23–51, 26nn.).

Hector's unit also appears in 577 (n.). As for the harnessing of the horses (27), there is no need to think of anything but Homeric chariot warfare. Aeneas warns of the risks should the vehicles get stuck in the Achaean trench (116–18n.).

(4) In 339–41 (339, 340–1nn.) Hector is equally deferential to the combined views of the coryphaeus and the Shepherd, who is no soldier. 'Weak leadership' and a propensity for peremptoriness, which Hector shows elsewhere (152–3, 264–341, 808–19nn.), do not exclude each other (indeed often go together), and a more active chorus of soldiers than in *Ajax* or *Philoctetes* needed something to say (cf. 131–6n.). Absolute realism was not upheld.

(5) In choosing a less obscure Trojan than Polydamas to caution Hector, our poet may have taken account of Aeneas' Balkan links (85–148n.). But Thrace rather than Macedon suggests itself in a play about Rhesus, who according to Hippon. fr. 72.7 *IEG* was Αἰνειῶν πάλμυς. The Iliadic tensions between Aeneas and Hector are omitted, or probably never thought of, as irrelevant to the plot.

(6) Emphasis on 'barbarian' valour is natural in a tragedy (the only one we possess) that portrays the Trojans on the brink of victory over the Greeks. But for the audience their optimism is always coloured by the knowledge that the dawning day will bring a decisive turning-point in the war (cf. ch. I). Individual Trojans do not look so good either: Dolon's bravery (154–223) can be assumed to have faltered in the face of Odysseus and Diomedes and Paris is easily hoodwinked by Athena (642–67).

The essential dominance of the Greek side throws a different light also on the Muse's anger towards Athena, which is as understandable as

---

38 For Liapis (p. 77) the 'Macedonian' interpretation would do so.
39 M. Fantuzzi, *JHS* 127 (2007), 161. Cf. R. D. Milns, *Historia* 20 (1971), 187.

it is futile. At 974–9 she can only anticipate the death of Athena's protégé Achilles (after he has killed Hector), and whether she threatens Athens with cultural decline depends on the text and interpretation of 948–9 (n.). It seems improbable that ambitious Macedonians of the mid-fourth century BC would have liked to be associated with the failing Trojan cause.

III. Authenticity and Date

1. External Evidence

When J. J. Scaliger laconically pronounced *Rhesus* spurious in 1600,[1] he could support his claim with one ancient piece of evidence. According to Hyp. (b) *Rh*. (64.25–6 = 430.23–4 Diggle), 'some' suspected that the play was not by Euripides because it rather showed a 'Sophoclean stamp' (τοῦτο τὸ δρᾶμα ἔνιοι νόθον ὑπενόησαν, Εὐριπίδου δὲ μὴ εἶναι· τὸν γὰρ Σοφόκλειον μᾶλλον ὑποφαίνειν χαρακτῆρα). Unfortunately, there remains no clue to the date or identity of these doubters, and despite some Sophoclean echoes in language and dramatic structure (pp. 31–9, 41), it is not clear what Σοφόκλειον … χαρακτῆρα was supposed to mean.[2]

Otherwise no indication survives that *Rhesus* was considered inauthentic in antiquity or Byzantine times. On the contrary, Hyp. (b) *Rh*. (64.26–7 = 430.24–5 Diggle) = Arist. fr. 626 Rose explicitly identifies the play with a genuine one of that name recorded in the *didascaliae* (ἐν μέντοι ταῖς διδασκαλίαις ὡς γνήσιον ἀναγέγραπται). This entry, which presumably caused the false attribution in Alexandria (below), must have been for a year between Euripides' first performance in 455 (*Peliades*) and 438 BC (*Alcestis*),[3] for Crates of Mallus is likely to have drawn on it[4] when excusing a supposed astronomical error in *Rh*. 528–31 as due to the poet's youth (527–31n.). The correct interpretation of the passage goes back to the Alexandrian Parmeniscus, who also knew the

---

[1] *M. Manili Astronomicon* …, Leiden 1600, 6–7: '*Nam ecce auctor Rhesi Tragoediae vetustissimus, qui sine dubio non est Euripides …*' (cf. 8). Seven years before M. A. Del Río (Delrius) had already attributed the play to 'Euripides II' (*Syntagma tragoediae latinae in tres partes distinctum*, Antwerp 1593, 22). For a brief review of the debate since then see Jouan, X–XV.

[2] Ritchie 11–15. To his cases of an author's χαρακτήρ being invoked in questions of authenticity (13) add Σ^A *Il*. 18.39–49 (IV 443.19–21 Erbse) ὁ τῶν Νηρεΐδων χορὸς προηθέτηται καὶ παρὰ Ζηνοδότῳ ὡς Ἡσιόδ<ε>ιον ἔχων χαρακτῆρα.

[3] Between these years Euripides competed in the 83rd Olympiad (448/7–445/4 BC) and won his first victory in 442/1 BC (DID D 1 60, D 3 *TrGF*), but we do not know with which plays.

[4] Taken from Aristotle's compilation or a full version of Aristophanes of Byzantium's hypothesis (65.48–58 = 431.45–432.53 Diggle). Cf. Pfeiffer, *History of Classical Scholarship* I, 242 and Kannicht on *TrGF* V.2 (60) ΡΗΣΟΣ.3–4.

play as Euripidean. His learning, seen also in the correct explanation of προταινί as Boeotian (523–5a n.), may have reached the ancestor of the V-scholia through Didymus.

In a similar way, Crates and Aristarchus are opposed by ΣΣ^V *Rh.* 5 and 540 on the order of the night-watches in 538–45 (n.). Crates again seems to have mentioned Euripides by name (Σ^V *Rh.* 5 [II 326.13–15 Schwartz = 78.7–9 Merro]), and given that Aristarchus' pupil Dionysodorus did the same in his *Errors in the Tragedians* (507b–9a n.), it is reasonable to assume with Ritchie (54) that the master, who perhaps also taught Parmeniscus, supported the ascription.

The remaining old scholia in V share the view of the competing scholars,[5] and in their often petty criticism of individual passages match those for the other 'Selection' plays.[6] There is certainly no evidence for a Hellenistic edition intended to prove *Rhesus* spurious, as Wilamowitz wished to reconstruct.[7]

If we grant that neither the great Euripides nor a namesake wrote the *Rhesus* we have, we must assume the existence of two homonymous plays, one of which disappeared very early on and was supplanted in the tradition by the other one. Most probably this happened in Alexandria, where, despite all efforts and the relatively good documentation for Athenian drama, the librarians did not always achieve satisfactory results. We hear of several texts that did not survive (οὐκ ἐσῴζοντο).[8] For the same reason presumably Ar. *Ran.* 1269/70 = A. fr. 238 could not be firmly located in Aeschylean lyrics,[9] whereas Cratinus' *Satyroi* and Eupolis' *Noumeniai* are mentioned only once each.[10] Conversely, the Medicean catalogue of Aeschylus records Αἰτναῖαι γνήσιοι and Αἰτναῖαι νόθοι (A. T 78 *TrGF*), that is, the Alexandrians had copies of both plays and

---

5   Cf. Σ^V *Rh.* 251 (II 332.7–8 Schwartz = 89.5 Merro) κέχρηται δὲ καὶ νῦν Εὐριπίδης τῇ παροιμίᾳ παρὰ τοὺς χρόνους and Σ^V *Rh.* 430 (II 337.14–19 Schwartz = 100 Merro), where *Or.* 220 is quoted as if by the same poet.
6   Ritchie 47–55.
7   *De Rhesi scholiis*, 10–12 = *KS* I, 9–12 and *Einleitung*, 155–6. The theory rests mainly on his unwarranted emendation of the probably misplaced (821–3n. with n. 292) Σ^V *Rh.* 41 (II 330.6–7 Schwartz = 82 Merro) τὸ χ ὅτι συνθέτως ἀναγινώσκεται (*sc.* πυραίθει) καὶ ὅτι οὐκ ἔστιν Εὐριπίδειος [ὁ στίχος] (del. Wilamowitz, i.e. 'because *the play* is not by Euripides') and has rightly been refuted by Porter (*Hermathena* 17 [1913], 366–8) and Ritchie (49–52).
8   So E. *Theristai*, a satyr-play (DID C 12 *TrGF* = Ar. Byz. Hyp. *Med.* 90.40–3 Diggle), Cratin. Χειμαζόμενοι (Hyp. I Ar. *Ach.* 2.4 Wilson [*PCG* IV, 244]), all but one or two of Lysippus' comedies (Lysipp. T 3 *PCG* = *IG* 14.1097.7–9 = *IG Urb. Rom.* 1.216.7–9) and an unknown, perhaps satyric, play connected in some way with E. *Oenomaus* and *Chrysippus* (Hyp. (g) *Phoen.* 81.6–7 Diggle).
9   Cf. ΣΣ$^{vett.}$ Ar. *Ran.* 1269a/b/c (III 1a 143 Chantry), Σ$^{rec.}$ 1269a (III 1b 211 Chantry).
10 Cratin. *Satyroi*: Hyp. A5 3.10–12 Jones–Wilson (*PCG* IV, 232). Eup. *Noumeniai*: Hyp. I Ar. *Ach.* 2.4–5 Wilson (*PCG* V, 424). In general see Fraenkel, *Rev.* 229–30.

found ways to distinguish the 'genuine' from the 'spurious'. Questions unsolved (and unsolvable) since antiquity are the authorship of several comedies[11] and in particular whether the famous 'atheistic' Sisyphus speech, which is partially preserved in Sextus Empiricus (*Adv. Math.* 9.54) and elsewhere, belongs to Euripides' satyric *Sisyphus* of 415 or an otherwise unattested play of that title by Critias (88 B 25 DK = *TrGF* 43 F 19; cf. *TrGF* V.2, 658–9).[12] Likewise, the tragedies *Tennes*, *Rhadamanthys* and *Pirithous* are doubted in the *Life of Euripides* (E. T 1 IA § 9 ~ IB § 5 *TrGF*), and for the last one there is independent evidence for confusion with Critias (Ath. 11.496b = Critias 88 B 17 DK = *TrGF* 43 F 2).[13] The ascription of *Prometheus Bound* to Aeschylus, on the other hand, may have been uncontested.[14]

There was thus ample scope for error in the attribution of plays – more than in the fourth century, when little systematic research on drama was done,[15] memories of performances were still fresher and only the odd book-trader, actor or producer may have tried to pass off an obscure or anonymous text as the (re-discovered?) work of a fifth-century classic. In the case of *Rhesus* the Alexandrians will have acquired at least one such nameless, or wrongly inscribed, copy and identified it with the lost Euripidean tragedy in the *didascaliae*. They may have been particularly eager to fill a gap among the poet's early plays, which by their very antiquity were most likely to have perished.[16]

---

11   Including four of Aristophanes (*Poiesis*, *Dionysos Nauagos*, *Nesoi*, *Niobos*), which 'some said were by [his contemporary] Archippus' (*Vit. Aristoph.* 1.59–61 *PCG*). Cf. Ritchie 24.
12   In the latter case the other fragments must follow, since 'it is ... most unlikely that both *Sisyphoi* survived the fifth century BC and were then quietly transmitted side by side' (R. Kannicht, in C. Mueller-Goldingen – K. Sier (eds.), ΛΗΝΑΙΚΑ: *Festschrift für Carl Werner Müller*, Stuttgart – Leipzig 1996, 27).
13   Whether a tetralogy *Tennes*, *Rhadamanthys*, *Pirithous*, *Sisyphus* should be given to Critias (Wilamowitz, *Analecta Euripidea*, 161–6; cf. *Einleitung*, 40–2, 'Memorandum', edd. J. M. Bremer – W. M. Calder III, *Mnemosyne* IV 47 [1994], 211–16) cannot be discussed here nor indeed decided from the extant data. 'Suffice to say that acceptance of Critias as author of the 42 lines considered above does not necessarily entail acceptance of *either* his further authorship of the disputed *Peirithous or* of the notion that the *Sisyphus* was written to accompany the above-mentioned tragedies' (M. Davies, *BICS* 36 [1989], 32). Cf. C. Collard, in J. A. López Férez (ed.), *Da Homero a Libanio ...*, Madrid 1995, 183–93 ~ *Selected Papers*, 56–68 and Collard–Cropp, *Euripides VIII. Fragments*, 629–35.
14   If, as West plausibly suggested (*Studies*, 67–72, *CQ* n.s. 50 [2000], 339 = *Hellenica* II, 229–30), Aeschylus' son Euphorion wrote and staged the play, or in fact the entire Prometheus trilogy, under his father's name and it was so entered in the *didascaliae*.
15   Apart from Aristotle and his pupil Dicaearchus. Previous efforts had primarily been directed at tragic mythography, e.g. Asclepiades of Tragilus' six books of Τραγῳδούμενα (below) and Philochorus' Περὶ τῶν Σοφοκλέους μύθων (cf. J. Rusten, *GRBS* 23 [1982], 361–2 with n. 22).
16   Cf. J. S. Scullion, in D. Cairns – V. J. Liapis (eds.), *Dionysalexandros. Essays ... in Honour of Alexander F. Garvie*, Swansea 2006, 188. According to Kannicht's (n. 12) and

III. Authenticity and Date 25

As has just been indicated, it is possible (though much less probable) that a spurious *Rhesus* had already before 300 BC become established under Euripides' name. Proof of this, and indeed of authenticity, has sometimes been derived from the quotation in Hyp. (b) *Rh*. (64.29–32 = 430.26–431.29 Diggle) of a one-verse iambic prologue fragment after a hypothesis ascribed to Dicaearchus (fr. 81 Wehrli = 114 Mirhady):

πρόλογοι δὲ διττοὶ φέρονται· ὁ γοῦν Δικαίαρχος ἐκτιθεὶς τὴν ὑπόθεσιν τοῦ Ῥήσου γράφει κατὰ λέξιν οὕτως·

Νῦν εὐσέληνον φέγγος ἡ διφρήλατος.[17]

Yet whereas Nauck's Δικαίαρχος for δικαίαν (VL: om. Q) is certain,[18] we can hardly be sure that Dicaearchus really wrote those alphabetically arranged plot summaries which in their original form invariably added the first line for identification and are known since Zuntz as *Tales from Euripides*.[19] It is far more plausible that Sextus Empiricus' attestation of Dicaearchan ὑποθέσεις τῶν Εὐριπίδου καὶ Σοφοκλέους μύθων (*Adv. Math.* 3.3 = Dic. fr. 78 Wehrli = 112 Mirhady) represents a case of later mythography falsely credited to a famous scholar.[20] Diggle, most recently, endorsed a date between the second century BC and the first

---

Scullion's (197–8 n. 7) calculations, only two (or three) of the fifteen (or sixteen) dramas by Euripides that did not reach Alexandria were tragedies, the others satyr-plays.

17 [E.] fr. 1108 N.² = E. fr. 660a N.²-Sn. = *TrGF* V.2 (60) ΡΗΣΟΣ, 642.8. A supplement for the next line, more suitable to the action of *Rhesus* than Ἕως διώκει ... (Snell, διώκουσ' Diggle) may be something to do with Nyx (J. Rusten, *GRBS* 23 [1982], 360 n. 17). For 'Night' driving a chariot cf. *Cho.* 660–1, A. fr. 69.6–7 and *Ion* 1150–1 (A. Fries, *Mnemosyne* IV 66 [2013], 816 with n. 4).

18 A. Nauck, *Aristophanis Byzantii Grammatici Alexandrini Fragmenta*, Halle 1848, 254. Recent attempts to defend the paradosis (A. Tuilier, *Sileno* 9 [1983], 11–28 [21–3], P. Carrara, *ZPE* 90 [1992], 35–44 [40–3]) do not convince. See V. Liapis, *GRBS* 42 (2001), 313–16, who then, however, follows Kirchhoff (*Philologus* 7 [1852], 563–4) and others in regarding the whole end of Hyp. (b) *Rh.* as Dicaearchan, on the basis of which he would reconstruct a lost work including both plot narratives and more theoretical dicussions.

19 Zuntz, *Political Plays*, 135, although Wilamowitz (*Analecta Euripidea*, 183–4, *Einleitung*, 134 n. 19, 170) had already deduced the existence of such a collection and compared it to *Lamb's Tales from Shakespeare*. As Sophoclean examples have also come to light (P. Oxy. 3653, 3013), 'narrative hypotheses' may now be a better title (van Rossum-Steenbeek, *Greek Readers' Digests?*, 1–2). Dicaearchan authorship was particularly defended by M. W. Haslam, *GRBS* 16 (1975) 149–74 (150–6) and W. Luppe, in J. Wiesner (ed.), *Aristoteles. Werk und Wirkung* I, Berlin – New York 1985, 610–12 and in W. W. Fortenbaugh – E. Schütrumpf (eds.), *Dicaearchus of Messana. Text, Translation, and Discussion*, New Brunswick – London 2001, 329–32.

20 J. Rusten, *GRBS* 23 (1982), 357–67, R. Kassel, in W. J. Aerts *et al.* (eds.), Σχόλια. *Studia ... D. Holwerda oblata*, Groningen 1985, 53–9 = *KS*, 207–14, Scullion (n. 16), 198 n. 9.

century AD, on the basis of the author's extensive use of 'Asianic' rhythmical clausulae.[21]

Nevertheless, the attestation of this and a second additional prologue in Hyp. (b) *Rh.* (64.33–65.47 = 431.30–44 Diggle), which the compiler (or his source) was able to define from autopsy as an actor's interpolation 'not worthy of Euripides', suggests that our *Rhesus* was revived at least twice in the fourth century BC. An audience 'brought up' on Euripidean expositions may have been irritated at the archaising opening parodos, which so perfectly sets a mood of disorder and suspense, but does not well prepare for the reversals of the plot (1–51n.), and the obvious solution was to supply an iambic speech or dialogue providing all the information that was missed. These revivals must have been a success – or the interpolations would not have got into circulation to survive in 'wild' copies until at least the second century BC. That Aristophanes of Byzantium did not know them can be deduced not only from our standard text, but also from the statement in his hypothesis that the sentry chorus 'delivered the prologue': Hyp. (c) *Rh.* 65.56–7 = 432.52–3 Diggle ὁ χορὸς συνέστηκεν ἐκ φυλάκων Τρωϊκῶν, οἳ καὶ προλογίζουσι. The Alexandrians did not as a rule omit passages they deemed spurious.[22]

The very possibility of multiple re-performances would lead us to place *Rhesus* relatively early in the fourth century, even if we are not bound by the notion that Dicaearchus knew it as Euripidean around 300 BC. A rough *terminus ante quem* (and evidence for an almost immediate non-theatrical interest in the play) may indeed be given by sources as different as vase-paintings and a scholarly text.

From the middle of the fourth century (ca. 360–340 BC) we have three splendid Apulian vessels with illustrations of Rhesus' death.[23] Their main pictures, showing Diomedes in flight or attack, while Odysseus is leading away the famous horses, follow *Iliad* 10. Yet one crater (Berlin, Antikensammlung, Inv. 1984.39) adds in the top right margin (next to

---

21 J. Diggle, in G. Bastianini – A. Casanova (eds.), *Euripide e i papiri* ..., Florence 2005, 27–67. A *terminus ante quem* is provided by the first-century AD P. Mil. Vogl. II 44 (Pack² = Mertens–Pack³ 398).
22 Pfeiffer, *History of Classical Scholarship* I, 113–15, 173–4. Cf. V. Liapis, *GRBS* 42 (2001), 318–19, also against the theory of Carrara (n. 18) that Aristophanes' note on the προλογίζων is a later addition. For the formulation cf. e.g. Ar. Byz. Hyp. (g) *Phoen.* 81.7–8 Diggle ὁ χορὸς συνέστηκεν ἐκ Φοινισσῶν γυναικῶν. προλογίζει δὲ Ἰοκάστη and Hyp. *Pers.* 3.7–8 West ἐνταῦθα δὲ προλογίζει χορὸς πρεσβυτῶν.
23 *LIMC* VIII.1/2 s.v. Rhesos 3, 4, 6. Cf. L. Giuliani, *Tragik, Trauer und Trost. Bildervasen für eine apulische Totenfeier*, Berlin 1995, 31–3, 94–102, *BICS* 41 (1996), 71–86 (with plts. 16–20), Jouan, LXI–LXIII, O. P. Taplin, *Pots & Plays. Interactions between Tragedy and Greek Vase-Painting of the Fourth Century B.C.*, Los Angeles 2007, 160–5, 283 (notes).

Athena) a female figure in pathetic pose and below her a horned man, whom conch and reed identify as a river god. Given the influence that Attic tragedy seems to have exerted on the south-Italian vase painters, the couple is most easily interpreted as Rhesus' divine parents, Strymon and the Muse, who were probably first introduced in our play (p. 13).

Secondly, a comment by Asclepiades of Tragilus (cf. n. 15), who may be the same as the tragic victor at the Lenaea of 352 BC (DID A 3b 54 *TrGF*), has with some plausibility been referred to *Rhesus*. The source is an almost identical note in Hesychius, Photius and the *Suda* on a fragmentary verse from Epicharmus (Hsch. ρ 272 Hansen ~ Phot. ρ 103 Theodoridis ~ *Suda* ρ 143 Adler):

Ῥῆσος ἀρχός, ὃς †ῥέει† τὰ θέσφατα· ἤτοι παρὰ τὴν ῥῆσιν εἴρηκεν, ἤ, ὡς Ἀσκληπιάδης ἐν ἕκτῳ Τραγῳδουμένων (*FGrHist* 12 F 5), ἄριστον αὐτὸν γεγονέναι ἀλήθειαν εἰπεῖν (Epich. fr. 206 *PCG*). ἐγένετο δὲ καὶ ἕτερος.

Ῥῆσος ἀρχός Schmidt: Ῥησόσαρχος Hsch: Ῥησός· ἀρχός Phot.: Ῥησίαρχος *Suda*   ῥέει Hsch: ἐρέει Suda: αἱρέσει Phot.: χρέει Schmidt, θροεῖ Liapis, <ἐ>ρ[ε]εῖ Hansen (contra metrum)   post θέσφατα add. παρ' Ἐπιχάρμῳ Phot., Suda   <διὰ τὸ> ἄριστον Jacoby

---

As it is unlikely that Asclepiades in his Τραγῳδούμενα wished to explain an obscure gloss from Sicilian comedy,[24] several authorities have thought of the Muse's prediction at *Rh.* 970–3.[25] Rhesus' future status as a heroic Bacchus prophet on Mt. Pangaeus (970–1, 972–3nn.) could indeed be alluded to in <διὰ τὸ> ἄριστον αὐτὸν γεγονέναι ἀλήθειαν εἰπεῖν, especially since no other dramatisation of the myth can safely be posited for Asclepiades' days. But absolute certainty is impossible.

It should be stated that this interpretation of the external evidence, with its consequences for the dating of *Rhesus* and the way it entered the Euripidean tradition, represents the *communis opinio* of those who regard the play as spurious. Liapis' theory that *Rhesus* was written for a Macedonian audience between 350 and 330 BC, which is untenable also on other grounds (pp. 18–21), requires him to dismiss Asclepiades and the Apulian vase and, more importantly, to assume that the two prologue fragments in Hyp. (b) *Rh.* belong to the genuine early work of Euripides

---

24 V. Liapis, *ZPE* 143 (2003), 20.
25 Kaibel on Epich. fr. 205, M. L. West, in Hansen's apparatus on Hsch. ρ 272 (of which mine is an abridged and adapted version). More hesitantly V. Liapis *ZPE* 143 (2003), 20–2.

and were transmitted through Dicaearchus.[26] Yet apart from the doubtful association of Dicaearchus with any kind of tragic hypotheses, it is hardly conceivable that this drama survived until the late fourth century BC (and with an alternative prologue in some copies), only to vanish soon after and become one of the very few Euripidean tragedies that did not reach Alexandria. Moreover, the second prologue seems specifically composed for our *Rhesus*, and not enough of the first is preserved to prove that it could not have been. It would require an extraordinary similarity of plot structure for the expositions to fit both plays and for the author of Hyp. (b) *Rh.* (or a predecessor) to attach them to the wrong one.[27]

To sum up, if the extant *Rhesus* is not by Euripides, it belongs in all likelihood to the first quarter or third of the fourth century BC. Evidently popular on stage, it remained current long enough for at least one copy to reach Alexandria, where (most probably) it was falsely identified as Euripidean. The edition by Aristophanes of Byzantium and the scholarly work we can glimpse through the hypotheses and scholia secured its place in the corpus until in late antiquity it became one of Euripides' 'select' plays (ch. III.4). Like the 'ἔνιοι' in Hyp. (b) *Rh.* (and as in the case of *Prometheus Bound*), modern scholars have to rely on internal criteria, from language, style and dramaturgy,[28] to show that *Rhesus* was not written by the man tradition claims.

2. Language and Style

Of the various internal grounds that can be advanced for or against the authenticity of a text language and style are often the most conclusive, but in the case of ancient literature hardest to assess on the basis of usually limited material for comparison. In particular, the pitfalls of judging by individual words and phrases, without taking account of the subject-matter, context or an element of chance, have been brilliantly (if very polemically) exposed by Douglas Young,[29] and for *Rhesus* we need only remember the changes that subsequent discoveries have caused in the eighteenth- and nineteenth-century lists of ἅπαξ λεγόμενα,

---

26 V. Liapis, *GRBS* 42 (2001), 328, in Θυμέλη, 173–7 ~ *JHS* 129 (2009), 85–6 and his commentary on Hyp. (b) *Rh.* (pp. 59–60, 62–5).
27 Ritchie 35–7 and also A. Fries, *Mnemosyne* IV 66 (2013), 815–16. In addition to Asclepiades and the vase painting, the possible reminiscence of *Rh.* 161–83 in Men. *Peric.* 271–91 (cf. p. 44 with n. 87) would have to be explained away.
28 It has long been shown that neither the stichic nor the lyric metres afford conclusive evidence to the dating and authorship of the play (cf. Fraenkel, *Rev.* 236–7, Liapis, lxiv–lxvii).
29 *G&R* 6 (1959), 96–108.

III. Authenticity and Date   29

ἅπαξ τραγῳδούμενα and expressions shared with one other (group of) tragedian(s) only.[30] Also, regarding our play, it is obvious that almost any 'intertextual' argument from a work later than the mid-fifth century BC entails a suggestion of *petitio principii*, if the genuine *Rhesus* of Euripides indeed belonged in that period (p. 22). Yet whereas such linguistic idiosyncrasies as the author's repetitiveness (a) and eclectic vocabulary (b) can only be described with an eye to general tragic practice, the sheer number, character and diversity of his poetic recollections (c) should suffice to settle the question of priority and establish a connection with post-classical drama (d).

(a) Repetition

Perhaps the most noticeable (and notorious) trait of the trimeter and, to a lesser extent, the tetrameter, anapaestic and lyric versification of *Rhesus*[31] is the high incidence of verbal repetition, which exceeds even what is found in Euripides[32] and only occasionally seems unavoidable (41–2, 125–6a, 135b–6nn.)[33] or to fulfil a specific function (149–50, 154–5, 543–5nn.). Entire phrases, moreover, tend to have equivalents in other drama and, whether then re-used or not, occupy the same metrical position before or after the main caesurae. Unfortunately, apart from certain set locutions,[34] we do not know how many of these, especially Euripidean, verse-openings and -ends (recorded throughout the commentary) formed part of a developed tragic *koine*,[35] as opposed to a single author's

---

30 Ritchie 143, 150–1, 170–1, 175, Fraenkel, *Rev.* 230. Cf. *Rh.* 214–15, 551–3 (ἰάν), 736–7nn.
31 M. Parry (*HSPh* 41 [1930], 96–7, 98 = *The Making of Homeric Verse*, 284–5, 286) notes how the irregular metres of choral song inhibit the formation of set expressions. He also warns against unthinkingly equating tragic iterations with traditional epic formulae (80–4, 97–114 = 272–5, 285–98).
32 See Ritchie 218–25, who compares to *Rhesus* collections of recurrent junctures in *Hippolytus* and *Bacchae*, without, however, specifiying their metrical positions or any artistic effect they might have.
33 Cf. Ritchie 218–19. The plentiful allusions to night and darkness, so intrinsic to the setting and atmosphere of our play, can be related to the frequency with which the similarly repetitive author of *Prometheus Bound* refers to the *skene* as 'rock', 'hill' or 'crag' (Griffith on *PV* 15).
34 Cf. e.g. *Rh.* 57 (56–8n.) ... Ἀργείων στρατόν, 577 (n.) τί δῆτ᾽ ἂν εἴη; 669 (668–9n.) Λαερτίου παῖ, 915 (915–16n.) ... εἰς Ἅιδου μολών.
35 A term coined by P. T. Stevens, *CR* n.s. 15 (1965), 270 (cf. H. D. F. Kitto, *YCS* 25 [1977], 318–19, Liapis, lviii–lix). Few of the 'fifth-century' half-lines which recur in the minor tragedians (Th. K. Stephanopoulos, *ZPE* 75 [1988], 3–38) may be identified as (semi-)conscious contextual borrowings: e.g. Chaerem. *TrGF* 71 F 30 ~ *Andr.* 1008, Theodect. *TrGF* 72 F 2.1 ~ E. *El.* 1278 (two hated mothers) and Theodect. *TrGF* 72 F 10.1–2 ~

recognisable predilections. One would be surprised, however, if Aristophanes' ληκύθιον-joke (*Ran.* 1198–1247) were not also aimed at this 'formulaic' quality in Euripides' style, which like his other mannerisms and relative simplicity of diction would have made exploitation by later contemporaries and successors all the easier.[36]

(b) Vocabulary

In its lexicon *Rhesus* shows a curious blend of such Euripidean plainness and a liking for the archaic and precious, which manifests itself not only in the poetic adaptations discussed under (c), but also in the more or less incidental use of remarkable words or phrases from different categories.

Like the other tragedians and lyric poets, the author of *Rhesus* employed a variety of epic and epic-style expressions. Some are shared with one or more of his predecessors, so that it is hardly possible to specify the source,[37] others were evidently suggested by the Homeric models for his plot (cf. 72–3, 233–5a, 509b, 557–8, 908–9nn.). An 'intertextual' relationship can also be detected at 29 (28–9n.) ... Λυκίων ἀγὸν ἀνδρῶν and, with reference to Achilles or Ajax, 492 (n.) θοῦρον, 494 (494–5n.) μηνίων and 461–3 (n.) ... ὑπομεῖναι. Similarly, both former and envisaged battles are marked as 'epic' by the appropriate language (408–10a, 477–8, 479, 480, 485–7nn.), while the Charioteer in his lament and messenger speech attempts in vain to meet heroic standards (756–803, 762–3a, 776–7nn.). In contrast, several verb-forms without parallel in tragedy or lyric seem merely intended to raise the overall stylistic level: 514 (513b–15n.) ἀμπείρας, 525 (523–5a n.) δέχθαι, 629 μεμβλωκότων, 811 (810b–12a n.) ἐξαπώσατε.

The same applies to the regular presence of words (especially compound adjectives and adverbs) which on our evidence were favourites of, or probably coined by, Aeschylus: e.g. 58 σύρδην, 77, 656, 737 τορῶς, 79, 158, 476 κάρτα, 222 ἀναιμάκτῳ, 390 προσήμενον, 646 πρευμενής, 724, 805 (nn.) δυσοίζων (-ου), 932 φιλαιμάτους, 962

Phoen. 3. Among the *adespota* (Th. K. Stephanopoulos, *ZPE* 73 [1988], 207–47) attribution to one of the 'big three' is often a possibility.

36 See P. T. Stevens, *CR* n.s. 15 (1965), 270. As regards diction, *Rh.* 42 (41–2n.) ὄρφναν, 164, 271 ... (κ)οὐκ ἄλλως λέγω, 351–2, 393, 923 μελῳδοῦ, μελῳδίας, 509 θάσσων, 625 κομψά, 662 (n.) φροῦδος, 722 φόβος μ' ἔχει, 750 φονίου and 974 ... τῆς θαλασσίας θεοῦ are sanctioned by comic parody (especially Aristophanes). Cf. D. Sansone, *BMCR* 2013.03.15.

37 E.g. *Rh.* 97 ἐπ' εὐσέλμων νεῶν, 255 οὐτάσει, 825 ἔβριξ', 827 μή μοι κότον ... θῇς and 932–3 φιλαιμάτους / ἀλκὰς κορύσσοντ', where see the commentary notes. Cf. A. C. Pearson, *CR* 35 (1921), 55.

μελάγχιμον. The list is supplemented by such unique formulations as 8 (n.) βλεφάρων γοργωπὸν ἕδραν (~ 554 ὄμματος ἕδραν), 260 (257b–60n.) κακόγαμβρον ... γόον, 288 (287–9n.) αὐτόρριζον ἑστίαν χθονός and 971 (970–1n.) ἀνθρωποδαίμων. Some of these may at least in part have Aeschylean precedents.[38]

Our poet's taste for the unusual is further seen in various rarities, including, as Fraenkel (*Rev.* 234) pointed out, words that have pre-fourth-century equivalents only in Euripides' latest plays. Thus two adjectives that once counted as ἅπαξ λεγόμενα (215 δίβαμος, 737 ἀμβλῶπες) are accompanied by e.g. 296 προυξερευνητάς (~ *Phoen.* 92 προυξερευνήσω), 426 ἀγχιτέρμων (~ S. fr. 384), 441 (440–2n.) ἐπεζάρει (= *Phoen.* 45), Boeotian προταινί (523–5a n.) and what appear to be medical terms at 711 (710–11n.) ὕπαφρον, 784–6 (n.) ἀρτηριῶν and 789 (n.) μυχθισμόν. In view of the last two classes, it is not surprising to find also Ionisms at 322 (322b–3n.) ἐξώστης, 633 (n.) ὑπάρχειν (with a predicative participle) and perhaps 881 (879–81n.) κελεύθου λεωφόρου.[39]

Owing to the theme of *Rhesus*, the low-style sector is particularly represented by military expressions paralleled in the historians: 6 προκάθηνται, 125 (125–6a n.) κατάσκοπον, 136 (135b–6n.) ναυστάθμων, 146, 673 ὁλκοῖσι (-ούς), 311 πελταστῶν, 521 (521–2n.) ξύνθημα, 595 λιπόντε Τρωϊκῶν ἐκ τάξεων, 604 ἐσδρομὴν ποιούμενον, 664 τάξιν φυλάξων, 768–9 κἀφεδρεύοντας νεῶν / πρύμναισι, 954 γῆς ἔφεδρον. By the same token, a number of colloquialisms (partly, one suspects, of the soldierly kind) cluster in the comic-satyric chasing scene (675–91, 680, 686nn.) and the speech of the humble Charioteer (759, 770–2, 784–6nn.), where they strikingly contrast with his 'epic' pretensions. Otherwise few words or turns of phrase can reasonably be assigned to that register: 87–9 τί χρῆμα ...; 149 ... οἳ πάρεισιν ἐν λόγῳ, 195 μέγας ἀγών (in lyrics), 285 φαῦλος, 574, 729, 885 ἔα (ἔα), 625 τρίβων (in a Euripidean reminiscence), 870 ἅλις, 874 αὖ. Most of these had entered tragic diction with Euripides (if not other mid- to late-fifth-century playwrights) and so do not contradict our poet's general quest for a high-flown style.

(c) Poetic Borrowings

What really distinguishes *Rhesus* from the body of surviving tragedy is the manner and extent to which it relies on other drama, epic and lyric poetry, ranging from the adaptation of whole scenes to the collocation of

---

38 Cf. A. C. Pearson, *CR* 35 (1921), 56 with n. 1, Fraenkel, *Rev.* 238.
39 Cf. Fraenkel, *Rev.* 239 and 445b–6n. (against the inclusion of ἡμέραν ... ἐξ ἡμέρας).

memorable words or passages, and including several instances from later Euripides and Sophocles. Naturally the divisions merge so that, for example, Odysseus' and Diomedes' entrance dialogue in 565–94 (n.) features such linguistic overlaps as may, in any authors who share a literary language, be due to the description of similar situations (570–1, 574–9, 574nn.). But we also find at the beginning a fine example of more specific lexical association (565–6n.).

Likewise 675–91 (n.) illustrates what may be called 'reverse composition' in that two successive *Rhesus* passages seem inspired by one model. The agitated choral imperatives at 675b (n.) βάλε βάλε βάλε· θένε θένε θένε and 685 (n.) †πέλας ἴθι παῖε πᾶς† can all be related to Ar. *Ach*. 280–3 (Χο.) οὗτος αὐτός ἐστιν, οὗτος· / βάλλε, βάλλε, βάλλε, βάλλε, / παῖε, παῖε τὸν μιαρόν. / οὐ βαλεῖς; οὐ βαλεῖς; and an analogous picture emerges if one compares 677/680 (680n.) λεῦσσε· τοῦτον αὐδῶ. / δεῦρο δεῦρο πᾶς and 730 (n.) σῖγα πᾶς ὕφιζ'· ... with Ar. *Ach*. 238–40 (Χο.) σῖγα πᾶς. ἠκούσατ', ἄνδρες, ἆρα τῆς εὐφημίας; / οὗτος αὐτός ἐστιν ὃν ζητοῦμεν. ἀλλὰ δεῦρο πᾶς / ἐκποδών. Without connection to a particular scene add *Rh*. 48 + 261–3 (nn.) ~ *IA* 171–7 (cf. pp. 34, 36), *Rh*. 970 (970–1n.) + 972 ~ *Cyc*. 293–4 and perhaps *Rh*. 949 + 952–3 (nn.) ~ *HF* 911–12.[40]

In order to elucidate our poet's 'intertextual' practice, it will nevertheless be well to take a systematic approach and, moving from large to smaller patterns, consider (i) 'one-to-one' scenic adaptations, (ii) scattered reminiscences of continuous tragic passages, (iii) 'mosaic-like combinations of borrowed expressions',[41] (iv) 'noun with attribute' phrases as a sub-category of the latter and (v) peculiarities of diction that appear to result from unconscious reception. Often we will discover contextual and purely verbal echoes side by side, and it should cause no surprise that war-plays and 'slices from the great Homeric banquets' (Ath. 8.347e ~ Eust. 1298.56–8 = A. T 112a, b *TrGF*) supply a significant proportion of its assumed sources. To judge by the number of parallels with A. *Myrmidons*, we might easily be able to expand the selection if more were preserved.[42]

(i) While different typological models lie behind the entry of Odysseus and Diomedes and their encounter with the chorus (above), other scenes

---

40   In *Rh*. 82 (n.) ... ἐν τροπῇ δορός + 819 τὸ μηδὲν εἶναι ... ~ *Ai*. 1275 ἤδη τὸ μηδὲν ὄντας ἐν τροπῇ δορός the second 'part' comes too late and is too common a phrase to be significant (cf. Ritchie 202–3).
41   Fraenkel, *Rev*. 233.
42   On *Myrmidons* see below (pp. 34–5 with n. 53). Another welcome reference to a lost drama which seems to have wider connections with our play is *Rh*. 967–9 (n.) ~ A. (?) fr. 99.13–14 (*Cares* = *Europa*). Cf. above (p. 14).

and choral odes in *Rhesus* were evidently inspired by a single fifth-century precedent. The clearest example is Athena's epiphany, which in structure and expression (rather than spirit and dramatic purpose) is heavily indebted to the *Ajax* prologue (595–674n.). A similar relationship exists between the 'Dawn-Song' in 527–64 (n.) and the first three stanzas of the *Phaethon* parodos (63–86 Diggle = E. fr. 773.19–42), although the lyrics were far more expertly converted into something new.[43] On a smaller scale, the third stasimon of *Ajax* (1185–1222) is probably echoed in the chorus' reverie of peace at 360–7 (n.), and we may also see the influence of *Bacchae* in Dolon's disguise (201–23n.) and the Shepherd's report of Rhesus' approach (264–341n.).

Much less can be said with regard to Sophocles' *Poimenes* (cf. 264–341, 342–79, 388–526nn.). Wilamowitz went too far in seeing there the fifth-century prototype of *Rhesus*,[44] especially since only one slight verbal parallel survives among its certain remains (770–2n.).[45] But he was right to observe the analogies between the Idaean Shepherd and the Goatherd who announces the arrival of Cycnus' army at Troy (S. frr. 502–4),[46] and also between the hero's boasts (S. frr. 500?, 501, 507?) and those of Hector, Dolon and Rhesus.[47] That our play may generally have been inspired by a tragedy on (or recounting) Cycnus' death is further suggested by Ar. *Ran.* 962–3, where 'Euripides' criticises 'Aeschylus' for having terrified his spectators 'by creating characters like Cycnus and Memnon with bells on the cheek-plates of their horses' (tr. Sommerstein). Aristophanes' κωδωνοφαλαροπώλους to describe the exotic Trojan allies arguably left its own trace in *Rh.* 306b–8 and 383–4 (nn.).[48]

(ii) Another category of scenic adaptation involves the openings of three, possibly four, tragedies which, like *Ajax* and *Poimenes*, resemble *Rhesus* in subject-matter and/or the basic situation.

---

43 With the help also of a choral-lyric reminiscence at *Rh.* 554–6 (n.) ~ Pi. *Pyth.* 9.23–5, Bacch. *Pae.* 4.76–8 and probably Alcm. 3 fr. 1.7 *PMGF*.
44 *De Rhesi scholiis*, 12 = *KS* I, 13 and, more reserved, *Hermes* 61 (1926), 282–3 n. 3, 284, 288 = *KS* IV, 409–10 n. 3, 411, 415.
45 A stronger linguistic connection would be established if S. fr. 859 ~ *Rh.* 33, 383–4 (nn.) could be firmly ascribed to *Poimenes*. See also S. fr. 515 ~ *Rh.* 380 (380–1n.).
46 So Wilamowitz (*De Rhesi scholiis* = *KS* I, 13, *Hermes* 61 [1926], 282 = *KS* IV, 409). It can hardly have been the Greeks, as Welcker and others surmised, since they did not arrive over land (Sommerstein, in *Sophocles. Selected Fragmentary Plays* II, 181, 203 [on fr. 502]).
47 Cf. Sommerstein (n. 46), 180–1, 204–6 (on frr. 500, 501, 507) and 388–526n. with n. 147.
48 See also ch. III.3 (p. 41) and 380–7n. on a possible chariot entry in A. *Memnon* and *Rhesus* and, for the overall pattern behind the theatrical representations of Cycnus, Memnon and Rhesus, Ritchie 99–100, M. P. Pattoni, *PapLup* 9 (2001), 313–31 and ch. II.1 (pp. 13–14).

Klyve (41–2) had already isolated from the many lexical and contextual echoes of *Seven against Thebes* a series that almost in order of appearance refers to the prologue (1–77) alone: *Rh.* 19 νυκτηγορίαν, 89 νυκτηγοροῦσι ~ *Sept.* 29 νυκτηγορεῖσθαι, *Rh.* 20–2 (n.) ~ *Sept.* 59–60, *Rh.* 514 πυλῶν ἐπ' ἐξόδοισιν ... ~ *Sept.* 33, 58, *Rh.* 632 κατόπτας ... στρατοῦ ~ *Sept.* 36, 41 (+ 369), *Rh.* 932 φιλαιμάτους ~ *Sept.* 45 φιλαίματον.[49] An equally strong tendency of this kind seems to exist in connection with *Persians*, where the anapaestic-lyric parodos (1–154) provided not only numerous salient words and phrases,[50] but also the notion of a vast army doomed to destruction with its overbold leader (264–341, 309–10nn.) and a model for bringing the chorus on stage at once (cf. p. 40 and 1–51n.).

The fact that this type of borrowing only works in one direction becomes relevant for the dating of *Rhesus* when a similar pattern emerges with regard to the disputed prologue anapaests of *Iphigenia in Aulis* (1–48 + 115–62):[51] *Rh.* 12 θρόει ~ *IA* 143 (?), *Rh.* 16 ~ *IA* 2–3, *Rh.* 274 πρὸ χειρῶν ... βαστάζομεν ~ *IA* 36 πρὸ χερῶν ... βαστάζεις and *Rh.* 529–30 ἑπτάποροι / Πλειάδες ~ *IA* 7–8 τῆς ἑπταπόρου / Πλειάδος. The impression that our poet used Euripides' final play – and knew it more or less as we do – is corroborated by several further analogies, especially with its parodos (*IA* 164–230): *Rh.* 48 + 261–3 ~ *IA* 171–7, *Rh.* 356 βαλιαῖσι πώλοις ~ *IA* 220–2 πώλους ... βαλιούς, *Rh.* 467 ... τῆς μακρᾶς ἀπουσίας ~ *IA* 651 μακρὰ ... ἡ 'πιοῦσ' ἀπουσία, 1172 ... διὰ μακρᾶς ἀπουσίας. By contrast, the occurrence of adjectival βασιλίς in *Rh.* 718 and *IA* 1306 may be coincidental, and the same applies to the conceptual parallel in *Rh.* 904–5 (n.) and *IA* 469–70.[52]

Among lost plays, it is interesting to observe that three out of five verbal or syntactical overlaps with A. *Myrmidons* come from its likewise

---

49 From only just outside the prologue note *Rh.* 290 (n.) ~ *Sept.* 79–80 and otherwise *Rh.* 49–51 (n.) ~ *Sept.* 651–2, *Rh.* 122 (n.) ~ *Sept.* 447–8 (cf. p. 35), *Rh.* 158 (158–9a n.) ~ *Sept.* 658 (+ *Eum.* 90), *Rh.* 306b–8 + 383–4 (nn.) ~ *Sept.* 385–6, *Rh.* 568b–9 (n.) ~ *Sept.* 245 + 249 (cf. p. 37), *Rh.* 770 (770–2n.) ~ *Sept.* 287 + 288–9 (cf. p. 37) and *Rh.* 796 (795b–6n.) ~ *Sept.* 593.

50 *Rh.* 30 (n.) σφαγίων ἔφοροι ~ *Pers.* 25 στρατιᾶς πολλῆς ἔφοροι, *Rh.* 58 (56–8n.) σύρδην ~ *Pers.* 54, *Rh.* 117 (n.) ἱππηλάται + 254, 763 (253–5a, 763b–4a nn.) πεδοστιβής (-εῖ) ~ *Pers.* 126–7 πᾶς ... ἱππηλάτας / καὶ πεδοστιβὴς λεώς (?), *Rh.* 311 τέλη ('divisions') ~ *Pers.* 47, *Rh.* 375 (375b–7n.) σὲ γὰρ οὔτις ὑποστάς ~ *Pers.* 87 δόκιμος δ' οὔτις ὑποστάς, *Rh.* 741 (n.) διόπων στρατιᾶς ~ *Pers.* 44 βασιλῆς δίοποι. For further reminiscences of *Persians* see below (p. 35–6) and 53–5, 72–3, 96–8, 290, 436–7, 471–2, 734–5nn.

51 The prologue question is reviewed by W. Stockert (ed.), *Euripides. Iphigenie in Aulis* I. *Einleitung und Text*, Vienna 1992, 66–79, to which add D. Kovacs, *JHS* 123 (2003), 77–103 (80–3, 101–2).

52 Cf. A. Fries, *CQ* n.s. 60 (2010), 348 with nn. 16–18 (also on *Seven against Thebes*).

anapaestic-lyric parodos (cf. 404–5, 557–8, 763b–4a nn.).[53] Given that we can only compare what exists, it would be imprudent to place too much weight on this; yet the use of the first two lines of the lyric part (A. fr. 132) in the parody of Aeschylean song at Ar. *Ran.* 1264–77 probably indicates that the passage was famous,[54] and it seems safe to state that the beginnings of texts are generally better remembered than the rest. Our poet would have been no exception to that rule.

(iii) Fraenkel based his case against the authenticity of *Rhesus* above all on the author's habit of combining notable expressions of different provenance, which in that form is not found in any of the 'three great tragedians'. He did not usually spell out the 'intertextual' relationship between the passages, so that further systematisation is possible. At times his collection will silently be supplemented.

Some examples of this 'mosaic-technique' show a contextual overlap with both supposed models. The Charioteer's grim depiction of Rhesus' death at 790–1 (n.) θερμὸς δὲ κρουνὸς δεσπότου παρὰ σφαγῆς / βάλλει με δυσθνῄσκοντος αἵματος νέου recalls both the murder of Agamemnon at *Ag.* 1389–90 and, in the irregular compound participle δυσθνῄσκοντος, that of Aegisthus at E. *El.* 842–3. 'Wily' Odysseus, connects 498–9 ἔστι δ' αἱμυλώτατον / κρότημ' Ὀδυσσεύς with *Ai.* 388–9 and S. fr. 913, of which the first supplied the superlative epithet and the second the disparaging noun (498b–500n.). Similarly, Achilles in 122 (n.) acquired expressions used elsewhere for proud or overconfident warriors (*Sept.* 447–8, *Ai.* 221/2, 1088 + *Or.* 1568), while in describing Odysseus at 713b–14 (n.) our poet may have thought of Orestes and Pylades on their way to kill Helen (*Or.* 1125 + 1271–2).

More often only one of the two (or three) identifiable source passages resembles *Rhesus* in content. When in 404–5 (n.) Hector accuses Rhesus of having failed him as an ally (σὺ δ' ἐγγενὴς ὢν βάρβαρός τε βαρβάρους / Ἕλλησιν ἡμᾶς προύπιες τὸ σὸν μέρος), the verb προπίνω, which in the same sense is previously found only in A. fr. 131.3 (*Myrmidons*), follows a variation of the contextually unrelated *IT* 31 ... βαρβάροισι βάρβαρος.[55] Rhesus justifies his delay with a Scythian attack and the generally difficult journey to Troy (424–42). The account takes much from *Persians* (cf. 388–453n.), including two impressive

---

53 On the first passage see further below and for the other correspondences 312–13, 814–15nn.
54 At the outset of the contest between 'Aeschylus' and 'Euripides' (Ar. *Ran.* 911–20) *Myrmidons* and *Niobe* are ridiculed for their silent 'opening-tableaux'. Cf. 'Scene and Setting', 114 and 1–51n. (p. 116).
55 The verse-end is varied again at 833 ... βάρβαρός τε βαρβάρου, where the nouns belong to different syntactical units.

'composite passages': *Rh.* 430–1 (n.) ~ *Pers.* 816–17 + *Alc.* 850–1 (*IT* 300) and *Rh.* 440–2 (n.) ~ *Pers.* 500–1 + *Phoen.* 45–6 + E. *El.* 820, *HF* 959.[56] An excellent specimen of literary 'purple patches' from outside tragedy being combined in such a way is *Rh.* 72–3 (n.) ~ *Il.* 8.512–15 + Pi. *Pyth.* 1.28 + Pi. *Isthm.* 8.49–50.

Even in the case of purely lexical adaptations a connection of thought can sometimes be detected. At 817–18a (n.) ἤτοι μάραγνά γ' ἢ καρανιστὴς μόρος / μένει σε δρῶντα τοιάδ' two notable words from the *Oresteia* come together in one line: cf. *Cho.* 375 διπλῆς ... τῆσδε μαράγνης δοῦπος and *Eum.* 186–7 καρανιστῆρες ... / δίκαι σφαγαί τε. The latter stems from Apollo's list of cruel punishments meted out in barbarian lands (*Eum.* 186–90), which also supplied a precedent for Rhesus' threat to impale Odysseus in 513–15 (512–17, 513b–15nn.). No such 'intertext' exists for 739–40 ποῦ δῆθ' Ἕκτωρ / τὸν ὑπασπίδιον κοῖτον ἰαύει; Yet the metrical association with *Ai.* 1408 τὸν ὑπασπίδιον κόσμον φερέτω may suggest that our poet also had in mind *Ai.* 1204 οὔτ' ἐννυχίαν τέρψιν ἰαύειν, where the epic verb is used in the same way (cf. 740n.).

(iv) In *CQ* n.s. 60 (2010), 345–51 I examined 'noun + attribute' collocations unique to *Rhesus*, in which each term can independently be traced to a common source. The intention was to defend 118 (n.) θραύσαντες ἀντύγων χνόας as an authorial conflation of S. *El.* 745–6 ἔθραυσε δ' ἄξονος μέσας χνόας, / κἀξ ἀντύγων ὤλισθε, but a persistent and generally perhaps less conscious form of poetic borrowing also emerged. This section will review the earlier finds and add two further examples of a similar kind.

In one variety of the pattern a choice adjective qualifies a noun which separately stands nearby in its closest or only extant parallel. Thus ναυσιπόρος ('seafaring') is restricted to *Rh.* 48 (n.) ναυσιπόρος στρατιά and *IA* 171–3 (ἔμολον ...) Ἀχαιῶν στρατιὰν ὡς ἐσιδοίμαν / Ἀχαιῶν τε πλάτας ναυσιπόρους ἡ- / μιθέων, and although it may also have occurred elsewhere,[57] other echoes of the *IA* parodos (cf. p. 34) suggest it was recalled from there and joined with the preceding στρατιά(ν). The same phenomenon (with 'composition') can be detected in *Rh.* 605–6 (n.)

---

56 Less obvious cases from other scenes are *Rh.* 690–1 (690, 691nn.) ~ *Or.* 1353–5 + *Cho.* 288–9 and *Rh.* 699–701 (699–701, 701nn.) ~ *Tro.* 187–9, 241–2 + *Hcld.* 84, although the latter may rather be a question of stock language used for a particular topic (cf. pp. 31–2). Similarly, thematically linked 'half-verse formulae' are joined at *Rh.* 871 ποῖ δὴ τράπωμαι δεσπότου μονούμενος ~ *Ba.* 1366 (ποῖ γὰρ τράπωμαι ...) + *Alc.* 380 (... δῆτα σοῦ μονούμενος) and perhaps *Rh.* 894 (893b–4n.) δόλιος Ὀδυσσεὺς ἀξίαν τείσει δίκην ~ *Phil.* 608 (δόλιος Ὀδυσσεύς ...) + *Med.* 802 (... τείσει δίκην).

57 Cf. Fraenkel, *Rev.* 235.

τὰς ... Ἕκτορος / ... καρατόμους σφαγάς ~ *Tro.* 562–6 (+ *Andr.* 399) and *Rh.* 618 (n.) ποταμίου κύκνου πτερόν ~ *Hel.* 215 + E. *El.* 151–2.

A second class of attributive collocations tends to involve unusual nouns. Here Fraenkel (*Rev.* 231) had already analysed 569 (568b–9n.) δεσμῶν ἀραγμὸν ἱππικῶν as a fusion of *Sept.* 245 ἱππικῶν φρυαγμάτων and 249 ἀραγμός, and Fantuzzi (*MD* 36 [1996], 183–5) did the same for 715 (715–16n.) ἀγύρτης τις λάτρις in semantic relation to *Od.* 4.245 οἰκῆϊ ἐοικώς and 4.247–8 ἄλλῳ δ' αὐτὸν φωτὶ ... ἤϊσκε / ΔΕΚΤΗΙ (taken to mean 'beggar' rather than as a proper name). Similarity of context also accounts for *Rh.* 276–7 (n.) ~ *Or.* 688–90, whereas *Rh.* 118 (n.) ~ S. *El.* 745–6 (above) is explicable by recollection of the famous 'fake' messenger speech in S. *El.* 680–763.

On the analogy of these, and especially the linguistically awkward 118, it may not be far-fetched to see in 111 (110b–11n.) νυκτὸς ἐν καταστάσει (with λαμπτῆρας preceding in 109) a somewhat muddled adaptation of *Ag.* 22–4 ὦ χαῖρε λαμπτήρ, νυκτὸς ἡμερήσιον / φάος πιφαύσκων καὶ χορῶν κατάστασιν / πολλῶν. More straightforwardly again 255b–7a (n.) τετράπουν / μῖμον ἔχων ἐπὶ γαίας / θηρός seems to echo both *Hec.* 1058–9 and A. fr. 57.8–11 (*Edoni*).

(v) Finally, some light may be thrown on other difficult expressions by supposing they betray mechanical adaptation or even misunderstanding of tragic material.

The clearest examples of this are probably 389 (388–9n.) παλαιᾷ σ' ἡμέρᾳ προσεννέπω, where reference to *Ai.* 624–5 παλαιᾷ ... ἔντροφος ἁμέρᾳ, / λευκῷ τε γήρᾳ μάτηρ explains rather than justifies the application of παλαιᾷ ... ἡμέρᾳ to Rhesus' last-minute appearance, and 770 (770–2n.) κἀγὼ μελούσῃ καρδίᾳ λήξας ὕπνου, which Fraenkel (*Rev.* 238) had recognised as a hasty reworking of *Sept.* 287 μέλει, φόβῳ δ' οὐχ ὑπνώσσει κέαρ (+ 288–9 γείτονες ... καρδίας / μέριμναι).

To these we may add *Rh.* 201 (201–2n.) ~ *Tr.* 262–3, *Rh.* 604 (603–4n.) λόγχῃ πλατεῖαν ἐσδρομὴν ποιούμενον ~ E. fr. 495.29–30 (*Captive Melanippe*) [λόγ]χῃ πλατείᾳ συοφόνῳ δι' ἥπατος / [παίσ]ας, *Rh.* 636–7a (n.) ~ *Cho.* 659–60, *Rh.* 780 (n.) ... δόξα τις παρίσταται ~ *OT* 911 ... δόξα μοι παρεστάθη (in a different sense) and *Rh.* 870 (n.) μὴ θνῇσχ·’ ἅλις γὰρ τῶν τεθνηκότων ὄχλος, which owes much of its peculiarity to the fact that μὴ θνῇσχ’ (~ *Alc.* 690, *IA* 1419) lacks a sense-defining adverbial supplement. On a more general level, the choral entrance-announcement for Aeneas at 85–6 (n.) is too close to *Hec.* 216–17 to be fully appropriate to the situation, while the Muse's 'mortal' pain at the loss of her son in 980–2 (980–2, 980nn.) may come from *Hyps.* fr. 60 ii.90–1 Bond = E. fr. 757.921–2.

(d) Conclusion and Outlook

The preceding enquiry should leave no doubt that, arguably from reading as well as theatre practice, our poet was familiar with the whole range of fifth-century drama and, alongside epic and lyric poetry, exploited even its most original language as a means to express his own thoughts and embellish the vernacular of his trade. Some of his poetic habits can also be related to post-classical tragedy, although comparison there is even more severely hampered than in the case of earlier works by the scarcity of what remains.

In a manner redolent of the *Rhesus* 'Dawn-Song' and the *Phaethon* parodos, Carcinus the Younger (*floruit* 380–76 BC)[58] largely followed the third stasimon of *Helen* (1301–68, especially 1301–37) when he composed his iambic account of Demeter's search for Kore in Sicily (Carc. II *TrGF* 70 F 5),[59] and it is instructive to see how two other passages contributed a resounding epithet and a useful 'verse-end formula' each: *Hel.* 517–19 ὡς Μενέλαος οὔ- / πω μελαμφαὲς οἴχεται / δι' ἔρεβος ~ Carc. II *TrGF* 70 F 5.3 δῦναί τε γαίας εἰς μελαμφαεῖς μυχούς[60] and *Cyc.* 95 πόθεν πάρεισι Σικελὸν Αἰτναῖον πάγον ~ Carc. II *TrGF* 70 F 5.6 καὶ γῆν μὲν Αἰτναίοισι Σικελίας πάγοις.

Parallels for our poet's 'mosaic' technique are harder to find in genuine fourth-century fragments than in certain actors' interpolations. The second iambic prologue to *Rhesus*, which is composed of various 'fifth-century' lines and half-lines,[61] provides an extreme example. More to the point, Fraenkel compared (supposed) insertions in *Phoenissae*[62] and the undoubtedly spurious end of *Seven against Thebes* (1005–78), where in addition to borrowings from the play itself,[63] the influence of *Antigone*

---

58 Carc. II *TrGF* 70 T 1 = *Suda* κ 394 Adler Καρκίνος ... Ἀθηναῖος ... ἤκμαζε κατὰ τὴν ρ' ὀλυμπιάδα (380/79–377/6 BC), πρὸ τῆς Φιλίππου βασιλείας τοῦ Μακεδόνος.
59 See Xanthakis-Karamanos, *Studies in Fourth-Century Tragedy*, 87–9, Th. K. Stephanopoulos, *ZPE* 75 (1988), 6–7 and Kannicht on *Hel.* 1306–7, 1321–2. Carcinus repeatedly visited Sicily (Timae. *FGrHist* 566 F 164 = D. S. 5.5.1), and our fragment is the first explicit witness for this relocation of the legend (Richardson, *Homeric Hymn to Demeter*, 76–7).
60 Cf. *Rh.* 962 οὐκ εἶσι γαίας ἐς μελάγχιμον πέδον. The adjective μελαμφαής does not occur elsewhere.
61 Th. K. Stephanopoulos, *ZPE* 73 (1988), 208. Cf. above (p. 26).
62 Fraenkel, *Rev.* 233. Cf. *Zu den Phoenissen*, especially 76–81, 82–3, 101–13, 117–18 and *Rh.* 149–94 (pp. 175–6 with n. 74), 728–55 (+ 'Metre') nn.
63 Cf. *Sept.* [1018–19] θεῶν πατρῴων, οὓς ἀτιμάσας ὅδε / στράτευμ' ἐπακτὸν ἐμβαλὼν ᾕρει πόλιν ~ *Sept.* 582–3 πόλιν πατρῴαν καὶ θεοὺς τοὺς ἐγγενεῖς / πορθεῖν, στράτευμ' ἐπακτὸν ἐμβεβληκότα and *Sept.* [1036–7] κοιλογάστορες / λύκοι ~ *Sept.* 496 κοιλογάστορος κύκλου (of Hippomedon's shield).

and *Phoen.* 1625–82⁶⁴ extends to the smallest matters of diction.⁶⁵ The difference from *Rhesus* lies in the straightforward transposition of a tragic motif (Creon's and Antigone's dispute over the burial of Polynices) to an earlier dramatisation of the same story and, as *mutatis mutandis* in *Phoenissae*, the all but exclusive concentration on the relevant sources for theatrical and linguistic inspiration alike. One would like to know how the celebrated playwrights of the fourth century treated the classic material.

3. Dramatic Technique

Rhesus is well known for rapid action and theatrical excitement, which must have been a major cause of its initial survival. As in its language, we observe, among several 'unconventional procedures' discussed in the commentary,⁶⁶ a highly idiosyncratic mixture of 'old-style' and 'progressive' elements, aimed apparently at indulging a later audience's tastes with a maximum of spectacle and naturalistic turns.

Both these objectives underlie the sentry chorus, which has been created against the testimony of *Il.* 10.416–20 φυλακὰς δ' ἃς εἴρεαι, ἥρως, / οὔ τις κεκριμένη ῥύεται στρατὸν οὐδὲ φυλάσσει. / ὅσσαι μὲν Τρώων πυρὸς ἐσχάραι ... / οἳ δ' ἐγρηγόρθασι φυλασσέμεναί τε κέλονται / ἀλλήλοις. Their role is the only suitable one in the circumstances.⁶⁷ It allows them to take an active part in the play and, together with their excitable character, easily motivates the direction and manner of their stage-movements. The much-criticised lack of military common sense in that *all* the watchmen go respectively to rouse Hector (1–51n.) and their Lycian relief (527–64n.)⁶⁸ would

---

64 Hutchinson (on *Sept.* 1005–78) persuasively argues for the priority of the *Phoenissae* scene, which he thinks genuine. But even an interpolation could have been used by a subsequent writer.
65 See *Sept.* [1007–8] Ἐτεοκλέα ... / θάπτειν ἔδοξε γῆς φίλαις κατασκαφαῖς + [1037–8] τάφον γὰρ αὐτῷ καὶ κατασκαφὰς ἐγώ / ... μηχανήσομαι ~ *Ant.* 920 ζῶσ' ἐς θανόντων ἔρχομαι κατασκαφάς + 891–2 ὦ τύμβος ... ὦ κατασκαφής / οἴκησις (Barrett, *Collected Papers*, 328–9), *Sept.* [1013–14] ~ *Phoen.* 1628–30 (1629b = *Ant.* 26b) + E. *El.* 896, *Sept.* [1028] + [1052–3] ~ *Phoen.* 1657 and *Sept.* [1045] ~ *Phoen.* 1656.
66 See 149–94n. (Dolon's entry and Hector's silence in 191–265), 264–341n. (the Shepherd staying on after delivering his message), 595–674n. (Paris played by a fourth actor) and 804–81n. (Hector's return from an unspecified direction and the Charioteer remaining on stage). The term 'unconventional procedures' is taken from J. P. Poe, *Philologus* 148 (2004), 21–33.
67 G. Björck, *Arctos* n.s. 1 (1954), 16–17, *Eranos* 55 (1957), 14, Ritchie 94–5.
68 Wilamowitz, *Hermes* 61 (1926), 286 = *KS* IV, 414. Cf. Burlando, *Reso*, 35 n. 25, Liapis, xli with n. 117.

either have passed unnoticed or been accepted as a piece of dramatic necessity.[69]

An archaising impression is given immediately by the anapaestic-lyric parodos, which does not resemble anything Euripidean and, for all its divergences in form and spirit, rather harks back to the choral openings of Aeschylus' *Persians, Supplices, Myrmidons, Nereids, Niobe* and especially perhaps the spurious *Prometheus Unbound* (1–51n.). Not for nothing, moreover, the first words of the turbulent, and possibly 'scattered' (σποράδην), epiparodos recall the Erinyes on the hunt (675–91, 675b nn.), and it may also be relevant that both *Myrmidons* and *Nereids* belong to the Iliadic(-Cyclic) Achilles trilogy[70] and show other connections with our play (cf. pp. 13–14, 34–5).

From the historical perspective, this handling of the chorus – almost as if our poet had followed Aristotle's precept that it 'should be treated as one of the actors, form an integral part of the whole and join in the action' (*Poet.* 1456a25–7 καὶ τὸν χορὸν δὲ ἕνα δεῖ ὑπολαμβάνειν τῶν ὑποκριτῶν, καὶ μόριον εἶναι τοῦ ὅλου καὶ συναγωνίζεσθαι) – may have been a reaction against its gradual loss of significance, and particularly Agathon's alleged introduction of ἐμβόλιμα ('interludes').[71] We need not believe in Aristotle's linear account of this decline (*Poet.* 1456a27–30), and there is good reason to think that, as in Middle Comedy, at least some of the post-classical tragic titles in the plural (e.g. Agatho *Mysoi*, Dicaeog. *Kyprioi*, Moschio *Pheraioi*, Lyc. *Marathonioi*) designate their, however detached, chorus.[72]

Another feature redolent of early tragedy is the neglect of the stage-building as part of the dramatic landscape ('Scene and Setting', 114 with n. 1).[73] In accordance with *Iliad* 8 and 10, Hector's sleeping-place in the temporary Trojan camp, which forms the centre of the action, is called εὐναί, κοῖται (1n.) and χάμευναι φυλλόστρωτοι (9n.) rather than 'hut' or 'tent' as in other military plays (cf. *Ai.* 3–4, *Hec.* 53, *Tro.* 32–3, *IA* 1, 12, 189–90)[74] and indeed also in *Rhesus* when the Greeks

---

69 Hector's accusation that the sentries let the enemies slip by (804–81, 808–19nn.), which is foreshadowed by their fear in 722–7 (692–727n.) and immediately followed by self-defence (820–32, 821–3nn.), perhaps hints at the 'problem'.
70 Cf. M. Fantuzzi, *Entretiens Hardt* LII, 142 n. 22, *JHS* 127 (2007), 162.
71 Cf. O. P. Taplin, *LCM* 1 (1976), 50.
72 Xanthakis-Karamanos, *Studies in Fourth-Century Tragedy*, 11, 12–13, 123.
73 See most recently S. Perris, *G&R* 59 (2012), 151–64 (especially 151–7, 160–1, 163–4). To his list of earlier literature (153 n. 11) add Wilamowitz, *Hermes* 61 (1926), 286 = *KS* IV, 413, G. Björck, *Arctos* n.s. 1 (1954), 16, P. Arnott, *Greek Scenic Conventions in the Fifth Century B.C.*, Oxford 1962, 100 and Klyve 104.
74 Perris (n. 73), 152 also considers Euripides' and Sophocles' *Palamedes*, which are set in the Greek camp. In Aeschylus' Achilles trilogy the acting area represents the interior of the hero's hut.

III. Authenticity and Date

are concerned (45, 61, 255). Likewise, the Trojans and their commander are said to rest in full armour by or under the cover of their shields (20–2, 123–4, 740nn.), while Rhesus has been assigned a bivouac (κατηύνασται) outside the ranks (611, 614). In contrast to *Eum.* 566–1047, however, where the presumably newly-invented *skene* fades into oblivion behind the Areopagus court,[75] the stage-building here retains its physical use as 'θεολογεῖον' for Athena and the Muse (595–674, 882–9nn.).

Given this archaising mise-en-scène, it would have been fitting for Rhesus to enter on a chariot, drawn by his splendid horses, at 380–7 (n.). To judge by Ar. *Ran.* 962–3 (… οὐδ' ἐξέπληττον αὐτούς, / Κύκνους ποιῶν καὶ Μέμνονας κωδωνοφαλαροπώλους), Aeschylus was famous for this device, which would have made particularly good sense on the pre-*skene* stage and, among his extant plays, is certainly found in *Persians* (155–8, 607–9) and *Agamemnon* (783–809, 906, 1039, 1054, 1070).[76] Yet, as is argued in the note above, we cannot be sure that *Rhesus* shared in the apparent fourth-century revival of chariot-borne arrivals. The text gives no conclusive evidence, and for strategic reasons our poet may not have wished to show the horses on stage. The vivid picture drawn by the Shepherd in 301–8 perhaps had to suffice.

Traces of new developments include the management of Athena, the Charioteer and the Muse. While Athena's mid-play epiphany as such appears to have had Aeschylean and Sophoclean as well as later Euripidean precedents (cf. 595–674n.), her transformation into another deity, Aphrodite, has often been regarded as impossible for the fifth century[77] and so far is paralleled only once in the mythical burlesque of Middle Comedy (642–74n.).

The multiple functions of the Charioteer as victim, messenger and accuser (728–55, 756–803, 804–81, 833–81nn.) also transcend the conventions of classical tragedy, as does the Muse, who unlike any other *deus ex machina* sings a strophic dirge from 'on high' (882–9, 890–914nn.). In terms of staging, however, an even bolder move may already have been attempted in *Prometheus Bound*, if the chorus of Oceanids (minor deities like the Muse) performed their 'flying' parodos and initial

---

75 Sommerstein, *Eumenides*, 33 (although see Garvie, *Choephori*, xlvi–xlvii against his claim that in the first half of that play the building was also ignored). West's case for a *skene* in *Aigyptioi* remains speculative (*Studies*, 169–70), and A. fr. 58 (*Edonoi*) ἐνθουσιᾷ δὴ δῶμα, βακχεύει στέγη need not mean that, contrary to *Bassarai*, Lycurgus' palace formed the background.
76 Cf. Taplin, *Stagecraft*, 43, 76.
77 So e.g. Fraenkel, *Rev.* 240–1, Liapis, xxxix.

conversation with Prometheus (*PV* 114–283) on the *skene*-roof or somehow suspended from the crane.⁷⁸

The two epiphanies in *Rhesus*, as well as the brief, 'purpose-oriented' entries of Aeneas (85–148n.) and Paris (595–641, 642–74nn.), also contribute to the play's very large number of speaking characters (11), which is matched only by the late-Euripidean, and much longer, *Phoenissae* (11) and *Orestes* (10).⁷⁹ By the same token, its structurally well-placed pair of messenger-scenes seems to follow *Iphigenia in Tauris* (238–343, 1284–1434), *Helen* (597–757, 1512–1618), *Phoenissae* (1067–1283, 1335–1479), *Orestes* (852–956, 1368–1536), *Bacchae* (660–774, 1024–1152) and, as we have it, *Iphigenia in Aulis* (414–542, 1532–1629) rather than isolated earlier examples of such doubling as Sophocles' *Trachiniae* (180–99 + 335–496, 734–820) and *Antigone* (223–331, 384–445, 1155–1256 + 1278–1346). The fact that our poet adopted these techniques from far more expansive plays goes some way towards explaining our impression of hectic and at times truncated action, although given the underlying concept of divine responsibility (ch. I), it may also be 'an index of the complexity of events and the separateness and weakness of each character's impact on the overall [plot].'⁸⁰

For lack of evidence we cannot tell how far the eclectic stagecraft of *Rhesus* was typical of post-classical tragedy. But various ancient sources suggest that the late fifth and fourth centuries saw an increasing preference for spectacle, both in new productions and in revivals of old plays (especially, it seems, Aeschylus).⁸¹ *Rhesus* is well placed in this development and appears to have been popular enough to be revived itself, albeit with a choice of two iambic prologues prefixed to the parodos. Whoever wrote them meant to add clarity without depriving the audience of the first exciting scene.

---

78 For useful reviews of how the scene could have been staged see Taplin, *Stagecraft*, 252–60, M. L. West, *JHS* 99 (1979), 136–9 ~ *Hellenica* II, 262–7 (who proposed several cranes) and Griffith on *PV* 128–92.

79 *Phoenissae* was known as πολυπρόσωπον or παραπληρωματικόν already in antiquity (Hyp. (b) and (c) *Phoen.* 77.7, 78.1–2 Diggle). *Helen* has nine speaking roles (like *Andromache*), if at 1627–41 we reject the second servant in favour of the coryphaeus (cf. 149–94n. [p. 174]), while the other extant 'three-actor' plays waver between five (*Eumenides*, *Philoctetes*) and eight.

80 Mastronarde on *Phoen.* 1308–479 (p. 511).

81 Taplin, *Stagecraft*, 39–49, 477–9. Among the most telling evidence is the comic ridicule of Xenocles, son of Carcinus, as mechanically adventurous (*TrGF* 21 TT 3a, c, 33 T 4b), Aristotle's famous censure of poets who seek to arouse 'tragic' emotions only through ὄψις (*Poet.* 1453b7–11) and the repeated references in the *Life of Aeschylus* to the monstrous effects he obtained (A. T 1 §§ 7, 9, 14 *TrGF*; cf. 675–91n. [p. 371 n. 250]). Note also the kind of interpolation mentioned in 380–7n.

4. *Rhesus* and the 'Euripidean Selection'

Although *Rhesus* had been edited in Alexandria under a famous poet's name, it might still have perished before reaching the medieval tradition. Yet by the second or third century AD it had become part of the 'Euripidean Selection', the standard repertoire of ten plays (comprising also *Alcestis, Medea, Hippolytus, Andromache, Hecuba, Troades, Phoenissae, Orestes* and *Bacchae*) that were a mainstay of the ancient and Byzantine school curricula and survive in a separate line of transmission together with 'old' scholia.[82] It is likely that this canon resulted from a prolonged and self-reinforcing reduction process rather than, as Wilamowitz supposed, the choice of a single influential school-master.[83] Of the 75 or so Euripidean dramas that the Alexandrians collected some will already have been better known and so perhaps received priority treatment from exegetes; conversely, the existence of appropriate, and regularly modified, commentaries is liable to increase the popularity of a text. In time the range of plays performed and widely read diminished until it focussed on the ten in question. Barrett further suggests that seven to ten dramas (we have seven each of Aeschylus and Sophocles) were the content of a late-antique codex.

Spectacular stage action apart, the qualities which ensured the pre-Hellenistic survival of *Rhesus* will also have recommended it to a reading audience: a varied plot based on a well-known episode from 'Homer', relatively easy language (despite its many idiosyncrasies) and its brevity compared with other tragedies. Deviations from *Iliad* 10 invited literary adaptation, while for the last two reasons it may have been preferred to Aeschylus' and Sophocles' now lost Homeric tragedies,[84] especially when it came to finding suitable texts for education. By the same token *Prometheus Bound* stood at the head of the Byzantine triad of Aeschylus,[85] and the *Batrachomyomachia* 'was adopted as a school text, to make a short and entertaining introduction to Homer'.[86]

It is to some extent possible to trace the progress of *Rhesus* into the 'Selection' and beyond by way of its ancient literary reception and

---

82 Apart from *Bacchae*, which is only carried by the 'alphabetic' branch (LP). See p. 49 and p. 53 n. 39.
83 Barrett, *Hippolytos*, 50–3. For Wilamowitz' view see *Einleitung*, 173–203 (especially 173–4, 195–203).
84 In particular Aeschylus' Achilles trilogy (*Myrmidons, Phrygians, Nereids*) and A. (?) *Cares = Europa*, on which see pp. 13–14. Also A. *Psychagogoi, Penelope, Ostologoi* and S. *Nausicaa = Plyntriai* (all based on the *Odyssey*). The latter has sometimes been regarded as a satyr-play, like A. *Proteus* and *Kirke*.
85 Cf. Wilamowitz, *Einleitung*, 195.
86 West, *Homeric Hymns*, 235. Cf. H. Wölke, *Untersuchungen zur Batrachomyomachie*, Meisenheim am Glan 1978, 28–44.

quotations in scholarly and other sources. For practical reasons the two categories will be treated separately, although they partly overlap in time and supplement each other.

(a) Literary Reception

A number of Greek and Latin authors, both poets and prose writers, show the influence of *Rhesus*, suggesting that the drama was familiar in literary circles. In some cases, notably Menander, Virgil and Longus, the allusions must also have been intended to be recognised by the audience or readers.

In pre-Alexandrian times already Menander may have referred to *Rhesus*, if Fantuzzi and Konstan are right to see an echo of the 'guessing-game' between Hector and Dolon (161–83) in *Peric.* 271–91.[87] There Moschion's slave Daos claims credit for the move of his master's beloved Glycera into the house of his foster mother and asks for a reward. After going through several options for a 'good life' (including the command of the Greek land forces), they settle on a cheese stall, and Moschion asks Daos to investigate the situation in the house (*Peric.* 295–6 εἰσιὼν δέ μοι σύ, Δᾶε, τῶν ὅλων κατάσκοπος / πραγμάτων γενοῦ ...). Despite obvious comic distortion, the subject matter of the debate and its connection with a 'spying mission' – κατάσκοπος occurs nine times in *Rhesus* (125–6a n.) – makes adaptation of the Dolon scene a distinct possibility.

Accius (170 – ca. 86 BC) perhaps also referred to *Rhesus*, although too little of his *Nyctegresia*, another tragedy based on *Iliad* 10, survives to tell whether any part of it came from our play.[88] More promising is a fragment from his *Antigone* (Acc. Ant. fr. III Dangel = IV *TRF*[3]), which bears a striking resemblance to *Rh.* 532–3 (n.).

In the first century BC Parthenius of Nicaea wrote his Ἐρωτικὰ Παθήματα, a collection of thirty-six mythological vignettes dedicated to C. Cornelius Gallus. His tale of Rhesus and Arganthone (no. 36) corresponds to our play in significant points (cf. p. 17), and there may even be a verbal echo in the δασμός ('tribute') the hero imposed on the peoples he conquered: *Rh.* 435 (434–5n.) ~ *Erot. Path.* 36.1. Both Parthenius and Asclepiades of Myrlea (who may have been the source) were

---

[87] M. Fantuzzi – D. Konstan, in E. Bakola *et al.* (eds.), *Greek Comedy and the Discourse of Genres*, Cambridge 2013, 256–74, especially 265–73. Cf. 149–94n. (p. 174 n. 71).
[88] Ritchie 45–7 against, by implication, G. Pacitti, *Maia* n.s. 15 (1963), 184–98. See also M. Dangel, *Accius. Oeuvres (fragments)*, Paris 1995, 295–6.

scholars, of whom first-hand acquaintance with Greek tragedy could be expected.

By far the most extensive (and subtle) adaptation of the material stems from Virgil. The relationship of *Iliad* 10, *Rhesus* and the Nisus and Euryalus episode in *Aen.* 9.176–458 has been the subject of comprehensive studies[89] and can only be outlined here. While 'Homer' remains the main source of the nocturnal adventure, during which Nisus and Euryalus (on their way to Aeneas through enemy territory) devastate the Rutulian camp, but eventually fall victim to recklessness and are killed by an arriving cavalry unit, *Rhesus* appears to be responsible for numerous details. The Charioteer's speech (756–803) especially provided Virgil with models for the careless (and drunken) disorder among the Rutulians (762–9n.), the deaths of Remus and Rhoetus (789, 793–5a nn.) and perhaps also Nisus' and Euryalus' reaction to the challenge of Volcens (774b–5n.), which itself resembles that of the chorus to Odysseus and Diomedes at 682 (n.). Before their capture Nisus had restrained his younger companion from further killing in much the same way as Athena does for the Greeks in 668–72 (668–9n.). At the outset of the expedition observe how Aletes' praise for Nisus and Euryalus (*Aen.* 9.247–50) reverses the expression, but not the sentiment, of *Rh.* 245b–9a (n.).

While it seems improbable that Ov. *Her.* 11.111 reflects *Rh.* 896–7 (895–8n.), the verbal similarities between both D. Chr. 55.14 and *Rh.* 854b–5 (n.) and Aristid. *Or.* 1.106 Lenz–Behr and *Rh.* 335 (n.) may at least be due to unconscious reminiscence. The first two passages especially are related in content, and the relevant part of the *Rhesus* lines (οὐδ' ἀφιγμένον ... ἦσαν) pervades the later lexicographical tradition (below). But coincidence in the choice of (rather ordinary) words cannot be ruled out.

Around 200 AD, finally, Longus transferred to the pastoral world the motif of Dolon's wolf-disguise. When the cowherd Dorkon plans to sneak up on Chloe dressed as a wolf, the actual donning of the hide (1.20.2) reads almost like a prose version of *Rh.* 208–11a (n.) – to the point that the military background of the scheme (cf. 201–23n.) is recalled in the comparison of the animal's 'gaping jaws' (χάσμα) with a hoplite's helmet (208–9n.). The near-homonymy Dolon – Dorkon will also have played a part.[90]

---

[89] B. Fenik, *The Influence of Euripides on Vergil's* Aeneid, diss. Princeton 1960, 54–96, (from where all parallels are taken), B. Pavlock, *TAPA* 115 (1985), 207–24 and, more reserved, A. König, *Die Aeneis und die griechische Tragödie – Studien zur imitatio-Technik Vergils*, diss. Berlin 1970, 89–108.

[90] For further details see M. P. Pattoni, *MD* 53 (2005), 83–123 (100–5) and Liapis on 208–15.

(b) Ancient and Medieval Quotations, Lexica

Owing to its small number of γνῶμαι and other generally applicable utterances, *Rhesus* is under-represented in the anthological tradition,[91] and for similar reasons presumably held no appeal to Plutarch or Athenaeus.[92] Quotations and scholarly allusions begin only with Nicanor in the second century AD[93] – that is when the 'Selection' was already in the ascendancy – and therefore, like our manuscripts and papyri (ch. IV), rather testify to the drama's relatively subordinate status within the canon. In the fourth and fifth centuries one verse each of *Rhesus* occurs in Ap(h)thonius and St. Basil of Caesarea,[94] while Orus in his Atticist lexicon quotes 854b–5 with an important textual variation.[95] Of Byzantine authors, Eustathius and Tzetzes used *Rhesus* passages in their commentaries and poetic works.[96]

Although *Rhesus* could probably never compete with plays like *Medea* or *Hippolytus*, let alone the Byzantine triad *Hecuba*, *Orestes* and *Phoenissae*,[97] it continued to be read and annotated for private and educational use. Witness to this are not only the 'old' scholia preserved in V, but also the combined lexicon of Cyril and Hesychius, which contains a large number of entries related to our play.[98] Most of these, especially in the Cyril part, are explanations of unusual words or phrases, excerpted

---

91 Only *Rh.* 105–8 (Stob. 4.13.8), *Rh.* 206 (Stob. 2.31.14 = Orio *Anth.* 1.7 [p. 42 Schneidewin] = [Men.] *Mon.* 718 Jäkel) and later *Rh.* 106–7 (Apostol. 13.51g [*CPG* II 588.18–19]), *Rh.* 182b–3 (Apostol. 18.34h [*CPG* II 727.20–1]) and the Byzantine gnomologies gV, gB and gE, which belong to the direct manuscript tradition (p. 52–3).

92 Since of the extant tragedies Plutarch does not cite *Agamemnon*, *Eumenides*, *Philoctetes* and *Helen* either (K. Ziegler, *RE* XXI.1 s.v. Plutarchos 2, col. 917), it is unsafe to assume with Klyve (28) that he regarded *Rhesus* as spurious or that, on account of such misgivings as voiced by the ἔνιοι (p. 22), it was absent from his Euripides texts.

93 Σ^A *Il.* 6.479–80 (II 212.19–23 Erbse), where *Rh.* 390–1a and *Il.* 13.352–3 are not quite rightly adduced to explain the loose accusative participle ἀνιόντα after εἴποι.

94 Ap(h)thonius *GL* VI 54.9–12 Keil (the metrical treatise that was combined with the *Ars Grammatica* of Marius Victorinus): *Rh.* 211, Bas. Caes. *leg. libr. gent.* 31.576 B–C Migne: *Rh.* 84 (garbled).

95 Orus B 77 Alpers = *Et. Gen.* (cod. B) s.v. ᾖσμεν (cf. p. 55). Codex A of the *Etymologicum Genuinum* omits the second half of *Rh.* 855 (ἀλλὰ μηχαναὶ τάδε), and in that form the passage is also found in the *Suda* (η 573 Adler) and the *Etymologicum Magnum* (439.3–4).

96 Cf. Eust. ad Dion. Perieg. 270 (I 138.9–11 Bernhardy = *GGM* II 264.17–19) ~ Σ Dion. Perieg. 270 (*GGM* II 442.20–1): *Rh.* 29, ad *Il.* 10.519–25 (822.2–5): *Rh.* 338? (n.), 802–3, 833–55, Tz. *Hist.* 4.969–70 Leone: *Rh.* 510–11, *Carm. Il.* (commentary) p. 65 Schirach: *Rh.* 618.

97 On the early popularity of the three plays (with slightly lower scores for *Hecuba*) see M. Heath, *BICS* 34 (1987), 41–3 ~ J. Mossman (ed.), *Oxford Readings in Classical Studies: Euripides*, Oxford 2003, 220–3 and Collard, *Hecuba*, 37–8.

98 See Diggle, *Euripidea*, 517 n. 27 (for the letter α) and my testimonial apparatus, the principles of which are explained in ch. V.

from a basic Euripides glossary that was meant to render the 'Selection' more accessible at a time when few in or outside school would have been familiar with all the intricacies of the tragic language. The fact that proportionately as well as in the absolute number of glosses *Rhesus* is surpassed only by the much longer and already prevalent *Orestes* and *Phoenissae* shows that it had a firm place in the late-antique curriculum.

The ancient and medieval history of *Rhesus*, as sketched at the beginning and end of this chapter on 'Authenticity and Date', provides a salutary reminder that dramatic and literary tastes change over time. Modern scholars who deny Euripidean authorship because of the play's poor quality usually fail to account for its survival not by chance, but as a canonised work of the most celebrated Greek tragedian. Authors like Virgil and Longus found in it aspects, even expressions, worth borrowing, while from the fourth century BC into the middle ages theatre-goers, schoolmasters and general readers would have appreciated it for some of the very features later condemned. *Prometheus Bound* represents a parallel in more than one way.

IV. Textual Tradition

Rhesus is one of the rarer plays in the 'Euripidean Selection', joining *Alcestis*, *Troades* and *Bacchae* in the relatively small number of sources in which it survives.[1] All or part of the text is transmitted in seven manuscripts worth quoting, which, despite a certain degree of contamination, fall into two distinct classes, OV(Va)(Hn) = Δ and L(P)Q = Λ. Their testimony is supplemented by the Ambrosian fragments Ao and Af, three papyri, the medieval gnomologies gV, gB and gE, the scholia and the probably twelfth-century tragic cento *Christus Patiens*. None of these sources can be disregarded, although pride of place goes to the manuscripts O, V (with its scholia), L (with Triclinius' corrections) and Q.

1. Manuscripts

The oldest manuscript of the play proper is O (Laurentianus plut. 31.10),[2] written by the industrious scribe Ioannikios, whose activity was initially redated by N. G. Wilson from the later thirteenth or early fourteenth century to the last third or quarter of the twelfth.[3] Subsequent research has suggested that he may have practised his craft as early as 1135–40,[4] in which case the date of his production (including O) might have to be raised by another decade or two.[5]

The codex comprises the 'Selection', except *Troades*, with two thirds of *Rhesus* (1–714) concluding the Euripidean part. Under the siglum K it

---

1   For the special case of *Bacchae* see p. 43 with n. 82.
2   A. Turyn, *The Byzantine Manuscript Tradition of the Tragedies of Euripides*, Urbana (Ill.) 1957 (repr. Rome 1970), 333–5, K. Matthiessen, *Studien zur Textüberlieferung der Hekabe des Euripides*, Heidelberg 1974, 39, D. J. Mastronarde – J. M. Bremer, *The Textual Tradition of Euripides' Phoinissai*, Berkeley 1982, 3.
3   N. G. Wilson, *Scrittura e Civiltà* 7 (1983), 161–76. In essence already *CR* n.s. 28 (1978), 336 and *JHS* 100 (1980), 219.
4   G. Vuillemin-Diem – M. Rashed, *Recherches de Théologie et Philosophie médiévales* 64 (1997), 136–98 (especially 157–80).
5   Before the invention of spectacles, Nigel Wilson reminds me, the career of an average scribe spanned a maximum of thirty years. See the dated manuscripts under individual names in M. Vogel – V. Gardthausen, *Die griechischen Schreiber des Mittelalters und der Renaissance*, Leipzig 1909.

is also a first-rate witness for the text of Sophocles.⁶ In *Rhesus* O stands close to V(Va), although numerous separative errors, individual or shared with L and/or Q,⁷ preclude any direct relationship. On the other hand, it alone is correct at 179 γ' (om. VΛ), 205 κλωπικοῖς, 236 Ἰλιάδας, 271 λέγω, 343 εἴργοι, 379 Θρῃκί, 431 (430–1n.) φόνος, 505 Ἰλίου, 536–7 ὅδε γ', 548 φοινίας, 560 (560–1n.) εἰσπαίσας, 595 λιπόντε, 601 οὔτ' ἄν, 619 κτανόντε, 635 θανεῖν (also in the margin of L) and 654 δ' (om. VΛ).⁸

V (Vaticanus gr. 909) from ca. 1250 to 1280⁹ is the only manuscript which contains all 'Selection' plays, except *Bacchae*, with substantial old scholia. Its text wavers between O and Λ,¹⁰ and several original leaves are missing. In *Rhesus* we lack 112–51, 551–630, 792–811 and 941–96,¹¹ which, as in some other places (*Hec.* 212–56, 712–1068, *Or.* 1205–1504), can be supplied from the fourteenth-century Va (Palatinus gr. 98),¹² a full unannotated copy of V. Together V and Va preserve the truth in almost thirty places, most notably 17 λόχος, 161 μέν, 175 (n.) Ἰλέως, 296 ὁδοῦ, 453 ὕστερος, 594 τύχῃ, 601 Ἀχιλλεύς, 669 κοιμίσαι and 718 Ἀτρειδᾶν. In using Va, however, one must bear in mind that its scribe emended or tried to emend many, especially metrical, errors in the iambics and anapaests of his exemplar, probably by a combination of collation, memory and his own conjectural efforts.¹³ The text of 941–96, moreover, stems not from V itself (already mutilated when Va

---

6 P. J. Finglass, *CQ* n.s. 58 (2008), 441–51 (on the triad).
7 E.g. 17 λόχος V: δόλος OQ, Tr³P²: δοῦλος <LP>, 161 μέν V: με OΛgVgB, *Chr. Pat.* 1964, 296 ὁδοῦ V: στρατοῦ OΛ, 601 ἀχιλλεύς Va: -έως OΛ, 702 ποίας VΛ: τίνος O (cf. Klyve 86 n. 181). Note also Ioannikios' propensity for committing the *vitium Byzantinum* (170, 218, 220, 265, 269, 290, 313, 331, 421, 426, 433, 503, 506, 606, 618, 635, 636).
8 Cf. Wecklein, *Textkritische Studien*, 68–70 (who wrote before the discovery of Π² and the gnomologies).
9 Turyn 90; cf. N. G. Wilson, *Gnomon* 38 (1966), 342, *CR* n.s. 16 (1966), 288 on the somewhat earlier date. Further descriptions in Matthiessen 46–7, Mastronarde–Bremer 3–4 (+ D. J. Mastronarde, *GRBS* 26 [1985], 106–8), Diggle, *Textual Tradition*, 6 and H.-C. Günther, *The Manuscripts and the Transmission of the Paleologan Scholia on the Euripidean Triad*, Stuttgart 1995, 225.
10 See above (n. 7) and Barrett, *Collected Papers*, 427.
11 The last folio (*Rh.* 899–940) had survived in a set of loose fragments and was reunited with the manuscript upon its discovery by H. Rabe (*RhM* N.F. 63 [1908], 419–22).
12 Turyn 91–2, Matthiessen 45–6.
13 Matthiessen 126–8 (for *Hecuba*). Examples in *Rhesus* (without rhythmical significance) are 398 (396–8n.) πολεμίῳ, 607 (n.) ἥξει and probably 887 νεόδμητον (νεόχμ- V: νεόκμ- Λ, recte), which also occurs in *Chr. Pat.* 1456. The metrical interests of our scribe are evident also from his insertion of pertinent notes and a brief treatise copied on foll. 1ʳ–3ᵛ.

was prepared), but from a closely related manuscript,[14] which seems to have avoided many trivial mistakes.[15]

The latest member of the Δ family, Hn (Hauniensis 417) of around 1475,[16] is for *Rhesus*, *Alcestis*, *Andromache* and *Troades* an apograph of Va and to be cited only exceptionally. At 131 (n.) μεταθέμενος, 694 (693–4n.) χέρα, 792 ὀρθὸς (-ῶς Ω) and 924 (924b–5n.) κἀτυφλώσαμεν it is correct against all earlier witnesses, but whether through scribal conjecture or a lucky accident remains difficult to decide in each case.[17] In 134 (κατόπταν OQ: -την <Va>HnL), where V is defective and Va illegible, the (wrong) reading of the latter can only be inferred from Hn.[18]

The other branch (Λ), which also transmits the 'alphabetic' plays, is above all represented by L (Laurentianus plut. 32.2), a vast miscellany of poetic works, written around 1310 for the personal use of Demetrius Triclinius.[19] Its Euripidean text, set out like the rest in two columns to be read across the page, shows the characteristics of two or, according to some, three different scribes,[20] the second of whom wrote *Rhesus*, *Ion*, *IT* and *IA* (foll. 119ʳ – 154ʳ) and was identified by Turyn (229–33) as Nikolaos Triklines, presumably a relative (younger brother?) of the famous scholar. Triclinius went over the text three times (Tr¹ – Tr³), performing the task of the corrector as well as applying his own conjectures or readings he found in other manuscripts. His understanding of metre (by the standards of his time) and the principle of strophic response prompted emendation particularly in the anapaestic and lyric sections, where remedies 'such as changes of spelling and word order, addition or omission of the article, prepositions, pronouns and particles like γε,

---

14 H. Rabe, *RhM* N.F. 63 (1908), 421–2. On the text source see Zanetto, ed. *Rhesus*, IX–X and, by implication, Diggle, *Euripidis Fabulae* III, 428, against Turyn (91), who had envisaged a congener of L.
15 Cf. *Rh*. 951 ἕκτορ Va: -ωρ Λ, 952 μάντεων Va: -εως Λ, 960 ξυμ- Va: συμ- Λ, 976 θρήνοις Va: -ους Λ, 987 πληροῦν Va: -οῦ Λ: -ου[Af, 993 στείχωμεν Va: -ομεν Λ. The tendency of the V scribe to write single instead of double consonants is relevant for the constitution of the text at 461–3 (n.).
16 See R. Prinz, *RhM* N.F. 30 (1875), 129–33, Turyn 329–33, Matthiessen 42 and B. Schartau, *Codices Graeci Haunienses. Ein deskriptiver Katalog des griechischen Handschriftenbestandes der Königlichen Bibliothek Kopenhagen*, Copenhagen 1994, 99–100.
17 For both phenomena in Hn and other late Euripides manuscripts see Diggle, *Euripidea*, 239, 243–4, 270–2.
18 Cf. Diggle, *Euripidea*, 324 with n. 8.
19 Turyn 222–58, Zuntz, *Inquiry*, 126–35, 144–51, 192, Matthiessen 39–40, Mastronarde-Bremer 7 and on the date also O. L. Smith, *C&M* 43 (1992), 219 n. 92.
20 Two: Turyn 229, less certain Zuntz, *Inquiry*, 103–4, 127–8, 134, 178; cf. N. G. Wilson, *Gnomon* 38 (1966), 336. Three: J. A. Spranger, *SIFC* n.s. 10 (1932), 321–4, P. G. Mason, *CQ* n.s. 4 (1954), 57–8, C. Collard, *SIFC* n.s. 35 (1963), 107–11 (= *Selected Papers*, 109–114, with 'Endnote 2006'), Matthiessen 39.

τε and even οὐκ ...'²¹ produced some successes, but more often (one suspects) led to further corruption. In *Rhesus* compare e.g. 715 βίον δ' ἐπαιτῶν εἰρπ' ἀγύρτης <τις> λάτρις (suppl. Tr¹) with 559 ταρβῶ· χρόνιος γὰρ ἄπεστιν, where the same insertion after γάρ (Tr³) was designed to remove a paroemiac, or the restoration of 549, 712, (715) and 716²² with the confusion created at 682, 685 and 702. L and Triclinius offer unique (or nearly unique) good readings also at 9 φυλλοστρώτους, 14 ἐνέπειν, 82 ὧδέ γ' (+ Π²), 322 ξυμπονοῦσιν, 326 αἱροῦσι, 665 δόκει, 734 ἐσιδών, 748–9 ἃ (four times), 753 κέλσαντ', 772 μετρῷ (+ Σⱽ), 784 θείνοντε, 816 νυν, 825 ἔβριξα (also presupposed by Σᵠ), 835 οὐδέν', 927 παρθενείαν and 942 κἀπιχρώμεθα. Many of these mean the absence of minor errors.

In P (Palatinus gr. 287 + Laurentianus Conv. Soppr. 172), a luxurious tragic collection produced about 1315–25,²³ the text of *Rhesus* was, like that of the 'alphabetic' plays, copied from L after Triclinius had revised it for the first time.²⁴ The manuscript is thus of limited use, except where L is illegible or Tr²/³ has changed the original (for better or for worse) beyond recovery.²⁵ At 561 P alone may attest the correct διόλωλε, whereas at 636 ἀλλ' ὧπερ ἥκεις ... a second hand changed ὥσπερ (Ω) into ὧπερ by erasing the σ and placing a circumflex slightly to the right of the ω. The learned rubricator Ioannes Catrares added one valid speaker assignation (594, also in VaQ) and perhaps an interesting γράφεται-variant (92).²⁶

Q (Harleianus 5743) of ca. 1500²⁷ contains *Trachiniae, Philoctetes*, the end of *Alcestis* (1029–1163), *Rhesus* and *Troades*. Notwithstanding some contamination from the first family, its Euripides up to *Tro.* 610 ultimately depends on an ancestor of L (or P's model respectively),²⁸ so

---

21 Zuntz, *Inquiry*, 194.
22 In some of these cases, notably 712, which is corrupt only in <L>P, the truth may go back to L's exemplar (cf. below on the importance of Q in this respect).
23 Turyn 258–64, Zuntz, *Inquiry*, 135–40 (with N. G. Wilson, *Gnomon* 38 [1966], 336–7), Matthiessen 41, Mastronarde–Bremer 8. For the dating see A. Turyn, *Codices graeci Vaticani saeculis XIII et XIV scripti annorumque notis instructi*, Vatican City 1964, 127 and O. L. Smith, *Mnemosyne* IV 35 (1982), 328, *C&M* 43 (1992), 198, 219 (among new information on the scribes and the advanced metrical notes on E. *Supplices* and the two Iphigeneia plays). *Rhesus* is found in the Vatican part.
24 Zuntz, *Inquiry*, 144–51, Diggle, *Euripidea*, 508–13.
25 Zuntz, *Inquiry*, 140, 148. Cf. *Rh.* 11, 49, 266, 345, 348, 531, 702, 706, 711, 733a, 734, 827, 907.
26 Cf. Zuntz, *Inquiry*, 136, 139, 289 and Diggle, *Euripidea*, 510–12, also on his other activities in P.
27 Turyn 288–98 (with Barrett, *Collected Papers*, 425), Zuntz, *Inquiry*, 144–51. Turyn's dating to about 1475 was revised by Wilson (*Gnomon* 38 [1966], 337), who identified the scribe as Gian Francesco Burana, born in 1474.
28 Cf. Diggle, *Euripidis Fabulae* II, vi–viii (on *Troades*).

that in *Rhesus* it again helps to reconstruct L, prior to any alterations by Tr¹.²⁹ Moreover, several peculiar or shared preservations of the truth make it a valuable witness in its own right.³⁰ The survival of a Triclinian reading in Q suggests that Triclinius found it in L's exemplar rather than conjecturing it himself.

2. Evidence from Lost Manuscripts

To the medieval history of the *Rhesus* text belong six further direct sources, which, though less important than the manuscripts and papyri, deserve attention.

The relevant part of the Ambrosianus F 205 inf. (Af)³¹ consists of thirty-eight paper folios of the thirteenth century, on which *Andr.* 1–102 and *Rh.* 856–84 + 985–9 are quoted among Homeric scholia. The poetic text, written continuously like prose, is often difficult, if not impossible, to decipher and offers nothing special, except that it confirms the weakly attested readings and/or conjectures at 881 (879–81n.) λεωφόρου and 883 (882–4n.) ἀνάγει and avoids some trivial errors of V(Va). The second part (*Rh.* 985–9) is particularly badly damaged.

A much later Milan manuscript supplements the testimony of VQ for the first argument (Hyp. (a) *Rh.*). Ambrosianus O 123 sup. (Ao),³² a composite codex of the early sixteenth century, transmits on fol. 32ʳ part of Hyp. (a) *Med.* (89.25–34 Diggle) and the said *Rhesus* piece. This stands close to Q, probably descending from the same ancestor of L, after Hyp. (a) *Rh.* had been added there from a V-type manuscript.³³ A far better text of the latter half, however, is given by Π¹.

Three Byzantine gnomologies preserve independent manuscript evidence for all or most of the 'Selection' plays, collecting passages of sententious or stylistic-rhetorical interest in the original verse order.³⁴ They do not usually offer new readings, but may add welcome support where other sources are scarce (especially in *Troades*, *Bacchae* and *Rhesus*, but also *Alcestis* and *Andromache*).³⁵ So the eleventh- or twelfth-century

---

29 Zuntz, *Inquiry*, 147–50 with 150–1 n. ¶. Cf. e.g. *Rh.* 262, 263, 682, 828, 830.
30 Diggle, *Euripidea*, 324–5, where add 43 (ναῶν VQ et L¹ᶜ vel Tr¹: νηῶν Lᵘᵛ: νεῶν O), 215 (εἶμι Q et Tr²ʳ: εἰμὶ L⁷P: εἰμι Δ), 354 (σὰν ἐφύτευσεν Q et Tr³: σὰν ἐφύτευσ' L: ἀνεφύτευσεν O: -σαν V), 412 (ὕστερος OQgV: -ον VLgE), 686 (ἢ Q: ἢ ΔL) and 994 (καὶ ξυμμαχίᾳ Q: καὶ συμμ- L: ξυμμαχίαν Va).
31 Turyn 341–2.
32 Turyn 296–8.
33 Zuntz, *Inquiry*, 144–5.
34 In general A. Meschini, *Helikon* 13–14 (1973–74), 349–62 (349–55).
35 K. Matthiessen, *Hermes* 94 (1966), 409–10.

Athous Vatopedi 36 (gV),³⁶ which in forty-seven excerpts covers *Rh.* 84–961, almost certainly antedates even O (making it the earliest medieval witness for the text of *Rhesus*) and often sides with it in truth (122 θράσει) or error (106, 161, 327, 583).³⁷ Vaticanus Barberini gr. 4 (gB) of around 1300 has fifty-eight lines from *Rh.* 7 to 980–2 and the early-fourteenth-century Escorialensis gr. X.1.13 (gE)³⁸ seventy-six lines from *Rh.* 39–40 to 980–2, each with scattered V-type scholia inherited from their respective exemplars.³⁹ Like gV these are more interesting for the transmission than the constitution of the text, with gB supporting Va only in 962 (μελάγχιμον) and gE supplying the syntactically possible, but unlikely, κυνηγέτης in 325 (325–6n.).

With about 250 passages quoted, the author of *Christus Patiens*⁴⁰ placed *Rhesus* fourth in order of utility after *Medea, Bacchae* and *Hippolytus* and before even the triad plays *Hecuba* and *Orestes*. On the evidence of the varied textual affiliations, his model preceded any major division, although most borrowings have been deliberately altered to suit their new context.⁴¹ Yet a demonstrably ancient (and correct) reading survived for *Rh.* 52 (n.), and other successful variants for 148, 249, 532–3, 658 (nn.) and perhaps 285 (n.).

---

36 G. A. Longman, *BICS* 4 (1957), 60–1, *CQ* n.s. 9 (1959), 129–41 (analysis and collation of the Euripidean part) and E. Lamberz, *Katalog der griechischen Handschriften des Athosklosters Vatopedi* I, Thessaloniki 2006, 156–62, who on the basis of the principal script (161) supports Christodoulou's dating to the middle of the eleventh century ('Επιστημονική Ἐπετηρὶς τῆς Φιλοσοφικῆς Σχολῆς τοῦ Πανεπιστημίου Ἀθηνῶν 26 [1977/8], 322–3 = Σύμμικτα κριτικά, Athens 1986, 30–1). After examining the samples on the CD-ROM accompanying Lamberz' catalogue, Nigel Wilson informs me that the mid- to late eleventh century is 'perfectly possible'.
37 In 482 (n.) the correct μή νυν (coni. Scaliger) for ... νῦν (ΩgBgE) is barely a variant.
38 On both compilations see Turyn 93–4 n. 151, Mastronarde–Bremer 173–4. Collations in K. Matthiessen, *Hermes* 93 (1965), 148–58 (gB) and *Hermes* 94 (1966), 398–410 (gE).
39 Including one on *Ba.* 344 in gB, the final proof that this play belonged to the 'Selection'.
40 Edited most recently by A. Tuilier, *La passion du Christ. Tragédie*, Paris 1969, who still falsely attributes it to Gregory of Nazianzus. On the dating to the eleventh or twelfth century see W. Hörandner, in E. Trapp et al. (eds.), *Studien zur Byzantinischen Lexikographie*, Vienna 1988, 183–202, also against the attempt of A. Garzya to prove that the extant manuscripts of the cento derive from an uncial source (*Sileno* 10 [1984] = *Studi ... Adelmo Barigazzi* I, 237–40, *ByzZ* 82 [1989], 110–13), and N. Vakonakis, *Das griechische Drama auf dem Weg nach Byzanz. Der euripideische Cento Christos Paschon*, Tübingen 2011, 97–103 (preceded by an overview of the discussion since the *editio princeps* of 1542).
41 Cf. 164, 285, 532–3, 875–6, 938–40 (n. 330) nn. and see F. Jouan, in U. Criscuolo – R. Maisano (eds.), *Synodia. Studia humanitatis Antonio Garzya ... dicata*, Naples 1997, 495–509. A. Döring (*Philologus* 23 [1866], 577–91) takes too many divergences for true variants.

3. Papyri

To judge by the small number of papyri (three) that have so far come to light, *Rhesus* was one of the less popular 'Selection' plays already in antiquity. In this respect it again sides with *Alcestis* (four) and *Troades* (one), but not apparently *Bacchae* (nine).

Π[1] (PSI XII 1286) of the second century AD[42] transmits Hyp. (a) *Rh.* from]υ κιν[δ- (63.11 -429.10 Diggle) to the end. After a fragmentary beginning, it gives a far more accurate and complete version of the text than the medieval sources (VQAo), not least because such 'accessory matter' tended to be less well protected from corruption. The papyrus was the earliest part found of the so-called *Tales from Euripides*. Its summary of *Rhesus* is followed by *Rhadamanthys* and *Scyrii*.

Π[2] (P. Achmîm 4 = P. Par. Suppl. gr. 1099.2)[43] from a fourth- or fifth-century AD papyrus codex presents *Rh.* 48–96 on either side of a single leaf. It introduces the certainly correct οὔτἂν for οὐκ ἂν (ΩgB) in 60 and supports 52 ἥκεις (above), 63 ἦ (coni. Cobet) and 78 πῦρ' αἴθειν (cf. 41–2n.). In addition, the corruptions at 51 (33, 49–51nn.), 54 (53–5n.) αἴρεσθαι and 59 (59–60a n.) †ξυνέσχοντ† are proved ancient.

Π[3] (P. Oxy. 4568), dated to the third century AD,[44] is a scrap of 3.8 × 5.8 cm, which has the openings of *Rh.* 839–47. Barely a complete word remains, with an obvious error in 841 (ηλθε[ν for ἦλθον Ω) and a peculiar alteration, perhaps by a second hand, in 846 (n.). Had the end of 847 and/or the beginning of 848 survived, we might have been better equipped with regard to †συμμάχων† / τῶν σῶν (847–8n.).

4. Scholia and Other Indirect Sources

Our relatively sparse scholia and glosses in V, L and Q[45] reveal no otherwise unknown truths. But they bear witness, through their text or interpretation, to the original readings in 177 (n.) ζῶντ' ἀποινᾶσθαι, 441 (440–2n.) ἐπεζάρει (though cf. below on Cyril / Hesychius) and 685 (n.) ἴστω and rightly agree with the minority in 772 μετρῷ, 825 ἔβριξ', 852 ἄν and 881 λεωφόρου (above). On three occasions they add a verse

---

42 Pack[2] 428 = Mertens–Pack[3] 454. Add F. Sisti, *BPEC* 27 (1979), 105–11 (109–11), W. Luppe, *Anagennesis* 2 (1982), 74–82 and van Rossum-Steenbeek, *Greek Readers' Digests?*, 17–18, 201–2.
43 Pack[2] = Mertens–Pack[3] 427. Cf. Wilamowitz, *Einleitung*, 215 with n. 186, P. Collart, *BIFAO* 31 (1931), 52–5, Turyn 97 n. 156, 313 n. 301.
44 By D. Obbink, who edited the piece in R. A. Coles *et al.* (eds.), *The Oxyrhynchus Papyri* LXVII, London 2001, 62. Cf. Mertens–Pack[3] 427.01.
45 (Re-)edited recently by Merro. Schwartz did not publish the notes in Q.

omitted by their manuscript (7, 781) or comment on it as if it was there (234). At 508 Σ^V offers the variant ἢ ἄστεος, intended to remove a clash with Homer's geography (507b–9a n.).

Among the late-antique and medieval quotations, the Atticist lexicon of Orus (~ *Et. Gen.* cod. B) has confirmed Musgrave's μηχαναί in 854 (854b–5n.). Otherwise Cyril / Hesychius supports the paradosis in 118 (n.) ἀντύγων χνόαι, adds to the evidence for 209 χάσμα and 514 ἀμπείρας and is probably the source of the relevant V- and Q-glosses on 441 (above), whether or not the note originally referred to *Rhesus* or *Phoen.* 45.

5. The Aldine

Together with most Euripidean plays, the first printed edition of *Rhesus* was published by Aldus Manutius in Venice (1503).[46] According to a persuasive study by M. Sicherl,[47] the exemplar in the non-triadic 'Selection' dramas was not P, as had long been presumed, but a lost copy of L and the editor most likely Ioannis Gregoropoulos (Aldus' corrector-in-chief) rather than his more famous fellow-Cretan, Marcus Musurus.

In general the text of the Aldine, which was to become the vulgate for the following three centuries, is of low quality. But several unique good readings, mostly small corrections, give it a place in the critical apparatus. In *Rhesus* note 90 τεύχεσιν (-σι Π²Ω), 99 (n.) χέρα (-ας Ω), 201 (201–2n.) <δ'>, 249 τις (cf. *Chr. Pat.* 1443: τίς Ω), 369 ἐς (εἰς Ω), 441 Παίονάς (παιόνας Ω), 525 (523–5a n.) δέχθαι (δέχεσθαι fere Ω), 906 Οἰνεΐδας (-είδας VL: -ίδας Q) and 909 (908–9n.) ἀριστοτόκοιο (-τοτόκου VL: -τόκου Q). Of these the epic δέχθαι and ἀριστοτόκοιο (in lyrics) are remarkable, but probably not beyond the conjectural ability of the Aldine editor.[48] By contrast, ὅποι for ὅπῃ in 689 may come from the manuscript that was taken as the basis for the print.

---

[46] *Alcestis, Medea, Hippolytus* and *Andromache* had already been printed by Janus Lascaris in Florence (ca. 1495). Aldus omitted the *Electra*.
[47] *RhM* N.F. 118 (1975), 205–25, partly superseded by M. Sicherl, *Griechische Erstausgaben des Aldus Manutius. Druckvorlagen, Stellenwert, kultureller Hintergrund*, Paderborn et al. 1997, 291–309.
[48] Cf. *Hec.* 1100, where ἀναπτάμενος in the exemplar Par. suppl. gr. 212 was corrected to the metrically required ἀμπτάμενος (M. Sicherl, *RhM* N.F. 118 [1975], 218–19 = *Griechische Erstausgaben*, 301–2). In *Rh.* 429 πορθμεῦσαι, also found in Q (-εύσων L: -εύσας Δ), has some claim to being right (428b–9n.).

V. The Edition

Despite a number of deviations, my Greek text and critical apparatus are heavily indebted to Diggle's magisterial edition of 1994. I have made no systematic collations of my own, but checked doubtful points in Q (from autopsy) and OLP from the published facsimiles of L and P[1] and, in the case of O and L, the excellent digital images that are now available on the website of the Biblioteca Medicea Laurenziana.[2] Likewise, P. Oxy. 4568 (Π³) has been consulted online[3] and its variants added to the apparatus.

Details of V and Va were kindly communicated to me by Prof. Diggle; for the remaining sources (including the distinction in L of corrections by Tr¹, Tr² and Tr³) I have relied on his apparatus, occasionally those of earlier editors (especially Murray and Wecklein) and the collations of gV, gB and gE made by Longman and Matthiessen. The photographs of gV which Longman said he left to the Bodleian Library[4] cannot be traced.

I quote P slightly more consistently when L is difficult or impossible to decipher, even if the correct reading is also attested in Q. On the other hand, I have been even more sparing than Diggle in the report of conjectures, naming only those that are printed in the text or considered very plausible alternatives. More can often be found in the commentary.

The testimonial apparatus lists direct quotations and close adaptations, primarily from *Christus Patiens*. Of Cyril / Hesychius I have included only those entries which, by virtue of being whole phrases, parsed forms or extremely rare or unique words, can be attributed to *Rhesus* without reasonable doubt.

---

1   J. A. Spranger (ed.), *Euripidis quae inveniuntur in codice Laurentiano Pl. XXXII, 2*, Florence 1920 and *id.* (ed.), *Euripidis quae in codicibus Palatino Graeco inter Vaticanos 287 et Laurentiano Conv. soppr. 172 (olim Abbatiae florentinae 2664) inveniuntur*, Florence 1939–46.
2   At http://opac.bmlonline.it/ (via 'manoscritti').
3   In high resolution via http://www.papyrology.ox.ac.uk/POxy/.
4   *CQ* n.s. 9 (1959), 135–6.

Text and Critical Apparatus

Conspectus Siglorum

I. Codices

1. Constanter Citati

O	Laurentianus plut. 31.10 (c. 1160): vv. 1–714
V	Vaticanus gr. 909 (c. 1250–80): vv. 1–111, 152–550, 631–791, 812–940
Va	Palatinus gr. 98 (saec. xiv): adhibetur ubi deficit V
L	Laurentianus plut. 32.2 (c. 1310)
Q	Harleianus 5743 (c. 1500)
Ao	Ambrosianus O 123 sup. (saec. xvi in.): argumentum (a)
Af	Ambrosianus F 205 inf. (saec. xiii): vv. 856–84, 985–9

2. Raro Memorantur

P	Palatinus gr. 287 (c. 1315–25): codicis L apographum
Hn	Hauniensis 417 (ca. 1475): codicis Va apographum

3. Codicum Familiae

Δ	consensus codicum OV(Va)(Hn)
Λ	consensus codicum L(P)Q
Ω	consensus codicum OVVaLQAoAf (vel quotquot adsunt)

II. Papyri

Π^1	PSI XII 1286 (saec. ii p. C.): argumenti (a) pars
Π^2	P. Achmîm 4 = P. Par. Suppl. gr. 1099.2 (saec. iv-v p. C.): vv. 48–96
Π^3	P. Oxy. 4568 (saec. iii p. C.): vv. 839–47 initia

III. Gnomologia

gV Athous Vatopedi 36 (saec. xi vel xii)
gB Vaticanus Barberini gr. 4 (c. 1300)
gE Escorialensis gr. X.1.13 (saec. xiv in.)

IV. Fontes Alii

Chr. Pat. Cento Byzantinus qui Christus Patiens (Χριστὸς Πάσχων) vocatur
EM Etymologicum Magnum
Et. Gen. Etymologicum Genuinum
Hsch. Hesychius
Orus Orus Grammaticus
Suda Etymologicum quod Suda vocatur

V. Sigla Cetera

A^{ac} A ante correctionem
$A^{(p)c}$ A post correctionem incertum qua manu factam
A^{1c} A post correctionem a prima manu factam
A^{1s} lectio in A a prima manu supra lineam scripta
A^2 lectio in A ab altera manu scripta (sive in textu sive supra lineam)
A^r lectio in A a rubricatore scripta
A^{gl} glossema in A
$^iA^{gl}$ lectio quam in textu invenisse glossatorem codicis A ex eius interpretatione colligitur
$A^{\gamma\rho}$ varia lectio in A cum nota γρ(άφεται) vel sim.
A^m A in margine
A^{uv} A ut videtur
$A^?$ A non certo legitur
(A) A a lectione memorata pusillum discrepat
[A] A non legibilis vel deest
<A> lectio in A non legibilis aliunde colligi potest
Tr^1, Tr^2, Tr^3 Demetrius Triclinius codicem L primo / secundo / tertio emendavit
Σ scholiasta, scholia
$Σ^A$ lectio quam disertim testatur scholiasta codicis A
$^lΣ^A$ lemma scholiastae codicis A

ⁱΣᴬ	lectio quam in textu invenisse scholiastam codicis A ex eius interpretatione colligitur
≠	lectio cum ceteris codicibus consentit contra lectionem vel coniecturam modo memoratam
※	littera erasa vel obliterata
[ ]	delenda censeo (sed in papyro supplementum significat)
{ }	delenda censeo (in papyro)
< >	inserenda censeo
† †	corruptela nondum sanata
add.	addidit, addiderunt
cl.	collato, collatis
coni.	coniecit, coniecerunt
corr.	correxit, correxerunt
del.	delevit, deleverunt
dist.	distinxit, distinxerunt
om.	omittit, omittunt
prob.	probavit, probaverunt
rest.	restituit, restituerunt
rett.	rettulit, rettulerunt
stat.	statuit, statuerunt
suppl.	supplevit, suppleverunt
trib.	tribuit, tribuerunt
v.l.	varia lectio

VI. Canticorum Metra

ᴗ	syllaba brevis
—	syllaba longa
×	syllaba anceps
ᴗ̱	longa in stropha, brevis in antistropha
◡̄	brevis in stropha, longa in antistropha
ᴗᴗ	duae breves ex resolutione in loco principi
ᴗ̱ᴗ̱	longa in stropha, duae breves in antistropha
ᴗᴗ̄	duae breves in stropha, longa in antistropha
⸚	longa in loco bicipiti
⌐	syllaba τρίσημος (pro — ᴗ)
|	finis vocabuli
||	finis periodi
|||	finis strophae
∫	vocabulum una syllaba transgreditur colorum iuncturam
~	respondet stropha antistrophae
∘∘	duae syllabae ancipites, dum ne ambae breves sint

::	mutatio personae
^	metrum seu versus catalecticus
an	metrum anapaesticum (⏖ ⏔ ⏖ ⏔)
ar	versus aristophaneus (– ᴗ ᴗ – ᴗ – –)
ar^{2c}	versus aristophaneus duobus choriambis auctus (– ᴗ ᴗ – – ᴗ ᴗ – – ᴗ ᴗ – ᴗ – –)
ba	metrum baccheum (ᴗ – –)
cho	choriambus (– ᴗ ᴗ –)
cr	creticus (– ᴗ –)
D	– ᴗ ᴗ – ᴗ ᴗ –
D^2	– ᴗ ᴗ – ᴗ ᴗ – ᴗ ᴗ –
δ	dochmius (⏒ ⏔ ⏔ ⏒ ⏔)
da	dactylus (– ᴗ ᴗ)
dod	dodrans (– ᴗ ᴗ – ᴗ –)
e	– ᴗ – (in dactylo-epitritis)
E	– ᴗ – × – ᴗ – (in dactylo-epitritis)
'enopl.'	versus 'enoplius'
gl	versus glyconeus (∘∘ – ᴗ ᴗ – ᴗ –)
gl^{2c}	versus glyconeus duobus choriambis auctus (∘∘ – ᴗ ᴗ – – ᴗ ᴗ – – ᴗ ᴗ – ᴗ –)
hδ	hypodochmius (– ᴗ – ᴗ –)
hi	versus hipponacteus (∘∘ – ᴗ ᴗ – ᴗ – –)
hi^c	versus hipponacteus choriambo auctus (∘∘ – ᴗ ᴗ – – ᴗ ᴗ – ᴗ – –)
hi^{2c}	versus hipponacteus duobus choriambis auctus (∘∘ – ᴗ ᴗ – – ᴗ ᴗ – – ᴗ ᴗ – ᴗ – –)
ia	metrum iambicum (× – ᴗ –)
^ia	– ᴗ – pro metro iambico
ia^	ᴗ – – pro metro iambico
^ia^	– – pro metro iambico
io	metrum ionicum (ᴗ ᴗ – –)
$2io^+$	dimeter ionicus cum anaclasi = versus anacreonteus (ᴗ ᴗ – ⏒ – ᴗ – –)
ith	versus ithyphallicus (– ᴗ – ᴗ – –)
kδ	dochmius Kaibelianus (× – ⏒ – ᴗ –)
lec	lecythium (– ᴗ – ⏒ – ᴗ –)
mol	molossus (– – –)
pe	penthemimeres (× – ᴗ – ×)
ph	versus pherecrateus (∘∘ – ᴗ ᴗ – –)
reiz	versus reizianus (× – ᴗ ᴗ – –)
sp	metrum spondaicum = ^ia^ vel e^ (– –)
tl	versus telesilleus (× – ᴗ ᴗ – ᴗ –)
tr	metrum trochaicum (– ᴗ – ×)

Ὑπόθεσις Ῥήσου

(a)

Ἕκτωρ τοῖς Ἕλλησιν ἐπικοιτῶν ἀκούσας αὐτοὺς †δείλλης†
πυρὰ καίειν ηὐλαβήθη μὴ φύγωσιν. ἐξοπλίζειν δὲ διεγνωκὼς
τὰς δυνάμεις μετενόησεν Αἰνείου συμβουλεύσαντος ἡσυχάζειν,
κατάσκοπον δὲ πέμψαντα δι' ἐκείνου τὴν ἀλήθειαν ἱστορῆσαι.
Δόλωνα δὲ πρὸς τὴν χρείαν ὑπακούσαντα †ἐκπέμπεσθαι†   5
< > τόπον εἰς τὴν παρεμβολὴν ἀφώρισεν αὐτῷ. ἐπιφανέντες
δὲ οἱ περὶ τὸν Ὀδυσσέα Δόλωνα μὲν ἀνῃρηκότες, ἐπὶ δὲ τὴν
Ἕκτορος κατηντηκότες σκηνὴν πάλιν ἀπέστρεφον οὐχ εὑρόντες
τὸν στρατηγόν. οὓς Ἀθηνᾶ κατέσχεν ἐπιφανεῖσα καὶ τὸν μὲν
Ἕκτορα ἐκέλευσε μὴ ζητεῖν, Ῥῆσον δὲ ἀναιρεῖν ἐπέταξε· τὸν 10
γὰρ ἐκ τούτου κίνδυνον ἔσεσθαι μείζονα τοῖς Ἕλλησιν, ἐὰν
βιώσῃ. τούτοις δὲ ἐπιφανεὶς μὲν ὁ Ἀλέξανδρος ἐπῃσθημένος τὴν
πολεμίων παρουσίαν, ἐξαπατηθεὶς δὲ ὑπὸ τῆς Ἀθηνᾶς ὡς δῆθεν
ὑπὸ Ἀφροδίτης ἄπρακτος ὑπέστρεψεν. οἱ δὲ περὶ τὸν Διομήδην
φονεύσαντες Ῥῆσον ἐπειγομένως ἐχωρίσθησαν. ἡ συμφορὰ δὲ τῶν 15
ἀνῃρημένων καθ' ὅλον ἐλαλήθη τὸ στράτευμα. παραγενηθέντος

---

codd.: (a) VQAo et inde a 11 ( ]υ κιν[δ-) Π¹; (b) et (c) VLQ (hoc ordine V; (b) post (d) LQ;
48–55 post (b), 56–8 post (a) Q); (d) OVLQ
  Inscriptio ὑπόθεσις ῥήσου V^r: ὑπ- τοῦ εὐριπιδείου ῥ- Q: εὐριπίδου ῥῆσος Ao   1
ἐπικοιτῶν Ao: ἐπὶ κ- V: ἐποικτῶν Q   δείλλης Q: om. VAo: δείλης Nauck, δι' ὅλης <τῆς
νυκτὸς> Kirchhoff (δι' ὅλης <νυκτὸς> Schwartz)   2 πυρὰ Nauck: πυρὰν QAo: πῦρ
V   ηὐλαβήθη Ao: εὐ- VQ   5–6 post ἐκπέμπεσθαι lac. stat. Morstadt: infinitivus incertum an corruptus sit (ἐκπέμπ< >εσθαι vel ἐκπέμ<ψας >εσθαι dubitanter West)   6 τόπον
V: τάττει Ao: om. Q   ἀφώρισεν VQ: ἀφορίσας Ao   7–8 ἐπὶ δὲ τὴν Ἕκτορος om. Ao   8
κατηντηκότες σκηνὴν Q: σκηνὴν Ao: κοίτην tum spat. vac. fere ix litt. V   ὑπέστρεφον Va,
coni. Schwartz   εὑρόντες VQ: εὗρον δὲ Ao   9 κατέσχεν ἐπιφανεῖσα QAo: ἐπι- κατέσχε
V   10 ἀναιρεῖν VQ: ἀνελεῖν Ao   ἐπέταξε VAo: -εν Q   11 ἔσεσθαι μείζονα QAo: μ-
ἔ- V: [Π¹]   11–12 ἐὰν βιώσῃ(ι) VQ: εἰ βιώσει Ao: [Π¹] (ἐὰν εἰς αὔριον βιῷ in Π¹ suppl.
Luppe cl. 600)   12 τούτοις QAo:]ς Π¹: τούτων V   δ επι[φανεὶς μὲν ὁ Ἀλέξανδρος] in
Π¹ suppl. Luppe: δὲ ἐπιφανεὶς ἀλ- Ω   12–13 επησθη[μένος τὴν πολεμίων παρ]ουσιαν in
Π¹ suppl. Gallavotti: ἐπίστασθαι (ἐπι tum spat. vac. fere vi litt. V) πολέμου (πολεμίων Kirchhoff) παρουσίαν Ω   13 ἐξαπ- VAo: ἐξηπ- Q: [Π¹]   τῆς Π¹: om. Ω   13–14 ὡς δῆθεν
ὑπὸ ἀφροδίτης fere Ω (ὑπ' Ao): [ὡς Ἀφροδίτ]ης in Π¹ suppl. Gallavotti   14 ὑπέστρεψεν Ω:
επεστρε[ψεν Π¹   τον Π¹: om. Ω   15 επειγομενως Π¹: om. Ω   η συμφορα δε Π¹: καὶ ἡ
σ- Ω   16 καθόλου Ao   ελαληθη Π¹: ἦλθε Ω   παραγενηθε[ντος Π¹: παραγενομένου Ω

δὲ Ἕκτορος ἵνα αὐτόπτης τῶν πεπραγμένων γένηται τετρωμένος
ὁ τῶν Ῥήσου πώλων ἐπιμελητὴς διὰ τοῦ Ἕκτορος τὸν φόνον
ἐνηργῆσθαι †ἐπινοεῖ†. τούτου δὲ ἀπολογουμένου τὴν ἀλήθειαν
αὐτοῖς ἐμήνυσεν ἡ Καλλιόπη νεκρὸν κομίζουσα τοῦ Ῥήσου τὸ   20
σῶμα. κατοδυρομένη δὲ καὶ τὸν ἐπιπλακέντα αὐτῇ Στρυμόνα
διὰ τὸ τοῦ παιδὸς πένθος καὶ τὸν ἐξ ἐκείνου γεγενημένον Ῥῆσον
οὐδ' Ἀχιλλέα φησὶν ἀδάκρυτον ἔσεσθαι, τῷ κοινῷ τῶν ἐπιφανῶν
θανάτῳ τὴν ἰδίαν παραμυθουμένη λύπην.

(b)

τοῦτο τὸ δρᾶμα ἔνιοι νόθον ὑπενόησαν, Εὐριπίδου δὲ μὴ εἶναι·   25
τὸν γὰρ Σοφόκλειον μᾶλλον ὑποφαίνειν χαρακτῆρα. ἐν μέντοι
ταῖς διδασκαλίαις ὡς γνήσιον ἀναγέγραπται, καὶ ἡ περὶ τὰ
μετάρσια δὲ ἐν αὐτῷ πολυπραγμοσύνη τὸν Εὐριπίδην ὁμολογεῖ.
πρόλογοι δὲ διττοὶ φέρονται. ὁ γοῦν Δικαίαρχος (fr. 81 Wehrli
= 114 Mirhady) ἐκτιθεὶς τὴν ὑπόθεσιν τοῦ Ῥήσου γράφει κατὰ   30
λέξιν οὕτως (E. fr. 1108 N.² = 660a N.²-Sn. = TrGF V.2, p. 642.8)·

Νῦν εὐσέληνον φέγγος ἡ διφρήλατος.

καὶ ἐν ἐνίοις δὲ τῶν ἀντιγράφων ἕτερός τις φέρεται πρόλογος,
πεζὸς πάνυ καὶ οὐ πρέπων Εὐριπίδῃ· καὶ τάχα ἄν τινες τῶν
ὑποκριτῶν διεσκευακότες εἶεν αὐτόν. ἔχει δὲ οὕτως (E. fr. 1109   35
N.² = TrGF II adesp. fr. 8 l = TrGF V.2, p. 642.12-22)·

---

17 τοῦ ἕκτορος Ao   αυτοπτης τ[ῶν] πεπραγμε[ν]ων γενηται Π¹: αὐτὸς περιγένηται (-γίνηται V) τῶν πεπραγμένων Ω   **18** τω[ν Ῥή]σου πωλων Π¹: τοῦ ῥήσου Ω   **18–19** δια τ[οῦ Ἕκ]τορος τον φ[όνο]ν ενηργησθα[ι ἐ]πινοει Π¹: δι' αὐτοῦ φησὶν (φησὶν Ao: φασὶν Q: om. spat. vac. relicto V) ἕκτορος τὸν (τὸν om. V) φόνον γεγενῆσθαι Ω: {διὰ τοῦ} Ἕκτορος <ἐπινοήσαντος> τὸν φόνον <φησὶν> ἐνεργῆσθαι (vel ... <ἐπινοήσαντος ἔφησε> τὸν φόνον ἐν-) Liapis   **19** τουτου δ Π¹: τοῦ δὲ ἕκτορος Ω   **20** εμηνυ[σε ἡ] καλλιοπη (vel εμηνυ[σεν]) Π¹ (suppl. Luppe): ἐμήνυσεν ἡ τοῦ ῥήσου μήτηρ ἡ μοῦσα Ω (ante μοῦσα spat. vac. fere v litt. V)   κομίζουσα Π¹QAo: κομίζειν V   το]υ ρησου Π¹: om. Ω   **21** κατοδυρομένη QAo: κατοδ[Π¹: κάποδ- V: κατοδυραμένη Wecklein (cf. arg. Tro. 179.12 Diggle)   **23** αχ[ιλέα Π¹⁷ (suppl. Gallavotti): ἀχιλ(λ)εῖ Ω (-λ- V)   φησὶν Ao: φασὶν VQ: [Π¹]   post ἔσεσθαι nihil Π¹: τὴν στρατείαν (haec om. V) τῷ(ι) κοινῷ(ι) τῶν ἐπιφανῶν (τῶν ἐπι om. spat. vac. relicto V) θανάτῳ(ι) τὴν ἰδίαν παραμυθομένη (-ην V) λύπην Ω

25 εὐριπίδου δὲ μὴ εἶναι V: ὡς οὐκ ὂν εὐριπίδου Λ   **26** τὸ V   μᾶλλον Λ: λον praemisso spat. vac. fere iii litt. V   ὑποφαίνειν Valckenaer: -νει Ω   **28** μετάρσια Λ: inter μετα et σια spat. vac. fere iii litt. V   δὲ Λ: δὲ ἐν αὐτῷ V   **29** Δικαίαρχος Nauck: δικαίαν VL: om. Q   **30** ἐκτιθεὶς V: ἐπιτιθεὶς Λ   **31** οὕτως VL: -ω Q   οὕτως· <Ῥῆσος, οὗ ἡ ἀρχή> Luppe (ZPE 84 [1990] 11–13), verisimiliter (lac. iam indic. Schwartz)   **32** alterius v. init. e.g. Ἕως διώκει Snell (διώκουσ' Diggle) cl. Ion 1158, potius fortasse Νὺξ Rusten (vide p. 25 n. 17)   **33** φέρεται Λ: φαίνεται V   **34** ἄν τινες L: ἀντὶ Q: ἂν V   **35** inter ὑποκρ et τῶν spat. vac. fere iii litt. V

Ὦ τοῦ μεγίστου Ζηνὸς ἄλκιμον τέκος
Παλλάς, τί δρῶμεν; οὐκ ἐχρῆν ἡμᾶς ἔτι
μέλλειν Ἀχαιῶν ὠφελεῖν στρατεύματα.
νῦν γὰρ κακῶς πράσσουσιν ἐν μάχῃ δορός, 40
λόγχῃ βιαίως Ἕκτορος στροβούμενοι.
ἐμοὶ γὰρ οὐδέν ἐστιν ἄλγιον βάρος,
ἐξ οὗ γ' ἔκρινε Κύπριν Ἀλέξανδρος θεάν
κάλλει προήκειν τῆς ἐμῆς εὐμορφίας
καὶ σῆς, Ἀθάνα, φιλτάτης ἐμοὶ θεῶν, 45
εἰ μὴ κατασκαφεῖσαν ὄψομαι πόλιν
Πριάμου, βίᾳ πρόρριζον ἐκτετριμμένην.

(c)

Ἀριστοφάνους ὑπόθεσις

Ῥῆσος παῖς μὲν ἦν Στρυμόνος τοῦ ποταμοῦ καὶ Τερψιχόρης
Μουσῶν μιᾶς, Θρᾳκῶν δὲ ἡγούμενος εἰς Ἴλιον παραγίνεται
νυκτός, στρατοπεδευομένων τῶν Τρώων παρὰ ταῖς ναυσὶ τῶν 50
Ἑλλήνων. τοῦτον Ὀδυσσεὺς καὶ Διομήδης κατάσκοποι ὄντες
ἀναιροῦσιν, Ἀθηνᾶς αὐτοῖς ὑποθεμένης· μέγαν γὰρ ἔσεσθαι
τοῖς Ἕλλησι κίνδυνον ἐκ τούτου. Τερψιχόρη δὲ ἐπιφανεῖσα τὸ
τοῦ παιδὸς σῶμα ἀνείλετο. ὡς ἐν παρόδῳ δὲ διαλαμβάνει καὶ
περὶ τοῦ φόνου τοῦ Δόλωνος. 55
  ἡ σκηνὴ τοῦ δράματος ἐν Τροίᾳ. ὁ χορὸς συνέστηκεν
ἐκ φυλάκων Τρωϊκῶν, οἳ καὶ προλογίζουσι. περιέχει δὲ τὴν
Νυκτεγερσίαν.

---

37 τέκος om. spat. vac. relicto V   38 τί δρῶμεν Morstadt: παρῶμεν VL: παρῶ παρῶμεν Q   39 στρατεύματα L: -ματι Q: στράτευμα V   40 μάχῃ Valckenaer: μακῇ L: μακρῷ V, -ρῇ V¹ᶜ?: μακαῇ Q   41 βιαίως Hermann: βιαίας Λ: βιαία V   42 οὐδέν ἐστιν Λ: οὐκ ἔνεστι V   ἄλγιον βάρος L: ἀλγίβαρος Q: βάβαρος V   43 οὗ γ' L: ὅτ' Q: ὅτ' V   ἔκρινε VQ: -να L   Ἀλέξανδρος Valckenaer: ἀλεξάνδρου Λ: ἀλέξαι V   44 προήκειν Valckenaer: προσήκειν Ω   45 Ἀθάνα Valckenaer: ἀθηνᾶ Ω   φιλτάτης Valckenaer: φίλτατ' fere Ω (φίλατ' V)   47 βίᾳ om. V
  Inscriptio ἀριστοφάνους ὑπόθεσις Vʳ: ὑπ- ῥήσου Λ   48–9 ῥῆσος παῖς ... μιᾶς Λ: ῥ- ... μιᾶς παῖς V   48 καὶ om. Q   50 στρατοπεδευομένων Wecklein: στρατευομένων Ω   τῶν L: om. VQ   52 αὐτοῖς VQ: om. L   52–3 μέγαν γὰρ (δὲ Q) ἔσεσθαι τοῖς ἕ- (τοῖς ἕ- om. V) κίνδυνον VQ: μέγας γὰρ ἔμελλεν ἔσεσθαι τοῖς ἕ- κίνδυνος L   54–5 ὡς ... δόλωνος L: om. VQ

(d)

τὰ τοῦ δράματος πρόσωπα· χορὸς φυλάκων, Ἕκτωρ, Αἰνείας,
Δόλων, ἄγγελος ποιμήν, Ῥῆσος, Ὀδυσσεύς, Διομήδης, Ἀθηνᾶ, 60
Πάρις, Ῥήσου ἡνίοχος, Μοῦσα.

59–61 personarum indicem hoc ordine L: fere eodem O (Πά- et Ῥή- ἡν- ante Ῥῆ-): χο- φυ- ὀδ- ἔκ- ἄγγ- ποι- αἰ- δό- διο- ῥῆ- ἀθ- ῥή- ἡν- πά- μοῦ- Vr: χο- φυ- ὀδ- ἔκ- διο- αἰ- ἀθ- δό- πά- ἀγγ- ποι- ῥή- ἡν- ῥῆ- μοῦ- Q (indice qualem prae se fert L transvorsum perlecto: vide p. 113)   Πάρις] Ἀλέξανδρος Wecklein   post indicem ὁ χορὸς προλογίζει O

Ῥῆσος

ΧΟΡΟΣ
    Βῆθι πρὸς εὐνὰς τὰς Ἑκτορέους· 1
    τίς ὑπασπιστῶν ἄγρυπνος βασιλέως
    ἢ τευχοφόρων;
    δέξαιτο νέων κληδόνα μύθων,
    οἳ τετράμοιρον νυκτὸς φυλακὴν 5
    πάσης στρατιᾶς προκάθηνται.
    ὄρθου κεφαλὴν πῆχυν ἐρείσας,
    λῦσον βλεφάρων γοργωπὸν ἕδραν,
    λεῖπε χαμεύνας φυλλοστρώτους,
    Ἕκτορ· καιρὸς γὰρ ἀκοῦσαι. 10

ΕΚΤΩΡ
    τίς ὅδ'— ἦ φίλιος φθόγγος; — τίς ἀνήρ;
    τί τὸ σῆμα; θρόει.
    τίνες ἐκ νυκτῶν τὰς ἡμετέρας
    κοίτας πλάθουσ'; ἐνέπειν χρή.
Χο. φύλακες στρατιᾶς. Εκ. τί φέρῃ θορύβῳ; 15
Χο. θάρσει. Εκ. θαρσῶ.
    μῶν τις λόχος ἐκ νυκτῶν; [Χο. οὐκ ἔστι. Εκ.] τί
    σὺ γὰρ†

---

2 cf. Chr. Pat. 1911   7 (γοργωπὸν ἕδραν) Hsch. (Cyr.) γ 850; cf. Chr. Pat. 1304   8 cf. Chr. Pat. 1996

Inscriptio εὐριπίδου ῥῆσος Λ: ὑπόθεσις ῥησου Δ (ante personarum indicem O)   1ⁿ Χο. aut L aut Tr⁽²⁷⁾: Χορὸς φυλάκων VQ: om. O   1 Βῆθι Diggle: βᾶθι fere Ω et Σⱽ   2 ὑπ' ἀσπιδῶν O   5 φυλακὴν Δ et Σⱽ: φρουρὰν Λ   6 πάσης στρατιᾶς Δ: π- σ- πόλεως τροίας Λ   7 habent ΔgB et ʸᵖΣᴸ et Chr. Pat. 1304: om. Λ   ὄρθου Δ et Chr. Pat.: ὤρθου ʸᵖΣᴸ: ὄρθρου gB   8 λύσιν Q   γοργοπὸν L   9 φυλλο- L: φυλο- Δ: φιλο- Q   10 ἕκτορα L   11 τίς ὅδ' ἢ (Barnes: ἦ V: ἡ O) φίλιος φθόγγος τίς ἀνήρ Δ: τίς ὅδ' εἶ φίλος φθέγμ' ὅστις ἀνήρ Q: τίς ἀνὴρ ὦ φίλος φθέγγ' ὅστις ἀνήρ <L>P: τίς ὅδ' ὦ φίλος εἶ φθέγγ' ὅστις ἀνήρ Tr³ parenthesin indic. Diggle   12 θρόει V: θροεῖ OΛ   13 τὰς ἀμέρας O   13–14 ταῖς ἡμετέραις | κοίταις Bothe   14 ἐνέπειν Tr²′³: ἐνν- Ω   17ⁿ (ante μῶν) nullam notam Δ: paragr. L: Χο. Q   17 λόχος V: δόλος OQ et Tr³P²: δοῦλος <LP>   17ⁿ (ante οὐκ) Χο. Δ: paragr. L: Ἕκ. Q   17 οὐκ ἔστι Λ: οὐκέτι Δ   17ⁿ (ante τί) Ἕκ. O: paragr. L: om. VQ   Χο. οὐκ ἔστι. Εκ. del. Dindorf   Χο. οὐκ ἔσθ', <Ἕκτορ>. Εκ. τί Jackson

φυλακὰς προλιπὼν κινεῖς στρατιάν,
εἰ μή τιν' ἔχων νυκτηγορίαν;
οὐκ οἶσθα δορὸς πέλας Ἀργείου 20
νυχίαν ἡμᾶς
κοίτην πανόπλους κατέχοντας;

Χο. ὁπλίζου χέρα, συμμάχων, στρ.
Ἕκτορ, βᾶθι πρὸς εὐνάς,
ὄτρυνον ἔγχος αἴρειν, 25
ἀφύπνισον. 25a
πέμπε φίλους ἰέναι ποτὶ σὸν λόχον,
ἁρμόσατε ψαλίοις ἵππους.
τίς εἶσ' ἐπὶ Πανθοΐδαν
ἢ τὸν Εὐρώπας, Λυκίων ἀγὸν ἀνδρῶν;
ποῦ σφαγίων ἔφοροι, 30
ποῦ δὲ γυμνήτων μόναρχοι
τοξοφόροι τε Φρυγῶν;
ζεύγνυτε κερόδετα τόξα νευραῖς.

Εκ. τὰ μὲν ἀγγέλλεις δείματ' ἀκούειν,
τὰ δὲ θαρσύνεις, κοὐδὲν καθαρῶς. 35
ἀλλ' ἢ Κρονίου Πανὸς τρομερᾷ
μάστιγι φοβῇ, φυλακὰς δὲ λιπὼν
κινεῖς στρατιάν; τί θροεῖς; τί σε φῶ
νέον ἀγγέλλειν; πολλὰ γὰρ εἰπὼν
οὐδὲν τρανῶς ἀπέδειξας. 40

Χο. πῦρ' αἴθει στρατὸς Ἀργόλας, ἀντ.
Ἕκτορ, πᾶσαν ἀν' ὄρφναν,

---

27 (ψαλίοις ἵππους) Hsch. (Cyr.) ψ 42 (ubi ἵππων bis codd., ἵππους Schmidt) **29** cf. Eust. ad Dion. Perieg. 270 (I 138.9–11 Bernhardy = GGM II 264.17–19) ~ Σ Dion. Perieg. 270 (GGM II 442.20–1) **33** (κερόδετα τόξα) Hsch. (Cyr.) κ 2352 **34** cf. Chr. Pat. 618 **35** cf. Chr. Pat. 620 **38–9** cf. Chr. Pat. 2180 **39** cf. Chr. Pat. 2186 **39–40** cf. Chr. Pat. 617 **41–2** cf. Chr. Pat. 96, 2194 **42** cf. Chr. Pat. 2003

20ⁿ Χο. O **22** κοίτην Dindorf: -αν Ω πανόπλοις O **23**ⁿ Χο. Σᴸ: om. Ω **23** συμμάχων Bothe (1803), denuo Hermann: σύμμαχον Ω **24** ἕκτωρ L **25** ὄτρυν' fortasse Tr¹ pot. qu. L ὄτρυνον ἔγχος bis O αἴρειν Badham: ἀείρειν Ω **27** ψαλίους O **28** Πανθοΐδαν Bothe: -οίδαν Ω **29** τῶν Q εὐρώτας V (≠ V² et Σⱽ) **32** δὲ O **33** τόξα γε Tr¹ νεβράδες O **34** ἀγγέλλεις OQ et Lᶦᶜ pot. qu. Tr¹: -έλεις VL **35** θρασύνεις Q **36** ἢ Heath ἦ Ω et ¹Σⱽ **37b–38a** del. Dobree cl. 18, fortasse recte **39** νέον δ' L? (≠ Lᶜ⁷P) ἀγγέλειν V **40** τρανῶς VΛ: -οῦς O: -ὲς gE ἀπέδεξας O **41** πῦρ' αἴθει Reiske: πῦρ' αἴθει O: πυραίθει VΛ et Σⱽ ἀργόλας OQ: -όλαος V: -έλας L

Ῥῆσος 69

διιπετῆ δὲ ναῶν
πυρσοῖς σταθμά. 43a
πᾶς δ' Ἀγαμεμνονίαν προσέβα στρατὸς
ἐννύχιος θορύβῳ σκηνάν, 45
νέαν τιν' ἐφιέμενοι
βάξιν· οὐ γάρ πω πάρος ὧδ' ἐφοβήθη
ναυσιπόρος στρατιά.
σοὶ δ', ὑποπτεύων τὸ μέλλον,
ἤλυθον ἄγγελος ὡς 50
μήποτέ τιν' ἐς ἐμὲ μέμψιν εἴπῃς.

Εκ. ἐς καιρὸν ἥκεις, καίπερ ἀγγέλλων φόβον·
ἄνδρες γὰρ ἐκ γῆς τῆσδε νυκτέρῳ πλάτῃ
λαθόντες ὄμμα τοὐμὸν ἀρεῖσθαι φυγήν
μέλλουσι· σαίνει μ' ἔννυχος φρυκτωρία. 55
ὦ δαῖμον, ὅστις μ' εὐτυχοῦντ' ἐνόσφισας
θοίνης λέοντα, πρὶν τὸν Ἀργείων στρατόν
σύρδην ἅπαντα τῷδ' ἀναλῶσαι δορί.
εἰ γὰρ φαεννοὶ μὴ †ξυνέσχον† ἡλίου
λαμπτῆρες, οὔτἂν ἔσχον εὐτυχοῦν δόρυ, 60
πρὶν ναῦς πυρῶσαι καὶ διὰ σκηνῶν μολεῖν
κτείνων Ἀχαιοὺς τῇδε πολυφόνῳ χερί.
κἀγὼ μὲν ἦ πρόθυμος ἰέναι δόρυ
ἐν νυκτὶ χρῆσθαί τ' εὐτυχεῖ ῥύμῃ θεοῦ·
ἀλλ' οἱ σοφοί με καὶ τὸ θεῖον εἰδότες 65
μάντεις ἔπεισαν ἡμέρας μεῖναι φάος

---

45 cf. Chr. Pat. 95, 2196   46–7 cf. Chr. Pat. 2198   48 (ναυσιπόρος) Hsch. (Cyr.) ν 145   50 cf. Chr. Pat. 2386–7   52 cf. Chr. Pat. 1249, 1870, 2299, 2389–90   53–4 cf. Chr. Pat. 2293–4, 2303–4   55 et 128 (φρυκτωρία) Hsch. (Cyr.) φ 935   59–60 cf. Chr. Pat. 2338–9   63 cf. Chr. Pat. 88, 2334   64 (ῥύμη) Hsch. (Cyr.) ρ 489?   65–6 cf. Chr. Pat. 2336–7   66 cf. Chr. Pat. 90

---

43 διιπετῆ Ω et Σ^VL: διειπ- Elmsley   ναῶν VQ et L^1c vel Tr^1: νηῶν L^uv: νεῶν O   πυρσοῖς Δ et Σ^V: -σοῖ Λ   44 ἀγαμεμνονίαν Δ: -είαν Λ   προσέβα OL: -έβη VQ   49 σοὶ δ' (Π^2) ΔQ: σὺ δ' <L>P: σοὶ γὰρ Tr^3   51 τιν' ἐς ἐμὲ μέμψιν Lindemann: τινα μ- εἰς ἔμ' (Π^2)Ω: ἐς ἐμέ τινα μ- Musgrave, denuo Bothe (1803)   εἴπῃ(ι)ς Π^2Δ et Tr^1: -εις Λ   52 ἥκεις Π^2 et Chr. Pat. 1870, 2389, 2390: ἦλθες Ω   ἀγγέλων V   53 ἄνδρες Elmsley: ἄ- Ω: α- Π^2   54 ἀρεῖσθαι Nauck: αιρεισθαι Π^2: αἴρεσθαι Ω   φυγήν Stephanus: φυγῆ(ι) ΟΛ: φ*υγῆ V (ras.): φυγη[Π^2   55 σημαίνει O   φυκταρία Q^γ   57 τῶν Q   ἀργεῖον O   58 σύρδην OLQ^γ: σύρσην V et Q^2:]υρδην Π^2: φύρδην Blomfield   59 ξυνέσχον fere Π^2ΔQgB (ξύν- VgB) et Chr. Pat. 2338: συν- L: 'ξέλειπον Wecklein   60 ουταν Π^2: οὐκ ἂν ΩgB   εὐτυχοῦν om. spat. vac. relicto Q   61 ναυσι Π^2 (≠ Π^2 man. sec.)   63 η Π^2, coni. Cobet: ἦν Ω et Chr. Pat. 88, 2334   64 εὐτυχεῖν O   65 με Π^2Λ: μοι Δ et L^1s   ἰδόντες V   66 ἔπεισαν Π^2Λ et Chr. Pat. 90, 2337: ἔφησαν Δ   μεῖναι Π^2Δ et Chr. Pat. 2337 (μίμνειν 90): εἶναι Λ

κἄπειτ' Ἀχαιῶν μηδέν' ἐν χέρσῳ λιπεῖν.
οἳ δ' οὐ μένουσι τῶν ἐμῶν θυοσκόων
βουλάς· ἐν ὄρφνῃ δραπέτης μέγα σθένει.
ἀλλ' ὡς τάχιστα χρὴ παραγγέλλειν στρατῷ 70
τεύχη πρόχειρα λαμβάνειν λῆξαί θ' ὕπνου,
ὡς ἄν τις αὐτῶν καὶ νεὼς θρῴσκων ἔπι
νῶτον χαραχθεὶς κλίμακας ῥάνῃ φόνῳ,
οἳ δ' ἐν βρόχοισι δέσμιοι λελημμένοι
Φρυγῶν ἀρούρας ἐκμάθωσι γαπονεῖν. 75

Χο. Ἕκτορ, ταχύνεις πρὶν μαθεῖν τὸ δρώμενον·
ἄνδρες γὰρ εἰ φεύγουσιν οὐκ ἴσμεν τορῶς.
Εκ. τίς γὰρ πῦρ' αἴθειν πρόφασις Ἀργείων στρατόν;
Χο. οὐκ οἶδ'· ὕποπτον δ' ἐστὶ κάρτ' ἐμῇ φρενί.
Εκ. πάντ' ἂν φοβηθεὶς ἴσθι δειμαίνων τόδε. 80
Χο. οὔπω πρὶν ἦψαν πολέμιοι τοσόνδε φῶς.
Εκ. οὐδ' ὧδέ γ' αἰσχρῶς ἔπεσον ἐν τροπῇ δορός.
Χο. σὺ ταῦτ' ἔπραξας· καὶ τὰ λοιπὰ νῦν σκόπει.
Εκ. ἁπλοῦς ἐπ' ἐχθροῖς μῦθος, ὁπλίζειν χέρα.
Χο. καὶ μὴν ὅδ' Αἰνέας καὶ μάλα σπουδῇ ποδός 85
στείχει, νέον τι πρᾶγμ' ἔχων φίλοις φράσαι.

ΑΙΝΕΙΑΣ
Ἕκτορ, τί χρῆμα νύκτεροι κατὰ στρατόν
τὰς σὰς πρὸς εὐνὰς φύλακες ἐλθόντες φόβῳ
νυκτηγοροῦσι καὶ κεκίνηται στρατός;

68–9a cf. Chr. Pat. 2327–9, 2341 **69b–70** cf. Chr. Pat. 2347–8 **72** cf. Chr. Pat. 2349 **73** cf. Chr. Pat. 2352 **74** cf. Chr. Pat. 2351 **76** cf. Chr. Pat. 2346 **77** cf. Chr. Pat. 2343 **78** cf. Chr. Pat. 2314 **79** cf. Chr. Pat. 2344, 2357 **83** cf. Chr. Pat. 600, 2375 **84** Bas. Caes. leg. lib. gent. 31.576 B–C Migne; Chr. Pat. 2373 **85–6** cf. Chr. Pat. 98–9, 1134–5 **87–9** cf. Chr. Pat. 2196–9

---

67 μηδέν' Π²Λ: μηδὲν Δ **68** θυοσκόων Δ: -όπων Λ: [Π²] **69** ὄρφνει V **70** παραγγέλειν V **72** νεώς Π²Λ: νεῶν Δ ἔπι Ω: εστι Π² **73** ῥάνοι O **74** δέσμιοι Π²VΛ et fere Chr. Pat. 2351 (-ος): δεσμίοις O λελημμένοι O et fere Chr. Pat. pars codd. (-ος): λελημ- Π² et fere Chr. Pat. pars codd. (-ος): λελη(ι)σμ- VΛ **75** γαπονεῖν fere Π²Δ (γᾶ π- V; γε Π²ᵐ man. sec.): γηπ- Λ **76** τὸ δρώμενον Ω et Π² man. sec. et Chr. Pat. 2346: πορωμενον Π² **77** ἄνδρες Matthiae: ἄ- Ω: [Π²] φευγωσιν Π² (≠ Π² man. sec.) τωρως Π² **78** τί O et Chr. Pat. 2314 pars codd. πυρ' αιθειν Π², coni Reiske: πῦρ αἴθειν V: πυραίθειν OΛ (πυρὰ αἴθειν Lᵍˡ) στρατῷ Morstadt **82** ὧδέ γ' Π²L: ὧδε δ' OQ: ὧδ' V ἐκ Q **84** ἁπλῶς ἐπ' ἐχθροὺς Basil. leg. lib. gent. (31.576 Migne) (≠ Chr. Pat. 2373) μῦθος Ω(gV)gB et Chr. Pat.: μυθοις Π²: θυμός Basil. ὁπλίζει Basil., Chr. Pat. pars codd. χέρα Π²ΔQgV et Σⱽ et Basil.: χέρας LgB: utrumque Chr. Pat. **85** ὅδ' Π²OΛ: οὐδ' V αἰνέας Π²ΔL: -είας Q et L¹ᶜ vel Tr⁽²⁷⁾ **86** ἔχων φίλοις fere Π²Ω (ἔχον L): ἔχων ἴσως Chr. Pat. 99, ἔ- ἴσως et ἴσως ἔ- 1135 **89** νυκ]τηγορευουσι Π² (≠ Π² man. sec.)

Ἐκ.   Αἰνέα, πύκαζε τεύχεσιν δέμας σέθεν.   90
Αἰ.   τί δ' ἔστι; μῶν τις πολεμίων ἀγγέλλεται
      δόλος κρυφαῖος ἑστάναι κατ' εὐφρόνην;
Ἐκ.   φεύγουσιν ἄνδρες κἀπιβαίνουσιν νεῶν.
Αἰ.   τί τοῦδ' ἂν εἴποις ἀσφαλὲς τεκμήριον;
Ἐκ.   αἴθουσι πᾶσαν νύκτα λαμπάδας πυρός·   95
      καί μοι δοκοῦσιν οὐ μενεῖν ἐς αὔριον,
      ἀλλ' ἐκκέαντες πύρσ' ἐπ' εὐσέλμων νεῶν
      φυγῇ πρὸς οἴκους τῆσδ' ἀφορμήσειν χθονός.
Αἰ.   σὺ δ' ὡς τί δράσων πρὸς τάδ' ὁπλίζῃ χέρα;
Ἐκ.   φεύγοντας αὐτοὺς κἀπιθρῴσκοντας νεῶν   100
      λόγχῃ καθέξω κἀπικείσομαι βαρύς·
      αἰσχρὸν γὰρ ἡμῖν, καὶ πρὸς αἰσχύνῃ κακόν,
      θεοῦ διδόντος πολεμίους ἄνευ μάχης
      φεύγειν ἐᾶσαι πολλὰ δράσαντας κακά.
Αἰ.   εἴθ' ἦσθ' ἀνὴρ εὔβουλος ὡς δρᾶσαι χερί.   105
      ἀλλ' οὐ γὰρ αὐτὸς πάντ' ἐπίστασθαι βροτῶν
      πέφυκεν· ἄλλῳ δ' ἄλλο πρόσκειται γέρας,
      σὲ μὲν μάχεσθαι, τοὺς δὲ βουλεύειν καλῶς·
      ὅστις πυρὸς λαμπτῆρας ἐξήρθης κλυών
      φλέγειν Ἀχαιούς, καὶ στρατὸν μέλλεις ἄγειν   110
      τάφρους ὑπερβὰς νυκτὸς ἐν καταστάσει.
      καίτοι περάσας κοῖλον αὐλώνων βάθος,
      εἰ μὴ κυρήσεις πολεμίους ἀπὸ χθονός

---

90 cf. Chr. Pat. 91   91 cf. Chr. Pat. 139   91–2 cf. Chr. Pat. 93–4   92 cf. Chr. Pat. 1913   94. cf. Chr. Pat. 2193, 2345   95 cf. Chr. Pat. 2316   102–4 cf. Chr. Pat. 2353–5   105–8 Stob. 4.13.8   105–9 cf. Chr. Pat. 2367–71   106–7 Apostol. 13.51g (CPG II 588.18–19)   111 cf. Chr. Pat. 2350   112 (αὐλώνων) Hsch. α 8317

---

90 πύκαζε Π²Λ et Chr. Pat. 91: πυκάζου Δ   τεύχεσιν Aldina: -σι Π²Ω   σέθεν (Π²)Δ: τὸ σὸν Λ   91 πολεμων Π² (≠ Π² man. sec.)   ἀγγέλλεται ΟΛ et Π² man. sec.: αγελλ- Π²: ἀγγέλ- V   92 δόλος Ω (cf. Chr. Pat. 1913): λόχος Chr. Pat. 94 (et P²ᵞᵖ vel Pᵞᵞᵖ): [Π²]   93 ἄνδρες Matthiae: ἄ- Ω: α- Π²   94 τοῦδ' Λ et Chr. Pat. 2345: τῶνδ' Δ: utrumque Chr. Pat. 2193:]δ' Π²   95 πᾶσαν Ω: πανος Π², πανας Π² man. sec.   νυκτος vel -ας Π²   λαμπαδα Π² (≠ Π² man. sec.)   96ⁿ Αἰ. Ο   96 καί μοι VΛ: κἀμοὶ Ο:]ι Π²   μενεῖν Portus: μένειν Ω: μενειν Π²   97 ἐκκέαντες OQ et Tr¹: ἐκκαίαντες V<L>   πῦρ V   99ⁿ Αἰ. Λ: om. Δ   99 ὁπλίζεις L   χέρα Aldina: -ας Ω   100ⁿ om. V   101 κἀπικήσομαι V   105 πρόβουλος Chr. Pat. 2367 (≠ Stob. 4.13.8)   ὡς δραστήριος F. W. Schmidt, ὡς δρᾶσαι χερί | <δυνατὸς ...> Diggle, alii alia (≠ Stob., Chr. Pat.)   106 ὡὑτὸς L⁷: ὁὑτὸς Q et P²: ὡὑτὸς V: αὐτὸς OgVgBgE et L¹ᶜ vel Tr¹: αὑτὸς vel αὐτὸς P: de Stob. et Chr. Pat. 2368 incertum   βροτῶν] βροτῶν βία gE; χερὶ Stob. (≠ Chr. Pat.)   107 γέρας] κακὸν γέρας O; χάρις Chr. Pat. 2369 pars codd. (≠ Stob.)   108 σοὶ ... τοῖς δὲ fere Chr. Pat. 2370 (τοῖσδε), coni. Stephanus (≠ Stob.)   109 κλυών West: κλύων Ω (item 286, 573, 858)   110 φλέγειν Musgrave: φεύγειν fere Ω (-εις Q) et Σᵛ   112 κοίλων αὐλόνων Q   113 κυρήσῃς Ο

φεύγοντας ἀλλὰ σὸν βλέποντας ἐς δόρυ,
νικώμενος μὲν οὔτι μὴ μόλῃς πάλιν· 115
πῶς γὰρ περάσει σκόλοπας ἐν τροπῇ στρατός;
πῶς δ' αὖ γεφύρας διαβαλοῦσ' ἱππηλάται,
ἢν ἄρα μὴ θραύσαντες ἀντύγων χνόας;
νικῶν δ' ἔφεδρον παῖδ' ἔχεις τὸν Πηλέως,
ὅς σ' οὐκ ἐάσει ναυσὶν ἐμβαλεῖν φλόγα, 120
οὐδ' ὧδ' Ἀχαιοὺς ὡς δοκεῖς ἀναρπάσαι·
αἴθων γὰρ ἀνὴρ καὶ πεπύργωται θράσει.
ἀλλὰ στρατὸν μὲν ἥσυχον παρ' ἀσπίδας
εὕδειν ἐῶμεν ἐκ κόπων ἀρειφάτων,
κατάσκοπον δὲ πολεμίων, ὅς ἂν θέλῃ, 125
πέμπειν δοκεῖ μοι· κἂν μὲν αἴρωνται φυγήν,
στείχοντες ἐμπέσωμεν Ἀργείων στρατῷ·
εἰ δ' ἐς δόλον τιν' ἤδ' ἄγει φρυκτωρία,
μαθόντες ἐχθρῶν μηχανὰς κατασκόπου
βουλευσόμεσθα· τήνδ' ἔχω γνώμην, ἄναξ. 130

Χο. τάδε δοκεῖ, τάδε μεταθέμενος νόει. στρ.
σφαλερὰ δ' οὐ φιλῶ στρατηγῶν κράτη.
τί γὰρ ἄμεινον ἢ ταχυβάταν νεῶν κατόπταν μολεῖν
πέλας ὅτι ποτ' ἄρα δαΐοις 135
πυρὰ κατ' ἀντίπρῳρα ναυστάθμων δαίεται;

Εκ. νικᾷς, ἐπειδὴ πᾶσιν ἁνδάνει τάδε.
στείχων δὲ κοίμα συμμάχους· τάχ' ἂν στρατός
κινοῖτ' ἀκούσας νυκτέρους ἐκκλησίας.

---

118 (ἀντύγων χνόας) Hsch. α 5546 ~ Suda α 2660 **125** cf. Chr. Pat. 1910 **128** (φρυκτωρία) vide ad 55 **130** cf. Chr. Pat. 1916, 2231 **134** vel 558 (κατόπταν) Hsch. (Cyr.) κ 1840 **137** cf. Chr. Pat. 498

---

115 οὔτι μὴ Cobet: τήνδ' οὐ μὴ L: τήνδε μὴ VaQ et Tr³: τήνδ' ἐμὴ O: τήνδε μὴ οὐ Schaefer (servato πόλιν) πάλιν Reiske: πόλιν Ω **116** περάσει ... στρατός ΔQ (-εις Va²): -εις ... δορός L σκόλωπας Q **118** ἄρα Va: ἄρα OΛ ἀξόνων Blaydes (≠ Hsch. α 5546; cf. Suda α 2660) χρόας O (≠ O¹ˢ) **121** διαρπάσαι Va (≠ Va²) **122** om. Q ἀνὴρ Valckenaer: ἁ- ΩgVgBgE πεπύρωται O θράσει OgV: χερί VaLgB: δορί gE **124** κόπων Λ: πόνων Δ **126** αἴρωνται Wecklein φυγήν Stephanus: -ῇ(ι) Ω **127** ἀργείῳ Q **128** εἰς Δ: ὡς Λ **129** κατασκόπου Λ: -ους Δ **130** βουλευσόμεθα L (≠ Tr¹) γνώμην ἄναξ VaΛ: προθυμίαν O: γνώμην ἐγώ Chr. Pat. 1916 et fere Chr. Pat. 2231 (-ης ἐγώ) **131** μεταθέμενος Hn, coni. Musgrave: μετατιθέμενος Ω **134** κατόπταν OQ: -την <Va>HnL: κατόπταν Hsch. κ 1840 utrum huc an ad 558 spectet incertum **135** ὅτι Λ: ὅθι Δ ἄρα Δ: ἆρ Λ **136** ἀντίπρωνα L (≠ Tr²/³) **137** νικᾷς Bothe -ᾶτ' Ω et Chr. Pat. 498 **138** κοίμα Pierson: κόσμει OΛ: σκόπει Va: cf. 662 **139** νυκτέρας O

Ῥῆσος 73

ἐγὼ δὲ πέμψω πολεμίων κατάσκοπον. 140
κἄν μέν τιν' ἐχθρῶν μηχανὴν πυθώμεθα,
σὺ πάντ' ἀκούσῃ καὶ παρὼν εἴσῃ λόγον·
ἐὰν δ' ἀπαίρωσ' ἐς φυγὴν ὁρμώμενοι,
σάλπιγγος αὐδὴν προσδοκῶν καραδόκει,
ὡς οὐ μενοῦντά μ'· ἀλλὰ προσμείξω νεῶν 145
ὁλκοῖσι νυκτὸς τῆσδ' ἐπ' Ἀργείων στρατῷ.
Αι. πέμφ' ὡς τάχιστα· νῦν γὰρ ἀσφαλῶς φρονεῖς.
σὺν σοὶ δ' ἔμ' ὄψῃ καρτεροῦνθ' ὅταν δέῃ.
Εκ. τίς δῆτα Τρώων οἳ πάρεισιν ἐν λόγῳ
θέλει κατόπτης ναῦς ἔπ' Ἀργείων μολεῖν; 150
τίς ἂν γένοιτο τῆσδε γῆς εὐεργέτης;
τίς φησιν; οὔτοι πάντ' ἐγὼ δυνήσομαι
πόλει πατρῴᾳ συμμάχοις θ' ὑπηρετεῖν.

ΔΟΛΩΝ
ἐγὼ πρὸ γαίας τόνδε κίνδυνον θέλω
ῥίψας κατόπτης ναῦς ἔπ' Ἀργείων μολεῖν, 155
καὶ πάντ' Ἀχαιῶν ἐκμαθὼν βουλεύματα
ἥξω· 'πὶ τούτοις τόνδ' ὑφίσταμαι πόνον.
Εκ. ἐπώνυμος μὲν κάρτα καὶ φιλόπτολις
Δόλων· πατρὸς δὲ καὶ πρὶν εὐκλεᾶ δόμον
νῦν δὶς τόσως ἔθηκας εὐκλεέστερον. 160
Δο. οὔκουν πονεῖν μὲν χρή, πονοῦντα δ' ἄξιον
μισθὸν φέρεσθαι; παντὶ γὰρ προσκείμενον
κέρδος πρὸς ἔργῳ τὴν χάριν τίκτει διπλῆν.
Εκ. ναί, καὶ δίκαια ταῦτα κοὐκ ἄλλως λέγω.
τάξαι δὲ μισθόν, πλὴν ἐμῆς τυραννίδος. 165
Δο. οὐ σῆς ἐρῶμεν πολιόχου τυραννίδος.

---

141 cf. Chr. Pat. 1913, 1917   146 (ὁλκοῖσι) vide ad 673   147–51 cf. Chr. Pat. 1931–5   154–6 cf. Chr. Pat. 1941–3   157 cf. Chr. Pat. 1945   159–60 cf. Chr. Pat. 1947   161–3 cf. Chr. Pat. 1964–6   164 cf. Chr. Pat. 1620   164–5 cf. Chr. Pat. 1968–70

---

142 σύμπαντ' Ο   λόγον Λ: -ους Δ   145 προσμείξω Murray: -μίξω fere Ω (-μίζω Q)   146 ὁλκοῖσιν Ο   στρατῶ(ι) Δ: -τόν Λ   147 πέμπε <L>, πέμπ' Tr$^{(27)}$ <P> (≠ P²)   148 δ' ἔμ' Bothe et Chr. Pat. 1932 pars codd.: δέ μ' Ω et Chr. Pat. codd. plerique   149 λόγω(ι) ΔQ: λόχω L et Q^{1s} 150 θέλει] τολμᾷ Chr. Pat. 1934 pars codd.   152 οὔτι L   154 πρὸς Ο (≠ O^{1c}) et Chr. Pat. 1941   160 τόσῳ σ' Ο   ἔθηκεν gV   161 οὔκουν Denniston: οὐκοῦν fere ΩgVgBgE (item 481, 543, 585, 633)   μὲν V: με ΟΛgVgB et Chr. Pat. 1964   162 προκείμενον Chr. Pat. 1965   164 λέγεις Chr. Pat. 1620 (cf. 1968–9), coni. Nauck   165 ἐμὴν τυραννίδα Nauck cl. 173   166 πολιόχου OQ: πολιούχου V: πολυόχου L

Εκ. σὺ δ' ἀλλὰ γήμας Πριαμιδῶν γαμβρὸς γενοῦ.
Δο. οὐδ' ἐξ ἐμαυτοῦ μειζόνων γαμεῖν θέλω.
Εκ. χρυσὸς πάρεστιν, εἰ τόδ' αἰτήσεις γέρας.
Δο. ἀλλ' ἔστ' ἐν οἴκοις· οὐ βίου σπανίζομεν. 170
Εκ. τί δῆτα χρῄζεις ὧν κέκευθεν Ἴλιον;
Δο. ἑλὼν Ἀχαιοὺς δῶρά μοι ξυναίνεσον.
Εκ. δώσω· σὺ δ' αἴτει πλὴν στρατηλάτας νεῶν.
Δο. κτεῖν', οὔ σ' ἀπαιτῶ Μενέλεω σχέσθαι χέρα.
Εκ. οὐ μὴν τὸν Ἰλέως παῖδά μ' ἐξαιτεῖς λαβεῖν; 175
Δο. κακαὶ γεωργεῖν χεῖρες εὖ τεθραμμέναι.
Εκ. τίν' οὖν Ἀχαιῶν ζῶντ' ἀποινᾶσθαι θέλεις;
Δο. καὶ πρόσθεν εἶπον· ἔστι χρυσὸς ἐν δόμοις.
Εκ. καὶ μὴν λαφύρων γ' αὐτὸς αἱρήσῃ παρών.
Δο. θεοῖσιν αὐτὰ πασσάλευε πρὸς δόμοις. 180
Εκ. τί δῆτα μεῖζον τῶνδέ μ' αἰτήσεις γέρας;
Δο. ἵππους Ἀχιλλέως· χρὴ δ' ἐπ' ἀξίοις πονεῖν
     ψυχὴν προβάλλοντ' ἐν κύβοισι δαίμονος.
Εκ. καὶ μὴν ἐρῶντί γ' ἀντερᾷς ἵππων ἐμοί·
     ἐξ ἀφθίτων γὰρ ἄφθιτοι πεφυκότες 185
     τὸν Πηλέως φέρουσι θούριον γόνον·
     δίδωσι δ' αὐτὸς πωλοδαμνήσας ἄναξ
     Πηλεῖ Ποσειδῶν, ὡς λέγουσι, πόντιος.
     ἀλλ' οὔ σ' ἐπάρας ψεύσομαι· δώσω δέ σοι,
     κάλλιστον οἴκοις κτῆμ', Ἀχιλλέως ὄχον. 190
Δο. αἰνῶ· λαβὼν δ' ἄν φημι κάλλιστον Φρυγῶν
     δῶρον δέχεσθαι τῆς ἐμῆς εὐσπλαγχνίας.
     σὲ δ' οὐ φθονεῖν χρή· μυρί' ἐστὶν ἄλλα σοι
     ἐφ' οἷσι τέρψῃ τῆσδ' ἀριστεύων χθονός.

---

181 cf. Chr. Pat. 1972 **182b–3** (χρὴ … δαίμονος) Apostol. 18.34h (CPG II 727.20–1) **185** cf. Chr. Pat. 1925 **189** cf. Chr. Pat. 1973, 2235

---

168 οὐδ' V: οὐκ ΟΛ **169** πάρεστιν Δ: γάρ ἐστιν Λ αἰτήσῃ V **170** σπανίζομεν βίου Ο **171** Ἴλιον OQ: -ος VL **174** χέρα Δ: -ας Λ **175** ἰλέως V: ἴλεον Ο: ὀϊλέως Λ παῖδά μ' VΛ: γε παῖδ' Ο ἐξαιτῇ V **177** ζῶντ' ἀποινᾶσθαι ⁱΣᴠᴸ: -τ' ἀποίνασθαι Ο: -τα ποινᾶσθαι VΛ et ⁱΣᵛ et ⁱΣᴸ **179** γ' Ο: om. VΛ λαβὼν Ο **180** δόμοις Q et Lˡˢ: -ους ΔL **181** δ' εἶτα Q (≠ Qˡᶜ) αἰτήσεις Λ et fere Chr. Pat. 1972 (ἀπ-): -σῃ Ο: -σει V **182** ἀχιλέως V μολεῖν Ο **183** προσβ- Q διαίμονος V **184** γ' Δ: τ' Λ **187** αὐτὸς Dobree: -τοὺς ΟΛ: -τὰς V πολο- Q **191** δ' ἄν Verrall: δέ Ω κάλλιστον φρυγῶν VΛ: τῆς ἐμῆς εὐσπλαγχνίας Ο **192** εὐσπλαχνίας V

Χο.	μέγας ἀγών, μεγάλα δ' ἐπινοεῖς ἑλεῖν·	ἀντ.
	μακάριός γε μὰν κυρήσας ἔσῃ.	196
	πόνος ὅδ' εὐκλεής· μέγα δὲ κοιράνοισι γαμβρὸν πέλειν.	
	τὰ θεόθεν ἐπιδέτω Δίκα,	
	τὰ δὲ παρ' ἀνδράσιν τέλειά σοι φαίνεται.	200
Δο.	στείχοιμ' ἄν· ἐλθὼν <δ'> ἐς δόμους ἐφέστιος	
	σκευῇ πρεπόντως σῶμ' ἐμὸν καθάψομαι,	
	κἀκεῖθεν ἥσω ναῦς ἔπ' Ἀργείων πόδα.	
Χο.	ἐπεὶ τίν' ἄλλην ἀντὶ τῆσδ' ἕξεις στολήν;	
Δο.	πρέπουσαν ἔργῳ κλωπικοῖς τε βήμασιν.	205
Χο.	σοφοῦ παρ' ἀνδρὸς χρὴ σοφόν τι μανθάνειν·	
	λέξον· τίς ἔσται τοῦδε σώματος σαγή;	
Δο.	λύκειον ἀμφὶ νῶτ' ἐνάψομαι δοράν	
	καὶ χάσμα θηρὸς ἀμφ' ἐμῷ θήσω κάρᾳ,	
	βάσιν τε χερσὶ προσθίαν καθαρμόσας	210
	καὶ κῶλα κώλοις τετράπουν μιμήσομαι	
	λύκου κέλευθον πολεμίοις δυσεύρετον,	
	τάφροις πελάζων καὶ νεῶν προβλήμασιν.	
	ὅταν δ' ἔρημον χῶρον ἐμβαίνω ποδί,	
	δίβαμος εἶμι· τῇδε σύγκειται δόλος.	215
Χο.	ἀλλ' εὖ σ' ὁ Μαίας παῖς ἐκεῖσε καὶ πάλιν	
	πέμψειεν Ἑρμῆς, ὅς γε φιλητῶν ἄναξ.	
	ἔχεις δὲ τοὔργον· εὐτυχεῖν μόνον σε δεῖ.	
Δο.	σωθήσομαί τοι καὶ κτανὼν Ὀδυσσέως	
	οἴσω κάρα σοι — σύμβολον δ' ἔχων σαφές	220
	φήσεις Δόλωνα ναῦς ἔπ' Ἀργείων μολεῖν —	

---

196 cf. Chr. Pat. 1975   **206** Stob. 2.31.14 = Orio Anth. 1.7 (p. 42 Schneidewin) = [Men.] Mon. 718 Jaekel; Chr. Pat. 1766   **208–11** cf. Longus 1.20.2   **209** (χάσμα θηρός) Hsch. (Cyr.) χ 224   **211** Ap(h)thonius GL VI 54.9–12 Keil

---

195 μέγας ΔQgE: μ- μὲν L   μεγάλας δ' Q   **196** μὰν Diggle: μὴν ΩgE   **197** ὅδ' Nauck: δ' Ω   μέγα Δ: μεγάλα Λ   **199** τὰ Bothe (1803), denuo Seidler: τὰ δὲ Ω   θεόθι ἐπί τῳ δίκᾳ O   **200** τάδε O   ἀνδράσιν Heath: -σι Ω: ἀνέρων Wecklein   τέλειά Λ: τέλεά Δ   **201** <δ> Aldina   ἀφ' ἑστίας Q   **203** κἀκεῖθεν ἥσω Δ: κεῖθεν δ' ἐφήσω Λ   **204** ἐπεὶ τίν' Δ et Q[1c]: ἐπεὶ τὴν τίν' Q: εἶπ'· ἦ τιν' L   **205**[n] om. O   **205** κλωπικοῖς O: κλοπτ- V: κλεπτ- Λ   **206** παρ'] πρὸς gV (≠ Stob. 2.31.14 = Orio anth. 1.7 = [Men.] sent. 718, Chr. Pat. 1766)   **207** ἔστι V   **208**[n] om. O   **208** νῶτ' ἐνάψομαι Cobet: νῶτον ἅψομαι Δ: νῶτα θήσομαι Λ   **209** χάσμα Δ et Q[1γρ] et Hsch. χ 224: σχῆμα Λ   ἐμῷ(ι) VΛ et O[1s]: αὐτῷ O   **212** πολεμίους Q   **215** εἰμὶ Q et Tr[2?]: εἰμὶ L[?P]: εἰμὶ Δ   **217** φιλητῶν Δ: φηλ- ΛgE   **218** μόνον σε δεῖ ΛgE: σὲ δεῖ μ- O: μ- σε χρή V   **219** τοι Diggle: τε VΛ et [1Σ]V: δὲ O: γε Wilamowitz   ὀδυσέως V   **220** δ' ἔχων σαφές fere VΛ (ἔχω Q): σαφὲς δ' ἔ- O

ἢ παῖδα Τυδέως· οὐδ' ἀναιμάκτῳ χερί
ἥξω πρὸς οἴκους πρὶν φάος μολεῖν χθόνα.

Χο. Θυμβραῖε καὶ Δάλιε καὶ Λυκίας   στρ. α
     ναὸν ἐμβατεύων   225
     Ἄπολλον, ὦ Δία κεφαλά, μόλε τοξή-
        ρης, ἱκοῦ ἐννύχιος
     καὶ γενοῦ σωτήριος ἀνέρι πομπᾶς
     ἁγεμὼν καὶ ξύλλαβε Δαρδανίδαις,   230
     ὦ παγκρατές, ὦ Τροΐας
     τείχη παλαιὰ δείμας.

     μόλοι δὲ ναυκλήρια καὶ στρατιᾶς   στρ. β
     Ἑλλάδος διόπτας
     ἵκοιτο καὶ κάμψειε πάλιν θυμέλας οἴ-   235
        κων πατρὸς Ἰλιάδας·
     Φθιάδων δ' ἵππων ποτ' ἐπ' ἄντυγα βαίη,
     δεσπότου πέρσαντος Ἀχαιὸν Ἄρη,
     τὰς πόντιος Αἰακίδᾳ   240
     Πηλεῖ δίδωσι δαίμων.

     ἐπεὶ πρό τ' οἴκων πρό τε γᾶς ἔτλα μόνος   ἀντ. α
     ναύσταθμα βὰς κατιδεῖν· ἄγαμαι
     λήματος· ἦ σπάνις αἰεὶ   245
     τῶν ἀγαθῶν, ὅταν ᾖ δυσάλιον ἐν πελάγει
     καὶ σαλεύῃ
     πόλις. ἔστι Φρυγῶν τις ἔστιν ἄλκιμος·

---

223 cf. Chr. Pat. 1944   244 et 602 (cf. 448, 582, 591, 673) (ναύσταθμα) Hsch. (Cyr.) v 147   249 cf. Chr. Pat. 1443

226–8 Δία Mantziou: δία V: δῖα ΟΛ   ἱκοῦ L. Dindorf: ἵκου fere Ω (ἥκ- Q)   ἐννύχιος VL: εὐνύχ- O: ἐνοίκ- Q   229–30 καὶ γενοῦ ... ἁγεμὼν Dindorf: ἁγεμὼν (ἀ- Tr²: ἡ- <L?>P) ... καὶ γενοῦ Ω   231 Τροΐας Lachmann: τροίας Ω   232 τεύχη Q   234 ἑλλάδος διόπτας Λ et Σ^V: om. Δ   235–7 κάμψειε Q: -ειεν Δ et Tr³ᵘᵛ: -οι L   πατρὸς Δ: πάτρας Λ   ἰλιάδας O: -δος VΛ   238 δ' ἵππων VΛ: οἴκων O   πότ' V: τότ' O: om. Λ   ἄντυγι V   239 ἀχαιὸν Δ et Σ^V: -ῶν Λ   240 ποντίας V   241 δαίμων OL: δαιμόνων Q: δόμων V   242–3 οἴκως Q   245 σπάνις αἰεὶ Diggle praeeunte Wilamowitz (ἀεὶ): σπάνια O: σπανία V² et Σ^V (quo accepto γᾶν vel γᾶς 256 Dindorf): πανία V: σπάνις Λ: σπάνις ἐστὶ Ritchie   246–7 δυσάλιον Δ et Σ^V: -ος Λ   248 σαλεύῃ V: -ει ΟΛ et Σ^V   249 τις Aldina (cf. Chr. Pat. 1443): τίς Ω

ἔνι δὲ θράσος 250
ἐν αἰχμᾷ· πόθι Μυσῶν ὃς ἐμὰν συμμαχίαν ἀτίζει;

τίν' ἄνδρ' Ἀχαιῶν ὁ πεδοστιβὴς σφαγεὺς   ἀντ. β
οὐτάσει ἐν κλισίαις, τετράπουν 255
μῖμον ἔχων ἐπὶ γαίας
θηρός; ἕλοι Μενέλαν, κτανὼν δ' Ἀγαμεμνόνιον
κρᾶτ' ἐνέγκοι
Ἑλένᾳ κακόγαμβρον ἐς χέρας γόον, 260
ὃς ἐπὶ πόλιν,
ὃς ἐπὶ γᾶν Τροΐαν χιλιόναυν ἤλυθ' ἔχων στρατείαν.

ΑΓΓΕΛΟΣ
    ἄναξ, τοιούτων δεσπόταισιν ἄγγελος
    εἴην τὸ λοιπὸν οἷά σοι φέρω μαθεῖν. 265
Εκ. ἦ πόλλ' ἀγρώσταις σκαιὰ πρόσκειται φρενί·
    καὶ γὰρ σὺ ποίμνας δεσπόταις τευχεσφόροις
    ἥκειν ἔοικας ἀγγελῶν ἵν' οὐ πρέπει.
    οὐκ οἶσθα δῶμα τοὐμὸν ἢ θρόνους πατρός,
    οἳ χρῆν γεγωνεῖν σ' εὐτυχοῦντα ποίμνια; 270
Αγ. σκαιοὶ βοτῆρές ἐσμεν· οὐκ ἄλλως λέγω.
    ἀλλ' οὐδὲν ἧσσόν σοι φέρω κεδνοὺς λόγους.
Εκ. παῦσαι λέγων μοι τὰς προσαυλείους τύχας·
    μάχας πρὸ χειρῶν καὶ δόρη βαστάζομεν.
Αγ. τοιαῦτα κἀγὼ σημανῶν ἐλήλυθα· 275
    ἀνὴρ γὰρ ἀλκῆς μυρίας στρατηλατῶν
    στείχει φίλος σοι σύμμαχός τε τῇδε γῇ.
Εκ. ποίας πατρῴας γῆς ἐρημώσας πέδον;
Αγ. Θρῄκης· πατρὸς δὲ Στρυμόνος κικλήσκεται.

---

253 (ἀτίζει) Hsch. (Cyr.) α 8083   265 cf. Chr. Pat. 2185   266 et 287 (ἀγρώσταις) cf. Hsch. α 844   272 Chr. Pat. 2184   274 (δόρη) Hsch. δ 2210   275 cf. Chr. Pat. 2190

250-2 (≠ 261-3) numerorum ratio incerta est   250 θάρσος Σ^V (≠ ^{i}Σ^V) et Tr^3 251-2 αἰχμᾷ(ι) O^{uvV}: -αῖς Λ   πόθι Hoffmann: ποτὶ Ω et ^{i}Σ^V 255 οὐτάσει ἐν VΛ: -σειεν O   256 γαίας Λ: γαίᾳ O: γαῖαν V (vide ad 245)   257-8 μενέλαον L   ἀγαμεμνόνιον V: -ειον OΛ   260 χέρας Λ: χεῖρας Δ   261 πόλιν O: πτόλιν V: πόλον Q: πῶλον L   262-3 Τροΐαν Dindorf: τροίαν Δ<L>Q: del. Tr^1 ἤλυθ' Δ et Tr^1: -θεν <L>Q   στρατείαν Heath: -τιάν Ω   264^n Ἄγγελος VΛ: Ποιμήν O   265 οἴην L   μαθεῖν φέρω O   266 ἦ fere OΛ (ἦ Q): ἢ VgV   ἀγρώσταις O<L>P: -ώταις V et Tr$^{2/3}$: -όταις Q: -ώτες gV   267 τευχεσφόροις Q   268 ἥκεις V   ἔοικας om. Q   269 πατρὸς θρόνους O   270 οἳ χρῆν fere Δ (χρὴν V): οἷς χρὴ Λ   γεγωνεῖν σ' ΔL: -εῖς Q   ποιμνίων O   271^n Ποιμήν O   271 λέγω O: -εις VΛ   274 δόρη VL et Σ^{VL}: δόρυ OQgE   276 ἀλκῆς Λ: ἀρχῆς Δ

Εκ. Ῥῆσον τιθέντ' ἔλεξας ἐν Τροίᾳ πόδα; 280
Αγ. ἔγνως· λόγου δὲ δὶς τόσου μ' ἐκούφισας.
Εκ. καὶ πῶς πρὸς Ἴδης ὀργάδας πορεύεται,
πλαγχθεὶς πλατείας πεδιάδος θ' ἁμαξίτου;
Αγ. οὐκ οἶδ' ἀκριβῶς· εἰκάσαι γε μὴν πάρα.
νυκτὸς γὰρ οὔτι φαῦλον ἐσβαλεῖν στρατόν, 285
κλύοντα πλήρη πεδία πολεμίας χερός.
φόβον δ' ἀγρώσταις, οἳ κατ' Ἰδαῖον λέπας
οἰκοῦμεν αὐτόρριζον ἑστίαν χθονός,
παρέσχε δρυμὸν νυκτὸς ἔνθηρον μολών.
πολλῇ γὰρ ἠχῇ Θρῄκιος ῥέων στρατός 290
ἔστειχε· θάμβει δ' ἐκπλαγέντες ἵεμεν
ποίμνας πρὸς ἄκρας, μή τις Ἀργείων μόλῃ
λεηλατήσων καὶ σὰ πορθήσων σταθμά,
πρὶν δὴ δι' ὤτων γῆρυν οὐχ Ἑλληνικήν
ἐδεξάμεσθα καὶ μετέστημεν φόβου. 295
στείχων δ' ἄνακτος προυξερευνητὰς ὁδοῦ
ἀνιστόρησα Θρῃκίοις προσφθέγμασιν·
Τίς ὁ στρατηγὸς καὶ τίνος κεκλημένος
στείχει πρὸς ἄστυ Πριαμίδαισι σύμμαχος;
καὶ πάντ' ἀκούσας ὧν ἐφιέμην μαθεῖν 300
ἔστην· ὁρῶ δὲ Ῥῆσον ὥστε δαίμονα
ἑστῶτ' ἐν ἵπποις Θρῃκίοις τ' ὀχήμασιν.
χρυσῇ δὲ πλάστιγξ αὐχένα ζυγηφόρον
πώλων ἔκλῃε χιόνος ἐξαυγεστέρων.
πέλτη δ' ἐπ' ὤμων χρυσοκολλήτοις τύποις 305
ἔλαμπε· Γοργὼν δ' ὡς ἐπ' αἰγίδος θεᾶς

280–1 cf. Chr. Pat. 2186–7 **282** cf. Chr. Pat. 2189 **284–5** cf. Chr. Pat. 2095–6 **285** cf. Chr. Pat. 2452 **287** (ἀγρώσταις) vide ad 264 **291** cf. Chr. Pat. 2138, 2467 **294–5** cf. Chr. Pat. 2449–50 **297** cf. Chr. Pat. 2443 **300** cf. Chr. Pat. 2455 **305** (cf. 371–2, 410, 487) (πέλτη) Hsch. (Cyr.) π 1364? (etiam Alc. 498 et alibi)

---

280 εἰς Τροίαν O **282** post 283 O **283** πλαγχθεὶς OL: πλαχ- VQ πλατείας V: -αις Λ: πατρῴας O θ' ἁμαξιτοῦ Stiblinus: τ' ἀμ- ΔL: ἀμαξίτοις Q **285** ἐσβαλεῖν Diggle (cf. Chr. Pat. 2096, 2452): ἐμβ- Ω **286** κλύοντα West: κλύοντα Ω (vide ad 109) **287** λέπας ΔL: ὅπας Q **288** αὐτόριζον Q **290** ῥέων στρατός VL: σ- ῥ- O: λέγων σ- Q **292** πρὸς Δ: ἐς Λ **293** πορθμήσων O **295** ἐδεξάμεθα L **296** προυξενευρητὰς O ὁδοῦ V: στρατοῦ OΛ **297** -φθέγμασιν scripsi post West: -φθέγμασιν Ω (item 608) **298** κεκλιμένος O **299** πριαμίδεσι V **302** ἑστῶτ' ἐν VΛ: ἑστῶθ' O ἵπποις (-σι Q) θρη(ι)κίοις τ' ὀχήμασιν (-σι L°P) Λ: ἱππείοισι θρη(ι)κίοις ὄχοις Δ **303** χρυσῇ Δ πλάστιγξ Λ: -ιξ V: -ιγγι O ζυγηφόρον Δ: -ων Λ **304** ἔκλυε Q χρόνος O εὐαυγεστέρων Blaydes **305** πέλτη Λ: -ῃ O: -ης V δ' Λ: τ' O: om. V ὤμων V τύποις OL et Q¹ᶜ: δίφροις V: ἵπποις Q **306** ἀπ' O θοᾶς V

χαλκῇ μετώποις ἱππικοῖσι πρόσδετος
πολλοῖσι σὺν κώδωσιν ἐκτύπει φόβον.
στρατοῦ δὲ πλῆθος οὐδ' ἂν ἐν ψήφου λόγῳ
θέσθαι δύναι' ἄν, ὡς ἄπλατον ἦν ἰδεῖν, 310
πολλοὶ μὲν ἱππῆς, πολλὰ πελταστῶν τέλη,
πολλοὶ δ' ἀτράκτων τοξόται, πολὺς δ' ὄχλος
γυμνῆς ἁμαρτῇ, Θρηκίαν ἔχων στολήν.
τοιόσδε Τροίᾳ σύμμαχος πάρεστ' ἀνήρ,
ὃν οὔτε φεύγων οὔθ' ὑποσταθεὶς δορί 315
ὁ Πηλέως παῖς ἐκφυγεῖν δυνήσεται.
Χο. ὅταν πολίταις εὐσταθῶσι δαίμονες,
ἕρπει κατάντης ξυμφορὰ πρὸς τἀγαθά.
Εκ. πολλούς, ἐπειδὴ τοὐμὸν εὐτυχεῖ δόρυ
καὶ Ζεὺς πρὸς ἡμῶν ἐστιν, εὑρήσω φίλους. 320
ἀλλ' οὐδὲν αὐτῶν δεόμεθ', οἵτινες πάλαι
μὴ ξυμπονοῦσιν ἡνίκ' ἐξώστης Ἄρης
ἔθραυε λαίφη τῆσδε γῆς μέγας πνέων.
Ῥῆσος δ' ἔδειξεν οἷος ἦν Τροίᾳ φίλος·
ἥκει γὰρ ἐς δαῖτ', οὐ παρὼν κυνηγέταις 325
αἱροῦσι λείαν οὐδὲ συγκαμὼν δορί.
Χο. ὀρθῶς ἀτίζεις κἀπίμομφος εἶ φίλοις·
δέχου δὲ τοὺς θέλοντας ὠφελεῖν πόλιν.
Εκ. ἀρκοῦμεν οἱ σῴζοντες Ἴλιον πάλαι.
Χο. πέποιθας ἤδη πολεμίους ᾑρηκέναι; 330
Εκ. πέποιθα· δείξει τοὐπιὸν σέλας θεοῦ.
Χο. ὅρα τὸ μέλλον· πόλλ' ἀναστρέφει θεός.

---

318 (κατάντης) Hsch. (Cyr.) κ 1296 (etiam Ar. Ran. 127)   327 (ἀτίζεις) Hsch. (Cyr.) α 8084   330–1 cf. Chr. Pat. 1767–8

---

308 κόδωσιν L (≠ Tr²/³)   309 ψήφῳ λόγου O   310 δύναι' ἄν Δ: δυναίμην Λ   311 ἱππῆς Dindorf: -εῖς ΩgE   πολλὰ δὲ gE   πέλη Q   312 πολλοί] πομποί O   δ' (prius) L: τ' ΔQgE   ἀστράκτων O   313 γυμνὸς Q   ἁμαρτῇ Wackernagel: ὁμαρτῇ(ι) Δ: ὁμαρτεῖ ΛgE et O¹ᶜ   στολὴν ἔχων O   318 ἕρπε O   ξυμ- VL: συμ- OQgV   τἀγαθά ΔgV: -όν Λ   322 ξυμπονοῦσιν L: -ῶσιν ΔQgB   323 ἔθραυε V: ἔθραυσε OgB: ἔφαυσε Λ   λαίφη VLgB: λαίφθη O: λέχη Q   μέγα OgBᵘᵛ   324 δ' om. V   τροία(ι) Δ: -ας Λ   325 κυνηγέτης gE, coni. Elmsley   326 αἱροῦσι L: αἴρουσι ΔQ   δουρί V   327 ἀτίζεις VΛ: ἀτιμάζεις gB: ἔλεξας OgV   κἀπίμομφος OΛgV: -μορφος VgBᵘᵛ   328 πόλιν ΩgB: φίλους gV   329 πάλαι Δ: πόλιν Λ   330 εἰρηκέναι V   331 δείξοι V (≠ Chr. Pat. 1768)   θεοῦ σέλας O (≠ Chr. Pat)

Εκ. μισῶ φίλοισιν ὕστερον βοηδρομεῖν. 333
ὃ δ' οὖν, ἐπείπερ ἦλθε, σύμμαχος μὲν οὔ, 336
ξένος δὲ πρὸς τράπεζαν ἡκέτω ξένων·
χάρις γὰρ αὐτῷ Πριαμιδῶν διώλετο. 338
Χο. ἄναξ, ἀπωθεῖν συμμάχους ἐπίφθονον. 334
Αγ. φόβος γένοιτ' ἂν πολεμίοις ὀφθεὶς μόνον. 335
Εκ. σύ τ' εὖ παραινεῖς καὶ σὺ καιρίως σκοπεῖς. 339
ὁ χρυσοτευχὴς δ' οὕνεκ' ἀγγέλου λόγων 340
Ῥῆσος παρέστω τῇδε σύμμαχος χθονί.

Χο. Ἀδράστεια μὲν ἁ Διὸς   στρ. α
  παῖς εἴργοι στομάτων φθόνον·
φράσω γὰρ δὴ ὅσον μοι
ψυχᾷ προσφιλές ἐστιν εἰπεῖν. 345
ἥκεις, ὦ ποταμοῦ παῖ,
ἥκεις ἐπλάθης Φιλίου πρὸς αὐλὰν
ἀσπαστός, ἐπεί σε χρόνῳ
Πιερὶς μάτηρ ὅ τε καλλιγέφυρος ποταμὸς πορεύει 350

Στρυμών, ὅς ποτε τᾶς μελῳ-   ἀντ. α
  δοῦ Μούσας δι' ἀκηράτων
δινηθεὶς ὑδροειδὴς
κόλπων σὰν ἐφύτευσεν ἥβαν.
σύ μοι Ζεὺς ὁ Φαναῖος 355
ἥκεις διφρεύων βαλιαῖσι πώλοις.
νῦν, ὦ πατρὶς ὦ Φρυγία,
ξὺν θεῷ νῦν σοι τὸν Ἐλευθέριον
Ζῆνα πάρεστιν εἰπεῖν.

---

335 cf. Aristid. Or. 1.106?   **338** cf. Eust. 822.2–5? (vide comm.)   **339** cf. Chr. Pat. 1968–9

333, 336–8, 334–5, 339–41 hoc ordine Nauck correcta personarum dispositione: 334–8 nuntio 339–41 choro trib. Δ, 334–5 choro 336–8 Hectori 339–41 choro L (praescriptis paragr.), 334–8 choro 339–41 Hectori Q   **336–8** del. West   **336** ὃ δ' Nauck: ὅδ' Ω   **337** ἱκέτω L   ξένον Q   **338** ἀπώλετο L   **335** ὀφθεὶς VΛ: ἐλθὼν O   post hunc versum fortasse lacuna statuenda   **339** κυρίως O (≠ Chr. Pat. 1969)   **340** δ' οὕνεκ' OΛ: οὖν ἐκ V   **341** παρέστω Λ: -έσται Δ et ⁱΣᵛ   **342ⁿ** om. V   **342** ἀδράστεια O et V¹ᵍ¹Tr³: -άστια V, -αστία LᵘᵛQ, utrumque Σᵛ   ἁ om. O   **343** εἴργοι O: -ει V: -οις Λ   **344** φράσον Q   **345** ἔστ' <L>P (≠ Tr³)   **347** φιλίου Λ: φρυγίαν Δ   **348** ἀσπαστός γ' <L>P (≠ Tr³)   **351** ταῖς Q   **352** διακράτων V   **354** σὰν ἐφύτευσεν Q et Tr³: σὰν ἐφύτευσ' L: ἀνεφύτευσεν O, -σαν V   **356** διφρεύων Δ: -σων Λ   **358** ἐλεύθερον V   **359** ἰδεῖν V

Ῥῆσος 81

ἆρά ποτ' αὖθις ἁ παλαι-   στρ. β
  ἁ Τροία τοὺς προπότας παναμερεύ-   361
σει θιάσους ἐρώτων
ψαλμοῖσι καὶ κυλίκων οἰνοπλανήτοις ἐπιδεξίοις ἁμίλ-
λαις κατὰ πόντον Ἀτρειδᾶν   365
Σπάρταν οἰχομένων Ἰλιάδος παρ' ἀκτᾶς;
ὦ φίλος, εἴθε μοι
σᾷ χερὶ καὶ σῷ δορὶ πράξας τάδ' ἐς οἶκον ἔλθοις.

ἐλθὲ φάνηθι, τὰν ζάχρυ-   ἀντ. β
  σον προβαλοῦ Πηλεΐδα κατ' ὄμμα πέλ-   371
ταν δοχμίαν πεδαίρων
σχιστὰν παρ' ἄντυγα, πώλους ἐρεθίζων δίβολόν τ' ἄκοντα πάλλων. σὲ γὰρ οὔτις ὑποστὰς   375
Ἀργείας ποτ' ἐν Ἥρας δαπέδοις χορεύσει·
ἀλλά νιν ἅδε γᾶ
καπφθίμενον Θρῃκὶ μόρῳ φίλτατον ἄχθος οἴσει.

ἰὼ ἰώ,   380
μέγας ὦ βασιλεῦ. καλόν, ὦ Θρήκη,
σκύμνον ἔθρεψας πολίαρχον ἰδεῖν.
ἰδὲ χρυσόδετον σώματος ἀλκήν,
κλύε καὶ κόμπους κωδωνοκρότους
παρὰ πορπάκων κελαδοῦντας.
θεός, ὦ Τροία, θεός, αὐτὸς Ἄρης   385
ὁ Στρυμόνιος πῶλος ἀοιδοῦ
Μούσης ἥκων καταπνεῖ σε.

368–9 cf. Chr. Pat. 2025   **370–1** cf. Chr. Pat. 2029, 2083   **371–2** (πέλταν) vide ad 305

---

360 Τροία Murray: τροία Ω   **361** τὰς O   **363** ψαλμοῖσι Canter: ψάλμασι Ω   οἰνοπλάντοις O   **364** ἐπιδεξίοις L. Dindorf (-αις iam Musgrave): ὑποδεξίοις O, -αις VΛ et $^i\Sigma^V$ **367** ἀκτᾶς VL: -άς Q: -ὰν O   **369** δόρατι V   ἐς Aldina: εἰς Ω   ἔλθης L (≠ L^{1c})   **370** προβαλοῦ OL: -βαλλοῦ Q: -λαβοῦ V   **372** πεδραίνων Q   **373** πώλους Reiske: κώλοις Λ: om. (una cum ἐρεθίζων) Λ   **379** καπφθίμενον Bothe (1803), denuo Elmsley: καταφθ- Ω   θρῃκὶ O: -κίω L: -κίων VQ   οἴσοι Q   **380b** θρήκη V   **381** πολίαρχον Δ: πολύ- Λ   **382** ἰδὲ Liapis: ἴδε Ω   **384** πορτάκων O   **386** στρυμόνειος V   **387** ἀναπνεῖ Hn   σε] σου West, σοι Feickert

ΡΗΣΟΣ
χαῖρ', ἐσθλὸς ἐσθλοῦ παῖ, τύραννε τῆσδε γῆς,
Ἕκτορ· παλαιᾷ σ' ἡμέρᾳ προσεννέπω.
χαίρω δέ σ' εὐτυχοῦντα καὶ προσήμενον 390
πύργοισιν ἐχθρῶν· συγκατασκάψων δ' ἐγώ
τείχη πάρειμι καὶ νεῶν πρήσων σκάφη.

Εκ. παῖ τῆς μελῳδοῦ μητέρος Μουσῶν μιᾶς
Θρῃκός τε ποταμοῦ Στρυμόνος, φιλῶ λέγειν
τἀληθὲς αἰεὶ κοὐ διπλοῦς πέφυκ' ἀνήρ. 395
πάλαι πάλαι χρῆν τῇδε συγκάμνειν χθονί
ἐλθόντα, καὶ μὴ τοὐπὶ σ' Ἀργείων ὕπο
Τροίαν ἐᾶσαι πολεμίῳ πεσεῖν δορί.
οὐ γάρ τι λέξεις ὡς ἄκλητος ὢν φίλοις
οὐκ ἦλθες οὐδ' ἤμυνας οὐδ' ἐπεστράφης. 400
τίς γάρ σε κῆρυξ ἢ γερουσία Φρυγῶν
ἐλθοῦσ' ἀμύνειν οὐκ ἐπέσκηψεν πόλει;
ποῖον δὲ δώρων κόσμον οὐκ ἐπέμψαμεν;
σὺ δ' ἐγγενὴς ὢν βάρβαρός τε βαρβάρους
Ἕλλησιν ἡμᾶς προύπιες τὸ σὸν μέρος. 405
καίτοι σε μικρᾶς ἐκ τυραννίδος μέγαν
Θρῃκῶν ἄνακτα τῇδ' ἔθηκ' ἐγὼ χερί,
ὅτ' ἀμφὶ Πάγγαιόν τε Παιόνων τε γῆν
Θρῃκῶν ἀρίστοις ἐμπεσὼν κατὰ στόμα
ἔρρηξα πέλτην, σοὶ δὲ δουλώσας λεών 410
παρέσχον· ὧν σὺ λακτίσας πολλὴν χάριν
φίλων νοσούντων ὕστερος βοηδρομεῖς.
οἱ δ' οὐδὲν ἡμῖν ἐγγενεῖς πεφυκότες,
πάλαι παρόντες, οἳ μὲν ἐν χωστοῖς τάφοις

---

388 cf. Chr. Pat. 2098, 2538   390–1a (χαίρω … ἐχθρῶν) Nic. ad Il. 6.479–80 (II 212.21–2 Erbse)   391 cf. Chr. Pat. 2099   399–400 cf. Chr. Pat. 1716–17   401 cf. Chr. Pat. 1719   403 cf. Chr. Pat. 1720   406–11 cf. Chr. Pat. 1721–6   410 (πέλτην) vide ad 305   413–14 cf. Chr. Pat. 1741–2

388ⁿ om. O, Ῥῆσος βασιλεύς O¹ᵐ   388 ἐσθλὸς ἐσθλοῦ παῖ Q et Chr. Pat. 2098, 2538: ἐ- ἐ- παῖς L: ἐσθλοῦ παῖ V: ἐσθλοῦ πατρὸς παῖ O   versum suspectum habuit Diggle   392 πρήσσων L   393 παῖ Δ: παῖς Λ   394 θρη(ι)κός ΔQ et Tr⁽³⁷⁾P²: παῖς L<P>   395 αἰεὶ Va: ἀεὶ ΩgVgBgE   πέφηκ' V   396 συγκάμειν V   397 τοὐπὶ σ' VΛ: τοὐπίσω O   398 πολεμίῳ Vaˡˢ, coni. Bothe: -ων Ω   399 φίλοις OL: -ος VQ   400 om. O   ἦλθες Λ: -ας V   401 κῆρυξ scripsi post Hermann et West: κῆρυξ Ω   402 ἐπέσκυψε V   403 ποῖον Λ: ποίων Δ (cf. Chr. Pat. 1720)   τε O   404 ἐγγενὴς VL: εὐγ- OQgE   τ' ὢν gE   βαρβάρους Λ: -ου ΔgE   408 παγαῖον O   409 ἀρίστοις Λ et Chr. Pat. 1724: -ους Δ   411 πολὺν Q   412 φίλων ΩgE: ἡμῶν gV (sed 411 ἐσθλῶν φίλων δὲ pro παρέσχον ὧν σὺ)   ὕστερος OQgV: -ον VLgE   βοηδρομεῖν V   413 ἐγγενεῖς VLQ: εὐγ- O: συγγ- Chr. Pat. 1741: ἐν γένει Valckenaer

Ῥῆσος 83

κεῖνται πεσόντες, πίστις οὐ σμικρὰ πόλει, 415
οἳ δ' ἔν θ' ὅπλοισι καὶ παρ' ἱππείοις ὄχοις
ψυχρὰν ἄησιν δίψιόν τε πῦρ θεοῦ
μένουσι καρτεροῦντες, οὐκ ἐν δεμνίοις
πυκνὴν ἄμυστιν ὡς σὺ δεξιούμενοι.
ταῦθ', ὡς ἂν εἰδῇς Ἕκτορ' ὄντ' ἐλεύθερον, 420
καὶ μέμφομαί σοι καὶ λέγω κατ' ὄμμα σόν.

Ρη. τοιοῦτός εἰμι καὐτός· εὐθεῖαν λόγων
τέμνω κέλευθον, κοὐ διπλοῦς πέφυκ' ἀνήρ.
ἐγὼ δὲ μεῖζον ἢ σὺ τῇσδ' ἀπὼν χθονός
λύπῃ πρὸς ἧπαρ δυσφορῶν ἐτειρόμην. 425
ἀλλ' ἀγχιτέρμων γαῖά μοι, Σκύθης λεώς,
μέλλοντι νόστον τὸν πρὸς Ἴλιον περᾶν
ξυνῆψε πόλεμον· Ἀξένου δ' ἀφικόμην
πόντου πρὸς ἀκτάς, Θρῇκα πορθμεύσων στρατόν.
ἔνθ' αἱματηρὸς πελανὸς ἐς γαῖαν Σκύθης 430
ἠντλεῖτο λόγχῃ Θρῇξ τε συμμιγὴς φόνος.
τοιάδε τοί μ' ἀπεῖργε συμφορὰ πέδον
Τροίας ἱκέσθαι σύμμαχόν τέ σοι μολεῖν.
ἐπεὶ δ' ἔπερσα, τῶνδ' ὁμηρεύσας τέκνα,
τάξας ἔτειον δασμὸν ἐς δόμους φέρειν, 435
ἥκω περάσας ναυσὶ Πόντιον στόμα,
τὰ δ' ἄλλα πεζὸς γῆς περῶν ὁρίσματα —
οὐχ ὡς σὺ κομπεῖς τὰς ἐμὰς ἀμύστιδας
οὐδ' ἐν ζαχρύσοις δώμασιν κοιμώμενος,
ἀλλ' οἷα πόντον Θρήκιον φυσήματα 440
κρυσταλλόπηκτα Παίονάς τ' ἐπεζάρει
ξὺν τοῖσδ' ἄυπνος οἶδα τλὰς πορπάμασιν.

415 cf. Chr. Pat. 1749   416–18 cf. Chr. Pat. 1743–5   419 (ἄμυστιν) Hsch. (Cyr.) α 3875 (etiam Cyc. 417, Ar. Ach. 1229)   426 (ἀγχιτέρμων) Hsch. (Cyr.) α 890?   435 (ἔτειον) Hsch. (Cyr.) ε 6525?   439 cf. Chr. Pat. 1747   441 (ἐπεζάρει) Hsch. (Cyr.) ε 4304 (etiam Phoen. 45)

415 μικρὰ Ο   πίστιν οὐ σμικρὰν Bothe   416 ἔν θ' ὅπλοισι V: ἐν ὅ- Ο: ἐνθάδ' ὅπλοις Λ   417 ἄησι V (≠ ¹Σᵛ)   δίψιόν τε] -ίοντες V (≠ Vᶜ)   418 μένουσι] οὐκ ἐν Ο   421 καὶ κατ' ὄμμασιν λέγω Ο   422ⁿ om. O   422 sic interpunxi post Nauck (vide ad 423)   423 τέμνω (vel τέμνειν) Nauck: τέμνων Ω   424 μείζον' L   426 λαὸς σκύθης Ο   428 ἀξένου (praestat Ἀξένου) Markland: εὐξ- Ω   429 πορθμεύσων L: -εύσας Δ: -εῦσαι Q, coni. Aldina, haud male   στρατόν om. Q   430 ἐς Δ: εἰς Λ   431 φόνος Ο: -ω(ι) VΛ, quo accepto Θρηκὶ συμ- Matthiae   432 ἀπῆγε V   433 μολεῖν τέ σοι Ο   435 ἔσειον Ο   440 πόντον Λ: -ιον Δ   441 κρυσταλό- V   -πηκτον vel -πήγα Kirchhoff   Παίονάς Aldina: παιόνας Ω   ἐπεζάρει Scaliger et ¹Vᵍˡ Qᵍˡ (ἐπεβάρει; cf. Hsch. ε 4304): -ζάτει Ω   442 ξὺν Λ: σὺν Δ   ἄυπνος οἶδα Δ: ἀόπλοις οἷα Λ   πορπάμασιν Porson: -πημ- Λ: -πάσμ- Δ

ἀλλ' ὕστερος μὲν ἦλθον, ἐν καιρῷ δ' ὅμως·
σὺ μὲν γὰρ ἤδη δέκατον αἰχμάζεις ἔτος
κοὐδὲν περαίνεις, ἡμέραν δ' ἐξ ἡμέρας 445
ῥίπτεις κυβεύων τὸν πρὸς Ἀργείους Ἄρη·
ἐμοὶ δὲ φῶς ἓν ἡλίου καταρκέσει
πέρσαντι πύργους ναυστάθμοις ἐπεσπεσεῖν
κτεῖναί τ' Ἀχαιούς· θἠτέρᾳ δ' ἀπ' Ἰλίου
πρὸς οἶκον εἶμι, συντεμὼν τοὺς σοὺς πόνους. 450
ὑμῶν δὲ μή τις ἀσπίδ' ἄρηται χερί·
ἐγὼ γὰρ ἔξω τοὺς μέγ' αὐχοῦντας δορὶ
πέρσας Ἀχαιούς, καίπερ ὕστερος μολών.

Χο. ἰὼ ἰώ. στρ.
φίλα θροεῖς, φίλος Διόθεν εἶ· μόνον 455
φθόνον ἄμαχον ὕπατος
Ζεὺς θέλοι ἀμφὶ σοῖς λόγοισιν εἴργειν.
τὸ δὲ νάϊον Ἀργόθεν δόρυ
οὔτε πρίν τιν' οὔτε νῦν
ἀνδρῶν ἐπόρευσε σέθεν κρείσσω. 460
πῶς μοι τὸ σὸν ἔγχος Ἀχιλλεὺς ἂν δύναιτο,
πῶς δ' Αἴας ὑπομεῖναι;
εἰ γὰρ ἐγὼ τόδε γ' ἦμαρ
εἰσίδοιμ', ἄναξ, ὅτῳ πολυφόνου 465
χειρὸς ἄποιν' ἄροιο σᾷ λόγχᾳ.

Ρη. τοιαῦτα μέν σοι τῆς μακρᾶς ἀπουσίας
πρᾶξαι παρέξω· σὺν δ' Ἀδραστείᾳ λέγω.
ἐπεὶ δ' ἂν ἐχθρῶν τήνδ' ἐλευθέραν πόλιν

---

443 cf. Chr. Pat. 1728   **447** cf. Chr. Pat. 1731   **448–50** cf. Chr. Pat. 1732–3   **448** (ναυστάθμοις) vide ad 244   **464–5** cf. Chr. Pat. 1785–6   **466** (ἄροιο Diggle) Hsch. (Cyr.) α 7362?

---

443 ὕστερος Cobet: -ον ΩgV et Chr. Pat. 1728   μὲν om. Q   εἰς καιρὸν Chr. Pat.   **446** ῥίπτεις Sallier: πίπτεις fere Ω (-ῃς O)   ἄρη OQ: -ην VL   **448** ναυστάθμοις Λ: -ους Δ   -πεσὼν Q   **449** θἠτέρᾳ Feickert et Chr. Pat. 1732 pars codd.: θ' ἠτ- Ω et Chr. Pat. codd. pler.: θατέρᾳ Brunck, vix recte   δ' Δ: τ' Λ   **451** ἄρηται L. Dindorf: αἴρηται V: αἱρεῖται O: αἱρέτω Q, αἱ- L   **452–3** ἥκω ... πέρσων Nauck, alii alia (vide comm.)   **452** μεγαλαυχοῦντας V   **453** ὕστερος V: -ον ΟΛ   **455** μόνος L   **457** θέλοι Λ: ἐθ- Δ   **459** τιν' οὔτε νῦν Nauck: οὔτε νῦν τιν' Ω   **460** ἐπόρευσεν L   **461–2** τὸ σὸν ἔγχος Ἀχιλλεὺς Wilamowitz: Ἀχιλλεὺς τὸ σὸν ἔγχος fere Ω (Ἀχιλεὺς V)   **464** τόδε γ' Hermann: τόδ' Ω: τόδ' ἔτ' Dindorf   **465** ὅτῳ Musgrave: ὅπως Ω   **466** ἄποιν' ἄροιο σᾷ Diggle: ἀποινάσαιο Δ: ἀπονάσαιο fere Λ (-όνα- Q, ≠ Q¹ᶜ)   λόγχᾳ OQ: -α VL   **467** post hunc versum lac. stat. Kovacs   **469** ἐπεὶ δ' ἂν Morstadt: ἐπειδὰν ΟΛ: ἐπειδ' ἂν δ' V: ἐχθρῶν δ' ἐπειδὰν Sansone

Ῥῆσος 85

θῶμεν θεοῖσί τ' ἀκροθίνι' ἐξέλῃς, 470
ξὺν σοὶ στρατεύειν γῆν ἔπ' Ἀργείων θέλω
καὶ πᾶσαν ἐλθὼν Ἑλλάδ' ἐκπέρσαι δορί,
ὡς ἂν μάθωσιν ἐν μέρει πάσχειν κακῶς.
Εκ. εἰ τοῦ παρόντος τοῦδ' ἀπαλλαχθεὶς κακοῦ
πόλιν νεμοίμην ὡς τὸ πρίν ποτ' ἀσφαλῆ, 475
ἦ κάρτα πολλὴν θεοῖς ἂν εἰδείην χάριν.
τὰ δ' ἀμφί τ' Ἄργος καὶ νομὸν τὸν Ἑλλάδος
οὐχ ὧδε πορθεῖν ῥᾴδι' ὡς λέγεις δορί.
Ρη. οὐ τούσδ' ἀριστέας φασὶν Ἑλλήνων μολεῖν;
Εκ. κοὐ μεμφόμεσθά γ', ἀλλ' ἅδην ἐλαύνομεν. 480
Ρη. οὔκουν κτανόντες τούσδε πάντ' εἰργάσμεθα;
Εκ. μή νυν τὰ πόρσω τἀγγύθεν μεθεὶς σκόπει.
Ρη. ἀρκεῖν ἔοικέ σοι παθεῖν, δρᾶσαι δὲ μή.
Εκ. πολλῆς γὰρ ἄρχω κἀνθάδ' ὢν τυραννίδος.
ἀλλ' εἴτε λαιὸν εἴτε δεξιὸν κέρας 485
εἴτ' ἐν μέσοισι συμμάχοις πάρεστί σοι
πέλτην ἐρεῖσαι καὶ καταστῆσαι στρατόν.
Ρη. μόνος μάχεσθαι πολεμίοις, Ἕκτορ, θέλω.
εἰ δ' αἰσχρὸν ἡγῇ μὴ συνεμπρῆσαι νεῶν
πρύμνας, πονήσας τὸν πάρος πολὺν χρόνον, 490
τάξον μ' Ἀχιλλέως καὶ στρατοῦ κατὰ στόμα.
Εκ. οὐκ ἔστ' ἐκείνῳ θοῦρον ἀντᾶραι δόρυ.
Ρη. καὶ μὴν λόγος γ' ἦν ὡς ἔπλευσ' ἐπ' Ἴλιον.
Εκ. ἔπλευσε καὶ πάρεστιν· ἀλλὰ μηνίων
στρατηλάταισιν οὐ συναίρεται δόρυ. 495
Ρη. τίς δὴ μετ' αὐτὸν ἄλλος εὐδοξεῖ στρατοῦ;
Εκ. Αἴας ἐμοὶ μὲν οὐδὲν ἡσσᾶσθαι δοκεῖ
χὠ Τυδέως παῖς· ἔστι δ' αἱμυλώτατον

---

487 (πέλτην) vide ad 305   494 cf. Chr. Pat. 2188   498 (αἱμυλώτατον) Hsch. (Cyr.) μ 1865 <αἱ>μυλώτατον· … (suppl. Latte) (etiam Ai. 388)

---

470 ἴωμεν Q   471 ξὺν Λ: σὺν Δ   τρατεύειν O   ἀργείων Δ: -αν Λ   476 ἦ Λ: ἢ Δ   πολλὴν Δ et ΄Σ^V: -οῖς Λ   ἂν θεοῖς ἂν Q (≠ Q^{1c})   477 ἄργους Q   478 ῥᾳδίως O   479 τούσδ' ΔQ: τούς γ' L   ἀριστέας VΛ: -εῖς O   480 κοὐ VΛ et Σ^V: οὐ O   ἀλλ' ἅδην O: ἀλλ' ἅδην V: ἀλλὰ δὴν Λ   481 οὔκουν: vide ad 161   πάντ' εἰργάσμεθα Q: πᾶν εἰργ- Δ: πάντ' εἰργάσμεθ' ἄν L: cf. Σ^V πάντα διεπραξάμεθα (διαπεπραξόμεθα Schwartz, διαπραξόμεθα Wilamowitz)   482 νυν gV, coni. Scaliger: νῦν ΩgBgE   πόρσω Dindorf: πόρρω ΩgVgBgE   483 ἔοικεν O   484 τυρρ- O (≠ O^{1c})   488^n om. L   488 ἕκτωρ L (≠ L^{1c} vel Tr^1)   491 ἀχιλέως V   492 ἔστιν Q   ἀντᾶραι Reiske: ἐντάξαι Ω   495 δορί O   496 τίς δὴ Λ: τίς δὲ V: τί δαὶ O   497 ἡσσᾶσθαι Dindorf: ἡττ- Ω   498 τυδέος Q

κρότημ' Ὀδυσσεὺς λῆμά τ' ἀρκούντως θρασύς
καὶ πλεῖστα χώραν τήνδ' ἀνὴρ καθυβρίσας· 500
ὃς εἰς Ἀθάνας σηκὸν ἔννυχος μολών
κλέψας ἄγαλμα ναῦς ἐπ' Ἀργείων φέρει.
ἤδη δ' ἀγύρτης πτωχικὴν ἔχων στολήν
ἐσῆλθε πύργους, πολλὰ δ' Ἀργείοις κακά
ἠρᾶτο, πεμφθεὶς Ἰλίου κατάσκοπος· 505
κτανὼν δὲ φρουροὺς καὶ παραστάτας πυλῶν
ἐξῆλθεν· αἰεὶ δ' ἐν λόχοις εὑρίσκεται
Θυμβραῖον ἀμφὶ βωμὸν ἄστεως πέλας
θάσσων· κακῷ δὲ μερμέρῳ παλαίομεν.

Ρη. οὐδεὶς ἀνὴρ εὔψυχος ἀξιοῖ λάθρα 510
κτεῖναι τὸν ἐχθρόν, ἀλλ' ἰὼν κατὰ στόμα.
τοῦτον δ' ὃν ἵζειν φῂς σὺ κλωπικὰς ἕδρας
καὶ μηχανᾶσθαι, ζῶντα συλλαβὼν ἐγώ
πυλῶν ἐπ' ἐξόδοισιν ἀμπείρας ῥάχιν
στήσω πετεινοῖς γυψὶ θοινατήριον. 515
λῃστὴν γὰρ ὄντα καὶ θεῶν ἀνάκτορα
συλῶντα δεῖ νιν τῷδε κατθανεῖν μόρῳ.

Εκ. νῦν μὲν καταυλίσθητι· καὶ γὰρ εὐφρόνη.
δείξω δ' ἐγώ σοι χῶρον, ἔνθα χρὴ στρατόν
τὸν σὸν νυχεῦσαι τοῦ τεταγμένου δίχα. 520
ξύνθημα δ' ἡμῖν Φοῖβος, ἤν τι καὶ δέῃ·
μέμνησ' ἀκούσας Θρῃκί τ' ἄγγειλον στρατῷ.
ὑμᾶς δὲ βάντας χρὴ προταινὶ τάξεων
φρουρεῖν ἐγερτὶ καὶ νεῶν κατάσκοπον
δέχθαι Δόλωνα· καὶ γάρ, εἴπερ ἐστὶ σῶς, 525
ἤδη πελάζει στρατοπέδοισι Τρωϊκοῖς.

---

499 (κρότημα) Hsch. κ 4209 (ad S. fr. inc. 913 rett. Valckenaer) **503–7** cf. Chr. Pat. 1734–8 **510–11** Tz. Hist. 4.969–70 Leone **514** (ἀμπείρας) Hsch. (Cyr.) α 3775 **515** (θοινατήριον) Hsch. (Cyr.) θ 626 (ubi θοινη-) **516** cf. Chr. Pat. 1438 **517** cf. Chr. Pat. 1440 **518** cf. Chr. Pat. 1815 **519–20** cf. Chr. Pat. 1629, 1813

---

499 ὀδυσεὺς V   θρασύν V   **500** καὶ] εἰς Hermann   **501** ἀθάνας V: ἀθ∗νᾶς O: -ηνᾶς Λ   **503** ἤδην O (≠ O[1c])   στολὴν ἔχων O   **504** ἀργείοις Δ: -ους Λ   **505** ἰλίου O: Ἴλιον VΛ   **506** πυλῶν ΟΛ et Chr. Pat. 1737: φρυγῶν V   π- παραστάτας O (≠ Chr. Pat.)   **507** αἰεὶ Λ: ἀεὶ Δ   **508** ἄστεως Λ: -ος Δ   ἢ ἄστεος v. l. in Σ[V]   **509** μερμαίρῳ O   **512** δ' om. V   ἵζειν VΛ: -εις O: -ει gB (om. φῂς σὺ)   σὺ ΟΛ: οὐ V   κλωπικὰς ἕδρας ΔgB -αῖς ... -αις Λ   **514** ἀμπείρας Δ et Hsch. α 3775: ἐμπ- fere Λ (-πύρ- Q)   **515** θήσω O   θοιναστήριον O   **517** πότμῳ V (≠ Chr. Pat. 1440)   **518**[n] notam erasam L   **518** καταυλίσθητι Kirchhoff: -ητε Ω et Chr. Pat. 1815   **522** δ' V   ἄγγελον Q   **523** τάξεως L   **525** δέχθαι Aldina: δέχεσθαι fere Ω (-θε O)

Χο. τίνος ἁ φυλακά; τίς ἀμείβει τὰν ἐμάν; πρῶτα   στρ.
  δύεται σημεῖα καὶ ἑπτάποροι
  Πλειάδες αἰθέριαι· μέσα δ' Αἰετὸς   530
    οὐρανοῦ ποτᾶται.
  ἔγρεσθε· τί μέλλετε; κοιτᾶν
  ἔξιτε πρὸς φυλακάν.
  οὐ λεύσσετε μηνάδος αἴγλαν;
  ἀὼς δὴ πέλας ἀὼς   535
  γίγνεται καί τις προδρόμων ὅδε γ' ἐστὶν ἀστήρ.

— τίς ἐκηρύχθη πρώτην φυλακήν;
— Μυγδόνος υἱόν φασι Κόροιβον.
— τίς γὰρ ἐπ' αὐτῷ; — Κίλικας Παίων   540
  στρατὸς ἤγειρεν, Μυσοὶ δ' ἡμᾶς.

— οὔκουν Λυκίους πέμπτην φυλακὴν
  βάντας ἐγείρειν
  καιρὸς κλήρου κατὰ μοῖραν;   545

  καὶ μὰν ἀίω· Σιμόεντος ἡμένα κοίτας   ἀντ.
  φοινίας ὑμνεῖ πολυχορδοτάτᾳ
  γήρυϊ παιδολέτωρ μελοποιὸν ἀ-
    ηδονὶς μέριμναν.   550
  ἤδη δὲ νέμουσι κατ' Ἴδαν
  ποίμνια· νυκτιβρόμου
  σύριγγος ἰὰν κατακούω.

---

532 cf. Chr. Pat. 1995   532–3 Acc. Ant. fr. IV TRF³ = III Dangel?; cf. Chr. Pat. 1855–
6   534–7 cf. Chr. Pat. 1997–8

---

529 ἑπτάπορος Q   530 πληϊάδες V   531 μέσα VQ et Tr³: μέσας O: μέσον <L?>P et Tr²   οὐράνιός γε <Tr¹⁷>P (≠ Tr²/³)   533 ἔξιτε Hartung (cl. Chr. Pat. 1855–6 ἔγρεσθ' ἔγρεσθε· τί, γυναῖκες, μέλλετε; | ἔξιτε): ἔγρεσθε Ω   534ⁿ ἡμιχ. O   534 λεύσετε V   535ⁿ ἡμιχ. L (≠ Tr³)   535 ἀὼς δὲ πέλας ἀὼς δὴ O   536–7 προδρόμων Musgrave: προδόμων Δ: πρὸ δόμων Λ   ὅδε γ' O: οὐδέ γ' V: ὅδε γὰρ Λ   ἀστήρ VΛ et Oᶜ (cf. Chr. Pat. 1998): ἀνήρ O et Tr¹ˢ   538ⁿ ἡμιχ. Ω   538 ἐκληρώθη Dobree   φυλακάν O   539ⁿ ἡμιχ. VQ et L¹ᶜ: paragr. L: om. O   539 μιγδόνος O   κόροιβον V et Σⱽ: -ρυβ- OΛ et Σⱽ ad 5   540ⁿ (ante τίς) ἡμιχ. O: paragr. VL: om. Q   (ante Κίλικας) paragr. VL: om. OQ   540 παίων Λ: παιῶν Δ et Σⱽ ad 5   541–2ⁿ (ante Μυσοὶ) nullam notam OQ: paragr. VL   543ⁿ ἡμιχ. O: paragr. VL: om. Q   543 οὔκουν: vide ad 161   544 μάντας ἐγείρει V   545ⁿ (ante κλήρου) ἡμιχ. O   546–7ⁿ paragr. VL: om. OQ   546–7 μὰν Diggle: μὴν Ω   ἡμέρα O   548 φοινίας O: φον- VΛ   θρηνεῖ ʸᵖΣⱽ   -χορδοτάταν O⁷ (≠ O¹ᶜ⁷)   549 παιδολέτωρ O et Tr³: ἁ π- VΛ   550 μελοποιὸν ... μέριμναν Dindorf (μέριμναν iam Reiske): -ὸς ... μέριμνα fere Ω (μελω- ... μέριμνᾳ Q)   552 νυκτιβρόμου Pierson: νυκτιδρόμου Δ: νυκτὶ δρ- Λ

θέλγει δ' ὄμματος ἕδραν
ὕπνος· ἅδιστος γὰρ ἔβα βλεφάροις πρὸς ἀῶ.   555

— τί ποτ' οὐ πελάθει σκοπός, ὃν ναῶν
Ἕκτωρ ὤτρυνε κατόπτην;
— ταρβῶ· χρόνιος γὰρ ἄπεστιν.
— ἀλλ' ἦ κρυπτὸν λόχον ἐσπαίσας   560
διόλωλε; †τάχ' ἂν εἴη† φοβερόν μοι.

— αὐδῶ Λυκίους πέμπτην φυλακὴν
βάντας ἐγείρειν
ἡμᾶς κλήρου κατὰ μοῖραν.

ΟΔΥΣΣΕΥΣ
Διόμηδες, οὐκ ἤκουσας — ἢ κενὸς ψόφος   565
στάζει δι' ὤτων; — τευχέων τινὰ κτύπον;
ΔΙΟΜΗΔΗΣ
οὔκ, ἀλλὰ δεσμὰ πωλικῶν ἐξ ἀντύγων
κλάζει σίδηρον· κἀμέ τοι, πρὶν ᾐσθόμην
δεσμῶν ἀραγμὸν ἱππικῶν, ἔδυ φόβος.
Οδ.   ὅρα κατ' ὄρφνην μὴ φύλαξιν ἐντύχῃς.   570
Δι.   φυλάξομαί τοι κἂν σκότῳ τιθεὶς πόδα.
Οδ.   ἢν δ' οὖν ἐγείρῃς, οἶσθα σύνθημα στρατοῦ;
Δι.   Φοῖβον Δόλωνος οἶδα σύμβολον κλυών.
Οδ.   ἔα·
εὐνὰς ἐρήμους τάσδε πολεμίων ὁρῶ.

554–6 cf. Chr. Pat. 1831, 1999–2001, 1820, 1850   558 (κατόπταν) vide ad 134   567 (ἐξ ἀντύγων) Hsch. (Cyr.) ε 3575 (etiam Ai. [1030])   570–1 cf. Chr. Pat. 1980–1   574 cf. Chr. Pat. 2031–2

---

554 θέλθει Q   555–6[n] (ante ὕπνος) Xo. O   555–6 βλεφάροις Musgrave (cf. Chr. Pat. 1820, 1850, 2000): -οισι Ω   ἀῶ Blaydes, Headlam: ἀοῦς Ω   557–9 om. L, add. L[lc] vel Tr[1] (559 denuo add. Tr[2], del. Tr[3])   557[n] ἡμιχ. ΔQ: om. ut vid. L[lc] vel Tr[1]   557 πελάθει ΔQ: -θῃ L[lc] vel Tr[1]: πλάθει Nauck   ὃν ναῶν om. Va   558 κατόπτην Wecklein: -ταν Ω: vide ad 134   559[n] nullam notam Ω   559 γάρ τις Tr[3]   ἄπεστιν ἐμπεσών O   560[n] paragr. L: om. ΔQ   560 ἦ Matthiae: ἢ Ω   εἰσπαίσας O: εἰσπεσὼν VaΛ   561 διόλωλε <L[?]>P: διόλωλεν Q et aut L aut Tr[3]: ὄλωλεν Va: διώλεσεν O   561[n] (ante τάχ') paragr. L   561 τυχ' Va — τάχ' ἂν [εἴη]· φοβερόν μοι Headlam, alii alia (vide comm.)   562[n] ἡμιχ. Ω: paragr. L: om. VaQ   565 οὐκ om. Va   ἢ κενὸς ΟΛ: ὡς ἧκε Va   568 σίδηρον Bothe (1803), denuo Paley: σιδήρου Ω   569 ἀραγμῶν Va   570 ὄρφνην Δ: -αν Λ et Chr. Pat.1980   571 τοι ΟΛ: τι Va: utrumque Chr. Pat. 1981   573 κλυών West: κλύων Ω (vide ad 109)

Ῥῆσος 89

Δι. καὶ μὴν Δόλων γε τάσδ' ἔφραζεν Ἕκτορος 575
κοίτας, ἐφ' ᾧπερ ἔγχος εἵλκυσται τόδε.
Οδ. τί δῆτ' ἂν εἴη; μῶν λόχος βέβηκέ ποι;
Δι. ἴσως ἐφ' ἡμῖν μηχανὴν στήσων τινά.
Οδ. θρασὺς γὰρ Ἕκτωρ νῦν, ἐπεὶ κρατεῖ, θρασύς.
Δι. τί δῆτ', Ὀδυσσεῦ, δρῶμεν; οὐ γὰρ ηὕρομεν 580
τὸν ἄνδρ' ἐν εὐναῖς, ἐλπίδων δ' ἡμάρτομεν.
Οδ. στείχωμεν ὡς τάχιστα ναυστάθμων πέλας.
σῴζει γὰρ αὐτὸν ὅστις εὐτυχῆ θεῶν
τίθησιν· ἡμῖν δ' οὐ βιαστέον τύχην.
Δι. οὔκουν ἐπ' Αἰνέαν ἢ τὸν ἔχθιστον Φρυγῶν 585
Πάριν μολόντε χρὴ καρατομεῖν ξίφει;
Οδ. πῶς οὖν ἐν ὄρφνῃ πολεμίων ἀνὰ στρατόν
ζητῶν δυνήσῃ τούσδ' ἀκινδύνως κτανεῖν;
Δι. αἰσχρόν γε μέντοι ναῦς ἐπ' Ἀργείων μολεῖν
δράσαντε μηδὲν πολεμίους νεώτερον. 590
Οδ. πῶς δ' οὐ δέδρακας; οὐ κτανόντε ναυστάθμων
κατάσκοπον Δόλωνα σῴζομεν τάδε
σκυλεύματ'; ἢ πᾶν στρατόπεδον πέρσειν δοκεῖς;
Δι. πείθεις· πάλιν στείχωμεν· εὖ δοίη τύχη.

ΑΘΗΝΑ
ποῖ δὴ λιπόντε Τρωϊκῶν ἐκ τάξεων 595
χωρεῖτε, λύπῃ καρδίαν δεδηγμένοι,
εἰ μὴ κτανεῖν σφῷν Ἕκτορ' ἢ Πάριν θεός
δίδωσιν; ἄνδρα δ' οὐ πέπυσθε σύμμαχον
Τροίᾳ μολόντα Ῥῆσον οὐ φαύλῳ τρόπῳ;
ὃς εἰ διοίσει νύκτα τήνδ' ἐς αὔριον, 600

577–81 cf. Chr. Pat. 2033–7   582 (ναυστάθμων) vide ad 244; cf. Chr. Pat. 2004, 2006, 2411   583–4 cf. Chr. Pat. 2040–1   587–8 cf. Chr. Pat. 1908–9   591 (ναυστάθμων) vide ad 244   594 cf. Chr. Pat. 2009, 2038   596 cf. Chr. Pat. 2005

---

575 ἔφραξεν Va   576 εἵλκισται Ο   577 ποι ΟΛ et Chr. Pat. 2033 pars codd. (πῃ vel που cett.): σοι Va   578ⁿ et 579ⁿ om. Va   579 ἕκτορ Q   νῦν δ' Ο et Chr. Pat. 2035   ἐπικρατεῖ Va   580 ηὕρομεν Dindorf: εὕρ- VaΛ: ἔβρ- Ο   581 τὸν Δ: τόνδ' Λ   582 ναυστάθμων Δ: -ου Λ   583 ὅστις ΔgV et Chr. Pat. 2040: ὅσπερ Λ   εὐτυχεῖ Ο   585 οὔκουν: vide ad 161   αἰνέαν Δ: -είαν Λ   586 μολόντε Canter: -όντες ΟΛ: -ῶντες Va   χρὴ Δ: χρῆν Λ   590 πολεμίοις Ο   591 δ' om. Va   δέδορκας Ο (≠ Ο¹ᶜ)   ναυστάθμω Va   593 ᾗ Q   594ⁿ Δι. VaQPʳ: om. OL   594 πείθεις Wilamowitz: πείθου Ω et Chr. Pat. 2038   δοίη Nauck (noluit Vater): δ' εἴη Ω et Chr. Pat. 2009, 2038   τύχῃ Va: τυχεῖν ΟΛ et Chr. Pat. 2009, 2038   595 λιπόντε Ο: -τες VaΛ: 'λιπόντε Bothe   596 κραδίαν Va (≠ Va¹ˢ)   δεδηγμένοι ΟΛ: -μένον Va: -μένῳ Wecklein   597 κατανεῖν Q (≠ Q²)   600 τήνδ' Reiske: τὴν Ω   ἐς αὔριον ΟΛ: ἐπαύριον Va

οὔτ' ἂν σφ' Ἀχιλλεὺς οὔτ' ἂν Αἴαντος δόρυ
μὴ πάντα πέρσαι ναύσταθμ' Ἀργείων σχέθοι,
τείχη κατασκάψαντα καὶ πυλῶν ἔσω
λόγχῃ πλατεῖαν ἐσδρομὴν ποιούμενον.
τοῦτον κατακτὰς πάντ' ἔχεις· τὰς δ' Ἕκτορος 605
εὐνὰς ἔασον καὶ καρατόμους σφαγάς·
ἔσται γὰρ αὐτῷ θάνατος ἐξ ἄλλης χερός.

Οδ. δέσποιν' Ἀθάνα, φθέγματος γὰρ ᾐσθόμην
τοῦ σοῦ συνήθη γῆρυν· ἐν πόνοισι γὰρ
παροῦσ' ἀμύνεις τοῖς ἐμοῖς ἀεί ποτε. 610
τὸν ἄνδρα δ' ἡμῖν ποῦ κατηύνασται φράσον·
πόθεν τέτακται βαρβάρου στρατεύματος;

Αθ. ὅδ' ἐγγὺς ἧσται κοὐ συνήθροισται στρατῷ,
ἀλλ' ἐκτὸς αὐτὸν τάξεων κατηύνασεν
Ἕκτωρ, ἕως ἂν νὺξ ἀμείψηται φάος. 615
πέλας δὲ πῶλοι Θρῃκίων ἐξ ἁρμάτων
λευκαὶ δέδενται, διαπρεπεῖς ἐν εὐφρόνῃ·
στίλβουσι δ' ὥστε ποταμίου κύκνου πτερόν.
ταύτας, κτανόντε δεσπότην, κομίζετε,
κάλλιστον οἴκοις σκῦλον· οὐ γὰρ ἔσθ' ὅπου 620
τοιόνδ' ὄχημα χθὼν κέκευθε πωλικόν.

Οδ. Διόμηδες, ἢ σὺ κτεῖνε Θρῄκιον λεών,
ἢ 'μοὶ πάρες γε, σοὶ δὲ χρὴ πώλους μέλειν.

Δι. ἐγὼ φονεύσω, πωλοδαμνήσεις δὲ σύ·
τρίβων γὰρ εἶ τὰ κομψὰ καὶ νοεῖν σοφός. 625
χρὴ δ' ἄνδρα τάσσειν οὗ μάλιστ' ἂν ὠφελοῖ.

Αθ. καὶ μὴν καθ' ἡμᾶς τόνδ' Ἀλέξανδρον βλέπω
στείχοντα, φυλάκων ἔκ τινος πεπυσμένον
δόξας ἀσήμους πολεμίων μεμβλωκότων.

Δι. πότερα σὺν ἄλλοις ἢ μόνος πορεύεται; 630

---

602 (ναυστάθμ') vide ad 244   **618** Tz. Carm. Il. (comm.) p. 65 Schirach; cf. Chr. Pat. 2058   **619** cf. Chr. Pat. 787

---

601 οὔτ' ἄν O: οὔτε Λ: [Va]   ἀχιλλεὺς Va: -έως OΛ   ἄν (alterum) om. Q   **602** μὴ <οὐ> Nauck   **603** εἴσω L (≠ L¹ᶜ vel Tr¹)   **606** σφαγὰς καρατόμους O   **607** ἔσται OΛ: ἥκει Va: ἥξει Va¹ˢ   **608**ⁿ om. O, Ὀδ. καὶ Δι. O¹ᵐ   **608** φθέγμ- Ω (vide ad 297)   **609** συνήθη Λ: -ους Δ   **611** ποῖ O   κατηύνασται Dindorf: -ευ- Ω (item 614, 762)   **613** ἧσται VaL: ἔσται O: ἧσθαι Q   **614** τάξεων Λ: -εως Δ   κατηύνασεν Dindorf: -ευ- Ω (vide ad 611)   **615** νὺξ Ω: νύκτ' Lenting   ἀμείψεται Oᵘᵛ (≠ O¹ᶜ?)   **617** δέδηνται Q   **618** στίλβουσι δ' OΛgB: -σιν Va   ὥστε Λ: ὥσπερ ΔgB et Chr. Pat. 2058   πτερὸν κύκνου O   **619** κτανόντε O: -τες VaΛ   **621** πωλικόν VaΛ: τρωικὸν O   **623** 'μοὶ VaL: μοι OQ   πάρες γε OΛ: πάρεχε Va: παράσχες Reiske, πάρες σφε Dobree   πώλους Δ: -ων Λ   **625** κομψά] σοφὰ Q   **626** ὠφελ* ῖ Q (≠ Q¹ᶜ)   **630** σὺν ΔQ: πρὸς L

| | Ῥῆσος | 91 |

Αθ. μόνος· πρὸς εὐνὰς δ', ὡς ἔοικεν, Ἕκτορος
χωρεῖ, κατόπτας σημανῶν ἥκειν στρατοῦ.
Δι. οὔκουν ὑπάρχειν τόνδε κατθανόντα χρή;
Αθ. οὐκ ἂν δύναιο τοῦ πεπρωμένου πλέον·
τοῦτον δὲ πρὸς σῆς χειρὸς οὐ θέμις θανεῖν. 635
ἀλλ' ᾧπερ ἥκεις μορσίμους φέρων σφαγάς
τάχυν'· ἐγὼ δὲ τῷδε σύμμαχος Κύπρις
δοκοῦσ' ἀρωγὸς ἐν πόνοις παραστατεῖν
σαθροῖς λόγοισιν ἐχθρὸν ἄνδρ' ἀμείψομαι.
καὶ ταῦτ' ἐγὼ μὲν εἶπον· ὃν δὲ χρὴ παθεῖν 640
οὐκ οἶδεν οὐδ' ἤκουσεν ἐγγὺς ὢν λόγου.

ΑΛΕΞΑΝΔΡΟΣ
σὲ τὸν στρατηγὸν καὶ κασίγνητον λέγω,
Ἕκτορ, καθεύδεις; οὐκ ἐγείρεσθαί σ' ἐχρῆν;
ἐχθρῶν τις ἡμῖν χρίμπτεται στρατεύματι,
ἢ κλῶπες ἄνδρες ἢ κατάσκοποί τινες. 645
Αθ. θάρσει· φυλάσσω σ' ἥδε πρευμενὴς Κύπρις.
μέλει δ' ὁ σός μοι πόλεμος, οὐδ' ἀμνημονῶ
τιμῆς, ἐπαινῶ δ' εὖ παθοῦσα πρὸς σέθεν.
καὶ νῦν ἐπ' εὐτυχοῦντι Τρωϊκῷ στρατῷ
ἥκω πορεύουσ' ἄνδρα σοι μέγαν φίλον, 650
τῆς ὑμνοποιοῦ παῖδα Θρήκιον θεᾶς
[Μούσης· πατρὸς δὲ Στρυμόνος κικλήσκεται].
Αλ. ἀεί ποτ' εὖ φρονοῦσα τυγχάνεις πόλει
κἀμοί, μέγιστον δ' ἐν βίῳ κειμήλιον
κρίνας σέ φημι τῇδε προσθέσθαι πόλει. 655
ἥκω δ' ἀκούσας οὐ τορῶς — φήμη δέ τις
φύλαξιν ἐμπέπτωκεν — ὡς κατάσκοποι
ἤκουσ' Ἀχαιῶν. χὣ μὲν οὐκ ἰδὼν λέγει,
ὃ δ' εἰσιδὼν μολόντας οὐκ ἔχει φράσαι·

---

645 et 678–9 codd. (κλῶπες) Hsch. (Cyr.) κ 3075   653 cf. Chr. Pat. 2601   654 cf. Chr. Pat. 2602   656–9 cf. Chr. Pat. 1874–7   658–9 cf. Chr. Pat. 1878

---

631 δ' Δ: om. Λ   632 ἥκει Q   633 οὔκουν: vide ad 161   καταθανόντα O   635 χειρὸς οὐ θέμις fere Δ (θέμις post θανεῖν O): οὐ θ- χερός Λ   θανεῖν O et aut L¹ᵐ aut Tr^m: κτανεῖν VΛ   636 ᾧπερ P²: ὥσπερ Ω   σφαγὰς φέρων O   638 ἀρωγοὺς Q   642ⁿ Ἀλέξανδρος ΔQ: Πάρις L (item 653, 663)   643 σ' ἐχρῆν O: σ' ἐχρή V: σε χρή Λ   644 ἡμῶν Q   στρατεύμασι O (≠ O¹ᶜ)   646 φυλάσσω Naber: -ει Ω   647 μέλλει O   652 del. Lachmann (cf. 279)   654 δ' O: om. VΛ   655 σέ VΛ: δέ O   658 ἰδὼν Lenting cl. Chr. Pat. 1876: εἰδὼς Ω   659 εἰσιδὼν OΛ et Chr. Pat. 1877: ὡς ἰδὼν V   μολῶντας V

ὧν οὕνεκ' εὐνὰς ἤλυθον πρὸς Ἕκτορος. 660
Αθ. μηδὲν φοβηθῇς· οὐδὲν ἐν στρατῷ νέον·
Ἕκτωρ δὲ φροῦδος Θρῇκα κοιμήσων στρατόν.
Αλ. σύ τοί με πείθεις, σοῖς δὲ πιστεύων λόγοις
τάξιν φυλάξων εἶμ' ἐλεύθερος φόβου.
Αθ. χώρει· μέλειν γὰρ πάντ' ἐμοὶ δόκει τὰ σά, 665
ὥστ' εὐτυχοῦντας συμμάχους ἐμοὺς ὁρᾶν·
γνώσῃ δὲ καὶ σὺ τὴν ἐμὴν προθυμίαν.
ὑμᾶς δ' αὐτῷ τοὺς ἄγαν ἐρρωμένους,
Λαερτίου παῖ, θηκτὰ κοιμίσαι ξίφη.
κεῖται γὰρ ἡμῖν Θρῄκιος στρατηλάτης 670
ἵπποι τ' ἔχονται, πολέμιοι δ' ᾐσθημένοι
χωροῦσ' ἐφ' ὑμᾶς. ἀλλ' ὅσον τάχιστα χρή
φεύγειν πρὸς ὁλκοὺς ναυστάθμων. τί μέλλετε
σκηπτοῦ 'πιόντος πολεμίων σῶσαι βίον;

Χο. ἔα ἔα· 675
βάλε βάλε βάλε· θένε θένε <θένε>.
τίς ἀνήρ;
λεῦσσε· τοῦτον αὐδῶ. 677
δεῦρο δεῦρο πᾶς. 680
τούσδ' ἔχω, τούσδ' ἔμαρψα 681
κλῶπας οἵτινες κατ' ὄρφνην τόνδε κινοῦσι στρατόν. 678–9
τίς ὁ λόχος; πόθεν ἔβας; ποδαπὸς εἶ; 682

---

660 cf. Chr. Pat. 1883   663–5 cf. Chr. Pat. 1806–8   667 cf. Chr. Pat. 1809, 1979   673 (cf. 146) (ὁλκοὺς ναυστάθμων) Hsch. (Cyr.) ο 590 ὁλκούς· ναυστάθμους, (ναυστάθμων) vide ad 244   678–9 codd. (κλῶπες) vide ad 645

---

660 εὐνὰς VΛ: ἦλθον O   662 κοιμήσων Δ: κοσμ- Λ   663 πείθοις O (≠ Chr. Pat. 1806)   δὲ πιστεύων Δ: τε πιστεύω Λ et Chr. Pat.   665 μέλειν OΛ: μέλλει V, -ειν V^{1c}gV: eandem varietatem Chr. Pat. 1808   δόκει L: δοκεῖ ΔQgV et Chr. Pat.   666 ὥστ' ΔgV: ὡς Λ   συμμάχους Ω: ἐς φίλους gV   668 δ' αὐτῷ fere VΛ (δ' αὐτῷ Q): μὲν αὐδῶ O   ἐρωμ- Q   669 κοιμίσαι V: κοιμῆσαι O: κομίσαι L: κοσμίσας Q, κοιμ- Q^{1c} 670 om. O   ὑμῖν Valckenaer   672 τάχιστα χρή Δ: -τ' ἐχρῆν Λ   675–91 lectio, personarum dispositio, versuum consecutio saepius incerta   675–82 inter hemichoria distribuit Bothe, inter singulos choreutas Arnoldt praeeunte Vater   675^n Xo. L: Xo. Λυκίων OQ et Σ^V: [V]: Ἡμ.^{α} Bothe   675a ἔα ἔα Λ: ἔααε V: om. O   675b βάλε ter Tr^1: βάλε quater ΔQ et Tr$^{2/3}$: βάλλε quater L   θένε ter Diggle: θένε bis ΔL: θάνε bis Q   676 ἀνήρ Murray: ἀ- Ω   τίς <ὅδ'> ἀνήρ Musgrave   677 λεῦσσε Diggle: λεύσ(σ)ετε Ω (-σσ- Λ, -σ- Δ): λεῦσσε λεῦσσε Hartung   αὐτῷ O   680–1 post 677 trai. Diggle   680^n ἡμιχ. O   678–9 κλῶπας Diggle: -ες Ω   ὄρφνην ΔL: -αν Q et Tr^1 κινοῦσι OΛ: κτεν- V   682 λόχος Δ: λόγος Λ   ἔβας· ποδαπὸς εἶ Δ: ἔβας πόδα πῶς εἶ <L>Q: σὸν φέρεις πόδα· πῶς εἶ Tr^1

Οδ.	οὔ σε χρὴ εἰδέναι. Ημ.ᵃ θάνῃ γὰρ σήμερον δράσας κακῶς·	
	οὐκ ἐρεῖς ξύνθημα, λόγχην πρὶν διὰ στέρνων μολεῖν;	
Οδ.	†ἴστω θάρσει. Ημ.ᵃ πέλας ἴθι παῖε πᾶς.†	685
Ημ.ᵝ	ἦ σὺ δὴ †'Ρῆσον† κατέκτας; Οδ. <μὴ> ἀλλὰ τὸν	
	κτενοῦντα σέ.	
Ημ.ᵝ	ἴσχε πᾶς τις. Ημ.ᵃ οὐ μὲν οὖν. Οδ. ἆ· φίλιον ἄνδρα μὴ	
	θένῃς.	
Ημ.ᵃ	καὶ τί δὴ τὸ σῆμα; Οδ. Φοῖβος. Ημ.ᵃ ἔμαθον· ἴσχε πᾶς	
	δόρυ.	
Ημ.ᵝ	οἶσθ' ὅπῃ βεβᾶσιν ἄνδρες; Οδ. τῇδέ πῃ κατείδομεν.	
Ημ.ᵃ	ἕρπε πᾶς κατ' ἴχνος αὐτῶν· ἢ βοὴν ἐγερτέον;	690
	ἀλλὰ συμμάχους ταράσσειν δεινὸν ἐκ νυκτῶν φόβῳ.	

Χο.	τίς ἀνδρῶν ὁ βάς;	στρ.
	τίς ὁ μέγα θρασὺς ἐπεύξεται	
	χέρα φυγὼν ἐμάν;	
	πόθεν νιν κυρήσω;	695
	τίνι προσεικάσω,	
	ὅστις δι' ὄρφνης ἦλθ' ἀδειμάντῳ ποδὶ	
	διά τε τάξεων καὶ φυλάκων ἕδρας;	
	Θεσσαλὸς ἢ	
	παραλίαν Λοκρῶν νεμόμενος πόλιν;	700
	ἢ νησιώτην σποράδα κέκτηται βίον;	
	τίς ἦν; πόθεν; ποίας πάτρας;	
	ποῖον ἐπεύχεται τὸν ὕπατον θεῶν;	

---

683 οὔ σε χρὴ εἰδέναι VQ (χρὴν V²): οὐκ ἐχρῆν σ' εἰδέναι Ο: οὐ χρὴ εἰδέναι σε L: εἰδέναι σ' οὐ χρή Heath   **683ⁿ** (ante θάνῃ) Ἡμ. Matthiae: om. Ω   **683** σήμερον om. V   **684ⁿ** nullam notam L: Χο. OQ: ἡμιχ. Tr²/³: paragr. V   **684** ξύν- Δ: σύν- Λ   λόγχων Q   **685** ἴστω Σᴸ (ἴστω ἵστασο) et ⁱVᵍˡQᵍˡ (ἀνίστασο), coni. Portus: ἴστω Ω   πέλας τις ἴθι Tr¹   παῖε bis O et Tr³ (tum πᾶς τὶς ἂν Tr³)   **686ⁿ** (ante ἦ) nullam notam O: ἡμιχ. VΛ   **686** ἦ fere Q (ἢ): ἦ ΔL   δὴ om. V   'Ρῆσον Ω: φίλους West   **686ⁿ** (ante ἀλλὰ) Ὀδ. O: om. VΛ   **686** <μὴ> Dindorf   κτενοῦντα VL: κταν- OQ   **687ⁿ** (ante ἴσχε) Χο. O: Ὀδ. VΛ   **687** ἴαχε V   τις L: om. ΔQ   **687ⁿ** (ante οὐ) ἡμιχ. ΔQ: Χο. L   **687** μὲν οὖν Reiske: μενῶ Ω   **687ⁿ** (ante ἆ) Ὀδ. Stiblinus: Χο. O: ἡμιχ. VΛ   **687** ἆ Musgrave: ἆ ἆ vel ἄ ἄ Ω   φίλιον O<L>PQ: φίλον V et Tr²/³   **688ⁿ** (ante καὶ) ἡμιχ. ΔQ: Χο. L   (ante ἔμαθον) ἡμιχ. VQ: Χο. O: paragr. L   **688** ἴαχε V   **689ⁿ** (ante οἶσθ') ἡμιχ. ΔQ: paragr. L   **689** ὅπῃ(ι) Ω: ὅπη in ὅπο aut ὅπο in ὅπη mut. Pᶜ: ὅποι Aldina   βεβήκασιν O   ἄνδρες O', coni. Matthiae: ἄ- VΛ   **689ⁿ** (ante τῇδε) Ὀδ. VQ: ἡμιχ. L: [O]   **689** τῇ(ι)δέ OL: πῇδέ V: τί δέ O   πῃ om. O   κατίδομεν O   **690ⁿ** (ante ἕρπε) Χο. O: om.VΛ   **690** αὐτοῦ O   **690ⁿ** (ante ἢ) Χο. VQ: ἡμιχ. O: paragr. L   **691ⁿ** nullam notam Λ: paragr. V: [O]   **691** ἐν Q   **692** om. Q   **692ⁿ** Χο. Tr³: paragr. L: om. V: [O]   **693** μέγας V   θρασὺς Madvig: θράσος Ω   **694** χέρα Hn, coni. Musgrave: χεῖρα Ω   **696** om. O   **697** δι' OL: δ' V   ὄρφνης Δ: -ας Λ   ἀδιμάντῳ Q   **702** πόθεν Hermann: πόθεν ἢ O: ἢ πόθεν ἐστὶν ἢ V: ἢ πόθεν ἐστὶν· ἐκ Q: γὰρ· ἢ πόθεν ἐστὶν· ἢ <L>P: ἢ πόθεν ἢ (del. etiam ἦν) Tr³   ποίας VΛ: τίνος O   **703** ποῖον Δ: ὁποῖον Λ   ἐπεύχεται Hermann: εὔχ- Ω: δ' εὔχ- Porson, Bothe (1803)

— ἆρ' ἔστ' Ὀδυσσέως τοὔργον ἢ τίνος τόδε;
εἰ τοῖς πάροιθε χρὴ τεκμαίρεσθαι· τί μήν; 705
— δοκεῖς γάρ; — τί μὴν οὔ;
— θρασὺς γοῦν ἐς ἡμᾶς.
— τίν' ἀλκὴν τίν' αἰνεῖς; — Ὀδυσσῆ.
— μὴ κλωπὸς αἴνει φωτὸς αἱμύλον δόρυ.

Χο. ἔβα καὶ πάρος ἀντ.
κατὰ πόλιν ὕπαφρον ὄμμ' ἔχων, 711
ῥακοδύτῳ στολᾷ
πυκασθείς, ξιφήρης
κρύφιος ἐν πέπλοις·
βίον δ' ἐπαιτῶν εἷρπ' ἀγύρτης τις λάτρις, 715
ψαφαρόχρουν κάρα πολυπινές τ' ἔχων·
πολλὰ δὲ τὰν
βασιλίδ' ἑστίαν Ἀτρειδᾶν κακῶς
ἔβαζε δῆθεν ἐχθρὸς ὢν στρατηλάταις.
ὄλοιτ' ὄλοιτο πανδίκως, 720
πρὶν ἐπὶ γᾶν Φρυγῶν ποδὸς ἴχνος βαλεῖν.

— εἴτ' οὖν Ὀδυσσέως εἴτε μή, φόβος μ' ἔχει·
Ἕκτωρ γὰρ ἡμῖν τοῖς φύλαξι μέμψεται.
— τί λάσκων; — δυσοίζων ...
— τί δρᾶσαι; τί ταρβεῖς; 725
— καθ' ἡμᾶς περᾶσαι ... — τίν' ἀνδρῶν;
— οἳ τῆσδε νυκτὸς ἦλθον ἐς Φρυγῶν στρατόν.

---

711 (ὕπαφρον) Hsch. υ 264? 719 (ἔβαζε) Hsch. ε 53 720 cf. Chr. Pat. 352, 1441

704ⁿ ἡμιχ. ΔQ: Χο. L 704 ὀδυσσέως Λ: -σ- Δ et LᶜP 705ⁿ nullam notam VΛ: ἡμιχ. Tr²/³: Χο. O 705 πάροιθε O⁷Λ: -εν V τί μήν O: τιμήν L: τί μή Q et Tr²: om. V 706ⁿ (ante δοκεῖς) ἡμιχ. O: paragr. VL: om. Q 706 δοκεῖ O 706ⁿ (ante τί) Χο. O: paragr. VL: spat. Q 706 τιμὴν L⁷P (≠ Tr²/³?) 707ⁿ ἡμιχ. O: paragr. VL: om. Q 707 ἐς Λ: εἰς Δ 708ⁿ (ante τίν') Χο. O: paragr. VL: om. Q 708 τίν' (prius) Δ: τίς Λ 708ⁿ (ante Ὀδ-) ἡμιχ. O: paragr. VL: spat. Q 708 ὀδυσσῆ VL: -σῆ O et LᶜP: -σσεῖ Q 709ⁿ paragr. VL: om. Q: [O] 709 αἱμύλον fere Λ (αἴμυλ- Q): -ου ΔgBgE 710ⁿ Χο. Tr³: paragr. VL: om. Q: [O] 711 πόλιν Δ et Tr²⁷: πτ- <L>PQ et Tr³ 712 ἐν ῥακ- <L>P (≠ Tr²/³) στολᾶ(ι) Δ: -ῇ(ι) Λ 714 κρύφιος Bothe (1824), denuo Morstadt: κρυφαῖος Ω 715 ἀγύρτης τις Tr¹: ἀγύρτης Λ: ἀγύρτις V λάτρης Q 716 κάρα Λ: κράτα V πολυπινές Tr⁽¹⁷⁾ˢ: -νῆ Ω 717 τὰν Λ V: τὴν Λ 718 ἀτρειδᾶν V: -ῶν Λ 720ⁿ notam erasam L: ἡμιχ. VQ 721 γᾶν Λ: γᾷ VgE 722ⁿ paragr. V: Χο. L: om. Q 722 ὀδυσσέως ΛP: -σ- V et Lᶜ 723ⁿ nullam notam Λ: paragr. V 723 μέμψεται Λ: -φεται V 724ⁿ (ante τί) paragr. VL: om. Q (ante δυσοίζων) paragr. VL: spat. Q 725–7ⁿ (quater) paragr. VL: om. Q 725 δρᾶσαι L. Dindorf: δρᾶς Ω: δρᾶς δὴ Tr¹

Ῥῆσος 95

ΗΝΙΟΧΟΣ
  ἰὼ ἰώ·
  δαίμονος τύχα βαρεῖα· φεῦ φεῦ.
Χο. ἔα ἔα·
  σῖγα πᾶς ὕφιζ'· ἴσως γὰρ ἐς βόλον τις ἔρχεται. 730
Ην. ἰὼ ἰώ·
  συμφορὰ βαρεῖα Θρηκῶν.   Χο. συμμάχων τις ὁ στένων.
Ην. ἰὼ ἰώ·
  δύστηνος ἐγὼ σύ τ' ἄναξ Θρηκῶν·
  ὦ στυγνοτάτην Τροίαν ἐσιδών,
  οἷόν σε βίου τέλος εἷλεν. 735
Χο. τίς εἶ ποτ' ἀνδρῶν συμμάχων; κατ' εὐφρόνην
  ἀμβλῶπες αὐγαὶ κοὔ σε γιγνώσκω τορῶς.
Ην. ποῦ τιν' ἀνάκτων Τρώων εὕρω;
  ποῦ δῆθ' Ἕκτωρ
  τὸν ὑπασπίδιον κοῖτον ἰαύει; 740
  τίνι σημήνω διόπων στρατιᾶς
  οἷα πεπόνθαμεν, οἷά τις ἡμᾶς
  δράσας ἀφανὴ φροῦδος, φανερὸν
  Θρηξὶν πένθος τολυπεύσας;
Χο. κακὸν κυρεῖν τι Θρηκίῳ στρατεύματι 745
  ἔοικεν, οἷα τοῦδε γιγνώσκω κλύων.
Ην. ἔρρει στρατιά, πέπτωκεν ἄναξ
  δολίῳ πληγῇ. ἆ ἆ ἆ ἆ,
  οἵα μ' ὀδύνη τείρει φονίου
  τραύματος εἴσω. πῶς ἂν ὀλοίμην; 750

736–7 cf. Chr. Pat. 2176–7   740 (κοῖτον ἰαύει) Hsch. (Cyr.) κ 3276, (ἰαύει) Hsch. (Cyr.) ι 97   744 (τολυπεύσας) Hsch. (Cyr.) τ 1101

728ⁿ Ἡνίοχος L. Dindorf: Οἰκέτης Ῥήσου in ras. Tr³: [L]: om. VQ   728a ἰὼ ἰώ Q: ἰώ VL   728b τύχῃ Kirchhoff   φεῦ φεῦ om. Q (≠ Qʳ)   729ⁿ Χο. Tr³: paragr. V et Tr³ (primitus) pot. qu. L: om. LᵘᵛQ   729 ἔα ἔα V et Qʳ: ἔα Λ   730 σῖγα L. Dindorf: σίγα VQ: σιγα L   730ⁿ (post πᾶς) nullam notam L. Dindorf: Χο. Ω: ἡμιχ. Tr³   730 ὕφιζ' Reiske praeeunte Barnes: ὕφιζος V: ὕβριζ' Λ   ἴσως γὰρ εἰς βόλον Q et Tr³: ἴσως γὰρ εἰσβολή L: εἰς βόλον γὰρ ἴσως V   731ⁿ paragr. V: ἡμιχ. L: om. Q   731 ἰὼ ἰώ V: ἰώ Λ: ὦ Tr¹   732ⁿ (ante συμμάχων) Χο. Hermann: (post συμ-) ἡμιχ. L, paragr. V: om. Q   732 τις Hermann: τίς Ω   733aⁿ paragr. V: Οἰκέτης in ras. Tr³: [L]: om. Q   733a ἰὼ ἰώ V: ἰώ Q et Tr³: ὦ <L>P   734 ὦ V et Tr²/³: ἰὼ <L>P: ὡς Q   στυγνοτάταν Q   ἐσιδών Tr³: εἰσ- <L>PQ: ἰδών V   737 τορῶς] γ' ὅλως Q (≠ Qᵞᵖ et Chr. Pat. 2177)   738ⁿ Οἰκέτης in ras. Tr³: [L]: ἡμιχ. VQ   738 Τρώων Diggle (Τρῴων iam Hermann): τρωϊκῶν Ω   741 σημήνω V et Tr³: σημανῶ <L>PQ   διόπων Portus: διοπῶν Tr³: δι' ὀπῶν V: διοπτῶν Λ   747ⁿ Ην. VQ: Οἰκέτης in ras. Tr³: [L]   748–9 ἆ quater L, ter Q: ἆ ter V   751 πῶς V: πῶς δ' Λ   ὀλοίμην VQ: -μαν L

χρῆν γάρ μ' ἀκλεῶς Ῥῆσόν τε θανεῖν,
Τροίᾳ κέλσαντ' ἐπίκουρον;
Χο. τάδ' οὐκ ἐν αἰνιγμοῖσι σημαίνει κακά·
σαφῶς γὰρ αὐδᾷ συμμάχους ὀλωλότας. 755

Ην. κακῶς πέπρακται κἀπὶ τοῖς κακοῖσι πρός
αἴσχιστα. καίτοι δὶς τόσον κακὸν τόδε·
θανεῖν γὰρ εὐκλεῶς μέν, εἰ θανεῖν χρεών,
λυπρὸν μὲν οἶμαι τῷ θανόντι — πῶς γὰρ οὔ; —
τοῖς ζῶσι δ' ὄγκος καὶ δόμων εὐδοξία· 760
ἡμεῖς δ' ἀβούλως κἀκλεῶς ὀλώλαμεν.
ἐπεὶ γὰρ ἡμᾶς ηὔνασ' Ἑκτόρεια χείρ,
ξύνθημα λέξας, ηὕδομεν πεδοστιβεῖ
κόπῳ δαμέντες, οὐδ' ἐφρουρεῖτο στρατός
φυλακαῖσι νυκτέροισιν οὐδ' ἐν τάξεσιν 765
ἔκειτο τεύχη πλῆκτρά τ' οὐκ ἐπὶ ζυγοῖς
ἵππων καθήρμοσθ', ὡς ἄναξ ἐπεύθετο
κρατοῦντας ὑμᾶς κἀφεδρεύοντας νεῶν
πρύμναισι· φαύλως δ' ηὕδομεν πεπτωκότες.
κἀγὼ μελούσῃ καρδίᾳ λήξας ὕπνου 770
πώλοισι χόρτον, προσδοκῶν ἑωθινήν
ζεύξειν ἐς ἀλκήν, ἀφθόνῳ μέτρῳ χερί.
λεύσσω δὲ φῶτε περιπολοῦνθ' ἡμῶν στρατόν
πυκνῆς δι' ὄρφνης· ὡς δ' ἐκινήθην ἐγώ,
ἐπτηξάτην τε κἀνεχωρείτην πάλιν. 775
ἤπυσα δ' αὐτοῖς μὴ πελάζεσθαι στρατῷ,
κλῶπας δοκήσας συμμάχων πλάθειν τινάς.
οἳ δ' οὐδέν· οὐ μὴν οὐδ' ἐγὼ τὰ πλείονα·
ηὗδον δ' ἀπελθὼν αὖθις ἐς κοίτην πάλιν.

---

754 cf. Chr. Pat. 155, 1637   755 cf. Chr. Pat. 1639   763 cf. Chr. Pat. 1852   770 cf. Chr. Pat. 1819, 1851, 2002   772 cf. Chr. Pat. 540

---

753 κέλσαντ' L: -τες V: κελεύσαντ' Q   754 ἐν om. Q   755 αὐδᾷ(ι) Λ: -ᾷς V   756ⁿ Ἡν. VQ: ἡμιχ. L   757 καὶ σοὶ gV   759 μὲν] γὰρ Q (≠ Q¹ᶜ)   762 ηὔνασ' Ἐκτόρεια χείρ Dindorf: εὔνασ' ἐκτορεία (-ία L?P, ≠ Lᶜ?) χείρ Λ: ἐκτορέα χείρ εὔνασε V   763 ξύν- Λ: σύν- V   ηὔδ- Dindorf: εὔδ- Ω (item 769, 779)   πεδοστιβεῖ Morstadt: -εῖς Ω et fere Chr. Pat. 1852 (-ής)   764 κόπῳ VQ: κόμπῳ L   765 τάξεσι(ν) Λ: -αισιν V   767 ἐπεύθετο Λ: ἐπύθ- V   768 ἡμᾶς Q   νεῶν Λ: νηῶν V   769 πρύμναισι Λ: -ησι V   ηὕδομεν Dindorf: εὐδ- Ω (vide ad 763)   770 μελλούσῃ Q   λήξας Λ et V¹ᶜ: ζήλας V   772 ἐς V: πρὸς Λ   μέτρῳ Lᵘᵛ et Σⱽ: μέτρω(ι) VQ et Trˡᵘᵛ P   773 λεύσω Q   στρατόν Λ: -ῷ V   776, 775, 780–1, 777–9 hoc ordine V¹ᶜ (litteris adscriptis)   775 -είτην Λ: -ήτην V   776 ἤπυσα Λ: ἀπ- V   αὐτοῖς Λ: -οὺς V   πελάζεσθαι Λ: πλάθειν V   778 οὐδ' V: οἶδ' Λ   779 ἐς V: εἰς Λ

καί μοι καθ' ὕπνον δόξα τις παρίσταται· 780
ἵππους γὰρ ἃς ἔθρεψα κἀδιφρηλάτουν
Ῥήσῳ παρεστὼς εἶδον, ὡς ὄναρ δοκῶν,
λύκους ἐπεμβεβῶτας ἑδραίαν ῥάχιν·
θείνοντε δ' οὐρᾷ πωλικῆς ῥινοῦ τρίχα
ἤλαυνον, αἳ δ' ἔρρεγκον ἐξ ἀρτηριῶν 785
θυμὸν πνέουσαι κἀνεχαίτιζον φόβῳ.
ἐγὼ δ' ἀμύνων θῆρας ἐξεγείρομαι
πώλοισιν· ἔννυχος γὰρ ἐξώρμα φόβος.
κλύω δ' ἐπάρας κρᾶτα μυχθισμὸν νεκρῶν·
θερμὸς δὲ κρουνὸς δεσπότου παρὰ σφαγῆς 790
βάλλει με δυσθνῄσκοντος αἵματος νέου.
ὀρθὸς δ' ἀνᾴσσω χειρὶ σὺν κενῇ δορός·
καί μ' ἔγχος αὐγάζοντα καὶ θηρώμενον
παίει παραστὰς νεῖραν ἐς πλευρὰν ξίφει
ἀνὴρ ἀκμάζων· φασγάνου γὰρ ᾐσθόμην 795
πληγῆς, βαθεῖαν ἄλοκα τραύματος λαβών.
πίπτω δὲ πρηνής· οἳ δ' ὄχημα πωλικόν
λαβόντες ἵππων ἵεσαν φυγῇ πόδα.
ἆ ἆ·
ὀδύνη με τείρει κοὐκέτ' ὀρθοῦμαι τάλας.
καὶ ξυμφορὰν μὲν οἶδ' ὁρῶν, τρόπῳ δ' ὅτῳ 800
τεθνᾶσιν οἱ θανόντες οὐκ ἔχω φράσαι
οὐδ' ἐξ ὁποίας χειρός. εἰκάσαι δέ μοι
πάρεστι λυπρὰ πρὸς φίλων πεπονθέναι.
Χο. ἡνίοχε Θρῃκὸς τοῦ κακῶς πεπραγότος,
μηδὲν δυσοίζου· πολέμιοι 'δρασαν τάδε. 805
Ἕκτωρ δὲ καὐτὸς συμφορᾶς πεπυσμένος
χωρεῖ· συναλγεῖ δ', ὡς ἔοικε, σοῖς κακοῖς.

---

789 (μυχθισμόν) Hsch. μ 2003   790 cf. Chr. Pat. 1081, 1085, 1219   794–6 cf. Chr. Pat. 1213–15   802–3 cf. Eust. 822.2–5   805 (δυσοίζου) Hsch. δ 2622 †δύσοιο· φοβοῦ? (vide comm. ad 804–5 n. 287)

---

781 om. spat. vac. relicto V, add. Σ^V   ἃς Λ: οὓς Σ^V   κἀδ- Q et Σ^V: καὶ ἐδ- <L?>: καὶ δ- L^lc vel Tr^1   783 ῥάχιν Λ: ῥοήν V   784 θείνοντε L: -τες VQ   δ' om. V   τρίχα om. V   785 ἔρρ- Nauck: ἐρ- Ω   ἀρτηριῶν Musgrave: ἀντηρίδων fere Ω (-αντ- VQ)   786 πνέουσαι Λ: πνεί- V   φόβην Reiske   787 ἀμείνων Q   788 ἐξόρμα Q   789 μυχθισμὸν V et Σ^L (in textu) et 'Σ^L (in marg.): -ῶν Λ   790 σφαγῆς Musgrave: -αῖς Ω et Σ^V, quo servato πάρα Hermann (παρὰ Λ, παρα- V et Σ^V), insolenti verborum ordine   792–835 om., 812–35 post 855 add. deinde del. V   792 ὀρθὸς Hn: -ῶς Ω   ἀναίσσω Q   794 νεῖραν Bothe: νείαιραν Ω: cf. Chr. Pat. 1213 νύσσει παραστὰς νειάτην πλευρὰν ξ-   πλευρὰν Va et Chr. Pat.: -οῦ Λ   795 ἀὴρ Q   805 πολέμιοι 'δρασαν Murray (π- δρῶσιν iam Lenting, δρᾶσαν West): πολεμίους δρᾶσαι Ω   806 συμφορᾶς VaL: -ᾷ Q: -ὰς Lenting, -ὰν Wecklein

Εκ. πῶς, ὦ μέγιστα πήματ' ἐξειργασμένοι,
μολόντες ὑμᾶς πολεμίων κατάσκοποι
λήθουσιν αἰσχρῶς καὶ κατεσφάγη στρατός,   810
κοὔτ' εἰσιόντας στρατόπεδ' ἐξαπώσατε
οὔτ' ἐξιόντας; τῶνδε τίς τείσει δίκην
πλὴν σοῦ; σὲ γὰρ δὴ φύλακά φημ' εἶναι στρατοῦ.
φροῦδοι δ' ἄπληκτοι, τῇ Φρυγῶν κακανδρίᾳ
πόλλ' ἐγγελῶντες τῷ στρατηλάτῃ τ' ἐμοί.   815
εὖ νυν τόδ' ἴστε — Ζεὺς ὀμώμοται πατήρ —
ἤτοι μάραγνά γ' ἢ καρανιστὴς μόρος
μένει σε δρῶντα τοιάδ', ἢ τὸν Ἕκτορα
τὸ μηδὲν εἶναι καὶ κακὸν νομίζετε.

Χο. ἰὼ ἰώ,   ἀντ.
†μέγας ἐμοὶ μέγας ὦ† πολίοχον κράτος   821
τότ' ἄρ' ἔμολον ὅτε σοι
ἄγγελος ἦλθον ἀμφὶ ναῦς πῦρ' αἴθειν·
ἐπεὶ ἄγρυπνον ὄμμ' ἐν εὐφρόνᾳ
οὔτ' ἐκοίμισ' οὔτ' ἔβριξ',   825
  οὐ τὰς Σιμοεντιάδας παγάς·
μή μοι κότον, ὦ ἄνα, θῇς· ἀναίτιος γὰρ
†ἔγωγε πάντων†.
εἰ δὲ χρόνῳ παρὰ καιρὸν
ἔργον ἢ λόγον πύθῃ, κατά με γᾶς   830
ζῶντα πόρευσον· οὐ παραιτοῦμαι.

---

808 cf. Chr. Pat. 2210   808–13 cf. Chr. Pat. 2305–10   815 cf. Chr. Pat. 2313   817 (μάραγνά γ' ἤ) Hsch. (Cyr.) μ 257   824 cf. Chr. Pat. 1840, 2003   824–6 cf. Chr. Pat. 2331–2   825 cf. Chr. Pat. 1853

---

811 ἐξηπύσατε Naber, alii alia (vide comm.)   812 τείσει <L?>, coni. Murray: τίσει Q et L¹ᶜ vel Tr¹ et Chr. Pat. 2309 codd. plerique: δώσει V et Chr. Pat. pars. codd.   816 νυν L: νῦν VQ   ὀμώμοται Buttmann: -όσται Ω   817 ἤτοι VQ et Tr¹ et Σᴸ: ἦ L   μάραγνά Barnes: μάραγνα Ω et Σᴸ   818 μένει V: μενεῖ Λ   820ⁿ om. Q   821 μοι Tr¹   μέγα σύ μοι μέγ' ὦ Nauck   πολίοχον Vater: -οῦχον Ω   822 ἔμολον V<L?>Q et Tr¹ˢ: ἔμολ' Tr¹   823 ἀμφὶ V<L?>Q: περὶ P et aut Tr¹ (≠ L) aut L (rescr. Tr²)   ναῦς Badham: ναυσὶ Ω   πῦρ' αἴθειν Reiske: πυραίθειν Ω   ἀργείων στρατόν quae post πυραίθειν habet Ω del. Badham, Kirchhoff (στρατόν iam del. Tr¹)   824 εὐφρόνᾳ Diggle: -η(ι) Ω et Chr. Pat. 1840, 2331   825 ἔβριξα L et ⁱΣᏫ: ἔβρισ' VQ et Chr. Pat. 1853, 2332   826 οὐ Hermann: οὐ μὰ Ω   Σιμοεντιάδας Hermann: -ίδας Ω   παγάς Badham: πη- Ω   827 ὦ ἄνα VQ: ὦ ἄναξ <L>P: ὦ 'ναξ Tr²/³   828 ἔγωγε V<L?>Q: ἐγὼ Tr¹   πάντων πάντῃ (praestat πάντα) ἔγωγε Nauck   829 παράκαιρον Vater   830 ἔργον V: ἔργ' L: ἔργα Q   με γᾶς Barnes: με γᾶ(ι) V<L?>Q: γᾶς με Tr¹   831–2 οὐ γὰρ Tr¹

Ῥῆσος 99

Ην. τί τοῖσδ' ἀπείλεις βάρβαρός τε βαρβάρου
γνώμην ὑφαιρῇ τὴν ἐμήν, πλέκων λόγους;
σὺ ταῦτ' ἔδρασας· οὐδέν' ἂν δεξαίμεθα 835
οὔθ' οἱ θανόντες οὔτ' ἂν οἱ τετρωμένοι
ἄλλον· μακροῦ γε δεῖ σε καὶ σοφοῦ λόγου,
ὅτῳ με πείσεις μὴ φίλους κατακτανεῖν,
ἵππων ἐρασθείς, ὧν ἕκατι συμμάχους
τοὺς σοὺς φονεύεις, πόλλ' ἐπισκήπτων μολεῖν. 840
ἦλθον, τεθνᾶσιν· εὐπρεπέστερον Πάρις
ξενίαν κατῄσχυν' ἢ σὺ συμμάχους κτανών.
μὴ γάρ τι λέξῃς ὥς τις Ἀργείων μολὼν
διώλεσ' ἡμᾶς· τίς ἂν ὑπερβαλὼν λόχους
Τρώων ἐφ' ἡμᾶς ἦλθεν, ὥστε καὶ λαθεῖν; 845
σὺ πρόσθεν ἡμῶν ἦσο καὶ Φρυγῶν στρατός.
τίς οὖν τέτρωται, τίς τέθνηκε †συμμάχων†
τῶν σῶν, μολόντων ὧν σὺ πολεμίων λέγεις;
ἡμεῖς δὲ καὶ τετρώμεθ', οἱ δὲ μειζόνως
παθόντες οὐχ ὁρῶσιν ἡλίου φάος. 850
ἁπλῶς δ' Ἀχαιῶν οὐδέν' αἰτιώμεθα.
τίς δ' ἂν χαμεύνας πολεμίων κατ' εὐφρόνην
Ῥήσου μολὼν ἐξηῦρεν, εἰ μή τις θεῶν
ἔφραζε τοῖς κτανοῦσιν; οὐδ' ἀφιγμένον
τὸ πάμπαν ᾖσαν· ἀλλὰ μηχαναὶ τάδε. 855
Εκ. χρόνον μὲν ἤδη συμμάχοισι χρώμεθα
ὁσόνπερ ἐν γῇ τῇδ' Ἀχαιικὸς λεώς,
κοὐδὲν πρὸς αὐτῶν οἶδα πλημμελὲς κλυών·
ἐν σοὶ δ' ἂν ἀρχοίμεσθα. μή μ' ἔρως ἕλοι

833–55 cf. Eust. 822.2–5   834 cf. Chr. Pat. 2324   835 cf. Chr. Pat. 273, 2323   837–8 cf. Chr. Pat. 2325–6   854b–5 (οὐδ' … τάδε) Orus B 77 Alpers = Et. Gen. (cod. B) s.v. ᾖσμεν, (οὐδ' … ᾖσαν) Et. Gen. (cod. A) s.v. ᾖσμεν, Suda η 573, EM 439.3; cf. D. Chr. 55.14

833ⁿ Ἡν. VQ: ἡμιχ. L   834 ἀφαιρῇ Chr. Pat. 2324   835 οὐδέν' L: οὐδὲν VQ et Chr. Pat. 2323   836 θανόντες V: μαθόντες Λ   841 ηλθε[Π³   842 σὺ om. Q   843 λέξῃ(ι)ς Λ: -εις V   ὥς τις VL: ὅστις Q   844 ἂν Nauck: δ' Ω, quo servato 845 ἦλθ' ἄν Beck   846 σὺ (Π³ᵃᶜ)VΛ: ου Π³ᵖᶜ (fortasse man. sec.)   847–8 συγγενῶν | τῶν σῶν vel ἐν λόχῳ | τῷ σῷ Murray   848 ὧν Bothe: ὡς Ω   849 μείζονα Elmsley   851 ἀχαιῶν Λ: -οὺς V   οὐδέν' Λ: οὐδὲν V   αἰτιώμεσθα Q   852 ἂν Q et Σᵛ: αὖ VL et ⁱΣᵛ   854 ἀφιγμένοι Q (≠ Orus B 77 Alpers = Et. Gen. AB, Suda η 573, EM 439.3)   855 ᾖ(ι)σαν VQ et ⁱΣᵛᴸ et Et. Gen., Suda, EM: ⁱΣᴸ: ἴσαν in ἴσαν aut ἴσ- in ἴσ- mut. Lˡᶜ vel Tr   μηχαναὶ Et. Gen. B (deest A), coni. Musgrave: -ᾶ(ι) Ω   857 ἀχαιικὸς Λ: -αϊκὸς VAf   858 κοὐδὲν VΛ: οὐδὲν gE: [Af]   πλημελὲς (-μμ- Lˡᶜ) οἶδα L   859 δ' ἂν ἀρχοίμε(σ)θα VL (-μεθα V): δ' ἄρ' ἀρχ- Q: δ' ἀρ[χοίμε]σθα Af⁇   ἕλῃ Q

τοιοῦτος ἵππων ὥστ' ἀποκτείνειν φίλους. 860
καὶ ταῦτ' Ὀδυσσεύς· τίς γὰρ ἄλλος ἄν ποτε
ἔδρασεν ἢ 'βούλευσεν Ἀργείων ἀνήρ;
δέδοικα δ' αὐτὸν καί τί μου θράσσει φρένας,
μὴ καὶ Δόλωνα συντυχὼν κατέκτανεν·
χρόνον γὰρ ἤδη φροῦδος ὢν οὐ φαίνεται. 865

Ην. οὐκ οἶδα τοὺς σοὺς οὓς λέγεις Ὀδυσσέας·
ἡμεῖς δ' ὑπ' ἐχθρῶν οὐδενὸς πεπλήγμεθα.
Εκ. σὺ δ' οὖν νόμιζε ταῦτ', ἐπείπερ σοι δοκεῖ.
Ην. ὦ γαῖα πατρίς, πῶς ἂν ἐνθάνοιμί σοι;
Εκ. μὴ θνῇσχ'· ἅλις γὰρ τῶν τεθνηκότων ὄχλος. 870
Ην. ποῖ δὴ τράπωμαι δεσπότου μονούμενος;
Εκ. οἶκός σε κεύθων οὑμὸς ἐξιάσεται.
Ην. καὶ πῶς με κηδεύσουσιν αὐθεντῶν χέρες;
Εκ. ὅδ' αὖ τὸν αὐτὸν μῦθον οὐ λήξει λέγων;
Ην. ὄλοιθ' ὁ δράσας· οὐ γὰρ †εἰς σὲ τείνεται† 875
γλῶσσ', ὡς σὺ κομπεῖς· ἡ Δίκη δ' ἐπίσταται.
Εκ. λάζυσθ'· ἄγοντες <δ'> αὐτὸν ἐς δόμους ἐμούς
οὕτως ὅπως ἂν μὴ 'γκαλῇ πορσύνετε.
ὑμᾶς δ' ἰόντας τοῖσιν ἐν τείχει χρεών
Πριάμῳ τε καὶ γέρουσι σημῆναι νεκρούς 880
θάπτειν κελεύθου λεωφόρου πρὸς ἐκτροπάς.

Χο. τί ποτ' εὐτυχίας ἐκ τῆς μεγάλης
Τροίαν ἀνάγει πάλιν ἐς πένθη
δαίμων ἄλλος, τί φυτεύων;
ἔα ἔα· 885

861–2 cf. Chr. Pat. 274–5   **866** cf. Chr. Pat. 2322, 2356   **868** cf. Chr. Pat. 2376   **873** cf. Chr. Pat. 1125   **875–6** cf. Chr. Pat. 276   **877** cf. Chr. Pat. 1446

---

860 τοσοῦτος Wecklein   **861** καὶ] ἦ Dawe   ὀδυσσεύς ΛAf: -σ- V: -σσέως Fix (cf. 704, 722)   **863** αὐτὸν ΛgE: -τῶν V: -τοῦ Af?   **864** κατέκτανεν Matthiae: κατακτάνη(ι) Ω   **866** ὀδυσέας V   **867** ἀπ' Q   **868** post 869 (ambos Hectori tributos) Af   **868** δ' οὖν ΛAf: δὲ V: δὴ Va: γοῦν Chr. Pat. 2376   **869ⁿ, 870ⁿ** om. Q   **869** ἐνθάνοιμι VL: θάν- Q:]άν- Af   **871** δὴ Porson: δὲ VΛ: ν[ῦν Af?   τράπωμαι VQ: -ομαι L: [Af]   **872** οἶκος VΛ: ὁ μαῖκος Af   **873** κηδεύσουσιν ΛAf?: -σωσιν V: utrumque Chr. Pat. 1125   **874** λέξων Af   interrogationis nota dist. Diggle   **875–6** ὄλοιθ' ὁ δράσας· ἡ Δίκη ἐπίσταται ceteris omissis Chr. Pat. 276   post 875 vel post 876 γλῶσσ' lacunam stat. West   **875** εἰς σὲ fere ΛAf (εἴς σε Q): εἰσέτι V   **877** <δ'> Morstadt (≠ Chr. Pat. 1446)   **878** 'γκαλῇ(ι) ΛAfᵘᵛ: κ- V   πορσύνεται Af   **881** κελεύειν Dobree: κελεύειν Ω   λεωφόρου Afᵘᵛ et Vᵍˡ, coni. Vater: λαοφόρου Λ, -ους V   **883** ἀνάγει Af, coni. Heath: ἄγει VL: ἄγοι Q   πένθη VΛ: πένθως pot. qu. -θος Af   **884** ἄλλος, τί Tyrwhitt: ἄλλό τι Λ: ἄλλοτε V]τι Af   **885** ἔα ἔα Dindorf: ἔα ἔα ὦ ὦ fere VQ et Tr³ (ἔα ἔα ω ω V): om. L

τίς ὑπὲρ κεφαλῆς θεός, ὦ βασιλεῦ,
τὸν νεόκμητον νεκρὸν ἐν χειροῖν
φοράδην πέμπει;
ταρβῶ λεύσσων τόδε πῆμα.

ΜΟΥΣΑ
ὁρᾶν πάρεστι, Τρῶες· ἡ γὰρ ἐν σοφοῖς 890
τιμὰς ἔχουσα Μοῦσα συγγόνων μία
πάρειμι, παῖδα τόνδ' ὁρῶσ' οἰκτρῶς φίλον
θανόνθ' ὑπ' ἐχθρῶν· ὅν ποθ' ὁ κτείνας χρόνῳ
δόλιος Ὀδυσσεὺς ἀξίαν τείσει δίκην.

ἰαλέμῳ αὐθιγενεῖ   στρ.
τέκνον σ' ὀλοφύρομαι, ὦ   896
 ματρὸς ἄλγος, οἵαν
ἔκελσας ὁδὸν ποτὶ Τροίαν·
ἦ δυσδαίμονα καὶ μελέαν
ἀπὸ μὲν φαμένας ἐμοῦ πορευθείς,   900
 ἀπὸ δ' ἀντομένου πατρὸς βιαίως.
ὤμοι ἐγὼ σέθεν, ὦ φιλία
φιλία κεφαλά, τέκνον, ὤμοι.

Χο. ὅσον προσήκει μὴ γένους κοινωνίαν
    ἔχοντι λύπης τὸν σὸν οἰκτίρω γόνον.   905

Μο. ὄλοιτο μὲν Οἰνείδας,   ἀντ.
    ὄλοιτο δὲ Λαρτιάδας,
     ὅς μ' ἄπαιδα γέννας
    ἔθηκεν ἀριστοτόκοιο·
    ἅ θ' Ἕλλανα λιποῦσα δόμον   910
    Φρυγίων λεχέων ἔπλευσε πλαθεῖσ',

887-8 cf. Chr. Pat. 1456   **894** cf. Chr. Pat. 277, 786   **904-5** cf. Chr. Pat. 1159-60, 1282-3

---

887 νεόκμητον Λ: νεόχμ- V: νεόδμ- Va et Chr. Pat. 1456   χειροῖν Valckenaer: χεροῖν Ω   **889** om. L   λεύσσων Q: -σ- V   **894** ὀδυσεὺς V   τείσει Murray: τίσει Ω et Chr. Pat. 277, 786   **899** ἦ fere Λ (ἢ Q): ἢ V   **900** ἀπὸ μὲν φαμένας Dindorf (cf. 934): ἀπομεμφομένας V: -μεμψαμένας L: -πεψαμένας Q et Tr^ls   **904** ὄσῃ (et 905 λύπῃ) Wecklein (≠ Chr. Pat. 1159)   γένος Q (≠ Chr. Pat. 1159, 1282)   **905** λύπης Kirchhoff: -η L: -ην VQ   οἰκτίρω Murray: -ει- Ω   **906** Οἰνείδας Aldina: -είδας VL: -ίδας Q   **907** Λαρτιάδας Heath: λαρτιάδης V: λαρτίδας <L>P: λαερτίδας Q et Tr³   **909** ἔθηκ' L (≠ Tr³)   ἀριστοτόκοιο Aldina: -τοτόκου VL: -τόκου Q   **910** Ἕλλανα Badham: ἑλένα Ω

†ὑπ' Ἰλίῳ ὤλεσε† μὲν σ' ἕκατι Τροίας,
φίλτατε, μυριάδας τε πόλεις
ἀνδρῶν ἀγαθῶν ἐκένωσεν.

ἦ πολλὰ μὲν ζῶν, πολλὰ δ' εἰς Ἅιδου μολών, 915
Φιλάμμονος παῖ, τῆς ἐμῆς ἥψω φρενός·
ὕβρις γάρ, ἥ σ' ἔσφηλε, καὶ Μουσῶν ἔρις
τεκεῖν μ' ἔθηκε τόνδε δύστηνον γόνον.
περῶσα γὰρ δὴ ποταμίους διὰ ῥοὰς
λέκτροις ἐπλάθην Στρυμόνος φυταλμίοις, 920
ὅτ' ἤλθομεν γῆς χρυσόβωλον ἐς λέπας
Πάγγαιον ὀργάνοισιν ἐξησκημέναι
Μοῦσαι μεγίστην εἰς ἔριν μελῳδίας
κλεινῷ σοφιστῇ Θρῃκὶ κατυφλώσαμεν
Θάμυριν, ὃς ἡμῶν πόλλ' ἐδέννασεν τέχνην. 925
κἀπεί σε τίκτω, συγγόνους αἰδουμένη
καὶ παρθενείαν, ἧκ' ἐς εὐύδρου πατρός
δίνας· τρέφειν δέ σ' οὐ βρότειον ἐς χέρα
Στρυμὼν δίδωσιν ἀλλὰ πηγαίαις κόραις.
ἔνθ' ἐκτραφεὶς κάλλιστα παρθένων ὕπο, 930
Θρῄκης ἀνάσσων πρῶτος ἦσθ' ἀνδρῶν, τέκνον.
καί σ' ἀμφὶ γῆν μὲν πατρίαν φιλαιμάτους
ἀλκὰς κορύσσοντ' οὐκ ἐδείμαινον θανεῖν·
Τροίας δ' ἀπηύδων ἄστυ μὴ κέλσαι ποτέ,
εἰδυῖα τὸν σὸν πότμον· ἀλλά σ' Ἕκτορος 935
πρεσβεύμαθ' αἵ τε μυρίαι γερουσίαι
ἔπεισαν ἐλθεῖν κἀπικουρῆσαι φίλοις.
καὶ τοῦδ', Ἀθάνα, παντὸς αἰτία μόρου —
οὐδὲν δ' Ὀδυσσεὺς οὐδ' ὁ Τυδέως τόκος

915–16 cf. Chr. Pat. 1338–9   **917** cf. Chr. Pat. 1341   **918** cf. Chr. Pat. 1344   **920** (φυταλμίοις) Hsch. φ 1066   **925** et 951 (ἐδέννασεν) Hsch. (Cyr.) ε 437   **926** cf. Chr. Pat. 1347   **928–30** cf. Chr. Pat. 1348–50   **933** cf. Chr. Pat. 1367   **935b–6** cf. Chr. Pat. 1368–9   **937** cf. Chr. Pat. 1371   **938** cf. Chr. Pat. 1661

---

912 ὅπου ὤλεσε Wilamowitz, ἀπὸ δ' ὤλεσε Henning (ἀπό τ' Wecklein), ἃ διώλεσε Jackson   σ' ἕκατι Bruhn: σε κατὰ Ω   **913** μυριάδος vel μυριάδων Ritchie   πόλεων Reiske   **915** ἦ fere Λ (ἦ Q) et Chr. Pat. 1338 pars codd.: ἢ V   **917** σφ' Q   **919** διὰ ῥοάς L. Dindorf: διαρροάς Ω   **920** ἐπλάθην Q   φυταλμίοις V   **922** ἐξησκημένοι L   **924** κλεινῷ Dobree: κείνω(ι) Ω: δεινῷ Valckenaer   κατυφλώσαμεν Hn: κἀκτ- Ω   **925** ἐδένναζεν Wecklein   **926** συγγόνως Q (≠ Q¹ᶜ)   **927** παρθενείαν L: -ίαν VQ   εὐύδρου Λ: εὔδ- V   **928** σ' VL: γ' Q   βρότειον Elmsley: βροτείαν Ω et Chr. Pat. 1348   ἐς χέρα V: ἐσχάραν Λ et Chr. Pat.   **932** φιλαίματος Q (≠ Q¹ᶜ)   **937** ἔπεισ' ἀνελθεῖν Q   κἀπικυρῆσαι V   **938** καὶ] σὺ Kirchhoff   **939** ὀδυσεὺς V   οὐδ' ὁ Λ: οὐδὲ V

ἔδρασε — δρῶσα μὴ δόκει λεληθέναι. 940
καίτοι πόλιν σὴν σύγγονοι πρεσβεύομεν
Μοῦσαι μάλιστα κἀπιχρώμεθα χθονί,
μυστηρίων τε τῶν ἀπορρήτων φανάς
ἔδειξεν Ὀρφεύς, αὐτανέψιος νεκροῦ
τοῦδ' ὃν κατέκτεινας σύ· Μουσαῖόν τε, σὸν 945
σεμνὸν πολίτην κἀπὶ πλεῖστον ἄνδρ' ἕνα
ἐλθόντα, Φοῖβος σύγγονοί τ' ἠσκήσαμεν.
καὶ τῶνδε μισθὸν παῖδ' ἔχουσ' ἐν ἀγκάλαις
θρηνῶ· σοφιστὴν δ' ἄλλον οὐκ ἐπάξομαι.
Χο. μάτην ἄρ' ἡμᾶς Θρήκιος τροχηλάτης 950
ἐδέννασ', Ἕκτορ, τῷδε βουλεῦσαι φόνον.
Εκ. ἤδη τάδ'· οὐδὲν μάντεων ἔδει φράσαι
Ὀδυσσέως τέχναισι τόνδ' ὀλωλότα.
ἐγὼ δὲ γῆς ἔφεδρον Ἑλλήνων στρατὸν
λεύσσων, τί μὴν ἔμελλον οὐ πέμψειν φίλοις 955
κήρυκας, ἐλθεῖν κἀπικουρῆσαι χθονί;
ἔπεμψ'· ὀφείλων δ' ἦλθε συμπονεῖν ἐμοί.
οὐ μὴν θανόντι γ' οὐδαμῶς συνήδομαι·
καὶ νῦν ἕτοιμος τῷδε καὶ τεῦξαι τάφον
καὶ ξυμπυρῶσαι μυρίαν πέπλων χλιδήν· 960
φίλος γὰρ ἐλθὼν δυστυχῶς ἀπέρχεται.
Μο. οὐκ εἶσι γαίας ἐς μελάγχιμον πέδον·
τοσόνδε νύμφην τὴν ἔνερθ' αἰτήσομαι,
τῆς καρποποιοῦ παῖδα Δήμητρος θεᾶς,
ψυχὴν ἀνεῖναι τοῦδ'· ὀφειλέτις δέ μοι 965

---

940 cf. Chr. Pat. 1411 943 (φανάς) Hsch. (Cyr.) φ 144 φάνας· ... ἢ τὰς ἐκλάμψεις (etiam Ion 550) 943-4 cf. Chr. Pat. 1387-9, 1400 946-7 cf. Chr. Pat. 1392-3 948-9 cf. Chr. Pat. 1373-6 951 (ἐδέννασ') vide ad 925 956 cf. Chr. Pat. 1406 959 (τεῦξαι) Hsch. (Cyr.) τ 695 (etiam E. fr. 370.91) 959-60 cf. Chr. Pat. 1378-9

---

940 ἔδρασε — δρῶσα Lenting: ἔδρασε δράσας Ω (cf. Chr. Pat. 1411 ἔδρας ἔδρασας κτλ.): ἔδρασ' — ἔδρασας Heath, quibus acceptis τοῦτ' pro τοῦδ' 938 Paley post hunc versum desinunt VVa; spat. vac. relicto rursus in novo folio incipit Va 942 κἀπιχρώμεθα L: -μεσθα Q: χρώμεθα Va 943 φανάς Lobeck et Chr. Pat. 1387, 1400 pars codd.: φάνας Ω 945 ὃν κατέκτεινας σύ Cobet: οὖν κατακτείνασα Va: οὕνεκα κτείνασα Λ: ὃν κατακτείνεις σύ Bothe, ὃν κατέκτανες σύ Seager 946 πλεῖσθον Q (≠ Q¹ᶜ) 949 ἐπάξομεν Paley (vide comm.) 950 τροχηλάτης Valckenaer: στρατηλάτης (idem error Phoen. 39 Rw): διφρηλάτης Portus 951 ἕκτορ Va: -ωρ Λ φόνων Lᵘᵛ<P> (≠ Lᶜᴾᶜ) 952ⁿ Εκ. Q: om. VaL 952 ἤδη Va: ἥ(ι)δειν Λ μάντεων Λ: -εως Λ 955 πέμπειν L (≠ Tr²/³) 959 ἕτοιμος Λ et Chr. Pat. 1378: ἑτοίμως Va 960 ξυμ- Va: συμ- Λ μυρίαν Wecklein: -ίων Ω et Chr. Pat. 1379 961 ἀποίχεται Vater 962 μελάγχιμον VagB: -χεῖμον Λ 965 ὀφειλέτης Q

τοὺς Ὀρφέως τιμῶσα φαίνεσθαι φίλους.
κἀμοὶ μὲν ὡς θανών τε κοὐ λεύσσων φάος
ἔσται τὸ λοιπόν· οὐ γὰρ ἐς ταὐτόν ποτε
ἔτ' εἶσιν οὐδὲ μητρὸς ὄψεται δέμας·
κρυπτὸς δ' ἐν ἄντροις τῆς ὑπαργύρου χθονός   970
ἀνθρωποδαίμων κείσεται βλέπων φάος,
Βάκχου προφήτης, ὅς γε Παγγαίου πέτραν
ᾤκησε, σεμνὸς τοῖσιν εἰδόσιν θεός.
ῥᾷον δὲ πένθος τῆς θαλασσίας θεοῦ
οἴσω· θανεῖν γὰρ καὶ τὸν ἐκ κείνης χρεών.   975
θρήνοις δ' ἀδελφαὶ πρῶτα μέν σ' ὑμνήσομεν,
ἔπειτ' Ἀχιλλέα Θέτιδος ἐν πένθει ποτέ.
οὐ ῥύσεταί νιν Παλλάς, ἥ σ' ἀπέκτανεν·
τοῖον φαρέτρα Λοξίου σῴζει βέλος.
ὦ παιδοποιοὶ συμφοραί, πόνοι βροτῶν·   980
ὡς ὅστις ὑμᾶς μὴ κακῶς λογίζεται
ἄπαις διοίσει κοὐ τεκὼν θάψει τέκνα.

Χο. οὗτος μὲν ἤδη μητρὶ κηδεύειν μέλει·
σὺ δ', εἴ τι πράσσειν τῶν προκειμένων θέλεις,
Ἕκτορ, πάρεστι· φῶς γὰρ ἡμέρας τόδε.   985

Εκ. χωρεῖτε, συμμάχους δ' ὁπλίζεσθαι τάχος
ἄνωχθε πληροῦν τ' αὐχένας ξυνωρίδων.
πανοὺς δ' ἔχοντας χρὴ μένειν Τυρσηνικῆς
σάλπιγγος αὐδήν· ὡς ὑπερβαλὼν τάφρον
τείχη τ' Ἀχαιῶν ναυσὶν αἶθον ἐμβαλεῖν   990
πέποιθα Τρωσί θ' ἡμέραν ἐλευθέραν
ἀκτῖνα τὴν στείχουσαν ἡλίου φέρειν.

---

968 cf. Chr. Pat. 1775   **972–3** cf. Asclep. Tragil. apud Hsch. ρ 272 ~ Phot. ρ 103 Theodoridis, Suda ρ 143 (FGrHist 12 F 5)   **973–5** cf. Chr. Pat. 1776–8   **975** cf. Chr. Pat. 1773   **983–5** cf. Chr. Pat. 1779–81   **990** (αἶθον) Hsch. (Cyr.) α 1878 (etiam E. Suppl. 208, A. R. 3.1304)   **991–2** cf. Chr. Pat. 1783–4, 2010–11

---

966 τιμῶσαι Q   **968** ἐς ταὐτόν VaL: ἔστ' αὐτόν Q   **969** ἔτ' … οὐδὲ Kirchhoff (ἔτ' iam L. Dindorf): οὔτ' … οὔτε Ω   **970** τῆς Musgrave: τῆσδ' Ω   **972** ὅς γε Matthiae: ὅς τε Q et Pᶜ: ὥστε VaL   **974** ῥᾷον Valckenaer, denuo Musgrave (1749): βαιὸν Ω et Chr. Pat. 1777   θαλασσίου L   **975** εἴσω Q   ἐκ κείνης Λ: ἐκείνης Va: utrumque Chr. Pat. 1773, 1778   **976** θρήνους Va: -ους Λ   σ' om. L   **977** ἀχιλέα Va   **981** καλῶς Va   **983** οὗτος Λ: οὕτως Λ   **985** ἕκτωρ Af   ἡμέρᾳ Q   **986** δ' VaAf: θ' Λ   ὁπλίζεσθε Q   **987** πληροῦν Va: -ου Λ: -ου[Af   αὐχένας VaL: -να Q: [Af]   **988** πανοὺς Reiske: πόνους Ω: [Af]   **989** ὑπερβαλὼν Lenting: -βάλλων Ω: [Af]   τάφρον Jacobs: στρατόν Ω: [Af]   **991** τρωσί VaL: τρωσίν Q

Χο. πείθου βασιλεῖ· στείχωμεν ὅπλοις
     κοσμησάμενοι καὶ ξυμμαχίᾳ
     τάδε φράζωμεν· τάχα δ' ἂν νίκην   995
     δοίη δαίμων ὁ μεθ' ἡμῶν.

---

993 στείχωμεν Va: -ομεν Λ   **994** καὶ ξυμμαχίᾳ Q: καὶ συμμ- L: ξυμμαχίαν Va   **995** νίκην Dindorf: -αν fere Ω   Subscriptio ὡδὶ τὸ τέρμα τῆς ῥήσου τραγῳδίας L: τέλος τοῦ εὐριπιδείου ῥήσου Q: τέλος Va

Commentary

The Hypotheses

Like many other Greek plays *Rhesus* is accompanied by a variety of prefatory material, although only V and Q preserve the entire set. This edition follows Diggle in reproducing the order exhibited by V. For details of the arrangement and transmission of the sections in the MSS see Zuntz, *Inquiry*, 144–6; on dramatic hypotheses in general Pfeiffer, *History of Classical Scholarship* I, 192–6, Zuntz, *Political Plays*, 129–46, Barrett, *Hippolytos*, 153–4 and van Rossum-Steenbeek, *Greek Readers' Digests?*, 1–52. Liapis (pp. 55–69) offers a full commentary on the *Rhesus* arguments, although his interpretation of Hyp. (b) needs to be viewed with caution (cf. Introduction, 25–6 with n. 18, 27–8).

Hypothesis (a)

The piece belongs to the *Tales from Euripides* or 'narrative hypotheses', which go back to a late-Hellenistic collection of plot summaries, arranged alphabetically according to the first letter of the play title (cf. pp. 25 and 54 on the papyrus that carries the second half of the text). The narratives do not give a true synopsis of the action (as we find in Hyp. (a) *Med.*), but recount the story in the past tense, passing over and expanding on scenes as was deemed expedient, for the benefit of 'persons unwilling or unable to go to the trouble of reading the originals' (Barrett, *Hippolytos*, 153). In the fifth or sixth century AD perhaps (when marginal commentaries also began to be inserted extensively) these epitomes were prefixed to the tragic texts in the editions, from where they entered the medieval tradition, including that of the 'alphabetical' plays.[1]

4–5. †ἐκπέμπεσθαι† < > τόπον εἰς τὴν παρεμβολὴν ἀφώρισεν αὐτῷ: Since the arrival of Rhesus and his acceptance as an ally by Hector could hardly have been omitted, something must have fallen out after the verb referring to Dolon's dispatch, as Morstadt (*Beitrag*, 70–1 n. 2)

---

[1] Cf. W. S. Barrett, *CQ* n.s. 15 (1965), 63 = *Collected Papers*, 444. Of the 'alphabetical' plays, complete or partial narrative hypotheses survive for *Cyclops, Heraclidae, Heracles, Iphigenia in Tauris, Ion* and *Helen* (preceded by Byzantine elaborations and added in P only by Ioannes Catrares). On the transmission of the material see Zuntz, *Inquiry*, 140–4.

indicated and Liapis ('Notes', 48) implied in his *exempli gratia* reconstruction of the sentence: Δόλωνα δὲ ὑπακούσαντα πρὸς τὴν χρείαν ἐκπέμψας <'Ρῆσον μετ' ὀλίγον ἀφικόμενον ἀπεδέξατο> τόπον εἰς τὴν παρεμβολὴν ἀφορίσας αὐτῷ. Here, however, the closing participial clause (ἀφορίσας Ao) seems to bear too much syntactical weight ('... he admitted Rhesus ... *and* demarcated a camping space for him') to be compatible with the style of the hypotheses (cf. van Rossum-Steenbeek 9 on the frequent use of circumstantial participles and genitive absolutes to express subordination). It is better to keep ἀφώρισεν (VQ).

Whether ἐκπέμπεσθαι is corrupt we cannot be sure. It may depend on a lost main verb, although the active would be more likely then. So perhaps the word combines fragments from before and in or after the lacuna, which appears to have been the reasoning behind Diggle's ... ἐκπέμψας θηρὸς τρόπον ... (an odd expression, apart from the fact that Dolon's animal disguise is too unimportant to have been mentioned in the hypothesis).[2] Martin West tentatively suggests ἐκπέμπ< >εσθαι or ἐκπέμ<ψας >εσθαι.

9. ἐὰν βιώσῃ: so VQ (εἰ βιώσει Ao). Π¹ is unavailable, but Luppe (*Anagennesis* 2 [1982], 78) very plausibly supplied ... τοῖς ῞Ελλη[σιν, ἐὰν εἰς αὔριον βιῷ. τούτοι]ς δ' ... (with the earlier root aorist of βιόω), on the analogy of the 'oracle' at *Rh.* 600 ὃς εἰ διοίσει νύκτα τήνδ' ἐς αὔριον. Cf. Liapis 55.

10–11. ὡς δῆθεν ὑπὸ Ἀφροδίτης is the reading of Ω (ὑπ' Ao). Π¹ has room only for [ὡς Ἀφροδίτ]ης (suppl. Gallavotti), but it seems less likely that the particle and preposition were added in the course of transmission than that the papyrus left them out.

14–15. διὰ τοῦ ῞Εκτορος τὸν φόνον ἐνηργῆσθαι †ἐπινοεῖ†: This is the version of Π¹, as against δι' αὐτοῦ φησὶν ῞Εκτορος τὸν φόνον γεγενῆσθαι (fere VQAo). While ἐνηργῆσθαι is evidently correct, ἐπινοεῖ cannot stand, for (1) both its meaning ('contrive, intend') and construction are inappropriate, (2) the present tense does not conform to the author's habit of writing (above) and (3) hiatus is admitted in the hypotheses only after prepositives (and δέ, where elision is possible). Haslam's simple ἐπενόει (*apud* van Rossum-Steenbeek 202) founders on (1) and (3), but Liapis ('Notes', 48–9) may be on the right track in assuming that the verb preserves traces of the original and combining it with φησίν (Ao) to e.g. ... {διὰ τοῦ} ῞Εκτορος <ἐπινοήσαντος> τὸν φόνον <φησὶν> ἐνεργῆσθαι or (removing what appears to be the only acceptable historic present) ... {διὰ τοῦ} ῞Εκτορος <ἐπινοήσαντος

---

[2] The fact that in *Rhesus* the wolf-costume is not part of Hector's orders (Liapis, 'Notes', 48) need not be an objection, since the hypotheses are not always faithful in their reports (cf. below on ll. 14–15, and see e.g. Barrett, *Hippolytos*, 153, Parker, *Alcestis*, 47).

ἔφησε> τὸν φόνον ἐνεργῆσθαι. Such an emendation, Liapis observes, would also represent accurately the Charioteer's allegation that Hector arranged for the killing of Rhesus (rather than carrying it out himself), although the epitomiser may here have been misled by the use of the second person singular in *Rh.* 835–42.

18–19. Π¹ concludes with … οὐδ' Ἀχιλλέα φησὶν ἀδάκρυτον ἔσεσθαι (Ἀχ[ιλέα suppl. Gallavotti). The MSS have Ἀχιλλεῖ and after ἔσεσθαι add τὴν στρατείαν τῷ κοινῷ τῶν ἐπιφανῶν θανάτῳ τὴν ἰδίαν παραμυθουμένη λύπην (τὴν στρατείαν om. V, τῶν ἐπι om. spat. vac. rel. V), which Diggle, following Zuntz (*Political Plays*, 142), did not print. More recently, in the light of his research on rhythmical clausulae in the narrative hypotheses (in *Euripide e i papiri*, 27–67), he has conceded that τῷ κοινῷ … λύπην 'may be genuine' (comparing the 'rhetorical flourish' at the end of the *Stheneboea* hypothesis) and accorded the same benefit of doubt to Ἀχιλλεῖ … τὴν στρατείαν (41 with n. 25). The latter is unlikely, given that it could easily be understood to mean 'for Achilles the campaign will not be without weeping either' (cf. Liapis on Hyp. (a) *Rh.* 19–22), but τῷ κοινῷ … λύπην should probably be retained.

Diggle (above) likewise disposes of Luppe's ἔφησε(ν) for φησίν in Π¹ (*Anagennesis* 2 [1982], 81), on account of the hiatus this would create. The question does not arise in the parallels adduced by Luppe: Hyp. (a) *Or.* 187.18–19 Diggle ἐπιφανεὶς δ' Ἀπόλλων Ἑλένην μὲν αὐτὸς ἔφησεν εἰς θεοὺς διακομίζειν and Hyp. *Rhadamanthys* … [τὰς θυγα-] | τέρας δ' αὐτοῦ θεὰς ἔφησε γ[ενέσθαι (where previous editors had wrongly read ἔφη).

Hypothesis (b)

With the authenticity question and alternative prologues, the learned note, which in its present form perhaps dates to the second century AD,[3] treats matters of literary history, like part of Hyp. *Pers.* (3.1–8 West), Hyp. (a) *Med.* (88.11–89.34 Diggle) and the end of the 'Aristophanic' hypothesis to *Hippolytus* (205.27–30 Diggle). It provides the clearest evidence for the origin and early transmission of *Rhesus* (Introduction, ch. III.1), although the material has suffered abridgement, most regrettably with regard to the argument for non-Euripidean authorship. This and at least the following references to the *didascaliae* and astronomical

---

[3] See H. Grégoire, *AC* 2 (1933), 97–8 for the apparent dependence of the astronomical remark (ll. 22–3) on commentaries resembling our scholia (cf. Σᵛ *Rh.* 528 [II 340.5–341.13 Schwartz = 105–7 Merro]).

detail (cf. n. 3) go back to high Hellenistic scholarship, mediated perhaps through Didymus (P. Carrara, *ZPE* 90 [1990], 36–7 with n. 9).

23. Δικαίαρχος: For Nauck's correction of the transmitted δικαίαν see Introduction, 25 with n. 18.

24. γράφει κατὰ λέξιν οὕτως: a set expression in scholiastic Greek, indicating a usually longer verbatim quotation. Schwartz (II 324) therefore posited a lacuna, which Luppe filled with <'Ρῆσος, οὗ ἀρχή>, the equivalent to the standard opening tag of the ancient narrative hypotheses (*ZPE* 84 [1990], 11–13). This is still short, but if one includes the iambic trimeter, not too far from the two-and-a-half-line Timaeus excerpt, introduced by οὕτως γράφων, in Σ^MV *Hec.* 131 (I 26.3–5 Schwartz). The view, most recently endorsed by Liapis (*GRBS* 42 [2001], 313–28), that all the rest of Hyp. (b) *Rh.* belongs to Dicaearchus (cf. Introduction, 25 n. 18) is rendered unlikely by its content and style of writing, which 'are ... typical of a later period of scholarship' (Ritchie 31).

Hypothesis (c)

This is a fragment of the hypothesis of Aristophanes of Byzantium (the heading was added by the rubricator in V). In their complete form these highly standardised introductions for the scholarly reader contained (1) a brief summary of the plot, (2) an indication of other dramatic treatments of the theme, (3) notes on the scene, the identity of the chorus and the prologist, (4) didascalic information (the date of the first performance, accompanying plays, choregos, the names of the competitors and the result of the contest, occasionally the play's position in the author's *œuvre*) and (5) a critical judgement.[4] In some hypotheses (3) is followed by a list of keywords, introduced by τὸ δὲ κεφάλαιον (*PV, OT, Ant.*) or ἡ δ' ὑπόθεσις (*Pers., Sept.*), which name the main parts of the action, although C. H. Moore (*HSPh* 12 [1901], 288 n. 1) has doubted that these go back to Aristophanes.

For *Rhesus* only (1) and (3) survive, and apparently a variation on the κεφάλαιον in the concluding statement περιέχει δὲ τὴν Νυκτεγερσίαν. The plot summary has been expanded by interpolation and rewriting, certainly in the passages that, against the testimony of the play, name Terpsichore as Rhesus' mother (cf. Th. O. H. Achelis, *Philologus* 73 [1914–16], 148 with n. 338c, who plausibly deletes παῖς μὲν ἦν ...

---

[4] See Pfeiffer, *History of Classical Scholarship* I, 192–6, Barrett, *Hippolytos*, 153, van Rossum-Steenbeek 32–4. The best-preserved examples of Aristophanic hypotheses are those to *Seven against Thebes, Philoctetes, Alcestis* and *Medea* (Zuntz, *Political Plays*, 131, 139–40 with n. 6).

ἡγούμενος, Zuntz, *Political Plays*, 140 with n. 1, Liapis 67–8). Its final sentence in L (om. VQ) about Dolon's murder being treated in passing (ὡς ἐν παρόδῳ δὲ διαλαμβάνει καὶ περὶ τοῦ φόνου τοῦ Δόλωνος) also looks peculiar for its lack of connection with the preceding and use of διαλαμβάνω + περί in an unparalleled sense.[5]

Hypothesis (d)

The *dramatis personae* (including the chorus) are listed in the order of appearance in the play. This, however, is correctly preserved only in L (and with small variations O). Q has succumbed to a common error by which the names 'written in [two] columns intended to be read vertically ... were ... instead read off horizontally' (Barrett, *Hippolytos*, 154). Cf. Diggle's apparatus on Hyp. (c) *Or.* (189.45–7) and for the same mistake also e.g. the lists for *Seven against Thebes* (p. 62 West) and *Phoenissae* (p. 81 Diggle). The rubricator of V has created (or copied out) untraceable confusion.

---

[5] Cf. A. L. Brown, *CQ* n.s. 37 (1987), 430 (who otherwise is too critical of the synopses). Liapis (on Hyp. (c) *Rh.* 50–1) quotes LSJ s.v. διαλαμβάνω III 7, which is different ('state distinctly').

The Play

Scene and Setting

The stage represents Hector's bivouac in the temporary camp which the Trojans set up at the end of *Iliad* 8. The *skene* is ignored, as part of the realistic setting on the open plain and perhaps a tribute to early-fifth-century dramatic technique (Introduction, 40–1).[1] Of the two *eisodoi*, the one to the audience's right leads to the main body of Trojans and further to the seashore with the Achaean ships; the one to the left leads to the Thracian camp, Troy and Mt. Ida, from which the Shepherd and Rhesus arrive (L. Battezzato, *CQ* n.s. 50 [2000], 367–8).

The time is indicated by *Rh.* 5–6 (n.) οἳ τετράμοιρον νυκτὸς φυλακὴν / πάσης στρατιᾶς προκάθηνται. This corresponds to the beginning of *Iliad* 10 in the same way as the choral song 527–64 (n.) adapts *Il.* 10.251–3 μάλα γὰρ νὺξ ἄνεται, ἐγγύθι δ' ἠώς, / ἄστρα δὲ δὴ προβέβηκε, παροίχωκεν δὲ πλέων νύξ / τῶν δύο μοιράων, τριτάτη δ' ἔτι μοῖρα λέλειπται (on Homer's three night watches as opposed to the five in *Rhesus* see 538–45n.). At 985 (983–5n.) the sunrise heralds the end of the nocturnal play.

Hector is first seen lying on his 'leaf-strewn couch' (9), surrounded by his attendants (2–3) in a sort of 'opening tableau' (cf. Taplin, *Stagecraft*, 134–6). Other tragedies that began with the parodos also had the main character silent on stage before: A. *Niobe*, *Myrmidons* (both mocked by 'Euripides' in Ar. *Ran.* 911–20) and the spurious *Prometheus Unbound* (O. P. Taplin, *HSPh* 76 [1972], 58–76). Hector is neither lost in grief (like Niobe and Achilles) nor has he been tormented for endless years, but perhaps our poet wished to show briefly the peace of the victorious night before rapid action initiates the fatal chain of events.

1–51. A chorus of Trojan sentries hurries in from the audience's right in order to wake Hector and tell him important news (1–10). Some agitated dialogue (11–22) is followed by a call to arms (23–33: strophe) and,

---

[1] Nevertheless, the chorus behave almost as if somebody had to be called out of the stage-building (2–3, 11–14nn.).

after further complaints from Hector (34–40), the actual report (41–51: antistrophe).

The anapaestic-lyric composition (below) leads the spectators *in medias res*. But it soon becomes clear that we have here a dramatisation of *Iliad* 10, which tells the story from the Trojan perspective. As the convocation of Hector's assembly at *Il.* 10.299–302 did not offer much material, our poet modelled his parodos on the 'Homeric' opening episode (*Il.* 10.1–202).[2] The watchfires and noise are transferred to the Greek camp (23–51, 41–3a, 41–2, 44–8nn.), the fearful commotion now lies on the Trojan side (15, 17–18, 36–7a nn.). Several echoes in language and content underline the inversion. In particular, the chorus' initial conversation with Hector matches Agamemnon's rousing of Nestor in *Il.* 10.73–101 (7, 11–14, 15nn.). Like the sentries, he had been worried by the activities in the enemy camp and found Nestor, as later Diomedes, sleeping in the open and under arms (20–2n.). Even the structural parallelism of *Iliad* 10 is to some extent reproduced in the choral song. For while the strophe recalls in greater detail the Greek preparations at the beginning of the book (23–51n.), the rally of their army described in the antistrophe mirrors the Trojan gathering that is shown on stage (R. S. Bond, *AJPh* 117 [1996], 265). And part of *Rh.* 44–8 probably depends on Dolon's assumption of a meeting by Agamemnon's ship at *Il.* 10.325–7.

Within this framework the parodos resembles a (Euripidean) messenger scene with many of its typical elements: the question for the addressee (2–6), a general announcement (4), a short counter-question, here multiplied in Hector's confusion (11–22), and the request for the full account in 38–9 (cf. Strohm 266–9, 273 with n. 1). But as in 728–55 (n.) the scheme is varied to give an effective picture of human fallibility and nocturnal tumult (Strohm 258–66, 272–3, H. Parry, *Phoenix* 18 [1964], 284–5, Introduction, 4–5). When the sentries finally get a chance to speak, they recommend action instead of telling the 'news in brief' (23–33),[3] and their message proper (41–51) mainly consists of visual and aural impressions, nothing sure (76–7, 79). This is far from the clear and well-structured report in anapaests that Hecuba receives from the Trojan Women about the imminent sacrifice of Polyxena (*Hec.* 105–40). Rather we may compare the Phrygian's aria (*Or.* 1368–1502), where regular iambic questions from the coryphaeus punctuate 'a not entirely σαφές account' (Willink on *Or.* 1366–1502). Similarly, at *Hec.* 658–725 (which moves from trimeters through mixed speech and lyric back to trimeters)

---

2   See Ritchie 64–5, R. S. Bond, *AJPh* 117 (1996), 265–6, Fantuzzi, in *I luoghi*, 244–56 and *Entretiens Hardt* LII, 148–51.

3   Strohm (273 n. 1) gives as a parallel *Med.* 1122–3 Μήδεια, φεῦγε φεῦγε, μήτε ναΐαν / λιποῦσ' ἀπήνην μήτ' ὄχον πεδοστιβῆ.

the usual introduction is transferred to a situation that for the moment cannot be clarified. The maidservant does not know how Polydorus died, and thus no messenger speech is to come (Strohm 267–8, 272–3).

Formally our scene is unlike any prologue we know. Of Euripides' plays only *Iphigenia in Aulis* (as it stands) and *Andromeda* begin with anapaests, but the former (*IA* 1–48 + 115–62) constitute a recitative (and later partly melic) actors' dialogue,[4] the latter (E. frr. 114–16) a monody of the heroine, interspersed with repetitions from the invisible Echo. For genuine opening parodoi we have to go back to Aeschylus: *Persians* (1–154), *Supplices* (1–175ef), *Myrmidons* (fr. 131), *Nereids* (fr. 150),[5] *Niobe* (cf. Ar. *Ran.* 911–15) and [A.] *Prometheus Unbound* (frr. 190–2). In *Persians* the Old Councillors can hardly supply more preliminary information, and in *Myrmidons*, *Niobe* (?) and *Prometheus Unbound* the chorus address a person already on stage ('Scene and Setting', 114). The last example may have been close to *Rhesus*, if the initial anapaests were followed not by regular song, but by an epirrhematic dialogue with Prometheus as in the parodos of *Prometheus Bound* (Griffith, *Prometheus Bound*, 287–8, 290). What remains unique in our case is the form and degree of interaction between chorus and actor, which sets the tone for the rest of the play (cf. Introduction, 39–40).

It is evident that no iambic prologue has been lost. Anything like the two fragments cited in Hyp. (b) 64.29–65.47 = *Rh.* 430.26–431.44 Diggle would have caused doublets and greatly impaired the effect of the parodos. Our poet aimed at 'novelty and excitement' (Taplin, *Stagecraft*, 63), for which he was willing to forgo absolute coherence of plot.[6] His view of men's incapacity to understand their world is likewise admirably introduced by the opening we have. Hectic movement that bears little fruit recurs in the epiparodos: 675–91 (n.).

1–10. The chorus' agitation is reflected in their speech. Short asyndetic clauses rarely occupy more than one anapaestic dimeter (note especially the sequence of disyllabic imperatives in 1 and 7–9), Hector is asked first to raise himself and then to open his eyes (7–8), and his name is postponed to an emphatic position at the beginning of the last verse (10). Some scholars thus wished to make the chorus enter σποράδην and/or to attribute different verses to different members or groups. But the marching anapaests, unlike perhaps the lyrics of 675–82 (675–91n.), favour an

---

4 On our poet's probable acquaintance with the whole passage see Introduction, 34.
5 See Radt's note and add M. L. West, *CQ* n.s. 50 (2000), 342 = *Hellenica* II, 234 to those who would assign the fragment to the prologue.
6 Rhesus' entry is prepared for by the Shepherd scene (264–341), but those of Odysseus and Diomedes (565), Athena (595) and Paris (641) 'are all deliberately surprising' (Taplin, *Stagecraft*, 63–4 n. 4).

ordered entrance, and the language displays even fewer signs of possible division than the introduction to the epiparodos. In 23–33 (23–51n.) asyndeton and *hysteron proteron* also mark the excitement of the chorus as a whole (cf. Hutchinson on *Sept.* 78–181 [pp. 56–7]).

1–6. 'Come to Hector's sleeping-place! Which of the king's squires or soldiers is awake? Let him receive a report of the disturbing news (from those) who are placed before the entire army on the fourth watch of the night.'

This is the transmitted text and punctuation, supported also by the scholia (cf. 1, 5–6nn.), which yield plausible syntax and an individually well-documented sequence of choral self-exhortation (1n.), proxy question for the recipient of the message (2–3, 4nn.) and explicit information on the speaker's identity (5–6n.). Several modern editors, however, have been worried by the 'unconnected' relative οἵ (5) – though their remedies all entail linguistic and interpretative problems of their own. Stiblinus' popular τις for τίς (2) not only 'offends by its position in the sentence [and] ... at the beginning of an anapaestic dimeter' (J. Diggle, *Eikasmos* 9 [1998], 44 n. 22), but also creates a weak alternative between one of Hector's shield-bearers (ὑπασπιστῶν) and the chorus (τευχοφόρων in this case) as bringers of the news: 1–6 Βᾶθι πρὸς εὐνὰς τὰς Ἑκτορέους / τις ὑπασπιστῶν ἄγρυπνος βασιλέως, / ἢ τευχοφόρων / δέξαιτο νέων κληδόνα μύθων / οἵ ... (Wecklein)[7] or, with an impossibly harsh parenthesis, Βᾶθι πρὸς εὐνὰς τὰς Ἑκτορέους / τις ὑπασπιστῶν ἄγρυπνος βασιλέως / ἢ τευχοφόρων / – δέξαιτο νέων κληδόνα μύθων – / οἵ ... (Zanetto). Others went further still. Paley and Feickert, for example, replace ἢ (3) with εἰ from the second *ed. Hervagiana* (1544) and so must accept a (potential) optative where ordinary usage from Homer on would have a subjunctive after αἴ κε / ἐάν (KG II 534–5 n. 16; cf. SD 631 on the strong hypothetical sense of this εἰ, which may justify the contruction here). No one has endorsed Nauck's transposition of verse 4 after 9 (*Euripideische Studien* II, 167) and his δέξαι τε for δέξαιτο, which brings an unwelcome end to the series of asyndeta (1–10n.). In view of all these objections, and other problematic variations on the paradosis (5–6n.), a slightly ill-prepared relative clause seems to be a tolerable deficiency, especially when it gains support from a doubtful *Phoenissae* passage (5–6, 12nn.).

1. Βῆθι πρὸς εὐνὰς τὰς Ἑκτορέους: a choral self-exhortation (cf. ΣΣ[V] *Rh.* 1 [II 326.2, 18–19 Schwartz = 77 a[1], a[2] Merro]) of the type 'stage-direction embodied in the text' (Collard on E. *Suppl.* 271(–2) βᾶθι, τάλαιν' ... / βᾶθι καὶ ἀντίασον γονάτων ἔπι χεῖρα βαλοῦσα). With

---

[7] In *Textkritische Studien* (1921/22) he returned to the paradosis, but with 5–6 ὅς ... προκάθημαι for allegedly better grammatical reference to the chorus.

verbs of motion also e.g. A. *Suppl.* 832, *HF* 119-20, 124-6 (parodos), S. fr. 314.64, 68, 190, 196, 201 (*Ichneutae*) and Ar. *Lys.* 302-3, 321 (the parodoi of the male and female semi-choruses respectively). See Schadewaldt, *Monolog und Selbstgespräch*, 215-16, Kaimio, *Chorus*, 129-37 and FJW on A. *Suppl.* 808-10 (III, p. 156). Similar imperatives occur in the 'comic-satyric' search-scene 675-91 (675b, 677, 685nn.).

βῆθι: Diggle for βᾶθι (Ω). The intrusion of Doric α in recitative anapaests is not uncommon (Diggle, *Textual Tradition*, 122). In *Rhesus* cf. 22, 538, 558, 734, 751, 995.

πρὸς εὐνὰς τὰς Ἑκτορέους: Owing to the central significance of Hector's bivouac ('Scene and Setting', 114), variants of this phrase occur throughout the play: 87-8 Ἕκτορ ... / τὰς σὰς πρὸς εὐνάς, 574 εὐνὰς ... τάσδε πολεμίων, 575-6 Ἕκτορος / κοίτας, 580-1, 605-6, 631, 660. The 'proper name' adjective Ἑκτορέους – with Aeolic -ρε- for *-ρι- (Chantraine, *GH* I, 170, *LfgrE* s.v. Νεστόρεος) and here uniquely of two terminations – immediately sets an epic tone (*Il.* 2.416, 10.46, 24.276, 579, *Il. Parv.* fr. 29-30.2 *GEF*). Similarly *Rh.* 44-5 Ἀγαμεμνονίαν ... σκηνάν, 258-9, 386, 762. For εὐναί of soldiers' temporary or permanent resting-places in the field cf. e.g. *Ag.* 559, Thuc. 3.112.3 and Pl. *Rep.* 415e4 (LSJ s.v. εὐνή I 2 b, S. Perris, *G&R* 59 [2012], 153-4 with n. 18).

2-3. Hector's attendants (below) are addressed first, according to protocol: cf. Xen. *An.* 2.3.2 οἳ δ' (*sc.* οἱ κήρυκες) ἐπεὶ ἦλθον πρὸς τοὺς προφύλακας, ἐζήτουν τοὺς ἄρχοντας. ἐπειδὴ δὲ ἀπήγγελλον οἱ προφύλακες, Κλέαρχος ... εἶπε τοῖς προφύλαξι κελεύειν τοὺς κήρυκας περιμένειν ἄχρι ἂν σχολάσῃ (Feickert on 2 [pp. 103-4]). Where the *skene* is involved, a messenger can ask those inside to fetch the desired person: *IT* 1284-7 (~ 1304-6), *Phoen.* 1067-9 ὠή, τίς ἐν πύλαισι δωμάτων κυρεῖ; / ἀνοίγετ', ἐκπορεύετ' Ἰοκάστην δόμων. / ὠὴ μάλ' αὖθις. The latter is followed by a call to Jocasta herself (*Phoen.* 1070-1),[8] as we have it for Hector in 7-10.

ὑπασπιστῶν ... βασιλέως: i.e. 'squires' (literally 'shield-bearers') or 'subordinate fighting comrades' (ΣΣ^{VL} *Rh.* 2 [II 326.5-6, 20-1 Schwartz = 77 a^1, a^2 Merro]), as at Pi. *Nem.* 9.34 Χρομίῳ ... ὑπασπίζων, Hdt. 5.111.1-4, *Hcld.* 216, *Phoen.* 1213 ἔρημος παῖς ὑπασπιστοῦ σέθεν (with Mastronarde), Xen. *An.* 4.2.20, *HG* 4.5.14, 4.8.39 and, of the whole infantry, A. *Suppl.* 182 ὄχλον ... ὑπασπιστῆρα (with FJW [II, pp. 147-8]). This term from hoplite warfare (Pritchett, *GSW* I, 49-51, Hanson, *Western Way of War*, 61-3) is easily transferred to the Homeric world, where anonymous 'attendants' are regularly charged with such

---

[8] Diggle, after Reeve (*GRBS* 13 [1972], 253-4 n. 21), deleted the lines. They are defended by Mastronarde on *Phoen.* 1070-1.

tasks as carrying arms (*Il.* 5.48, 6.52–3, 7.121–2, 13.600, 709–11). On the social range of the epic θεράπων see P. A. L. Greenhalgh, *BICS* 29 (1982), 81–90, and H. van Wees, in I. Morris – B. Powell (eds.), *A New Companion to Homer*, Leiden 1997, 670–3.

The juncture ὑπασπιστῶν ... βασιλέως, reminiscent as it is of the later technical term for the personal guards of the Macedonian kings (ὑπασπισταὶ οἱ βασιλικοί), may or may not have a northern Greek connection (Introduction, 19, 20).

For Hector as βασιλεύς ('monarch') see 388–9n.

ἄγρυπνος: Cf. *Rh.* 824 ἄγρυπνον ὄμμ' and *PV* 358 ἀλλ' ἦλθεν αὐτῷ Ζηνὸς ἄγρυπνον βέλος (on which see further 8, 824–6nn.). Like ἀγρυπνέω ('Thgn.' 471) and ἀγρυπνία (Ar. *Lys.* 27), the adjective does not recur in poetry before the Hellenistic age.

τευχοφόρων: here 'ordinary soldiers' (ΣΣ^{VL} *Rh.* 2 [II 326.6, 21 Schwartz = 77 a^1, a^2 Merro]) and so probably referring to the more distant members of Hector's λόχος (26n.). τευχοφόρος is a metrical variant form of τευχεσφόρος (*Cho.* 627, E. *Suppl.* 654, *Rh.* 267), with o- instead of s-stem composition (Schwyzer 440; cf. KB II 331–2), as in ἀνθοφόρος (Ar. *Ran.* 441/2, later) as against ἀνθεσφόρος (*Ba.* 703, *IA* 1544) and σακοφόροι (Hsch. σ 80 Hansen) as against σακεσφόρος (Bacch. 13.104, *Ai.* 19, *Phoen.* 139).

4. δέξαιτο: The subject is Hector (from 1 Ἑκτορέους and 2 βασιλέως). The third (as well as second) person optative expressing a polite command is mainly epic (KG I 229–30, SD 322) and so may add the appropriate tone here. Attic examples of the idiom are few: Xen. *An.* 3.2.37 εἰ μὲν οὖν ἄλλο τις βέλτιον ὁρᾷ, ἄλλως ἐχέτω· εἰ δὲ μή, Χειρίσοφος μὲν ἡγοῖτο ... τῶν δὲ πλευρῶν ἑκατέρων δύο τὼ πρεσβυτάτω στρατηγὼ ἐπιμελοίσθην, 6.6.18 τούτου ἕνεκα μήτε πολεμεῖτε Λακεδαιμονίοις σῴζοισθέ τε (v.l. σῴζεσθέ τε) ἀσφαλῶς, ὅποι θέλει ἕκαστος and, with a proverbial force, Ar. *Vesp.* 1431 ἔρδοι τις ἣν ἕκαστος εἰδείη τέχνην, Pl. *Rep.* 362d6 οὐκοῦν ... ἀδελφὸς ἀνδρὶ παρείη. Ritchie (181) wrongly adds *PV* 1047, 1048 and 1050 (concessive).

νέων κληδόνα μύθων: Cf. *Hel.* 1250 ὦ ξένε, λόγων μὲν κληδόν' ἤνεγκας φίλην (LSJ s.v. κληδών II 1), *Med.* 173–5 πῶς ἂν ... / ... μύθων τ' αὐδαθέντων / δέξαιτ' ὀμφάν and *Tro.* 230–1 καὶ μὴν ... ὅδ' ... / κῆρυξ,[9] νεοχμῶν μύθων ταμίας, where νεοχμός (like νέος here) has the familiar sense of 'unexpected, strange, disagreeable' (cf. 589–90n.).

5–6. The (natural) position of the sentries mirrors that of the Greeks at *Il.* 10.126–7 ἀλλ' ἴομεν· κείνους δὲ κιχησόμεθα πρὸ πυλάων / ἐν φυλάκεσσ', ἵνα γάρ σφιν ἐπέφραδον ἠγερέεσθαι (~ 10.180–93).

---

[9] For the accent see 401–3n.

οἵ ... προκάθηνται: The lack of an antecedent, such as παρ' ἡμῶν (ΣΣ^V *Rh.* 4, 5 [II 326.19, 327.17 Schwartz = 77, 79 Merro]) or τούτων (cf. KG I 357–8, 394–5, SD 94–5), is much harsher than with other 'substantival' relative clauses (KG II 352, 401, 440, SD 640), but mitigated somewhat by our expectation of hearing the source of the news. A telltale parallel exists in the possibly interpolated *Phoen.* 1602–4 πέμπει δέ με / μαστὸν ποθοῦντα θηρσὶν ἄθλιον βοράν· / οὗ σῳζόμεσθα,[10] where 'the antecedent ... has to be inferred from πέμπει ... βοράν' (Pearson on 1604).

Klyve's supplement <παρὰ τῶν φυλακῶν> before οἵ is weak and not borne out by the variants φυλακήν (Δ et Σ^V) and φρουράν (Λ) at the end of 5. Although the words could indeed annotate each other (cf. Hsch. φ 918, 972 Hansen–Cunningham), φυλακήν is more likely to be right. Unlike φρουρά (LSJ s.v. I 2), it is well-attested in the sense 'watch of the night' (LSJ s.v. φυλακή I 4) and recurs thus at 527, 538 and 543 = 562. Λ also copied πόλεως Τροίας into the middle of 6.

τετράμοιρον ... φυλακήν: 'the fourth watch' out of five (538–45, 540–2nn.), as if it was τὴν τετάρτην ... (Σ^V *Rh.* 5 [II 326.10–13, 327.3–4, 13–19 Schwartz = 78–9.4–7, 14–15, 25–31 Merro]). Properly, τετράμοιρος, a classical *hapax*, ought to mean 'fourfold' (i.e. 'having four parts': cf. *Ag.* 872 χθονὸς τρίμοιρον χλαῖναν and Xen. *An.* 7.2.36, 7.6.1, *HG* 6.1.6 τετραμοιρία = 'fourfold pay') or 'a quarter' (i.e. 'the fourth part of four': cf. Nic. *Th.* 106, 712 (τὸ) τετράμορον, with ΣΣ 106a, 710–13 τετράμοιρον). But the required sense comes close to (τὸ) δίμοιρον = 'two thirds' (i.e. 'two parts out of three'), first found in A. *Suppl.* 1069–70 τὸ βέλτερον κακοῦ / καὶ τὸ δίμοιρον αἰνῶ (LSJ s.v. δίμοιρος I 1). Presumably our poet also wished to refer to the allotment of shifts to the different contingents: 538–45 and especially 545 = 564 (543–5n.) κλήρου κατὰ μοῖραν.

προκάθηνται: a military verb particularly (LSJ s.v. I 2), and not attested anywhere else in poetry.

7–8. For the *hysteron proteron* see 1–10, 23–51 and 25–5a nn.

7. ὄρθου κεφαλὴν πῆχυν ἐρείσας: an adaptation of *Il.* 10.80 ὀρθωθεὶς δ' ἄρ' ἐπ' ἀγκῶνος, κεφαλὴν ἐπαείρας, as was already noted by Σ^V *Rh.* 7 (II 327.25–6 Schwartz = 79 Merro). In tragedy cf. *Ag.* 2–4 (φρουρᾶς ...) ἣν κοιμώμενος / στέγαις Ἀτρειδῶν ἄγκαθεν κυνὸς δίκην / ἄστρων κάτοιδα νυκτέρων ὁμήγυριν (with Fraenkel on 3) and, for the language, *Alc.* 388 ὄρθου πρόσωπον ..., *Hcld.* 635 ἔπαιρέ νυν σεαυτόν,

---

[10] All or part of the *Phoenissae* exodos (1582–1766) has been considered spurious, and 1604–7 in particular were deleted by Hartung. Cf. Fraenkel, *Zu den Phoenissen*, 89–90, M. D. Reeve, *GRBS* 13 (1972), 463 and, for the defence, Mastronarde on *Phoen.* 1604.

ὄρθωσον κάρα, *Hipp.* 198 ... ὀρθοῦτε κάρα, *Ba.* 933 (Ritchie 205). Also 789 (n.) ἐπάρας κρᾶτα.

8. λῦσον βλεφάρων γοργωπὸν ἕδραν: literally 'Open the grim-eyed seat of your lids'. Unlike λύω in this application (LSJ s.v. I 1 b), the periphrasis βλεφάρων ... ἕδραν for 'eyes' has no parallel except 554–6 (n.) θέλγει δ᾽ ὄμματος ἕδραν / ὕπνος· ἄδιστος γὰρ ἔβα βλεφάροις πρὸς ἀῶ. It can hardly be compared to *Tro.* 556–7 Περ- / γάμων ἕδρας (Ritchie 213) or E. *El.* 458 περιδρόμῳ ... ἴτυος ἕδρᾳ (with Denniston), nor do we get help from e.g. Pl. *Tim.* 67b5 περὶ τὴν τοῦ ἥπατος ἕδραν and 72c 1–2 ἡ δ᾽ αὖ ... ἕδρα σπλάγχνου (LSJ s.v. ἕδρα I 3). Hermann (*Opuscula* III, 292) suggested lexical conflation of *Hipp.* 290 στυγνὴν ὀφρῦν λύσασα and E. *El.* 739–41 (λέγεται ...) στρέψαι θερμὰν ἀέλιον / χρυσωπὸν ἕδραν ἀλλάξαν- / τα. Hsch. γ 850 Latte γοργωπὸν ἕδραν· φοβερὰν [καὶ] καθέδραν. ἢ ὄψιν shows an early need of elucidation.

Hector's 'Gorgon's eyes' go back to *Il.* 8.348–9 Ἕκτωρ ... / Γοργοῦς ὄμματ᾽ ἔχων, which also inspired Parthenopaeus at *Sept.* 537 γοργὸν δ᾽ ὄμμ᾽ ἔχων (~ *Phoen.* 146–7). γοργωπός perhaps comes from *PV* 356 ἐξ ὀμμάτων δ᾽ ἤστραπτε γοργωπὸν σέλας, where ἄγρυπνος follows in 358 (cf. 2–3n.). But Euripides was also fond of this and related adjectives: *Suppl.* 322 γοργὸν ὄμμ᾽ (Wecklein for γοργὸν ὡς L; cf. Diggle, *Studies*, 12–13, where add West, *Studies*, 311–12 on the text of *PV* 901–3), *HF* 131–2 γοργῶπες αἵδε ... / ὀμμάτων αὐγαί, 868, 990, 1266, *Ion* 210, *Or.* 260–1, *Hyps.* fr. 18.3 Bond = E. fr. 754a.3. In general see Leumann, *Homerische Wörter*, 154–5.

9. χαμεύνας φυλλοστρώτους: Despite the very different context, one is reminded of the bed of leaves Odysseus assembled for himself in *Od.* 5.482–91.

χάμευνα (for the accentuation see Fraenkel on *Ag.* 1540, Radt on S. fr. 175) is a mainly poetic noun, which denotes a humble couch (*Ag.* 1540, E. fr. 676.1 [*Sciron*], Ar. *Av.* 816) or, as here, an open bivouac (cf. 852–3 χαμεύνας ... Ῥήσου, Theoc. 13.33–5, A. R. 3.1193, 4.883).

The previously unattested φυλλόστρωτος may have been coined after *Cyc.* 386–7 ἔπειτα φύλλων ἐλατίνων χαμαιπετῆ / ἔστρωσεν εὐνὴν πλησίον πυρὸς φλογί (ἔστρωσεν Pierson: ἔστησεν L). A third-declension form occurs in Theoc. *Ep.* 3.1 Gow φυλλοστρῶτι πέδῳ.

10. Ἕκτορ: 1–10n.

καιρὸς γὰρ ἀκοῦσαι: Cf. E. fr. 727a.66 .]μω[.] ἀκοῦσαι καιρὸς [... For the semantic range of καιρός see Barrett on *Hipp.* 386–7, J. R. Wilson, *Glotta* 58 (1980), 177–204, *CQ* n.s. 31 (1981), 418–20, W. H. Race, *TAPA* 111 (1981), 197–213 and M. Trédé, *Kairos. L'à-propos et l'occasion ...*, Paris 1992, especially 25–73.

11–14. Hector wakes. His first reply mirrors, and adapts to his excitable character, Nestor's confident questions at *Il.* 10.82–5 τίς δ᾽ οὗτος κατὰ νῆας ἀνὰ στρατὸν ἔρχεαι οἶος / νύκτα δι' ὀρφναίην, ὅτε θ' εὕδουσι βροτοὶ ἄλλοι, / ἠέ τιν' οὐρήων διζήμενος, ἤ τιν' ἑταίρων; / φθέγγεο, μηδ' ἀκέων ἐπ' ἔμ' ἔρχεο. τίπτε δέ σε χρεώ; Thoas displays similar irritation at the messenger's repeated attempts to call him out of the temple: *IT* 1307–8 τίς ἀμφὶ δῶμα θεᾶς τόδ' ἵστησιν βοήν, / πύλας ἀράξας καὶ ψόφον πέμψας ἔσω; (cf. 2–3n.).

11. τίς ὅδ' – ἦ φίλιος φθόγγος; – τίς ἀνήρ; This is the text of Δ, with Barnes' ἦ for ἤ (V: ἡ O) and Diggle's parenthesis (*Euripidea*, 429 n. 40), which fits Hector's confusion even better than the traditional punctuations τίς ὅδ'; ἦ φίλιος φθόγγος; τίς ἀνήρ; (e.g. Paley, Jouan) or τίς ὅδ'; ἦ φίλιος φθόγγος· τίς ἀνήρ; (Wecklein, Murray, Porter). For the framing question Diggle compares *Or.* 1269–70 τίς ὅδ' ... πολεῖ ... ἀνήρ; and *Ba.* 578–9 τίς ὅδε, τίς πόθεν ὁ κέλαδος / ἀνά μ' ἐκάλεσεν Εὐίου;

Zanetto and Feickert read τίς ὅδ'; ἦ φίλος εἶ; φθέγγου, τίς ἀνήρ with Barnes (II [1694], 109), and after the Aldine (τίς ὅδ' ὦ φίλος εἶ; φθέγγου τίς ἀνήρ;) and Tr³ (τίς ὅδ' ὦ φίλος εἶ φθέγγ' ὅστις ἀνήρ;). But the errors in Λ rather point to Δ as the original than *vice versa* (Paley on 11), and *Il.* 10.85 φθέγγεο (taken up in 12 θρόει and 14 ἐνέπειν χρή) is not sufficient an argument for preferring φθέγγου to φθόγγος.

φίλιος φθόγγος: 'a friendly voice' as against an enemy's: *Rh.* 687 ἅ· φίλιον ἄνδρα μὴ θένῃς, *PV* 128–30 μηδὲν φοβηθῇς· φιλία γὰρ ἅδε τάξις / ... / προσέβα τόνδε πάγον, *Hec.* 858–9, E. *Suppl.* 372–3, Lyc. 1242. This usage of φίλιος is common in the historians (LSJ s.v. I 1), but does not seem to occur anywhere else in poetry.

12. τί τὸ σῆμα; similarly *Hyps.* fr. 57.10 Bond = E. fr. 758a.10 τί τὸ σῆμα [, where, however, σῆμα would mean an ordinary 'sign' (Bond). In the sense 'watchword' it appears only here and in 688.

θρόει: In anapaests also *IA* 143 εὔφημα θρόει (cf. Stockert, *IA* I, 79 n. 376, Introduction, 34), although it may be coincidence that this imperative is otherwise confined to lyrics (*PV* 608, *Or.* 187).

Ritchie (290–1) wishes to add <(Χο.) Φοῖβος· θάρσει>, which from a subsequent note in the margin would have produced 16 (16–19n.), since no reply is given and the dramatically relevant watchword revealed only at 521. But nothing must interrupt Hector's breathless speech, and θάρσει would seem just as 'pointless' here as allegedly after 15. For unanswered questions in tragedy Fraenkel (*Rev.* 235) quotes *Phoen.* 376–8, which for precisely this reason were deleted by Usener (*RhM* N.F. 23 [1868], 155–6 = *KS* I, 141).[11] It may have been ordinary fourth-century technique.

---

[11] Diggle follows him, whereas Mastronarde rather feebly defends the lines (*Contact and Discontinuity*, 121–4 ~ on *Phoen.* 376–8, 376).

13–14. ἐκ νυκτῶν: 'at night'. Cf. *Rh*. 17, 691 (n.), Thgn. 460, *Cho*. 288, Hp. *Morb. Sacr*. 15.4 and Xen. *Cyr*. 8.5.12. The idiom goes back to *Od*. 12.286–7 ἐκ νυκτῶν δ' ἄνεμοι χαλεποί, δηλήματα νηῶν, / γίνονται, where both the plural and the preposition retain part of their original force (Heubeck on *Od*. 12.286, Garvie on *Cho*. 288; 'out of the night', with verbs of motion, is still possible in modern English). Analogous formations are Archil. fr. 122.3 *IEG* ἐκ μεσαμβρίης, S. *El*. 780 ἐξ ἡμέρας (with Finglass) and e.g. fr. tr. adesp. 7.3, Xen. *Cyr*. 1.4.2 ἐκ νυκτός.

τὰς ἡμετέρας / κοίτας πλάθουσ': Our poet has a penchant for πελάζω and its cognates: 213 τάφροις πελάζων καὶ νεῶν προβλήμασιν, 347, 526, 557–8 (n.) τί ποτ' οὐ πελάθει σκοπός ...; 776, 777, 910–11 (n.), 920. Bothe's ταῖς ἡμετέραις / κοίταις (II [1826], 84) need not be adopted in view of *Andr*. 1166–7 καὶ μὴν ὅδ' ἄναξ ἤδη φοράδην / ... δῶμα πελάζει and maybe *OC* 1059–61 ἦ που τὸν ἐφέσπερον / πέτρας νιφάδος πελῶσ' / Οἰάτιδος ἐκ νομοῦ (codd.: εἰς νομόν Hartung).[12]

15. '*Cho*. The army's guards. *Hect*. Why are you carried away by alarm?'

The earliest extant cases of speaker change between two anapaestic metra are *Med*. 1397, 1398 and 1402; then *Ba*. 1372, 1379 (with Dodds on 1372–92), *OC* 173 and *IA* 3, 16, 140 – all, as here, in passages of high suspense. *Rhesus* allows the same in 540 and even divided metra (and feet?) in 16, 17–18 and 560–1 (nn.).

τί φέρῃ θορύβῳ; In addition to noise, which could wake up others, θόρυβος here implies a degree of panic, as Hector suspects in 36–7 (Fantuzzi, in *Ancient Scholarship*, 42–6). Similarly Aeneas in 87–9 and, for the Greeks, 44–5 πᾶς δ' Ἀγαμεμνονίαν προσέβα στρατός /... θορύβῳ σκηνάν (cf. 44–8n.).

The meaning of φέρῃ wavers between 'being carried along' and 'being carried away', but with 16–18 left standing (16–19n.) the latter has more force. Of various mental states cf. *Hipp*. 197 μύθοις δ' ἄλλως φερόμεσθα, *Andr*. 729 ἄγαν προνωπὴς ἐς τὸ λοιδορεῖν φέρῃ, *HF* 1246 ποῖ φέρῃ θυμούμενος; and *Hel*. 1642 ἐπίσχες ὀργὰς αἷσιν οὐκ ὀρθῶς φέρῃ. The metaphor lies in 'motion over which one has no control' (Barrett on *Hipp*. 191–7 [p. 198]), either by waves, winds or bolting horses (LSJ s.v. φέρω B I 1; *Cho*. 1023–4 [with Garvie], *PV* 883–4).

16–19. '*Cho*. Have no fear! *Hect*. I have no fear. There is no ambush by night, is there? [*Cho*. No. *Hect*.] I mean, why have you left your posts and disturb the army if you do not have some message at night?'

---

12 See Kamerbeek on *OC* 1059–64, Ll-J/W, *Sophoclea*, 247 and, in favour of the change, Jebb on *OC* 1059 ff. At *Phil*. 1146–50 read ὦ πτανοὶ θῆραι χαροπῶν τ' / ἔθνη θηρῶν, οὓς ὅδ' ἔχει / χῶρος οὐρεσιβώτας, / φυγᾷ μηκέτ' ἀπ' αὐλίων / ἐλᾶτ' (μηκέτ' Auratus: μ' οὐκέτι codd., ἐλᾶτ' Canter: πελᾶτ' codd.).

Lines 16–18 have long aroused suspicion, not least because 17 is clearly corrupt. Diggle deletes the whole passage, at the possible price of a lacuna after 15 to prevent a hiatus that would mark period-end without catalexis and sense-pause (West, *GM* 95). Yet apart from 18 ~ 37b–8a (n.), it is hard to explain the intrusion of the lines, which are consistent with 34–5 and Aeneas' opening questions at 87–9 and 91–2. Thus, far from being a scribal reconstruction (Ritchie 290–1), 16 (Χο.) θάρσει. (Εκ.) θαρσῶ should be retained as one of several echoes of the dubious anapaestic prologue of *Iphigenia in Aulis* (Introduction, 34) and 17–18 emended to restore the metre. The easiest, and generally accepted, solution is Dindorf's excision of 17 ... (Χο.) οὐκ ἔστι (Λ: οὐκέτι Δ) (Εκ.) ... (III.2 [1840], 589), which anyone who missed an answer could have added.[13] Jackson (*CQ* 35 [1941], 45 n. 1 ~ *Marginalia Scaenica*, 12–13), less plausibly perhaps in this hectic dialogue, expands to ... (Χο.) οὐκ ἔσθ' <Ἕκτορ>. (Εκ.) τί σὺ γάρ ... It is no objection that in either case there remains but a faint metron-diaeresis between ἐκ and νυκτῶν. The phenomenon is paralleled at *Phil.* 162 δῆλον ἔμοιγ' ὡς | φορβῆς χρείᾳ, and even bolder overlaps are found in *Pers.* 47 δίρρυμά τε καὶ | τρίρρυμα τέλη and *HF* 449 δακρύων ὡς οὐ | δύναμαι κατέχειν (cf. Griffith, *Authenticity of PV*, 70–1, L. P. E. Parker, *CQ* n.s. 8 [1958], 86).[14] Attempts that avoid the licence require more severe changes not warranted by the surrounding text (see Wecklein, *Appendix*, 48).

16. (Χο.) θάρσει. (Εκ.) θαρσῶ: Cf. *IA* 2–3 (Αγ.) στεῖχε. (Πρ.) στείχω ... / ... (Αγ.) σπεῦδε. (Πρ.) σπεύδω (16–19n.). The inner-metric *antilabe* (15n.) is paralleled in *Tr.* 976–7 (Πρ.) ... ἀλλ' ἴσχε δακὼν / στόμα σόν. (Υλ.) πῶς φῄς, γέρον; ἦ ζῇ; 981–2, 991 and the partly corrupt *IA* 149 (Πρ.) ἔσται. (Αγ.) κλήθρων δ' †ἐξόρμα (lyric anapaests).

17–18. μῶν τις λόχος ἐκ νυκτῶν; is resumed in 91–2 μῶν τις πολεμίων ἀγγέλλεται / δόλος κρυφαῖος ἑστάναι κατ' εὐφρόνην; and the words of 577 ... μῶν λόχος βέβηκέ ποι; For μῶν (i.e. contracted μὴ οὖν) introducing apprehensive and/or surprised questions see Barrett on *Hipp.* 794, who contests the traditional assertion (e.g. KG II 525) that with this particle the speaker invariably expects a negative answer.

λόχος: 'ambushing party', as in 560 and e.g. *Il.* 8.521–2 φυλακὴ δέ τις ἔμπεδος ἔστω, / μὴ λόχος εἰσέλθῃσι πόλιν λαῶν ἀπεόντων (LSJ s.v. λόχος I 3 a, *LfgrE* s.v. B 3).

---

[13] Taplin (*PCPS* n.s. 23 [1977], 126) refuted the idea of οὐκ ἔστι being an intrusive stage-direction (Murray, apparatus 17, followed by Zanetto, *Ciclope, Reso*, 136).

[14] *PV* 172 καί μ' οὔτι μέλι | γλώσσαις πειθοῦς ἐπαοιδῇσιν and [A.] fr. 192.4 (*P. Lyom.*) λίμναν παντο | τρόφον Αἰθιόπων, if sound, have a 'quasi-caesura' within the compound (West, *GM* 95 n. 56). For Ar. *Pax* 1002, *Av.* 523 and 536 see Dunbar on *Av.* 523 and 534–8.

Only V is right here. The other MSS read δόλος (OQ et Tr³P²: δοῦλος <LP>), which may be an uncial misreading or a gloss. Conversely, a variant λόχος is attested at 92 (91–2n.).

ἐκ νυκτῶν: 13–14n.

τί σὺ γὰρ ...; For the postponement of γάρ see *GP* 95–6. Its sense is causal-progressive (*GP* 81–2, 85): 'I mean, why ...' or 'Why else then ...'

φυλακὰς προλιπὼν κινεῖς στρατιάν: one of our poet's recurrent formulations: 37b–8a (n.) φυλακὰς δὲ λιπὼν / κινεῖς στρατιάν, 89 ... καὶ κεκίνηται στρατός, 138–9 τάχ' ἂν στρατός / κινοῖτ', 678–9 κλῶπας οἵτινες ... τόνδε κινοῦσι στρατόν. There is a realistic fear of panic – at night and close to the enemy (Thuc. 7.80.3). Cf. 15, 20–2, 36–7a, 691nn.

19. νυκτηγορίαν: This is our earliest attestation of the rare noun (cf. LSJ s.v.), which was probably formed after *Sept.* 28–9 λέγει μεγίστην προσβολὴν Ἀχαιΐδα / νυκτηγορεῖσθαι κἀπιβούλευσιν πόλῃ ('to discuss by night').[15] The link is reinforced by νυκτηγοροῦσι in 89 and a number of other references to the prologue of *Seven against Thebes* (Introduction, 34).

20–2. 'Do you not know that we are lying near the Argive host in full armour all night?'

The Trojans sleep ready for battle (cf. 123–4, 740), as do the Greeks in *Il.* 10.74–9, 150–6, with the enemy camp nearby (*Il.* 9.232–3, 10.100–1, 160–1, 221–2). The words recall *Sept.* 59–60 ἐγγὺς γὰρ ἤδη πάνοπλος Ἀργείων στρατός / χωρεῖ and so an essential point of comparison between the two plays: both Troy and Thebes have been under siege for a while, and the commander-in-chief employs a scout.

δορὸς ... Ἀργείου: a favourite juncture of Euripides. Frequently, as here, δόρυ stands for the entire host: *Hcld.* 500 (Ἀργείων Elmsley: -εῖον L), 674, 834, 842, *Tro.* 8, *Phoen.* 1080, 1086, 1094 (Diggle, *Euripidea*, 442 n. 4, Mastronarde on *Phoen.* 1086).

νυχίαν ... / κοίτην ... κατέχοντας: Cf. *Ag.* 1539–40 πρὶν τόνδ' ἐπιδεῖν ἀργυροτοίχου / δροίτης κατέχοντα χάμευναν, of Agamemnon's bath, called κοίταν ... ἀνελεύθερον in *Ag.* 1518 (Denniston–Page on 1539–40).

For the 'Doric' κοίταν (Ω), corrected by Dindorf (III.2 [1840], 589), see 1n.

---

[15] It is possible that νυκτηγορία for the Greek meeting in 'Arist.' fr. 159 Rose (*Aporemata Homerica*) = Porph. ad *Il.* 10.194 ff. (I 145.22–146.4 Schrader) = Σ^(B*) *Il.* 10.198 (III 431.25–432.3 Dindorf) was inspired by our play (Fantuzzi, in *Ancient Scholarship*, 43 n. 10, 52–3). But Fantuzzi goes too far in suggesting that '*Rhesus* adopts a pre-'Aristotelian' interpretation of the assembly of *Iliad* 10 in terms of anti-panic caution' (53). See also 138–9 (n.).

23–51. Instead of answering Hector's questions, the chorus call for mobilisation in a strophe that shows no sign of their slowing down. As in 1–10 (n.), few of their highly asyndetic orders exceed one verse,[16] and absolute logic is not always observed (25–5a n.). It takes another indignant cue from Hector (34–40n.) before the tension is relieved. The antistrophe tells in well-ordered form what has excited the sentries so much: watchfires in the Achaean camp and a rally in front of Agamemnon's hut.

The ode continues to offer detailed reminiscences of 'Homer'. At a deeper level than the parodos as a whole (1–51n.), most of the chorus' instructions to Hector mirror the activities of the Greek chiefs in *Il.* 10.29–179: 'take up your arms' (*Rh.* 23 ~ *Il.* 10.29–37, 131–5, 148–9, 177–9), 'rouse your friends and allies' (*Rh.* 23–26, 31–3 ~ *Il.* 10.53–6, 72–3, 108–13, 125, 136–79) and even the respectful addresses in 28–9 (n.). Their observations, moreover, correspond exactly to those of Agamemnon at *Il.* 10.11–13 ἤτοι ὅτ' ἐς πεδίον τὸ Τρωϊκὸν ἀθρήσειεν, / θαύμαζεν πυρὰ πολλά, τὰ καίετο Ἰλιόθι πρό, / αὐλῶν συρίγγων τ' ἐνοπὴν ὅμαδόν τ' ἀνθρώπων. Only the sounds of joy are replaced with such reactions as would be expected of a defeated host (44–8n.).

Metre

23–33 ~ 41–51. Aeolo-iambic, merging into dactyls and dactylo-epitrite. The last colon is exceptional (33/51n.), an exotic flourish perhaps to crown an unusually vivid scene.

34–40. Recitative anapaests (continued).

23	41	⏑ – – | ⏑ ⏑ | – ⏑ – |	*gl* |
24	42	– – | – ⏑ | ⏑ – – |	*ph* |
25	43	⏑ – ⏑ – ⏑ | – – |	*ia ia*ˏ |
25a	43a	⊽ – ⏑ – ||	*ia* ||
26	44	– ⏑ ⏑ – ⏑ ⏑ – | ⏑ ⏑ – ⏑ ⏑ |	*4da* |
27	45	– ⏑ ⏑ – | ⏑ ⏑ – | ⏓ – |	*D²* (contr.) |
28	46	⏑ – ⏑ ⏑ – ⏑ ⏑ – |	⏑ *D* |
29	47	– ⏑ – – – | ⏑ ⏑ – | ⏑ ⏑ – – |	*e – D –* |
30	48	– ⏑ ⏑ – | ⏑ ⏑ – |	*D* |
31	49	– ⏑ – – – | ⏑ – ⏓ |	*E* ⏓ |
32	50	– ⏑ ⏑ – ⏑ ⏑ –	*D*
33	51	– ⏑ ⏑ ⏖ ⏑ ⏑ ⏑ | – ⏑ | – – |||	*D* (res.) ⏑ – – |||

---

[16] Willink ('Cantica', 23 n. 8 = *Collected Papers*, 562 n. 8) accordingly suggests 'more staccato punctuation' than printed by e.g. Diggle, 'with colons after χέρα (23), εὐνάς (24), αἴρειν (25a), ἀφύπνισον (25b), λόχον (26) and ἵππους (27)'.

Notes

25–25a/43–43a   The lines were rightly separated by Wilamowitz (*GV* 287–8 n. 2), Ritchie (297) and Willink ('Cantica', 23–4 = *Collected Papers*, 562–3). 'Bacchiacs' (*ia*$_\wedge$) are all but invariably preceded or, as here, followed by word-end, i.e. stand first or last in a 'minor period' (L. P. E. Parker, *CQ* n.s. 26 [1976], 20 with n. 17).[17] The syntax of 25–25a ὄτρυνον ἔγχος αἴρειν, ἀφύπνισον also supports the division.

27/45   An ambiguous colon, effecting the transition from pure dactyls to dactylo-epitrite, and 'harmonised' with each by word-break after the third princeps (cf. Parker, *Songs*, 49–50). The context favours contracted D^2 or $4da_\wedge$ (Dale, LM^2 43) over a 'dragged' ibycean (– ⌣ ⌣ – ⌣ ⌣ – – –), such as Euripides liked to combine with 'enoplians' (Schroeder[2] 167, 182; cf. Willink, 'Cantica', 24 = *Collected Papers*, 563). But we have no certain means of deciding between the two, nor whether any difference would have been felt. A rare length in other tragedy (Parker on *Alc.* 568–605 *Metre* [p. 171]), the 'prolonged hemiepes' (D^2) recurs at 244 ~ 255, 899 ~ 910 (contr.) and 902 ~ 913.

33/51   Analysis must start from the strophe, which, unlike the antistrophe, shows no obvious sign of textual corruption (33, 49–51nn.). The pattern of word-ends and the link by synartesis with 32 ~ 50 (ὡς), suggest further dactylo-epitrites, and resolved *D* (cf. Pi. *Isthm.* 3/4.63 [proper name]) + *ba* (527–64 'Metre' 536–7/555–6 n.) seems more likely than Willink's equally unique – ⁓*e*⁓ ⌣ *e* – ('Cantica', 25 = *Collected Papers*, 564).[18] Diggle (*Studies*, 20), followed by Feickert, envisages syncopated iambics ($_\wedge ia\ _\wedge ia\ ia_\wedge$) or '*cr cr ba*', but apart from creating split resolution in 33, this would leave us with the impossible sequence – ⌣ ⌣⌣ ⌣⌣ ⌣ – (Parker, *Songs*, 47). Nothing is gained by Zanetto's admission of *Responsionsfreiheit* between the paradosis of 33 and 51 ($_\wedge ia\ _\wedge ia\ ia_\wedge$ ~ $_\wedge ia\ ia\ ia_\wedge$), a dubious licence anyway among syncopated and full iambotrochaics in tragedy (Diggle, *Euripidea*, 314, against West, *GM* 103–4; cf. West, *Studies*, 109–10). For a summary of the treatments applied to our lines see G. Pace, *QUCC* n.s. 60 (1998), 133–5.

23–4. ὁπλίζου χέρα: 23–51n. The mainly Euripidean phrase (*Alc.* 34–5, *Phoen.* 267, *Or.* 926, 1222–3) reappears in 84 and 99 (n.).

---

17   There is no argument here about the date of the play, as Willink wishes to see in Ritchie. Stinton's observations on the rarity of ⌣ – – – ⌣ – ⌣ – and its virtual restriction to Aeschylus and later Euripides (*BICS* 22 [1974], 88–95 = *Collected Papers*, 119–28) mainly concern verse-openings and such exceptional cases of synartesis as listed by Parker (20 n. 17).

18   Fully resolved *e* (⌣⌣ ⌣ ⌣⌣) sometimes occurs in Pindar's 'freer dactylo-epitrite', as described by K. Itsumi, *Pindaric Metre. The 'Other Half'*, Oxford 2009 (especially 50, 98, 150–1, 354, 389, 434–6).

συμμάχων / ... βᾶθι πρὸς εὐνάς: 1, 23–51nn. With συμμάχων for σύμμαχον (Ω) Bothe (5 [1803], 283) and Hermann (*Opuscula* III, 300) restored metre and syntax.

Ἕκτορ: The emphatic vocative (1–10n.) has the same position in the antistrophe (42). On such 'isometric echoes' see 131–6 ~ 195–200 'Metre' (p. 167), 454–66 ~ 820–32 'Metre' (p. 293) and 722n.

25–5a. Cf. 23–51 'Metre' 25–25a/43–43a n. In their haste the sentries request arming before the allies are awake (1–10, 23–51nn.).

25. ὄτρυνον ἔγχος αἴρειν: Given the context (23–51n.), as well as the rarity of epic ὀτρύνω in tragedy, this may indeed be an allusion to *Il*. 10.54–5 ἐγὼ δ᾽ ἐπὶ Νέστορα δῖον / εἶμι καὶ ὀτρυνέω ἀνστήμεναι (Ritchie 65). Cf. 557–8 (n.).

Badham's αἴρειν (*Philologus* 10 [1855], 336) should be read here, with Doric ναῶν (VQ et L¹ᶜ vel Tr¹: νηῶν Lᵘᵛ: νεῶν O) in 43. Porter, Ammendola, Schroeder[2] (166), Zanetto (9, 66) and Pace (*Canti*, 21–2) retain ἀείρειν (Ω) with synizesis.[19] But while the form itself is widely attested in tragic lyrics and anapaests (e.g. *Pers*. 660, *Sept*. 759, *Ag*. 1525, *Alc*. 450, *Andr*. 848, E. *El*. 873, *Tro*. 99, fr. tr. adesp. 482.5; Diggle, *Studies*, 65), it invites suspicion of 'scribal epicism' when not required by metre. Cf. *Tr*. 216–17 αἴρομαι οὐδ᾽ ἀπώσομαι / τὸν αὐλόν (αἴρομαι οὐδ᾽ Lloyd-Jones: ἀείρομ᾽ οὐδ᾽ codd.), with Ll-J/W, *Sophoclea*, 157, *Second Thoughts*, 91.[20]

25a. ἀφύπνισον: a rare verb in classical Greek (cf. Eup. fr. 205.1 *PCG* ἀφυπνίζεσθαι < > χρὴ πάντα θεατήν, Pherecr. fr. 204 *PCG*), but recommended by Atticist lexica (Phryn. *Ecl*. 195 Fischer, [Hdn.] *Philet*. 53 Dain, Moeris α 124 Hansen).

26. πέμπε φίλους ἰέναι ποτὶ σὸν λόχον: 'Send for your friends to join your company.' On this rendering, absolute πέμπω, 'send word' (LSJ s.v. I 3), governs an infinitive clause as at Xen. *HG* 3.1.7 ... πέμπουσιν οἱ ἔφοροι ἀπολιπόντα Λάρισαν στρατεύεσθαι ἐπὶ Καρίαν, *IA* 360–2 καὶ πέμπεις ... / ... σῇ δάμαρτι παῖδα σήν / δεῦρ᾽ ἀποστέλλειν (~ *IA* 98–100, 115–19) or, identifying the messenger, *Il*. 24.117–19 αὐτὰρ ἐγὼ Πριάμῳ μεγαλήτορι Ἶριν ἐφήσω, / λύσασθαι φίλον υἱὸν ἰόντ᾽ ἐπὶ νῆας Ἀχαιῶν, / δῶρα δ᾽ Ἀχιλλῆϊ φερέμεν, τά κε θυμὸν ἰήνῃ (with *BK* on 118) and *Rh*. 955–6 (954–6n.) τί μὴν ἔμελλον οὐ πέμψειν φίλοις / κήρυκας, ἐλθεῖν κἀπικουρῆσαι χθονί; The alternative (e.g. Kovacs,

---

[19] As do Wecklein and Dale (*MATC* I, 95) without it. The result is an awkward 'hendecasyllable' (⏑ – – ⏑ – ⏑ ⏑ – – ⏓ ⏑ –), which entails (possible) -ὕπν- in 25 and Attic νεῶν in 43 (Willink, 'Cantica', 24 n. 11 = *Collected Papers*, 563 n. 11).

[20] *Ant*. 417–18 καὶ τότ᾽ ἐξαίφνης χθονός / τυφὼς ἀείρας σκηπτόν, the only example in iambic trimeters, may just add another Homeric touch to the Guard's account (Griffith on 417–18). Lloyd-Jones and Wilson adopt Radermacher's ἀγείρας, but see *Hyps*. fr. I ii.39 Bond = E. fr. 752 f.39 ἀειρόμενοι χθ[ον (with Bond on 39).

Feickert, Liapis), namely to take φίλους as the object of πέμπε and ἰέναι as an infinitive of purpose (cf. *Od.* 14.396–7 ἕσσας με χλαῖνάν τε χιτῶνά τε εἵματα πέμψαι / Δουλίχιόνδ' ἰέναι, Thuc. 4.132.3) is less natural in the context. We expect Hector's people to be encamped with him (577), and his 'friends and allies' (Paley on 26) to require a summons (*Il.* 10.299–302).

λόχον: 'armed band', 'body of troops' (LSJ s.v. λόχος I 3 b; cf. 577, 682, 844). The sense is post-Homeric,[21] by extension either of the old 'ambushing party' (17–18n.), or by secondary derivation from *λέχω, 'lay' (Björck, *Alpha Impurum*, 292, comparing Swedish *lag*, 'company', and *lägga*, 'lay').

27. 'Fit the horses with bridles!'

In temporary camps the unyoked horses were tied to their chariots at night, to have them close by in an emergency. Of the Trojans cf. *Il.* 8.543–4, *Rh.* 567–8a (n.) and of Rhesus *Il.* 10.473–5, *Rh.* 616–17 (n.).

ψαλίοις: a type of noseband, for which the modern technical term is 'cavesson', but here *pars pro toto* for the bridles, as in *HF* 380–2 τεθρίππων τ' ἐπέβα / καὶ ψαλίοις ἐδάμασσε πώ- / λους Διομήδεος and, metaphorically, *Cho.* 961–2, *PV* 54.

The ψάλιον consisted of two U-shaped metal bands, one of which sat on the horse's nose, the other near the back of its lower jaw. They were connected by vertical bars and provided means to attach the headgear, reins and/or a separate lead rope. Used with or without a bit, the device would increase control over the animal by preventing unwanted movements of the head or mouth (J. K. Anderson, *JHS* 80 [1960], 3–6, *Ancient Greek Horsemanship*, 60–1, M. A. Littauer, *Antiquity* 43 (1969), 291–5 with fig. 3 = M. A. Littauer – J. H. Crouwel, *Selected Writings on Chariots, other Early Vehicles, Riding and Harness*, Leiden *et al.* 2002, 491–5 with fig. 3 and plt. 208).

28–9. The polite appellations probably reflect *Il.* 10.67–9 (Agamemnon to Menelaus) φθέγγεο δ', ᾗ κεν ἴῃσθα, καὶ ἐγρήγορθαι ἄνωχθι, / πατρόθεν ἐκ γενεῆς ὀνομάζων ἄνδρα ἕκαστον, / πάντας κυδαίνων ... (Ritchie 65, Fantuzzi, in *Entretiens Hardt* LII, 149–51, *I luoghi*, 252–3; cf. *Il.* 10.87, 144, 159). Zeus' son Sarpedon gets the matronymic, where a god's name would be out of place.

Πανθοΐδαν: Polydamas or Euphorbus.[22] The former plays a greater part in the *Iliad* and serves as a model for Aeneas in 105–30 (n.). Here,

---

21 At *Od.* 20.49–50 εἴ περ πεντήκοντα λόχοι μερόπων ἀνθρώπων / νῶϊ περισταῖεν 'ambush' fits as well as elsewhere in epic (Björck, *Alpha Impurum*, 291–2; *LfgrE* s.v. B 3).

22 Panthous' third son, Hyperenor, is 'a mere cipher' (Janko on *Il.* 14.511–2), whose death at Menelaus' hands (*Il.* 14.516–19) becomes a convenient motive for Euphorbus' fatal challenge to the Greek chief (*Il.* 17.24–42 [with Edwards on 24–8, 33–42]).

however, the famous patronym (e.g. *Il.* 13.756, 14.450, 18.250) is all that matters.

Bothe's reinterpretation of the MSS' Πανθοίδαν (5 [1803], 284) leaves an ordinary *D*-colon in responsion with 46. On the tetrasyllabic form see also West, ed. *Iliad* I, XXIII–XXIV.

τὸν Εὐρώπας: Sarpedon. *Il.* 6.198–9 make him a son of Zeus and Laodamia, whereas the common (and perhaps older) tradition gives him to Europa, the mother also of Minos and Rhadamanthys: e.g. 'Hes.' fr. 140 M.–W. = Bacch. fr. 10 Sn.–M. (Σ^D *Il.* 12.397 [p. 392 van Thiel]),[23] 'Hes.' fr. 141.11–14 M.–W., Hellanic. *FGrHist* 4 F 94 (Σ^V *Rh.* 29 [II 327.22–4 Schwartz = 79 Merro]), A. (?) fr. 99.15–23 (*Cares* = *Europa*). The last passage is of particular interest for inviting comparison with the grieving Muse (cf. 882–9, 967–9nn., Introduction, 13–14).

Λυκίων ἀγὸν ἀνδρῶν: taken literally from *Il.* 7.13 (= 17.140) Γλαῦκος δ' Ἱππολόχοιο πάϊς, Λυκίων ἀγὸς ἀνδρῶν. For Sarpedon cf. *Il.* 5.647 Σαρπηδὼν Λυκίων ἀγός and 16.541 (~ 16.490) ... Σαρπηδών, Λυκίων ἀγὸς ἀσπιστάων, which comes shortly after a reference to Polydamas Πανθοίδης (*Il.* 16.535).

Tragic metre rarely accepts Homeric phrases of more than two words: *Med.* 425 ὤπασε θέσπιν ἀοιδάν (= *Od.* 8.498), *Phaeth.* 243 Diggle = E. fr. 781.30 δι' ἀπείρονα γαῖαν (~ e.g. *Il.* 7.446, *Od.* 17.418). See M. Parry, *HSPh* 41 (1930), 97–8 = *The Making of Homeric Verse*, 285–6, who cites Andromache's elegy (*Andr.* 103–16) as the obvious exception.

30. ποῦ σφαγίων ἔφοροι; i.e. the μάντεις (66) normally in charge of pre-battle σφάγια. These were pure blood-sacrifices, performed in the field, for some last-minute divination and appeasement of the gods (Pritchett, *GSW* I, 109–15, III, 83–90, M. H. Jameson, in V. D. Hanson [ed.], *Hoplites: The Classical Greek Battle Experience*, London – New York 1991, 197–227, Liapis on 30 [with further literature]). The practice is not in Homer, but freely transferred back to the Heroic Age by tragedy: *Sept.* 230–1, *Hcld.* 399–409, 673, 819–22 (all with Wilkins), *Phoen.* 174 (with Mastronarde), 1109–12 (1104–40 del. Morus), *Or.* 1603.

ἔφοροι ('overseers') evokes *Pers.* 25 στρατιᾶς πολλῆς ἔφοροι rather than A. *Suppl.* 674–5 ἐφόρους γᾶς / ἄλλους, *OC* 145 ὦ τῆσδ' ἔφοροι χώρας or fr. tr. adesp. 39 ἔφορος οἰάκων. For other references to *Persians*, especially its parodos, see Introduction, 34 with n. 50.

31. γυμνήτων μόναρχοι: 'leaders of the light-armed troops'. Cf. *Rh.* 312–13 πολὺς δ' ὄχλος / γυμνῆς ἁμαρτῇ (where the more specialised archers are also mentioned separately), *Phoen.* 1147 γυμνῆτες ἱππῆς ἁρμάτων τ' ἐπιστάται and, for the first time in Greek literature, Tyrt.

---

[23] Cf. Σ^T *Il.* 12.292–3 (III 359.49–50 Erbse) with apparatus, Σ^A *Il.* 12.307 (III 362.20–1 Erbse).

fr. 11.35–8 *IEG* ὑμεῖς δ', ὦ γυμνῆτες, ὑπ' ἀσπίδος ἄλλοθεν ἄλλος / πτώσσοντες μεγάλοις βάλλετε χερμαδίοις / δούρασί τε ξεστοῖσιν ἀκοντίζοντες ἐς αὐτούς, / τοῖσι πανόπλοισιν πλησίον ἱστάμενοι (otherwise prose). Tyrtaeus' description resembles that of the Locrian archers and slingers at *Il.* 13.712–22 (with Janko on 712–18).

The unique application of μόναρχος here may suggest that every contingent of Trojan allies was led by their respective 'king' (Porter, Feickert on 31). But perhaps it is just a lofty alternative to the common military use of ἄναξ: *Pers.* 383 ναῶν ἄνακτες (with Garvie on 378–9, 382–3), E. *Suppl.* 680–1 Φόρβας, ὃς μοναμπύκων ἄναξ / ἦν.

32–3. The peoples of the East had a reputation for archery, which already in the *Iliad* is more closely associated with the Trojans (F. H. Stubbings, in *Companion to Homer*, 518). Our poet appropriately gives the men 'Asiatic' bows (33n.) and, since Trojans are speaking, eschews the typical Greek contempt for their use in war (*Il.* 11.385–95 [with Hainsworth], *Ai.* 1120, Bond on *HF* 161, Garvie on *Pers.* 26; cf. 312–13, 510–11nn.).

32. τοξοφόροι: substantival, as in Hdt. 1.103.1 ... καὶ πρῶτος διέταξε χωρὶς ἑκάστους εἶναι, τούς τε αἰχμοφόρους καὶ τοὺς τοξοφόρους καὶ τοὺς ἱππέας (and there only in classical prose). Elsewhere τοξοφόρος is an epithet of archer gods or nations: e.g. *Il.* 21.483, Ar. *Thesm.* 970 (Artemis), *h.Ap.* 13, 126, Pi. *Ol.* 6.59 (Apollo), *Tro.* 804 (Heracles), Pi. *Pyth.* 5.41, Call. (?) fr. 786 Pf. (Cretans), Hdt. 9.43.2, 'Sim.' *Ep.* 46.2 *FGE*, Arist. *Ep.* 1.2 *FGE* = fr. 674.8 Rose (Persians / Medes), Nonn. *D.* 20.225 (Arabs).

Φρυγῶν: 'Trojans', as mostly in tragedy at least since Aeschylus (fr. 446) and generally in *Rhesus*. Cf. E. Hall, *ZPE* 73 (1988), 15–18, *Inventing the Barbarian*, 38–9. The Homeric Phrygians represent a separate allied force (*Il.* 2.862–3, 3.184–90, 10.431, 16.718–9; cf. *h.Ven.* 111–16).

33. 'Span the horn-bound bows with strings.'

ζεύγνυτε κερόδετα τόξα νευραῖς: The verse does not respond with the paradosis at 51 (49–51n.). Emendation here, as was attempted already by Tr¹ τόξα <γε> (Diggle, *Euripidea*, 513), could produce regular syncopated iambics (∧*ia ia ia*∧), but this is probably not what our poet desired (23–51 'Metre' with 33/51 n.), and there are no other reasons to change the text. Dale's ζεύγνυτ' εὖ (*MATC* I, 95) and Willink's ζεύγνυτ' ὦ ('Cantica', 25 = *Collected Papers*, 564) both interrupt the rhythm after 32 ~ 50, while Ritchie's τὰ (298) looks unduly specific in an ode that employs the article only where necessary (29 τὸν Εὐρώπας, 49 τὸ μέλλον). The state of 51, on the other hand, is easily explained by simplification of word-order and script.

κερόδετα: a *hapax* formed after χρυσόδετος (382) and the like. The meaning 'bound with horn' (cf. Σ^L *Rh.* 33 [II 328.19–20 Schwartz = 80

Merro] τὰ κερουλκά, τὰ ὑπὸ κεράτων δεδεμένα) refers to the 'composite' or 'Asiatic' bow, whose stave was fitted with keratin on the inside and sinew on the outside to increase the flexibility, range and penetration of the weapon (Lorimer, *Homer and the Monuments*, 276–7, 290–2, 298, F. H. Stubbings, in *Companion to Homer*, 518–20, Snodgrass, *Arms and Armour of the Greeks*, 39–40). In Homer Pandarus' bow (*Il.* 4.105–13) and maybe that of Odysseus (*Od.* 21.393–5) are meant to be of that type. More clearly *Or.* 268 δὸς τόξα μοι κερουλκά, δῶρα Λοξίου and, also of the Trojans, S. fr. 859 φίλιπποι καὶ κερουλκοί ('drawing horn-tipped bows'), / σὺν σάκει δὲ κωδωνοκρότῳ παλαισταί (cf. 383–4n.).

34–40. Hector is angry at the lack of solid information. His exclamations and further impatient questions sum up what the audience too will think about the action so far.

34–5. For the antithesis Klyve compares *Pers.* 215–16 οὔ σε βουλόμεσθα μῆτερ οὔτ' ἄγαν φοβεῖν λόγοις / οὔτε θαρσύνειν, which comes immediately after another potential model for our lines (below).

δείματ' ἀκούειν: i.e. the chorus' frightened call to arms. A final-consecutive infinitive is more frequent with θαῦμα, but note *Pers.* 210–11 ταῦτ' ἐμοί τε δείματ' ἔστ' ἰδεῖν, / ὑμῖν τ' ἀκούειν and Hdt. 6.112.3 τέως δὲ ἦν τοῖσι Ἕλλησι καὶ τὸ οὔνομα τὸ Μήδων φόβος ἀκοῦσαι (KG II 15, SD 364–5).

τὰ δὲ θαρσύνεις: Cf. 16 (Χο.) θάρσει. (Εκ.) θαρσῶ (with 16–19n.).

κοὐδὲν καθαρῶς prefigures 40 οὐδὲν τρανῶς ἀπέδειξας and 77 ... οὐκ ἴσμεν τορῶς. Of the three adverbs καθαρῶς comes closest to ordinary Attic speech (LSJ s.v. καθαρός II 4) and in other tragedy occurs only at *Hcld.* 1055 (with Wilkins on 1053–5, against Barrett's suspicion of these lines).

36–7a. 'Why – are you frightened by the scourge of Cronus' descendant, Pan, which induces trembling fear?'

This is the earliest evidence for Pan being credited with causing 'panics' – those sudden, and generally groundless, terrors which could befall an army 'both at night and in daytime' (Aen. Tact. 27.1; cf. e.g. Hdt. 4.203.3, Thuc. 4.125.1, *Ba.* 302–5, *Rh.* 15, 17–18, 138–9, 691 [nn.], Pritchett, *GSW* III, 45, 162–3, E. L. Wheeler, *GRBS* 29 [1988], 153–88, P. Borgeaud, *Recherches sur le dieu Pan*, Geneva 1979, 137–75 = *The Cult of Pan in Ancient Greece*, Chicago – London 1988, 88–116, 228–39).[24] Our poet cast the thought into the traditional metaphor of the scourge: *Il.* 12.37 Ἀργεῖοι δὲ Διὸς μάστιγι δαμέντες (with Hainsworth), 13.812 (with Janko on 312–16). Cf. West, *EFH* 116, Fantuzzi, in *I luoghi*, 253–4 and on τρομερᾷ / μάστιγι below.

---

[24] Contrast individual 'Panic' frenzy at e.g. *Med.* 1171–3 καί τις γεραιὰ προσπόλων, δόξασά που / ἢ Πανὸς ὀργὰς ἤ τινος θεῶν μολεῖν, / ἀνωλόλυξε and *Hipp.* 141–4.

ἀλλ' ἦ: Heath (*Notae sive lectiones*, 94) for ἀλλ' ἤ (Ω, ¹Σ^V [corr. Schwartz]), with which it tends to be confused (*GP* 28; cf. 560–1n.). ἀλλ' ἦ 'puts an objection in interrogative form, giving lively expression to a feeling of surprise or incredulity' (*GP* 27). It normally introduces a reply, but may also come later, as here, when the thought is developed by the speaker himself (Barrett on *Hipp*. 858–9).

Κρονίου Πανός: Pan did not have a fixed genealogy in myth (cf. Roscher III.1, 1379–80). With Zeus as his father (Epimenid. 3 B 16 DK = Σ^V *Rh*. 36 [II 329.6–7 Schwartz = 81.6–8 Merro], Σ^vet. Theoc. 1.3/4 c [28.1–3 Wendel]), Κρόνιος could be παππωνυμικόν (Σ^V *Rh*. 36 [II 329.10 Schwartz = 81.10–11 Merro]), although this is not the ordinary way of referring to gods (unlike e.g. Achilles Αἰακίδης). More probably thus our poet followed a tradition ascribed to Aeschylus that (one of two) Pan(s) was Cronus' son: Σ^V *Rh*. 36 (II 329.10–11 Schwartz = 81.11–12 Merro) + Σ^vet. Theoc. 4.62/63 d.e (153.9–12 = 154.4–7 Wendel) = A. fr. 25b (one of the two *Glaukoi*), S. fr. 136 (*Andromeda*). In any case the epithet points to the antiquity of the Arcadian god (Σ^V *Rh*. 36 [II 329.8–10 Schwartz = 81.8–10 Merro]). Cf. Wilamowitz, *SPrAW* IV (1929), 40 = *KS* V.2, 164.

τρομερᾷ / μάστιγι: In addition to *Il*. 12.37–8 and 13.812 (above), note *Sept*. 608 πληγεὶς θεοῦ μάστιγι παγκοίνῳ 'δάμη, *Ag*. 642 διπλῇ μάστιγι, τὴν Ἄρης φιλεῖ, *PV* 682 μάστιγι θείᾳ ... ἐλαύνομαι and later Nonn. *D*. 10.4 οἰστρηθεὶς ... μανιώδεϊ Πανὸς ἱμάσθλη, 10.13 Πανιάδος Κρονίης ... δοῦπος ἱμασθλῆς. For active τρομερός ('shiver-inducing') cf. Ar. *Av*. 950 κλῇσον ... τὰν τρομερἀν, κρυερἀν (*sc.* πόλιν) and A. R. 4.53 τρομερῷ δ' ὑπὸ δείματι πάλλετο θυμός.

37b–8a. φυλακὰς δὲ λιπὼν / κινεῖς στρατιάν was athetised by Dobree (*Adversaria* II [1833], 87 = IV [1874], 84) as a doublet of 18, and numerous editors have followed him. Yet 'the abandonment of their posts by the sentinels is prominent in Hector's mind' (Porter on 37; cf. 808–19n.), and so is the fear of nocturnal commotion in the camp (15, 17–18, 138–9nn.). Possibly, therefore, the phrase belongs to our poet (e.g. Ammendola on 36–7, D. Ebener, *WZRostock* 12 [1963], 205, Jouan 9 n. 12), rather than to someone who inserted a marginal note (Klyve on 16–18). A similar repetition in [652] (n.) ~ 279 looks more firmly like an interpolation, while 150 ~ 155 and 543–5 ~ 562–5 are unexceptionable for their literary and dramatic function in the text (149–50, 154–5, 543–5nn.).

38b–40. The words and sentence structure, if not the tone, recall *Tro*. 153–5 Ἑκάβη, τί θροεῖς; τί δὲ θωΰσσεις; / ποῖ λόγος ἥκει; διὰ γὰρ μελάθρων / ἄιον οἴκτους οὓς οἰκτίζῃ.

οὐδὲν τρανῶς ἀπέδειξας: 34–5n. Strohm (258 n. 3) here quotes *Ai*. 23 ἴσμεν γὰρ οὐδὲν τρανές, ἀλλ' ἀλώμεθα, where human knowledge is similarly impaired by night (cf. 595–674, 656–60nn., Introduction, 4–5).

Unlike its adjective, τρανῶς ('clearly') is attested three more times in classical tragedy (*Ag.* 1371 *Eum.* 45, E. *El.* 758).

41–3a. The tell-tale watchfires (1–51, 23–51nn.) are effectfully contrasted with the darkness of night (Klyve on 42–3). For the colometry at 43 see 23–51 'Metre' 25–25a/43–43a n.

41–2. πύρ' αἴθει στρατὸς Ἀργόλας: Cf. 78 τίς γὰρ πύρ' αἴθειν πρόφασις Ἀργείων στρατόν; and 822–3 (821–3n.) ... ὅτε σοι / ἄγγελος ἦλθον ἀμφὶ ναῦς πύρ' αἴθειν. Reiske's πύρ' αἴθει(ν) (*Animadversiones*, 86) for the 'false' compound πυραίθει(ν) (KB II 260, 336–7, Schwyzer 726; cf. 790–1n.) in all three passages is confirmed by O's πῦρ' αἴθει here, as well as 78 πυρ' αιθειν (Π²) and the double accent in the papyrus of Call. fr. 228.13 Pf. (πύραιθεῖν, corr. Pfeiffer).

Ἀργόλας: a poetic variant of Ἀργεῖος, also attested in E. fr. 630 and Ar. fr. 311.1 *PCG*.

Ἕκτορ: 23–4n.

πᾶσαν ἀν' ὄρφναν: 'all through the dark night'. The preposition here is essentially local, as at *Il.* 14.80 οὐ γάρ τις νέμεσις φυγέειν κακόν, οὐδ' ἀνὰ νύκτα, with its residue of a quasi-material conception of night: 'out into the dark' (R. Dyer, *Glotta* 52 [1974], 34; cf. 696–8, 774a nn.). This view is reinforced by *Il.* 8.553–63 (~ 10.11–13), which emphasise the quantity and distribution of the Trojan watchfires (1–51, 23–51nn.) and the way ὄρφνη tends to denote darkness or obscurity rather than the time of night (e.g. Thgn. 1077–8 ὄρφνη γὰρ τέταται· πρὸ δὲ τοῦ μέλλοντος ἔσεσθαι / οὐ ξυνετὰ θνητοῖς πείρατ' ἀμηχανίης, Pi. *Ol.* 1.71, *Hcld.* 857–8, *Ion* 955). So Ritchie (181) is rightly critical about classing our phrase as a Homerism only on the basis of 'temporal' ἀνὰ νύκτα in *Il.* 14.80 (A. C. Pearson, *CR* 35 [1921], 56). For a comparable use of 'spatial' ἀνά in Attic he cites Thuc. 3.22.1 ἀνὰ τὸ σκοτεινὸν μὲν οὐ προϊδόντων αὐτῶν (LSJ s.v. ἀνά C I 2, SD 441).

Our poet's sevenfold use of ὄρφνη (also 69, 570, 587, 678–9, 697, 774) to stress the fact that is sinisterly dark (Ritchie 218–19) was probably inspired by *Il.* 10.83, 276, 386 νύκτα δι' ὀρφναίην (cf. Hainsworth on *Il.* 10.41). In classical tragedy only Euripides has the word (seven times), and it may be relevant that it also occurs in the 'Euripidean' monody at Ar. *Ran.* 1331 (cf. 662, 750–1a nn. and Introduction, 29–30 with n. 36). The adjective ὀρφναῖος, however, is found in *Ag.* 21 (with Fraenkel).

43–3a. '... and the mooring places of the ships are gleaming with torches.'

διιπετῆ: a word of uncertain sense and etymology (cf. *DELG* s.v. διιπετής). Our poet follows Euripides and others who took it to mean 'bright', 'clear', 'translucent': *Ba.* 1267 (ὁ αἰθὴρ) λαμπρότερος ἢ πρὶν καὶ διιπετέστερος (P, testt.: διει- Elmsley), *Hyps.* fr. I iv.31 Bond =

E. fr. 752h.31 στατῶν γὰρ ὑδάτων [ν]άματ' οὐ διειπετῆ and, apparently of fire, E. fr. 815 δμωσὶ<ν> δ' ἐμοῖσιν εἶπον ὡς †ταυτηρίαις / πυρίδες καὶ διηπετῆ κτεῖναι† (= Erot. δ 27 Nachmanson).[25] In Homer it only occurs in the verse-end formula ... διιπετέος ποταμοῖο (*Il.* 16.174, 17.263, 21.268, 326, *Od.* 4.477, 581, 7.284; cf. 'Hes.' fr. 320 M.–W.), where ancient scholars explained it as 'fallen from Zeus' (i.e. 'rain-fed')[26] or, after Euripides, as λαμπρός, διαυγής (e.g. ΣΣ^AbT *Il.* 16.174, 17.263 [IV 204.49–205.64, 380.90–2 Erbse], ΣΣ *Od.* 4.477, 7.284 [II 315.79–317.21 Pontani + I 348.10–11 Dindorf], Hsch. δ 1535, 1784 Latte). Yet it is doubtful whether a dative δι(ε)ι- (= διϝεί) could convey the ablatival notion present in the first definition (cf. later διοπετής: *IT* 977–8 διοπετὴς ... ἄγαλμ', E. fr. 971 ὁ δ' ... διοπετὴς ὅπως / ἀστὴρ ἀπέσβη). With an old locative (= διϝί), and the second part derived from πέτομαι instead of πίπτω, we could translate 'flying in the sky', although the origin from an Indo-European or Egyptian notion of celestial rivers is again disputed (see recently West, *IEPM* 350–1, R. Drew Griffith, *AJPh* 118 [1997], 353–362). In any case, this is how the poet of the *Homeric Hymn to Aphrodite* understood the word (4 οἰωνούς ... διιπετέας) and Alcman may have been inspired to the comparison in 3 fr. 3.65–7 *PMGF* [ἀλλὰ τὸ]ν πυλεῶν' ἔχοισα / [ὤ] τις αἰγλά[ε]ντος ἀστήρ / ὠρανῶ διαιπετής (= *δια-, 'flying along': G. O. Hutchinson, *Greek Lyric Poetry*, Oxford 2001, 109). From that passage and/or possibly a lost one that applied δι(ε)ιπετής to a meteor (~ E. fr. 971 [above]), it is easy to see how the association with 'brightness' or 'clarity' evolved.

The spelling διειπετής (Elmsley on *Ba.* 1266) is found in *Hyps.* P. Oxy. 852 (II–III AD),[27] Hsch. δ 1535 Latte (above) and recommended by the Alexandrian Zenodorus: Porph. ad *Il.* 16.174 (129.14–16 Sodano), *Od.* 4.477 (II 48.1–2 Schrader) = Σ *Od.* 4.477 (II 316.7–8 Pontani) Ζηνόδωρος δὲ διιπετῆ τὸν διαυγῆ ἀποδίδωσι· διὰ τοῦτο καὶ γράφει διειπετῆ διὰ τῆς ει διφθόγγου. If it was already current in fifth-century Athens (cf. the genuine dative-compound Διειτρέφης [*LGPN* II s.v., Threatte II 230; Ar. *Av.* 798 (with Dunbar), 1442]), it could be what

---

25 On Hp. *Mul.* 1.24 (VIII 64.5–6 Littré) ἦν δὲ ὁ γόνος ἀπορρέῃ διιπετής, καὶ μὴ λήγῃ, οὐ μίσγεται ἀσπασίως τῷ ἀνδρί. Cf. Emp. 31 B 100.8–9 DK ὥσπερ ὅταν παῖς / κλεψύδρῃ παίζουσα διειπετέος (Diels: δι- ZMil.) χαλκοῖο, where, despite Bollack (*Empédocle* III.2, Paris 1969, 485–6), the better-attested δι' εὐπετέος seems impossible.
26 There may be a fifth-century precedent, if A. Henrichs (*HSPh* 79 [1975], 100–2 with n. 37) is right to find Democritean wording in Phld. *Piet.* P. Herc. 1428 fr. 16 (1–6 και [| θέρος εν ... [. . . . .] | χε[ι]μὼν καὶ ἔ[αρ καὶ] | μεθόπωρον [κ]αὶ πά[ν]- | τα ταῦτα ἄν<ω>θεν δι- | ειπετῆ γε<ί>νεται ...).
27 Cf. B. P. Grenfell – A. S. Hunt, *The Oxyrhynchus Papyri* VI, London 1908, 21: '... ει and ι are unusually correctly written ...' This proves nothing for the original text, but rules out simple iotacism, which presumably accounts for διειπετῆ in Phld. *Piet.* P. Herc. 1428 fr. 16.5–6 Henrichs (n. 26) and one MS at Hp. *Mul.* 1.24 (n. 25).

Euripides and our poet wrote. But the MSS and other evidence favour διι-, which a cautious editor may wish to retain (M. Fantuzzi, *BMCR* 2006.02.18, on 43).

ναῶν / ... σταθμά: like our poet's favourite ναύσταθμα (135b–6n.). ναῶν is correct (25n.).

44–8. For the enemy noises (θορύβῳ) that worry the Trojans see 1–51 and 23–51nn. In *Il.* 9.1–15 the Greeks succumb to Φύζα (Panic), 'sister of chilling Φόβος' (2), before Agamemnon calls the host to assembly, and Dolon assumes something like that at *Il.* 10.325–7 τόφρα γὰρ ἐς στρατὸν εἶμι διαμπερές, ὄφρ᾽ ἂν ἵκωμαι / νῆ᾽ Ἀγαμεμνονέην, ὅθι που μέλλουσιν ἄριστοι / βουλὰς βουλεύειν, ἢ φευγέμεν ἦε μάχεσθαι. Our poet may have looked at both passages in transferring his council back to the camp from the open field of *Il.* 10.194–273.

44–7a. Ἀγαμεμνονίαν: 1n. (πρὸς εὐνὰς τὰς Ἑκτορέους).

προσέβα ... / ... θορύβῳ: Cf. 15 (n.) ... τί φέρῃ θορύβῳ;

νέαν τιν᾽ ἐφιέμενοι / βάξιν: 'eager for some new announcement' or, in view of the accusative instead of the regular genitive object with ἐφίεμαι, 'long for, desire' (LSJ s.v. ἐφίημι B II 2, SD 105; cf. 300 καὶ πάντ᾽ ἀκούσας ὧν ἐφιέμην μαθεῖν), perhaps rather '*urging* some new announcement' (D. J. Mastronarde, *ElectronAnt* 8 [2004], 28, Liapis on 44–7). Yet the difference in meaning is slight, and maybe ἐπι- could acquire such force as to demand an accusative, or at least tolerate one, when it suited the metre.[28]

βάξις is here just 'speech', 'utterance' (cf. S. fr. 314.371–2 [*Ichneutae*] στρέφου, λυγίζου τε μύθοις, ὁποίαν θέλεις / βάξιν εὕρισκ᾽ ἀπόψηκτον, S. *El.* 637–8 [of a prayer], *Med.* 1374), although perhaps with an air of authority, as from an oracle (Porter on 46, 47, Ammendola on 46).

48. ναυσιπόρος στρατιά has a near-precedent at *Ag.* 987 ναυβάτας στρατός. But our phrase was probably inspired by *IA* 171–3 (ἔμολον ...) Ἀχαιῶν στρατιὰν ὡς ἐσιδοίμαν / Ἀχαιῶν τε πλάτας ναυσιπόρους ἡ- / μιθέων, the only other passage where ναυσιπόρος, 'seafaring', occurs and, by extension, also refers to the Greek στρατιά (A. Fries, *CQ* n.s. 60 [2010], 348; cf. Introduction, 34, 36 and 261–3n.).

49–51. Fear of royal disapproval is common among tragic messengers (e.g. *Ant.* 223–43, *Ba.* 668–71 and especially *Sept.* 651–2 ὡς οὔποτ᾽ ἀνδρὶ τῷδε κηρυκευμάτων / μέμψῃ). But nowhere are the consequences

---

[28] *OT* 766 ἀλλὰ πρὸς τί τοῦτ᾽ ἐφίεσαι; differs by involving a neuter pronoun (KG I 310 n. 5, 352 n. 10), and at Xen. *Ages.* 11.14 ἐκεῖνος γοῦν οὐκ ἀπεῖπε μεγάλην καὶ καλὴν ἐφιέμενος <δόξαν, ἔστε> (suppl. Marchant) τὸ σῶμα φέρειν ἐδύνατο τὴν τῆς ψυχῆς αὐτοῦ ῥώμην the corruption may exceed the lacuna.

so disproportionate to the news. For had the sentries stayed on their posts, the enemy spies could not have entered the Trojan camp.

ὑποπτεύων τὸ μέλλον: Cf. 79 (n.) οὐκ οἶδ'· ὕποπτον δ' ἐστὶ κάρτ' ἐμῇ φρενί. Like its adjective, ὑποπτεύω is mainly a prose word and otherwise limited to spoken verse: S. *El.* 43, *IT* 1036, Epich. fr. 113.10 *PCG* (cf. [Theoc.] 23.10). Here it suits the character and content of the soldiers' song.

ἤλυθον: The epic aorist appears nowhere in Aeschylus and only once in Sophocles (*Ai.* 234 [recitative anapaests]), whereas Euripides freely uses it in lyric and sometimes also non-lyric parts: *Med.* 1108 (recitative anapaests), *IA* 1339, 1349 (4tr$_\wedge$), *El.* 598, *Tro.* 374, fr. 451.2 (3ia). Cf. Neophr. fr. 1.1 (3ia), *Rh.* 263 (lyric), 660 (3ia). For the 'collective' singular see KG I 85, SD 242–3.

ὡς / μήποτέ τιν' ἐς ἐμὲ μέμψιν εἴπῃς: 23–51 'Metre' 33/51, 33nn. The text of Lindemann (*Emendationes*, 7) offers 'slightly [more] agreeable word-divisions' (Diggle, *Studies*, 20) than the reconstruction of Musgrave (on 23) and Bothe (5 [1803], 285): μήποτ' ἐς ἐμέ τινα μέμψιν εἴπῃς. It also accords better with the idea that the transmitted μήποτέ τινα μέμψιν εἰς ἔμ' εἴπῃς (Π²Δ et Tr¹: -εις Λ) arose when μέμψιν was placed to follow unelided τινα.

52–84. After hearing the chorus' observations, Hector quickly changes his mind about their nocturnal interruption. Oblivious of the rally at Agamemnon's hut (44–7), he infers that the watchfires must be a trick – one frequently employed by historical generals to win time for retreat under the enemy's eyes by feigning normal activities in the camp (e.g. Hdt. 4.134.3–135.2, Thuc. 7.80.1–3, Plb. 9.5.7, Jos. *AJ* 13.178).[29] So for different reasons Hector himself comes round to proposing an attack (70–5), and it now falls to the coryphaeus to assume a warning tone in the brief stichomythia that concludes the exchange (76–84).

Much of the material for Hector's speech stems from that of his epic self at *Il.* 8.497–541 (53–5, 56–69, 72–3nn.).[30] But with subtle changes and allusions to other Iliadic episodes woven in (56–69, 56–8, 60b–2, 65–9, 82–3, 84nn.), our poet adapted it to the new situation and his own idea of the Trojan chief. In contrast to *Rhesus*, the Homeric Hector graciously gives in to dusk, despite his confidence that he was about to destroy the Achaean ships (*Il.* 8.498–502, 529–41). The Trojan fires were meant to

---

[29] Cf. R. Goossens, *Euripide et Athènes*, Brussels 1962, 299 n. 71, M. Fantuzzi, *CPh* 100 (2005), 269 with n. 3, in *I luoghi*, 245 with n. 10, *Ancient Scholarship*, 45 n. 14, Liapis on 41 ff. (p. 84).

[30] So already Hermann (*Opuscula* III, 285): '*Oratio Hectoris v. 57 seqq. adumbrata est ex Iliad.* θ *498 seqq.*' Cf. Ritchie 65.

prevent the enemy from escaping, or to catch them in the attempt and take revenge (*Il.* 8.507–16). Here their presence on the other side arouses Hector's suspicion and provokes him to threaten similar measures in related words: 72–5 (72–3n.). One important addition to the speech is the seers, who have persuaded Hector not to prolong fighting into the night. The way he treats them recalls his attitude to Polydamas (56–69, 65–9, 84nn.), shortly before Aeneas assumes the role of this prudent counsellor (85–148n.). For the first time also we see an apparently wise suggestion courting disaster when continued battle would have forestalled the Greek spying attack.

Two other leitmotifs are introduced or reinforced in this passage. Like the seers, Hector's repeated invocations of 'god / fate' and εὐτυχία (56–8, 60b–2, 63–4nn.) prefigure the later 'intrusions of the supernatural order into our play' (Rosivach 54–5, 64–5). Moreover, by evoking Zeus and his deceptive support for Troy, they bring out the delusion which lies at the base of Hector's confidence. So it is fitting that his call to arms takes up that of the unthinking chorus (70–1, 84nn.), while the coryphaeus in giving sound advice falls back on the calm but uncertain message of the antistrophe: 77, 79 (n.).

52. In commending the chorus on their timely arrival, Hector treats them as just the dramatic persona they are (Introduction, 39–40). His words also reflect the topos, usually uttered by the messenger himself, that there is no reward for delivering bad news (*Pers.* 253 ὤμοι, κακὸν μὲν πρῶτον ἀγγέλλειν κακά, *Ag.* 636–49, *Ant.* 276–7, *Phoen.* 1214–18, fr. tr. adesp. 122; cf. *Andr.* 1084, *Hec.* 511–17). The diction resembles *Tro.* 238 Ταλθύβιος ἥκω καινὸν ἀγγελῶν λόγον (~ *Phoen.* [1075]) and *Hcld.* 656 τί γὰρ βοὴν ἔστησας ἄγγελον φόβου;

ἐς καιρὸν ἥκεις: 10n. The combination of (εἰς) καιρόν with a verb of motion is typical of Euripides (Ritchie 251–2). Π² confirms ἥκεις (*Chr. Pat.* 1870, 2389, 2390), which also has the appropriate 'resultative' sense: *Tro.* 238 (above), Alexis fr. 151.1 *PCG*, *Hyps.* fr. 60 i.27 Bond = E. fr. 757.858 (with Bond), E. fr. 495.7–9 (*Captive Melanippe*) τὼ δ' ... / ἥσθησαν, εἶπόν θ'· 'εἶα συλλάβεσθ' ἄγρα[ς]· / καιρὸν γὰρ ἥκετ''· οὐδ' ὑπώπτευον [δόλον], where note the proximity of ὑποπτεύω (49–51n.). In view of ἤλυθον in 50 and perhaps similar phrases with ἐλθεῖν (*Tro.* 744, *Hel.* 479, 1081), the corruption into ἦλθες (Ω) was easy.

καίπερ ἀγγέλλων φόβον: 'although you are bringing a message of fear'. Cf. *Hcld.* 656 (above), *OT* 917 ... ἢν φόβους λέγῃ (LSJ s.v. φόβος II 2) and also *Rh.* 34 τὰ μὲν ἀγγέλλεις δείματ' ἀκούειν.

53–5. The thought has been adapted from *Il.* 8.508–11 ὥς κεν ... / καίωμεν πυρὰ πολλά, σέλας δ' εἰς οὐρανὸν ἵκῃ, / μή πως καὶ διὰ νύκτα κάρη κομόωντες Ἀχαιοί / φεύγειν ὁρμήσωνται ἐπ' εὐρέα νῶτα θαλάσσης (~ *Il.* 10.308–12, [147] = 327) and perhaps Agamemnon's own desire to flee at *Il.* 8.242–4 and 9.27–8 (M. Fantuzzi, *CPh* 100 [2005], 269). For camp-fires masking withdrawal see 52–84n.

νυκτέρῳ πλάτῃ: 'by oar at night'. While πλάτη is frequently *pars pro toto* for 'ship' (Breitenbach 174), its basic meaning remains visible in this idiom: *Phil.* 220–1,[31] 355–6, *Tro.* 877–8, *IT* 241–2 ἥκουσιν ἐς γῆν, κυανέας Συμπληγάδας / πλάτῃ φυγόντες, *Or.* 54–5, E. fr. 846 = Ar. *Ran.* 1206–8.

ἀρεῖσθαι φυγήν / μέλλουσι: The expression, all but repeated at 126 (126b–7n.) harks back to *Pers.* 480–1 ναῶν δὲ ταγοὶ τῶν λελειμμένων σύδην / κατ' οὖρον οὐκ εὔκοσμον αἴρονται φυγήν (with σύδην echoed in *Rh.* 58 σύρδην). Pace (in *Scritti Gallo*, 453–4), Feickert (on 54), Fantuzzi (*CPh* 100 [2005], 268–9 n. 2) and Liapis ('Notes', 51–2) err on the side of conservatism in preferring αἴρεσθαι (Ω) to Nauck's ἀρεῖσθαι (*Hermes* 24 [1889], 450).[32] In references to the immediate future there is often little difference between μέλλω with present and future infinitive (LSJ s.v. II, KG I 179, SD 293–4), and critical method here favours the latter. Of αἴρειν / ἀείρειν, '[t]enses with ἀρ- tend when they resemble a pres[ent] to be corrupted to or towards it' (Barrett on *Hipp.* 198; cf. Wecklein, *Textkritische Studien*, 14–15, FJW on A. *Suppl.* 342). Π² already has the hybrid αιρεισθαι (cf. e.g. *OT* 1225 ἀρεῖσθε O**a**t: αἰρ- vel αἱρ- **lrp**, *Tr.* 491 ἐξαρούμεθα Z**o**t: ἐξαιρ- cett.).

Similarly, Stephanus' φυγήν (*Annotationes*, 115, 116) for φυγῇ (fere Ω: φυγη[Π²) is not only supported by *Pers.* 481 … αἴρονται φυγήν, Max. Astrol. 350 αἴροιτο φυγήν and Porph. *Abst.* 2.29.2 φυγὴν … ἀράμενος, but would also have easily been corrupted that way after πλάτῃ. Otherwise, the dative could stand with intransitive-passive αἴρεσθαι, 'put to sea' (Barrett, *Collected Papers*, 258 n. 69, Pace, in *Scritti Gallo*, 454–5, who quotes *Med.* 938 ἡμεῖς μὲν ἐκ γῆς τῆσδ' ἀπαροῦμεν φυγῇ).

σαίνει μ' ἔννυχος φρυκτωρία: 'Their nocturnal beacons are fawning on me', i.e. '… are trying to mislead me' (52–84n.). Properly of a dog that wags its tail, (προσ)σαίνω denotes a strong (sensual) appeal to a person's feelings and often, as here, implies deceit: Hes. *Th.* 769–74, Pi. *Pyth.* 2.82–3, *Pers.* 97/8–9 (with Garvie on 93–100 [p. 85]), *Ag.* 725/6, 795–8, *Cho.* 194, 420–2, S. frr. 577.3–4 885 (LSJ s.v. σαίνω III 4, R. M. Harriott, *CQ* n.s. 32 [1982], 11–15).

φρυκτωρία, like φρυκτός, mainly refers to beacon-fires (*Ag.* 33, 490, S. fr. 432.6, Ar. *Av.* 1161, Thuc. 3.22.8). The sense is appropriate, since to the Trojans they *signal* a ruse.

---

31 For the text see Dawe, *STS* III, 52, Ll-J/W, *Sophoclea*, 184, *Second Thoughts*, 105.
32 Previously among the marginalia in his working copy of *Euripidis tragoediae* … (³1871). Cf. J. Družinina, *Hyperboreus* 5 (1999), 254.

56–69. Our poet extrapolates from *Il.* 8.487 Τρωσὶν μέν ῥ' ἀέκουσιν ἔδυ φάος and the epic Hector's conviction that he could have defeated the Greeks that day: *Il.* 8.498–501 (cf. 52–84n.). The idea to carry on fighting at night (and indeed to plan an attack) presumably comes from Agamemnon's comment at *Il.* 10.100–1 δυσμενέες δ' ἄνδρες σχεδὸν εἵαται, οὐδέ τι ἴδμεν, / μή πως καὶ διὰ νύκτα μενοινήσωσι μάχεσθαι, while Hector's contempt for seers (65–9n.) mirrors his reaction to Polydamas at *Il.* 12.231–50 (with Hainsworth). See also Ritchie 65, Fantuzzi, *CPh* 100 (2005), 269–70 and in *I luoghi*, 256–9.

56–8. 'Oh fate, you who have robbed me in my success, (robbed) a lion of his feast, before in one swoop I could destroy the whole Argive army with my spear!'

This sounds like a pettier version of Achilles in *Il.* 22.15–20 ἔβλαψάς μ', Ἑκάεργε, θεῶν ὀλοώτατε πάντων, / ἐνθάδε νῦν τρέψας ἀπὸ τείχεος· ἦ κ' ἔτι πολλοί / γαῖαν ὀδὰξ εἷλον, πρὶν Ἴλιον εἰσαφικέσθαι. / νῦν δ' ἐμὲ μὲν μέγα κῦδος ἀφείλεο, τοὺς δ' ἐσάωσας / ῥηϊδίως, ἐπεὶ οὔ τι τίσιν γ' ἔδδεισας ὀπίσσω. / ἦ σ' ἂν τεισαίμην, εἴ μοι δύναμίς γε παρείη. The lion imagery recalls the extended simile at *Il.* 15.630–8, which illustrates Hector's raging in the Achaean camp. In *Ag.* 827–8 the victorious Greeks become like 'a flesh-eating lion', which jumps over the walls of Troy and licks 'its fill of royal blood'.

ὦ δαῖμον: Here for the first time in *Rhesus* (perceived) success or failure is attributed to supernatural agency (Rosivach 54–5, 64–5), and one remembers the volatile favours of the Iliadic gods. But Fantuzzi (*CPh* 100 [2005], 270–2) considers a more tangible epic source. Our poet may have read *Il.* 8.500–1 as ἀλλὰ πρὶν κνέφας ἦλθε, τὸ νῦν ἐσάωσε μάλιστα / Ἀργείους καὶ νῆας, ἐπεὶ Διὸς ἐτράπετο φρήν, like Zenodotus (Σ^A *Il.* 8.501 [II 381.19–22 Erbse]),[33] instead of 501 ... ἐπὶ ῥηγμῖνι θαλάσσης. If so, he skilfully blurred the connection, for Hector continues to believe in Zeus' support (60b–2, 63–4nn.).

εὐτυχοῦντ': 52–84, 665–7nn.

θοίνης λέοντα: Cf. 325–6 ἥκει γὰρ ἐς δαῖτ', οὐ παρὼν κυνηγέταις / αἱροῦσι λείαν ... and, for θοίνη and its cognates of animals 'feasting' on human flesh, *Hec.* 1070–2 (where it amounts to cannibalism), E. frr. 145, 792 (with Kannicht's apparatus) and *Rh.* 515 (513b–15n.) πετεινοῖς γυψὶ θοινατήριον. The simile (on the form of which see Liapis on 56–8) here alleviates the grimness of the idea.

---

[33] Cf. Σ^A *Il.* 10.45 (III 12.50–1 Erbse) καὶ ὅτι τὸ ἡμιστίχιον ὁ Ζηνόδοτος μετήνεγκεν ἐπὶ τὸν Ἕκτορος λόγον κατὰ τὴν κόλον μάχην.

Ἀργείων στρατόν: With three repetitions (78, 127, 146) our poet matches *Phoenissae* (711, 732, 1099, 1188)[34] in the application of this common line end (821–3n.). Cf. A. C. Pearson, *CR* 35 (1921), 58.

σύρδην: See 53–5n. (ἀρεῖσθαι φυγήν / μέλλουσι). The adverb, from σύρω, 'drag / trail along', is previously attested only at *Pers.* 53–4 Βαβυλὼν δ' ἡ πολύχρυσος / πάμμικτον ὄχλον πέμπει σύρδην ('in a long trailing line' [Broadhead]; cf. Garvie on *Pers.* 54). Here it acquires a violent note, as a lion perhaps would drag its prey, or a river sweep everything away with it (LSJ s.v. σύρω 2, Feickert on 58, Liapis on 56–8).[35] Herodotus and others use κατασύρω for the ravaging of cities in war (LSJ s.v. I 1).

Blomfield (*Aeschyli Persae* ..., Cambridge ¹1814, on 54) proposed φύρδην, 'in utter confusion', which seems less apposite to the present text. But it also occurs in *Persians* (812), and together with σύρω (and ὦ δαῖμον) at S. fr. 210.37–9 (*Eurypylus*). Against φύρδην (Schütz) in *Pers.* 54 see Garvie on 54.

τῷδ' ... δορί: Ritchie (235–6) notes the Euripidean character of such disyllabic, and often pleonastic, datives. Again they are more frequent in *Rhesus* than in any other tragedy.

59–62. The syntax resembles *Alc.* 357–62 εἰ δ' Ὀρφέως μοι γλῶσσα καὶ μέλος παρῆν / ... 360 κατῆλθον ἄν, καί μ' οὔθ' ὁ Πλούτωνος κύων / οὔθ' οὑπὶ κώπῃ ψυχοπομπὸς ἂν Χάρων / ἔσχ' ἄν, πρὶν ἐς φῶς σὸν καταστῆσαι βίον (Ritchie 243–4).

59–60a. 'For if the sun's radiant lights had not †restrained me† ...

φαεννοὶ ... ἡλίου / λαμπτῆρες: Cf. *Ion* 1516 ἐν φαενναῖς ἡλίου περιπτυχαῖς. Euripides most often applied φαεννός to the sun, stars or the sky as a whole: *Cyc.* 353, *Andr.* 1086, *El.* 727–8, *Ion* 1071–2, *Phoen.* 84, *Ba.* 631, *Phaeth.* 5 Diggle = E. fr. 771.5, E. fr. 919.2.

λαμπτήρ, which is non-Attic in origin (Fraenkel on *Ag.* 22), does not otherwise refer to solar rays, but cf. *Ion* 1467 ἀελίου δ' ἀναβλέπει λαμπάσιν (*sc.* ὁ δόμος) and later Nonn. *D.* 2.189 νύχιοι λαμπτῆρες ... Σελήνης. See also Liapis on 59–62 and West, *IEPM* 195–6.

†ξυνέσχον†: Σ^V *Rh.* 59 (II 330.29 Schwartz = 83 Merro) explains with δύντες ἐπέσχον. Yet this is hard to justify, for (1) συνέχω does not mean 'detain, hold back' in classical Greek (LSJ s.v. I 4, 6) and (2) in the schema *res ponitur pro defectu rei* (KG II 569–70) the negative action ascribed to the subject still reflects its original force (e.g. the sun

---

34 Unless the corrupt *Phoen.* 710–11 is emended in such a way as to eliminate Ἀργείων στρατόν (see Diggle's apparatus and Mastronarde on 710–11).

35 On Homeric river similes see H. Fränkel, *Die homerischen Gleichnisse*, Göttingen 1921, 25–8, especially *Il.* 5.87–94 (Diomedes advances like a winter torrent) and 5.597–600 (Diomedes turns away from Hector like a man from a fast-flowing river).

can illuminate or darken the earth [Cic. *N. D.* 2.49],[36] winds can rouse and calm the sea [*Ai.* 674–5]). So critics were right to suspect corruption, most likely from ἔσχον in the following line (Kirchhoff, I [1855], 551). The best suggestion so far is Wecklein's 'ξέλειπον (*SBAW* I [1897], 484), which not only carries the appropriate durative verbal aspect, but could also have been taken by our poet from S. *El.* 17–19 ὡς ἡμὶν ἤδη λαμπρὸν ἡλίου σέλας / ἑῷα κινεῖ φθέγματ᾽ ὀρνίθων σαφῆ / μέλαινά τ᾽ ἄστρων ἐκλέλοιπεν εὐφρόνη. Feickert's μή μ᾽ ἔπαυσαν (~ *Il.* 18.267–8 νῦν μὲν νὺξ ἀπέπαυσε ποδώκεα Πηλείωνα / ἀμβροσίη) founders on (2) above and is probably too far removed from the initial ξύν-. Kovacs, by accepting Heimsoeth's 'ξανεῖσαν (*De Madvigii Hauniensis adversariis criticis commentatio altera*, Bonn 1872, vii-viii), implausibly makes the sunbeams 'slacken' or 'relax' (LSJ s.v. ἐξανίημι II 1; of wind *Phil.* 639 ἐπειδὰν πνεῦμα τοὐκ πρῴρας ἀνῇ).

For further discussion see Liapis, 'Notes', 52–3 and E. Magnelli, *Eikasmos* 10 (1999), 101–4 (who improbably offers εἰ γὰρ φαεννοὺς μὴ ξύνεσχεν ἥλιος / λαμπτῆρας).

60b–2. Hector had threatened to burn the Greek ships and kill the men at *Il.* 8.180–2 (~ 14.44–7). The attempt is foiled for the moment when Agamemnon, with Zeus' support, manages to inspire a counter-attack (*Il.* 8.217–349).

οὔτἂν: i.e. οὔτοι + ἄν (Π²: οὐκ ἄν ΩgB). The particle τοι here emphasises the negation (*GP* 537, 543–4) and adds an emotional note to the whole (Feickert on 60). For its position 'early in the apodosis of a conditional sentence' see *GP* 547.

ἔσχον: 'check', as in the third person plural at E. *El.* 851–2 οἱ δ᾽, ἐπεὶ λόγων / ἤκουσαν, ἔσχον κάμακας. Also *Od.* 22.70 οὐ γὰρ σχήσει ἀνὴρ ὅδε χεῖρας ἀάπτους.

εὐτυχοῦν δόρυ: 52–84, 56–8nn. At 319–20 πολλούς, ἐπειδὴ τοὐμὸν εὐτυχεῖ δόρυ / καὶ Ζεὺς πρὸς ἡμῶν ἐστιν, εὑρήσω φίλους Hector openly ascribes his success to Zeus. The words echo *Hec.* 18 (ἕως μὲν οὖν ...) Ἕκτωρ τ᾽ ἀδελφὸς οὑμὸς εὐτύχει δορί and *Tro.* 1162 Ἕκτορος ... εὐτυχοῦντος ἐς δόρυ.

τῇδε πολυφόνῳ χερί: 56–8n. (τῷδ᾽ ... δορί). Apart from *Rh.* 465–6 πολυφόνου / χειρός, the adjective occurs only at *HF* 419–21 τάν τε ... / πολύφονον κύνα Λέρνας / ὕδραν. But it looks regular, and Fraenkel (*Rev.* 235) suggests it may not have been rare.

63–4. 'And I was eager to hurl my spear by night and use the impetus of good fortune the god had sent.'

---

36 Thus already *Il.* 8.485–6 ἐν δ᾽ ἔπεσ᾽ Ὠκεανῷ λαμπρὸν φάος ἠελίοιο, / ἕλκον νύκτα μέλαιναν ἐπὶ ζείδωρον ἄρουραν.

ἦ: Π², coni. Cobet (*VL²*, 593) Later ἦν (Ω, *Chr. Pat.* 88, 2334) often replaces the old Attic ἦ (i.e. contracted ἦα) and should only be kept when metre opposes the change (Barrett on *Hipp.* 700, Kannicht on *Hel.* 992, Parker on *Alc.* 655). Cf. 642–3n. for the similar issue of χρῆν as against ἐχρῆν.

πρόθυμος: 665–7n.

ἰέναι δόρυ also concludes the line at *Phoen.* 1247.

χρῆσθαί τ' εὐτυχεῖ ῥύμῃ θεοῦ: Zeus comes to mind again (56–8, 60b–2nn.), rather than an impersonal 'god' or 'fate' (M. Fantuzzi, *CPh* 100 [2005], 270–1 with n. 6, Liapis on 63–4). The same applies to 103 θεοῦ διδόντος, 582–4, 995b–6 (nn.).

The expression is best compared to Plut. *Caes.* 53.3 τρεψάμενος δὲ τούτους, ἐχρῆτο τῷ καιρῷ καὶ τῇ ῥύμῃ τῆς τύχης (~ *Mar.* 28.9 ῥύμῃ μιᾷ τύχης). Our poet may have been the first to employ ῥύμη ('impetus, force, rush') metaphorically (cf. Dem. 21.99 ἀλλ' ἁπλῶς οὕτως ἠτίμωται τῇ ῥύμῃ τῆς ὀργῆς καὶ τῆς ὕβρεως τῆς Μειδίου). Unattested in early epic and lyric, the word occurs several times in Old and Middle Comedy (Ar. *Nub.* 407, *Pax* 86, *Av.* 1182 [paratragic], *Eccl.* 4, Antiph. fr. 55.2 *PCG*) and has been suggested at A. fr. 451p 59.5] . υσμ[|] . σρύμ[. (ῥύμ[η Snell).

65–9. Hector berates his seers for misinterpreting the signs, just as at *Il.* 12.195–250 he prefers his own supposed knowledge of Zeus' will (~ *Il.* 11.200–9) to Polydamas' caution over the eagle omen in the field (52–84, 56–69, 84nn.).[37] Scepticism about diviners and their art was traditional (952–3n.) and did not necessarily betray the foolish or impious (A. D. Nock, *PAPhS* 85 [1942], 476–7 = *Essays on Religion and the Ancient World*, Oxford 1972, 541–2, K. J. Dover, *JHS* 93 [1973], 63–4).[38] Here deference proves a fatal mistake, as the Trojans will learn in the course of the night.

65–6. οἱ σοφοί ... καὶ τὸ θεῖον εἰδότες: The bitter-sarcastic tone recalls E. fr. 795 (*Philoctetes*) τί δῆτα ... / σαφῶς διόμνυσθ' εἰδέναι τὰ δαιμόνων, / ... / ὅστις γὰρ αὐχεῖ θεῶν ἐπίστασθαι πέρι, / οὐδέν τι μᾶλλον οἶδεν ἢ πείθειν λέγων (with Müller,[39] Collard). σοφός is a regular epithet of seers: *Sept.* 382–3 θείνει δ' ὀνείδει μάντιν Οἰκλείδην σοφόν, / σαίνειν μόρον τε καὶ μάχην ἀψυχίᾳ,[40] *OT* 484, *Ant.* 1059,

---

[37] Note also *Il.* 15.718–25 (with Janko), where he blames unnamed 'elders' for keeping him from the ships for so long.

[38] Often in fact μαντοσύνη is opposed to the veracity of the gods (*Il.* 24.220–4, *OT* 498–503, E. *El.* 399–400, *Hel.* 744–57 [as it stands], *Phoen.* 954–9).

[39] C. W. Müller (ed.), *Euripides. Philoktet: Testimonien und Fragmente*, Berlin – New York 2000.

[40] Spoken by the Scout. But the situation resembles *Rhesus* in that Tydeus, 'raging and eager for battle' (380), is discouraged by Amphiaraus from crossing the Ismenus on account of unfavourable sacrifices.

Ba. 179, 186 (Teiresias), *Med.* 686 (Pittheus), *IT* 662–3 (Calchas), *Hcld.* 856–7. Cf. Liapis on 65–7.

με ... ἔπεισαν: Enclitics tend to assume the earliest possible position in their clause (J. Wackernagel, *IF* 1 [1892], 333–436 = *KS* I, 1–104; cf. Diggle, *Textual Tradition*, 59 with n. 33); hence the separation of με from its verb, to which Paley (on 65) objected. Δ offers the inferior μοι ... ἔφησαν (μοι et L¹ˢ).

Our poet often employed πείθω (a favourite verb of Euripides) to signal a wrong and potentially fateful decision or conviction on a human character's part. Cf. 330–1, 594 (nn.), 663, 838, 937, 991 (989b–92n.), 993 (Strohm 260 n. 4, 264 with n. 4).

ἡμέρας ... φάος: Cf. E. fr. 443.1 ὦ λαμπρὸς αἰθὴρ ἡμέρας θ' ἁγνὸν φάος.

68–9a. θυοσκόων: here equivalent to μάντεις (66), as at *Il.* 24.221 ἢ' οἳ μάντιές εἰσι θυοσκόοι ἢ' ἱερῆες (~ *Od.* 21.145, 22.318, 321). The formation (θύος + *(σ)κοϝός) suggests 'a person who inspected the flame or smoke of a sacrificial fire' (Fraenkel on *Ag.* 87 τίνος ἀγγελίας πειθοῖ περίπεμπτα θυοσκεῖς; cf. West's apparatus). But the verb already indicates an extension of meaning towards other forms of divination from burnt offerings (D. H. 1.30.3 θυοσκόοι = *haruspices*) or the act of sacrificing as such (*Ba.* 224 πρόφασιν μὲν ὡς δὴ μαινάδας θυοσκόους).

69b. This is one of the rare γνῶμαι in our play (Introduction, 46 with n. 91). On 'fugitives' (below) cf. S. fr. 63 δῆλον γάρ· ἐν δεσμοῖσι δραπέτης ἀνήρ / κῶλον ποδισθεὶς πᾶν πρὸς ἡδονὴν λέγει (Stob. 4.19.29).

ἐν ὄρφνῃ: 41–2n.

δραπέτης: 'runaway' (Hdt. 3.137.2, Pi. fr. 134 Sn.–M., *Ai.* 1285, *Hcld.* 140, *IT* 1341, Ar. *Ach.* 1187) and, more specifically, 'runaway slave' (Hdt. 6.11.2, Ar. *Av.* 760; cf. *Or.* 1499, Men. *Asp.* 398, *Carch.* 35). *Sisyphus Drapetes* was the title of an Aeschylean satyr-play, which presumably dealt with Sisyphus' escape from Hades.

70–5. Hector's exhortation shows a surprising number of verbal overlaps with *HF* 1006–12 ... πίτνει δ' ἐς πέδον πρὸς κίονα / νῶτον πατάξας ... / ... / 1010 ἡμεῖς δ' ... / 1009 σὺν τῷ γέροντι δεσμὰ σειραίων βρόχων / 1011 ἀνήπτομεν πρὸς κίον', ὡς λήξας ὕπνου / μηδὲν προσεργάσαιτο τοῖς δεδραμένοις (the end of Heracles' mad rage). Cf. 70–1, 72–3, 74–5nn.

70–1. The *hysteron proteron* (71) and the choice of words hark back to 23–5a ὁπλίζου χέρα, συμμάχων, / Ἕκτορ, βᾶθι πρὸς εὐνάς, / ὄτρυνον ἔγχος αἴρειν, / ἀφύπνισον (52–84n.).

ἀλλ': here marking the 'transition from arguments for action to a statement of the action required' (*GP* 13–15).

τεύχη πρόχειρα λαμβάνειν: For πρόχειρος of weapons 'at hand' see *Hcld.* 726–7 ἀλλ' ἐμοὶ πρόχειρ' ἔχων / τεύχη κόμιζε, *Phil.* 747–8 πρόχειρον εἴ τί σοι, τέκνον, πάρα / ξίφος χεροῖν, E. *El.* 695–6, *Hel.* 1563–4 (with Diggle's apparatus), Thuc. 4.34.1 and Xen. *Cyr.* 4.2.32. Our passage allows it to be attributive or predicative. The former ('to grasp their arms that lie to hand') evokes the Homeric practice of keeping one's weapons close by (20–2, 740, 762–9nn.), the latter ('to take their arms to hand') appeals for its 'dynamic' note: *Ag.* 1651–2 (Αιγ.) εἶα δή, ξίφος πρόκωπον πᾶς τις εὐτρεπιζέτω. / (Χο.) ἀλλὰ κἀγὼ μὴν πρόκωπος ..., *Or.* 1478 ὁ δὲ ξίφος πρόκωπον ἐν χεροῖν ἔχων.

λῆξαί θ' ὕπνου Cf. *HF* 1011 ... ὡς λήξας ὕπνου (70–5n.). The verse-end recurs in 770 (770–2n.).

72–3. '... so that even if someone is leaping on his ship, he may be spear-split in his back and sprinkle the boarding-ladders with blood.'

This couplet is perhaps the most extravagant result of our poet's 'mosaic' compositional technique (Introduction, 35–7). The gory details and basic syntactical structure stem from *Il.* 8.512–15 μὴ μὰν ἀσπουδεί γε νεῶν ἐπιβαῖεν ἔκηλοι, / ἀλλ' ὥς τις τούτων γε βέλος καὶ οἴκοθι πέσσῃ, / βλημένος ἠ' ἰῷ ἢ' ἔγχεϊ ὀξυόεντι / νηὸς ἐπιθρῴσκων, where the end has even literally been worked into *Rh.* 72 (below). This is followed by a very poetic trimeter (73), the first half of which indicates lexical influence from Pi. *Pyth.* 1.28 στρωμνὰ δὲ χαράσσοισ' ἅπαν νῶτον ποτικεκλιμένον κεντεῖ.[41] In addition, ῥάνῃ φόνῳ perhaps harks back to Pi. *Isthm.* 8.49–50 (Achilles) ὃ καὶ Μύσιον ἀμπελόεν / αἵμαξε Τηλέφου μέλανι ῥαίνων φόνῳ πεδίον, the only other passage that combines these words for bloodshed. Moreover, as Liapis (on 72–3) points out, there is no certain instance of ῥαίνω in classical tragedy (although ἐκραίνω occurs at *Tr.* 781 and *Cyc.* 402).[42]

ὡς ἄν: The use of ὡς ἄν and ὅπως ἄν in tragedy has been examined by J. F. Dobson, *CR* 24 (1910), 143–4, who concludes (144) that they properly 'express a purpose of the speaker which is capable of fulfilment in the future.' Cf. KG II 375, 385–6, SD 665, 671, 673, *Rh.* 420, 473, 878 (877–8n.).

καὶ νεὼς θρῴσκων ἔπι: similarly 100 ... κἀπιθρῴσκοντας νεῶν, where metre allows the retention of Homeric ἐπιθρῴσκω (LSJ s.v. I), instead of the simple verb with ἐπί postponed after its noun.[43] Both

---

41 The eruption of Etna (*Pyth.* 1.15–28) was one of the best-known Pindaric episodes in antiquity. Cf. e.g. *PV* 351–72, Carc. II *TrGF* 70 F 5.6–7, [Longin.] *De Subl.* 35.4, Favorinus' unfavourable comparison of Verg. *Aen.* 3.570–7 with Pi. *Pyth.* 1.21–6 (Gell. 17.10 ~ Macr. 5.17.7–14) and Strabo 5.4.9 = Posidon. fr. 39 Theiler.

42 The date and exact status of fr. tr. adesp. 90 are unknown. It may be comic paratragedy.

43 This rather than 'anastrophic tmesis', which is already rare in Homer (KG I 531, SD 425) and in genuine tragic verse restricted to *Pers.* 873/4 αἱ κατὰ χέρσον ἐληλαμέναι πέρι

passages also recall *Pers.* 357–60 ὡς εἰ μελαίνης νυκτὸς ἵξεται κνέφας, / Ἕλληνες οὐ μενοῖεν, ἀλλὰ σέλμασιν / ναῶν ἐπανθορόντες ἄλλος ἄλλοσε / δρασμῷ κρυφαίῳ βίοτον ἐκσωσοίατο and 457 ναῶν ἐξέθρῳσκον. The former may be another adaptation of *Il.* 8.512–15 and itself have been in our poet's mind.

νῶτον χαραχθείς: Apart from Pi. *Pyth.* 1.28 χαράσσοισ' … νῶτον (above), cf. *HF* 1007 νῶτον πατάξας … (70–5n.) and also *Ai.* 110 νῶτα φοινιχθείς. The best tragic parallel for this 'physical' sense of χαράσσω is *Phil.* 267 ἀγρίῳ χαράγματι (of Philoctetes' wound). Ritchie (214) wrongly quotes *Med.* 155–6 εἰ δὲ σὸς πόσις καινὰ λέχη σεβίζει, / κείνῳ τόδε μὴ χαράσσου and the uncertain S. fr. 684.1–3 ἔρως γὰρ … / … καὶ θεῶν ἄνω / ψυχὰς ταράσσει (v.l. χαράσσει).

κλίμακας: 'boarding-ladders', as in e.g. *IT* 1351, 1382 βὰς ἐς θάλασσαν κἀπὶ κλίμακος θορών, *Hel.* 1570 κλιμακτῆρας, Theoc. 22.30 (with Gow).

74–5. Hector's plans for the survivors reverses 'the stereotype of the servile Phrygian' (Liapis on 74–5, with reference to his note on 31).

οἳ δ' answers 72 τις αὐτῶν. Likewise Lys. 19.59 ἔτι τοίνυν καὶ ἰδίᾳ τισὶ τῶν πολιτῶν … συνεξέδωκε θυγατέρας καὶ ἀδελφάς, τοὺς δ' ἐλύσατο ἐκ τῶν πολεμίων, τοῖς δ' … (KG II 265–6 n. 4, SD 188, GP 166).

ἐν βρόχοισι δέσμιοι λελημμένοι: Although common tragic words, βρόχος and δεσμός (or their derivatives) are found together only in Euripides: *HF* 1009 (cf. 70–5n.), 1035, *IT* 1411 and especially *Ba.* 615 οὐδέ σου συνῆψε χεῖρας δεσμίοισιν ἐν βρόχοις;

λελημμένοι (fere Π²O, *Chr. Pat.* 2351 pars codd.) represents the form that in tragedy has largely replaced εἰλημμέναι as the regular perfect passive of λαμβάνω (*Ag.* 876, S. fr. 750, *Ion* 1113, *Ba.* 1102, *IA* 363; cf. *Cyc.* 433, Ar. *Eccl.* 1090). VΛ's λελη(ι)σμένοι perhaps arose by association with war booty, but the same error occurs at *Ba.* 1102 (λελημμένος Π⁷, coni. Musgrave: λελησμ- P).

Φρυγῶν: 32n.

ἐκμάθωσι: '… may learn *thoroughly*' (LSJ s.v. I) sounds very cynical.

γαπονεῖν: a poetic synonym of γεωργεῖν (176n.). Earlier, only γαπόνος appears at E. *Suppl.* 419–22 ὁ γὰρ χρόνος μάθησιν ἀντὶ τοῦ τάχους / κρείσσω δίδωσι. γαπόνος δ' ἀνὴρ πένης, / εἰ καὶ γένοιτο μὴ ἀμαθής, ἔργων ὕπο / οὐκ ἂν δύναιτο πρὸς τὰ κοίν' ἀποβλέπειν, which, to judge by the surrounding μαθ- words, may be the source of our

---

πύργον (πέρι Heath: περὶ fere Ω) and, despite Barrett (on *Hipp.* 548–9), *Phil.* 343 ἦλθόν με νηὶ ποικιλοστόλῳ μέτα.

verb. 'Doric' γα- takes precedence over γη- or γεω- in tragic compounds (Björck, *Alpha Impurum*, 114–16, 331–2, R. Renehan, *Greek Textual Criticism*, Cambridge [Mass.] 1969, 117–18).

77. οὐκ ἴσμεν τορῶς: Cf. 656 ἥκω δ' ἀκούσας οὐ τορῶς and 737 κοὔ σε γιγνώσκω τορῶς. On τορός ('piercing' or mostly 'clear', 'accurate') see J. de Roos, in J. M. Bremer *et al.* (eds.), *Miscellanea tragica in honorem J. C. Kamerbeek*, Amsterdam 1976, 323–31. The adjective and adverb are Aeschylean – with fifteen instances (+ four in *PV*), as opposed to one in Euripides (*Ion* 696) and none in Sophocles. The combination with negatives here is unique for classical Greek and also rare later (e.g. Call. fr. 398 Pf., Plut. *De Pyth. or.* 22.405b).

78. τίς γὰρ ... πρόφασις ...; 'Well, what other reason ...?' (*GP* 81–2, 85, FJW on A. *Suppl.* 586, *Rh.* 17–18n.).

πῦρ' αἴθειν: 41–2n.

Ἀργείων στρατόν: 56–8n. Morstadt's στρατῷ (*Beitrag*, 16) would make the construction regular (cf. LSJ s.v. πρόφασις I 2), but cf. 107–8 ἄλλῳ δ' ἄλλο πρόσκειται γέρας, / σὲ μὲν μάχεσθαι, τοὺς δὲ βουλεύειν καλῶς (Porter on 78) and KG II 26–7 n. 2, SD 376–7.

79. Syntax and verse-rhythm resemble E. *El.* 644 συνῆχ'· ὕποπτος οὖσα γιγνώσκει πόλει.

ὕποπτον resumes 49 (49–51n.) ὑποπτεύων τὸ μέλλον. Euripides liked the somewhat prosaic ὕποπτος (*Andr.* 1088, *Hec.* 1135, *El.* 345, 644, *HF* 1120, *IT* 1334, *Phoen.* 1210). In other early poetry only ὑπόπτης at *Ag.* 1637 and *Phil.* 136.

κάρτ' (also 158, 476) is all but restricted to tragedy and Ionic prose (LSJ s.v.; cf. FJW on A. *Suppl.* 450, Dunbar on Ar. *Av.* 342). Aeschylus has more cases (32) than Sophocles (17) and Euripides (12) together.

80. πάντ' ἂν φοβηθεὶς ἴσθι δειμαίνων τόδε can hardly disguise its relationship with *Hipp.* 519 πάντ' ἂν φοβηθεῖσ' ἴσθι. δειμαίνεις δὲ τί;

In both places the participle with ἄν represents an independent potential optative (KG I 242–3, SD 407). On the juxtaposition of φόβος (general 'fear') and δεῖμα (the actual dread) see Dale and Kannicht on *Hel.* 312.

82–3. Surprise at Hector's deeds is voiced by Agamemnon in *Il.* 10.47–50 οὐ γάρ πω ἰδόμην οὐδ' ἔκλυον αὐδήσαντος, / ἄνδρ' ἕνα τοσσάδε μέρμερ' ἐπ' ἤματι μητίσασθαι, / ὅσσ' Ἕκτωρ ἔρρεξε διίφιλος υἷας Ἀχαιῶν / αὔτως, οὔτε θεᾶς υἱὸς φίλος οὔτε θεοῖο.

82. ἐν τροπῇ δορός: 'when the battle turned' or 'in their army's rout' (Morwood), depending on the metaphorical interpretation of δόρυ (20–2n.). In any event, inspiration seems to have come from *Ai.* 1275 ἤδη τὸ μηδὲν ὄντας ἐν τροπῇ δορός, which likewise refers to the hard-pressed Greeks. Similar phrases are *Ag.* 1237 ... ὥσπερ ἐν μάχης τροπῇ, *Ant.* 674–5 ἥδε (*sc.* ἡ ἀναρχία) συμμάχου δορός / τροπὰς καταρρήγνυσι and, phonetically, *Rh.* 116 (n.) ... ἐν τροπῇ στρατός (ΔQ: δορός L).

83. σὺ ταῦτ' ἔπραξας· καὶ τὰ λοιπὰ νῦν σκόπει: a proud affirmation, and a warning not to risk 'by hasty action ... what has been already done' (Paley on 83).

84. Hector reasserts his decision to fight (52–84, 70–1nn.) in a tone that recalls *Il.* 12.243 εἷς οἰωνὸς ἄριστος, ἀμύνεσθαι περὶ πάτρης. The closest linguistic parallel is *Alc.* 519 διπλοῦς ἐπ' αὐτῇ μῦθος ἔστι μοι λέγειν, followed by *Cho.* 554 ἁπλοῦς ὁ μῦθος· τήνδε μὲν στείχειν ἔσω, *Phoen.* 469 ἁπλοῦς ὁ μῦθος τῆς ἀληθείας ἔφυ and E. fr. 253.1 ἁπλοῦς ὁ μῦθος· μὴ λέγ' εὖ ... (Ritchie 244).

St. Basil (*leg. libr. gent.* 31.576 B–C Migne) quotes the verse as ἁπλοῦς ἐπ' ἐχθροὺς θυμὸς ὁπλίζει χέρα. Whether the errors are his or, in part at least, MSS variants is impossible to tell (Liapis on 84). See further Introduction, 46.

ὁπλίζειν χέρα: 23–4, 99nn.

85–148. Aeneas arrives in haste from the direction of the Trojan camp (to the audience's right) in order to find out about the nocturnal tumult (85–9). When Hector reveals his intention to attack the supposedly fleeing Greeks (90–104), he condemns this impetuosity in a detailed speech and recommends gathering intelligence first (105–30). The chorus support him with extraordinary vigour (131–6), and Hector agrees to dispatch a scout (137–48).

The formal purpose of the scene is to bring the story back onto the Homeric track. Unlike his epic counterpart (*Il.* 10.303–12), Hector is far too agitated to retract his course and propose the spying mission himself, but, in the way of Agamemnon at *Il.* 10.37–41, needs a more level-headed companion to lead him there (Ritchie 66). The conflict between military θάρσος and εὐβουλία is a familiar theme in ancient literature (Mastronarde on *Phoen.* 746) and further exemplified by Odysseus and Diomedes later in the play (565–94n.). Here Aeneas' role comes closest to that of Polydamas, whose invariably prudent advice to the Iliadic Hector informs the first two thirds of Aeneas' speech (105–30n.). The same passage also betrays influence from *Phoen.* 697–747, where Creon opposes a number of incautious strategies which Eteocles suggests employing against the Argive host (105–30n.).

The opening dialogue between the Trojan leaders (87–104) mirrors the parodos in that it is now Hector who utters a seemingly random call to arms (90), and Aeneas has to worm solid information out of him. This reversal is underlined with linguistic echoes in Aeneas' questions (87–9, 91–2nn.) and Hector's explanation of what the sentries saw (95–8n.).

The obstinacy with which he adheres to his understanding of the situation thus remains before the audience's eyes, even after he has converted to Aeneas' strategy (137–46n.). In that way it contrasts all the more sharply with his uncharacteristic respect for public opinion (131–6n.). The last order for Aeneas to 'go and calm the allies' (138) could not be further removed from the earlier cries for battle, which paradoxically would have saved the Trojans' day (Strohm 258–9; cf. 52–84, 65–9nn.).

If one asks why our poet chose Aeneas and not Polydamas to counsel Hector, the easiest answer is that he wished for a more distinguished Trojan than Panthous' son, who has no life outside the *Iliad* and may have been a Homeric invention (cf. M. Schofield, *CQ* n.s. 36 [1986], 18–19, Hainsworth on *Il.* 12.60). As a warrior Aeneas is second only to Hector and often mentioned in the same breath (e.g. *Il.* 5.467–8, 6.75–9, 17.513), while his advisory role shines through in the appellation Τρώων βουληφόρε: *Il.* 5.180, 13.463, 17.485, 20.83 (Janko on 13.219–20). In addition, he may owe his inclusion in *Rhesus* to a Thracian link. Whether he actually has an indigenous name (von Kamptz, *Homerische Personennamen*, 283–4, *LfgrE* s.v. Αἰνείας E) and originated in that area or, more probably, was adopted as the eponym of places like Aenus and Aenia in historical times (N. M. Horsfall, in J. N. Bremmer – N. M. Horsfall [eds.], *Roman Myth and Mythography*, London 1986, 12–13), it may be sufficient that by the early fourth century BC he was firmly connected with sites in Macedon and Thrace (cf. Introduction, 14–16, 19, 20).

85–6. Comments upon hurried movement and/or the anticipation of news being brought are typical features of tragic entry announcements (e.g. *Pers.* 247–8 τοῦδε γὰρ δράμημα φωτὸς Περσικὸν πρέπει μαθεῖν, / καὶ φέρει σαφές τι πρᾶγος ἐσθλὸν ἢ κακὸν κλυεῖν, *Sept.* 369–71, 372–4, *PV* 941–3, *Med.* 269–70, 1118–20, *Hipp.* 1151–2, *Tro.* 230–2, *Ba.* 212–14). Our couplet looks like *Hec.* 216–17 καὶ μὴν Ὀδυσσεὺς ἔρχεται σπουδῇ ποδός, / Ἑκάβη, νέον τι πρὸς σὲ σημανῶν ἔπος, and imitation is supported by the fact that, far from having anything to report, Aeneas turns out to seek information himself (Taplin, *Stagecraft*, 147 n. 3). Cf. Klyve 44–5, who rightly doubts the idea of a conscious game with the audience's expectations.

καὶ μήν, normally followed by a form of ὅδε, became the standard marker for new stage arrivals in later drama (*GP* 356, 586, Taplin, *Stagecraft*, 147–8, G. Wakker, in *NAGP*, 227–9, J. Diggle, *CQ* n.s. 47 [1997], 98). Cf. 627–9.

Αἰνέας: The 'unepic' name form, as in *Il.* 13.541 (*metri gratia*) and Pi. *Ol.* 6.88 (cf. Barrett, *Collected Papers*, 148), fits better in iambics and would thus have been preferred by the tragedians (*Rh.* 90, 585 and, without synizesis, S. fr. 373.1).

καί: intensifying μάλα (*GP* 317–18, Paley, Porter on 85).

σπουδῇ ποδός: Apart from *Hec.* 216–17 (above), cf. *Andr.* 879–80 καὶ μὴν ὅδ' ἀλλόχρως τις ἔκδημος ξένος / σπουδῇ πρὸς ἡμᾶς βημάτων πορεύεται (βημάτων Brunck: δωμάτων codd. et gB).

στείχει: Often in entrance announcements the verb of motion stands at the beginning of the second verse (*Cho.* 10–12, 16–18, *OC* 311–13, *Phoen.* 196–7). Euripides has a penchant for στείχω (e.g. *Alc.* 611–13, *Med.* 46–8, *Hcld.* 49–51, *Tro.* 707–8, *Or.* 459–61), Cf. 627–9, 806–7 (n.), Ritchie 251, J. Diggle, *CQ* n.s. 47 (1997), 98–9.

87–9. 'Hector, why have the guards come fearfully through the army at night to your resting-place? What are they debating at night? And why has the army been disturbed?'

Aeneas' question combines those of Hector at 13–14, 15 and 17–19 (16–19, 17–18, 19nn.). The condensed and somewhat illogical syntax gives a sense of urgency and excitement.

τί χρῆμα: If νυκτηγοροῦσι is transitive, as at *Sept.* 28–9 (cf. 19n.), τί χρῆμα here wavers between pronominal ('what?') and adverbial ('why?'). Both usages are colloquial in origin, and the latter appears in Euripides only (Stevens, *CEE* 21–2, Collard, 'Supplement', 361, Ritchie 252, Fraenkel on *Ag.* 1306).

τὰς σὰς πρὸς εὐνάς: 1n.

νυκτηγοροῦσι: 19n. Unlike its noun, νυκτηγορέω is not otherwise attested in Greek.

καὶ κεκίνηται στρατός: 17–18n.

90. Hector's reaction corresponds to that of the chorus who at 23–33 called him to arms before telling the facts (23–51, 85–148nn.).

Αἰνέα: 85–6n.

πυκάζε τεύχεσιν δέμας σέθεν appears to take all its words from *Hcld.* 720–5 ὅπλων μὲν ἤδη τήνδ' ὁρᾷς παντευχίαν, / φθάνοις δ' ἂν οὐκ ἂν τοῖσδε σὸν κρύπτων δέμας· / ... / ... εἰ δὲ τευχέων φοβῇ βάρος, / νῦν μὲν πορεύου γυμνός, ἐν δὲ τάξεσιν / κόσμῳ πυκάζου τῷδ'. For πυκάζω ('cover') of protective armour see also *Il.* 10.271 δὴ τότ' Ὀδυσσῆος πύκασεν κάρη ἀμφιτεθεῖσα (*sc.* ἡ κυνέη). With δέμας σέθεν as little more than a reflexive pronoun here, the active form (Π²Λ, *Chr. Pat.* 91), not the middle (Δ), is desired. Cf. *Pers.* 456–7 αὐτημερὸν φάρξαντες εὐχάλκοις δέμας / ὅπλοισι, *Hcld.* 721 (above), *Phoen.* 1242 ἤδη δ' ἔκρυπτον σῶμα παγχάλκοις ὅπλοις (Barrett on *Hipp.* 131–4).

91–2. 'What is it? Surely the message is not that the enemy have set up some hidden stratagem in the night?'

Aeneas' second question is an extended version of 17 μῶν τις λόχος ἐκ νυκτῶν; (16–19, 17–18, 85–148nn.).

τί δ' ἔστι; a standard line-opening in post-Aeschylean[44] drama, 'conveying surprise' (*GP* 175) and often followed by a more precise question. With μῶν τι(ς) cf. *Hcld*. 795 τί δ' ἔστι; μῶν τι κεδνὸν ἠγωνίζετο; and *Hipp*. 1160–1 τί δ' ἔστι; μῶν τις συμφορὰ νεωτέρα / δισσὰς κατείληφ' ἀστυγείτονας πόλεις;

μῶν: 17–18n.

δόλος κρυφαῖος ἑστάναι: similarly *Rh*. 578 (n.) ἴσως ἐφ' ἡμῖν μηχανὴν στήσων τινά and E. *El*. 983–4 ἀλλ' εἰ τὸν αὐτὸν τῇδ' ὑποστήσων δόλον / ᾧ καὶ πόσιν καθεῖλεν †Αἴγισθον κτανών†. The variant λόχος (*Chr. Pat.* 94 et P²ᵞᵖ vel Pʳᵞᵖ; cf. Zuntz, *Inquiry*, 149, Diggle, *Euripidea*, 510–12) would be too specific here and probably arose by analogy with 17 (17–18n.).

κατ' εὐφρόνην recurs in the same metrical position at 736 and 852 (also *Pers*. 221, E. fr. 107.1). Our poet has three further instances of εὐφρόνη (literally 'the kindly time') as a synonym for 'night' (518, 617, 824).

93. φεύγουσιν ἄνδρες κἀπιβαίνουσιν νεῶν: Both here and in 100 φεύγοντας αὐτοὺς κἀπιθρῴσκοντας νεῶν the phrasing resembles Zeus' intention for a new Trojan attack on the Achaeans at *Il*. 15.63 (ὄφρ' ...) φεύγοντες δ' ἐν νηυσὶ πολυκλήϊσι πέσωσιν.[45] The slight *hysteron proteron* marks Hector's obsession with a possible enemy escape.

κἀπιβαίνουσιν νεῶν: an even closer echo of *Il*. 8.512 μὴ μὰν ἀσπουδεί γε νεῶν ἐπιβαῖεν ἔκηλοι than *Rh*. 72 (72–3n.) ... καὶ νεὼς θρῴσκων ἔπι and 100 (above). Otherwise, before *Rhesus*, Herodotus writes ἐπιβαίνειν ἐπὶ νεός (6.43.2, 8.118.1).

94. Klyve compares Thoas' suspicious question at *IT* 1164 τί τοὐκδιδάξαν τοῦτό σ'; ἢ δόξαν λέγεις; But a better parallel is probably *Ag*. 272 τί γὰρ τὸ πιστόν; ἔστι τῶνδέ σοι τέκμαρ; Unlike Aeneas, the Old Argives will be convinced by Clytaemestra's interpretation of the fire-beacons: *Ag*. 352 ἐγὼ δ' ἀκούσας πιστά σου τεκμήρια.

95–8. In further imitation of the parodos (85–148n.), Hector repeats the chorus' observation at 41–2. His circular speech and use of the verb δοκέω (96) belie its status as an ἀσφαλὲς τεκμήριον.

95. λαμπάδας πυρός: For a similar tautologous 'genitive of material' see Theodect. *TrGF* 72 F 10.1–2 ὦ καλλιφεγγῆ λαμπάδ' εἰλίσσων φλογός / Ἥλιε.

96–8. The sentence-structure, wording and content again evoke *Pers*. 357–60 (quoted in 72–3n.).

---

44 But see *Ag*. 1306 (with Fraenkel), *Cho*. 885 (with Garvie) τί δ' ἔστι χρῆμα;
45 Especially if the sequel, *Il*. 15.64–77 Πηλείδεω Ἀχιλῆος. ὃ δ' ..., is omitted with Zenodotus (Σᴬᵀ *Il*. 15.64 [IV 23.58–60, 62–3 Erbse] ~ Eust. 1006.2–4). West follows Hentze in deleting 64–71 (cf. his apparatus on 64–77).

οὐ μενεῖν ἐς αὔριον: The preposition here retains its full force, as in *Rh.* 600 ὃς εἰ διοίσει νύκτα τήνδ' ἐς αὔριον, *Od.* 11.350–1 ξεῖνος δὲ τλήτω ... / ἔμπης οὖν ἐπιμεῖναι ἐς αὔριον, Hes. *Op.* 410 and Call. *Aet.* fr. 43.16 Harder καὶ τῶν οὐδὲν ἔμεινεν ἐς αὔριον (cf. *Od.* 7.318, Ar. *Eq.* 661, Alexand. Com. fr. 3.1 *PCG*: 'for tomorrow'). Elsewhere it has often become meaningless: e.g. *Il.* 8.538 ἠελίου ἀνιόντος ἐς αὔριον (with Kirk), *OC* 567–8, S. fr. 593.2, *Alc.* 320, Nicoch. fr. 18.1 *PCG*, Men. *Epitr.* 379, Pl. *Crit.* 43d5 (LSJ s.v. εἰς II 2).

Portus' μενεῖν (*Breves Notae*, 69) for μένειν (Ω: μενειν Π²) is recommended by the future infinitive ἀφορμήσειν (98).

ἐκκέαντες: i.e. the old Attic aorist of καίω (< epic ἔκη(ϝ)α, by quantitative metathesis), which is attested only in the masculine participle (cf. *Ag.* 849, S. *El.* 757 [Brunck: καί- OV: κεί- PT: κη(ι)- cett.], Ar. *Pax* 1133, *IG* I³ 476.47–8, 271 [408/7 BC]; Threatte II 529) and appealed to dramatists as metrically convenient and perhaps more traditional than καυσ-. It 'was easily corrupted [as in V<L>] owing to its unfamiliarity' (Finglass on S. *El.* 757).

πύρσ': The heteroclitic accusative plural is unique (LSJ s.v. πυρσός (A) I, II 2).

ἐπ' εὐσέλμων νεῶν: 'on their well-benched (or 'well-decked') ships' (LSJ s.v. εὔσελμος, *LfgrE* s.v. ἐΰσσελμος B, Hoekstra on *Od.* 13.101). For this standard epic phrase in tragedy cf. *IT* 1383–4 ἔθηκ' ἀδελφήν <τ'> ἐντὸς εὐσέλμου νεώς / τό τ' οὐρανοῦ πέσημα (εὐσέλμου Pierson: εὐσήμου L) and fr. tr. adesp. 463 σωτῆρες εὐσέλμων νεῶν. Stesichorus probably first used the trisyllabic form at *Palinod.* fr. 192.2 *PMGF* (= Pl. *Phaedr.* 243a9) οὐδ' ἔβας ἐν νηυσὶν εὐσέλμοις (after which Haslam [*QUCC* 17 (1974), 44] supplied <ποκα>, for the sake of metre; Blomfield read ἐϋσσέλμοις).

99. 'And in reaction to this you are taking up arms. With what intention?

Aeneas' comment on Hector's premature order to prepare for war (90) is metaphorical, rather than literally indicating a silent (and probably incomplete) arming-scene on stage (Taplin, *Stagecraft*, 160; cf. Klyve on 99, Wilkins on *Hcld.* 720–47).

ὡς τί δράσων: a set locution, especially in Euripides. Ritchie (252) cites *Alc.* 537 ὡς δὴ τί δράσων τόνδ' ὑπορράπτεις λόγον; and *Med.* 682 σὺ δ' ὡς τί χρῄζων τήνδε ναυστολεῖς χθόνα; but see also *IT* 557 ... ὡς τί δὴ θέλων; and *Tr.* 160 ἀλλ' ὥς τι δράσων εἷρπε, *Hel.* 1038 ὡς δή τι δράσων χρηστὸν ἐς κοινόν γε νῷν, *Ai.* 326, *Med.* 93. The ὡς is comparative in origin: 'like someone about to do what ...?' (KG II 90–1, 520).

πρὸς τάδ' goes with ὁπλίζῃ χέρα. For the meaning ('in reaction / response to that') cf. A. *Suppl.* 302 τί δῆ<τα> πρὸς ταῦτ' ἄλοχο<ς>

ἰσχυρὰ Διός; (with FJW on 249 [II, p. 203]) and E. *El.* 274 τί δῆτ' Ὀρέστης πρὸς τάδ', Ἄργος ἦν μόλῃ; (τάδ' Camper: τόδ' L). Also Diggle, *Studies*, 38.

ὁπλίζῃ χέρα Most editors retain the MSS' χέρας. But the singular (Aldine) is supported by 23 and 84 and the fact that generally in this phrase the number of χείρ matches that of the people concerned: *Alc.* 34–5 νῦν δ' ἐπὶ τῇδ' αὖ / χέρα τοξήρη φρουρεῖς ὁπλίσας, *Phoen.* 267, *Or.* 926, 1222–3 ἡμεῖς δ' ... / ... ὁπλιζώμεσθα φασγάνῳ χέρας, Opp. *Hal.* 5.258–9, Nonn. *D.* 1.295, *Orac. Sib.* 14.72. An exception is Lyc. 916–17 (Heracles) ὅς ποτε ... / ... ῥαιβῷ χεῖρας ὥπλισε Σκύθῃ (where metrical considerations apply).

100–1. φεύγοντας αὐτοὺς κἀπιθρῴκσοντας νεῶν: 72–3, 93nn.

κἀπικείσομαι βαρύς: *sc.* αὐτοῖς – according to the rule that, regardless of case, the object of two verbs need be expressed only once (KG II 562–3, SD 708–9). So LSJ (s.v. ἐπίκειμαι II 2) are wrong to class the word as 'absolute' here, and the same applies to the remaining passages in their list, except Theoc. 22.90–1.

βαρύς is given special emphasis by its final position in both line and clause. Cf. e.g. *Pers.* 828, *PV* 77, *Ant.* 767, *Tr.* 1202, *Cyc.* 678, *Hec.* 722.

102–4. 'For it is disgraceful for us and, in addition to the disgrace, disastrous as well to let the enemy run away without battle, when the god is handing them to us, the enemy who have done us so much harm.'

The overall sentiment matches *Il.* 21.437–8 (Poseidon to Apollo) τὸ μὲν αἴσχιον, αἴ κ' ἀμαχητεί / ἴομεν Οὔλυμπόνδε Διὸς ποτὶ χαλκοβατὲς δῶ (Klyve on 102). Hector expects an easy victory, as he transfers to the new expedition his trust in the gods' / Zeus' support (63–4n.).

αἰσχρὸν γὰρ ἡμῖν, καὶ πρὸς αἰσχύνῃ κακόν: In addition to shame, Hector mainly seems to think of material loss, and scholars have long compared Hor. *Carm.* 3.5.26–7 *flagitio additis* / *damnum*. With regard to physical pain cf. Hes. *Op.* 211 νίκης τε στέρεται πρός τ' αἴσχεσιν ἄλγεα πάσχει (with West on 210–11), *Cyc.* 670 (Χο.) αἰσχρός γε φαίνῃ. (Κυ.) κἀπὶ τοῖσδέ γ' ἄθλιος and, in a version equivalent to the English 'add insult to injury', the Charioteer at 756–7a (n.) κακῶς πέπρακται κἀπὶ τοῖς κακοῖσι πρός / αἴσχιστα. For αἰσχρόν in situations where 'martial prestige is at stake' see Cairns, *Aidōs*, 59–60, 181–3.

θεοῦ διδόντος: probably not absolute ('when the god grants the opportunity'), but with πολεμίους as object to διδόντος as well as φεύγειν ἐᾶσαι. Similarly e.g. *Pers.* 293–4 ὅμως δ' ἀνάγκη πημονὰς βροτοῖς φέρειν / θεῶν διδόντων, *Sept.* 719 θεῶν διδόντων οὐκ ἂν ἐκφύγοις κακά, *Hipp.* 1433–4 ἀνθρώποισι δέ / θεῶν διδόντων εἰκὸς ἐξαμαρτάνειν and especially *IA* 701–2 (Αγ.) ... ὁ Πηλεὺς δ' ἔσχε Νηρέως κόρην. / (Κλ.) θεοῦ διδόντος ἢ βίᾳ θεῶν λαβών; For δίδωμι, 'hand over, deliver up', cf. *Il.* 23.21 Ἕκτορα ... δώσειν κυσὶν ὠμὰ δάσασθαι (LSJ s.v. II 1 with Suppl. [1996]).

105–30. Aeneas' speech falls into three parts: 1. criticism of Hector's rashness (105–11), 2. the likely consequences of his plan if the Greeks fight back (112–22), and 3. advice for a safer course of action (123–30). This is the Iliadic 'rebuke pattern' in its simplest form (Fenik, *Typical Battle Scenes*, 109, 120–1, 206), which also underlies Polydamas' tactical warnings at *Il.* 12.61–79, 211–29, 13.726–47 and 18.254–83 (cf. C. Moulton, *Hermes* 109 [1981], 2). Of these, our poet primarily excerpted the first and third, and it is probably no coincidence that they remain closest to the basic scheme.

In the sequence of thoughts, Aeneas' characterisation of Hector as brave but imprudent combines Polydamas' very similar opening at *Il.* 13.726–33 with the authorial comment of *Il.* 18.252 that Polydamas excelled in wisdom, Hector in valour (105–8, 107b–8nn.). Next comes the bipartite account of what could face the army in the Achaean camp. If they meet with opposition and are forced to retreat, the spiked ditch will pose a serious obstacle to the charioteers, as Polydamas warns in *Il.* 12.61–74, and the Trojans learn to their peril at *Il.* 16.367–71 (110b–18, 112–15, 112, 116–18nn.). Yet if they succeed Achilles will rise to defend the ships. This takes us back to *Il.* 13.726–47, which ends with the prospect of the hero's return (13.744–7), and to *Il.* 18.254–83, occasioned by his first appearance (119–22, 120–1, 122nn.).

It emerges that, together with the earlier allusions to the 'eagle omen' (52–84, 56–69, 65–9, 84nn.), our poet adapted all four strategic interventions of Polydamas. Hector alternately takes and rejects the advice, as he does in *Rhesus* with the seers and Aeneas. Indeed *Il.* 12.61–79 and 13.726–47 'pleased' the general, a reaction that is almost parodied in *Rh.* 137 (n.).

A tragic precedent will complete the picture. At *Phoen.* 697–747 Creon and Eteocles are confronted with the Argive intention to encircle Thebes (710–11).[46] The young commander proposes 1. an instant sortie (712–23), 2. a night attack (724–7), 3. an assault at meal-time (728–31), and 4. to overrun the enemy with chariots (732–3). Creon dismisses each tactic as too dangerous, and at least two of his objections have equivalents in our speech (115, 116–18nn.). Finally, as he develops his own plan of placing seven leaders at the seven gates (*Phoen.* 734–47), he demands they be selected for prudence (εὐβουλία) as well as courage (θάρσος), 'for each is worthless if separated from the other': *Phoen.* 746–7 ~ *Rh.* 105 (n.). The reminiscence would have been caused by the similarity of

---

46 On the text see 56–8n. (p. 141 n. 34).

context and the known risks of night raids, crossing ditches, rivers and the like. In both *Rhesus* and *Phoenissae* the new strategy becomes essential for the tragedy to unfold.

105–8. The lines are quoted in Stobaeus (4.13.8) among other tragic reflections on the λόγος-ἔργον antithesis in war. But the immediate model is Polydamas at *Il.* 13.726–33 Ἕκτορ, ἀμήχανός ἐσσι παραρρητοῖσι πιθέσθαι. / οὕνεκά τοι περὶ δῶκε θεὸς πολεμήϊα ἔργα, / τούνεκα καὶ βουλῇ ἐθέλεις περιίδμεναι ἄλλων; / ἀλλ' οὔ πως ἅμα πάντα δυνήσεαι αὐτὸς ἑλέσθαι· / ἄλλῳ μὲν γὰρ ἔδωκε θεὸς πολεμήϊα ἔργα, / [...] / ἄλλῳ δ' ἐν στήθεσσι τιθεῖ νόον εὐρύοπα Ζεύς / ἐσθλόν. In his speech, as here, 'the priamel softens the rebuke by granting that one cannot be good at everything' (Janko on *Il.* 13.726–47). Further uses and variants of this maxim are discussed at 105, 106–7a, 107b–8nn.

105. 'Would that you were as good a man in counsel as in action!'

No Homeric hero fully achieves the ideal of *Il.* 9.443 μύθων τε ῥητῆρ' ἔμμεναι πρηκτῆρά τε ἔργων, either because of his age or because the gods do not distribute their gifts evenly among men (F. Solmsen, *TAPA* 85 [1954], 1–4, H. D. Kemper, *Rat und Tat* ..., diss. Bonn 1960, 13–22, BK on *Il.* 1.258). In a comparable situation (cf. 105–30n.) both virtues are required of a military leader at *Phoen.* 746–7 (Ετ.) θάρσει προκρίνας ἢ φρενῶν εὐβουλίᾳ; / (Κρ.) ἀμφότερ'· ἓν ἀπολειφθὲν γὰρ οὐδὲν θατέρου (Wecklein: ἀμφότερον ... θάτερον fere codd.).

εἴθ' ἦσθ' ἀνὴρ εὔβουλος ὡς δρᾶσαι χερί: The formulation is reminiscent of *Hcld.* 731 εἴθ' ἦσθα δυνατὸς δρᾶν ὅσον πρόθυμος εἶ,[47] but differs from it in that an 'expression of ability' has to be supplied with the infinitive (Matthiae, VIII [1824], 10, *GG* II³ [1835], 1238). This seems possible if we think of εὔβουλος as separable into ἀγαθὸς βουλήν, from which the adjective could also be taken to govern δρᾶσαι χερί (F. W. Schmidt, *Kritische Studien zu den griechischen Dramatikern* II, Berlin 1886, 370). The ellipse would still be harsher than at e.g. Pi. *Ol.* 6.16–17 ποθέω στρατιᾶς ὀφθαλμὸν ἐμᾶς / ἀμφότερον μάντιν τ' ἀγαθὸν καὶ δουρὶ μάρνασθαι,[48] though not extraordinary enough perhaps (for our poet) to posit corruption. Suitable remedies at any rate are hard to find. Schmidt's δραστήριος (370), adopted by Wecklein, is a

---

[47] Σ^V *Rh.* 105 (II 330.16–17 Schwartz = 85 Merro) already cites S. fr. 896 εἴθ' ἦσθα σώφρων ἔργα τοῖς λόγοις ἴσα, which may, however, be truncated or corrupt (Pearson and Radt nn.).

[48] In *Or.* 717–18 ὦ πλὴν γυναικὸς οὕνεκα στρατηλατεῖν / τἄλλ' οὐδέν, ὦ κάκιστε, τιμωρεῖν φίλοις, cited by Matthiae (above), the first infinitive (without article) parallels the accusative of respect τἄλλ'.

Euripidean favourite (*Hel.* 992,⁴⁹ E. frr. 54.4, 688.4; of things *Ion* 985, 1185, *Or.* 1554),⁵⁰ but improbable palaeographically (unless a scribe filled in a partly illegible verse). Bothe's θρασὺς χερί (5 [1803], 286) unduly stresses and generalises Hector's boldness (cf. *Ai.* 1142 ἄνδρ' ... γλώσσῃ θρασύν), while Porter's δράσας χερί (on 105) looks too specifically at earlier deeds. Lexical change is avoided with Diggle's lacuna after 105. He suggests ... ὡς δρᾶσαι χερί / <δυνατός ...> on the analogy of *Hcld.* 731 (above) and E. fr. 7a.1–2 ἀνὴρ γὰρ ὅστις χρημάτων μὲν ἐνδεής, / δρᾶσαι δὲ χειρὶ δυνατός, Kovacs *exempli gratia* 105a–b ... ὡς δρᾶσαι χερί / <ἰταμῇ πρόθυμος τοὺς ἐναντίους κακῶς> (where ἰταμός is suspect for tragedy).⁵¹ Yet the meaning of the words is complete as they stand, and any addition (also if we wrote 105a–b εἴθ' ἦσθ' ἀνὴρ εὔβουλος ὡς <... / ...> δρᾶσαι χερί) would disproportionately expand on Hector's skills in war. It appears that our poet tried to fit into a single line *Il.* 13.727–8 οὕνεκά τοι περὶ δῶκε θεὸς πολεμήϊα ἔργα, / τούνεκα καὶ βουλῇ ἐθέλεις περιίδμεναι ἄλλων; (105–8n.) and thereby compressed the syntax a little beyond the norm.

εὔβουλος: For the value of εὐβουλία in war add e.g. *Pers.* 749–50, E. *Suppl.* 161 (with Collard), *Phoen.* 721 καὶ μὴν τὸ νικᾶν <γ'> ἐστι πᾶν εὐβουλίας, E. fr. 200, Hdt. 7.10δ.1–2. Unlike its noun, εὔβουλος is rare in tragedy (*Cho.* 696, *OC* 947, E. fr. 472e.51).

106–7a. ἀλλ' οὐ γὰρ ... / πέφυκεν: In addition to *Il.* 13.729 (quoted in 105–8n.), cf. e.g. *Il.* 4.320, 23.670–1 οὐδ' ἄρα πως ἦν / ἐν πάντεσσ' ἔργοισι δαήμονα φῶτα γενέσθαι (with Richardson), *Od.* 8.167–77 and Pi. *Nem.* 1.25–8.

ἀλλ' οὐ γάρ: For ἀλλά (...) γάρ, 'but then / as a matter of fact ...', see *GP* 100–1. It here marks the non-fulfilment of the preceding wish (*GP* 104).

αὐτὸς ... βροτῶν: The partitive genitive with ὁ αὐτός, which was severely criticised by Hermann (*Opuscula* III, 301) and Fraenkel (*Rev.* 238), is paralleled in S. *El.* 916–17 τοῖς αὐτοῖσί τοι / οὐχ αὑτὸς αἰεὶ δαιμόνων παραστατεῖ (οὐχ αὑτὸς Brunck: οὐκ αὐτὸς codd.)⁵² and *Phoen.* 86–7 χρῆν δ' ... οὐκ ἐᾶν βροτῶν / τὸν αὐτὸν αἰεὶ δυστυχῆ καθεστάναι, where Markland's and Valckenaer's βροτῶν for βροτὸν has been found in the MS Ab (early 14ᵗʰ century) and another one at Σ Dion.

---

49 Diggle deletes *Hel.* 991–5 with Schenkl (991–2 already Hartung) and Reeve (*GRBS* 14 [1973], 154–5). The lines are defended by Dale (on 993), Burian (991–5) and Allan (991–5) and silently retained by Kannicht.
50 Unlike Hartung's δράστης (17 [1852], 28, 122), which is not attested in tragedy and has only very late credentials for the required sense (LSJ s.v. δρήστης I 1, 2).
51 Only at A. fr. 282 = Ar. *Ran.* 1291 κυρεῖν παρασχὼν ἰταμαῖς κυσὶν ἀεροφοίτοις. It becomes frequent in Middle and New Comedy (LSJ s.v. ἰταμός).
52 The same error runs through most witnesses at *Rh.* 106.

Thr. *GrGr* I.3 289.20–1 Hilgard (cf. Diggle's apparatus and Mastronarde on *Phoen*. 86). The sense and construction are analogous to θεῶν τις (as against θεός τις) and the like (KG I 338–40, SD 116).

107b–8. The general truth of *Il*. 13.730 + 732–3 that some are better in battle, others in council (105–8n.) is applied to Hector and Polydamas at *Il*. 18.252 ἀλλ' ὃ μὲν ἂρ μύθοισιν, ὃ δ' ἔγχεϊ πολλὸν ἐνίκα.

ἄλλῳ δ' ἄλλο πρόσκειται γέρας: The formulation, if not the sense, resembles *PV* 229–30 εὐθὺς δαίμοσιν νέμει γέρα / ἄλλοισιν ἄλλα. Gygli-Wyss (*Polyptoton*, 137–42) qualifies Wackernagel's assertion that 'one of the features of the figure of speech polyptoton is that ... the nominative must precede an oblique case' (*Lectures on Syntax*, 644 = *Vorlesungen über Syntax* II, 194; cf. KG II 602, Feickert on 107). Rather, in most cases, the subject would come first anyway, and writers are free to change the order for stylistic and/or metrical reasons.

σὲ μὲν μάχεσθαι, τοὺς δὲ βουλεύειν καλῶς depends on γέρας without attraction to the dative ἄλλῳ (KG II 24–7, SD 367–8). σοὶ μὲν ... τοῖς δέ (fere *Chr. Pat.* 2370, coni. Stephanus, *Annotatione*s, 116) oversimplifies the construction.

109–10a. 'You got carried away upon hearing that the Achaeans are burning fire-beacons ...'

ὅστις: The antecedent is best extracted from ἦσθ' (105), with 'the three intervening lines forming a kind of parenthesis' (Porter on 109).

πυρὸς λαμπτῆρας: See 59–60a n. (φαεννοὶ ... ἡλίου / λαμπτῆρες) and, for the pleonastic genitive, 95n. The noun is employed for 'watchfires' also at *Ai*. 285–6 ἡνίχ' ἕσπεροι / λαμπτῆρες οὐκέτ' ἦθον (with Finglass on 585–7).

ἐξήρθης: 'to be excited, agitated' (LSJ s.v. ἐξαίρω III 3), as e.g. S. *El*. 1460–1 ὡς εἴ τις αὐτῶν ἐλπίσιν κεναῖς πάρος / ἐξῇρετ' ἀνδρὸς τοῦδε and in the active Thgn. 630, *Ai*. 1066, *Hipp*. 322 τί γὰρ τὸ δεινὸν τοῦθ' ὅ σ' ἐξαίρει θανεῖν; *Alc*. 346–7 (LSJ s.v. I 3). ἐπαίρω (189) is more common in this sense, especially in prose.

κλυών: As a participle dependent on an aorist verb (expressing Hector's reaction to the news), this should also be recognised and accented as an aorist with West (*BICS* 31 [1984], 177–8). Our MSS invariably give the (secondary) present κλύω in such infinite or non-indicative forms. Similarly 286, 573, 858 (nn.).

φλέγειν: Musgrave (*Exercitationes*, 94 = II [1778], on 110). Zanetto alone among recent editors retains the transmitted φεύγειν (-εις Q) and construes like Σ^V *Rh*. 109 (II 330.18–331.1 Schwartz = 85 Merro) ὅστις πυρὸς λαμπτῆρας κλύων ἐξήρθης Ἀχαιοὺς φεύγειν (*Ciclope, Reso*, 138 n. 13). But although, against Porter (on 110), κλύω with accusative object of an indirect perception may be acceptable (KG I 360 n. 8, SD 106–7), ἐξαίρομαι in the the pregnant sense 'to be excited (by the belief that ...)'

with accusative and infinitive seems impossible (Thuc. 1.25.4 ναυτικῷ δὲ καὶ πολὺ προύχειν ἔστιν ὅτε ἐπαιρόμενοι, quoted by Zanetto, has the simple infinitive, and that restriction also applies to ἐξαίρω).[53] Confusion of the two verbs was easy, especially since forms of φεύγω or φυγή appear in the same position at 93, 98, 100, 104 and 114 (Porter on 110). For transitive φλέγω, 'cause to flame, kindle', cf. *Sept.* 513 (Ζεὺς ...) διὰ χερὸς βέλος φλέγων, fr. tr. adesp. 90.2 καὶ πυρὸς φλέξον μένος and *Tro.* 319–21 ἐγὼ δ' ... / ἀναφλέγω πυρὸς φῶς / ἐς αὐγάν.

110b–18. At *Il.* 12.61–74 Polydamas advises Hector not to attempt the Achaean wall and ditch with chariots. His objections include the structure of the earthwork, which would make it hard to move and fight (*Il.* 12.63–6), and particularly the risk it would pose if the army was routed (*Il.* 12.71–4). Aeneas here naturally emphasises the latter (112–15n.) and leaves the physical details to illustrate the disaster he fears (116–18n.).

110b–11. '... and you intend to lead the army out over the ditch at dead of night.'

τάφρους ὑπερβάς (plural for singular) means the Greek fortifications, as do 112 (n.) κοῖλον αὐλώνων βάθος, 213 τάφροις πελάζων and, most clearly, 989–90 (989b–92n.) ὡς ὑπερβαλὼν τάφρον / τείχη τ' Ἀχαιῶν. Mastronarde wrongly compares our lines to *Phoen.* 714 ἐκτὸς τάφρων τῶνδ', ὡς μαχουμένους τάχα for 'the rashness of crossing one's *own* defensive trench before one is certain of victory' (my emphasis). The Trojans did not have a fortified camp in the open field.

νυκτὸς ἐν καταστάσει: an elaborate periphrasis for 'at night'. The juncture is intelligible, but difficult to explain from the ordinary use of κατάστασις, 'state', 'condition' (LSJ s.v. II 2). Fraenkel (*Rev.* 237) rightly rejects Ritchie's (214) comparison of *Med.* 1197 ὀμμάτων ... κατάστασις (the 'normal condition' of Medea's eyes) and *Hipp.* 1296 ἄκουε, Θησεῦ, σῶν κακῶν κατάστασιν ('the state of your misfortunes'), and at [Pl.] / [Luc.] *Halc.* 4 μετὰ μικρὸν δὲ θαυμαστή τις κατάστασις εὐδίας ἐγένετο (Feickert on 111) the attribute makes all the difference.[54] Perhaps *Ag.* 22–4 ὦ χαῖρε λαμπτήρ, νυκτὸς ἡμερήσιον /

---

53 Paley's assumption of an ellipse ἐλπίδι (on 105) is even harsher and not supported by passages like S. *El.* 1460–1 ὡς εἴ τις αὐτῶν ἐλπίσιν κεναῖς πάρος / ἐξῇρετ' ἀνδρὸς τοῦδε, Thuc. 1.81.6 μὴ γὰρ δὴ ἐκείνῃ γε τῇ ἐλπίδι ἐπαιρώμεθα ὡς ταχὺ παυσθήσεται ὁ πόλεμος and [Lys.] 9.21 τίνι γὰρ ἐπαρθέντα ἐλπίδι δεῖ με συμπολιτεύεσθαι. An equivalent to ἐλπίζω (with present infinitive) = 'deem, suppose that ...' (LSJ s.v. 3) would be needed.

54 *Halcyon* or *On Metamorphosis* is a late-Hellenistic 'Socratic' dialogue, which Nicias of Nicaea (*apud* Ath. 11.506c) and Favorinus (*apud* D. L. 3.62) ascribed to Leon the Academic (otherwise unknown). Feickert also cites Hyp. fr. 205 δεῖ τὴν ἐκ τῆς οἰκίας ἐκπορευομένην ἐν τοιαύτῃ καταστάσει εἶναι τῆς ἡλικίας, ὥστε τοὺς ἀπαντῶντας πυνθάνεσθαι, μὴ τίνος ἐστὶ γυνή, ἀλλὰ τίνος μήτηρ, where τοιαύτῃ adds suitable emphasis.

φάος πιφαύσκων καὶ χορῶν κατάστασιν / πολλῶν ('Oh welcome, beacon, you show the light of day by night and signal the institution of many dancing choruses …'), where νυκτός and κατάστασις, as well as λαμπτήρ, occur in the same positions (and mark a similar contrast between light and dark), exerted some influence (cf. Liapis on 109–11, Introduction, 37). 'At dead of night' or, more accurately, 'while the night is established' (LSJ s.v. ἵστημι B III 4), conveys the meaning here.

112–15. Aeneas' general warning of a Trojan defeat follows the pattern of *Il.* 12.71–4 εἰ δέ χ' ὑποστρέψωσι, παλίωξις δὲ γένηται / ἐκ νηῶν, καὶ τάφρῳ ἐνιπλήξωμεν ὀρυκτῇ, / οὐκέτ' ἔπειτ' ὀΐω οὐδ' ἄγγελον ἀπονέεσθαι / ἄψορρον προτὶ ἄστυ ἑλιχθέντων ὑπ' Ἀχαιῶν. In *Il.* 12.223–7, the 'bird omen' speech (56–69, 65–9nn.), Polydamas again predicts heavy losses and a chaotic retreat, which becomes reality at *Il.* 16.367–71 (cf. 116–18n.).

112. 'But having crossed the hollow depth of the trench …'

The expression implies some of the difficulties envisaged by Polydamas in *Il.* 12.61–3 Ἕκτορ τ' ἠδ' ἄλλοι Τρώων ἀγοὶ ἠδ' ἐπικούρων, / ἀφραδέως διὰ τάφρον ἐλαύνομεν ὠκέας ἵππους. / ἡ δὲ μάλ' ἀργαλέη περάαν (~ *Il.* 12.52–4). For the construction of the Achaean ditch see 116–18n.

καίτοι 'introduces an objection … of the speaker's own, which tends to invalidate, or cast doubt upon, what he has just said' (*GP* 556).

περάσας κοῖλον αὐλώνων βάθος: Cf. 110b–11n. (τάφρους ὑπερβάς). The use of αὐλών (generally 'hollow') for τάφρος may be an Aeschylean borrowing (fr. 419) both here and at Carc. II *TrGF* 70 F 1d (*Achilles*) βαθεῖαν εἰς αὐλῶνα περίδρομον στρατοῦ. Sophocles has the word, which in poetry can be masculine and feminine, in *Tr.* 100 Ποντίας αὐλῶνας ('straits') and fr. 549.2 ('creeks'), Euripides not at all. The 'deep' trench goes back to *Il.* 7.440–1 ἔκτοσθεν δὲ βαθεῖαν ἐπ' αὐτῷ τάφρον ὄρυξαν, / εὐρεῖαν μεγάλην.

113–14. κυρήσεις πολεμίους: The accusative (other than of a neuter pronoun or adjective) is rare with κυρέω: *Sept.* 699 βίον εὖ κυρήσας (with Hutchinson on 698–701), *Hec.* 698 ἐπ' ἀκταῖς νιν κυρῶ θαλασσίαις, *Rh.* 695 πόθεν νιν κυρήσω, Opp. *Hal.* 1.34 (LSJ s.v. I 3 a, falsely adding *Hipp.* 746–7, where the participle is of κυρόω, KG I 350 n. 9).

ἀλλὰ σὸν βλέποντας ἐς δόρυ: 'This is indeed the situation which greets H[ector] when he gets into the Greek camp at *Il.* 13.145–8' (Klyve on 114). For the language, reminiscent of hoplite warfare (Tyrt. fr. 12.10–12 *IEG*), cf. E. *Suppl.* 318–19 οὗ δ' ἐς κράνος βλέψαντα καὶ λόγχης ἀκμήν / χρῆν ἐκπονῆσαι δειλὸς ὢν ἐφηυρέθης, E. *El.* [377–8] and *HF* 163–4 ἀλλ' ὃς μένων βλέπει τε κἀντιδέρκεται / δορὸς ταχεῖαν ἄλοκα τάξιν ἐμβεβώς (with Bond on 164).

115. '… if you are defeated, you will never return again.'

The risk of utter destruction is particularly high at night, as Creon points out to Eteocles at *Phoen.* 725 εἴπερ σφαλείς γε δεῦρο σωθήσῃ πάλιν (with Mastronarde on 724–31). One may add that the Greeks would here be fighting in their own camp.

νικώμενος μέν is answered by 119 νικῶν δ'. Both times we have 'present for perfect', as often with that verb (KG I 136–7, SD 274).

οὔτι μὴ μόλῃς πάλιν: The MSS give the unmetrical τήνδ' οὐ μὴ μόλῃς πόλιν (L), or τήνδε μὴ μόλῃς πόλιν (fere ΔQ et Tr³ [τήνδ' ἐμὴ O]), which neither as a prohibition nor as a positive statement of anxiety ('I fear you may ...') makes any sense. Wecklein, Murray, Diggle, Kovacs and Liapis (cf. 'Notes', 53–4) thus read Cobet's οὔτι μή (*VL²*, 583) with Reiske's πάλιν for πόλιν (*Animadversiones*, 86–7), all others τήνδε μὴ οὐ μόλῃς πόλιν (G. H. Schaefer, *Euripidis Tragoediae* III, Leipzig 1811, 85). This is only a step away from the paradosis on the assumption that, as often, μὴ οὐ in synizesis was reduced to μή, and οὐ then wrongly reinserted in the L(P)-branch from an earlier corrector's interlinear note (Feickert on 115, Mastronarde *apud* M. Fantuzzi, *BMCR* 2006.02.18, on 115). Yet a strong future denial with οὐ μή (KG II 221–2, SD 317) rather than the milder expression of fear or suspicion with μὴ οὐ (KG I 224, SD 317)[55] is desired in Aeneas' urgent attempt to dissuade Hector from his plan. Also, τήνδε ... πόλιν ill suits the setting on the Trojan plain and could as well be a scribe's as the poet's reminiscence of *Il.* 12.73–4 οὐκέτ' ἔπειτ' ὀΐω οὐδ' ἄγγελον ἀπονέεσθαι / ἄψορρον προτὶ ἄστυ (cf. Jouan 61 n. 28, Fantuzzi [above]). Once πάλιν (~ ἄψορρον) had become πόλιν (cf. e.g. *Sept.* 613, *OC* 426, E. *Suppl.* 460), it was easy to supply τήνδε for clarification, which then corrupted the negatives in various ways. Apart from *Phoen.* 725 (above), Cobet's and Reiske's text has a parallel at *IA* 1464 ... καὶ πάλιν γ' οὐ μὴ μόλω.

116–18. The Trojans do break the poles (not axles) of their chariots when they take headlong flight through the Greek ditch in *Il.* 16.367–71. Polydamas especially warned of the pointed stakes (σκόλοπες) that lined its inner crest: *Il.* 12.63–4 ~ 12.54–7 (with Hainsworth). The 'causeways', γέφυραι (117n.), are not mentioned in the *Iliad*, but at 12.118–19 εἴσατο γὰρ νηῶν ἐπ' ἀριστερά, τῇ περ Ἀχαιοί / ἐκ πεδίου νίσοντο σὺν ἵπποισιν καὶ ὄχεσφιν 'the poet seems to envisage some means of passing the ditch in front of the gate' (Hainsworth), and the same must be true whenever men and/or chariots cross it without apparent trouble

---

[55] This is found in tragedy only at *Tro.* 981–2 μὴ ἀμαθεῖς ποίει θεάς / τὸ σὸν κακὸν κοσμοῦσα, μὴ <οὐ> πείσῃς σοφούς (suppl. Seidler). More commonly independent μή + subjunctive of something that *may* happen (above): A. *Suppl.* 357 (with FJW on 375–8), 399–400, *Ag.* 131–4, 341–2 (with Fraenkel on 341), *Alc.* 315–16, *HF* 1399, *Or.* 776 (μὴ <οὐ> Brunck).

(*Il.* 8.254–5, 10.194, 198, 564). Perhaps our poet thought of *Il.* 15.357–8, where Apollo 'made a large and wide causeway' (... γεφύρωσεν δὲ κέλευθον / μακρὴν ἠδ' εὐρεῖαν ...) for the Trojans by kicking in the spoil-heaps on either side of the trench.

A deep ford is the problem that Eteocles recognises in *Phoen.* 730 βαθύς γέ τοι Διρκαῖος ἀναχωρεῖν πόρος (with Mastronarde on 730–1).

116. περάσει ... ἐν τροπῇ στρατός: so rightly ΔQ (-εις Va²). L has περάσεις ... δορός, doubtless by reminiscence of 82 (n.) ... ἐν τροπῇ δορός.

σκόλοπας: 116–18n. The plural in the sense 'palisade' is Homeric (*Il.* 7.441, 8.343, 9.350, 12.55, 63, 15.1, 344 [all of the Achaean fort], *Il.* 18.177, *Od.* 7.45 [the townwalls of Troy and Scheria]) and in other classical literature occurs only at Hdt. 9.97 and Xen. *An.* 5.2.5 (LSJ s.v. σκόλοψ I 1). Euripides refers to σκόλοψ as an instrument for impaling (*El.* 898, *IT* 1430, E. fr. 878).[56]

117. γεφύρας: Most broadly, in Homer, 'γέφυρα ... is a mound of earth either along or across a ditch or river-bed' (Kirk on *Il.* 5.87–8). So 'causeways' seem to be meant here (116–18n.) rather than separately constructed 'bridges' over the moat.

διαβαλοῦσ': 'pass over, cross' with an accusative of space (LSJ s.v. I 2).

ἱππηλάται ('charioteers') again evokes epic, where ἱππηλάτα is a 'quasi-title of old and legendary heroes' (*LfgrE* s.v. B). Aeschylus uses the word adjectivally at *Pers.* 126–7 πᾶς γὰρ ἱππηλάτας / καὶ πεδοστιβὴς λεώς ('cavalry and infantry'), and a trace of it presumably remains in A. fr. 36b 4.3].ηλάτην (ἱππηλάτην Siegmann), ascribed by Lobel to *Glaucus Potnieus*, the third play of the tetralogy that included *Persians*.

118. '... without shattering the axle-boxes of their chariots.'

ἢν ἄρα μή: sc. διαβάλωσι. There have long been objections to this unique variant of εἰ μὴ ἄρα (*nisi forte*), which itself is unattested in drama. But none of the conjectures (Wecklein, *Appendix*, 49) or reinterpretations (like ἢν ἄρα, μή = εἴπερ ἄρα, μή, 'if at all, without ...' [Wilamowitz, *Hermes* 61 (1926) 288 = *KS* IV, 415]) are convincing, and it seems that we must accept the expression here (Fraenkel, *Rev.* 239; cf. Liapis on 117–18). For ἆρα as a metrical equivalent to ἄρα in poetry see LSJ s.v. ἆρα A II and *GP* 44–6.

θραύσαντες ἀντύγων χνόας: M. Magnani (*Paideia* 56 [2001], 107–11) well exposed the difficulties of this phrase, which had already received a (rather desperate) note in Cyr. / Hsch. α 5546 Latte ἀντύγων

---

[56] *Ba.* 982–4 μάτηρ πρῶτά νιν λευρᾶς ἀπὸ πέτρας / †ἢ σκόλοπος† ὄψεται / δοκεύοντα is corrupt (Dodds on 982–4). For σκολοπισμός see *Rh.* 512–17n.

χνόαι· αἱ περιφέρειαι τοῦ ἅρματος, οἱ τροχοί (~ *Suda* α 2660 Adler ἀντιγόχνοιαι [ἀντυγ- M^ec]: οἱ τροχοὶ τοῦ ἅρματος). For while ἄντυξ, 'chariot-rail' (LSJ s.v. I 2), could by metonymy stand for the vehicle as such (*Rh.* 238 [n.], Call. *Dian.* 140–1), it is strange to see it in that function here, where χνόαι ('naves' or 'axle-boxes') denotes precisely a part of the whole. Blaydes (*Adversaria Critica*, 2 ~ *Analecta Tragica*, 128) proposed ἀξόνων on the model of *Sept.* 153 ἔλακον ἀξόνων βριθομένων χνόαι, S. *El.* 745–6 ἔθραυσε δ' ἄξονος μέσας χνόας, / κἀξ ἀντύγων ὤλισθε and Ar. *Nub.* 1264–5 ... ὦ τύχαι θραυσάντυγες / ἵππων ἐμῶν (~ Xenocl. I *TrGF* 33 F 2 + T 1). But the error is not easily explained, unless indeed S. *El.* 745–6 comes in from scribal reminiscence or a gloss. Most likely, therefore, and given the antiquity of the transmitted text, the expression goes back to the poet himself, who recalled Sophocles' celebrated account of Orestes' 'death' (*El.* 680–763) and joined the key terms of its climax in an unusual way (A. Fries, *CQ* n.s. 60 [2010], 345–51, Introduction, 36).

119–22. If they are victorious, the Trojans will have to face Achilles, who will not idly watch the destruction of the camp (cf. *Il.* 9.650–5). This is also Polydamas' fear when he advises Hector to rally his men at *Il.* 13.744–7 ἦ γὰρ ἐγώ γε / δείδω, μὴ τὸ χθιζὸν ἀποστήσωνται Ἀχαιοί / χρεῖος, ἐπεὶ παρὰ νηυσὶν ἀνὴρ ἆτος πολέμοιο / μίμνει, ὃν οὐκέτι πάγχυ μάχης σχήσεσθαι ὀΐω. Similarly, in his last speech, Polydamas (unsuccessfully) proposes to return to the city because Achilles has re-emerged and will now fight to the end (*Il.* 18.254–83).

119. νικῶν δ': 115n. (νικώμενος μέν).

ἔφεδρον: a sporting metaphor, which presents Achilles as a formidable (and well-rested) opponent. The ἔφεδρος was a wrestler, boxer or pancratiast who had drawn a bye and 'sat by' a fight, ready to take on the winner in the following round: e.g. Pi. *Nem.* 4.96, *Cho.* 866–8 (with Garvie), Ar. *Ran.* 791–4, Xen. *An.* 2.5.10 (LSJ s.v. II 4). In comparison with *Phoen.* 1095 ἐφέδρους <δ'> ἱππότας ('reserve'), the word gains special emphasis here, as one man is said to be 'waiting for' an entire host.

Later in the play ἔφεδρος (954) and ἐφεδρεύω (768) appear in the non-technical sense of a 'besieging' army (768–9, 954–6nn.).

120–1. The relative clause perhaps echoes *Il.* 13.747 (ἀνὴρ ἆτος πολέμοιο) ... ὃν οὐκέτι πάγχυ μάχης σχήσεσθαι ὀΐω (119–22, 122nn.).

ναυσὶν ἐμβαλεῖν φλόγα: Cf. *Rh.* 990 (989b–92n.) ... ναυσὶν αἶθον ἐμβαλεῖν and, for the verse-end alone, *Alc.* 4 ... στέρνοισιν ἐμβαλὼν φλόγα. Aeneas did not hear Hector's threat against the ships at 60–2, but it is easy to assume that he voiced this more than once.

Ἀχαιοὺς ὡς δοκεῖς ἀναρπάσαι: For ἀναρπάζω in the sense 'seize by storm' or 'ravage' (people) see Hdt. 8.28 οἳ δὲ ὡς ἀναρπασόμενοι τοὺς Φωκέας φερόμενοι ἐσέπεσον ἐς τοὺς ἀμφορέας, 9.59.2, *Batr.* 264

οὗτος ἀναρπάξαι βατράχων γενεὴν ἐπαπείλει, D. H. 5.22.3, 5.44.4, 7.4.1 (LSJ s.v. ἀναρπάζω III).

122. 'For the man is fiery and of towering boldness.'

The verse combines, and translates into tragic language, Polydamas' descriptions of Achilles at *Il.* 13.746 ἀνὴρ ἆτος πολέμοιο and 18.262 οἷος ἐκείνου θυμὸς ὑπέρβιος.

αἴθων γὰρ ἀνήρ: Of the human temperament αἴθων, 'fiery, burning', is first attested in *Sept.* 447–8 ἀνὴρ ... / αἴθων ... λῆμα and *Ai.* 221/2 ἀνδρὸς αἴθονος (with Finglass on 221/2–222/3), 1088 αἴθων ὑβριστής, all of which could have been in our poet's mind (cf. Fraenkel, *Rev.* 231, Hutchinson on *Sept.* 448). One also thinks of the many fire similes that are applied to Homeric heroes, especially perhaps *Il.* 13.53 (~ 13.330, 688, 17.88, 18.154, 20.423) φλογὶ εἴκελος (ἀλκήν) and, of Achilles, *Il.* 20.371–2 τοῦ δ' ἐγὼ ἀντίος εἶμι, καὶ εἰ πυρὶ χεῖρας ἔοικεν, / εἰ πυρὶ χεῖρας ἔοικε, μένος δ' αἴθωνι σιδήρῳ (H. Fränkel, *Die homerischen Gleichnisse*, Göttingen 1921, 49–52).

For the etymology and semantics of αἴθων (< αἴθομαι, αἴθω) see O. Levaniouk, *HSPh* 100 (2000), 25–51 (26–36), who argues convincingly that 'fiery, burning' (LSJ s.v. I) takes precedence over all other meanings which have been assigned to the word (LSJ s.v. II of metals: 'flashing, glittering', III of animals: 'red-brown, tawny').

καὶ πεπύργωται θράσει: literally 'and towers in boldness' (cf. LSJ s.v. πυργόω II). The closest parallels are *Or.* 1567–8 οὗτος σύ ... / Μενέλαον εἶπον, ὃς πεπύργωσαι θράσει, *HF* 238 ... οἷς πεπύργωσαι λόγοις (with Bond) and *Pers.* 192 χἣ μὲν τῇδ' ἐπυργοῦτο στολῇ (of a horse). In all these places 'lofty pride' is the predominant notion, although here at least it gives cause for real concern. So Ajax is called a πύργος in *Od.* 11.556 (~ Callin. fr. 1.18–21 *IEG*). Cf. A. W. H. Adkins, *HSPh* 81 (1977), 74 with n. 48, H. Bernsdorff, *ZPE* 158 (2006), 3 and, for the motif in general, West, *IEPM* 454–5.

Murray, Porter[1], Zanetto and Jouan read καὶ πεπύργωται χερί (VaLgB) on the hypothesis (stated by the first two)[57] that θράσει intruded from *Or.* 1568. But the instrumental dative with πυργόω always refers to an external 'force' (add E. *Suppl.* 997–8, Ion *TrGF* 19 F 63.1 and Ar. *Pax* 749–50 to the examples quoted), and in view also of *Il.* 18.262 οἷος ἐκείνου θυμὸς ὑπέρβιος (above), our poet would have had no reason to change the phrase. Yet the process of corruption may have been the same, since χερί stands at the end of *Or.* 1567.

123–4. 'No, let us allow the army to sleep quietly by their shields (and rest) from the toils of deadly warfare.'

---

57 In his second edition ('Addenda et Corrigenda', liv) Porter comes to favour θράσει (OgV).

ἀλλά: 70–1n. Aeneas suggests the exact opposite of Hector's 'call for action'.

παρ' ἀσπίδας / εὕδειν: Cf. 20–2 (n.) οὐκ οἶσθα δορὸς πέλας Ἀργείου / νυχίαν ἡμᾶς / κοίτην πανόπλους κατέχοντας; and 739–40 ποῦ δῆθ' Ἕκτωρ / τὸν ὑπασπίδιον κοῖτον ἰαύει; Unlike the Thracians in our play (762–9, 792nn.), the Trojans keep their equipment well-ordered and ready for use (cf. *Il.* 10.75–7, 150–3, 471–3).

ἐκ κόπων ἀρειφάτων: '(to get a rest) from ...', as implied in εὕδειν. More clearly S. *El.* 231 οὐδέ ποτ' ἐκ καμάτων ἀποπαύσομαι.

For ἀρείφατος in tragedy cf. *Eum.* 913–14 τῶν ἀρειφάτων ... / ... ἀγώνων, A. fr. 146b καὶ καρτερὸς γὰρ καὶ ᴗ – ἀρείφατος (~ fr. 147 ἀρείφατον λῆμα?), E. *Suppl.* 603–4 ἀρείφατοι / φόνοι and E. fr. 741a]. .π[. . . .]ω.[. .]ῳς ἀρείφατο[ς] τισ̣[. Epic ἀρηίφατος means 'slain in war' (*Il.* 19.31, 24.415, *Od.* 11.41, Heraclit. 22 B 24 DK,[58] Opp. *Hal.* 3.562), and while the dramatists used the word almost like ἄρειος (Sideras, *Aeschylus Homericus*, 50, Collard on E. *Suppl.* 603–7), we need not suppose that the second element lost all its force. Some association with 'killing' probably remained (Porter on 124 [with 'Addenda et Corrigenda' ([2]1929), lv], FJW on A. *Suppl.* 633).

Klyve (on 124) prefers πόνων (Δ) to κόπων (Λ). The latter indeed appears as a gloss on πόνος and the like (FJW on A. *Suppl.* 209), but must be the *lectio difficilior* here. In 763–4 the Thracians are said to have slept πεδοστιβεῖ / κόπῳ δαμέντες.

125–30. On Aeneas' role in proposing to send out a spy and its relationship to *Iliad* 10 see 85–148n. In tragedy cf. *Sept.* 36–8 σκοποὺς δὲ κἀγὼ καὶ κατοπτῆρας στρατοῦ / ἔπεμψα, τοὺς πέποιθα μὴ ματᾶν ὁδῷ· / καὶ τῶνδ' ἀκούσας οὔ τι μὴ ληφθῶ δόλῳ and *Hcld.* 337–8 πρῶτα μὲν σκοπούς / πέμψω πρὸς αὐτόν, μὴ λάθῃ με προσπεσών.

125–6a. κατάσκοπον δὲ πολεμίων: likewise 140 (n.) ... πολεμίων κατάσκοπον and 809 ... πολεμίων κατάσκοποι (of the Greeks, i.e. with a subjective genitive). Owing mainly to its theme (Ritchie 218), *Rhesus* has six further cases of κατάσκοπος (129, 505, 524, 592, 645, 657), which, like κατασκοπή and κατασκοπέω, probably entered later dramatic idiom from prose. Cf. *Phil.* 45, *Hec.* 239 (= *Rh.* 505), *Hel.* 1607, *Ba.* 838, 916, 956, 981, fr. tr. adesp. 712.13,[59] Lyc. 784, Ar. *Thesm.* 588 (paratragic), Antiph. fr. 274.2 *PCG*, Men. *Peric.* 295 (Pritchett, *GSW* I, 130, who is wrong to say that κατάσκοπος occurs once in Homer).

---

[58] Cf. [Heraclit.] 22 B 136 DK = *Orac. Chald.* 159.2 des Places ψυχαὶ ἀρηίφατοι καθερώτεραι ἢ ἐνὶ νούσοις.

[59] This piece has also been assigned to iambus, but see *TrGF* II, 297. Fr. tr. adesp. 733 fr. a 14 (= *FGrHist* 153 IV 7.10) does not preserve, or never has been, original tragic verse.

126b–7. κἂν μὲν αἴρωνται φυγήν: 53–5n. Wecklein in his edition (~ *Textkritische Studien*, 14) wrote ἄρωνται, but the durative aspect of the present is desired here. The MSS' φυγῇ, corrected by Stephanus (*Annotationes*, 116), may have arisen after 54 ... ἀρεῖσθαι φυγῇ (φυγήν Stephanus) or from θέλῃ in 125.

Ἀργείων στρατῷ: 56–8n.

128–30a. ἐς δόλον τιν': Cf. 91–2 ... μῶν τις πολεμίων ἀγγέλλεται / δόλος κρυφαῖος ἑστάναι κατ' εὐφρόνην;

φρυκτωρία: 53–5n.

130b. τήνδ' ἔχω γνώμην, ἄναξ: Such short, affirmative statements often conclude a speech in drama: e.g. *Ag.* 582, A. fr. 47a.21 (*Diktyoulkoi*) πάντ' ἔχει[ς] λόγον, *Eum.* 710, *Or.* 1203 εἴρηται λόγος, *Phil.* 389 λόγος λέλεκται πᾶς, Men. *Epitr.* 292 εἴρηκα τόν γ' ἐμὸν λόγον (Collard, 'Supplement', 376). Cf. Athena at 640 καὶ ταῦτ' ἐγὼ μὲν εἶπον.

O's τήνδ' ἔχω προθυμίαν makes no sense here. The phrase fills the same position in *Alc.* 1107, followed by 1108 νίκα νυν· οὐ μὴν ἁνδάνοντά μοι ποιεῖς, which shares two words with *Rh.* 137 νικᾷς, ἐπειδὴ πᾶσιν ἁνδάνει τάδε.

131–6 ~ 195–200. This is the first of two pairs of separated but responding stanzas in *Rhesus*. Yet unlike 454–66 ~ 820–32 (n.), which spans nearly half the play, the present pair remains confined to one 'act' (85–223). Among other tragic instances of divided song (*Hipp.* 362–72 ~ 669–79, *Or.* 1353–65 ~ 1537–48, *Phil.* 391–402 ~ 507–18, *OC* 833–43 ~ 876–86),[60] the closest in form and function is *Phil.* 391–402 ~ 505–18, where twice within the long first epeisodion (*Phil.* 219–675) the chorus support Neoptolemus (cf. *Phil.* 146–9 ὁπόταν δὲ μόλῃ / δεινὸς ὁδίτης τῶνδ' οὐκ μελάθρων, / πρὸς ἐμὴν αἰεὶ χεῖρα προχωρῶν / πειρῶ τὸ παρὸν θεραπεύειν). Similarly here the sentries intervene at important stages in the plot (Ritchie 328). With Aeneas' proposal to dispatch a spy the action is about to take a major turn (85–148n.), and it will be the passionate strophe that tips the scales (131–6, 137–46nn.). The antistrophe, on the other hand, comes when everything is settled (or so it appears). The chorus praise Dolon for his audacity and the glorious reward he has secured. Only a touch of scepticism hints at the disaster ahead (195–200n.).

---

[60] The phenomenon is far more frequent in comedy (West, *GM* 80). Passages like *Sept.* 369–652, where three strophic pairs near-symmetrically alternate with the Scout's descriptions of the Seven and Eteocles' replies, or *Ag.* 1401–47, where two choral remarks (1407–11 ~ 1426–30) punctuate Clytaemestra's iambic speeches, are perhaps better regarded as epirrhematic compositions (Ritchie 330). But one may add to the cases above S. fr. 314.243–50 ~ 290–7 and 329–37 ~ 371–9 from the satyric *Ichneutae*.

It is noteworthy, though not surprising, that most separated odes in tragedy belong to the iambo-dochmiac class. Like many astrophic lyrics ('act-dividing' or not), their individual stanzas are designed as spontaneous outbursts in response to the preceding scene or speech, and the audience, after hearing the strophe, will not automatically expect an antistrophe to follow later in the play. One partial exception to this 'rule' is *Rh.* 454–66 ~ 820–32, which combines iambo-dochmiacs with a longer dactylo-epitrite run.

Metre

131–6 ~ 195–200. Dochmio-iambic (cf. above). Apart from the slightly unusual verse 131 (131/195n.), the composition is plain, with strict metrical responsion throughout. The two most common forms of dochmiac (⏑⏕–⏑– and ⏑–––⏑–) predominate.

131	195	⏑⏕–⏑⏕⏑⏕–⏑–∣	2δ∣
132	196	⏑⏕–⏑–∣⏑–––⏑–∣	δ∣δ∣
133–4	197–8	⏑⏕–⏑–⏑⏕–⏑–⏑–––⏑–∣	3δ∣
135	199	⏑⏕⏑⏕⏑–⏑–∣	2ia∣
136	200	⏕⏑–⏑–⏑–⏑–––⏑–∥∣	˰ia ia (lec) δ ∥∣

Notes

131/195 The strophe (131) has split resolution in the final element of the first dochmiac, which is very rare, especially in forms other than ⏑⏕ ⏕⏑⏕ (L. P. E. Parker, *CQ* n.s. 18 [1968], 267–8, Diggle, *Euripidea*, 378 n. 53, with *HF* 1070, *Tro.* 253 and maybe *Andr.* 842). Equally notable, if of less rhythmical import, is the four-syllable 'overlap' between the two dochmiacs (τάδε δοκεῖ, τάδε με∣ταθέμενος νόει), caused by the long participle and paralleled only at *Sept.* 692–3 ... ἵμερος ἐξοτρύ- / νει πικρόκαρπον ἀνδροκτασίαν τελεῖν, *Phoen.* 176 (though see Diggle's apparatus and Mastronarde [p. 177]) and again *HF* 1070 ἀπόκρυφον δέμας ὑπὸ μέλαθρον κρύψω (making it closest in shape to our line).[61]

---

[61] Unless we read and divide with Willink (*CQ* n.s. 38 [1988], 96 = *Collected Papers*, 113–14): *HF* 1068/9–70 (Χο.) ὦ πρέσβυ. (Αμ.) σῖγα σῖγα, παλίντροπος ἐξεγειρόμενος στρέφεται· / φέρ', ἀπόκρυφα (Willink: -ον L) δέμας ὑπὸ μέλαθρον κρύψω. Changing ἀπόκρυφον avoids creating by emendation split resolution in iambics or a *dochmius Kaibelianus*, depending on whether one takes 1070 φέρ', ... as *2ia mol* or *kδ δ*. But the adjective seems better with δέμας, and it is in any case not clear that the usual colometry is inadmissible because of placing period-end after 'hortatory' φέρε (Wilamowitz) in 1069.

The responding word-end after the second long (131 τάδε δοκεῖ | ... ~ 195 μέγας ἀγών | ...) may be the reason why some have preferred (or envisaged) the analysis ˌia | lec (cf. Schroeder² 167, Ritchie 299, Dale, MATC III, 150, Zanetto 66). 'But the sequel should leave us in no doubt that the verse is dochmiac' (Willink, 'Cantica', 26 n. 19 = Collected Papers, 565 n. 19).

133–4/197–8 The continuous run of dochmiacs makes line-division a mere typographical choice.

135/199 Willink ('Cantica', 26 = Collected Papers, 565) calls this a 'characteristic "sub-dochmiac" iambic dimeter (tolerant of split resolutions)'. But while cola of the shape ⏑ ⏑⏑ ⏑ ⏑⏑ ⏑ – ⏑ – are indeed frequent with dochmiacs (West, GM 112), nothing invites us to believe that the context would make them more susceptible to 'splits'. Of the cases Willink cites (also ed. Orestes, 113 and CQ n.s. 49 [1999], 420 = Collected Papers, 289), some are textually suspect or admit of alternative scansions (Sept. 157 ~ 165, Or. 329 ~ 345, 1253 ~ 1273),⁶² others have no (real) split resolutions at all (Ag. 1091 ~ 1096, Cho. 155, Hipp. 878,⁶³ Hec. 1031, Rh. 693 ~ 711). Moreover, the phenomenon occurs in various surroundings.

136/200 The line should be taken as ˌia ia (lec) δ, not δ ia | ˌia with Conomis (Hermes 92 [1964], 46), Diggle, Kovacs, Liapis and, hesitantly, Pace (Canti, 24) and Feickert. ⏑ – ⏑ – – ⏑ – is not unusual (especially in Aeschylus), but never, it seems, ends a stanza or ode. And if the lecythion here is iambic instead of catalectic trochaic (see West, GM 99–100), there is no objection to having it run over in synartesis, as also, against Diggle, at E. El. 1153–4 ~ 1161–2 ˌia ia (lec)] δ (Willink, 'Cantica', 26 = Collected Papers, 565–6). For the clausular dochmiac preceded by 2ia | or lec | cf. Cho. 944–5 and Med. 1281 ~ 1292.

As in Rh. 454–66 ~ 820–32 (p. 293), response extends to the wording with a series of structural and/or phonetic echoes, doubtless reflecting musical phrases: 131 τάδε ... τάδε ~ 195 μέγας ... μεγάλα, 134 κατόπταν μολεῖν ~ 198 γαμβρὸν πέλειν, 136 δαίεται ~ 200 φαίνεται. Also, Rh. 131 ~ 195 may be included in the list of examples where word-repetition in dochmiacs does not (quite) follow a specific pattern (Diggle, Euripidea, 296–7, 376–8).⁶⁴

---

62 See L. P. E. Parker, CQ n.s. 18 (1968), 241–2, 253 and Diggle, apparatus Or. 329–30, 345–6.
63 I.e. with Willink's colometry at Hipp. 877–8 βοᾷ βοᾷ δέλτος ἀλασ- / τα· πᾷ φύγω βάρος κακῶν; / ἀπὸ γὰρ ὀλόμενος οἴχομαι (CQ n.s. 49 [1999], 420 = Collected Papers, 289; cf. Diggle, Euripidea, 475–6 n. 158). The split would be virtually non-existent between ἀπό and γάρ.
64 It falls short of Diggle's category (c) (Euripidea, 377) in that the words repeated from the beginning do not conclude their respective dochmiacs.

131–6. Like *Phil.* 391–402 ~ 507–18 and *Rh.* 454–66, this choral strophe replaces the normal two- or three-trimeter comment after a major speech. As such, it stands out for its bias and the freedom with which the sentries criticise Hector's judgement. Their lack of deference, especially for a chorus of soldiers, has been considered dramatically superfluous and even a reflection of Macedonian army ἰσηγορία (cf. Introduction, 19, 20; also Liapis on 137). But Hector is bound to accept Aeneas' plan (or the plot could not return to *Iliad* 10), and by giving the chorus a vital role, our poet characterises his general as not only rash, but also susceptible to pressure from below (85–148, 137–46nn.). We shall see manifestations of both traits throughout the play.

131. τάδε δοκεῖ, τάδε … νόει: Dawe's δόκει (*apud* Diggle) would reinforce the chorus' appeal (and the linguistic parallelism), but the imperative of this verb usually takes an infinitive construction (e.g. *PV* 436–7, S. *El.* 312–13, *Alc.* 53, *Rh.* 665, 940; implied at Ar. *Thesm.* 208), and we should expect a reaction to Aeneas' speech first. Cf. Liapis, 'Notes', 54.

μεταθέμενος: 'change one's mind, retract' (LSJ s.v. μετατίθημι II 4 a). Hn alone is right here against Ω's μετατιθέμενος (Introduction, 50).

132. 'I do not like a general excercising his authority in a way that risks disaster.'

The sentries turn into personal criticism what has been expressed in a gnomic fashion or context at *Phoen.* 599 ἀσφαλὴς γάρ ἐστ' ἀμείνων ἢ θρασὺς στρατηλάτης, E. *Suppl.* 508–9 σφαλερὸν ἡγεμὼν θρασύς / νεώς τε ναύτης (with Collard on 508b–10) and E. fr. 194.3–4 ἐγὼ γὰρ οὔτε ναυτίλον φιλῶ / τολμῶντα λίαν οὔτε προστάτην χθονός. Their exceptional frankness (131–6n.) is reminiscent of Archil. fr. 114 *IEG* οὐ φιλέω μέγαν στρατηγὸν οὐδὲ διαπεπλιγμένον / οὐδὲ βοστρύχοισι γαῦρον οὐδ' ὑπεξυρημένον, / ἀλλά μοι σμικρός τις εἴη καὶ περὶ κνήμας ἰδεῖν / ῥοικός, ἀσφαλέως βεβηκὼς ποσσί, καρδίης πλέως (where note the verbal overlaps with our passages in the first and fourth line). For another Archilochian echo see 166n.

σφαλερά: i.e. 'likely to make one stumble / trip' (LSJ s.v. σφαλερός I), since the chorus fear that Hector will lead the army astray (cf. 110–11). But with persons especially it is often difficult to distinguish between this active sense of σφαλερός and the middle-passive 'ready to fall, uncertain, fallible' (cf. LSJ s.v. II, III, Stockert on *IA* 21).

δ' stands for γάρ as not infrequently in poetry and very seldom in prose (*GP* 169–70). Cf. 182, 618, 626, 635, 647, 852, 965.

στρατηγῶν κράτη comes close to βίη Ἡρακληείη and the like (KG I 280–1): 'generals in their position of authority'. For κράτος more directly of powerful individuals see 821–3n.

133–6. 'For what is better than to have a swiftly-pacing spy go near the ships (to see) why the enemy are burning watch-fires in front of their naval station?'

133–5a. ταχυβάταν: a *hapax*, albeit of regular formation. Cf. A. fr. 280 (Hsch. α 8338 Latte) αὐριβάτας, 'swift-striding', *Pers.* 1072, Bacch. 3.48 ἁβροβάτης, 'soft-stepping', and also e.g. [Arist.] *Phgn.* 813a 7, 9 ταχυβάμων. It may have been in tragic use before *Rhesus*.

κατόπταν: 631–2n. Given the form, Hsch. κ 1840 Latte κατόπταν· κατάσκοπον belongs either here or to 557–8 ναῶν / ... κατόπτην (Wecklein: -ταν Ω).

135b–6. ὅτι ποτ' ἄρα ... / ... δαίεται: The indirect question, which easily attaches to the verbal noun κατόπταν (Porter on 134 ff.), seems to have been inspired by *Il.* 9.75–7 μάλα δὲ χρεὼ πάντας Ἀχαιούς / ἐσθλῆς καὶ πυκινῆς (*sc.* βουλῆς), ὅτι δήϊοι ἐγγύθι νηῶν / καίουσιν πυρὰ πολλά. The particle ἄρα adds a sense of urgency or excitement (*GP* 39–40, LSJ s.v. B 2).

κατ' ἀντίπρῳρα: 'in front of' or 'face to face' (LSJ s.v. ἀντίπρῳρος 2). Compounds with πρῷρα were often used 'metaphorically to indicate simply the forward end of something' (Fraenkel on *Ag.* 235). Yet in the context here, and despite the fact that ships were drawn ashore stern first, one also recalls the literal meaning, common in the historians, 'with the prow towards' (LSJ s.v. 1; cf. Denniston on E. *El.* 846). For κατά (with accusative), 'along, opposite', see LSJ s.v. B I 3, KG I 477–8, SD 473–4 and e.g. *Rh.* 371, 421 κατ' ὄμμα, 409, 491, 511 κατὰ στόμα.

ναυστάθμων for the Achaean naval camp recurs in 244, 448, 582, 591, 602 and 673. The accusatives at 244 and 602 prove it to be neuter as in Thuc. 3.6.2 and presumably 6.49.4 ναύσταθμον δὲ ἐπαναχωρήσαντας. Later a masculine form is attested and the preferences of authors vary. As a technical term the word is otherwise confined to prose.

δαίεται: The assonance with δαΐοις is noteworthy (Feickert on 135), particularly since καίεται, after *Il.* 9.77 (above), would have scanned as well (and was indeed conjectured by Hartung [17 (1852), 123]). It is unclear, however, whether δάϊος and δαίω are related (*GEW, DELG* s.v. δήιος) and/or whether the ancients saw them that way.

137–46. Hector betrays his military weakness by giving in not to Aeneas' (apparently) sound advice, but to the majority of the ranks (85–148, 131–6nn.). His entire response, moreover, is built on Aeneas' plan for action (123–30), except that the inverse position and extended treatment of a possible enemy escape (126–7 ~ 143–6) show that this topic is still foremost in his mind. Numerous verbal echoes (140, 141–2, 143–5a, 145b–6nn.) bear further witness to his lack of independent thought.

137. νικᾷς: Bothe (5 [1803], 288) for νικᾶτ' (Ω, *Chr. Pat.* 498). With this very small change, rejected by Zanetto (Feickert) and Jouan,[65] our verse becomes an appropriate first reply to Aeneas' speech (Bothe; cf. M. Fantuzzi, *BMCR* 2006.02.18, on 137) and largely conforms to the rule that 'characters do not ... allude to what is said in choral odes' (Stevens, *Andromache*, 114, who notes *OT* 216 as an exception). The expression follows E. *Suppl.* 947–8 νικᾷς. μένειν χρὴ τλημόνως· λέγει γὰρ εὖ / Θησεύς and *Hyps.* fr. 20/21.13 Bond = E. fr. 754b.13 [ν]ικᾷ[ς]· ἐῶ δὴ τοῦτ[ό] <γ'>· ἀλλ̣ [ἀ]πέρχομαι (init. suppl. Wilamowitz). In both these passages the speaker gracefully concedes a point after brief discussion, which throws into even sharper relief the bathos in Hector's change of mind.

ἐπειδὴ πᾶσιν ἁνδάνει τάδε: 'since everybody agrees on this.' The verb brings out the contrast with *Il.* 12.80 = 13.748 ὣς φάτο Πουλυδάμας, ἅδε δ' Ἕκτορι μῦθος ἀπήμων (105–30n.). ἁνδάνω of collective opinion seems to be Herodotean: 4.145.5 Λακεδαιμονίοισι δὲ ἕαδε δέκεσθαι τοὺς Μινύας ἐπ' οἷσι θέλουσι αὐτοί, 4.153, 4.201.2, 6.106.3, 9.19.1 (LSJ s.v. ἁνδάνω II with Suppl. [1996], where Hdt. 7.172.1 and 9.5.2 belong under I).

138–9. Hector remains preoccupied with the idea that the army could have been disturbed by their nocturnal assembly (17–18, 87–9nn.). Fear of creating a commotion recurs in 'Arist.' fr. 159.9–12 Rose (*Aporemata Homerica*)[66] as one reason why at *Il.* 10.194–253 the Greek chiefs meet outside the wall (cf. Fantuzzi, in *I luoghi*, 254–5 and *Ancient Scholarship*, 49–53, who improbably advocates a common source for *Rhesus* and 'Aristotle').

κοίμα: Pierson (*Verisimilium* I, 81). OΛ's κόσμει (σκόπει Va) is wrongly defended by Ammendola (on 138–9), Ebener (*WZRostock* 12 [1963], 205) and Zanetto (*Ciclope, Reso*, 139). As at 662 Ἕκτωρ δὲ φροῦδος Θρῇκα κοιμήσων στρατόν (Δ: κοσμ- Λ), the idea of 'putting to rest, calming' is needed here, and κοσμέω in a military context generally means 'order' or 'marshal' troops (LSJ s.v. I 1, Liapis on 138–9). The error may be a simple misreading or an unconscious alteration to a more common phrase.

τάχ' ἂν στρατός / κινοῖτ': 17–18n.

---

[65] Bothe's two German translations of Euripides with textual notes seem to have been unknown to editors before D. Sansone (*GGA* 230 [1978], 237, *QUCC* n.s. 1 [1979], 157–9). Cf. Diggle, *Euripidea*, 518–23.

[66] Porph. ad *Il.* 10.194 ff. (I 146.1–4 Schrader) = Σ^(B*) *Il.* 10.198 (III.432.1–3 Dindorf). Cf. Σ^T *Il.* 10.194 (III 38.57–8 Erbse) ἀλλ' ἐν τῷ στρατεύματι νυκτὸς συνιόντες θόρυβον ἂν ἐκίνησαν, Σ^A *Il.* 10.194 (III 38.64–6 Erbse) διέβη διὰ τῆς τάφρου, ἵνα μὴ θόρυβος ἐν τῷ στρατοπέδῳ γίνηται, τὴν μὲν σύνοδον ὁρώντων, τὴν δὲ αἰτίαν ἀγνοούντων, Porph. ad *Il.* 10.194 ff. (I 146.26–7 Schrader).

140. πέμψω πολεμίων κατάσκοπον: Cf. 125–6 κατάσκοπον δὲ πολεμίων ... / πέμπειν δοκεῖ μοι (137–46nn.). For κατάσκοπος see 125–6a n.

141–2. 'And if we learn of some trick on the enemy's part, you will hear everything and be present to know the report.'

κἂν μέν τιν' ἔχθρων μηχανὴν πυθώμεθα resumes 129 μαθόντες ἐχθρῶν μηχανάς (137–46nn.).

σὺ πάντ' ἀκούσῃ καὶ παρὼν εἴσῃ λόγον: a somewhat tautological variation on the idea that first-hand knowledge is preferable to a later report: *Pers.* 266–7 καὶ μὴν παρών γε κοὐ λόγους ἄλλων κλυών /... φράσαιμ' ἄν (with Garvie), *Cho.* 851–4 (Diggle, *Euripidea*, 81 n. 60). The participle παρών in such cases nearly equals αὐτός, which may or may not also be present (P. von der Mühll, *MH* 19 [1962], 202–3). Cf. 179 (n.) καὶ μὴν λαφύρων γ' αὐτὸς αἱρήσῃ παρών.

Almost the reverse formulation is found at 640–1 (n.) ... ὃν δὲ χρὴ παθεῖν / οὐκ οἶδεν οὐδ' ἤκουσεν ἐγγὺς ὢν λόγου.

λόγον: i.e. the spy's report. λόγους (Δ) perhaps goes back to a scribe who thought of the following 'deliberations' (cf. Liapis on 140–2).

143–5a. 'But if they are rushing off in flight and put to sea, listen out, expecting the trumpet to sound, since I shall not wait.'

ἐὰν δ' ἀπαίρωσ' ἐς φυγὴν ὁρμώμενοι: Cf. 126 ... κἂν μὲν αἴρωνται φυγήν (137–46n.). ἐς φυγήν here goes with ὁρμώμενοι, as in e.g. Hdt. 7.179 προϊδόντες δὲ οὗτοι τὰς νέας τῶν βαρβάρων ἐς φυγὴν ὥρμησαν, Thuc. 3.112.5, Xen. *HG* 5.3.2 and Tim. *Pers.* fr. 791.173–5 *PMG* = Hordern ὁ δὲ ... ὡς ἐσ- / εἶδε Βασιλεὺς εἰς φυγὴν ὁρ- / μῶντα παμμιγῆ στρατόν.

σάλπιγγος αὐδὴν προσδοκῶν καραδόκει: so also Hector at 988–9a (n.) πανοὺς δ' ἔχοντας χρὴ μένειν Τυρσηνικῆς / σάλπιγγος αὐδήν. In tragedy the use of the σάλπιγξ to sound the charge or to call the Athenians to assembly (*Eum.* 567–70) is transferred to the Heroic Age, although Σ^AbT *Il.* 18.219 (IV 474.17–20, 475.36–7, 40–2 Erbse) and Σ^AGeT *Il.* 21.388 (V 216.30–217.35 Erbse) correctly observe that Homer does not grant his own knowledge of the instrument to his characters (West, *Ancient Greek Music*, 119; cf. P. Krentz, in V. D. Hanson [ed.], *Hoplites: The Classical Greek Battle Experience*, London – New York 1991, 113, 115–6).

αὐδή rarely refers to 'sounds other than the human voice' (Liapis on 143–5). But the trumpet's signal just replaces a verbal call to arms.

καραδόκει: 'wait for' (< κάρα + √dek̑, 'receive with outstretched head'?). The verb is frequent in Euripides (never Aeschylus or Sophocles), both in this neutral sense and with the extended notion of 'waiting for the outcome of (e.g. a battle) before deciding how to proceed' (LSJ s.v., Mastronarde on *Med.* 1117). The wording here resembles *Med.* 1116–17 φίλαι, πάλαι τοι προσμένουσα τὴν τύχην / καραδοκῶ τἀκεῖθεν οἳ προβήσεται and *Hel.* 739–40 μένειν τ' ἐπ' ἀκταῖς τούς τ' ἐμοὺς καραδοκεῖν / ἀγῶνας οἳ μένουσί μ'.

ὡς οὐ μενοῦντά μ': For the accusative absolute with 'subjective' ὡς and the participle of a non-impersonal verb see KG II 95–6, SD 402–3. Unequivocal tragic parallels are rare: *OT* 100–1 ἀνδρηλατοῦντας, ἢ φόνῳ φόνον πάλιν / λύοντας, ὡς τόδ' αἷμα χειμάζον πόλιν, *Ion* 964–5 σοὶ δ' ἐς τί δόξ' ἐσῆλθεν ἐκβαλεῖν τέκνον; / – ὡς τὸν θεὸν σώσοντα τόν γ' αὐτοῦ γόνον, *Phoen.* 1461–2 ἡμεῖς μὲν ὡς νικῶντα δεσπότην ἐμόν, / οἳ δ' ὡς ἐκεῖνον. S. *El.* 882 (with Finglass) and *Phoen.* 714 (with Mastronarde) allow other analyses, while *OC* 380–1 and *Hcld.* 693 are corrupt (Ll-J/W, *Sophoclea*, 227–9, *Second Thoughts*, 120–1,[67] Diggle, *Euripidea*, 225–6, Wilkins on *Hcld.* 693).

145b–6. Hector just expands on Aeneas at 127 στείχοντες ἐμπέσωμεν Ἀργείων στρατῷ (137–46n.).

προσμείξω: 'I will go close up to (their slipways)': Thuc. 3.22.1 ἔπειτα προσέμειξαν τῷ τείχει τῶν πολεμίων, 7.70.2 ἐπειδὴ δὲ οἱ ἄλλοι Ἀθηναῖοι προσέμισγον τῷ ζεύγματι (LSJ s.v. προσμείγνυμι II 3). Murray restored the classical -μείξ- for -μίξ- (LSJ s.v. μείγνυμι A I [morphology], West, ed. *Aeschylus*, XLVIII, Threatte II, 623–4).

νεῶν / ὁλκοῖσι: similarly 673 (672b–3a n.) πρὸς ὁλκοὺς ναυστάθμων. The ὁλκοί were channels or stone slips for drawing up or launching ships, not 'windlasses', as in LSJ s.v. I 1. Cf. Hdt. 2.154.5 ἐξ ὧν δὲ ἐξανέστησαν χώρων ἐν τούτοισι δὴ οἵ τε ὁλκοὶ τῶν νεῶν ... τὸ μέχρι ἐμεῦ ἦσαν, 2.159.1, Thuc. 3.15.1 καὶ ὁλκοὺς παρεσκεύαζον τῶν νεῶν ἐν τῷ Ἰσθμῷ ὡς ὑπεροίσοντες ἐκ τῆς Κορίνθου ἐς τὴν πρὸς Ἀθήνας θάλασσαν, A. R. 1.375 ἐν δ' ὁλκῷ ξεστὰς στορέσαντο φάλαγγας, and see L. Casson, *Ships and Seamanship in the Ancient World*, Princeton ¹1971, Baltimore – London ²1995, 363–4. In *Il.* 2.153 the οὐροί ('trenches, channels') must be cleared out before the ships can be put to sea again.

ἐπ' Ἀργείων στρατῷ: 56–8n. Both ἐπί with dative (Δ) and with accusative (Λ) can be used 'in hostile sense' (LSJ s.v. B I 1 c, C I 4, KG I 503, 505, SD 468, 470), but the former is expected when the goal of motion has already been specified with νεῶν / ὁλκοῖσι.

147–8. νῦν γὰρ ἀσφαλῶς φρονεῖς harks back to 132. Strohm (259) compares the rather more chilling *Ba.* 924 (Dionysus to Pentheus) ... νῦν δ' ὁρᾷς ἃ χρή σ' ὁρᾶν.

---

[67] R. Renehan's objection (*CPh* 87 [1992], 373) that πέδον 'refers specifically to the *surface* of the earth' and so cannot denote the soil in which one is buried, is not invalidated by E. *Suppl.* 829 κατά με πέδον γᾶς ἕλοι and *Rh.* 962 οὐκ εἶσι γαίας ἐς μελάγχιμον πέδον. In both places the idea of 'going below' remains.

δ' ἔμ': The implied contrast with Hector favours the emphatic pronoun (Bothe [II (1826), 90], *Chr. Pat.* 1932 pars codd.) over the enclitic δέ μ' (Ω, *Chr. Pat.* 1932 codd. pler.). See Feickert on 148 and, for the use of the different forms in general, KG I 557, SD 186–7.

149–94. After Aeneas' departure, Hector asks for a volunteer to spy on the Greeks (149–53). Dolon agrees on the condition that he be given a suitable reward (154–63). The following dialogue (164–83) reveals that Achilles' horses are the object of his desire. Hector politely grants the wish, although he himself had set an eye on the splendid pair (184–94).

Together with 201–23 (n.) the scene dramatises Hector's assembly in *Il.* 10.299–337. Several points and expressions have direct equivalents in the epic (149–50, 154–5, 156–7a, 186, 189b–90nn.), while at the same time our poet adapted the material to suit his own literary and theatrical needs (cf. Ritchie 67). Most importantly, Dolon himself here raises the subject of a reward (161–2a, 162b–3nn.). In that way, he gives a clearer impression of being driven by gain (although Hector admits that he is only demanding his due), and his request initiates the elaborate 'guessing-game' (below), which like a priamel leads up to his fantastic goal (182–3n.). Hector, by contrast, advertises the expedition as a patriotic service (151, 152–3nn.). This new motif – developed perhaps from *Il.* 10.421–2 Τρωσὶν γὰρ ἐπιτραπέουσι φυλάσσειν· / οὐ γάρ σφιν παῖδες σχεδὸν εἵαται οὐδὲ γυναῖκες (Strohm 259, 265)[68] – helps to elevate not only his own status and that of the mission, but also Dolon's compared to *Iliad* 10. Before we notice his mercenary streak, a natural ability for δόλος (as reflected in his name) and 'love for his city' replace mere swiftness (*Il.* 10.316 ἀλλὰ ποδώκης) as qualifications for the undertaking (158–9a n.). In addition, our poet has suppressed the potentially prejudicial fact that he was the only son among five sisters (*Il.* 10.317),[69] while keeping allusions to his father's nobility and wealth (159b–60, 169–70, 170, 178nn.). One wonders whether his ugliness (*Il.* 10.316) was represented by the mask (Jouan, XXIX).

Characterisation by way of Homeric reminiscence continues in the negotiations about the reward. They are modelled on the proxy exchange between Agamemnon and Achilles in *Il.* 9.115–61 / 225–306 / 308–429, where the latter is offered and rejects in turn gold (*Rh.* 169–70, 170, 178nn.), treasures (171–2n.), spoils (171–2, 179nn.), a royal bride (167–

---

[68] Cf. particularly *Il.* 15.494–9. On 'Patriotism in the Homeric World' see P. A. L. Greenhalgh, *Historia* 21 (1972), 528–37.
[69] Cf. Σ^T *Il.* 10.317 (III 67.85–6 Erbse) ὡς γυναικοτραφὴς δειλὸς ἦν καὶ ῥιψοκίνδυνος (~ Eust. 808.49–50). The adjective ῥιψοκίνδυνος recalls *Rh.* 154–5 (n.) ἐγὼ ... τόνδε κίνδυνον θέλω / ῥίψας κατόπτης ναῦς ἐπ' Ἀργείων μολεῖν.

8, 167nn.) and political power short of the king's position (165–6n.). Both quarrel and contestants lack the Iliadic dimensions, but Hector shows himself a 'better Agamemnon' for being able to subordinate his desire for Achilles' horses (184n.) to the benefit of Troy (M. Fantuzzi, in *I luoghi*, 260–1; cf. R. S. Bond, *AJPh* 117 [1996], 258).[70] The 'guessing-game' itself is more familiar from comedy than extant tragedy (e.g. Ar. *Ach.* 414–31, *Vesp.* 71–88, *Ran.* 52–67) as a means of playing with the audience's expectations and keeping them in suspense as to the actual result.[71]

The scene therefore serves a dual purpose. It has powerful stage-effects and offers a more balanced picture of Hector and Dolon than *Il.* 10.299–337. They are not equals (167–8n.), but neither is Dolon wholly debased, nor does Hector live up to his Homeric self. The comparison with *Iliad* 9 also reduces to proportion the Trojan aspirations for that night. A scouting mission will not win the war, and Dolon in particular overrates himself.

Two questions of stagecraft are of interest here: 1. Where does Dolon come from? and 2. Does Hector stay or leave after 194?

The first can confidently be answered in favour of an entry by an *eisodos*. To have Dolon present already as part of Hector's silent retinue would lead to a procedure unparalleled in Greek drama (Ritchie 113–14; cf. J. P. Poe, *Philologus* 148 [2004], 26). 'Minor characters do not step out of their anonymity just like that, as it were, in order to become a well-defined *dramatis persona* for one short scene' (Kannicht on *Hel.* 1621–41 [p. 423]). In *Helen* this is one of several arguments against the introduction of a male servant instead of the chorus-leader (L) to bar Theoclymenus' way into the palace (1626–41), and Danaus in A. *Suppl.* 1–176, Cassandra in *Ag.* 810–1072 and Alcestis' son in *Alc.* 233–393, all of whom could have been identified before they are named or speak, do not support such a practice either (contrary to Liapis on 154 ff.; cf. S. Perris, *G&R* 59 [2012], 157–8).

A conventional side-entry, by contrast, presents no serious problems. Hector's words can easily be imagined to reach the backstage area, which to the audience's right represents the Trojan camp (Ritchie 114–

---

70 On the 'communal' aspect of Agamemnon's and Achilles' conflict see W. Allan and D. Cairns, in N. Fisher – H. van Wees (eds.), *Competition in the Ancient World*, Swansea 2011, 113–46 (especially 121–30).

71 Cf. M. Fantuzzi – D. Konstan, in E. Bakola *et al.* (eds.), *Greek Comedy and the Discourse of Genres*, Cambridge 2013, 256–74, who relate the device to the 'series of false guesses or assumptions' that feature in several Euripidean plays (e.g. *Alc.* 512–21, 803–21, *Hec.* 667–82) and detect a possible allusion to our scene in Men. *Peric.* 271–91 (Introduction, 44).

15). His initial appeal at 149–50 (n.) τίς δῆτα Τρώων οἳ πάρεισιν ἐν λόγῳ / θέλει ... μολεῖν; resembles that of Apollo for help with searching his stolen cattle at S. fr. 314.39–40 (*Ichneutae*) ἀλλ᾽ εἴτε ποι]μὴν εἴτ᾽ ἀγρωστή[ρων τις ἢ / μαριλοκαυ]τῶν ἐν λόγῳ παρ[ίσταται (suppl. Diggle, Wilamowitz).[72] After four more lines Silenus, followed by the satyr-chorus (63), bursts in. Similarly, Hector's repetitions here may partly be designed to give Dolon time to arrive. Even for slower *eisodos* entries five to seven lines seem to have sufficed, if the newcomer was already becoming visible during the call and spoke his first words before reaching centre-stage. Note *HF* 514–19 (with Bond), *Hyps.* fr. 60 i.16–21 Bond = E. fr. 757.847–52 and Ar. *Ach.* 566–72 (with Olson, lxix). There remains the slight peculiarity of an entry just after another major character (i.e. Aeneas) exited within the same epeisodion. Poe (*Philologus* 148 [2004], 30) compares *Ai.* 989 / 1047, *Phil.* 1260 / 1263 and *Or.* 716 / 729,[73] the last two in late-fifth-century plays and with equally few intervening lines. Our poet also used the device for Paris' surprise appearance at 642 (595–641n.; cf. O. P. Taplin, *GRBS* 12 [1971], 41–2 n. 38).

With 190 Hector falls silent until he is addressed by the Shepherd in 264. The text gives no sign of a departure (J. P. Poe, *Philologus* 148 [2004], 27–8) and, unlike at 526, he has no off-stage business to attend to. From a dramaturgical perspective it is also desirable that he should stay. All messages and arrivals in *Rhesus* are directed at Hector's εὐναί, except that, for good or ill, he misses the first three in the second half (Strohm 264–5, 269–70). This long-term contrast would be spoilt if after an unmotivated exit he had to return just in time to hear the news of Rhesus' approach. That simultaneous entries from different directions are rare and usually better accounted for (Taplin, *Stagecraft*, 148–9, 177 with n. 1) is perhaps less relevant in an author who with the alternative solution too seems to have sacrificed convention to theatrical effect.

For Hector's long silence Ritchie (117) adduces *Hcld.* 720–83 (Alcmena), E. *Suppl.* 381–512 + 513b–733 (Adrastus), *HF* 252–331 (Lycus), 1214–1404 (Amphitryon) and *Phoen.* 1356–1583 (Creon). The first bears some resemblance to our case as Alcmena watches the ancient Iolaus being led into battle (720–47), remains for the choral song (748–83) and then immediately receives the Messenger from the field (784–891). But only *Phoen.* 1356–1583 is similarly ill-rooted in the dramatic action. Creon fades into complete oblivion while the Messenger gives his report to the chorus and Antigone and Oedipus sing their lament. It is likely

---

[72] Alternatives for the end of 40 are Vollgraff's πάρ[εστ᾽ ἀνήρ (*Mnemosyne* n.s. 42 [1914], 83) or πάρ[εστι νῦν / πάρ[εστί που (*Mnemosyne* n.s. 43 [1915], 72).

[73] *Or.* 714–16 are interpolated and/or corrupt. Pylades is announced by Orestes (725–8) before he initiates the new dialogue at 729. Cf. Paris in *Rh.* 627–41 / 642 (below).

therefore that his presence in 1308–1581 (at least) was interpolated by someone able to tolerate the formal awkwardness for the pathos of bringing Menoeceus' grieving father on stage (Fraenkel, *Zu den Phoenissen*, 71–86).[74] If a fourth-century audience was more indulgent in this respect, our poet may have had his choice. Hector momentarily recedes to the margin so as to be in place when required again. The little choral strophe in 195–200 probably helped to structure the rearrangement of characters in the acting space (cf. Taplin, *Stagecraft*, 52–3).

149–53. Our poet has reduced *Il.* 10.303–12 to the simple question for a volunteer (149–94n.). Hector's threefold repetition (with anaphoric τίς) and the growing impatience he betrays in 152–3 (n.) perhaps mirror the Trojans' reserve at *Il.* 10.313 ὣς ἔφαθ'· οἱ δ' ἄρα πάντες ἀκὴν ἐγένοντο σιωπῇ (Ritchie 67). The lines also cover (part of) Dolon's way onto stage (149–94n. [p. 175]).

149–50. Hector's initial appeal corresponds almost exactly to *Il.* 10.303 τίς κέν μοι τόδε ἔργον ὑποσχόμενος τελέσειεν + 307–8 ὅς τίς κε τλαίη ... / νηῶν ὠκυπόρων σχεδὸν ἐλθέμεν ἔκ τε πυθέσθαι. And as in *Il.* 10.319–20 Ἕκτορ, ἔμ' ὀτρύνει κραδίη καὶ θυμὸς ἀγήνωρ / νηῶν ὠκυπόρων σχεδὸν ἐλθέμεν ἔκ τε πυθέσθαι, the central words are resumed by Dolon in 154–5 (n.).

τίς δῆτα: For this use of δῆτα see *GP* 270. The particle 'denotes that the question springs out of something which another person (or, more rarely, the speaker himself) has just said' (*GP* 269).

οἳ πάρεισιν ἐν λόγῳ: 'who are at hand to hear my words', as at S. fr. 314.39–40 (cited in 149–94n. [p. 175]), Ar. *Ach.* 513 ... φίλοι γὰρ οἱ παρόντες ἐν λόγῳ, *Av.* 30 ... ὦνδρες οἱ παρόντες ἐν λόγῳ (LSJ Suppl. [1996] s.v. λόγος VI 3 a) and, similarly, *Rh.* 641 (640–1n.) ... ἐγγὺς ὢν λόγου. The parallels support λόγῳ (ΔQ) against λόχῳ (LQ¹ˢ) and by their distribution suggest that the idiom has colloquial roots (A. Meschini, in *Scritti Diano*, 217). Confusion of λόγος and λόχος, found in the reverse sense in 682 (n.), was particularly easy in the context here, and with Hector's unit already mentioned in 26.

κατόπτης: 631–2n.

ναῦς ἔπ' Ἀργείων μολεῖν: Cf. 155, 221, 589 and, with different verbs, 203 ... ᾖσω ναῦς ἔπ' Ἀργείων πόδα, 502 ... ἄγαλμα ναῦς ἔπ' Ἀργείων

---

74 Following a suggestion by Di Benedetto and after H. Leidloff, *De Euripidis Phoenissarum argumento atque compositione*, Holzminden 1863, 24. Some of the supposed additions resemble *Rhesus* in their derivative technique: *Phoen.* 1310–11 ~ *OC* 1254–6, *Phoen.* 1315–16 ~ *Ant.* 1258 + 1297, *Phoen.* 1348–9 ~ *Ant.* 1281–2 + S. *El.* 1189 (Fraenkel 76–81, 82–3; cf. Introduction, 38–9). Mastronarde's defence of the passage (on *Phoen.* 1308–1479, 1308–53) does not convince.

φέρει. The juncture comes from *Tro.* 954 (χρῆν μ' …) λιποῦσαν οἴκους ναῦς ἔπ' Ἀργείων μολεῖν (~ *Andr.* 401 αὐτὴ δὲ δούλη ναῦς ἔπ' Ἀργείων ἔβην) and could, in *Rhesus* at least, be an attempt to reproduce the Iliadic (θοὰς / κοίλας) ἐπὶ νῆας Ἀχαιῶν (cf. Fenik, *Iliad X*, 27–8 n. 1).

151. τῆσδε γῆς εὐεργέτης: The patriotic motivation to the spying mission is new (149–94n.) and much invoked in the course of this scene (152–3, 154–5, 157b, 158–9a, 230b, 242–4a nn.). Of the dramatists, Euripides was especially fond of εὐεργέτης / -ις and εὐεργετέω.

152–3. Apart from giving Dolon time to appear (149–94, 149–53nn.), Hector's outburst at the lack of volunteers characterises him again as hot-tempered and prone to ill-conceived responses (as if he was expected to go reconnoitring himself!). He remains a long way from the heroic leader of the *Iliad*.

πόλει πατρῴᾳ συμμάχοις θ' ὑπηρετεῖν: 149–94, 151nn.

154–5. 'I am willing to run this risk for our land and to go as a spy to the Argive ships.'

ἐγὼ … θέλω / … κατόπτης ναῦς ἔπ' Ἀργείων μολεῖν: 149–50n. The repetition and choice of words imitate epic formular style. For κατόπτης see 631–2nn.

πρὸ γαίας: likewise *Ion* 278 and E. fr. 360.39 (of human sacrifice). Dolon soon abandons patriotism and openly asks for a 'worthy reward'.

τόνδε κίνδυνον … / ῥίψας: a dicing metaphor (cf. Σ^V *Rh.* 155 [II 331.17–18 Schwartz = 85 Merro] προκινδυνεύσας. ἀπὸ τῶν κύβων ἡ μεταφορά and e.g. Phryn. *PS* 29.1–2 de Borries, Phot. κ 733 Theodoridis),[75] as also in 183 (182–3n.) ψυχὴν προβάλλοντ' ἐν κύβοισι δαίμονος and 445b–6 (n.) … ἡμέραν δ' ἐξ ἡμέρας / ῥίπτεις κυβεύων τὸν πρὸς Ἀργείους Ἄρη. The formulation here has equivalents in *Hcld.* 148–9 ἢ κίνδυνον ἐξ ἀμηχάνων / ῥίπτοντες, E. fr. 402.6–7 κίνδυνον μέγαν / ῥίπτοντες and Xen. *Mem.* 1.3.9 τῶν … ῥιψοκινδύνων. Similarly, *Sept.* [1028] ἐγώ σφε θάψω κἀνὰ κίνδυνον βαλῶ. Prose authors seem to prefer ἀναρρίπτω (LSJ s.v. II).

156–7a. Dolon's confidence resembles *Il.* 10.324–7 σοὶ δ' ἐγὼ οὐχ ἅλιος σκοπὸς ἔσσομαι οὐδ' ἀπὸ δόξης· / τόφρα γὰρ ἐς στρατὸν εἶμι διαμπερές, ὄφρ' ἂν ἵκωμαι / νῆ' Ἀγαμεμνονέην, ὅθι που μέλλουσιν ἄριστοι / βουλὰς βουλεύειν, ἢ φευγέμεν ἠὲ μάχεσθαι (~ *Il.* 10.307–12), although the phrasing is closer to *Il.* 10.211–12 (Nestor) ταῦτά τε πάντα πύθοιτο καὶ ἂψ εἰς ἡμέας ἔλθοι / ἀσκηθής.

157b. 'It is on these conditions that I take upon myself this task.'

---

[75] The explanations show that if there is some (etymological) link between κίνδυνος and dice / dicing (*GEW*, *DELG* s.v. κίνδυνος; J. Knobloch, *Glotta* 53 [1975], 78–80), it had been forgotten by the second century AD.

ἐπὶ τούτοις sums up Dolon's part of the promise (i.e. that he will undertake the expedition for his land and not return until he has learnt all he can) and thus 'already establishes the basis for a contract' (Jouan 61 n. 39). This notion is lost if, with Liapis (on 156–7), we take ἐπί as an indication 'of an end or purpose' (LSJ s.v. B III 2).

τόνδ' ὑφίσταμαι πόνον: In a different martial context cf. E. Suppl. 188–9 πόλις δὲ σή / μόνη δύναιτ' ἂν τόνδ' ὑποστῆναι πόνον and 344–5 ὅθ' ἡ τεκοῦσα ... / πρώτη κελεύεις τόνδ' ὑποστῆναι πόνον.

158–9a. 'You are well named indeed, and you love your city, Dolon.'

Hector's etymological pun is an unusual way of identifying a new character who has not been named. 'Dolon' implies δόλος, which not only makes him an ideal choice as a spy, but also suggests that he was at some point invented for that role (cf. Hainsworth on Il. 10.314, Rh. 201–23n.). On the ancient belief that a name reflects, or should reflect, the nature of its bearer see Dodds on Ba. 367, M. Griffith, HSPh 82 (1978), 84 n. 5 and on PV 85–6, Garvie on Pers. 65–72.

ἐπώνυμος μὲν κάρτα adapts Sept. 658 ἐπωνύμῳ δὲ κάρτα, Πολυνείκει λέγω (~ Eum. 90 ... κάρτα δ' ὢν ἐπώνυμος). But the expression is typical of name-etymologies from Homer on (LSJ s.v. ἐπώνυμος I 1). In tragedy see also e.g. Sept. 405, 829–31, A. Suppl. 45–8 (νῦν δ' ἐπικεκλομένα ...) Ζηνὸς ἔφαψιν – ἐπωνυμίᾳ δ' ἐπεκραίνετο μόρσιμος αἰών / εὐλόγως, Ἔπαφον δ' ἐγέννασεν (with FJW on 45 [II, pp. 43–5]), PV 848–51, Ai. 430–1, S. fr. 965, Phoen. 636–7, E. fr. 696.11–13. The practice became something of a mannerism – to the point that it attracted comic parody: Ar. Ran. 1192, frr. 342 PCG (~ E. fr. 182), 373 PCG (~ IT 32–3) and perhaps Anaxil. fr. 35 PCG (Rau, Paratragodia, 210–11, Kannicht on Hel. 13–5).

κάρτα (79n.) emphasises the appropriateness of the etymology, as do words like ὀρθῶς, ἀληθῶς and εὐλόγως elsewhere (W. Headlam, On Editing Aeschylus. A Criticism, London 1891, 140–3, Diggle on Phaeth. 225 [p. 146], Collard on E. Suppl. 496–7a).

φιλόπτολις: See 149–94, 151nn. and, on φιλόπ(τ)ολις as a fifth- and fourth-century term of praise, Liapis on 158–60.

Epic -πτολις stands metri causa, always in the nominative or accusative singular, and in iambo-trochaic dialogue at the end of the line. The same applies to πτόλις, which does not occur in Sophocles (Page on Med. 641, FJW on A. Suppl. 699).

159b–60. Dolon's reputable descent comes from Il. 10.314–15 (~ 378–81), where he is the son of the wealthy herald Eumedes. It would have been pointless to hint at the less favourable details (149–94n.), although our poet lowered the 'Homeric' standard (Il. 10.212–13, 307) by having Hector promise enhanced εὔκλεια for volunteering alone. At 197 the chorus more adequately speak of a πόνος ... εὐκλεής.

δὶς τόσως ... εὐκλεέστερον: 'twice as glorious'. Cf. *Rh.* 281 ἔγνως· λόγου δὲ δὶς τόσου μ' ἐκούφισας, 757b (n.) ... καίτοι δὶς τόσον κακὸν τόδε and especially *Med.* 1193–4 πῦρ δ' ... / ... μᾶλλον δὶς τόσως ἐλάμπετο (with Mastronarde on 1194). Unlike Aeschylus, Euripides appears to have avoided using τόσος or τόσως without δίς (cf. *Cyc.* 147, *Med.* 1047, 1134, *Hcld.* 293, *Hec.* 392, *El.* 1092, fr. 995).[76] This may also be true of Sophocles' trimeters, if one can tell from a single instance (*Ai.* 277 δὶς τόσ' ... κακά) as against one other in lyrics (*Ai.* 184 τόσσον).

161–2a. 'Well, ought one not to undertake a task and in undertaking it win a worthy reward?'

As Dolon is best seen to move from the general to the specific, the expression should not personally be referred to him with με (OΛgVgB, *Chr. Pat.* 1964) for μέν (V). The syntax resembles *IT* 810 οὔκουν λέγειν μὲν χρὴ σέ, μανθάνειν δ' ἐμέ; and *Phoen.* 979 οὔκουν σὲ φράζειν εἰκός, ἐκπονεῖν δ' ἐμέ;

οὔκουν: Denniston (*GP* 436). The MSS have οὐκοῦν as introducing a statement ('surely, then ...'), which does not readily follow the previous sentence and, in any case, is too tame for Dolon here. Between interrogative οὐκοῦν and οὔκουν, the latter is livelier and, with a few exceptions, perhaps to be restored in drama thoughout (*GP* 430–6). Likewise 481, 543, 585, 633.

ἄξιον / μισθὸν φέρεσθαι: Cf. *Il.* 10.304 (Hector speaking) μισθὸς δέ οἱ ἄρκιος ἔσται and *Rh.* 182 (Dolon) χρὴ δ' ἐπ' ἀξίοις πονεῖν.

162b–3. 'For the profit attached to every action doubles (literally 'generates as double') the satisfaction.'

This is how most scholars understand the text. Dolon accepts εὔκλεια as one benefit to be gained from the spying expedition, but, as becomes clear in 182–3 (n.), he really just wants a material reward. His mercenary attitude and desire for the biggest possible gift tell against Palmer (*CR* 4 [1890], 229), Porter (on 163) and Pearson (*CQ* 11 [1917], 57–8), who see here an appeal for mutual recognition and translate χάριν with 'favour'. Yet Pearson correctly noted the linguistic similarity to passages like *Ai.* 522 χάρις χάριν γάρ ἐστιν ἡ τίκτουσ' ἀεί, *OT* 231–2 τὸ γὰρ / κέρδος τελῶ 'γὼ χἠ χάρις προσκείσεται and *OC* 1483–4 μηδ' ἄλαστον ἄνδρ' ἰδὼν / ἀκερδῆ χάριν μετάσχοιμί πως. Perhaps our poet was inspired by such topical formulations and used them to somewhat startling effect.

---

76 At *Med.* 725, whether genuine or not, τοσόνδε (BOCDE) offers itself as an alternative to τόσον γε (fere AVP: τὸ σόν γε L). Cf. C. Austin – M. D. Reeve, *Maia* 22 (1970), 14, Collard on E. *Suppl.* [899–900].

Or he genuinely wished Dolon to sound ambiguous in an attempt to win Hector to his course.[77]

τίκτει: Apart from *Ai.* 522 (above), cf. *Sept.* 437 καὶ τῷδε κέρδει κέρδος ἄλλο τίκτεται.

164. κοὐκ ἄλλως λέγω: '... and I do not deny it'. Cf. *Rh.* 271 ... οὐκ ἄλλως λέγω, *Hec.* 302, E. *El.* 1035, *Hel.* 1106, *Or.* 709 and also *Sept.* 490 ... οὐκ ἄλλως ἐρῶ, E. *El.* 226 ... καὶ τάχ' οὐκ ἄλλως ἐρεῖς. Euripides' predilection for this phrase is reflected in Ar. *Ran.* 1140 ('Aeschylus' to 'Euripides') ... οὐκ ἄλλως λέγω (Ritchie 206–7, who adds Ar. *Eccl.* 440 ... τίς δὲ τοῦτ' ἄλλως λέγει;). Cf. Introduction, 30 n. 36.

The parallels tell against Nauck's ... κοὐκ ἄλλως λέγεις (II[1] [1854], XXII), for which he relied on *Chr. Pat.* 1620 ναὶ καὶ δίκαιον τοῦτο, κοὐκ ἄλλως λέγεις and 1968 ... κοὐκ ἄλλως σκοπεῖς.[78] Hector should utter a strong affirmation, not politely agree with his interlocutor ('Yes ... and your words are not beside the point'). Likewise 271 (λέγω O: λέγεις VΛ).

165–6. Hector instantly excludes the (unrealistic) prize of his royal power (388–9n.).[79] In the negotiations of *Il.* 9.121–61 / 260–99 / 378–92 (cf. 149–94n.), Agamemnon finally offers Achilles a provincial kingdom (*Il.* 9.149–56) before admonishing him to respect his higher rank (160–1). Odysseus wisely omits this condition (291–9), although Achilles exploits the point in rejecting a princess bride: *Il.* 9.388–92 ~ *Rh.* 168 (167–8n.). Cf. R. S. Bond, *AJPh* 117 (1996), 257–8.

165. δέ: for οὖν or δή (*GP* 170), as in *Ba.* 1118–20 ἐγώ τοι, μῆτερ, εἰμί, παῖς σέθεν / Πενθεύς ... / οἴκτιρε δ' ὦ μῆτέρ με.

πλὴν ἐμῆς τυραννίδος: Nauck (II[1] [1854], XXII ~ *Euripideische Studien* II, 170) offered πλὴν ἐμὴν τυραννίδα on the analogy of 173 ... σὺ δ' αἴτει πλὴν στρατηλάτας νεῶν. But there the accusative is more natural as 'the implied object of αἴτει' (Liapis, 'Notes', 55). And we need not avoid the repetition with τυραννίδος in 166.

166. οὐ σῆς ἐρῶμεν ... τυραννίδος: For the wording cf. Archil. fr. 19.3 *IEG* ... μεγάλης δ' οὐκ ἐρέω τυραννίδος. See also 132n.

πολιόχου: '... which guards the city'. The adjective recurs in 821 (Chorus to Hector) †μέγας ἐμοὶ μέγας ὦ† πολίοχον κράτος (Vater: πολιοῦχον Ω), where it retains part of its association with tutelary deities (821–3n.). Here this notion is uniquely transferred to the abstract

---

77 Strictly speaking, Liapis (on 162–3) is right that διπλοῦς does not mean 'mutual, reciprocal'. But the sense is implied at *Ant.* 14 μιᾷ θανόντοιν ἡμέρᾳ διπλῇ χερί (i.e. Eteocles and Polynices).
78 Followed by *Chr. Pat.* 1969 σύ τ' εὖ παραινεῖς καὶ σὺ καιρίως λέγεις (~ *Rh.* 339). As often, the excerptor slightly altered the original for his text (Introduction, 53).
79 Σ[V] *Rh.* 165 (II 331.18–19 Schwartz = 85 Merro) comments γελοῖον τὸ οἴεσθαι ὅτι βασιλείαν αἰτήσει.

τυραννίς. Feickert (on 166) suspects an allusion to Hector's name, which since antiquity has been connected with ἔχω, 'hold, rule, keep safe' (von Kamptz, *Homerische Personennamen*, 26, 171, 261–2, Wathelet, *Dictionnaire des Troyens* I, 472, II, 1304–5). Cf. Pl. *Crat.* 393a1–b6 and the play on Athena πολιοῦχος at Ar. *Thesm.* 1136–41 Παλλάδα ... 1140 ἣ πόλιν ἡμετέραν ἔχει / καὶ κράτος φανερὸν μόνη.

Outside *Rhesus*, the form πολίοχος for πολιοῦχος (here V: πολυόχου L) is attested in Pi. *Dith.* 4 fr. 70d.38–9 Sn.–M. [καὶ π]ολίοχον Γλαυ- / [κώπιδ]α and *Inscr. Cret.* 4.171.14 (III BC). On Πολίοχος and Πολιοῦχος as proper names see *LGPN* II s.vv. and G. Pace, *QUCC* n.s. 65 (2000), 131 n. 19.

167–8. At *Il.* 9.141–8 ~ 283–90 Agamemnon promises Achilles one of his three daughters in wedlock, but the latter refuses with the deeply ironic suggestion that Agamemnon look for someone 'more princely' (βασιλεύτερος) than himself: *Il.* 9.388–92. The idea that one should not marry above one's station is a commonplace for both men and women (e.g. Alcm. fr. 1.16–17 *PMGF*, Pi. *Pyth.* 2.34–6, *PV* 887–93, S. fr. 353, E. *El.* 930–7, E. frr. 214, 502) and gives Dolon an elegant excuse to reject Hector's offer (Feickert on 168). In 197–8 (n.) the chorus will doubt the wisdom of demanding Achilles' horses instead.

167. 'Well then, marry and become related to Priam's family.'

σὺ δ' ἀλλά opens a fresh proposal (of equal merit). Formally, δ' ἀλλά 'is always followed by an imperative ... and nearly always preceded by σύ' (*GP* 10).

Πριαμιδῶν γαμβρὸς γενοῦ: Cf. *Il.* 9.142 (Agamemnon speaking) γαμβρός κέν μοι ἔοι and 284 (Odysseus) γαμβρός κέν οἱ ἔοις (167–8n.). In our passage γαμβρός need not mean more than 'relative by marriage' (Liapis on 167).

168. ἐξ ἐμαυτοῦ μειζόνων γαμεῖν: 'to take a wife of nobler stock than myself'. Cf. Thgn. 189–90 καὶ ἐκ κακοῦ ἐσθλὸς ἔγημε / καὶ κακὸς ἐξ ἀγαθοῦ and especially *Andr.* 1279 κᾆτ' οὐ γαμεῖν δῆτ' ἔκ τε γενναίων χρεών,[80] Xen. *Hier.* 1.28 τῷ τοίνυν τυράννῳ ... ἀνάγκη ἐκ μειόνων γαμεῖν (LSJ s.v. γαμέω I 1). With ἀπό or παρά also e.g. *Hcld.* [299], *Andr.* 974–5, *Or.* 1676–7, Pl. *Plt.* 310c10.

169–70. 'Ten talents of gold' are among the treasures that Agamemnon initially offers to give Achilles: *Il.* 9.122b, 126 = 264b, 268 (cf. *Il.* 19.247). In his response to Odysseus, the hero summarily dismisses all material gifts (*Il.* 9.378–87) and insinuates that he and his family themselves are rich (*Il.* 9.364–7, 400). On the wealth of Dolon's father see 149–94, 159b–60, 170nn.

---

80 Diggle follows Stevens in deleting *Andr.* 1279–82. The lines are defended by A. H. Sommerstein, *CQ* n.s. 38 (1988), 243–6.

169. χρυσὸς πάρεστιν (Δ) must be read. Λ's χρυσὸς γὰρ ἔστιν arose by confusion of Π and Γ, and Zanetto is wrong to take it as *lectio difficilior* on the assumption that with γάρ Hector expresses his assent: 'Yes, you are right to refuse to marry above your station; but if you want gold, you only need to ask for it' (*Ciclope, Reso*, 140 n. 22). If we render the paradosis by Denniston's simple 'Not, for …' (*GP* 73-4), the lack of connection with Dolon's statement becomes obvious.

εἰ τόδ' αἰτήσεις γέρας: similarly 181 τί δῆτα μεῖζον τῶνδέ μ' αἰτήσεις γέρας;

170. ἀλλ' ἔστ' ἐν οἴκοις: 'No, I have gold at home', with ἀλλά simply expressing opposition (*GP* 7). For the fact cf. *Il.* 10.378-9 ἔστι γὰρ ἔνδον / χαλκός τε χρυσός τε πολύκμητός τε σίδηρος and for the language *Rh.* 178 ἔστι χρυσὸς ἐν δόμοις.

οὐ βίου σπανίζομεν: The expression is ordinary Greek (e.g. Hdt. 1.196.5), but may here have a Euripidean ring: E. *Suppl.* 240 οἱ δ' … σπανίζοντες βίου, *El.* 235 οὔ που σπανίζων τοῦ καθ' ἡμέραν βίου; E. fr. 285.11-12, *Hec.* 11-12 ἵν' … / τοῖς ζῶσιν εἴη παισὶ μὴ σπάνις βίου. In other tragedy only *OT* 1460-1 ἄνδρες εἰσίν, ὥστε μὴ / σπάνιν ποτὲ σχεῖν … τοῦ βίου. The words σπάνις, σπάνιος and σπανίζω are on the whole much rarer (or non-existent) in Aeschylus and Sophocles than in Euripides.

O's οὐ σπανίζομεν βίου is the first of several instances of the *vitium Byzantinum* in that MS (Introduction 49 n. 7).

171-2. Hector's new question perhaps corresponds to the other valuables (tripods, cauldrons, prize-winning horses) Agamemnon has in store for Achilles (*Il.* 9.122a, 123-4 = 264a, 265-6). In Agamemnon's speech this is followed by the promise of spoils (*Il.* 9.135-40 ~ 277-82), a topic which Dolon himself raises as the first explicit step to his desired reward (149-94n.).

171. τί δῆτα: 149-50n.

ὧν κέκευθεν Ἴλιον presumably echoes *Il.* 22.118 ἀλλ' … ὅσα τε πτόλις ἥδε κέκευθεν, where Hector considers surrendering Helen, the goods Paris stole and half of Troy's wealth (~ *Il.* 18.511-12). Ἴλιον (OQ), not Ἴλιος (VL), is the preferred tragic form, except in the epicising *Andr.* 103 (LSJ s.v. Ἴλιος I, Diggle, *Euripidea*, 324 n. 9). For κέκευθε(ν) see also 620b-1n.

172. ξυναίνεσον: 'promise, grant'. Cf. *Ag.* 483-4 γυναικὸς αἰχμᾷ / πρὸ τοῦ φανέντος χάριν ξυναινέσαι (with Fraenkel on 484), Xen. *An.* 7.7.31 οἱ δὲ Λακεδαιμόνιοι διὰ τὸ δεῖσθαι τῆς στρατιᾶς συναινέσωσιν αὐτοῖς ταῦτα, *Cyr.* 8.5.20 (LSJ s.v. συναινέω 2). Our passage provides a particularly good example of how the basic meaning of the verb, 'agree with, consent' (LSJ s.v. 1), develops when the action responds to a request (H. L. Ahrens, *Philologus* Suppl. 1 [1860], 532).

173. πλὴν στρατηλάτας νεῶν: 165n. Here πάντα is omitted as an 'antecedent' to πλήν, as in e.g. *OT* 118 θνῄσκουσι γάρ, πλὴν εἷς τις and 369–70 (Τε.) εἴπερ τί γ' ἐστὶ τῆς ἀληθείας σθένος. / (Οι.) ἀλλ' ἔστι, πλὴν σοί. The Greek commanders could fetch enormous ransoms: 177 (n.).

174. 'Kill them. I do not demand that you keep your hand off Menelaus.'

Dolon *may* understand Hector's motive to be primarily vengeance, but given his aim, the reply looks more like another rejection of conventional wealth. Thus at 176 (n.) he cannot seriously believe that high-ranking captives should work the fields.

Both syntax and verse-rhythm recall E. *Suppl.* 385 Θησεύς σ' ἀπαιτεῖ πρὸς χάριν θάψαι νεκρούς.

Μενέλεω σχέσθαι χέρα: For metrical reasons the simplex ἔχομαι replaces ἀπέχομαι in this common phrase (*Od.* 22.316 ἀλλά μοι οὐ πείθοντο κακῶν ἄπο χεῖρας ἔχεσθαι, Emp. 31 B 141 DK, A. *Suppl.* 755–6 οὐ μὴ ... / ... ἡμῶν χεῖρ' ἀπόσχωνται, πάτερ, *Eum.* 350, Antiph. fr. 27.16 *PCG*, Crates Com. fr. 19.2 *PCG*, Pl. *Smp.* 213d3–4, 214d3–4). χέρα (Δ), rather than χέρας (Λ), connotes a powerful martial blow.

175. οὐ μήν ('Surely ... not ...?') 'introduces, tentatively and half incredulously, an alternative suggestion' (*GP* 334). Likewise *Alc.* 518 οὐ μὴν γυνή γ' ὄλωλεν Ἄλκηστις σέθεν;

τὸν Ἰλέως παῖδα: the 'lesser' Ajax. Ἰλέως (V: ἴλεόν O) is preferable to Οἰλέως (Λ ὀϊλ-). Diggle, among recent editors, followed by Kovacs and (for *Rhesus*) Jouan, adopts the latter both here and at *IA* 193 and 263 (ὀϊλ- L). But the contraction of Homeric Ὀῑλ- (< ϝιλ-) into Οἰλ- is odd and significantly perhaps not attested by our MSS. As in Pi. *Ol.* 9.112 Αἴαν ... Ἰλιάδα (v.l. ὀϊλ-), their epicising and unmetrical Ὀϊλέως is the likely response of scribes not familiar with the form in Ἰλ- (also < ϝιλ-). This further occurs in the *Iliou Persis* (Arg. p. 146 (1) *GEF*),[81] 'Hes.' fr. 235.1 M.–W., Stes. fr. 226 *PMGF* and Lyc. 1150 and probably gained some currency in pre-Aristarchean Iliadic texts (cf. Nickau, *Zenodotos*, 36–42). The tragedians then had ample precedent for a variant of cretic or spondaic shape and no need to create one of their own. Fantuzzi (*CPh* 100 [2005], 272–3) is inconsistent when he defends Ἰλέως here, but does not equally strongly support the conjecture Ἰλ- by England and Wilamowitz (*GV* 283 n. 1) at *IA* 193 and 263.

---

[81] In view of the standard Homeric Ὀϊλεύς, Proclus would hardly have written Ἰλ- in *prose*, if it had not stood in his epic text. And cf. the inscription ΑΙΑΣ ΙΛΙΑΔΕΣ on an early-sixth-century Attic amphora picturing another scene from the *Iliou Persis*, Polyxena's death (H. B. Walters, *JHS* 18 [1898], 282–8 ~ *LIMC* I.1/2 s.v. Aias II 8).

ἐξαιτεῖς: ΟΛ. Most editors adopt ἐξαιτῇ (V), which they take to mean 'demand / ask for yourself' (LSJ s.v. ἐξαιτέω II 1). Yet there are no parallels for this sense with an infinitive construction, as opposed to the more urgent and humble 'beg, implore' (*Med*. 969–71 ἀλλ', ὦ τέκν' ... / πατρὸς νέαν γυναῖκα ... / ἱκετεύετ', ἐξαιτεῖσθε μὴ φεύγειν χθόνα, *Hec.* 49–50, *Ba.* 360–3). For the active cf. *OT* 1255–7 φοιτᾷ γὰρ ἡμᾶς / ἔγχος ἐξαιτῶν πορεῖν, / γυναῖκά τ' οὐ γυναῖκα, μητρῴαν δ' ὅπου / κίχοι διπλῆν ἄρουραν οὗ τε καὶ τέκνων.

176. The verse recalls 74–5, where the question of ransom (173, 174, 177nn.) did not occur. Its plain, sententious style also contrasts with Hector's elaborate threat.

γεωργεῖν is the prose alternative to γαπονεῖν (75). In drama γεωργός appears at A. fr. 46a.18 (ascribed to the satyr-play *Diktyoulkoi*), and γεωργέω at Ar. *Lys.* 1173, *Eccl.* 592, 651 and Ar. fr. 102.1 *PCG*. See Björck, *Alpha Impurum*, 115, 330–1.

χεῖρες εὖ τεθραμμέναι: The participial attribute is a set expression, which also belongs to everyday speech: E. *El.* 64–5 τί γὰρ τάδ' ... ἐμὴν μοχθέω χάριν / πόνους ἔχουσα, πρόσθεν εὖ τεθραμμένη, E. fr. 111.2–3, Diod. Com. 3.3–4 *PCG* (both gnomic), Pl. *Rep.* 496b2, D. S. 3.43.1, Apollon. *Lex. Hom.* 79.13 Bekker εὐπηγέες· εὖ τεθραμμένοι.

177. 'Which of the Achaeans then do you want to hold to ransom alive?'

ζῶντ' ἀποινᾶσθαι: The correct word-division is preserved in O (ζῶντ' ἀποίνασθαι [*sic*]) and implied in the explanations of Σ^V *Rh.* 177 (II 331.3–5 Schwartz = 85 Merro) ἄποινα λέγεται τὰ λύτρα ... τίνα οὖν, φησί, τῶν Ἀχαιῶν λύτρα λαβὼν βούλει ἀπολῦσαι and Σ^L *Rh.* 177 (II 331.30 Schwartz = 86 Merro) ἢ ἀπεμπολεῖν. The middle ἀποινάομαι from ἀποινάω, 'release for a ransom' (Hsch. α 6362 Latte ἀποινᾶν· ἀπολυτροῦν),[82] is attested only here and at 464–6 (n.) τόδε γ' ἦμαρ / ... ὅτῳ πολυφόνου / χειρὸς ἀποινάσαιο λόγχᾳ (fere codd.), where both metre and sense betray corruption and Diggle (*Euripidea*, 515–17) ingeniously wrote ... ἄποιν' ἄροιο σᾷ λόγχᾳ. Yet given the present context and the frequency of ἄποινα in Homer (*Iliad* only), it seems strange that ζῶντα ποινᾶσθαι gained such ground in the other MSS and scholia (cf. especially Σ^L *Rh.* 177 [II 331.30 Schwartz = 86 Merro] ἀντὶ τοῦ τιμωρεῖσθαι).[83]

---

[82] *An. Gr.* I 210.6 Bekker ἀποινᾶν· ἄποινα λαμβάνειν from a collection of rhetorical glosses probably refers to Dem. 23.28 (a law) τοὺς δ' ἀνδροφόνους ἐξεῖναι ἀποκτείνειν ἐν τῇ ἡμεδαπῇ ... λυμαίνεσθαι δὲ μή, μηδὲ ἀποινᾶν and its explanation at 23.33 τὸ δὲ μηδ' ἀποινᾶν μὴ χρήματα πράττεσθαι ('to exact compensation')· τὰ γὰρ ἄποινα χρήματα ὠνόμαζον οἱ παλαιοί (LSJ s.v. ἄποινα II 1).

[83] Ποινάομαι (with an accusative object) is found only in *IT* 1433. But ποινή would have been familiar.

At *Il.* 24.686–7 Hermes states that Priam's life would be worth three times the amount he gave for Hector's body. Fighting heroes (and spies) are not spared for ransom on the Iliadic battlefield (Pritchett, *GSW* V, 246).

178. καὶ πρόσθεν εἶπον: For the syntax cf. A. *Suppl.* 398–9 εἶπον δὲ καὶ πρίν, οὐκ ἄνευ δήμου τάδε / πράξαιμ' ἄν (with FJW on 389), and for the tone and words *OC* 932–3 εἶπον μὲν οὖν καὶ πρόσθεν, ἐννέπω δὲ νῦν, / τὰς παῖδας ὡς τάχιστα δεῦρ' ἄγειν τινά. The parataxis makes Dolon sound all the more impatient.

ἔστι χρυσὸς ἐν δόμοις: 169–70, 170nn. The verse ends like *Med.* 542 εἴη δ' ἔμοιγε μήτε χρυσὸς ἐν δόμοις.

179–80. This new exchange shows significant overlaps with *Ag.* 577–9 Τροίαν ἑλόντες δήποτ' Ἀργείων στόλος / θεοῖς λάφυρα ταῦτα τοῖς καθ' Ἑλλάδα / δόμοις ἐπασσάλευσαν ἀρχαῖον γάνος (Fraenkel, *Rev.* 232). The practice of hanging up enemy arms and armour in temples is often referred to in poetry: e.g. *Il.* 7.82–3, *Sept.* 277–8, *Hcld.* 695–9, *Andr.* 1121–2, E. *El.* 6–7, 1000–1, *Tro.* 573–6, Hdt. 5.95.1–2 (= Alc. fr. 401B b, test. 467 Voigt). Cf. Pritchett, *GSW* III, 277–95, V, 132–3 and Liapis on 180 (with further literature).

179. καὶ μὴν ... γ' marks the transition to a new point (*GP* 351–2). With μήν Hector asserts the truth of his proposition, which he may reasonably believe to counter Dolon's expectations. See below (παρών) and in general G. Wakker, in *NAGP*, 209–31 (especially 213–16, 226–7, 229–30).

λαφύρων: The distinction of Hsch. λ 440 Latte (~ Phot. λ 121 Theodoridis, *Suda* λ 158 Adler) between λάφυρα as 'what is taken from the enemy when still alive' and σκῦλα as 'spoils from the dead' (cf. 591–3, 619–20a nn.) is largely confirmed by Pritchett (*GSW* I, 54–8, V, 132–47). Outside tragedy (*Sept.* 278, 479, *Ag.* 578, *Ai.* 93, *Tr.* 645, *HF* 417, *Tro.* 1124) the word has one mid-fifth-century attestation in the Argive inscription *SIG* 56.9 = 42B.9 Meiggs–Lewis φαλύρον (*sic*).

παρών emphasises αὐτός and the fact that Dolon is offered the privilege of choosing 'in person' his part of the spoils (cf. 141–2n.). Similarly Agamemnon to Achilles at *Il.* 9.139 (~ 281) Τρωϊάδας δὲ γυναῖκας ἐείκοσιν αὐτὸς ἑλέσθω.

180. θεοῖσιν ... πασσάλευε πρὸς δόμοις: Fraenkel (on *Ag.* 579) notes that 'this is a less harsh expression than' the double dative at *Ag.* 578–9 θεοῖς ... / δόμοις ἐπασσάλευσαν (cf. 179–80n.). Here δόμοις (QL^{1s}) is *lectio difficilior* to δόμους (ΔL) and further protected by *PV* 56 ... πασσάλευε πρὸς πέτραις. The error has numerous parallels in our MSS (FJW on A. *Suppl.* 793 [III, pp. 142–3]).

181. τί δῆτα: 149–50n.

μ' αἰτήσεις γέρας: 169n.

182–3. 'The horses of Achilles. For one must work for a worthy reward, if one hazards one's life in fortune's game of dice.'

Dolon's final revelation comes as a surprise, despite (or because of?) the extended build-up compared to his prompt request at *Il.* 10.321–3 ἀλλ' ἄγε μοι τὸ σκῆπτρον ἀνάσχεο καί μοι ὄμοσσον, / ἦ μὲν τοὺς ἵππους τε καὶ ἅρματα ποικίλα χαλκῷ / δωσέμεν, οἳ φορέουσιν ἀμύμονα Πηλείωνα. By reminding Hector of the risks and the need for 'a worthy reward' (154–5, 161–3), he confirms his materialistic approach to the task.

ἵππους Ἀχιλλέως stands out for its initial position, followed by metrical and syntactical pause.

δ': 132n.

ψυχὴν προβάλλοντ' ἐν κύβοισι δαίμονος: This hardly reaches the grandeur of *Il.* 9.322 (Achilles) ἀεὶ ἐμὴν ψυχὴν παραβαλλόμενος πολεμίζειν. With προβάλλω cf. *OT* 744–5 ἔοικ' ἐμαυτὸν εἰς ἀράς / δεινὰς προβάλλων ἀρτίως οὐκ εἰδέναι.

ἐν κύβοισι δαίμονος: While Greek commonly uses dicing metaphors for the uncertainties of luck and chance, their frequency in *Rhesus* (154–5n.) may reflect the sense that this was a favourite soldiers' game (Klyve on 183). For the gods throwing dice on human affairs cf. *Sept.* 414 ἔργον δ' ἐν κύβοις Ἄρης κρινεῖ (also in a military setting), S. fr. 895 ἀεὶ γὰρ εὖ πίπτουσιν οἱ Διὸς κύβοι and *HF* 1227–8 ὅστις εὐγενὴς βροτῶν / φέρει †τὰ τῶν θεῶν γε† πτώματ' οὐδ' ἀναίνεται (with Wilamowitz and Bond on 1228).

184. 'Ah, but you are my rival in desire for the horses.'

At *Il.* 17.485–90 Hector declares his longing for Achilles' steeds, shortly after Apollo had rebuked him for pursuing this aim (17.75–81) and we learnt from Zeus that they were not his to possess (17.448–50). By introducing the motif here, our poet not only suggests that Dolon has overreached himself, but also reveals in Hector a touch of greed. The audience is supposed to remember this when in 859–60 he has to defend himself against the charge of having killed Rhesus ἵππων ἐρασθείς (839). See 833–81n.

καὶ μὴν ... γ': In statements that raise an objection to the last speaker's words καὶ μὴν (... γε) acquires an adversative force (Jebb on *Ai.* 531, *GP* 357–8, G. Wakker, in *NAGP*, 217–18, 224–5). So also 492–3 and 574–5.

ἐρῶντι ... ἀντερᾷς: The juxtaposition of simple and compound verb underlines the almost erotic competition for Achilles' horses. For the figure of speech and syntax here cf. *Alc.* 1103 νικῶντι μέντοι καὶ σὺ συννικᾷς ἐμοί (Ritchie 241). Also Liapis on 184 (with further references).

In the sense 'rival in love' (as against 'love in return') ἀντεράω / -έραμαι is not attested again until Plutarch (*Lyc.* 18.4, *De soll. an.* 18

972d) and Lucian (*Musc. Enc.* 10). But ἀντεραστής occurs in e.g. Ar. *Eq.* 733, Xen. *Cyn.* 1.7, Pl. *Rep.* 521b5, Men. *Sam.* 26.

185–8. As already seen by Σ^V *Rh.* 185 (II 331.6–7 Schwartz = 86 Merro), the tale of Achilles' horses is extracted from *Il.* 16.149–51 Ξάνθον καὶ Βαλίον, τὼ ἅμα πνοιῇσι πετέσθην, / τοὺς ἔτεκε Ζεφύρῳ ἀνέμῳ ἅρπυια Ποδάργη, / βοσκομένη λειμῶνι παρὰ ῥόον Ὠκεανοῖο and 23.276–8 ἴστε γάρ, ὅσσον ἐμοὶ ἀρετῇ περιβάλλετον ἵπποι. / ἀθάνατοί τε γάρ εἰσι, Ποσειδάων δ' ἔπορ' αὐτούς / πατρὶ ἐμῷ Πηλῆϊ, ὃ δ' αὖτ' ἐμοὶ ἐγγυάλιξεν (+ *Il.* 16.154, 866–7, 17.443–4). Aeneas' team (*Il.* 5.265–72) and Adrestus' stallion Arion (*Il.* 23.346–7 ~ *Thebaid* fr. 11 *GEF*) boast comparable divine pedigrees (cf. R. Janko, *CQ* n.s. 36 [1986], 51–5 and on *Il.* 16.149–50, Richardson on *Il.* 23.346–7).

185. ἐξ ἀφθίτων ... ἄφθιτοι πεφυκότες: The polyptoton underlines the equal nature of parents and offspring (Gygli-Wyss, *Polyptoton*, 92–3, Liapis on 185–6, with many parallels).

In view of the Homeric background (185–8n.), it is natural that Achilles' horses are here described as male, whereas at 238–41 our poet follows the lyric-tragic convention of making teams feminine, regardless of their individual members' sex (Barrett on *Hipp.* 231, Finglass on S. *El.* 703–4; cf. *Rh.* 356, 616–17, 781, 785–6 of Rhesus' steeds). Such small inconsistencies are common in drama and hardly entered an audience's mind (Mastronarde on *Phoen.* 26). Cf. 355–6 (βαλιαῖσι πώλοις), 686nn.

186. τὸν Πηλέως φέρουσι θούριον γόνον recalls *Il.* 10.323 (τοὺς ἵππους τε καὶ ἅρματα) ... οἳ φορέουσιν ἀμύμονα Πηλείωνα (cf. 182–3n.) ~ *Il.* 2.770 ἵπποι θ', οἳ φορέεσκον ἀμύμονα Πηλείωνα. From the Trojan perspective θούριος ('impetuous') well replaces ἀμύμων. The adjective (epic θοῦρος) is traditionally applied to Ares (e.g. *Il.* 5.30, 35, 355, Tyrt. fr. 12.34 *IEG*, *Ai.* 612, E. *Suppl.* 579, *Phoen.* 240) and, by extension, to ferocious warriors or their equipment: *Ai.* 212, 1213 (Ajax),[84] *Rh.* 492 (n.).

187–8. δίδωσι δ' ... πόντιος: Cf. *Il.* 23.277–8 (185–8n.) and *Rh.* 238–41 Φθιάδων δ' ἵππων ... / ... / τὰς πόντιος Αἰακίδᾳ / Πηλεῖ δίδωσι δαίμων. For the 'perfective' present in both tragic passages see KG I 134–5, SD 272 and A. Rijksbaron, *Grammatical Observations on Euripides' Bacchae,* Amsterdam 1991, 1–4 with n. 7. With δίδωσι(ν) *Eum.* 7–8, *OT* 1173, *Hec.* 1133–4, E. *El.* 34–5 and *Ba.* 43–4.

αὐτός: Dobree's conjecture (*Adversaria* II [1833], 87 = IV [1874], 84) is superior to the paradosis αὐτούς (OΛ) or αὐτάς (V) for stressing the animals' special nature as Poseidon's gift. Indeed in *Il.* 23.277–8 (above) some MSS read αὐτός for αὐτούς, by analogy with *Il.* 2.827 Πάνδαρος, ᾧ καὶ τόξον Ἀπόλλων αὐτὸς ἔδωκεν.

---

84 Cf. *Rh.* 122 (n.), where Achilles and Ajax share the epithet αἴθων.

πωλοδαμνήσας: Unlike at 624 πωλοδαμνήσεις δὲ σύ ('you shall bring the horses under control'), the verb here bears its ordinary sense 'to break in young horses'. It is first found metaphorically in *Ai*. 548–9 ἀλλ' αὐτίκ' ὠμοῖς αὐτὸν ἐν νόμοις πατρός / δεῖ πωλοδαμνεῖν, but otherwise belongs to fourth-century and later prose.

ὡς λέγουσι: Phrases of this kind mark a statement 'as being beyond the speaker's direct knowledge' (FJW on A. *Suppl*. 230 [II, p. 186]) and may lend 'the authority of tradition' to mythical and often miraculous events (T. C. W. Stinton, *PCPS* n.s. 22 [1976], 65 = *Collected Papers*, 242–3). There is usually no scepticism implied.

189a. ἐπάρας: 'stir up, excite' (LSJ s.v. ἐπαίρω II 1). ἐλπίδι or the like can be understood (109–10a n. with n. 53).

189b–90. δώσω δέ σοι / ... Ἀχιλλέως ὄχον adapts Hector's initial promise of the finest Greek team and chariot in return for the spying expedition: *Il*. 10.305–6 δώσω γὰρ δίφρον τε δύω τ' ἐριαύχενας ἵππους, / οἵ κεν ἄριστοι ἔωσι θοῆς ἐπὶ νηυσὶν Ἀχαιῶν.

ὄχος (literally 'carriage, chariot') here refers to the team alone, as at *Hipp*. 1229 φόβῳ τέτρωρον ἐκμαίνων ὄχον and E. *El*. 1135–6 ἀλλὰ τούσδ' ὄχους, ὀπάονες, / φάτναις ἄγοντες πρόσθεθ'. So also *Rh*. 621 (620b–1n.) ὄχημα ... πωλικόν, 797–8 (n.) ὄχημα πωλικόν / ... ἵππων and more often ἅρμα (LSJ s.v. I 3).

κάλλιστον οἴκοις κτῆμ': Cf. 620 κάλλιστον οἴκοις σκῦλον ... The near-repetition stresses the analogy between Rhesus' and Achilles' horses.

191–2. 'Thank you. And I say that, if I were to get them, I would receive the finest gift among the Phrygians in return for my courage.'

αἰνῶ: 'a one-word formula of approval' (Bond on *HF* 275), which sounds rather dry in response to Hector's noble concession. The idiom is especially Euripidean: *Alc*. 1093 αἰνῶ μὲν αἰνῶ, *HF* 275, *IT* 1486, E. fr. 603.1 (context uncertain) and, with the less poetic ἐπαινῶ, *HF* 1235, *IA* 440, Ar. *Ach*. 485 (paratragic), *Ran*. 508, S. fr. 282.1 (*Inachus*). For the two verbs expressing thanks in general see J. H. Quincey, *JHS* 86 (1966), 133–58 (133–5, 144–58) and 647–8n.

δ' ἄν: Verrall (*apud* Murray) for δέ. With ἄν added, we arrive at an indirect potential hypothetical period, where the protasis is represented by the participle λαβών. Otherwise no satisfactory meaning could be elicited from the text.

Φρυγῶν: 32n.

τῆς ἐμῆς εὐσπλαγχνίας: almost like English 'for my guts' (εὔσπλαγχνος = 'with healthy inwards': [Hp.] *Prorrh*. II 6, 11). The noun is not elsewhere attested in classical Greek, but εὔσπλαγχνος appears, already in the figurative sense (cf. LSJ s.v. σπλάγχνον II), at A. fr. dub. 451c.33–4. To judge by similar tragic -σπλαγχνος compounds

(Ritchie 155), it was rare, so that our poet perhaps coined εὐσπλαγχνία after precisely this source.

193–4. Dolon ends with a characteristically bold and condescending 'consolation', to which Hector does not respond (Strohm 259). The dramaturgy of his silence is discussed in 149–94n. (pp. 175–6).

ἐφ' οἷσι τέρψῃ: By contrast to other verbs of feeling, τέρπομαι does not usually take ἐπί + dative (KG I 440 n. 10, 502, SD 168, 467). Feickert (on 194) compares Luc. *DMort.* 22.6 ἐγὼ δὲ μάλα ἐτερπόμην ἐπ' αὐτοῖς.

τῆσδ' ἀριστεύων χθονός: With the non-personal partitive (or local) genitive, ἀριστεύω here merges from 'to be best / bravest' (LSJ s.v. I) into 'hold a leading position, rule' (cf. ἄρχω, κρατέω and the like). The construction has a late-fourth-century parallel in the *lex sacra* preceding Isyllus' Epidaurian Paean: Isyll. 14–15 (*CA* 133 = Furley–Bremer II 181) οἵ κεν ἀριστεύωσι πόληος τᾶσδ(ε) Ἐπιδαύρου / λέξασθαί τ' ἄνδρας.

195–200. The antistrophe to 131–6 (131–6 ~ 195–200, 131–6nn.) is placed between Dolon's dialogue with Hector (149–94) and his prolonged exit into 'battle' (201–23). Its praise for the spy and the fortune that, it is hoped, lies in store for him cannot be separated from the greatness and glory of his enterprise, which elevates the scouting mission to a heroic feat and so prepares the ground for Dolon's boast at 219–23 (n.) that he will capture Odysseus' or Diomedes' head (R. S. Bond, *AJPh* 117 [1996], 259, 260–1). However, in contrast to the retrospective first stasimon (224–63n.), the chorus also strike a more serious chord, as they chide the arrogance of turning down a Priamid's hand (197b–8n.). On the whole, therefore, we get the impression of a miniature victory-ode (Strohm 259), which highlights the disproportion between Dolon, his task and the reward he has asked for it. Getting the promise of Achilles' horses will remain his sole 'exploit', while (with his help) another splendid team is to be taken that night.

Metre

131–6 ~ 195–200n.

195. μέγας ἀγών: 'Great is the contest'. Euripides often used μέγας / μέγιστος ἀγών, both literally and in metaphorical sense (*Med.* 235, *Hipp.* 496, *Hec.* 229, *Hel.* 843, 1090, *Phoen.* 860, *Ba.* 975, *IA* 1003–4, 1254). The expression is colloquial to judge by various comic examples (Ar. *Nub.* 957, *Pax* 276, *Ran.* 883, Pl. Com. fr. 46.10 *PCG* μείζων ἀγών, Men. *Sam.* 95 οὐ ... μέτριος ἀγών) and e.g. Hdt. 7.104.3, 7.209.2,

Thuc. 2.89.10 (all in direct speech) and Pl. *Rep.* 608b4. For Sophocles cf. *OC* 587 ὅρα γε μήν· οὐ σμικρός, οὐχ, ἀγὼν ὅδε.

ἐπινοεῖς: The verb is not otherwise attested in tragedy, but ἐπίνοια ('intention, purpose') occurs at *Med.* 760 and *Phoen.* 408 (with Mastronarde). In *Ant.* 389 it means 'afterthought, second thoughts' (LSJ s.v. ἐπίνοια II).

196. μακάριός γε μὰν ... ἔσῃ: '(Yet) truly you will be blessed'. In the fifth century BC only Pindar (*Pyth.* 5.46), Aristophanes and Euripides have μακάριος and, unlike μάκαρ, always of men or their affairs (M. McDonald, *ICS* 4 [1979], 27–33). With γε μάν (Diggle for μήν in lyrics) the statement is marked as mildly adversative (G. Wakker, in *NAGP*, 224–6, where our passage fits better than under 'progressive' γε μήν [226–7 with n. 39]).

197a. πόνος ὅδ' εὐκλεής: Nauck's ὅδ' (II[1] [1854], XXII) for the MSS' δ' creates an elegant asyndeton (cf. 199–200n.) and exact metrical responsion with 133a τί γὰρ ἄμεινον ἢ ... The connection remains causal.

197b–8. 'Still it is a great thing to become the kinsman of rulers.'

The sudden return to the subject of a royal marriage, which Dolon declined in 167–8 (n.), has perplexed scholars who failed to assign full adversative value to δέ and thus saw here either a gross poetic infelicity (Strohm 262 n. 2) or textual corruption in γαμβρὸν πέλειν (J. F. Gaertner, *Hermes* 131 [2003], 500). Yet as an oblique warning the remark makes perfect sense. Despite their enthusiasm, the chorus wonder whether Dolon has not gone too far in pressing for Achilles' team, instead of accepting the first, and most generous, offer Hector made.

μέγα δὲ ... πέλειν: For μέγα (σμικρόν / φαῦλον) with infinitive see Wilkins on *Hcld.* 21–2. The idiom recurs in 285 νυκτὸς γὰρ οὔτι φαῦλον ἐσβαλεῖν στρατόν, but otherwise belongs to Euripides only of the tragedians. In the present context, note especially *Tro.* 259 οὐ γὰρ μέγ' αὐτῇ βασιλικῶν λέκτρων τυχεῖν;

199–200. 'Let Justice see to what comes from the gods; what lies with men seems fulfilled for you.'

The prospect of glory and a marvellous reward leaves nothing to be desired, although the outcome of Dolon's mission still depends on the gods. Jouan and Zanetto, among others, translate 'As to what comes from the gods, let Justice watch over you, as to ...'.[85] But it is unnatural to make τὰ δὲ παρ' ἀνδράσιν adverbial (parallel to τὰ θεόθεν), and ἐπίδοι rather than ἐπιδέτω would be expected in the wish (Paley on 199,

---

85 This rendering also lies behind FJW on A. *Suppl.* 1 (II, p. 6), where our passage joins several Aeschylean examples (and one from Herodotus) of ἐφοράω 'with a connotation of protecting'.

200). Moreover, while Dike may be assumed to determine which fate Dolon deserves, she has no place as protector of a spying expedition. Hermes will appropriately be invoked for that in 216–17.

τὰ θεόθεν: Bothe (5 [1803], 288) and Seidler (*De versibus dochmiacis*, 61 n.*) reduced Ω's τὰ δέ. In contrast to 197a (n.), the scribal attempt to remove asyndeton destroys the metre here.

τὰ δὲ παρ' ἀνδράσιν: Heath (*Notae sive lectiones*, 95) for ἀνδράσι (Ω), which does not scan. Wecklein (*SBAW* I [1897], 478) also offered παρ' ἀνέρων. But exact correspondence with τὰ θεόθεν is unnecessary and not even desired if a difference in rank is to be observed between gods and men as distributors of boons (cf. Feickert on 200).

201–23. Before his departure Dolon explains to the curious and astonished chorus how he is planning to approach the Greek camp in a wolf's disguise (201–15). The sentries dispatch him with a tell-tale good wish (216–18), which elicits one last, extravagant boast (219–23). We will not see Dolon on stage again.

Formally the scene resembles *Ba.* 821–46, where Dionysus prepares to lure Pentheus to his death by tempting him to spy on the maenads in women's dress. There is nothing of the dark and twisted psychology here, but Dolon too will go to his doom in what should have been the perfect camouflage (201–2n.). Each time, moreover, the subject of disguise is introduced in a similar way (204, 206nn.) and then described, as it were, from head to toe (*Rh.* 208–11a ~ *Ba.* 831–5). Most significantly, perhaps, Pentheus invokes the need for a 'military reconnaissance' sortie (*Ba.* 838 ὀρθῶς· μολεῖν χρὴ πρῶτον ἐς κατασκοπήν)[86] to justify his desire to see the Bacchic rites (Dodds on *Ba.* 821–38).

Dolon's animal costume goes far beyond the donning of a wolf-skin and marten's cap in *Il.* 10.333–5 (208–11a n.) and has provoked ridicule since Σ[V] *Rh.* 210 (II 331.8–9 Schwartz = 86–7 Merro) ἀπίθανον τετραποδίζειν αὐτὸν ὡς τοὺς λύκους· οὐδὲ γὰρ Ὅμηρος διὰ τοῦτο τὴν λυκῆν αὐτῷ περιτίθησιν. Yet it was no invention on our poet's part. Three Attic vase-paintings of the early fifth century BC already show the spy thus fully attired, and one even crawling on all fours (Paris, Louvre CA 1802 [~ 480–460 BC]).[87] Of special interest is a fragmentary red-figure cup attributed to Onesimus (Paris, Cab. Méd. 526 [part], 743, 553, L. 41 [~ 500–490 BC]),[88] which shows the encounter with Odysseus and Diomedes. On the far right Athena appears by Diomedes' side, while

---

[86] Cf. *Ba.* 916, 956, 981. The words κατασκοπή and κατάσκοπος are rare in drama. *Rhesus* has eight cases of the latter for both the Trojan and the Achaean spies (125–6a n.).
[87] *LIMC* III.1 s.v. Dolon B 2 (p. 661), III.2 (p. 525).
[88] *LIMC* III.1 s.v. Dolon E 11 (p. 662), III.2 (p. 526).

on the far left Hermes (cf. 199–200, 216–17nn.) is leaving Dolon to his fate.[89] It seems, therefore, that we have in Dolon's mimicry a genuine early variant of the myth, for which *Rhesus* happens to be our only literary source.[90] If and how it relates to *Iliad* 10 is impossible to tell (Fenik, *Iliad X*, 59–60), but it may well be older and ultimately reflect some ritual or werewolf tale (cf. Jouan, XXX with n. 58, S. H. Steadman, *CR* 59 [1945], 7). As an ancient military ruse, animal disguise is attested by Jos. *BJ* 3.190–2 ὁ μέντοι γε Ἰώσηπος πρὸς τῷδε τῷ στρατηγήματι καὶ ἕτερον ἐπενόησεν ... ἕρπειν τὰ πολλὰ παρὰ τὰς φυλακὰς κελεύσας τοῖς ἐξιοῦσιν καὶ τὰ νῶτα καλύπτειν νάκεσιν, ὡς εἰ καὶ κατίδοι τις αὐτοὺς νύκτωρ, φαντασίαν παρέχοιεν κυνῶν (Musgrave on *Rh.* 208). The attempt also failed.

The dramatic prominence given to Dolon's camouflage foreshadows the recurrent use of the wolf-motif thoughout the play, especially regarding Odysseus and Diomedes, who take the hide (591–3, 780–8nn.). More immediately, its description in terms of both a Homeric arming scene (208–11a n.) and the way Heracles puts on his lion-skin (208–9n.) contributes to Dolon's transformation into an overconfident warrior, which was begun in the preceding choral song (195–200n.) and culminates in the hope that he will kill an Achaean chief (219–223n.). It is a characteristic paradox that the man who receives a farewell like King Aegeus after granting Medea sanctuary (216–17n.) will engage in the distinctly unheroic activity of prowling around in the dark. No single Iliadic fighter is compared to a wolf, the emblem of trickery and sneak attacks (W. Richter, *RE* Suppl. XV s.v. Wolf, col. 966, R. Buxton, in J. N. Bremmer [ed.], *Interpretations of Greek Mythology*, London – Sydney 1987, 64–5, Janko on *Il.* 16.156–63).[91] Unsurprisingly, then, Longus was inspired by our account for Dorkon's treacherous attempt on Chloe (cf. 208–11a n.).

---

89 See J. A. K. Thomson, *CR* 25 (1911), 238–9 (whose undue trust in a reconstruction of Dolon's head with a helmet pervades the literature). The third vessel, an intact cup by the Dokimasia Painter of about 490–480 BC (St. Petersburg, Ermitage Б 1452), depicts the same scene without the gods (*LIMC* III.1 s.v. Dolon E 13 [p. 662], III.2 [p. 527]). Some scholars add a contemporary Attic black-figure oenochoe (Oxford, Ashm. Mus. G 251), but there the wolf-skin is merely tied round Dolon's shoulders, and he seems to be wearing a skull-cap (*LIMC* III.1 s.v. Dolon 12 [p. 662], III.2 [p. 526]). In general, Wilamowitz, *De Rhesi scholiis*, 11 = *KS* I, 11 and F. Lissarague, *RA* n.s. 1 (1980), 3–30.
90 Too little of Eubulus' comedy *Dolon* survives (frr. 29–31 *PCG*) to determine whether he appeared in it in disguise (Porter, xi).
91 Cf. also Σ^bT *Il.* 10.23 (III 8.45–7 Erbse) Μενέλαον δὲ ὡς ἥττω παρδαλῆν ἐνδύει, Δόλωνα δὲ ὡς δειλὸν καὶ ἐπὶ λαθρίδιον πρᾶξιν ὁρμῶντα λυκέαν (with Hainsworth on *Il.* 10.334–5).

It has been suggested that Dolon acts out the movements while he describes his disguise and four-footed walk (Burnett, 'Smiles', 22, R. S. Bond, *AJPh* 117 [1996], 260, Burlando, *Reso*, 63–4), like the Pythia in *Eumenides* and Polymestor in *Hecuba* (211b–12n.). But anything beyond a few gestures would look absurd and ruin the delicate balance our poet draws between the elevated and base. More probably, Odysseus' and Diomedes' entry with the wolf-skin mirrors what in Dolon's case we never see.

201–3. 'I will go. I will return to my hearth at home and equip my body with suitable attire, and from there I will set out for the Argive ships.'

201–2. στείχοιμ' ἄν: For the first-person potential optative expressing a fixed resolve see KG I 233, SD 329, and cf. 835–7 οὐδέν' ἂν δεξαίμεθα / ... / ἄλλον. Euripides has several cases of στείχοιμ' ἄν at line-opening (*El.* 669, *Ion* 418, 668, *Ba.* 515, 845)[92] and the last one in a context similar to ours (201–23n.). Sophocles avoids 'formulaic' style at *Ant.* 1108 ὧδ' ὡς ἔχω στείχοιμ' ἄν.

ἐλθὼν <δ'> ἐς δόμους ἐφέστιος: Ritchie (201) denied any direct influence of *Tr.* 262–3 ὅς αὐτὸν ἐλθόντ' ἐς δόμους ἐφέστιον, / ξένον παλαιὸν ὄντα by referring to *Med.* 713 δέξαι δὲ χώρᾳ καὶ δόμοις ἐφέστιον and the general frequency in tragedy of ἐφέστιος ('at one's hearth') following a form of δόμοι or δώματα (cf. Davies on *Tr.* 262). However, the case for (somewhat imperfect) verbal borrowing (Fraenkel, *Rev.* 232; cf. Introduction, 37), is strengthened by the observation that ἐφέστιος is far less relevant to changing garb than to being a guest – let alone a suppliant (A. *Suppl.* 365, *Eum.* 577, 669, *Cyc.* 371, *Med.* 713) or a man going to greet his household gods (*Ag.* 851–3).[93] Also, in view of *Il.* 10.333–6, one may doubt whether Dolon will return home (i.e. to Troy) at all, and the words become entirely improbable for a mere bivouac (Porter on 201: 'The poet seems to ignore the fact that Dolon is in camp').[94] Perhaps he at first thought of *Ba.* 843a–6, where Pentheus leaves for his palace (ἐς οἴκους) to get dressed as a maenad, as it turns out (201–23n.).

<δ'> (Aldine) removes the unwanted asyndeton in the paradosis.

σκευῇ ... σῶμ' ἐμὸν καθάψομαι: Cf. *Rh.* 208 (208–9n.) λύκειον ἀμφὶ νῶτ' ἐνάψομαι δοράν, Arch. *Ep.* 19.2 Gow–Page *GPh* ὁ πρὶν ὑπαὶ

---

[92] *Ion* 981 (L) is uncertain, since uniquely 'the words' would not 'indicate an immediate intention to depart' (Diggle, *Studies*, 101 n. 1). Various remedies have been proposed.

[93] With Karsten's ἐφέστιος for ἐφεστίους in 851. *Od.* 23.55 ἦλθε μὲν αὐτὸς ζωὸς ἐφέστιος (compared by LSJ s.v. ἐφέστιος I) is different in that the adjective alone connotes 'home'.

[94] Feickert (on 201) is wrong to speak of Trojan 'tents', which are nowhere mentioned in the play. Words like εὐναί, κοῖται and χάμευναι (9, 852) indicate the setting in an open camp (Introduction, 40–1).

μίτραις κῶλα καθαψάμενος (of a race-horse), S. fr. 314.225–6 (*Ichneutae*) νεβρίνῃ καθημμέν[ο]ς / δορᾷ (LSJ s.v. καθάπτω I 2: '*equip* by fastening or hanging on') and E. fr. 752.1–3 = Ar. *Ran*. 1211–13 Διόνυσος, ὃς θύρσοισι καὶ νεβρῶν δοραῖς / καθαπτὸς ἐν πεύκῃσι Παρνασσὸν κάτα / πηδᾷ. On σκευή, 'dress, attire', in tragedy see Collard on E. *Suppl*. 1054.

203. ἥσω ... πόδα: The idiom recurs in 797–8 οἳ δ' ... / ... ἵεσαν φυγῇ πόδα. Barrett on *Hipp*. 542–4 (p. 262) examines this 'less restricted use' of ἵημι in tragedy and also quotes E. *El*. 799 δμῶες πρὸς ἔργον πάντες ἵεσαν χέρας. Later, note Diosc. *Ep*. 16.10 Gow–Page *HE* ἐς τὸν ἑὸν τύμπανον ἧκε χέρας.

ναῦς ἔπ' Ἀργείων: 149–50n.

204. 'Why, what other dress will you wear instead of this?'

The coryphaeus' question and its virtual repetition in 207 (n.) resemble those of Pentheus at *Ba*. 828 τίνα στολήν; ἦ θῆλυν; ἀλλ' αἰδώς μ' ἔχει and 830 στολὴν δὲ τίνα φῂς ἀμφὶ χρῶτ' ἐμὸν βαλεῖν; (201–23n.).

ἐπεὶ τίν' ἄλλην ... στολήν; The logical connection is as follows: 'You say you want to go home and put on a garb to suit your purpose. For (ἐπεί) what other dress ...?' (Ammendola on 204). More regularly, such questions explain why something has just been said (FJW on A. *Suppl*. 330), but cf. *Cho*. 212–14 (Ορ.) εὔχου τὰ λοιπά, τοῖς θεοῖς τελεσφόρους / εὐχὰς ἐπαγγέλλουσα, τυγχάνειν καλῶς. / (Ηλ.) ἐπεὶ τί νῦν ἕκατι δαιμόνων κυρῶ; for a similar use in dramatic dialogue.

205. κλωπικοῖς ... βήμασιν: 'stealthy movements'. κλωπικός (properly 'thievish') occurs only here and in 512, unless, against Fraenkel (*Rev*. 230) and all modern editors, we accept it in Pl. *Crat*. 408a1 as a variant for the equally unparalleled κλοπικός (A. Meschini, in *Scritti Diano*, 218–19).[95] It is possible, therefore, that our poet coined the word himself, after the contemporary fashion of forming (pseudo-)technical adjectives in -ικός (cf. Liapis on 205). Λ has κλεπτικοῖς (cf. Pl. *Rep*. 334b4 and later), which accords less well with κλῶπες later in the play (644–5n.). See also 503–5n.

206. σοφοῦ παρ' ἀνδρὸς χρὴ σοφόν τι μανθάνειν: Cf. Pentheus at *Ba*. 824 εὖ γ' εἶπας αὖ τόδ'· ὥς τις εἶ πάλαι σοφός (201–23n.). In view of *Ba*. 178–9 (Cadmus to Teiresias) ὦ φίλταθ', ὡς σὴν γῆρυν ᾐσθόμην κλυών / σοφὴν σοφοῦ παρ' ἀνδρός and the secure position παρά holds in both the direct and indirect tradition (below), σοφοῦ πρὸς ἀνδρός (gV) should not be preferred with Liapis ('Notes', 57).

---

[95] One would indeed have to examine the Platonic MSS tradition to determine whether κλωπ- is a true *varia lectio* or a 'conjecture' perpetuated from the Aldine through the early editions and lexica.

Apart from 105–8 (n.), this is the only *sententia* in our play that found its way into the anthological tradition: Stob. 2.31.14, Orion *Anth.* 1.7 (p. 42 Schneidewin), [Men.] *Mon.* 718 Jäkel. Cf. Introduction, 46.

207. λέξον· τίς ἔσται ...; The division into command and direct question, when the verse could also be taken as a single sentence, suits the chorus-leader's excitement and perhaps general soldiers' diction. For the largely subjective editorial choice involved see FJW on A. *Suppl.* 460.

σαγή (properly 'pack, baggage') has come to denote all sorts of 'equipment' (LSJ s.v. I) and refers to a disguise also at *Cho.* 560–1 ξένῳ γὰρ εἰκώς, παντελῆ σαγὴν ἔχων, / ἥξω ... ἐφ' ἑρκείους πύλας. But the usual sense in drama is 'military gear' (*Pers.* 240, *Sept.* 126, 391, *HF* 188 and, of the panoply, *Ant.* 107 πανσαγίᾳ, S. fr. 1092 [with Radt], Ar. fr. 881 *PCG*, Men. fr. 570 *PCG*), which Dolon exploits in the following account of how he will 'arm' himself (208–11a n.).

208–11a. Just as *Il.* 10.333–5 αὐτίκα δ' ἀμφ' ὤμοισιν ἐβάλλετο καμπύλα τόξα, / ἕσσατο δ' ἔκτοσθεν ῥινὸν πολιοῖο λύκοιο, / κρατὶ δ' ἔπι κτιδέην κυνέην, ἕλε δ' ὀξὺν ἄκοντα may be called 'a truncated arming ... scene' (Hainsworth on *Il.* 10.333–7), our poet adheres to the Homeric pattern in his description of Dolon's wolf-disguise (R. S. Bond, *AJPh* 117 [1996], 259). Deviations from the standard order, 1. greaves, 2. corslet, 3. sword, 4. shield, 5. helmet, 6. spear (Kirk on *Il.* 3.330–8), are due to the fact that Dolon will don not a panoply, but an animal skin, which it is practical to put round first the torso (208: corslet), then the head (209: helmet), and finally the arms and shins (210–11a: greaves).[96] The usual weapons are not mentioned here for the simple reason that they would spoil the stratagem.

Together with *HF* 361–3 (below) our text seems to have been the model for Dorkon's scheme at Longus 1.20.2–3 λύκου δέρμα μεγάλου λαβὼν ... περιέτεινε τῷ σώματι ποδῆρες κατανωτισάμενος ὡς τούς τε προσθίους πόδας ἐφηπλῶσθαι ταῖς χερσὶ καὶ τοὺς κατόπιν τοῖς σκέλεσιν ἄχρι πτέρνης καὶ τοῦ στόματος τὸ χάσμα σκέπειν τὴν κεφαλὴν ὥσπερ ἀνδρὸς ὁπλίτου κράνος. ἐκθηριώσας δὲ αὐτὸν ὡς ἔνι μάλιστα ... (201–23, 208–9, 210–11a nn., Introduction, 45). For wolf-imagery and the tradition of Dolon's disguise see likewise 201–23n. and Introduction, 5.

---

[96] Realism also lies behind the Homeric system. With the corslet on it would have been difficult to stoop and fasten the greaves, and the sword- and shield-straps might have got caught in the helmet's plume (Kirk on *Il.* 3.330–8, *BK* on *Il.* 3.328–338, Hanson, *The Western Way of War*, 77). In *Sept.* 675–6 Eteocles asks for his greaves as the first item to be put on.

208–9. The opening couplet has long been recognised as an imitation of *HF* 361–3 πυρσῷ δ' ἀμφεκαλύφθη / ξανθὸν κρᾶτ' ἐπινωτίσας / δεινοῦ χάσματι θηρός[97] (~ 465–6 στολήν τε θηρὸς ἀμφέβαλλε σῷ κάρᾳ / λέοντος, ᾗπερ αὐτὸς ἐξωπλίζετο), which affords the only classical parallel for χάσμα = 'gaping mouth' (LSJ s.v. II with Suppl. [1996], Wilamowitz on *HF* 363, R. Renehan, *CPh* 80 [1985], 154). Both passages probably shaped the words of Longus 1.20.2 (cf. 208–11a n.).

ἀμφὶ νῶτ' ἐνάψομαι: Cobet (*VL*[2], 583). The transmitted ἀμφὶ νῶτον ἅψομαι (Δ: νῶτα θήσομαι Λ), still kept by Wecklein, Porter, Ammendola and Zanetto (Feickert), is possible but unidiomatic Greek. ἐνάπτομαι and ἐνῆμμαι regularly appear of putting on or wearing clothes: Hdt. 7.69.1 Αἰθίοπες δὲ παρδαλέας τε καὶ λεοντέας ἐναμμένοι, *HF* 549 θανάτου τάδ' ἤδη περιβόλαι' ἐνήμμεθα (Scaliger: ἀν- L), Ar. *Nub.* 72, *Av.* 1250, *Ran.* 430, *Eccl.* 80, fr. 264.1 *PCG* ὁ χορὸς δ' ὠρχεῖτ' ἂν ἐναψάμενος δάπιδας καὶ στρωματόδεσμα, D. Chr. 7.32, Luc. *Herc.* 1, *Tim.* 6 (LSJ s.v. ἐνάπτω I 2) and in particular also Eust. on Dion. Per. 939 (I 286.27–31 Bernhardy = *GGM* II 383.31–5) ἐνάπτεσθαι δὲ καὶ καθάπτεσθαι λέγομεν τὰ μὴ ζώνῃ διαλαμβανόμενα, μηδὲ τὸ σῶμα ὅλον ἐνδύοντα, ἀλλὰ μέρος τι σκέποντα καὶ ἄφετα ἐξαρτώμενα, οἷον πήραν λεοντῆν ἢ παρδαλέην. There should be no objection to the addition of a prepositional phrase here. Singular νῶτον and νῶτα alternate in poetry.

With Cobet's conjecture 208 joins 986 as the only other iambic trimeter in *Rhesus* where elision creates a (weakened) medial caesura. See Ritchie 285–6 and in general West, *GM* 82–3, Diggle, *Euripidea*, 473–4 with n. 151.

χάσμα θηρός: In later Greek (where χάσμα, 'jaws, gaping mouth', is common) cf. especially Plut. *Mar.* 25.10 οἱ δ' ἱππεῖς ... ἐξήλασαν λαμπροί, κράνη μὲν εἰκασμένα θηρίων φοβερῶν χάσμασι καὶ προτομαῖς ἰδιομόρφοις ἔχοντες. Hsch. χ 224 Hansen–Cunningham χάσμα θηρός· ὄψις θηρός, [...] πρόσωπον explains the synecdoche.

210–11a. Again a strong influence can be seen on Longus 1.20.2 ὡς τούς τε προσθίους πόδας ἐφηπλῶσθαι ταῖς χερσὶ καὶ τοὺς κατόπιν τοῖς σκέλεσιν ἄχρι πτέρνης (cf. 208–11a n.).

βάσιν ... προσθίαν: 'the fore-feet', as in e.g. Hdt. 2.69.2 περὶ τοὺς ἐμπροσθίους πόδας (v.l. προσθίους), 4.60.1, Xen. *Cyn.* 4.1 σκέλη τὰ

---

[97] Diggle (*PCPS* n.s. 20 [1974], 6–8 + *Studies*, 48–9) wrote δεινοῦ for δεινῷ (L). R. Renehan (*CPh* 80 [1985], 155–6) defends the paradosis, with Wilamowitz' interpretation of δεινῷ χάσματι θηρός as an explanatory apposition to πυρσῷ, 'firebrand, torch' (LSJ s.v. (A) I). But this metaphor for a 'tawny mane' is strained, and L(P) show further assimilative errors in this ode at 64, 372, 376, 377, 396, 398, 412 and 441 (cf. M. L. West, *Textual Criticism and Editorial Technique*, Stuttgart 1973, 23–4).

πρόσθια μικρά, 9.19 and Longus 1.20.2 (above). Simple βάσις meaning 'foot' first occurs in *Phil.* 1378–9. Otherwise note *Hec.* 836–7 εἴ μοι γένοιτο φθόγγος ἐν βραχίοσιν / ... καὶ ποδῶν βάσει, E. fr. 540.2–3 ... ὑπὸ λεοντόπουν βάσιν / καθέζετ᾽ and *IA* [421] θηλύπουν βάσιν.

211b–12. τετράπουν μιμήσομαι / λύκου κέλευθον: Although 'Dolon the Wolf' never appears on stage, and we may doubt he went to great, if any, mimetic efforts here (201–23n.), it is worth noting that the only surviving cases of a dramatic entry on all fours are the terrified Pythia at *Eum.* 34–8 (Taplin, *Stagecraft*, 363, Sommerstein on 33) and Polymestor, blinded, at *Hec.* 1056–9 ὤμοι ἐγώ, πᾷ βῶ ... / τετράποδος βάσιν θηρὸς ὀρεστέρου / τιθέμενος ἐπὶ χεῖρα καὶ ἴχνος; The latter shows pertinent verbal overlaps with our passage and its lyric 'repetition' in 255b–7a (n.) ... τετράπουν / μῖμον ἔχων ἐπὶ γαίας / θηρός (Collard on *Hec.* 1056–1106, 1058–9 ~ in J. A. López Férez [ed.], *Estudios actuales sobre textos griegos* ..., Madrid 1991, 165, 167).

LSJ s.v. κέλευθος III quote *Tro.* 887–8 πάντα γὰρ δι᾽ ἀψόφου / βαίνων κελεύθου κατὰ δίκην τὰ θνήτ᾽ ἄγεις as a parallel for the sense 'walk, gait'. But a local interpretation ('For proceeding on a silent path you direct all mortal affairs in accordance with justice') seems preferable; cf. Bacch. 9.47–8 στείχει δι᾽ εὐρείας κελε[ύ]θου / μυρία πάντα φάτις.

δυσεύρετον: The adjective is surprisingly rare in classical Greek: *PV* 816, *Ba.* 1221 (del. Nauck), Xen. *Mem.* 3.14.7, *Vect.* 4.13.

213. τάφροις ... καὶ νεῶν προβλήμασιν: the Achaean trench and wall (110b–11, 989b–92nn.). For πρόβλημα with an objective genitive, 'defence for ...' (LSJ s.v. II 1), cf. *Sept.* 539–40 ἐν χαλκηλάτῳ / σάκει, κυκλωτῷ σώματος προβλήματι.

πελάζων: 13–14n.

214–15. 'But when I set foot on empty land, I shall walk on two legs. That is how my ruse is constructed.'

ὅταν δ᾽ ἔρημον χῶρον ἐμβαίνω ποδί: Euripides often used ἐμβαίνω with the accusative (properly of direction): *Cyc.* 91–2 ἄξενόν τε γῆν (Jacobs: στέγην L) / τήνδ᾽ ἐμβεβῶτες (with Seaford on 91), *Alc.* 1000–1, *Hec.* 921–2, *Suppl.* 987–9 (metaphorical) and *El.* 1288 σὺ δ᾽ Ἰσθμίας γῆς αὐχέν᾽ ἐμβαίνων ποδί, which illustrates his further habit of combining a verb of motion with ποδί or πόδα (Diggle, *Studies*, 36–7). *Rhesus* has several other such pleonastic datives (Ritchie 235–6; cf. 56–8n.).

δίβαμος: Like ἀμβλώψ (736–7n.), this had been a *hapax* until a Euripidean attestation emerged in P. Oxy. 2461 fr. 1.15 = E. fr. 472b.32 (*Cretans*) τετρ]ασκελὴς γὰρ ἢ δίβαμ[ος ἔρχεται; (Ritchie 150 n. 1, Fraenkel, *Rev.* 230; cf. Introduction, 31). The ending -βαμος is a metrical alternative to -βάμων also at Pi. *Pyth.* 9.18 ἰστῶν παλιμβάμους ...

ὀδούς.⁹⁸ For the latter cf. particularly τετραβάμων, 'four-footed', in the lyric E. *El.* 476 τετραβάμονες ἵπποι, *Tro.* 516, *Hel.* 376, *Phoen.* 792 (corrupt) and 808.

τῇδε σύγκειται δόλος: Dolon's confident summary (130b, 640–1n.) ends with the very word that recalls his name (158–9a n.).

216–17. The coryphaeus' invocation bears a striking similarity to that for Aegeus at *Med.* 759–60 ἀλλά σ' ὁ Μαίας πομπαῖος ἄναξ / πελάσειε δόμοις (Strohm 259), which throws into relief the great hopes that rest on the spy (G. Paduano, *Maia* n.s. 25 [1973], 20, Burlando, *Reso*, 57, *Rh.* 201–23n.). Hermes is here called upon as both divine escort (πομπαῖος) and god of deceit (δόλιος). Cf. *Cho.* 726–9 (~ 812–18), S. *El.* 1395–7 ὁ Μαίας δὲ παῖς / Ἑρμῆς σφ' ἄγει δόλον σκότῳ / κρύψας πρὸς αὐτὸ τέρμα κοὐκέτ' ἀμμένει (with Jebb and Finglass on 1395–6), *Phil.* 133 Ἑρμῆς δ' ὁ πέμπων δόλιος ἡγήσαιτο νῷν (with Jebb) and Ar. *Pl.* 1157–60. An early-fifth-century Attic vase-painting shows him deserting Dolon as he falls into the Achaeans' hands (201–23n.).

ἀλλά: When ἀλλά introduces a wish or prayer in reply, '[t]here is no strong break-off ... [it] merely marks a gentle transition from the known present to the unknown and desired future, corresponding very closely with the English 'well'" (*GP* 15–16).

ὅς γε φιλητῶν ἄναξ: Hermes is the 'prince of thieves' also at *h.Merc.* 174–5 ... ἤτοι ἐγώ γε / πειρήσω – δύναμαι – φιλητέων ὄρχαμος εἶναι, 292 ἀρχὸς φιλητέων κεκλήσεαι ἤματα πάντα and the dubious Chian verse-inscription *EG* 1108 Ἑρμῆν τὸν κλέπτην τις ὑφείλετο· θερμὸς ὁ κλέπτης, / ὃς τῶν φιλητέων ᾤχετ' ἄνακτ[α] φέρων. Elsewhere φιλήτης and φιλητεύω (on the spelling see below) are just as naturally applied to the god: *h.Merc.* 66–7, 159, 446, Hippon. fr. 79.10 *IEG*, S. fr. 314.340 (*Ichneutae*), Hellanic. *FGrHist* 4 F 19b (Garvie on *Cho.* 1001–3).

Editors prefer to read φηλητῶν (ΛgE) here. But φιλ- (Δ) is confirmed by the pun in Hellanic. *FGrHist* 4 F 19b τ[ῶν] δὲ γίγνεται Ἑρμ[ῆς] φιλήτης, ὅτι αὐτῇ φιλησίμ[ως] συνεκοιμ[ᾶτο], as well as *Foed.Delph. Pell.* I B 8, II A 13 (= 328a Schwyzer) φιλατίας (III BC) and several papyri and learned works (LSJ s.v. φιλήτης with Suppl. [1996]). It seems, then, that this was the accepted form, despite the apparent connection with φηλόω (*Ag.* 492, E. *Suppl.* 243), φήλωμα (Antipho Soph. 87 B 71 DK) and the like. 'No satisfactory explanation of the matter has yet been given' (West on Hes. *Op.* 375).

---

98 Hsch. χ 650 χορταιόβαμος· ὁ Σειληνός and Hsch. χ 651 Hansen–Cunningham χορταιοβάμων· χορταῖον τὸ ἔνδυμα τοῦ Σειληνοῦ probably derive from a single gloss on χορταιοβάμων (W. & L. Dindorf, in *ThGL* s.v. χορταῖος 8.1602 B), which has become fr. tr. adesp. 601.

218. ἔχεις δὲ τοὔργον: 'You know what you must do', like *Phil.* 789 ἔχετε τὸ πρᾶγμα ('You know what is the matter'). In general see LSJ s.v. ἔχω (A) A I 9 'possess mentally, understand'.

εὐτυχεῖν μόνον σε δεῖ: Cf. *Hel.* 1424 ... τῆς τύχης με δεῖ μόνον. The parallel favours δεῖ (OΛgE) over χρή (V). Both verbs occur with little or no noticeable difference and are often confused by scribes (Barrett on *Hipp.* 41, R. Renehan, *Greek Textual Criticism*, Cambridge [Mass.] 1969, 129–34, Diggle, *Textual Tradition*, 123). For 'leave-taking formulae' such as this see Collard on E. *Suppl.* 1182.

219–23. Dolon's parting words are full of dramatic irony. The preposterous claim that he will kill Odysseus or Diomedes is taken even further in 254–60, where the chorus hope that he will murder Menelaus or Agamemnon (and bring Helen his head). Together the passages foreshadow the fall of a would-be hero (G. Paduano, *Maia* n.s. 25 [1973], 19–20, R. S. Bond, *AJPh* 117 [1996], 260–1), who will himself lose his head in a gruesome way (*Il.* 10.455–7).

On decapitation in epic (and Greek myth generally) see 257b–60n. and Liapis on 219–23 (p. 124).

219–22a. σωθήσομαί τοι: 'Be assured that ...'. Diggle's τοι (*Euripidea*, 513–15) for τε (VΛ et ¹Σᵛ: δὲ O) has rightly been adopted by Kovacs and Jouan. A more confident statement than 'Yes, I will both come safe home and kill Odysseus ...' (Parker on *Alc.* 420–1 [p. 139]) is desired, and unlike γε (Wilamowitz, *apud* Murray) or δή (Liapis, 'Notes', 58 and on 219–23), τοι regularly stands 'in response to a command' (*GP* 541); cf. 570–1 (Οδ.) ὅρα ... μὴ φύλαξιν ἐντύχῃς. / (Δι.) φυλάξομαί τοι ... The error is easy and common, whether or not the particle precedes καί (Diggle, *Euripidea*, 314–15).

Ὀδυσσέως / ... κάρα ... ἢ παῖδα Τυδέως: 'Odysseus' head ... or that of Tydeus' son' (cf. Σᵛ *Rh.* 219 [II 331.10–11 Schwartz = 87 Merro]). The change of construction is explicable both by the long parenthesis (below) and the tendency in Greek to 'default' obliques into the accusative case. Our example follows the pattern of *comparatio compendiaria*, where for the sake of brevity a part of the whole is related to another whole: *Il.* 17.51 κόμαι Χαρίτεσσιν ὁμοῖαι, 21.191, Theoc. 20.25 ὄμματά μοι γλαυκᾶς χαροπώτερα πολλὸν Ἀθάνας, Thuc. 1.71.3 δι' ὅπερ καὶ τὰ τῶν Ἀθηναίων ... ἐπὶ πλέον ὑμῶν κεκαίνωται (KG II 310–11, SD 99). And it may have helped that often in tragedy κάρα stands in periphrasis for a person (LSJ s.v. (A) 3, Griffith on *Ant.* 1, *Rh.* 226a, 902–3nn.). We see here the literal reverse, as it were.[99]

---

[99] E. *El.* 855–7 ἔρχεται δὲ σοί / κάρα 'πιδείξων οὐχὶ Γοργόνος φέρων / ἀλλ' ὃν στυγεῖς Αἴγισθον, adduced by Feickert (on 222), is not parallel if, as it seems, κάρα ... οὐχὶ

σύμβολον δ' ἔχων σαφές / φήσεις Δόλωνα ναῦς ἔπ' Ἀργείων μολεῖν: Like 939–40a (938–40n.) οὐδὲν δ' Ὀδυσσεὺς οὐδ' ὁ Τυδέως τόκος / ἔδρασε, this cannot be recognised as a parenthesis in *writing* until the main sentence is resumed in 222. Similarly E. *El.* 787–9 ἀλλ' ἴωμεν ἐς δόμους – / καὶ ταῦθ' ἅμ' ἠγόρευε καὶ χερὸς λαβών / παρῆγεν ἡμᾶς – οὐδ' ἀπαρνεῖσθαι χρεών, *Phoen.* 163–7 (with Mastronarde on 167), *Or.* 1516, *IA* 391–4.

σύμβολον δ' ἔχων σαφές: The same words are used at *Phil.* 403–4 ἔχοντες ... σύμβολον σαφές / λύπης πρὸς ἡμᾶς ... πεπλεύκατε (where λύπης is a defining genitive). The head of Odysseus (or Diomedes) will be a visible 'token' that Dolon's has reached the Greek ships (cf. Willink on *Or.* 1130).

Δόλωνα: The spy and would-be assassin proudly refers to himself in the third person. Cf. *Il.* 1.240 ἦ ποτ' Ἀχιλλῆος ποθὴ ἵξεται υἷας Ἀχαιῶν (with *BK*), 4.354, 8.22, 11.761, and see West on Hes. *Th.* 22.

ναῦς ἔπ' Ἀργείων μολεῖν: 149–50n.

222b–3. ἀναιμάκτῳ: 'bloodless, unstained with blood' (LSJ s.v. with Suppl. [1996]). Before *Rhesus* the adjective is found in A. *Suppl.* 196 and *Phoen.* 264. It may be an Aeschylean coinage.

πρὶν φάος μολεῖν χθόνα: Cf. *Alc.* 1145–6 πρὶν ἄν ... / ... τρίτον μόλῃ φάος and *Ag.* 766–7 ... ὅτε τὸ κύριον μόλῃ / φάος.

224–63. Dolon's departure is marked with a lively song that moves from a traditional cletic hymn to Apollo (224–32) and prayers for success on the scouting expedition (233–41) to praise for Dolon's valour (242–52) and the wish that he may kill (one of) the Achaean generals (253–63).[100] The symmetric pattern, which 'mirrors the development of D[olon]'s mission' in the preceding episode 'from that of a spy ... to that of an assassin ...' (Klyve on 224–263 [p. 186]), is underlined by sentence structure (both antistrophes end with a relative clause pertaining to the prehistory of the Trojan War) and the unusual syntactical bridge between the first antistrophe and the second strophe (242–4a n.). To a considerable extent, moreover, the chorus repeat sentiments from Dolon's conversations with Hector (149–94) and the coryphaeus (201–23) – in more or less the original order and words (233–6, 240–1, 242–4a, 255b–7a, 257b–60nn.). Apart from the 'cletic hymn' to Rhesus at 342–79 (n.), two Euripidean examples for this type of 'scene-reflecting' song particularly come to mind (Ritchie 338). The first stasimon of *Alcestis* (435–75) not only summarises the heroine's fate so far, but in celebrating her virtue

---

Γοργόνος together are opposed to ... Αἴγισθον (G. Gellie, *BICS* 28 [1981], 11 n. 12, D. Kovacs, *CPh* 82 [1987], 139–41, Cropp on E. *El.* 855–7).

100 Cf. Kranz, *Stasimon*, 264, Klyve on 224–63 (pp. 186–7) and Feickert on 224–63 (p. 153).

also provided thematic and verbal precedents for our ode (242–4a, 245b nn.). *Hcld*. 353–80 similarly recalls the *agon* between Demophon and the Argive Herald in lyric form (Wilkins on *Hcld*. 353–80). Like the sentries' hymn, these stasima conclude the first movement of their plays and so indirectly prepare for an advance in the plot. In *Hcld*. 353–80 we observe a comparable (if more immediate and not absolute) contrast between the confidence of the chorus and the following ruination of their hopes (cf. M. R. Halleran, *Stagecraft in Euripides*, London – Sydney 1985, 53–4, 56).

This παρὰ προσδοκίαν quality of both *Rh*. 224–63 and 342–79 (above) recalls Sophocles' famous 'odes of false preparation': *Ai*. 693–718, *OT* 1086–1109, *Ant*. 1115–54 and *Tr*. 633–62 (Kranz, *Stasimon*, 213–14, 264). Placed right at the dramatic turning point, they express various degrees of choral delusion. Our songs join *Tr*. 633–62 (and *HF* 763–814) in that for the moment 'there is good reason for rejoicing' (Bond on *HF* 763–814). But as in *Ai*. 693–718 and especially *Ant*. 1115–54, we also have here divine invocations which remain unanswered (A. Henrichs, in M. Griffiths – D. J. Mastronarde [eds.], *Cabinet of the Muses. Essays ... in Honor of Thomas G. Rosenmeyer*, Atlanta 1990, 266). Apollo no more comes to help Troy than Dionysus his city Thebes (*Ant*. 1122–5, 1135–9), and Rhesus is prevented by Athena from fulfilling his promise as a 'saviour god' (cf. C. W. Keyes, *CPh* 24 [1929], 207 ~ *TAPA* 59 (1928), xxviii and Rosivach 63–4 on the role of fate behind Apollo's and Athena's interventions). In the long run, therefore, the chorus' fervour will be recognised as just another manifestation of their (and indeed all human characters') inability to understand the order of events. Meanwhile Trojan expectations are raised further by the arrival of the Idaean Shepherd (264) and Rhesus himself (388).

Metre

224–32 ~ 233–41. Dactylo-epitrites with the typically Attic admixture of iambics (Dale, LM^2 180–1, West, *GM* 132–3, Parker, *Songs*, 88–9). Cf. the 'Dawn-Song' (527–37 ~ 546–56) and the Muse's monody, which recalls several metrical features of this ode (890–14 'Metre').

242–52 ~ 253–63. A blend of dactylo-epitrites, iambo-choriambic and aeolic metres, not unlike that of the parodos (23–33 ~ 41–51). On the difficult sequence that ends the stanzas see 250–2/261–3n.

As in the second stasimon of *Troades* (799–859), the preponderance of dactylo-epitrite in both strophic pairs may to some degree reflect their 'epic' content (Klyve on 224–263 [p. 186]; cf. Collard on *Hec*. 905–52 [p. 177]). The fact that it was also a favourite metre of choral-lyric hymns (West, *GM* 76) makes it doubly appropriate to this song.

224	233	⌴ – ⌣ | – – ⌣ ⌣ | – ⌣ ⌣ – |	⌴ *e D* |
225	234	– ⌣ – ⌣ – – |	*ith* |
226–8	235–7	⌣ – ⌣ | – – – ⌣ ⌣ – | ⌣ ⌣ – – ‑ | ⌣ ⌣ | – ⌣ ⌣ – ||	⌣ *e* – *D* – *D* ||
229	238	– ⌣ – | – – ⌣ ⌣ – ⌣ ⌣ | – – |	*e* – *D* – |
230	239	– ⌣ – | – – ⌣ ⌣ – ⌣ ⌣ – |	*e* – *D* |
231	240	– – ⌣ ⌣ | – ⌣ ⌣ – |	– *D* |
232	241	– – | ⌣ – ⌣ | – – |||	– *ith* (*ia ia*ˆ) |||
242–3	253–4	⌣ – ⌣ – – | ⌣ ⌣ – ⌣ – | ⌣ – |	*ia cho ia* |
244	255	– ⌣ ⌣ – ⌣ ⌣ – | ⌣ ⌣ – |	*D*² |
245	256	– ⌣ ⌣ – ⌣ ⌣ | – – |	*D* – |
246–7	257–8	– ⌣ ⌣ – | ⌣ ⌣ – | ⌣ – ⌣ ⌣ – ⌣ ⌣ – |	*D* ⌣ *D* |
248	259	– ⌣ – – ||	*e* – ||
249	260	⌣ ⌣ – ⌣ ⌣ – ⌣ | – ⌣ – ⌣ – ||	'enopl.' (*tl ia*) ||
250	261	⌣⌣⌣ ⌣ | ⌣⌣⌣ |	~*cr*~ |
251–2	262–3	⌣ ⌴ – | ⌣ ⌣ – – ⌣ ⌣ – – ⌣ ⌣ – | ⌣ – – |||	*hi*²ᶜ |||

Notes

224/233 For the juxtaposition of *e*- and *D*-cola without link-anceps or word-division cf. *Tr.* 94 ~ 103 (⌣ *e* ∫ *D*),[101] *Andr.* 1011–12 ~ 1020–1 (– *D* – *e* ∫ *D*), E. fr. 303.4 (⌣ *e* ∫ *D*) and in less purely dactylo-epitrite contexts (so that the *e*-unit could also be regarded as iambic) *Hel.* 1107 ~ 1122 (⌵ *e* ∫ *D*), 1145–6 (– *E* ∫ *D*) and *Phaeth.* 272–3 Diggle = E. fr. 781.63–4 (⌣ *e* ∫ *D* ∫ *ia* ˆ*ia*ˆ). In our passage we do not have 'dove-tailing', but word-end after a longer overlap of three syllables.

226–8/235–7 This is really one long verse so that it does not matter whether (with most editors) we divide after the link-syllable or before (Willink, 'Cantica', 27 = *Collected Papers*, 566).

231–2/240–1 Taken together, the lines resemble the 'Archilochian dicolon' × *D* × \| *ith* \|\| (Willink, 'Cantica', 27 = *Collected Papers*, 566). But the responding word-end after – *D* suggests that our poet envisaged two separate entities, showing the characteristic interplay between blunt and pendent. For similar clausulae to (partly) dactylo-epitrite stanzas cf. *PV* 429–30 ~ 434–5, 534–5 ~ 543–4, S. fr. 476 = Ar. *Av.* 1337–9, *Med.*

---

[101] There is a weaker break between ⌣ e and *D*. See West, *GM* 134 n. 144.

419–20 ~ 430–1, *Hec.* 931–2 ~ 941–2. See also Dale, *LM²* 180–1, West, *GM* 132 with n. 141, 133 and Parker, *Songs*, 88–9, 90, 260–1.

242–3/253–4 'Lyric trimeters in which a choriamb appears as either the first or second metron seem to be distinctively tragic' (Parker, *Songs*, 79). Cf. 342–79 'Metre' 347/356n. on '*ia cho ia*ₐ'.

244/255 Our poet has a liking for the 'prolonged hemiepes' (23–51 'Metre' 27/45n.).

249/260 The ambiguous colon connects the preceding dactylo-epitrite with the mainly aeolo-choriambic sequence of 250–2 ~ 261–3 (n.). K. Itsumi (*BICS* 38 [1991–1993], 250, 255) sharply distinguishes between 'enoplian' and aeolic metres, which do not often occur together. Our length is paralleled at *IT* 1245–6 ~ 1270–1 (aeolo-choriambic). Euripides has several cases of telesillean (= acephalous glyconic) with resolved half-base, especially in his later plays: *Hec.* 635 ~ 644, 905 ~ 914, 926 ~ 936, *El.* 708 ~ 722, 727 ~ 737, *Ion* 468–9 ~ 488–9, *Hel.* 1113 ~ 1128, 1119 ~ 1134, 1314 ~ 1332, 1342 ~ 1358, *IA* 582, 1049 ~ 1071, 1051 ~ 1073, *Hyps.* fr. 8/9.10 Bond = E. fr. 753c.16 (J. A. J. M. Buijs, *Mnemosyne* IV 39 [1986], 70–1).[102]

250–2/261–3 Although the text is basically sound (251b–2, 261–3nn.), one cannot be sure about the metre here. The present colometry was suggested to me by Laetitia Parker. One fully resolved cretic (cf. *IT* 881), followed by a pendent version of the 'greater asclepiad' (hi^{2c}),[103] seems less odd than the isolated dochmiac (?) ⏑ ⏑ ⏑ ⏑ ⏑ ⏑ ⏒ (+ 2 *cho ar*) in the division of Murray, Ritchie (304–5), Dale (*MATC* I, 97), Diggle and Kovacs: 250–2 ἔνι δὲ θράσος ἐν αἰχ- / μᾷ· πόθι Μυσῶν ὃς ἐμὰν / συμμαχίαν ἀτίζει; ~ 261–3 ὃς ἐπὶ πόλιν, ὃς ἐπὶ / γᾶν Τροΐαν χιλιόναυν / ἤλυθ' ἔχων στρατείαν. Also, it places first in successive cola the corresponding repetitions ἔνι δὲ ... ἐν ... and ὃς ἐπὶ ... ὃς ἐπὶ ... (cf. 249b–51a, 454–66 'Metre' 460–2/826–7nn.). Of other notable approaches, Ritchie (301–4) has made an effective case against Wilamowitz' 'enoplion' in synartesis with two resolved choriambics (*GV* 583–4), while Dale, in her alternative analysis (*MATC* I, 97 n. 250–2), prefixes 251–2 ~ 262–3 ⏑ ⏒ 2*cho* + *ar* (i.e. hi^{2c}) with a peculiar combination of ⏑ ⏑ – ⏑ ⏑ – ⏑ (249 πόλις ... τις ~ 260 Ἑλένα κακόγαμβρον) and a resolved glyconic (250 ἔστιν ... θράσος ~ 260 ἐς χέρας ... πόλιν).[104]

---

[102] Of the two plausible comic examples (Ar. *Thesm.* 1020, *Eccl.* 972 ~ 975b), the former stands in a parody of Euripidean monody, the latter in a sort of paraclausithyron (Parker, *Songs*, 442–3, 546–9).

[103] In drama choriambic expansion of aeolic cola is 'particularly Sophoclean' (West, *GM* 118). The analysis of the last verse was in principle prefigured by Schroeder² and Dale (below).

[104] Likewise Schroeder² (168), except that, with certain older editors, he leaves an intolerable

Willink ('Cantica', 28–31 = *Collected Papers*, 567–70) notes the 'symmetrical sense-pause' after 249 ... ἄλκιμος ∥ ~ 260 ... γόον ∥, but then needs major textual changes in 250–2 ~ 261–3 to produce a very improbable stretch of ionics.

224–6a. Hymns typically open with a series of vocatives, which call upon the respective god by name and one or more titles 'designating his function, his location, or his descent from other gods' (FJW on A. *Suppl.* 524–6 [II, pp. 406–7]; cf. H. Lloyd-Jones, *JHS* 83 [1963], 85 = *Academic Papers* II, 174, Furley–Bremer, *Greek Hymns* I, 52–6). The closest tragic parallel to our strophe is probably *Hipp.* 61–71. It consists almost entirely of invocations, but the address 'Artemis' is also left to a middle position (cf. e.g. Sapph. fr. 1.1–2 Voigt, Anacr. fr. 348.1–3 *PMG*, [Pi.]? *Ol.* 5.17–18, Ar. *Pax* 974–6), and vocatives with ὦ recur at the end of the ode (231–2n.). References to a god's location often assume the shape of a relative or participial clause: *Il.* 1.37–9 κλῦθί μοι, Ἀργυρότοξ', ὃς Χρύσην ἀμφιβέβηκας / Κίλλάν τε ζαθέην, Τενέδοιό τε ἶφι ἀνάσσεις, / Σμινθεῦ, Pi. *Pyth.* 1.39 Λύκιε καὶ Δάλοι' ἀνάσσων Φοῖβε Παρνασσοῦ τε κράναν Κασταλίαν φιλέων, [Pi.]? *Ol.* 5.17–18, *Ant.* 1118–25, *Hipp.* 67–9, Ar. *Nub.* 596–7 (Norden, *Agnostos Theos*, 166–76; cf. 224–5, 351b–4nn.). Two of the three traditional epithets here bear a special relationship to the plot (224–5n.).

224–5. Θυμβραῖε: Thymbra, known primarily for its shrine of Thymbraean Apollo (below), is mentioned in *Il.* 10.430–1 πρὸς Θύμβρης δ' ἔλαχον Λύκιοι Μυσοί τ' ἀγέρωχοι / καὶ Φρύγες ἱππόδαμοι καὶ Μηίονες ἱπποκορυσταί. According to Dionysodorus of Troizen (507b–9a n.) and Strabo (13.1.35 [598 C. 10–11 = III 572 Radt]), it lay on the Scamander, fifty stades (about 9 km) away from classical Troy (i.e. Hisarlık). Hesychius' ten stades (θ 868 Latte) go back to the belief of Demetrius of Scepsis that Homer's city occupied the site of the so-called 'Village of the Ilians': Demetr. frr. 20–8 Gaede (~ Strabo 13.23–42). Cf. J. M. Cook, *The Troad* ..., Oxford 1973, 117–18.

In pre-Hellenistic Greek Θυμβραῖος recurs only at *Rh.* 508 Θυμβραῖον ἀμφὶ βωμὸν ἄστεως πέλας. But it may have featured in lost plays – above all S. *Troïlus* (frr. 618–35), which dealt with Achilles' killing of the titular hero by the Thymbraean altar. The story was recounted in the *Cypria* (Arg. p. 78 (11) *GEF*), at least alluded to by Ibycus (fr. 224.7–10 *PMGF*) and became popular with Greek vase-painters early on (Richardson and *BK* on *Il.* 24.257).

---

mid-verse hiatus in the antistrophe by failing to divide after 248 ... σαλεύῃ ~ 259 ... ἐνέγκοι.

Δάλιε: The first explicit reference to Delos as the birth-place of Apollo is *h.Ap.* 14–18,[105] although Odysseus' comparison of Nausicaa's beauty to that of the Delian palm tree (*Od.* 6.162–9) already presupposes a cult (Richardson on *h.Ap.* 16–18). Apollo entered the island around 1000 BC with the Ionian Greeks, but received a major sanctuary only in the second half of the sixth century BC.

Λυκίας / ναὸν ἐμβατεύων: 'haunting your temple in Lycia'. Cf. *Pers.* 447–9 νῆσός τίς ἐστι ... / ... ἣν ὁ φιλόχορος / Πὰν ἐμβατεύει ποντίας ἀκτῆς ἔπι, *OC* 678–80, E. fr. 696.2–3, Cratin. fr. 359 *PCG* ~ fr. tr. adesp. 185a χαῖρ' ὦ ... / Πάν, Πελασγικὸν Ἄργος ἐμβατεύων (LSJ s.v. ἐμβατεύω I with Suppl. [1996]). For such participial (or relative) clauses, giving a god's favoured abode(s) as part of an invocation, see 224–6a n. and also Barrett on *Hipp.* 61–71 (p. 170).

Apollo had a famous shrine in Lycian Patara, with an oracle that took over from Delos in the winter months (Hdt. 1.182.2, Verg. *Aen.* 4.143–4).[106] But the place-name here also evokes his epithet Λύκ(ε)ιος, which already in the first half of the fifth century BC could variously be understood as meaning 'wolfish' (< λύκος) or 'Lycian' (FJW on A. *Suppl.* 686 [III, pp. 49–50]).[107] Whatever the correct derivation (cf. Nilsson, *GGR* I³, 536–8, F. Graf, *Nordionische Kulte* ..., Rome 1985, 220–6), it is sufficient to observe that Apollo is called upon to protect 'Dolon the Wolf' (note especially 208 λύκειον ... δοράν) and that the Lycians (i.e. 'wolf-men'?) are Trojan allies in both the *Iliad* and *Rhesus*: 543–5 ~ 562–4 (nn.). By his conspicuous absence (224–63n.), the god will become λυκοκτόνος to his charge; cf. S. *El.* 6–7 αὕτη δ', Ὀρέστα, τοῦ λυκοκτόνου θεοῦ / ἀγορὰ Λύκειος (with Finglass), S. H. Steadman, *CR* 59 (1945), 8, Feickert on 224 (p. 156).

---

105 Unless Thgn. 5–10 is earlier. On the basis of historical allusions in the poems, West (*Studies in Greek Elegy and Iambus*, Berlin – New York 1974, 65–71) puts Theognis in the seventh to sixth century BC, while our late-antique and medieval sources give a *floruit* between the 59th and 57th Olympiads (552–41 BC). The date of the composite *Hymn to Apollo* is likewise disputed (Richardson, *Three Homeric Hymns*, 13–15).

106 T. R. Bryce (*CJ* 86 [1990], 144–9) claims that Hdt. 1.182.2 does not prove the existence of an Apollo cult in Lycia prior to the fourth century BC (whence *Rhesus* must be spurious) because 'in referring to the oracle, Herodotos leaves the god in residence unnamed' (146). But the opposite is likely to be true. Delphic Apollo could simply be ὁ θεός in the *Histories* (e.g. 1.19.2, 4.157.2, 7.148.2, 8.122), and at *Alc.* 112–18 (with Dale and Parker) the audience was expected to draw the right inference from a mention of Lycia alongside the oracle of Zeus Ammon in Thebes (~ Hdt. 1.182.2). See further A. W. Parke, *The Oracles of Apollo in Asia Minor*, London et al. 1985, 185–93.

107 The third (now largely discredited) ancient 'etymology' from *lyk-* ('light') appears to go back to the early Stoics (Cleanthes *SVF* I F 541, Antip. *SVF* III F 36), although Apollo had long been identified with Helios / the sun (Diggle on *Phaeth.* 225 [pp. 147–8]). See D. E. Gershenson, *Apollo the Wolf-god* (*JIES* Suppl. 8), McLean (VA) 1991, 17–19, 131–3.

226a. ὦ Δία κεφαλά: 'great son of Zeus' (Morwood). Mantziou's reinterpretation (*Dodone* 14 [1985], 100–1) of the transmitted δία (V: δῖα ΟΛ) is supported by Σ^V *Rh*. 226 (II 331.24–5 Schwartz = 87 Merro) ὦ ἀπὸ τοῦ Διὸς κεφαλή. It introduces to the list of Apollo's titles (224–6a n.) a welcome note on his paternal descent (LSJ s.v. δῖος II 'of Ζεύς') and avoids the abnormal application of δῖος in the sense 'divine, noble' (LSJ s.v. I) to a higher male god (as opposed to goddesses and illustrious humans of either sex).[108] Yet one cannot but feel that ὦ Δία κεφαλά stretches the boundaries of Greek idiom. For whereas κεφαλή (and κάρα) are common in emotional addresses from Homer on (902–3n.), the combination with an epithet denoting physical origin here would seem to put greater stress than usual on the synecdoche. The opening of a second-century AD hymn to Asclepius inscribed in his Athenian sanctuary (*IG* II² 4514.1–5 τάδε σοι ζάκορος φίλιος λέγω, / Ἀσκληπιὲ Λητοΐδου πάι. / πῶς χρύσεον ἐς δόμον ἵξομαι / τὸν σόν, μάκαρ ὦ πεποθημένε, / θεία κεφαλά ...) does not necessarily constitute independent evidence. Its author, a certain Diophantos of Sphettos, may have read *Rhesus* and interpreted ΔΙΑ just as the medieval scribes and most modern scholars did.

The long α in Δία, found also in A. *Suppl*. 4–5 Δίαν ... χθόνα (Seidler: δῖαν M), does not conform to the etymology of the word (< δίϝ-ι̯α; cf. Sanskrit *divya-*, 'heavenly'), but has a precedent in the 'hyper-Ionic' δίη at Hes. *Th*. 260 and 'Hes.' frr. 70.10, 169.2 M.–W. See West, *Theogony*, 80 and Liapis on 226–7.

226b–8. μόλε ... ἱκοῦ: For the imperatives see 370–2a n.

τοξήρης: 'furnished with your bow', as, likewise of Apollo, *Alc*. 34–5 νῦν δ' ἐπὶ τῇδ' αὖ / χέρα τοξήρη φρουρεῖς ὁπλίσας. In *HF* 188 τοξήρη σαγήν and 1062–3 ἔκανε δὲ ψαλμῷ / τέκεα τοξήρει (our only other instances of the word) the suffix -ήρης (< ἀραρίσκω) has lost much of its force (cf. 713b–14n.).

ἐννύχιος: Cf. 44–5 προσέβα ... / ἐννύχιος and 501 (501–2n.) ... ἔννυχος μολών. 'Apollo is not a god who comes much by night' (Klyve on 227; cf. Liapis on 226–7).[109] There may be a sinister echo of Apollo at *Il*. 1.47 ὃ δ' ἤϊε νυκτὶ ἐοικώς.

229–30a. '... and be a saving guide to the man on his mission ...'

The expression is reminiscent of Dionysus' bitterly ironic address to Pentheus at *Ba*. 965 ἕπου δέ· πομπὸς εἶμ' ἐγὼ σωτήριος (with Dodds

---

108 Mantziou (101 n. 1) adduces Q. S. 8.290 δῖον Ἄρηα as a (very late) exception. For the stylistic rule see J. Wackernagel, *Progr. Gött*. (1912), 26–7 n. 2 = *KS* II, 993–4 n. 2 and West on Hes. *Th*. 991.
109 His intervention at *Il*. 10.515–22 is an emergency response and, significantly, comes too late (Hainsworth on *Il*.10.515–22).

on 963–5). For analogies between Dolon's and Pentheus' spying expeditions see 201–23, 201–2, 204, 206nn.

καὶ γενοῦ ... / ἀγεμών: Dindorf (*PSG*¹, xx-xxi = III.2 [1840], 597) corrected the MSS' ἀγεμὼν... / καὶ γενοῦ (ἀ- Tr²: ἡ- <L?>P). Similar inversion of line-beginnings occurs at *Hel.* 680–1 Πάριν ... / Κύπρις (Reiske: κύπριν ... / πάριν L), *IA* 448–9 ἅπαντά ... / ἄνολβα (Musgrave: ἄνολβα ... / ἅπαντα L), 844–5 (FJW on A. *Suppl.* 309–11 [II, p. 252], Diggle, *Euripidea*, 493 with n. 12) and maybe *OC* 1234–5 (but see Ll-J/W, *Sophoclea*, 252, *Second Thoughts*, 132). Zanetto alone among recent editors preserves the MSS' order, writing καὶ πόνου for the then isolated καὶ γενοῦ. Yet apart from his dubious comparison with *Med.* 946 συλλήψομαι δὲ τοῦδέ σοι κἀγὼ πόνου (apparatus 230, *Ciclope, Reso*, 143 n. 33), this gives a feeble addition to πομπᾶς (cf. Liapis, 'Notes', 58–9) and clumsily juxtaposes word- and sentence-connecting καὶ in 230.

γενοῦ belongs to the language of prayer: Anacr. fr. 357.9–10 *PMG*, *Sept.* 128–34, *Cho.* 1–2 Ἑρμῆ χθόνιε ... / σωτὴρ γενοῦ μοι ξύμμαχός τ' αἰτουμένῳ, 18–19, S. *El.* 1379–81 νῦν δ', ὦ Λύκει' Ἄπολλον ... / ... γενοῦ πρόφρων / ἡμῖν ἀρωγὸς τῶνδε τῶν βουλευμάτων, *Alc.* 223–4, E. *Suppl.* 628–31.

πομπᾶς: 'mission, journey'. Our nearest tragic parallel is the syntactically difficult *Sept.* 613 (ἀνδράσιν ...) τείνουσι πομπὴν τὴν μακρὰν πάλιν μολεῖν.

230b. καὶ ξύλλαβε Δαρδανίδαις: Dolon's venture becomes centrally important to the Trojan cause (149–94, 224–63nn.). 'The confidence that the god will take his share in fighting or working alongside man is deeply rooted in Greek religious feeling' (Fraenkel on *Ag.* 811 [II, p. 373]; cf. Kranz, *Stasimon*, 68–9).

231–2. The appellations mirror and reinforce those at the beginning of the strophe (224–6a n.). By mentioning Apollo's service to Laomedon (below), the chorus at once honour the god's achievement and remind him of his special relationship with Troy.

ὦ ... ὦ: For the emphatic repetition cf. 357–8 νῦν, ὦ πατρὶς ὦ Φρυγία, / ... νῦν (with 249b–51a n.).

παγκρατές: a poetic epithet of 'gods and divine or quasi-divine beings' to express their power (Fraenkel on *Ag.* 1648). It is mostly used of Zeus (e.g. Bacch. frr. 14 + 57.4–5 Sn.–M., *Sept.* 255, *Eum.* 918, A. fr. 168.14–15. . παντοκρα[τ ... / Ζηνί, *PV* 389, *Phil.* 679, S. fr. 684.4–5, Ar. *Thesm.* 368–9), but see *Ai.* 675 (Sleep), *Phil.* 986–7 (Hephaestus' fire), *OC* 609 (Time), Ar. *Thesm.* 317 (Athena), Bacch. 11.44 (Hera) and *Dith.* 3.25–6 (Moira).

Τροίας / τείχη παλαιὰ δείμας: According to *Il.* 21.441–57 (see Richardson), Poseidon built the city walls, while Apollo tended

Laomedon's cattle. But the standard version of the tale (already alluded to in *Il.* 7.452–3)[110] is that both gods participated in the construction work: 'Hes.' fr. 235.4–5 M.–W., Pi. *Ol.* 8.31–52, *Andr.* 1109–18, *Tro.* 4–7, Hellanic. *FGrHist* 4 F 26 (a/b). Occasionally in tragedy Poseidon's name is omitted in favour of the chief divine supporter of Troy (*Tro.* 814, 1174, *Hel.* 1511, *Or.* 1387–9). Nowhere is there better reason than here.

It may be coincidence that the words most closely resemble *Il.* 21.446 ἤτοι ἐγὼ Τρώεσσι πόλιν πέρι τεῖχος ἔδειμα (above).

Τροίας: Lachmann (*De choricis systematis*, 154–5 n.) for Τροίας (Ω), which spoils metre and responsion. On the form and prosody (⌣ ⌣ –) see Radt on Pi. *Pae.* 6.75. In tragedy it is required also at *Rh.* 262 and 360 (261–3, 360–2a nn.). *Ai.* 1190 is too corrupt to be certain about Wilamowitz' Τροΐαν (*GV* 511) as against Τρωίαν (Ahrens) or the transmitted Τροίαν (see Finglass on 1190).

233–6. 'May he come to the naval station and arrive as a spy on the Greek army, and may he turn back to the Trojan altars of his father's house.'

The chorus expand their simple prayer to Hermes in 216–17 (n.) to one for success as well as a safe return (224–63n.). Its first half (233–5a μόλοι … ἵκοιτο) recalls not only *Il.* 10.562–3 τόν ῥα διοπτῆρα στρατοῦ ἔμμεναι ἡμετέροιο / Ἕκτωρ τε προέηκε, but also 149–50 ~ 154–5 from the preceding epeisodion (224–63n.) and indeed 133–5 τί γὰρ ἄμεινον ἢ ταχυβάταν νεῶν / κατόπταν μολεῖν / πέλας (…); Dolon's family (235b–6) was praised at 159b–60 (n.).

233–5a. ναυκλήρια: In Dem. 23.211, Plut. *Apophth. Lacon.* 48.234f and P. Oxy. 87.7 (IV AD) ναυκλήριον is the property of a shipowner (ναύκληρος). Here also it need not mean more than 'ships', as ναυκληρία for a single vessel in *Hel.* 1519 (Ritchie 158; cf. Liapis on 233–6). But the shift to ναύσταθμα (135b–6n.) is possible, given 'the extended meaning of the root ναυκληρ- found elsewhere in tragedy' (Mastronarde on *Med.* 527): A. *Suppl.* 177, S. fr. 430, *Hipp.* 1224 ναύκληρος ('captain, master'), *Sept.* 652 ναυκληρεῖν ('command like a ship's captain'), S. fr. 143.1, *Alc.* 112, *Med.* 527, *Hel.* 1589 ναυκληρία ('voyage').

καὶ στρατιᾶς / Ἑλλάδος διόπτας / ἵκοιτο: Apart from *Il.* 10.562 (cf. 233–6n.), this is our only attestation of διόπτης (-τήρ), 'spy, scout', before the imperial period (Plut. *Galb.* 24.1, D. C. 78.14.1), although Ar.

---

110 On the athetesis of *Il.* 7.443–64 by Zenodotus, Aristophanes and Aristarchus (ΣΣ^AT *Il.* 7.443–64 [II 290.69–291.80 Erbse]) see Nickau, *Zenodotos*, 51–2, 178–80. Σ^bT *Il.* 7.464 (II 293.28–30 Erbse) notes that it would be 'strange' (ἄτοπον) to have line 465 follow immediately upon 442.

Ach. 435 ὦ Ζεῦ διόπτα ('through-seer') καὶ κατόπτα πανταχῇ probably plays on the sense. For the verb cf. *Il.* 10.449–51 (Odysseus to Dolon) εἰ μὲν γάρ κέ σε νῦν ἀπολύσομεν ἠὲ μεθῶμεν, / ἦ τε καὶ ὕστερον εἶσθα θοὰς ἐπὶ νῆας Ἀχαιῶν, / ἠὲ διοπτεύσων ἢ ἐναντίβιον πτολεμίξων and Xen. *Cyr.* 8.2.10.

235b–7. The connection with 216–17 and Dolon's respected home was pointed out at 233–6n. If he were to die, his father would lose his sole male heir.

κάμψειε πάλιν: Cf. *Ba.* 1225–6 πάλιν δὲ κάμψας εἰς ὄρος κομίζομαι / τὸν κατθανόντα παῖδα μαινάδων ὕπο – another allusion to Pentheus' story (201–23, 229–30a nn.)?

θυμέλας: a Euripidean favourite (*Suppl.* 64, *El.* 713, *Ion* 46, 114, 161, 228, *IA* 152). The original meaning 'place of fire' = 'hearth' (< θύω) is always traceable and foremost in A. *Suppl.* 669, *IA* 152, as well as here (A. S. F. Gow, *JHS* 32 [1912], 213–38). Other literary (and non-technical) cases are Pratin. fr. 708.2 *PMG* = *TrGF* 4 F 3.2 τίς ὕβρις ἔμολεν ἐπὶ Διονυσιάδα πολυπάταγα θυμέλαν; and Aristonous *h.Hestia* 16–17 (*CA* 165 = Furley–Bremer II 38) λιπαρόθρονον / ἀμφὶ σὰν θυμέλαν (~ *Eum.* 806 λιπαροθρόνοισιν ἡμένας ἐπ' ἐσχάραις).

Ἰλιάδας: so O. Corruption into Ἰλιάδος (VΛ) was all but inevitable after πατρός (Δ).

238. Φθιάδων δ' ἵππων: Achilles' team (182–3, 185–8nn.), which is considered feminine, even though the individual horses are male (185n.). Phthia in south-east Thessaly was the home of Peleus and his son.

ἐπ' ἄντυγα: As in Call. *Dian.* 140–1 καὶ ἄντυγες, αἵ τέ σε ῥεῖα / θηητὴν φορέουσιν ὅτ' ἐς Διὸς οἶκον ἐλαύνεις (118n.), 'chariot' is the only suitable meaning. Porter (on 118) notes that in all other passages quoted for 'chariot' by LSJ s.v. ἄντυξ II 1 (where add *Hipp.* 1231) 'the notion 'chariot-*rail*' is to be traced'. Cf. A. Fries, *CQ* 60 (2010), 345 with n. 3.

239. δεσπότου: Hector. The choice of word 'underlines the slavish attitude which the guards have towards' their commander (Klyve on 239). In a military context cf. E. *Suppl.* 635–7 ᾑρέθην γὰρ ἐν μάχῃ / ᾗν οἱ θανόντες ἑπτὰ δεσπόται λόχων / ἠγωνίσαντο ῥεῦμα Διρκαῖον πάρα. Euripides was exceedingly fond of δεσπότης (Ritchie 190, Liapis on 237–41).

Ἀχαιὸν Ἄρη: 'the Achaean war-might' – a common tragic metonymy: *Pers.* 85–6 ἐπάγει δουρικλυτοῖς ἀν- / δράσι τοξόδαμνον Ἄρη (with Garvie on 81–6 [p. 78]), 951, *Hcld.* 275–6, 290, *Andr.* 105–6, *Phoen.* 1081–2, *IA* 237, 283, 764–5 (Breitenbach 176). See also e.g. Tim. *Pers.* fr. 791.116–18 *PMG* = Hordern οὐ γὰρ ἂ[ν Τμ]ῶλον οὐδ' / ἄστυ Λύδιον [λι]πὼν Σαρδέων / ἦλθον ["Ε]λλαν' ἀπέρξων Ἄρ[η (perhaps after Aeschylus).

240–1. τὰς πόντιος Αἰακίδᾳ / Πηλεῖ δίδωσι δαίμων: a minor variation on 187–8 (n.) δίδωσι δ' αὐτὸς πωλοδαμνήσας ἄναξ / Πηλεῖ Ποσειδῶν, ὥς λέγουσι, πόντιος. Cf. 224–63n.

τὰς: 185, 238nn. The ὅ ἥ τό relative (KG I 587–8, SD 642–3, Barrett on *Hipp*. 525–6) prevents hiatus.

242–4a. ἐπεί: The logical connection is with the preceding prayers for protection by Apollo and complete success. Similarly *Med*. 759–63 ἀλλά σ' ὁ Μαίας πομπαῖος ἄναξ / πελάσειε δόμοις ... / ... ἐπεὶ / γενναῖος ἀνήρ, / Αἰγεῦ, παρ' ἐμοὶ δεδόκησαι (cf. 216–17n.).

Such 'enjambement' rarely occurs between antistrophe and strophe: *Ant*. 1137, *Tr*. 647 and, continuing the main sentence, *Sept*. 750, *Ag*. 176, 238 (with Fraenkel), *Phil*. 707 (FJW on A. *Suppl*. 49 [II, p. 47]). Cf. the extraordinary 'choral-lyric' overrun at 350–1 (348b–51a n.).

πρό τ' οἴκων πρό τε γᾶς: This resumes the patriotic motifs of 151–3 (151n.) and Dolon's response at 154–5. See 224–63n.

ἔτλα μόνος: Cf. with similar choral praise *Alc*. 460–3 σὺ γάρ, ὦ μόνα ... / σὺ τὸν αὐτᾶς / ἔτλας <ἔτλας> πόσιν ... ἀμεῖψαι / ... ἐξ Ἅιδα (224–63n.) and, perhaps mildly paratragic, Ar. *Thesm*. 544–5 ... ἥτις μόνη τέτληκας / ὑπὲρ ἀνδρὸς ἀντειπεῖν ὅς ...

ναύσταθμα: 135b–6n.

244b–5a. ἄγαμαι / λήματος: 'I marvel at his courage'. Elsewhere in serious poetry ἄγαμαι + genitive is found only at *Alc*. 603 σοφίας ἄγαμαι. In comedy cf. Ar. *Ach*. 489 ἄγαμαι καρδίας (with Olson), *Av*. 1744a, Eup. fr. 349 *PCG* and Phryn. Com. fr. 10.1 *PCG*. By contrast, λῆμα has an elevated ring (Pi. *Pyth*. 8.45, *Nem*. 1.57, *Pers*. 55, *Sept*. 447–8, *Ag*. 123–4, A. fr. 146b + 147). Places like *Cyc*. 596 πέτρας τὸ λῆμα κἀδάμαντος ἕξομεν, Ar. *Nub*. 457, *Ran*. 463 and 898 λῆμα δ' οὐκ ἄτολμον ἀμφοῖν ('Aeschylus' and 'Euripides') support rather than discount this impression.

245b–9a. 'There is always a shortage of good men, when it is sunless on the sea and the city is tempest-tossed.'

The sentiment was perhaps adapted in Verg. *Aen*. 9.247–50 *di patrii, quorum semper sub numine Troia est, / non tamen omnino Teucros delere paratis, / cum talis animos iuvenum et tam certa tulistis / pectora* (Introduction, 45).

245b. ἦ σπάνις αἰεί: Diggle, after Wilamowitz' σπάνις ἀεί (*apud* Murray). The transmitted text (σπάνις Λ: σπανία V² et Σ^V [πανία V]: σπάνια O) does not correspond with 256 μῖμον ἔχων ἐπὶ γαίας. Most editors accept σπανία and change the antistrophe to ἐπὶ γᾶν or ἐπὶ γᾶς with Dindorf (*PSG*¹, XXI = III.2 [1840], 598). But σπανία, which recurs only at D. S. 24.1.4, Hsch. σ 1402 Hansen and Phot. σ 437 Theodoridis is an improbable *lectio difficilior* for the usual σπάνις (LSJ s.v. I, II), and γαίας in 256 is otherwise likely to be right (255b–7a n.). Compared to

Ritchie's σπάνις ἐστί (301), Wilamowitz' solution includes the last letter of the variants and perhaps better prepares for the indefinite ὅταν in 246–7. But certainty is impossible. In any case σπάνια (O) may preserve the original accentuation.

Both wording and sentiment recall *Alc.* 473–4 τὸ γὰρ (a wife like Alcestis) / ἐν βιότῳ σπάνιον μέρος, again from the first stasimon of that play (cf. 224–63, 242–4a nn.).

ἦ: affirmative, as mainly in poetry (*GP* 280, G. Wakker, in *NAGP*, 209–10, 218–23, 229–30).

246–9a. The 'Ship of State in distress' (Collard on E. *Suppl.* 267–9a) is a pervasive metaphor in Greek poetry (and prose).[111] The version here betrays influence from *OT* 22–4 πόλις γὰρ ... ἄγαν / ἤδη σαλεύει κἀνακουφίσαι κάρα / βυθῶν ἔτ' οὐχ οἵα τε φοινίου σάλου (~ *Ant.* 162–3 ἄνδρες, τὰ μὲν δὴ πόλεος ἀσφαλῶς θεοί / πολλῷ σάλῳ σείσαντες ὤρθωσαν πάλιν). Ritchie (201–2), as usual, dismisses the connection. But the only other attestation of σάλος (or σαλεύω) in this context is Lys. 6.49 καὶ ἐπιστάμενος ἐν πολλῷ σάλῳ καὶ κινδύνῳ τὴν πόλιν γενομένην, which may in turn have been inspired by *Ant.* 162–3.

ὅταν ᾖ δυσάλιον: Commentators have long compared Xen. *Cyn.* 8.1 ὅταν ... ᾖ βόρειον. Klyve (on 247) advocates Hutchinson's δυσαλίῳ. As with δυσάλιος (Λ), however, it would be odd to describe the city as being actually 'on the sea'. The picture does not tend to be so explicit. For δυσάλιος, 'sunless', cf. *Eum.* 396 δυσάλιον κνέφας and later Moschio *TrGF* 97 F 6.5–6 (βροτοί) ... δυσηλίους / φάραγγας ἐνναίοντες.

249b–52. Dolon is a particularly bad example when it comes to defending the Trojans against the (contemporary) Greek prejudice of oriental ἀνανδρία. We are thus reminded once more that his venture is bound to fail (Feickert on 251).

249b–51a. ἔστι ... ἔστιν ... / ἔνι ... / ἐν: Like Euripides (and to a lesser degree Sophocles) our poet was fond of such emphatic anadiplosis: 231 ὦ ... ὦ, 261–2 ὃς ἐπί ... / ὃς ἐπί, 346–7 ἥκεις ... / ἥκεις, 357–8, 385, 396, 535, 579 (n.), 720, 821 (821–3n.), 902–3 (Ritchie 237–9, Willink, 'Cantica', 31 with n. 27 = *Collected Papers*, 570 with n. 27). On the colometry see 224–63 'Metre' 250–2/261–3n.

249b. Φρυγῶν: 32n.

250–1a. 'There is in us courage in battle.'

θράσος: In a positive sense ('courage') the tragedians chose freely between θάρσος and θράσος according to metrical convenience, whereas

---

[111] It presumably goes back to Archilochus (frr. 105, 106 *IEG*) and Alcaeus (frr. 6, 208.1–9 Voigt) and is used with greatest effect by Aeschylus in *Seven against Thebes* (cf. Hutchinson on *Sept.* 62–4). See also *Rh.* 322–3 (321–3n.) ἡνίκ' ἐξώστης Ἄρης / ἔθραυε λαίφη τῆσδε γῆς μέγας πνέων.

the negative ('over-boldness, rashness, insolence') already seems restricted to θράσος (Fraenkel on *Ag.* 803–4 [II, p. 364], Diggle on *Phaeth.* 92). The distinction becomes absolute in later Greek.

ἐν αἰχμᾷ should be taken with θράσος, not ἔνι, which would produce the less satisfactory meaning 'There is courage in our spear-points'. Cf. *HF* 157–8 ὃ δ' ἔσχε δόξαν ... / θηρῶν ἐν αἰχμῇ (with Bond on 158) and 436–7 εἰ δ' ἐγώ ... / δόρυ ... ἔπαλλον ἐν αἰχμᾷ. For the attributive use of prepositional phrases see 567–8a n. (πωλικῶν ἐξ ἀντύγων).

251b–2. 'Where is the Mysian who scorns to have me as an ally?'

πόθι: Hoffmann's conjecture (*NJbbClPh* 8 [1862], 598–9) has rightly been approved by most scholars. The scholia (Σ^V *Rh.* 251 [II 332.4–333.10 Schwartz = 89–90 Merro]) have a long note on the proverb ἔσχατος Μυσῶν (Magn. fr. 5 *PCG*, Philem. fr. 80 *PCG*, Pl. *Tht.* 209b7–8, Men. frr. 54, 153, 658 *PCG*, Cic. *Flacc.* 65),[112] which is assumed to lie behind the MSS' ποτὶ Μυσῶν ὅς ... (cf. Σ^V *Rh.* 252 [II 333.11–14 Schwartz = 90 Merro] ὁ τὴν ἐμὴν συμμαχίαν ἀτίζων ... πρὸς Μυσῶν ... ἐστὶν ἢ ὡς εἰπεῖν ἔσχατος καὶ οὐδενὸς λόγου ἄξιος. οἷον· Μυσός ἐστιν ὁ ἀτιμάζων ἡμᾶς, ἢ ἀδόκιμος παρὰ τὴν παροιμίαν). But ποτί / πρός + genitive cannot easily be understood in a local sense ('in the direction of, towards'), unless the context clearly suggests so (W. H. Porter, *CQ* 11 [1917], 159 – against A. C. Pearson, *CQ* 11 [1917], 58–9, who had quoted *Il.* 10.430 πρὸς Θύμβρης δ' ἔλαχον Λύκιοι Μυσοί τ' ἀγέρωχοι and *Od.* 21.347 οὔθ' ὅσσοι νήσοισι πρὸς Ἤλιδος ἱπποβότοιο [LSJ s.v. πρός A I 2]). The same applies to the use 'of origin or descent' (LSJ s.v. πρός A I 5), while 'on the side of' (LSJ s.v. πρός A III 2, where add *Rh.* 320) does not express a sufficiently close connection, as its advocate Meschini (*AFLPad* 1 [1976], 177–8) herself seems to feel. With πόθι, by contrast, we get a straightforward question of the sort 'Where's the Ally now who says we're not doing our bit?' (W. H. Porter, *CQ* 11 [1917], 159). That the Mysians are named as Trojan allies in 541 (540–2n.) does not mean that our poet could not also have alluded to the proverb here (N. Wecklein, *NJbbClPh* Suppl. n.s. 7 [1873–5], 410–11; cf. A. C. Pearson, *CQ* 12 [1918], 79). But there is a difference between an open slight and a statement of pride and military competition,[113] which the audience may have interpreted in more than one way.

Homeric πόθι / ποθι for ποῦ / που (Schwyzer 619, 627, 628) is rare in tragedy and always lyric: *Ai.* 885, *Tr.* 98, *Phoen.* [1718–19], *Ba.* 556.

---

[112] Cf. *App. Prov.* II 85 (*CPG* I 411–12), which has the same source as part of our scholion (A. C. Pearson, *CQ* 11 [1917], 59). Also 'Diogenian.' II 47 (*CPG* II 25).

[113] The relationship between Troy and her allies was not free of animosities (319–26, 762–9, 859a nn.). In our play these are personified by Rhesus and his Charioteer (Strohm 265).

ἀτίζει: a mainly poetic verb, which after Homer (*Il.* 20.166 'to disregard') serves as a metrical alternative to ἀτιμάζω (cf. FJW on A. *Suppl.* 733, Parker on *Alc.* 1037). Also 327 ὀρθῶς ἀτίζεις κἀπίμομφος εἶ φίλοις (VΛ: ἀτιμάζεις gB: ἔλεξας OgV).

253–5a. πεδοστιβής: 'earth-treading' (763b–4a n.), with particular reference to Dolon's four-footed gait (211b–12, 255b–7a nn.). Similarly A. *Suppl.* 1000 καὶ κνώδαλα πτεροῦντα καὶ πεδοστιβῆ and E. fr. 472e.17–18 (*Cretans*) ... οὕνεκ' εἰς] πεδοστιβῆ / ῥινὸν καθισ.[... (i.e. Daedalus' wooden cow).

οὐτάσει: The epic verb, '[o]riginally of wounds inflicted by striking or thrusting' (Barrett on *Hipp.* 684), is appropriate in this context.

255b–7a: '... as he imitates on the ground a four-footed animal?'

τετράπουν / μῖμον ἔχων ἐπὶ γαίας / θηρός: This lyric echo of 211–12 comes even closer to *Hec.* 1058–9 τετράποδος βάσιν θηρὸς ὀρεστέρου / τιθέμενος ἐπὶ χεῖρα καὶ ἴχνος (211b–12, 224–63nn.). An early parallel for μῖμος, 'imitation', is found in A. fr. 57.8–11 (*Edoni*) ταυρόφθογγοι δ' ὑπομυκῶνταί / ποθεν ἐξ ἀφανοῦς φοβεροὶ μῖμοι, / τυπάνου δ' εἰκών, ὥσθ' ὑπογαίου / βροντῆς, φέρεται βαρυταρβής (G. F. Else, *CPh* 53 [1958], 74–6, Ritchie 161), where the further assonance of ὑπογαίου ~ ἐπὶ γαίας suggests that this passage was also in our poet's mind. The action noun with ἔχω ('to be engaged in') follows a familiar pattern: e.g. *Il.* 9.1 ὣς οἳ μὲν Τρῶες φυλακὰς ἔχον, 10.515, *Ai.* 564 δυσμενῶν θήραν ἔχων (LSJ s.v. ἔχω (A) A I 2 a).

ἐπὶ γαίας: See 245b n. The 'long' form γαια- is universally transmitted here (γαίας Λ: γαία O: γαῖαν V) and appears *metri gratia* in the similar expression of *Alc.* 869 ἐπὶ γαίας πόδα πεζεύων (Willink, 'Cantica', 29 = *Collected Papers*, 568). Moreover, corruption of γαια- into γα- or γη- appears to be more frequent (and natural) than the reverse (Denniston on E. *El.* 678, Kannicht on *Hel.* 1642–5, where add e.g. *Ba.* 64 γαίας Bothe: γᾶς Π⁹LP).

257b–60. 'May he kill Menelaus, may he slay Agamemnon and put his head in Helen's hands to make her weep for her evil brother-in-law ...'

In their final reference to the previous scene (224–63n.), the chorus transfer to the Greek commanders Dolon's already fantastic boast of 219–22 (219–23n.) σωθήσομαί τοι καὶ κτανὼν Ὀδυσσέως / οἴσω κάρα σοι ... / ... / ἢ παῖδα Τυδέως. Decapitation of corpses is envisaged, but never carried out in the *Iliad* (cf. Edwards on *Il.* 17.38–40, 18.176–7). Klyve (on 260) primarily compares Euphorbus' threat to Menelaus at *Il.* 17.36–40 χήρωσας δὲ γυναῖκα μυχῷ θαλάμοιο νέοιο, / ἀρητὸν δὲ τοκεῦσι γόον καὶ πένθος ἔθηκας. / ἦ κέ σφιν δειλοῖσι γόου κατάπαυμα γενοίμην, / εἴ κεν ἐγὼ κεφαλήν τε τεὴν καὶ τεύχε' ἐνείκας / Πανθόῳ ἐν χείρεσσι βάλω καὶ Φρόντιδι δίῃ. Several words and phrases there recur in our passage, and like Dolon, Euphorbus is a minor warrior whose overconfidence prefigures an early death (Edwards on *Il.* 17.51–2 [p. 68]; cf. W. H. Friedrich, *Verwundung und Tod in der Ilias* ..., Göttingen 1956, 58 = *Wounding and Death in the Iliad* ..., London 2003, 45–6, C. Segal, *The Theme of the Mutilation of the Corpse in the Iliad*, Leiden 1971, 20–1). As with impalement (512–17, 513b–15nn.), it is likely that a (post-)classical audience would have considered such cruelty to the dead more characteristic of barbarians than Greeks (Hall, *Inventing the Barbarian*, 25–6, 158–9).

Ἀγαμεμνόνιον: 1n. (πρὸς εὐνὰς τὰς Ἑκτορέους).

κακόγαμβρον ... γόον: an accusative in apposition to the sentence, describing 'that in which the action of [the] verb ... results' (Barrett on *Hipp.* 752–7 ὦ λευκόπτερε Κρησία / πορθμίς, ἃ ... / ... / ἐπόρευσας ἐμὰν ἄνασσαν ὀλβίων ἀπ' οἴκων / κακονυμφοτάταν ὄνασιν – very similar, but giving a judgement, not a result). Cf. KG I 284–5, SD 86–7, 617–18 and Diggle, *Euripidea*, 191–3, 223–4 with many examples (e.g. *Il.* 11.27–8 ἴρισσιν ἐοικότες, ἅς τε Κρονίων / ἐν νέφεϊ στήριξε, τέρας μερόπων ἀνθρώπων, *Ag.* 1419–20, S. *El.* 964–6, *Or.* 842–3, 961–2).

κακόγαμβρος is a *hapax*, which like χιλιόναυς (261–3n.) or the 'proper name' adjectives (above) belongs to the class that replace a genitive attribute (KG I 261–2, SD 176–8). It may or may not have been coined for this place. The whole juncture sounds Aeschylean.

261–3. Both syntax and vocabulary betray the influence of *IA* 173–7 (Ἀχαιῶν ... ἡ- / μιθέων), οὓς ἐπὶ Τροίαν / ἐλάταις χιλιόναυσιν / ... Μενέλαον <θ'> / ... / ἐνέπουσ' Ἀγαμέμνονά τ' ... στέλλειν, where the same context (*IA* 171–3) had already supplied *Rh.* 48 (n.) ναυσιπόρος στρατιά (A. Fries, *CQ* n.s. 60 [2010], 348 with n. 16, Introduction, 34, 36). See also below on στρατεία for στρατιά ('army').

ὃς ἐπὶ ... / ὃς ἐπί: 249b–51a n. Like the object of κτανών (257–8), the antecedent is extracted from Ἀγαμεμνόνιον.

γᾶν Τροίαν: Dindorf (III.2 [1840], 599) for Ω's Τροίαν (231–2n.). Willink ('Cantica', 30 = *Collected Papers*, 569) objects to the expression 'Troy land' instead of 'Trojan land'. But attribute and apposition are interchangeable with πόλις (Τροία e.g. *Od.* 11.510, *Eum.* 457; Τρῳάς *Andr.* 970, *IT* 442), and *IA* 173 ἐπὶ Τροίαν (above) would seem to support our text. For a town giving its name to the surrounding country cf. E. fr. 515.1 (*Meleager*) Καλυδὼν μὲν ἥδε γαῖα.

χιλιόναυν ... στρατείαν: The round number of 1000 ships that went to Troy is first found in *Ag.* 45 στόλον Ἀργείων χιλιοναύτην (with Fraenkel). To the Euripidean parallel at *IA* 174 (above) add *Andr.* 106, *IT* 139–41 and *Or.* 351–2. Similarly also *IT* 10 χιλίων νεῶν στόλον and *IA* 354–5 νεῶν / χιλίων ἄρχων.

Heath (*Notae sive lectiones*, 95) corrected the transmitted στρατιάν. The two words tend to be variants in the sense 'campaign', 'but στρατεία = *army, expeditionary force* is very rare' (LSJ s.v. στρατεία 5). Significantly, another passage from *Iphigeneia in Aulis* can be adduced: *IA* 495 ἴτω στρατεία διαλυθεῖσ' ἐξ Αὐλίδος.

ἤλυθ': 49–51n.

264–341. A Shepherd arrives from Mt Ida in order to tell Hector that Rhesus is on his way to Troy. After some initial confusion (264–83), he recounts in great detail the advent of the Thracian lord and his mighty host (284–316). When Hector, angry at Rhesus' delay, refuses to accept him as an ally, both the chorus-leader and the Shepherd intervene to change his mind (317–41).

If we disregard the parodos (1–51n.), this is the first of two unusual messenger scenes in our play, although closer parallels can be found for the Idaean Shepherd (below) than for Rhesus' tormented charioteer (728–55, 756–803, 804–81, 833–81nn.). Like him, however, the Shepherd remains on stage after delivering his message to assume a small, but decisive, role in advancing the plot (333–41, 334–5, 340–1nn.).

The introductory dialogue is built on Hector's double misunderstanding of the 'general announcement' (264–5, 271–2nn.), which apart from characterising him again as rash and somewhat impatient with his inferiors (267–8, 270nn.; cf. Rosivach 56), seems to have no other purpose than to increase the audience's expectation of the report. His assumption that – at this time and place – the Shepherd wishes to inform him about the state of his flocks is far from such poignant examples as *Hcld.* 646–53, *Hipp.* 1164–5 or *Hec.* 505–7 (Strohm 270) and would be dismissed as sheer poetic folly, did not the Messenger's gentle irony (266, 281nn.) show it in the appropriate light.[114]

After the 'summary report' (276–7n.) resolving the tension over what has happened, the narrative itself concentrates on the process of Rhesus' arrival (282–3, 284–6nn.), moving from a mainly aural to a visual mode of description and culminating in the splendid picture of the hero leading his innumerable host (301b–13). While Rhesus' 'godlike' appearance (301) has been adapted from *Il.* 10.436–41 and particularly such Aeschylean passages as foreshadow the fall of an overconfident warrior (301b–8, 303–4, 305–6a, 306b–8nn.), the Thracian 'roll-call' (309–10, 311–13nn.) appears to owe something also to the catalogue of Xerxes'

---

[114] Wilamowitz (*Hermes* 61 [1926], 282 n. 3 = *KS* IV, 409 n. 3) suggests that Hector tries to prevent 'peasant talk' of the kind we hear from the Goatherd and chorus of herdsmen in S. *Poimenes* (frr. 502 + 505). On the possible connection of this drama with *Rhesus* see below.

forces in the parodos of *Persians* (1–64 + 65–139). Like Rhesus' army they are vast and terrifying to behold – and doomed with him to a disastrous end (cf. Introduction, 34).

In general, Strohm (270–1) compares the Herdsman from Mt. Cithaeron in *Bacchae* (660–774), who with the Theban women's Dionysiac frenzy reports an event not yet completed behind the scene. Both messengers see divine forces at work, and several verbal echoes of the Herdsman's speech (*Ba.* 677–774) and Pentheus' immediate reaction to it (*Ba.* 778–86) support the link (cf. 287–9, 301b–2, 303–4, 311–13, 327–8nn.). Unfortunately, too little of Sophocles' *Poimenes* is left to determine how much the Goatherd and his announcement of Cycnus (S. frr. 502–4) influenced our poet's concept of the scene (Introduction, 33 with n. 46). The probably interpolated messenger-speech at *IA* 414–39, which proclaims the approach of Clytaemestra and Iphigeneia to the Greek camp, may or may not be later than *Rhesus*.

Within the play the scene looks both ahead and back. Apart from introducing Rhesus as a semi-divine warrior prince (301b–8, 301b–2nn.) and Trojan answer to Achilles (314–16, 335nn.), it gives a foretaste of the *agon* (388–526n.) and later quarrels between Trojans and allies in Hector's dispute with the coryphaeus and Shepherd about Rhesus' status at Troy (276–7, 319–26, 333–41nn.). Yet the episode also recalls the way Hector let himself be persuaded by Aeneas and the chorus to dispatch a scout instead of attacking the Greeks at once (333–41n.). He gives in to reason, or what appears to be such, too fast to be fully convincing as the commander-in-chief (H. D. F. Kitto, *YCS* 25 [1977], 335, 336; cf. Rosivach 55, 56–60, 61).

264–5. As good tidings are rare in tragedy, this 'general announcement' (1–51, 264–341nn.) is best compared to *Hcld.* 784–5 δέσποινα, μύθους σοί τε †συντομωτάτους / κλύειν ἐμοί τε τῷδε καλλίστους φέρω†, where probable remedies are Hartung's ... σοί τε καλλίστους φέρω / κλύειν ἐμοί τε συντομωτάτους λέγειν or Wecklein's ... σοί τε καλλίστους φέρω / κλύειν λέγειν τε τῷδε συντομωτάτους. The Shepherd's joviality may be a veiled request for a reward, which would be exceptional coming in his very first words (cf. Wilkins on *Hcld.* 784–7). The sentiment itself is the reverse of the fear of punishment for bringing bad news (49–51n.).

οἷά σοι φέρω μαθεῖν: With an object signifying the content of the message, φέρω alone often means 'bring news of, report': *Pers.* 248 καὶ φέρει σαφές τι πρᾶγος ἐσθλὸν ἢ κακὸν κλυεῖν, *Sept.* 40, *Ag.* 638–9, *Ai.* 789–90, *Ant.* 1172, *Phoen.* 1072–3, 1337, *IA* 1536–7 (LSJ s.v. φέρω A IV 4). Contrast 272 ἀλλ' οὐδὲν ἧσσόν σοι φέρω κεδνοὺς λόγους.

266. πόλλ' ... σκαιά: Cf. 271 σκαιοὶ βοτῆρές ἐσμεν. 'Euripides uses σκαιός far more than the other tragedians' (Bond on *HF* 283). Applied to persons, the adjective – properly 'left, on the left hand' (LSJ s.v. I) – has a range of figurative meanings, which Bond defines as (a) aesthetically repulsive, (b) intellectually stupid, (c) morally deficient, and (d) socially 'ignorant'. Hector accuses the Shepherd of (b) and (d), while the latter is prepared to admit only to (b). He may be uneducated, but he knows that it is both the right time and occasion for the news he brings (271–2, 275–7).

ἀγρώσταις: 'countrymen, peasants', as in 287 and e.g. A. fr. 46c.5 (*Diktyoulkoi*?), S. frr. 94 (*Alexandros*), 314.39 (*Ichneutae*) [. . . . . . ποι]μὴν εἴτ' ἀγρώστη[‑ ⏑ ‑] (ἀγρωστή[ρων τις ἢ suppl. Wilamowitz, ἀγρώστη[ς ἤ τις ὤν Vollgraff), *HF* 377 (with Bond). Some read ἀγρώταις (V et Tr²/³) in our passage. This 'regular' form (cf. Schwyzer 451–2, *DELG* s.v. ἀγρός col. 2) is attested in Hdn. I 74.19–75.1 Lentz, Steph. Byz. α 49 Billerbeck (= Hdn. II 292.8–9 Lentz) and *Ba.* 564 σύναγεν θῆρας ἀγρώτας (LP: ἀγρώστας Blaydes; cf. Anaxil. fr. 12.2 *PCG*). But the unanimous paradosis in 287 (above) as well as most other passages that have the word suggests that ἀγρώστ- (O<L>P) is what our poet wrote. Q's ἀγρόταις (cf. *Or.* 1270, where ἀγρότας is required by metre) does not scan.

The double dative ἀγρώσταις ... φρενί follows the σχῆμα καθ' ὅλον καὶ μέρος (KG I 289–90, SD 81, 189–90 n. 5, Diggle, *Euripidea*, 365 n. 4).

πρόσκειται: 'belongs to, is attached to'. Of permanent qualities e.g. *Ant.* 1242–3 δείξας ἐν ἀνθρώποισι τὴν ἀβουλίαν / ὅσῳ μέγιστον ἀνδρὶ πρόσκειται κακόν, *Hipp.* 970 τὸ δ' ἄρσεν αὐτοὺς ὠφελεῖ προσκείμενον (with Barrett on 966–70), fr. tr. adesp. 1b (b) βραχεῖ λόγῳ δὲ πολλὰ πρόσκειται σοφά (LSJ s.v. πρόσκειμαι III 1).

267–70. Hector's 'proof' for the preceding statement – καὶ γὰρ σύ ... (*GP* 66–7, 108) – mocks the Shepherd with deliberately pompous speech (267–8, 270nn.).

267–8. ποίμνας ... ἀγγελῶν: 'bring news of ...' (LSJ s.v. ἀγγέλλω I 3). Porter (on 268) notes the epic touch in ἀγγέλλω with the bare accusative of 'person', comparing *Od.* 14.122–3 οὔ τις κεῖνον ἀνὴρ ἀλαλήμενος ἐλθών / ἀγγέλλων πείσειε γυναῖκά τε καὶ φίλον υἱόν (+ 14.120 εἴ κέ μιν ἀγγείλαιμι ἰδών) 'The distinction of usage' may be clearer than Ritchie (182) feels and contribute to Hector's elevated style (267–70n.).

δεσπόταις τευχεσφόροις: In contrast to *Cho.* 627 ἐπ' ἀνδρὶ τευχεσφόρῳ (Agamemnon), E. *Suppl.* 654 τευχεσφόρον ... λαόν and *Rh.* 3 (2–3n.) τευχοφόρων, the adjective here has a pregnant sense: '... when they are in full arms' (Jouan 63 n. 71). The juxtaposition of the phrase with ποίμνας is ironic.

270. γεγωνεῖν: 'tell out, proclaim'(LSJ s.v. γέγωνα 3) with accusative and participle, on the analogy of ἀγγέλλω and its kind (KG II 52–3, 72, SD 394, 395, 397). Again both verb and construction are intentionally grand (Porter on 270; cf. 267–70n.).

εὐτυχοῦντα ποίμνια: The flocks are prospering, just as the Trojans are currently thought to be (52–84, 665–7nn.). O's ποιμνίων looks like a correction by someone who took σ' as the subject of εὐτυχοῦντα. The genitive of respect with εὐτυχέω is late (LSJ s.v. I 1).

271–2. As he was misunderstood by Hector, the Shepherd repeats his 'general announcement' (264–5n.), but not clearly enough to resolve the matter. No parallel exists for this technique being used mainly to build up tension through delay (264–341n.).

271. Liapis (on 271–2) aptly compares the 'concessive' Men. *Georg.* fr. 5.1 Sandbach εἰμὶ μὲν ἄγροικος, καὐτὸς οὐκ ἄλλως ἐρῶ.

σκαιοὶ βοτῆρές ἐσμεν: 266n.

οὐκ ἄλλως λέγω: 164n. The second person (λέγεις VΛ) is pointless here.

272. ἀλλ' ... σοι φέρω κεδνοὺς λόγους: Cf. 264–5n. (οἷά σοι φέρω μαθεῖν).

273–4. 'Stop telling me about the state of your farmyard! We bear in our hands (the burden of) battles and spears.'

παῦσαι λέγων: Euripides alone of the tragedians employs 'the imperative παῦσαι with a participle in a sharp prohibition' (Ritchie 253): *Alc.* 707, *Hipp.* 706 παῦσαι λέγουσα ..., *IT* 1437, *Ion* 1410, *Or.* 1625, *Ba.* 809 ... σὺ δὲ παῦσαι λέγων, *IA* 496, E. fr. 188.2. With a genitive note especially E. *El.* 1123 = *Ion* 650 παῦσαι λόγων τῶνδ' ... As a part of everyday speech (presumably), the idiom is frequent in comedy.

τὰς προσαυλείους τύχας: 270n. προσαύλειος ('near to / in reference to the farmyard') is a *hapax*. On the formation see SD 517 (5).

μάχας πρὸ χειρῶν καὶ δόρη βαστάζομεν: Our poet may have had in mind E. *El.* 695–6 φρουρήσω δ' ἐγώ / πρόχειρον ἔγχος χειρὶ βαστάζουσ' ἐμῇ and *IA* 35–6 δέλτον ... / τήνδ' ἣν πρὸ χερῶν ἔτι βαστάζεις (Introduction, 34). In itself, however, βαστάζω (a poetic verb in archaic and classical Greek) is usual of weapons: *Alc.* 40, Hermipp. fr. 47.1–2 PCG βασιλεῦ σατύρων, τί ποτ' οὐκ ἐθέλεις / δόρυ βαστάζειν (...); Men. *Epit.* 324, Theoc. 16.78 ἤδη βαστάζουσι Συρακόσιοι μέσα δοῦρα (with Gow on 16.78–9), Plb. 2.24.16, D. H. 8.64.3. The object μάχας here is prefixed by slight zeugma (cf. KG II 570–1, SD 710).

πρὸ χειρῶν goes with βαστάζομεν (above). Similarly also *Ant.* 1279 τὰ μὲν πρὸ χειρῶν τάδε φέρεις (... κακά), *Tro.* 1207–8 καὶ μὴν πρὸ χειρῶν αἵδε σοι σκυλευμάτων / Φρυγίων φέρουσι κόσμον ἐξάπτειν νεκρῷ.

δόρη: This accusative plural (instead of δόρατα) is previously attested in A. fr. 74.7 and Theopomp. Com. fr. 26 *PCG*. It seems to be an Attic formation, by false analogy as from an s-stem; cf. ΣΣ^(V ~ L) *Rh*. 274 (II 333.21–2, 30–1 Schwartz = 91 a¹, a² Merro) ἀπὸ γενικῆς τῆς δόρεος καὶ δόρεα καὶ δόρη ὡς βέλεα βέλη. The occurrence in tragedy of a dative singular δόρει (< *δόρεϝι) probably helped: A. frr. 99.20 (Π: δορί Wecklein), 129 and, *metri gratia* restored for δορί, A. *Suppl*. 846, *OC* 620, 1314, 1386. Cf. Call. *Aet*. fr. 137a.10 Harder . . . . .]αιανι .[.]ν ἦν ὑπὸ πάντα δόρε[ι].

As in the Theopompus fragment (= Poll. VII 158), some sources here wrongly read δόρυ (OQgE).

275. τοιαῦτα: i.e. information relating to warfare (Paley).

276–7. 'For a man who commands an army of vast might is approaching, a friend to you and an ally to this land.'

The Shepherd's 'report in brief' (1–51, 264–341nn.) shares several words with *Or*. 688–90 ἥκω γὰρ ἀνδρῶν συμμάχων κενὸν δόρυ / ἔχων, πόνοισι μυρίοις ἀλώμενος, / σμικρᾷ σὺν ἀλκῇ τῶν λελειμμένων φίλων – especially ἀλκή ('armed might') and μυρίος, which stand together here (Klyve on 276). The result is the opposite of what is being said (or claimed) by Menelaus in a context that seems comparable enough to have caused the echo (A. Fries, *CQ* n.s. 60 [2010], 350, Introduction, 37).

ἀλκῆς: Apart from *Or*. 688–90 (above), note *Or*. 711–12 ἀλκῇ δέ σ' οὐκ ἄν, ᾗ σὺ δοξάζεις ἴσως, / σώσαιμ' ἄν and e.g. Hdt. 4.132.1 εἰκάζων ... τοὺς δὲ ὀϊστοὺς ὡς τὴν ἑωυτῶν ἀλκὴν παραδιδοῦσι. Δ's ἀρχῆς presumes a meaning not found until the *Septuagint* (LSJ s.v. ἀρχή II 5 '*command*, i.e. *body of troops*').

στρατηλατῶν here governs a genitive, as in *HF* 61 στρατηλατήσας κλεινὰ Καδμείων δορός. With a dative cf. E. *El*. 321, 917, *Ba*. 52.

φίλος σοι σύμμαχός τε τῇδε γῇ introduces the main point of conflict in the relationship between Hector and Rhesus (264–341n.). For the expression cf. *Ai*. 1052–3 ὀθούνεκ' αὐτὸν ἐλπίσαντες οἴκοθεν / ἄγειν Ἀχαιοῖς ξύμμαχόν τε καὶ φίλον.

278. πατρῴας γῆς ... πέδον: Cf. S. fr. 202 ἀλλ' ὦ πατρῴας γῆς ἀγυιαίου πέδον, E. fr. 558.1–2 Ὦ γῆς πατρῴας χαῖρε φίλτατον πέδον / Καλυδῶνος and also *Ag*. 503 πατρῷον οὖδας Ἀργείας χθονός. The periphrasis γῆς ... πέδον is typical of tragedy (FJW on A. *Suppl*. 316 [II, p. 255], where add *Hel*. 525). Our only comic example (Ar. *Nub*. 573) occurs in a high-flown cletic hymn. Similarly 962 (n.).

ἐρημώσας: With πέδον cf. *Andr*. 314 κεἰ μὴ τόδ' ἐκλιποῦσ' ἐρημώσεις πέδον (of a sacred precinct). Here the verb suggests that the leader of the enormous army has left his country 'empty' of young men (cf. *Pers*. 718 θούριος Ξέρξης, κενώσας πᾶσαν ἠπείρου πλάκα) and so unprotected in case of war. Rhesus fought regular battles with neighbouring tribes (406–11, 426–35, 932–3).

279. πατρὸς δὲ Στρυμόνος κικλήσκεται: 'He is called the son of Strymon', with a genitive of origin, as in e.g. Pi. *Pyth.* 3.67 ἤ τινα Λατοΐδα κεκλημένον ἢ πατέρος, Ar. *Vesp.* 151 ὅστις πατρὸς νῦν Καπνίου κεκλήσομαι, *Rh.* 298 ... καὶ τίνος κεκλημένος, Theoc. 24.103–4, Hdt. 6.88 (KG I 374–5, SD 124). On the river-god Strymon (instead of Eioneus in *Iliad* 10) as Rhesus' father see 348–54, 386, 394, 919–31 and Introduction, 13 with n. 10. The present clause is repeated by interpolation, it seems, in 652 (n.).

280. Ῥῆσον: This is the first mention of Rhesus in our play.

τιθέντ' ἔλεξας ἐν Τροίᾳ πόδα: In poetry (and very rarely prose) verbs of saying may take a participle instead of the infinitive if the statement is marked as a fact (KG II 72 n. 2, SD 394). τιθέντ' ... πόδα here bears the strong sense 'is setting foot (in Troy)', for which cf. A. *Suppl.* 31–2 πρὶν πόδα χέρσῳ τῇδ' ἐν ἀσώδει / θεῖναι (from a ship), *Ag.* 906–7 μὴ χαμαὶ τιθείς / τὸν σὸν πόδ' ... Ἰλίου πορθήτορα and, of movements in fighting and/or dance, *Eum.* 294–5 (with Sommerstein on 292–6), *Ba.* 862–4. Part of this can also still be felt at *Rh.* 571 (n.) φυλάξομαί τοι κἂν σκότῳ τιθεὶς πόδα, while elsewhere in Euripides the idiom has become a mere periphrasis for 'walk': *Andr.* 545–6, *Suppl.* 171–2 (with Collard), *IT* 32–3, *Hel.* 1528, *Phoen.* [1721], E. fr. 124.2–5 ~ Ar. *Thesm.* 1099–1101.

O's εἰς Τροίαν is a simplifying error (perhaps from a gloss). The pregnant construction of ἐν with dative and a verb of motion signifies 'both *motion to* and subsequent *position in* a place' (LSJ s.v. ἐν A I 8; cf. KG I 540–2, SD 155–6, 455–6, 457).

281. 'Exactly. You have spared me an explanation twice as long.'

The Shepherd's laconic reply appears to mock both Hector's earlier failure to understand and the usual desire of tragic messengers to convey their news as quickly and succinctly as possible (cf. *Hcld.* 784–5 [quoted in 264–5n.], Collard on E. *Suppl.* 638b–40).[115] One may compare the Servant at E. *El.* 770 τέθνηκε· δίς σοι ταῦθ', ἃ γοῦν βούλῃ, λέγω, following Electra's suspicious questions about his identity and the credentials of his report (765). No such irony applies to *Ag.* 628–9 ἔκυρσας ὥστε τοξότης ἄκρος σκοποῦ, / μακρὸν δὲ πῆμα ξυντόμως ἐφημίσω,

---

[115] In E. *Suppl.* 638–9 λόγου δέ σε / μακροῦ ἀπολύσω Herwerden's conjecture (*Mnemosyne* 5 [1877], 36) is preferable to L's ἀποπαύσω (Diggle, *Euripidea*, 61 n. 11). The paradosis could only mean 'I shall save you from much talking, i.e. from the need to ask many questions' (Morwood on E. *Suppl.* 638–9), which would leave the expectation of brevity with the addressee.

where Agamemnon's trusted Herald confirms that Menelaus was caught in a storm.

ἔγνως (literally 'you have got it') is frequent in Euripides: *Andr.* 881–3, 920, *El.* 617, *Ion* 1115, *Phoen.* 983, *Or.* 1131. But cf. *Tr.* 1221, Nausicr. fr. 1.5 *PCG* – Γλαῦκον λέγεις. – ἔγνωκας < > and also A. *Suppl.* 467 ξυνῆκας and *Or.* 752 αἰσθάνῃ. In general Ritchie 253–4.

δὶς τόσου: 159b–60n.

282–3. 'And how is it that he has strayed from the broad highway in the plain and is coming towards the pasture-lands of Mt. Ida?'

Messenger-speeches tend to be triggered by a πῶς-question (or the like), as the addressee wishes to know *how* the fact already reported came to pass (Kannicht on *Hel.* 597–604, de Jong, *Narrative in Drama*, 32–4; cf. e.g. *Pers.* 446 ποίῳ μόρῳ δὲ τούσδε φῇς ὀλωλέναι; *Tr.* 884–7, *Med.* 1134 λέξον δέ· πῶς ὤλοντο; *Hipp.* 1171). Our poet here skilfully varies the scheme. While it would be senseless to enquire into the manner of Rhesus' coming (276–7), the question about his detour via Mt. Ida offers itself as a starting-point for the Shepherd's colourful report (284–6n.).

καὶ πῶς πρὸς Ἴδης ὀργάδας πορεύεται, / πλαγχθεὶς πλατείας πεδιάδος θ' ἁμαξιτοῦ; The π(λ)-alliteration is remarkable, although no special purpose seems to be intended. Ritchie (241–2) compares 139 (?), 286, 393, 545 and, as a rhetorical exception, 383–4 (n.) κλύε καὶ κόμπους κωδωνοκρότους / παρὰ πορπάκων κελαδοῦντας.

πρὸς Ἴδης ὀργάδας: Chantraine (*DELG* s.v. ὀργή) defines ὀργάς (*sc.* γῆ) as '*terre grasse, humide et fertile, mais qui en général n'est pas cultivé*' (cf. Harpocr. I 224.13–14 Dindorf ὀργὰς καλεῖται τὰ λοχμώδη καὶ ὀρεινὰ χωρία καὶ οὐκ ἐπεργαζόμενα). The word, which also came to denote sacred land, is first attested towards the end of the fifth century: *IG* I² 325.18 (414/13 BC), E. *El.* 1163–4 ὀρεία τις … λέαιν' ὀργάδων / δρύοχα νεμομένα, *Ba.* 340 … ἐν ὀργάσιν and 445 … πρὸς ὀργάδας (Fraenkel, *Rev.* 234).

πεδιάδος: In view of 286 κλυόντα πλήρη πεδία πολεμίας χερός, 'in the plain' (LSJ s.v. πεδιάς II) is preferable to 'flat, level' (LSJ s.v. I). Cf. *Ant.* 417–20 καὶ τότ' ἐξαίφνης χθονός / τυφὼς ἀγείρας σκηπτόν … / πίμπλησι πεδίον, πᾶσαν αἰκίζων φόβην / ὕλης πεδιάδος.

θ' ἁμαξιτοῦ: Stiblinus for τ' ἁμαξιτοῦ (ΔL: ἁμαξίτοις Q). The unaspirated form would be archaic (Wackernagel, *Sprachliche Untersuchungen*, 46, B. Forssman, *Untersuchungen zur Sprache Pindars*, Wiesbaden 1966, 8–11; cf. West, ed. *Iliad*, XVII). It is partly transmitted also at *OT* 716 and 730.

284–6. 'I do not know for sure. But I can make a guess. It is no small matter to bring an army into the country by night, when one has heard that the plain is full of enemy troops.'

Just as Hector does not ask a typical 'πῶς-question' (282–3n.), the Shepherd's reply only superficially resembles the general statement with which many, especially non-Euripidean, messengers introduce their account: e.g. *Sept.* 39–40 Ἐτεόκλεες ... / ἥκω σαφῆ τἀκεῖθεν ἐκ στρατοῦ φέρων, 375–6, *Ai.* 719, S. *El.* 680 (with Finglass on 680, 681), *OT* 1237–40, *Ant.* 407, 1192–5, *Tr.* 749, *OC* 1586, *Hcld.* 799, *Phoen.* 1356–7, 1427. The result is a more natural transition to the narrative than usual – comparable to *Ant.* 248–77, where the Guard cannot tell who buried Polynices (248–52), but proceeds to describe the discovery and consequences of the deed (253–77).

Diggle (*Euripidea*, 515) is wrong to criticise the passage as 'illogical', for (in the reverse order of his arguments) 1. γάρ in 285 does not explain οὐκ οἶδ' ἀκριβῶς (284), but follows 'an expression denoting the giving ... of information' (*GP* 59; cf. 285n.), 2. that Rhesus 'has heard that the plain is full of enemy troops' (286) belongs to the Shepherd's inference and need not be true (although in fact it is: 390–2, 396–403, 444–53) and 3. Rhesus may have 'borne the troubles of a night-time arrival with a very light heart',[116] but the Shepherd does not know this, nor will we miss information about Rhesus' actual reasons for coming via Mt. Ida (a convenient place to meet such an enthusiastic messenger). It is thus neither necessary nor desirable to read *intransitive* ἐσβαλεῖν in 285 and refer the sentence to the frightened Shepherd ('For it is no small matter to come upon an army by night ...'). Yet with στρατόν as the object ('to bring in an army') the verb may still be right (285n.).

284. οὐκ οἶδ' ἀκριβῶς· εἰκάσαι γε μὴν πάρα: Cf. 800–3 καὶ ξυμφορὰν μὲν οἶδ' ὁρῶν, τρόπῳ δ' ὅτῳ / τεθνᾶσιν οἱ θανόντες οὐκ ἔχω φράσαι /... εἰκάσαι δέ μοι / πάρεστι. In contrast to the Charioteer, however, the Shepherd lacks precise knowledge only about some subsidiary fact, and his speculations serve no purpose beyond this speech.

εἰκάσαι ... πάρα: In addition to 802–3 (above), cf. *Cho.* 976–7 ὡς ἐπεικάσαι πάθει / πάρεστιν, *OC* 1503–4 πάντα γὰρ ... / ... εἰκάσαι πάρα, S. fr. 269c.22 (with Radt on 21–24) and *Hel.* 421–2 αὐτὰ δ' εἰκάσαι / πάρεστι ναὸς ἐκβόλοις ἀμπίσχομαι.[117]

γε μήν: 196n.

285. γάρ: See 284–6n. In contrast to many other messenger-speeches, the particle here does not introduce the story proper (I. J. F. de Jong,

---

[116] That in 426–42 Rhesus complains 'of the extreme difficulties he has had to face on his way to Troy' (Liapis, 'Notes', 62) is a different story. There seem to have been no problems after crossing the Hellespont.

[117] *Sept.* 356 †τί† ἐκ τῶνδ' εἰκάσαι †λόγος† πάρα is severely corrupt. See Hutchinson on 356, West, *Studies*, 112–13 and Sommerstein, *Aeschylus* I, 188–9 (apparatus and n. 46).

in *NAGP*, 180–1; cf. 762–3a n.), but merely marks νυκτὸς ... στρατόν as the 'object' of εἰκάσαι. Similarly *Pers.* 254–5 ὅμως δ' ἀνάγκη πᾶν ἀναπτύξαι πάθος, / Πέρσαι· στρατὸς γὰρ πᾶς ὄλωλε βαρβάρων, *Ag.* 266–7, *OT* 345–9, *Phil.* 915–16, *Cyc.* 313–15, *Hec.* 1180–2, Ar. *Pl.* 76–8.

οὔτι φαῦλον ἐσβαλεῖν στρατόν: Cf. E. *El.* 760 ... οὔτοι βασιλέα φαῦλον κτανεῖν and, for the Euripidean quality of the construction, 197b–8n. Euripides was also among the first authors, and the only one of the three tragedians, to use the 'everyday' φαῦλος and its noun extensively (32 cases as against one in Aeschylus and two in Sophocles: *Pers.* 520, S. frr. 41, 771.3). *Rhesus* has it again at 599 and 769.

ἐσβαλεῖν στρατόν: Diggle (*Euripidea*, 515) for ἐμβαλεῖν ... (Ω). His interpretation as 'to come upon' cannot be upheld (284–6n.), also because 'intransitive εἰσβάλλω is normally followed by an accusative denoting the *place* or *area* entered' (*Cyc.* 99, *Hipp.* 1198, *Andr.* 968, *Ba.* 1045, *Phaeth.* 168 Diggle = E. fr. 779.1), not a person or personal collective like στρατόν (Liapis, 'Notes', 62). Both ἐμβάλλω and εἰσβάλλω, however, are used (with or without στρατιάν or the like) for 'to throw an army into' = 'make an inroad, invade' (LSJ s.vv. ἐμβάλλω II 1, εἰσβάλλω I, II 1). Of these the latter seems to be the more common and also bears the neutral sense 'to bring in', which is required here: Hdt. 2.14.2 τότε σπείρας ἕκαστος τὴν ἑωυτοῦ ἄρουραν ἐσβάλλει ἐς αὐτὴν ὗς, E. *El.* 78–9 ἐγὼ δ' ἅμ' ἡμέρᾳ / βοῦς εἰς ἀρούρας ἐσβαλὼν σπερῶ γύας. The corruption of ἐσβ- to ἐμβ- is paralleled at Hdt. 4.125.4 (which has ἐμβ- in the same paragraph), 5.15.1 and 9.13.2 (cf. LSJ s.v. ἐμβάλλω II 1). For our passage *Chr. Pat.* 2096 μορφῇ γὰρ οὔτι φαῦλον εἰσβαλεῖν τινά (~ 2452 ... εἰσβαλεῖν ἔφην) may or may not represent a MSS variant. In any event the author altered the meaning and construction to suit his own text.

286. This is the only trimeter in *Rhesus* with more than one resolution, inspired perhaps by *Med.* 1321–2 τοιόνδ' ὄχημα πατρὸς Ἥλιος πατήρ / δίδωσιν ἡμῖν, ἔρυμα πολεμίας χερός (Ritchie 267–8; cf. Klyve on 286). For the π-alliteration see 282–3n.

κλυόντα: so West rightly for present κλύοντα (Ω) because the participle 'is subordinated to an aorist main verb denoting a simultaneous or consequent action' and 'a single specific occasion of cognition is in question' (*BICS* 31 [1984], 177, 178). Cf. 109–10a n.

287–9. 'But he frightened us peasants, who live among the crags of Ida in our land's ancestral dwellings, as he came to the thickets at night, the haunts of wild animals.'

ἀγρώσταις: 266n.

κατ' Ἰδαῖον λέπας: Here λέπας is employed 'not in the older sense ... of a naked cliff or summit ... but rather [as] a collective term for the broken country where forest, rock, and upland pasture mix' (Dodds on *Ba*. 677–8 (Αγ.) ἀγελαῖα μὲν βοσκήματ' ἄρτι πρὸς λέπας / μόσχων ὑπεξήκριζον; cf. 264–341n.). So also *Andr*. 295, E. fr. 411.2 Ἰδαῖον (...) λέπας, *Phoen*. 24, *Ba*. 751–2, 1045. Differently 921–2a (n.) χρυσόβωλον ἐς λέπας / Πάγγαιον.

αὐτόρριζον ἑστίαν χθονός: literally 'the self-rooted hearth of our land' (i.e. 'where we put down our roots'), and so probably an allusion to Dardanus' ancient foundation at the foot of Mt. Ida: *Il*. 20.216–18 κτίσσε δὲ Δαρδανίην, ἐπεὶ οὔ πω Ἴλιος ἱρή / ἐν πεδίῳ πεπόλιστο, πόλις μερόπων ἀνθρώπων / ἀλλ' ἔθ' ὑπωρείας οἴκεον πολυπίδακος Ἴδης, Hellanic. *FGrHist* 4 F 25a. This interpretation, which most scholars have adopted from the Renaissance on, is supported by A. *Suppl*. 370–2 (Chorus to Pelasgus) σύ τοι ... / πρύτανις ἄκριτος ὤν / κρατύνεις βωμόν, ἑστίαν χθονός and several places where ἑστία denotes a geographical focal point: E. fr. 944 καὶ Γαῖα μῆτερ· Ἑστίαν δέ σ' οἱ σοφοί / βροτῶν καλοῦσιν ἡμένην ἐν αἰθέρι,[118] Call. *Del*. 325 ἱστίη ὦ νήσων εὐέστιε, χαῖρε μὲν αὐτή, Plb. 5.58.4, D. S. 4.19.2 (LSJ s.v. ἑστία I 5; cf. Feickert on 288). αὐτόρριζος is first found here, and not again before the first century BC. It usually means 'together with the roots' (e.g. D. S. 4.12.5, Babr. 36.1–2), but 'self-rooted' recurs at Opp. *Hal*. 2.464–6 (of the swordfish) καὶ τῷ μὲν ὑπὲρ γένυν ἐστήριξεν /... αὐτόρριζον ... / φάσγανον and Nonn. *D*. 40.469–70 αἷς ἔνι θάλλει / ἥλικος αὐτόρριζον ... ἔρνος ἐλαίης, *Par*. 1.64, 19.224. In view of the Aeschylean parallel for ἑστίαν χθονός (above), Fraenkel (*Rev*. 238) may be right to associate the word with the same poet (who has numerous αὐτο- compounds). Cf. *PV* 1046–7 χθόνα δ' ἐκ πυθμένων αὐταῖς ῥίζαις / πνεῦμα κραδαίνοι (~ *Il*. 9.541–2 πολλὰ δ' ὅ γε προθέλυμνα χαμαὶ βάλε δένδρεα μακρά / αὐτῇσιν ῥίζῃσιν). Pindar applied ῥίζα to an aboriginal place: *Pyth*. 4.15 (Cyrene) ἀστέων ῥίζαν ... μελησιμβρότων, 9.8 (Libya) ῥίζαν ἀπείρου τρίταν (LSJ s.v. ῥίζα II 1).

Other renderings are less convincing. Paley's 'on the very foot of the mountain' is feeble and not borne out by the later usage of αὐτόρριζος. J. T. Sheppard (*CR* 28 [1914], 87–8) compares Hsch. α 8492 Latte (~ fr. tr. adesp. 201) αὐτόχθων ἑστία· ἡ τοῦ Χείρωνος παρόσον ἐν τοῖς ὄρεσι διῆγεν[119] and assigns to the shepherds 'a hearth rock-rooted on the mountains', if they do not actually live in caves (cf. Σ^V *Rh*. 288 [II 333.25–6 Schwartz = 91 Merro], Liapis on 287–9). That the latter contradicts 273

---

118 Cf. W. Burkert, *Weisheit und Wissenschaft: Studien zu Pythagoras, Philolaos und Platon*, Nuremberg 1962, 296–7 = *Lore and Science in Ancient Pythagoreanism*, Cambridge (Mass.) 1972, 317–18 and Collard–Cropp, *Euripides* VIII. *Fragments*, 527–9 n. 1.
119 He might have added *PV* 300–1 πετρηρεφῆ / αὐτόκτιτ' ἄντρα (i.e. that of Oceanus) and S. fr. 332 (= Hsch. α 8426 Latte) αὐτοκτίστους δόμους.

τὰς προσαυλείους τύχας and 293 need not be an objection (185n.). But the description of humble peasant abodes seems less apposite here than a modest expression of pride in the land of Troy.

δρυμὸν ... ἔνθηρον: an accusative of direction (KG I 311–12, SD 67–8). For ἔνθηρον note *Il.* 8.47 Ἴδην ... πολυπίδακα, μητέρα θηρῶν (cf. *Il.* 14.283, 15.151, *h.Ven.* 68) and, in terms of language, S. fr. 314.221–2 (*Ichneutae*) θῆρες, τί [τό]νδε χλοερὸν ὑλώδη πάγον / ἔγ[θ] ηρον ὡρμήθητε σὺν πολλῇ βοῇ;

290. Θρήικιος ῥέων στρατός: The verb ῥέω suggests a great multitude of men (as described in 309–13) that inexorably moves forward like a stream. It here recalls *Sept.* 79–80 μεθεῖται στρατὸς ... / ῥεῖ πολὺς ὅδε λεὼς πρόδρομος ἱππότας and the equivalent use of ῥεῦμα at *Pers.* 88 μεγάλῳ ῥεύματι φωτῶν, 412 ῥεῦμα Περσικοῦ στρατοῦ, *Ant.* 128–9 καί σφας ἐσιδὼν / πολλῷ ῥεύματι προσνισομένους (itself echoing Aeschylus) and *IT* 1437 ῥεῦμά ... στρατοῦ. In a non-military context see E. fr. 146.1 < × – ⏑ > πᾶς δὲ ποιμένων ἔρρει λεώς.

Within the narrative, Θρήικιος ... στρατός anticipates information gained only as the army drew nearer and could be overheard (294–5). But the Shepherd had already mentioned their provenance and that Rhesus was their lord (279–81).

291b–3. 'And struck with alarm, we drove our flocks to the heights, in case any of the Argives was coming to plunder and to destroy your folds ...'

The shepherds' worries are realistic. Achaean raids were common (Feickert on 293), and on one occasion Aeneas only just escaped Achilles, who had come after the Trojan cattle grazing on Mt. Ida: *Il.* 20.90–1 (with Edwards on 89–93), 20.187–90, *Cypria* (Arg. p. 78 (11) *GEF*). For peasants and their livestock mountains presented a natural refuge in case of an invasion (V. D. Hanson, *Warfare and Agriculture in Classical Greece*, Pisa [1]1983, 95–7 ~ Berkeley *et al.* [2]1998, 114–16).

θάμβει: essentially 'astonishment, awe'. The connotation of 'alarm' is even stronger in *Hec.* 177–9 μᾶτερ μᾶτερ, τί βοᾷς; τί νέον / καρύξασ' οἴκων μ' ὥστ' ὄρνιν / θάμβει τῷδ' ἐξέπταξας; To the discussion of the word family by FJW on A. *Suppl.* 570 add ἀθαμβής, 'devoid of awe', i.e. 'reckless, fearless', in e.g. Ibyc. 286.11 *PMGF*, Phryn. Trag. *TrGF* 3 F 2, Bacch. 15.58, Lyc. 558, Plut. *Lyc.* 16.4 (Jebb on Bacch. 14[15].57–8, M. Nöthiger, *Die Sprache des Stesichorus und des Ibycus*, Zurich 1971, 177–8) and Democritus' ideal of philosophical ἀθαμβίη (68 A 169, B 4, 215, 216 DK).

πρὸς ἄκρας: For ἄκρα, 'summit, height', cf. Alc. fr. 48.13 Voigt ...]ν κὰτ ἄκρας (?), S. fr. 271.1–2 ῥεῖ γὰρ (sc. ὁ Ἴναχος) ἀπ' ἄκρας / Πίνδου Λάκμου τ', *Or.* 871, Thuc. 7.3.3.

μή τις Ἀργείων μόλῃ: Like 843 ... ὥς τις Ἀργείων μολών, this is a variation on ... ναῦς ἔπ' Ἀργείων μολεῖν (149–50n.). The object clause μή τις ... σταθμά depends on θάμβει ... ἐκπλαγέντες as a verbal expression of fear.

λεηλατήσων: literally 'to drive away booty' (λεία + ἐλαύνω), and so particularly of (or including) cattle: e.g. *Ai.* 342–3, *Hec.* 1142–3, Xen. *Cyr.* 1.4.17, *HG* 2.4.4. It is combined with πορθέω at *Hell. Oxy.* 24.1, 24.6 Chambers, Plb. 4.26.4 and Plut. *Cam.* 23.1.

294–7. Reassured by the sound of non-Greek voices (294–5), the Shepherd goes to question the foreign explorers – in Thracian (296–7). The fact that different peoples speak different languages or dialects, or that individuals speak more than their native tongue (see already *Il.* 2.803–4, 867, 4.437–8, *Od.* 19.175, *h.Ven.* 113–16) is conventionally ignored in tragedy, except when calling attention to it 'serves some special purpose' (FJW on A. *Suppl.* 118–19 = 129–30, who refer to Thomson and Fraenkel on *Ag.* 1061).[120] The Shepherd's proficiency here is probably meant to reflect not only the alleged racial ties between Thracians and Phrygians (below), but also the pan-barbarian opposition to the Greeks, which Hector and Rhesus' charioteer invoke (404–5, 833–4nn.). In that latter sense linguistic (and dialectal) variance is played out at *Pers.* 401–7 and *Sept.* 169–70 (with Hutchinson on 170).

The Phrygians were known to have migrated into Anatolia from the Balkans and Thrace: Hdt. 7.73, Xanth. *FGrHist* 765 FF 14, 15, Strabo 10.3.16 (cf. P. Carrington, *AS* 27 [1977], 117–26). They did not, however, speak a common language; indeed Thracian and Phrygian may not even belong to the same Indo-European sub-group (R. D. Woodard – C. Brixhe, in R. D. Woodard [ed.], *The Cambridge Encyclopedia of the World's Ancient Languages*, Cambridge 2004, 12, 780). Genuine 'Thracians in Asia' were the Bithynians and related tribes (Pherecyd. *FGrHist* 3 F 27, Hdt. 1.28, 3.90.2, 7.75.2, Xen. *An.* 6.4.1–2). Their area of settlement along the Propontis and south-western Black Sea was close enough to the Troad to allow for contact on various levels. A Trojan peasant speaking Thracian, therefore, was conceivable also in historical times.

294–5. One may compare Philoctetes' relief at finally hearing Greek: *Phil.* 234–5 ὦ φίλτατον φώνημα· φεῦ τὸ καὶ λαβεῖν / πρόσφθεγμα τοιοῦδ' ἀνδρὸς ἐν χρόνῳ μακρῷ (Klyve on 294).

---

[120] On bilingualism in Greek literature generally see J. Werner, in P. Händel – W. Meid (eds.), *Festschrift für Robert Muth* ..., Innsbruck 1983, 583–95 and Faulkner on *h.Ven.* 113–16.

πρὶν δή: 'until (indeed) …', as in *Andr.* 1145–8 ἐν εὐδίᾳ δέ πως / ἔστη … δεσπότης … / πρὶν δή τις ἀδύτων ἐκ μέσων ἐφθέγξατο / δεινόν τι καὶ φρικῶδες, Hdt. 1.13.2, 4.157.2, Thuc. 1.118.2, 3.29.1, 3.104.6 (*GP* 220). The use of πρίν with the indicative depending on an affirmative clause in the past is rare (KG II 453–4, SD 655), and often a negative force can still be detected in the main verb, a predicative adjective or in thought (cf. Jebb on *OT* 776). In tragedy it also occurs at A. fr. 83 (?), *PV* 480–3, *OT* 775–8, *Alc.* 127–9, *Med.* 1171–5, *Hec.* 130–40, *IA* 489–90 and *Rh.* 568–9. All except the last example mark a decisive turning point in the narrated action (Dawe on *OT* 776).

δι' ὤτων … / ἐδεξάμεσθα: 'received with our ears' = 'heard'. Cf. *Ba.* 1086–7 αἳ δ' ὠσὶν ἠχὴν οὐ σαφῶς δεδεγμέναι / ἔστησαν ὀρθαὶ καὶ διήνεγκαν κόρας, E. *El.* 110–11 ἤν τι δεξώμεσθ' ἔπος / ἐφ' οἷσι … τήνδ' ἀφίγμεθα χθόνα, and, for δι' ὤτων / ὠτός, *Cho.* 56, 451, S. *El.* 737, 1437, *OT* 1387, *Ant.* 1188, S. fr. 858.2, *Med.* 1139, *Rh.* 565–6 ἢ κενὸς ψόφος / στάζει δι' ὤτων, Theoc. 14.27.

καὶ μετέστημεν φόβου: similar verse-ends in *Eum.* 900 … καὶ μεθίσταμαι κότου, *Alc.* 21 … καὶ μεταστῆναι βίου, *Hel.* 856 … καὶ μεταστήτω κακῶν and *Ba.* 944 … ὅτι μεθέστηκας φρενῶν.

296–7. 'And I went and asked those scouting a path ahead for their lord, addressing them in Thracian.'

ἄνακτος depends on ὁδοῦ or possibly προυξερευνητὰς ὁδοῦ together. There is no need to alter the text, as Kovacs did by adopting Morstadt's ἔναντα (*Beitrag*, 20 n. 2), and several other scholars have proposed (Wecklein, *Appendix*, 50, to which add his own ἀν' αὐτούς [*SBAW* I (1897), 494]). The Shepherd may assume that the army was led by a 'lord' – or ἄνακτος is spoken with hindsight, like 290 (n.) … Θρῄκιος ῥέων στρατός.

προυξερευνητάς: The noun is a *hapax*. But προυξερευνάω occurs at *Phoen.* 92 (the Old Servant to Antigone) ἐπίσχες, ὡς ἂν προυξερευνήσω στίβον, which probably inspired the formation here (Fraenkel, *Rev.* 231, 234, against Ritchie 150, 207). For military scouting (cf. Xen. *Cyr.* 5.4.4, 6.3.2 προδιερευνάω, διερευνητής) the verb is used in Aen. Tact. 15.5 πρὸ δὲ αὐτῶν δεῖ πρώτους τοὺς ὑπάρχοντας ἱππέας καὶ κούφους ἐξιέναι, μηδὲ τούτους <ἀτάκτους>, προεξερευνῶντάς τε καὶ προκαταλαμβάνοντας τὰ ὑψηλὰ τῶν χωρίων. See further F. S. Russell, *Information Gathering in Classical Greece*, Ann Arbor 1999, 10–22.

ὁδοῦ: so rightly V. στρατοῦ (ΟΛ) cannot meaningfully be construed with either ἄνακτος or προυξερευνητάς and may easily have intruded from the context. στρατόν or -ός stand at the end of 285 and 290.

Θρῃκίοις προσφθέγμασιν: 294–7n. πρόσφθεγμα, 'address', is frequent in tragedy and mainly used in the plural, as here: e.g. *Ag.* 903,

Cho. 876, A. fr. 47a.7 (*Diktyoulkoi*), *Ai.* 500, *Phil.* 235, *Hcld.* 573, *Hec.* 413, *Or.* 75, E. fr. 309a. For the double γ (as also in 608 φθέγγματος) see West, ed. *Aeschylus*, LII.

298–9. The Shepherd asks the traditional question for the general's name and descent, leaving out the country of origin, which he has already established (294–7). The information was imparted to the audience at 278–81.

τίνος κεκλημένος: 279n.

σύμμαχος: The leader of an army not speaking Greek (294–5n.) can be assumed to be an ally.

300–1a. ὧν ἐφιέμην μαθεῖν: The relative pronoun is governed by ἐφιέμην, with a genitive, as usual (44–7a n.), and μαθεῖν follows either as an epexegetic infinitive (Bruhn, *Anhang*, § 137, SD 361–2), or we explain the whole construction by attraction of the object to the main verb (KG II 276–7 with n. 1). So also Pl. *Rep.* 437b1–2 τὸ ἐφίεσθαί τινος λαβεῖν and e.g. *h.Cer.* 283–4 οὐδέ τι παιδός / μνήσατο τηλυγέτοιο ἀπὸ δαπέδου ἀνελέσθαι, Pi. *Ol.* 3.33–4 (δένδρεα ...) τῶν νιν γλυκὺς ἵμερος ἔσχεν ... / ... φυτεῦσαι, *Med.* 1399–1400 ὤμοι, φιλίου χρῄζω στόματος / παίδων ὁ τάλας προσπτύξασθαι.

301b–8. Rhesus' description is largely based on *Il.* 10.436–41 τοῦ δὴ καλλίστους ἵππους ἴδον ἠδὲ μεγίστους· / λευκότεροι χιόνος, θείειν δ' ἀνέμοισιν ὁμοῖοι. / ἅρμα δέ οἱ χρυσῷ τε καὶ ἀργύρῳ εὖ ἤσκηται· / τεύχεα δὲ χρύσεια πελώρια, θαῦμα ἰδέσθαι, / ἤλυθ' ἔχων· τὰ μὲν οὔ τι καταθνητοῖσιν ἔοικεν / ἄνδρεσσιν φορέειν, ἀλλ' ἀθανάτοισι θεοῖσιν. But while Dolon there presents him as little more than a valuable target (to save himself by offering useful information: *Il.* 10.442–5), the Shepherd expresses genuine wonder, which foreshadows the 'deification' of Rhesus in the chorus' eyes (264–341, 301b–2nn.). Details of the reworking and other passages that influenced the report are discussed in 301b–2, 303–4, 305–6a, 306b–8nn.

301b–2. ὁρῶ δέ: With this introduction 'the Messenger not only stresses the fact that he was an eyewitness, but through his use of the historic present also asks our special attention for *what* he has seen and is about to recount' (de Jong, *Narrative in Drama*, 44). Cf. E. *Suppl.* 651–3 ἀμφὶ δ' Ἠλέκτρας πύλας / ἔστην θεατὴς πύργον εὐαγῆ λαβών. / ὁρῶ δὲ ... (where note ἔστην in the preceding line), *Or.* 871, *Ba.* 680 (cf. 264–341n.) and, marking a fresh start in the story, *Phoen.* 1165, *Or.* 879. In a way, all that the Shepherd had said so far was preliminary to his portrayal of Rhesus' approach.

ὥστε δαίμονα: In contrast to *Il.* 10.436–41 (301b–8n.), the comparison with a god here comes first and refers to Rhesus' entire appearance. The wording is not far from the epic δαίμονι ἶσος (e.g. *Il.* 5.438, 16.705, 786, *h.Cer.* 235) – whereas the chorus later all but identify Rhesus with

Zeus and Ares (Ritchie 69, Fenik, *Iliad X*, 26–7 n. 3; cf. 355–6, 357–9, 385–7nn.).

Comparative ὥστε is common in tragedy, and usually (as here and in 618) the verb has to be supplied from the main clause. Examples of full comparative clauses are few and often doubtful (*GP* 526–7, Ruijgh, *Te épique*, 991–8, Diggle, *Euripidea*, 321–3). Cf. 972–3n.

ἑστῶτ' ἐν ἵπποις Θρηκίοις τ' ὀχήμασιν: Λ's text (apart from ἵπποισι Q, ὀχήμασι LᶜP) gains support from *Il.* 4.366 = 11.198 (of Diomedes and Hector respectively) ἑσταότ' ἔν θ' ἵπποισι καὶ ἅρμασι κολλητοῖσιν, which our poet evidently wished to recall. Editors before Murray preferred to read ἐν ἱππείοισι Θρηκίοις ὄχοις (Δ), with the horses expressed by an adjective, as in 416 παρ' ἱππείοις ὄχοις and *Hcld.* 845 ἵππειον δίφρον. But apart from losing the Homeric echo, the presence of two parallel epithets with ὄχοις is awkward, especially since Θρηκίοις is likely to qualify the horses as well as the chariot (cf. 616–17 πέλας δὲ πῶλοι Θρηκίων ἐξ ἁρμάτων / λευκαὶ δέδενται). The mistake is a simplifying one by a scribe perhaps who was puzzled by the separate mention of animals and vehicle. This is regular in epic (or ἵππω / -οι alone stands for 'horses and chariot'), but in tragedy recurs only at *IA* 83 ἵπποις τε πολλοῖς ἅρμασίν τ' ἠσκημένοι.[121]

303–4. 'And a golden collar enclosed the yoke-bearing necks of his horses, gleaming whiter than snow.'

χρυσῆ ... πλάστιγξ: Properly the 'scale of a balance', πλάστιγξ is here used for the collar that joined the horses to the yoke and allowed them to draw the chariot (Anderson, *Ancient Greek Horsemanship*, 3, 108 with plts. 14a, 16, 19, 31c). The metaphor arose by similarity. Hanging ready from the outer ends of the yoke, the collars could be likened to the scales of a balance (*GEW*, *DELG* s.v. πλάστιγξ); conversely ζυγόν / ζυγός ('yoke') came to denote various kinds of crossbars and specifically the beam of a balance or the balance itself (LSJ s.v. ζυγόν IV a). Porter (on 303) appropriately cites Pl. *Rep.* 550e7 ὥσπερ ἐν πλάστιγγι ζυγοῦ κειμένου ἑκατέρου.

The same basic meaning for πλάστιγξ has been recognised at *Cho.* 288–90 καὶ λύσσα καὶ μάταιος ἐκ νυκτῶν φόβος / κινεῖ, ταράσσει, καὶ διωκάθει πόλεως / χαλκηλάτῳ πλάστιγγι λυμανθὲν δέμας, where an allusion to human scapegoats and the metal collar employed 'in execution by *apotympanismos*' appears to be made (Sommerstein,

---

[121] From the dubious iambic prologue (*IA* 49–114). E. *Suppl.* 660–2 ἱππότην <δ'> ὄχλον / ... / ... ἁρμάτων δ' ὀχήματα and *Phoen.* 522 ζεύγνυσθε δ' ἵππους, πεδία πίμπλαθ' ἁρμάτων (cited, among others, by Stockert on *IA* 83) are not equivalent. The first opposes cavalry and chariots, and in the second horses and chariots again appear in different clauses, not as a unity or *hendiadys*.

Aeschylus II, 249 n. 64; cf. L. Battezzato, *SCO* 42 [1992], 71–4, West, apparatus 290).¹²² Our poet may even have had the passage in mind, given that *Cho.* 288–9 shares several words also with *Rh.* 691 (n.). The more widespread ζεύγλη, 'half-collar', and λέπαδνα, 'yoke-straps' (J. Wiesner, *Arch. Hom.* F 18–19, 53–5, 106–7), at any rate did not scan.

χρυσῆ adapts *Il.* 10.438 ἅρμα δέ οἱ χρυσῷ τε καὶ ἀργύρῳ εὖ ἤσκηται (301b–8n.) and so refers to gold decoration, as presumably also of Rhesus' armour at *Il.* 10.439 (305–6a, 340–1, 370–2a nn.). Hera's chariot, by contrast, has a yoke and yoke-straps 'of gold' (*Il.* 5.729–31). The precious metal is characteristic of divine accoutrements (West, *EFH* 112, *IEPM* 153–4).

αὐχένα ζυγηφόρον / πώλων: Cf. A. fr. dub. 465.1 πώλους ... ζυγηφόρους, *Hipp.* 1183 ἐντύναθ' ἵππους ἅρμασι ζυγηφόρους and *HF* 121 †ζυγηφόρον πῶλον†. Later prose has ζυγοφόρος: Plut. *De cup. div.* 2.524a, [Athan.] *In nat. praec.* 28.905.38–9 Migne τὸν ζυγοφόρον ... αὐχένα (of an ox). For ᾱ (η) instead of ο in nominal o-stem composition see Schwyzer 438–9 with 439 n. 1.

The *enallage* produced by ζυγηφόρον (Δ) is preferable to ζυγηφόρων (Λ). Either reading, however, could have arisen by assimilation.

χιόνος ἐξαυγεστέρων: Rhesus' horses are λευκότεροι χιόνος in *Il.* 10.437 (301b–8n.), make Nestor compare them to sunrays (*Il.* 10.547) and shine though the night like a swan's plumage at 616–18 (616–17, 618nn.). Only 356 ἥκεις διφρεύων βαλιαῖσι πώλοις deviates, perhaps from literary reminiscence (185, 355–6nn.).

ἐξαυγής (with intensifying ἐξ-) is a *hapax* formed like e.g. τηλαυγής, διαυγής and εὐᾱγής (< εὐαυγής). There is no reason to write εὐαυγεστέρων with Blaydes (*Adversaria critica*, 4), although *Ba.* 661–2 (Κιθαιρῶν' ...) ἵν' οὔποτε / λευκῆς χιόνος ἀνεῖσαν εὐαγεῖς βολαί (εὐαυγεῖς Hemsterhuys, ἐξαυγεῖς Elmsley) remains worth quoting (264–341n.).

305–6a. 'On his shoulders his shield flashed with images inlaid with gold.'

Following *Il.* 10.439 τεύχεα δὲ χρύσεια πελώρια (301b–8, 340–1, 382nn.), Rhesus is equipped with a gold-decorated Thracian *pelte*, like Telamon at E. fr. 530.1–2 (*Meleager*) Τελαμὼν δὲ χρυσοῦν αἰετὸν πέλτης ἔπι / πρόβλημα θηρός (*sc.* ἔχων) and Diomedes, lord of the flesh-eating horses, at *Alc.* 498 Ἄρεος, ζαχρύσου Θρῃκίας πέλτης ἄναξ (~

---

122 *Apotympanismos* (practised in Athens) 'involved clamping the criminal by the neck, wrists and ankles to a large board and standing the board up ... in such a way that the condemned man's feet did not reach the ground; he would then be left degradingly and agonizingly exposed, with no one permitted to come near him, probably until sunset when, if still alive, he would be strangled by tightening the neck clamp' (Sommerstein, *Aeschylus* I, 437 n. 17).

Rh. 370–2a [n.]). In reality this small crescent-shaped shield was made of wood or wicker-work and covered with animal skin (often painted). Yet despite Aristotle *apud* Σ^V *Rh.* 311 (II 334.1–7 Schwartz = 92 Merro) = fr. 498 Rose, a thin layer of bronze is also attested (Xen. *An.* 5.2.29), which in 'poetic fantasy' (Parker on *Alc.* 498) could have been replaced with gold. Later in *Rhesus* the *pelte* tends to be described in terms of the much larger and heavier hoplite shield (311–13, 383–4, 408–10a, 485–7nn.).

χρυσοκολλήτοις τύποις: i.e. figures of beaten metal inlaid with gold (LSJ s.vv. τύπος IV, χρυσόκολλος, -κόλλητος). Even more perhaps than Telamon's *pelte* (above), one recalls the blazons of the 'Seven' so elaborately described by the Scout in the course of *Sept.* 369–685; cf. particularly the gold-plated ones of Capaneus (434) and Polynices (644–5, 660–1). At *Phoen.* 1130–1 σιδηρονώτοις δ' ἀσπίδος κύκλοις ἐπῆν / γίγας (κύκλοις Π¹: τύποις ΩΧΖΤ^Z) the reading of the ancient wood tablet seems preferable to that of the MSS (J. M. Bremer, *Mnemosyne* IV 36 [1983], 300–1). Otherwise Mastronarde on *Phoen.* 1130.[123]

It is (for once) unlikely that χρυσοκολλήτοις here was borrowed from the Sun's chariot at *Phoen.* 2 χρυσοκολλήτοισιν ... δίφροις (e.g. Fraenkel, *Rev.* 234). *Phoen.* 1–2 are deleted by Haslam (*GRBS* 16 [1975], 149–74) as virtually unattested before the medieval tradition and stylistically otiose in combination with *Phoen.* 3 (cf. Mastronarde on *Phoen.* [1–2]). If the lines are early, their absence from ancient testimonia and papyri may indicate simply that they were not widely current (and probably unknown to Aristophanes of Byzantium), but they have perhaps a better claim to a later date. χρυσόκολλος and -κόλλητος were regular in drama: S. fr. 378.3, E. fr. 587 (of a sword hilt), Antiph. frr. 105.2, 234.2 *PCG* (both paratragic). Similarly λιθοκόλλητος at *Tr.* 1261 and Men. fr. 275.1 *PCG* and ῥινοκόλλητος at S. fr. 314.375 (*Ichneutae*).

V has δίφροις for τύποις (ἵπποις Q), either by scribal recollection of *Phoen.* 2 (above) or from a marginal or interlinear parallel (Klyve on 305).

306b–8. 'And a bronze Gorgon as on the goddess' aegis was attached to the horses' foreheads and rang forth terror with many bells.'

The narrative returns to the chariot in the widest sense: *Il.* 10.438 (301b–8n.). For the fearful noise of horse-trappings cf. e.g. the chorus at *Sept.* 123–4 διάδετοι δὲ < – > γενυῶν ἱππίων / μινύρονται φόνον χαλινοί (with West's apparatus and *Studies*, 105) and 206–7 ἱππικῶν τ' ἄπυεν / πηδαλίων διαστόμια, πυριγενετᾶν χαλινῶν. More specifically our poet seems to have recalled *Sept.* 385–6 ὑπ' ἀσπίδος δὲ τῷ / χαλκήλατοι κλάζουσι κώδωνες φόβον, both here and at 383–4

---

123 *Phoen.* 1104–40 has been excised by Morus. Whether (partly) genuine or not, the passage was inspired by *Sept.* 369–685.

(n.).¹²⁴ His portrayal of a mighty foreign warrior bound to be killed at Troy was traditional, to judge by Ar. *Ran.* 962–3 ('Euripides' to 'Aeschylus') οὐδ' ἐξέπληττον αὐτούς, / Κύκνους ποιῶν καὶ Μέμνονας κωδωνοφαλαροπώλους (cf. Introduction, 33, 41).

ὡς ἐπ' αἰγίδος θεᾶς: i.e. Athena, who in classical times is mainly associated with the aegis (as a kind of shawl, usually lined with snakes and bearing the Gorgoneion [*Il.* 5.738–42] in the middle). In Homer the aegis – a shield of metal and/or covered with goat-skin (αἰγ-)? – belongs to Zeus, who shakes it in anger (*Il.* 4.166–8). Athena uses it to spur on the Greeks (*Il.* 2.446–54), and Apollo to lead the Trojans into battle and rout the Achaeans (*Il.* 15.229–30, 308–11, 318–27, 360–6). So also the Gorgon's heads on the frontlets of Rhesus' horses are meant to frighten the enemy with the flash of polished bronze and the clang of the bells (fastened to the bridles and maybe the harness) as the animals move. Like a god (301b–2n.) going before his host, Rhesus will cause panic merely by being seen (and heard): 335 (n.) φόβος γένοιτ' ἂν πολεμίοις ὀφθεὶς μόνον.

The Gorgoneion was probably as common on horse frontlets (E. Pernice, *Griechisches Pferdegeschirr im Antiquarium der Königlichen Museen*, Berlin 1896, 28)¹²⁵ as it was as a device on shields and other pieces of armour from the seventh century on (*LIMC* IV.1/2 s.v. Gorgo, Gorgones A 19, 72–4, 87, 89, B 147–9, 151, E 156–193, F 194–228). For the nature and various etymologies of the aegis see *LfgrE* s.v. αἰγίς E, B, Kirk on *Il.* 2.446–51, Janko on *Il.* 15.18–31 (p. 230), 308–11, Edwards on *Il.* 17.593–6.

ἐκτύπει φόβον: an internal accusative, as in *Sept.* 123–4, 385–6 (above) and *Rh.* 567–8a (n.) οὔκ, ἀλλὰ δεσμὰ πωλικῶν ἐξ ἀντύγων / κλάζει σίδηρον.

309–10. The impression of an uncountable army (cf. 276 ἀλκῆς μυρίας) is first given in the introduction to the Achaean catalogue at *Il.* 2.488–90. Tragic examples include *Pers.* 39–40 καὶ ἐλειοβάται ναῶν ἐρέται / δεινοὶ πλῆθός τ' ἀνάριθμοι and the exchange between Iolaus and Hyllus' Servant at *Hcld.* 668–9 πόσον τι πλῆθος συμμάχων πάρεστ' ἔχων; / – πολλούς· ἀριθμὸν δ' ἄλλον οὐκ ἔχω φράσαι. In phrasing our verses resemble *Pers.* 429–30 κακῶν δὲ πλῆθος, οὐδ' ἂν εἰ δέκ' ἤματα / στοιχηγοροίην, οὐκ ἂν ἐκπλήσαιμί σοι, where the 'host of

---

124 Aeschylus' description of the 'Seven' was well-known (305–6a n. with n. 123), and that of Tydeus stands first. *Sept.* 384–5 is parodied at Ar. *Ach.* 964–5 (cf. Olson).
125 Cf. K. Schumacher, *Großherzogliche Vereinigte Sammlungen zu Karlsruhe: Beschreibung der Sammlung antiker Bronzen*, Karlsruhe 1890, no. 782 with plts. XVI, XXII, Daremberg–Saglio s.v. 'frontale', E. Kunze, *VIII. Bericht über die Ausgrabungen in Olympia*, Berlin 1967, 191, 195 with plt. 73.

troubles' stems from the vast number of Persian soldiers that fell (Garvie on 429–32).

ἐν ψήφου λόγῳ / θέσθαι: 'count by reckoning with pebbles', i.e. by using an abacus for exact computation (Paley on 309, Porter on 309–10). The periphrasis with θέσθαι (LSJ s.v. τίθημι B II 3) is unique and perhaps a little awkward in style (Fraenkel, *Rev.* 238). More regularly *Ag.* 570 ... ἐν ψήφῳ λέγειν and in particular λογίζομαι (ταῖς) ψήφοισ(ι) in Hdt. 2.36.4, Ar. *Vesp.* 656 and Thphr. *Char.* 14.2. *Med.* 532 ἀλλ' οὐκ ἀκριβῶς αὐτὸ θήσομαι λίαν, where τίθεμαι alone means 'set down, reckon' (LSJ s.v. τίθημι A II 9 b), should not be compared.

δύναι' ἄν: Δ has the correct generalising second person singular ('you / one could not ...') with repeated ἄν (KG I 246–7, SD 306 with n. 1). The corruption into δυναίμην (Λ) is partly paralleled at *Phoen.* 407 (corr. Markland).

ὡς ἄπλατον ἦν ἰδεῖν: causal-exclamatory: 'so overwhelming it was to look upon' (KG II 370–1, Barrett on *Hipp.* 877–80). The literal sense of ἄπλατος is 'unapproachable' (α + the root stem πλη- / πλα- of πελάζω), with a connotation of 'terrible, monstrous' (LSJ s.v. 1), which also suits an enormous host: Lyc. 569 ἄλλων δ' ἄπλατον χειρὶ κινήσει νέφος (of the Greeks coming to Troy). For a thing 'too great for sense to grasp' (Porter on 309–10) cf. Archestr. fr. 190.8–9 *SH* (describing Phoenician wine) εὐώδης μέν σοι δόξει τοῦ Λεσβίου εἶναι / μᾶλλον, ἔχει γὰρ τοῦτο χρόνου διὰ μῆκος ἄπλατον.

311–13. The Shepherd's synopsis can profitably be compared to *Ba.* 781–5 κέλευε πάντας ἀσπιδηφόρους / ἵππων τ' ἀπαντᾶν ταχυπόδων ἐπεμβάτας / πέλτας θ' ὅσοι πάλλουσι καὶ τόξων χερὶ / ψάλλουσι νευράς, ὡς ἐπιστρατεύσομεν / βάκχαισιν (cf. 264–341n.). Both times 'the military relationships of the time of writing ... are obviously projected onto those of a distant past' (Best, *Thracian Peltasts*, 12), but whereas Pentheus musters a typical Greek army, that of Rhesus reflects Thracian conditions, with the cavalry taking pride of place and peltasts supplanting the regular hoplite forces. It would be mistaken, therefore, to think here of the Thracian mercenaries whom the Athenians employed as light-armed skirmishing troops, let alone, as Liapis does, the later Macedonian peltasts with their somewhat larger and heavier shields (cf. Introduction, 19). We are dealing with poetic fiction, not absolute historical fact.

πολλοὶ μὲν ... πολλὰ ... / πολλοὶ δ' ... πολὺς δ': The anaphora emphasises the vastness of Rhesus' army (Ammendola on 309–13). With lexical variation cf. *Phoen.* 113 (Πολυνείκης ...) πολλοῖς μὲν ἵπποις, μυρίοις δ' ὅπλοις βρέμων. For further effect 'connexion is varied with asyndeton' (*GP* 164).

311. ἱππῆς: Dindorf (*PSG*[1], 222) restored the classical Attic form of the nominative plural (ἱππεῖς ΩgE). In drama cf. E. *Suppl.* 666 ἱππεῦσι δ' ἱππῆς ἦσαν ἀνθωπλισμένοι, *Phoen*. 1146–7 τί μέλλετ' ἄρδην πάντες ἐμπίπτειν πύλαις, / γυμνῆτες ἱππῆς ἁρμάτων τ' ἐπιστάται; 1191, Ar. *Eq.* 225, 242.

πελταστῶν τέλη: 'divisions of peltasts'. Likewise *Pers*. 47 δίρρυμά τε καὶ τρίρρυμα τέλη (with Garvie: 'squadrons of two-poled and three-poled chariots') and, in a broader sense, already *Il.* 10.470 αἶψα δ' ἐπὶ Θρηκῶν ἀνδρῶν τέλος ἷξον ἰόντες (LSJ s.v. τέλος I 10 a; cf. G. C. Richards, *CQ* 10 [1916], 196).

While Thracian peltasts are first mentioned by Thucydides (e.g. 2.29.5, 4.28.4, 5.6.4, 7.27.1), the Athenians appear to have been familiar with them from at least the latter half of the sixth century BC (Best, *Thracian Peltasts*, 4–16, who adds vase-paintings to the description of Xerxes' Thraco-Bithynian allies at Hdt. 7.75.1; cf. 312–13n.). The use of the term thus provides no *terminus post quem* for the composition of *Rhesus* (Ritchie 83, 157), even apart from the Macedonian interpretation rejected in 311–13n.

312–13. ἀτράκτων τοξόται: 'shooters of arrows'. Our poet may have been inspired by A. fr. 139.2 (*Myrmidons*) πληγέντ' ἀτράκτῳ τοξικῷ τὸν αἰετόν,[126] although ἄτρακτος, 'arrow', also occurs at *Tr.* 714, *Phil.* 290, Thuc. 4.40.2 (below) and later Leon. Tarent. *Ep.* 92.4 Gow–Page *HE*. Originally the word means 'spindle', probably from an unattested IE verb 'to twist, rotate', which also lies behind Sanskrit *tarku-* ('spindle'), Greek ἀτρεκής ('*unumwunden*') and Latin *torquere* (*GEW*, *DELG* s.v. ἄτρακτος). The metaphorical use for 'arrow' developed from similarity of form and movement (around its own axis). There is no sense of contempt involved, except perhaps at Thuc. 4.40.2 (a Spartan to an Athenian) ἀπεκρίνατο αὐτῷ πολλοῦ ἂν ἄξιον εἶναι τὸν ἄτρακτον, λέγων τὸν ὀιστόν, εἰ τοὺς ἀγαθοὺς διεγίγνωσκε, where 'spindle' (a female instrument) stresses the prejudice of the cowardly archer (Hornblower on Thuc. 4.40.2; cf. 32–3n.).

ὄχλος / γυμνής: i.e. slingers, stone- and/or javelin-throwers, mentioned separately from the archers, as at 31 (n.) ποῦ δὲ γυμνήτων μόναρχοι;

ἁμαρτῇ: 'together, at once'. Diggle and Kovacs rightly follow Wackernagel (*Sprachliche Untersuchungen*, 70–1) in writing ἁμαρτῇ for Attic (?) ὁμαρτῇ here (Δ: ὁμαρτεῖ ΛgE et O¹ᶜ) and at *Hec.* 839. Aristarchus read ἁμαρτή in Homer (*Il.* 5.656, 18.571, 21.162, *Od.* 22.81),[127] and for archaic and classical Attic ἁμαρτῇ is attested at Sol. fr. 33.4 *IEG*, *Hcld.*

---

126 Achilles' retelling of a 'Libyan' animal fable was famous. Ar. *Av.* 808 gives the moral (~ A. fr. 139.4–5), and the whole fragment is quoted by the scholia on the preceding line. Numerous other sources transmit part of the passage or allude to it (Radt, *TrGF* III, 252–6).

127 On this form see J. Wackernagel, *Gött. Nachr.* (1902), 742 n. 1 = *KS* I, 132 n. 1, Schwyzer 550 and West's apparatus on *Il.* 5.656.

138 (L: ὁμ- Tr²) and *Hipp.* 1195 (Π⁸ [III BC]: ὁμ- ΩVΛ). The far more frequent verb seems to have made a fuller change early on, given that we have 17 undisputed cases of ὁμαρτ- in tragedy (including three augmented forms: *PV* 678, *OC* 1647, *Ion* 1151) as against one possible of ἁμαρτ- at E. fr. 680 (= Hsch. α 3456 + 3457 Latte). See also Barrett on *Hipp.* 1194–7.

Θρηκίαν ἔχων στολήν: The dress of strangers tends to be commented on as part of their national identification: A. *Suppl.* 234–7 ποδαπὸν ὅμιλον τόνδ' ἀνελληνόστολον / πέπλοισι βαρβάροισι κἀμπυκώμασιν / χλίοντα προσφωνοῦμεν; οὐ γὰρ Ἀργολίς / ἐσθὴς γυναικῶν οὐδ' ἀφ' Ἑλλάδος τόπων (with FJW on 234, 235), A. fr. 61 = Ar. *Thesm.* 136–42, *Hec.* 734–5, *Hyps.* fr. I iv.11–14 Bond = E. fr. 752h.11–14, Ar. fr. 311 *PCG* and, of Greeks, *Phil.* 223–4, *Hcld.* 130–1 (with Wilkins).

Thracian warriors typically wore a knee-length tunic covered by a heavy patterned cloak (ζειρά), soft leather boots and on their heads a fox-skin cap with earflaps (ἀλωπεκίς) – all primarily designed for protection against the cold. The accounts of Herodotus (7.75.1) and Xenophon (*An.* 7.4.4) are confirmed by artistic representations from the later sixth century on (Best, *Thracian Peltasts*, 6–8 with plts. 2, 3, 4 and, for further literature, Liapis on 311–13).

314–16. The implicit comparison between Rhesus and Achilles (as well as sometimes Ajax and Diomedes) becomes another *leitmotif*. After 335 (n.), it is resumed by the chorus (370–4, 460–2), Rhesus himself (491, 496–8), Athena (600–4) and the Muse (974–7), stressing Rhesus' martial prowess and the Trojans' reverent trust in him. Cf. G. Paduano, *SCO* 23 (1974), 19–21.

φεύγων ... ἐκφυγεῖν: This collocation 'plays upon the conative aspect of the present and the complexive aspect of the aorist reinforced by ... the preposition ('get away', 'succeed in escaping')' (Mastronarde on *Phoen.* 1216 ἢν μή γε φεύγων ἐκφύγῃς πρὸς αἰθέρα). So in particular also Ar. *Ach.* 177 δεῖ γάρ με φεύγοντ' ἐκφυγεῖν Ἀχαρνέας and Pl. (?) *Hp. Ma.* 292a6–7 ... ἂν μὴ ἐκφύγω φεύγων αὐτόν.

οὔθ' ὑποσταθεὶς δορί: Cf. 375b–7 (n.) σὲ γὰρ οὔτις ὑποστὰς / Ἀργείας ποτ' ἐν Ἥ- / ρας δαπέδοις χορεύσει. The 'first' aorist passive (ὑποσταθ-) looks like a concession to metre, when otherwise the intransitive middle ὑπέστην is the rule (LSJ s.v. ὑφίστημι B with IV 1 'resist, withstand'; cf. Fraenkel, *Rev.* 239). Similarly e.g. ἀνθίσταμαι (LSJ s.v. ἀνθίστημι II 1, 3 'stand against, withstand, resist'), which in classical times has ἀντισταθ- only at Hdt. 5.72.2.

The coupling with φεύγω in our line is natural: *Cyc.* 198–200 οὐ δῆτ'· ἐπεὶ τἂν μεγάλα γ' ἡ Τροία στένοι, / εἰ φευξόμεσθ' ἕν' ἄνδρα, / μυρίον δ' ὄχλον / Φρυγῶν ὑπέστην πολλάκις σὺν ἀσπίδι, *Phoen.* 1470–1, Thuc. 1.144.4, 4.54.2, Plut. *Demetr.* 25.1.

317–18. 'When the gods stand firm for our citizens, fortune moves easily towards success.'

This kind of translation suits both the context and the Greek better than anything implying a rapid change from misfortune (ξυμφορά) to good luck (τἀγαθά). 'The chorus mean, that Hector's recent success, showing the favour of heaven to the Trojans, has now been crowned by this second piece of luck, the arrival of a powerful ally' (Paley on 317). Yet unlike their commander, they remain conscious of the mutability of fate (332) and eventually are forced to recant their optimistic statement here: 882–4 (n.) τί ποτ' εὐτυχίας ἐκ τῆς μεγάλης / Τροίαν ἀνάγει πάλιν ἐς πένθη / δαίμων ἄλλος, τί φυτεύων;

Initially the expression resembles *Pers.* 601 ὅταν δ' ὁ δαίμων εὐροῇ ..., and most words are used in comparable ways elsewhere (below). But one may wonder whether the whole *sententia* is in the best of Greek tragic style (Fraenkel, *Rev.* 238).

εὐσταθῶσι: 'to be steady, stable' (LSJ s.v. 1), attested only here in classical Greek. The sense corresponds to that of ἵσταμαι at Xen. *HG* 5.2.23 τούτου γὰρ γενομένου τάς τε οὔπω προσκεχωρηκυίας πόλεις στῆναι ἂν καὶ τὰς βεβιασμένας ἧττον ἂν συμμαχεῖν (LSJ s.v. ἵστημι Β ΙΙ 2), rather than Plut. *Aet. Rom.* 72.281b πνευμάτων δ' ὄντων οὐκ εὐσταθοῦσιν οἱ ὄρνιθες (of Roman augury), which commentators tend to quote. Paley and Feickert (on 317) suspect an allusion also to the belief that the gods leave a city which has fallen or is about to fall. Note particularly *Sept.* 217–18 ἀλλ' οὖν θεούς / τοὺς τῆς ἁλούσης πόλεος ἐκλείπειν λόγος and 318–20 καὶ πόλεως ῥύτορες <ἔστ'> / εὔεδροί τε στάθητ' / ὀξυγόοις λιταῖσιν (with Hutchinson on 318–19). Other examples in Hutchinson on *Sept.* 304.

ἕρπει: for the course of time or events also e.g. Pi. *Nem.* 7.67–8 ὁ δὲ λοιπὸς εὔφρων / ποτὶ χρόνος ἕρποι, *Ai.* 1087 ἕρπει παραλλὰξ ταῦτα (i.e. good and bad fortune) and *IT* 476–7 πάντα γὰρ τὰ τῶν θεῶν / ἐς ἀφανὲς ἕρπει κοὐδεὶς οἶδ' οὐδεὶς †κακόν†.

κατάντης: literally 'downwards', implying quick and easy movement on a way (Ar. *Ran.* 127), not the tipping of a balance, as Palmer (*CR* 4 [1890], 229) and others surmised. The word is again unique in tragedy. But its opposite προσάντης occurs metaphorically at *Med.* 303–5 σοφὴ γὰρ οὖσα, τοῖς μέν εἰμ' ἐπίφθονος / [...] / τοῖς δ' αὖ προσάντης ('adverse, an obstacle'), 381, *IT* 1012–13 and *Or.* 790, while ἄναντες (for ἀνέντες) has been proposed at *HF* 122 (see Bond on 121–3). Ritchie (215) adds *Alc.* 500 σκληρὸς γὰρ αἰεὶ καὶ πρὸς αἶπος ἔρχεται (i.e. Heracles' δαίμων).

ξυμφορά: without a qualifying epithet in a good sense, as in *Ag.* 24, S. *El.* 1230 (with Finglass) and Sim. fr. 512 = 1 Poltera πῖνε πῖν' ἐπὶ συμφοραῖς (quoted in Ar. *Eq.* 406). συμφορά 'in itself [is] neither good nor bad but used most frequently of unfavourable events' (Fraenkel on *Ag.* 24).

319–26. Confident as ever, Hector greets the news of Rhesus' approach with a variation on the commonplace that friends are abundant in success (Feickert on 320). The indignant little speech foreshadows the first part of the *agon* (388–526, 388–453nn.), where Hector berates Rhesus for coming late, despite the many embassies he had sent: 399–403 (cf. the Muse at 935–7). Tensions between the Trojans and their allies occasionally surface in the *Iliad* and may have been a feature of the older epic tradition (Edwards on *Il.* 17.219–32; cf. 251b–2, 762–9, 859a nn.).

319–20. ἐπειδὴ τοὐμὸν εὐτυχεῖ δόρυ: 60b–2n.

καὶ Ζεὺς πρὸς ἡμῶν ἐστιν: Cf. 52–84, 317–18nn. and, for Hector's failure to understand that the tide of war will turn, 983–96, 995b–6nn.

321–3. 'But we do not need those who have not toiled with us all the long time that the violent winds of Ares were blowing with full force and rending the sails of our ship of state.'

321b–2a. οἵτινες πάλαι / μὴ ξυμπονοῦσιν: For πάλαι with a present tense for an action that continues from the past into the present (KG I 134–5, SD 273–4, LSJ s.v. I 1) cf. 329, 396 and 414. Only L has the correct indicative ξυμπονοῦσιν (ξυμπονῶσιν ΔQgB) with μή in a generalising relative clause (KG II 185–6, 422).

322b–3. ἡνίκ' ἐξώστης Ἄρης / ἔθραυε λαίφη τῆσδε γῆς μέγας πνέων: As in *Sept.* 62–4 σὺ δ' ὥστε ναὸς κεδνὸς οἰακοστρόφος / φάρξαι πόλισμα, πρὶν καταιγίσαι πνοάς / Ἄρεως (with Hutchinson), the 'Ship of State' image (246–9a n.) is here amalgamated with that of Ares' breath as a furious gale. The latter recurs twice in *Seven against Thebes* (112–15, 343–4 [~ *Ant.* 135–7, of Capaneus]) and has a precedent in the comparison of Ares to a storm-wind at *Il.* 20.51 αὖε δ' Ἄρης ἑτέρωθεν, ἐρεμνῇ λαίλαπι ἶσος (although the formula is also applied to humans: *Il.* 11.747 ... κελαινῇ λαίλαπι ἶσος, 12.375). It contrasts with the gentle, fragrant breeze of more benevolent gods, which is given a twist in 385–7 (n.).

ἐξώστης of a wind that drives ships off course (Σ^V *Rh.* 322 [II. 334.10–11 Schwartz = 93 Merro], LSJ s.v. ἐξώστης 2) seems to be an Ionism: Hdt. 2.113.1, Hp. *VM* 9.4 (E. Fraenkel, *Nomina agentis* I, 241; cf. Fraenkel, *Rev.* 239, *Rh.* 810b–12a n.). The verb, however, was regularly so used in Attic: *Cyc.* 278–9 πνεύμασιν θαλασσίοις / σὴν γαῖαν ἐξωσθέντες ἥκομεν, Κύκλωψ, Thuc. 2.90.5, 7.52.2, 8.104.4 (LSJ s.v. ἐξωθέω II).

ἔθραυε λαίφη: As θραύω ('break in pieces, shatter') is not entirely fitting for sails, there may be an echo of *Eum.* 553–7 τὸν ἀντίτολμον δέ φαμι ... 555b ξὺν χρόνῳ καθήσειν / λαῖφος, ὅταν λάβῃ πόνος, / θραυομένας κεραίας ('the yard-arm', i.e. the crossbeam from which the sail was hung). V's 'durative' imperfect is correct (ἔθραυε OgB: ἔφαυσε Λ).

μέγας πνέων: Cf. Thuc. 6.104.2 καὶ ἁρπασθεὶς ὑπ' ἀνέμου ... ὃς ἐκπνεῖ ταύτῃ μέγας and, of a person identifying himself with a storm, Ar. *Eq.* 430 ἔξειμι γάρ σοι λαμπρὸς ἤδη καὶ μέγας καθιείς. Tragic instances of (ἀνα)πνέω with μέγα / μεγάλα are metaphorical (*Andr.* 189, *Tro.* 1277, *Ba.* 640).

324. ἦν refers to the time at which Rhesus professed his allegiance.

325–6. 'For he has come to the feast, without helping the hunters catch the prey or sharing our toils with his spear.'

The hunting metaphor looks proverbial, although it entered only the medieval gE (325). As the thought returns to the literal world of fighting, λεία acquires a trace of its ordinary meaning 'booty' (LSJ s.v. (B) 1), suggesting that Hector does not wish to share the spoils (and glory) of a war he believes he has won alone (cf. Feickert on 326).

κυνηγέταις: Elmsley[1] (on *Hcld.* 694) proposed κυνηγέτης, which is also now found in gE. But unlike at *Hcld.* 694 πῶς οὖν ὁπλίτης τευχέων ἄτερ φανῇ; (ὁπλίτης Elmsley: -ταις L), the dative is more trenchant here (it was the Trojans who did all the hard work). Moreover, an assimilative error seems likelier with παρών in the same line.

οὐδὲ συγκαμὼν δορί: Cf. Hector at 396–7 πάλαι πάλαι χρῆν τῇδε συγκάμνειν χθονί / ἐλθόντα.

327–8. ἀτίζεις: 251b–2n.

κἀπίμομφος: here active, 'inclined to blame' (LSJ s.v. ἐπίμομφος I). The adjective is passive ('blameable, unlucky') at *Ag.* 551–3 ταῦτα δ' ἐν πολλῷ χρόνῳ / τὰ μέν τις ἂν λέξειεν εὐπετῶς ἔχειν, / τὰ δ' αὖτε κἀπίμομφα and, if correct, *Cho.* 829–30 καὶ πέραιν' / οὐκ ἐπίμομφον ἄταν (see West's apparatus and Garvie on *Cho.* 827–30).

δέχου δέ: In view of 301 ὥστε δαίμονα (301b–8, 301b–2nn.), Strohm (270 with n. 5) compares the Herdsman at *Ba.* 769–70 τὸν δαίμον' οὖν τόνδ', ὅστις ἔστ', ὦ δέσποτα, / δέχου πόλει τῇδ' (264–341n.).

329. The nearest parallel is *Alc.* 383 ἀρκοῦμεν ἡμεῖς οἱ προθνῄσκοντες σέθεν. Ritchie (202 n. 1) fails to see the difference hinted at by Dale (on *Alc.* 383), namely that ἀρκέω here means 'suffice' not only in numerical terms, but also in the sense 'to be strong enough' (cf. *Hcld.* 574–6 καὶ δίδασκέ μοι / τοιούσδε τούσδε παῖδας, ἐς τὸ πᾶν σοφούς, / ὥσπερ σύ, μηδὲν μᾶλλον· ἀρκέσουσι γάρ). But he rightly draws attention to the use of the article, which puts special emphasis on the person(s) concerned (Feickert on 329).

πάλαι: 321b–2a n. Λ's πόλιν intruded from the end of 328.

330–1. πέποιθας ... / πέποιθα: Hector's misguided confidence is sustained to the end: 989b–92 (n.) ὡς ... / ... ναυσὶν αἴθον ἐμβαλεῖν / πέποιθα Τρωσί θ' ἡμέραν ἐλευθέραν / ἀκτῖνα τὴν στείχουσαν ἡλίου φέρειν. For the ominous connotations of πείθω in *Rhesus* see 65–6n.

τοὐπιὸν σέλας θεοῦ: Cf. *Med.* 352 ἡ 'πιοῦσα λαμπὰς ... θεοῦ, E. *Suppl.* 469 ... πρὶν θεοῦ δῦναι σέλας and *Tro.* 860 ὦ καλλιφεγγὲς ἡλίου σέλας τόδε. Euripides had a penchant for attributive ἐπιών ('coming, following') and periphrases for sun- or daylight. The former is exemplified also by *Alc.* 173–4 τοὐπιόν / κακόν, *IT* 313, *Or.* 1659, *IA* 651, E. frr. 135.2, 1073.6,[128] the latter by *Alc.* 722 τὸ φέγγος ... τοῦ θεοῦ, *Hcld.* 749–50, *Ion* 1467 ἀελίου ... λαμπάσιν and *Or.* 1025. Diggle (on *Phaeth.* 6, *Euripidea*, 405–6) cites further tragic cases for Ἥλιος being replaced with θεός (properly 'the relevant god', i.e. the sun).

332. πόλλ' ἀναστρέφει θεός: 317–18, 882–4nn. The idea of the gods 'turning over' the affairs of men is frequent in Euripides: E. *Suppl.* 331 ὁ γὰρ θεὸς πάντ' ἀναστρέφει πάλιν (with πέποιθα preceding, as here), *Hipp.* 981–2, *Andr.* 1007–8 ἐχθρῶν γὰρ ἀνδρῶν μοῖραν εἰς ἀναστροφήν / δαίμων δίδωσι, E. fr. 301.1, *Hel.* 712–13 εὖ δέ πως πάντα στρέφει (*sc.* ὁ θεός) / ἐκεῖσε κἀκεῖσ' ἀναφέρων, E. fr. 536. Elsewhere *Eum.* 650–1 (Zeus) τὰ δ' ἄλλα πάντ' ἄνω τε καὶ κάτω / στρέφων τίθησιν (with Sommerstein). Cf. Collard on E. *Suppl.* 330–1a and Liapis on 330–2 on the underlying 'Wheel of Fortune' image.

333–41. The transmitted line order and speaker distributions make no sense. 333 must belong to Hector (Ω), and 334–5, given to the coryphaeus and the Shepherd respectively, would follow well. But 336–8, which L alone rightly assigns to Hector, are no cogent reply to the preceding objections and at any rate cannot come immediately before Hector's (Q) final decision to accept Rhesus as an ally (339–41).

Nauck's transposition of 336–8 after 333 (*Euripideische Studien* II, 171–3) is the easiest solution. Hector still disapproves of tardy friends (333), but in order perhaps to avert the wrath of Zeus Ξένιος concedes admitting Rhesus as a guest (336–7n.). Further advice by the chorus-leader and the Shepherd (334–5n.) – for 339 (n.) σύ τ' ... καὶ σύ ... refers to two different persons – then persuades him to take the second step (339–41). If his change of mind seems even more abrupt than in the Aeneas scene (264–341n.), the imperfection must probably be laid at our poet's door. But it is possible that a few lines were lost after 335 (n.), which in the way of *Il.* 16.278–83 (Patroclus) and 18.197–238 (Achilles) expanded on the fear Rhesus would strike into the Greek host.[129] Apart from making Hector's reaction more plausible, a short speech by the

---

[128] His rarer use of literal ἐπιών (attributive and predicative) is discussed in 673b–4n.

[129] Klyve (on 336–41 [pp. 225–6]) had already placed a lacuna *before* 335 'containing a speech ... spoken by the messenger, pleading for the acceptance of Rh[esus] as an ally'. Yet as with Rosivach's (58 n. 12) idea to keep the MSS order and assume a gap between 336–8 and 339–41, it is difficult to see how this could have avoided repeating much that has already been said. And the asyndeton is no argument against 335 being a 'one-liner' (or the beginning rather than the end of a longer utterance).

Shepherd would also fit the type of messenger who stays on to influence the course of the play (804–81n.). On the other hand, our poet may have intended a single put-down remark like that of Iolaus at *Hcld.* 687 οὐδεὶς ἔμ' ἐχθρῶν προσβλέπων ἀνέξεται.

Zanetto's transposition (cf. *Ciclope, Reso*, 145–6 n. 46) can be rejected at once. Placing 336–8 after 328 and giving 338 (punctuated as a question) to the coryphaeus does nothing to improve the logic of the passage. 329–35 awkwardly follow 338 (which is not answered by 329), and 'Hector's capitulation in 336–7 ... would come as a complete surprise after only two lines of argumentation by the chorus (327–8)' (Liapis, 'Notes', 66). The creation of straight stichomythia is a negligible advantage.

West (*apud* Klyve on 336–41 [p. 225]) proposed to treat 336–8 and 339–41 as alternative versions, one of which he would delete. From the subsequent ode it is evident that 336–8 could not stand on their own, since the chorus express hopes in Rhesus too high for him to have been admitted merely as a guest (Klyve). Without those lines the discussion would in a clear and coherent fashion centre on the question of military allegiance, and if there was a lacuna of the kind discussed above, Hector's turn-about would appear no less abrupt than in Nauck's correction of the paradosis. But it is difficult to explain how 336–8 could have entered the text, unless a redactor (desiring further conflict perhaps) interpolated them for a revival of the play.[130] This, however, would have worked only after 333, bringing us back to the order restored by Nauck. Short of conclusive evidence, it seems best to accept it as what our poet wrote.

333. 'I hate it if a man comes too late to help his friends.'

Hector's summary complaint, which he repeats almost literally at 411b–12 (n.), resembles Ar. *Ran.* 1427–8 ~ E. frr. [886] [887] ('Euripides' on Alcibiades) μισῶ πολίτην, ὅστις ὠφελεῖν πάτραν / βραδὺς πέφανται (Hamaker: φανεῖται R, *Suda* σ 511: πέφυκε VAKL). The second versehalf echoes *Phoen.* 1432–3 ... Ὦ τέκν', ὑστέρα βοηδρόμος / πάρειμι. Euripides liked βοηδρόμος (also *Hcld.* 339, *El.* 963, *Or.* 1290/1) and βοηδρομέω (*Hcld.* 121, *Hipp.* 776, *Or.* 1356, 1476, 1510, 1622), which elsewhere before the Imperial period is found only in A. fr. 46c.6 (*Diktyoulkoi*?) and, perhaps as Euripidean imitations (Liapis on 333), Lyc. 923 and Ezek. 232. Its use here remains true to the basic 'run in response to a call for help' (Willink on *Or.* 1288–91).

336–7. ὃ δ' οὖν is Nauck's idiomatic reinterpretation of the transmitted ὅδ' οὖν (*Euripideische Studien* II, 173), in which he rightly prefers

---

130 One would not wish to ascribe the incongruous MSS text to our poet. Where alternative versions coalesce (e.g. Ar. *Ran.* 1251–60, 1431a/b, 1437–53), the confusion usually arose in the early tradition.

to leave the demonstrative accented (cf. West, ed. *Aeschylus*, XLIX). For 'permissive' δ' οὖν (with a second- or third-person imperative) see *GP* 466–7; in mid-speech also *OC* 1205 and Ar. *Lys*. 491. The tone is petulant here, condescending in 868 σὺ δ' οὖν νόμιζε ταῦτ', ἐπείπερ σοι δοκεῖ.

ξένος ... πρὸς τράπεζαν ... ξένων: The polyptoton, here emphasised by the way it frames the line, expresses the mutual ties (and duties) of hospitality: *Cho*. 702–3 τί γὰρ / ξένου ξένοισίν ἐστιν εὐμενέστερον (~ Hdt. 7.237.3), *Eum*. 660–1 ἢ δ' ἅπερ ξένῳ ξένη / ἔσωσεν ἔρνος, *IA* [604–6] and, in general, Denniston on E. *El*. 337, Gygli-Wyss, *Polyptoton*, 64–8, 112–15, 127 with n. 3, West, *IEPM* 113–14

For τράπεζαν ... ξένων cf. *Od*. 14.158 = 17.155 ξενίη ... τράπεζα and *Ag*. 401/2 ξενίαν τράπεζαν. See also 841b–2n.

338. 'For he has utterly lost the gratitude of Priam's sons.'

The sentiment corresponds to Men. fr. 702 *PCG* ἅμ' ἠλέηται καὶ τέθνηκεν ἡ χάρις / ἣν δεόμενος τότ' ἀθάνατον ἕξειν ἔφη, the first verse of which became proverbial early on (*PCG* VI.2, 347). This, and not our passage, appears to be alluded to in Eust. 822.4–5 (on *Il*. 10.519–25) ὀκνοῦσι γὰρ ἴσως ὑπερκινδυνεῦσαι τῶν νεηλύδων, ὧν οὐδὲν αὐτοὶ ἀπώναντο. καὶ εἰ τοῦτο, ἄρα συντέθνηκε κατὰ τὴν παροιμίαν ἡ ἐκ τῶν Τρώων χάρις τῷ 'Ρήσῳ (cf. Introduction 46 with n. 96).

διώλετο: ΔQ. Liapis alone prefers L's ἀπώλετο, on the ground that διόλλυμαι tends to emphasise 'the role of an external agency', while (ἀπ)όλλυμαι 'can mean merely "to cease to exist, to fail"' ('Notes', 67). But the stronger verb is desired here, suggesting that Rhesus himself has forfeited Hector's gratitude (Paley on 338). Cf. *Pers*. 589–90 βασιλεία γὰρ διόλωλεν ἰσχύς (i.e. through Xerxes' failure) as against the 'neutral' S. fr. 920 ἀμνήμονος γὰρ ἀνδρὸς ὄλλυται χάρις, *Hcld*. 437–8 εἰ θεοῖσι δὴ δοκεῖ τάδε / πράσσειν ἔμ', οὔτοι σοί γ' ἀπόλλυται χάρις and E. fr. 736.5–6 ἡ δ' ἐν ὀφθαλμοῖς χάρις / ἀπόλωλ', ὅταν τις ἐκ δόμων ἀνὴρ θάνῃ.

334–5. For the need to divide the couplet between two speakers see 333–41n. The sententious admonition not to scorn allies (334) suits the coryphaeus, who had already said as much in 327–8. And the Shepherd has personal experience of Rhesus' fearsome effect (287–9, 306–8). See Nauck, *Euripideische Studien* II, 172–3.

334. ἐπίφθονον: *sc*. ἐστίν ('it is hateful ...'). Cf. *Hcld*. 202–3 ... καὶ γὰρ οὖν ἐπίφθονον / λίαν ἐπαινεῖν ἐστι and Ar. *Eq*. 1274 λοιδορῆσαι τοὺς πονηροὺς οὐδέν ἐστ' ἐπίφθονον. The arrogance of rejecting an ally was likely to arouse resentment in both men and gods (Liapis on 334). See further 342–5, 342–3, 455b–7nn.

335. Two particular epic precedents exist. At *Il*. 16.278–83 Patroclus frightens the Trojans in Achilles' panoply, and at *Il*. 18.197–238 the hero himself achieves that end, supernaturally enhanced by Athena in aspect and voice. Our poet thus resumes the connection of Rhesus with Achilles (314–16n.) in a way that intimates divine support for him.

It is possible that Aelius Aristides recalled *Rhesus* in *Or.* 1.106 Lenz–Behr (of Darius' Persians) τοσαύτη δ' ἦν ὑπερηφανία τῆς παρασκευῆς καὶ τῶν ποιουμένων, ὥστ' ἐξαρκεῖν ἐδόκει τοῖς βαρβάροις ὀφθῆναι μόνον (Vater on 325; cf. Introduction, 45).

φόβος: 'an object of fear', as in e.g. A. *Suppl.* 479 ὕψιστος γὰρ ἐν βροτοῖς φόβος (i.e. Zeus), *OC* 1651–2 ὡς δεινοῦ τινος / φόβου φανέντος οὐδ' ἀνασχέτου βλέπειν, *Or.* 1518 ὧδε κἂν Τροίᾳ σίδηρος πᾶσι Φρυξὶν ἦν φόβος; (FJW on A. *Suppl.* 479) and *Rh.* 52 (n.) ... καίπερ ἀγγέλλων φόβον. The Iliadic parallels (above) tell against capitalising the noun with, tentatively, Liapis ('Notes', 67–8).

ὀφθείς: VΛ. O's ἐλθών arose from ἦλθε in 336.

339. 'You give good advice, and you consider <what is advantageous> in time.'

σύ τ' ... καὶ σύ: 333–41, 334–5nn. The choice of words suggests that the chorus-leader is addressed first. Usually the last speaker gets that privilege and/or a clarifying vocative is added: *IT* 655–6 ἔτι γὰρ ἀμφίλογα δίδυμα μέμονε φρήν, / σὲ πάρος ἢ σ' ἀναστενάξω γόοις (i.e. Pylades – Orestes), 1079 (Orestes – Pylades), *OT* 637 οὐκ εἶ σύ τ' οἴκους σύ τε, Κρέον, τὰς σὰς στέγας, *Ant.* 724–5, 1340–4, *Phoen.* 568 (cf. Nauck, *Euripideische Studien* II, 172 n. 1). But on stage a turn of the head or some other gesture would have sufficed.

καιρίως σκοπεῖς: For absolute σκοπέω, 'look to, consider', with an adverb or adverbial phrase cf. *Phoen.* 155 ὃ καὶ δέδοικα μὴ σκοπῶσ' ὀρθῶς θεοί (with Mastronarde), Pl. *Smp.* 219a1–2 ἀλλ' ... ἄμεινον σκόπει, μή σε λανθάνω οὐδὲν ὢν and probably A. *Suppl.* 232 σκοπεῖτε κἀμείβεσθε τόνδε τὸν τ<ρ>όπον (with FJW).

Some scholars refer the phrase to the Shepherd's observation of Rhesus' coming: '... and you were keeping your eyes open at the right time' (Morwood). But neither the context nor the tense of the verb recommend this view.

340–1. χρυσοτευχής: a *hapax*, which may have been coined for the occasion after *Il.* 10.439 τεύχεα δὲ χρύσεια (305–6a n.). Note the equally unparalleled E. *Suppl.* 999 χαλκεοτευχέος Καπανέως.

οὕνεκ' ἀγγέλου λόγων 'in view of what the messenger said', as at *Tro.* 912–13 τῶν σῶν δ' οὕνεχ' ... λόγων / δώσω τόδ' αὐτῇ (Klyve on 340–1). The alternative, namely to refer the clause to χρυσοτευχής alone ('as far as the messenger's words are concerned') has been discounted by Pearson (*CQ* 11 [1917], 60 + *CQ* 12 [1918], 79) on the ground that elsewhere this idiom indicates an entirely objective cause: e.g. S. *El.* 786–7 νῦν δ' ἕκηλά που / τῶν τῆσδ' ἀπειλῶν οὕνεχ' ἡμερεύσομεν, *Phil.* 774, *OC* 22, *Hipp.* 421–3 ἀλλ' ... / ... οἰκοῖεν πόλιν / κλεινῶν

Ἀθηνῶν, μητρὸς οὕνεκ' εὐκλεεῖς, *Hel.* 885–6, *Phoen.* 865–6, *Or.* 84 (LSJ s.v. ἕνεκα I 2). And while one need not perhaps be so strict (cf. W. H. Porter, *CQ* 11 [1917], 159–60), a half-sarcastic remark on Rhesus' golden armour seems to be less relevant here than a (grudging) recognition of his potential value for Troy.

On οὕνεκα as a preposition in drama see LSJ s.v. II, Barrett on *Hipp.* 453–6 and West, ed. *Aeschylus*, XLIX.

342–79. Even more than 224–63 (n.) this joyous ode which greets Rhesus' imminent arrival shows the elements of a cletic hymn (cf. Fenik, *Iliad X*, 26–7 n. 3, Furley–Bremer, *Greek Hymns* I, 50–63). After an apotropaic prayer to Adrasteia (342–5, 342–3nn.) and declaring their intention to sing Rhesus' praise (344–5n.), the chorus 'invoke' him as the son of the Thracian river god Strymon, whose waters impregnated a virgin Muse (346–8a, 348b–51a, 351b–4nn.). The so-called 'eulogy' distinguishes Rhesus with titles derived from different aspects of Zeus and with his dramatically most important attribute, the marvellous horses (355–6, 357–9nn.).

In the second strophe we get a nostalgic picture of Troy enjoying the pleasures of peace (360–7n.), which the chorus hope Rhesus will restore (368–9n.). This develops out of his identification with Zeus Ἐλευθέριος (357–9n.) and in the hymn takes the place of the usual myth and/or here inapplicable reminder of the god's previous service. The actual 'prayer' occupies the final stanza – forcefully introduced by ἐλθὲ φάνηθι (370–2a n.). As in the Shepherd's imagination (315–16), Rhesus is to confront Achilles and thus, it is implied, to defeat the Greeks once and for all (370–5a, 373b–5a, 375b–7nn.). The confident imperatives and future indicatives (370, 377, 379) leave no doubt of the chorus' trust at this point; contrast their misgivings in face of his arrogance upon arrival in 454–66 (n.).

Linguistically the hymnic style is evoked by anaphora (346–8a, 357–9nn.), a descriptive relative clause (351b–4n.), second-person invocations (355–6n.) and, reflecting choral-lyric rather than tragic practice, the syntactical overlap between the first strophe and antistrophe (348b–51a n.). All these set the tone for the unprecedented identification of a mortal with Zeus and, in the following anapaests, Ares 'himself' (385–7n.).

By casting Rhesus' arrival in the light of a divine epiphany, the chorus not only surpass the Shepherd's excited description – including the epicising ὥστε δαίμονα in 301 (301b–2n.) – but also their earlier exaltation of Dolon (224–63), who after all required the help of Apollo and Hermes to succeed (cf. Klyve on 342–87 [pp. 229–31]). In the course of the ode both the Trojan hopes and the audience's expectation of Rhesus reach their peak, although for the latter sinister undercurrents again come in.

The dazzling Thracian will no more 'return home' (367–9; cf. 450)[131] than the hapless Dolon (235–7), and instead of witnessing symposia again, Troy will suffer the fate envisaged for the Greeks (357–9, 375b–7nn.).

If we had the choral response to Memnon's arrival in A. *Memnon* (cf. 380–7n.) or to that of Cycnus in S. *Poimenes* (264–341, 388–526nn.), we might find that our poet went out of his way to elevate Rhesus before his fall (certainly with the lavish titles he bestowed on him). Yet it is not hybris and divine φθόνος that will prove his doom. Rhesus is as potent as the chorus wish and he himself will maintain, and has to die because Athena will not let him have his way (Klyve on 342–87 [p. 231]).

Metre

342–50 ~ 351–9. A sequence of aeolic, iambo-choriambic and dactylo-epitrite cola with an aristophanean clausula. The pattern again resembles the parodos (23–33 ~ 41–51) and in Euripides especially *Tro.* 1060–70 ~ 1071–81 (Ritchie 306–7). On the frequent combination of these metres see also West, *GM* 118–20.

360–9 ~ 370–9. Primarily iambo-choriambic and aeolic. With the colometry given here a 'dove-tailed' iambo-choriambic period (360–2/370–2n.) is followed by a variation on that scheme (363–5/373–5n.) and two aeolic elements with a iambo-choriambic close. But it is possible that the rhythm turns to ionic in the middle (363–5/373–5, 366–7/376–7nn.).

342	351	– – – ⏑ ⏑ | – ⏑ –	gl ⌠
343	352	– | – – | ⏑ ⏑ – ⏑ – |	gl |
344	353	⏓ – – ⏑ ⏑ – – |	ph |
345	354	– – | – ⏑ ⏑ – ⏑ | – – |	hi |
346	355	⏒ – | – ⏑ ⏑ – – ||	ph ||
347	356	– – | ⏑ – – | ⏑ ⏑ – ⏑ – – |	ia cho ia∧ |
348	357	– – ⏑ ⏑ – ⏑ ⏑ – |	– D |
349	358	– ⏑ – | – – | ⏑ ⏑ – ⏑ ⏑ –	e – D |
350	359	– ⏑ ⏑ – ⏑ – – |||	ar |||
360	370	– ⏑ ⏑ – ⏑ | – ⏑ –	cho ia ⌠
361	371	– | ⏑ ⏑ – | – ⏑ ⏑ – | ⏑ – ⏑ –	cho | cho | ia ⌠
362	372	– | ⏑ ⏑ – | ⏑ – – |	cho | ia∧ (ar) |
363	373	– – ⏑ – ⏑ ⏑ – – ⏑ ⏑ –	– – ⏑ 2cho ⌠
364	374	– | ⏑ ⏑ – ⏑ – ⏑ –	cho ia ⌠

---

[131] At least not in the intended way. Rhesus' ascension to heroic cult in Thrace is unforeseeable at this stage.

365	375	$-\mid\cup\cup-\cup\mid\cup--\mid$	$D-\mid$
366–7	376–7	$---\cup\cup--\cup\cup-\mid\cup--\parallel$	$hi^c \parallel$
368	378	$-\cup\cup\mid-\cup-\mid$	$dod\mid$
369	379	$-\cup\cup--\cup\cup--\cup\cup-\cup\mid--\parallel\mid$	$3cho\ ia_\wedge\ (ar^{2c})\parallel\mid$

Notes

344/353 The strophe shows correption between δή and ὅσον. The phenomenon does not often involve monophthongs (West, *GM* 12). In drama cf. particularly Ar. *Vesp.* 1065 δὴ αἴδ' – 'highly unusual in trochaics' (Parker, *Songs*, 247) because 'the shortened syllable is practically always preceded or followed by a naturally short syllable' (West, *GM* 11).

347/356 For choriambic trimeters in tragedy see 224–63 'Metre' 242–3/253–4n. The first exponent of *ia cho ia*$_\wedge$ is Anacr. fr. 384 *PMG*. Like other pendant cola, the verse need not be clausular (cf. *Ag.* 141, *Ant.* 806 ~ 823, *Med.* 432 ~ 439, *Hel.* 1452 ~ 1466).

350/359 The aristophanean, which is not elsewhere appended to dactylo-epitrite (Parker, *Songs*, 83), echoes the closing rhythm of 347 ~ 356 (above).

360–2/370–2 Various divisions are possible, not least because of the regular word-ends after the choriambs. The standard arrangement is *cho ia cho* | *cho* | *ia* ∫ *cho* | *ia*$_\wedge$ |, but the double 'dove-tailing', by which the initial colon (*cho ia*) is first expanded (*cho* | *cho* | *ia*), then reduced (*cho* | *ia*$_\wedge$), may be preferable also in view of the parallel evolution that seems to obtain in 363–5 ~ 373–5 (below).

363–5/373–5 This is the colometry of Murray, Schroeder² (168) and Parker (unpublished notes). At the relatively small price of leaving the unidentifiable $--\cup$[132] at the beginning of 363 ~ 373, it produces another stretch of 'dove-tailed' iambo-choriambics (360–2/370–2n.), ending in a pendant hemiepes ($D-$), which combines equally well with the following aeolic (cf. West, *GM* 100–2, 104, 118–20). All other editors since Wilamowitz (*GV* 586–7) have adopted an ionic interpretation (in accordance with the word-divisions): *ia 2io* | *2io*⁺ (*anacr*) | *io*$_\wedge$ *io* |. For a sequence of iambo-choriambic, ionic and aeolic West (*GM* 126–7) compares *Ag.* 681–98 ~ 699–716 and 737–49 ~ 750–62. Yet in both those strophic pairs the ionic element is more pronounced and separated from the rest by period-ends (so admitting of no alternative analysis).[133] The

---

[132] Not a 'palimbacchiac', which is a syncopated form of trochaic ($\cup--\cup$). It is impossible to tell whether the first long of our unit is anceps or not.

[133] The first criterion at least also applies to his other instances of 'interweaved' ionics. *Sept.* 321–32 ~ 333–44 and *Ba.* 556–75 simply begin with that metre.

potentially ambiguous colon 366 ~ 376 (below), which rounds off the period, also favours aeolo-choriambic over ionic. Nevertheless it frequently remains difficult, if not impossible, to decide between iambo-choriambic / aeolic and ionic (Dale, *LM²* 143–7, West, *GM* 127, Parker, *Songs*, 63–4). For all we can tell, our poet may have preferred mixing metres to a regular series of related types.

In 363 (362b–5a n.) Canter's ψαλμοῖσι for ψάλμασι (Ω) restores responsion. As a iambo-choriambic prefix – ⏑ ⏑ is meaningless and could not be answered by – – ⏑. And if the line was *ia 2io*, we would have correspondence between *cho* and *ia*, certain examples of which are rare and not attested in an ionic context (Parker, *Songs*, 78, 151, 237–8, 369; cf. West, *GM* 105).

366–7/376–7 The verse should not be divided with Murray, Schroeder² (168), Diggle and Kovacs. It is best taken as a colon of the 'asclepiad' family (*hi^c*), as e.g. *Ai.* 630 ~ 641 and, with two internal choriambs, *Rh.* 251–2 ~ 262–3 (224–63 'Metre' 250–2/261–3n.). In a more obviously ionic setting one could also regard it as contracted *2io* + ⏑ ⏑ – ⏑ – – ||. But '– x̄ – is very much commoner as aeolic opening than ⏓ – – as ionic' (Dale, *LM²* 144), which unequivocally occurs only at *Sept.* 321 ~ 333 and *Ba.* 81 (responding to ⏑ ⏑ – – in 97).

342–5. 'May Adrasteia, the daughter of Zeus, keep (divine) envy from my mouth. For I shall say all that my soul finds pleasing to utter.'

In true Pindaric fashion the chorus seek to avert such misfortune as may come from their glorification of Rhesus: *Ol.* 13.24–6 (cited in 455b–7n.), *Pyth.* 8.71–2, 10.19–22, *Isthm.* 7.39 ἀείσομαι χαίταν στεφάνοισιν ἁρμόζων· ὁ δ' ἀθανάτων μὴ θρασσέτω φθόνος (cf. Kranz, *Stasimon*, 264). The idea that excessive (self-)praise, as a form of ὕβρις, is liable to arouse the gods' ill-will is deep-rooted in archaic and classical Greek thought (Nilsson, *GGR* I³, 736–40). See also *Ag.* 903–4 τοιοῖσδέ τοί νιν / ἀξιῶ προσφθέγγμασιν, / φθόνος δ' ἀπέστω (with Fraenkel on 904) and *Rh.* 455b–7 (n.) μόνον / φθόνον ἄμαχον ὕπατος / Ζεὺς θέλοι ἀμφὶ σοῖς λόγοισιν ἔργειν, 468 ... σὺν δ' Ἀδραστείᾳ λέγω.

342–3. Ἀδράστεια: Originally a Phrygian mountain goddess (*Phoronis* fr. 2.1–4 *GEF* < ... > ἔνθα γόητες / Ἰδαῖοι, Φρύγες ἄνδρες, ὀρέστερα οἰκί' ἔναιον, / ... / εὐπάλαμοι θεράποντες ὀρείης Ἀδρηστείης, A. fr. 158.2–3) with a shrine near Cyzicus (Strab. 12.8.11, 13.1.13), Adrasteia was admitted to public cult at Athens some time before 429 BC (Parker, *Athenian Religion*, 172, 195, 197). Around that date she also surfaces in invocations against the effects of arrogant speech (*PV* 936, Pl. *Rep.* 451a4–5, [Dem.] 25.37, Men. *Peric.* 304) – like Nemesis, the personification of public and divine disapproval: e.g. Pittac. 10 ε 5 DK, S. *El.* 792 (with Finglass), *Phoen.* 182–4, Pl. *Leg.* 717d1–3. How this identification, which was first explicitly made in Antim. fr. 131 Matthews = 53 Wyss, came to pass we cannot tell. Nothing is known about Adrasteia's Athenian cult, and hardly more about the much older and autochthonous one of Nemesis at Rhamnus (Parker, *Polytheism and Society*, 406–7). It may be that the popular etymology of her name as ἀναπόδραστος ('not to be escaped') already played a part, although it is not attested before the Hellenistic age, when the early Stoics equated her with Fate (H. Posnansky, *Nemesis und Adrasteia* ..., Breslau 1890, 72–5, 88–90, West, *Orphic Poems*, 195–6 with n. 63). The explanation at any rate appears in the scholarly tradition: Ael. Dion. ν 5 Erbse (= Eust. 355.36–7) ἕτεροι δὲ τὴν Νέμεσιν Ἀδράστειαν εἶπον καλεῖσθαι διὰ τὸ τῆς θείας δίκης ἀναπόδραστον, Hsch. α 1190 Latte (= Phot. α 384 Theodoridis, *Suda* α 523 Adler) Ἀδράστεια· ἡ Νέμεσις, ἣν οὐκ ἄν τις ἀποδράσειεν.

It is possible that Adrasteia bore oriental associations here and at 468, spoken by Rhesus (e.g. Porter on 342, Jouan 65 n. 93, Liapis on 342–3). But given the frequent appeals to her also by Greeks, this is not a necessary assumption.

μέν: This is our sole example in lyric of 'inceptive' μέν without an answer expressed or implied (cf. *GP* 382–4, Fraenkel on *Ag*. 1). Similarly *Ag*. 40, the opening of the anapaestic parodos.

ἁ Διὸς / παῖς: As a daughter of Zeus Adrasteia recurs only at Plut. *De sera num. vind*. 25.564e Ἀδράστεια ... Ἀνάγκης καὶ Διὸς θυγάτηρ, which follows the tradition of Plato and the Stoics, where she became not only a judge of the departed souls (Pl. *Phdr*. 248c2–e5), but also the power of Fate itself (Posnansky, *Nemesis und Adrasteia*, 71 n. 1; cf. above). Our poet presumably created an *ad hoc* genealogy on the analogy of Dike, who fulfils a similar role as divinely authorised watcher over human affairs (Feickert on 342). That Adrasteia is thought to act on Zeus' behalf is shown by the chorus' prayer at 455–7 (342–5, 454–66, 455b–7nn.). On Adrasteia as one of Zeus' nurses (Call. *Iov*. 47–8, A. R. 3.133, 'Apollod.' 1.1.6 [1.5]; cf. Σ^V *Rh*. 342 [II 334.15–16 Schwartz = 93 Merro]) and the origin of this idea in a late-fifth-century Orphic theogony see West, *Orphic Poems*, 72, 122–4, 127–8, 131–2, 158.

στομάτων: 'the mouth as the organ of speech' (LSJ s.v. στόμα I 2), or 'lips' to do justice to the plural. In any case we need not understand 'speech, utterance', as in e.g. *OT* 671–2 τὸ γὰρ σὸν ... ἐποικτίρω στόμα / ἐλεινόν.

344–5. φράσω γὰρ δὴ ... εἰπεῖν: an emphatic explanation after the apotropaic prayer (cf. *GP* 243). φράσω is an ordinary rather than an 'encomiastic' or 'performative' future, as Liapis (on 344–5) would prefer.

μοι / ψυχᾷ: Cf. 266 ἀγρώσταις ... φρενί for this form of σχῆμα καθ᾽ ὅλον καὶ μέρος.

προσφιλές: The word is common in tragedy, but used in lyrics and with an infinitive only here.

346–8a. ἥκεις ... / ἥκεις: 249b–51a n. Here epanalepsis at the beginning of two successive cola (cf. Diggle, *Euripidea*, 370) 'helps create a mood of jubilant impatience in view of Rhesus' imminent arrival' (Liapis on 346–8). Similarly 357–8 (357–9n.) νῦν, ὦ πατρὶς ὦ Φρυγία, / ... νῦν σοι ... and 385–7 (n.) θεός, ὦ Τροία, θεός ... καταπνεῖ σε. Ritchie (238–9) lists general tragic examples of iteration after an apostrophe.

The verb occupies the same initial position in the corresponding 355–6 σύ μοι Ζεὺς ὁ Φαναῖος / ἥκεις ...

ὦ ποταμοῦ παῖ: The obligatory hymnic address at once identifies the 'god' (Rhesus) and his genuinely divine father (Strymon). Cf. 224–6a, 226a, 342–79nn.

ἐπλάθης: 13–14n. Forms of this poetic intransitive passive aorist recur in 911 and 920 (910–11, 919–20nn.). To the passages cited there add *Hec.* 890 and probably *Phil.* 727–8 ἵν' ὁ χάλκασπις ἀνὴρ θεοῖς / πλάθη †πᾶσι† (πλάθη QR, coni. Bergk: -θῃ G^pc: -θει G^ac rell.).

Φιλίου πρὸς αὐλάν: 'to the hall of the Friendly God', i.e. the royal palace of Troy, where Rhesus will be received as a friend. For (Zeus) Φίλιος cf. e.g. *Andr.* 602–4 (Ἑλένην ...) ἥτις ἐκ δόμων / τὸν σὸν λιποῦσα Φίλιον ἐξεκώμασεν / νεανίου μετ' ἀνδρὸς εἰς ἄλλην χθόνα, Ar. *Ach.* 730 ναὶ τὸν Φίλιον, Pherecr. fr. 102.4 *PCG*, Pl. *Euthphr.* 6b3–4, *Phdr.* 234e 2 πρὸς Διὸς φιλίου, Men. fr. 53 *PCG* (LSJ s.v. φίλιος I 2). The fact that Φίλιος is more often (and in earlier sources) mentioned alone can be interpreted in two ways. It is possible that this Zeus had long been familiar in the domestic sphere and so could be referred to only by this epithet (Parker, *Athenian Religion*, 241–2). But it may also be that he was originally an independent deity (ὁ Φίλιος θεός), who as protector of friendship and family bonds (φιλία) tied in with the sociomoral aspects of Zeus (especially that of Ξένιος) and in time was subsumed by him (Wilamowitz, *GV* 585, Nilsson, *GGR* I³, 808–10).

Older editors (and Klyve) prefer Φρυγίαν (Δ), a weak alternative, which may go back to a gloss, an associative error or a scribe's interpretation of a (partly) illegible reading.

ἀσπαστός occurs only here in tragedy, as does ἀσπασίως at *Ag.* 1555. Both adjectives are particularly epic.

348b–51a. To say that Rhesus is sent by Strymon and his Pierian mother (which turns out to be wrong: 899–901, 934–5) is an elegant way of expanding on his divine origin and leading into the colourful account of his conception (351b–4n.). With Strymon's name in single-word enjambment placed prominently at the head of the antistrophe, the sentence continues over the stanza boundary in a way that is unique for drama (cf. 242–4a n.), but has many parallels in Pindar and Bacchylides: e.g. Pi. *Ol.*

2.95, 10.55, *Pyth.* 12.17, *Nem.* 9.31, Bacch. 1.124, 5.151 (Kranz, *Stasimon*, 263, Ritchie 333–6).[134]

Πιερὶς μάτηρ: one of the Muses, who remains unidentified throughout the play. On her place in the mythical tradition and the confusion about her name in later scholarly texts see Introduction, 13.

καλλιγέφυρος: 'with beautiful bridges'. The word is a *hapax*, like many poetic καλλι- compounds (which in tragedy tend to be found in lyrics). Of rivers also καλλιδίνης (*HF* 368), καλλιδόναξ (*Hel.* 493), and καλλιπάρθενος (*Hel.* 1) as well as the more widespread καλλίναος (*Med.* 835).

Our poet probably alludes to the well-known Strymon bridge on the north-western side of Amphipolis, which played a crucial part in Brasidas' attack on the city in 424 BC (Thuc. 4.103.4, 4.108.1). Remains of its wooden structure were excavated in 1972 (cf. B. Isaac, *The Greek Settlements in Thrace until the Macedonian Conquest*, Leiden 1986, 55 with n. 284, Hornblower on Thuc. 4.103.4 [II, pp. 329–30]). It has nothing to do with the bridges Xerxes had built across the Strymon near Ennea Hodoi (Hdt. 7.24, 7.114.1)

351b–4. '... who swirling once in watery form through the virginal lap of the sweet-singing Muse begat your youthful vigour.'

Even more than in the previous clause the chorus speak as if they *perform* a hymn, not like a body of Trojan night-watchmen in the field. In a wider framework, but with less attention to 'detail', the story of Rhesus' conception is told again by the Muse at 919–20 (n.). Here especially the picture recalls *Od.* 11.241–4, where Poseidon visits Tyro in the guise of the river-god Enipeus, and a large wave surrounds the couple. More often in hymns we hear of the birth of a god or hero, but the parental union is described at e.g. *h.Merc.* 3–10, *h.Hom.* 33.4–6 (Dioscuri), Alc. fr. 308 Voigt and Isyll. *Pae. Epid.* 48–51 (*CA* 134 = Furley–Bremer II 183).

For relative clauses identifying a god's cult places or favourite haunts see 224–6a n. Other aspects so expressed included his genealogy, as here and in the first three examples quoted above (cf. Norden, *Agnostos Theos*, 168–76, *Rh.* 342–79n.).

τᾶς μελῳ- / δοῦ Μούσας: Cf. *Rh.* 393 παῖ τῆς μελῳδοῦ μητέρος Μουσῶν μιᾶς, 921–3 ὅτ' ἤλθομεν ... / ... / Μοῦσαι μεγίστην εἰς ἔριν μελῳδίας and, at the same metrical position, *IT* 1104–5 κύκνος μελῳ- / δὸς Μούσας (θεραπεύει). Euripides and Aristophanes were the first to use μελῳδός, μελῳδία (923–4a n.) and μελῳδέω.

---

[134] Ritchie tries to play down the import of the device. But the halting effect remains, even if both stanzas are syntactically intelligible on their own (as is also the case at *Pyth.* 12.17, *Nem.* 9.31 and *Isthm.* 6.35).

δι' ἀκηράτων ... κόλπων: similarly Zeus at *Hel*. 1145–6 πτανὸς γὰρ ἐν κόλποις σε Λή- / δας ἐτέκνωσε πατήρ (LSJ s.v. κόλπος I 2 c). For ἀκήρατος, 'undefiled, untouched, pure' (< κηραίνω), in a sexual context cf. *Tro*. 675–6 ἀκήρατον δέ μ' ... / πρῶτος τὸ παρθένειον ἐζεύξω λέχος, *Or*. 575, *IA* 1083, Pl. *Leg*. 840d5–6.

ὑδροειδής: another *hapax*, which emphasises Strymon's natural (as opposed to human or animal) form when he attacked the Muse (Liapis on 351–4, who also compares Ov. *Met*. 3.342–4). With δινηθείς the wording resembles *Ion* 95–6 τὰς Καστάλιας ἀργυροειδεῖς / ... δίνας (~ *IA* 751–2).

σὰν ... ἥβαν: i.e. 'you, a vigorous young man'. For similar periphrases of the type βίη Ἡρακληείη see 132 and 762–3a nn.

355–6. 'You have come to me as Zeus the 'Bringer of Light', driving your chariot with your dappled mares.'

σύ μοι: Emphatic (and repeated) second-person addresses are again typical of hymns. Cf. 369 σᾷ χερὶ καὶ σῷ δορί, 375 σὲ γὰρ ..., and see Norden, *Agnostos Theos*, 149–60, West, *IEPM* 310–11.

The dative is properly one 'of advantage' with Ζεὺς ὁ Φαναῖος ('... the Bringer of Light for me'). Cf. below.

Ζεὺς ὁ Φαναῖος is not attested anywhere else. But Apollo was worshipped as Φαναῖος on Chios (e.g. Hsch. φ 141 Hansen–Cunningham ~ Achae. *TrGF* 20 F 35), where his temple stood close to the harbour and promontory of Φάναι (Strab. 14.1.35). Both the place name and title have correctly been derived from φανή or φαναί, 'torch(es)' – most recently by Liapis (*CQ* n.s. 57 [2007], 382–5 and on 355–6). But whether he is justified in making wide-ranging assumptions about the use of ritual torches and mystic elements in the cults of Apollo Φαναῖος and Zeus is another question. Most of the parallels he adduces (*CQ* n.s. 57 [2007], 386–94) are late and/or relate to the fringes of the Greek world. It may be more promising after all to think of the Chian φαναί as 'beacons' for guiding ships safely into the harbour named after them (O. Crusius, *Die Delphischen Hymnen. Untersuchungen über Texte und Melodien*, Göttingen 1894, 16 n. 24). In that case our poet would have transferred the epithet to Zeus, one of whose many functions was to be a Σωτήρ (cf. Parker, *Athenian Religion*, 238–41) and whose sons Castor and Polydeuces brought light to ships in distress (Alc. fr. 34.9–12 Voigt). Likewise Rhesus (in his dazzling armour) could become a 'light of salvation' for the hard-pressed Trojans (cf. West, *EFH* 253, *IEPM* 482), without suggesting mystic release as the soon-to-be ἀνθρωποδαίμων and 'prophet of Bacchus' in a Pangaean cave: 970–3 (962–82n.).

Ultimately we do not know what connotations Φαναῖος bore for a fifth- or fourth-century Greek. But in view of (Zeus) Φίλιος in 347 (346–8a n.) and the straightforward association of Rhesus with Zeus

Ἐλευθέριος (357–9n.) and Ares (385–7n.), it would be strange to find a heavily 'laden' epithet here. The chorus' hopes for delivery from their present plight are clear in any case.

ἥκεις: 346–8a n.

διφρεύων βαλιαῖσι πώλοις: Cf. *Andr.* 1010–12 ὦ Φοῖβε ... / καὶ πόντιε κυανέαις ἵπποις διφρεύ- / ων ἅλιον πέλαγος. In classical Greek (δια)διφρεύω is found only in Euripides (also *Andr.* 108, *Suppl.* 991, *Or.* 991, E. fr. 114.3 = Ar. *Thesm.* 1067), although Sophocles has διφρευτής (*Ai.* 857).

Rhesus' horses serve as his 'hymnic attribute' (342–79n.). Here alone they are said to be dappled instead of gleaming white (303–4n.), the sort of minor contradiction all tragedians commit (185, 686nn.). In this case it may be due to *IA* 220–2 πώλους ... / ... / λευκοστίκτῳ τριχὶ βαλιούς (Hermann, *Opuscula* III, 293), from the parodos that also seems to lie behind *Rh.* 48 and 261–3 (nn.). Apart from Achilles' immortal stallion Βαλίος (*Il.* 16.149, 19.400), the adjective is not otherwise applied to horses.

For the gender of the team see again 185n.

357–9. The structure and diction of this emotional address to the fatherland (cf. 380–1, 385–7) recalls *Hcld.* 867–8 (Chorus) ὦ Ζεῦ τροπαῖε, νῦν ἐμοὶ δεινοῦ φόβου / ἐλεύθερον πάρεστιν ἦμαρ εἰσιδεῖν. The sentries now all but identify Rhesus with Zeus of Freedom (below). Yet their hopes will turn out to be as ill-founded as Hector's at 991–2 (989b–92n.) πέποιθα Τρωσί θ' ἡμέραν ἐλευθέραν / ἀκτῖνα τὴν στείχουσαν ἡλίου φέρειν.

νῦν ... νῦν: 346–8a n.

ὦ πάτρις ὦ Φρυγία: The emphatic repetition of 'vocative' ὦ, usually between the noun and its attribute, is as old as Homer: *Il.* 6.55 ὦ πέπον, ὦ Μενέλαε, 17.238 (KG I 49–50). In tragedy note especially the metrically identical *Tro.* 601 ὦ πάτρις, ὦ μελέα and 1082 ὦ φίλος, ὦ πόσι μοι (Ritchie 238).

ξὺν θεῷ ... σοι ... πάρεστιν εἰπεῖν: 'with the favour of the god ...' Cf. *Rh.* 468 ... σὺν δ' Ἀδραστείᾳ λέγω, *Med.* 625 = Ar. *Pl.* 114 σὺν θεῷ δ' εἰρήσεται and the common apotropaic formula σὺν θεῷ εἰπεῖν (e.g. S. fr. 479.1–2, Pl. *Tht.* 151b3–4, *Prt.* 317b7, *Lg.* 858b2). The chorus seek further protection against divine φθόνος (342–5, 342–3nn.) before pronouncing the name of Zeus Ἐλευθέριος when Troy is still under siege (Liapis on 357–9).

τὸν Ἐλευθέριον / Ζῆνα: Zeus Ἐλευθέριος was the god who guarded a community against foreign and domestic oppression. His cult developed in the first half of the fifth century in response to the Persian Wars (first at Plataea: Thuc. 2.71.2–4) and the overthrow of the Sicilian tyrannies (Pi. *Ol.* 12.1–2, D. S. 11.72.2). At Athens at least he became an aspect of the much older Zeus Σωτήρ and between ca. 430 and 410 BC acquired a splendid stoa with cult statue on the west side of the agora (K. Raaflaub, *Die Entdeckung der Freiheit* ..., Munich 1985, 125–47 ~ *The Discovery of Freedom in Ancient Greece*, Chicago – London 2004, 102–17, W. S. Barrett, *JHS* 93 [1973], 23–35 = *Collected Papers*, 78–97, especially 28–35 = 86–96). His mention here is 'anachronistic', although already in *Il.* 6.526–9 Hector could hope that Zeus would let the Trojans set up a 'mixing bowl of freedom' (κρητῆρα ... ἐλεύθερον) to the gods when the Greeks had been expelled.

360–7. 'Shall ancient Troy ever again spend all day in toasting company, with songs of love and drinking contests, in which the wine circles from left to right, when the sons of Atreus have gone over the sea to Sparta from the shore of Ilium?'

The joys of feasting and the symposium are regularly opposed to the grimness of war: Pi. *Pyth.* 10.29–46 (of the Hyperboreans, who live in a sort of paradise), Bacch. *Pae.* 4.61–80, *Phoen.* 784–92, E. frr. 369, 453 (cf. West, *Ancient Greek Music*, 13–14). But our passage appears to be connected with the third stasimon of *Ajax* (1185–1222), where the Salaminian sailors (another chorus of simple soldiers) bemoan the absence of drink, music and love in much the same way as the sentries here (*Ai.* 1199–1205) and eventually wish they were at home in Attica (1216–22). Correspondingly, the Trojans hope for the Greeks to depart so that they can resume their previous life.

The language of the passage is notable for its compression and large number of otherwise unattested compound adjectives and verbs (360–2a, 362b–5a nn.).

360–2a. ἁ παλαι- / ἁ Τροΐα: Cf. 231–2 (n.) ὦ Τροΐας / τείχη παλαιὰ δείμας, likewise with trisyllabic Τροΐα (here restored by Murray). The article can stand in tragic lyrics and anapaests with a geographical name that also has an attribute (FJW on A. *Suppl.* 634).

τοὺς προπότας ... θιάσους: literally 'the toast-drinking companies (of revellers)'. This is our sole example of προπότης (< προπίνω, 'drink a toast to'). It may have been coined for the occasion, although its common formation and 'subject-matter' means that it could have been more widespread. The article implies that at least in the chorus' vision (day-long) merrymaking was a usual feature of Troy in peace.

παναμερεύ- / σει: 'spend all day in, maintain all day long' (transitive, like many verbs in –εύω). All three tragedians have intransitive ἡμερεύω, 'spend the day' or 'pass one's days' (LSJ s.v. 1, 2), but the παν- compound is found only here. The respective adjectives and adverb (πανημέριος, πανήμερος, πανῆμαρ) are largely epic and more than once used with regard to extended meals: *Od.* 12.23–4 (Circe to Odysseus and his companions after their return from Hades) ἀλλ' ἄγετ' ἐσθίετε βρώμην καὶ πίνετε οἶνον / αὖθι πανημέριοι, Cratin. fr. 149 *PCG* (*Odyssēs*) ἦσθε πανημέριοι χορταζόμενοι γάλα λευκόν, / πυὸν δαινύμενοι κἀμπιμπλάμενοι πυριάτῃ and, of the eagle that will come to 'feast on' Prometheus' liver, *PV* 1024 ἄκλητος ἕρπων δαιταλεὺς πανήμερος (~ Hes. *Th*. 525 ὅσον πρόπαν ἦμαρ ἔδοι τανυσίπτερος ὄρνις). Likewise πρόπαν ἦμαρ at *Il*. 1.601–2 (= *Od*. 19.424–5) and *Od*. 9.161–2 (= 9.556–7, 10.183–4, 476–7, 12.29–30).

362b–5a. ἐρώτων / ψαλμοῖσι belong together as 'love-songs accompanied by the sound of the lyre', parallel to κυλίκων ... ἁμίλλαις (datives of attendant circumstance). On Canter's ψαλμοῖσι for ψάλμασι (Ω) see 342–79 'Metre' 363–5/373–5n. Originally the 'plucking' or 'twanging' (ψάλλω) of a string, ψαλμός could denote the tune of a stringed instrument already in the first half of the fifth century (Pi. fr. 125.3 Sn.–M., Phryn. Trag. *TrGF* 3 F 11, A. fr. 57.7). As a dedicated word for this ψάλμα is first found in Phld. *Ep*. 21.1 Gow–Page *GPh* (I BC) and remains very rare both in later antiquity and in Byzantine times (especially compared to ψαλμός = 'Psalm'). The error most likely arose by confusion of οι and α in early minuscule script (where they did not write accents).

On song and instrumental music at the symposium see West, *Ancient Greek Music*, 25–6, 348–9.

οἰνοπλανήτοις: again a *hapax*. It is hard to tell whether the verbal part is from passive-intransitive πλανάομαι (as usual in such compounds) or transitive πλανάω, but the latter seems easier in direct application to ἁμίλλαις, whose 'action' it should describe. 'Causing the wine to wander' then is more natural than 'causing (the mind) to wander with wine' (Σ^V *Rh*. 360 [II 336.9–10 Schwartz = 96 Merro]), especially with ἐπιδεξίοις (below). Nonnus has νοοπλανής, 'leading the mind astray' (e.g. *D*. 4.197, 9.44, 29.69, 42.168).

ἐπιδεξίοις: L. Dindorf (in *ThGL* III, col. 1568) for ὑποδεξίοις (O: -αις VΛ et ¹Σ^V).[135] 'From left to right' was the standard (since propitious) direction in which wine was served, cups circled and any other symposiastic activities took place: e.g. *Il*. 1.597–8 αὐτὰρ ὃ τοῖς ἄλλοισι θεοῖς ἐνδέξια πᾶσιν / οἰνοχόει γλυκὺ νέκταρ ἀπὸ κρητῆρος ἀφύσσων, *Od*. 21.141–2, Eup. fr. 354 *PCG* ὅταν δὲ δὴ πίνωσι τὴν ἐπιδέξια (*sc*. κύλικα), fr. 395 *PCG*, Dionys. Eleg. frr. 1, 4 *IEG*, Critias 88 B 1.7 DK προπόσεις ἐπὶ δεξιὰ νωμῶν, 88 B 6.1–8 (= fr. 6.1–7 *IEG*), 88 B 33 DK.

The transmitted ὑποδεξ- has little to recommend it. In its only other literary occurrence (Hdt. 7.49.3) ὑποδέξιος defines a harbour as 'able to receive, capacious, ample' (LSJ s.v.), and Σ^V *Rh*. 364 (II 336.11 Schwartz

---

135 Musgrave (on 364) had already conjectured ἐπιδεξίαις. But the adjective is normally of two terminations, and the form in -αις would jar with οἰνοπλανήτοις.

= 96 Merro), Photius (υ 191 Theodoridis) and the *Suda* (υ 475 Adler) gloss it with ὑποδεκτικός ('of / for receiving') or ὑποδοχεύς ('receiver, host'). Transferred to κυλίκων ... ἁμίλλαις it would have to mean not 'able to receive (a lot of wine)', as the *Rhesus* scholiast understood it, but 'receiving, hospitable to (the Trojan warriors)' for the *enallage* to work in its ordinary way (G. Pace, in *Scritti Gallo*, 455–8).[136] This, however, is impossibly weak and places too much emphasis on the supposed victory celebrations (360–7n.). That attributive ἐπιδέξιος (as opposed to the adverbial neuter plural ἐπιδέξια or ἐπὶ δεξιά) and ἐνδέξιος (LSJ s.v. I 1) do not elsewhere occur in the sense 'from left to right' does not seem a fatal objection.

366–7. Σπάρταν: Menelaus' home is mentioned here probably because it was the abduction of Helen that triggered the Trojan War. But Stesichorus (fr. 216 *PMGF*) and Simonides (fr. 549 *PMG* = 276 Poltera) also placed Agamemnon there. Cf. Liapis on 360–7 (p. 165).

368–9. ὦ φίλος: The 'nominative for vocative' in words that also form a vocative of their own (otherwise 388–9n.) is common in poetry and often without special significance. But φίλος appears to be different in that the nominative (mainly substantival in use) marks a more serious or emotional tone (M. L. West, *Glotta* 44 [1966], 139–44; cf. J. Svennung, *Anredeformen* ..., Uppsala 1958, 199–208). Both criteria, in addition to metrical considerations, fit the present case, which comes close to an appeal for help to a 'friendly' god: *Sept.* 174–9 ἰὼ φίλοι δαίμονες, / λυτήριοί <τ'> ἀμφιβάντες πόλιν / δείξαθ' ὡς φιλοπόλεις, / μέλεσθέ θ' ἱερῶν / δαμίων, μελόμενοι δ' ἀρήξατε (with Hutchinson on 174), *Cyc.* 73–5 †ὦ φίλος ὦ φίλε Βακχεῖε / ποῖ οἰοπολεῖς / ξανθὰν χαίταν σείεις;† (with Seaford on 73, 73–4).[137] Contrast Ar. *Ach.* 568 ἰὼ Λάμαχ', ὦ φίλ', ὦ φυλέτα (370–2a n.).

σᾷ χερὶ καὶ σῷ δορὶ πράξας τάδ': In view of 464–6 εἰ γὰρ ἐγὼ τόδε γ' ἦμαρ / εἰσίδοιμ' ... ὅτῳ πολυφόνου / χειρὸς ἄποιν' ἄροιο σᾷ λόγχᾳ (454–66, 464–6nn.), it is probably no coincidence that the expression here resembles *Ag.* 111 πέμπει ξὺν δορὶ καὶ χερὶ πράκτορι θούριος ὄρνις, where πράκτωρ means not just 'doer', but 'exactor, avenger' (LSJ s.v. II 3, Fraenkel on *Ag.* 111). The passage was famous (cf. Ar. *Ran.* 1289) and also seems to have inspired an early-fourth-century Attic funerary epigram: *CEG* 2 488 (ii).3–4 [κ]τ<ώ>μενον εὔκλειαν [δ]ορὶ καὶ χερὶ τόνδε πρὸς ἀ[ν]δρός / †...† ὤλεσε θοῦρος Ἄρ<ης>. For the pairing

---

136 She quotes V. Bers, *Enallage and Greek Style*, Leiden 1973, 3: 'In the vast majority of examples one can make some sense of the adjective taken with the governing substantive.' This is the same as saying that one must 'think of the substantives as coalescing into a single compound' (Wilamowitz on *HF* 468, adapted by Fraenkel on *Ag.* 504).

137 The general sense is not obscured by the corruption. To the possible remedies in Diggle's apparatus add ὦ φίλος ὦναξ Βακχεῖε (Willink, *apud* D. Kovacs, *Euripidea*, Leiden *et al.* 1994, 146–7).

of χείρ and δόρυ see also *Andr.* 523–5 ὦ πόσις πόσις, εἴθε σὰν / χεῖρα καὶ δόρυ σύμμαχον / κτησαίμαν, Πριάμου παῖ and for the (repeated) second-person address 355–6n.

ἐς οἶκον ἔλθοις: 447–53n.

370–5a. 'Come, appear, hold before you your richly gilded shield as you face Peleus' son, raising it aslant along the bifurcating chariot-rail, urging on your horses and brandishing your two-pronged spear.'

The chorus wish Rhesus to engage Achilles in single combat (342–79n.). Both heroes are imagined as fighting from their chariots – a rare scene in Homer (*Il.* 5.9–26, 8.112–29, 16.372–83), where the vehicle is mainly employed to carry a warrior into or out of battle (Lorimer, *Homer and the Monuments*, 325, M. A. Littauer – J. H. Crouwel, *Antiquity* 57 (1983), 187–92 = *Selected Writings on Chariots, other Early Vehicles, Riding and Harness*, Leiden et al. 2002, 53–61). In language the passage is largely 'Euripidean' (370–2a, 372b–3a nn.), with an epic touch at the end (373b–5a n.). Ar. *Lys.* 563 portrays an insolent Thracian mercenary as πέλτην σείων κἀκόντιον ὥσπερ ὁ Τηρεύς.

370–2a. ἐλθὲ φάνηθι: Both imperatives (and others like them) are typical of cletic hymns: e.g. Sapph. fr. 1.5 Voigt ἀλλὰ τυίδ' ἔλθ', 25 (Aphrodite), Pi. *Dith.* 3 fr. 70c.9 Sn.–M. (Dionysus), Alc. fr. 34.1–4 Voigt Δεῦτέ μοι ...] ... 3b προ[φά]νητε, Κάστορ / καὶ Πολύδε[υ]κες (cf. 355–6n.), *Pers.* 668, *Ai.* 694–7, *HF* 494 (Megara to Heracles) ἄρηξον, ἐλθέ· καὶ σκιὰ φάνηθί μοι, *Ba.* 1017–20, *Rh.* 226–8. Aristophanes parodies the usage at *Ach.* 566–7 ἰὼ Λάμαχ' ... / βοήθησον ... φανείς (368–9n.). Cf. West, *IEPM* 318–20.

τὰν ζάχρυσον ... πέλταν: 305–6a n. The epithet presumably comes from *Alc.* 498 Ἄρεος, ζαχρύσου Θρηκίας πέλτης ἄναξ. It is also found at *Rh.* 439 ἐν ζαχρύσοις δώμασιν and, referring to the Taurians, *IT* 1111–12 ζαχρύσου ... δι' ἐμπολᾶς. As an intensive prefix the tragedians adopted Aeolic ζα- (= δια-) from Homer. Other formations of their own are ζαπληθής (*Pers.* 316), ζάπυρος (*PV* 1083) and, as a certain conjecture, ζάχρειος (A. *Suppl.* 194).[138]

προβαλοῦ: i.e. in attack or defence (LSJ s.v. προβάλλω B III 1). Of a shield also *Carm. Pop.* 856.3–4 *PMG* λαιᾷ μὲν ἴτυν προβάλεσθε, / δόρυ δ' εὐτόλμως πάλλοντες (ascribed to Tyrtaeus by Σ D. Chr. 2.59, who quotes the poem, and Tz. *Hist.* 1.695–702 Leone) and Xen. *Mem.* 3.8.4 ἀσπὶς καλὴ πρὸς τὸ προβάλλεσθαι.

κατ' ὄμμα: Apart from *Ant.* 760–1, κατ' ὄμμα(τα), 'face to face, in the face', is confined to Euripides: *Andr.* 1064 κρυπτὸς καταστὰς ἢ κατ'

---

138 At *PV* 792 West (*Studies*, 308) wrote πόντον παρὰ ζάφλοισβον for the transmitted πόντον (-ου) περῶσα φλοῖσβον. But see S. R. West, *Hermes* 125 (1997), 377–8 in favour of Girard's πόντον περῶσ' ἄφλοισβον (i.e. the Russian steppe).

ὄμμ' ἐλθὼν μάχῃ; 1117, *El*. 910, *Or*. 288–9, *Ba*. 469 (Ritchie 211, where delete *Tr*. 102 [Chorus to Helios] εἴπ', ὦ κρατιστεύων κατ' ὄμμα). Cf. *Rh*. 420–1 ταῦθ' ... / ... λέγω κατ' ὄμμα σόν and 409 (408–10a n.), 491, 511 κατὰ στόμα.

372b–3a. δοχμίαν πεδαίρων: The crescent-shaped *pelte* was naturally held 'aslant' the upper body for protection. See Best, *Thracian Peltasts*, plts. 1b, 1c, 2, 3 and e.g. *LIMC* I 1/2 s.v. Amazones I A 41, 62, I C 242, I E 303.

Euripides employed πεδαίρω as an elevated form of μεταίρω in *HF* 819, 872 (both with Bond) and *Phoen*. 1027. The Aeolo-Doric πεδ- is unattested for Sophocles, but Aeschylus has πεδάρσιος (*Cho*. 846), πεδάορος (*Cho*. 590), πεδαίχμιος (*Cho*. 589)[139] and πέδοικος (fr. 246d). Of these the first recurs in *PV* 269, 710, 916 and Ar. *Av*. 1197 = fr. tr. adesp. 47.1. Mastronarde (on *Phoen*. 1027) notes the all but complete restriction in tragedy to 'words from the root of ἀείρω'.

σχιστὰν παρ' ἄντυγα: The chariot-rail is called 'divided' probably because it branches out in two parts from the front of the breastwork. Hence also the plural in *Il*. 11.535 = 20.500 ... καὶ ἄντυγες αἳ περὶ δίφρον, 21.37–8 ὃ δ' ἐρινεὸν ὀξέϊ χαλκῷ / τάμνε νέους ὄρπηκας, ἵν' ἅρματος ἄντυγες εἶεν (it would have been hard to find a branch long enough for a single rail) and e.g. [Hes.] *Sc*. 64, S. *El*. 746, *Rh*. 567 (567–8a n.). Hera's chariot may be subject to 'divine doubling': *Il*. 5.728 δοιαὶ δὲ περίδρομοι ἄντυγές εἰσιν. See Lorimer, *Homer and the Monuments*, 326, J. Wiesner, *Arch. Hom*. F 15–16, 103–4 and Kirk on *Il*. 5.727–8.

373b–5a. πώλους ἐρεθίζων: Reiske's πώλους for κώλοις (*Animadversiones*, 88) eliminates the absurd picture of Rhesus trying to incite Achilles with some kind of war dance (cf. Σ^V *Rh*. 374 [II 336.26–7 Schwartz = 97 Merro] ... ἀνακρούων. οἱ γὰρ πολεμοῦντες κινοῦσι τοὺς πόδας, Feickert on 373). Musgrave (*Exercitationes*, 144) compared *Ba*. 148 πλανάτας ἐρεθίζων.

The phrase is absent in Δ, whence ΣΣ^V *Rh*. 372, 373 (II 336.13–16 Schwartz = 96 Merro) explain ἄντυξ as shield-rim.

δίβολόν τ' ἄκοντα πάλλων has an epic flavour. In particular note *Il*. 3.18–19 (of Paris) δοῦρε δύω κεκορυθμένα χαλκῷ / πάλλων (with Kirk on 18) and Pi. *Nem*. 3.44–5 (the boy Achilles hunting wild animals) χερσὶ θαμινά / βραχυσίδαρον ἄκοντα πάλλων.

Scholars since Vater (on 361 [pp. 168–9]) have explained δίβολον ... ἄκοντα by means of Σ^BD Pi. *Nem*. 6.50/85b (III 112.5–9 Drachmann)

---

[139] In *Cho*. 589–91 βλάπτουσι καὶ πεδαίχμιοι / λαμπάδες πεδάοροι / πτανά τε καὶ πεδοβάμονα the choice of πεδαίχμιοι was probably motivated by πεδάοροι (a metrical necessity) and πεδοβάμονα (Garvie on *Cho*. 588–91 [p. 206]). πεδάοροι (cf. Alc. fr. 315 Voigt) is Portus' correction of M's non-existent πεδάμαροι.

οὐκ ἐκ παραδρομῆς δὲ ζάκοτον εἶπε τὸ δόρυ τοῦ Ἀχιλλέως ... ἀλλ᾽ ὅτι ἰδιαίτερον παρὰ τὰ ἄλλα κατεσκεύαστο. δίκρουν γάρ, ὥστε δύο ἀκμὰς ἔχειν καὶ μιᾷ βολῇ [ὥστε] δισσὰ τὰ τραύματα ἀπεργάζεσθαι (cf. below). The reference is to Achilles' famous spear, which only he could wield (*Il.* 16.141–2), and which in the *Little Iliad* had two points (*Il. Parv.* fr. 5.2 *GEF* δίκροος αἰχμή). Like Aeschylus (fr. 152) and Sophocles (fr. 152), our poet may have followed this tradition here, ironically giving such a weapon to Achilles' would-be defeater. A linguistic model is suggested by Hsch. τ 1350 Hansen–Cunningham τρίβολον ἄκοντα· τρίαιναν, where the lemma looks like an excerpt from tragedy or lyric (MLW). Conversely, *PV* 925 ἢ τρίκροον αἰχμὴν τὴν Ποσειδῶνος σκεδᾷ echoes the wording of *Il. Parv.* fr. 5.2 *GEF* (above), if West is right so to correct Ω's τρίαιναν αἰχμήν (*Studies*, 312–14).

On bident spears in ancient myth and reality see A. B. Cook, *Zeus* ... II.1, Cambridge 1925, 799–806 and K. DeVries, in B. Cohen (ed.), *Not the Classical Ideal* ..., Leiden *et al.* 2000, 352–3 with fig. 13.7 (a fifth-century Phrygian warrior).

δίβολον: i.e. 'scoring two hits at once'. To Hsch. τ 1350 Hansen–Cunningham τρίβολον ἄκοντα add the ἀμφώβολοι ... βουπόροι ('double-pointed ox-piercing spits') which are hurled as missiles at *Andr.* 1133–4 (with Stevens on 1133, 1134).

375b–7. 'For no one who resists you shall ever (again) dance in the grounds of Argive Hera.'

This grim vision for Argos (Agamemnon's capital) contrasts with the anticipated Trojan festivities (360–7n.).

σὲ γάρ: 355–6n. γάρ gives the motive for the 'prayer': 'For (you are so powerful that) ...' See *GP* 60–2 and 608–9a n.

οὔτις ὑποστάς: Cf. *Rh.* 315 (of Achilles) οὔθ᾽ ὑποσταθεὶς δορί (314–16, 342–79nn.), *Phoen.* 1470 κοὐδεὶς ὑπέστη and above all *Pers.* 87–9 δόκιμος δ᾽ οὔτις ὑποστὰς / μεγάλῳ ῥεύματι φωτῶν / ὀχυροῖς ἕρκεσιν εἴργειν (with Garvie on 87–92), which takes up Rhesus' association with Xerxes and his host (290, 264–341nn.).

Both dative and accusative occur with ὑφίσταμαι, 'resist, withstand' (LSJ s.v. ὑφίστημι B IV 1). They stand together in *HF* 1349–50 ταῖς συμφοραῖς γὰρ ὅστις οὐχ ὑφίσταται / οὐδ᾽ ἀνδρὸς ἂν δύναιθ᾽ ὑποστῆναι βέλος.

Ἀργείας ... ἐν Ἥρας δαπέδοις: The Argolid was Hera's original home (Nilsson, *GGR* I³, 427–8) and Argos that of her most eminent sanctuary (situated some 7.5 km north-east of the city, near Mycenae). Its main annual festival was the *Heraia* or *Hekatombaia*, which included a sacrificial procession, the presentation of a πέπλος by local maidens, athletic contests (W. Burkert, *Homo Necans* ..., Berlin – New York 1972, 182–4 = Berkeley *et al.* 1983, 162–4 [English], Cropp on E. *El.* 173–4) and no doubt ample opportunity for music and dance (cf. E. *El.* 178–80 οὐδ' ἱστᾶσα χοροὺς / Ἀργείαις ἅμα νύμφαις / εἱλικτὸν κρούσω πόδ' ἐμόν). Any fifth- or fourth century Athenian would have had this occasion in mind.

In the Trojan legend Hera's stock-epithet Ἀργεία / Ἀργείη (FJW on A. *Suppl.* 299) also expresses her partiality for the Greeks. Cf. *Il.* 4.8 = 5.908, *Tro.* 23–4 (Poseidon speaking) νικῶμαι γὰρ Ἀργείας θεοῦ / Ἥρας Ἀθάνας θ', αἳ συνεξεῖλον Φρύγας.

δαπέδοις: Euripides had a liking for δάπεδον (< √dm̥ + πέδον), 'house floor' or maybe rather 'the flattened ground on which one can build' (Schwyzer 358 with n. 10, 426, *DELG* s.v.). Like other post-Homeric writers, he primarily applied it to 'the floor or ground of a temple or its precinct ... usually with a gen[itive] or adj[ective] of a deity' (Barrett on *Hipp.* 230), and almost always in lyrics: *Hipp.* 228–30 δέσποιν' ... Ἄρτεμι ... / ... / εἴθε γενοίμαν ἐν σοῖς δαπέδοις, *Andr.* 117, E. *Suppl.* 271, *Tro.* 539–41, *Ion* 121, 576, *Or.* 330, E. fr. 955h. The only other certain instance in tragedy is in *Cho.* 798 (wavering between 'house-floor' and 'race-track').

378–9. καπφθίμενον: Bothe (5 [1803], 293) for Ω's unmetrical καταφθίμενον (κατφθίμενον already Musgrave on 378). Cf. E. *Suppl.* 984 κλεινήν τ' ἄλοχον τοῦ καπφθιμένου and *El.* 1298–9 τῇδέ τ' ἀδελφῷ / τῆς καπφθιμένης (with Elmsley's short form in both places). On apocope in tragedy see KB I 180.

φίλτατον ἄχθος: a poignant oxymoron. The notion reverses Achilles' self-reproach at *Il.* 18.104 ἀλλ' ἧμαι παρὰ νηυσὶν ἐτώσιον ἄχθος ἀρούρης (with Edwards).

380–7. As Rhesus with his retinue approaches from the left *eisodos* (i.e. the direction of Mt. Ida), he receives the kind of extended choral address in anapaests which since Aeschylus tended to accompany grandiose chariot entries: *Ag.* 783–809, E. *El.* 988–97, *Tro.* 568–76 (addressed in bitter irony to the captive Andromache and Astyanax), *IA* [590–7 + 598–606] (below); cf. the brief trochaics at *Pers.* 155–8. It is possible that Rhesus was also meant to arrive on his chariot (Taplin, *Stagecraft*, 43, 74–8, 287–8; cf. Liapis on 380–7). The device became fashionable again in the fourth century – a number of 'classic' tragedies received imitative interpolations[140] – and the verbal parallels between Ar. *Ran.* 961–3

---

140 *Eum.* 405 (Wilamowitz, *Einleitung*, 154 n. 63, Taplin, *Stagecraft*, 47, 77, 388–90, Sommerstein on *Eum.* 404–5) and *IA* 590–634 (cf. Barrett on *Hipp.* 1102–50 [p. 368 n. 1], Taplin, *Stagecraft*, 77 n. 1). According to Σ^MTAB *Or.* 57 (I 103.14–17 Schwartz), 'some actors' also perverted *Orestes* by giving Helen a procession from Nauplia, either before the prologue or, as Willink (on 57 ff.) reasonably contends, at 71.

and *Rh.* 306b–8 and 383–4 (nn.) suggest that, if there was a pompous chariot entry in A. *Memnon*, our poet would have followed the lead (cf. Taplin, *Stagecraft*, 77, 422–3).

On the other hand, it may have been counter-productive to show the horses, which almost certainly do not come on stage with Odysseus and Diomedes (670–1a n.). There is also no indication of a vehicle in the text, except for the Shepherd's description in 301–8 (this in contrast to the extant plays mentioned above), and in 383–4 (n.) the bells on Rhesus' horse-trappings (306–8) have been transferred to his conspicuous shield. Perhaps, therefore, the exotic hero alone was considered impressive enough and, as at *Ag.* 258–63 (Clytaemestra) and *Or.* 348–55 (Menelaus), the honorific greeting applied to his entry on foot. Likewise it is unclear whether at A. *Suppl.* 234 Pelasgus appears with the horses and chariots depicted by Danaus in 180–3. As in our play, they are not referred to again (and no further comment signals their approach) so that 'indeed the words may be a substitute for any attempt at staging' (Taplin, *Stagecraft*, 201, FJW on A. *Suppl.* 180–3).

The hymnic mode continues in the opening address as 'great king' (380–1n.) and those to Thrace and Troy, which mask third-person predications of the 'god' (cf. Norden, *Agnostos Theos*, 163–6). Imperatives, half general and half directed at the chorus themselves, signal the appearance of Rhesus in essentially the way he was described by the Shepherd (382, 383–4nn.).[141] The long-awaited hero is now actually seen (ἰδέ) and heard (κλύε).

380–1. 'Hail, hail, o great king! A fine cub you have reared, o Thrace, an obvious ruler of cities.'

ἰὼ ἰώ could be *extra metrum* or an initial anapaestic monometer. The former seems more probable, as also at *OC* 140, *Andr.* 1226, *Tro.* 164, 172, 187, 1118, 1251.

μέγας ὦ βασιλεῦ: Cf. the exalted choral address to Hector at 820–1 (821–3n.) ἰὼ ἰώ, / †μέγας ἐμοὶ μέγας ὦ† πολίοχον κράτος. Among anapaestic greetings see *Ag.* 783–4 ἄγε δὴ βασιλεῦ, Τροίας π<τ>ολίπορθ᾽, / Ἀτρέως γένεθλον and E. *El.* 988 ἰώ, βασίλεια γύναι χθονὸς Ἀργείας. Sommerstein (*Sophocles. Selected Fragmentary Plays* II, 181, 203–4) also compares S. fr. 515 (*Poimenes*) ἰὼ βαλλήν (lyric, or indeed anapaestic).

The title μέγας ... βασιλεῦ(ς) is redolent of oriental, especially Persian, royalty, but was also applied to Zeus in Pi. *Ol.* 7.34. For βασιλεύς alone of Zeus cf. e.g. *Pers.* 532 and *Ag.* 355. μέγας is a common epithet of Greek gods.

---

141 Except that he (like his attendants) probably also wears the Thracian ζειρά (440–2n. [p. 286]).

ὦ Θρῄκη: 357–9n.

σκύμνον: especially a lion's cub (LSJ s.v. 1). The notion suits a king and mighty warrior. So Achilles mourns over Patroclus like a lion whose young have been seized by a hunter (*Il.* 18.318–23), and oracles or dreams foreshadow the birth of powerful men as lions: Hdt. 5.92β.3 (Cypselus of Corinth), 6.131.2 (Pericles), Ar. *Eq.* 1037–44 (Cleon). In tragedy cf. *Ai.* 985–7 οὐχ ὅσον τάχος / δῆτ' αὐτὸν ἄξεις δεῦρο, μή τις ὡς κενῆς / σκύμνον λεαίνης δυσμενῶν ἀναρπάσῃ; (with Garvie on 986–7, Finglass on 985–7), E. *Suppl.* 1222–3 (with Collard), *Andr.* 1169–70 and perhaps *Or.* 1213 (Hermione). The use of 'animal' words for young human beings is characteristically Euripidean (Breitenbach 153, Ritchie 232, West on *Or.* 1213). See also 386 (385–7n.) ὁ Στρυμόνιος πῶλος.

πολίαρχον ἰδεῖν: a common type of epexegetic infinitive (KG II 15 with n. 13, SD 364), which tends to stand last in dramatic spoken verse. The best syntactic parallel is *Sept.* 644 χρυσήλατον ... ἄνδρα τευχηστὴν ἰδεῖν, where, despite Hutchinson, the word-order marks τευχηστήν, not χρυσήλατον, as the predicative with ἰδεῖν.

Our poet may well have got πολίαρχος, 'ruler (of a city), prince', from Pi. *Nem.* 7.84–5 λέγοντι γὰρ Αἰακόν νιν (Zeus) ... φυτεῦσαι, / ἐμᾷ μὲν πολίαρχον εὐωνύμῳ πάτρᾳ. It is the only earlier attestation of this very rare word (cf. Call. *Iov.* 73–4), and Zeus, with whom Rhesus was twice compared in the ode, is the recipient of the praise.

382. 'See his body-armour, enriched with gold!'

ἰδέ: It is sensible to follow Liapis (on 382–4) in printing the Attic oxytone accentuation (cf. Hdn. I 431.5 Lentz, Σ^A *Il.* 1.85 [I 33.78–34.80 Erbse]) instead of epic ἴδε. The same applies to the unelided lyric cases in A. *Suppl.* 350, *Tr.* 222, *OC* 1463, *Alc.* 398 and *Or.* 1541. At S. fr. 1131.7 (= P. Oxy. 1083 fr. 2) editors have always read ἰδέ.

χρυσόδετον: 'bound with gold', i.e. 'with golden adornments attached' (Mastronarde on *Phoen.* 805, LSJ s.v. 2). Cf. 305 (305–6a n.) χρυσοκολλήτοις τύποις. Of arms or armour also Alc. fr. 350.1–2 Voigt ἐλεφαντίναν / λάβαν τῶ ξίφεος χρυσοδέταν, Bacch. *Pae.* 4.69–70 ἐν δὲ σιδαροδέτοις πόρπαξιν αἰθᾶν / ἀραχνᾶν ἱστοὶ πέλονται, *Sept.* 161 κόναβος ... χαλκοδέτων σακέων, *Rh.* 33 (n.) κερόδετα τόξα.

σώματος ἀλκήν: In the sense 'protection, (means of) defence' ἀλκή is applied to rocks at A. *Suppl.* 351–4 λυκοδί<ω>κτον ὡς δάμαλιν ἀμ πέτραις / ἠλιβάτοις, ἵν' ἀλ- / κᾷ πίσυνος μέμυκε φρά- / ζουσα βοτῆρι μόχθους (with FJW on 352) and to an altar at A. *Suppl.* 731, 832 and *Eum.* 257.

383–4. 'Hear too the boastful jingle of the bells which ring out from his shield band!'

To the parallels from Aeschylus (*Sept.* 385–6) and Aristophanes (*Ran.* 962–3) discussed at 306b–8 (n.) add S. fr. 859 (of the Trojans) φίλιπποι καὶ κερουλκοί, / σὺν σάκει δὲ κωδωνοκρότῳ παλαισταί, which, if rightly attributed to *Poimenes* by Hartung (*Sophokles. Fragmente*, Leipzig 1851, 33), could hardly have been spoken in contempt (Pearson on S. fr. 859). On a practical reason for having the bells on Rhesus' shield instead of his horse-trappings here see 380–7n.

The series of κ-sounds mirrors the cacophonous jingle of the armour. See Ritchie 241–2 and *Rh.* 282–3n.

κλύε καί: If καί connects χρυσόδετον ... ἀλκήν and κόμπους κωδωνοκρότους, we need not speak of postponement here. The imperatives ἰδέ and κλύε are subsumed under 'verbs of sensory perception'.

κωδωνοκρότους: Apart from S. fr. 859.2 (above), this is the only surviving attestation of the adjective.

παρὰ πορπάκων: The πόρπαξ was a bronze band on the inside of the hoplite shield (often covering the full diameter), through which the bearer passed his left arm up to the elbow. With the hand he then grasped a handle in the form of a leather thong or cord (ἀντιλαβή) near the right-hand rim of the shield (A. M. Snodgrass, *Early Greek Arms and Armour*, Edinburgh 1964, 61–6 with plt. 26, *Arms and Armour of the Greeks*, 53, 95 with plts. 18–19). The πόρπαξ could be ornamented (P. Ducrey, *Guerre et guerriers dans la Grèce antique*, Paris 1985, 49–51 with plt. 29 = *Warfare in Ancient Greece*, New York 1986, 47, 50 with plt. 29) and in myth at least also be equipped with bells. Their place inside the shield is paralleled at *Sept.* 385–6 ὑπ' ἀσπίδος δὲ τῷ / χαλκήλατοι κλάζουσι κώδωνες φόβον (above), where the variant δ' ἔσω (MQ²) for δὲ τῷ represents an associative error or a gloss on ὑπ' ἀσπίδος.

Our poet seems to transfer to Rhesus' *pelte* the language appropriate for a hoplite shield (305–6a n.), although it is possible that the arm-strap and handle of the Thracian targe (see Best, *Thracian Peltasts*, plts. 1b, 2 and Appendix B) also came to be designated by πόρπαξ and ἀντιλαβή. Mythical heroes in tragedy often wielded hoplite shields (cf. especially *Tro.* 1194–6 ὦ καλλίπηχυν Ἕκτορος βραχίονα / σῴζουσ' ... / ὡς ἡδὺς ἐν πόρπακι σῷ κεῖται τύπος, *Hel.* 1376, *Phoen.* 1126–7),[142] and at *Ai.* 574–6 Ajax's famous tower-shield (σάκος) anachronistically has its τελαμών ('shoulder-strap') replaced with a πόρπαξ (Kannicht on *Hel.* 1375–81, Finglass on *Ai.* 574–6 [pp. 306–7]).

The plural πορπάκων here is explicable only as a poetic licence, suggested perhaps by the numerous bells (κόμπους κωδωνοκρότους ... κελαδοῦντας).

385–7. 'A god, o Troy, a god, Ares himself, the colt born of Strymon and the songstress Muse, has come and breathes upon you!'

---

142 On the textual status of *Phoen.* 1104–40 see 305–6a n. (p. 231 n. 123).

After Zeus Φαναῖος and Ἐλευθέριος (355–6, 357–9nn.) Rhesus is equated with Ares, who in the *Iliad* also stands on the Trojans' side. If 387 ... καταπνεῖ σε is essentially correct (below), our poet has tried to convert Ares' destructive blowing (322b–3n.) into something beneficial for Troy. One is reminded of Homeric gods breathing μένος or θάρσος into their protégés (e.g. *Il.* 10.482, *Od.* 24.520) as well as the sweet odour which accompanies deities (e.g. *PV* 114–15, *Med.* 835–45, *Hipp.* 1391–3). Cf. Richardson on *h.Cer.* 238 and 275 ff.

The war god was traditionally associated with Thrace (*Il.* 13.301, *Od.* 8.361–2, *OT* 190–7, *Ant.* 969–76, *Alc.* 498, *Hec.* 1088–90). Yet his name, like that of Enyalios and Dionysus, already appears on Mycenean tablets and may come from Greek ἀρή, 'ruin, harm' (Janko on *Il.* 13.301–3, 14.484–5). The Greek tendency to regard more violent gods as immigrants (cf. also Hall, *Inventing the Barbarian*, 151) goes hand in hand with their readiness to adopt such from other peoples.

The whole passage goes far beyond the usual epic or epic-style comparison of a ferocious warrior to Ares (e.g. *Il.* 7.208, 11.295, 16.784, A. fr. 74.10).

θεός ... θεός: an excited repetition, typical of invocations: e.g. *Bacch.* 3.21–2 θεὸν θ[εό]ν τις / ἀγλαϊζέθω γὰρ ἄριστος ὄλβων, *Sept.* 566–7 (but see Hutchinson on 565–7), S. fr. 314.100 (*Ichneutae*) θεὸς θεὸς θεὸς θεός, *HF* 772–3. Yet the closest parallels are Verg. *Aen.* 6.46 *deus ecce deus* and Ov. *Met.* 15.677 *en deus est, deus est*, both of which mark epiphanies and may go back to ritual calls. '*Die überall zugrundeliegende Vorstellung ist, daß durch die Wiederholung die Richtigkeit oder Dringlichkeit des Wortes betont wird*' (Norden on Verg. *Aen.* 6.46). Cf. West, *IEPM* 106.

ὦ Τροία: 357–9n.

ὁ Στρυμόνιος πῶλος ἀοιδοῦ / Μούσης: literally 'Strymon's colt by the songstress Muse'. For (semi-)divine parents being indicated by a 'proper-name adjective' (1n.) for the father and a genitive of possession (or origin) for the mother cf. Pi. *Ol.* 2.12 ἀλλ' ὦ Κρόνιε παῖ Ῥέας and A. *Suppl.* 314 τί<ς> οὖν ὁ Διὸς πόρτις εὔχεται βοός; (with FJW). The tone seems more elevated than in the case of the double genitive at *Tr.* 644 ὁ γὰρ Διὸς Ἀλκμήνας κόρος.

πῶλος: another 'young animal' word (380–1n.), appropriate for the leader of the 'horse-loving' Thracians. While πῶλος is far more often used of young (unmarried) women than men (LSJ s.v. I 3; cf. J. Gould, *JHS* 100 [1980], 53), there is no need to assume with Roux (*REG* 87 [1974], 68–70) that in the latter it indicates weakness, especially when it merely stands for 'offspring', as here.[143]

---

[143] In *Cho.* 794–9 (where Zeus is asked to help the 'colt' Orestes in the 'chariot-race' to avenge his father) and *Phoen.* 947–8 it is probably meant to arouse sympathy (E. Petrou-

καταπνεῖ σε: It is a matter of dispute whether the paradosis (Ω: ἀναπνεῖ Hn) can in fact mean 'breathes upon you', given that the only certain parallel for καταπνέω with a spatial accusative (cf. LSJ s.v. κατά B I 2) is Hld. 3.2.1 αἱ δὲ κανᾶ πεμμάτων τε καὶ θυμιαμάτων κανηφοροῦσαι τὸν τόπον εὐωδίᾳ κατέπνεον. In *Med.* 836–8 τὰν Κύπριν κλῄζουσιν ... / χώρας καταπνεῦσαι μετρίας ἀνέμων / ἡδυπνόους αὔρας the genitive χώρας is Reiske's very reasonable correction of the MSS' χώραν, while elsewhere a dative (of interest) designates the person(s) positively or negatively affected by the verb: Ar. *Lys.* 551–2 ἀλλ᾽ ἥνπερ ὅ <τε> γλυκύθυμος Ἔρως χἠ Κυπρογένει᾽ Ἀφροδίτη / ἵμερον ἡμῖν (Bentley: ἡμῶν codd.) ... καταπνεύσῃ, Pl. Com. fr. 189.15 *PCG* ... μή σοι νέμεσις θεόθεν καταπνεύσῃ (~Archestr. fr. 146.3–4 *SH* = 16.3–4 Olson–Sens).[144]

The evidence is insufficient to judge all possible constructions of καταπνέω in classical Greek (cf. Page on *Med.* 839–40). If we were to emend the pronoun, σου (West) seems preferable to Feickert's σοι (on 387), which may carry the personification of Troy too far.

Nothing comes from changing the verb. Verrall's καταπλεῖ (*The 'Medea' of Euripides*, London 1881, 120–3), endorsed by Porter, is impossibly flat, not to mention the doubtful accusative of direction it would have to take (cf. Jouan 66 n. 109). Collard's κατέχει (*apud* Klyve on 387), which he proposed after *Hec.* 1088–90 αἰαῖ ἰὼ Θρῄκης ... / ... Ἄρει κάτοχον γένος (cf. Polyaen. 1.20.1 οἳ δὲ κάτοχοι ἐκ Μουσῶν καὶ Ἄρεως ... Μεγαρεῖς κατὰ κράτος ἐνίκων), makes better sense, except that we do not want the durative notion of 'possession' or 'inspiration' by a god, when Rhesus has barely entered the stage. ἀναπνεῖ (Hn) is hardly convincing in the causative sense 'gives you time to recover breath' (Paley on 388).

388–526. At first sight the confrontation between Hector and Rhesus looks like a Euripidean *agon* of the strictest form (for which see C. Collard, *G&R* 22 [1995], 62 = J. Mossman [ed.], *Oxford Readings in Classical Studies. Euripides*, Oxford 2003, 69). It occupies the whole second *epeisodion*, and initially opposes two speeches of almost equal length (393–421 + 422–53), which show several verbal and rhetorical echoes of the *agones* of *Alcestis*, *Medea* and *Phoenissae* (388–453n.). The lack of a

---

nias, *Funktion und Thematik der Bilder bei Aischylos*, Göttingen 1976, 110–11, 170–1). For Menoeceus the requirement of ritual purity may also play a part (Mastronarde on *Phoen.* 947).

144 The same is to be supplied at *h.Cer.* 236a–8 Δημήτηρ / ... / ἡδὺ καταπνείουσα (i.e. on Demophon) and *Ag.* 105–6 ... ἔτι γὰρ θεόθεν καταπνείει (or -πνεύει?) / πειθώ, μολπᾶν ἀλκάν, ξύμφυτος αἰών (for which see Fraenkel on *Ag.* 106 and M. L. West, *Lexis* 17 [1999/2000], 43–4).

two- or three-line choral comment after Hector's speech has a parallel in E. *Suppl.* 409–25 + 426–62 – the first part of the famous 'political' double *agon* between Theseus and the Theban Herald (E. *Suppl.* 399–580). In both places the device is entirely natural. Just as the mothers of the Seven have nothing to say to the Herald's attack on democracy, so Rhesus' lateness has never been a problem for the chorus. At the same time the conflict becomes more pronounced.

The similarity ends when the chorus answer Rhesus' defence (or rather his final promise to defeat the Greeks) with a characteristically energetic song (454–66n.). Likewise we have no dialogue, stichomythic or otherwise, to continue the debate in a livelier style. Instead the following irregular discussion (about as long as the two 'set speeches' together) brings up, but never quite resolves, a series of new points before the contestants leave in apparent harmony (467–526n.). The reason for this unique pattern[145] lies in the subject-matter of the *agon*, which unlike any other does not relate to the central dramatic question. In the great order of events Rhesus' tardiness is of no consequence, particularly since he has already been accepted as an ally (Ritchie 89–90). Once he had explained himself, therefore, all that would have remained for Hector was to give his assent – a lame conclusion prevented by the chorus and Rhesus' ever more outrageous plans and demands.

Like most *agones* in Euripides, the scene does nothing to advance the plot. Its purpose is to present Rhesus, who was so eagerly anticipated and whose fate will dominate the rest of the play (Ritchie 90–1). In that respect it seems clear that our poet intended him to be seen as a genuinely powerful, if increasingly overconfident, warrior. Rather than being a *miles gloriosus*, as has often been maintained,[146] he is modelled on the Aeschylean Xerxes (cf. 388–453n.), the Argive heroes in *Seven against Thebes* (305–6a, 306b–8nn.) and apparently such boastful foreign warriors as Cycnus in S. *Poimenes* (especially fr. 501).[147] Yet it is difficult to assess how the audience, who in part at least would have been familiar with not only the dramatic precedents, but also the tradition of Rhesus' *aristeia* and possibly the invincibility oracle (Introduction, 11–12), would have interpreted what they heard. They could not know that Athena would

---

[145] As analysed by J. Duchemin, *L'ΑΓΩΝ dans la tragédie grecque*, Paris ²1968, 81 and M. Lloyd, *The Agon in Euripides*, Oxford 1992, 7–8.

[146] First by Valckenaer, *Diatribe*, 97, 103–5. See further Ritchie 96–7, Liapis, xlv with n. 133 (literature) and on 447–9. Lamachus in Ar. *Acharnians* parodies some of Rhesus' prototypes.

[147] Cf. Introduction, 33. From Hector's comment in S. fr. 498 that 'it is pleasant to tire oneself out and exercise one's arms' Sommerstein deduces a scene in which Cycnus, like Rhesus at 451–3 and 488, offered to engage the Greeks alone (*Sophocles. Selected Fragmentary Plays* II, 180, 206).

confirm the threat (600–4n.) and, in view of the chorus' warning note in 455–7 (454–66, 455b–7nn.), may have expected Rhesus to suffer for the hybris he displays (cf. 342–79n.). Hector's reactions in 467–526 (n.) at any rate show that he has in more than one way overstepped the line.

388–453. The *agon* is introduced in a natural way. As a newcomer Rhesus extends a polite greeting to the Trojan commander (388–92), which by the very mention of his late arrival, however, was bound to arouse the charge of neglect (compare Pheres' good intentions in *Alc.* 614–28 and the brusque provocation of Jason in *Med.* 446–64). Hector's speech (393–421) is well-structured: a short proem professing frankness and honesty (393–5) is followed by the accusation (396–8) and a long narrative (399–419), in which the reasons for Hector's claim to support alternate with variations on the original complaint (405, 411–12, 418–19). The conclusion (420–1) returns to the topic of candour, as it does in Polynices' speech at *Phoen.* 469–96 (394b–5, 420–1nn.).

The strictly military nature of the conflict in *Rhesus* did not lend itself to the raising of complex questions about duty and ingratitude for favours done. Yet apart from the opening device, we find several verbal and rhetorical echoes of Achilles' speech in *Il.* 9.308–429 (312–43) as well as the *agones* in *Alcestis* (614–733) and *Medea* (446–622) – all of which deal with these issues in highly emotional and unsettling situations. See *Rh.* 399–400 (n.) ~ *Alc.* 658–9, *Rh.* 411b–12 (n.) ~ *Alc.* 660–1, *Rh.* 406–12 (406–11a, 411b–12nn.) ~ *Il.* 9.315–32, *Med.* 476–90, *Rh.* 413–18 (n.) ~ *Il.* 9.321–43 and, in the respective replies, *Rh.* 438–40 (438–9, 440–2nn.) ~ *Med.* 555–9.

Rhesus' defence (422–53) opens with a partly verbatim echo of Hector's introduction and peroration, a feature we find in subtler form with Eteocles in *Phoen.* 503 (422–3n.). But subsequently he does not answer the accusations point by point – only the generalising charge of drunken indulgence is addressed: 418b–19 ~ 438–9 (nn.). Instead Rhesus gives an account of the difficulties he encountered on his way to Troy, including a war against the Scythians, which as a probably invented episode corresponds to the Thracian one Hector said he had won for him (406–11a, 426–42nn.). The whole narrative stands in the tradition of Aeschylean 'travelogues', with the report of Xerxes' ill-fated homeward journey in *Pers.* 480–514 as a certain model (440–2n.; cf. 53–5, 56–8nn.). Other verbal and contextual references (430–1, 436–7nn.) confirm the evocation of the Persian king in Rhesus (cf. 264–341, 290, 375b–7nn.): his north-to-south crossing of the Bosporus really 'becomes a Xerxes expedition in reverse' (Burnett, 'Smiles', 182 n. 57).

A consequence of our poet's choice of sources, and his interweaving of rare words from elsewhere, is that the passage acquires a (perhaps overly) grandiose ring. It is as if the tale of Rhesus' hardship was set up as 'epic' – to match not only the great Persian march, but also the ten-year Trojan War he has come to end in a day (443–53). Apart from the Muse's version of his rise in Thrace (930–3, 932–3nn.), this is all we will ever hear of his martial exploits.

388–9. 'Greetings, noble son of a noble father, ruler of this land, Hector! It is late in the day that I am addressing you.'

Diggle was tempted to delete 388 as an addition to the vocative Ἕκτορ in the following line. But not all extended apostrophes in drama result from interpolation. Of the examples quoted by Haslam (in G. W. Bowersock *et al.* [eds.], *Arktouros. Hellenic Studies presented to Bernard M. W. Knox* ..., Berlin – New York 1979, 100) and Willink (on *Or.* 71–2), *Hec.* 953 should certainly remain (cf. Collard and Matthiessen on 953), and *Or.* 72 itself 'would be abrupt on its own' (West on 71). This is even truer of *Rh.* 389. However self-possessed, Rhesus could hardly omit some honorific epithet or apposition for Hector. *Or.* 852–4 [ὦ τλῆμον, ὦ δύστηνε τοῦ στρατηλάτου] / Ἀγαμέμνονος παῖ, πότνι' Ἠλέκτρα, λόγους / ἄκουσον οὕς σοι δυστυχεῖς ἥκω φέρων (852 del. Paley) illustrates the difference between a necessary and an unnecessary expansion.[148]

ἐσθλὸς ἐσθλοῦ παῖ: In tragedy the combination of a nominative adjective with a vocative noun, or *vice versa*, is restricted to special cases (cf. 368–9n., Finglass on *Ai.* 89–90, 641/2, 923–4). So here παῖ (ΔQ, *Chr. Pat.* 2098, 2538) with ἐσθλός, which has no vocative in classical Greek, is right. L's παῖς would be most unusual in an address (Diggle, *Euripidea*, 317, 324 n. 10), especially if metre plays no part, as it does in the only possible dramatic instance at *OC* 188–9 ἄγε νυν σύ με, παῖ<ς> (Musgrave), / ἵν' ἂν ... (cf. Ll-J/W, *Sophoclea*, 223). In 393 no one doubts παῖ (Δ) against παῖς (Λ), in 916 Φιλάμμονος παῖ is transmitted unanimously.

Δ's unmetrical variations of the whole phrase are easily explained. ἐσθλοῦ παῖ (V) arose by haplography and ἐσθλοῦ πατρὸς παῖ (O) by intrusion of a gloss and/or reminiscence of *Phil.* 96 ἐσθλοῦ πατρὸς παῖ ...

τύραννε τῆσδε γῆς: Cf. 165–6 and 484. In *Rhesus* Hector (not Priam) is the ruler of Troy. At 2, 886 and 993 the chorus call him βασιλεύς, a title which in fifth-century tragedy was reserved for actual monarchs (Hutchinson on *Sept.* 804).

The verse-end all but recurs in [E.] fr. 1132.4 (*Danae*) ... τύραννος τῆσδε γῆς, possibly from our play. But it looks as if it was a standard one.

---

[148] Liapis ('Notes', 70–1) adds that the addresses suspected to be spurious follow the pattern 'ὦ + vocative', while *Rh.* 388 has χαῖρ' and no ὦ. Cf. M. L. West, *Glotta* 44 (1966), 142 n. and on Hes. *Th.* 964.

παλαιᾷ ... ἡμέρᾳ is difficult and, rather than being a colloquialism (Jouan 66 n. 110), may be owed to mechanical adaptation of *Ai.* 624–5 ἦ που παλαιᾷ μὲν ἔντροφος (codd.: συν- Nauck) ἀμέρᾳ, / λευκῷ τε γήρᾳ μάτηρ (A. Fries, *CQ* n.s. 60 [2010], 351, Introduction, 37). With παλαιός conveying the notion that time has itself grown old (cf. Barrett on *Hipp.* 907–8, Kannicht on *Hel.* 625–9, J. de Romilly, *Time in Greek Tragedy*, Ithaca [NY] 1968, 42–9), we need to think of 'a period during which [Rhesus'] presence might have been expected' (Porter on 388–9), and ἡμέρα in the sense 'state or time of life' (cf. LSJ s.v. I 2) comes closest to that idea. *OC* 1138 ἐς τόδ' ἡμέρας ('up to this time') lacks this relative specificity, and at *Hel.* 628–9 περί τ' ἐπέτασα χέρα φίλιον ἐν μακρᾷ / φλογὶ φαεσφόρῳ, to which Kannicht on 625–9 (pp. 183–4) hesitantly refers, φαεσφόρος 'suggests ... repeated dawns' (Allan on *Hel.* 627–9).

προσεννέπω: 'to address (by name)'. The verb, which is often used in divine invocations (e.g. Pi. *Isthm.* 6.17, *Ag.* 162, *Ai.* [857], *Hipp.* 99), has formal overtones. See especially E. *El.* 552 ὅμως δὲ χαίρειν τοὺς ξένους προσεννέπω, *Tro.* 48–50 (Athena to Poseidon) ἔξεστι τὸν γένει μὲν ἄγχιστον πατρός / μέγαν τε δαίμον' ἐν θεοῖς τε τίμιον, / λύσασαν ἔχθραν τὴν πάρος, προσεννέπειν; and *Hel.* 1165–8 ὦ χαῖρε, πατρὸς μνῆμ' ... / ... / ἀεὶ δέ σ' ... / Θεοκλύμενος παῖς ὅδε προσεννέπω, πάτερ (προσεννέπω Lenting: -ει L).

390–1a. χαίρω plays on χαῖρ' (388). For the construction with an accusative and participle(s) cf. *Hipp.* 1339–40 τοὺς γὰρ εὐσεβεῖς θεοί / θνῄσκοντας οὐ χαίρουσι, E. fr. 673, *Ai.* 136 σὲ μὲν εὖ πράσσοντ' ἐπιχαίρω and *Phil.* 1314 ἥσθην πατέρα τὸν ἀμὸν εὐλογοῦντά σε (KG I 298–9 with n. 6, SD 395, Finglass on *Ai.* 136).

εὐτυχοῦντα: 56–8n.

προσήμενον / πύργοισιν ἐχθρῶν: 'besieging ...', as of the Erinyes at *Ag.* 1191–2 ὑμνοῦσι δ' ὕμνον δώμασιν προσήμεναι / πρώταρχον ἄτην (with Fraenkel on 1191). Aeschylus was fond of πρόσημαι in its various shades of meaning (LSJ s.v. I).

The towers belong to the fortifications which the Greeks built after the first Iliadic day of battle (*Il.* 7.337–43, 436–41). For the trench and wall see 110b–11, 116–18, 989b–92nn.

391b–2. συγκατασκάψων ... / τείχη: 'to help you demolish their walls'. Cf. *Rh.* 603 (603–4n.) τείχη κατασκάψαντα (also of Rhesus), Andoc. 1.101 οὐδ' ἐναυμάχησας ἐναντία τῇ πόλει, οὐδὲ συγκατέσκαψας τὰ τείχη ...; Strabo 12.4.3 and Lyc. 222 συγκατασκάπτην ('joint-destroyer'). In *Phoen.* 884 and *Or.* 735 the prefix σύν- refers to the object of the verb and may add some intensive force.

νεῶν ... σκάφη: 'the hulls of their ships'. So also *Ai.* 1278 ναυτικὰ σκάφη (in the same context as here), *Pers.* 418–19 ὑπτιοῦτο δέ / σκάφη νεῶν, *Cyc.* 467, *Tro.* 538–9 and *Hel.* 1543–4. Elsewhere in Euripides the phrase is essentially a periphrasis for 'ship': *Cyc.* 85, 702, *Tro.* 686, 1049, *IT* 742, 1345.

Setting fire to Protesilaus' ship marks the zenith of Hector's *aristeia* at *Il.* 16.122–4. Cf. 60b–2, 120–1, 989b–92nn.

393–4a. By greeting Rhesus with all the grandeur that befits a foreign prince, Hector forestalls potential charges of discourtesy and 'places the encounter on an official plane' (Jouan 27 n. 112). His designation of Rhesus' parents takes up the chorus at 349–52 and 386–7.

τῆς μελῳδοῦ μητέρος: 351b–4n. Of the other tragedians only Euripides uses μητέρος and μητέρι (instead of μητρός, μητρί) in spoken verse (Ritchie 179). Metrical considerations no doubt apply, but the forms may also have a more elevated tone: E. *El.* 1243, 1267, *Or.* 423, 504, 580, 798, 1589 (all of Clytaemestra killed by Orestes), *HF* 843 (Lyssa identifying her divine mother, Nyx), *IA* 669, 909 (the latter in an invocation).

Μουσῶν μιᾶς: For indefinite εἷς (μία, ἕν) with a partitive genitive see Dodds on *Ba.* 917 and Kannicht on *Hel.* 6–7 (p. 18). Our passage belongs to the category 'where something is predicated of one member of a group which by its nature can be true of only one' (Dodds). Cf. *Il.* 14.275–6 ἣ μὲν ἐμοὶ δώσειν Χαρίτων μίαν ὁπλοτεράων, / Πασιθέην, Pi. *Nem.* 4.65 (of Peleus) ἔγαμεν ὑψιθρόνων μίαν Νηρεΐδων, *Ion* 1–3 and *Hel.* 6–7. Differently *Rh.* 891 (890–2a n.) Μοῦσα συγγόνων μία.

394b–5. '... it is my custom always to speak the truth, and I am not a duplicitous man.'

Hector opens his speech like Polynices at *Phoen.* 469 ἁπλοῦς ὁ μῦθος τῆς ἀληθείας ἔφυ (cf. 388–453, 420–1nn.), which itself imitates A. fr. 176 (*Hoplōn Krisis*) ἁπλᾶ γάρ ἐστι τῆς ἀληθείας ἔπη. But whereas Euripides proceeds with 'an attack on sophistic conceptions of truth and on positive evaluations of rhetoric' (Mastronarde on *Phoen.* 469–72), traditional honesty is the issue both here and in Rhesus' answer at 422–3 (n.). Klyve, Feickert and Sansone (*BMCR* 2013.03.15, on 394–5) refer to *Il.* 9.312–14 (Achilles to Odysseus) ἐχθρὸς γάρ μοι κεῖνος ὁμῶς Ἀΐδαο πύλῃσιν, / ὅς χ' ἕτερον μὲν κεύθῃ ἐνὶ φρεσίν, ἄλλο δὲ εἴπῃ· / αὐτὰρ ἐγὼν ἐρέω ὥς μοι δοκεῖ εἶναι ἄριστα (~ Achilles at *IA* 926–7 ἐγὼ δ' ... / ... ἔμαθον τοὺς τρόπους ἁπλοῦς ἔχειν).

κοὐ διπλοῦς πέφυκ' ἀνήρ: likewise 423. In the sense ' duplicitous, treacherous' διπλοῦς is first attested in Archil. fr. 196a.36 *IEG* σὺ] μὲν γὰρ οὔτ' ἄπιστος οὔτε διπλόη (which LSJ s.v. IV 2 with Suppl. [1996] do not quote). Elsewhere e.g. Xen. *HG* 4.1.32 and *Tro.* 287 διπτύχῳ γλώσσᾳ (of Odysseus). Cf. Latin *duplex* (*OLD* s.v. 6 b).

The verse-end ... πέφυκ' ἀνήρ (first or third person singular) is typical of Euripides: *Med.* 294, *Hcld.* 2, *Hipp.* 1031, 1075, 1191, *Or.* 540, frr. 325.1, 425.1. Ritchie (207–8) notes that in *Hippolytus*, as here, an entire half-line (... εἰ κακὸς πέφυκ' ἀνήρ) is repeated with rhetorical effect.

396–8. πάλαι πάλαι: 321b–2a n. For the emphatic doubling of πάλαι cf. Ar. *Av.* 921 πάλαι πάλαι δὴ τήνδ' ἐγὼ κλήζω πόλιν and perhaps E. fr. 579 †Λάϊε† πάλαι δή σ' ἐξερωτῆσαι θέλων, / σχολή μ' ἀπεῖργε (Λάϊε Σᵇ *Il.* 2.353a¹ Erbse, om. alii: πάλαι Nauck).

τῇδε συγκάμνειν χθονί: a 'sardonic' reply to συγκατασκάψων in 391 (Liapis on 396–8). The expression resumes 326 ... οὐδὲ συγκαμὼν δορί.

τοὐπὶ σ': 'in so far as it depended on you'. So also *Alc.* 666 τέθνηκα γὰρ δὴ τοὐπὶ σ', *Or.* 1345 σώθηθ' ὅσον γε τοὐπ' ἔμ', *IA* 1557–8, Xen. *Cyr.* 1.4.12 and *Rh.* 405 ... τὸ σὸν μέρος. Where the implied subject of the phrase 'has no power to influence the situation' (Parker on *Alc.* 666), the meaning is simply 'as far as regards ...': e.g. *Ant.* 889 ἡμεῖς γὰρ ἀγνοὶ τοὐπὶ τήνδε τὴν κόρην, *Hec.* 514 ἡμεῖς δ' ἄτεκνοι τοὐπὶ σ' (Hecuba addressing the dead Polyxena).

πολεμίῳ ... δορί: The transmitted πολεμίων ... δορί (by assimilation from Ἀργείων) was corrected by the scribe of Va (above the line) and Bothe (II [1826], 103). Ar. *Ach.* 1192/3 (Lamachus) διόλλυμαι δορὸς ὑπὸ πολεμίου τυπείς parodies πολέμιον (...) δόρυ (or *vice versa*) as a standard juncture in tragedy (cf. *Sept.* 416, *Ai.* 1013 and, with δόρυ for 'armed force' or 'war', *Sept.* 216, E. fr. 370.83).

399–403. Hector's frequent embassies to Rhesus (implicit in 321–6, 333) have a model in *Il.* 17.220–2 κέκλυτε, μυρία φῦλα περικτιόνων ἐπικούρων. / οὐ γὰρ ἐγὼ πληθὺν διζήμενος οὐδὲ χατίζων / ἐνθάδ' ἀφ' ὑμετέρων πολίων ἤγειρα ἕκαστον, which is followed by a bitter comment on what it costs Troy to support her allies with provisions and conciliatory gifts: *Il.* 17.225–6 ~ *Rh.* 403 (n.). In the *Little Iliad* Priam sent for Eurypylus to come to his aid (Σ *Od.* 11.520 [II 517.15–17 Dindorf] = Acusil. fr. 40a Fowler), and the same is attested for Memnon from the early fourth century on (Ctes. *FGrHist* 688 F 1 [pp. 441–2] = D. S. 2.22.2,[149] Q. S. 2.34–7). See West, *Epic Cycle*, 144 with n. 22, 190–1, Introduction, 13–14.

For the Charioteer (839–41) and the Muse (935–7) the entreaties become the main cause of Rhesus' death, compelling Hector to defend himself (954–7). Parthenius incorporated the motif into his tale of Rhesus and Arganthone (*Erot. Path.* 36.4) – probably directly from our play (Introduction, 17, 44–5).

399–400. 'For you cannot say it was because your friends failed to call you that you did not come or defend or spare a thought for us.'

---

[149] The story is alluded to in Pl. *Lg.* 685c2–d2 and Cephalio *FGrHist* 93 F 1 (pp. 441–2).

For the rhetorical structure of the sentence Ritchie (92 n. 3) compares *Alc.* 658–9 οὐ μὴν ἐρεῖς γέ μ' ὡς ἀτιμάζοντα σόν / γῆρας θανεῖν προύδωκας (where ὡς is also followed by a negative participial phrase). By denoting what the subject can or should not do the future indicative shows part of its modal force (KG I 173, 175–6, SD 290–2).

ἄκλητος: 'uncalled, unbidden', here with a dative of the agent (φίλοις OL: -ος VQ). Of military allies the word is paralleled in Thuc. 6.87.2 φαμὲν γὰρ ... ξύμμαχοι δὲ καὶ νῦν καὶ πρότερον τοῖς ἐνθάδε ὑμῶν ἀδικουμένοις οὐκ ἄκλητοι, παρακληθέντες δὲ ἥκειν.

οὐκ ἦλθες οὐδ' ἤμυνας οὐδ' ἐπεστράφης: a rising tricolon (according to Behaghel's Law of Increasing Terms), in which the verbs form a climactic sequence. That Rhesus did not even *think* of the beleaguered Trojans (οὐδ' ἐπεστράφης) is arguably his worst omission in Hector's eyes. For ἐπιστρέφομαι, 'turn the mind towards, pay attention to, regard', cf. e.g. Thgn. 439–40 νήπιος, ὃς τὸν ἐμὸν μὲν ἔχει νόον ἐν φυλακῆσιν, / τῶν δ' αὐτοῦ †κἰδιον† οὐδὲν ἐπιστρέφεται, *Phil.* 598–9 τίνος δ' Ἀτρεῖδαι τοῦδ' ἄγαν οὕτω ... / ... ἐπεστρέφοντο πράγματος χάριν (...;), Dem. 10.9, 23.136 and ἐπιστροφή of the '*attention paid to* a person or thing' (LSJ s.v. II 3 a). Like other verbs of caring ἐπιστρέφομαι usually takes a genitive (KG I 365–6 with n. 13, SD 108–9).

401–3. 'For what Phrygian herald or embassy of elders did not come and urge you to defend our city? What gifts of honour did we neglect to send you?'

In an urgent appeal the double rhetorical question (with ποῖον merely a variation for τίς) has a precedent in *Andr.* 299–300 τίν' οὐκ ἐπῆλθε, ποῖον οὐκ ἐλίσσετο / δαμογερόντων βρέφος φονεύειν; Similarly *Ai.* 1012–16, *OT* 420–3, *Hcld.* 440–1, *Phoen.* 878–9 (869–80 del. Fraenkel) Theoc. 2.90–1 (Liapis on 401–3).

401–2. κήρυξ: Cf. 955–6 τί μὴν ἔμελλον οὐ πέμψειν φίλοις / κήρυκας ...; (399–403n.). On the acute accent in the nominative singular see G. Hermann, *De emendandae ratione Graecae grammaticae*, Leipzig 1801, 71, West, ed. *Aeschylus*, XLVIII and Barrett, *Collected Papers*, 285 n. 1.

γερουσία for πρεσβεία recurs elsewhere only at 936 (cf. 399–403n.). While it may be that this small (and metrically useful) shift in meaning was suggested by Priam's Council of Elders at *Il.* 3.146–53 (Jouan 27 n. 115), the fact that γέρων and πρέσβυς are synonyms probably also played a part (Liapis on 401–3).

Φρυγῶν: 32n.

ἐπέσκηψεν: The same verb, literally 'make to lean (or fall) upon' and so 'lay it upon one, ask earnestly, enjoin' (LSJ s.v. ἐπισκήπτω II 1, 2), is used by the Charioteer in 839–40. In other tragedy e.g. *Pers.* 103–6 (Μοῖρ' ...) ἐπέσκηψε ... Πέρσαις / πολέμους πυργοδαΐκτους / διέπειν,

PV 663–6, *Ai.* 752–4 and, with accusative and infinitive (as here), *Alc.* 365–7.

403. Rhesus was induced by presents – like the other allies, who did not fight for their homes and families: *Il.* 17.223–6 ἀλλ' ἵνα μοι Τρώων ἀλόχους καὶ νήπια τέκνα / προφρονέως ῥύοισθε φιλοπτολέμων ὑπ' Ἀχαιῶν· / τὰ φρονέων δώροισι κατατρύχω καὶ ἐδωδῇ / λαούς, ὑμέτερον δὲ ἑκάστου θυμὸν ἀέξω (399–403n.). The material strain put on Troy by the long war is evident also from *Il.* 9.401–3 and especially Hector's reply to Polydamas at 18.288–92 (Hainsworth on *Il.* 9.401–3, Edwards on 17.223–6, 18.290–2).

ποῖον δὲ δώρων κόσμον οὐκ ἐπέμψαμεν; literally 'Which honour (consisting) of gifts ...' This sense of κόσμος (LSJ s.v. II 2) is a metaphorical extension of 'ornament, decoration', which itself goes back to the original '(good) order' (H. Diller, in *Festschrift Bruno Snell ...*, Munich 1956, 57–9, J. Kerschensteiner, *Kosmos. Quellenkritische Untersuchungen zu den Vorsokratikern*, Munich 1962, 7–8, 20–3). For similar applications of the word cf. *Tro.* 1207–8 καὶ μὴν ... αἵδε σοι σκυλευμάτων / Φρυγίων φέρουσι κόσμον ἐξάπτειν νεκρῷ and *Phaeth.* 88–90 Diggle = E. fr. 773.44–6 κόσμον δ' ὑμεναίων δεσποσύνων / ἐμὲ καὶ τὸ δίκαιον ἄγει καὶ ἔρως / ὑμνεῖν (with Diggle on 87–8).[150] κόσμος ('finery') and δῶρα occur together at *Med.* 972–3.

ποῖον (Λ) is *lectio difficilior* for ποίων (Δ; cf. *Chr. Pat.* 1720 οἵων δὲ δώρων ...). Both syntax and metrical structure of the question correspond to *Hcld.* 441 ποῖον δὲ γαίας ἕρκος οὐκ ἀφίγμεθα; (cf. 401–3n.).

404–5. 'But you, for your part, a barbarian of a kindred race, betrayed us fellow-barbarians to the Greeks.'

Thracians and Phrygians were thought to be related (294–7n.). Equally common, at least in tragedy, was the pan-barbarian idea to which Hector appeals (below).

σὺ δ' ἐγγενὴς ὤν: For the language cf. fr. tr. adesp. 536 μέτοικε σύ / <οὐ>δ' ἐγγενὴς ὢν τήνδε δουλώσας ἔχεις.

ἐγγενής (frequent in Sophocles) easily corrupted into εὐγενής (OQgE): *Rh.* 413 ἐγγενεῖς (VLQ: εὐγ- O), S. *El.* 1328 (pars codd.), fr. tr. adesp. 536 (ἐγγ- Valckenaer: εὐγ- codd. Stob. 3.40.8) and *vice versa* probably *OT* 1225 (εὐγενῶς Hartung: ἐγγ- codd.).

βάρβαρός τε βαρβάρους: Similar verse-ends appear in *Rh.* 833 (833–4n.) ... βάρβαρός τε βαρβάρου and *IT* 31 ... βαρβάροισι βάρβαρος. Euripides was particularly fond of nominal polyptota (Denniston on

---

[150] It is not quite clear from Diggle's discussion that κόσμον ἐπέων for 'poetry' (to which, after Page, he traces the restored κόσμον δ' ὑμεναίων) essentially denotes 'an ordered and metrically defined sequence of ἔπεα' (Noussia-Fantuzzi on Sol. fr. 2.2 G.–P.^{2} = 1–3.2 *IEG*). But the meaning in *Phaethon* remains 'songs in honour of our master's marriage'.

E. *El.* 337, Collard on E. *Suppl.* 42–4) and first applied them to the names of peoples: *Hcld.* 139 Ἀργεῖος ὢν γὰρ αὐτὸς Ἀργείους ἄγω, *Hec.* 137–40 ὡς ἀχάριστοι / Δαναοὶ Δαναοῖς τοῖς οἰχομένοις / ὑπὲρ Ἑλλήνων / Τροίας πεδίων ἀπέβησαν (Gygli-Wyss, *Polyptoton*, 127 with n. 4). For βάρβαρος this implies a bond of kinship (and thus loyalty owed) between all foreigners as opposed to the Greeks. See Hall, *Inventing the Barbarian*, 161, 195, to whose list of passages add *Hel.* 863–4 Τροίας δὲ σωθεὶς κἀπὸ βαρβάρου χθονός / ἐς βάρβαρ' ἐλθὼν φάσγαν' αὖθις ἐμπεσῇ.

The easiest explanation for βαρβάρου in ΔgE is the loss of a letter at line-end.

Ἕλλησιν ἡμᾶς προύπιες was probably inspired by A. fr. 131.1–4 (*Myrmidons*) τάδε μὲν λεύσσεις, φαίδιμ' Ἀχιλλεῦ, / δοριλυμάντους Δαναῶν μόχθους, / οὓς σὺ π[ροπιν – ⏑ –] εἴσω / κλισίας.[151] Both times we have προπίνω, which does not otherwise occur in drama, in the metaphorical sense 'make a drinking-present of', i.e. 'give away, betray' (LSJ s.v. II 2, 3), and the overall situations can be compared. At the beginning of Aeschylus' play the chorus of Myrmidons rebuke Achilles for indulging his wrath and leaving the Greeks to their fate (Fraenkel, *Rev.* 231; cf. Introduction, 34–5).

Nevertheless one may also see here an allusion to the Thracians' notorious drunkenness (Liapis on 404–5) in rhetorical anticipation of 418–19.

τὸ σὸν μέρος: likewise e.g. *Ant.* 1062 οὕτω γὰρ ἤδη καὶ δοκῶ τὸ σὸν μέρος; *OC* 1366 and *Tr.* 1215, *Hcld.* 678 … τοὐμὸν μέρος (LSJ s.v. μέρος III 2). Cf. 396–8n. (τοὐπὶ σ').

406–11a. With the omission of Hector's part in it, Rhesus' fight for supremacy over Thrace is also alluded to by the Muse at 930–3 (n.). But despite a pertinent remark in Σ^AD *Il.* 10.435 (p. 355 van Thiel = I 364.4–5 Dindorf), we cannot be sure that this, like the hero's other pre-Trojan exploits (426–42n.), featured in earlier versions of the myth (Introduction, 11–12). Our poet perhaps invented the episode to give Hector a further powerful claim on Rhesus' support (957 ἔπεμψ'· ὀφείλων δ' ἦλθε συμπονεῖν ἐμοί).

In *Il.* 9.315–32 Achilles reminds the Greek envoys of his ceaseless fighting and the many raids he undertook on behalf of Agamemnon (cf. D. Sansone, *BMCR* 2013.15.03, on 394–5). Similarly Medea in her *agon* speech lists all the favours she has done Jason (*Med.* 476–87) and for which she would have wished to receive the proper reward (388–453, 411b–12nn.).

---

[151] So P. Oxy. 2163, supplementing Ar. *Ran.* 992 and Harpocr. I 259.10–260.3 Dindorf. Blomfield (*Aeschyli Persae* …, Cambridge ¹1814, XIV) had already conjectured οὓς σὺ προπίνεις, to which Taplin (*HSPh* 76 [1972], 66 n. 27) plausibly added θάσσων.

406–7. 'And yet with this hand of mine I raised you from a petty kingdom to be the great ruler of the Thracians.'

καίτοι: 112n. 'Surprise' is the foremost notion here and at 941.

μικρᾶς ἐκ τυραννίδος: 'abstract for concrete', as in *Cho.* 405, 973–4 ἴδεσθε χώρας τὴν διπλῆν τυραννίδα / πατροκτόνους τε δωμάτων πορθήτορας, S. fr. 345 μηροῖς ὑπαίθων τὴν Διὸς τυραννίδα and Hdt. 8.137.2 ἦσαν δὲ τὸ πάλαι καὶ αἱ τυραννίδες τῶν ἀνθρώπων ἀσθενέες χρήμασι, οὐ μοῦνον ὁ δῆμος (LSJ s.v. τυραννίς II 2). In general KG I 10–12.

τῇδ' ... **χερί:** By surrounding ἐγώ the phrase stresses the active role Hector played, instead of just being a pleonastic dative (56–8, 214–15nn.).

408–10a. ἀμφί: 'around, somewhere in'. Cf. *Rh.* 477 τὰ δ' ἀμφί τ' Ἄργος καὶ νομὸν τὸν Ἑλλάδος and especially *Andr.* 215–16 εἰ δ' ἀμφὶ Θρῄκην τὴν χιόνι κατάρρυτον / τύραννον ἔσχες ἄνδρ' (LSJ s.v. C I 2, Mastronarde on *Phoen.* 825).

Παγγαιόν τε Παιόνων τε γῆν: Mt. Pangaeus lies on the east side of the lower Strymon. On its rich mineral resources and consequent importance for Athens see 921–2a n.

The Paeonians were a Thraco-Illyrian people whose area of settlement stretched from the Axius in north-eastern Macedon as far as the Strymon. In both Homer and *Rhesus* they are independent Trojan allies (538–45, 540–2nn.), and our poet is vague enough here to avoid a conflict of statements (cf. Feickert on 408). His geographic boundaries merely indicate the size of Rhesus' eventual rule.

Θρηκῶν ἀρίστοις ἐμπεσών: so rightly Λ (~ *Chr. Pat.* 1724 ἐθνῶν ἀρίστοις ἐμπεσών). Δ's ἀρίστους is probably a mere copying error.

κατὰ στόμα: 'face to face'. Cf. *Rh.* 491, 511 and e.g. *Cho.* 573, *Hcld.* 801, Hdt. 8.11.1, Xen. *An.* 5.2.26 (LSJ s.v. στόμα I 3 g).[152] Also *Rh.* 371 (370–2a n.), 421 κατ' ὄμμα.

ἔρρηξα πέλτην: 'broke their shields' (Σ^V *Rh.* 410 [II 337.24 Schwartz = 98 Merro]), not with most commentators (and LSJ s.v. πέλτη I 2) metonymically for '... ranks of peltasts' (Liapis on 408–10 ~ *JHS* 129 [2009], 73 with n. 15). The phrase is modelled on *Il.* 20.267–8 (~ 21.164–5) οὐδὲ ... / ῥῆξε σάκος of Achilles' indestructible divine shield (Morstadt, *Beitrag*, 23–4 n. 1). For the distributive singular here see KG I 14–15 and SD 42.

411b–12. 'For these (favours) you have spurned your great debt of gratitude, and when your friends are in trouble, you come to our help too late.'

---

[152] *Phaeth.* 246–7 Diggle = E. fr. 781.33–4 πᾶσι τοῖς κατὰ στόμα / θεοῖς should be deleted from LSJ. Read κατὰ σταθμά (Blass) or κατὰ στέγας (Rau).

Words and rhetoric resemble Admetus' demand for parental recognition at *Alc.* 660–1 ... κἀντὶ τῶνδέ μοι χάριν / τοιάνδε καὶ σὺ χὴ τεκοῦσ' ἠλλαξάτην (less close Medea at *Med.* 488–90), while Achilles begins with the Achaeans' lack of gratitude in *Il.* 9.316–17 ... ἐπεὶ οὐκ ἄρα τις χάρις ἦεν / μάρνασθαι δηίοισιν ἐπ' ἀνδράσι νωλεμὲς αἰεί (+ 318–19). Cf. 388–453, 406–11a nn.

λακτίσας πολλὴν χάριν: literally 'you have kicked ...'. So also *Ag.* 381–4 οὐ γάρ ἐστιν ἔπαλξις / ... ἀνδρί / λακτίσαντι μέγαν Δίκας βωμὸν εἰς ἀφάνειαν, *PV* 651–2 σὺ δ' ... μὴ ἀπολακτίσῃς λέχος / τὸ Ζηνός and *Eum.* 110 καὶ πάντα ταῦτα λὰξ ὁρῶ πατούμενα (with Sommerstein).

ὕστερος βοηδρομεῖς: 333n. Personal ὕστερος (OQgV) is required in the sense 'later, too late' (LSJ s.v. A II 2, 3), whence also 443 (n.) ἀλλ' ὕστερος μὲν ἦλθον ... (corr. Cobet) and 453 ... καίπερ ὕστερος μολών (-ος V: -ον OΛ). The (adverbial) accusative here (VLgE) was easy after 333 ... ὕστερον βοηδρομεῖν. V even continues with the infinitive.

413–18. Hector's complaint that the Trojans and their other allies have endured the hardships of war, while Rhesus led an easy life (and now has come to receive a share in the spoils: 325–6) has a precedent in Achilles' accusation of Agamemnon as only ever having profited from his exploits (*Il.* 9.321–43). Cf. D. Sansone, *BMCR* 2013.03.13 and 388–453n.

413–14a. δ': strongly adversative (*GP* 166–7), contrasting 404–5.

ἡμῖν ἐγγενεῖς πεφυκότες: Cf. *OC* 1167–8 ὅρα κατ' Ἄργος εἴ τις ὑμῖν ἐγγενής / ἔσθ', and see 404–5n. Many editors before Murray read Valckenaer's ἐν γένει (*Diatribe*, 105 n. 7), which, however, seems to be restricted to family ties: *Cho.* 287, *OT* 1016, 1430, *Alc.* 904, Dem. 23.72, 57.28, [Dem.] 47.70, 60.7. Unfortunately, the text of Dicaeog. *TrGF* 52 F 1b.3 ἢ τοῖς †ἀνάγκης ἐν γένει πεφυκόσιν† is insecure.

πάλαι: 321b–2a n.

414b–15. ἐν χωστοῖς τάφοις: '... in grave mounds', such as were heaped over the pyre or, in the case of major individual heroes, the urn or coffin containing their bones: *Il.* 6.418–19, 7.328–37, 23.234–57, 24.788–801 (Hector), *Od.* 11.74–8, 12.11–15, 24.71–84 (Achilles and Patroclus), *Rh.* 959 (959–60n.) καὶ νῦν ἕτοιμος τῷδε καὶ τεῦξαι τάφον. Cf. M. Andronikos, *Arch. Hom.* W 32–4, 107–21.

χωστός ('heaped up') occurs only here in classical Greek (later e.g. Lyc. 698, 1064, Plb. 4.61.7, Strabo 11.2.7). But it may have been current to judge by the compounds in *Cho.* 351–2 πολύχωστον ... τάφον and *Ant.* 848–9 πρὸς ἔργμα (v.l. ἕρμα) τυμβόχωστον ἔρ- / χομαι τάφου ποταινίου. The verb χόω is also regular in tragedy.

πίστις οὐ σμικρὰ πόλει ('no small pledge of loyalty to our city') echoes the second half of *Hipp.* 1037 ὅρκους παρασχών, πίστιν οὐ σμικράν, θεῶν, which comes shortly after 1031 (= 1075, 1191) ... εἰ κακὸς πέφυκ' ἀνήρ (cf. 394b–5n.). For the nominative in apposition to the sentence, expressing a judgement, cf. e.g. *Tro.* 489–90 τὸ λοίσθιον δέ, θριγκὸς ἀθλίων κακῶν, / δούλη γυνὴ γραῦς Ἑλλάδ' εἰσαφίξομαι (KG I 284, SD 617). This is preferable to Bothe's πίστιν οὐ σμικρὰν πόλει (5 [1803], 293), which, following nominatives, would signify a result (257b–60n.).

416–18a. '... whereas others stand fast in armour and by their horse-drawn chariots, patiently enduring the wind's cold blasts and the sun-god's thirsty flame ...'

The pairing of winter cold and summer heat resembles the account of the Argive Herald at *Ag.* 563–6 χειμῶνα δ' εἰ λέγοι τις οἰωνοκτόνον, / οἷον παρεῖχ' ἄφερτον Ἰδαία χιών, / ἢ θάλπος, εὖτε πόντος ἐν μεσημβριναῖς / κοίταις ἀκύμων νηνέμοις εὕδοι πεσών (Paley on 417). But one also recalls Odysseus' account of a freezing night before Troy at *Od.* 14.471–502 (especially 475–7). For the language here cf. E. fr. 78a (below).

παρ' ἱππείοις ὄχοις: 301b–2n. The phrase may go back to *Il.* 5.794 ηὖρε δὲ τόν γε ἄνακτα παρ' ἵπποισιν καὶ ὄχεσφιν, just as A. *Suppl.* 183 ξὺν ἵπποις καμπύλοις τ' ὀχήμασιν (with FJW) has more closely been adapted from *Il.* 4.297 (= 5.219, 9.384, 12.119, 18.237) σὺν ἵπποισιν καὶ ὄχεσφιν. Similarly *Il.* 5.107 πρόσθ' ἵπποιιν καὶ ὄχεσφιν. Mycenean Greek has feminine *i-qi-ja* meaning 'chariot' (LSJ Suppl. [1996] s.v. ἵππιος IV).

ψυχρὰν ἄησιν: The noun otherwise appears only at E. fr. 78a (*Alcmeon*) ὡς ἄπεπλον, ὦ δύστηνε, σῶμ' ἔχεις σέθεν. / – ἐν τοῖσδ' ἄησιν καὶ θέρος διέρχομαι (where Phot. α 448 Theodoridis glosses ἄησιν with χειμῶνα) and *Phaeth.* 255 Diggle = E. fr. 781.46 καπνοῦ μέλαιν' ἄησις. More commonly ἄημα in Aeschylus (*Ag.* 1418, *Eum.* 905), Sophocles (*Ai.* 674) and later poetry (e.g. Call. *Aet.* fr. 75.36 Harder, Nonn. *D.* 2.529 φεύγων ψυχρὸν ἄημα νιφοβλήτοιο Βορῆος).

δίψιόν τε πῦρ θεοῦ: 'thirsty' because the blazing summer sun drains all moisture from the land. Cf. Opp. *Hal.* 3.47–8 εὖ δὲ φέροι ... δίψιον ὥρην / Σειρίου (unless this generally means 'parched'), Nonn. *D.* 1.237 δίψιος ... κύων (i.e. Sirius), 12.287. Conversely, dry ground has traditionally been called (πολυ)δίψιος: e.g. *Il.* 4.171 πολυδίψιον Ἄργος, *Alc.* 560, *Ag.* 495 διψία κόνις, *Ant.* 246–7 (with Griffith on 245–7), 429, Call. *Aet.* fr. 137c.10 Harder [Σ]πάρτη δ[ί]ψιον ἄστυ γε . […].

For θεός = 'the sun-god' see 330–1n. (τοὐπιὸν σέλας θεοῦ).

418b–19. '... not (reclining) on soft bedding, like you, and toasting one another in many deep draughts.'

Heavy drinking (of beer and undiluted wine) was a vice traditionally ascribed to northern barbarians: Archil. fr. 42 *IEG* (Thracians and Scythians), Anacr. fr. 356 (b) *PMG*, Ar. *Ach.* 141, Hdt. 6.84, Pl. *Leg.* 637d2–e7 (who observes that it does not diminish their martial prowess), Call. *Aet.* fr. 178.11–12 Harder, Hor. *Carm.* 1.36.13–14 *neu multi Damalis meri / Bassum Threicia vincat amystide.* Cf. Hall, *Inventing the Barbarian*, 18, 133–4.

The 'bedding' here also implies a charge of luxuriousness, which Rhesus includes in his defence at 438–9 (n.).

πυκνὴν ἄμυστιν is an internal accusative with δεξιούμενοι (below), in which πυκνός marks a frequently repeated action (LSJ s.v. A II 2; cf. 438–9n.). ἄμυστις – from ἀμυστί (< α privative + μύω), 'without closing one's mouth' (Schwyzer 623 with n. 10) – denotes (1) a long draught and (2) a cup that lends itself to being drained at one go: Ath. *Epit.* XI 783d (III 22.15–19 Kaibel), Σ^V *Rh.* 419 (II 337.6–10 Schwartz = 99 a¹ Merro) and, for further references, Kassel–Austin on Cratin. fr. 322 *PCG*. Both meanings have been advocated here.[153] But the first better suits the grammatical construction, and the passage from a play *Auge*, quoted by Σ^V *Rh.* 419 (above) in support of 'cup', actually favours a series of deep draughts: σὺν τῷ βαθείας καὶ πυκνὰς ἕλκουσι τὰς ἀμύστιδας (~ *Cyc.* 416–18 ὁ δ' … / ἐδέξατ' ἔσπασέν <τ'> ἄμυστιν ἑλκύσας / κἀπήνεσ').[154] Likewise at Ar. *Ach.* 1229 καὶ πρός γ' ἄκρατον ἐγχέας ἄμυστιν ἐξέλαψα predicative 'in one draught, without taking breath' is preferable to a separate object 'cup' (Olson).

δεξιούμενοι: literally 'greeting (one another) with the right hand' (LSJ s.v. δεξιόομαι I with Suppl. [1996]). Of toasting also Men. *Dysc.* 948 ἐδεξιοῦτ' αὐτοῖς κύκλῳ. The symposiastic order was from left to right (362b–5a n.).

420–1. Like Polynices at *Phoen.* 494–6 ταῦτ' αὔθ' ἕκαστα, μῆτερ, οὐχὶ περιπλοκάς / λόγων ἀθροίσας εἶπον ἀλλὰ καὶ σοφοῖς / καὶ τοῖσι φαύλοις ἔνδιχ', ὡς ἐμοὶ δοκεῖ, Hector resumes the introductory theme of his speech (388–453, 394b–5nn.). Mastronarde (on *Phoen.* 494–6) ob-

---

[153] So Σ^V *Rh.* 419 (II 337.25–6 Schwartz = 99 a² Merro) = Hsch. α 3875 Latte τὴν συνεχῆ πόσιν opposes the main scholiast's preferred interpretation. Also Σ^L *Rh.* 419 (II 337.27 Schwartz = 99 a³ Merro) ἄμυστις εἶδος ποτηρίου and Σ^V *Rh.* 438 (II 338.22 Schwartz = 101 Merro) τὰς φιάλας as against Σ^P *Rh.* 419 (99 a⁴ Merro) συνεχῆ πότον (Merro: πότου P).

[154] As to the play title, ἐν Αὔγῃ is Hermann's (*Opuscula* V, 189) palmary emendation of ἐν αὐτῇ (V). But it is not clear whether the lines belong to Euripides' tragedy of that name (in which case we would have to restore trimeters by accepting Hermann's lacuna between ἕλκουσι and τὰς ἀμύστιδας) or, as iambic dimeters, to a homonymous comedy by Eubulus or Philyllius (Kassel–Austin, *PCG* V, 199). The surrounding text allows either view (cf. Merro 207–8, where add that the similarity to *Cyc.* 416–18 may be coincidence – or support Euripidean authorship of the fragment). All we can safely say is that the scholiast (or his source) was struck by the parallel occurrence of πυκνός.

ταῦθ'... / ... μέμφομαί σοι: 'This I blame you for', as in Ar. *Nub.* 525–6 ταῦτ' οὖν ὑμῖν μέμφομαι / τοῖς σοφοῖς (LSJ s.v. μέμφομαι 2). The internal accusative pronoun (as always with μέμφομαι τινί τι) here doubles as a 'proper' accusative object to λέγω (cf. KG II 561–3, SD 708–9).

ὡς ἄν: 72–3n.

καὶ λέγω κατ' ὄμμα σόν: 370–2a n. In particular cf. E. *El.* 910 (Electra to the murdered Aegisthus) θρυλοῦσ' ἅ γ' εἰπεῖν ἤθελον κατ' ὄμμα σόν and Ar. *Ran.* 626 αὐτοῦ μὲν οὖν, ἵνα σοι κατ' ὀφθαλμοὺς λέγῃ.

422–3. 'I am like this myself; I cleave a straight path in my speech, and I am not a duplicitous man.'

While Rhesus almost literally repeats Hector's declaration of sincerity in 394–5, Eteocles recalls his brother only vaguely, and with no express acknowledgement, at *Phoen.* 503 ἐγὼ γὰρ οὐδέν, μῆτερ, ἀποκρύψας ἐρῶ (388–453, 394b–5, 420–1nn.). Yet in both cases we have a *captatio benevolentiae* for the defence: Rhesus will speak the truth, and Eteocles must be excused if he is too blunt (cf. Mastronarde on *Phoen.* 503).

εὐθεῖαν λόγων / τέμνω κέλευθον: Two metaphors converge in this phrase. The 'path of words' was common in poetry and prose from Homer on (cf. West, *IEPM* 43–4)[155] and so was the association of 'straightness' with justice and, more generally, honesty (LSJ s.vv. εὐθύς A 2, ἰθύς (A) I 2, Liapis on 422–3; especially *Hipp.* 491–2 ὡς τάχος διιστέον, / τὸν εὐθὺν ἐξειπόντας ἀμφὶ σοῦ λόγον). Verbal inspiration may have come from E. fr. 124.2–5 (*Andromeda*) ~ Ar. *Thesm.* 1099–1101 διὰ μέσου γὰρ αἰθέρος / τέμνων κέλευθον πόδα τίθημ' ὑπόπτερον / ... / Περσεύς,[156] with a similar expression already used figuratively at A. *Suppl.* 806–7 ἀμφυγᾶς τίν' ἔτι πόρον / τέμνω γάμου λυτῆρα; (for the text see FJW on 806). The origin of this idiom lay in 'cutting a road' (LSJ τέμνω (A) VI 2 a, J. Chadwick, *Lexicographica Graeca* ..., Oxford 1996, 276–7: Thuc. 2.100.2 ὁδοὺς εὐθείας ἔτεμε) rather than ploughing, as could be the case with places like *Od.* 3.174–5 πέλαγος ... / τέμνειν, 13.88, *h.Cer.* 383

---

[155] Pindar and Bacchylides greatly elaborated this theme. Cf. e.g. Pi. *Ol.* 1.110 ἐπίκουρον εὑρὼν ὁδὸν λόγων, *Pyth.* 11.38–9 ἦρ' ... κατ' ἀμευσίπορον τρίοδον ἐδινάθην, / ὀρθὰν κέλευθον ἰὼν τὸ πρίν, *Nem.* 6.45–6, *Isthm.* 3/4.19–21, Bacch. 5.31–3, 9.47–8, (O. Becker, *Das Bild des Weges* ..., Berlin 1937, 68–85, M. R. Lefkowitz, *HSPh* 67 [1963], 243 with n. 44 = *First-Person Fictions. Pindar's Poetic 'I'*, Oxford 1991, 27 with n. 44, Maehler [1982] on Bacch. 5.31).

[156] *Phoen.* 1–2 are rightly deleted by Haslam (cf. 305–6a n.). A possible source for the first verse is [E.] *Ep.* 1.1 (478 *EG*) ὦ τὸν ἀγήραντον πόλον αἰθέρος Ἥλιε τέμνων (M. W. Haslam, *GRBS* 16 [1975], 173 n. 83).

βαθὺν ἠέρα τέμνον ἰόντες (Mastronarde on *Phoen.* 1 [p. 142], Dunbar on Ar. *Av.* 1398–1400, J. Chadwick, *BICS* 39 [1994], 7).

Despite E. fr. 124.3 (above), Nauck's τέμνω (less likely τέμνειν) for the MSS' τέμνων (*Euripideische Studien* II, 173–4) seems inescapable here, since explanations after τοιοῦτος or τοιόσδε normally follow in an asyndetic main clause (infinitive at *IA* 502–3). To his list of examples (*Cyc.* 524 τοιόσδ' ὁ δαίμων· οὐδένα βλάπτει βροτῶν, *Or.* 895–6 [895–7 del. Dindorf], E. fr. 196.1–3) Liapis added *Andr.* 173–6, E. *Suppl.* 881–7 and E. fr. 322.1–3 ('Notes', 71–2), while no satisfactory parallel for the participle exists (*Ag.* 312–13 τοιοίδε τοί μοι λαμπαδηφόρων νόμοι, / ἄλλος παρ' ἄλλου διαδοχαῖς πληρούμενοι is a distributive apposition to the sentence [Fraenkel on 313, KG II 107, SD 403–4]). The corruption was easy by assimilation to the preceding εὐθεῖαν λόγων.

κοὐ διπλοῦς πέφυκ' ἀνήρ: 394b–5n.

424–5. 'I was more vexed, more distressed by sorrow in my heart, than you at being absent from this land.'

ἐγὼ δέ: The particle here 'marks the transition from the introduction ... to the opening of the speech proper' (*GP* 170–1). So especially after ἐγώ (e.g. *Ant.* 1196, *Alc.* 681, *Phoen.* 473).

μεῖζον: thus rightly ΔQ. The neuter plural (L) is not used as an adverb.

τῆσδ' ἀπὼν χθονός goes with both δυσφορῶν and, as a phrasal verb of feeling, λύπῃ ... ἐτειρόμην (KG II 53–4, SD 392–3).

λύπῃ πρὸς ἧπαρ ... ἐτειρόμην recalls *Il.* 22.242 ἀλλ' ἐμὸς ἔνδοθι θυμὸς ἐτείρετο πένθεϊ λυγρῷ (~ *Od.* 2.70–1), *Od.* 1.340–2 ταύτης δ' ἀποπαύε' ἀοιδῆς / λυγρῆς, ἥ τέ μοι αἰὲν ἐνὶ στήθεσσι φίλον κῆρ / τείρει (cf. 750–1a, 799nn.) and, in the juxtaposition of λύπη and ἧπαρ, *Ag.* 791 δῆγμα δὲ λύπης οὐδὲν ἐφ' ἧπαρ προσικνεῖται. By the early fifth century BC the liver had come to be regarded as the organ affected by deep emotions: also *Ag.* 432 πολλὰ δ' οὖν θιγγάνει πρὸς ἧπαρ, *Cho.* 271–2, *Eum.* 135, *Ai.* 938 χωρεῖ πρὸς ἧπαρ, οἶδα, γενναία δύη (with Kamerbeek, Finglass), *Hipp.* 1070 (with Barrett on 1070–1), E. *Suppl.* 599 ὥς μοι ὑφ' ἥπατι †χλωρὸν δεῖμα ταράσσει†.[157]

There is no need to suspect πρὸς ἧπαρ here (Nauck, *Euripideische Studien* II, 174) or to take it attributively with λύπη (cf. Feickert on 425). Previous motion 'towards' the liver can easily be deduced from ἐτειρόμην (LSJ s.v. πρός C I 2 a, KG I 540–1, 543–4, SD 433–4 on the 'pregnant' use of prepositions).

---

[157] The likeliest remedies are Hartung's ... χλωρόν <τι> δεῖμα θράσσει (θράσσει iam Markland), with θάρσος in 609, and Diggle's ὡς χλοερόν μοι ὑφ' ἥπατι δεῖμα θάσσει (*GRBS* 14 [1973], 50–2 = *Euripidea*, 68–70), taking up Murray's θάσσει and a corrector of P who wrote δεῖμα χλοερόν. See also Collard on 598–9.

δυσφορῶν: a forceful verb (W. S. Barrett, in R. Carden [ed.], *The Papyrus Fragments of Sophocles*, Berlin – New York 1974, 217–18, Hutchinson on *Sept.* 780 '... may denote being swept along by sinister or painful feelings ... by madness, grief, or rage'), which here, however, looks like a verse filler.

426–42. As in the case of Rhesus' Thracian battles (406–11a n.), there is no evidence that this Scythian war was anything but our poet's invention – which Parthenius took over in *Erot. Path.* 36.1 λέγεται δὲ καὶ Ῥῆσον, πρὶν ἐς Τροίαν ἐπίκουρον ἐλθεῖν, ἐπὶ πολλὴν γῆν ἰέναι προσαγόμενόν τε καὶ δασμὸν ἐπιτιθέντα (434–5n., Introduction, 17, 44–5). Similarly, Menelaus excuses himself with the necessity to defend Sparta in *Andr.* 732–8, and Polymestor in *Hec.* 962–7 declares that, when Hecuba came to the Greek camp, he had been away in inland Thrace (Burnett, 'Smiles', 30 with n. 52 [p. 181]).[158]

The Scythians lived beyond the Danube, whose lower stretch our poet appears to regard as the north-eastern border of Rhesus' realm (as it was for the historical kingdom of the Odrysae). Thus if they attacked him by the Bosporus (cf. 436–7n.), 'they were alarmingly deep into his territory' (Liapis on 428–9). Rhesus' apparent detour to the Black Sea also fits his arrival via Mt. Ida to the south-east of Troy (284–6n.).

426–8a. 'But a country bordering on mine, the Scythian people, started a war on me as I was about to make the journey across to Ilium.'

ἀγχιτέρμων: 'near the border, neighbouring' (LSJ s.v.). Before *Rhesus* the adjective is attested only at S. fr. 384 ὦ Λῆμνε Χρύσης τ' ἀγχιτέρμονες πάγοι (ἀγχιτέρμονος Blaydes). Later Theodect. *TrGF* 72 F 17.1, Lyc. 729, 1130 and, in prose, Xen. *Hier.* 10.7 τὰς <δ'> ἀγχιτέρμονας πόλεις. Pollux (6.113) calls it διθυραμβώδης ('dithyrambic in style, high-flown').

Σκύθης λεώς: The apposition of a people's name to the country they inhabit (ἀγχιτέρμων γαῖά μοι) seems to be unparalleled.

νόστον τὸν πρὸς Ἴλιον: here simply 'journey ...' (Σ^V *Rh.* 427 [II 337.11–13 Schwartz = 100 Merro]), as in *IT* 1111–12 ζαχρύσου δὲ δι' ἐμπολᾶς / νόστον βάρβαρον ἦλθον, *IA* 965–6 ἔδωκά τἂν Ἕλλησιν, εἰ πρὸς Ἴλιον / ἐν τῷδ' ἔκαμνε νόστος, 1261. Also νοστέω at *Hel.* 428, 474, 891, Ar. *Ach.* 28–9, Pherecr. fr. 87.2 *PCG*.

ξυνῆψε πόλεμον: Cf. Hdt. 1.18.2 ὁ τὸν πόλεμον ... συνάψας, Thuc. 6.13.2 and, with the subject designating an external cause, *Hel.* 53–5 ἡ δὲ πάντα τλᾶσ' ἐγώ /... δοκῶ προδοῦσ' ἐμόν / πόσιν συνάψαι πόλεμον Ἕλλησιν μέγαν (LSJ s.v. συνάπτω A II 1 b).

---

158 *Hec.* 962 σὺ δ', εἴ τι μέμφῃ τῆς ἐμῆς ἀπουσίας could stand for Hector's entire speech. Note also the verbal resemblance in *Rh.* 467–8 τοιαῦτα μέν σοι τῆς μακρᾶς ἀπουσίας / πρᾶξαι παρέξω.

Euripides was extremely fond of συνάπτω in nearly all its applications. Though used by the other dramatists and once by Pindar (*Pyth.* 4.247), the verb does not seem to have been part of the poetic tradition.

428b–9. Ἀξένου ... / πόντου πρὸς ἀκτάς: Diggle and Kovacs rightly read ἀξένου (better Ἀξένου) for the MSS' εὐξένου with Markland (*Euripidis dramata Iphigenia in Aulide et Iphigenia in Tauris*, London ¹1771, 242–3) – as also in *HF* 410, *IT* 124–5, 395, 1388–9 and *Andr.* 1262 (Cobet). Even if one disputes the need for consistency in any given author or genre, Ἄξενος is the more poignant in all these places[159] and would easily have been replaced by the later 'default' form. Cf. Pi. *Pyth.* 4.203–4 ἐπ' Ἀξείνου στόμα ... / ἤλυθον (ἀξειν- codd. pler.: εὐξ- C), and see n. 159, Bond on *HF* 410.

Since Vasmer (1921)[160] the original Greek Ἄξε(ι)νος for the Black Sea, first attested in Pi. *Pyth.* 4.203 (above), has been linked with common Iranian **axšaina-*, 'dark-coloured', which is represented by Avestan *axšaēna-*, Old Persian *axšaina-* (marking the turquoise) and various terms for 'blue', 'greenish' or 'dark gray' in related languages (R. Schmitt, in H. M. Ölberg *et al.* [eds.], *Sprachwissenschaftliche Forschungen. Festschrift für Johann Knobloch* ..., Innsbruck 1985, 409–12, who notes, however, the lack of first-hand evidence that the word was used of the Black Sea).[161] False etymology as 'inhospitable' then led to the euphemistic change into Εὔξεινος, probably indeed by Ionian settlers (Strabo 7.3.6), as the vocalism suggests (W. S. Allen, *CQ* 41 [1947], 88; cf. Bond on *HF* 410). Hecataeus may have been the earliest author to use that name (*FGrHist* 1 FF 18a, b).

Θρῆκα πορθμεύσων στρατόν: so L and most editors. But the final-consecutive infinitive πορθμεῦσαι (Q, Aldina) is attractive and has been adopted by Paley and Feickert (on 429). To the latter's argument of *lectio difficilior* and the fact that an analogous pair of variants can be found at *Med.* 1303 ἐμῶν δὲ παίδων ἦλθον ἐκσώσων βίον (codd. pler.: ἐκσῶσαι

---

159 Including at *Andr.* 1260–2 Ἀχιλλέα / ... δόμους ναίοντα νησιωτικούς / Λευκὴν κατ' ἀκτὴν ἐντὸς Ἀξένου πόρου, where Achilles' blessed existence contrasts with the 'inhospitable' sea. So also *IT* 438 Ἄξεινον κατὰ πόντον was 'corrected' to εὐξ- only by Triclinius, and at Pi. *Nem.* 4.49–50 ἐν δ' Εὐξείνῳ πελάγει φαενvὰν Ἀχιλεύς / νᾶσον West (*apud* Henry on 49) plausibly conjectured Ἀξένῳ. Cf. S. R. West, *G&R* 50 (2003), 157.

160 M. Vasmer, 'Osteuropäische Ortsnamen: I. Das Schwarze Meer', *Acta ...Universitatis Dorpatensis* B. 1.3 (1921), 3–6 = *Schriften zur slavischen Altertumskunde und Namenkunde* I, Berlin 1971, 103–5.

161 An English adaptation in W. Leschhorn *et al.* (eds.), *Hellas und der Griechische Osten ... Festschrift für Peter Robert Franke ...*, Saarbrücken 1996, 219–24 = *Selected Onomastic Writings*, New York 2000, 158–63. Cf. *Encyclopaedia Iranica* IV s.v. 'Black Sea', 310.

HOP²: [Π⁵])¹⁶² one may add that πορθμεῦσαι would account even better for πορθμεύσας in Δ (on its genesis from the future participle see 452–3n. with n. 168). The infinitive survives in *IT* 937–8 (Op.) Φοίβου κελευσθεὶς θεσφάτοις ἀφικόμην. / (Ιφ.) τί χρῆμα δρᾶσαι; (Elmsley: δράσειν L: δράσων idem Elmsley) and *Phaeth.* 97–8 Diggle = E. fr. 773.53–4 λισσομένα προσέβαν ὑμέναιον ἀεῖσαι / φίλον (cf. KG II 16–17, SD 362, Diggle, *Euripidea*, 324).

430–1. 'There the spear drew thick streams of Scythian blood, (to run) into the ground, and Thracian gore mixed up with it.'

This grim depiction of the battle was clearly influenced by the Ghost of Darius' prophecy of Plataea at *Pers.* 816–17 τόσος γὰρ ἔσται πελανὸς αἱματοσφαγής / πρὸς γῇ Πλαταιῶν Δωρίδος λόγχης ὕπο. But our poet supplanted the unique and not universally transmitted αἱματοσφαγής (v.l. αἱματοσταγής – but see Garvie on 816–17) with the more familiar and metrically easier αἱματηρός, which qualifies πελανός in the otherwise unrelated *Alc.* 850–1 (Heracles of Death drinking sacrificial blood) ἢν δ' οὖν ἁμάρτω τῆσδ' ἄγρας καὶ μὴ μόλῃ / πρὸς αἱματηρὸν πελανόν. The result of this 'non-slavish' form of borrowing (Fraenkel, *Rev.* 232; cf. Introduction, 35–6) still sounds disproportionate for Rhesus' peripheral war (388–453n.).

ἔνθ': Like its temporal counterpart in 930, this marks a new development in the tale and so is demonstrative rather than relative. The usage is rare outside epic (LSJ s.v. ἔνθα I 1, 2). Certainly in drama only A. *Suppl.* 30–6 ἀρσενοπληθῆ δ' ἑσμὸν ὑβριστὴν Αἰγυπτογενῆ ... ξὺν ὄχῳ ταχυήρει / πέμψατε πόντονδ' · ἔνθα δὲ λαίλαπι χειμωνοτύπῳ, / ... ὄλοιντο, although *Andr.* 21 and *Phoen.* 657 (at the beginning of a choral antistrophe) can hardly be different. See FJW on A. *Suppl.* 33.

αἱματηρὸς πελανός: Apart from *Alc.* 850–1 (above), cf. *IT* 300 ὥσθ' αἱματηρὸν πέλαγος ἐξανθεῖν ἁλός, with predicative αἱματηρόν and the near-homophone πέλαγος at the same metrical position. πελανός can be 'any thick liquid substance' (LSJ s.v. I) and is applied to blood also in *Eum.* 265 ἐρυθρὸν ... πελανόν (where, as in *Alcestis*, the ritual connotation is important). It is a favourite word of Aeschylus and Euripides (Fraenkel on *Ag.* 96, Parker on *Alc.* 851).

Θρῇξ τε συμμιγὴς φόνος: O alone has φόνος here. On the basis of VΛ's φόνῳ, Matthiae (VIII [1824], 23, on 428) wrote Θρηκὶ συμμιγὴς φόνῳ. But Θρῇξ τε is much less likely to have arisen by anticipation

---

162 In *Phil.* 645–6 ἀλλ' εἰ δοκεῖ, χωρῶμεν, ἔνδοθεν λαβών / ὅτου σε χρεία καὶ πόθος μάλιστ' ἔχει the sequence of a plural verb and singular participle should probably be kept (Ll-J/W, *Sophoclea*, 193–4; cf. Sommerstein on *Eum.* 142, Dunbar on Ar. *Av.* 202–4). Page's λαβεῖν for λαβών (*PCPS* n.s. 6 [1960], 51) at any rate would destroy the reference of ἀλλ' ... χωρῶμεν to the departure from Lemnos discussed before.

(following λόγχῃ especially) than φόνῳ as a dative falsely supplied with συμμιγής (cf. *Sept.* 739–40 ὦ πόνοι δόμων / νέοι παλαιοῖσι συμμιγεῖς κακοῖς, S. fr. 398.3, Antiph. fr. 55.7–8 *PCG*).

In classical Greek συμμιγής is restricted 'to poets and poetic prose' (Dunbar on Ar. *Av.* 771–2).

432–3. τοι serves to emphasise the truth of what Rhesus has just explained. If translated at all, parenthetic 'you (must) know' would convey the point (*GP* 537–40).

πέδον / Τροίας: a 'Euripidean' juncture (*Andr.* 11, 58, *Or.* 522). Sophocles has Τροίας πεδία / -ίον five times in *Philoctetes* (920, 1297, 1332, 1376, 1435). Also *Hec.* 140 Τροίας πεδίων.

434–42. Nearly the whole long sentence hinges on ἥκω as the main verb: Rhesus negotiated all obstacles as quickly as possible and now 'has come'.

434–5. 'But when I had sacked them, having taken their children as hostages and set an annual tribute to bring to my home …'

τῶνδ' resumes the object of ἔπερσα (i.e. the Scythians), which has to be supplied from the context. For this 'anaphoric' use of ὅδε (rare in prose) cf. e.g. *Sept.* 424, *PV* 904, *Ai.* 28, *Hec.* 427 (KG I 646–7, SD 209).

ὁμηρεύσας: transitive, 'to take as a hostage', only here (cf. 360–2a n.), though Aen. Tact. 10.23 has the middle in the sense 'give hostages'. It is also our sole poetic attestation of the verb, save for *Ba.* 296–7 ὅτι θεᾷ θεός (Dionysus) / Ἥρᾳ ποθ' ὠμήρευσε (with Dodds) and Antiph. fr. 115.2 *PCG* (cf. Fraenkel, *Rev.* 234). The noun ὅμηρος is found in *Alc.* 870, *Or.* 1189, *Ba.* 293, Ar. *Ach.* 327 and *Lys.* 244.

The purpose of the hostages was to ensure that the Scythians accepted submission (Σ^V *Rh.* 434 [II 338.20–1 Schwartz = 100 Merro]) and paid their annual tribute. Similarly e.g. Thuc. 1.108.3, 1.115.3, 3.90.4 and, in general, M. Amit, *RFIC* 98 (1970), 129–47, Olson on Ar. *Ach.* 326–7.

τάξας ἔτειον δασμὸν … φέρειν follows in asyndeton to mark the rapid sequence of events (Feickert on 435). Lenting's τάξας <τ'> (*Animadversiones*, 74) would spoil that effect.

Unlike φόρος for 'tribute, payment' (LSJ s.v. 1, 2), δασμός has a poetic heritage from epic and elegiac 'division' (< *δατ-σμος < δατέομαι: *Il.* 1.166, Hes. *Th.* 425, *h.Cer.* 86, 'Thgn.' 678) to 'tribute' in *OT* 36, *OC* 635 and S. fr. 730c.15. Of prose authors Xenophon alone made widespread use of the word. In particular see *An.* 5.5.10 διὸ καὶ δασμὸν ἡμῖν φέρουσιν οὗτοι τεταγμένον and *Cyr.* 8.6.8 δασμοὺς μέντοι συνέταξεν ἀποφέρειν καὶ τούτους.

The relative infrequency of δασμός suggests that Parth. *Erot. Path.* 36.1 (quoted in 426–42n.) goes back to our passage instead of representing a separate tradition. 'But Parthenius speaks in very unspecific terms, and makes Rhesus sound like a second Achilles, winning over cities to his side before he joins the Greeks at Troy' (Lightfoot, *Parthenius*, 555–6).

436–7. In addition to Xerxes' return to Persia (388–453n.), we are reminded here of his fateful 'yoking' of the Hellespont at *Pers.* 65–72, 108–13, 721–4, 736–8 and 745–50 (cf. Hdt. 7.33–6, 8.117.1, 9.114.1). Darius I had the Bosporus bridged to bring his army across to Scythia (Hdt. 4.83–9).

ἥκω: 434–42n.

Πόντιον στόμα was a regular periphrasis for the Bosporus. Cf. e.g. *Pers.* 879 στόμωμα Πόντου, Pi. *Pyth.* 4.203 ἐπ' Ἀξείνου στόμα, Hdt. 4.81.3 ἐπὶ στόματι τοῦ Πόντου, 4.85.3, Thuc. 4.75.2, A. R. 1.2, 4.1002 (Gow on Theoc. 22.28).

τὰ δ' ἄλλα ... γῆς ... ὁρίσματα: 'the other territories', as in *Hec.* 16 ἕως μὲν οὖν γῆς ὄρθ' ἔκειθ' ὁρίσματα (Troy and the Troad) and *Tro.* 375 οὐ γῆς ὅρι' ἀποστερούμενοι. 'Words meaning 'boundaries' ... are commonly used with a gen[itive] of a country in contexts of leaving or entering ...; since in these contexts ὅροι χώρας differs little from χώρα, it was no long step to treating it as an equivalent of χώρα in any context' (Barrett on *Hipp.* 1158–9 γῆς τέρμονας Τροζηνίας). So also *Hipp.* 1459 ὦ κλείν' Ἀφαίας Παλλάδος θ' ὁρίσματα (Ἀφαίας Fitton: ἀθῆναι vel ἀθηνῶν codd.) and properly *Andr.* 968 ὃς πρὶν τὰ Τροίας ἐσβαλεῖν ὁρίσματα.

438–9. '... no deep draughts on my part, as you loudly claim, nor resting on beds in all-golden palaces ...'

The syntactic structure of Rhesus' reply to 418–19 recalls *Med.* 555–7 (Jason to Medea) οὐχ, ᾗ σὺ κνίζῃ, σὸν μὲν ἐχθαίρων λέχος / ... / οὐδ' εἰς ἅμιλλαν πολύτεκνον σπουδὴν ἔχων (Ritchie 244–5; cf. 388–453, 440–2nn.). But it presents a very harsh anacoluthon, in which the expected participle (δεξιούμενος from 419) is omitted and its object transferred to the parenthesis ὡς σὺ κομπεῖς. Attempts to posit a lacuna after 438 (Vater on 425) or otherwise to emend the text have failed,[163] so that we are left with the assumption that '[t]he anacoluthon ... is authorial' (Liapis, 'Notes', 73).

A closer parallel than *Ba.* 683–8 ηὗδον δὲ πᾶσαι σώμασιν παρειμέναι / ... 686 ... οὐχ ὡς σὺ φῄς / ᾠνωμένας κρατῆρι καὶ λωτοῦ ψόφῳ / θηρᾶν καθ' ὕλην Κύπριν ἠρημωμένας (cited by Porter), where

---

[163] See Wecklein, *Appendix*, 51 and Liapis, 'Notes', 72–3. The best proposal is Musgrave's ἑλκύσας for τὰς ἐμάς (on 438), on the analogy of *Cyc.* 417 ... ἄμυστιν ἑλκύσας and indeed the *Auge* fragment in Σ^V *Rh.* 419 (418b–19n. with n. 154). But the corruption would be difficult to explain. With its contemptuous undertone (below), τὰς ἐμάς does not look like a gloss (for glossing with possessive pronouns see M. L. West, *BICS* 26 [1979], 107 and *BICS* 31 [1984], 186).

the accusative and infinitive follows more easily on the verb of speaking (cf. Bruhn, *Anhang*, § 176, Jebb on *Tr.* 1238–9), is Theoc. 12.12–14 δίω δή τινε τώδε μετὰ προτέροισι γενέσθην / φῶθ', ὁ μὲν εἴσπνηλος ('lover'), φαίη χ' Ὠμυκλαϊάζων, / τὸν δ' ἕτερον πάλιν, ὥς κεν ὁ Θεσσαλὸς εἴποι, ἀίτην ('beloved'). There the apposition has been 'attracted' into the second parenthesis to produce a formally identical result.

ὡς σὺ κομπεῖς: For the exact phrase cf. *Rh.* 875–6 (n.) ὄλοιθ' ὁ δράσας· οὐ γὰρ †εἰς σὲ τείνεται† / γλῶσσ', ὡς σὺ κομπεῖς ... and *Or.* 570–1 δράσας δ' ἐγώ / δείν', ὡς σὺ κομπεῖς, τόνδ' ἔπαυσα τὸν νόμον.[164] Porter (on 438) does well to distinguish our passages from the regular (metaphorical) sense of κομπέω, 'to brag, boast' (LSJ s.v. II). Applied to human speech, the original 'din' or 'clash' (LSJ s.v. I) just as easily covered a loud proclamation or complaint.

The verb has a direct object also at *PV* 947 ... οὕστινας κομπεῖς γάμους (LSJ s.v. II 2).

τὰς ἐμὰς ἀμύστιδας: 418b–19n. The plural was implied in 419 πύκνην ἄμυστιν. With the possessive pronoun, however, it also reflects Hector's contempt (cf. 866–7n.).

ἐν ζαχρύσοις δώμασιν: 370–2a n. (τὰν ζάχρυσον ... πέλταν). Golden halls are a standard symbol of excessive (non-Greek) luxury: e.g. *Pers.* 3–4 καὶ τῶν ἀφνεῶν καὶ πολυχρύσων ἑδράνων φύλακες, 159 χρυσεοστόλμους δόμους, *Hel.* 928 Φρυγῶν ... πολυχρύσους δόμους (Hall, *Inventing the Barbarian*, 80–1, 127–8). In a wholly 'barbarian' context they are set against the austerity of the Trojan field (416–18a n.).

440–2. 'No, I know what frozen blasts press heavily upon the Thracian sea and the Paeonians, having sleeplessly endured them in this cloak.'

'Thrace was notorious for its snow and harsh winters' (Olson on Ar. *Ach.* 138–40).[165] For Rhesus' justification, which is added in the same way as that of Jason at *Med.* 559–65 ἀλλ' ὡς ... (388–453, 438–9nn.), our poet had again recourse to *Persians* – to produce a 'mosaic passage' similar to 430–1 (n.). The adjective κρυσταλλόπηκτος is unique, like its parallel form κρυσταλλοπήξ, applied to the Strymon in *Pers.* 500–1 (cf. 388–453n.). By contrast, ἐπεζάρει (below) occurs elsewhere only in the much later *Phoen.* 45–6 ... ὡς δ' ἐπεζάρει / Σφὶγξ ἁρπαγαῖσι πόλιν ... (at the same verse position), while πορπάματα, 'cloak held by a clasp (πόρπη)' is restricted to the ends of E. *El.* 820 and *HF* 959. On the technique of supplementing a contextual echo with external material see

---

[164] *Or.* 564–71 were deleted by Kovacs (*Euripidea Tertia*, 88–90). Yet δείν' at least could refer to Tyndareus' entire speech (Di Benedetto on 571).

[165] In Ar. *Ach.* 136–9 Theoros excuses his long absence in Thrace with bad weather conditions. The whole country was covered†snow and the rivers had frozen over.

Introduction, 35–6, Fraenkel, *Rev.* 231, 233 and, for our lines in particular, A. Fries, *CQ* n.s. 60 (2010), 346–7 with nn. 11, 12.

It would be possible (as some scholars do) to connect τλάς predicatively with οἶδα: 'No, I know that such frozen blasts as press heavily upon the Thracian sea ... I have sleeplessly endured in this cloak' (KG II 50–2, SD 394; cf. G. Pace, *Lexis* 27 [2009], 183–4, 185). But the circumstantial participle makes the statement more intense.

πόντον Θρήκιον (Λ: πόντιον Δ) seems to refer to the northern Aegean (rather than the Black Sea), which bore this designation from Homer on: *Il.* 23.229–30 οἳ δ' ἄνεμοι πάλιν αὖτις ἔβαν οἶκόνδε νέεσθαι / Θρηΐκιον κατὰ πόντον (i.e. Boreas and Zephyros, who blow from Thrace: *Il.* 9.4–6), Hdt. 7.176.1 ἐκ τοῦ πελάγεος τοῦ Θρηκίου. This also accords better with the mention of the Paeonians, whose land lies west of Mt. Pangaeus. So Rhesus generally speaks of the hardships of his journey now. Cf. Liapis on 440–2.

φυσήματα / κρυσταλλόπηκτα corresponds to 417 ψυχρὰν ἄησιν. The epithet, 'congealed to ice, frozen', is used here with the same 'looseness of expression' as English speaks of '*frozen* blasts' (Porter on 441), unless, as a compound verbal adjective, it was meant to bear the causative sense 'making freeze over' (Feickert on 441, Liapis on 440–2 [p. 189]). Kirchhoff's κρυσταλλόπηκτον or -πῆγα (I [1855], 556, on 430) would resolve the ambiguity and bring the expression even closer to *Pers.* 500–1 (above). But they leave the Paeonians strangely unaffected (except by ordinary storms) and weaken the 'competition' for the greatest discomfort in the field.

φυσήματα of strong winds is paralleled at *Tro.* 78–9 καὶ Ζεὺς μὲν ὄμβρον καὶ χάλαζαν ἄσπετον / πέμψει δνοφώδη τ' αἰθέρος φυσήματα and probably E. fr. 370.40 (*Erechtheus*) φόνια φυσήματ' (with Cropp). Yet with πόντον preceding in the same line we also get a phonetic similarity to the foaming sea at *Hipp.* 1211 ... ποντίῳ φυσήματι. Euripides alone of the other tragedians has the word.

Παίονάς τ': 408–10a n. The upper-case initial and correct accentuation were given in the Aldine (παιόνας Ω)

ἐπεζάρει is J. J. Scaliger's restoration of the MSS' non-existent ἐπεζάτει (cf. C. Collard *CQ* n.s. 24 [1974], 249), which gains support from Σ^VQ *Rh.* 441 (II 338.23 Schwartz ~ 101 Merro) ἐπεβάρει, ἔβλαπτεν (ἔβλαπτεν om. Q) and Hsch. ε 4304 Latte ἐπεζάρει· ἐπεβάρει, ἐπέκειτο AS. ἐπεκράτει (where the *codex unicus* of Hesychius also seems to give -ζάτει). The true meaning and etymology of the verb are obscure. Apart from *Phoen.* 45–6 (above), it is attested in Σ *Od.* 22.9–12 (II 707.4–5 Dindorf) ἄφνω συνέβη χρῆμα συὸς μεγάλου ἐπιζαρῆσαι (v.l. ἐπιβαρῆσαι) τοῖς τοῦ Ἀγκαίου χωρίοις and, taken from some ancient text, the lemma of Hsch. ε 4303 Latte (= Phot. ε 1390 Theodoridis) ἐπεζάρηκεν. 'Fall upon' or 'oppress' is clearly how authors and grammarians understood the word. The statement in Eust. 381.19–20 and 909.27–8 that it was Arcadian is not supported by the sound-patterns of this dialect (cf. Mastronarde on *Phoen.* 45).

ξὺν τοῖσδ' ... πορπάμασιν probably refers to the Thracian cloak called ζειρά (312–13n.), which Rhesus may be wearing on top of his armour (Liapis on 440–2 [p. 190]).

Porson (*Appendix* II, in J. Toup, *Emendationes in Suidam et Hesychium* ... IV, Oxford ²1790, 439–40; cf. G. Pace, *Lexis* 27 [2009], 185–6) corrected the paradosis πορπήμασιν (Λ) and -πάσμ- (Δ). πορπάματα (always plural) belongs to the derivatives of feminine a-stem nouns (πόρπη) which show Doric vocalisation also in spoken verse (Nauck, *Euripideische Studien* II, 175, Björck, *Alpha Impurum*, 139–42, *Rh.* 513b–15n.). Thus the unanimous tradition at E. *El.* 820 and *HF* 959, as well as *PV* 61 πόρπασον and 141 προσπορπατός.

For ξύν (σύν) of clothing worn cf. Thuc. 2.70.3 and Xen. *An.* 4.5.33 (LSJ s.v. σύν A 4, KG I 466, SD 489). The old Attic ξύν (Λ) should be accepted on the premise that the MSS would hardly have replaced the later form (Barrett on *Hipp.* 40). Contrary to the evidence of inscriptions, from which ξυν(-) had all but disappeared by 400 BC (Threatte I 553–4, II 768), *Rhesus* has an equal number of ξυν(-) and συν(-) in metrically indifferent positions. Especially telling is the variable use as a preposition (148, 468 σύν, 358, 471 ξύν),[166] since ξυν- survived longer in literary texts.

443. The first verse-half is almost identical to Ar. *Eccl.* 381 ἀλλ' ὕστερος νῦν ἦλθον, ὥστ' αἰσχύνομαι (another reason to leave that line as it is transmitted in most MSS?). It may also have occurred in lost tragedies.

ἀλλ': in opposition to the preceding excuse, and so partly assentient (cf. *GP* 16–20): 'But I *did* come late ...'

ὕστερος: Cobet (*Mnemosyne* 11 [1862], 435–6) for ὕστερον (ΩgV, *Chr. Pat.* 1728). See 411b–12n. At Ar. *Eccl.* 381 (above) one MS also has ὕστερον.

ἐν καιρῷ: 10, 52nn. Liapis favours ἐς καιρόν (after *Chr. Pat.* 1728 εἰς καιρόν) because '[t]ragic idiom seems to prefer ἐς καιρόν after verbs of motion' ('Notes', 73). However, the passages he cites (*Ai.* 1168–9 καὶ μὴν ἐς αὐτὸν καιρὸν οἵδε πλησίοι / πάρεισιν, *Hipp.* 899–900, *Hec.* 665–6, *HF* 701, *Hel.* 1081 ἐς καιρὸν ἦλθε, τότε δ' ἄκαιρ' ἀπώλλυτο, *Phoen.* 106, *Or.* 384, *Rh.* 52) all concern a new and/or urgent situation, often marking the entry of the character who has come 'in time' to learn

---

[166] In 471 the MSS again disagree (ξὺν Λ: σὺν Δ). Cf. 59 (59–60a n.) †ξυνέσχον† (συν- L), 684, 763.

and possibly act on it. Rhesus, by contrast, claims to have arrived 'at the right time' to end a war that has already lasted for ten years (444–50). The distinction seems to be less pronounced between ἐς δέον (*OT* 1416, *Ant.* 386, *Alc.* 1101) and temporal ἐν δέοντι (*Alc.* 817, *Or.* 211–12, E. fr. 727c.39), more so again between εἰς καλόν and ἐν καλῷ (cf. Stevens, *CEE* 28).

If the above distinction is right, εἰς καιρόν does not suit *Chr. Pat.* 1728 either. It probably stems from a MS of *Rhesus* where ἐν καιρῷ had been corrupted to the commoner phrase.

444. αἰχμάζεις: Unlike αἰχμή, the verb is rare. Properly 'to throw the spear' (*Il.* 4.324), it acquired the general sense of 'fight': *Pers.* 755–6 τὸν δ' ἀνανδρίας ὕπο / ἔνδον αἰχμάζειν ('play the warrior at home'), *Ai.* 97, *Tr.* 355 and absolute also Men. *Sam.* 628–9 εἰς Βάκτρα ποι / ἢ Καρίαν διέτριβον αἰχμάζων ἐκεῖ. Cf. Sideras, *Aeschylus Homericus*, 76.

445b–6. '… day after day you cast the dice in war against the Argives.'

Our poet liked the dicing metaphor (154–5, 182–3nn.). Here cf. especially E. *Suppl.* 329–31 Κάδμου θ' ὁρῶσα λαὸν εὖ πεπραγότα / ἔτ' αὐτὸν ἄλλα βλήματ' ἐν κύβοις βαλεῖν / πέποιθ' (with Collard on 330–1a) and *Hell. Oxy.* 4.2 Chambers (below).

ἡμέραν δ' ἐξ ἡμέρας occurs at the same position in Henioch. fr. 5.13 *PCG*. Similarly Hdt. 9.8.1 ἐξ ἡμέρης ἐς ἡμέρην and A. R. 1.861 εἰς ἦμαρ … ἐξ ἤματος. 'Such phrases convey in all Greek literature the notion of succession, continuity' (Headlam on Herod. 5.85 ἑορτὴν ἐξ ἑορτῆς; cf. Gow on Theoc. 18.15, Gygli-Wyss, *Polyptoton*, 69–71). It should thus be excluded from Fraenkel's list of possible Ionisms (*Rev.* 239).

ῥίπτεις … τὸν πρὸς Ἀργείους Ἄρη: Sallier's ῥίπτεις (*Histoire de l'Académie royale des inscriptions et belles-lettres* 5 [1729], 125) is correct. With the transmitted πίπτεις (which may have been suggested by the 'fall' of dice) Rhesus' comment would be intolerably negative (Liapis on 444–6) and the construction of κυβεύων unclear (LSJ s.v. II 1, Porter and Liapis take it as transitive. But at Antip. Sid. *Ep.* 32.13–14 and Mel. *Ep.* 15.2 Gow–Page *HE* the object is what is 'set at stake', which cannot well be said about 'the war against the Argives'. Hence Feickert's accusative of respect). In the reconstructed text we have an internal accusative ('cast a throw in war …'), as in 154–5 (n.) τόνδε κίνδυνον … / ῥίψας and the parallels given there. Absolute κυβεύων reinforces the notion of dicing. Cf. *Sept.* 414 (quoted in 182–3n.), where Ares himself casts the dice of war.

On Ἄρης by metonymy for war see LSJ s.v. II 1 (and cf. 239n.). Whatever the truth at *Il.* 5.909 παῦσασαι βροτολοιγὸν Ἄρην ἀνδροκτασιάων (with West's apparatus), Ἄρη (OQ) is the correct accusative in Attic and

Ἄρην (VL) a common error. This form, on the analogy of fourth-century and later -ην for -η in s-stem names (cf. Collard on E. *Suppl.* 928–9, Mastronarde on *Phoen.* 72), is never required by metre and appears to be absent from Attic inscriptions (LSJ s.v. Ἄρης I, Threatte II 274).

κυβεύων: our only tragic example of the verb, although S. fr. 947.2 has κυβευτής. In the context of war also *Hell. Oxy.* 4.2 Chambers Ἀθηναῖοι δὲ πυ | [θ]όμενοι τὰ περὶ τῆς μάχης τοῖς μὲν | [σ]τρατηγοῖς ὠργίζοντο καὶ χαλεπῶς εἶ | [χο]ν ὑπολαμβάνοντες προπετῶς αὐ | [το]ὺς ἀνελέσθαι τὸν κίνδ[υ]νον καὶ κυ | [βε]ῦσαι περὶ ὅλης τῆς πόλεως.

447–53. Without knowing it, Rhesus promises to fulfil the chorus' wish at 368–9, although they hardly expected him to succeed in one day. The boast probably reflects the *aristeia* Rhesus enjoyed before his death in Pindar's version of the myth (Introduction, 11–12, 595–641n.). The contradiction with his lengthy Scythian war (Valckenaer, *Diatribe*, 104–5) is likely to have passed unnoticed (Liapis on 447–9).

447–9a. φῶς ἐν ἡλίου: For φῶς (ἡλίου) = 'day' cf. *Pers.* 261 καὐτὸς δ᾽ ἀέλπτως νόστιμον βλέπω φάος – after the Odyssean formula ... νόστιμον ἦμαρ ἰδέσθαι / ἴδηαι (3.233, 5.220, 6.311, 8.466) and also conveying a sense of salvation (Garvie on *Pers.* 261). In other such tragic periphrases (330–1n.) the notion of day*light* remains stronger.

καταρκέσει: 'will be *fully* sufficient' (LSJ s.v.). The verb is very rare and in other drama found only at S. fr. 86.1 παῦσαι· καταρκεῖ τοῦδε κεκλῆσθαι πατρός.

πύργους: 390–1a n.

ναυστάθμοις ἐπεσπεσεῖν: 135b–6n. Δ's ναυστάθμους was an easy error between πύργους and Ἀχαιούς and given that ἐπεισπίπτω can also take the accusative, as at *HF* 34 ... τήνδ᾽ ἐπεσπεσὼν πόλιν. Liapis (on 447–9) seems too hasty in calling the dative 'prosaic' on account of that single tragic parallel. At *OC* 915, *Hec.* 1042 and *Ba.* 753 the verb stands absolute.

449b–50. θἠτέρᾳ: *sc.* ἡμέρᾳ. This form (found in *Chr. Pat.* 1732 cod. Vat. gr. 481) rather than Brunck's θατέρᾳ (*Euripidis tragoediae quatuor ...*, Strasbourg 1780, 372, on *Hipp.* 905) should be read for θ᾽ ἡτέρᾳ in Ω and the other MSS at *Chr. Pat.* 1732 (cf. Feickert on 449, Liapis on 449–50). In crasis of ἕτερος with the definite article Attic has ἅτερ- and θἅτερ- (from original ἅτερος: Schwyzer 401) in the masculine and neuter, while in the feminine (other than the nominative plural) only ἡτερ- and θἡτερ- are attested in inscriptions (Threatte I 431, II 345–7) and were declared correct by Pausanias the Atticist (θ 2 Erbse). Intermittent cases of feminine α-forms in 'classical' MSS (e.g. at *OT* 782, *Tr.* 272, *Hipp.* 894, Ar. *Ach.* 789, Henioch. fr. 5.16–17 *PCG* = Stob. 4.1.27) have no evidential value. In the later fourth century BC (it seems) θάτερος came to be seen as a legitimate alternative to ἕτερος, first in the masculine and neuter (Theophr. *Vent.* 53, Men. *Mis.* 164, fr. 491 *PCG* ὁ θάτερος, Lyc. 590, D. S. 14.22.5 τὸ δὲ θάτερον μέρος) and later also in the feminine (Luc. *Bacch.* 2, *JTr.* 11, *Icar.* 14, Hld. 1.2.2, 3.4.6). All three gender forms are common in late-antique and Byzantine Greek and could therefore have been introduced into our MSS (ἅτερος of three endings also occasionally appears). It follows that feminine ἅτερ- and θᾱτερ- should not be accepted in classical Attic texts, let alone be introduced against the tradition.

πρὸς οἶκον εἶμι: Cf. 368–9 ὦ φίλος, εἴθε μοι / ... πράξας τάδ' ἐς οἶκον ἔλθοις (447–53n.).

συντεμὼν τοὺς σοὺς πόνους: 'having cut short ...' Similarly S. fr. 941.16–17 πάντα τοι συντέμνεται / Κύπρις τὰ θνητῶν καὶ θεῶν βουλεύματα and, of a pregnancy, Hdt. 5.41.2 τοῦ χρόνου συντάμνοντος.

451. ὑμῶν δὲ μή τις ἀσπίδ' ἄρηται χερί: Cf. 488 (n.) μόνος μάχεσθαι πολεμίοις ... θέλω and, for the expression, 492 (n.) οὐκ ἔστ' ἐκείνῳ θοῦρον ἀντᾶραι δόρυ, 495 ... οὐ συναίρεται δόρυ. Of beginning a war e.g. *Hcld.* 313–14 καὶ μήποτ' ἐς γῆν ἐχθρὸν αἴρεσθαι δόρυ / μέμνησθέ μοι τήνδ', *Phoen.* 433–4, *Ba.* 788–9.

L. Dindorf (I [1825], 490 ~ W. Dindorf, III.2 [1840], 607) rightly wrote ἄρηται, since we do not want the durative aspect of Q's αἰρέτω (cf. Liapis, 'Notes', 74) and otherwise the aorist subjunctive is required in prohibitions (KG I 220, SD 315). On the corruption of ἀρ- into αἰρ- (V) or αἱρ- (OL) see 53–5n.

452–3. 'For I shall have the mightily proud Achaeans vanquished with my spear, latecomer though I am.'

†**ἔξω†** ... / **πέρσας:** The only way to understand the MSS text is as a case of ἔχω + aorist participle to express a permanent result (Feickert on 452).[167] This is otherwise unattested in the future (KG II 61–2, W. J. Aerts, *Periphrastica* ..., Amsterdam 1965, 128–60), but would lend a strong and effective conclusion to Rhesus' boasts.

Emendation in any case is difficult (cf. Liapis, 'Notes', 73–5). Nauck's ἥκω ... πέρσων (II[1] [1854], XXIII) presupposes a simple error by assimilation in πέρσας (after αὐχοῦντας in 452 or πέρσαντι in 448)[168] and the less easy corruption of ἥκω into ἔξω, but becomes somewhat tautologous with ... καίπερ ὕστερος μολών (though not intolerably so for our poet?). Kirchhoff's ἔγωγ' ἀρήξω, which would resemble the

---

167 He adduces Vater (on 439), who did not in fact advocate this solution. Hermann (*Opuscula* III, 304) had already refuted the idea that ἔχω could here mean 'stay, keep back' (LSJ s.v. (A) A II 9), on the ground that the Greeks were not attacking ('*Non enim cohibendi erant, qui non instabant*'). Cf. Liapis, 'Notes', 74.

168 Cf. *Rh.* 428–9 ἀξένου δ' ἀφικόμην / πόντου πρὸς ἀκτάς, Θρῇκα πορθμεύσων στρατόν (L: πορθμεύσας Δ), unless πορθμεῦσαι is to be read there (428b–9n.).

beginning of *Eum*. 232 ἐγὼ δ' ἀρήξω τὸν ἱκέτην τε ῥύσομαι, founders less on the absence of an explicit object[169] than on the fact that Rhesus does not merely want to 'succour' (Nauck, *Euripideische Studien* II, 174). Diggle (*apud* Jouan) and Kovacs (*Euripidea Tertia*, 147) independently proposed ἥξω ... πέρσας, which makes sense only if the main emphasis can fall onto the notion of the participle. This is not the case to judge by e.g. *Alc*. 488 κτανὼν ἄρ' ἥξεις ἢ θανὼν αὐτοῦ μενεῖς; *Hec*. 930–2, *Tro*. 460–1 and *Rh*. 156–7 καὶ πάντ' Ἀχαιῶν ἐκμαθὼν βουλεύματα / ἥξω (Liapis, 'Notes', 75). Of Diggle's other two suggestions, ἐξαρκέσω γὰρ ... πέρσας ('For I shall succour <you> by vanquishing ...') attracts the same doubts as Kirchhoff's reading, whereas ἀρκῶ (Holzner)[170] ... πορθεῖν is not only too far from the paradosis, but also ill accords with ... καίπερ ὕστερος μολών. Nothing is gained by deleting 452–3 with Herwerden (*RPh* 18 [1894], 84–5) or, better, 451–3 (451 could hardly end the speech on its own). The lines do not look like an addition, and one would still have to account for the text as it stands. If an interpolator could write ἔξω ... πέρσας, perhaps our poet could too.

τοὺς μέγ' αὐχοῦντας ... / ... Ἀχαιούς: Cf. *Hcld*. 353 εἰ σὺ μέγ' αὐχεῖς, E. fr. 1007 αὐχοῦσιν μέγα, *Andr*. 463 μηδὲν τόδ' αὔχει and also Xerxes at Hdt. 7.103.2 (of the Spartans willing to confront a Persian army ten times the size of their own) εἰ δὲ τοιοῦτοί τε ἐόντες καὶ μεγάθεα τοσοῦτοι ... αὐχέετε τοσοῦτον, ὅρα μὴ μάτην κόμπος ὁ λόγος οὗτος εἰρημένος ᾖ (Ritchie 211–12). For the meaning of αὐχέω (properly 'feel confident') see Fraenkel on *Ag*. 1497, Barrett on *Hipp*. 952–5 and Kannicht on *Hel*. 1366–8.

δορί (56–8n.) is to be construed with πέρσας rather than μέγ' αὐχοῦντας. Cf. *Rh*. 472 ... ἐκπέρσαι δορί and 478 ... πορθεῖν ... δορί.

καίπερ ὕστερος μολών: 411b–12, 443nn.

454–66. Impressed with Rhesus' words and appearance, the chorus sing a brief song of praise and exhortation. It is unusual not only for replacing the regular trimeter comment after an *agon* speech (388–526n.), but also, as Hermann (*Opuscula* III, 304, 308–9) demonstrated, for responding metrically with the sentries' own defence against the charge of laxity in 820–32 (n.).[171]

---

[169] At S. *El*. 1197 οὐδ' οὑπαρήξων οὐδ' ὁ κωλύσων πάρα; the dative object of οὑπαρήξων (i.e. Electra) has to be supplied from the preceding line.

[170] E. Holzner, *Studien zu Euripides*, Prague 1895, 108–9, whose πέρσων is an unidiomatic complement.

[171] This relationship between the stanzas has only ever been questioned by Pace (*QUCC* n.s. 65 [2000], 127–29, *Canti*, 41–3, 56–9) and Jouan (LXX, 48 n. 245, 74 n. 246), who 'with uncritical tolerance of [metrical and linguistic] anomalies' (Willink, 'Cantica', 33 = *Collected Papers*, 572) keep the MSS text and colometry in both 454–66 and 820–32.

The phenomenon of separated stanzas in drama has been discussed in 131–6 ~ 195–200n. In extant tragedy only *Hipp.* 362–72 ~ 669–79 with its intervening spoken passages, choral song (*Hipp.* 525–64) and semi-lyric *amoibaion* (*Hipp.* 565–600) can be compared to the present case. Yet it has often been felt (e.g. by Wilamowitz, *GV* 587, Ritchie 331, 332–3) that the extraordinary interval of 354 lines in this short play and the fact that it includes *two* lyric pieces (527–64, 675–82) as well as the temporary absence of the chorus (565–674) set *Rhesus* apart from anything known in Greek drama.

In both its structure and language the strophe echoes the preceding 'Hymn to Rhesus' (342–79), but is altogether more cautious in tone (cf. Klyve on 388–526 [p. 261]). Instead of invoking Adrasteia, as in 342–3 (342–5, 342–3nn.), the chorus pray that her father Zeus may not be angered by Rhesus' boastful speech (455b–7n.). The following accolade (458–63) repeats the desired confrontation with Achilles and other, unnamed warriors (370–9), though partly in rhetorical questions (with a potential optative) rather than imperatives and statements in the future indicative (cf. 342–79n.). Only the final wish (464–6) corresponds exactly to 368–9 (n.).

It appears, therefore, that for all their admiration the chorus are somewhat sceptical of Rhesus' ambitions (447–53) or, in other words, our poet felt that such excessive self-praise could not go unrestrained (just as Hector provides a corrective in the dialogue to come). Even if we are to take Rhesus seriously and he will fall victim only to divine whim (342–79, 388–526nn.), our sense of foreboding is further heightened by this ode.

Metre

454–66 ~ 820–32. With the analysis and colometry adopted here we get a slightly unusual combination of dochmiacs with larger stretches of dactylo-epitrite metres (cf. Wilamowitz, *GV* 587). Yet the transition is made elegantly through the trimeter in 457 ~ 823 (beginning like a dochmiac of the form $-\cup\cup-\cup-$), a common 'enoplian' colon (458/824n.) and the lecythion (= E) at 459 ~ 825. Towards the end the rhythm returns to the earlier iambo-choriambics (466/832n.).

454	820	⏑⏑⏑–∣	˜cr ∣
455		⏑⏑⏑– ∣ ⏑– ∣ ⏑⏑⏑–⏑– ∣	2δ ∣
821		†⏑⏑⏑– ∣ ⏑⏑–† ∣ ⏑⏑⏑–⏑– ∣	
456	822	⏑⏑ ⁞ ⏑⏑⏑ ∣ ⏑⏑–∥	˜δ vel kδ ? ∥
457	823	–⏑⏑ ∣ –⏑–⏑–⏑ ⁞ –– ∣	cho ia ia͜ ∣
458	824	⏑⏑–⏑⏑ ∣ –⏑–⏑–∥	'enopl.' ∥

292   Commentary

459	825	– ⏑ – ⏑ ¦ – ⏑ – ¦	*lec* (= *E*) ¦
460	826	– – ⏑ ⏑ – ⏑ ⏑ – | – – |	– *D* | – – |
461–2	827	– – | ⏑ ⏑ – ⏑ ⏑ – ⏒ – ⏑ – – ||	– *D* ⌣ *e* – ||
463		– ⏒ – ⏑ ⏑ – – ||	*D* (contr.) – ||
828		†⏑ – ⏑ – –†||	
464	829	– ⏑ ⏑ – | ⏑ ⏑ – ⏑ |	*D* ⏑ |
465	830–1	– ⏑ – ⏑ – | ⏑ – | ⏑⏑ ⏑ – |	*lec* | ⌣*cr* (= *E* | ⌣*e*) |
466	832	– ⏑ | ⏑ – ⏑ – ⏑ – – – |||	*cho ia* ˰*ia*˰ |||

Notes

454/820   ἰώ ἰώ responding with itself could also be *extra metrum*. But the resolved cretic neatly foreshadows the opening rhythm of the following verse.

455/821   For a possible solution to the textual problems and lack of response see 821–3n.

456/822   Despite Conomis (*Hermes* 92 [1964], 30), the perfect correspondence, which even extends to word-ends, would seem to indicate that both lines are basically sound (for a textual interpretation of 822 see 821–3n.). The sequence ⏑ ⏑ ⏑ ⏑ ⏑ ⏑ ⏑ – is further attested among (iambo-)dochmiacs at *Eum.* 158 ~ 165, *HF* 1058 ἀδύνατ' ἀδύνατά μοι and *Tro.* 311 μακάριος ὁ γαμέτας (~ 328 τυχαῖς. ὁ χορὸς ὅσιος) and usually interpreted as a resolved *dochmius Kaibelianus*.[172] Alternatively, and in view of the word-divisions here, one could regard the colon as a dochmiac with two shorts for initial (or, at *Tro.* 311, second) *anceps* (Wilamowitz, *GV* 405, 588, L. P. E. Parker, *CQ* n.s. 18 [1968], 261 n. 3, *Songs*, 66). But other possible examples of ⌣δ in tragedy are rare, and many scholars hesitate to admit it at all (especially Barrett, Add. on *Hipp.* 670 [p. 434], Diggle, *Euripidea*, 100–1, 167 with n. 28, 315). A well-balanced, if sceptical, record is given by R. Renehan, *CPh* 87 (1992), 344–6, and individual passages are defended by Bond on *HF* 878, Kannicht on *Hel.* 670 ('Metrik' [p. 180]), 670–1 and Dodds on *Ba.* 997–1001.

458/824   This colon, later named 'cyrenaic', also occurs in (iambo-) dochmiac settings at E. *El.* 586, 588, *HF* 1188, *Ion* 1448 and *Phaeth.* 276

---

[172] Diggle (in his respective apparatuses) offers to turn *HF* 1058 into an ithyphallic (ἀδύνατ' ἀδύνατ'· οἴμοι) and *Tro.* 311 ~ 328 into 2ia (<⏑ –> μακάριος ὁ γαμέτας ~ τυχαῖς. ὁ χορὸς ὅσιος <ὅσιος>), but does not quote *Eum.* 158 ~ 165. At *Sept.* 782 ~ 789 the length appears in an iambo-dactylic context, and another analysis than as dochmiac may be desired (Hutchinson on 720–91 [pp. 162–3], though his scansion of 781–2 ~ 788–9 as a short form of the 'archilochian' does not appeal either).

Diggle = E. fr. 781.66.[173] Elsewhere Euripides has the 'dragged' version
⏑ ⏑ – ⏑ ⏑ – ⏑ – – – (*Ion* 1494, *Hel.* 657, 680, 681, *Hyps.* fr. 64.94 Bond = E. fr. 759a.1615; cf. *Tr.* 647 ~ 655, and see Dale, *LM²* 171, Diggle, *Euripidea*, 107, 393).

460–2/826–7 Wilamowitz' colometry (*GV* 587–8), which in the strophe also happens to be that of the MSS, has found favour with several scholars, most recently Liapis (on 454–66 'Metre' [p. 196]). At the small cost of transposing the name Ἀχιλ(λ)εύς in 461 (461–3n.), he obtained straightforward dactylo-epitrites (for – *D* | – – | cf. Pi. *Pyth.* 1.2, Ar. *Eccl.* 576b and, in general, 527–64 'Metre' 527–8/546–7n.), corresponding rhetorical and metrical break in strophe and antistrophe and more prominent positions for the verbal echo πῶς μοι ~ μή μοι (below) and the anaphora πῶς μοι ... / πῶς δ' ... in 461–2. Compared to the traditional division of e.g. Wecklein, Murray, Diggle and Kovacs (460–1 ... σέθεν κρείσσω. πῶς μοι ‖ Ἀχιλεὺς ... δύναιτο ~ 826–7 ... παγάς· μή μοι ‖ κότον ... θῆς ...), this also removes one period-end after the long verse 460 ~ 826 (– *D²* (contr.) | – – ‖?).

463/828 Our poet was fond of contracted *D*-cola. Cf. 535 ~ 554 (*D* – |) and 27 ~ 45, 899 ~ 910 (*D²*). The antistrophe here is incurably corrupt (827–8n.).

466/832 A rare clausular colon, which otherwise is found only at *HF* 1024 (again in juxtaposition to dochmiacs) and has variously been interpreted as *cho ia* ‸*ia*‸ or δ + ⏑ – – – (Diggle, *Euripidea*, 107–8, 395 with n. 108, 516). Yet here, where the preceding line is better taken as *lec* | ⁓*cr* (= *E* | ⁓*e*) than *hδ* | δ and – ⏑ ⏑ – ⏑ – ⏑ – – – may be seen to echo 457 ~ 823 (*cho ia ia*‸), the iambo-choriambic analysis seems preferable.

The responsion between 454–66 and 820–32, at least musically recognisable over the long distance, is underlined with a series of both strict and more liberal 'isometric echoes': 454 = 820 ἰὼ ἰώ, 455 φίλα ... φίλος ~ 821 †μέγας ... μέγας†, 457 Ζεὺς θέλοι ἀμφὶ σοῖς λόγοισιν εἴργειν ~ 823 ἄγγελος ἦλθον ἀμφὶ ναῦς πῦρ' αἴθειν (sentence structure), 459 οὔτε ... οὔτε ~ 825 οὔτ' ... οὔτ', 461 (460) πῶς μοι ~ 827 (826) μή μοι, 464 εἰ γάρ ~ 829 εἰ δέ. Among the other divided songs in tragedy this is proportionally matched only by *Rh.* 131–6 ~ 195–200 (n.). On such verbal correspondences in general see Bond on *HF* 763 ff. and West, *GM* 5 (with further literature).

---

173 Diggle (*TrGFS*) creates two further specimens at *Hyps.* 276 (fr. 64 ii.91 Bond = E. fr. 759a.1612) and *Antiope* V.54a ἀλαλάζεται̣[ἁ στ]έγα (= E. fr. 223.83 ἀλαλάζεται̣[στ]έγα [suppl. Blass] with Kannicht's apparatus). A form with contracted first biceps appears to be in evidence at *Ai.* 399 ~ 416 (Ritchie 310 with n. 2, Finglass on *Ai.* 348–429 [p. 240]).

455a. φίλα θροεῖς: 'You speak welcome words.' Cf. e.g. *Tr.* 373 ... εἰ δὲ μὴ λέγω φίλα, *Hec.* 517, E. *Suppl.* 634, 643, Hdt. 7.104.1 οὐ φίλα τοι ἐρέω.

φίλος Διόθεν εἶ: For the concept of a 'god-sent deliverer' – here from the supreme patron deity of Troy – Liapis (on 455) compares *Cho.* 939–41 ἔλασε δ' εἰς τὸ πᾶν / ὁ πυθόχρηστος φυγάς / θεόθεν εὖ φραδαῖσιν ὡρμημένος (the chorus after Orestes' killing of Aegisthus and Clytaemestra), which presumably inspired S. *El.* 69–70 (Orestes) σοῦ γὰρ ἔρχομαι / δίκῃ καθαρτὴς πρὸς θεῶν ὡρμημένος.

455b–7. 'Only may Zeus supreme wish to keep away irresistible resentment concerning your words.'

On the relationship of this invocation to that in 342–3 see 454–66n. The closest literary precedent is Pi. *Ol.* 13.24–6 ὕπατ' εὐρὺ ἀνάσσων / Ὀλυμπίας, ἀφθόνητος ἔπεσσιν / γένοιο χρόνον ἅπαντα, Ζεῦ πάτερ.

Nothing has been lost after 455–7, as Wilamowitz (*GV* 587–8) and Zanetto (ed. *Rhesus*, 33, 68, *Ciclope, Reso*, 149 n. 64) presumed. Instead, after 821–3 (n.) we should delete the universally transmitted Ἀργείων στρατόν.

μόνον: often in asyndeton to express 'a reservation or an important prerequisite' (Liapis on 455–7). In wishes to divinities also e.g. *Cho.* 244–5 <μόνον> Κράτος τε καὶ Δίκη ξὺν τῷ τρίτῳ / πάντων μεγίστῳ Ζηνὶ συγγένοιτό μοι, *Phil.* 528–9, *Hipp.* 522–3, E. *Suppl.* 1229–30 and Ar. *Av.* 1315 τύχη μόνον προσείη. Cf. Headlam on Herod. 2.89 and FJW on A. *Suppl.* 1012.

φθόνον ἄμαχον ... / ... θέλοι ... εἴργειν: Cf. 343 εἴργοι ... φθόνον (above). In tragedy ἄμαχος, 'unconquerable, irresistible', is restricted to lyrics and perhaps had an Aeschylean ring: *Pers.* 90, 856, *Ag.* 733, 769, *Cho.* 55 (otherwise only *Ant.* 799). But the comedians used it in spoken verse (e.g. Ar. *Lys.* 253, Antiph. fr. 7 *PCG*, Eub. fr. 117.2 *PCG*, Men. *Dysc.* 193, 775, 870), and it also occurs in prose (LSJ s.v. I with Suppl. [1996]).

ὕπατος / Ζεύς: Like Aeschylus and the lyric poets (Fraenkel on *Ag.* 55), but not, to our evidence, Sophocles and Euripides, our poet followed Homer in calling Zeus ὕπατος here and in 703 (n.). Cf. *Il.* 19.258, *Od.* 19.303 (*et al.*) θεῶν ὕπατος καὶ ἄριστος, *Il.* 8.31, *Od.* 1.45 ... ὕπατε κρειόντων, *Il.* 5.756, 8.22, 17.339 Ζῆν' ὕπατον Κρονίδην (μήστωρα).

458–60. 'Neither before nor now have the ships from Argos brought (here) any man superior to you.'

Feickert (on 460) aptly compares *Ai.* 418–26 (Ajax) ὦ Σκαμάνδριοι / γείτονες ῥοαί / ... / οὐκέτ' ἄνδρα μὴ / τόνδ' ἴδητ' ... / ... / οἷον οὔτινα / Τρωΐα στρατοῦ / δέρχθη χθονὸς μολόντ' ἀπὸ / Ἑλλανίδος. While shameless self-aggrandisement (Finglass on *Ai.* 421–6) is not at issue here, we know that the chorus' high hopes and panegyric have no basis in fact. They duly think of Achilles and Ajax in 461–3 (n.).

τὸ δὲ νάϊον ... δόρυ: The expression recalls epic δόρυ (...) νήϊον (*Il.* 15.410, 17.744, *Od.* 9.384, A. R. 3.582) and νήϊα δοῦρα (*Od.* 9.498, *h.Ap.* 403, A. R. 2.79), though all of these refer to the ship's planks. Metonymic δόρυ of the whole vessel is first attested in Sim. fr. 543.10 *PMG* = 271.9 Poltera and becomes very frequent in tragedy. Here the entire fleet is meant, as presumably also by *IA* 1494 δόρατα ... νάϊ' (Hartung [ναΐα]: δάϊα L).

οὔτε πρίν τιν' οὔτε νῦν: Nauck (II¹ [1854], XXIII) for οὔτε πρὶν οὔτε νῦν τιν' (Ω). This is the easiest, and no doubt correct, way to create responsion with 825. It 'postulates only that τιν was skipped after πριν and later restored in the wrong place' (Willink, 'Cantica', 37 = *Collected Papers*, 576).

461–3. In our play Rhesus is regularly contrasted with Achilles (314–16n.). To stress their meaning, the chorus here add Ajax – by all accounts 'the *second* best fighter among the Greeks at Troy' (Finglass on *Ai*. 421–6). Athena does likewise at 601–2, and when Hector has to tell Rhesus that Achilles is out of reach, he names Ajax (along with Diomedes) as coming next (497–8a n.).

πῶς μοι τὸ σὸν ἔγχος Ἀχιλλεὺς ἂν δύναιτο / ... ὑπομεῖναι; With Wilamowitz' colometry (454–66 'Metre' 460–2/826–7n.) it is necessary to change the transmitted word-order πῶς μοι Ἀχιλεύς (V: -λλ- OΛ) τὸ σὸν ἔγχος ... in order to avoid hiatus after the second position in the verse. Apart from the metrical and rhetorical advantages of this arrangement (discussed above), there may also be a textual argument. While in Euripidean anapaests and lyrics epic Ἀχιλ- is *lectio difficilior* for Ἀχιλλ- (*Hec.* [94], 108, 128, *El.* 439, *IT* 436–7, *IA* 124, 128),[174] it need not be the original here. The scribe of V had a tendency to write single for double consonants (with Ἀχιλλ- also 182, 491, 977;[175] cf. *Tro.* 39, 264, 575, 623, 1124, *Or.* 1657). The same could have happened in the present passage, after Ἀχιλλεύς had been misplaced in an early source (either to normalise the word-order or because it was left out and wrongly reinserted from a note).

In other tragedy ὑπομένω is found only at *OT* 1322–3 ('stay behind, endure'). The sense 'hold out against' goes back to Homer: *Il.* 5.498 (= 15.312), 14.488–9 ὃ δ' οὐχ ὑπέμεινεν ἐρωήν / Πηνελέωιο ἄνακτος, 16.814–15, 17.174 (Hector to Glaucus) ὅς τ' ἐμὲ φῂς Αἴαντα πελώριον οὐχ ὑπομεῖναι.

---

174 The form does not occur in other tragedy (Ritchie 179). At *IA* 207 metre favours λαιψηροδρόμον Ἀχιλλέα (Hermann: -ιλῆα L). See Diggle, *Euripidea*, 470–1.
175 V is defective from *Rh.* 941, but the reading appears in its apograph Va.

464–6. 'May I see that day, o lord, on which you exact retribution for his murderous hand with your spear.'

Similar wishes for salvation are uttered by the chorus of satyrs at *Cyc.* 437–8 ὦ φίλτατ', εἰ γὰρ τήνδ' ἴδοιμεν ἡμέραν / Κύκλωπος ἐκφυγόντες ἀνόσιον κάρα and that of Greeks at Ar. *Pax* 346 εἰ γὰρ ἐκγένοιτ' ἰδεῖν ταύτην μέ ποτε τὴν ἡμέραν (i.e. on which to enjoy the pleasures of peace again).

εἰ γὰρ ἐγὼ τόδε γ' ἦμαρ / εἰσίδοιμ': The MSS' τόδ' ἦμαρ does not respond with παρὰ καιρόν or παράκαιρον (Vater) in 829. To restore the missing element, Hermann's τόδε γ' ἦμαρ (*Opuscula* III, 304) is preferable to Dindorf's τόδ' ἔτ' ἦμαρ (*PSG*², 182), which creates an unduly despondent tone ('May I yet see that day ...'). Changing the antistrophe instead would entail various metrical difficulties (829–32n.).

For 'assentient or approving' γάρ in wishes see *GP* 92–3 with n. 1 and *Cyc.* 437–8, Ar. *Pax* 346 (above).

ὅτῳ: Musgrave (on 466, 7) for ὅπως (Ω). Neither a temporal clause (LSJ s.v. ὅπως A I 7) nor a final-consecutive one (Paley on 466, G. Pace, *QUCC* n.s. 65 [2000], 134, Jouan 30 n. 139) has a place here. The optative (below) is due to attraction of mood, as in e.g. *Tr.* 953–5 εἴθ' ἀνεμόεσσά τις γένοιτ' ... αὔρα, / ἥτις μ' ἀποικίσειεν ἐκ τόπων (KG I 255–6, SD 642, Bruhn, *Anhang*, § 136).

πολυφόνου / χειρός: 60b–2n. The owner of the 'murderous hand' (Achilles or Ajax) is left deliberately unclear. As often χείρ effectively stands for the hand's action or acts (LSJ s.v. IV).

ἄποιν' ἄροιο σᾷ λόγχᾳ: Diggle's brilliant emendation (*Euripidea*, 515–17) solves all the metrical and linguistic problems presented by the transmitted ἀποινάσαιο λόγχα (ἀποιν- Δ: ἀπον- LQ[1c]: ἀπόν- Q, λόγχα OQ: -α VL) and presupposes the easiest possible way of corruption. Hartung (17 [1852], 137) had already seen that instead of the verb ἀποινάομαι, which in 177 (n.) means 'hold to ransom', we need ἄποινα ('compensation, requital') and wrote ἄποινα σᾷ φέροις (or λάβοις) λόγχα to respond with 832. Yet Diggle's ἄροιο is the more idiomatic verb and requires only that an original αποιναροιο was conflated with σαι inserted above the line. In its support he quotes *Il.* 1.159–60 τιμὴν ἀρνύμενοι Μενελάῳ σοί τε ... / πρὸς Τρώων, S. *El.* 33–4 ὅτῳ τρόπῳ πατρός / δίκας ἀροίμην τῶν φονευσάντων πάρα and *Hec.* 1073–4 ἀρνύμενος λώβας λύμας τ' ἀντίποιν' / ἐμᾶς, ὦ τάλας. Hsch. α 7362 Latte ἄροιο· λάβοις, ἀπενέγκοιο may well refer to our passage.

467–526. Despite the unbroken tension between Hector and Rhesus, this scene is not part of the formal *agon* (388–526n.). The exchange it portrays covers three main points: 1. Rhesus' plan to carry the war into

Greece (467–84), 2. the battle dispositions for the following day (485–98a) and 3. the 'problem' of Odysseus (498b–517). With Hector's arrangements for the rest of the night (418–26) the plot somewhat abruptly returns to *Iliad* 10.

As in the final part of Rhesus' speech (443–53), and perhaps incited by the flattery of the chorus, we observe him trying to assert his claim to leadership. The new war, which he proposes both as 'compensation' for his delay (467–8) and to take revenge on the Greeks (473),[176] is meant to be a joint venture (471 ξὺν σοί ...), and he even seems to remember his status as an *ally* to Troy: 469–70 ἐπεὶ δ' ἂν ... / θῶμεν ... Once he has been turned down, however, he reverts to his former arrogance in restating, and adding a new option to, the battle position he wishes to hold (488, 489–90, 491nn.). We may presume also that it was not his business to interfere with the treatment of potential captives (510–17).

Hector is justly sceptical about the Greek campaign, especially since their war has not yet been won (482). In opposing the idea he assumes the same role of prudent warner which Aeneas and the chorus had previously played for him (52–84, 85–148nn.) – not entirely out of character, given his ready acceptance of their advice and the fact that Rhesus' plan is on a very different scale from continuing a successful attack at night. The reverse relationship between the scenes is underlined by a series of verbal and contextual reminiscences (477–8, 482, 483nn.; Klyve on 388–526 [p. 262]).

The discussion of battle order, together with that of Achilles' wrath, is heavily indebted to Iliadic sources (485–7, 494–5, 497–8a nn.).[177] On a more general level the ensuing review of Greek heroes and the way it develops into the lengthy treatment of Odysseus is vaguely reminiscent of the τειχοσκοπία (*Il.* 3.161–242), where Antenor likewise recounts an earlier, albeit peaceful, visit of the archtrickster to Troy (*Il.* 3.203–24).[178] In *Rhesus* the succession of stealthy blows dealt to the city and its inhabitants offers a preparation for the second half of the play (498b–509, 501–2, 503–7a, 507b–9a nn.). Our growing anticipation in this *epeisodion* reaches its peak when Hector encamps the Thracians as in *Iliad* 10 and asks the chorus to wait for Dolon's return (519–20, 523–6, 523–5a nn.).

In the course of the conversation Hector cuts Rhesus short twice (cf. Liapis on 485–7 and 518). But the invasion of Greece he finds at least

---

[176] The thought that the Trojans may have turned the tables recurs in Verg. *Aen.* 2.192–4 and 11.285–7, as an allusion to Rome's later conquest of Greece (Klyve on 471–2, Liapis on 422–53).

[177] Several other Homerisms cluster mainly in the first half of the scene (cf. Introduction, 30). Perhaps the subject-matter of Odysseus' adventures was considered 'epic' enough.

[178] See Klyve on 388–526 (p. 262).

worth discussing, and we may take his brisk change of subject in 484–5 as an expedient response to the preceding affront (Rosivach 59–60). Rhesus' fancy of impaling Odysseus, by contrast, he passes over in silence (518–26), as if he did not want to be associated with such cruelty (512–17, 513b–15nn.). The idea would also have alienated a largely Greek audience, who as a result may have viewed Odysseus' plot with greater sympathy (as an act of pre-emptive self-defence). We noticed a similar 'technique', and source of dramatic irony, in Dolon's promise to bring back Odysseus' or Diomedes' head (219–23, 257b–60nn.).

467–8. 'Such things I shall allow you to exact (from me) in return for my long absence. I say this with (the approval of) Adrasteia.'

Nothing seems to be amiss here. With πρᾶξαι in the sense 'exact' (LSJ s.v. πράσσω VI) and τῆς μακρᾶς ἀπουσίας as a genitive of price or exchange (below), the statement neatly summarises Rhesus' promise to vanquish the Greeks in a single day (447–53). Kovacs' argument for a lacuna after 467 (*Euripidea Tertia*, 147–8) rests on several wrong premises, most importantly that the declaration contradicts 447–53 and so should point forward to the plans for an attack on Greece itself (469–73). Yet apart from the difficulty of seeing such an contradiction, τοιαῦτα (μέν) is more naturally resumptive (KG I 646, J. Wackernagel, *Glotta* 7 [1916], 194–5 n. 1 = *Sprachliche Untersuchungen*, 34–5 n. 1), and μέν especially calls for a complement (other than ... σὺν δ' Ἀδραστείᾳ λέγω). Hence Morstadt's ἐπεὶ δ' ἄν for ἐπειδάν (fere Ω) in 469, which is impossible also on metrical grounds (469–70n.).

There is little merit in Liapis' attempt ('Notes', 77) to revive Musgrave's πρᾶξιν παρέξω (*Exercitationes*, 94–5 ~ II [1778], 408): 'These things I shall offer you as a compensation for my long absence' or, with his own τοιάνδε for τοιαῦτα (Ω), 'This compensation I shall offer you ...'. If one suspects the paradosis (Diggle, apparatus 468), it seems best to accept Kovacs' lacuna and *exempli gratia* supplement (τοιαῦτα μέν σοι τῆς μακρᾶς ἀπουσίας, / <ἣ δυσχεραίνεις, ἄξι' ὠφελήματα> / πρᾶξαι παρέξω ...), with anaphoric τοιαῦτα μέν and ἐπεὶ δ' ἄν.

τῆς μακρᾶς ἀπουσίας / πρᾶξαι παρέξω: For the genitive of price or exchange (KG I 377–8, SD 127) with πράσσω or its noun cf. Pl. *Grg.* 511e1–3 ταύτης τῆς μεγάλης εὐεργεσίας ... δύο δραχμὰς ἐπράξατο (*sc.* ἡ κυβερνητική), *Eum.* 320 πράκτορες αἵματος ... ἐφάνημεν and S. *El.* 953 φόνου ... πράκτορ' ... πατρός. Otherwise e.g. *Med.* 534–5 μείζω γε μέντοι τῆς ἐμῆς σωτηρίας / εἴληφας ἢ δέδωκας, ὡς ἐγὼ φράσω (Ritchie 249).

The line-end ... τῆς μακρᾶς ἀπουσίας is Euripidean in character: *Hec.* 962–3 (Polymestor to Hecuba) σὺ δ', εἴ τι μέμφῃ τῆς ἐμῆς ἀπουσίας, / σχές (cf. 426–42n. with n. 158), *IA* 651 μακρὰ γὰρ ἡμῖν ἡ 'πιοῦσ' ἀπουσία, 1172 ... διὰ μακρᾶς ἀπουσίας.

σὺν δ' Ἀδραστείᾳ λέγω: 342–5, 342–3, 455b–7nn. The indicative verb lends confidence to an otherwise reverent formula. Cf. *Med.* 625–6 νύμφευ'· ἴσως γάρ, σὺν θεῷ δ' εἰρήσεται, / γαμεῖς τοιοῦτον ὥστε θρηνεῖσθαι γάμον (with Mastronarde on 625, 626), Ar. *Pl.* 114–16, *Rh.* 357–9 (n.).

469–73. Whatever other motives we may ascribe to Rhesus for wishing to continue the war on Greek soil (467–526, 471–2nn.), he professes the well-known principle that one should help one's friends and harm one's enemies. See further 483 (n.) and generally M. W. Blundell, *Helping Friends and Harming Enemies* ..., Cambridge 1989, 26–59, especially 26–31 with n. 21.

469–70. ἐπεὶ δ' ἄν: Morstadt (*Beitrag*, 25 n. 2). The transmitted ἐπειδάν (ΟΛ: ἐπειδ' ἄν δ' V) cannot stand because 1. we need δέ to balance μέν in 467 (467–8n.) and 2. the final syllable of ἐπειδάν (ἐπειδή + ἄν) is long. The second criterion is decisive also at *Sept.* 734–5 ἐπεὶ δ' ἄν αὐτοκτόνως / αὐτοδάϊκτοι θάνωσι, where most older editors read ἐπειδάν (M² et codd. pler.). V's text here acknowledges the first (unless it is a simple copying error).

Sansone's ἐχθρῶν δ' ἐπειδὰν ... (*BMCR* 2013.03.15, on 469), for which he compares *Eum.* 647 ἀνδρὸς δ' ἐπειδὰν αἷμ' ... and Eup. fr. 172.7 *PCG* ... ἐκεῖ δ' ἐπειδὰν κατίδω τιν' ἄνδρα presupposes two stages of corruption instead of one (i.e. the regularisation of word order and loss of δ').

θῶμεν ... ἐξέλῃς: The use of person and number here is good rhetoric. Hector has to keep (some of) his privileges at Troy, if he is to be persuaded to join a new campaign. Contrast 451–3, 488 (467–526n.), and see Liapis on 469–70.

ἀκροθίνι': Usually in the plural, ἀκροθίνια denotes the topmost or best part of a heap (< ἀκρός + θίς) and thus the choicest spoils or first fruits to be offered to the gods (LSJ s.v. ἀκροθίνιον with Suppl. [1996], Mastronarde on *Phoen.* 203, 281–2). For their 'selection' cf. Hdt. 8.121.1 πρῶτα μέν νυν τοῖσι θεοῖσι ἐξεῖλον ἀκροθίνια ἄλλα τε καὶ τριήρεας τρεῖς Φοινίσσας and Xen. *Cyr.* 7.5.35 πρῶτον μὲν τοὺς μάγους καλέσας, ὡς δοριαλώτου τῆς πόλεως οὔσης ἀκροθίνια τοῖς θεοῖς καὶ τεμένη ἐκέλευσεν ἐξελεῖν.

471–2. It may not be coincidence that the language resembles *Pers.* 177–8 (the Queen has had frequent dream visions) ἀφ' οὗπερ παῖς ἐμὸς στείλας στρατόν / Ἰαόνων γῆν οἴχεται πέρσαι θέλων and 234 πᾶσα γὰρ γένοιτ' ἂν Ἑλλὰς βασιλέως ὑπήκοος (cf. Paley on 474). If Rhesus is consistently portrayed as a would-be Xerxes (264–341, 290, 375b–7, 388–453nn.), his intended invasion of Greece also fits the theme.

ξὺν σοί: 467–526n. The words emphatically stand at the beginning of the main clause and a new line. On ξύν (Λ) as against σύν (Δ) see 440–2n.

γῆν ἔπ' Ἀργείων ... / ... πᾶσαν ... Ἑλλάδ': Whereas Argos and Hellas are formally distinct in 477 (477–8n.), this cannot be the case here. At best 'all Hellas' includes the 'land of the Argives' (i.e. the Peloponnese), as it would at *Pers.* 234 (above).

γῆν ἔπ' Ἀργείων adapts our poet's favourite mid-verse formula ... ναῦς ἔπ' Ἀργείων ... (149–50n.).

ἐκπέρσαι δορί: Cf. *Pers.* 178 ... πέρσαι θέλων (above). The redundant dative is Euripidean in style (56–8, 452–3nn.). Likewise Hector at 478 πορθεῖν ... δορί.

473. ὡς ἄν: 72–3n.

ἐν μέρει: 'in turn'. Cf. *Eum.* 198 ἄναξ Ἄπολλον, ἀντάκουσον ἐν μέρει, 436, *Cyc.* 253, *Hcld.* 182, Ar. *Av.* 1228. Elsewhere in drama (never Sophocles) the juncture is found in the sense 'alternately, one after another': e.g. *Ag.* 332, 1192 (with Fraenkel), *Eum.* 586, *Cyc.* 180, *Andr.* 216, *Hec.* 1130, Ar. *Vesp.* 1319.

475–6. πόλιν νεμοίμην: Cf. 700 νεμόμενος πόλιν. But the expression is standard from Homer on.

ἦ κάρτα: 79n. ἦ κάρτα only occurs in tragedy (particularly Aeschylus) and always at the beginning of an iambic trimeter: A. *Suppl.* 452, *Ag.* 592, 1252, *Cho.* 929, *Eum.* 213, A. fr. 78a.3, *Ai.* 1359, 1278, *Alc.* 811, *Hipp.* 412 and perhaps *Tr.* 379 (with Davies and Ll-J/W, *Sophoclea*, 159). At S. *El.* 312 read Meineke's καὶ κάρτα, followed by a stop (Finglass on 312 with n. 23).

For affirmative ἦ (+ adverb) introducing a conditional apodosis see *GP* 281.

477–8. 'But the regions around Argos and the pastures of Hellas are not as easy to ravage with the spear as you say.'

In 112–22 Aeneas had warned Hector of the risks if he attacked the Greek camp at night. The wording of 121 in particular resembles 478 (below).

In addition we may see here another oblique reference to *Persians* (471–2n.). Xerxes and his army learnt to their cost that Greece was difficult to subdue (cf. particularly *Pers.* 230–45).

τὰ δ' ἀμφί τ' Ἄργος καὶ νομὸν τὸν Ἑλλάδος: 408–10a n. The present phrase looks like an adaptation of the Odyssean formula ... καθ' (ἄν') Ἑλλάδα καὶ μέσον Ἄργος (1.344, 4.726, 816, 15.80), which combines two originally separate territories – Ἑλλάς used to designate Peleus' Thessalian kingdom (and by extension northern Greece), while Ἄργος stands for the Peloponnese – to represent '... the whole of Greece' (S. R. West on *Od.* 1.344; cf. Hoekstra on 15.80). Yet Liapis (on 477–8) puts too much emphasis on the distinction here. It is simply a way of taking up πᾶσαν ... Ἑλλάδ' in 472 (471–2n.).

νομὸν τὸν Ἑλλάδος: With the article so placed the attributive genitive qualifies its noun as a specimen of its kind (KG I 618, who cite e.g. Hdt. 5.50.1 ἀπὸ θαλάσσης τῆς Ἰώνων). For νομός, 'pastures, (fertile) land, region', cf. Pi. *Ol.* 7.33 ἐς ἀμφιθάλασσον νομόν (i.e. Rhodes), *OC* 1061 Οἰάτιδος ἐκ νομοῦ (codd.: εἰς νομόν Hartung) and possibly S. fr. 284 (*Inachus*) < ... > πατὴρ δὲ ποταμὸς Ἴναχος / τὸν ἀντίπλαστον νομὸν ἔχει κεκμηκότων (Ellendt: νόμον ἔχει Porson: ἔχει νόμον cod. Hsch. α 5460 Latte). In general LSJ s.v. II 1 with Suppl. (1996).

οὐχ ὧδε πορθεῖν ῥᾴδι' ὡς λέγεις δορί: Cf. 120–1 ὅς σ' οὐκ ἐάσει ... / οὐδ' ὧδ' Ἀχαιοὺς ὡς δοκεῖς ἀναρπάσει (above). For πορθεῖν ... δορί see 471–2n.

479. 'Do they not say that these who have come here are the Greeks' most valiant men?'

ἀριστέας ... Ἑλλήνων recalls the Homeric ... ἀριστῆες (-ας) Παναχαιῶν, especially as it is used at *Il.* 7.73 (Hector addressing the Greeks) ὑμῖν δ' ἐν γὰρ ἔασιν ἀριστῆες Παναχαιῶν. For this reason and because forms of ἀριστεύς are *lectio difficilior* in tragedy (cf. Parker on *Alc.* 920–1 [pp. 236–7], Finglass on *Ai.* 1304–7) VΛ's ἀριστέας[179] should not be changed to ἀρίστους with Cobet (*VL*², 583–4). ΣΣⱽ *Rh.* 479 and 481 (II 338.5, 12 Schwartz = 102, 103 Merro) obviously substituted the regular word. On the synizesis of ε and α in ἀριστέας see 85–6n. (Αἰνέας).

A similar echo may be found in *Med.* 4–6 μηδ' ἐρετμῶσαι χέρας / ἀνδρῶν ἀριστέων οἳ τὸ πάγχρυσον δέρος / Πελίᾳ μετῆλθον, where Wakefield's ἀριστέων (ἀρίστων codd. et Σᴮ) is supported by the fact that the Argonauts are called ἀριστῆες in Apollonius of Rhodes (e.g. 1.70, 2.301, 3.21, 4.106) and Theoc. 13.17 (Porson on *Med.* 5). This is likely to go back to the epic tradition.

480. 'Yes, and we find no fault with them, but we are pressing them well enough.'

κοὐ μεμφόμεσθά γ': *sc.* αὐτοῖς (LSJ s.v. μέμφομαι 3 'to be dissatisfied with, find fault with').[180] Cf. Σⱽ *Rh.* 480 (II 338.6, 8–9 Schwartz = 102–3 Merro) καὶ οὐκ ἐκφαυλίζομεν αὐτούς.

For καὶ ... γε in affirmative answers cf. A. *Suppl.* 296, 313, *PV* 931, *OT* 771–2, Ar. *Nub.* 1068. 'The effect of γε ... is to stress the addition made by καί' (*GP* 157).

---

179 In O the later accusative plural ἀριστεῖς intruded (cf. Schwyzer 563, 575, Threatte II 247–8).
180 Ignoring this usage, Liapis (on 480) takes the verb absolutely, which makes no sense: 'Yes, and we are not complaining ...' (i.e. because we are resisting well so far).

ἀλλ' ἅδην ἐλαύνομεν: another Homerism. The phrase goes back to *Il.* 13.315 οἵ μιν ἅδην ἐλόωσι καὶ ἐσσύμενον πολέμοιο (~ 19.423 οὐ λήξω, πρὶν Τρῶας ἅδην ἐλάσαι πολέμοιο), as is confirmed by the echo of *Il.* 13.307–9 in *Rh.* 485–7 (n.). For that reason (and because of Hector's success on the previous day) we should take ἐλαύνω transitively and ἅδην of the Greeks being harried 'to their fill' (cf. Σ^V *Rh.* 480 [II 338.6–8 Schwartz = 102–3 Merro] ἀλλὰ πάντα κινοῦμεν πρὸς τὸ ἀποστῆσαι αὐτούς, ὁμόσε ἐλαύνομεν αὐτοῖς καὶ πολεμοῦμεν). Rhesus' question in 481 (n.) then follows naturally: 'So having killed these, shall we not have completed our work?'

The second explanation in Σ^V *Rh.* 480 (II 338.8–11 Schwartz = 103 Merro), which most modern critics adopt (with variations), makes the verb intransitive (i.e. '... we are driven to our fill of them'). But apart from contradicting Hector's attitude (above), this is based on a misconception of *Od.* 5.290 ἀλλ' ἔτι μέν μίν φημι ἅδην ἐλάαν κακότητος – already found, it seems, in Tyrt. fr. 11.10 *IEG* ἀμφοτέρων δ' ἐς κόρον ἠλάσατε and Sol. fr. 4c.2 *IEG* οἳ πολλῶν ἀγαθῶν ἐς κόρον [ἠ]λάσατε. Hartung's ἐλαύνομαι (17 [1852], 138–9) merely tries to exonerate our poet (and his scholiast) from that 'mistake'.

The lack of a genitive here may be due to an interpretation of *Il.* 13.315 that construed πολέμοιο with ἐσσύμενον ('... although he is rushing for war') instead of ἅδην. The latter is proved correct by *Od.* 5.290 and e.g. *Il.* 5.388 ... Ἄρης ἆτος πολέμοιο (~ Hes. *Th.* 714),[181] but the question was raised by Nicanor (Σ^A *Il.* 13.315 [III 459.81–4 Erbse]), and Hsch. α 1096 Latte excerpted ἅδην ἐλόωσιν alone.

ἅδην is usually explained as a fossilised accusative of *ἅδη, 'satiety' (*DELG*, *LfgrE* s.v. E); hence 'to satiety, to one's fill'. It is cognate with Latin *satis, satur* (< √*seh$_2$-) and so should have an aspirate in Attic. Tragic MSS tend to give ἅδην (cf. *Ag.* 828, *Ion* 975, *Hel.* 620), probably under the influence of epic, where psilosis may apply.[182]

481. οὔκουν: 161–2a n. An animated question seems more appropriate than a statement with οὐκοῦν (Ω).

πάντ' εἰργάσμεθα: Editors are divided between πάντ' (Λ) and πᾶν (Δ), but the former is supported by 605 (605–6n.) τοῦτον κατακτὰς πάντ' ἔχεις and maybe the neuter plurals in 482 (Liapis, 'Notes', 78). See also Σ^V *Rh.* 481 (II 338.13 Schwartz = 103 Merro) πάντα διαπεπραξόμεθα

---

[181] In *Il.* 19.422–3 (above) πολέμοιο could in theory go with οὐ λήξω. But the word order tells against this, and no ancient scholar suggested it.
[182] See West, ed. *Iliad* I, XVI (with literature). Aristarchus advocated ἅδην in epic, according to a dubious rule (Σ^AbT *Il.* 5.203 [II 32.28–30 Erbse]; cf. Σ *Od.* 5.290 [I 273.26–8 Dindorf]). This intermittently appears in Homeric MSS.

(Schwartz: διαπραξάμεθα V: -πραξόμεθα Wilamowitz) and Xen. *An.* 1.8.12 κἂν τοῦτ' ... νικῶμεν, πάνθ' ἡμῖν πεποίηται.

In references to the future the perfect tense vividly anticipates a verbal action as already completed (KG I 150, SD 287). So especially in conditional periods: cf. *Phil.* 75–6 ὥστ' εἴ με τόξων ἐγκρατὴς αἰσθήσεται, / ὄλωλα, E. *El.* 686–7 (685–9 del. Nauck), *Or.* 940–1, Xen. *An.* 1.8.12 (above). L here impossibly offers πάντ' εἰργάσμεθ' ἄν.

482. 'Now do not set your sight on what is far away, neglecting what is close at hand.'

Hector's warning, like that of the chorus in 76 (467–526n.), is fully rooted in the situation, with τἀγγύθεν referring to the Trojan War and τὰ πρόσω to Rhesus' plans for a Greek campaign. Yet the expression is proverbial, and it was included in the gnomologia gV, gB and gE. One may compare Pi. *Pyth.* 3.21–3 ἔστι δὲ φῦλον ἐν ἀνθρώποισι ματαιότατον, / ὅστις αἰσχύνων ἐπιχώρια παπταίνει τὰ πόρσω, / μεταμώνια θηρεύων ἀκράντοις ἐλπίσιν.

μή νυν: Enclitic νυν (gV, coni. Scaliger) is normal in injunctions (LSJ s.v. νῦν II 3, SD 570–1, Fraenkel on *Ag.* 937). But νῦν (ΩgBgE) can hardly count as an error, given that the ancients accentuated the word according to vowel length and that in the 'weakened' sense especially the υ may be either long or short (indeterminable here by position). It is rather a question of interpreting the MSS evidence (cf. P. J. Finglass, *Mnemosyne* IV 60 [2007], 269–73).

τὰ πόρσω τἀγγύθεν: The same juxtaposition (though of place, not time) was restored by Valckenaer (*Diatribe*, 32–3 with n. 4) at *Phaeth.* 6–7 Diggle = E. fr. 772 θερμὴ δ' ἄνακτος φλὸξ ὑπερτέλλουσα γῆς / καίει τὰ πόρσω, τἀγγύθεν δ' εὔκρατ' ἔχει. Cf. also S. fr. 858.3 πρόσω δὲ λεύσσων, ἐγγύθεν δὲ πᾶς τυφλός and *Ion* 585–6 οὐ ταὐτὸν εἶδος φαίνεται τῶν πραγμάτων / πρόσωθεν ὄντων ἐγγύθεν θ' ὁρωμένων.

Dindorf (III.2 [1840], 608) corrected the transmitted πόρρω here, which is the form used in Attic comedy and prose. Tragic and lyric πόρσω was regularly corrupted into πόρρω or πρόσω (Diggle on *Phaeth.* 7, Finglass on S. *El.* 213).

483. Rhesus' accusation is an insult to the man who in 102–4 (n.) regarded it as shameful not to act and whose extraordinary, if sometimes misdirected, valour was praised by Aeneas in 105 (n.). But Hector remains true to his current placatory self.

παθεῖν, δρᾶσαι: a frequent antithesis in this context. Cf. e.g. *Cho.* 314 'δράσαντι παθεῖν', τριγέρων μῦθος τάδε φωνεῖ, *OC* 271 ὅστις παθὼν μὲν ἀντέδρων, 953, S. frr. 223b, 962, *Andr.* 438; also Paley on 483.

484. πολλῆς ... τυραννίδος: The only parallel for τυραννίς in the territorial sense seems to be Liv. 38.14.12 *Quinque et viginti talenta* *tyrannidem tuam exhaurient?* (LSJ s.v. τυραννίς II 3, *OLD* s.v. 1 b). But βασιλεία is so used at e.g. Xen. *Cyr.* 8.8.1,[183] and D. S. 20.25.2.

According to *Il.* 24.544–5 (cf. Richardson on 543–6, *BK* on 544–5), the kingdom of Troy extended to Lesbos (in the south), Phrygia (in the east) and the Hellespont (in the north). On Hector as the regent see 388–9n.

γάρ: assentient: 'Yes, for …' (*GP* 73–4). Likewise 579 and, dissentient, 683 (n.).

ἄρχω appears to play on ἀρκεῖν in the preceding line (Porter on 483–4).

485–7. 'But you may rest your shield and position your army either on the left or on the right wing or in the middle of the allied forces.'

Among the Achaeans, Meriones asks Idomeneus where he intends to fight at *Il.* 13.307–9 Δευκαλίδη, πῆ ταρ μέμονας καταδῦναι ὅμιλον; / ἢ᾽ ἐπὶ δεξιόφιν παντὸς στρατοῦ, ἦ᾽ ἀνὰ μέσσους, / ἦ᾽ ἐπ᾽ ἀριστερόφιν; They choose the left side as the weaker (*Il.* 13.309–10, 326–7), while in *Rhesus* the question is never decided (cf. Burnett, 'Smiles', 31, Liapis on 485–7). Yet it soon becomes irrelevant anyway, and it is doubtful whether anyone would have noticed the omission by the end of the scene.

ἀλλ᾽ here marks 'a break-off in the thought' and the introduction of another thought (*GP* 8, Parker on *Alc.* 1034).

εἴτε λαιὸν εἴτε δεξιὸν κέρας: 'This probably depends on the sense of the passage, and so may be resolved into a cognate accusative', as in *Hcld.* 671 … καὶ δὴ λαιὸν ἕστηκεν κέρας and E. *Suppl.* 657–8 καὶ τοὺς σὺν αὐτῷ δεξιὸν τεταγμένους / κέρας (Paley on 485). Less likely, in all three passages, the noun phrase could be understood predicatively. At any rate there is a slight zeugma here.

ἐν μέσοισι συμμάχοις: For a group of persons cf. *Ba.* 221 θιάσοις ἐν μέσοισιν and 259 ἐν βάκχαισι … μέσαις.

πέλτην ἐρεῖσαι: Despite the lack of a complement, the sense appears to be that Rhesus is 'to bring [his shield] in support of the others' (Paley on 485) in close formation: *Il.* 13.131 = 16.215 ἀσπὶς ἄρ᾽ ἀσπίδ᾽ ἔρειδε and especially Tyrt. fr. 11.31 *IEG* καὶ πόδα πὰρ ποδὶ θεὶς καὶ ἐπ᾽ ἀσπίδος ἀσπίδ᾽ ἐρείσας (LSJ s.v. ἐρείδω I 2). Morstadt (*Beitrag*, 23–4 n. 1), by contrast, compares *Il.* 22.97 ἀσπίδ᾽ ἐρείσας – i.e. Hector leaning his shield against a wall tower before his duel with Achilles. Similarly the hoplite would often have to support the weight of his shield (whose place the *pelte* here takes) by resting its upper rim on his left shoulder (Hanson, *Western Way of War*, 65–70; cf. Liapis on 485–7).

---

[183] Whether or not Xenophon wrote the appendix on the decline of Persia after Cyrus' death (*Cyr.* 8.8), it can hardly be later than 330 BC without referring to the victory of Alexander the Great.

Either way the phrase forms a *hysteron proteron* with καταστῆσαι στρατόν. Σ^V *Rh.* 485 (II 339.1–2 Schwartz = 103 Merro) is wrong to interpret πέλτην as 'ranks of peltasts' here. But as at 410 (408–10a n.), where the scholium is correct, several modern scholars have followed it.

καταστῆσαι στρατόν: a bare technical term after the Homerism: Cf. e.g. Xen. *An.* 1.10.10 καὶ δὴ βασιλεὺς ... κατέστησεν ἀντίαν τὴν φάλαγγα (LSJ s.v. καθίστημι A II 1).

488. μόνος μάχεσθαι πολεμίοις ... θέλω: 467–526n. A variation on 451 (n.), the demand runs counter to the epic motif that a hero cannot do it all by himself: *Il.* 12.409–12 (Sarpedon speaking) ὦ Λύκιοι, τί ταρ ὧδε μεθίετε θούριδος ἀλκῆς; / ἀργαλέον δέ μοί ἐστι καὶ ἰφθίμῳ περ ἐόντι / μούνῳ ῥηξαμένῳ θέσθαι παρὰ νηυσὶ κέλευθον. / ἀλλ' ἐφαμαρτεῖτε (with Hainsworth), 20.354–9 (with Edwards) and, within a rebuke, 16.620–2.

489–90. The expression, which effectively reverses 391b–2 (n.) συγκατασκάψων δ' ἐγώ / τείχη πάρειμι καὶ νεῶν πρήσων σκάφη, is impossibly condescending. See Paley on 489 and 467–526n.

μὴ συνεμπρῆσαι νεῶν / πρύμνας: In classical literature συνεμπίμπρημι is attested only here, and nowhere else in this verb, it seems, does συν- refer to a joint agent (as opposed to recipient of the action). It was probably coined for the occasion – after Iliadic ἐμπρήθω for burning the ships.

The whole phrase is echoed in 768–9 κἀφεδρεύοντας νεῶν / πρύμναισι. By coincidence perhaps νεῶν (...) πρύμν- (or *vice versa*) is all but confined to Euripides: *Hec.* 539–40, *Tro.* 1047, *Ion* 1243, *IA* 1319–20.

πονήσας τὸν πάρος πολὺν χρόνον resumes 444–6.

491. Ἀχιλλέως καὶ στρατοῦ: Only the 'best of the Achaeans' will be good enough for Rhesus (cf. 467–526n.). Given his regular pairing with Achilles (314–16, 461–3nn.) and ἐκείνῳ (i.e. Achilles) in 492, the phrase cannot be taken as a hendiadys ('Achilles' army').

κατὰ στόμα: 408–10a n.

492. θοῦρον ... δόρυ: 'your furious spear'. The stock epithet of Ares was used of Achilles in 186 (n.) τὸν Πηλέως ... θούριον γόνον. In its epic form it here well designates (the weapon of) his would-be opponent, who was all but identified with the war-god in 385–7 (n.).

Of military gear cf. *Eum.* 627–8 οὔ τι θουρίοις / τόξοις ἐκηβόλοισιν ὥστ' Ἀμαζόνος, *Il.* 11.32 (with Hainsworth), 20.162 ἀσπίδα θοῦριν and, by analogy, *Il.* 15.308 (of Apollo) ἔχε δ' αἰγίδα θοῦριν.

ἀντᾶραι: Reiske (*Animadversiones*, 89). The verb is appropriate for initiating hostilities: e.g. Thuc. 1.53.2 ὅπλα ἀνταιρόμενοι and, in the first century AD (?), 'Anon.' *Ep.* 40.1–2 *FGE* Ἕκτορι μὲν Τροίῃ συγκάτθανεν, οὐδ' ἔτι χεῖρας / ἀντῆρεν Δαναῶν παισὶν ἐπερχομένοις (LSJ s.v. ἀνταίρω I). The MSS' ἐντάξαι (which is otherwise attested only in late Greek) ought to mean 'arrange (light-armed men and hoplites) alternately' or 'insert (men) alternately' (LSJ s.v. ἐντάσσω I 2). Its presumed use for 'put in the way of (one's opponent)' cannot be justified with ἐνστάτης for ἀντιστάτης in *Ai.* 104 (cf. Paley, Porter, Feickert on 492), which is easily derived from ἐνίσταμαι, 'stand in the way, resist, block' (LSJ s.v. ἐνίστημι B IV 1). Note also 451 (n.).

493. καὶ μὴν ... γ': 184n.

494–5. 'He has sailed and is here. But in his wrath against the generals he does not raise his spear to help them.'

With μηνίων especially, the allusion to the central theme of the *Iliad*, Achilles' wrath, is unmistakable. His withdrawal from battle is recommended by Thetis at *Il.* 1.421–2 and put into practice at *Il.* 1.488–92. Hector cannot know (but the audience may remember) that Agamemnon's attempt at reconciliation failed in that same night (cf. Feickert on 494).

μηνίων will at least have evoked *Il.* 1.1. In the *Iliad* μῆνις, and even more its derivatives, characterise 'the mutual anger between Achilles and Agamemnon' (G. Nagy, *The Best of the Achaeans* ..., Baltimore – London ¹1979, ²1999, 73; cf. *LfgrE* s.vv. μῆνις B 188.23–40, μηνίω B 189.41–50 on the distribution and possible sacral connotations of the words). The strong 'semantic Homerism' (FJW on A. *Suppl.* 975) is reinforced by a metrical one in that the present stem here retains its primary short ι (Schwyzer 727, *BK* on *Il.* 2.769). In tragedy this is paralleled only in the lyric *Hipp.* 1145–6 (cf. Sim. fr. 572.1 *PMG* = 290 Poltera).[184] For a collection of epic verb forms in *Rhesus* see 523–5a n. (δέχθαι).

οὐ συναίρεται δόρυ: 451, 492nn.

496. 'Well then, who else after him is of high repute in the army?'

τίς δή: so Λ (τίς δὲ V; τί δαὶ O), with 'connective' δή marking 'the progression from one idea to a second of which the consideration naturally follows' (*GP* 239). O's text need not represent original τί<ς> δαί (Liapis, 'Notes', 78–9), and while 'colloquial' δαί (*GP* 262–4) will often be *lectio difficilior* in tragedy (Stevens, *CEE* 45–6, West, *Studies*, 258, 314), its tone does not seem appropriate here (contrast the lively 'transitional' *Ion* 275 εἶέν· / τί δαὶ τόδ'; ἆρ' ἀληθὲς ἢ μάτην λόγος;). As in other passages where τί δαί is an inferior or impossible reading (*Hec.*

---

[184] *Eum.* 101 (3ia) ends in μηνίεται, and despite Ritchie (288), it is likely that the present tenses in *OC* 965 and 1274 have an 'Attic' long ι in anceps position (cf. W. Schulze, *Quaestiones Epicae*, Gütersloh 1892, 351 with n. 3, Wackernagel, *Sprachliche Untersuchungen*, 140).

1256, E. *El.* 244, 978, 1303, *IA* 1447 and perhaps E. *El.* 1116, *IA* 1443), the extreme frequency of the juncture in Aristophanes (eleven times in the 'triad' alone) may have aided confusion.

εὐδοξεῖ: Unlike εὔδοξος and εὐδοξία (760n.), the verb is first attested here and in fourth-century prose (e.g. Xen. *HG* 1.1.31, *Mem.* 3.6.16, Dem. 8.20, 20.142, Aeschin. 2.66, 118, 172). Also probably Men. *Asp.* 4 ὤμην γὰρ εὐδο[ξο]ῦντα καὶ σωθέντα σε (with Gomme–Sandbach on εὐδο[ξο]ῦντα rather than Austin's εὐδο[κο]ῦντα).

Hec. 294–5 opposes ἀδοξοῦντες (again our earliest example of the verb) to οἱ δοκοῦντες, 'men of repute' (LSJ s.v. δοκέω II 5 with Suppl. [1996]).

497–8a. The relative ranking of Ajax and Achilles was traditional: *Il.* 2.768–9 ἀνδρῶν αὖ μέγ' ἄριστος ἔην Τελαμώνιος Αἴας – / ὄφρ' Ἀχιλεὺς μήνιεν, 7.226–32, 13.321–5. For further references see West, *Making of the Iliad*, 121; also *Ai.* 1338–41, *Rh.* 461–3 (n.). Diomedes is famed for his divinely supported *aristeia* in *Iliad* 5, although his mention here seems primarily intended as a preparation for Odysseus and their joint venture which will result in Rhesus' death (498b–509, 501–2, 503–7a nn.).

ἡσσᾶσθαι: Dindorf (III.2 [1849], 608) for ἡττᾶσθαι (Ω). Tragedy and Attic literary prose up to (and including) Thucydides generally wrote σσ instead of native ττ, no doubt under Ionic influence. Our verb in particular constitutes a false Ionism (as opposed to genuine ἐσσοῦσθαι). See Schwyzer 316, 317, J. Wackernagel, *Hellenistica*, Göttingen 1907, 14–15 = *KS* II, 1045–6 and W. S. Allen, *Vox Graeca* ..., Cambridge ³1987, 13.

498b–509. Hector's denunciation of Odysseus combines a typical piece of stage-abuse (498b–500n.) with the recounting of two episodes that technically belong to the final stages of the Trojan War: the theft of the Palladion (501–2n.) and Odysseus' spying expedition to Troy in a beggar's disguise (503–7a n.). Both featured in the *Little Iliad* and as single exploits of a furtive kind not only exemplify Odysseus' post-Iliadic character, but also foreshadow the coming attack, which will involve both homicide and theft (cf. 503–7a n.).

The paradigmatic function of the stories is underlined by the fact that Hector tells them in reverse order to the *Little Iliad*. The more 'recent' Palladion theft also took place at night and (as the audience will remember) with the help of Diomedes, who is here suppressed. In this context it seems all the more likely that the capture of Helenus is alluded to in 507b–9a (n.).

With respect to the first account, the 'mythical anachronism' was already criticised by Σ^V *Rh.* 502 (II 339.10–11 Schwartz = 104 Merro). Cf. Introduction, 13.

498b–500. 'Then there is a most wily piece of work, Odysseus, sufficiently bold in spirit and a man who has inflicted the greatest number of insults on this land.'

Odysseus is introduced with strong language, part of which belonged to the common stock (below). Tragedy did not often present him in a favourable light (W. B. Stanford, *The Ulysses Theme* ..., Oxford ²1968, 102–17, Willink on *Or.* 1403).

αἱμυλώτατον / κρότημ' appears to be compounded from *Ai.* 388–9 τὸν αἱμυλώτατον, / ἐχθρὸν ἄλημα and S. fr. 913 ≏ πάνσοφον κρότημα, Λαέρτου γόνος (Fraenkel, *Rev.* 232). Elsewhere in tragedy αἱμύλος refers to Odysseus at *Rh.* 709 (n.), E. fr. 715.1 and maybe fr. tr. adesp. 564d (with Kannicht–Snell, where for the idea that Odysseus is addressed add Th. K. Stephanopoulos, *ZPE* 73 [1988], 235), but never in the superlative and/or with an abusive noun in -μα. In the latter category κρότημα is unique to our passages. The word denotes the result of hammering (< κροτέω), i.e. an intricately worked bronze tool or artefact and so figuratively a cunning man; cf. Σ^V *Rh.* 499 (II 339.8 Schwartz = 104 Merro) οἷον συγκρότημα, μηχάνημα, Σ^UEAP Theoc. 15.48–50c (310.1–3 Wendel) κεκροτημένοι· ... ἐθάδες πανούργων ἔργων. ἡ δὲ μεταφορὰ ἀπὸ τοῦ κεκροτημένου χαλκοῦ. It has to be distinguished from κρόταλον ('clapper'), which stresses 'the 'sound' aspect of κροτεῖν' (A. A. Long, *Language and Thought in Sophocles* ..., London 1968, 115 n. 13) and is applied to Odysseus at *Cyc.* 104 ('rattle, chatterbox').

With κρότημα as an image from craft compare also *Ai.* 379–80 ἰὼ πάνθ' ὁρῶν, ἁπάντων τ' ἀεὶ / κακῶν ὄργανον, τέκνον Λαρτίου and *Phil.* 927–8 (Philoctetes to Neoptolemus) ὦ ... πανουργίας / δεινῆς τέχνημ' ἔχθιστον (Finglass on *Ai.* 379–80).[185] For neuters in -μα used to characterise (and often denounce) persons in drama see Long (above), 114–20, Collard, 'Supplement', 370–1 and Barrett, *Collected Papers*, 351–64.

λῆμά τ' ... θρασύς: Cf. *Sept.* 447–8 ἀνὴρ ... / αἴθων ... λῆμα (Polyphontes). Odysseus is θρασύς also in 707.

ἀρκούντως: largely a prose word. In other tragedy (and all poetry) only *Cho.* 892 σὲ καὶ ματεύω· τῷδε δ' ἀρκούντως ἔχει (with Garvie), *Hec.* 318 ... πάντ' ἂν ἀρκούντως ἔχοι and S. *El.* 354 ἐπαρκούντως. It here provides 'a sardonic touch' (Liapis on 498–500), i.e 'more than sufficiently'.

καὶ πλεῖστα χώραν τήνδ' ἀνὴρ καθυβρίσας: As transmitted, the clause continues λῆμά τ' ... θρασύς in apposition to Ὀδυσσεύς. But

---

[185] In a positive sense already 'Hes.' fr. 198.3 M.–W. υἱὸς Λαέρταο πολύκροτα μήδεα εἰδώς. The adjective is a variant on πολύτροπον at *Od.* 1.1. See *LfgrE* s.v. πολύκροτος B 2, D.

Hermann's εἷς for καὶ (*Opuscula* III, 304–5) is attractive in view of the frequent collocation of εἷς (ἀνήρ) and a superlative (945b–7n.), especially as we have it at *Pers.* 326–8 Συέννεσίς τε ... / ... εἷς ἀνὴρ πλεῖστον πόνον / ἐχθροῖς παρασχών. The corruption would have been easy after the then single τε (*GP* 497–8) connecting predicative αἱμυλώτατον κρότημ' and λῆμα ... θρασύς. A possible objection is that εἷς ἀνήρ usually stands together.

Another common error, the intrusion of a form of ὅδε with a locality (FJW on A. *Suppl.* 79), is presupposed by Boissonade's earlier εἷς for τήνδ' (IV [1826], 289), which leaves the syntax as in the MSS text. But Hermann (above) rightly observed that the demonstrative is desired here.

501–2. In the *Little Iliad* (Arg. p. 122 (4) *GEF* + *Il. Parv.* fr. 11 *GEF*) Odysseus and Diomedes entered Troy at night to steal the Palladion, a statuette of Athena standing upright in arms, which guaranteed the safety of the city (cf. L. Ziehen, *RE* XVIII.3 s.v. Palladion, coll. 171–4, E. Penkova, *LIMC* II.1 'Athena' A 7, C. A. Faraone, *Talismans and Trojan Horses* ..., New York 1992, 4, 7, 21). According to Verg. *Aen.* 2.166 (~ 9.151), this entailed their killing the guards on the acropolis to gain access to the goddess' shrine.

Our poet ascribes the venture to Odysseus alone in order to highlight his depravity in the Trojans' eyes and to prepare for the leading role he will play in the invasion of their camp. By the same token the chorus identify him, and not Diomedes, as the prime suspect in this case (692–727n.). The Palladion theft is recalled at 709 (n.) μὴ κλωπὸς αἴνει φωτὸς αἱμύλον δόρυ.

With some changes the episode was dramatised in Sophocles' *Lakainai* (S. frr. 367–9a). See Pearson, *The Fragments of Sophocles* II, 34–6, *Rh.* 503–7a n. and, for a reconstruction of the epic version, West, *Epic Cycle*, 199–203.

εἰς Ἀθάνας σηκόν: Properly σηκός ('enclosure') denotes a sacred precinct 'without any roofed building' (Jebb on *Phil.* 1327 ff.), often a hero's burial place or cultic site. But the tragedians also used it more losely for 'shrine': cf. *Ion* 300 σηκοῖς ... Τροφωνίου (i.e. his cave), *Phoen.* [1751–2], fr. tr. adesp. 424 ἁγνὸν εἰς σηκὸν θεοῦ.

Doric Ἀθάνα (V) is the regular trisyllabic form (tetrasyllabic Ἀθηναία) in tragic dialogue as in lyric verse (Björck, *Alpha Impurum*, 132–5, 201–2, 242–3, Barrett on *Hipp.* 1120–5 [p. 374]). Later Attic Ἀθηνᾶ (fere ΟΛ) is a frequent 'simplifying' mistake (*Sept.* 487, *Phil.* 134, *Hcld.* 350, 934, *Tro.* 979, *Ion* 1529, E. fr. 369.4).

ἔννυχος μολών: 226b–8n. The adjective appears also in 55 ἔννυχος φρυκτωρία and 788 (787–8n.) ἔννυχος ... φόβος.

ναῦς ἔπ' Ἀργείων φέρει: 149–50n.

503–7a. Unlike the other episodes (501–2, 507b–9a nn.), the so-called 'Ptôcheia' is repeated in more elaborate form (and with many verbal echoes) by the chorus to support their idea that it was Odysseus who had slipped by their lines: 710–21 (n.). Apart from the *Little Iliad* (cf. Arg. p. 122 (4) *GEF* + *Il. Parv.* frr. 8–10 *GEF*), it was told by Helen at *Od.* 4.242–64. Our poet deviates from both sources in that he does not have Odysseus disfigure himself (*Od.* 4.244) or receive disfiguring blows from Thoas (*Il. Parv.* fr. 8 *GEF*), perhaps because it did not suit his notion of 'the self-serving master of wiles' (Liapis on 498–509 [p. 206]).[186] He also omitted as irrelevant the encounter with Helen, but not the killing of Trojan guards (*Od.* 4.257–8, *Il. Parv.* Arg. p. 122 (4) *GEF*). Whether or not the latter was 'suggested by the *Doloneia* if that already existed' (West, *Epic Cycle*, 199), in the reverse order of events here it shows that Odysseus is capable of combining reconnaissance with a violent assault on the enemy (cf. 498b–509, 501–2nn.).

A reference to Euripides' idiosyncratic version at *Hec.* 239–50 is found in 505 (503–5n.) and possibly 711 (710–11n.). Of other dramatic treatments we cannot be sure. Very little is left of Ion's *Phrouroi* (*TrGF* 19 FF 43a–49a), and the same is true of S. *Lakainai* (501–2n.), which appears to have conflated the 'Ptôcheia' and the Palladion theft. According to Aristotle (or his interpolator) in *Poet.* 1459b6, there also existed a tragedy *Ptôcheia* (fr. tr. adesp. 8k), unless this was identical with *Lakainai* or *Phrouroi* (Radt, *TrGF* IV, 328–9).

503–5. 'And he had already entered our walls as a vagabond, dressed in beggar's clothes, and uttered many curses against the Argives – when he had been sent as a spy on Ilion.'

ἤδη: indicating an action previous to the last one spoken about (KG II 120–1; cf. LSJ s.v. ἤδη I 1).

ἀγύρτης: Cf. 715 (715–16n.) ... ἀγύρτης τις λάτρις. Properly ἀγύρτης (< ἀγείρω) denotes a priest or prophet who collects gifts for his deity. It is derogatory, as the once acceptable custom had turned into fraudulence and mere beggary under an honourable pretext: e.g. *Ag.* 1273–4 (Cassandra) κακουμένη δέ, φοιτὰς ὡς ἀγύρτρια, / πτωχὸς τάλαινα λιμοθνὴς ἠνεσχόμην (with Fraenkel on 1273), *OT* 388–9, Hp. *Morb. Sacr.* 1.4, Pl. *Rep.* 364b5–7 (cf. W. Burkert, *RhM* N.F. 105 [1962], 36–55, particularly 50–5, on a similar development in γόης, ἀλαζών and φέναξ). Our passages are the first and by far the earliest where the word does not bear any 'sacral' connotations (see, however, *Od.* 19.284 χρήματ' ἀγυρτάζειν, 'to collect guest-gifts', also of Odysseus). An ex-

---

186 On the alternative influence of *Od.* 13.397–403 (~ 13.429–38) on Odysseus' disguise in *Rh.* 710–21 see 710–21, 710–11, 712–13a, 715–16 (ψαφαρόχρουν) nn.

cellent late parallel is Hld. 2.19.1 ἐλευσόμεθα δ' οὖν ὅμως εἰς πτωχοὺς καὶ τοὺς διὰ τροφὴν ἀγύρτας ἑαυτοὺς μεταπλάσαντες.[187]

πτωχικὴν ἔχων στολήν receives a lyric reworking at 712–13a (n.) ῥακοδύτῳ στολᾷ / πυκασθείς ... Like other adjectives in -ικός (205n.), πτωχικός was more at home in comedy and prose than in tragedy, although it may have stood in E. fr. 727a.30 (*Telephus*) × – ⏑ – × πτω]χὸς ὢν οὐ πτω[χ ⏑ – (πτω[χικά Kannicht: πτω[χικῶς Snell). Otherwise note especially Lycurg. 86 λαβόντα πτωχικὴν στολήν – of the mythical Athenian king Kodros, who similarly deceived the enemy in a beggar's disguise.

πολλὰ δ' Ἀργείοις κακά / ἠρᾶτο: The repetition at 717–19 (n.) πολλὰ δὲ τὰν / βασιλίδ' ἑστίαν Ἀτρειδᾶν κακῶς / ἔβαζε δῆθεν ἐχθρὸς ὢν στρατηλάταις confirms that the imprecations were intended to make Odysseus look like a Greek defector, even without the (self-inflicted) disfigurement, which our poet suppressed (503–7a n.). Despite Fantuzzi (*MD* 36 [1996], 180–2), it is probable that this detail also came from the 'Ptôcheia' rather than the story of Sinon in the *Little Iliad* or *Iliou Persis*. At Plut. *Sol.* 30.1 Solon calls Peisistratos (who had used the same ruse to simulate an enemy attack) a bad 'Homeric' *Odysseus*, and other sources support this association (cf. West, *Epic Cycle*, 197 with n. 42). Yet it may be that Odysseus was an early doublet of Sinon here.

For ἀράομαι (τινί τι), 'imprecate, curse', cf. e.g. *Sept.* 632–3 ... πόλη / οἵας ἀρᾶται καὶ κατεύχεται τύχας, *PV* 912, *OC* 951–2, *Alc.* 714. Λ here has Ἀργείους, by assimilation to πύργους or false analogy with verbs of saying which take a double accusative.

πεμφθεὶς Ἰλίου κατάσκοπος echoes *Hec.* 239 (Hecuba to Odysseus) οἶσθ' ἡνίκ' ἦλθες Ἰλίου κατάσκοπος (503–7a n.). On κατάσκοπος see 125–6a n.

506–7a. φρουροὺς καὶ παραστάτας πυλῶν: Unless this is a hendiadys ('the guards standing by the gates'), we must assume a distinction between other sentries (within the city walls) and the gatekeepers (Liapis on 506–7, who compares the clearer *Tro.* 956 πύργων πυλωροὶ κἀπὸ τειχέων σκοποί).

In the sense 'standing by, defender of (something)' παραστάτης does not occur anywhere else (LSJ s.v. I). Similarly φρουρός has only two parallels in surviving drama (*Ion* 22, *Hel.* 1673), although it may have been more frequent in Ion's *Phrouroi* (503–7a n.). Whatever restrictions the playwrights appear to have felt about φρουρός, they did not extend to its verb and other words from that stem.

ἐξῆλθεν balances ἐσῆλθε in 504.

---

[187] Σ[V] *Rh.* 503 (II 339.25–6 Schwartz = 104 Merro) ἀγύρτης ἀπὸ τοῦ συνάγειν καὶ ἀγείρειν τροφήν. ἐπαίτης need not be more than an inference from the line itself.

507b–9a. Odysseus could always be expected to be lurking in ambush (cf. his false account to Eumaeus at *Od.* 14.468–506). If we are to think of a specific plot, it can only be the capture of Helenus, which in the *Little Iliad* preceded both the 'Ptôcheia' and the Palladion theft and was probably a prerequisite for the latter: Arg. p. 120 (2) *GEF* μετὰ ταῦτα Ὀδυσσεὺς λοχήσας Ἕλενον λαμβάνει and, in greater detail, *Phil.* 604–7(9) ... μάντις ἦν τις εὐγενής, / ... / Ἕλενος, ὃν οὗτος νυκτὸς ἐξελθὼν μόνος / ... / δόλοις Ὀδυσσεὺς εἷλε (Housman: δόλῳ K: δόλιος rell.).[188] The original location of the attack is unclear. But if it was not Mt. Ida or Arisbe (as in later sources), the Thymbraean altar, which is also where Achilles slew Troilus (224–5n.), seems a plausible choice (West, *Epic Cycle*, 180 with nn. 17, 18).

The acts of the Doloneia are mentioned alongside Helenus and the theft of the Palladion at Ov. *Met.* 13.98–100 (Ajax speaking) *conferat his Ithacus Rhesum imbellemque Dolona / Priamidenque Helenum rapta cum Pallade captum; / luce nihil gestum, nihil est Diomede remoto.* Cf. 498b–509n.

ἐν λόχοις ... θάσσων: similarly 512 ἴζειν ... κλωπικὰς ἕδρας. The versatile λόχος (17–18, 26nn.) here means 'ambush' in the sense 'place for lying in wait' (LSJ s.v. I 1, *LfgrE* s.v. B 1a). A possible model is *Il.* 13.284–5 οὔτέ τι λίην / ταρβεῖ (*sc.* ὁ ἀγαθός), ἐπειδὰν πρῶτον ἐσίζηται λόχον ἀνδρῶν. Similarly Hes. *Th.* 174 εἷσε δέ μιν κρύψασα λόχῳ (i.e. Earth her son Cronus).

θάσσω is a favourite verb of Euripides (21 secure instances). Aristophanes exploited this in *Thesm.* 889–90 ('Euripides' speaking) τί δαὶ σὺ θάσσεις τάσδε τυμβήρεις ἕδρας / φάρει καλυπτός, ὦ ξένη;[189] Otherwise only *OT* 161 and Ar. *Vesp.* 1482 (again paratragic).

Θυμβραῖον ἀμφὶ βωμὸν ἄστεως πέλας: On Thymbra and the sanctuary of Thymbraean Apollo see 224–5n. The complaint of Dionysodorus (in *Errors in the Tragedians*) that the site lay fifty stades away from Troy and thus could not be described as being 'near the city' (Σ[V] *Rh.* 508 [II 339.13–16 Schwartz = 104 Merro]) is learned pedantry getting the better of literary perception (and common sense). In order to appear as a constant threat, Odysseus needed to be placed in the vicinity of Troy, whether or not our poet had a clear topography in mind and could have expected his audience to do so. Probably neither was the case.

---

[188] On the choice of reading and in favour perhaps of δόλιος see 893b–4n. with n. 309.
[189] Mette ascribed the lines to Aeschylus' *Niobe* (A. fr. **157a). But given the speaker's identity and the very detailed parody of *Helen* in Ar. *Thesm.* 855–919, it is more likely to be a paratragic confection with a nod to Euripidean style.

Prompted by the ancient criticism, the V-scholiast, or one of his sources, conjectured ἢ ἄστεος πέλας (with the epic genitive that is falsely in Δ).

509b. κακῷ ... μερμέρῳ: 'a baneful evil'. This is our only example of epic μέρμερος in drama and perhaps the earliest one of its application to a person rather than, in the neuter plural, to actions in war (or the doings of women): *Il.* 8.453 πολέμοιό τε μέρμερα ἔργα, 10.48 τοσσάδε μέρμερ' ... μητίσασθαι, 289, 524 θηέοντο δὲ μέρμερα ἔργα (the massacre in the Thracian camp), 11.502, 21.217, Hes. *Th.* 603 μέρμερα ἔργα γυναικῶν (*LfgrE* s.v. μέρμερα B). The precise meaning and etymology of the word are uncertain, but it may be related to μέριμνα, i.e. 'causing anxiety' and hence 'grievous, baneful' (*GEW*, *DELG* s.v. μέρμερος; cf. Hsch. μ 876 Latte, Σ^A *Il.* 10.48 [III 12.60–1 Erbse]).

No doubt the threefold occurrence of μέρμερα in *Iliad* 10 (above) influenced our poet's choice. If there was such a need, its un-epic use of a person here may have been mitigated by the fact that grammatically it refers to a substantivised neuter adjective.[190] Later see especially Lyc. 949 τεύξει ... μερμέραν βλάβην (i.e. the Trojan Horse).

510–17. In his reply Rhesus expresses the usual heroic contempt for covert actions (510–11n.) before fastening on the Palladion theft and threatening Odysseus with the most gruesome death for the sacrilege (512–17n.). There is obvious dramatic irony, combined perhaps with an anticipatory moral judgement (Morwood on 510), in that Rhesus himself will soon fall victim to the man he denounces.

510–11. While epic saw some merit in ambushes and the men who executed them (*Il.* 13.276–91, *Od.* 14.468–506), traditional warrior ethics demanded meeting the enemy 'face to face', κατὰ στόμα (408–10a n.). Regarding Odysseus, note especially Antisth. *Ai.* 5 νῦν δ' οὐκ ἔστιν ὃ διαφέρει πλέον ἐμοῦ καὶ τοῦδε. ὁ μὲν γὰρ οὐκ ἔστιν ὅ τι ἂν δράσειε φανερῶς, ἐγὼ δὲ οὐδὲν ἂν λάθρᾳ τολμήσαιμι πρᾶξαι and, outside war, *Phil.* 88–91 (Neoptolemus) ἔφυν γὰρ οὐδὲν ἐκ τέχνης πράσσειν κακῆς, / ... / ἀλλ' εἴμ' ἑτοῖμος πρὸς βίαν τὸν ἄνδρ' ἄγειν / καὶ μὴ δόλοισιν.

ἀνὴρ εὔψυχος: Cf. *Hel.* 852 εὔψυχον ἄνδρα. Both εὔψυχος and εὐψυχία are first found in Aeschylus (*Pers.* 326, 394). Later they became widespread in Attic prose, while of the tragedians only Euripides shows numerous cases of the noun and one more of the adjective (*Andr.* 764). In *HF* 157–64 εὐψυχία is twice denied to the archer who strikes from afar (cf. 32–3, 312–13nn.).

512–17. Despite the noble denunciation of secrecy and the fact that the Greeks too had severe punishments for sacrilegious theft (below),

---

[190] Μέρμερος is attested as a proper name in *Il.* 14.513 and *Od.* 1.259. The adjective is employed directly of a person in Pl. (?) *Hp. Ma.* 290e4.

Rhesus' plans would hardly have endeared him to the audience (cf. 467–526n.). Impalement of the living or (parts of) the dead body was considered the utmost cruelty in Greece, not least presumably because of the 'prolonged public exposure of the corpse' (Parker, *Miasma*, 47 with n. 53). It was, however, practised by Near Eastern peoples like the Persians and Medes (e.g. Hdt. 1.128.2, 3.159.1, 4.43.6, 7.238.1, 9.78.3, Thuc. 1.110.3) and so became a characteristic of 'barbarian' behaviour (cf. Hall, *Inventing the Barbarian*, 158–9, 205). Hence Apollo telling the Erinyes they belong where impalement, among other atrocities, is committed (*Eum.* 186–90) and the remark of Orestes in E. *El.* 896–8 that his sister may cast out Aegisthus' body or put it on a stake 'as a spoil for the birds'.

In the context of temple robbery, Thoas in *IT* 1429–30 envisages impalement for Orestes and his party as an alternative to throwing them over a cliff, which in some Greek states was the penalty for this crime (Parker, *Miasma*, 45 with n. 47, 46–7, 170 with n. 150).[191] The theft of the Palladion is declared sacrilege at Antisth. *Ai.* 2–3 and 6.

512–15. 'This man who you say sits in thievish ambushes and plots – I will capture him alive, impale him along the spine and set him up outside the city gates to be a feasting-place for the winged vultures.'

512–13a. ἵζειν ... κλωπικὰς ἕδρας: Cf. 507–9 and, for κλωπικός, 205 (n.). The adjective here evokes the Palladion theft, which seems to be foremost in Rhesus' mind.

μηχανᾶσθαι: absolute, as in *Od.* 4.822–3 δυσμενέες γὰρ πολλοὶ ἐπ' αὐτῷ μηχανόωνται / ἱέμενοι κτεῖναι, πρὶν πατρίδα γαῖαν ἱκέσθαι (LSJ s.v. μηχανάομαι A I 2).

513b–15. πυλῶν ἐπ' ἐξόδοισιν: i.e. for maximum visibility. The phrase comes from *Sept.* 58 πυλῶν ἐπ' ἐξόδοισι τάγευσαι τάχος, which itself is a repetition of *Sept.* 33–4 ... πυλῶν ἐπ' ἐξόδοις / μίμνοντες. On 'scattered' references to the prologue of *Seven against Thebes* see Introduction, 33–4.

ἀμπείρας ῥάχιν: Cf. *Eum.* 189–90 καὶ μύζουσιν οἰκτισμὸν πολύν / ὑπὸ ῥάχιν παγέντες – from the same notable passage (*Eum.* 186–90) that seems to have influenced *Rh.* 817 (817–18a n.). 'Execution by impalement' involved 'driving a sharp stake through the body from near the base of the spine' (Sommerstein on *Eum.* 186–90 [p. 115]). Here ῥάχιν specifies τοῦτον (512) according to the σχῆμα καθ' ὅλον καὶ μέρος (266n.).

ἀναπείρω, properly 'fix (meat) on a spit' (LSJ s.v. I), is also used for impalement (of the head) at Hdt. 4.103.3 (describing the Taurians' treat-

---

[191] In fourth-century Athens convicts for such offences were executed, their bodies left unburied outside the borders of Attica and their property confiscated by the state.

ment of their dead enemies) ἀποταμὼν ἕκαστος κεφαλὴν ἀποφέρεται ἐς τὰ οἰκία, ἔπειτα ἐπὶ ξύλου μεγάλου ἀναπείρας ἱστᾷ ... The participle here with 'epic-poetic' apocope (cf. *Il.* 2.426 σπλάγχνα ... ἀμπείραντες) is correctly preserved in Δ and Hsch. α 3775 Latte. Corruption into ἐμπ- (fere Λ) was helped by the fact that ἐμπείρω occurs in the same sense in later Greek (LSJ s.v. I 2). Likewise 'Megarian' ἀμπεπαρμένον at Ar. *Ach.* 796 (ἀμπ- Elmsley: ἐμπ- codd.).

πετεινοῖς γυψὶ θοινατήριον: Among the birds (and other beasts) that would have preyed on unburied corpses vultures are singled out at *Il.* 4.237, 11.161–2, 16.836, 18.271, 22.42–3 and *Tro.* 599–600. The earliest Greek example of this literary topos (West, *EFH* 215–16, *IEPM* 476 with n. 87, 491–2) is *Il.* 1.4–5 αὐτοὺς δὲ ἑλώρια τεῦχε κύνεσσιν / οἰωνοῖσί τε πᾶσι. With a variant δαῖτα for πᾶσι, favoured also by Zenodotus (*apud* Ath. 1.12e-f), this inspired A. *Suppl.* 800–1 κυσὶν δ' ἔπειθ' ἕλωρα κἀπιχωρίοις / ὄρνισι δεῖπνον (cf. FJW on 800–1, M. L. West, *Studies in the Text and Transmission of the Iliad*, Munich – Leipzig 2001, 173 with n. 1) and, directly or indirectly, a series of similar passages in tragedy (and *nomos*): *Ant.* 29–30 (~ *Phoen.* [1634]), *Hec.* 1077, *Ion* 504–6 πτανοῖς ... / θοίναν θηρσί τε φοινίαν / δαῖτα (cf. 903–5, 1494–6), Tim. *Pers.* fr. 791.137–8 *PMG* = Hordern ἔνθα κείσομαι οἰκτρός, ὀρ- / νίθων ἔθνεσιν ὠμοβρῶσι θοινά. Our poet stands in this tradition and perhaps had *Ion* (and Timotheus) in mind.

The unique θοινατήριον, literally 'feasting-place' (G. Björck, *Eranos* 55 [1957], 10), is a substantivised neuter adjective (cf. Schwyzer 467, 470), based on θοινατήρ ('giver of a feast'), which itself is found only in *Ag.* 1502. For the irregular long α in tragic derivatives of θοίνη and other nouns (440–2n.) see Nauck, *Euripideische Studien* II, 175 and Björck, *Alpha Impurum*, 139–42, 223 (Hsch. θ 626 Latte writes θοινητήριον). O's θοιναστήριον has a parallel in εὐναστηρ- for εὐνατηρ- at *Tr.* 918 and *Or.* 590.

516–17. θεῶν ἀνάκτορα: in the same metrical position *Tro.* 15–16 ἔρημα δ' ἄλση καὶ θεῶν ἀνάκτορα / φόνῳ καταρρεῖ ... Euripides was fond of ἀνάκτορον (< ἄναξ, ἀνάκτωρ) for a god's shrine (also *Andr.* 43, 117, 1111, 1157, *Suppl.* 88, *Tro.* 85, 330, *IT* 66, 636, *Ion* 55–6). Elsewhere before *Rhesus* only S. fr. 757.4 and Hdt. 9.65.2.

συλῶντα: 'despoil'. Of temple robbery cf. e.g. *Pers.* 809–10 οἳ γῆν μολόντες Ἑλλάδ' οὐ θεῶν βρέτη / ᾐδοῦντο συλᾶν οὐδὲ πιμπράναι νεώς, E. fr. 328.3 θεῶν συλᾶν βρέτη, Hdt. 6.19.3, 8.33 (LSJ s.v. 2).

τῷδε κατθανεῖν μόρῳ: Tragedy regularly has μόρος, 'fate (of death)', in this kind of expression. V's πότμῳ is a curiously high-style variant, prompted perhaps by recollection of epic πότμος for 'evil destiny' and particularly 'death' (Liapis on 516–17; cf. LSJ s.v. I 1). Similarly at *Pers.* 444 τεθνᾶσιν αἰσχρῶς δυσκλεεστάτῳ μόρῳ some MSS read πότμῳ, which West and Sommerstein accept as *lectio difficilior*.[192] The two words are paired in *Hec.* 695–6 τίνι μόρῳ θνῄσκεις, τίνι πότμῳ κεῖσαι, / πρὸς τίνος ἀνθρώπων;

518–26. On Hector's breaking off the discussion see 467–526n. In addition to redirecting the plot towards *Iliad* 10 (467–526, 519–20, 523–6nn.), this short 'coda' motivates the exits of first Hector and Rhesus (526), then the chorus (564) to leave the stage empty for Odysseus and Diomedes.

518. καταυλίσθητι: 'make camp, bivouac', as at Xen. *An.* 7.5.15, Plut. *Pyrrh.* 27.2 and, in a non-military setting, *Phil.* 30 ὅρα καθ' ὕπνον μὴ καταυλισθεὶς κυρῇ. Diggle is probably right to accept Kirchhoff's singular imperative (I [1855], 556, on 507) for the transmitted καταυλίσθητε. It readily curtails Rhesus' exposition and suits the ensuing addresses to him alone.

καὶ γάρ: explanatory, with καί meaning 'in fact' (*GP* 108–9). So also 525–6 καὶ γάρ, εἴπερ ἐστὶ σῶς, / ἤδη πελάζει στρατοπέδοισι Τρωϊκοῖς.

εὐφρόνη: 91–2n.

519–20. The placement of the Thracian contingent apart from the Trojans and their other allies accords with *Il.* 10.434 Θρήϊκες οἵδ' ἀπάνευθε νεήλυδες, ἔσχατοι ἄλλων. So also Athena's description in 613–15.

νυχεῦσαι: 'pass the night'. The verb says nothing about sleep or wakefulness, although the latter is implied in its other three (four) occurrences: E. *El.* 181 δάκρυσι νυχεύω, *Hyps.* fr. 8/9.13–14 Bond = E. fr. 753c.19–20, Nic. fr. 74.8 Gow–Scholfield, *Ant.* 782–4 "Ερως ... / ὃς ἐν μαλακαῖς παρειαῖς / νεάνιδος ἐννυχεύεις.[193] Similarly ἰαύω (740n.) and the prosaic νυκτερεύω, 'spend the night in the open' (LSJ Suppl. [1996] s.v. a).

τοῦ τεταγμένου δίχα: Cf. 614 ἐκτὸς ... τάξεων. Like the plural of τάξις ('rank of soldiers') there and in 523, 595 (595–8a n.) and 698, the semi-substantivised τεταγμένου (*sc.* στρατοῦ) loosely refers to an encamped army. The Thracians will not keep such good order (762–9n.).

521–2. We finally learn the Trojan watchword, which Hector did not allow the chorus to give after 12 (n.). It will be instrumental to Odysseus' and Diomedes' success.

---

[192] West (apparatus) refers to *Pers.* 446 ποίῳ μόρῳ δὲ τούσδε φῂς ὀλωλέναι; But the same sort of repetition is found in the preceding exchange between the Messenger (436–7) and the Queen (439–40). It seems better to regard πότμῳ as a gloss (Garvie on *Pers.* 441–6).

[193] In E. *Suppl.* 1135 ποῦ λοχευμάτων χάρις Musgrave's restoration of the nonsensical πολυχευμάτων (L) is preferable to Triclinius' ποῦ νυχευμάτων ... ('sleepless nights'). See Collard on 1135–8.

ξύνθημα also appears in 572, 684 and, with reference to our lines, 762–3a (n.) ἐπεὶ γὰρ ἡμᾶς ηὔνασ' Ἑκτόρεια χείρ, / ξύνθημα λέξας. Unlike σῆμα (12, 688) and σύμβολον (573), this is the regular term for 'watchword' (e.g. Hdt. 9.98.3, Thuc. 7.44.4, Xen. *An.* 1.8.16, 6.5.25, 7.3.39, *Phoen.* 1140, fr. tr. adesp. 365). For other military applications of these words see LSJ s.vv. and Willink on *Or.* 1130.

Φοῖβος: Divine watchwords are well attested in historical times (add Xen. *Cyr.* 3.3.58 and 7.1.10 to the Herodotus and *Anabasis* passages cited above). Since they were meant to put the army under the respective god's protection, there is great irony in that 'Phoebus', one of the chief supporters of Troy, will soon assist the Greeks: 573, 688 (with 675–91n.), C. W. Keyes, *CPh* 24 (1929), 207 ~ *TAPA* 59 (1928), xxviii, Rosivach 64. We also recall the chorus' (abortive) prayer to Apollo for Dolon's safety in 224–63 (n.).

ἤν τι καὶ δέῃ: '… if (indeed) you should need it'. For εἰ (τι) καί in this sense cf. *PV* 342–3 μάτην γὰρ … / … πονήσεις, εἴ τι καὶ πονεῖν θέλεις, and see *GP* 303.

μέμνησ' ἀκούσας: 'remember it, now that you have heard it …', i.e. with ἀκούσας as an ordinary circumstantial instead of a supplementary participle. Likewise *Ag.* 830 τὰ δ' εἰς τὸ σὸν φρόνημα, μέμνημαι κλυών (with Fraenkel).

523–6. As it happens, the sentries will not return to their posts. Yet this is the first time that we hear of Dolon since his departure in 223 and, from Hector's sceptical conclusion (525–6), get the impression that all may not be well. The chorus specify their premonition in 557–61 (n.).

523–5a. 'But you must go in front of the lines to keep watch wakefully and receive Dolon, our spy upon the ships.'

ὑμᾶς δέ: i.e. the chorus.

προταινὶ τάξεων: Parmeniscus' claim that προταινί is Boeotian (Σ^V *Rh.* 523 [II 340.3–4 Schwartz = 105 Merro]) is confirmed by the occurrence of προτηνί (with later Boeotian spelling) in three fourth- to third-century BC inscriptions from Thespiae (*IG* VII 1739.14, *BCH* 21.554/557.2) and Thebes (*IG* VII 2406.7). There, however, the word is used as a temporal adverb (= πρότερον), in accordance with its likely derivation from locative-dative πρὸ ται-νί (*sc.* ἀμέρᾳ), 'before this day' (F. Bechtel, *Die Griechischen Dialekte* I, Berlin 1921, 309–10, C. D. Buck, *The Greek Dialects*, Chicago 1955, §§ 123, 136.1). It seems, therefore, that our poet has misapplied a metrically convenient dialect gloss (Schwyzer 619 n. 3, Liapis on 523–5) on the analogy of πάρος, (ἐμ)πρόσθεν and the like (cf. Ritchie 159). Unfortunately, we cannot determine the origin of Hsch. π 3966 Hansen προταίνιον· πρὸ μικροῦ (~ 3967 προταίνιον· παλαιόν, where the text is uncertain), but the Doric (?) parallel form ποταίνιος, 'fresh, new, unexpected' (LSJ s.v. 1, 2), occurs several times in tragedy and satyr-play (*Cho.* 1055, *Eum.* 282, *PV* 102, A. frr. 46b.6 (?), 78a.69, *Ant.* 849, S. fr. 149.5). Its adverb is attested in 'Zon.' π 1571.9 Tittmann ποταινί· προσφάτως.

ἐγερτί: Cf. *Ant.* 413–14 ἐγερτὶ κινῶν ἄνδρ' ἀνὴρ ἐπιρρόθοις / κακοῖσιν (i.e. the guards keeping vigil over Polynices' body) and Heraclit. 22 B 63 DK ἔνθα δ' ἐόντι ἐπανίστασθαι καὶ φύλακας γίνεσθαι ἐγερτὶ ζώντων καὶ νεκρῶν. But the primary model would have been the Greek sentries at *Il.* 10.182 ἀλλ' ἐγρηγορτεὶ σὺν τεύχεσιν εἴατο πάντες, with that unique adverb based on the perfect stem (Schwyzer 623, Hainsworth on *Il.* 10.180–2).

νεῶν κατάσκοπον / ... Δόλωνα: similarly 557–8 (n.) ναῶν / ... κατόπτην and 591–2 ναυστάθμων / κατάσκοπον Δόλωνα. For κατάσκοπος see 125–6a n.

δέχθαι: The epic infinitive (cf. *Il.* 1.23, 377, *h.Ven.* 140) suits the context. It was restored in the Aldine (cf. Introduction, 55) from the unmetrical δέχεσθαι (VΛ: -θε O), which appears to be an old gloss. Similar verbal epicisms are μηνίων (494–5n.), ἀμπείρας (513b–15n.), μεμβλωκότων (627–9n.) and ἐξαπώσατε (810b–12a n.).

525b–6. καὶ γάρ: 518n.

πελάζει: 13–14n.

στρατοπέδοισι Τρωϊκοῖς: plural for singular also in *Rh.* 811 κοὔτ' εἰσιόντας στρατόπεδ' ἐξαπώσατε and Xen. *An.* 7.3.34.

527–64. The sentries' 'Dawn-Song' is widely recognised as the finest piece of lyric in *Rhesus*. Following the time-scale of *Il.* 10.251–3 ἀλλ' ἴομεν· μάλα γὰρ νὺξ ἄνεται, ἐγγύθι δ' ἠώς, / ἄστρα δὲ δὴ προβέβηκε, παροίχωκεν δὲ πλέων νύξ / τῶν δύω μοιράων, τριτάτη δ' ἔτι μοῖρα λέλειπται (cf. 527–31, 535–7nn.), its strophe (527–37) and antistrophe (546–56) give a vivid, and very poetical, picture of the sights and sounds commonly held to accompany daybreak. For the tired soldiers they are of special significance as signs that their period of guard duty is drawing to a close. The connection with the plot is strengthened by the brief anapaestic dialogues on the rota of night-watches (538–45, 562–4nn.) and Dolon's alarming failure to return (557–61n.).

This 'dramatic' quality distinguishes our ode from the parodos of Euripides' *Phaethon* (63–101 Diggle = E. fr. 773.19–58),[194] with which it shares several motifs and expressions (527–30, 532–3, 535–7, 546–50, 551–3nn.; cf. G. H. Macurdy, *AJPh* 64 [1943], 408–16, Ritchie 255–6, Diggle on *Phaeth.* 63–101 [pp. 95–6]). Merops' maidservants also de-

---

[194] Dated from the trimeter resolution rate to 'within a few years of 420' (Diggle, *Phaethon*, 47–9; cf. M. Cropp – G. Fick, *Resolutions and Chronology in Euripides: the Fragmentary Tragedies*, London 1985, 87).

scribe dawn mainly in visual and aural terms, but apart from the stars and the nightingale's song (*Phaeth.* 63–70 Diggle = E. fr. 773.19–26), these are not based on immediate observation, and the whole (imagined) bustle of early morning life merely serves as a foil for their own activities in preparation for Phaethon's wedding.[195] The sentries, moreover, with their keen personal interest in determining the time for relief, pay much more attention to the celestial bodies, which incidentally signal an hour somewhat prior to that in *Phaethon* (Fraenkel on *Ag.* 826 [II, 381 n. 2]; cf. Diggle [above] and H. D. Jocelyn, *PCPS* n.s. 17 [1971], 70 with n. 3 for the gap recorded between the first light here and sunrise at 985, 992).[196]

Each ode thus perfectly suits the character and respective situation of its chorus, and even without invoking Euripides' 'obsession with astronomy' (Hyp. (b) *Rh.* 64.27–8 = 430.25–6 Diggle), we should be hard put to tell the original from the imitation. It is not surprising, however, that our poet felt attracted by a piece which in the third century BC already formed part of a Euripidean anthology (Diggle, *Phaethon,* 34 + *AC* 65 [1996], 191) and was later to inspire the parodos of Seneca's *Hercules Furens*.[197]

Formally, the watchmen's song resembles the parodoi of *Alcestis* (77–135) and *Antigone* (100–61), the 'only two other passages in tragedy where the chorus delivers both lyric and anapaestic sections' (Parker on *Alc.* 77–135 [p. 70 (~ 68)]; cf. Dale on *Alc.* 91 and *Rh.* 527–64 'Metre' 538–45 + 557–64n.). But it also foreshadows the epirrhematic structure of the epiparodos proper (692–727n.), in which the sentries, as it were, discuss the result of their collective departure. Inappropriate as this would be outside drama (Introduction, 39–40), their weariness gives a realistic impression. The small hours are the the most difficult for guards 'torn from their regular sleeping cycle' (cf. already *Il.* 10.97–9, 181–2, 192–3), and any stratagem like that of the Greeks would concentrate on them (F. S. Russell, *Information Gathering in Classical Greece*, Ann Arbor 1999, 36–7).

---

195 Cf. M. Hose, *Studien zum Chor bei Euripides* I, Stuttgart 1990, 129–31 on the ode's priamel structure.
196 Some knowledge of astronomy was recommended for soldiers, not least for the purpose of regulating night-watches (Xen. *Mem.* 4.7.4; cf. Plb. 9.14.5–15.15). But in practice more reliable results were obtained by the use of a water-clock: Aen. Tact. 22.24–5 (with Whitehead [pp. 159–60], P. Pattenden, *RhM* N.F. 130 [1987], 164–74), Veget. *Epit. rei mil.* 3.8.17.
197 See Diggle on *Phaeth.* 63–101 (pp. 96–7), J. G. Fitch (ed.), *Seneca's Hercules Furens. A Critical Text with Introduction and Commentary*, Ithaca – New York 1987, on 125–204 (pp. 158–63) and M. Billerbeck (ed.), *Seneca. Hercules Furens. Einleitung, Text, Übersetzung und Kommentar*, Leiden et al. 1999, on 125–204 (pp. 241–5).

Metre

527–537 ~ 546–556. Dactylo-epitrites with one irregular colon at 530–1 ~ 549–50. The analysis of the lines as *4da* + *ith* (530–1/549–50n.) removes the most pertinent metrical similarities with *Alc.* 568–77 + 588–96 ~ 578–87 + 597–605 (Ritchie 314–15) as well as *Alc.* 435–44 ~ 445–54 and *Rh.* 895–903 ~ 906–914 (890–914 'Metre' nn.). Yet the former two still share the sequence $D^{(2)}$ ⏑ – – (536–7/555–6n.), and the latter ends in ⏓⏓ *D* – ||| (903 ~ 914 with 890–914 'Metre' 903/914n. and Diggle, *Euripidea*, 207).

538–545 + 557–564. Recitative anapaests. As often in such epirrhematic structures, neither metre nor changes of speaker (538–45, 557–64nn.) correspond exactly. Cf. e.g. *Cho.* 306–14, 340–4, 372–9, 400–9, 476–8 (West, *GM* 79), *Phil.* 144–9, 159–68, 191–200, *OC* 138–49, 170–5, 188–91 and, in wholly choral systems, *Ant.* 110–16, 127–33, 141–7, 155–61, *Alc.* 77–85, 93–7, 105–11, [131–5]?.

527–8	546–7	⏓⏓ – ⏑⏑ – | ⏑⏑ – ⏒ | – ⏑ – | – – ||	⏓⏓ D ⏒ | e | – – ||
529	548	– ⏑ – | – – ⏑ ⏑ – ⏑ ⏑ – |	e | – D |
530	549	– ⏑ ⏑ | – ⏑ ⏑ – | ⏑ ⏑ – ⏑ ⏑	*4da*
531	550	– ⏑ – | ⏑ – – ||	*ith* ||
532	551	⏓ – ⏑ | ⏑ – ⏑ ⏑ – – |	⏓ D – |
533	552	– ⏑ ⏑ | – ⏑ ⏑ – |	D |
534	553	– – ⏑ ⏑ – ⏑ ⏑ – – |	– D – |
535	554	– ⏔ – ⏑ ⏑ | – – |	D (contr.) – |
536–7	555–6	– ⏑ – – – ⏑ ⏑ – | ⏑ ⏑ – ⏑ – – |||	e – D ⏑ – – |||

Notes

527–8/546–7 The rhythm – ⏑ – – – – (*e* – – or '*cr sp*') concludes dactylo-epitrite sequences in *Phaeth.* 235 ~ 244 Diggle = E. fr. 781.22 ~ 31 and E. fr. 911.3–4, and also appears in such a context at *Tro.* 515 ~ 535 (Diggle, *Euripidea*, 392–3; cf. 149–50, 207). Occasional 'spondees' belong to dactylo-epitrites from the beginning: at verse-end Ibyc. fr. 287.4 *PMGF*, Pi. *Pyth.* 1.2, 9.2, Ar. *Eccl.* 576b and, with Wilamowitz' text and colometry, *Rh.* 460 ~ 826 (454–66 'Metre' 460–2/826–7n.). Cf. Dale, *LM*² 181–2, West, *GM* 53 with n. 60, 71, 73, 132, Parker, *Songs*, 86–7.

530–1/549–50 Diggle, as also Ritchie (314–15) and Willink ('Cantica', 39 = *Collected Papers*, 578) divides – ⏑ ⏑ – ⏑ ⏑ – \| ⏑ ⏑ – ⏑ ⏑ – ⏑ – ⏑ – – (*D* \| '*enopl.*' [890–914 'Metre' 900–1/911–12n.]) on the ground that '[i]n dactylic lengths the clausular – ⏑ – ⏑ – – does not abut directly on to dactyls ending in double short' (*Euripidea*, 395 n. 107; cf. 361). But acatalectic tetrameters are followed by syncopated iambics at *Ant.* 339–41 ~ 350–2 (*4da* | *4da* | ˌ*ia*ˌ + *ith*), *Cyc.* 610–11, 615–16,[198] *Andr.* 293–4 ~ 301–2, *Ba.* 159–60 and maybe *Hyps.* fr. 64 ii.90–2 Bond = E. fr. 759a.1611–13[199] (Mastronarde on *Phoen.* 1581 [p. 561]), and taken together our lines form the familiar 'Archilochian dicolon' *4da* + *ith* (Archil. frr. 188–92 *IEG*; cf. Wilamowitz, *GV* 589, Schroeder² 170, Dale, *LM*² 181–2). The lack of diaeresis between the dactyls and the ithyphallic in the antistrophe is prefigured by Archil. fr. 191.1 *IEG* τοῖος γὰρ φιλότητος ἔρως ὑπὸ καρδίην ἐλυσθείς and, more clearly, Antig. *Ep.* 1.9 *FGE* (V BC)[200] τῶν ἐχορήγησεν κύκλον μελίγηρυν Ἱππόνικος (with Page on 9–10 μελίγηρυν), while the regular 'tetrameter caesura' after – ∪ ∪ – ∪ ∪ – | helps to accommodate the verse to its dactylo-epitrite surroundings.[201]

536–7/555–6 The line is metrically equivalent to *Ant.* 585 ~ 596 (*e* – *D* ∪ – – ||). For a 'bacchiac' appended to a *D*-colon in dramatic dactylo-epitrites see also S. fr. 591.2–3 and, in 'freer' moves, A. *Suppl.* 539 ~ 548 (*D* | ∪ – – |), *Alc.* 436 ~ 446 (– *D* | ∪ – – |) and 568 ~ 578 (*e* – *D*² ∪ – – ||).

527–31. 'Whose watch is it? Who is taking over from me? The first constellations are setting, and the Pleiades of the seven tracks are in the sky. The Eagle flies in mid-heaven.'

The syntax and astronomy of these verses have caused much confusion among scholars ancient and modern. Σᵛ *Rh.* 528 (II 340.5–17 Schwartz = 105.1–106.14 a¹ Merro) chides Crates of Mallus[202] for failing to understand αἰθέριαι (530) predicatively and thus accusing 'Euripides' of youthful ignorance in celestial affairs. For the Eagle could

---

198 Ussher's and Seaford's interpretation of *Cyc.* 611 and 616 (*lec* = ˌ*ia ia*) as trochaic is not supported by the word-ends.
199 I.e. *4da* | *lec* (or *2*ˌ*ia*) | *2*ˌ*ia*. Diggle (*Hyps.* 275–7 *TrGFS*) takes the lines as *D* | '*cyren.*' | ˌ*ia pe*.
200 A dithyrambic poet, otherwise unknown. 'Guesses' at his date 'have ranged from 490 to 480 B.C. ... to the end of the century ... If the lines are a true reflection of the style of Antigenes, it would seem fair comment that he was much more like Bacchylides than Timotheus, and that the first half of the century is the likelier' (Page, *FGE*, 11).
201 Laetitia Parker also points out that 530–1 ~ 549–50 could be seen as a longer version of 527/8 ~ 546/7, if, instead of *e* | – – || with 'link-anceps' (527–8/546–7n.), the sequence ⌣ | – ∪ – | – – || there passed for some sort of iambic compound. But any attempt to make this rhythmically equivalent to – ∪ – ∪ – – (i.e. ⌣ – ∪ – – ⌐ = ⌐ ∪ – ∪ –) remains speculative, and we simply do not know how to distinguish ... ∪ ∪ – ∪ ∪ + *ith* from a possible unsyncopated 'enoplion' ∪ ∪ – ∪ ∪ – ∪ – – (with – ∪ ∪ throughout).
202 I.e. Crates fr. 89 Broggiato. There is a pun on the scholar's name (11–12 Schwartz = 106.7–8 a¹ Merro = 12–14 Broggiato): καὶ ταῦτα μὲν ὁ Κράτης. ἔοικε δὲ ὑπὸ τῆς φράσεως ἀμφιβόλου <οὔσης> κεκρατῆσθαι.

not culminate when the Pleiades are setting. The scholiast's view is supported by Parmeniscus (Σ^V *Rh.* 528 [II 340.17–341.3 Schwartz = 106.14–107.28 a¹ Merro], perhaps from his treatise Πρὸς Κράτητα),[203] whose further explanation of πρῶτα ... σημεῖα as the first degrees of Scorpio (Σ^V *Rh.* 528 [II 340.17–23 Schwartz = 106.14–20 a¹ Merro]) has most recently been endorsed by Feickert (on 528–37). While this is astronomically conceivable, one should remember that Parmeniscus' claim rests solely on a mutilated fragment from Cleostratus' *Phaenomena* / *Astrologia* (6 B 1 DK): ἀλλ' ὁπόταν τρίτον ἦμαρ ἐπ' ὀγδώκοντα μένῃσι / <Ἀρκτοφύλαξ φαίνων, τότε δὴ σημήϊα πρῶτα> / σκορπίου εἰς ἅλα πίπτει ἅμ' ἠοῖ φαινομένηφι (lac. stat. Boll: suppl. Diels). Likewise, Euctemon's calendar records the heliacal setting of Scorpio by way of its 'first stars',[204] and Hipparchus in his commentary on Aratus regularly explains τίνες ἀστέρες ἑκάστου τῶν ἄστρων ('constellations') πρῶτοί τε καὶ ἔσχατοι ἀνατέλλουσιν ἢ δύνουσι (*In Arat.* 1.1.10). Yet none of these passages suggests that πρῶτα ... σημεῖα alone could point to a specific star group or indeed reflect a technical term (E. J. Webb, *JHS* 41 [1921], 77–80).[205] It appears, therefore, that our poet chose to be just as vague as *Il.* 10.251–2 μάλα γὰρ νὺξ ἄνεται ... / ἄστρα δὲ δὴ προβέβηκε (527–64n.) before mustering some notable constellations and heavenly bodies to indicate more precisely the hour of the night. Cf. *IA* 6–8 (with Stockert [pp. 161–4] on a similar astronomical problem) and [Sapph.] fr. mel. adesp. 976 *PMG* δέδυκε μὲν ἁ σελάνα / καὶ Πληϊάδες, μέσαι δέ / νύκτες, παρὰ δ' ἔρχεθ' ὥρα· / ἐγὼ δὲ μόνα καθεύδω.

527–30. ἀμείβει: literally 'takes (mine) in exchange' (LSJ s.v. ἀμείβω A I 2). The vocabulary recalls *Il.* 9.471 οἳ μὲν ἀμειβόμενοι φυλακὰς ἔχον and, much later, Q. S. 8.498–9 Δαναοὶ δὲ νεῶν προπάροιθεν ἴαυον / αἰὲν ἀμειβόμενοι φυλακάς.

πρῶτα / ... σημεῖα: i.e. the stars or constellations that would set first towards dawn in that particular night (Jouan 69 n. 162) and so mark the end of the chorus' watch (cf. Σ^V *Rh.* 528 [II 340.14 Schwartz = 106.10–11 a¹ Merro, II 341.2–3 Schwartz = 107.27 a¹ Merro]). There is no need to to look for greater detail here, although 'it may no doubt be possible, from the *data* supplied by the Pleiades and the Eagle, to find out what

---

203 So doubtfully M. Breithaupt, *De Parmenisco grammatico*, Leipzig 1915, 30 (on fr. 16), 34 (on fr. 17).
204 Euct. *Parap.* Pisc. 29 (23 March) ἐν δὲ τῇ κθ' τοῦ Σκορπίου οἱ πρῶτοι ἀστέρες δύνουσιν (A. Rehm, *Das Parapegma des Euktemon*, Heidelberg 1913, 23 = W. K. Pritchett – B. L. van der Waerden, *BCH* 85 [1961], 17–52 [36]). For brief accounts of the fixed-star phases see D. R. Dicks, *Early Greek Astronomy to Aristotle*, London 1970, 10–16 and West, *Works and Days*, 379–80.
205 The same objection applies to Liapis' identification of πρῶτα ... σημεῖα as the constellation Bootes and, more specifically, its brightest star Arcturus (on 527–36 [pp. 219–20]).

these setting stars were or should have been' (E. J. Webb, *JHS* 41 [1921], 75). Cf. 527–31n.

σημεῖα for constellations as heavenly 'indicators' has a clearer precedent in *Ion* 1156–7 Ὑάδες τε, ναυτίλοις / σαφέστατον σημεῖον (LSJ s.v. σημεῖον I 2) than, if rightly restored, Cleostrat. 6 B 1 DK (527–31n.). More often the 'epic' σῆμα is used in this way: *Il*. 22.30 λαμπρότατος μὲν ὅ γ᾽ ἐστί, κακὸν δέ τε σῆμα τέτυκται (i.e. Sirius), Parm. 28 B 10.1–2 DK, S. fr. 432.3 οὐράνιά τε σήματα (with Radt) and e.g. Arat. 10–13, 167–71, 233–4. The notion recurs in Latin *signum* (*OLD* s.v. 13).

καὶ ἑπτάποροι / Πλειάδες αἰθέριαι: If we follow Σ^V *Rh*. 528 and Parmeniscus in mentally supplying εἰσίν (cf. 527–31n.), we achieve reasonable astronomy and avoid an otherwise redundant epithet with Πλειάδες (contrast E. *El*. 467–8 ἄστρων τ᾽ αἰθέριοι χοροί, / Πλειάδες, Ὑάδες). Unlike *Phaeth*. 65–6 Diggle = E. fr. 773.21–2 ὑπὲρ δ᾽ ἐμᾶς κεφαλᾶς / Πλειά[δων πέφευγε χορός],²⁰⁶ then, where the Pleiades stand for the fading stars in general (Diggle on *Phaeth*. 66; cf. *Or*. 1005–6, E. fr. 124.2–5 ~ Ar. *Thesm*. 1099–1101), the present passage indicates their heliacal rising in late May (Hes. *Op*. 383–4 [with West], 571–3; Kidd on Arat. 254–267, 265). This would match the ancient tradition that Troy fell in Thargelion: e.g. *Il. Parv*. fr. 14 *GEF* (with n. 43), D. H. 1.63.1, (Fraenkel on *Ag*. 826 [II, 380–2], A. Grafton – N. M. Swerdlow, *CQ* n.s. 36 [1986], 212–18). But it is doubtful whether our poet thought so far or could have expected the audience to take the hint.

The language is reminiscent of late Euripides: *El*. 467–8 (above), *Or*. 1005 ἑπταπόρου τε δραμήματα Πλειάδος and, at the same metrical position in anapaests, *IA* 6–8 ἀστὴρ ... / σείριος ἐγγὺς τῆς ἑπταπόρου / Πλειάδος ἄσσων. First attested as a river-name in *Il*. 12.20 and Hes. *Th*. 341 (with West on 337–70), ἑπτάπορος became a stock epithet for the Pleiades: e.g. Arat. 257, Antip. Sid. *Ep*. 33.4 Gow–Page *HE*, Nonn. 2.17, 8.76, 47.702.²⁰⁷ The seven stars of the cluster, only six of which are usually visible to the naked eye (Arat. 257–8 [with Kidd on 254–67, 258]), were identified with the seven daughters of Atlas (Hes. *Op*. 383, 'Hes.' fr. 169 M.–W., Sim. fr. 555.3–5 *PMG* = 20.3–5 Poltera, A. fr. 312), and various myths evolved about their catasterisation (W. and H. Gundel, *RE* 21.2 s.v. Pleiaden, coll. 2495–8, West on Hes. *Op*. 383–4).

V's epic-ionic Πληϊάδες is unparalled in tragedy and should not be introduced here with Zanetto and, more hesitantly, Pace (*Canti*, 45–6).

---

206 E.g. suppl. Diggle: Πλειὰ[ς ἐκλείπει σκοτίᾳ] Wilamowitz prob. Lloyd-Jones (*CR* n.s. 21 [1971], 344 = *Academic Papers* I, 455–6).

207 Cf. (of the planets) *h.Hom*. 8.6–7 (Ares) πυραυγέα κύκλον ἑλίσσων / αἰθέρος ἑπταπόροις ἐνὶ τείρεσιν. On the author of this late work (Proclus or some earlier Neoplatonist like Porphyry) see M. L. West, *CQ* n.s. 20 (1970), 300–4 (+ *Homeric Hymns*, 17, 189 n. 53) and Th. Gelzer, *MH* 44 (1987), 150–67.

Apart from producing undesirable metre (530–1 ~ 549–50 $_\wedge ia\ cho$ + '*enopl*.'), it would force us to read VΛ's γήρυϊ ἃ παιδολέτωρ in 549 and thus to accept a highly dubious case of consonantalised iota at word-end.[208]

531. μέσα δ' ... οὐρανοῦ: i.e. 'due south', as in Hes. *Op.* 609–10 εὖτ' ἂν δ' Ὠρίων καὶ Σείριος ἐς μέσον ἔλθῃ / οὐρανόν and the later technical term μεσουρανέω, 'culminate'. Adverbial μέσον / μέσα with a genitive has one classical parallel at *Or.* 982–4 τὰν οὐρανοῦ / μέσον χθονός <τε> τεταμέναν / ... / πέτραν (~ *Il.* 5.769 = 8.46 μεσσηγὺς γαίης τε καὶ οὐρανοῦ ἀστερόεντος). For the MSS variants in our line see Zuntz, *Inquiry*, 149–50.

Ἀιετός: This is the first Greek reference to the Babylonian constellation Eagle outside a calendar (Democr. 68 B 14 [143.11–13] DK = Gem. *Calend.* Sagitt. 16 [222.9–11 Manitius = 103.12–14 Aujac], Euct. *Parap.* Canc. 28, Sagitt. 15, Capric. 7, Taur. 30 [14, 19, 20, 25 Rehm = 33, 34, 35, 36 Pritchett–van der Waerden]). Willink (*CQ* n.s. 21 [1971], 351 = *Collected Papers*, 61–2) and O. Wenskus (*Astronomische Zeitangaben von Homer bis Theophrast*, Stuttgart 1990, 84) see it as a bad omen for Troy (cf. e.g. *Il.* 8.247–52, 12.200–29, *Ag.* 134–8), the great 'bird of Zeus', which prominently sits right on the equator (Kidd on Arat. 313, referring to 522–3). As with the rising Pleiades (527–30n.), however, this portentous connotation can at best be secondary, and a purely temporal reading remains to be preferred.

ποτᾶται: The Eagle 'flies' like a real bird (cf. Manil. *Astr.* 1.343–5). Non-frequentative ποτάομαι (LSJ s.v. 1) is typical of tragedy, especially the lyrics: A. fr. 275.1 ἐρωδιὸς ... ὑψόθεν ποτώμενος, *Sept.* 85 (βοᾷ) ποτᾶται, A. *Suppl.* 656–8, *Ag.* 576 (3ia), S. fr. 476 = Ar. *Av.* 1337–9, *Hipp.* 1272–3. Note also ἐκποτάομαι (LSJ s.v., where add E. *El.* 175–8) and ὑπερποτάομαι (Lyc. 17).

532–3. ἔγρεσθε, falsely repeated in 533 (below), could here be an aorist imperative like ἔγρεο in *Il.* 10.159 ἔγρεο Τυδέος υἱέ· τί πάννυχον ὕπνον ἀωτεῖς; (followed by another urgent question), *Od.* 15.46, 23.5 and perhaps ἐγρέσθω in Sapph. et Alc. fr. S 286 col. iii.4 *SLG*. But it is normally taken as a present and connected with *Phaeth.* 73–4 Diggle =

---

[208] 'Synecphonesis and Consonantalization of Iota in Greek Tragedy' is treated by A. Kapsomenos, in E. M. Craik (ed.), *Owls to Athens. Essays on Classical Subjects Presented to Sir Kenneth Dover*, Oxford 1990, 321–30. But most of his examples are controversial, and the only two 'parallels' for the phenomenon occurring in final position do not bear examination. At *Pers.* 850 ὑπαντιάζειν †ἐμῷ παιδὶ† πειράσομαι there is no reason to make concessions for the variant παιδὶ ἐμῷ, when the possessive pronoun could be a gloss (West, *Studies*, 88–90; cf. his apparatus), and *OT* 865–7 ἔργων τε πάντων, ὧν νόμοι πρόκεινται / ὑψίποδες, †οὐρανίαν / δι' αἰθερα† τεκνωθέντες (fere codd.: οὐρανίᾳ 'ν / αἰθέρι Enger) presents independent metrical and linguistic problems (L. P. E. Parker, *CQ* n.s. 18 [1968], 253; cf. Ll-J/W, *Sophoclea*, 100).

E. fr. 773.29–30 ἔγρονται δ' εἰς βοτάναν / ξανθᾶν πώλων συζυγίαι. For this rare secondary form of ἐγείρω / ἐγείρομαι (from precisely the poetic medio-passive aorist ἐγρέσθαι) cf. also Call. *Hec.* fr. 260.67–8 Pf. (= 288.67–8 *SH* = 74.26–7 Hollis) ἔγρει καί τιν' ἔχοντα παρὰ πλόον οἰκίον ἄξων / τετριγὼς ὑπ' ἄμαξαν, Opp. *Hal.* 2.204, 5.241, Q. S. 5.610 and Nonn. *Par.* 11.82. It has been conjectured at Ibyc. fr. 303 (b) *PMGF* ἆμος ἄυπνος κλυτὸς ὄρθρος ἐγείρησιν (ἔγρησιν Page) / ἀηδόνας and Sopat. fr. 10.3 *PCG* (cf. R. Kassel, *ZPE* 128 [1999], 30 with n. 12).

τί μέλλετε; looks ahead to 534 οὐ λεύσσετε μηνάδος αἴγλαν; as the immediate reason for the chorus' impatience. Similar sequences, based on sound rather than sight, occur in *Sept.* 99–100 τί μέλλομεν ἀγάστονοι; / ἀκούετ' ἢ οὐκ ἀκούετ' ἀσπίδων κτύπον; *Hec.* 1094 κλύει τις ἢ οὐδεὶς ἀρκέσει; τί μέλλετε; *Phoen.* 298–300 κλύεις, ὦ τεκοῦσα τόνδε μᾶτερ; / τί μέλλεις (...); (all lyric) and E. *El.* 747–57 (Χο.) ἔα ἔα· / φίλαι, βοῆς ἠκούσατ' ... 757 (Ἑλ.) σφαγὴν αὐτεῖς τῇδέ μοι· τί μέλλομεν; The close link between the two questions refutes O's assignation of 534 to a semi-chorus (cf. Hutchinson on *Sept.* 98–108).

κοιτᾶν / ἔξιτε πρὸς φυλακάν: Hartung's ἔξιτε (17 [1852], 66, 142) replaces ἔγρεσθε (Ω), which yields good Greek (*HF* 1048–50 μὴ / τὸν εὔδι' ἰαύονθ' / ... εὐνᾶς / ἐγείρετε), but does not correspond with 552. The reading is based on *Chr. Pat.* 1855–6 ἔγρεσθ' ἔγρεσθε· τί, γυναῖκες, μέλλετε; / ἔξιτ' ἄπιτε βαιὸν ὡς πρὸς τὴν πόλιν, where double ἔγρεσθε need not mirror a faulty text (cf. *Chr. Pat.* 2000–1 ἄδιστος ἄδιστος γὰρ ἐν τοῖς βλεφάροις / ἐνδὺς ἔβα ... ~ *Rh.* 555–6 ἄδιστος γὰρ ἔβα βλεφάροις πρὸς ἀῶ). It may gain further support from *exsurgite* (~ κοιτᾶν ἔξιτε) in Acc. *Ant.* fr. IV *TRF*³ = III Dangel *Heus, vigiles, properate, expergite / pectora tarda sopore, exsurgite.* The couplet, from a scene that seems to have adapted S. *Ant.* 249–77 and given this 'wake-up call' to the πρῶτος ... ἡμεροσκόπος of *Ant.* 253 (O. Ribbeck, *Die römische Tragödie im Zeitalter der Republik*, Leipzig 1875, 484, M. Dangel, *Accius. Oeuvres (fragments)*, Paris 1995, 363), looks nearly like a poetic translation of *Rh.* 532–3 (cf. Jouan 33 n. 163) and so comes closer to our play than anything remaining of the *Nyctegresia* (Introduction, 44).

534. 'Do you not see the bright shine of the moon?'

μηνάδος αἴγλαν: 'It is not explained how [this] proclaims the approach of dawn' (Porter on 534), nor is this necessary in a poetic text (cf. 527–30n.). Still, several scenarios have been proposed. Of these a setting moon would be possible if μηνάδος ... αἴγλαν stood in periphrasis for 'the bright moon' (Paley on 532). The opposite has rightly been excluded by Liapis (on 534) on the ground that 'only a very new moon would rise just before dawn, and it would be unlikely to be referred to as 'bright''. Those who see here a variety of *res ponitur pro defectu rei* ('the *fading* light of the moon' [KG II 569–70]) unduly strain the resources of the text, especially since darkness will prevail to the end of the play (985 φῶς γὰρ ἡμέρας τόδε). *Chr. Pat.* 1997–8 οὐ λεύσετ᾽ (*sic*) ἐς μηνάδος αἴγλαν παμφαῆ; / ἀὼς πέλας, ἀώς ... remains equally indistinct.

μηνάς is a unique, metrically convenient, parallel formation to μήνη (Schwyzer 508). For similar 'pairs', with little or no difference in sense, cf. πέλεια – πελειάς (mostly plural), οἴνη – οἰνάς ('vine': Ion fr. 26.4 *IEG*, Simm. *Ep.* 2.2 Gow–Page *HE*, 'wine': Nic. *Alex.* 355, 444), πόρνη – πορνάς (in late church authors) and also αἷμα – αἱμάς ('stream of blood': *Phil.* 696). δειράς is probably unrelated to δειρή (Schwyzer 507 with n. 7, *GEW*, *DELG* s.v. δειράς).

535–7. 'Dawn indeed is near, dawn is coming, and this star is one of her precursors.'

ἀὼς δὴ πέλας, ἀὼς / γίγνεται adapts *Il.* 10.251 ἐγγύθι δ᾽ ἠώς (527–64, 527–31nn.) to tragic idiom and metre, but is also reminiscent of *Phaeth.* 63–4 Diggle = E. fr. 773.19–20 ἤδη μὲν ἀρτιφανὴς / Ἀὼς ἱ[ππεύει] κατὰ γᾶν (with Diggle on 63, for other such references to the coming day in tragedy).

The phrase should be punctuated and translated as above, not with πέλας ... γίγνεται run together. For ἀὼς ... γίγνεται cf. *Ag.* 264–5 εὐάγγελος μέν, ὥσπερ ἡ παροιμία, / ἕως γένοιτο μητρὸς εὐφρόνης πάρα, Thuc. 4.32.2 ἅμα δὲ ἕῳ γιγνομένῃ, 4.67.3, 7.81.1, Xen. *An.* 2.4.24, Pl. *Prt.* 311a5 (LSJ s.v. γίγνομαι I 2 a 'of times of day').

δή reinforces the first ἀώς and so the character of the whole clause as the conclusion to be drawn from the previously observable 'signs' (*GP* 213–14, G. Wakker, *Conditions and Conditionals* ..., Amsterdam 1994, 351 n. 100 = *NAGP*, 216 n. 17). Similarly e.g. *Pers.* 433–4 αἰαῖ, κακῶν δὴ πέλαγος ἔρρωγεν μέγα / Πέρσαις τε καὶ πρόπαντι βαρβάρων γένει (the Queen upon hearing about the battle of Salamis), *Sept.* 655, Ar. *Thesm.* 1227–9, *Eccl.* 1163.

καί τις προδρόμων ὅδε γ᾽ ἐστὶν ἀστήρ: Musgrave (*Exercitationes*, 95 ~ II [1778], on 538) for the MSS' προδόμων (Δ: πρὸ δόμων Λ).[209] The phrase probably echoes Ion fr. 745 *PMG* ἀοῖον ἀεροφοίταν / ἀστέρα μείναμεν, ἀελίου / λευκᾷ πτέρυγι (λευκοπτέρυγα Bentley) πρόδρομον, the beginning of a dithyramb well enough known to be alluded to in Ar. *Pax* 835–7. For πρόδρομος, 'precursor', cf. also Ar. fr. 346.1 *PCG* ἠπίαλος πυρετοῦ πρόδρομος and Eub. fr. 75.13 *PCG* δείπνου πρόδρομον ἄριστον (LSJ s.v. I 3). In other tragedy the adjective tends to mean 'rushing forward': *Sept.* 80 (with Hutchinson), 211, *Ant.* 108. The Herald at *IA* [424–5] ἐγὼ δὲ πρόδρομος ... / ἥκω combines the notions of speed and advance movement.

---

[209] Note the reverse error at A. fr. 388.2 and *Phoen.* 296.

Again the star in question is not specified (cf. 527–30, 534nn.), but as in Ion fr. 745 *PMG* (above), Venus presents itself.

538–45. With a view to naming the overdue relief contingent, the chorus now recall the rota of night watches as established by lot (543–5n.). The transmitted speaker distribution in this lively anapaestic dialogue, which roughly corresponds to 557–64 (n.), largely coincides with what can be deduced from the text. Division into semi-choruses would be the most economic solution, but utterances by up to four individual choreutae cannot be ruled out (Liapis on 538–45).

The generally accepted order of night-watches, already advocated by Aristarchus (Σ^V *Rh.* 540 [II 341.15–16 Schwartz = 107 Merro]),[210] is 1. Paeonians, 2. Cilicians, 3. Mysians, 4. Trojans, 5. Lycians. There is hardly a problem in transferring the leadership of Mygdon's son Coroebus from the Phrygians to the Paeonians (539n.), nor does the fact that the Cilicians are not said to have roused the Mysians affect our understanding of the passage (Feickert on 538–45). Crates of Mallus, by contrast, who assigns the first watch to the Phrygians (οἱ περὶ Κόροιβον), the second to the Paeonians and then equates the Cilicians with the Mysians for the third (Σ^V *Rh.* 5 [II 326.13–327.4 Schwartz = 78.7–15 Merro][211] = Crates fr. 88.21–30 Broggiato), is severely criticised in the remaining Σ^V *Rh.* 5 (II 327.4–15 Schwartz = 78.15–27 Merro). Even apart from the erroneous reference to the Mysians of Thrace (*Il.* 13.4–7) – Crates meant the Anatolian branch (*Il.* 2.858–61) located near the Homeric Cilicians around Thebe (*Il.* 6.395–7, 414–16) – one does not see why our poet should have confused these peoples (540–2n.) or, if he did, why he expressed himself in such unclear terms. Moreover, a guard turn taken by the Phrygians under Coroebus would contradict their identification with the Trojans elsewhere in *Rhesus* (32n.).

Except for the Cilicians, who do not play an important part in the *Iliad* (540–2n.), all the Trojan allies here are also mentioned in *Il.* 10.428–31 πρὸς μὲν ἁλὸς Κᾶρες καὶ Παίονες ἀγκυλότοξοι / καὶ Λέλεγες καὶ Καύκωνες δῖοί τε Πελασγοί· / πρὸς Θύμβρης δ' ἔλαχον Λύκιοι Μυσοί τ' ἀγέρωχοι / καὶ Φρύγες ἱππόδαμοι καὶ Μῄονες ἱπποκορυσταί. Dolon's list again largely 'tallies with that of the 'middle distant' allies named in the Trojan Catalogue' (Hainsworth on *Il.* 10.428–31; cf. *Il.* 2.840–77, *Rh.* 539, 540–2, 543–5nn.).

Σ^V *Rh.* 5 (II 326.7–10 Schwartz = 77.1–78.4 Merro) records a set of five night watches already for Stesichorus (fr. 268 *PMGF*) and, depending on the reconstruction of the text, also Simonides (fr. 644 *PMG* = 317 Poltera), while Homer divided night and day into three parts: *Il.*

---
210 Cf. Σ^V *Rh.* 541 (II 341.17–18 Schwartz = 107 Merro).
211 Cf. Σ^V *Rh.* 540 (II 341.14–15 Schwartz = 107 Merro).

10.252–3 παροίχωκεν δὲ πλέων νύξ / τῶν δύο μοιράων, τριτάτη δ' ἔτι μοῖρα λέλειπται (cf. Σ^A *Il.* 10.252 [III 48.16–49.1 Erbse] τριφύλακος γὰρ ἦν καθ' Ὅμηρον ἡ νύξ),[212] *Od.* 12.312, 14.483, *Il.* 21.111 ἔσσεται ἤ' ἠὼς ἢ δείλη ἢ μέσον ἦμαρ. In real life the number of shifts probably depended on the circumstances (e.g. Xen. *Cyr.* 5.3.44, Aen. Tact. 1.8, 22.4–5), but four are specially attested (Aen. Tact. 18.21, Arr. *An.* 5.24.2, Curt. 7.2.19) and became standard in the Roman army (Prop. 4.4.63–4, Veget. *Epit. rei mil.* 3.8.17; cf. Plin. *N.H.* 10.21.47).

538. 'Who was summoned to take the first watch'?

ἐκηρύχθη has been variously derived from (a) κηρύσσω τινί τι, which in the passive retains its accusative object, while the dative of the person is turned into a nominative (KG I 125, SD 241; cf. Thuc. 1.126.11 οἱ τῶν Ἀθηναίων ἐπιτετραμμένοι τὴν φυλακήν); or (b) κηρύσσω τινά with an accusative of direction (πρώτην φυλακήν), analogous to e.g. *Il.* 2.51 (~ 443) κηρύσσειν ἀγορήνδε (πόλεμόνδε) κάρη κομόωντας Ἀχαιούς and 10.195 Ἀργείων βασιλῆες, ὅσοι κεκλήατο βουλήν (LSJ s.v. κηρύσσω II 1 with Suppl. [1996]). The first construction is unparalleled with κηρύσσω, but may still be easier than the second, since in order to serve as a 'goal of motion', φυλακή should carry a notion of place, as do ἀγορή, πόλεμος and βουλή above (cf. *BK* on *Il.* 2.51). This, however, does not apply here where the order, not the position, of the watches is at issue.

Dobree's ἐκληρώθη (*Adversaria* II [1833], 87 = IV [1874], 84), taken as middle in sense (cf. Schwyzer 760–1, Wackernagel, *Vorlesungen über Syntax* I, 137–9 = *Lectures on Syntax*, 179–81), would reduce the linguistic difficulty. But the error would be hard to explain in this context, which also favours the paradosis on independent grounds: the κῆρυξ (implied in the verb) probably oversaw the drawing of the lots (cf. *Il.* 7.181–9) and subsequently proclaimed its result (Liapis on 538).

539. Μυγδόνος υἱόν ... Κόροιβον: Coroebus first appears in the *Little Iliad* (fr. 24 *GEF* = Paus. 10.27.1, describing Polygnotus' murals in the Cnidian Lesche at Delphi). He came to Troy to marry Cassandra (cf. Verg. *Aen.* 2.341–6) and died fighting within the city walls, at the hands of varying Greek heroes. His father Mygdon ruled over the Phrygians (*Il.* 3.184–9), whom according to Pausanias (10.27.1) the poets called 'Mygdones' after him. In view of his non-Greek name (von Kamptz, *Homerische Personennamen*, 135, 328–9) and the 'conspicuous' tomb he possessed near Stektorion (Paus. 10.27.1), it would not have been

---

[212] For this notorious couplet, of which 253 was omitted by Zenodotus and athetised by Aristophanes and Aristarchus, see West's apparatus (with literature), Hainsworth on *Il.*10.253 and Nickau, *Zenodotos*, 54–5.

difficult to regard him as the eponym of Mygdonia on the south coast of the Propontis (cf. Horsfall on Verg. *Aen*. 2.342). The original branch of the Thracian tribe which gave the region its name settled east of the river Axius, whence Mygdon's son could have become the leader of the neighbouring Paeonians (Vater on 526 [p. 208]; cf. Ammendola on 538–39 and Porter on 539).

As another late ally unable to save Troy, Coroebus bears some similarity to Rhesus and may thus have been brought in here against chronology.

540–2. τίς γὰρ ἐπ' αὐτῷ; For this use of 'progressive' γάρ in a question, by which the speaker, 'having been satisfied on one subject, wishes to learn something further' (*GP* 81), cf. e.g. *Ag*. 630–1, *Ai*. 99–101 (Ἀθ.) τεθνᾶσιν ἄνδρες, ὡς τὸ σὸν ξυνῆκ' ἐγώ. / (Αι.) θανόντες ἤδη τἄμ' ἀφαιρείσθων ὅπλα. / (Αθ.) εἶέν· τί γὰρ δὴ παῖς ὁ τοῦ Λαερτίου; *IT* 531–3, Ar. *Av*. 298–9 (*GP* 82–3). The general force of the particle appears to be resultative: 'Because so-and-so is the case, I now ask ...' (KG II 335–6).

Κίλικας probably refers to (or would have been taken to refer to) the historical Cilicians of south-eastern Asia Minor, not the small Iliadic people inhabiting the Adramyttian plain (*Il*. 6.395–7). Despite Hector's marriage to Andromache, the daughter of their king Eetion, they are never mentioned as Trojan allies and get sad prominence only as victims of one of Achilles' raids (especially *Il*. 1.366–9, 6.414–28; cf. Kirk on 6.395–7).

Παίων / στρατός: Under a different leader, this host is introduced at *Il*. 2.848–50 αὐτὰρ Πυραίχμης ἄγε Παίονας ἀγκυλοτόξους / τηλόθεν ἐξ Ἀμυδῶνος, ἀπ' Ἀξιοῦ εὐρὺ ῥέοντος, / Ἀξιοῦ, οὗ κάλλιστον ὕδωρ ἐπικίδναται αἶαν. Pyraichmes falls in battle with Patroclus (*Il*. 16.287–8) and is replaced by Asteropaios, who claims the river Axius as his grandfather (*Il*. 21.140–3, 157–60) and puts up a remarkable fight with Achilles (*Il*. 21.139–204). After his death the Paeonians retreat in confusion (*Il*. 21.205–11).

Μυσοὶ δ' ἡμᾶς: For the Mysians (occupying northern central Asia Minor) see *Il*. 2.858–61 (with Kirk on 858). Their counterparts from opposite the Propontis, who were later called Μοισοί or *Moesi*, did not take part in the Trojan war: *Il*. 13.4–7 (with Janko).

The Trojans are serving on the fourth watch, as they themselves stated in 5–6 (n.).

543–5. 'Then is it not high time to go and rouse the Lycians to take the fifth watch according to the lot's apportionment?'

These verses are almost literally repeated at 562–4 (n.), where they mark the chorus' exit and, together with the present passage, give the effect of an ephymnium.

οὔκουν: 161–2a n. V and O here have οὐκ οὖν, on which see *GP* 424, 439–40.

Λυκίους: The Lycians are not only the most significant Trojan allies in the *Iliad*, but also among the geographically remotest and therefore stand at the very end of the Catalogue: *Il*. 2.876–7 Σαρπηδὼν δ' ἦρχεν Λυκίων καὶ Γλαῦκος ἀμύμων / τηλόθεν ἐκ Λυκίης, Ξάνθου ἄπο δινήεντος. Sarpedon is mentioned in 29 (28–9n.). As in 224–6 (224–5n.) Λυκίας / ναὸν ἐμβατεύων / Ἄπολλον, the audience may here have been reminded of 'wolf-men', at least on the second occasion (562–4), when the chorus had just been discussing Dolon's fate (557–61n.).

πέμπτην φυλακήν: literally 'as the fifth', perhaps with a final undertone comparable to that of ἐπί with the accusative of a noun of action: cf. e.g. Hes. *Op*. 20 ἥ τε καὶ ἀπάλαμόν περ ὅμως ἐπὶ ἔργον ἔγειρεν, *Od*. 12.439 ἦμος δ' ἐπὶ δόρπον ἀνὴρ ἀγορῆθεν ἀνέστη, Xen. *Cyr*. 1.2.9 ὅταν δὲ ἐξίῃ βασιλεὺς ἐπὶ θήραν (LSJ s.v. ἐπί C III 1). This would still differ from a true accusative of direction (Feickert on 545), which might be possible with ἐγείρω, but seems again ruled out here by πέμπτην (538n.).

καιρός: 10n.

κλήρου κατὰ μοῖραν probably reflects contemporary Greek army practice, although no other information on the subject survives. For the Romans cf. Plb. 6.35.11, 6.36.1 (cavalry-men doing allotted rounds) and especially Jos. *BJ* 5.510–11 τὴν τρίτην (*sc*. φυλακήν) δ' ἔλαχον οἱ τῶν ταγμάτων ἡγεμόνες. διεκληροῦντο δ' οἱ φύλακες τοὺς ὕπνους, καὶ δι' ὅλης νυκτὸς περιῄεσαν κατὰ [τὰ] διαστήματα τῶν φρουρίων.

546–50. 'Listen – I hear her! The nightingale, killer of her son, is sitting in her blood-stained nest by the Simois and singing her sorrowful melody with a voice of so many notes.'

Among the sounds accompanying daybreak, the nightingale's song is also mentioned at *Phaeth*. 67–70 Diggle = E. fr. 773.23–6 μέλπει δὲ δένδρεσι λεπ- / τὰν ἀηδὼν ἁρμονίαν / ὀρθρευομένα γόοις / Ἴτυν Ἴτυν πολύθρηνον (with Diggle on 70 [pp. 101–2] + *AC* 65 [1996], 193–4). More often in tragedy it transcends pure scene-description by serving – on the model of *Od*. 19.518–24 – as a paradigm of female grief and lamentation: e.g. A. *Suppl*. 57–76, *Ag*. 1140–9, *Ai*. 624–34, S. *El*. 103–9, 147–9, 1074–7, *Hel*. 1107–12 (A. Barker, in P. Murray – P. Wilson [eds.], *Music and the Muses. The Culture of 'Mousikē' in the Classical Athenian City*, Oxford 2004, 189–91).

The Attic tale of Aēdōn-Procne was already known to Hesiod (*Op*. 568–9 [with West on 568], fr. 312; cf. Sapph. fr. 135 Voigt) and received its canonical form in S. *Tereus* (frr. 580–595b). On this, and the possible variant behind *Od*. 19.518–24 (Σ *Od*. 19.518 [II 683.19–27 Dindorf] = Pherecyd. *FGrHist* 3 F 124 = fr. 124 Fowler), see P. M. C. Forbes Irving, *Metamorphosis in Greek Myths*, Oxford 1990, 248–9 and A. H. Sommerstein – D. Fitzpatrick, in *Sophocles. Selected Fragmentary Plays* I, 142–9 (*Tereus*).

The 'violent beauty of the Nightingale passage' (G. H. Macurdy, *AJPh* 64 [1943], 410) should not be understood as foreshadowing the deaths and sufferings that inform the latter part of our play. As in *Phaethon*, its significance is restricted to the immediate context of the ode. Cf. Diggle on *Phaeth.* 70 (pp. 100–1) and Collard on *Phaeth.* 63–101 (p. 226).

καὶ μάν: 'calling attention to something just seen or heard' (*GP* 356–7; cf. G. Wakker, in *NAGP*, 227–9), as in e.g. *Sept.* 245 καὶ μὴν ἀκούω γ' ἱππικῶν φρυαγμάτων, *Andr.* 820–1, *Ion* 201–2, Ar. *Ran.* 285. Typical of drama, this usage of καὶ μήν is closely akin to that in entry announcements (85–6n.).

The MSS have καὶ μήν. Diggle introduced the Doric form appropriate to lyrics.

Σιμόεντος ἡμένα κοίτας / φοινίας: the same combination of a spatial-cognate accusative (with verbs of 'resting') and a partitive-local genitive as at *OT* 161 Ἄρτεμιν, ἃ κυκλόεντ' ἀγορᾶς θρόνον εὐκλέα θάσσει (with Dawe² on 161). Each case construction, if separate, is common in tragedy. For the accusative see e.g. *Ag.* 182–3 δαιμόνων ... / ... σέλμα σεμνὸν ἡμένων, *OT* 2, *Phil.* 144–5, *Andr.* 117, E. *Suppl.* 987 (KG I 313–14 n. 13, SD 76), for the genitive Pi. *Pyth.* 4.56 Νείλοιο πρὸς πῖον τέμενος Κρονίδα ('to the rich precinct of Cronus' son by the Nile'), *Phil.* 489, *Ion* 154–5 φοιτῶσ' ἤδη λείπουσίν τε / πτανοὶ Παρνασοῦ κοίτας, 892, *Hyps.* fr. I iv.21, 24–5 Bond = E. fr. 752h.21, 24–5.

Poetic (and real) nightingales favour river-banks: Alcm. (?) fr. 10 (a).6–7 *PMGF* ἄκουσα τᾶν ἀηδ[όνων ταὶ] / παρ' Εὐρώτα [ῥοαῖσ(ι) ... (suppl. Page), A. *Suppl.* 62–4 ἀηδόνος, / ἅτ' ἐπὶ χλωρῶν ποταμῶν [τ'] εἰργομένα / πενθεῖ νέον οἶτον ἠθέων (with FJW on 63 and for the text West, *Studies*, 129–30), [Mosch.] 3.9–10, Ant. Lib. 11.11. Here her nest is 'blood-stained' – not from the battles raging before Troy (G. H. Macurdy, *AJPh* 64 [1943], 410, Feickert on 547), but, implicitly, from the murder of her child.[213]

ὑμνεῖ: Σ^V *Rh.* 547 (II 341.21–2 Schwartz = 108 Merro) records θρηνεῖ as a γράφεται-variant. This could stand with μελοποιὸν ... μέριμναν (below), but looks rather like a gloss by someone who, like the scholiast, took κοίτας φοινίας to be the object of the verb. See also Liapis, 'Notes', 79–80.

---

213 There is nothing 'odd' about this lyric blend of imagery and thus no need to take κοίτας φοινίας as the blood-stained river-bed of the Simois (Liapis on 546–50). This usage of κοίτη, moreover, is very late.

πολυχορδοτάτᾳ / γήρυϊ emphasises the variety of the nightingale's song, already famed at *Od.* 19.521 ἥ τε θαμὰ τρωπῶσα χέει πολυδευκέα φωνήν (Diggle on *Phaeth.* 67 f. with further references). Cf. especially *Med.* 196–7 μούσῃ καὶ πολυχόρδοις / ᾠδαῖς, *Lyr. adesp.* fr. 947 (b) *PMG* μή μοι καταπαύετ᾽ ... / τερπνοτάτων μελέων ὁ καλλιβόας πολύχορδος αὐλός (with 'strings' for 'notes', as here) and Theoc. 16.44–5 εἰ μὴ θεῖος ἀοιδὸς ὁ Κήιος αἰόλα φωνέων / βάρβιτον ἐς πολύχορδον. To the audience πολύχορδος may also have suggested the (notorious) intricacies of the 'New Music': Pherecr. fr. 155 *PCG*, Pl. *Rep.* 399c7–d5, Phaenias fr. 32 Wehrli, Artemon fr. 11 *FHG* IV 342, [Plut.] *De mus.* 18.1137a–b, 20–21.1137f (probably after Aristoxenus). See Denniston *apud* Page on *Med.* 196 and in general West, *Ancient Greek Music*, 356–72. Barker (in *Music and the Muses*, 185–204) takes the Nightingale in Ar. *Birds* as an emblem of that 'new' style.

παιδολέτωρ / ... **ἀηδονίς:** Cf. particularly S. *El.* 107 τεκνολέτειρ᾽ ... ἀηδών (where the adjective is a *hapax*) and, perhaps under Euripidean influence, Nonn. *D.* 48.748 Πρόκνη παιδολέτειρα (~ *Med.* 848–9 σε ... / τὰν παιδολέτειραν). Feminine παιδολέτωρ also occurs in *Sept.* 726 and *Med.* 1393 (again of Medea). It may be an Aeschylean coinage, taken over by Euripides (Ritchie 167).

Apart from, perhaps, the metaphor at Archil. fr. 263 *IEG* (= Hsch. α 1501 Latte), this is the only case of ἀηδονίς for ἀηδών before the Hellenistic age: Theoc. 8.38, Call. *Lav. Pall.* 94, *Aet.* fr. 1.16 Pf. ἀ[ηδονίδες] δ᾽ ὧδε μελιχρ[ό]τεραι (suppl. Housman, prob. Pfeiffer), Noss. *Ep.* 10.3 Gow–Page *HE*, Posidipp. *Ep.* 37.6 Austin–Bastianini. Similarly ἀδονίς in Theoc. *Ep.* 4.11 Gow and [Mosch.] 3.46.

μελοποιὸν ... μέριμναν: Dindorf (III.2 [1840], 611) for the MSS' μελοποιὸς ... μέριμνα (μελω- ... μέριμνᾳ Q), which is impossible to construe. μέριμνα as the subject of ὑμνεῖ and ἡμένα cannot be excused by reference to Bacch. 19.8–11 ὕφαινέ νυν ... / ... τι καινὸν / ... / εὐαίνετε Κηΐα μέριμνα (i.e. the poet), and the chain of three attributes (including adjectival ἀηδονίς!) that would depend on the single noun seems intolerable. Placing μελοποιὸς ... μέριμνα in apposition to παιδολέτωρ / ... ἀηδονίς (D. Ebener, *WZRostock* 12 [1963], 205) is ruled out by the word-order (Feickert on 550), and the problem of metaphorical μέριμνα for the nightingale's (as opposed to a human poet's) compositional pursuits would remain. Both interpretations, moreover, entail taking Σιμόεντος as an isolated local genitive with ἡμένα and κοίτας φοινίας as the object of ὑμνεῖ.[214]

---

[214] Thus Σ^V *Rh.* 547 (II 341.19–22 Schwartz = 108 Merro). Whether the latter is due to sheer proximity or the fact that no other accusative was available, we cannot tell. There is in

Reiske (*Animadversiones*, 89) had already written μέριμναν, but Dindorf's text (adopted by Murray, Diggle, Kovacs, Feickert and Liapis) achieves a better distribution of epithets. The error was easy – from the preceding nominatives as well as, perhaps, the more natural application of μελοποιός to the 'maker of the song' (LSJ s.v. I). Note, however, *Hec.* 917–18 χοροποιὸν / θυσίαν ('sacrifice leading to dances'). At *Hipp.* 1428–9 ἀεὶ δὲ μουσοποιὸς ἐς σὲ παρθένων / ἔσται μέριμνα (a possible model of our passage) the adjective retains its proper force.

It may be significant that μέριμνα occurs (in a different context) at *Phaeth.* 87 Diggle = E. fr. 773.43. On our poet's fondness for adjectives in -ποιός see 651n.

551–3. 'And they are already grazing their flocks on Mount Ida. I plainly hear the voice of the shepherd's pipe, sounding through the night.'

In both expression and content these lines closely resemble *Phaeth.* 71–6 Diggle = E. fr. 773.27–32 σύριγγας δ' οὐριβάται / κινοῦσιν ποιμνᾶν ἐλάται ... 75 = 31 ἤδη δ' εἰς ἔργα κυνα- / γοὶ στείχουσιν θηροφόνοι, which also come immediately after the nightingale motif at *Phaeth.* 67–70 Diggle = E. fr. 773.23–6 (546–50n.).

ἤδη δέ: Cf. *Phaeth.* 75 Diggle = E. fr. 773.31 (above). On the time-scale of *Rhesus*, it is the shepherds whose activities merit comment.

νυκτιβρόμου / σύριγγος likewise acknowledges the early hour. Pierson's νυκτιβρόμου (*Verisimilium* I, 33–4) for νυκτιδρόμου (Δ: νυκτὶ δρόμου Λ) has won general acceptance, despite being a new formation after βαρύβρομος and its kind (e.g. *Hel.* 1351 βαρύβρομον αὐλόν, *Ba.* 156, Ar. *Nub.* 313, Arch. *Ep.* 17.5 Gow–Page *GPh* βοὰν αὐλοῖο μελίβρομον). Pace (in *Scritti Gallo*, 458–9), who wishes to preserve the thinly-attested νυκτιδρόμος (Orph. *H.* 9.2, *SB* 4127.14), must either, by *hypallage*, take the genitive with ἰάν or write νυκτιδρόμον and in any case achieves much weaker sense in a stanza that deals with the *sounds* of early dawn (527–64n.). The confusion of β and δ is rare, but not unheard of (FJW on A. *Suppl.* 547, 599, where add particularly *HF* 1212 δρόμον Reiske: βρόμον L) For βρέμω and its cognates in the context of music see also Pi. *Nem.* 11.7 λύρα δέ σφι βρέμεται καὶ ἀοιδά, S. fr. 314.284 (*Ichneutai*) φ]θέγγμα μηχανῇ βρέμ[⌣], *Ba.* 160–1, *Pae. Delph.* 1.12 (*CA* 85 = Furley–Bremer II 85), *h.Merc.* 452 ἱμερόεις βρόμος αὐλῶν and S. fr. 513 (*Poimenes*).

By the later fifth century both σῦριγξ and σύριγγες could be used to denote the 'multiple-stem' panpipe (West, *Ancient Greek Music*, 109–10 with n. 122). Willink's assertion that at *Or.* 145–6 ἆ ἆ σύριγγος ὅπως πνοὰ / λεπτοῦ δόνακος, ὦ φίλα, φώνει μοι (and elsewhere in

---

any case no hint that the scholiast(s) read μέριμναν or μερίμνας, as Paley (on 547) supposed.

Euripides) the singular meant a simple reed-pipe, is disproved by *PV* 574 κηρόπλαστος ... δόναξ ('made with wax', i.e. held together by it, as the parts of the pan-pipe were).

ἰάν: a rare word. Cf. *Pers.* 937 κακομέλετον ἰάν, Hdt. 1.85.2 (oracle), *Hipp.* 585 ἰὰν μὲν κλύω, σαφὲς δ' οὐκ ἔχω, where Weil's emendation of ᵞᵖΣ^NB *Hipp.* 585 (II 75.13 Schwartz) ἰωὰν (ἰαχὰν ΩVΛ) was confirmed by P. Oxy. 2224, and *OT* 1219 ἰὰν χέων Burges: ἰαχέων codd. (see Ll-J/W, *Sophoclea*, 108).

κατακούω: The compound is found only here in tragedy. But Liapis (on 551–3) notes the contextually similar dialogue in Ar. *Ran.* 312–13 ... (Δι.) οὐ κατήκουσας; (Ξα.) τίνος; / (Δι.) αὐλῶν πνοῆς.

554–6. 'Sleep casts its spell over the seat of my eyes; for it comes upon their lids most sweetly towards dawn.'

The antistrophe ends with a reminiscence of Pi. *Pyth.* 9.23–5 τὸν δὲ σύγκοιτον γλυκύν / παῦρον ἐπὶ γλεφάροις / ὕπνον ἀναλίσκοισα ῥέποντα πρὸς ἀῶ. Others also praised the pleasure of early-morning sleep: Alcm. 3 fr. 1.7 *PMGF* [ὕπνον ἀ]πὸ γλεφάρων σκεδ[α]σεῖ γλυκύν (apparently), Bacch. *Pae.* 4.76–8 οὐδὲ συλᾶται μελίφρων / ὕπνος ἀπὸ βλεφάρων / ἀῷος ὃς θάλπει κέαρ (ἀῷος Blass: ἆμος vel ἇμος Stob. 4.14.3), Mosch. 2.2–4 (Aphrodite sent Europa a dream) νυκτὸς ὅτε τρίτατον λάχος ἵσταται, ἐγγύθι δ' ἠώς, / ὕπνος ὅτε γλυκίων μέλιτος βλεφάροισιν ἐφίζων / λυσιμελὴς πεδάᾳ μαλακῷ κατὰ φάεα δεσμῷ,[215] Luc. *Merc.Cond.* 24 ἕωθέν τε ὑπὸ κώδωνι ἐξαναστὰς ἀποσεισάμενος τοῦ ὕπνου τὸ ἥδιστον ... On the military realism of our lines see further 527–64n.

θέλγει ... / ὕπνος: In Greek literature the concept of sleep as 'spellbinding' goes back to *Il.* 24.343–4 (of Hermes) εἵλετο δὲ ῥάβδον, τῇ τ' ἀνδρῶν ὄμματα θέλγει / ὧν ἐθέλῃ, τοὺς δ' αὖτε καὶ ὑπνώοντας ἐγείρει (= *Od.* 5.47–8 ~ 24.2–4). Note also *Or.* 211 ὦ φίλον ὕπνου θέλγητρον, *IA* 142 μήθ' ὕπνῳ θελχθῇς and, of a divinely imposed trance, *Il.* 13.434–5 τὸν τόθ' ὑπ' Ἰδομενῆϊ Ποσειδάων ἐδάμασσεν / θέλξας ὄσσε φαεινά.

ὄμματος ἕδραν: By contrast with 8 (n.) λῦσον βλεφάρων γοργωπὸν ἕδραν (where 'the ... seat of your lids' = 'eyes'), periphrastic ἕδρα has here lost most of its force. The virtual repetition may have been aided by βλεφάροις in the following line.

βλεφάροις: Musgrave (on 556). Ω's βλεφάροισι is an epicising slip.

πρὸς ἀῶ: The MSS' πρὸς ἀοῦς was independently corrected by Blaydes (*Adversaria*, 7) and Headlam (*CR* 15 [1901], 102), the latter citing Pi. *Pyth.* 9.23–5 (above). Cf. further Ar. *Eccl.* 312 πρὸς ἕω, Theoc.

---

[215] Note the various adaptations from Homer, which account not only for the similarities with our passage, but also with *Rh.* 535–7 (n.).

18.55 πρὸς ἀῶ and e.g. Ar. *Lys.* 1089, *Eccl.* 20 πρὸς ὄρθρον (LSJ s.v. πρός C II). The genitive is not used in that temporal sense.

557–64. As in 538–45 (n.), the section is divided between semichoruses or single choreutae. The MSS run together 557–9, but change of speaker after 558 is indicated by the metrical pause (paroemiac). In 561 L has a paragraphos before †τάχ' ἂν εἴη† φοβερόν μοι. If the text is essentially correct, the comment would suit the speaker of 559. But more extensive corruption cannot be ruled out (560–1n.).

However we assign the utterances, the 'ephymnium' 543–5 ~ 562–4 (nn.) belongs to the same group or person.

557–61. While the chorus even verbally recall Hector's order to watch out for Dolon (cf. 557–8n.), their weariness prevents them from acting on it. Far from being mere characterisation, however, the dialogue will again remind the audience of the spy's fate and so prepare for the imminent entry of Odysseus and Diomedes (Fantuzzi, in *Entretiens Hardt* LII, 155).

557–8. The anxious query takes up Hector at 524–6. Its syntax, however, mirrors *Il.* 10.561–3 τὸν τρεισκαιδέκατον σκοπὸν εἵλομεν ἐγγύθι νηῶν, / τόν ῥα διοπτῆρα στρατοῦ ἔμμεναι ἡμετέροιο / Ἕκτωρ τε προέηκε καὶ ἄλλοι Τρῶες ἀγαυοί, and there are other points of contact with 'Homer' and Aeschylus (below).

τί ποτ' οὐ πελάθει: Given the rarity of πελάθω (LSJ s.v.), this may be a reminiscence of A. fr. 132 (*Myrmidons*) = Ar. *Ran.* 1264–5 (+ 1267/71/75/77) Φθιῶτ' Ἀχιλλεῦ, τί ποτ' ἀνδροδάικτον ἀκούων, / ἰή, κόπον οὐ πελάθεις ἐπ' ἀρωγάν; inspired either by *Frogs* or indeed primary acquaintance with *Myrmidons* (cf. Introduction, 34–5 with n. 53). Nauck's πλάθει (II[3] [1871], XXXIV) then probably misses the point. Exact metrical response with 538 need not be restored, nor do we require the same verb as at 13–14 (n.). On the contrary, πελάθει would even be closer in sound to 526 πελάζει.

σκοπός in the sense 'spy' or 'scout' is regularly used in *Iliad* 10 (38, 324, 342, 526, 561), but rare later (LSJ s.v. I 3,[216] Pritchett, *GSW* I, 129). It is combined with κατόπτης (-τήρ) at *Sept.* 36–7 σκοποὺς δὲ κἀγὼ καὶ κατοπτῆρας στρατοῦ / ἔπεμψα.

ναῶν / ... κατόπτην: 523–5a n. At 133–5a (n.) τί γὰρ ἄμεινον ἢ ταχυβάταν νεῶν / κατόπταν μολεῖν / πέλας (...); the genitive depends on πέλας.

Wecklein rightly wrote κατόπτην (-ταν Ω), which would easily have been 'doricised' under the influence of the preceding lyric (cf. 1n.).

ὤτρυνε: 25n. The double accusative (with ἰέναι to be supplied) is paralleled in *Il.* 10.37–8 τίφθ' οὕτως, ἠθεῖε, κορύσσεαι; ἦ τιν' ἑταίρων /

---

216 *Tro.* 956 belongs under I 2 'lookout-man', 'watcher'.

ὀτρυνέεις Τρώεσσιν ἔπι σκοπόν; where Nicias' ἔπι σκοπόν (*apud* Hdn. I 232.16–17, II 69.5–6 Lentz = Σ^A *II.* 10.38 [III 10.9–10 Erbse]) for ἐπίσκοπον or ἐπισκοπόν (cf. West's apparatus) is perhaps supported by σκοπός here in 557. Similarly 642–3n. with n. 245.

559. χρόνιος: Unlike the epic-style adverbial accusative χρόνον (865n.), predicative χρόνιος, 'for a long time', is well established in tragedy (LSJ s.v. I 2; especially *IA* 1098–9 ἐξῆλθον οἴκων προσκοπουμένη πόσιν, / χρόνιον ἀπόντα).

560–1. 'Can he have run into a hidden ambush and perished? †Perhaps so.† I am afraid.'

ἀλλ' ἦ: 36–7a n. Here ἀλλ' ἦ, restored by Matthiae (VIII [1824], 28) for the MSS' ἀλλ' ἤ conveys the speaker's natural reluctance to accept that Dolon may be dead.

λόχον: 17–18n.

ἐσπαίσας ('burst, rush in') is rare in drama and elsewhere: *OT* 1252 βοῶν γὰρ εἰσέπαισεν Οἰδίπους, Xenarch. fr. 1.3 *PCG* ἀλάστωρ τ' εἰσπέπαικεν Πελοπιδῶν, Ar. *Pl.* 804–5 ἡμῖν γὰρ ἀγαθῶν σωρὸς εἰς τὴν οἰκίαν / ἐπεισπέπαικεν οὐδὲν ἠδικηκόσιν[217] and probably also *Or.* 1315 στείχει γὰρ ἐσπαίσουσα δικτύων βρόχους (Wecklein cl. *Rh.* 560: ἐσπεσοῦσα codd [Π^16]).[218] The aorist and future invited corruption into forms of -πίπτειν. At *OT* 1252 most MSS read εἰσέπεσεν by phonetic confusion of αι and ε (cf. Dawe, *STS* I, 257), and in our passage O alone has the nearly correct εἰσπαίσας (if with ἐμπεσών attached to 559). VaΛ's εἰσπεσών will be another intrusive gloss, unless iotacism produced *εἰσπέσας, which someone then 'improved' to εἰσπεσών.

†τάχ' ἂν εἴη† (OΛ: τύχ' Va)[219] is too long by two syllables (⏑ –), but no fully satisfactory emendation has yet been made. Most recent editors accept Headlam's διόλωλε; – τάχ' ἄν· φοβερόν μοι (*CR* 15 [1901], 103), which neatly restores metre and sense. 'Absolute' τάχ' ἄν in reply has contemporary parallels at Pl. *Sph.* 255c12 and *Rep.* 369a8, and could have prompted a scribe or corrector to supply εἴη for 'clarification'. L's inner-metric *antilabe* (16n.) also suits the excited, colloquial tone of the passage and, by approximate response with 540–1, leaves 562–4 to the same speaker as 543–5 (cf. 557–64n.). One may object, however, to the

---

217 Fr. com. adesp. 439 Kock (LSJ s.v. ἐπεισπαίω with Suppl. [1996]) is now Archil fr. 124 (a) *IEG* and the verb confined to the surrounding text (Ath. *Epit.* 7–8).
218 Willink's objection (on *Or.* [1315–16]) that '… ἐσπαίσουσα is an unnaturally violent v[er]b in this context' is countered by e.g. *Od.* 22.468–9 ὡς δ' ὅτ' ἂν ἢ κίχλαι τανυσίπτεροι ἠὲ πέλειαι / ἕρκει ἐνιπλήξωσι and Call. *Aet.* fr. 75.36–7 Harder τὸ δ' ἄημα … ᾧ τε θαμεινοί / πλήσσονται λινέαις ὄρτυγες ἐν νεφέλαις (with Harder on 37), whether or not *Or.* 1315–16 are to be excised as an actors' interpolation (Diggle). The aorist participle at any rate is impossible, and ἐσπεσόντος lurks in 1312.
219 For the error see FJW on A. *Suppl.* 458 (II, p. 363).

general weakness of τάχ' ἄν. So Herwerden (*RPh* n.s. 18 [1894], 85) wrote διόλωλε τάλας; φοβερόν μοι – in fine tragic idiom (e.g. *Ai.* 838 ὡς διόλλυμαι τάλας, *Alc.* 391, *Hipp.* 1350), though perhaps with too much pity for Dolon. Hermann's διόλωλε; τάχ' ἄν <δ'> εἴη φανερόν (*Opuscula* III, 306), expanded by Diggle into διόλωλε; τάχ' ἄν <δ'> εἴη <φανερόν. / – καὶ μὴν τόδε γ' ἦν> φοβερόν μοι, merely transfers the 'weakness' to the entire sentence, not to mention the extreme rarity in tragedy of τάχα ('soon') with a potential optative (*Ai.* 1147–9 is a probable example). If, like Diggle, one wishes to give φοβερόν μοι a subject, West's τὸ πᾶν (after *PV* 126 πᾶν μοι φοβερὸν τὸ προσέρπον) might be considered. τάχ' ἄν was familiar to scholiasts and could have occurred to a scribe here when faced with some illegible letters.

On the whole, Headlam's solution remains the best, but as deeper corruption cannot be ruled out, Diggle's *obeli* are the appropriate response.

562–4. See 543–5 and 557–64nn. The statement with αὐδῶ reinforces the sentries' intention to call for relief. As far as the Trojans are concerned, Dolon is forgotten until 863–5.

After the sentries have left in the direction of the Trojan camp, the stage remains empty for a short while, before Odysseus and Diomedes enter by the same *eisodos*. The interval is necessary to avoid the impression that the two parties run into each other, but it also serves the important structural purpose of accentuating the dramatic turning point (Liapis, xxxvii-xxxviii and on 565–674). A technical parallel exists in *Alc.* 860, where Heracles, on his way to bring Alcestis back to life, must not meet Admetus and presumably the chorus (cf. below) returning from her funeral, and a brief gap in the action is much more likely than that Heracles simply exits 'on the 'wrong' side; and probably no one in the audience noticed the incongruity' (Taplin, *Stagecraft*, 385 n. 2).

The temporary departure of the chorus in mid-play (called μετάστασις by Poll. 4.108) is rare, but not unprecedented in fifth-century tragedy. In *Eum.* 231–43, the earliest surviving example,[220] it helps to indicate the change of scene and, more importantly, visualises the Erinyes' continuous pursuit on the Atridae's ancient trail of blood (Taplin, *Stagecraft*, 380–1). Later, as here, the device mainly enables the playwright to put on a scene that could not be enacted in front of the chorus: *Ai.* 815–65

---

[220] A fragmentary papyrus hypothesis assigned to A. *Aitn(ai)ai* (P. Oxy. 2257 fr. 1.5–14 = *TrGF* III, 126–7, A. fr. 451t 1) records no less than five scene-changes there, but whether and how they coincided with exits and re-entries of the chorus or choruses cannot be established (Taplin, *Stagecraft*, 416–18). S. *Achilleos Erastai*, a satyr play, and probably *Troïlus* (*TrGF* IV, 165–6, 453) are mentioned at the opening of the same note (after a possible reference to *Eumenides*, ingeniously restored by Lobel) and may thus also have involved a shift of location.

(Ajax' suicide),²²¹ *Alc.* 747–860 (Heracles' decision to save Alcestis)²²² and *Hel.* 386–514 (Menelaus' first entry and conversation with Theoclymenus' doorkeeper).²²³ *Rhesus*, however, is unique both formally and with regard to the plot in that the chorus depart after the equivalent of an act-dividing song (Taplin, *Stagecraft*, 376) and that their behaviour – all the worse for being in defiance of Hector's order at 523–5 – actually helps the enemy ruse (Burnett, 'Smiles', 36, G. Paduano, *Dioniso* 55 [1984–85], 267).

565–94. Onto the vacated stage sneak Odysseus and Diomedes, with the novel (and doomed) intention of killing Hector in his bed (574–6, 580–1 – probably suggested by *Il.* 10.406–8 + 414–16, where Odysseus asks after, and Dolon betrays, Hector's location).²²⁴ When they cannot find the Trojan commander, a brief discussion about the reasons (577–9) and their strategic options (580–93) ends with the decision to return to the ships (594).

The entry of two characters talking is rare in classical drama: *Phil.* 730, *IT* 67 (below), E. fr. 62a.5 and, in 'mid-conversation', *Phil.* 1222, *Hipp.* 601, *IA* 303, Ar. *Nub.* 1214, *Av.* 801, *Lys.* 1, *Ran.* 830 (O. P. Taplin, *GRBS* 12 [1971], 40, *Stagecraft*, 363–4; cf. Liapis on 565 ff.). The dialogue of the Greeks here at once reveals their uncharacteristic timidity (565–9 [568b–9n.], 577–8), as well as the more traditional contrast (exemplified by e.g. *Il.* 10. 383–4 + 446–57, 502–6) between Diomedes' warlike impetuosity and the calmer prudence of his companion (cf. 582–94, 582–4, 589–90nn.). Yet as with the advice Aeneas and the chorus give Hector in 85–148 (n.), Odysseus' apparently wiser plan to retreat is bound for disaster, except that in his case Athena will intervene to share her superior knowledge of Rhesus' arrival (Strohm 260 n. 4, G. Paduano, *SCO* 23 [1974], 25–6, Rosivach 61–3; cf. 595–674, 595–641nn.).

---

221 J. S. Scullion (*Three Studies in Athenian Dramaturgy*, Stuttgart – Leipzig 1994, 109–28) rejects a scene change in the latter half of the play. But see Finglass, *Ajax*, 14–20 and on 815–65 (p. 379).
222 Parker (on *Alc.* 746) offers some reasons why the chorus might stay, receding into the background of the acting area.
223 The view advocated by Ritchie (118–19) and others, that in *Phaethon* the chorus followed Clymene into the palace at 226 Diggle = E. fr. 781.13 and re-entered at 270 Diggle = E. fr. 781.61, cannot be upheld (Diggle, *Phaethon*, 150, Taplin, *Stagecraft*, 376).
224 Less likely, our poet over-interpreted Odysseus' prayer to Athena at *Il.* 10.281–2 δὸς δὲ πάλιν ἐπὶ νῆας ἐϋκλεῖας ἀφικέσθαι, / ῥέξαντας μέγα ἔργον, ὅ κε Τρώεσσι μελήσει, as did Aristarchus, according to Σ^A *Il.* 10.282 (III 61.37 Erbse) <μέγα ἔργον:> Ἀρίσταρχος τὸ φονεῦσαι τὸν Ἕκτορα (Liapis on 575–6). In theory the Alexandrian could even have got the idea from *Rhesus*.

The scene amounts to a second prologue (Fantuzzi, *Entretiens Hardt* LII, 156–9). A series of relevant echoes (discussed in the commentary) suggests that it was modelled on a combination of Orestes' and Pylades' cautious entry in *IT* 67–122, the arrival of Odysseus and Neoptolemus on Lemnos (*Phil.* 1–49) and, to a lesser degree, Polynices' secret return to Thebes at *Phoen.* 261–73 + 361–4 (cf. G. Björck, *Eranos* 55 [1957], 15, Strohm 263 n. 6, Mastronarde on *Phoen.* 261–442, 269). In addition, the 'clash of temperaments' between Odysseus and Diomedes reproduces on a smaller scale heroic motifs from *Il.* 8.130–58.

565–6. 'Diomedes, did you not hear – or is there a meaningless noise trickling through my ears? – a din of armour?'

Odysseus' opening words bear a striking similarity to E. *El.* 747–8 φίλαι, βοῆς ἠκούσατ', ἢ δοκῶ κενή / ὑπῆλθέ μ', ὥστε νερτέρας βροντῆς Διός; (Ritchie 245) as well as, closer to the present situation, *Phoen.* 269 ὠή, τίς οὗτος; ἢ κτύπον φοβούμεθα; S. fr. 61 (*Acrisius*) βοᾷ τις, ὤ· ἀκούετ'; ἢ μάτην ὑλῶ; / ἅπαντα γάρ τοι τῷ φοβουμένῳ ψοφεῖ (of which the first line is quoted as a parallel to *Phoen.* 269–71 in gB) and perhaps S. fr. 314.204 (*Ichneutae*) οὐ[κ ε]ἰσακο[ύε]ις, ἢ κεκώφη[σαι, ψόφον;] (suppl. Wilamowitz). For the vivid interlace of two independent questions by 'διὰ μέσου' parenthesis note also e.g. *Cyc.* 121 σπείρουσι δ' – ἢ τῷ ζῶσι; – Δήμητρος στάχυν; *Hipp.* 685–6, *Hel.* 1579–80 and *Ba.* 649 (KG II 602 n. 5, Diggle, *Studies*, 115–16, R. Renehan, *CPh* 87 [1992], 341–2).

στάζει δι' ὤτων finds its nearest parallel in Pi. *Pyth.* 4.136–8 πραῢν δ' Ἰάσων / μαλθακᾷ φωνᾷ ποτιστάζων ὄαρον / βάλλετο κρηπῖδα σοφῶν ἐπέων (with Braswell on 136–7). The image of sound as a liquid also lies behind *OT* 1386–7 ἀλλ' εἰ τῆς ἀκουούσης ἔτ' ἦν / πηγῆς δι' ὤτων φραγμός, Ar. *Thesm.* 18 ἀκοῆς δὲ χοάνην ('funnel') ὦτα διετετρήνατο, Pl. *Phdr.* 235c8–d1 and *Rep.* 411a5–8.

Metaphorical (-)στάζω in tragedy is largely confined to lyrics: *Ag.* 179–80 στάζει δ' ... πρὸ καρδίας / μνησιπήμων πόνος (with Fraenkel on 179), *Ant.* 959–60 οὕτω τᾶς μανίας δεινὸν ἀποστάζει / ἀνθηρόν τε μένος, *Hipp.* 525–6 Ἔρως, Ἔρως, ὁ κατ' ὀμμάτων / στάζων πόθον (with Barrett); in iambic trimeters cf. S. fr. 373.2–3 (of Aeneas) ἐπ' ὤμων πατέρ' ἔχων κεραυνίου / νώτου καταστάζοντα βύσσινον φάρος. For δι' ὤτων see 294–5n.

567–8a. 'No, it is harnesses, which hang from the rails of the horse-drawn chariots, sounding their clang of iron.'

For the practice of fastening one's unyoked horses to the chariot for the night see 27 and 616–17nn. In the permanent Greek camp, where no precautions for an emergency sortie are required, the captured team of Rhesus will be bound to the manger near Diomedes' hut (*Il.* 10.566–9).

πωλικῶν ἐξ ἀντύγων recalls *Ai.* 1030 (Hector) … πρισθεὶς ἱππικῶν ἐξ ἀντύγων, from the most likely interpolated end of Teucer's first speech (see Finglass on *Ai.* [1028–39]), except that ἀντύγων here is a genuine plural. Following *Il.* 5.262 (= 322) ἐξ ἄντυγος ἡνία τείνας and *Il.* 10.474–5 ~ *Rh.* 616–17 (n.), the phrase goes attributively with δεσμά in a manner comparable to e.g. *Pers.* 611 βοός τ' ἀφ' ἁγνῆς λευκὸν εὔποτον γάλα, E. *El.* 794 λουτροῖσι καθαροῖς ποταμίων ῥείθρων ἄπο and *IT* 162 παγάς τ' οὐρειᾶν ἐκ μόσχων. Cf. Diggle, *Studies*, 28–9, 69 (where the governing nouns are *verbal* abstracts), Willink on *Or.* 982–4 (βῶλον ἐξ Ὀλύμπου) and 829–32n.

The form of the ἄντυξ is discussed in 372b–3a n.

κλάζει σίδηρον: Cf. *Sept.* 385–6 ὑπ' ἀσπίδος δὲ τῷ / χαλκήλατοι κλάζουσι κώδωνες φόβον (LSJ s.v. κλάζω 3, KG I 309, SD 76–7), which in different ways also seems to have inspired *Rh.* 306b–8 and 383–4 (nn.).

σίδηρον is Bothe's (5 [1803], 296) and Paley's (on 568) simple correction of the MSS' σιδήρου. As a verb of sounding, κλάζω can hardly take a genitive on the analogy of ὄζω, πνέω and the like (KG I 356–7, SD 128–9), and other analyses (cf. Liapis, 'Notes', 82) do not appeal either.

568b–9. 'Fear came over me too, before I realised that it was the clatter of horse-trappings.'

Both expression and content resemble *Sept.* 245 καὶ μὴν ἀκούω γ' ἱππικῶν φρυαγμάτων and 249 δέδοικ'· ἀραγμὸς δ' ἐν πύλαις ὀφέλλεται. The latter supplies the rare ἀραγμός (LSJ s.v. with Suppl. [1996], where add E. fr. 631.1–2), while δέδοικ' may be echoed in ἔδυ φόβος (cf. *Sept.* 240 ταρβοσύνῳ φόβῳ). It is instructive to relate the Greek heroes' alarm at ultimately harmless enemy noises to that of the shy Theban chorus girls at the arrival of the Argive host (cf. A. Fries, *CQ* n.s. 60 [2010], 347–8, Introduction, 37).

τοι: 'Revealing the speaker's emotional or intellectual state (present or past)', as often when intensifying a personal pronoun (*GP* 541–2). Of fear also e.g. *Hipp.* 433, *Or.* 544.

πρὶν ᾐσθόμην: For πρίν with the indicative depending on an affirmative sentence in the past see 294–5n.

570–1. This couplet betrays influence from both *IT* 67–8 (Ορ.) ὅρα, φυλάσσου μή τις ἐν στίβῳ βροτῶν. / (Πυλ.) ὁρῶ, σκοποῦμαι δ' ὄμμα πανταχῇ στρέφων (Ritchie 245) and *Phil.* 30–1 (Οδ.) ὅρα καθ' ὕπνον μὴ καταυλισθεὶς κυρῇ. / (Νε.) ὁρῶ κενὴν οἴκησιν ἀνθρώπων δίχα, of which the latter verse seems in turn to be mirrored in 574 (n.). The dramatic situation in each case is similar (565–94n.).

570. Odysseus' warning acknowledges the situation of *Rhesus*. In *Il.* 10.416–20 the Greeks learn from Dolon that there is no regular watch. Cf. Introduction, 39.

κατ' ὄρφνην: 41–2n.

571. τοι: 'In response to a command' (*GP* 541): 'I *will* take care ...' See also 219–22a n.

τιθεὶς πόδα: 280n. The strong sense 'plant the foot, step', as opposed to simple 'walk', is appropriate to the Achaeans' careful movements in the dark.

572–3. While the audience will have had visual confirmation of Dolon's death in the wolf-skin Odysseus is carrying (591–3n.), this is the first explicit hint at his interception. The betrayal of the watchword, in addition to Hector's position (cf. 565–94n.), is another innovation for the sake of the plot. In 675–91 (n.) it will help the Achaeans escape.

ἢν δ' οὖν ἐγείρῃς; 'But if you *do* wake anyone ...?' 'εἰ δ' οὖν ... is particularly used when a speaker hypothetically grants a supposition which he denies, doubts, or reprobates' (*GP* 464–5). The particles after εἰ emphasise the adversative conditional clause (Paley on *Ag.* 1009 [1042]; cf. Fraenkel on *Ag.* 676).

σύνθημα: 521–2n.

Φοῖβον ... σύμβολον: 521–2n. The development of σύμβολον from a physical token of identification to 'prearranged signal, watchword' (LSJ s.v. III 4 with Suppl. [1996]) is easy to understand. But the usage is rare and found only here in classical Greek.

κλυών: 109–10a, 286nn. The knowledge of the watchword stems from 'one particular communication' (M. L. West, *BICS* 31 [1984], 177). So also 858 κοὐδὲν πρὸς αὐτῶν οἶδα πλημμελὲς κλυών.

574–9. The Greeks' arrival at Hector's bivouac looks like an adaptation of *Phil.* 26–42, where a cautious rather than fearful Odysseus asks Neoptolemus about Philoctetes' temporarily deserted cave. More generally, the passage also recalls Orestes and Pylades discussing the layout of Artemis' precinct in *IT* 69–76. Cf. 570–1, 574nn.

574–6. With this exchange contrast Odysseus' confident statement in *Il.* 10.477–8 οὗτός τοι, Διόμηδες, ἀνήρ, οὗτοι δέ τοι ἵπποι, / οὓς νῶϊν πίφαυσκε Δόλων, ὃν ἐπέφνομεν ἡμεῖς.

574. 'Oh, I see this bivouac of the enemy here is deserted.'

ἔα: *extra metrum*. Mostly ἔα 'expresses the speaker's surprise [Σ^A *PV* 114 ἐκπλήξεως ἐπίρρημα] at some novel, often unwelcome, impression on his senses' (Fraenkel on *Ag.* 1256–7 [III, p. 580 n. 4]; cf. Page on *Med.* 1004, Stevens on *Andr.* 896, *CEE* 33 n. 81, Collard, 'Supplement', 362). Etymologically it is thus likely to be a composite interjection (SD 599–600, Kannicht on *Hel.* 71), 'a gasp of astonishment, perhaps representing the sound of a sharp intake of breath' (Dodds on *Ba.* 644), rather than a fossilised imperative of ἐάω. As a colloquialism it is much more common in Euripides than in Aeschylus and Sophocles.

εὐνὰς ἐρήμους τάσδε πολεμίων ὁρῶ: 1n. With ὁρῶ here supply οὔσας (KG II 66–7). The wording recalls *Phil.* 31 (Νε.) ὁρῶ κενὴν οἴκησιν ἀνθρώπων δίχα and 34 (Ὀδ.) τὰ δ' ἄλλ' ἐρῆμα, κοὐδέν ἐσθ' ὑπόστεγον; (574–9n.).

575–6. 'Yet Dolon declared this to be Hector's bivouac, against whom my sword is drawn.'

καὶ μὴν ... γε: 184n.

τάσδ' ἔφραζεν Ἕκτορος / κοίτας: 1n. Add again οὔσας, as in 574 (n.) and on the model of *Od.* 19.477 πεφραδέειν ἐθέλουσα φίλον πόσιν ἔνδον ἐόντα, *Alc.* 812, 1012–13, *Hel.* 827, *IA* 802–3 and *Rh.* 952–3 οὐδὲν μάντεων ἔδει φράσαι / Ὀδυσσέως τέχναισι τόνδ' ὀλωλότα. Probably because of the verb's primary sense 'show, make known' (LSJ s.v. I 1), rather than 'declare, tell' the accusative and infinitive does not occur before the first century BC.

ἐφ' ᾧπερ ἔγχος εἵλκυσται τόδε: similarly *Il.* 1.194 εἵλκετο δ' ἐκ κολεοῖο μέγα ξίφος ... (from the famous passage in which Athena prevents Achilles from killing Agamemnon) and *Ant.* 1232–3 ξίφους / ἕλκει διπλοῦς κνώδοντας. Diomedes naturally has his sword at the ready, as Polynices does on his way through Thebes: *Phoen.* 267–8, 363–4 (cf. 565–94n.).

577. 'Now, what can that mean? The company has not gone off somewhere, has it?'

τί δῆτ' ἂν εἴη; an impatient question (Dale on *Hel.* 91) with near-formulaic status in later tragedy and comedy: *IA* 843, Ar. *Eccl.* 24, 348–9 τί δῆτ' ἂν εἴη; μῶν ἐπ' ἄριστον γυνή / κέκληκεν αὐτὴν τῶν φίλων; *Thesm.* 847, *Pl.* 1152. But see also E. *Suppl.* 558 πῶς οὖν ἂν εἴη; (with Collard on 558–63).

δῆτα in questions is always continuative. The particle largely belongs to lively dialogue and is therefore, apart from Plato, exceedingly rare outside drama (*GP* 269–70).

μῶν: 17–18n. The question here expresses both alarm and surprise.

λόχος: Hector's company, as at 26 (n.).

578. Diomedes' assumption is symptomatic of the role real or imagined treachery plays in our drama (Rosivach 65–7 with n. 35).

μηχανὴν στήσων τινά: Cf. *Andr.* 995–6 τοία γὰρ αὐτῷ μηχανὴ πεπλεγμένη /... ἕστηκεν φόνου, and see 91–2n. (δόλος κρυφαῖος ἑστάναι).

579. θρασὺς ... θρασύς: The emphatic placement of a mostly disyllabic word at the beginning and end of an iambic trimeter is Euripidean: *Alc.* 722 φίλον τὸ φέγγος τοῦτο τοῦ θεοῦ, φίλον, *Hcld.* 307, *Hipp.* 327, *Ba.* 963, E. fr. 414.1 φειδώμεθ' ἀνδρῶν εὐγενῶν, φειδώμεθα (Nauck, *Euripideische Studien* II, 184, Ritchie 238).[225] Note also *Hcld.* 225

---

[225] *IT* 991–3 and *IA* 1026, added by Ritchie, can be dismissed. The former is very probably corrupt and the latter falls with the rejection of Murray's strange punctuation.

βλέψον πρὸς αὐτούς, βλέψον – ἕλκεσθαι βίᾳ and E. fr. 548.1 νοῦν χρὴ θεᾶσθαι, νοῦν … Sophocles has two comparable instances in frr. 210.46 (lyric) and 753, Aeschylus none.

γάρ: 484n.

580–1. For the sentiment at this stage of the exploit cf. *IT* 94–7 σὲ δ' ἱστορῶ, / Πυλάδη … / τί δρῶμεν; ἀμφίβληστρα γὰρ τοίχων ὁρᾷς / ὑψηλά (565–94n.).

τί δῆτ' … δρῶμεν; another type of set question in drama (cf. 577n.). With γάρ in the next sentence explaining why it was asked note also E. *El.* 967–9 (Ορ.) τί δῆτα δρῶμεν; μητέρ' ἦ φονεύσομεν; / (Ελ.) … / (Ορ.) φεῦ· / πῶς γὰρ κτάνω νιν, ἥ μ' ἔθρεψε κἄτεκεν; and *Phoen.* 740 τί δῆτα δρῶμεν; ἀπορίαν γὰρ οὐ μενῶ (Mastronarde on *Phoen.* 1615). Otherwise e.g. *Cho.* 899 Πυλάδη, τί δράσω; (like E. *El.* 967 at a critical point in the plot), *Phil.* 757, *IT* 1188, Ar. *Pax* 263, *Ran.* 277.

ηὕρομεν: Dindorf (III.2 [1840], 611) for εὕρ- (Ω), since the dramatists apparently never omitted the temporal augment in spoken verse (KB II 18). In our case the frequent scribal error was probably assisted by the post-classical shortening of ηυ- in the imperfect, aorist and perfect tenses of verbs beginning with αυ- and ευ- (Threatte I 384–5, II 482–3, 486; cf. Lautensach, *Augment*, 47–9). Likewise 611 (611–12n.), 614, 762, 763, 769, 779.

ἐν εὐναῖς: 1n.

ἐλπίδων δ' ἡμάρτομεν: so also *Med.* 498 (plural for singular).

582–94. Despite the very different situation, which perhaps first recalls *IT* 102–4 (Ορ.) ἀλλὰ πρὶν θανεῖν νεὼς ἔπι / φεύγωμεν, ᾗπερ δεῦρ' ἐναυστολήσαμεν. / (Πυλ.) φεύγειν μὲν οὐκ ἀνεκτὸν οὐδ' εἰώθαμεν (565–94, 589–90nn.), this part of the dialogue resembles *Il.* 8.138–56, where after a checking thunderbolt from Zeus Nestor suggests to Diomedes retreat for much the same reason as Odysseus gives here (582–4n.). Diomedes recognises the value of the advice (*Il.* 8.146), but shrinks from acting on it for fear that Hector may gloat over his apparent cowardice: *Il.* 8.147–50 ~ *Rh.* 589–90 (n.). Nestor then reassures him (*Il.* 8.153–6 ~ *Rh.* 591–3) and turns the chariot without further ado (*Il.* 8.157–8). Contrast the express consent of Diomedes in *Rh.* 594 (n.).

582–4. In addition to *IT* 102–3 (582–94n.), cf. Nestor at *Il.* 8.139–44 'Τυδείδη, ἄγε δὴ αὖτε φόβονδ' ἔχε μώνυχας ἵππους. / ἦ οὐ γινώσκεις ὅ τοι ἐκ Διὸς οὐχ ἕπετ' ἀλκή; / νῦν μὲν γὰρ τούτῳ (i.e. Hector) Κρονίδης Ζεὺς κῦδος ὀπάζει / σήμερον· ὕστερον αὖτε καὶ ἡμῖν, αἴ κ' ἐθέλησιν, / δώσει. ἀνὴρ δέ κεν οὔ τι Διὸς νόον εἰρύσσαιτο / οὐδὲ μάλ' ἴφθιμος, / ἐπεὶ ἦ πολὺ φέρτερός ἐστιν' (582–94n.). The notion that fighting is pointless when a god supports the other side (583–4) also surfaces in *Il.* 2.111–16, 5.601–6, 9.18–23, 14.69–73, 16.119–21 and 20.97–8 (Fenik, *Typical Battle Scenes*, 164, 222).

ναυστάθμων: 135b–6n. As the word is always plural in *Rhesus*, Δ's ναυστάθμων (-ου Λ) must be adopted.

εὐτυχῆ: 52–84, 665–7, 882–4nn.

τύχην: perhaps a wordplay on εὐτυχῆ, rather than just an inevitable repetition.

585–6. The victims here are not chosen at random. Aeneas is the greatest Trojan warrior after Hector (85–148n.), whereas Paris gained obvious notoriety as the instigator of the whole conflict. Both, moreover, appear as characters in the play.

οὔκουν: 161–2a n. A statement (οὐκοῦν Ω) would be out of place here.

ἐπ' Αἰνέαν: For this form of the name, rather than epic Αἰνείας, in tragedy (and Pindar) see 85–6n.

Φρυγῶν: 32n.

μολόντε: Canter's correction of μολόντες (Ω) is obvious in view of the dual participles at 590, 591, 595, 619 and 784 (784–6n.), which are all found in at least one MS and, except for 595 and 619, sanctioned by metre.

χρή: Despite Liapis ('Notes', 83), there is no choice between χρή (Δ) and χρῆν (Λ), since Diomedes is not considering what they ought to be doing, but what they should do next. 'The scribes of our manuscripts, or their exemplars, had a strange tendency to corrupt χρή into χρῆν' (Kannicht on *Hel*. 1405–9).

καρατομεῖν: At *Alc*. 1118 καὶ δὴ προτείνω, Γοργόν' ὡς καρατομῶν the present participle is Lobeck's correction of the impossible καρατόμω(ι) in the MSS and scholia (II 243.15–17 Schwartz). See Dale and Parker on *Alc*. 1118, Fraenkel, *Rev*. 235 and, for καρατόμος in *Rhesus* (and the issue of beheading), 605–6n. The verb recurs in Lyc. 313, but otherwise is uncommon before the first century AD.

587–8. The first part of Odysseus' question (πῶς οὖν ... ζητῶν) looks like an echo of Nestor at *Il*. 10.82–4 τίς δ' οὗτος κατὰ νῆας ἀνὰ στρατὸν ἔρχεαι οἶος / νύκτα δι' ὀφναίην ... / ἠέ τιν' οὐρήων διζήμενος, ἤ τιν' ἑταίρων; Similarly Odysseus himself in *Il*. 10.141–2 τίφθ' οὕτω κατὰ νῆας ἀνὰ στρατὸν οἶοι ἀλᾶσθε / νύκτα δι' ἀμβροσίην, ὅ τι δὴ χρειὼ τόσον ἵκει;

πῶς οὖν: ' Well, how ...?', with 'progressive' οὖν marking a new stage in the sequence of thought (*GP* 425–6).

ἐν ὄρφνῃ: 41–2n.

πολεμίων ἀνὰ στρατόν: As a verse-end ἀνὰ στρατόν is Euripidean (*Hec*. 1110, *Phoen*. 1275, *IA* 538).

τούσδ': The strong deictic ὅδε can be applied to persons not on stage, but 'vividly present to the speaker's thought' (H. Lloyd-Jones, *CR* n.s. 15 [1965], 242 = *Academic Papers* I, 398). Cf. Taplin, *Stagecraft*, 150–2, with Diggle (*CR* n.s. 29 [1979], 208), who adds that properly then the character(s) in question should have been mentioned before.²²⁶

589–90. In contrast to Pylades at *IT* 104–17 (cf. 582–94n.), who rightfully contradicts Orestes' proposal to flee with reference to their honour (104, 114–15), Apollo's oracle (105) and the long journey they have undertaken for it (116–17), Diomedes here displays the same sort of 'heroic shame over prudent retreat' as his epic self in *Il.* 8.146–50 ναὶ δὴ ταῦτά γε πάντα, γέρον, κατὰ μοῖραν ἔειπες, / ἀλλὰ τόδ' αἰνὸν ἄχος κραδίην καὶ θυμὸν ἱκάνει· / "Ἕκτωρ γάρ ποτε φήσει ἐνὶ Τρώεσσ' ἀγορεύων, / 'Τυδεΐδης ὑπ' ἐμεῖο φοβεόμενος ἵκετο νῆας.' / ὥς ποτ' ἀπειλήσει· τότε μοι χάνοι εὐρεῖα χθών (with Kirk, who compares Hector's reply to his wife in *Il.* 6.441–3). Yet in the absence of any understanding for the other's concern, the couplet here merely helps to emphasise Diomedes' rashness in *Rhesus* (565–94n.).

αἰσχρόν γε μέντοι: likewise *Or.* 106 αἰσχρόν γε μέντοι προσπόλους φέρειν τάδε, with γε μέντοι 'introducing an objection in dialogue' (*GP* 412). For military αἰσχύνη see 102–4, 756–7a nn.

ναῦς ἔπ' Ἀργείων μολεῖν: 149–50n.

δράσαντε μηδὲν πολεμίους νεώτερον: '… without having done the enemies any harm'. The closest dramatic parallels are *Ba.* 362–3 (κἀξαιτώμεθα …) τὸν θεὸν μηδὲν νέον / δρᾶν and the paratragic (or perhaps even genuinely tragic) Ar. *Eccl.* 338 ὃ καὶ δέδοικα μή τι δρᾷ νεώτερον (cf. *Med.* 37, *Phoen.* 155, 263–4). But the euphemism is common in poetry and prose (LSJ s.vv. νέος II 2, νεώτερος II 1, cf. 4n.). νεώτερος in this application has almost entirely lost its comparative force (KG II 306–7, SD 184–5).

591–3. Odysseus is prepared to leave it at Dolon's killing for that night. In terms of stagecraft, we learn from his reply that he is carrying Dolon's wolf-skin – perhaps worn around his shoulders like Heracles' lion skin – as a visible token of the deed. In view of 780–8 (780–8, 781–3, 787–8nn.), Ritchie (70, 76–7) and others suppose that he has actually donned it as a disguise, but in that case it would be more difficult to remove the costume unobtrusively before 675 so that the chorus and Hector (863–5) remain unaware of their scout's death (cf. S. H. Steadman, *CR* 59 [1945], 6–7, Feickert on 593). The notion of Liapis (on 565 ff.) that Diomedes is wearing the hide rests on the unfounded assumption that he does not reappear with Odysseus in 675–91 (n.) and is also less probable on linguistic grounds (below). The epic Achaeans immediately

---

226 At *Sept.* 631–2 τὸν ἕβδομον δὴ τόνδ' (fere codd.: τόν τ' Blomfield) ἐφ' ἑβδόμαις πύλαις / λέξω, τὸν αὐτοῦ σὸν κασίγνητον the paradosis can be saved as preparing for the apposition (Hutchinson on 631; cf. SD 209).

dedicate the spoils to Athena and place them on a tamarisk to be collected on their return (*Il.* 10.458–68, 526–30).

πῶς δ' οὐ δέδρακας; expressing an obvious objection to the preceding δράσαντε μηδὲν (... νεώτερον). Likewise e.g. S. *El.* 922–3 (Ηλ.) οὐκ οἶσθ' ὅποι γῆς οὐδ' ὅποι γνώμης φέρῃ. / (Χρ.) πῶς δ' οὐκ ἐγὼ κάτοιδ' ἅ γ' εἶδον ἐμφανῶς; and *Phil.* 249–50 (Nauck, *Euripideische Studien* II, 176, Liapis on 591–3).

ναυστάθμων / κατάσκοπον Δόλωνα: 523–5a n. (νεῶν κατάσκοπον / ... Δόλωνα). For ναυστάθμων see 135b–6n.

τάδε / σκυλεύματ': The use of ὅδε ('this here') supports Odysseus as the wearer of the wolf-skin. Cf. Diomedes referring to his sword as ἔγχος ... τόδε (576) and the contrast between 'yours' and 'mine' in *Od.* 5.343–7 (Ino to Odysseus) εἵματα ταῦτ' ἀποδὺς σχεδίην ἀνέμοισι φέρεσθαι / κάλλιπ' ... / ... / τῇ δέ, τόδε κρήδεμνον ὑπὸ στέρνοιο τάνυσσαι / ἄμβροτον (KG I 641–3, SD 208, 209–10).

Whereas σκυλεύω, 'strip / despoil a slain enemy', is well attested in classical Greek, the noun (always plural) appears only once in Thucydides (4.44.5) and six times in Euripides (*El.* 314, *Tro.* 18, 1207, *Ion* 1145, *Phoen.* 857, 1475). On σκῦλον (-α) see 179 and 619–20a nn.

594. Wilamowitz (*De Rhesi scholiis*, 9 = *KS* I, 8) was right to attribute the line to Diomedes with VaQP[r] (no change of speaker marked in OL) and to write πείθεις instead of πείθου (Ω), since Athena's question in 595–8 shows that the two Greeks are already on the retreat and must thus have reached an explicit agreement. Comparable cases of this '*tragoediae consuetudo*' at or near the end of a scene are *Rh.* 339–41, 663–4 σύ τοί με πείθεις, *Cho.* 781–2 ἀλλ' εἶμι καὶ σοῖς ταῦτα πείσομαι λόγοις· / γένοιτο δ' ὡς ἄριστα σὺν θεῶν δόσει, E. *El.* 985–7 and *IT* 118–19 (Ορ.) ἀλλ' εὖ γὰρ εἶπας, πειστέον· χωρεῖν χρεών, / ὅποι ... (with the same kind of double asyndeton as here, effecting a conclusive matter-of-fact tone).

πείθεις: See above. As elsewhere in *Rhesus*, the verb invites the suspicion that a wrong decision has been made (65–6n.).

εὖ δοίη τύχη: Nauck (II[1] [1854], XXII, *Euripideische Studien* II, 175–6), after Vater (on 578), correcting the grammatically and idiomatically dubious MSS variants εὖ δ' εἴη τυχεῖν (ΟΛ, *Chr. Pat.* 2009, 2038) and εὖ δ' εἴη τύχῃ (Va). Cf. *OT* 1080–1 τῆς Τύχης ... / τῆς εὖ διδούσης, *OC* 642 ὦ Ζεῦ, διδοίης τοῖσι τοιούτοισιν εὖ, 1435, *Alc.* 1004 χαῖρ', ὦ πότνι', εὖ δὲ δοίης, *Andr.* 750, *Or.* 667. On the presumably substantival use of εὖ in εὖ διδόναι and similar phrases see Fraenkel on *Ag.* 121 τὸ δ' εὖ νικάτω.

595–674. This startling central scene comprises two separate strands of action, held together by Athena's purpose and continuous presence on stage. Introduced as a divinity to check the Achaeans' retreat and redirect them against Rhesus (of whose arrival they could not have learnt from Dolon), she is soon seen to demonstrate her support by distracting Paris in Aphrodite's guise (642–67) and, as in *Iliad* 10, urging the Greeks to escape while they can (668–74n.). The result is an intricate and highly idiosyncratic combination of four themes particularly familiar from Homer: divine epiphany, assistance (both foreshadowed in *Iliad* 10), transformation and deceit.

Athena's sudden, unannounced apparition must have surprised the audience as much as the characters on stage. Epiphanies rarely occur in the middle of a play. Our only surviving instance is Iris and Lyssa in *HF* 815–73,[227] a scene that almost like a 'second prologue' prepares for the fundamental reversal of Heracles' fortune. Consequently, the goddesses do not, as Athena here, interact with any of the characters, but merely talk to each other and (implicitly) the chorus, who in 815–21 had fearfully greeted their arrival. In lost tragedies Lyssa, probably on Dionysus' order (Dodds, *Bacchae*², xxx-xxxi), appeared in A. *Xantriae* (fr. 169) ἐπιθειάζουσα ταῖς Βάκχαις, and in a papyrus fragment attributed to S. *Niobe* (fr. 441a) Apollo speaks, while Artemis is killing the heroine's daughters.[228] Athena's outburst in S. *Ajax Locrus* (fr. 10c) also seems to fit best in an intermediate position.[229] The most notorious case, A. *Psychostasia* (*TrGF* III, 374–6), must be handled with care, for even if we do not follow Taplin (*Stagecraft*, 431–3) in totally rejecting the testimonial evidence, there is no proof that Zeus' weighing of the souls took place in mid-play and not rather during the prologue.[230]

Like so many tragic deities, Athena most likely appears 'on high', stepping into sight on top of the *skene*; contrast the Muse, who uses the *mechane* (882–9n.). This is indicated by the suddenness of her entry and departure, which would be much diminished if she just walked up one of the *eisodoi* (D. J. Mastronarde, *Cl. Ant.* 9 [1990], 275;[231] cf. S. Perris, *G&R* 59 [2012], 155 n. 23, 160–1). Since, moreover, the two sides at stage level represent the ways to the opposing Greek and Thracian camps, such an arrangement would conflict with the notion that she pre-

---

227 Dionysus' off-stage revelation of his divinity in *Ba.* 576–603 with the following narrative to the chorus of maenads (604–41) also resembles an epiphany (cf. Bond on *HF* 815 ff.).
228 See W. S. Barrett, in R. Carden, *The Papyrus Fragments of Sophocles*, Berlin 1974, 171–235 (particularly 184–5).
229 D. Fitzpatrick, in *Shards from Kolonos*, 251–2, 258 and hesitantly already M. W. Haslam, in P. J. Parsons *et al.* (eds.), *The Oxyrhynchus Papyri* XLIV, London 1976, 2.
230 So U. v. Wilamowitz-Moellendorff, *Aischylos. Interpretationen*, Berlin 1914, 58–9, 246, followed by W. Nestle, *Die Struktur des Eingangs in der attischen Tragödie*, Stuttgart 1930, 36, H. J. Mette, *Der verlorene Aischylos*, Berlin 1963, 112, M. L. West, *CQ* n.s. 50 (2000), 345 = *Hellenica* II, 238 and Fantuzzi, *Entretiens Hardt* LII, 170.
231 His alternative suggestion that she comes through a concealed side-door can be ruled out.

sumably comes straight down from Olympus (cf. R. S. Bond, *AJPh* 117 [1996], 269, although he confuses the directions of the camps).

A raised position – more obviously outside the characters' vision – would also add a physical dimension to Athena's invisibility, which cannot simply be due to the imaginary darkness. At 608–9 Odysseus identifies her by her voice, as he does in the *Ajax* prologue, where Athena is ἄποπτος, 'out of sight' (15), and we have other reasons for placing her 'on high'.[232] Similarly, at *Hipp.* 1391–3 (cf. Barrett on 1283) Hippolytus recognises Artemis only by her divine fragrance. In Paris' case we lack decisive verbal clues as to whether he sees Athena or not, since her self-introduction as Cypris (646) could be interpreted either way. But the poet's obvious intention of creating a distorted mirror image of the previous scene (642–74n.) and the fact that she cannot possibly change costume on stage clearly point to the latter. Her 'transformation' then need not have been more than a modulation of voice and perhaps a few characteristic poses and gestures for the audience's pleasure.[233]

Ever since Valckenaer (*Diatribe*, 111) the prologue of *Ajax* (1–133) has been identified as the chief model for this scene. Apart from the general situation and various verbal echoes (A. D. Nock, *CR* 44 [1930], 173–4; cf. 608–10, 608–9a, 609b–10, 637b–9, 642–3, 649–50, 653–4a, 656–60, 668–9nn.), the episodes are almost identical in structure and sometimes comparable in content. Both open with a thirteen-line speech of Athena, which leads into dialogue with Odysseus and in our play also Diomedes (*Ai*. 1–90, *Rh*. 595–641). The first part of each conversation (*Ai*. 1–65, *Rh*. 595–626) mainly conveys information about the enemy, while the second (*Ai*. 66–90, *Rh*. 627–41) prepares for the following deception scenes. During Athena's exchange with Paris (*Rh*. 642–67) the Achaeans are naturally absent, but in *Ai*. 91–117 Odysseus also recedes into the background, ignored by the goddess and invisible to the bewitched Ajax. When her victims have left in reliance on their divine 'ally', Athena briefly returns to her protégés (*Ai*. 118–33, *Rh*. 668–74), before the choruses (re-)enter in the parodos and epiparodos respectively.

---

232 See e.g. D. Seale, *Vision and Stagecraft in Sophocles*, Chicago 1982, 176 n. 3, D. J. Mastronarde, *Cl. Ant.* 9 (1990), 278.
233 Cf. Wilamowitz, *Hermes* 61 (1926), 287 = *KS* IV, 414, Strohm 261, Burnett, 'Smiles', 39 and R. S. Bond, *AJPh* 117 (1996), 270. Vater's idea (*Vindiciae*, lv), revived by Taplin (*Stagecraft*, 366 n. 1) and Burlando (*Reso*, 81, 83, 84 n. 52), that Athena was represented as a disembodied voice has rightly been rejected by Ritchie (128–9) and others. There would be no parallel for such a procedure, and our poet is most unlikely to have missed the opportunity for a spectacular epiphany in mid-play. Moreover, this would not solve the problem of the fourth actor (595–641n.) because someone would have had to deliver Athena's lines from off-stage (L. Battezzato, *CQ* n.s. 50 [2000], 371).

The parallel helps to establish Odysseus' dominance in the team and special relationship to Athena, which are not yet fully developed in *Iliad* 10 (609b–10, 668–74nn.). Otherwise comparison merely highlights the substantial differences in dramatic function and spiritual impact between the two scenes. Naturally for a prologue, most explanations given in *Ai.* 1–65 are aimed at the audience as well as Odysseus, whereas in *Rhesus* the only thing that is new to all is the hero's genuine importance for the war (595–641, 600–4nn.). The Athena of *Ai.* 1–133 is severe and remote, a manifestation of divine power over men, which moves Odysseus to pity his greatest enemy. In our passage she may seem less dignified or even capricious, but the way she controls friend and foe alike goes far beyond *Ajax* and all else we know from epic and fifth-century tragedy (Strohm 260–1, 262–3; cf. e.g. Fenik, *Iliad X*, 23–4).

595–641. In bringing the story back to *Iliad* 10, Athena formally resembles the 'complete-reversal *dei ex machina*' of *Philoctetes* and *Orestes*, who intervene at the last possible minute to prevent an outcome that would be contrary to the mythical tradition (cf. Willink, *Orestes*, xxix–xxx). Neoptolemus and Philoctetes especially would have departed for the wrong destination, had not Heracles reminded them of Zeus' purposes. But while in these plays the aberration comes from the human characters' disposition and their failure or unwillingness to perceive the truth (A. Spira, *Untersuchungen zum Deus ex machina bei Sophokles und Euripides*, Kallmünz 1960, 144–5, 157), Odysseus and Diomedes here lack factual knowledge, which (as the plot is conceived) can only be supplied by a god.

The first part of this scene (595–626) can be seen as a dramatisation of *Il.* 10.433–41, with allusions to *Il.* 10.278–9, 463–4, 474–5, 479–81, 482–501 and 544–63 interspersed (609b–10, 611–12, 616–21, 616–17, 620b–1, 622–3, 624–6nn.). In Athena's mouth, however, Dolon's betrayal is turned into a divine order to kill Rhesus (and steal his horses), enhanced by her revelation that for the final success of the Greeks he must not survive the night. This adaptation of the oracle in Σ^{AD} *Il.* 10.435 (Introduction, 12, 600–4n.) may come as a surprise, validating as it does Rhesus' martial boasts in 447–53 (cf. 388–526n.), but it suits Athena's repeated references to fate (597–8, 605–7, 634–7) and was doubtless meant to give Rhesus' death a more elevated note.

As an instigator of the main attack Athena owes something to Pindar's version (fr. 262 Sn.–M.), where on Hera's orders she initiated the entire night-raid after Rhesus' one-day *aristeia* had done considerable harm to the Greeks (Introduction, 11–12). If our poet had this episode in mind (and the author of the second spurious prologue certainly had), the need to replace that unsuitable motivation may have been another reason to insert the 'oracle'.

The second section (627–41) leads up to Paris' arrival and Athena's outrageous scheme. Here the question arises whether the whole scene could be played with three actors or a fourth was required for the Trojan. Battezzato in an re-examination of this much-discussed problem (*CQ* n.s. 50 [2000], 367–73) convincingly argues for the latter, taking into consideration the local division of the backstage area and the actors' movements this entails. With the conventional number, Paris' role could only be played by Odysseus, who might leave after 626. However, as the Thracian and the Trojan camps are to be imagined on the audience's left and right respectively, the actor would not only have to change costume, but also walk to the opposite *eisodos*, which seems impossible within fifteen or – for the reverse procedure between 664 and 675 (681, in Diggle's order, at the latest) – even fewer iambic trimeters.[234] At A. *Suppl.* 951–80 the Egyptian Herald has 29 lines (iambics and recitative anapaests) to return as Danaus from the other side, and the actor of the Nurse and the Old Man in *Trachiniae* needs to cover only half the distance during the choral ode 947–70.[235] The change from Electra to the Phrygian in *Or.* 1353–68 just requires going in and out of the *skene*, while again a sung strophe intervenes (cf. Pickard-Cambridge, *DFA*² 147, Willink on *Or.* 1350–2).

The use of a fourth actor may not have been without precedent. Pylades' crucial lines at *Cho.* 900–2 would be infinitely more effective if he uttered them suddenly as Orestes' ever-silent companion (Taplin, *Stagecraft*, 353–4),[236] and in *Oedipus Coloneus* a supernumerary would help to avoid the distribution of Theseus' part among two or more likely all three regular actors. But Ismene's long silence in 1099–1555 suggests she was there represented by an extra, and for lack of conclusive evidence the possibility of role-splitting cannot be ruled out (e.g. Pickard-Cambridge, *DFA*² 142–4, G. Sifakis, in A. Griffiths [ed.], *Stage Directions: Essays ... in Honour of E. W. Handley*, London 1995, 19–21).

If Odysseus' actor does not play Paris, he probably remains on stage after 626 despite Athena's second-person dialogue with Diomedes. A brief recess to the margin would be preferable to a totally unmotivated

---

234 The problem had already been noted by K. Schneider (*RE* Suppl. VIII s.v. Ὑποκριτής, coll. 191–2), who rejects the three-actor rule, and Bond (*AJPh* 117 [1996], 270 n. 28), who offered no further comment.

235 The Nurse enters the palace at 946, while the Heracles procession becomes visible at 964. But the Old Man need not have been among the first, and song offers more opportunities for delay than spoken verse.

236 For the traditional opinion that Pylades and the Servant were played by the same actor see e.g. Garvie, *Choephori*, xlix. Poll. 4.109–10 is too corrupt and probably unreliable to permit further conclusions with regard to *Memnon* (cf. *TrGF* III, 236–7).

(and formally ill-contrived)²³⁷ exit, especially since we should expect the pair to remain together. So also the Charioteer at 773–5 λεύσσω δὲ φῶτε περιπολοῦνθ' ἡμῶν στρατόν / πυκνῆς δι' ὄρφνης· ὡς δ' ἐκινήθην ἐγώ, / ἐπτηξάτην τε κἀνεχωρείτην πάλιν (O. Menzer, *De Rheso Tragoedia*, diss. Berlin 1867, 41–2; cf. Liapis on 624–6).

595–8a: '*Where* are you going, leaving the Trojan ranks, stung in the heart by pain that a god does not grant you to kill Hector or Paris?'

λιπόντε Τρωϊκῶν ἐκ τάξεων: The pregnant use of intransitive λείπω with ἐκ is unusual, but can be compared to that of ἀπολείπω in Thuc. 3.10.2 ἀπολιπόντων μὲν ὑμῶν ἐκ τοῦ Μηδικοῦ πολέμου, 5.4.4 ἀπολιπόντες ἐκ τῶν Συρακουσῶν, Pl. *Phd.* 112c 3–4 ὅταν τε αὖ ἐκεῖθεν μὲν ἀπολίπῃ (*sc.* τὸ ὕδωρ), *Phd.* 78a10–b1 and *Gorg.* 497c5 (KG I 545 with n. 4c). It is also found metaphorically at *HF* 133 τὸ δὲ κακοτυχὲς οὐ λέλοιπεν ἐκ τέκνων and probably S. *El.* 513–15 οὔ τί πω / ἔλιπεν ἐκ τοῦδ' οἴκου / πολύπονος αἰκεία, where see Finglass (on 514) for οἴκου as against the variant οἴκους, favoured by Dawe and Bond (on *HF* 133). We therefore need not strain the syntax and verse pattern here by taking ἐκ τάξεων with χωρεῖτε (Vater on 579, Dindorf, Paley, Ammendola and, more hesitantly, Porter on 595) or emend λιπόντε so as to facilitate this construction.²³⁸

While τάξεων ('ranks of soldiers') is here used of an encamped army (cf. 519–20n.), the whole expression looks similar to (ἐκ)λείπω τὴν τάξιν (e.g. Hdt. 5.75.3, And. 1.74), which may suggest that, paradoxically, Athena equates the Achaeans' retreat with desertion.

λύπῃ καρδίαν δεδηγμένοι: Cf. *Alc.* 1100 ... λύπῃ καρδίαν δηχθήσομαι, Ar. *Ach.* 1 ὅσα δὴ δέδηγμαι τὴν ἐμαυτοῦ καρδίαν (with Olson), *Vesp.* 374–5 ὡς ἐγὼ τοῦτόν γ' ... ποιή- / σω δακεῖν τὴν / καρδίαν, *Ag.* 1470–1 κράτος ... / καρδιόδηκτον ἐμοί, Hdt. 7.16α.2 ἐμὲ δὲ ... οὐ τοσοῦτον ἔδακε λύπη, Pl. *Symp.* 218a2–7. For earlier examples of 'getting stung in the heart (as by an insect)', see West on Hes. *Th.* 567 and *Op.* 450–1, 799.

Wecklein's tentative δεδηγμένω, accepted by Kovacs, gains support from the similar errors in 586 (585–6n.), 595, 619 and 784 and would make the alternation of numbers as regular as in Ar. *Av.* 42–8. But there is no fixed rule with regard to this phenomenon (KG I 73), and duals are combined with plural participles in e.g. *Il.* 5. 244–5 ἄνδρ' ὁρόω κρατερὼ

---

237 J. P. Poe, *Philologus* 148 (2004), 28–9, who does, however, follow Battezzato (369) in sending Odysseus off at 626.

238 Bothe's 'λιπόντε (3 [1824], 365–6), 'having failed / fallen short (of your duty)', for which cf. Ar. *Pl.* 859 ... ἤνπερ μὴ 'λλίπωσιν αἱ δίκαι, would come closest to the paradosis. Less convincing proposals are listed by Wecklein, *Appendix*, 52.

ἐπὶ σοὶ μεμαῶτε μάχεσθαι, / ἵν' ἀπέλεθρον ἔχοντας, 11.621–3, 16.218–19 (where metrical considerations do not apply) and Xen. *Mem.* 1.2.33. See also KG I 70 and SD 50 on dual nouns with plural adjectives.

εἰ μὴ … / δίδωσιν: conditional instead of a substantival clause with ὅτι after a verb, or verbal phrase, expressing emotion (KG II 369–70, LSJ s.v. εἰ B V).

598b–9. Athena's bare rhetorical question contrasts with the shepherd's elaborate account of Rhesus' arrival in 284–316 (264–341n.).

οὐ φαύλῳ τρόπῳ: 'in grand style', referring to Rhesus' appearance (301–8) as well as his enormous army (309–13), for which cf. *Phoen.* 112–13 οὐ γάρ τι φαύλως ἦλθε Πολυνείκης χθόνα, / πολλοῖς μὲν ἵπποις, μυρίοις δ' ὅπλοις βρέμων. Comparable phrases with τρόπῳ denoting 'modes of behaviour which one regulates oneself' (Bond on *HF* 282) end the lines at *Med.* 751 … ἑκουσίῳ τρόπῳ, *Hel.* 1547 … ποιητῷ τρόπῳ, Ar. *Thesm.* 961 (4tr_ lyr.) … χορομανεῖ τρόπῳ and Lyc. 1400 … ἀστεργεῖ τρόπῳ. *Sept.* 282–4 ἐγὼ δέ γ' ἄνδρας ἓξ ἐμοὶ ξὺν ἑβδόμῳ / ἀντηρέτας ἐχθροῖσι τὸν μέγαν τρόπον / εἰς ἑπτατειχεῖς ἐξόδους τάξω μολών is difficult and perhaps corrupt (Hutchinson on 283). On the Euripidean character of φαῦλος see 285n.

600–4. These lines recall the oracle that promised invincibility to Rhesus and his horses if they took Trojan water and food (Introduction, 12, 595–641n.). But in true Iliadic manner the magic element in the condition has largely been suppressed (Fenik, *Iliad X*, 15 n. 4, 16, 26, J. Griffin, *JHS* 97 [1977], 40), and in the apodosis (note the cautious potential optative) Athena speaks of a great *aristeia* as envisaged by the Shepherd (315–16, 335), the chorus (370b–9, 461–3) and Rhesus himself (particularly 391–2, 447–53, 461–3), rather than the superhuman qualities ascribed to him in the second stasimon (355, 358–9, 370a) and the ensuing anapaests (385–7). The result is a superficially realistic tone more in keeping with *Iliad* 10 and Pindar's version (Introduction, 11–12, 595–641n.), from which the *aristeia*-motif seems to derive.

600. διοίσει νύκτα τήνδ': 'lives through …', as in e.g. Hdt. 3.40.2 καί κως βούλομαι … οὕτω διαφέρειν τὸν αἰῶνα (LSJ s.v. διαφέρω I 2). The verb is uniquely absolute in 982 (981–2n.) ἄπαις διοίσει.

ἐς αὔριον: 'until tomorrow'. Cf. 96 (96–8n.) … οὐ μένειν ἐς αὔριον.

601–2. The diction resembles 461–3 (n.) πῶς μοι τὸ σὸν ἔγχος Ἀχιλλεὺς ἂν δύναιτο, / πῶς δ' Αἴας ὑπομεῖναι; For the pairing of Rhesus and Achilles see 314–16n.

Ἀχιλλεύς: Va alone preserves the truth. All other MSS have Ἀχιλλέως by assimilation.

μή: Nauck's μὴ <οὐ> (II³ [1871], XXXIV) would give the regular construction with a verb of preventing, but note the unemendable *OT* 1387–8 οὐκ ἂν ἐσχόμην / τὸ μὴ ἀποκλῇσαι τοὐμὸν ἄθλιον δέμας, with Denniston-Page on *Ag.* 1169–71 (citing A. C. Moorhouse, *CQ* 34 [1940], 70–7), Davies on *Tr.* 90–1 and KG II 216–18 n. 9 h, n.

ναύσταθμ': 135b–6n.

603–4. 'after utterly destroying the walls and with his spear making a broad gap for invasion inside the gates.'

τείχη κατασκάψαντα: Cf. 391b–2 (n.) συγκατασκάψων ... / τείχη, *OC* 1421 πάτραν κατασκάψαντι, *Tro.* 1263 κατασκάψαντες Ἰλίου πόλιν, Thuc. 4.109.1 Μεγαρῆς ... τὰ μακρὰ τείχη ... κατέσκαψαν ... ἐς ἔδαφος, Lys. 12.40 and Isoc. 14.35. The basic meaning of the verb, 'dig up' (Thphr. *HP* 4.13.5), is still present at *Ag.* 525–6 Τροίαν κατασκάψαντα τοῦ δικηφόρου / Διὸς μακέλλῃ (cf. Fraenkel on 525 ff., Denniston-Page on 525) and Ar. *Nub.* 1486–8 καὶ σμινύην φέρων / ... / τὸ τέγος κατάσκαπτ'.

λόγχῃ πλατεῖαν ἐσδρομὴν ποιούμενον: Before *Rhesus*, ἐσδρομή is attested only in Thuc. 2.25.2 and afterwards not again until the first century BC. But the periphrasis here follows a familiar pattern (KG I 106) and can be compared to προσβολὴν (-ὰς) ποιοῦμαι in e.g. Hdt. 3.158.1, 4.128.3 and Thuc. 5.61.4. Understanding the noun as denoting the result of the action ('gap for invasion': cf. Schwyzer 422, Barrett, *Collected Papers*, 329), rather than the action itself, also helps to mitigate its use with πλατύς, which in its literal sense does not otherwise qualify a genuine abstract. Nevertheless, one may wonder whether our poet had in mind a verse-opening like E. fr. 495.29–30 (*Captive Melanippe*) [λόγ]χῃ πλατείᾳ συοφόνῳ δι' ἥπατος / [παίσ]ας.

605–7. The lines refer back to and elaborate on 597–8, where Athena had indirectly confirmed Odysseus' assertion (583–4) that Hector is divinely protected and thus not fated to die at their hands. For the reason of this re-direction Fenik (*Iliad X*, 24 n. 2) compares *Il.* 5.669–76. There Odysseus ponders whether he should pursue the wounded Sarpedon or attack the main body of Lycians, and Athena turns his mind towards the latter because it was not μόρσιμον for him to kill 'the powerful son of Zeus' (*Il.* 5.674–5). In 634–5 Diomedes will receive a similar warning with regard to Paris.

605–6. 'If you kill him, you will have everything. So leave aside Hector's sleeping-place and (the idea of) killing him by decapitation.'

τοῦτον κατακτὰς πάντ' ἔχεις: For both expression and content cf. *Ant.* 497–8 (Αν.) θέλεις τι μεῖζον ἢ κατακτεῖναί μ' ἑλών; / (Κρ.) ἐγὼ μὲν οὐδέν· τοῦτ' ἔχων ἅπαντ' ἔχω and *Rh.* 481 (n.) οὔκουν κτανόντες τούσδε πάντ' εἰργάσμεθα;

The 'present for future' (KG I 137–9, SD 273, FJW on A. *Suppl.* 405–6) mainly stands in oracles and prophecies (e.g. Pi. *Ol.* 8.42, *Ag.* 126, Ar. *Eq.* 1086–7, Hdt. 7.140.2) and 'for rhetorical emphasis' in the apodosis of hypothetical periods or with a conditional participle (e.g.

Cho. 509, *Phil.* 117, *Andr.* 381, Hdt. 6.109.6). Here we have both, as in *PV* 511–13 οὐ ταῦτα ταύτῃ Μοῖρά πω τελέσφορος / κρᾶναι πέπρωται, μυρίαις δὲ πημοναῖς / δύαις τε καμφθεὶς ὧδε δεσμὰ φυγγάνω and 524–5 τόνδε γὰρ σῴζων ἐγώ, / δεσμοὺς ἀεικεῖς καὶ δύας ἐκφυγγάνω.

This use of the present is particularly rare with durative verbs. In addition to *Ant.* 498 (above), note *Pers.* 211–14 παῖς ἐμός / πράξας μὲν εὖ θαυμαστὸς ἂν γένοιτ' ἀνήρ, / κακῶς δὲ πράξας – οὐχ ὑπεύθυνος πόλῃ, / σωθεὶς δ' ὁμοίως τῆσδε κοιρανεῖ χθονός, Hdt. 6.109.6, 7.140.2 and Thuc. 6.91.3 (with FJW quoted above).[239]

τὰς δ' ... / εὐνάς: 1n.

καρατόμους σφαγάς: With Ἕκτορος belonging to it, this phrase perhaps developed from reminiscence of *Tro.* 562–6 σφαγαὶ δ' ἀμφιβώμιοι / Φρυγῶν ἔν τε δεμνίοις / καράτομος ἐρημία / νεανίδων στέφανον ἔφερεν / Ἑλλάδι κουροτρόφον (the end of the poignant ode on the fall of Troy) and *Andr.* 399 σφαγὰς ... Ἕκτορος τροχηλάτους. Yet the adjective is active (καρατόμος) rather than passive here, as in E. fr. 228a.10 ... ὃς ἐλθὼν Γοργόνος καρατόμος and Lyc. 187 ... Ἑλλάδος καρατόμον (i.e. Iphigenia), the only other instances if we exclude Kayser's dubious καρατόμα in *Ag.* 1091. Cf. A. Fries, *CQ* n.s. 60 (2010), 349 with n. 19, Introduction, 36–7 and, for the verb, 585–6n.

Both Greeks and Trojans in *Rhesus* speak of beheading their enemies (dead or alive), although the verbal borrowing here and in 585–6 seems to make it more of a coincidence for Odysseus and Diomedes than for Dolon in 219–23 and 257b–60 (nn.). σφαγή in its various applications is a favourite of Euripides, who has 49 certain cases as opposed to six in Aeschylus (+ *PV* 863) and seven in Sophocles.

607. ἔσται: ΟΛ. Liapis ('Notes', 83) draws attention to ἥξει (Va¹ˢ). But this merely restores the future tense to Va's ἥκει, which looks like a scribal replacement (in V or some earlier copy) of the correct reading (ἥκει γάρ opens the line at *Rh.* 325, *Ag.* 522, *Phil.* 758, *Hel.* 1200, *Or.* 53). The Va-copyist was given to emending his text (Introduction, 49).

ἐξ ἄλλης χερός: i.e. Achilles.

608–10. In content Odysseus' greeting resembles *Ai.* 14–17 ὦ φθέγγμ' Ἀθάνας, φιλτάτης ἐμοὶ θεῶν, / ὡς εὐμαθές σου, κἂν ἄποπτος ᾖς ὅμως, / φώνημ' ἀκούω καὶ ξυναρπάζω φρενί / χαλκοστόμου κώδωνος ὡς Τυρσηνικῆς, whereas its syntax has a Euripidean flavour (608–9a, 609b–10nn.).

608–9a. δέσποιν' Ἀθάνα: likewise E. *Suppl.* 1227. The title (for Athena also e.g. *Ai.* 38, E. fr. 370.118, Ar. *Pax* 271) expresses the humil-

---

[239] Xen. *An.* 4.7.3 τῇ γὰρ στρατιᾷ οὐκ ἔστι τὰ ἐπιτήδεια, εἰ μὴ ληψόμεθα τὸ χωρίον is different in that the main clause refers to the present and future alike (KG I 138).

ity of men before the gods (Barrett on *Hipp*. 88–9). On Doric Ἀθάνα in spoken verse see 501–2n.

γάρ explains the vocative, i.e. why Odysseus knows who has just spoken. Cf. *OC* 891 ὦ φίλτατ', ἔγνων γὰρ τὸ προσφώνημά σου and especially *Hec*. 1114–15 ὦ φίλτατ', ἠσθόμην γάρ, Ἀγάμεμνον, σέθεν / φωνῆς ἀκούσας (*GP* 69, 80, 581, Barrett on *Hipp*. 88–9).

ἠσθόμην: 'recognise (a voice)', as again in the first person singular aorist at *Hec*. 1114–15 (above) and *Ba*. 178–9 ὦ φίλταθ', ὡς σὴν γῆρυν ἠσθόμην κλυών / σοφὴν σοφοῦ παρ' ἀνδρός (cf. Mastronarde on *Phoen*. 141–4). In both these passages and *OC* 891 (above) the speaker is blind and so, like Odysseus here, unable to see his interlocutor.

609b–10. Athena's unfailing support for Odysseus is also acknowledged at the end of his first speech in the *Ajax* prologue: *Ai*. 34–5 πάντα γὰρ τά τ' οὖν πάρος / τά τ' εἰσέπειτα σῇ κυβερνῶμαι χερί. But verbally our passage comes closer to *Il*. 10.278–9 ἥ τέ μοι αἰεί / ἐν πάντεσσι πόνοισι παρίστασαι (~ *Od*. 13.300–1; cf. e.g. *Il*. 23.782–3, *Od*. 20.47–8). For the development and implications of this unique bond between the hero and his patron goddess see M. W. M. Pope, *AJPh* 81 (1960), 113–35 (particularly 119–24) and, from a radically unitarian perspective, W. B. Stanford, *The Ulysses Theme* ..., Oxford ²1968, 25–42.

γάρ refers to συνήθη, supposing an ellipse: 'The sound of your voice is familiar to me because ...' (*GP* 65–6).

ἀεί ποτε: also 653–4a (n.) ἀεί ποτ' εὖ φρονοῦσα τυγχάνεις πόλει / κἀμοί. In poetry ἀεί ποτε is virtually confined to drama, with more occurrences in Euripides (8) than in all other extant tragedy together (*Ai*. 320, *Ant*. 456, Critias *TrGF* 43 F 7.10,[240] Sclerias? *TrGF* 213 F 2.3). In view of our scanty evidence, one must not lay too much weight on such an inconspicuous phrase, but it may add another Euripidean touch to the language of this passage.

611–12. Odysseus' double question adapts his more general prayer to Athena at *Il*. 10.463–4 ἀλλὰ καὶ αὖτις / πέμψον ἐπὶ Θρηκῶν ἀνδρῶν ἵππους τε καὶ εὐνάς.

κατηύνασται: a regular, but unique perfect form of εὐνάζω and its compounds. Dindorf (III.2 [1840], 612) restored the reduplication, which is not omitted in drama and only very rarely shortened before the third century BC (Lautensach, *Augment*, 47–9, 181–2, Threatte I 385, II 486). Cf. 580–1n.

πόθεν: almost equivalent to ποῦ after a common Greek idiom, which defined a place by direction or movement from a starting point. Cf. e.g. *Rh*. 695 πόθεν νιν κυρήσω; *OC* 503–5 (Ισ.) ... τὸν τόπον δ' ἵνα / χρῆσται

---

[240] A papyrus fragment (P. Oxy. 2078) ascribed to *Pirithous*, of which the authorship has since antiquity been disputed between Euripides and Critias. See Introduction, 24.

μ' ὑπουργεῖν, τοῦτο βούλομαι μαθεῖν. / (Χο.) τοὐκεῖθεν ἄλσους ... τοῦδ', E. *Suppl.* 756–8, S. *Tr.* 938–9 ἀλλὰ πλευρόθεν / πλευρὰν παρεὶς ἔκειτο πόλλ' ἀναστένων, *IT* 1348–9 (ὁρῶμεν ...) τοὺς νεανίας / ... πρύμνωθεν ἑστῶτας νεώς. Expressions like *PV* 714 λαιᾶς ... χειρός and *Cyc.* 681 ποτέρας τῆς χερός (also adduced by Paley and Porter) are probably partitive local genitives and do not belong in this category (KG I 385, SD 112).

613–15. Athena's description echoes Hector at 519–20 (n.). After 526 he led Rhesus and his retinue down the left *eisodos*, opposite the direction to the Trojan camp.

613. ἧσται: 'is encamped', as in 846 σὺ πρόσθεν ἡμῶν ἧσο καὶ Φρυγῶν στρατός and e.g. *Il.* 18.509 τὴν δ' ἑτέρην πόλιν ἀμφὶ δύω στρατοὶ εἵατο λαῶν, E. *Suppl.* 357 παρ' ὅπλοις ... ἥμενος.

614–15. '... but Hector has allocated him a resting-place outside the ranks, until night passes into daylight.'

ἐκτὸς ... τάξεων: 519–20n. (τοῦ τεταγμένου δίχα).

κατηύνασεν: 580–1n.

ἕως ἂν νὺξ ἀμείψηται φάος: The transmitted νύξ should be retained and ἀμείψηται then explained as 'shall have taken light in exchange for itself', i.e. 'shall have given place to day' (Paley on 615), or, with Porter (on 615), as an extension of the verb's physical sense 'pass into' (LSJ s.v. ἀμείβω B II 2). In any case one may compare fr. tr. adesp. 692 col. II 14–16 ἵνα τε Νὺξ δ[ιαμε]ίβεται (Radt: ἀ[π- Schubart) / τὰ[ν φαες] | φόρον αἴγλαν / ἀοῖον [ἂ]ν' αἰθέρα, / φέρε[ι δ' ἁ] | μέριον φάος – from an ode that has variously been ascribed to the fourth century, the Hellenistic age or, in view of its similarities to *Phaeth.* 63–6 Diggle = E. fr. 773.19–22, even Euripides himself (Radt, *TrGF* II, 284; cf. M. Fantuzzi, *BMCR* 2006.02.18, on 615).

Diggle, Kovacs and Liapis (cf. 'Notes', 83–4) accept Lenting's νύκτ' (*Animadversiones*, 75) while also understanding daylight to supplant the night. But with φάος as subject this would require a genitive as in e.g. *Il.* 11.547 γόνυ γουνὸς ἀμείβων, *Hel.* 1186–7 πέπλους μέλανας ... / λευκῶν ἀμείψασ' and 1533 ἔργου δ' ἔργον ἐξημείβετο (KG I 378, SD 127). At *Med.* 1266–7 καὶ ζαμενὴς (Porson: δυσμενὴς codd.) <φόνου> / φόνος ἀμείβεται Diggle rightly prefers Wecklein's <φόνου> to Hermann's and Weil's <φόνον>, endorsed by Dodds (*Humanitas* 4 [1952], 15–18), on the ground that ἀμείβομαι with the accusative cannot possibly mean 'succeed' or 'being succeeded by' without a connotation of requital or exchange (*CQ* n.s. 34 [1984], 63 = *Euripidea*, 293–4). This sense of reciprocity is clearly present in our paradosis, but would be as alien to Lenting's text as it is to *Med.* 1266–7, and some spatial notion as 'to pass *out* through' (LSJ s.v. ἀμείβω B II 2, Garvie on *Cho.* 965–6) would again have to be employed.

616–21. Unlike Dolon in *Il.* 10.436–41, Athena centres her description on Rhesus' marvellous horses. We are ironically reminded of *Il.* 10.544–63, where Nestor wonders whether a god has given them to the two Achaeans (he mentions Zeus and Athena) and Odysseus explains how they captured them themselves.

616–17. πέλας δὲ πῶλοι Θρηκίων ἐξ ἁρμάτων / λευκαὶ δέδενται adapts *Il.* 10.474–5 'Ρῆσος δ' ἐν μέσῳ ηὗδε, παρ' αὐτῷ δ' ὠκέες ἵπποι / ἐξ ἐπιδιφριάδος πυμάτης ἱμᾶσι δέδεντο. Yet the vocabulary is closer to Hippon. fr. 72.5–6 *IEG* ἐπ' ἁρμάτων τε καὶ Θρεϊκίων πώλων / λευκῶν (... ἀπηναρίσθη 'Ρῆσος). For the gender of the team-horses see 185n. and for the practice of tying them to the chariot 27, 567–8a nn.

Θρηκίων ἐξ ἁρμάτων: Cf. also 302 (301b–2n.) ... Θρηκίοις τ' ὀχήμασιν. The chariot is described more fully in *Il.* 10.438 ~ *Rh.* 303–4, 306b–8 (nn.).

διαπρεπεῖς ἐν εὐφρόνῃ: 'conspicuous in the night' (cf. 91–2n.). Normally διαπρεπής is used in the more figurative sense 'distinguished, magnificent' (LSJ s.v.),[241] but see perhaps Chaerem. *TrGF* 71 F 1.2 στίλβοντα λευκῷ †χρώματι διαπρεπῆ (which could be a linguistic imitation of *Rh.* 616–18). Also the verb in the famous Pi. *Ol.* 1.1–2 ... ὁ δὲ χρυσὸς αἰθόμενον πῦρ / ἅτε διαπρέπει νυκτὶ μεγάνορος ἔξοχα πλούτου. The gleaming white horses are meant to act as a signpost for the Greeks.

618. δ': 132n.

ὥστε ποταμίου κύκνου πτερόν: For comparative ὥστε (Λ: ὥσπερ ΔgB, *Chr. Pat.* 2058) in tragedy see 301b–2n. With ποτάμιος uniquely applied to a swan, the following phrase may be a conflation of *Hel.* 215 χιονόχρῳ κύκνου πτερῷ (metrically identical, but with an epithet which in the genitive here would not scan) and E. *El.* 151–2 κύκνος ἀχέτας / ποταμίοις παρὰ χεύμασιν, where the adjective stands close by, but not in conjuction with, κύκνος (A. Fries, *CQ* n.s. 60 [2010], 349, Introduction, 36–7).

In *Il.* 10.437 and *Rh.* 304 Rhesus' horses are said to be whiter than snow. Elsewhere in drama the swan or its plumage is associated with the white hair of age: *HF* 110–11, 692–4, *Ba.* 1365, Ar. *Vesp.* 1064–5 and presumably *PV* 795, where the Graiae, who like Cycnus ('Hes.' fr. 237 M.–W.) were 'white-haired from birth' (Hes. *Th.* 270–1), are called κυκνόμορφοι (Griffith on *PV* 794–6, Bond on *HF* 110). *Or.* 1385–6 is too corrupt to make anything of the MSS' κυκνόπτερον (-πτέρου Scaliger) with reference to Helen's face.

619–20a. κάλλιστον οἴκοις σκῦλον: similarly 190 (189b–90n.) κάλλιστον οἴκοις κτῆμ' ... (of Achilles' chariot). The present passage

---

[241] The *Antiope* passage quoted there (now E. fr. 185.2) belongs under διαπρέπω.

is perhaps echoed in *IA* [1629] κάλλιστά μοι σκῦλ' ἀπὸ Τροίας ἑλών (i.e. Agamemnon), the last line of the late-antique addition to the play (*IA* 1578–1629, on which see M. L. West, *BICS* 28 [1981], 73–8 = *Hellenica* II, 318–25).

Normally σκῦλα denotes captured arms and armour (to be) dedicated in temples (cf. 179n.), although like σκυλεύματα (591–3n.) it can also refer to war-booty in general (*Or.* 1434; cf. Pritchett, *GSW* I, 55–6, V, 132–47). The unusual singular here must be due to the fact that the prospective loot consists of one specific item, i.e. the pair of horses regarded as a team. Likewise Aristopho fr. 11.8–9 *PCG* τὰς δὲ πτέρυγας / ἃς εἶχε (*sc.* ὁ Ἔρως) τῇ Νίκῃ φορεῖν / ἔδοσαν, περιφανὲς σκῦλον ἀπὸ τῶν πολεμίων, Plut. *Aem.* 21.1 (the sword Cato Licinianus lost in battle) and metaphorically E. *El.* 896–7 (Aegisthus) ὃν ... θηρσὶν ἁρπαγὴν πρόθες, / ἢ σκῦλον οἰωνοῖσιν.

The word is found several times in Euripides and twice in Sophocles (*Phil.* 1428, 1431), but not in Aeschylus.

620b–1. 'For nowhere else does the earth hold such a team of chariot-horses.'

Athena's comment is reminiscent of Nestor at *Il.* 10.550 ἀλλ' οὔ πω τοίους ἵππους ἴδον οὐδ' ἐνόησα (cf. 616–21n.). But the wording is peculiar, for the epic-poetic κεύθω properly means 'cover, conceal, shelter' (171, 872nn.), and these notions remain with the perfect in the sense 'contain' (LSJ s.v. κεύθω I 1). Perhaps our poet again thought of *Il.* 22.118 ἀλλ' ... ὅσα τε πτόλις ἥδε κέκευθεν and/or took out of context a phrase like *Od.* 3.16 ὅπου κύθε γαῖα – of Odysseus, presumed dead (Liapis on 619–21).

ὄχημα ... πωλικόν: Cf. 797–8 (n.) ὄχημα πωλικόν / ... ἵππων. In both passages ὄχημα is by extension used of the chariot-team, as at S. *El.* 740 κάρα ... ἱππικῶν ὀχημάτων, *Alc.* 66–7 ἵππειον ... ὄχημα, *Hipp.* 1355–6, *Phaeth.* 173 Diggle = E. fr. 779.6 and Tim. *Pers.* fr. 791.190–1 *PMG* = Hordern. See also 189b–90n.

622–3. The couplet is modelled on *Il.* 10.479–81 (Odysseus to Diomedes) ἀλλ' ἄγε δὴ πρόφερε κρατερὸν μένος· οὐδέ τί σε χρή / ἑστάμεναι μέλεον σὺν τεύχεσιν, ἀλλὰ λύ' ἵππους· / ἠὲ σύ γ' ἄνδρας ἔναιρε, μελήσουσιν δ' ἐμοὶ ἵπποι. But the alternatives come in reverse order.

Θρήκιον λεών: For a body of soldiers λαός (Attic λεώς) goes back to the *Iliad* (LSJ s.v. λαός I 1, *LfgrE* s.v. B 2; cf. 856–8n.). On the social implications of the term in epic and archaic to classical literature see J. Haubold, *Homer's People – Epic Poetry and Social Formation*, Cambridge 2000 (particularly 153–60).

ἢ 'μοὶ πάρες γε (OΛ) is probably sound. γε most frequently follows disjunctives and other connecting particles 'to define more sharply the new idea introduced' (*GP* 119–20; cf. KG II 173). It therefore emphasises 'μοί here rather than the imperative, which would indeed be difficult to maintain (*GP* 125, Diggle, *Studies*, 22). The postponement of the particle is rare, but well attested in Homer and fifth-century drama (*GP* 150). If one wishes to emend, Reiske's παράσχες (*Animadversiones*, 90) seems more attractive than Dobree's somewhat too specific πάρες σφε (*Adversaria* II [1833], 87 = IV [1874], 85).

σοὶ δὲ χρὴ πώλους μέλειν: so rightly Δ, after *Il.* 10.481 (above). Λ's πώλων would make μέλειν impersonal, the usual construction in prose.

624–6. The decision corresponds to *Il.* 10.482–501, where Diomedes' killing and Odysseus' handling of the horses are described in detail.

624. πωλοδαμνήσεις: 187–8n.

625. 'For you are well versed in subtleties and a clever thinker.'

This judgement about Odysseus shows remarkable verbal overlaps with *Med.* 686 σοφὸς γὰρ ἀνὴρ καὶ τρίβων τὰ τοιάδε (of Pittheus) and E. fr. 473 φαῦλον, ἄκομψον, τὰ μέγιστ' ἀγαθόν, / πᾶσαν ἐν ἔργῳ περιτεμνόμενον / σοφίαν, λέσχης ἀτρίβωνα (of Heracles).

τρίβων ... τὰ κομψά: With an accusative of respect τρίβων is paralleled only in *Med.* 686 (above), where, however, the neuter pronoun may help the construction. Elsewhere it takes a genitive on the analogy of ἔμπειρος and the like: e.g. *Cyc.* 519–20 (Odysseus speaking) Κύκλωψ, ἄκουσον· ὡς ἐγὼ τοῦ Βακχίου / τούτου τρίβων εἰμ', ὃν πιεῖν ἔδωκά σοι, *Ba.* 717 τρίβων λόγων, Ar. *Nub.* 869, *Vesp.* 1429, Hdt. 4.74.

Both τρίβων and κομψός occur in Euripides alone of the tragedians (although Sophocles has κομψεύω at *Ant.* 324). The former is colloquial (Stevens, *CEE* 50–1, J. Taillardat, *Les images d'Aristophane*, Paris 1965, 229 n. 3) and seems to be used here in ironic approval, as at *Cyc.* 519–20 (above). κομψός apparently belongs to a higher linguistic register. It has the same ambivalence of meaning as English 'smart', with the pejorative tone prevailing in genuine Euripides (cf. Collard on E. *Suppl.* 426, 'Supplement', 375–6). In a positive sense of 'Euripides' in Ar. *Thesm.* 93 (cf. Introduction 29–30 with n. 36).

νοεῖν σοφός: The infinitive is rare with σοφός: S. fr. 524.7 ... εὖ φρονεῖν σοφώτερος, *Med.* 580 ... σοφὸς λέγειν (~ E. fr. 189.2) and, by implication, *Hipp.* 986–7 ἐγὼ δ' ἄκομψος εἰς ὄχλον δοῦναι λόγον, / ἐς ἥλικας δὲ κὠλίγους σοφώτερος.

626. 'For one must station a man where he can be of greatest use.'

For this maxim Porter and others compare Ar. *Vesp.* 1431 ἔρδοι τις ἣν ἕκαστος εἰδείη τέχνην, a proverb still familiar to the Romans (Cic. *Att.* 5.10.3 *o illud verum* 'ἔρδοι τις ...'!, *Tusc.* 1.41 *quam quisque norit artem, in hac se exerceat*; cf. Hor. *Ep.* 1.14.44, Prop. 2.1.46, Cic. *Off.* 1.114). Feickert (on 626) adds Xen. *Cyr.* 8.5.15 ἀλλὰ καὶ τὸ διασπᾶν ... τακτικὸν ἡγεῖτο, καὶ τὸ τιθέναι γε τὸ μέρος ἕκαστον ὅπου μάλιστα ἐν ὠφελείᾳ ἂν εἴη and, less well, E. fr. 184 (*Antiope*) ἐν τούτῳ <γέ τοι> / λαμπρός θ' ἕκαστος κἀπὶ τοῦτ' ἐπείγεται / ... / ἵν' αὐτὸς αὐτοῦ τυγχάνει βέλτιστος ὤν (reconstructed from Pl. *Grg.* 484e4–7).

δ': 132n.

627–9. Athena sees Alexandros approach (still off-stage as Diomedes' next question proves) and warns the Achaeans. For this 'actional' entrance announcement (J. P. Poe, *HSPh* 94 [1992], 130–1) and the ensuing dialogue, which leads to the departure of the 'endangered' characters, cf. S. *El.* 1428–36 and, with fewer similarities, E. *El.* 962–87.

καὶ μήν ... τόνδ': For this 'formula' in entrance announcements see 85–6n.

στείχοντα: 85–6n.

δόξας ἀσήμους: 'indistinct rumours' (cf. 656–9). The basic meaning of ἄσημος in all its applications is that 'there is nothing to σημαίνειν, to indicate, what it is' (Barrett on *Hipp.* 269).

μεμβλωκότων: The epic perfect (*Il.* 4.11, 24.73, *Od.* 17.190) is attested nowhere else in classical Greek. On such verb forms in *Rhesus* see 523–5a n. (δέχθαι).

631–2. πρὸς εὐνὰς δ' ... Ἕκτορος: 1n. δέ quite often takes the third position after prepositional phrases involving a noun without article or a pronoun (KG II 268, *GP* 185–6).

κατόπτας ... στρατοῦ: Cf. *Sept.* 36 ... κατοπτῆρας στρατοῦ, 369 κατόπτης ... στρατοῦ (at the same verse-position) and *Rh.* 233–4 (233–5a n.) στρατιᾶς / Ἑλλάδος διόπτας. For a spy κατόπτης further appears in *Hel.* 1175, *Rh.* 134 (133–5a n.), 150, 155 and 558. At *Sept.* 41 αὐτὸς κατόπτης δ' εἴμ' ἐγὼ τῶν πραγμάτων the word has its original meaning 'eyewitness' (Pritchett, *GSW* I, 130), although military espionage remains implied.

633. 'Does he not then have to be the first to die?'

οὔκουν: 161–2a n.

ὑπάρχειν ... κατθανόντα: a curious expression, since ὑπάρχω as a full verb[242] normally stresses the initiative of the subject-agent (LSJ s.v. A, B I 1, T. C. W. Stinton, *Euripides and the Judgement of Paris*, London 1965, 14 with n. 4 = *Collected Papers*, 27 with n. 4); so literally 'Does he not then have to take the lead in dying?' With a predicative participle it is otherwise attested only in Hdt. 6.133.1 πρόφασιν ἔχων ὡς οἱ Πάριοι ὑπῆρξαν πρότεροι στρατευόμενοι τριήρεϊ ἐς Μαραθῶνα ἅμα τῷ Πέρσῃ, 7.8β.2, 9.78.2, Xen. *An.* 2.3.23 and 5.5.9, whence Fraenkel

---

[242] Feickert (on 633), as more hesitantly Vater (617) and Ammendola (633), takes ὑπάρχειν ... κατθανόντα as a mere periphrasis for κατθανεῖν (LSJ s.v. ὑπάρχω B I 5, KG I 38–9 n. 3, Schwyzer 811–12). But this would be rather weak in this context and hardly to the point.

(*Rev.* 239) suspected it to be an Ionism. Paley (on 633) notes that '[u]sually ὑπάρχειν conveys the idea of some wrong or benefit, committed or received, which serves as the motive for further action in requital'. This is true in most instances (including all the ones cited), but need not be the case (*Andr.* 274–6 ἦ μεγάλων ἀχέων ἄρ' ὑπῆρξεν ... ὁ Μαί- / ας τε καὶ Διὸς τόκος, Pl. *Tim.* 41c8).

635. τοῦτον δὲ πρὸς σῆς χειρὸς οὐ θέμις θανεῖν: 605–7n. The formulation resembles *OT* 376–7 (Teiresias to Oedipus) οὐ γάρ σε μοῖρα πρός γ' ἐμοῦ πεσεῖν, ἐπεὶ / ἱκανὸς Ἀπόλλων, ᾧ τάδ' ἐκπρᾶξαι μέλει (376 σε ... γ' ἐμοῦ Brunck: με ... γε σοῦ P. Oxy. 22, codd.).

Text and word-order here are reconstructed from Δ, where V has ... χειρὸς οὐ θέμις ... and O θανεῖν (cf. L¹ᵐ vel Trᵐ: κτανεῖν VΛ), albeit in penultimate position by a characteristic display of the *vitium Byzantinum* (Introduction, 49 n. 7). Liapis ('Notes', 84) favours τοῦτον δὲ πρὸς σῆς οὐ θέμις χε<ι>ρὸς θανεῖν (after Λ). But this would leave the verse with only a weak (penthemimeral) caesura, whereas Δ's reading adds a strong hephthemimeres.

δέ: 132n.

636–9. Before her fateful deception of Hector Athena commands a similar 'division of duties' between Achilles and herself: *Il.* 22.222–3 ἀλλὰ σὺ μὲν νῦν στῆθι καὶ ἄμπνυε, τόνδε δ' ἐγώ τοι / οἰχομένη πεπιθήσω ἐναντίβιον μαχέσασθαι.

636–7a. 'But for whom you have come bringing slaughter appointed by fate, make haste (*sc.* to bring it)!'

By a rare inversion of the usual finite verb and (mostly aorist) participle of intransitive ταχύνω (e.g. *Ai.* 1164–6 ἀλλ' ... ταχύνας / σπεῦσον κοίλην κάπετόν τιν' ἰδεῖν / τῷδ', *OT* 861), μορσίμους φέρων σφαγάς must here also be understood with τάχυν' (Paley on 637); cf. Hp. *Mul.* 3.222 ταχύνειν δὲ χρὴ ἐκκαθαίροντα and imperatival ἀνύω in Ar. *Vesp.* 1168 ἄνυσόν ποθ' ὑποδησάμενος, *Av.* 241, *Pl.* 413 and Pherecr. fr. 44.1 *PCG*. Still the transition between the relative and the main clause seems extremely harsh, and one is tempted to suspect influence from *Cho.* 659–60 (τοῖσι κυρίοισι δωμάτων) / πρὸς οὕσπερ ἥκω καὶ φέρω καινοὺς λόγους. / τάχυνε δ', ...

Kovacs prints ἀλλ' οἵπερ ἥξεις. But his criticism of the paradosis as unclear (*Euripidea Tertia*, 148–9) is unfounded, if one takes ἥκεις to refer to Diomedes' arrival in the Trojan camp. Moreover, ᾧπερ (fere P² ᾧπερ: ὥσπερ Ω) creates a welcome antithesis with τοῦτον in 635 (D. J. Mastronarde, *ElectronAnt* 8 [2004], 21–2), and ταχύνω (unlike σπεύδω) does not mean 'hasten on one's way'. Liapis ('Notes', 84–5) succumbs to a similarly over-literal reading of the MSS text.

637b–9. σύμμαχος ... παραστατεῖν: Athena employs σύμμαχος equally deceptively in *Ai.* 90 τί βαιὸν οὕτως ἐντρέπῃ τῆς συμμάχου; –

prompting Ajax' misguided reply in 91–2 ὦ χαῖρ' Ἀθάνα, χαῖρε Διογενὲς τέκνον, / ὡς εὖ παρέστης. Note also his request in *Ai.* 117–18 τοῦτο σοὶ δ' ἐφίεμαι, / τοιάνδ' ἀεί μοι σύμμαχον παρεστάναι.

παραστατεῖν (as παρέστης and παρεστάναι in *Ai.* 92 and 118) is reminiscent of Homeric παρίσταμαι for the presence and assistance of a god (cf. P. Pucci, *AJPh* 115 [1994], 24). The latter half of the sentence (ἀρωγὸς ... παραστατεῖν) in particular echoes the language that in 609b–10 (n.)[243] described the relationship between Athena and Odysseus, preparing for the ironic mirror scene between Paris and his supposed patroness.

σαθροῖς λόγοισιν ... ἀμείψομαι: 'I will reply ... with unsound words' (anticipating Paris' address to the absent Hector in 642–5). σαθρός is a medical metaphor (LSJ s.v. 1), which has three parallels in Euripides: *Hec.* 1189–90 ἀλλ' εἴτε χρήστ' ἔδρασε χρήστ' ἔδει λέγειν, / εἴτ' αὖ πονηρά τοὺς λόγους εἶναι σαθρούς, *Suppl.* 1064 τί φῄς; τί τοῦτ' αἴνιγμα σημαίνει σαθρόν; (with Collard) and, of moral depravity, *Ba.* 487 τοῦτ' ἐς γυναῖκας δόλιόν ἐστι καὶ σαθρόν. Elsewhere in the fifth century it occurs only in Pi. *Nem.* 8.34 κῦδος ... σαθρόν and Hdt. 6.109.5.

ἐχθρὸν ἄνδρ': Cf. 585–6 τὸν ἔχθιστον Φρυγῶν / Πάριν.

640–1. 'And that is my word; but the one to be affected does not know nor has he heard, in spite of being near to our conversation.'

καὶ ταῦτ' ἐγὼ μὲν εἶπον: For this type of 'formula', ending a (usually longer) speech, see 130b n.

ὃν δὲ χρὴ παθεῖν / οὐκ οἶδεν οὐδ' ἤκουσεν: Paris is the subject of both the infinitive and the main verbs. The expression is awkward (Fraenkel, *Rev.* 238), more for the antithesis between ὃν δὲ χρὴ παθεῖν and καὶ ταῦτ' ἐγὼ μὲν εἶπον than for the *hysteron proteron* οἶδεν ... ἤκουσεν.

λόγου has sometimes been taken with ἤκουσεν instead of ἐγγύς, which is grammatically possible (*Hec.* 967 λέγουσα μύθους ὧν κλύων ἀφικόμην, Thuc. 4.37.1 τοῦ κηρύγματος ἀκούσαντες, 5.44.1 ἀκούσαντες τῆς ... ἀγγελίας [KG I 358, SD 107]), but almost certainly ruled out by the word-order. ἐγγὺς ὢν λόγου then may be regarded as a variation on 149 (149–50n.) ... οἳ πάρεισιν ἐν λόγῳ in the sense that λόγου is short for 'where we were talking'.

The blissfully ignorant Paris recalls Ajax, who by Athena's designs cannot see Odysseus (*Ai.* 69–70, 83–5) and knows nothing of their plot against him. But there is no hint at divine 'magic' here, and the remark

---

[243] Of the Homeric parallels quoted there cf. especially also *Il.* 23.782–3 ἢ τὸ πάρος περ / μήτηρ ὣς Ὀδυσῆϊ παρίσταται ἠδ' ἐπαρήγει.

was most likely meant to remind the audience that the actual conditions on stage had no consequences for the story told.

642–74. Nowhere in epic and fifth-century drama does a god masquerade as another god. If not invisible or in their own form, they appear to men as a mortal comrade (e.g. Aphrodite in *Il.* 3.383–95, Athena in *Il.* 4.86–104, 22.226–47) or a stranger like Hermes in *Il.* 24.347–469, Athena in *Od.* 7.19–81 and 13.221–88, Dionysus in *Bacchae* or Hera, who in A. fr. 168.16–30 (ascribed to *Xantriae*) meets the chorus in the guise of a begging priestess. Our nearest equivalent is Dionysus in Ar. *Frogs*, inadequately dressed up as the immortalised Heracles.[244] Yet the mid-fourth-century comic poet Amphis had Zeus transform himself into Artemis before seducing Callisto, who later blames the goddess for the result (Amphis fr. 46 *PCG*; cf. A. Henrichs, in J. N. Bremmer [ed.] *Interpretations of Greek Mythology*, London – Sydney 1987, 262). A similar twist must have been intended here, where Athena likewise assumes a diametrically opposed identity in order to achieve her ends. This would suit the heyday of mythical parody (ca. 400–350 BC), although one may wonder how provocative, especially in a tragedy and with Athena as the protagonist, it was meant and perceived to be.

The interlude, which replaces a choral song or epirrhematic dialogue to cover the time of the Achaeans' absence, serves to maintain the suspense and translates into action Athena's personal involvement with the Greeks (Ritchie 125–6; cf. 670–1a n.). The encounter of Paris, 'the most hated of the Phrygians' (585–6n.), with his supposed patroness ironically reflects Odysseus' relationship to Athena (637b–9, 653–4a nn.) and thus recalls the Iliadic antinomy between the two goddesses (*Il.* 5.330–3, 350–1, 428–30, 21.423–33). In particular we are reminded of Aphrodite's rescue operation in *Il.* 3.373–82, her only successful intervention in the war (654b–5n.), and Athena's final deception of Hector in *Il.* 22.222–305 (cf. 636–9n.). As a smaller-scale version of the latter her scheme here deprives the Trojans of a mighty ally and potential victory (600–4n.), just as Hector's death seals the fall of the city (R. S. Bond, *AJPh* 117 [1996], 268). There is thus no doubt which tutelage prevails, and the 'divine comedy' of Athena's transformation becomes merely another, essentially epic, way to express the gods' superiority.

---

244 The notion is touched on in E. *El.* 979 ἆρ' αὔτ' ἀλάστωρ εἶπ' ἀπεικασθεὶς θεῷ; (Apollo) and *Or.* 1666–9 ὦ Λοξία μαντεῖε, σῶν θεσπισμάτων / οὐ ψευδόμαντις ἦσθ' ἄρ' ἀλλ' ἐτήτυμος. / καίτοι μ' ἐσῄει δεῖμα, μή τινος κλύων / ἀλαστόρων δόξαιμι σὴν κλύειν ὄπα.

642–3. Hermann (*Opuscula* III, 287) aptly refers to Zeus' malicious dream-figure speaking at *Il.* 2.23–5 (= 60–2) εὕδεις, Ἀτρέος υἱὲ δαΐφρονος ἱπποδάμοιο· / οὐ χρὴ παννύχιον εὕδειν βουληφόρον ἄνδρα, / ᾧ λαοί τ' ἐπιτετράφαται καὶ τόσσα μέμηλεν.[245]

σὲ τὸν ... λέγω: 'The abrupt acc[usative] calls the person's attention in a rough and harsh way' (Jebb on *Ant.* 441). Normally a descriptive apposition follows, whereas the verb of address may also be omitted (Barrett on *Hipp.* 1283–4). With a vocative following, as here, cf. *Med.* 271–3 σὲ τὴν σκυθρωπὸν καὶ πόσει θυμουμένην, / Μήδει', ἀνεῖπον τῆσδε γῆς ἔξω περᾶν / φυγάδα. Otherwise e.g. *PV* 944–6 σὲ τὸν σοφιστήν ... τὸν πυρὸς κλέπτην λέγω, *Ai.* 71–3, S. *El.* 1445–6 (with Finglass), *Hel.* 546–8 (with Kannicht), *Ba.* 912–13, Ar. *Av.* 274, *Ran.* 171.

Ἕκτορ: As usual, the name of the person addressed off-stage is supplied (cf. Dodds on *Ba.* 912–14).

σ' ἐχρῆν (O) should not be reinterpreted as σε χρῆν. The 'false' augment with χρῆν most probably arose on the analogy of ἔδει, when in instances such as ours ΣΕΧΡΗΝ (ΜΕΧΡΗΝ, ΔΕΧΡΗΝ) were read as σ' ἐχρῆν (μ' ἐχρῆν, δ' ἐχρῆν). This form, apparently still avoided by Aeschylus and Sophocles, is metrically sanctioned several times in Euripides (e.g. *Andr.* 395, *Suppl.* 174, *Ion* 1314), Old Comedy (Ar. *Ach.* 540, *Pax* 135, *Av.* 364, Pl. Com. fr. 71.5 *PCG*) and later drama (frr. tr. adesp. 1b (g).20, 81.2,[246] Alexis fr. 150.9 *PCG*, Men. *Peric.* 748, *Sam.* 551) and may thus also be recognised in uncertain cases. See Barrett on *Hipp.* 1072–3 (with sensible advice for treating the MSS evidence), Kannicht on *Hel.* 80.

644–5. ἡμῖν ... στρατεύματι: For this type of apposition cf. Pi. *Ol.* 2.14–15 εὔφρων ἄρουραν ἔτι πατρίαν σφίσιν κόμισον / λοιπῷ γένει, *Ol.* 9.98–9 σύνδικος δ' αὐτῷ Ἰολάου / τύμβος ἐνναλία τ' Ἐλευσὶς ἀγλαΐαισιν and *Ba.* 336 (ἵνα ...) ἡμῖν τε τιμὴ παντὶ τῷ γένει προσῇ (KG I 430 n. 2, SD 189–90 with n. 5).

κλῶπες ἄνδρες: Cf. 678–9, 709 (n.) κλωπὸς ... φωτός, 777 κλῶπας ... συμμάχων ... τινάς and 205 (n.), 512 κλωπικός. The noun and its cognates are relatively common in classical prose, but rare in poetry: *Cyc.* 223 λῃσταί τινες κατέσχον ἢ κλῶπες χθόνα; *Alc.* 766, probably S. fr. 314.68 (*Ichneutae*) and later e.g. Lyc. 658, 1303.

κατάσκοποί τινες: 125–6a n.

646. φυλάσσω: Naber (*Mnemosyne* n.s. 10 [1882], 4–5) for φυλάσσει (Ω). The first person calls attention to the speaker's presence and is often found in divine self-introductions: *Rh.* 890–2 ἡ γὰρ ... Μοῦσα ...

---

[245] *Il.* 2.23 is punctuated as a question in a number of MSS, and the *Rhesus* passage perhaps favours this interpretation.
[246] I.e. *TrGF* V.2 (60) ΡΗΣΟΣ 642.13, the second spurious prologue to *Rhesus*.

πάρειμι, *Hipp.* 1285 Λητοῦς δὲ κόρη σ' Ἄρτεμις αὐδῶ (with Barrett), *Andr.* 1232 ἥκω Θέτις λιποῦσα Νηρέως δόμους, *Hel.* 1643–4, *Ba.* 1–2, 1340–1. Moreover, ἥδε for ἐγώ here precludes a third-person verb, as is metrically guaranteed in E. *El.* 1238–9 δίπτυχοι δέ σε / καλοῦσι μητρὸς συγγόνοι Διόσκοροι. Cf. *OT* 41 ἱκετεύομέν σε πάντες οἵδε πρόστροποι, *Hel.* 1168 Θεοκλύμενος παῖς ὅδε προσεννέπω (Lenting: -ει L), πάτερ (with Dale) and *Or.* 1626 Φοῖβός σ' ὁ Λητοῦς παῖς ὅδ' ἐγγὺς ὢν καλῶ.

The same (very easy) corruption occurs at *Or.* 1226, where Herwerden's and Cobet's καλῶ is confirmed by Σ^M (I 210.27 Schwartz) ἀντὶ τοῦ· καλεῖ σε, and perhaps Ar. *Ach.* 406 and E. *El.* 1238–9.[247] In *Alc.* 167, *Hipp.* 1285 and *Or.* 1626 the MSS are divided.

πρευμενής: an Aeschylean favourite (thirteen references), taken over by Euripides: *Hec.* 538, *Tro.* 739, *Or.* 119, 138.[248] Note also Ar. fr. 21 *PCG* = fr. tr. adesp. 70a (a tragic quotation in disguise?). The word is applied to supernatural beings in *Pers.* 685, A. *Suppl.* 210, *Eum.* 236, *Hec.* 538 and *Or.* 119.

647–8. In the mouth of Athena pretending to be Aphrodite the reference to the Judgement of Paris is deeply ironical. She has indeed not 'forgotten the 'honour' Paris did her when he rejected her in favour of' the goddess of love (Liapis on 647–8).

δ': 132n.

οὐδ' ἀμνημονῶ: so at the same verse-position *Eum.* 24. Similarly *IT* 361 ... κακῶν γὰρ τῶν τότ' οὐκ ἀμνημονῶ.

ἐπαινῶ ... σέθεν: That ἐπαινέω as an expression of thanks does not in itself convey the idea of polite refusal (despite e.g. LSJ s.v. III) has been shown by Quincey (*JHS* 86 [1966], 133–58 [152–6]), who gives abundant evidence for its use in acceptance contexts. The construction with the nominative participle has a parallel in *Cyc.* 549 χάριν δὲ τίνα λαβών σ' ἐπαινέσω;

649-[52]. In fact Rhesus went to Troy after repeated embassies and presents sent by Hector (399–403n.). Athena's lie is to win Paris' confidence and remind the audience of the deed she is covering up.

649–50. 'And now that the Trojan army is favoured by fortune, I have come bringing you a great ally ...'

καὶ νῦν ἐπ' εὐτυχοῦντι Τρωϊκῷ στρατῷ / ἥκω: The structure and rhythm of 649 bear some resemblance to *Ai.* 3 καὶ νῦν ἐπὶ σκηναῖς σε ναυτικαῖς ὁρῶ.

---

247 In the former passage καλεῖ with appositional ἐγώ at verse-end may express a certain pomposness on the part of Dicaeopolis. In the latter Cobet's μητρὸς καλοῦμεν (*Mnemosyne* 5 [1856], 246) is more difficult for the change of word-order involved. But his comparison with *Hel.* 1643–4 is striking.

248 *Hec.* 540 is corrupt from 538. The adjective has further been conjectured at *Phaeth.* 269 Diggle = E. fr. 781.60, though all recent editors read Bekker's εὐμενεῖς.

ἐπ' εὐτυχοῦντι ... στρατῷ (52–84, 665–7, 882–4nn.) is best taken with Paley and others as a definition of the attendant circumstances (LSJ s.v. ἐπί B I 1 i, KG I 501–2, SD 468), since ἐπί with dative, dependent on ἥκω πορεύουσ', in a friendly sense would be hard to parallel (in S. *El.* 84–5 Tournier's ταῦτα γὰρ φέρειν / νίκην τέ φημι for the MSS' φέρει / νίκην τ' ἐφ' ἡμῖν ... has won general approval). The basic sense of the preposition ('upon') is also strongly felt here. Hence Porter's 'And now to crown the success of the Trojan host, I am come ...'

651. τῆς ὑμνοποιοῦ παῖδα Θρήκιον θεᾶς: similarly 964 τῆς καρποποιοῦ παῖδα Δήμητρος θεᾶς, with the perhaps newly-coined adjective καρποποιός (963–5a n.). Here ὑμνοποιός is previously found only in E. fr. 556.1 (*Oedipus*) and, as a noun, E. *Suppl.* 180 (with Collard on 180–1a). Our poet also has μελοποιός in 550 and παιδοποιός in 980 (n.).

[652]. The verse is essentially the same as 279 and was therefore deleted by Lachmann (*De mensura*, 43–4). In itself there is nothing wrong with adding Rhesus' paternal descent to his maternal one (cf. 348–54, 386–7, 393–4 and, for the structure, Xen. *Cyr.* 1.2.1 Πατρὸς μὲν δὴ ὁ Κῦρος λέγεται γενέσθαι Καμβύσου Περσῶν βασιλέως ... μητρὸς δὲ ὁμολογεῖται Μανδάνης γενέσθαι), and in an author so prone to reuse his own words mere duplication may not seem a decisive argument. Yet of the three repetitions comparable in length, 150 ~ 155 and 543–5 ~ 562–4 serve a particular purpose (149–50, 154–5, 543–5nn.), whereas 37b–8a (n.) has perhaps rightly been athetised by Dobree. Here Μούσης looks like a gloss on τῆς ὑμνοποιοῦ ... θεᾶς, after which a scribe would have filled the line with a familiar phrase. But as in the case of 37b–8a absolute certainty cannot be attained.

653–4a. ἀεί ποτ' ... / κἀμοί: For ἀεί ποτε see 609b–10n. This may be another ironic echo of Odysseus' reply to Athena in those lines (cf. 637b–9n.)

654b–5. '... and the greatest treasure in life I claim to have secured for my city by deciding in your favour'.

κειμήλιον: originally 'stored-up object of value'. Apart from *Phaeth.* 56 = E. fr. 773.12 (with Diggle), tragic usage of the word is always metaphorical (S. *El.* 437–8, *Hcld.* 591–2, E. fr. 362.4).

κρίνας σέ: of the Judgement of Paris also *Tro.* 927–8 Ἥρα δ' ὑπέσχετ' Ἀσιάδ' Εὐρώπης θ' ὅρους / τυραννίδ' ἕξειν, εἴ σφε κρίνειεν Πάρις. For κρίνω, 'decide in favour of, prefer', see LSJ s.v. II 7 with Suppl. (1996) and Wilkins on *Hcld.* 197.

τῇδε προσθέσθαι πόλει: perhaps taken from *Hcld.* 156–7 Ἄργους τοσήνδε χεῖρα τήν τ' Εὐρυσθέως / ἰσχὺν ἅπασαν τῇδε προσθέσθαι πόλει (with Wilkins on 157). Add Hdt. 1.53.1 to his parallels for προστίθεμαι, 'acquire as a friend / ally'.

The Homeric Aphrodite is no great help to the Trojans. She rescues Paris in *Il.* 3.373–82 (cf. 642–74n.), but her other two interventions end in disgrace (*Il.* 5.311–430, 21.415–33).

656–60. Odysseus in the *Ajax* prologue is in a similar situation as to assessing Ajax's guilt (*Ai.* 23 ἴσμεν γὰρ οὐδὲν τρανές, ἀλλ' ἀλώμεθα), but his eyewitness at least knows what he has seen: *Ai.* 29–31 καί μοί τις ὀπτὴρ αὐτὸν εἰσιδὼν μόνον / πηδῶντα πεδία σὺν νεορράντῳ ξίφει / φράζει τε κἀδήλωσεν (of which the nominative participle and first main verb recur in *Rh.* 659). The unreliability of Paris' information (cf. 628–9) makes him a particularly easy victim of Athena's persuasion (Paley on 656).

656–8a. ἀκούσας οὐ τορῶς: 77n. Of uninformed talk (among sailors) also *Ag.* 632 οὐκ οἶδεν οὐδεὶς ὥστ' ἀπαγγεῖλαι τορῶς (i.e. whether Menelaus is dead or alive).

φήμη δέ τις / φύλαξιν ἐμπέπτωκεν: 'a rumour has arisen among the watchmen'. Cf. Ar. *Lys.* 858–9 κἂν περὶ ἀνδρῶν γ' ἐμπέσῃ / λόγος τις, Pl. *Rep.* 354b6–7, *Lg.* 799d4–5 ἀτόπου γὰρ τὰ νῦν ἐμπεπτωκότος λόγου περὶ νόμων, Thphr. *Char.* 2.2 (LSJ s.v. ἐμπίπτω 3 b).

κατάσκοποι / ... Ἀχαιῶν: 125–6a n.

658b–9. 'And one man says so having laid no eye on them, while another, who has seen them come, cannot give particulars.'

ἰδών (*Chr. Pat.* 1876, Lenting, *Animadversiones*, 75) gives the appropriate antithesis to εἰσιδών (cf. Nauck, *Euripideische Studien* II, 177). Corruption into εἰδώς (Ω) was easy in this context and is paralleled at Ar. *Ran.* 714 ἰδὼν δὲ τάδ' (Bentley: εἰδὼς codd.) and E. *Suppl.* 1044 φράζετ' εἰ κατείδετε (Elmsley: κατοίδατε L). Conversely *Rh.* 65 καὶ τὸ θεῖον εἰδότες (Π²ΟΛ: ἰδόντες V).

οὐκ ἔχει φράσαι: *sc.* αὐτούς (KG II 562). The construction with a personal object is the same as in *Od.* 14.2–3 ᾗ οἱ Ἀθήνη / πέφραδε δῖον ὑφορβόν ('point out, show the way to'). This Homeric sense of φράζω recurs in 853–4, while the verse-end itself is all but repeated in 801 (800–2a n.).

660. εὐνὰς ἤλυθον πρὸς Ἕκτορος: The word-order 'noun, verbal part, preposition, genitive attribute' corresponds to *Sept.* 185 βρέτη πεσούσας πρὸς πολισσούχων θεῶν. At A. *Suppl.* 638 τὸν ἀρότοις θερίζοντα βροτοὺς ἐν ἄλλοις FJW (on 637–8) perhaps rightly prefer ἐν ἄλλων (Kraus), meaning that Ares reaps harvests of men 'in fields ploughed by others' (Sommerstein, *Aeschylus* I, 373 n. 131). Fraenkel on *Ag.* 964 discusses various other types of divided prepositional phrase.

For Hector's εὐναί see 1n. and for ἤλυθον 49–51n.

661. μηδὲν φοβηθῇς: Cf. *PV* 128 (opening the parodos), Ar. *Av.* 654 and, with an accusative object, *Andr.* 993–4 τὸν δ' Ἀχιλλέως / μηδὲν φοβηθῇς παῖδ'. Later Ezek. *Exag.* 127.

οὐδὲν ἐν στρατῷ νέον: 'new' in the sense of 'untoward' (4, 589–90nn.). This is Athena's second lie after 649-[52] (n.), which instantly fulfils its purpose of lulling Paris into a false sense of security.

662. φροῦδος (again 743, 814 and 865) is extremely frequent in Euripides. Note also Ar. *Ach.* 470 ('Euripides' speaking) and *Ran.* 1343 in the parody of Euripidean song (Introduction, 29–30 with n. 36; cf. 41–2, 750–1a nn.).

Θρῇκα κοιμήσων στρατόν: Only κοιμήσων (Δ) suits the context (519–20, 614, 762). Λ's κοσμήσων replicates the prevalent error at 138 (138–9n.).

663–4. σύ τοί με πείθεις: 65–6n. τοι intensifies σύ (cf. 568b–9n.) and thus, by expressing all Paris' confidence in 'Aphrodite', adds a fine touch of tragic irony.

τάξιν φυλάξων: 'to keep my station'. Cf. Xen. *Cyr.* 5.3.43 ἡ τάξις φυλακτέα (where, however, τάξις could also mean 'marching order') and D. H. 11.24.3 κατηγορηθέντες … τάξιν μὴ φυλάττειν.

ἐλεύθερος φόβου: similarly *Hec.* 869 ἐγώ σε θήσω τοῦδ' ἐλεύθερον φόβου and *Hcld.* 867–8 δεινοῦ φόβου / ἐλεύθερον … ἦμαρ.

665–7. For these 'unsound words' (639) to the retreating Paris Feickert (on 665) compares Electra's more open 'farewell' to Clytaemestra in E. *El.* 1139–46, which also begins with an ominous χώρει.

εὐτυχοῦντας συμμάχους ἐμούς: On the deceptive use of σύμμαχος see 637b–9n. There may be a further point in that εὐτυχέω and εὐτυχής have so far exclusively been applied to the Trojans or their affairs (cf. 52–84n. and 270, 390, 583, 649).

τὴν ἐμὴν προθυμίαν: Of a god's set purpose or will cf. *Hipp.* 1329–30, 1417, *Andr.* 1252, *Ion* 1385 and elsewhere Gorg. *Hel.* 6. Both προθυμία and πρόθυμος (63) are Euripidean favourites (Liapis on 63–4, 667).

668–74. After Paris' departure Athena addresses the returning Greeks. In *Il.* 10.509–11 it is Diomedes, the leader of the expedition, whom she warns to make a quick escape to the ships before 'another god' wakes up the Trojans. The choice of Odysseus here follows from his dominance in the play and, as regards the present scene, our poet's dependence on the *Ajax* prologue.

668–9. ὑμᾶς δ' αὐτῶ: Wecklein wished to delete δ', but the change of addressees should be marked, as in e.g. *Hipp.* 1431, *IT* 1446 and, more explicitly, E. *Suppl.* 1213, *Hel.* 1662.

αὐτέω rarely takes an infinitive. The only classical parallel is E. *El.* 723–6 νεόμενος δ' / εἰς ἀγόρους αὐτεῖ / τὰν κερόεσσαν ἔχειν / χρυσεόμαλλον κατὰ δῶμα ποίμναν.

τοὺς ἄγαν ἐρρωμένους could be a reminiscence of *Il.* 10.503–6, where Diomedes is not yet prepared to content himself with Rhesus' horses and the death of thirteen Thracians, including the king (cf. 670–

1). But ἄγαν suggests that, contrary to their earlier caution or even timidity, the Achaeans are now being carried away by blood lust (Fenik, *Iliad X*, 21–2 n. 4, who after Valckenaer, *Diatribe*, 111 compares Verg. *Aen.* 9.354 *sensit enim nimia caede atque cupidine ferri*). On the relationship between the Nisus-Euryalus episode (Verg. *Aen.* 9.176–458) and our play see Introduction, 45.

Adjectival ἐρρωμένος, like its verb, is essentially a prose word (in poetry only *PV* 65, 76 and a few times in comedy). For the meaning 'eager, enthusiastic' cf. e.g. Thuc. 2.8.1 ἀλλ' ἔρρωντο ἐς τὸν πόλεμον οὐκ ἀπεικότως, 2.8.4, Lys. 13.31, Cratin. fr. 452 *PCG* = Phryn. *PS* p. 10.14–17 de Borries and, for the opposite, Thuc. 3.15.2 οἱ δὲ ἄλλοι ξύμμαχοι ... ἐν καρποῦ ξυγκομιδῇ ἦσαν καὶ ἀρρωστίᾳ τοῦ στρατεύειν

Λαερτίου παῖ: Note Athena at *Ai.* 1 ὦ παῖ Λαρτίου, although this formula is not rare (as an address *Phil.* 87, *Hec.* 402, *Ai.* 380 τέκνον Λαρτίου, otherwise *Ai.* 101, *Phil.* 1286, 1357). For the singular vocative directed at a representative of two or more persons see Diggle, *Euripidea*, 506.

θηκτὰ κοιμίσαι ξίφη: No exact parallel exists, but κοιμάω and (κατα)κοιμίζω are used in various metaphorical ways: e.g. *Od.* 12.169 κοίμησε δὲ κύματα δαίμων (cf. *Eum.* 832, *Ai.* 674–5), *Ag.* 1247 εὔφημον ... κοίμησον στόμα, Nicopho fr. 15 *PCG*, Phryn. Com. fr. 25 *PCG* ἔπειτ' ἐπειδὰν τὸν λύχνον κατακοιμίσῃ, *Phoen.* 183–4 σύ ... / μεγαλαγορίαν ὑπεράνορα κοιμίζεις (LSJ s.vv. κοιμάω I 2, κοιμίζω 1, κατακοιμίζω I).

670–1a. κεῖται ... ἡμῖν: '... lies dead at our hands' (LSJ s.v. κεῖμαι I 4 a). With ἡμῖν (dative of agent) Athena associates herself with the Achaeans, as she had already done in 627 (καθ' ἡμᾶς) and as the Muse will complain in 938–40 (n.), 944–5 and 978. Valckenaer's ὑμῖν here (*Diatribe*, 111 n. 8) would obliterate this nuance and spoil the subtle contrast with 671–2 πολέμιοι ... / χωροῦσ' ἐφ' ὑμᾶς: Odysseus and Diomedes are in danger of being caught, not so the goddess (Fenik, *Iliad X*, 25 with n. 1).

ἵπποι τ' ἔχονται: The horses are not mentioned again until 797–8. It is highly improbable that they were shown on stage, as Battezzato (*CQ* n.s. 50 [2000], 371 with n. 30), Feickert (on 668–74, 671, 672, 674) and others maintain. Their splendid sight, 'conspicuous in the night' (617), would have elicited a comment from the chorus and proved a serious obstacle to Odysseus' deception. The visual inconsequence may well have passed unnoticed in the vigorous action of the following scene.

672b–3a. ἀλλ' ὅσον τάχιστα χρή / φεύγειν πρὸς ὁλκοὺς ναυστάθμων adapts Athena's order at *Il.* 10.509–10 νόστου δὴ μνῆσαι, μεγαθύμου Τυδέος υἱέ, / νῆας ἔπι γλαφυράς, μὴ καὶ πεφοβημένος ἔλθῃς (cf. 668–74n.).

ἀλλ': 70–1n.

πρὸς ὁλκοὺς ναυστάθμων: an elaborate periphrasis for the naval camp: Σ^V *Rh.* 673 (II 341.26 Schwartz = 108 Merro) πρὸς τὰ ναύσταθμα. For the ὁλκοί ('slipways') see 145b–6n. and for ναύσταθμα 135b–6n.

673b–4. τί μέλλετε / ... σῶσαι βίον; In the sense 'hesitate, delay' μέλλω normally governs a present infinitive (LSJ s.v. III). At *Phoen.* 299–300 τί μέλλεις ὑπώροφα μέλαθρα περᾶν / θιγεῖν τ' ὠλέναισι τέκνου; and Thuc. 1.124.1 μὴ μέλλετε Ποτειδεάταις τε ποιεῖσθαι τιμωρίαν ... καὶ τῶν ἄλλων μετελθεῖν τὴν ἐλευθερίαν. the aorist stands only second in a pair, but there seems to be no objection in principle to it. Maybe ὀκνέω, which easily takes both constructions, exerted some influence.

σκηπτοῦ 'πιόντος πολεμίων: The metaphor of a 'thunderbolt' (cf. Σ^V *Rh.* 674 [II 341.27–8 Schwartz = 108 Merro]) or 'whirlwind' seems rather strong here. Elsewhere σκηπτός is so applied to disasters of universal impact (*Pers.* 715 λοιμοῦ ... σκηπτός, *Andr.* 1046 σκηπτὸς σταλάσσων Δαναΐδαις φόνον ['the storm-cloud of war'], Dem.18.194 ὁ συμβὰς σκηπτός [Philip's invasion of Greece]), or to single persons in comic exaggeration (Antiph. fr. 193.11 *PCG*, Men. *Sam.* 556).

Euripides had a penchant for ἐπιών, but he mostly used it attributively and in the sense 'succeeding, future' (cf. 330–1n.). Literally only *Ion* 323 ... οὑπιών τ' ἀεὶ ξένος, half so *Or.* 630 ... οὑπιὼν ἡμῖν λόγος (see Willink on 630–1) and with an abstract object probably *Tro.* 119 ἐπιοῦσ' αἰεὶ δακρύων ἐλέγους (ἐπιοῦσ' Musgrave: ἐπὶ τοὺς VPQΣ).

675–91. The chorus return (via the right *eisodos*) in a menacing search for potential intruders and soon intercept Odysseus and Diomedes, who are on their way back from the Thracian camp (675–82). After a brief skirmish Odysseus effects their escape by giving the Trojan watchword and sending the guards on a wrong track (683–91).

Not surprisingly perhaps, this lively dramatisation of *Il.* 10.523–4 Τρώων δὲ κλαγγή τε καὶ ἄσπετος ὦρτο κυδοιμός / θυνόντων ἄμυδις (Ritchie 72), which gives wily Odysseus a brief *aristeia* in a positive counterpart to Dolon's off-stage interception and death (572–3, 591–3nn.), has caused the greatest variety of critical opinion. While the presence of a silent Diomedes can hardly be denied in view of 681 + 678–9 τούσδ' ἔχω, τούσδ' ἔμαρψα / κλῶπας οἵτινες ...,[249] the order of lines, the speaker distribution and text, especially in the partly corrupt 685–6 (n.), must to some degree remain conjectural. The present reading assumes, on the basis of 687 (n.), a division into two semi-choruses, of

---

249 Liapis (on 681/678–9) does not succeed in explaining away the plurals. Battezzato (*Lexis* 22 [2004], 279) adds that Diomedes' failure to reappear would give the impression that he never left Rhesus' quarters.

which the more lenient is already inclined to believe Odysseus' first assurance in 685 (n.) and, by accepting his reply to their further question in 686 (n.), unintentionally assists his stratagem. Regarding the lyric astrophon, one may also follow Bothe (5 [1803], 264–5) in recognising different voices at least in 675a–b, 676 and 677–82 or even, with Murray, Liapis (on 675–91 [p. 254]) and others, give the verses to individual singers. Both ways of staging would heighten the realism of the performance (particularly if it was done σποράδην),[250] but the final proof from language is lacking.

With its hasty movement and disjointed language the chorus' return mirrors their opening anapaests and first strophe of the parodos proper. Other hunting- or search-scenes, cast in the form of an (initially) astrophic epiparodos, appear in *Eumenides* (254–75) and *Ajax* (866–78), but as a whole our passage is unlike anything else in extant Greek tragedy. In fact the combination of violent physical contact and trochaic dialogue between chorus and actors most closely resembles the battle-scenes of Old Comedy, above all Ar. *Ach.* 280–327 (+ 204–40),[251] with which there are even verbal parallels (675b, 680, 685nn.).[252] The song can further be compared to S. fr. 314.64–78, 100–123, 176–202 (*Ichneutae*) and *Cyc.* 656–62 – the latter again preceding Odysseus' escape (689–91, 689nn.). Cf. Rau, *Paratragodia*, 26–7.

---

250 A scattered entry would probably be unexampled in fifth-century tragedy (Hutchinson on *Sept.* 78–181 [pp. 56–7]). Yet if reports like *Vit. Aesch.* 9 (*TrGF* III, T A 1) τινὲς δέ φασιν ἐν τῇ ἐπιδείξει τῶν Εὐμενίδων σποράδην εἰσαγαγόντα τὸν χορὸν τοσοῦτον ἐκπλῆξαι τὸν δῆμον ὡς τὰ μὲν νήπια ἐκψῦξαι, τὰ δὲ ἔμβρυα ἐξαμβλωθῆναι refer to later revivals (cf. Introduction, 42 with n. 81), this may not have been unusual in the fourth century.
251 Despite repeated allusions to searching in the fragments of E. *Telephus* (E. fr. 727a fr. 1.8, 11, fr. 14.1), it is unlikely that, as Ritchie (129–30) wants to believe, this was acted out in a scene which may have inspired *Acharnians* or *Thesm.* 597–614 + 655–87 (E. W. Handley – J. Rea, *The* Telephus *of Euripides*, London 1957, 35–6, C. Preiser, *Euripides: Telephos. Einleitung, Text und Kommentar*, Hildesheim 2000, 433).
252 Cf. Wilamowitz, *GV* 265 and Th. Drew-Bear, *AJPh* 89 (1968), 397. The only other scene where a tragic chorus comes to grips with the actors on stage seems to be *OC* 813–86 (835, 856–7). In A. *Suppl.* 825–910 the Egyptians probably do not lay hands on the Danaids before 808, and the coryphaei of *Agamemnon* (1650–3) and *Heracles* (252–74) merely threaten. At *Hel.* 1627–41 the identity of Theoclymenus' opponent is disputed (M. Kaimio, *Physical Contact in Greek Tragedy. A Study of Stage Conventions*, Helsinki 1988, 65–78). In favour of the chorus-leader (L) see 149–94n. (p. 174).

Metre

675–82. Dochmio-iambic, interspersed with 'cretics' and trochaics. This suits the chorus' agitation (cf. e.g. *Eum.* 254–75, *Ai.* 866–78, 879–90 [~ 925–36]) and runs smoothly into the trochaic tetrameters catalectic of 683–91 (680–1n.).

675	ἔα ἔα· ‖	*extra metrum* ‖
675b	∪ ∪∪ ∪∪ ∪ ∪∪ | ∪∪ ∪ – ‖	δ | ⌣*cr* ‖
676	∪ – – |	*ia*ˆ |
677	– ∪ – ∪ – – |	*ith* |
680	– ∪ – ∪ – |	*hδ* |
681	– ∪ – | – ∪ – ∪ |	*cr* | *tr* |
678–9	– ∪ – ∪ – ∪ – – | – ∪ – – – – ∪ – ‖	4*tr*ˆ ‖
682	∪∪ ∪ – | ∪∪ ∪ – | ∪∪ ∪ – ‖	3 ⌣*cr* ‖

Notes

675 The exclamation could also be iambic (*OC* 1478, *Hcld.* 73, *HF* 815) or cretic (*PV* 687, opening a dochmiac *Cho.* 870),[253] but apart from *Hcld.* 73 and *HF* 815, double ἔα in Euripides always stands extra metrum, and the same applies to *Rhesus* (cf. 729, 885). See Page on *Med.* 1004.

675b The analysis is due to L. P. E. Parker, *CQ* n.s. 18 (1968), 266–7 with 267 n. 3. It is preferable to that of Diggle, implied in his reconstruction of the line as βάλε βάλε βάλε· θένε θένε <θένε> (675b n.), and Liapis (on 675–91 'Metre' [p. 255]) as a trochaic dimeter, which would entail two divided resolutions, as well as the very rare phenomenon of a full trochee with short anceps at verse-end merging into iambic rhythm (L. P. E. Parker, in *Owls to Athens*, 332–7). Pace (*Canti*, 47–8) combines ... θένε θένε. τίς ἀνήρ; to a doubtful form of dochmiac (cf. N. C. Conomis, *Hermes* 92 [1964], 27–8)[254] with an equally dubious split resolution before the second long anceps.

676–7 τίς ἀνήρ (for the text see 676n.) forms a self-contained bacchiac question, as in e.g. *Ai.* 873 τί οὖν δή; 875 ἔχεις οὖν; 897 τί δ' ἔστιν; *OC* 512 ~ 524 (each set off by change of speaker), and should therefore be detached from 677.

680–1 On the metrical implications of Diggle's transposition see 680–1n. The sequence *cr* (*tr*ˆ) *tr* is paralleled in *Eum.* 324 ~ 337, *Cyc.*

---

[253] *PV* 114 is ambiguous (West, ed. *Aeschylus*, 505, Griffith on *PV* 114–19).
[254] *Sept.* 109 is defended by Hutchinson. On *Hel.* 694–5 see Diggle, *Euripidea*, 184–6.

608, *Ba.* 578, 584 and *IA* 258 ~ 270 (cf. Diggle, *Euripidea*, 424 n. 19, Liapis on 675–91 'Metre' [pp. 255–6]).²⁵⁵

675b. βάλε βάλε βάλε· θένε θένε <θένε>: Cf. *Eum.* 130 λαβέ. λαβέ. λαβέ. λαβέ. φράζου (the Erinyes dreaming of being hounds on the trail), Ar. *Ach.* 280–3 οὗτος αὐτός ἐστιν, οὗτος· / βάλλε, βάλλε, βάλλε, βάλλε, / παῖε, παῖε τὸν μιαρόν. / οὐ βαλεῖς; οὐ βαλεῖς; and, perhaps under Aristophanic influence, Xen. *An.* 5.7.21 (~ 5.7.28) συγκαθήμενοι δ' ἔξωθεν τῶν ὅπλων ἐξαίφνης ἀκούομεν θορύβου πολλοῦ Παῖε παῖε, βάλλε βάλλε, καὶ τάχα δὴ ὁρῶμεν πολλοὺς προσθέοντας λίθους ἔχοντας ἐν ταῖς χερσί, τοὺς δὲ ἀναιρουμένους. Such lines of imperatives generally indicate urgency (Arnott on Alexis fr. 207.1) and here even amount to a war-cry (Dover on Ar. *Nub.* 1508; cf. West, *IEPM* 478). Like the Acharnians, who are hurling stones, the sentries are prepared to hit (βάλε) and strike (θένε) anyone with their spears.

A similar confusion in the MSS as to the number and 'tense' of the imperatives occurs at Ar. *Ach.* 281. Diggle's triple θένε balances triple βάλε (Tr¹), but is not inevitable, if we reject his analysis of the verse as trochaic (675–91 'Metre' 675b n.).

676. τίς ἀνήρ; The article (Murray) relates the question to the implied object of the preceding verbs and removes an unparalleled dochmiac with strong rhetorical pause in the second resolved long: ... θένε θένε. τίς ἀνήρ; (cf. L. P. E. Parker, *CQ* n.s. 18 [1968], 267 with n. 3). Musgrave's τίς <ὅδ'> ἀνήρ; (on 678) would give another cretic, but the deictic seems too specific in view of the ensuing τοῦτον αὐδῶ.

677. λεῦσσε (Diggle) or λεῦσσε λεῦσσε (Hartung, 17 [1852], 81 n. 9) is expected after the preceding singulars, as in *OC* 118–22 ὅρα· ... [λεύσσατ' αὐτὸν,] (del. Dawe) προσδέρκου, προσφθέγγου, / προσπεύθου πανταχᾷ, Ar. *Thesm.* 663–6 εἶα νῦν ἴχνευε καὶ μά- / τευε τάχυ πάντ', ... / πανταχῇ δὲ ῥῖψον ὄμμα, / καὶ ... / πάντ' ἀνασκόπει καλῶς, probably *Eum.* 254/5 ὅρα ὅρα μάλ' αὖ· λεῦσσε τό<πο>ν πάντα (rest. West [*Studies*, 276–7]) and numerous other strings of choral self-exhortation (Kaimio, *Chorus*, 121–37; cf. 1n.). Cases like *Od.* 3.332 ἀλλ' ἄγε τάμνετε μὲν γλώσσας, Ar. *Ach.* 366 ἰδοὺ θεᾶσθε or *Ran.* 1378 ἴθι δή, παρίστασθον, where the first imperative is fossilised (KG I 84–5, SD 245, 583–4, 609–10), do not support the transmitted λεύσ(σ)ετε.

---

255 F. Lourenço (*JHS* 120 [2000], 136 n. 24) may be right to reject *Phoen.* 655b ~ 674b (cf. Mastronarde on 656 'Metre' [p. 334], 655bis, 674bis–75), but his analysis of *Ba.* 578 and 584 as (iambic) lecythia is unlikely. *Hel.* 352 and *IA* 1288 are metrically and/or textually uncertain, and *Hel.* 358 depends on Diggle's conjecture.

τοῦτον αὐδῶ: 'This man I mean'. Cf. *Hipp*. 352 Ἱππόλυτον αὐδᾷς; *Alc*. 106 †τί τόδ' αὐδᾷς;†, *Ion* 552 ἐθιάσευσ', ἢ πῶς τάδ' αὐδᾷς; and *Phil*. 852 οἶσθα γὰρ ὃν αὐδῶμαι.

680–1. By transposing these lines after 677, Diggle much improved the sequence of 675–82, without damaging our impression of headless confusion. For not only does 680 (n.) δεῦρο δεῦρο πᾶς now adjoin the opening imperatives, but we also have 678–9 (n.) κλῶπας οἵτινες κατ' ὄρφνην τόνδε κινοῦσι στρατόν follow more naturally on the plural pronouns in 681 τούσδ' ἔχω, τούσδ' ἔμαρψα (In dramaturgical terms the sentries are drawing nearer before they realise that a second intruder is lurking in the dark). Moreover, while there can be no metrical objection to the transmitted 681–2 ... τούσδ' ἔμαρψα. / τίς ὁ λόχος ... (– ⏑ – ⏑ | ⏑⏑ ⏑ – with strong rhetorical pause after the full trochee, for which cf. *Ba*. 589–90, *OC* 1708–9 and L. P. E. Parker, in *Owls to Athens*, 332–7), the trochaic tetrameter catalectic of 678–9 better continues 681b and, via 682, leads up to the stichic use of the verse.

680. δεῦρο δεῦρο πᾶς: Cf. Ar. *Ach*. 239–40 ἀλλὰ δεῦρο πᾶς / ἐκποδών, with the same quasi-verbal use of δεῦρο (Wackernagel, *Vorlesungen über Syntax* I, 71 = *Lectures on Syntax*, 99, Olson on Ar. *Ach*. 239–40), and Ar. *Pax* 301 δεῦρο πᾶς χώρει προθύμως εὐθὺ τῆς σωτηρίας, *Av*. 1186 χώρει δεῦρο πᾶς ὑπηρέτης. The connection of πᾶς (τις) with a second person singular imperative is colloquial (KG I 85–6, Collard, 'Supplement', 370) and here probably reproduces genuine soldiers' diction. Cf. 685 †πέλας ἴθι παῖε πᾶς†, 687 (n.), 688, 690, 730.

678–9. κλῶπας: 644–5n. Diggle's accusative further smoothes the syntax, but even with his verse order (680–1n.) one may look for another one-line exclamation and so keep κλῶπες with a full stop after ἔμαρψα: 'Thieves – whoever they are who are disturbing our army in the darkness!'

κατ' ὄρφνην: 41–2n.

τόνδε κινοῦσι στρατόν: 17–18n.

682. τίς ὁ λόχος; πόθεν ἔβας; ποδαπὸς εἶ; a military version of the Homeric τίς πόθεν εἰς ἀνδρῶν; πόθι τοι πόλις ἠδὲ τοκῆες; (e.g. *Od*. 1.170, 10.325, 14.187). Closer to the standard pattern are *Rh*. 702 τίς ἦν; πόθεν; ποίας πάτρας; A. fr. 61 = Ar. *Thesm*. 136 (Lycurgus to the captive Bacchus) ποδαπὸς ὁ γύννις; τίς πάτρα; τίς ἡ στολή; *Ion* 258–9 (quoted in 702n.) and Ar. fr. 307 *PCG* (*Pax II*) πόθεν τὸ φῖτυ; τί τὸ γένος; τίς ἡ σπορά; The brisk tone of the sentries is reinforced by the diaereses after each cretic, a rhythm tragedy tends to avoid (Dale, *LM*² 101).

It is possible that we have here the ultimate source of Verg. *Aen*. 9.376–7 *state viri. quae causa viae? quive estis in armis? / quove tenetis iter?* (cf. Introduction, 45).

λόχος: 26n. λόγος (Λ) shows hardly more than confusion of χ and γ (C. W. Willink, *CQ* n.s. 39 [1989] 52 n. 32 = *Collected Papers*, 143 n. 32, Diggle, *Euripidea*, 371–2). Likewise A. *Suppl.* 676/7 γυναι- / κῶν λόχους (Sophianus: λόγους M) and, conversely, *Rh.* 149 (149–50n.).

683–91. Although the whole scene seems more indebted to comedy and satyr-play (675–91n.), there is nothing untragic in having trochaic tetrameters catalectic indicate excitement and rapid motion. Euripides in his later plays particularly employed the 'running verse' (Arist. *Rhet.* 1409a1, Σ[vet.] Ar. *Ach.* 204a [I 1b.35–6 Wilson], Heph. 78.4–6 Consbruch) for hurried actors' entries: *Ion* 1250–60 (an agitated dialogue between Creusa and the chorus), *Or.* 729, 1506, 1549–53, *IA* 1338 (cf. *OC* 887–90). Frequent speaker changes, which the long verse accommodates more easily than the iambic trimeter, increase the vigour and harshness of the conversation. For further detail on the history and character of the tragic tetrameter see W. Krieg, *Philologus* 91 (1936), 42–51, M. Imhof, *MH* 13 (1956), 125–43, Th. Drew-Bear, *AJPh* 89 (1968), 385–405 and Willink on *Or.* 729–806.

683. '*Od.* You do not need to know that. *Cho.*[¹] Yes, I do. For otherwise you will die today as a malefactor.'

The MSS leave the whole verse to Odysseus, in which case θανῇ γὰρ σήμερον δράσας κακῶς is at best an empty taunt. Matthiae (VIII [1824], 52) thus assigned the latter half to a semi-chorus, with γάρ implying the new speaker's dissent (*GP* 74–5). Cf. Ar. *Nub.* 1440 σκέψαι δὲ χἀτέραν ἔτι γνώμην. – ἀπὸ γὰρ ὀλοῦμαι ('Now consider yet another point. – No, for that will be the end of me.').

χρὴ εἰδέναι: The synizesis has no exact parallel, unless Kaibel's εἴμειν or εἶμεν is correct at Epich. fr. 178 *PCG* ἀλλὰ χρὴ †ἡμῖν† ἕν τε λῆμα πᾶσι καὶ λῆσιν μίαν. Junctures like μὴ εἰδέναι (e.g. *Ant.* 33, *Tr.* 321, *Hipp.* 1335, *Ion* 313) or ἢ εἰδότος (*IT* 1048), which involve prepositives, are not really equivalent, and other such irregular synizeses also appear to be much rarer in tragedy (only E. *Suppl.* 638–9 λόγου δέ σε / μακροῦ ἀπολύσω [Herwerden: ἀποπαύσω L[uv]: 'πο- Tr¹]) than in Homer, Aeolic lyric and comedy (KB I 228–9, Schwyzer 400–1, West, *GM* 13–14). Yet the fact that χρή is a monosyllable (cf. Barrett, *Collected Papers*, 349–50 n. 85) may alleviate the peculiarity so that Heath's εἰδέναι σ' οὐ χρή (*Notae sive lectiones*, 97) need not perhaps be entertained.

684. Diggle's tentative transposition of the question before 683 should be resisted, for (a) οὔ σε χρὴ εἰδέναι is a much more suitable reply to 682 and (b) the challenge can only follow Odysseus' refusal to identify himself.

ξύνθημα: 521–2n.

685–6. These verses are the touchstone for the interpretation of the entire scene. The first one fits well in the context, but is metrically corrupt

(685n.), while the second makes no sense as transmitted (686n.). Among the many explanations and conjectures that have been proposed, Diggle suggested deleting the lines on the ground that they would not be missed ('*si abessent, non desiderarentur*'). Yet it is hard to see why 686 with its puzzling mention of Rhesus should have been interpolated (cf. L. Battezzato, *Lexis* 22 [2004], 284 n. 23), and the action would hardly become livelier or more 'physical' with the addition of 685.[256] It seems preferable, therefore, to accept both as part of the original text. The solution adopted here requires only minimal change in 686. Nothing new is ventured on 685.

685. '*Od.* †Stop! Have no fear. *Cho.¹* Come near, strike, everyone!†'

While sense, grammar and speaker distribution are unexceptionable, this line cannot be left to stand as any form of syncopated trochaics (Ritchie 73, 294, Zanetto, ed. *Rhesus*, 69), let alone dochmiacs (Feickert on 685). Attempts to restore a regular tetrameter go back as far as Triclinius' inept πέλας τις ἴθι (Tr¹) and παῖε παῖε πᾶς τίς ἄν (Tr³), but with little beyond *exempli gratia* solutions for the second verse-half (cf. Wecklein, *Appendix*, 53, to which add Kovacs' (Οδ.) ἴστ<ασ'> ὦ θάρσει πελάζων. (Χο.) παῖε <παῖε> [~ O, Tr³] πᾶς <ἀνήρ>), agnostic *obeli* are in place.

†ἴστω θάρσει: Portus (*Breves notae*, 70): ἴστω Ω. The contracted imperative of middle ἴσταμαι (A. fr. 273a.2, *Ai.* 775, *Phil.* 893, Ar. *Eccl.* 737, Cratin. fr. 250.1 *PCG*) is at least as old as Σ^L *Rh.* 685 (109 a² Merro) ἴστω. ἴστασο and must also be what lies behind the glosses ἀνίστασο in V and Q (II 342.11 Schwartz = 109 a¹ Merro). Yet with θάρσει (cf. 16, 646) it would be difficult to fit into the metre, even if there were some significance in the fact that both forms appear close to each other at *Phil.* 893–4 (Νε.) ἔσται τάδ'· ἀλλ' ἴστω τε καὐτὸς ἀντέχου. / (Φι.) θάρσει· τό τοι σύνηθες ὀρθώσει μ' ἔθος.

πέλας ἴθι παῖε πᾶς†: 680, 687nn. Whatever the exact words, we see here yet another echo of comic 'battle cries' in general (e.g. Ar. *Eq.* 247 παῖε παῖε τὸν πανοῦργον, 251–2, *Nub.* 1508, *Vesp.* 456 + 458) and Ar. *Ach.* 282 παῖε, παῖε τὸν μιαρόν (codd.: παῖε πᾶς Bergk) in particular. Cf. 675–91, 675b, 680, 730nn.

686. '*Cho.²* Did you kill †Rhesus†? *Od.* No, but the one who meant to kill you.'

The present speaker attribution (= O) suggests itself if one essentially accepts and reads the text as it stands (685–6n.) and takes seriously the division into semi-choruses indicated by 687 (n.). Short of the latter, most

---

[256] Liapis, who supports the excision, takes 685 as a botched imitation of Ar. *Ach.* 282, which could as well have been in our poet's mind (675–91, 685nn.). He fails to account for 686 (cf. 'Notes', 86–8).

modern editors have followed Murray in dividing the line between Odysseus (ἦ σὺ δὴ Ῥῆσον κατέκτας;) and the chorus (ἀλλὰ τὸν κτενοῦντα σέ ... [sc. κτενῶ]).[257] This, however, implies an unnatural aposiopesis and raises the question – not answered by temporary absent-mindedness (Porter, xiv and on 686) or Jouan's '*Initiative hardie (ou désespérée)* ...' (41 n. 208) – why Odysseus should mention the deed at all.[258] Still more dubiously, Ritchie (73–4) and Zanetto (ed. *Rhesus*; cf. *Ciclope*, *Reso*, 155 n. 87) write (Ἡμ.ᵝ) ἦ σὺ δὴ Ῥῆσον κατέκτας; (Ἡμ.ᵅ) ἀλλὰ τὸν κτενοῦντά σε, assuming that, against our poet's habit of spelling out costume divergences from the epic (208–11a, 591–3nn.), Odysseus had probably taken and donned Rhesus' armour to be mistaken for him by the less aggressive part of the chorus.[259]

ἦ σὺ δὴ †Ῥῆσον† κατέκτας; Although 'golden' Rhesus, who has arrived with such pomp and circumstance (284–316, 340, 382–4), may be thought the obvious victim for nocturnal marauders, the proper name here seems unduly specific and, for the full dramatic effect of the Charioteer's 'message', not even desired as a witty anticipation. Unless, therefore, the question constitutes a rather more consequential poetic inconsistency than usual (185, 355–6nn.),[260] it is likely to harbour corruption, and the easiest solution would be that, perhaps aided by the accusative singular in the answer, an explanatory gloss Ῥῆσον (cf. Diggle, *Euripidea*, 459 n. 79) has displaced a broader term. West's φίλους gains support from 687 ... ἆ· φίλιον ἄνδρα μὴ θένῃς, 838 ... μὴ φίλους κατακτανεῖν and 860 ... ὥστ' ἀποκτείνειν φίλους.

<μὴ> ἀλλά: 'No (don't say that), but (rather) ...' Dindorf's supplement (*PSG*⁵, 9) restores the colloquial expression, which apart from *Cho.* 918, Pl. *Men.* 75b1 and Pl. (?) *Alc. I* 114e1, is elsewhere confined to

---

[257] The actual distribution was anticipated by Musgrave (on 688), who prints a conjecture in the first half of the verse, and Nauck (II³ [1871], 332). Cf. L. Battezzato, *Lexis* 22 (2004), 280–1 with n. 12.

[258] The fact that the sentries do not react appropriately and later know nothing of Rhesus' death (Porter, xiv; cf. Mastronarde, *Contact and Discontinuity*, 81) could theoretically be attributed to their over-excitement and go unnoticed in the course of the play.

[259] Feickert, with elaborate stage-directions (89; cf. on 675–91, 675–82, 683–91, 683, 685, 686, 689), leaves this role to Diomedes, an idea Battezzato (*Lexis* 22 [2004], 279–80, 281–2) would endorse, *if* the armour were shown on stage. Battezzato's main contention that Diomedes speaks 683(a) and 685a, only to be superseded by Odysseus in 686b–91, founders on the difficulty of having one character answer a question addressed to another. *Phil.* 974 and 1293 are different in that Odysseus interrupts from outside, and so is *PV* 589, since Zeus, provided that he and not Prometheus is the recipient of the preceding line (Mastronarde, *Contact and Discontinuity*, 115–16; cf. Griffith on 588), would not be expected to reply to Io.

[260] Note also *Alc.* 249 ≠ 177–8, 911–25 (with Dale and Parker on 248–9), *Or.* 1075–7 ≠ 765 (Willink on 1075), E. *El.* 164 ≠ 160, 279, 1160 and perhaps *Hipp.* 1183 ≠ 1212, 1229 (Barrett on 1183).

Aristophanes: *Ach.* 458, *Ran.* 103, 611, 745, 751 and, also simply contradictory, *Av.* 109–10 μῶν ἡλιαστά; – μάλλα θατέρου τρόπου, / ἀπηλιαστά, *Thesm.* 646 οὐκ ἐγγεταυθί. – <μ>ἀλλὰ δεῦρ' ἥκει πάλιν (*GP* 4–5, Collard, 'Supplement', 367).

687–8. The only other trochaic tetrameters catalectic with more than one *antilabe* in tragedy come from the late fifth-century *Philoctetes* (1407)[261] and *Orestes* (1525).

687. ἴσχε πᾶς τις: The number of choral πᾶς (τις) imperatives in this and the following scene (680n.), as well as other such (pseudo-)military orders in e.g. *Ag.* 1651 (Aegisthus to his attendants) εἶα δή, ξίφος πρόκωπον πᾶς τις εὐτρεπιζέτω, Ar. *Av.* 1190/1–2 (Χο.) ... ἀλλὰ φύλαττε πᾶς / ἀέρα περινέφελον and 1196 ἄθρει δὲ πᾶς κύκλῳ σκοπῶν, support the ascription to a semi-chorus (Χο. Ο) rather than Odysseus, who has not yet established his 'authority' over the men. The refusal οὐ μὲν οὖν (below) then indicates, more poignantly, a brief disagreement between the sentries as to their captive's trustworthiness (675–91n.).

οὐ μὲν οὖν: Reiske (*Animadversiones*, 90) for the transmitted οὐ μενῶ. In this juncture οὖν emphasises adversative μέν (*GP* 475).

ἄ: here an expression of protest ('Stop!'), followed by a prohibition, as in *OT* 1147 ἄ, μὴ κόλαζε, πρέσβυ, τόνδ', *Phil.* 1300, *Alc.* 526, *Hipp.* 503 (with Barrett on 503–4), *Hel.* 445 (with Kannicht) and Ar. *Pl.* 127, 1052. It is often doubled, which may have given rise to the MSS error, corrected by Musgrave (on 689). For further details see 747–9n.

φίλιον ἄνδρα: On φίλιος, 'friendly', as opposed to '(of an) enemy', see 11n. Σ[V] *Rh.* 683 (II 342.10–11 Schwartz = 108 Merro) notes Ὀδυσσεὺς ὑποκρίνεται εἶναι Τρωικός.

688. καὶ ... δή in questions usually expresses surprise (*GP* 211). Here it is rather indignation or impatience: 'Well, and what *is* the watchword?'

σῆμα: 12, 521–2nn.

Φοῖβος: 521–2n.

ἴσχε πᾶς δόρυ: 680, 687nn.

689–91. Odysseus' last trick formally reverses the more typical misdirection of a character by the chorus-leader: *Cyc.* 675–88 (below), *IT* 1293–1301, Ar. *Thesm.* 1217–26.

689. The situation and wording most closely resemble *Cyc.* 684–5 (Χο.) καί σε διαφεύγουσί γε. / (Κυ.) οὐ τῇδέ πῃ, τῇδ' εἶπας; (Χο.) οὔ· ταύτῃ λέγω (cf. Seaford on 685). It makes little difference which semichorus speaks οἶσθ' ὅπῃ βεβᾶσιν ἄνδρες;

---

[261] Dawe is probably right to delete 1402–3 and retain 1407–8 with a lacuna and some further corruption (*STS* III, 136–7; cf. West, *GM* 91). But Dindorf's *Binneninterpolation*, accepted by most modern editors, does not affect the speaker distribution either.

ὅπῃ, 'which way' (S. fr. 314.166–7 [*Ichneutae*] εἰ μὴ ... ἐξιχνεύσε[τε] / τὰς βοῦς ὅπῃ βεβᾶσι ..., Ar. *Ach*. 198, *Ai*. 867–8 πᾷ πᾷ / πᾷ γὰρ οὐκ ἔβαν ἐγώ;), is favoured by the MSS and seems both more relevant and a better preparation for τῇδέ πῃ than ὅποι (Aldina, ὅπο P vel P^c), 'to what destination'. The two words tend to be confused.

690–1. Leaving this couplet to a single speaker (with Λ) avoids having an opposition pending at the end of the scene. ἀλλά in 691 then becomes 'self-correcting' (*GP* 7–8).

690. ἔρπε πᾶς: 680, 687nn.

ἢ βοὴν ἐγερτέον; Cf. *Or*. 1353–5 ἰὼ ἰὼ φίλαι, / κτύπον ἐγείρετε, κτύπον καὶ βοὰν / πρὸ μελάθρων, ὅπως ὁ πραχθεὶς φόνος / μὴ δεινὸν Ἀργείοισιν ἐμβάλῃ φόβον, where the final clause shares two further words with *Rh*. 691 (below). The βοή is a 'formal cry for help ... which a person in distress must utter if he is to merit assistance' (Diggle, *Euripidea*, 480 with n. 178).

691. At *Il*. 10.420–1 the allies are also said to be asleep. Here the coryphaeus probably fears that waking them might cause a nocturnal panic (15, 17–18, 36–7a nn.), which is difficult to suppress and hence dangerous (δεινόν).

ἀλλὰ ... ταράσσειν δεινὸν ἐκ νυκτῶν φόβῳ: In addition to the possible echo of *Or*. 1354–5 (690n.), the formulation may have been influenced by *Cho*. 288–9 καὶ λύσσα καὶ μάταιος ἐκ νυκτῶν φόβος / κινεῖ, ταράσσει. For ἐκ νυκτῶν, 'at night', see 13–14n.

692–727. After the Greeks' narrow escape the chorus eagerly follow the 'new' track (689–90) in pursuit of their elusive quarry. Baffled at first as to the identity of the bold intruder (692–703), they soon settle on Odysseus as a likely candidate (704–9) and, in the antistrophe, underpin this claim with their recollection of his spying expedition to Troy (710–21). Yet certainty is neither attainable nor practically relevant for these sentries so that in 722–7 they merely conclude with an anticipation of Hector's wrath (808–19n.).

With its recitative-style choral epirrhemata this epiparodos proper structurally resembles *Rh*. 527–64 and *Alc*. 86–111 (the centre part of the parodos), where only the anapaestic tail-pieces do not correspond in length and changes of speaker (cf. 527–64n.). Among the tragic 'search-scenes' (675–91n.), one may also compare the ode and semi-lyric lamentation-*amoibaia* between the chorus and Tecmessa in *Ai*. 879–90 + 891–914 ~ 925–36 + 936–60 (Ritchie 295). This likewise starts with excited τίς-questions in the strophe (*Ai*. 879–87 ~ *Rh*. 692–6) and gains support as a possible source from the echoes of the *Ajax* prologue in 595–674 (n.).

Metre

692–703 ~ 710–21. Iambo-dochmiac. As in e.g. *Sept.* 98–107 (100, 103, 106), *Alc.* 213–25 ~ 226–37 (221 ~ 233) and *HF* 875–921 (880, 894, 905), there seems to be no emotional difference between the regular lyrics and the iambic trimeters (with Attic vocalisation) in 697 ~ 715 and 701 ~ 719 (cf. Bond on *HF* 875–921, Willink, 'Cantica', 41 = *Collected Papers*, 579). Still their mode of delivery is debated, and some have seen them closer to spoken verse (especially Dale, *LM*² 207–8; more reserved Fraenkel, *Agamemnon* III, p. 539, Denniston–Page on *Ag.* 1072–1330 [p. 165], Barrett, *Collected Papers*, 388, 390, 392–3).

704–9 ~ 722–7. Iambic trimeters enclosing bacchiacs / syncopated iambics. In contrast to the irregular anapaests at 538–45 + 557–64 (nn.), the distribution of speakers here responds exactly, although their respective number (three at least in 704–9, two in 722–7) cannot be firmly established (cf. Liapis on 704–9, 704–5, 722–7, who improbably follows Paley and Wilamowitz in dividing 704–5 and 722–3 between two choreutae).

692	710	⏑ – – ⏑ – |	δ |
693	711	⏑ ⏑⏑ ⏑ ⏑⏑ ⏑ – ⏑ – |	2ia |
694	712	⏑ ⏑⏑ – ⏑ – |	δ |
695	713	⏑ – – | ⏑ – – |	ia∧ | ia∧ |
696	714	⏑ ⏑⏑ – ⏑ – ||	δ ||
697	715	⏒ – ⏑ – – | – ⏑ – – – – ⏑ – ||	3ia ||
698	716	⏑ ⏑⏑ – ⏑ – | ⏒ ⏑⏑ – ⏑ – |	δ | δ |
699	717	– ⏑ ⏑ – |	cho |
700	718	⏑ ⏑⏑ – ⏑ – | ⏑ ⏕ – ⏑ – ||	δ | δ ||
701	719	⏒ – ⏑ – ⏒ | ⏕ ⏑ – ⏒ – ⏑ – ||	3ia ||
702	720	⏑ – ⏑ – ⏒ – ⏑ – |	2ia |
703	721	⏒ ⏑⏑ – ⏑ – | ⏑ ⏑⏑ – ⏑ – ||	δ | δ ||
704	722	:: – – ⏑ – – | – ⏑ – ⏑ – ⏑ – ||	3ia ||
705	723	– – ⏑ – ⏓ | – ⏑ – ⏒ – ⏑ – ||	3ia ||
706	724	:: ⏑ – – | :: ⏑ – – |	ia∧ | ia∧ |
707	725	:: ⏑ – – | ⏑ – – |	ia∧ | ia∧ |
708	726	:: ⏑ – – | ⏑ – – | :: ⏑ – – |	ia∧ | ia∧ | ia∧ |
709	727	:: – – ⏑ – ⏒ | – ⏑ | – ⏑ – ⏑ – |||	3ia |||

Notes

699–700/717–18 The single choriamb preceding two dochmiacs is noteworthy. A partial parallel exists in *Hipp.* 1275 (δ | *cho*). See Barrett on *Hipp.* 1268–82 (pp. 392–3).

706–8/724–6 For such bacchiacs, sharply divided by rhetorical pause or even change of speaker, cf. *Sept.* 104 τί ῥέξεις; προδώσεις, παλαίχθων, *Eum.* 788–90, *Or.* 173 (Χο.) ὑπνώσσει. (Ηλ.) λέγεις εὖ ~ 194 (Χο.) δίκαι μέν. (Ηλ.) καλῶς δ' οὔ, *Ba.* 1177, 1181–2 ~ 1193, 1197–8 (West, *Studies*, 46 n. 49 ~ *BICS* 30 (1983), 70, Parker, *Songs*, 449).

692. τίς ἀνδρῶν ὁ βάς; The 'periphrasis' with a substantival predicative participle (KG I 592 n. 4, 594, G. Björck, ΗΝ ΔΙΔΑΣΚΩΝ. *Die periphrastischen Konstruktionen im Griechischen*, Uppsala 1940, 90–1, W. J. Aerts, *Periphrastica* ..., Amsterdam 1965, 21–2, 41–2) is almost as widespread in drama as it is elsewhere. Cf. *Pers.* 95–6, *Ag.* 1506, *Ant.* 248 τίς ἀνδρῶν ἦν ὁ τολμήσας τάδε; *Alc.* 530 τίς φίλων ὁ κατθανών; *Hipp.* 449 (FJW on A. *Suppl.* 571–2 with further examples) and in comedy e.g. Ar. *Nub.* 133 τίς ἐσθ' ὁ κόψας τὴν θύραν;

693–4. 'Who is this mightily bold fellow, who will boast of having escaped my grasp?'

Sense and syntax are restored by Madvig's θρασύς (*Adversaria critica* I, 271) for θράσος (Ω). ἐπεύξεται then governs the participle instead of an impossible accusative object, and there is no need to interpret ὁ as the relative pronoun ὅ, which in the masculine singular is already rare in Homer and probably unparalleled in tragedy (KG I 587–8, Barrett on *Hipp.* 525–6).

For the form of the question cf. *Il.* 1.552 ποῖον τὸν μῦθον ἔειπες; *Phil.* 601 τίς ὁ πόθος αὐτοὺς ἵκετ'; and *OC* 205 τίς ὁ πολύπονος ἄγῃ; (KG I 626 n. 1, LSJ s.v. τις, τι Β I 2). As in the preceding line, the article indicates familiarity with the subject.

μέγα θρασύς: Adverbial μέγα for μάλα intensifying an adjective goes back to epic (on a possible origin see Leumann, *Homerische Wörter*, 119–20). It is almost completely absent from choral lyric (FJW on A. *Suppl.* 141 = 151), but regularly appears in tragedy (e.g. A. *Suppl.* 141, *PV* 647, *OT* 1343, *Alc.* 742) and some (mock-)elevated comic passages (Ar. *Nub.* 291, Cratin. fr. 360.1 *PCG*, fr. com. adesp. 1110.8 *PCG*).

ἐπεύξεται / ... φυγών: The only other instance of ἐπεύχομαι, 'boast', with a predicative participle (cf. KG II 72 n. 2, SD 394) is Pl. *Sph.* 235c5–7 πάντως οὔτε οὗτος οὔτε ἄλλο γένος οὐδὲν μή ποτε ἐκφυγὸν ἐπεύξηται τὴν τῶν οὕτω δυναμένων μετιέναι καθ' ἕκαστά τε καὶ ἐπὶ πάντα μέθοδον. In Homer the verb normally follows a personal military triumph (A. Corlu, *Recherches sur les mots relatifs à l'idée de prière: d'Homère aux tragiques*, Paris 1966, 133–4), whereas later all sorts of reasons may be supplied (*h.Ven.* 48, 286–7, *Ag.* 1262, 1394, 1474, *Eum.* 58, *IT* 508, *Rh.* 703). It is a nice touch of irony that the actual intruders have just escaped a second time – and with more to boast of than having entered the camp unseen.

χέρα ... ἐμάν: so Hn and Musgrave (on 696). χεῖρα (Ω) would produce an equally correct dochmiac in responsion with 712, but corruption into the prose form is more likely than the reverse. At 887 Valckenaer's χειροῖν for χεροῖν (*Diatribe*, 116) is metrically necessary.

695. πόθεν νιν κυρήσω; literally 'Starting from what point shall I find him?'. On this use of πόθεν, where we would expect ποῦ, see 611–12n.

696–8. τίνι προσεικάσω: 'To whom shall I compare him ...?', i.e. 'Who can he possibly be, who ...?'. προσεικάζω ('compare, liken, refer to') here gets a sense of equation, as in *Sept.* 430–1 τὰς δ' ἀστραπάς τε καὶ κεραυνίους βολάς / μεσημβρινοῖσι θάλπεσιν προσήκασεν, *Ag.* 1131 κακῷ δέ τῳ προσεικάζω τάδε and also *Hel.* 68–70 τίς τῶνδ' ἐρυμνῶν δωμάτων ἔχει κράτος; / Πλούτῳ γὰρ οἶκος ἄξιος προσεικάσαι / βασίλειά τ' ἀμφιβλήματ' εὔθριγκοί θ' ἕδραι. See P. M. Smith, *On the Hymn to Zeus in Aeschylus' Agamemnon*, Chico 1980, 8–12, 79–91, who claims that 'identification by comparison' underlies nearly all uses of the verb.

In a way analogous to *Cho.* 12–15 ποίᾳ ξυμφορᾷ προσεικάσω; ('To what misfortune shall I refer them?') / πότερα δόμοισι πῆμα προσκυρεῖ νέον, / ἢ πατρὶ τὠμῷ τάσδ' ἐπεικάσας τύχω / χοὰς φερούσαις νερτέροις μειλίγματα; the chorus' question prepares for their own suggestions at 699–701 and 704.

δι' ὄρφνης: 41–2n. The local force of διά, 'through (and out of) the dark', is a remnant of the ancient view, found in many languages, that night and darkness were substances, which could cover or occupy a space (R. Dyer, *Glotta* 52 [1974], 31–6). Similarly 773–4 (774n.) λεύσσω δὲ φῶτε περιπολοῦνθ' ἡμῶν στρατόν / πυκνῆς δι' ὄρφνης.

ἀδειμάντῳ ποδί: a frequent tragic *enallage*, 'whereby the feet of moving persons are assigned qualities properly pertaining to their owners' (Liapis on 696–8, who quotes e.g. *Ag.* 907 τὸν σὸν πόδ' ... Ἰλίου πορθήτορα, *Ant.* 1144 μολεῖν καθαρσίῳ ποδί and *Alc.* 611–12 καὶ μὴν ὁρῶ σὸν πατέρα γεραιῷ ποδί / στείχοντ'). Apparently a highly poetic word, ἀδείμαντος occurs only four times before *Rhesus* (Pi. *Nem.* 10.17, *Isthm.* 1.12, *Pers.* 162, *Cho.* 771) and very rarely in later Greek (e.g. Nonn. *D.* 22.35 ποσσὶν ἀδειμάντοισι).

διά τε τάξεων: 519–20n.

699–701. Ritchie (246–7) notes certain syntactical and phraseological affinities with *Tro*. 187–9 τίς μ' Ἀργείων ἢ Φθιωτᾶν / ἢ νησαίαν ἄξει χώραν / δύστανον πόρσω Τροίας; and 241–2 αἰαῖ, τίν' ἢ Θεσσαλίας πόλιν Φθιάδος εἶπας ἢ / Καδμείας χθονός; See also the elaborate chain of queries in *Hec*. 447–74.

Besides evoking three major Greek heroes (Achilles from Phthia / Thessaly, Ajax Locrus and the islander Odysseus) the chorus' suspicions reflect fifth-century and later Athenian ideas of who could be credited with a bold and treacherous night-raid (699–700, 701nn; cf. Ammendola on 699–701, Porter on 701).

699–700. Θεσσαλός: The Thessalians were proverbially untrustworthy (Σ$^{recc.}$ Ar. *Pl*. 521g [III 4b.141 Chantry] 'αἰεὶ γὰρ τὰ Θετταλῶν ἄπιστα'; cf. E. fr. 422, Dem. 1.21–2, 23.112 and, on the political incidents that inspired this belief, H.-J. Gehrke, *Stasis* ..., Munich 1985, 185–9). Aristophanes (*Pl*. 520–1) accuses them, perhaps not unreasonably (Sommerstein on 521, 524), of habitual ἀνδραποδισμός, the kidnapping and selling of free persons or other people's slaves.

παραλίαν Λοκρῶν νεμόμενος πόλιν: Both East and West Locrians had a long-standing reputation for banditry (Thuc. 1.5.3, *Hell. Oxy*. 21.3 Chambers) and piracy (Thuc. 2.32.2; cf. Thuc. 2.26.1, D. S. 12.44.1), which in antiquity included seaborne attacks on coastal settlements (P. de Souza, *Piracy in the Graeco-Roman World*, Cambridge 1999, 1–42). On νεμόμενος πόλιν see 475–6n.

701. ἢ νησιώτην σποράδα κέκτηται βίον; Cf. *Hcld*. 84 οὐ νησιώτην, ὦ ξένοι, τρίβω βίον (Iolaus' reply to the chorus' questions on his homeland) and for adjectival νησιώτης e.g. Pi. *Pyth*. 9.54–5 λαὸν ... νασιώταν, *Pers*. 390 νησιώτιδος πέτρας, *Tr*. 658 νασιῶτιν ἑστίαν. Of the tragedians Euripides especially liked to use nouns as attributes (KG I 272–3); in -της also *Hcld*. 699 ὁπλίτην κόσμον, 800, *El*. 443 μόχθους ἀσπιστάς (with Denniston on 443–4) and *Ion* 1373 οἰκέτην βίον. Likewise *Rh*. 715 (715–16n.) ἀγύρτης τις λάτρις.

σποράδα suggests an isolated, backward life (especially Arist. *Pol*. 1252b23–4 σποράδες γάρ· καὶ οὕτω τὸ ἀρχαῖον ᾤκουν), whether or not the islands themselves were meant to be 'scattered through the Aegean' (Porter on 701; cf. Pi. *Pae*. 5.38–40 [fr. 52e Sn.–M. = D5 Rutherford] καὶ σποράδας φερεμήλους / ἔκτισαν νάσους ἐρικυδέα τ' ἔσχον / Δᾶλον).[262] Islanders often suffered contempt from the mainland Greeks: e.g. Sol. fr. 2 *IEG*, *Hcld*. 84 (above), *Andr*. 14–15 τῷ νησιώτῃ Νεοπτολέμῳ δορὸς

---

[262] From Hellenistic times on αἱ Σποράδες is attested as a general term to cover the Aegean islands other than the Cyclades. Ascriptions varied in detail, and Virgil (*Aen*. 3.126–7) could still write *sparsasque per aequor / Cycladas*. Its use for the Dodecanese alone is modern (O. Maull – L. Bürchner, *RE* III A 2 s.v. Sporaden, coll. 1857, 1871).

γέρας / δοθεῖσα (with Stevens), Hdt. 8.125.2, Thuc. 6.77.1, Dem. 23.211. Here suspicions of piracy, for which cf. Thuc. 1.8.1, [Dem.] 58.56 and Plut. *Cim.* 8.3–5, may again play a part.

702. τίς ἦν; πόθεν; ποίας πάτρας; 682n. The series of interrogatives is paralleled in *Ion* 258–9 τίς δ' εἶ; πόθεν γῆς ἦλθες; ἐκ ποίας πάτρας / πέφυκας; and E. *El.* 779–80 τίνες / πόθεν πορεύεσθ' ἔστε τ' (Musgrave: πορεύεσθέ τ' L) ἐκ ποίας χθονός; (cf. Diggle, *Studies*, 98).

Hermann (*Opuscula* III, 307) restored syntax and metre by removing the miscellaneous unmetrical additions in both MSS families, which look like successive attempts to 'fill up' the asyndetic text.

703. 'Whom does he declare to be the highest of the gods?'

ποῖον ἐπεύχεται / τὸν ὕπατον θεῶν; *sc.* εἶναι. Both ἐπεύχεται (Hermann, *Opuscula* III, 307) and ποῖον <δ'> εὔχεται (Porson on *Phoen.* 892, Bothe, 5 [1803], 297) restore normal dochmiac responsion with 721,[263] but the former is preferable for keeping the asyndetic sequence of the previous line. For (ἐπ)εύχομαι, 'declare', with accusative and infinitive cf. particularly *IT* 508 τὸ κλεινὸν Ἄργος πατρίδ' ἐμὴν ἐπεύχομαι (*sc.* εἶναι) and Pi. *Pyth.* 4.97–8 Ποίαν γαῖαν ... εὔχεαι / πατρίδ' ἔμμεν; The notion of personal pride inherent in either verb from Homer on (693–4n.) seems fitting here, where the different appellations of Zeus appear to correspond to national distinctions (Paley on 703; cf. below). Yet possibly an undertone of the sacral sense is to be discerned as well.

τὸν ὕπατον θεῶν: i.e. Zeus, to judge by 456–7 (455b–7n.) ὕπατος / Ζεύς. Murray (*The Rhesus of Euripides*, Oxford 1913, 64), followed by Liapis (on 703), quotes Hdt. 5.66.1 for the idea that someone's tribal affiliations may be deduced from a god his relatives worship (Carian Zeus in this case). But in general the identification of a man by his religion was not common in ancient Greece, perhaps because it mattered little to their form of polytheism by which name a deity was addressed (cf. J. Assmann, in S. Budick – W. Iser [eds.], *The Translatability of Cultures* ..., Stanford 1996, 25–36, especially 31–2, 34–5). Σ^V *Rh.* 703 (II 342.13 Schwartz = 109 Merro) paraphrases with ποῖός ἐστιν αὐτῷ πάτριος θεός;

704. ἆρ' ἔστ' Ὀδύσσεως τοὔργον ἢ τίνος τόδε; See 722n.

705. εἰ τοῖς πάροιθε χρὴ τεκμαίρεσθαι: Cf. *Alc.* 239–40 τοῖς τε πάροιθεν / τεκμαιρόμενος and *OT* 915–16 οὐδ' ὁποῖ' ἀνήρ / ἔννους τὰ καινὰ τοῖς πάλαι τεκμαίρεται.

---

[263] Zanetto and Pace (*Canti*, 51, 53) retain Δ's ποῖον εὔχεται as a hypodochmiac. However, the only example of this colon with a resolved first long (or perhaps rather a standard dochmiac of the form ⏑ ⏑⏑ – ⏑ – corresponding with a hypodochmiac) is *IA* 246 Καπανέως τε παῖς (~ 235 καὶ κέρας μὲν ἦν), which besides involving a proper name, comes from a passage of doubtful Euripidean authorship.

τοῖς πάροιθε refers to the Palladion theft, the 'Ptôcheia' and the unidentified ambush by the Thymbraean altar, which (against epic chronology) Hector recalled in 501–9 (498b–509, 501–2, 503–7a, 503–5, 507b–9a nn.). The 'Ptôcheia' will gain further room in the antistrophe (710–21n.).

τί μήν; 'What else indeed?', meaning 'Of course'. See *GP* 333, Fraenkel on *Ag.* 672, G. Wakker, in *NAGP*, 214–15 n. 13 and, for the supposedly Sicilian origin of this expression, A. F. Garvie, *Aeschylus' Supplices: Play and Trilogy*, Cambridge 1969, 54–5, FJW on A. *Suppl.* 999.

706. δοκεῖς γάρ; 'What! You think so?'. γάρ lends the question a surprised and incredulous tone, implying doubt about the justification of the previous speaker's words (*GP* 77–8).

τί μὴν οὔ; sc. δοκῶ. The only other case of this elliptical answer is S. *El.* 1280 ξυναινεῖς; – τί μὴν οὔ (Seidler: μὴ codd.); On μήν see Wakker (705n.).

707. θρασύς: 498b–500n. (λῆμά τ' ... θρασύς).

γοῦν: 'at any rate', introducing a 'part proof' argument for Odysseus' responsibility. Cf. e.g. *OC* 319–20 οὐκ ἔστιν ἄλλη. φαιδρὰ γοῦν ἀπ' ὀμμάτων / σαίνει με προσστείχουσα, *Alc.* 693–4 and *IT* 72–3 (*GP* 451–2).

708. 'Cho.³ What (act of) valour are you praising? Whom? Cho.¹ Odysseus.'

Ὀδυσῆ: likewise Pi. *Nem.* 8.26, based on *Od.* 19.136 Ὀδυσῆ (+ *Il.* 4.384 Τυδῆ, 15.339 Μηκιστῆ). It may be coincidence that the only tragic parallels for this contracted accusative singular come from Euripides: *El.* 439 Ἀχιλῆ (Heath: -λλῆ L), *Phaeth.* 237 Diggle = E. fr. 781.24 βασιλῆ (with J. Diggle, *AC* 65 [1996], 197). At *Alc.* 25 Diggle and Parker adopt ἱερέα (BˢLˢ) instead of ἱερῆ (BOVLP) in dialogue verse.

709. κλωπὸς ... φωτός: 644–5n. In the light of 705 (n.), κλωπός must also allude to the theft of the Palladion (cf. 502 κλέψας). Accordingly, φώς here has a contemptuous undertone, as more often does ἄνθρωπος in prose: e.g. Lys. 4.19 διὰ πόρνην καὶ δούλην ἄνθρωπον, 30.28 καὶ ἑτέρους ἀνθρώπους ὑπογραμματέας (KG I 272, LSJ s.v. ἄνθρωπος I 4). The same applies to ἄνδρες in 645 (cf. Ar. *Pax* 1120 τένθης ... κάλαζων ἀνήρ).

αἱμύλον δόρυ: For αἱμύλος ('wily') of Odysseus in tragedy see 498b–500n. Here the epithet is transferred from the man to his weapon, as in e.g. *Pers.* 320–1 Ἀμφιστρεύς ... πολύπονον δόρυ / νωμῶν, *Hcld.* 500 ... ἐχθρὸν Ἀργείων δόρυ (Elmsley: ἀργεῖον L), 932–3 ὅτ' ἐκ Μυκηνῶν πολυπόνῳ σὺν ἀσπίδι / ἔστειχε (with Wilkins on 932).

710–21. Continuing the series of verbal reminiscences in the previous lines (707, 709nn.), this second account of the 'Ptôcheia' draws heavily on the vocabulary and syntax of 503–7a (n.). Note 711, 716 ~

503 ἔχων ('with'), 712 στολᾷ ~ 503 στολήν, 715 ἀγύρτης τις λάτρις ~ 503 ἀγύρτης, 717–19 πολλὰ δὲ τὰν / βασιλίδ᾽ ἑστίαν Ἀτρειδᾶν κακῶς / ἔβαζε ~ 504–5 πολλὰ δ᾽ Ἀργείοις κακά / ἤρατο. In addition to *Od.* 4.244–58 and the Cyclic tradition (*Il. Parv.* Arg. p. 122 (4) + frr. 8–10 *GEF*), there appears to be influence here from Athena's transformation of Odysseus into a beggar in *Od.* 13.397–403 + 429–38. See M. Fantuzzi, *MD* 36 (1996), 182–3 and *Rh.* 710–11, 712–13a, 715–16nn.

710–14. 'In the past too he came into our city, rheumy-eyed, wrapped in ragged clothes, with a sword hidden under his cloak.'

710–11. πάρος: 498b–509, 705nn.

ὕπαφρον: 'dim with tears, rheumy' (cf. Hsch. υ 264 Hansen–Cunningham ... τὸ ὑγρασίαν ἔχον ἐμφερῆ ἀφρῷ) and so perhaps referring to conjunctivitis (a very common disease also associated with living in squalid conditions), like Latin *lippus*. This seems the most natural interpretation of the adjective here, which can be supported with ὕπαφρος, 'frothy', in Gal. *Cris.* 1.5 (p. 78.4–5 Alexanderson) πτύσματα ... ὕπαφρα, Σ^bT *Il.* 14.16 (III 565.48–9 Erbse) τὸ πέλαγός ... τὸ μηδέπω ὕπαφρον γενόμενον ἐκ κυμάτων παφλαζόντων (cf. Eust. 964.50), probably Hp. *de Arte* 10.5 (fifth or fourth century BC) and ὑπαφρίζω, 'to foam a little', in e.g. Eust. 586.8–9. The more frequent rendering 'hidden, secret' (Σ^L *Rh.* 711 [II 342.27–8 Schwartz = 109 a² Merro] ὕπαφρος ὁ μὴ φανερός, ἐκ μεταφορᾶς τῶν ὑπ᾽ ἀφρὸν νηχομένων, ἢ τῶν ὑφάλων πετρῶν αἷς ἐπανθεῖ ἀφρός, Σ^V *Rh.* 711 [109 a¹ Merro] ὕπουλον; cf. e.g. Hsch. υ 264 Hansen–Cunningham, Phot. υ 84 Thedoridis, Erot. υ 10 Nachmanson²⁶⁴) may in fact be due to mis- or overinterpretation of the prefix (Jouanna on Hp. *de Arte* 10.5 [p. 261]). Σ^L *Rh.* 711 (II 342.29 Schwartz = 109 a² Merro) ἢ ὁ καταπληκτικός, ὁ μανικός shows that some here understood the word to be the neuter of ὑπάφρων, 'slightly stupid' (Hdt. 4.95.2).

If the above explanation is right, ὕπαφρον ὄμμ᾽ ἔχων can be taken to mirror the effect of Athena's action at *Od.* 13.433 (~ 401) κνύζωσεν δέ οἱ ὄσσε πάρος περικαλλέ᾽ ἐόντε ('she dimmed his eyes ...'; cf. Hsch. κ 3148 Latte κνυζοί· οἱ τὰ ὄμματα πονοῦντες). Hermann (on *Hec.* 238, 239) had already compared it to *Hec.* 240–1 ὀμμάτων τ᾽ ἄπο / φόνου σταλαγμοὶ σὴν κατέσταζον γένυν (cf. 503–7a n.).

712–13a. ῥακοδύτῳ στολᾷ / πυκασθείς seems to have been phrased after *Od.* 22.488 ῥάκεσιν πεπυκασμένος εὐρέας ὤμους. In the *Odyssey* ῥάκος and ῥάκεα (which do not appear in the *Iliad*) almost exclusively refer to Odysseus' beggar disguise on Ithaca (e.g. 13.434, 14.342, 349, 512). Regarding the 'Ptôcheia', cf. Ar. *Vesp.* 351 εἶτ᾽ ἐκδῦναι ῥάκεσιν κρυφθεὶς ὥσπερ πολύμητις Ὀδυσσεύς.

---

264 On ὕποφρον (*sic*) ~ S. frr. 236, 312. See Radt's apparatus and Pearson on 236.

ῥακόδυτος, 'dressed in rags' or here 'ragged', is elsewhere attested only in Hsch. κ 331 Latte κακοείμονας (*Od.* 18.41)· ῥακκοδύτους (*sic*). But Patristic and Byzantine Greek has ῥακοδυτέω ('beg'), ῥακοδύτης ('beggar') ans the collateral ῥακενδυτ-.

713b–14. ξιφήρης / κρύφιος ἐν πέπλοις: literally 'secretly equipped with a sword under his cloak'. Cf. *Or.* 1125 κρύπτ' ἐν πέπλοισι τοισίδ' ἕξομεν ξίφη, 1271–2 κεκρυμμένας / θήρας ξιφήρεις αὐτίκ' ἐχθροῖσιν φανεῖ, both of the plot to kill Helen, whose important role in the 'Ptôcheia' our poet suppressed (503–7a n.). For a more natural use of predicative κρύφιος see *Hec.* 993 καὶ δεῦρό γ' ὡς σὲ κρύφιος ἐζήτει μολεῖν and *HF* 598 ὥστ' ... κρύφιος εἰσῆλθον χθόνα.

In ξιφήρης, which is not safely attested before Euripides (also *Andr.* 1114, *El.* 225, *Ion* 1153, 1258, *Phoen.* 363, *Or.* 1346, 1627) and does not recur until the first century BC, the kinship with ἀραρίσκω is still apparent, while elsewhere -ήρης has mostly lost its meaning (Wilamowitz on *HF* 243, J. Wackernagel, *Progr. Univ. Basel* (1889), 41 = *KS* II, 937). Cf. 226b–8n. (on τοξήρης).

κρύφιος: Bothe (3 [1824], 366) and Morstadt (*Beitrag*, 41) for the unmetrical κρυφαῖος (Ω). *Kaibeliani* (*k*δ) in 'responsion' with normal dochmiacs are generally emended away (e.g. *Sept.* 233a ~ 239a, *OT* 657b ~ 686b, *Or.* 147b ~ 160b). This quite frequent MSS error may in part be due to the same tendency that caused unrecognised dochmiacs to be filled up to make iambic trimeters, however imperfect (Fraenkel on *Ag.* 478 with n. 2, Dodds on *Ba.* 1188 and, for *k*δ, Willink on *Or.* 1246–85 [p. 288]).

715–16. 'And begging his bread he crept around, a vagabond menial, his head all rough and dirty.'

βίον δ' ἐπαιτῶν: Cf. *OC* 1364 ἄλλους ἐπαιτῶ τὸν καθ' ἡμέραν βίον and *Hel.* 790–1 (Με.) τοῖσδ' (*sc.* τοῖς πυλώμασιν), ἔνθεν ὥσπερ πτωχὸς ἐξηλαυνόμην. / (Ελ.) οὔ που προσῄτεις βίοτον; In classical Greek ἐπαιτέω, originally 'ask in addition' (*Il.* 23.593), is otherwise attested only in *OT* 1416 and S. *El.* 1124 (middle), both times meaning 'request urgently', while later it becomes common for beggary. See LSJ s.v. 2 and especially the agent noun ἐπαίτης.

εἷρπ': in the literal sense ('creep around') also *Sept.* 17–19 ἢ γὰρ νέους ἕρποντας εὐμενεῖ πέδῳ / ... / ἐθρέψατ' and, of the lame Philoctetes, *Phil.* 206–7 φθογγά του στίβον κατ' ἀνάγ- / καν ἕρποντος ('dragging along').

ἀγύρτης τις λάτρις: For ἀγύρτης in the sense 'vagabond' see 503–5n. and for λάτρις, hired servant' (as against the much rarer 'slave'), Wilamowitz on *HF* 823. The latter is popular with Euripides, as is the placing of one noun in an attributive relationship to an other (701n.).

It is tempting to suggest that our poet created his begging 'vagabond menial' from a combination of *Od.* 4.245 σπεῖρα κάκ' ἀμφ' ὤμοισι βαλών, οἰκῆϊ ἐοικώς and its probable doublet 4.247–8 ἄλλῳ δ' αὐτὸν φωτὶ κατακρύπτων ἤϊσκε / Δέκτῃ. In that case he would have been a precursor of Aristarchus, who understood ΔΕΚΤΗΙ to mean ἐπαίτῃ ('beggar'), whereas in the *Little Iliad*, we are told, it was a proper name: Σ *Od*. 4.248 (II 254.84–9 Pontani) = *Il. Parv*. fr. 9 *GEF*. Cf. S. R. West on *Od*. 4.246–9, M. Fantuzzi, *MD* 36 (1996), 183–5, A. Fries, *CQ* n.s. 60 (2010), 349–50 (+ Introduction, 37), West, *Epic Cycle*, 196–7.

ψαφαρόχρουν: most likely 'with rough skin, scabby', though not necessarily implying baldness ($Σ^V$ *Rh*. 716 [II 342.4 Schwartz = 110 Merro]). The word appears only here and was probably coined for the occasion. Many adjectives in -χρως (-χροος, -χρωτος), often without direct reference to the skin, are first attested in Euripides, especially in the lyrics of his later plays: e.g. *Hel*. 215 χιονόχρῳ κύκνου πτερῷ, *Phoen*. 322–3 λευκόχροα ... κόμαν, *Hel*. 1502–3 κυανόχροά τε κυμάτων / ῥόθια πολιὰ θαλάσσας, *Phoen*. 308–9 κυανόχρωτι χαί- / τας πλοκάμῳ (Mastronarde on *Phoen*. 138).

A possible model is ψαφαρόθριξ, 'rough-haired' (of sheep), in *h.Pan*. 32. ψαφαρός ('powdery, crumbling') is generally rare in poetry before Hellenistic times: only *Sept*. 323 ψαφαρᾷ σποδῷ and maybe Pl. Com. fr. 126 *PCG* ψαφαρόν = ἀπαλόν. Later cf. especially Nic. *Ther*. 369 καὶ τόθ' ὅγ' ἐν χερσῷ τελέθει ψαφαρός τε καὶ ἄχρους (i.e. the χέρσυδρος, an amphibious snake).

Fantuzzi (*MD* 36 [1996], 182–3) sees here an allusion to Odysseus' miraculous ageing at the hands of Athena in *Od*. 13.431–2 ξανθὰς δ' ἐκ κεφαλῆς ὄλεσε τρίχας, ἀμφὶ δὲ δέρμα / πάντεσσιν μελέεσσι παλαιοῦ θῆκε γέροντος. If so *Od*. 13.430 (~ 398) κάρψε μέν οἱ χρόα καλὸν ἐνὶ γναμπτοῖσι μέλεσσι (with κάρφω = 'dry up, wither': cf. Hes. *Op*. 575, Archil. fr. 188.1–2 *IEG*) should also be taken into account.

πολυπινές: another classical *hapax*. For πίνος, 'filth' (on clothes or the body), cf. *OC* 1259, E. *El*. 305 and A. R. 2.200–1 (of Phineus) πίνῳ δέ οἱ αὐσταλέος χρώς / ἐσκλήκει. Similar compound adjectives in drama are δυσπινής (*OC* 1597, Ar. *Ach*. 426 ~ fr. tr. adesp. 42), κακοπινής (*Ai*. 381, metaphorically of Odysseus) and εὐπινής, 'tidy', in E. fr. 494.11 and Cratin. fr. 455 *PCG*.

717–19. The mythical background of Odysseus' denunciations (by which he pretends to be a Greek deserter) is discussed in 503–5n.

πολλὰ δὲ τὰν / βασιλίδ' ἑστίαν Ἀτρειδᾶν κακῶς / ἔβαζε: The construction with the adverb is equivalent to πολλὰ ... κακὰ ἔβαζε (KG I 295, 323–4). βάζω governs a double accusative also at *Il*. 9.58–9 ἀτὰρ πεπνυμένα βάζεις / Ἀργείων βασιλῆας, 16.207 ταῦτά μ' ... θάμ' ἐβάζετε and *Hipp*. 118–19 εἴ τις σ' ... / μάταια βάζει.

Adjectival βασιλίς is paralleled in *IA* 1305–6 Ἥρα δὲ Διὸς ἄνακτος / εὐναῖσι βασιλίσιν (*sc*. τρυφῶσα). See 701n. and Introduction, 34.

δῆθεν: 'as if …', implying falsehood. The particle rarely precedes the phrase it qualifies, but cf. *PV* 986 ἐκερτόμησας δῆθεν ὥσ<τε> παῖδά με, *Tr.* 381–2 'Ἰόλη 'καλεῖτο, τῆς ἐκεῖνος οὐδαμά / βλάστας ἐφώνει δῆθεν οὐδὲν ἱστορῶν, *Or.* 1119 ἔσιμεν ἐς οἴκους δῆθεν ὡς θανούμενοι and Thuc. 1.127.1 τοῦτο δὴ τὸ ἄγος οἱ Λακεδαιμόνιοι ἐκέλευον ἐλαύνειν δῆθεν τοῖς θεοῖς πρῶτον τιμωροῦντες (*GP* 265–6).

720–1. 'I wish he had perished, perished as he deserved, before setting foot on the Phrygians' land!'

ὄλοιτ' ὄλοιτο: In curses ὄλοιο has become so stereotyped that the optative can be used for an unrealisable wish in the past (KG I 228, SD 322). Likewise A. *Suppl.* 867–71 εἰ γὰρ δυσπαλάμως ὄλοιο / δι' ἀλίρρυτον ἄλσος / … ἀλαθεὶς / Συρίαισιν αὔραις, *Hipp.* 407–9 ὡς ὄλοιτο παγκάκως / ἥτις πρὸς ἄνδρας ἦρξατ' αἰσχύνειν λέχη / πρώτη θυραίους and *Hel.* 1215 ὅπου κακῶς ὄλοιτο, Μενέλεως δὲ μή (with Kannicht on 1214–5). The anadiplosis has a match in *Ion* 705 (referring to the present).

πρὶν ἐπὶ γᾶν Φρυγῶν ποδὸς ἴχνος βαλεῖν: The clause is Euripidean in style. Cf. *IT* 752 μήποτε κατ' Ἄργος ζῶσ' ἴχνος θείην ποδός, *El.* 1344 δεινὸν γὰρ ἴχνος βάλλουσ' ἐπὶ σοί (i.e. the Erinyes) and for ποδὸς ἴχνος = 'foot' also *HF* 125, *Tro.* 3, *Ion* 792, *Phoen.* 105 and E. fr. 530.7 (Ritchie 209–10).

Φρυγῶν: 32n.

722. The verse echoes 704 with almost corresponding word-ends and Ὀδυσσέως at the same metrical position. Likewise 24 ~ 42 Ἕκτορ (with 23–4n.).

εἴτ' οὖν … εἴτε: 'Whether, in point of fact, … or …', with οὖν marking indifference (*GP* 418–19). The combination is typical of tragedy and Plato.

φόβος μ' ἔχει (or φόβος ἔχει με) also appears in A. *Suppl.* 379, *Ag.* 1243, S. fr. 314.278 (*Ichneutae*), *Med.* [356], *Or.* 1255 and *Hyps.* fr. 64 ii.76 Bond = E. fr. 759a.1597. In Euripides the periphrasis of a verb of feeling by way of its abstract noun with ἔχει (LSJ s.v. ἔχω (A) A I 8) has almost become a mannerism. Add *Hec.* 970, *Or.* 460 (~ 101), *Ba.* 828 (+ A. fr. 132c.12) αἰδώς μ' ἔχει, *HF* 515, *IA* 837, Ar. *Thesm.* 904 ('Euripides' speaking) ἀφασία μ' ἔχει, and see Kannicht on *Hel.* 558.

724. δυσοίζων: a very rare verb, attested elsewhere only in *Ag.* 1316 οὔτοι δυσοίζω θάμνον ὡς ὄρνις φόβῳ and *Rh.* 805 (804–5n.) μηδὲν δυσοίζου. Both etymology and meaning are disputed, but it seems easiest to explain it as an irregular compound of οἴζω (< οἰοί: A. D. *Adv.* 128.7 Schneider; cf. Schwyzer 716 on -ζω as a mode of verbifying interjections that end in vowels), which denotes a sharp cry of distress or here rather indignation (Σ^V *Rh.* 724 [II 342.16–17 Schwartz = 110 Merro] βλασφημῶν. ἢ ὀργιζόμενος καὶ λοιδορῶν). See further A. Debrunner,

IF 21 (1907), 273 and Fraenkel on *Ag.* 1316, who not quite justly compares the verbal adjective δυσβάϋκτος (< βαύζω, βαύ) in *Pers.* 574.

725. τί δρᾶσαι: L. Dindorf's correction (I [1825], 492 ~ W. Dindorf, III.2 [1840], 617–18) of the MSS' τί δρᾷς; (... δρᾷς δή; Tr¹) is supported by the infinitive περᾶσαι in the following line. Wilamowitz' τί δράσας; (on *HF* 540), accepted by Porter and Kovacs ('At what ill fortune?'), can also be excluded for semantic reasons, since in this and similar questions δρᾶν always refers to a *physical* action by its subject (e.g. *HF* 540, 1136, 1187, *Or.* 849). Cf. D. J. Mastronarde, *ElectronAnt* 8 (2004), 22.

727. ἐς Φρυγῶν στρατόν: 32n. Similarly 846 Φρυγῶν στρατός.

728–55. Both metrically and in terms of content this 'interlude' forms a transition between the preceding, almost entirely lyric search-scene and the narrative-agonistic episode of 756–881. The sentries, still groping in the dark at first in the hope of catching an intruder (730), meet Rhesus' badly injured Charioteer instead and with painful slowness, which again betrays their lack of visual (736–7) and mental (745–6) perception, make out his nationality and preoccupation. The humble Thracian meanwhile – a substitute for the king's cousin Hippocoon (< ἵππος + κοέω: 'he who looks after horses'), who in *Il.* 10.518–22 is woken by Apollo to discover the slaughter in the camp (Ritchie 74–5) – is so absorbed in his grief and agony that he does not even react to the coryphaeus' question in 736. In this emotional isolation[265] he resembles characters like Xerxes in *Pers.* 908–16, Oedipus in *OT* 1307–18, Creon in *Ant.* 1261–9, Antigone in *Phoen.* 1485–1529 and especially the mortally wounded Hippolytus (*Hipp.* 1347–88) with his comic counterpart Lamachus (Ar. *Ach.* 1190–1234),[266] whose respective lamentations offer some striking verbal and structural similarities (731–2, 733, 734–5, 750–1a nn.). Nearly all these entries, including the parody in *Acharnians*, are preceded by an account of the catastrophic events off-stage (in *Persians* it is the prediction of Plataea by the Ghost of Darius), while here the Charioteer himself will bring the news of the Thracian disaster: 756–803 (n.). With the relatively uniform introductions to Euripidean messenger-speeches (1–51n.) the present passage shares only an equivalent of the 'general announcement' (728b, 732a), the 'information in brief' (735, 742–4, 747–8, 752–3) and

---

[265] Mastronarde, *Contact and Discontinuity*, 77 n. 6. For the following examples cf. 21 n. 7, 22 with n. 14 and 25 n. 28. The Phrygian Slave in *Orestes*, while sharing certain traits with the Charioteer (804–81, 866–7nn.) and being unable to give the entire story (*Or.* 1498–9), does recognise the presence of the chorus (1375) and replies properly to most of their questions (1393, 1425, 1453, 1473).

[266] The scene parodies the final appearance of pain-stricken characters (and θρῆνοι) in general, but Hippolytus is the obvious Euripidean example. See also Rau, *Paratragodia*, 142–4.

the 'question for the addressee' (738–40) – all in so free an order and arrangement as not even the (semi-)lyric compositions of *HF* 910–21, *Ba.* 1024–42 and *Phoen.* 1335–55 display.²⁶⁷ Moreover, the chorus-leader fails to ask for a detailed report after 755, which gives the impression that the following speech is still directed at no one in particular (Strohm 272 with n. 2).

Influenced as it seems by two different scene types, the Charioteer's entry at once points to his double function as victim and messenger so as to prepare for his unusually subjective narrative²⁶⁸ and stubborn belief in the Trojans' guilt. Yet the reminiscence of great tragic heroes in misery adds a somewhat incongruous note, although it may have been intended to raise the Thracian's importance and pathos, even beyond such individual figures as the Guard in *Ant.* 223–331 and 384–445.

Metre

Given the trochaic tetrameters catalectic of 730 and 732, the Charioteer's lyric opening line 728b is best regarded with Diggle as a syncopated trochaic trimeter (*tr tr* | '*sp*' ||) after extra-metric ἰώ ἰώ (cf. 731 and 733a)²⁶⁹ or perhaps even a trochaic dimeter with φεῦ φεῦ again *extra metrum* (for other analyses see Willink, 'Cantica', 41–2 = *Collected Papers*, 580).²⁷⁰ His longer outbursts are set in recitative anapaests (733–5, 738–44, 747–53: cf. e.g. *Pers.* 908–16 and *Hipp.* 1347–69), to which the coryphaeus responds with pairs of iambic trimeters (736–7, 745–6, 754–5). Formally this alternation of actor's laments and choral spoken verse most closely resembles such semi-lyric *amoibaia* as *Ag.* 1072–1113 (the first four strophic pairs of the Cassandra-scene), *OT* 1313–68 or indeed *Pers.* 249–89, where Xerxes' messenger adheres to iambics while the shocked chorus reply in dochmiacs. Likewise in *HF* 910–21, *Ba.* 1024–42 and *Phoen.* 1335–55, which like our passage begins with 4tr_∧, although most of the remainder (1338–53) should go with 1308–34

---

267 The lines are most likely distorted by interpolation (Fraenkel, *Zu den Phoenissen*, 71–86). Cf. 149–94n. (pp. 175–6) with n. 74.
268 On the subjectivity of Euripidean messenger-speeches see de Jong, *Narrative in Drama*, 63–116. Cf. also 756–61n.
269 In view of the preceding two instances of extra-metric ἰώ ἰώ (and especially the unambiguous 731), there is no need to see in 728b a first anapaestic monometer, as Diggle (*Euripidea*, 119) seems to suggest.
270 Liapis takes 728b as non-lyric (with Kirchhoff's τύχη for τύχα), a trochaic tetrameter catalectic cut short by φεῦ φεῦ, as 'the charioteer, for some time now in the throes of pain, is unable to fill out' the line. But such 'realism' is alien to Greek tragedy. The sequence of lyric, recitative anapaests and iambic trimeters adequately represents the Charioteer's regaining mastery of himself.

(n. 267), it is the recipients of the news who burst into short snatches of song.[271] The reverse pattern here underlines again the exceptional status of the victim-messenger.

728b. δαίμονος τύχα βαρεῖα: Cf. *Med.* 671 ἄπαιδές ἐσμεν δαίμονός τινος τύχῃ, *Hipp.* 831–3 πρόσωθεν δέ ποθεν ἀνακομίζομαι / τύχαν δαιμόνων ἀμπλακίαισι τῶν / πάροιθέν τινος, *IT* 865 + 867 and E. fr. 37. In this type of expression τύχη denotes the intervention of a known or unknown deity (LSJ s.v. I 1 a) with advantageous (e.g. Pi. *Ol.* 8.67, *Pyth.* 8.53, *Nem.* 4.6–8) or detrimental effect upon men.

τύχα βαρεῖα also occurs in *Sept.* 332 βαρείας τοι τύχας προταρβῶ, *Ai.* 980 ὤμοι βαρείας ἆρα τῆς ἐμῆς τύχης, *Hipp.* 818–19 (with Barrett on 818–20), E. *El.* 300–1 and *Phaeth.* 93–4 Diggle = E. fr. 773.49–50 (with Diggle on 94). Similarly *Rh.* 731–2 (n.) ἰὼ ἰώ· / συμφορὰ βαρεῖα Θρῃκῶν.

729. ἔα ἔα: in Euripides nearly always *extra metrum* (675–82 'Metre' 675n.). On the meaning and etymology of ἔα see 574n.

730. 'Crouch down in silence, everyone! Perhaps somebody is falling within the cast of our net.'

σῖγα πᾶς ὕφιζ': Cf. 680, 687 (nn.) and, in a very similar situation, Ar. *Ach.* 238 σῖγα πᾶς. ἠκούσατ', ἄνδρες, ἆρα τῆς εὐφημίας; L. Dindorf's σῖγα (I [1825], 492 ~ W. Dindorf, III.2 [1840], 618) for σίγα (VQ: σιγᾷ L) is required by syntax and metre – an easy corruption with parallels in e.g. Ar. *Ach.* 238 (above), *Hec.* 532 and *Or.* 140. On σῖγα, especially in imperatives, see E. Schwyzer, *Glotta* 12 (1923), 27–8 = *KS* 483–4.

ὕφιζ' is Reiske's correction (*Animadversiones*, 91), after Barnes (129), of the transmitted ὕφιζος (V) or ὕβριζ' (Λ). The verb is unique in classical Greek, except for the transitive Ionic aorist participle ὑπείσας in Hdt. 3.126.2 and 6.103.3. The same applies to ὑφιζάνω (*Phoen.* 1382–3 ἀλλ' ὑφίζανον κύκλοις, / ὅπως σίδηρος ἐξολισθάνοι μάτην, Aristotle and late).

ἴσως γὰρ ἐς βόλον τις ἔρχεται is reminiscent of *Ba.* 848 ... ἀνὴρ ἐς βόλον καθίσταται and E. fr. 62d.29 ... εἰς βόλον γὰρ ἂν πέσοι and may be a proverbial fishing metaphor (C. B. Sneller, *De Rheso Tragoedia*, Amsterdam 1949, 68 n. 1). Cf. Herod. 7.75–6 ὡς, ἤν τι μὴ νῦν ἡμῖν ἐς βόλον κύρσῃ, / οὐκ οἶδ' ὅκως ἄμεινον ἡ χύτρη πρήξει and Hdt. 1.62.4 (oracle) ἔρριπται δ' ὁ βόλος, τὸ δὲ δίκτυον ἐκπεπέτασται, / θύννοι δ' οἰμήσουσι σεληναίης διὰ νυκτός.

---

[271] On all the preceding compositions and the division of lyric and non-lyric (iambic) metres between the characters see Barrett, *Collected Papers*, 386–419 (especially 389, 392–3, 398, 406–8, 409–10, 411).

731–2. Syntax and speaker assignments were restored by Hermann (*Opuscula* III, 307). Most MSS read and divide ἰὼ ἰώ· / συμφορὰ βαρεῖα Θρῃκῶν συμμάχων / τίς ὁ στένων; But συμμάχων fits better in a statement initiating the chorus' lengthy realisation process (728–55n.); cf. 736 and 755. By the same token, ἰὼ ἰώ ... Θρῃκῶν cannot belong to them (Liapis on 732).

ἰὼ ἰώ· / συμφορὰ βαρεῖα Θρῃκῶν: For the wording cf. especially Tim. *Pers.* fr. 791.187 *PMG* = Hordern <ἰ>ὼ βαρεῖα συμφορά, which imitates *Pers.* 1043–4 ὀτοτοτοτοῖ· / βαρεῖά γ' ἅδε συμφορά. The resemblance to Ar. *Ach.* 1204 ὢ συμφορὰ τάλαινα τῶν ἐμῶν κακῶν (Ritchie 3) and 1210 τάλας ἐγὼ ξυμβολῆς βαρείας is also noteworthy (728–55n.).

On the exclamatory nominative (as in 728b and 733b) see KG I 46 and SD 65–6; after ἰώ (ἰώ) e.g. *Pers.* 1073, *Sept.* 994, *Ai.* 893, *Tro.* 1118–19, *Ion* 912.

733. δύστηνος ἐγώ is a set-phrase in anapaestic laments (*Pers.* 908–10, *OT* 1307/8, *Med.* 96, *Hipp.* 239, 1348, *HF* 448, *Tro.* 112), but here, before σύ τ' ἄναξ Θρῃκῶν, it gains special significance by suggesting that the Charioteer is more concerned with his own fate than that of his master. Cf. 752 (752–3n.) χρῆν γάρ μ' ἀκλεῶς Ῥῆσόν τε θανεῖν.

734–5. 'O you who looked on Troy (that proved) most hateful (to us), what a death has taken you away!'

ὦ στυγνοτάτην Τροίαν ἐσιδών: Liapis (on 734–5) probably rightly suspects an echo of *Pers.* 974–6 (Xerxes speaking) ἰώ, ἰώ μοι· / τὰς ὠγυγίους κατιδόντες / στυγνὰς Ἀθάνας. In both places στυγνός bears an anticipatory sense equivalent to that of πικρός in e.g. *Od.* 17.447–8 στῆθ' ... ἐμῆς ἀπάνευθε τραπέζης, / μὴ τάχα πικρὴν Αἴγυπτον καὶ Κύπρον ἴδηαι (v.l. ἵκηαι), *Phil.* 355–6 κἀγὼ πικρὸν Σίγειον οὐρίῳ πλάτῃ / κατηγόμην and *Hec.* 772 ἐνταῦθ' ἐπέμφθη πικροτάτου χρυσοῦ φύλαξ (LSJ s.v. πικρός III 1 '... of what yields pain instead of expected pleasure', FJW on A. *Suppl.* 1033 [III, p. 319]).

ὦ στυγνοτάτην could be a reminiscence of *Hipp.* 1355 ὦ στυγνὸν ὄχημ' ἵππειον ... (cf. 728–55n.), but similar apostrophes are found in *Pers.* 472 (ὦ στυγνὲ δαῖμον) and *Phil.* 1348 (ὦ στυγνὸς αἰών).

736–7. 'Which of our allies are you? My vision is dimmed at night, and I cannot make you out clearly.'

κατ' εὐφρόνην: 91–2n.

ἀμβλῶπες αὐγαί: Photius (α 1164 Theodoridis) has given us an interesting parallel in E. fr. 397a (*Thyestes*) ἀμβλώπας αὐγὰς ὀμμάτων ἔχεις σέθεν (Reitzenstein: ἀμβλωπὰς bz). He further attests ἀμβλώψ (rather than ἀμβλωπός: *Eum.* 955, E. frr. 155a ἀμβλωπὸς ὄψις, 386a, Critias 88 B 6.11 DK = fr. 6.10 *IEG*) for Sophocles (fr. 1001), Ion (*TrGF* 19 F 53a) and Plato the Comedian (fr. 254 *PCG*). Like δίβαμος (214–15n.), this form of the adjective had previously been a *hapax* (Ritchie 151, 210, Fraenkel, *Rev.* 230).

Bare αὐγαί, 'eyes', is paralleled in *h.Merc.* 361, A. (?) fr. 99.13 (*Cares = Europa*)[272] ἀλλ' οὐκ ἐν αὐγαῖς ταῖς ἐμαῖς ζόη σφ' ἔχει, *Andr.* 1179–80 … †εἰς τίνα / δὴ φίλον αὐγὰς βαλὼν τέρψομαι;†[273] and, figuratively, Pl. *Rep.* 540a6–8 καὶ ἀναγκαστέον ἀνακλίναντας τὴν τῆς ψυχῆς αὐγὴν εἰς αὐτὸ ἀποβλέψαι τὸ πᾶσι φῶς παρέχον. The metaphor from the 'rays' or 'beams' of one's eyes (LSJ s.v. αὐγή 1, 5) is clearest where ὀμμάτων (-ος) is added: *Ai.* 69–70 (with Finglass), *HF* 132, *Phoen.* 1564, E. fr. 397a (above), Licymn. fr. 771.2 *PMG* and also *Hec.* 1102–5 Ὠαρίων ἢ Σείριος ἔνθα πυρὸς φλογέας ἀφίησιν / ὄσσων αὐγάς.

τορῶς: 77n.

738. Τρώων: Diggle for Τρωϊκῶν (Ω), since internal corretion of a long vowel or diphthong – except with comic αὐτηί, τουτῳί, ἐκεινηί and the like (West, *GM* 12; cf. J. W. White, *The Verse of Greek Comedy*, London 1912, 367) – would be unacceptable in Attic drama. Hermann (*Opuscula* III, 307) had already written Τρῴων, but the genitive of the people's name is regular with ἄναξ in this sense: e.g. *Rh.* 406–7 μέγαν / Θρηκῶν ἄνακτα, *Sept.* 39 Καδμείων ἄναξ, A. *Suppl.* 328, 616, S. *El.* 482–3, *Alc.* 510.

740. τὸν ὑπασπίδιον κοῖτον ἰαύει: Metre and syntax are almost identical with *Ai.* 1408 τὸν ὑπασπίδιον κόσμον φερέτω (the body-armour) from the difficult anapaestic ending of that play (see Finglass on 1402–20, 1416–17, 1418–20). Direct borrowing is further suggested by the general rarity of ὑπασπίδιος (*Il.* 13.158, 807, 16.609 … ὑπασπίδια προποδίζων / προβιβάντι / προβιβάντος, Asius fr. 13.7 *GEF* … ὑπασπίδιον πολεμιστήν), which here must mean that Hector passed the night fully armed under the cover of his shield: cf. 20–2, 123–4 (nn.). Likewise *Od.* 14.479 (of a Greek ambushing party caught in bad weather) εὗδον δ' εὔκηλοι, σάκεσιν εἰλυμένοι ὤμους and, with the shields as head-rests, *Il.* 10.150–2 βὰν δ' ἐπὶ Τυδείδην Διομήδεα· … / … ἀμφὶ δ' ἑταῖροι / ηὗδον, ὑπὸ κρασὶν δ' ἔχον ἀσπίδας.

κοῖτον ἰαύει combines two other essentially epic words. κοῖτος ('bed, sleep') is first and extensively attested in the *Odyssey* (cf. Hes. *Op.* 574), but in other drama occurs only at A. fr. 78c.7 (*Theoroi*?)]ῳ τε κο[ίτ]ῳι καὶ κακαῖς δ[υσ]αυλίαις. The original sense of ἰαύω, 'pass the night – in sleep or wakefulness' (*LfgrE* s.v. B 1; cf. 519–20n.), is also still

---

[272] The ascription of the fragment is not above suspicion (cf. *TrGF* III, 218), and West (*CQ* n.s. 50 [2000], 347–50 = *Hellenica* II, 241–6) went so far as to attribute the entire play to Aeschylus' son, Euphorion.

[273] The metrical corruption, for which see L. P. E. Parker, *CQ* n.s. 16 (1966), 23 and Diggle's apparatus on 1179–80, does not affect the substance of the text.

felt here, as in *Ai.* 1204 οὔτ' ἐννυχίαν τέρψιν ἰαύειν. At *HF* 1049–50 τὸν εὕδι' ἰαύονθ' (Reiske: εὖ διαύοντα L) / ὑπνώδεά τ' and *Phoen.* 1537–8 δεμνίοις / δύστανος ἰαύων it simply means 'rest in bed'.

741. διόπων στρατιᾶς: '(of) the army's commanders' (< διέπω, as in e.g. *Il.* 2.207 ὣς ὅ γε κοιρανέων δίεπε στρατόν). For the noun, restored here by Portus (*Breves Notae*, 71), cf. especially *Pers.* 44 βασιλῆς δίοποι (with Garvie), again in recitative anapaests. It is elsewhere attested as A. fr. 232 (*Sisyphus*), E. fr. 447 (*Hippolytus I*)[274] and, of a ship's supervisor or captain (cf. A. fr. 269 ἀδίοπον), in Hp. *Epid.* 5.74.1 and 7.36.1 (ca. 350 BC). Although Aristophanes of Byzantium (fr. 338 Slater) and Erotian (δ 2 Nachmanson) classed the word as Attic, it may have carried an epic tone, given the verb from which it is derived.

742b–4. '... what someone has done to us unseen and then vanished, while the misfortune he has accomplished for the Thracians is plain to see.'

οἷά ... ἀφανῆ ... φανερὸν / ... πένθος: This chiastic juxtaposition has exact parallels in *Hipp.* 1286–9 Θησεῦ, τί τάλας τοῖσδε συνήδῃ, / παῖδ' οὐχ ὁσίως σὸν ἀποκτείνας / ψεύδεσι μύθοις ἀλόχου πεισθείς / ἀφανῆ· φανερὰν δ' ἔσχεθες ἄτην and E. *El.* 1190–2 ἰὼ Φοῖβ', ἀνύμνησας δίκαι' / ἄφαντα, φανερὰ δ' ἐξέπρα- / ξας ἄχεα (δίκαι' Murray: δίκαν L, ἄφαντα Elmsley: ἄφατα L), whence we should not write ἀφανής with Dobree (*Adversaria* II [1833], 87 = IV [1874], 85). For φανερὸν ... πένθος cf. also *Ion* 945 φανερὰ ... κακά, *Phoen.* 1513 τοιάδ' ἄχεα φανερά and 1565 τῶν μὲν ἐμῶν τεκέων φανερὸν κακόν.

φροῦδος: 662n.

τολυπεύσας: literally 'wind off, unravel' (a skein of wool, τολύπη: Ar. *Lys.* 586, S. fr. 1102). Except for *Od.* 19.137 οἳ δὲ γάμον σπεύδουσιν· ἐγὼ δὲ δόλους τολυπεύω, where we have an allusion to Penelope's web, the metaphor is already dead in Homer (Janko on *Il.* 14.85–7 ... οἷσιν ἄρα Ζεύς / ἐκ νεότητος ἔδωκε καὶ ἐς γῆρας τολυπεύειν / ἀργαλέους πολέμους; cf. *Il.* 24.7–8 and the verse-end formula ... ἐπεὶ πόλεμον τολύπευσε(ν) / -α in *Od.* 1.238, 4.490, 14.368 and 24.95). The verb is very rare after Homer and adds yet another epicism to the Charioteer's

---

[274] The traditional order of the two *Hippolyti*, established from a short note in the hypothesis by Aristophanes of Byzantium, has been questioned (J. C. Gibert, *CQ* n.s. 47 [1997], 85–97) or even reversed on the basis of metrical evidence and new papyrus finds of a hypothesis to Ἱππόλυτος (κατα)καλυπτόμενος (G. O. Hutchinson, *ZPE* 149 [2004], 15–28, O. Zwierlein, *Lucubrationes Philologae* 1. *Seneca*, Berlin 2004, 57–90, especially 84–5). Against all three, however, Luppe (*Philologus* 142 [1998], 174 n. 3, *ZPE* 151 [2005], 11–14 + *ZPE* 156 [2006], 38) argues cogently for keeping the relative position, if not the date, of the extant play, whereas Cropp and Fick (*ZPE* 154 [2005], 43–5) doubt the evidential value of slightly lower resolution rates (compared to *Alcestis*, *Medea* and *Heraclidae*) in this case.

lament (740, 741, 750–1a nn.). Similarly ἐκτολυπεύω (from [Hes.] *Sc.* 44?) at *Ag.* 1032–3 οὐδὲν ἐπελπομέ- / να ποτὲ καίριον ἐκτολυπεύσειν (with Fraenkel on 1033).

745–6. 'Some evil seems to be falling on the Thracian host, according to what I understand from this man's words.'

κυρεῖν ... / ἔοικεν: Despite Paley (on 745), there is nothing exceptional about ἔοικα with a present infinitive (LSJ s.v. II 1). The latter, though perhaps slightly surprising after the aorist and perfect forms in 735 and 742–4, here seems to emphasise the lasting effects of the recent attack (Ammendola on 745–46) and point to further trouble ahead. Cf. *Cho.* 13 πότερα δόμοισι πῆμα προσκυρεῖ νέον (Orestes seeing Electra and the chorus in mourning). κυρέω with a personal dative is otherwise restricted to Sophocles: *Tr.* 291 ἄνασσα, νῦν σοι τέρψις ἐμφανὴς κυρεῖ, *OC* 1289–90 καὶ ταῦτ᾽ ἀφ᾽ ὑμῶν, ὦ ξένοι, βουλήσομαι / καὶ τοῖνδ᾽ ἀδελφαῖν καὶ πατρὸς κυρεῖν ἐμοί.[275]

οἷα depends on both γιγνώσκω and κλύων. The clause is causal-exclamatory in origin (cf. 309–10n.).

747–9. ἔρρει στρατιά: similarly *Pers.* 732 Βακτρίων δ᾽ ἔρρει πανώλης δῆμος.

δολίῳ πληγῇ: The adjective suggests Odysseus' agency (893b–4n.). Feminine δόλιος mostly stands for metrical reasons: Bacch. 17.116 δόλιος Ἀφροδίτα, *Cyc.* 449, *Tro.* 530, *IT* 859 (δόλιον Hartung: δολίαν ὅτ᾽ L), *Hel.* 20, 238, 1589. But see *Alc.* 33–4 Μοίρας δολίῳ / σφήλαντι τέχνῃ, where, as here, euphony may have played a part (cf. Kannicht on *Hel.* 335).

On Euripides' fondness for using three-termination adjectives with two terminations see further W. Kastner, *Die griechischen Adjektive zweier Endungen auf* -ΟΣ, Heidelberg 1967, especially 95–99, 114 and Diggle, *Euripidea*, 167, 186, 262.

ἆ ἆ ἆ ἆ: a cry of physical anguish as in 799 ἆ ἆ (*extra metrum*) and, again fourfold, *Phil.* 732 and 739. On the different denotations of the interjection – urgent protest, astonishment (*HF* 629, *Ba.* 586, 596), mental distress (A. *Suppl.* 162, *Ag.* 1087) – see the works cited in 687n. and also Dodds on *Ba.* 810–12, E. Schwentner, *Die primären Interjektionen in den indogermanischen Sprachen* ..., Heidelberg 1924, 7, Ll-J/W, *Second Thoughts*, 66.

750–1a. 'How the pain of my bloody wound afflicts me deep within!'

The expression is partly repeated in 799 (n.) ὀδύνη με τείρει κοὐκέτ᾽ ὀρθοῦμαι τάλας. It recalls *Il.* 15.60–1 λελάθῃ δ᾽ ὀδυνάων / αἵ νῦν

---

[275] *Hec.* 214–15 ἀλλὰ θανεῖν μοι / συντυχία κρείσσων ἐκύρησεν belongs to an actors' interpolation (211–15 del. Wilamowitz). For the metrical difficulty in 215 see Diggle, *Euripidea*, 315.

μιν τείρουσι κατὰ φρένας, *Od.* 9.440–1 ἄναξ ... ὀδύνῃσι κακῇσι / τειρόμενος, Ar. *Ach.* 1205 ἰὼ ἰὼ τραυμάτων ἐπωδύνων, *Hipp.* 1351 διά μου κεφαλῆς ᾄσσουσ' ὀδύναι and 1370–1 αἰαῖ αἰαῖ· / καὶ νῦν ὀδύνα μ' ὀδύνα βαίνει, which is also followed by a wish for death (1372–7, 1385–8). Cf. 728–55n.

φονίου: a favourite of Euripides (cf. Liapis on 750–1), as Aristophanes seems to have recognised in *Ran.* 1337. See 41–2, 662nn. and Introduction, 29–30 with n. 36.

εἴσω should be taken absolutely ('inside the body'), as in Pl. *Rep.* 407d4–5 τὰ δ' εἴσω διὰ παντὸς νενοσηκότα σώματα and epic ἔνδοθι (ἐντός) of various deep feelings at *Il.* 1.243–4 σὺ δ' ἔνδοθι θυμὸν ἀμύξεις / χωόμενος, 22.242 ἀλλ' ἐμὸς ἔνδοθι θυμὸς ἐτείρετο πένθεϊ λυγρῷ, 10.10 τρομέοντο δέ οἱ φρένες ἐντός, *Od.* 2.315, 8.577, 19.377–8 and especially A. R. 3.761–2 ἔνδοθι δ' αἰεί / τεῖρ' ὀδύνη (Medea's love-induced fear for Jason). Note also τὰ ἐντός, 'the inner parts' (LSJ s.v. ἐντός II with Suppl. [1996]), and Latin *intus* (*TLL* s.v. 103.52–76).

The only tragic parallel for this use of the adverb is *Ag.* 1343 ὤμοι, πέπληγμαι καιρίαν †πληγὴν ἔσω†, where scholars have long suspected corruption and Vetta (*GIF* 5 [1974], 162–4) in particular assumed the intrusion of a 'didascalic' gloss (cf. Σ^B *Med.* 96 [II 149.16 Schwartz] τάδε λέγει Μήδεια ἔσω οὖσα). Yet with πληγῇ in 749 and another echo of Agamemnon's death in 790–1 (n.), it is probable that our lines were also influenced by Aeschylus and that the passages hence support each other. Formulations like *Il.* 16.340 (~ 21.117–18) πᾶν δ' εἴσω ἔδυ ξίφος, E. *El.* 1221–3 ἐγὼ μὲν ... / φασγάνῳ κατηρξάμαν / ματέρος ἔσω δέρας μεθείς, *Ion* 767–8 διανταῖος ἔτυπεν ὀδύνα με πλευ- / μόνων τῶνδ' ἔσω and *Hel.* 354–6 ἢ ξιφοκτόνον διωγμὸν / αἱμορρύτου σφαγᾶς / αὐτοσίδαρον ἔσω πελάσω διὰ σαρκὸς ἅμιλλαν are made easier by the genitive or verb of motion they contain (Denniston–Page on *Ag.* 1343, M. Vetta, *GIF* 5 [1974], 159–64, who both falsely join εἴσω with φονίου τραύματος here).

751b. πῶς ἂν ὀλοίμην; another topos in anapaestic laments (cf. 733n.). So also *Alc.* 864, *Med.* 97 and, more expansively, E. *Suppl.* 795–7 μελέα / πῶς ἂν ὀλοίμην σὺν τοῖσδε τέκνοις / κοινὸν ἐς Ἅιδην καταβᾶσα; (Ritchie 211). For desperate 'wish-questions' with πῶς ἄν see 869n.

752–3. The sentiment is further developed in 758–61 (n.). As in 733 (n.), the Charioteer puts himself before his master, no matter that the order μ' ... Ῥῆσόν τε is dictated by Behaghel's Law of Increasing Terms.

ἀκλεῶς: likewise 761 (n.). Earlier tragic instances of ἀκλεῶς and its adjective all belong to Euripides: *Or.* 786 ἰτέον, ὡς ἄνανδρον ἀκλεῶς κατθανεῖν, *Hcld.* 623–4 ἀκλεής ... δόξα, *Hipp.* 1028, *IA* 18 (if genuine). It is not clear whether fr. tr. adesp. 665.21 comes from a fourth-

Τροίᾳ κέλσαντ' ἐπίκουρον: '... after he had landed in Troy as your ally'. In view of the verbal affinities with E. *El.* 135–9 ἔλθοις δὲ πόνων .../ ... λυτήρ, /... πατρί θ' αἱμάτων / αἰσχίστων ἐπίκουρος ('avenger'), Ἄρ- / γει κέλσας πόδ' ἀλάταν (where κέλλω is uniquely transitive in tragedy: FJW on A. *Suppl.* 330–2), it seems preferable to take Τροίᾳ here with κέλσαντ' rather than ἐπίκουρον (Kovacs, Liapis on 752–3). Elsewhere in *Rhesus* the verb has its regular construction with a prepositional phrase or an accusative of direction (895–8, 934–5a nn.).

754–5. ἐν αἰνιγμοῖσι ... / σαφῶς: a very common antithesis in fifth-century and later literature: e.g. *Ag.* 1178–83 καὶ μὴν ὁ χρησμὸς οὐκέτ' ἐκ καλυμμάτων / ἔσται δεδορκὼς ... 1183b φρενώσω δ' οὐκέτ' ἐξ αἰνιγμάτων, *PV* 609–10 λέξω τορῶς σοι πᾶν ὅπερ χρῄζεις μαθεῖν, / οὐκ ἐμπλέκων αἰνίγματ', ἀλλ' ἁπλῷ λόγῳ, 833–5, *IA* 1146–7, Aeschin. 3.121 and, conversely, A. *Suppl.* 464 αἰνιγματώδες τοὔπος· ἀλλ' ἀπ<λ>ῶς φράσον, Alexis fr. 242.6–7 *PCG*, Anaxil. fr. 22.23 *PCG*, Pl. *Ep.* 332d6–7. Further examples in FJW on A. *Suppl.* 464.

As regards tragedy, αἰνιγμός (for αἴνιγμα) is unique to our passage save for *Phoen.* 1353 Σφιγγὸς αἰνιγμοῖς, which is very probably part of an interpolation (see Fraenkel, *Zu den Phoenissen*, 83–4 [cf. n. 267] and Diggle's apparatus on 1308 ff.). The first unquestionably genuine instance is Ar. *Ran.* 61.

σημαίνει κακά: an inflectable Euripidean verse-end: *Hec.* 512 ... σημανῶν κακά, *HF* 1230 ... σημαίνεις κακά, *Ion* 945 ... σημαίνω κακά.

756–803. In a movement comparable to that employed in scenes where the same situation is presented first 'emotionally' in lyrics, then 'rationally' in dialogue verse,[276] the Charioteer turns from his sung and spoken trochaics (728b, 732a) and recitative anapaests (733–5, 738–44, 747–53) to regular iambic discourse. Among tragic messenger speeches, however, his account of Rhesus' death stands out for its extreme subjectivity (728–55n. with n. 268) and narrow perspective. Himself a victim of the nocturnal slaughter, he can only speak from direct perception and, with his failure to anticipate the attack (773–9), his belated and clumsy attempts to defend the camp (792–8) and his ignorance of the actual circumstances and perpetrators of the deed (800–3), he becomes the most obvious exponent in the play of human short-sightedness and inefficiency (Strohm

---

[276] E.g. *Ag.* 1072–1330 (with Fraenkel, *Ag.* III, p. 623), *OT* 1307–1415, *Alc.* 244–392, *Med.* 96–266, *Hipp.* 198–430. Cf. Schadewaldt, *Monolog und Selbstgespräch*, 143–4, Zanetto, *Ciclope, Reso*, 155–6 n. 91, Finglass on S. *El.* 254–309.

271–2, J. Barrett, *Staged Narrative. Poetics and the Messenger in Greek Tragedy*, Berkeley – London 2002, 189).

After a lengthy reflection on failed heroism harking back to 752–3 (756–7a, 758–61, 761, 762–3a nn.), the report proper confirms the return to the substance of *Iliad* 10, observed previously in the adaptation of Hippocoon's lament (728–55n.). This manifests itself in the all but exclusive interest in Rhesus' horses, which is certainly appropriate to the faithful Charioteer, but turns the king into little more than a source of splendid booty: *Il.* 10.463–4 ἀλλὰ καὶ αὖτις / πέμψον ἐπὶ Θρῃκῶν ἀνδρῶν ἵππους τε καὶ εὐνάς, 477–81, 488–501, 520 (cf. Burnett, 'Smiles', 34–5, Barrett, *Narrative*, 173).[277] The temporary marginalisation of Rhesus in favour of his servant's more immediate pathos is clearest in 780–8 (n.), the translation of *Il.* 10.494–7 into the only dream related by a 'messenger' on stage, and 790–1 (n.), where even his final moments appear as a grisly experience of the Charioteer (Barrett, *Narrative*, 181–2). Moreover, by a slight change in the Thracians' attitude towards self-protection (762–9n.), our poet manages to combine a first hint at the narrator's resentments against his hosts with a sense that Rhesus invited his fate.

When it comes to his own foiled attack and injury (792, 793–5a, 797–8, 799nn.), the Charioteer reverts to his earlier penchant for epic language (740, 741, 742b–4, 750–1a nn.), as if to corroborate the Thracian's lack of glory (756–61) by giving an ironic commentary on Homeric prowess. In addition, his groan at 799 almost literally takes up 749–51 and so reinforces the unique juxtaposition of message and lament.

756–61. Among introductions to tragic messenger speeches (284–6n.), the length and character of this passage are matched only by the Maidservant's reflections on Alcestis' excellence in *Alc.* 152–7. Both this woman and the Charioteer act as 'substitute messengers' and are in their respective ways perhaps more than usually affected by the incidents they are going to recount.

756–7a. 'We have suffered a disastrous blow and, over and above disaster, disgrace as well.'

Construction and wording are almost identical with 102 (102–4n.) αἰσχρὸν γὰρ ἡμῖν, καὶ πρὸς αἰσχύνῃ κακόν. But in contrast to Hector, the Charioteer is more concerned with physical suffering and, as Liapis (on 756–7) observes, foregrounds it over heroic shame. This also distinguishes him from other major characters in tragedy, such as Eteocles in *Sept.* 683–5 εἴπερ κακὸν φέροι τις, αἰσχύνης ἄτερ / ἔστω· μόνον

---

[277] I do not, however, agree with their respective ironic interpretations of the play.

γὰρ κέρδος ἐν τεθνηκόσιν· / κακῶν δὲ καἰσχρῶν οὔτιν' εὐκλείαν ἐρεῖς, Iolaus in *Hcld*. 449–50 χρῆν χρῆν ἄρ' ἡμᾶς ἀνδρὸς εἰς ἐχθροῦ χέρας / πεσόντας αἰσχρῶς καὶ κακῶς λιπεῖν βίον and Cadmus in *Ba*. 1305–7 ὅστις ... / τῆς σῆς τόδ' ἔρνος, ὦ τάλαινα, νηδύος / αἴσχιστα καὶ κάκιστα κατθανόνθ' ὁρῶ.

κακῶς πέπρακται: likewise *Med*. 364 κακῶς πέπρακται πανταχῇ· τίς ἀντερεῖ;

πρός after κἀπὶ τοῖς κακοῖσι is redundant and probably not more than a convenient verse-filler (Fraenkel, *Rev*. 238). Elsewhere this particular use of adverbial πρός is restricted to the phrases πρὸς δ' ἐπὶ τοῖς (A. fr. 146a) and καὶ πρὸς ἐπὶ τούτοις (Ar. *Pl*. 1001, Anaxil. fr. 24 *PCG*).

757b. 'And this is an evil twice as great.'

A similarly formulated question is asked by Tecmessa at *Ai*. 277 ἆρ' ἐστὶ ταῦτα δὶς τόσ' ἐξ ἁπλῶν κακά; meaning that Ajax, relieved from his madness, has started to torment himself as well as his family.

καίτοι: 'logical', marking the transition from minor to major premise in an incomplete syllogism (*GP* 561–4, especially ii). The particle seems to have no adversative force here.

δὶς τόσον κακόν: 159b–60n.

758–61. The wish for a glorious death in battle, if die one must, is a heroic commonplace from Homer on (e.g. *Il*. 22.304–5) and often contrasted with the prospect or reality of a less favourable end that brings no honour to the family: e.g. *Od*. 1.234–43, 14.365–71, 24.28–34, *Cho*. 345–53 + 494, *Andr*. 1181–5 (cf. Garvie on *Cho*. 345–53, Liapis on 758–60). Despite Ritchie (227), there is thus nothing specially Euripidean about the sentiment here, although certain phraseological resemblances can be discerned (758, 759, 760, 761nn.).

758. εἰ θανεῖν χρεών: Versions of this conditional clause appear several times in Euripides: *Hipp*. 442 (~ *HF* 147, *Ion* 1120) ... εἰ θανεῖν αὐτοὺς χρεών, *IT* 1004–5 ... οὐδέ σ' εἰ θανεῖν χρεών / σώσασαν, *Phoen*. [1745] ... εἰ με καὶ θανεῖν ... χρεών; cf. *Cyc*. 201 εἰ θανεῖν δεῖ, *Hcld*. 443 (~ *Or*. 50) εἴ με χρὴ θανεῖν. Aeschylus and Sophocles offer nothing of the sort, unless fr. tr. adesp. 626 (32 εἰ καὶ θανεῖν χρὴ ...) belongs to the latter.

759. On such strong subjective affirmations about the feelings or perceptions of the dead see K. J. Dover, *Greek Popular Morality in the Time of Plato and Aristotle*, Oxford 1974, 243, who quotes S. *El*. 400 πατὴρ δὲ τούτων, οἶδα, συγγνώμην ἔχει and E. *El*. 684 πάντ', οἶδ', ἀκούει τάδε πατήρ· στείχειν δ' ἀκμή.

λυπρὸν μὲν οἶμαι: Ritchie (245–6) notes the syntactical similarity to the opening of *Alc*. 353–4 ψυχρὰν μέν, οἶμαι, τέρψιν, ἀλλ' ὅμως βάρος / ψυχῆς ἀπαντλοίην ἄν. Parenthetical οἶμαι (μέν) is more frequent in Euripides (also *Alc*. 565, *Med*. 311, 331, 588, *Hcld*. 511, 670,

968, *Hipp.* 458, *El.* 1124, *Ba.* 321, *IA* 392) than in all other extant tragedy together: *Cho.* 758 οἴομαι (spoken by the Nurse), *PV* 758, 968, *Ant.* 1051, *Phil.* 498, S. fr. 583.4. It mostly has a colloquial ring (Stevens, *CEE* 23–4, Collard, 'Supplement', 361).

πῶς γὰρ οὔ; 'How could it not be?', i.e. 'of course' (cf. *GP* 86). This is likewise at least conversational in tone and, especially in reply to a previous speaker's words, exceedingly common in Plato. In tragedy it occurs in parenthesis at *Cho.* 753–4 (again from the Nurse's speech) and S. *El.* 1307. Cf. also S. *El.* 911 πῶς γάρ; and perhaps *OT* 567, S. fr. 730e.5 πῶς δ' οὐ(χί); (Collard, 'Supplement', 368).

760. καὶ δόμων εὐδοξία: For εὐδοξία with a possessive genitive cf. Sim. fr. 531.6–7 *PMG* = 261.5–6 Poltera ἀνδρῶν ἀγαθῶν ὅδε σηκὸς οἰκέταν εὐδοξίαν / Ἑλλάδος εἵλετο. In poetry the noun, but not its adjective, is virtually confined to choral lyric (also Pi. *Pyth.* 5.8, *Nem.* 3.40, *Pae.* 14.31 [fr. 52o Sn.–M. = S3 Rutherford]) and Euripides (*Med.* 627, *Hec.* 956, *Suppl.* 779, *Tro.* 643, possibly E. fr. 237.3); later only [Men.] *Mon.* 270 Jäkel. On εὐδοξέω see 496n.

761. ἡμεῖς δ' ἀβούλως κἀκλεῶς ὀλώλαμεν: The formulation resembles *Hipp.* 1028 ἦ τἄρ' ὀλοίμην ἀκλεὴς ἀνώνυμος and *IA* 17–18 ζηλῶ δ' ἀνδρῶν ὃς ἀκίνδυνον / βίον ἐξεπέρασ' ἀγνὼς ἀκλεής (752–3n.). Yet strictly speaking, ἀβούλως here is causal, 'through (our own) foolishness' (cf. S. *El.* 398 καλόν γε μέντοι μὴ 'ξ ἀβουλίας πεσεῖν), while ἀκλεῶς acquires an almost consecutive sense: *ita ut inglorii simus* (KG II 115, SD 414 c). The incomplete correspondence is mitigated by the unifying force of the privative prefix (Fraenkel on *Ag.* 412 [II, p. 217] and, for other such juxtapositions, Richardson on *h.Cer.* 200 [p. 221]).

In view of the relative frequency of ἀβουλία and ἄβουλος (which Sophocles seems to like), ἀβούλως is surprisingly rare in fifth-century literature: Hdt. 3.71.3, Pherecr. fr. 152.6 *PCG*, *Hcld.* 152 (Kirchhoff: ἀβούλους L); cf. Hdt. 7.9β.1 ἀβουλότατα. After our passage it does not recur until Polybius and Diodorus Siculus.

762–9. The Charioteer freely admits to their neglect of basic emergency precautions, which at last betrays Rhesus' gullibility and utter incompetence as a military leader. The somewhat reproachful tone in 767b–9a (as if the Trojans alone had failed to protect their auxiliaries) foreshadows his later accusations and probably mirrors Dolon's misgivings at the lack of allied night-watches in *Il.* 10.420–2. The epic Thracians, however, have arranged their weapons and horses in perfect order (*Il.* 10.471–3 οἳ δ' ηὗδον καμάτῳ ἀδηκότες, ἔντεα δέ σφιν / καλὰ παρ' αὐτοῖσι χθονὶ κέκλιτο εὖ κατὰ κόσμον, / τριστοιχεί· παρὰ δέ σφιν ἑκάστῳ δίζυγες ἵπποι) and even the goads (766b–7a n.) are in their proper place: *Il.* 10.500–1 (Odysseus drives Rhesus' team with his bow) ἐπεὶ οὐ μάστιγα φαεινήν / ποικίλου ἐκ δίφροιο νοήσατο χερσὶν ἑλέσθαι.

Rhesus here appears to have influenced Verg. *Aen*. 9.316–19 *passim somno vinoque per herbam / corpora fusa vident, arrectos litore currus, / inter lora rotasque viros, simul arma iacere, / vina simul* (cf. Introduction, 45).

762–3a. ἐπεὶ γάρ: Many dramatic narratives, and especially Euripidean messenger speeches, open with an ἐπεί-clause, which usually alludes to some earlier event or universally shared presupposition of the play: e.g. *Tr*. 899–946 (900), *OC* 1586–1669 (1590), *Med*. 1136–1230, *IT* 260–339, *Ion* 1122–1228, *Phoen*. 1090–1199; cf. *OT* 1237–85 (1241) ὅπως γάρ. The allocation of sleeping quarters had motivated Hector's departure with Rhesus at 526, and ἡμᾶς may indicate that the Charioteer was also there as a member of the latter's entourage. Cf. *Andr*. 1085 ἐπεὶ τὸ κλεινὸν ἤλθομεν Φοίβου πέδον, E. *El*. 774, *IT* 1327, *Hel*. 1526–30 and *Ba*. 1043–4 (A. Rijksbaron, in J. M. Bremer *et al*. [eds.], *Miscellanea tragica in honorem J. C. Kamerbeek*, Amsterdam 1976, 293–308, Ritchie 253).

γάρ marks the entire report as explanation for the preceding ἡμεῖς δ' ἀβούλως κἀκλεῶς ὀλώλαμεν. More often in this position it comes after 'an expression denoting the giving ... of information' (284–6, 285nn.). So e.g. *Ai*. 748–9 τοσοῦτον οἶδα καὶ παρὼν ἐτύγχανον. / ἐκ γὰρ συνέδρου καὶ τυραννικοῦ κύκλου (...), S. *El*. 680–1, *Alc*. 157–8, *Hcld*. 799–800, *PV* 827–9 and maybe also *Phoen*. 1427–8 (P. J. Finglass, *Mnemosyne* IV 58 [2005], 561–4).

ηὔνασ': 580–1n.

Ἑκτόρεια χείρ: a metrically convenient, epicising periphrasis for Ἕκτωρ (contrast Bacch. 13.151–4 ἐναριζ[ο]μ[έν]ων / [δ' ἔρ]ευθε φώτων / [αἵμα]τι γαῖα μέλα[ινα] / [Ἑκτορ]έας ὑπὸ χει[ρός]), although χείρ may imply that he *pointed out* the Thracian resting-places (Paley on 762; cf. 519 δείξω δ' ἐγώ σοι χῶρον ...), just as e.g. 'strength' is suggested by the noun in βίη Ἡρακληείη or the action of coming in *Or*. 1216–17 σὺ μέν νυν ... παρθένου δέχου πόδα (i.e. Ἑρμιόνην). See KG I 280–1.

For the irregular prosody of Ἑκτόρειᾰ, restored by Dindorf (III.2 [1840], 619), cf. Ar. *Eccl*. 1029 καὶ ταῦτ' ἀνάγκη μοὐστί; – Διομήδειά γε and perhaps Pi. *Ol*. 10.15–16 τράπε δὲ Κύκνεια μάχα καὶ ὑπέρβιον / Ἡρακλέα (Κύκνεια Hermann: κύκνεα codd.: Κυκνεία byz.).[278] The ori-

---

[278] St. Byz. α 570 Billerbeck νῆσος Ἀχίλλεια, *EM* 451.51 βασίλεια χείρ and 461.44–5 Πολυδεύκεια χείρ, Ἀγαμεμνόνεια give doubtful evidence, especially since Hdn. II 454.15 Lentz has Πολυδευκεία χείρ καὶ Ἀγαμεμνονεία ναῦς in the same context. A. Meschini (*AFLPad* 1 [1976], 180) further cites A. D. *Coni*. 233.7–9 Schneider ἦν οὖν καὶ τὸ εὐήνωρ, <ἀφ' οὗ> κτητικὴ παραγωγὴ ἔπιπτεν εὐηνόρεια ὡς Ἑκτόρεια κ .. ρεια

gin of this phenomenon is obscure, but a possible explanation is offered by W. Kastner (*Die griechischen Adjektive zweier Endungen auf* -ΟΣ, Heidelberg 1967, 63–4). Noting the tendency of proper name adjectives to avoid feminine forms in -εία and -ία, he deduced a poetic licence to replace them with substantival formations in -ιᾰ, as illustrated by the coexistence of epic δῖα θεάων / γυναικῶν and δῖα θεά (*Il.* 10.290; cf. e.g. *Il.* 1.141 εἰς ἅλα δῖαν, 14.347 χθὼν δῖα) and the occasional attributive use of βασίλεια in Attic drama (*Pers.* 623, E. *El.* 988, Ar. *Pax* 974). Cf. A. Meschini *AFLPad* 1 (1976), 182–3 and Liapis on 762–4. Barrett (*Collected Papers*, 187 n. 197) prefers to speak of analogy.

ξύνθημα λέξας: The participle goes κατὰ σύνεσιν with Ἑκτόρεια χείρ, as in *Il.* 11.690–1 ἐλθὼν γὰρ ἐκάκωσε βίη Ἡρακληείη / τῶν προτέρων ἐτέων and *Od.* 16.476–7 μείδησεν δ' ἱερὴ ἲς Τηλεμάχοιο / ἐς πατέρ' ὀφθαλμοῖσιν ἰδών. On ξύνθημα see 521–2n.

763b–4a. ηὕδομεν πεδοστιβεῖ / κόπῳ δαμέντες: '... we slept, overcome by the toils of our march'. This probably adapts the authorial statement about the Thracians at *Il.* 10.471 οἳ δ' ηὗδον καμάτῳ ἀδηκότες (762–9n.), although with Morstadt's πεδοστιβεῖ (*Beitrag*, 45) for the transmitted πεδοστιβεῖς (below) the construction comes closer to *Il.* 10.2 (= 24.678) ηὗδον παννύχιοι, μαλακῷ δεδμημένοι ὕπνῳ. Cf. also *Rh.* 123–4 (n.) ἀλλὰ στρατὸν ... / εὕδειν ἐῶμεν ἐκ κόπων ἀρειφάτων.

The textual change is necessary, for πεδοστιβής ('earth-treading') always implies at least a capacity for locomotion (cf. *Pers.* 127 πεδοστιβὴς λεώς, *Med.* 1123 ὄχον πεδοστιβῆ, *Hel.* 1516 πεδοστιβεῖ ποδί, E. fr. 670.3–4 ὑγρὰ δὲ μήτηρ, οὐ πεδοστιβὴς τροφός / θάλασσα and 253–5a n.) and could thus not possibly be applied to persons lying sprawled on the ground (769). Despite Liapis (on 762–4), an equivalent to its combination with κόπος here seems to exist in A. fr. 131.2 (*Myrmidons*) δοριλυμάντους Δαναῶν μόχθους (literally 'the toils of the Danaans resulting from the destruction by spears').

ηὕδομεν: 580–1n.

764b–5a. οὐδ' ἐφρουρεῖτο στρατός / φυλακαῖσι νυκτέροισιν: similarly *Cyc.* 689–90 τηλοῦ σέθεν / φυλακαῖσι φρουρῶ σῶμ' Ὀδυσσέως τόδε.

765b–6a. οὐδ' ἐν τάξεσιν / ἔκειτο τεύχη: '... nor was our armour laid out in order', with the plural τάξεσιν referring to the different sets of weapons (KG I 19 n. 3). Liapis (on 764–7 ~ 'Notes', 91) misunderstands the word as 'ranks' (cf. 519–20n.); hence his emendation οὐκ ἐν τεύχεσιν ἔκει<ν>το τάξεις, where τάξεις looks doubtful both in itself and in view of the following non-personal subject πλῆκτρα.

καὶ πρακτόρεια, εὐηνορέα (Schneider: -όρεια Ab) καὶ ἔτι Ἰωνικῶς εὐηνορ<έη>, ὡς Ἑκτορέη.

766b–7a. πλῆκτρά τ' οὐκ ἐπὶ ζυγοῖς / ἵππων καθήρμοσθ': The custom of leaning one's goad against the yoke is illustrated by *Il.* 23.510 (Diomedes after the chariot-race) κλῖνε δ' ἄρα μάστιγα ποτὶ ζυγόν. On *Il.* 10.500–1 see 762–9n.

πλῆκτρον in the sense 'goad, whip', occurs only here, but the association is obvious (LSJ s.v. 'anything to strike with'), and *Suda* κ 1338 Adler Κέντρα: τὰ τῶν ἵππων πλῆκτρα (cf. κ 1344) need not be based on these lines.

For the pluperfect καθήρμοσθ' of a state resulting from a (non-) action preceding ηὕδομεν in 763 Liapis (on 764–7) compares *Il.* 10.151–3 ἀμφὶ δ' ἑταῖροι / ηὗδον ... ἔγχεα δέ σφιν / ὄρθ' ἐπὶ σαυρωτῆρος ἐλήλατο (i.e. Diomedes' companions).

768–9. κἀφεδρεύοντας νεῶν / πρύμναισι: 489–90n. ἐφεδρεύω is exceedingly rare in poetry, and in its military use ('lie in wait, besiege') confined to our passage. But note *Or.* 1627 σύ θ' ὃς ξιφήρης τῇδ' ἐφεδρεύεις κόρῃ (with Willink).

φαύλως δ' ηὕδομεν πεπτωκότες: rounding off the preliminaries in ring-composition with 763–4 ηὕδομεν πεδοστιβεῖ / κόπῳ δαμέντες (Liapis on 762–4 [p. 277]). For ηὕδομεν (εὕδ- Ω) see 580–1n. and for φαύλως 285n. The meaning here is 'carelessly, thoughtlessly' (LSJ s.v. φαῦλος II 3).

770–2. 'And I awoke from sleep in heart-felt concern and with generous hand measured out fodder for the horses, expecting to yoke them for a battle at dawn.'

μελούσῃ καρδίᾳ λήξας ὕπνου: Personal μέλω, 'care for, take an interest in' (LSJ s.v. B), hardly ever has an non-personal subject (for a very late instance see Q. S. 4.500 ἱππασίῃ μεμελημένον ἦτορ), and Fraenkel (*Rev.* 238) was probably right in suspecting that our poet composed the phrase from *Sept.* 287 (Χο.) μέλει, φόβῳ δ' οὐχ ὑπνώσσει κέαρ (+ 288–9 γείτονες δὲ καρδιᾶς / μέριμναι), where μέλει answers Eteocles' preceding request for 'a better prayer' (265–81), but could easily have been mistaken for another predicate with κέαρ (A. Fries, *CQ* n.s. 60 [2010], 350; cf. Introduction, 37).

λήξας ὕπνου, which may itself be an echo of οὐχ ὑπνώσσει in *Sept.* 287 (Fraenkel, *Rev.* 238), comes from *HF* 1011 (cf. 70–5, 70–1nn.).

ἑωθινήν / ... ἐς ἀλκήν: 'for the purpose of ...', as in e.g. *Hel.* 1379 προὔργου δ' ἐς ἀλκὴν σῶμ' ὅπλοις ἠσκήσατο and *Il.* 8.375–6 ὄφρ' ἂν ἐγὼ ... / τεύχεσιν ἐς πόλεμον θωρήξομαι (LSJ s.v. εἰς A V 2). The text is that of V. Λ's πρός may be possible (LSJ s.v. C III 3 a), but most likely arose by assimilation to προσδοκῶν in 771 (Liapis on 770–2 ~ 'Notes', 91–2).

Unlike ἀλκή, 'battle, fight', which is regular in non-Sophoclean tragedy (and also occurs at 933), ἑωθινός is elsewhere attested in the genre only at S. fr. 502 (*Poimenes*) ἑωθινὸς γάρ ... / θαλλὸν χιμαίραις προσφέρων νεοσπάδα, / εἶδον στρατὸν στείχοντα παραλίαν πέτραν (Liapis on 770–2). On the (possible) connections between *Poimenes* and *Rhesus* see Introduction, 33 and 264–341, 388–526, 383–4nn.

ἀφθόνῳ μετρῷ χερί comes closest to *Med.* 612 ... ὡς ἕτοιμος ἀφθόνῳ δοῦναι χερί. Note also Pi. *Ol.* 2.93–5 φίλοις ἄνδρα μᾶλλον / εὐεργέταν πραπίσιν ἀφθονέστερόν τε χέρα / Θήρωνος, S. *El.* 457–8 ὅπως τὸ λοιπὸν αὐτὸν ἀφνεωτέραις / χερσὶ στέφωμεν and, for further parallels, FJW on A. *Suppl.* 958.

μετρέω, 'measure out (particularly provisions)', is a domestic term well-suited to this context and the attentive Charioteer. Cf. Hes. *Op.* 349 εὖ μὲν μετρεῖσθαι παρὰ γείτονος (with West), Ar. *Ach.* 548 σιτίων μετρουμένων, *Eq.* 1009 περὶ τῶν μετρούντων τἄλφιτ' ἐν ἀγορᾷ κακῶς, *Av.* 580 (LSJ s.v. III 3).

774a. πυκνῆς δι' ὄρφνης: 'through the thick darkness', as if this consisted of a substance which could be close-packed as in a cloud: *Il.* 5.751, 8.395 πυκινὸν νέφος, 16.298, Hes. *Op.* 553, E. fr. 330.4 ... συντιθεὶς πυκνὸν νέφος, *Phoen.* 250–1 (metaphorical). On ὄρφνη and traces of a quasi-material conception of night in Greek see 41–2, 696–8nn.

774b–5. Together with 778 (οἳ δ' οὐδέν) this looks like the model of Nisus and Euryalus in Verg. *Aen.* 9.377–8 *nihil illi tendere contra, / sed celerare fugam in silvas et fidere nocti* (Introduction, 45).

κἀνεχωρείτην πάλιν: In a similar narrative and situation cf. *IT* 264–5 ἐνταῦθα δισσοὺς εἶδέ τις νεανίας / βουφορβὸς ἡμῶν, κἀνεχώρησεν πάλιν.

776–7. 'And I called to them not to draw near our army, believing that some marauders from our allies had come.'

ἤπυσα: an originally epic word, which is not elsewhere found in tragic spoken verse. It occasionally governs a personal dative (e.g. *Ai.* 879–87 τίς ἂν δῆτά μοι ... ἀπύοι; *Ba.* 984 μαινάσιν δ' ἀπύσει, A. R. 4.230), but the infinitive, though easy on analogy with other verbs of saying, is again unique to this place.

κλῶπας ... συμμάχων ... τινάς: 644–5n. In suspecting his allies of theft (no doubt a well-known offence in army camps of all times) the Charioteer first explicitly shows his deep-rooted mistrust of the Trojans (cf. 802b–3n.). He 'does not even consider the possibility of a Greek venture into [their] camp' (Liapis on 776–7).

778–9. 'But they gave no response. I in my turn did not say anything further, but went back to bed and slept.'

The laconic tone of this couplet, enhanced by the double verbal ellipsis in 778, reflects the Thracian's fatal indifference to the intruders and aptly prepares for the horrors to come.

οἳ δ' οὐδέν: *sc.* e.g. ἡμείβοντο (Paley).

οὐ μὴν οὐδ' marks progression in negative statements (*GP* 338–9).

τὰ πλείονα: *sc.* ἔλεγον or εἶπον. The article, which sounds redundant to the modern ear, implies 'the more I might have said'. Cf. especially *Phil.* 576 μή νύν μ' ἔρῃ τὰ πλείον', *OC* 36–7 πρὶν νῦν τὰ πλείον' ἱστορεῖν, ἐκ τῆσδ' ἕδρας / ἔξελθ', *Med.* 609 ὡς οὐ κρινοῦμαι τῶνδέ σοι τὰ πλείονα (with Page), and see KG I 636–7, Liapis on 778–9.

ηὗδον: 580–1n.

αὖθις ἐς κοίτην πάλιν: The same phrase fills the second half of *Alc.* 188.

780–8. The Charioteer's lively allegoric dream has a precedent in Rhesus' highly 'condensed' nightmare of Diomedes at *Il.* 10.494–7 ἀλλ' ὅτε δὴ βασιλῆα κιχήσατο Τυδέος υἱός, / τὸν τρεισκαιδέκατον μελιηδέα θυμὸν ἀπηύρα, / ἀσθμαίνοντα· κακὸν γὰρ ὄναρ κεφαλῆφιν ἐπέστη / τὴν νύκτ', Οἰνείδαο πάϊς, διὰ μῆτιν Ἀθήνης[279] and can likewise be regarded as synchronous with the events that caused it. Unlike the foreboding dreams of other tragedy therefore (*Pers.* 181–99, *Cho.* 32–6, 526–34, S. *El.* 417–25, *Hec.* 1–58, 68–91, *IT* 42–55 – all received by women),[280] its significance is limited to this single episode, where it helps to maintain the dire atmosphere of human half-knowledge and inefficiency (Strohm 271–2, R. Lennig, *Traum und Sinnestäuschung bei Aischylos, Sophokles, Euripides,* diss. Tübingen 1969, 313).

The animal symbolism, thinly disguising Odysseus and Diomedes as marauding wolves, takes up a whole series of allusions centring around Dolon's costume (201–23, 224–5, 543–5nn.; cf. S. H. Steadman, *CR* 59 [1945], 6–8, Burlando, *Reso,* 66–71 and, in general, West, *IEPM* 450–1), which eventually falls into his enemies' hands (591–3n.) and may be thought to transfer part of its nature to them. Given the ancient reputation of wolves as tricksters (201–23n.), it is hardly coincidence that both here and in *Hec.* [90–1] (above) Odysseus, the grandson of Autolycus, is represented by that beast.

780. δόξα τις παρίσταται is evidently meant to recall the Homeric στῆ δ' ἄρ' ὑπὲρ κεφαλῆς ... (*Il.* 2.20, 59, 23.68, 24.682, *Od.* 4.803,

---

[279] The lines have caused much confusion among scholars ancient and modern. A succinct account of their problems and likeliest interpretation (with reference to earlier works) is given by A. H. M. Kessels, *Studies in the Dream in Greek Literature,* diss. Utrecht 1973, 30–3.

[280] Much emphasis has been put on the observation that, while Iliadic dreamers are always male, structurally important dreams in the *Odyssey* and tragedy (see also *Eum.* 94–139 and *PV* 645–57) usually occur to women (W. S. Messer, *The Dream in Homer and Greek Tragedy,* New York 1918, 8, 27–8, 51, 65; cf. J. Hundt, *Der Traumglaube bei Homer,* Greifswald 1935, 42 n. 7). However, as Kessels (n. 279), 113–15 points out, the Homeric discrepancies can reasonably be ascribed to the different roles the sexes play in each poem, whereas hardly enough of Greek tragedy survives to judge whether our epic-based passage constitutes a remarkable deviation from the 'norm'.

6.21) and similar expressions used of dreams and related nocturnal apparitions, especially *Il.* 10.496–7 (780–8n.), *Od.* 20.93–4 δόκησε δέ οἱ κατὰ θυμόν / ἤδη γινώσκουσα παρεστάμεναι κεφαλῆφι, *Hec.* 30–1 νῦν δ' ὑπὲρ μητρὸς φίλης / Ἑκάβης ἀΐσσω and ἐπιστῆναι in e.g. Hdt. 1.34.1, 2.139.1, 2.141.3 and numerous later writers (LSJ s.v. ἐφίστημι B III 1; cf. E. R. Dodds, *The Greeks and the Irrational*, Berkeley 1951, 105–6 with nn. 17 and 18). Yet most, if not all, of these passages feature anthropomorphic dream-figures or deities (who can literally be said to stand at somebody's head or side), not complex symbolic dreams as here or at *Od.* 19.535–53. Further doubts as to the exact applicability of our phrase are aroused by the fact that in *OT* 911 we find δόξα μοι παρεστάθη with παρίσταμαι bearing its regular metaphorical meaning 'come to one's mind' (LSJ s.v. παρίστημι B IV; cf. Pl. *Phd.* 66b1–2 οὐκοῦν ἀνάγκη ... παρίστασθαι δόξαν τοιάνδε τινὰ τοῖς γνησίως φιλοσόφοις, ὥστε ...). From there our poet may have adapted the words, aided by their corresponding verse position and the changeable sense of δόξα, 'thought' and 'fancy, vision' (*Ag.* 274–5, 420–1, *Cho.* 1051, 1053).

781–3. 'For I saw, it seemed to me, as in a dream, (two) wolves, which had climbed onto the seats on the backs of the horses I tended and used to drive standing next to Rhesus.'

ἵππους ... ἑδραίαν ῥάχιν: The σχῆμα καθ' ὅλον καὶ μέρος is rare of animals (SD 81c). At *Il.* 16.467–8 ὁ δὲ Πήδασον οὔτασεν ἵππον / ἔγχεϊ δεξιὸν ὦμον and *Od.* 10.161 τὸν δ' (*sc.* ἔλαφον) ἐγὼ ἐκβαίνοντα κατὰ κνῆστιν μέσα νῶτα / πλῆξα (KG I 289–90) the deaths of the horse and stag are subsequently described in almost human terms (Janko on *Il.* 16.467–9, Heubeck on *Od.* 10.162–5).

γάρ: explanatory after a statement (780) equivalent to 'an expression denoting the giving ... of information' (284–6n.); similarly e.g. Hdt. 1.59.1 Ἱπποκράτεϊ γὰρ ἐόντι ἰδιώτῃ καὶ θεωρέοντι τὰ Ὀλύμπια τέρας ἐγένετο μέγα· θύσαντος γὰρ αὐτοῦ τὰ ἱρά ... and Pl. *Ap.* 40a2–5 ἐμοὶ γάρ, ὦ ἄνδρες δικασταί ... θαυμάσιόν τι γέγονεν. ἡ γὰρ εἰωθυῖά μοι μαντικὴ ἡ τοῦ δαιμονίου ... (*GP* 60).

ἅς: 185n.

ὡς ὄναρ δοκῶν: *sc.* ὁρᾶν. Cf. *Pers.* 188 (of the Queen's dream) ὡς ἐγὼ 'δόκουν ὁρᾶν, *Ag.* 423 εὖτ' ἂν ἐσθλά τις δοκῶν ὁρᾶν and, with adverbial ὄναρ (LSJ s.v. II), *Cyc.* 8 φέρ' ἴδω, τοῦτ' ἰδὼν ὄναρ λέγω; and *IT* 518 ὡς μήποτ' ὤφελόν γε μηδ' ἰδὼν ὄναρ. On Greeks 'seeing' rather than 'having' dreams see especially G. Björck, *Eranos* 44 (1946), 306–14 (311–14), Kessels (n. 279), 135–7, 138–43 and Arnott on Alexis fr. 274.1. δοκέω is even more common in this context (Garvie on *Cho.* 527).

ἐπεμβεβῶτας: of riders or (more often) warriors fighting from a chariot also e.g. [Hes.] *Sc.* 195 = 324 δίφρου ἐπεμβεβαώς, Pi. *Nem.* 4.29

ἡροάς τ' ἐπεμβεβαῶτας ἱπποδάμους and ἐπεμβάτης at E. *Suppl.* 585, 685, *Ba.* 782 (below) and, metaphorically, Anacr. fr. 417.6 *PMG*.

ἐπεμβαίνω, 'step upon, mount', usually governs a genitive or dative (LSJ s.v. I 1). The accusative here is unique in classical Greek,[281] although one may compare ἐμβαίνω, 'step into', at *Cyc.* 91–2 (οὐκ ἴσασι ...) ἄξενόν τε γῆν / τήνδ' ἐμβεβῶτες and *Hec.* 921–2 ναύταν ... ὅμιλον / Τροίαν Ἰλιάδ' ἐμβεβῶτα, as well as ἐπιβαίνω, 'mount', at [Hes.] *Sc.* 286 νῶθ' ἵππων ἐπιβάντες.

ἑδραίαν ῥάχιν: literally 'the spine that provides a seat (for the rider)'. ἑδραῖος (which in other poetry is found only at *Andr.* 266 and Ar. *Thesm.* 663/4, meaning 'seated'), does not recur in that sense. But ἡ ἕδρα τοῦ ἵππου is used in Xen. *Eq. Mag.* 4.1, *Eq.* 5.5 and 12.9 as a technical term for the horse's back that carries the rider, and if this was at all common, the adjective here, together with ἐπεμβεβῶτας (cf. *Ba.* 782 ἵππων τ' ... ταχυπόδων ἐπεμβάτας), may help to give the 'wolves' their strangely human touch.

784–6. 'And whipping the horses' furry hide with their tails, they drove them on, while the mares snorted, breathing forth rage from their nostrils, and threw their manes back (i.e. reared up) in panic.'

θείνοντε echoes the dual participles for Odysseus and Diomedes at 586 (585–6n.), 590, 591, 595 and 619. Note further in this speech 773 φῶτε περιπολοῦνθ' ἡμῶν στρατόν and 775 ἐπτηξάτην τε κἀνεχωρείτην πάλιν.

ῥινοῦ: here the skin of living animals, as in Hes. *Op.* 515 καί τε διὰ ῥινοῦ βοὸς ἔρχεται (*sc.* ὁ Βορέας) and [Hes.] *Sc.* 426–8 λέων ὣς σώματι κύρσας, / ὅς τε μάλ' ἐνδυκέως ῥινὸν κρατεροῖς ὀνύχεσσι / σχίσσας ὅττι τάχιστα μελίφρονα θυμὸν ἀπηύρα. This use of ῥινός is not found in Homer (LSJ s.v. II 1) and also apparently remained unpopular later.

αἳ δ': 185n.

ἔρρεγκον: The snorting of spirited or frightened horses is referred to in e.g. *Il.* 4.227 καὶ τοὺς μὲν θεράπων ἀπάνευθ' ἔχε φυσιόωντας, 16.506–7, *Sept.* 245 (~ S. *El.* 717), 461–4 and 475. But ῥέγκω, which normally means 'snore', rather belongs to the comic register (Ar. *Eq.* 103–4, 115, *Nub.* 5, 11, Eup. fr. 289 *PCG* – of an aulos mouth-piece) and elsewhere in tragedy occurs only at *Eum.* 53 ῥέγκουσι δ' οὐ πλατοῖσι φυσιάμασιν, where the Pythia is lost for words to describe the Erinyes

---

281 At *Ba.* 1061 ὄχθων δ' ἔπ' ἀμβὰς ἐς ἐλάτην ὑψαύχενα (ἔπ' ἀμβὰς Bruhn: ἐπ' ἐμβὰς P, ἐς Heath: εἰς P) the Aldine offers ὄχθον δ' ἐπέμβας, which could be fitted into the sentence by combination with Musgrave's and Tyrwhitt's ἢ 'λάτην. But Dodds (on 1061) rightly remarks that this is farther from the paradosis than Bruhn's proposal, and also accords less well with the topographical details given in 1048 and 1051–2.

in Apollo's temple (A. H. Sommerstein, in A. Willi [ed.], *The Language of Greek Comedy*, Oxford 2002, 160, 167).

Against Paley (on 785), the transmitted ἔρεγκον, corrected by Nauck (II¹ [1854], XXIII), cannot be justified by reference to Homeric ἔρεζον, ἐράπτομεν and the like, that is the epic and lyric[282] licence of writing ρ instead of ρρ after the augment or in composition when a short syllable is required by metre.

ἐξ ἀρτηριῶν: perhaps ἀπὸ κοινοῦ with ἔρρεγκον as well as θυμὸν πνέουσαι (cf. Σ^VL *Rh.* 785 [II 342.5, 29–30 Schwartz = 112 Merro] ἐκ τῶν μυκτήρων ποιὸν ἦχον ἀπετέλουν). On the basis of *Tr.* 1054–5 πλεύμονός τ' ἀρτηρίας / ῥοφεῖ ξυνοικοῦν (i.e. the Nessus-shirt 'devouring' Heracles' 'bronchial tubes'), Musgrave (on 787) wrote ἀρτηριῶν, 'windpipes', which can easily be extended to denote the horses' nostrils. The MSS' ἀντηρίδων is most unlikely to be right. But those who wish to defend it will have to derive it from ἀντῆρις (not ἀντηρίς as in LSJ s.v. II),[283] a synonym of θυρίς, 'window', attested only in *Suda* α 2648 Adler (s.v. ἀντήρεις).

θυμὸν πνέουσαι: 'breathing rage', for which cf. *Ba.* 620 (of Pentheus) θυμὸν ἐκπνέων, *Sept.* 52–3 σιδηρόφρων γὰρ θυμὸς ... / ἔπνει λεόντων ὣς ἄρη δεδορκότων, *Phoen.* 454 θυμοῦ πνοάς and Ar. *Ran.* 1016–17 ἀλλὰ πνέοντας ... θυμοὺς ἑπταβοείους. These and similar expressions like κότον or μένος πνεῖν (*Cho.* 33, 952, *Eum.* 840–1 = 873–4, S. *El.* 610) go back to the Homeric μένεα / μένος πνείοντες (e.g. *Il.* 2.536, *Od.* 22.203) and may originate in a belief that connected emotion with the act of breathing (R. B. Onians, *The Origins of European Thought* ..., Cambridge 1951 = ²1954, 49–50, 53–6, Dodds on *Ba.* 620, Mastronarde on *Phoen.* 454 and, for further literature, Liapis on 784–6).

κἀνεχαίτιζον φόβῳ: With intransitive ἔρρεγκον preceding and no object expressed, the sense 'and threw back their manes (i.e. reared up) in panic' is more natural than Paley's '... tried to shake them off ...', for which he compared Pentheus on his fir-tree at *Ba.* 1072 ... φυλάσσων μὴ ἀναχαιτίσειέ νιν. By a curious coincidence, the (secondary) transitive of ἀναχαιτίζω seems only to occur in various metaphorical senses (LSJ s.v. I 2 with Suppl. [1996]). Contrast, of horses, D. H. 5.15.2 καὶ τοὺς

---

282 E.g. Pi. *Pyth.* 4.178, 6.37, *Ai.* 134 (recitative anapaests), *Ant.* 950, *Ba.* 154, 568. More Pindaric examples are listed in P. Maas, *Epidaurische Hymnen* (SKGG 9.5), Halle/Saale 1933, 10 with n. 5 and H. Maehler (ed.), *Pindari Carmina cum Fragmentis, Pars II. Fragmenta. Indices*, Leipzig 1989, 188.

283 The words are rightly distinguished by A. K. Orlandos – I. N. Travlos, Λεξικὸν Ἀρχαίων Ἀρχιτεκτονικῶν Ὅρων, Athens 1986, since whereas ἀντηρίς is related to ἀντερείδω (hence properly 'stay, support'), ἀντῆρις must be a substantival feminine of ἀντήρης, expanding on the sense 'opposite, facing' (i.e. the street).

ἐπιβάτας ἀναχαιτίσαντες ἀποσείονται and 12.5.2 ὃς ἀναχαιτίσας ῥιπτεῖ τὸν ἐπιβάτην.

Reiske's φόβην (*Animadversiones*, 91), probably intended to remove the repetition with φόβος in 788, would give the sentence a rather weak ending. The construction, however, has good, if late, parallels in Hld. 2.35.1 (of a confident young man) ὀρθὸς τὸν αὐχένα καὶ ἀπὸ τοῦ μετώπου τὴν κόμην πρὸς τὸ ὄρθιον ἀναχαιτίζων and Philostr. *Her*. 31.1 (of Ajax Locrus) καὶ ἀναχαιτίζων τὴν κομήν (cf. Liapis, 'Notes', 92).

787–8. Homeric sleepers usually awake immediately after the 'departure' of the dream: e.g. *Il*. 2.41, *Od*. 4.839–40, 6.48–9 (cf. E. Lévy, *Ktèma* 7 [1982], 26–7). To the Charioteer this happens quite realistically through fear and, as with Achilles trying to embrace Patroclus' ghost (*Il*. 23.99–102), his active efforts to fend off the 'wolves'. See Messer (n. 280), 15–16 with n. 48, 97–8.

ἔννυχος γὰρ ἐξώρμα φόβος: Platnauer (*Eranos* 62 [1964], 73), missing an accusative object with ἐξώρμα (as in e.g. *Pers*. 45–6, *IT* 1437, Ar. *Thesm*. 659, Thuc. 6.6.2), wished to read δέ μ' for γάρ. But the ellipsis is nothing out of the ordinary and has an almost exact parallel in Pl. *Pol*. 294e5–7 διὸ δή γε καὶ ἴσους πόνους νῦν διδόντες ἀθρόοις, ἅμα μὲν ἐξορμῶσιν, ἅμα δὲ καὶ καταπαύουσι δρόμου καὶ πάλης καὶ πάντων τῶν κατὰ τὰ σώματα πόνων.

For ἔννυχος ... φόβος in relation to a nightmare cf. *Cho*. 32–5, 288 μάταιος ἐκ νυκτῶν φόβος, 929, fr. tr. adesp. 626.37 [φό]βος τις ... δεῖμά τ' ἔννυχον and also *Cho*. 523–4 ἔκ τ' ὀνειράτων / καὶ νυκτιπλάγκτων δειμάτων (with Garvie on 523–5), S. *El*. 410 ἐκ δείματός του νυκτέρου (with Finglass) and *Hec*. 69–70 τί ποτ' αἴρομαι ἔννυχος οὕτω / δείμασι φάσμασιν;

789. 'And when I lifted my head, I heard the moans of dying men.'

The verse presumably represents a combination of *Il*. 10.483–4 τῶν δὲ στόνος ὤρνυτ' ἀεικής / ἄορι θεινομένων and 10.519–21 ὃ δ' (Hippocoon) ἐξ ὕπνου ἀνορούσας, / ὡς ἴδε χῶρον ἐρῆμον ... / ἄνδράς τ' ἀσπαίροντας ἐν ἀργαλέῃσι φονῇσιν (Ritchie 77) and may itself have inspired Verg. *Aen*. 9.332–3 *tum caput ipsi aufert domino truncumque relinquit / sanguine singultantem* (Introduction, 45).

ἐπάρας κρᾶτα: Cf. *Hec*. 499–500 ἀνίστασ' ... καὶ μετάρσιον / πλευρὰν ἔπαιρε καὶ τὸ πάλλευκον κάρα, E. *Suppl*. 289 ἔπαιρε λευκὸν κρᾶτα ... and *Tro*. 98–9 ἄνα, δύσδαιμον· πεδόθεν κεφαλὴν / ἐπάειρε δέρην <τ'>. In this form and context, however, the phrase particularly recalls Nestor roused by Agamemnon at *Il*. 10.80 ὀρθωθεὶς δ' ἄρ' ἐπ' ἀγκῶνος, κεφαλὴν ἐπαείρας (7n.).

μυχθισμόν: a very rare word, which basically seems to have denoted a forced passage of air through the nostrils: Hp. *Coac*. 509 τὰ μετὰ μυχθισμοῦ ἔξω ἀναφερομένα πνεύματα, 529 μυχθῶδες ... πνεῦμα,

Eust. 440.22–5 (on *Il.* 4.20 αἳ δ' ἐπέμυξαν Ἀθηναίη τε καὶ Ἥρη), 1965.48–50 (on *Od.* 24.416 μυχμῷ). From there the step to 'moan, groan' is not far: Σ^V *Rh.* 789 (II 342.6–7 Schwartz = 112 a¹ Merro) ποιὸν ἦχον καὶ στεναγμὸν μετὰ πνοῆς γινόμενον; cf. e.g. *PV* 742–3 (Ἰώ) ἰώ μοί μοι, ἐέ. / (Πρ.) σὺ δ' αὖ κέκραγας κἀναμυχθίζῃ, *Eum.* 117–20 (Χο.) 'μυγμός' / (Κλ.) μύζοιτ' ἄν ... / (Χο.) 'μυγμός' (with Sommerstein on 117), D. S. 17.11.5, 17.92.3 (of wounded men or a dog). But a connotation of 'the laboured breathing of those who cannot rightly be described either as living or as dead' (A. C. Pearson, *CQ* 11 [1917], 61) probably remained.

νεκρῶν: of dying men, as in Antipho 2.4.5 νεκροῖς ἀσπαίρουσι συντυχόντα and perhaps Thuc. 2.52.2 ... ἀλλὰ καὶ νεκροὶ ἐπ' ἀλλήλοις ἀποθνῄσκοντες ἔκειντο καὶ ἐν ταῖς ὁδοῖς ἐκαλινδοῦντο καὶ περὶ τὰς κρήνας ἁπάσας ἡμιθνῆτες τοῦ ὕδατος ἐπιθυμίᾳ (where Gomme's <καὶ> before ἀποθνῄσκοντες deserves consideration).

790–1. 'And a warm jet of fresh blood hit me from the slaughter of my master, who was dying in agony.'

Ritchie (77) may be right in tracing the idea for κρουνὸς ... αἵματος νέου to *Il.* 10.484 ἐρυθαίνετο δ' αἵματι γαῖα, but above all we find here a combined echo of Clytaemestra's gloating words over Agamemnon's dead body at *Ag.* 1389–90 κἀκφυσιῶν ὀξεῖαν αἵματος σφαγήν / βάλλει μ' ἐρεμνῇ ψακάδι φοινίας δρόσου and the Messenger's description of the dying Aegisthus at E. *El.* 842–3 πᾶν δὲ σῶμ' ἄνω κάτω / ἤσπαιρεν ἠλέλιζε δυσθνῄσκων φόνῳ (ἠλέλιζε Schenkl: ἠλάλαζεν L, δυσθνῄσκων Paley: -θνῆσκον L). Apart from the presumably interrelated similarity of language and context, however, no special point is recognisable in this piquant juxtaposition, while Sophocles in his adaptation of *Ag.* 1389–90 at *Ant.* 1238–9 καὶ φυσιῶν ὀξεῖαν ἐκβάλλει ῥοήν / λευκῇ παρειᾷ φοινίου σταλάγματος skilfully retained some of the distorted overtones for Haemon's and Antigone's 'bloody marriage' (J. L. Moles, *LCM* 4 [1979], 179–89, A. H. Sommerstein, in A. Willi [ed.], *The Language of Greek Comedy*, Oxford 2002, 154).

θερμὸς ... κρουνὸς ... αἵματος νέου: Cf. *Hec.* 566–8 ὃ δ' οὐ θέλων τε καὶ θέλων οἴκτῳ κόρης / τέμνει σιδήρῳ πνεύματος διαρροάς· / κρουνοὶ δ' ἐχώρουν.

δεσπότου παρὰ σφαγῆς: Musgrave (on 792). A genitive is needed, since the transmitted δεσπότου παρὰ σφαγαῖς would almost certainly have to be taken with με ('And a warm jet of newly-shed blood strikes me, [as I lay] close to my slaughtered master ...' [Paley]) and thus require a participle like κείμενον to clarify the connection. Hermann's δεσπότου πάρα (*Opuscula* III, 308) with σφαγαῖς ... αἵματος νέου going together as 'slaughters (i.e. spurts) of fresh blood' has the seeming advantage of bringing sense and syntax even closer to *Ag.* 1389–90 (cf. Denniston–

Page on 1389, A. Meschini, in *Scritti Diano*, 224–6), but doubts are cast on this conjecture by the fact that, except at verse-end, with ὑπέρ and forms in -αι, postposition of un-elided disyllabic prepositions is unexampled in Greek tragic trimeters (Denniston on E. *El.* 574).

δυσθνῄσκοντος: borrowed from E. *El.* 843 δυσθνῄσκων (above). The word contradicts analogy, since verbs of this type are usually formed from a corresponding compound noun or adjective and end in -έω (KB II 260, 336–7 with n. 2, Schwyzer 726). Yet the adjectival nature of the participle may soften the incongruity (cf. Fraenkel, *Rev.* 231, with earlier literature), as supposedly also in formations like *Pers.* 574 δυσβάϋκτον (724n.) and Hsch. δ 2671 Latte δυστοπάζοντες· δυσχερῶς ὑπονοήσαντες.

Euripides himself may have got δυσθνῄσκων from Aeschylus, if Enger was right to read δυσθνῄσκουσα (for συν-) at *Ag.* 819–20 ... δυσθνῄσκουσα δέ / σποδὸς προπέμπει πίονας πλούτου πνοάς. The conjecture much improves the sense of the passage and has been adopted by Page and Sommerstein.

792. ὀρθὸς δ' ἀνᾴσσω: Cf. *Od.* 21.118–19 (of Telemachus) ἦ, καὶ ἀπ' ὤμοιϊν χλαῖναν θέτο φοινικόεσσαν / ὀρθὸς ἀναΐξας, ἀπὸ δὲ ξίφος ὀξὺ θέτ' ὤμων, *Hel.* 1600–1 ὀρθοὶ δ' ἀνῇξαν πάντες, οἳ μὲν ἐν χεροῖν / κορμοὺς ἔχοντες ναυτικούς, οἳ δὲ ξίφη, *Phoen.* 1460 ἀνῇξε δ' ὀρθὸς λαὸς εἰς ἔριν λόγων and *Ba.* 692–3 αἳ δ' ἀποβαλοῦσαι θαλερὸν ὀμμάτων ὕπνον / ἀνῇξαν ὀρθαί. In each case the movement initiates vigorous (and often decisive) action, whereas all the Charioteer manages is to receive a serious blow (Liapis on 792).

χειρὶ σὺν κενῇ δορός: a natural consequence of the disarray in which the Thracians kept their equipment (765–6).

The genitive is usual with κενός (LSJ s.v. II 1, KG I 401–2; cf. especially *Or.* 688–9 ἥκω γὰρ ἀνδρῶν συμμάχων κενὸν δόρυ / ἔχων), but there appears to be no other example of a preposition standing between its noun, an attribute *and* another substantive depending on the latter.

793–5a. 'And while I was peering around and looking for a weapon, a man in his prime stood beside me and struck me in the lower flank with his sword.'

αὐγάζοντα: In most case αὐγάζω / -ομαι means 'see distinctly' or 'look upon' (LSJ s.v. I; cf. West on Hes. *Op.* 478: 'I suppose the essential idea is 'fix the gaze on' a particular object'), but the sense required here can perhaps be derived from a 'conative' force of the present participle: 'And as I strove to catch sight of my spear ...' (Porter on 793–4). In fifth-century tragedy, the verb is largely, if not exclusively, lyric (*Phil.* 217–18, *Hec.* 637, *Hel.* 1317, *Ba.* 596; S. fr. 659.6 [3ia] is dubious), although later its use was extended to iambic trimeters (Lyc. 71, 941, 1082) and even prose.

παίει παραστάς ... ξίφει was presumably suggested by *Il.* 10.489 ὅν τινα Τυδείδης ἄορι πλήξασκε παραστάς (Ritchie 77). One may also compare Rhoetus' violent death in Verg. *Aen.* 9.347–8 *pectore in adverso totum cui comminus ensem / condidit adsurgenti et multa morte recepit* (Porter on 793–4; cf. Introduction, 45).

νεῖραν ἐς πλευράν: so Bothe (3 [1824], 366) for the unmetrical νείαιραν ἐς πλευράν (Ω), to which, unlike Pierson's νειάτην πλευράν (*Moeridis Atticistae Lexicon Atticum*, Leiden 1759, 268; cf. *Chr. Pat.* 1213 νύσσει παραστὰς νειάτην πλευρὰν ξίφει) or Dobree's νείατ' ἐς πλευρά (*Adversaria* II [1833], 88 = IV [1874], 85), it could easily have been corrupted under epic influence (below). νεῖρα is a unique contraction of the old feminine adjective νείαιρα (Schwyzer 475, 503)[284] and appropriately applied to the lower area of the trunk: cf. *Il.* 5.857 νείατον ἐς κενεῶνα, the standard νείαιρα γαστήρ for 'abdomen' in Homer (*Il.* 5.539, 616, 16.465, 17.519) and the Hippocratic corpus, and also νείαιρα alone at Hp. *Coac.* 579, Call. *Aet.* fr. 43.15 Harder and perhaps Nic. *Alex.* 20 (Gow–Scholfield on 19 ff.). Another interesting parallel exists in Hp. *Int.* 27 τάδε οὖν πάσχει· ἐς τὸ ἧπαρ ὀδύνη ὀξέη ἐμπίπτει, καὶ ὑπὸ τὰς νεάτας πλευρὰς (the lowest ribs) καὶ ἐς τὸν ὦμον ... (dated to 400/390 BC by J. Jouanna, *Hippocrate. Pour une archéologie de l'école de Cnide*, Paris 1974, 513).

ἀνὴρ ἀκμάζων: similarly *Pers.* 441 Περσῶν ὅσοιπερ ἦσαν ἀκμαῖοι φύσιν and *Sept.* 10–11 καὶ τὸν ἐλλείποντ' ἔτι / ἥβης ἀκμαίας. The verb ἀκμάζω (often in the present participle) is otherwise confined to prose, apart from its impersonal use at *Sept.* 98 ἀκμάζει βρετέων ἔχεσθαι and *Cho.* 726/7 νῦν γὰρ ἀκμάζει Πειθὼ δολία<ν> ξυγκαταβῆναι.

795b–6. 'For I felt the blow of his sword, as I received the deep furrow of my wound.'

φασγάνου ... / πληγῆς: Cf. *Andr.* 1074–5 (of Neoptolemus) τοιάσδε φασγάνων πληγὰς ἔχει / Δελφῶν ὑπ' ἀνδρῶν καὶ Μυκηναίου ξένου. Compared to other tragedy, Euripides was exceedingly fond of φάσγανον (Liapis on 795–6).

γάρ explains ἀκμάζων: 'I call him so because ...' (609b–10n.).

βαθεῖαν ἄλοκα τραύματος: Essentially the same metaphor appears in *Cho.* 25 ὄνυχος ἄλοκι νεοτόμῳ, whereas *HF* 164 δορὸς ταχεῖαν ἄλοκα, adduced as the primary parallel by Ritchie (211), is more likely to designate a 'swathe' cut into hoplite ranks by the enemy spears (Bond

---

[284] Wellauer's νείρᾳ (after Portus' νείρῃ) at *Ag.* 1479 ἐκ τοῦ γὰρ ἔρως αἱματολοιχὸς †νείρει† τρέφεται(·) is very uncertain (Denniston–Page on 1477–80, West, *Studies,* 222), and Hsch. ν 245 Latte νειραί· κατωτάται. οἳ δὲ κοιλίας τὰ κατώτατα belongs to a secondary adjective (cf. Hsch. ν 246 Latte νειρὴ κοιλίη· κοιλία ἐσχάτη) attested also in the masculine (Lyc. 896) and neuter (Hsch. ν 247 Latte νειρόν· σφοδρόν. ἔσχατον).

on 164, taking up Wilamowitz' reaping imagery). βαθεῖαν ἄλοκα here most probably goes back to the famous *Sept.* 593–4 (of Amphiaraus) βαθεῖαν ἄλοκα διὰ φρενὸς καρπούμενος, / ἐξ ἧς τὰ κεδνὰ βλαστάνει βουλεύματα (cf. Pl. *Rep.* 362a8–b1 and West's extensive testimonial apparatus).

797–8. πίπτω δὲ πρηνής: 'And I fell on my face', an epic juncture unique in tragedy, which is normally used of warriors being wounded or falling in battle: e.g. *Il.* 6.306–7 ἄξον δὴ ἔγχος Διομήδεος, ἠδὲ καὶ αὐτόν / πρηνέα δὸς πεσέειν, 12.395–6, 16.378–9, 17.300, [Hes.] *Sc.* 365 (*LfgrE* s.v. πρηνής B 1a). It is thus ironically at odds with the Charioteer's ineffectual efforts (cf. 756–803n.).

ὄχημα πωλικόν / ... ἵππων belongs together, despite the tautologous accumulation of attributes (e.g. Paley on 797, Fraenkel, *Rev.* 237–8). For ὄχημα, 'team', see 620b–1n. and especially Tim. *Pers.* fr. 791.190–1 *PMG* = Hordern τετρά<ορ>ον ἱπ- / πων ὄχημ'.

ἵεσαν φυγῇ πόδα: 203n. Comparable expressions for flight appear in *OT* 467–9 ὥρα νιν ἀελλάδων / ἵππων σθεναρώτερον / φυγᾷ πόδα νωμᾶν, E. *Suppl.* 718 ... ἔτρεψαν ἐς φυγὴν πόδα, *Ba.* 436–7 ὁ θὴρ δ' ὅδ' ἡμῖν πρᾷος οὐδ' ὑπέσπασεν / φυγῇ πόδ' and E. fr. 495.32–3 [κἀντεῦ]θεν ἡμεῖς ... / [κοῦφον] πόδ' ἄλλος ἄλλοσ' εἴχομεν φυγῇ.

799. ἆ ἆ / ὀδύνη με τείρει: a slight variation of 749–50 ἆ ἆ ἆ ἆ, / οἵα μ' ὀδύνη τείρει (747–9, 750–1a nn.), with another, contextually more neutral, epicism after 797 (797–8n.). For the structural meaning of the repetition see 756–803n.

κοὐκέτ' ὀρθοῦμαι τάλας: Cf. *Phil.* 820 τὸ γὰρ κακὸν τόδ' οὐκέτ' ὀρθοῦσθαί μ' ἐᾷ, where Kamerbeek (on 819, 20) sees an ambiguity between ὀρθοῦμαι, 'to rise / stand upright' and 'to be restored to health'.

800–2a. The Guard in *Antigone* shows a similar lack of knowledge regarding the 'perpetrator' of Polynices' first burial: *Ant.* 238–9 τὸ γὰρ / πρᾶγμ' οὔτ' ἔδρασ' οὔτ' εἶδον ὅστις ἦν ὁ δρῶν (cf. 245–7, 248–9, 252). If he and his comrades were inattentive or asleep, no such hint is given before 411–14 (Griffith on 253), and the uncanny nature of the nocturnal event (249–58) even leads the coryphaeus to suspect divine intervention (278–9, with Griffith's note and his comments on 256, 376–440, 421). Yet in contrast to *Rhesus* (and *Iliad* 10), this is always left unclear to characters and audience alike, which creates tension and depth beyond the two reports.

τρόπῳ δ' ὅτῳ / τεθνᾶσιν οἱ θανόντες οὐκ ἔχω φράσαι: almost a parody on the classical messenger speech, which is precisely concerned with *how* things came to pass and often triggered by a πῶς-question (282–3n.).

οὐκ ἔχω φράσαι (cf. 659 ... οὐκ ἔχει φράσαι) is a rather frequent verse-end in Euripides (*Hcld.* 669, *Ion* 540 [4 tr_∧], 803) and comedy (Ar.

Ran. 60, *Eccl.* 333; cf. Alexis fr. 222.7 *PCG* … οὐκ ἔχοιμ' ἄν <σοι> φράσαι, Men. *Peric.* 333 … οὐκ ἔχω τουτὶ φράσαι). Its plain, matter-of-fact tone (e.g. Hdt. 4.53.5 μούνου δὲ τούτου τοῦ ποταμοῦ καὶ Νείλου οὐκ ἔχω φράσαι τὰς πηγάς, δοκέω δέ, οὐδὲ οὐδεὶς Ἑλλήνων, *Tr.* 401 Εὐβοιίς· ὧν δ' ἔβλαστεν οὐκ ἔχω λέγειν) here exemplifies the abrupt reversal from the colourful, poetic narrative of the Thracian disaster.

802b–3. The final remark, foreshadowed in 777 (776–7n.), prepares for the Charioteer's more serious charges against Hector in 833–55, 866–7, 873 and 875–6. Again there is a parallel with *Ant.* 259–67, where in their first surprise and fear the guards accuse each other of having performed the funeral rites for Polynices.

εἰκάσαι δέ μοι / πάρεστι: 284n.

804–81. No sooner has the coryphaeus rejected the Charioteer's allegation (804–5) than Hector returns, with bitter reproaches against the sentries who let the spies slip by (808–19). After the chorus' lyric defence (820–32), Hector in turn is accused of having planned the attack out of desire for Rhesus' horses (833–55). Unable to convince the Charioteer that Odysseus may be the culprit, he nevertheless has him led to his palace for care (856–81).

This second *agon* scene after 388–526 (388–526, 388–453, 467–526nn.) has been much criticised, both for appearing dramatically superfluous (G. Björck, *Arctos* n.s. 1 [1954], 17–18, *Eranos* 55 [1957], 16–17, H. D. F. Kitto, *YCS* 25 [1977], 341; cf. Ritchie 93–4) and its supposedly bad stage management regarding the Charioteer (e.g. F. Hagenbach, *De Rheso Tragoedia*, diss. Basel 1863, 25, Burnett, 'Smiles', 35; cf. Ritchie 131–2). Unusually indeed, the 'victim-messenger' (who must have collapsed for the moment at 799) does not exit upon delivering his speech to the chorus, but stays on to engage in further conversation with Hector. In this he particularly resembles the Phrygian in *Or.* 1506–36, while the fact that he gives a new turn to the plot brings him closer to the Idaean Shepherd (264–341n.) and the Old Man in *Trachiniae*, who recedes into the background after 180–99, waiting to offer his fateful assistance in 335–496 (Taplin, *Stagecraft*, 89, J. P. Poe, *Philologus* 148 [2004], 24–5 with n. 20).[285]

The entire parallel, yet chiastic, pair of disputes is centred on Hector in his successive functions of accuser and accused. Unlike the situation confronting him, he has not changed at all (808–19n.) and thus throws

---

285 Other 'lingering' messengers like the Old Servant in *Hel.* 597–624 + 700–60 (with Kannicht on 597–760) or the Argive in E. *Suppl.* 634–777 (Strohm 269 with nn. 3, 4) do not play a dramatic role either. The Pedagogue in S. *El.* 660–803 is a special case of an established character delivering a 'fake message'.

into even sharper relief the human characters' limitations of judgement. In fact neither his nor the Charioteer's charges lack a core of truth (808–19, 833–81nn.), but compared to the Muse's superior knowledge they remain weak attempts at interpreting the events, which serve to illustrate the persisting confusion and, in a mirror-image of the quarrel between Hector and Rhesus, the disintegration of the Trojan and allied forces (Strohm 262, 264–5, G. Paduano, *SCO* 23 [1974], 28–30; cf. Ritchie 131–2). From this latter perspective we may understand the Charioteer's premature removal (877–81) as a means not only to preserve medical realism and prevent the audience from dividing their sympathy between him and the grieving Muse (Ritchie 131), but also to leave a bitter note by making the suspicion that Hector killed for gain live on in one man (Burnett, 'Smiles', 35; cf. Rosivach 71–2 on Hector's real part in the causal chain that led to Rhesus' death).

Hector's return presents the only really puzzling staging-problem in *Rhesus*. For it is unclear how he learnt of the Thracian disaster (806–7) and indeed from which direction he arrives. By convention it should be the *eisodos* leading to the Thracian camp (i.e. where he left at 526), but this would suggest that he was present when Rhesus and his comrades were killed. Perhaps, therefore, our poet had him re-enter from the other side, inviting his audience to think that in the meantime Hector had gone back to the Trojans. In view of the undefined backstage area (Introduction, 40–1, 'Scene and Setting', 114), this seems to be the lesser inconsistency, although doubts about such a step remain.[286] See also Liapis, xli and on 808 ff.

804–5. 'Charioteer of the Thracian who has fared so ill, do not distress yourself. The enemy has done that.'

ἡνίοχε: the only 'first-foot dactyl' in *Rhesus*. Cf. Ritchie 265–6, 268, who with Zieliński (*Tragodumenon libri tres* II, Cracow 1925, 145) regards ἡνίοχε as 'almost equivalent to a proper name' and thus liable to create an exception.

τοῦ κακῶς πεπραγότος: another apparently Euripidean verse-end: *Alc.* 246 ὁρᾷ σε κἀμέ, δύο κακῶς πεπραγότας, 961, *Tro.* 608 ... τοῖς κακῶς πεπραγόσιν, E. frr. 81.1, 130.1, 165.1, 957. Similarly also E. fr. 908b.1 ὦ δυστυχεῖν φύς καὶ κακῶς πεπραγέναι, *HF* 707 (~ *Or.* 87) ἄναξ, διώκεις μ' ἀθλίως πεπραγότα and, paratragic, Ar. *Nub.* 1269 ἄλλως τε μέντοι καὶ κακῶς πεπραγότι, *Pax* 1255 οἴμ', ὦ κρανοποί', ὡς ἀθλίως πεπράγαμεν.

---

[286] According to Arist. *Poet.* 1455a26–9, a play by Carcinus II was 'hissed off' the stage because of some contradiction in a character's movements. Cf. *TrGF* I, 211–12.

μηδὲν δυσοίζου: On the most probable etymology and original sense of δυσοίζω (< οἴζω, 'to give a cry of distress / dismay') see 724n. If one of the corrections for the second verse-half (below) is correct, something like 'do not utter such accusations' might be expected here. However, the vulgate 'do not distress yourself' is perhaps easier to justify on the assumption that the middle shifted part of the emphasis from the 'physical activity (of crying out)' to the emotional state of the subject (KG I 102–3), as possibly in S. fr. 269c.47 (*Inachus*) οἴζομαι λα . . . . ριμ[in a context of fear.[287] Other, less dynamic middles of onomatopoeic verbs in –ζω occur in *Ag.* 1236–7 ὡς δ᾽ ἐπωλολύξατο / ἡ παντότολμος, S. fr. 534.5–7 τομάς, / ἃς ἥδε βοῶσ᾽ ἀλαλαζομένη (ὀλολυζομένη Ellendt) / γυμνὴ χαλκέοις ἧμα δρεπάνοις, *Ba.* 67 Βάκ- / χιον εὐαζομένα and 592–3 Βρόμιος <ὅδ᾽> ἀλα- / λάζεται στέγας ἔσω.

πολέμιοι ''δρασαν τάδε: If we assume the corruption lies here and not with δυσοίζου, as e.g. Valckenaer (*Diatribe*, 108–9) and Musgrave (on 808) suspected, Murray's emendation of πολεμίους δρᾶσαι (Ω) is superior to Lenting's πολέμιοι δρῶσιν (*Animadversiones*, 76), which in the absence of any nearby past-tense or temporal adverb / conjunction to indicate a historic present (KG I 132–4, SD 271–2) could only be taken as 'present for perfect': 'the enemies are the doers' (cf. Feickert on 804). Yet doubt is cast on ''δρασαν by the fact that neither tragedy nor comedy offer certain examples of prodelided ε after -οι, except in the exclamation οἲ 'γώ (M. Platnauer, *CQ* n.s. 10 [1960], 142).[288] Alternatively, one may consider unaugmented δρᾶσαν (West) as a deliberate epicism or 'Aeschyleism' outside a messenger speech. Cf. 811 (810b–12a n.) ἐξαπώσατε and perhaps *Cho.* 930 κάνες τὸν οὐ χρῆν (κάνες γ᾽ ὄν M: ἔκανες ὄν vel γ᾽ ὄν Pauw).

The accusative and infinitive was an easy error on the analogy of 724–5 – δυσοίζων ... / – τί δρᾶσαι; ... (cf. Porter on 805). Zanetto retains it, believing after Σ^Q *Rh.* 805 (112 Merro) δυσοίζου· ὑπόπτευε that

---

[287] Hsch. δ 2622 Latte †δύσοιο· φοβοῦ, which in view of the wrongly transmitted δυσοίζου for δυσοίζοντος (Schmidt, δυσοίζυος vel δυσοιζο<μέν>ου Latte) in the preceding lemma may conceal a reference to our line, is of little evidential value, since the explanation (cf. Hsch. δ 2620 Latte) could also have been deduced from *Ag.* 1316 οὔτοι δυσοίζω θάμνον ὡς ὄρνις φόβῳ (724n.). Moreover, the other glosses on the active in Hsch. δ 2619, 2620, 2621 and ε 537 Latte (δυσχεραίνω, ὑπονοέω, ὑποπτεύω, οἰωνίζομαι) seem to betray confusion with the stem of οἴομαι (*GEW*, *DELG* s.v.).

[288] *Pers.* 310 νικώμενοι κύρισσον ἰσχυρὰν χθόνα and 490–1 ἔνθα δὴ πλεῖστοι θάνον / δίψῃ τε λιμῷ τ᾽ would testify to the contrary only if, like Diggle in the case of prodelision after -ει and -αι (*Euripidea*, 56 n. 7, 61), we strictly applied the rule of Lautensach (*Augment*, 166–8) and Page (on *Med.* 1141) that in tragic messenger speeches the syllabic augment is hardly ever omitted save at the beginning of a line. But no recent editor of Aeschylus, not even Page himself, has done so.

μηδὲν δυσοίζου could bear the sense of πίστευε. But the gloss is simply based on the lexicographical tradition (n. 287).

806–7. συμφορᾶς πεπυσμένος: For the genitive of the thing heard cf. *Il.* 15.224 μάλα γάρ κε μάχης ἐπύθοντο καὶ ἄλλοι, S. *El.* 35 χρῆ μοι τοιαῦθ' ὁ Φοῖβος ὧν πεύσῃ τάχα, Lyc. 821 ... κληδόνων πεπυσμένος (KG I 358 with n. 5, SD 107 ε) and, of indirect perception (as here), *Od.* 13.256 πυνθανόμην Ἰθάκης, 14.321 ἔνθ' Ὀδυσῆος ἐγὼ πυθόμην and *Ant.* 1182 κλυοῦσα παιδός (KG I 360–1 n. 9 b, SD 106 β). The accusatives συμφοράς (Lenting, *Animadversiones*, 76) or συμφοράν (Wecklein) would give the regular construction, as in e.g. *Ag.* 261 σὺ δ' εἴ τι κεδνὸν εἴτε μὴ πεπυσμένη, 1098–9 and *Tr.* 141–2 (KG I 360 n. 8, SD 106–7 δ).

χωρεῖ: On the verb of motion at the beginning of the second (or third) line of an entrance announcement see 85–6n. With χωρέω also S. *El.* 1432, *Tr.* 870 and *Phoen.* 444.

συναλγεῖ δ' ... σοῖς κακοῖς: Cf. *PV* 288 ταῖς σαῖς δὲ τύχαις, ἴσθι, συναλγῶ and Moschio *TrGF* 97 F 9.10 τύχαις συναλγῶν (LSJ s.v. συναλγέω I 3).

808–19. With Hector's outburst the sentries finally get the censure they anticipated in 722–7 and, in a different context, tried to avoid by the very action that opened the camp to the Achaean attack: 49–51 (n.) σοὶ δ', ὑποπτεύων τὸ μέλλον, / ἤλυθον ἄγγελος ὡς / μήποτέ τιν' ἐς ἐμὲ μέμψιν εἴπῃς (cf. 820–32, 821–3nn.). Hector's accusations, like his own later identification of Odysseus as the culprit (861–5), are thus partly justified and will remain unchallenged when the Charioteer interrupts at 833.

Throughout the speech Hector gives his old impression of a rash, at times inconsiderate commander (Introduction, 20), who far from showing the expected sympathy for the Charioteer (807) is mainly concerned with the shame he and all Trojans will incur from the enemy: 808–10 (...) λήθουσιν αἰσχρῶς, 814–15 (n.), 819 τὸ μηδὲν καὶ κακόν (Rosivach 68 with nn. 40, 41). In this futile appeal to heroic standards, however, the allies are united (cf. 765–803n.) so as to create an ever more lasting image of human failure and defeat.

808–10a. 'You, who brought about the greatest calamities, how did the enemy spies slip past you unobserved, to your disgrace ...'

μέγιστα πήματ' ἐξειργασμένοι: Cf. *Hcld.* 959–60 (of Eurystheus) χρῆν γὰρ οὐχ ἅπαξ / θνῄσκειν σε πολλὰ πήματ' ἐξειργασμένον and *Pers.* 785–6 ἅπαντες ἡμεῖς ... / οὐκ ἂν φανεῖμεν πήματ' ἔρξαντες τόσα.

πολεμίων κατάσκοποι: 125–6a n.

λήθουσιν: resultative present (literally: 'Why did the enemy spies remain unseen ...?'), as e.g. φεύγω, 'I have taken flight = live in banishment' and νικῶ, 'I have vanquished = hold the field' (KG I 136–7 c, SD 274. 6).

αἰσχρῶς: here 'adverb of judgement' as more often in statements: e.g. *Andr.* 575–6 ῥῦσαί με πρὸς θεῶν· εἰ δὲ μή, θανούμεθα / αἰσχρῶς μὲν ὑμῖν, δυστυχῶς δ' ἐμοί, γέρον, E. *Suppl.* 529–30 ἠμύνασθε πολεμίους καλῶς, / αἰσχρῶς δ' ἐκείνοις (KG II 115–16, SD 414 d).

810b–12a. '... and the army has been massacred, and you beat them back neither when they were entering the camp nor when they were leaving it?'

καὶ κατεσφάγη στρατός: an affective hyperbole; cf. *Hipp.* 17–18 παρθένῳ ξυνὼν ἀεί / κυσὶν ταχείαις θῆρας ἐξαιρεῖ χθονός, *Hel.* 73–4 ἥ μ' ἀπώλεσεν / πάντας τ' Ἀχαιούς and 597–8 Μενέλαε, μαστεύων σε κιγχάνω μόλις, / πᾶσαν πλανηθεὶς τήνδε βάρβαρον χθόνα (with Kannicht). This and the anacoluthon after πῶς express Hector's indignation.

ἐξαπώσατε: from ἐξαπωθέω, a unique and possibly epicising compound, in which both preverbs retain their force ('thrust away out of'). Cf. *Od.* 5.372 εἵματα δ' ἐξαπέδυνε, 12.306–7 καὶ ἐξαπέβησαν ἑταῖροι / νηός, 22.443–4 εἰς ὅ κε πασέων / ψυχὰς ἐξαφέλησθε (weakened in S. *El.* 1157, but not fr. tr. adesp. 296.2), and see SD 428–9, 462.

The verb has often been suspected, most recently by Liapis ('Notes', 94–5), who comes to posit a crux. Conjectures like Paley's ἐξαπεώσατε (on 811)[289] or Herwerden's ἐξεώσατε (*Exercitationes criticae*, 140) address the absence of a syllabic augment, whereas Naber's newly-formed ἐξηπύσατε, 'you called (them) out' (cf. ἤπυσα in 776 [776–7n.]) deals with the fact that logically ἐξαπώσατε fits εἰσιόντας much better than ἐξιόντας. Regarding the augment, however, one may argue that – unlike perhaps in S. fr. 479.1, where λιμὸν ... ἔπαυσε (Herwerden) for ... ἀπῶσε (Eust. 228.6) is now generally accepted – the epic-Ionic (and late) aorist here is protected by the striking series of verbal Homerisms earlier in *Rhesus* (523–5a n.), as well as the cognate Ionic noun ἐξώστης in 322 (322b–3n.). In terms of syntactic 'logic' then, οὔτ' ἐξιόντας can easily be explained with Porter (on 811) and Mastronarde (*ElectronAnt* 8 [2004], 22) as a careless addition born out of Hector's anger or, grammatically, as supplementing εἰσιόντας to an example of polar expression which either emphasises the action as a whole ('during the entire invasion') or simply adds up to the sense 'not at all' (Kemmer, *Polare Ausdrucksweise*, 218–22, 227; cf. e.g. Hes. *Th.* 759–61 οὐδέ ποτ' αὐτούς /

---

[289] With an irregular synizesis in the fifth 'foot' of the iambic trimeter (J. M. Descroix, *Le trimètre iambique*, Macon 1931, 32–3).

Ἥλιος φαέθων ἐπιδέρκεται ἀκτίνεσσιν / οὐρανὸν εἰσανιὼν οὐδ' οὐρανόθεν καταβαίνων).

812b–13. τείσει δίκην: so also 893b–4 (n.) ὅν ποθ' ὁ κτείνας χρόνῳ / δόλιος Ὀδυσσεὺς ἀξίαν τείσει δίκην. The verse-end is common in Euripides: *Med.* 767, 802 ... ὃς ἡμῖν σὺν θεῷ τείσει δίκην, where, as here, the MSS are divided between the later form τίσει (corr. Murray: cf. Threatte I 190, II 536–8, 654, West, ed. *Iliad* I, XXXV–VI) and δώσει, *Suppl.* 733, *El.* 260 ... Ὀρέστη μή ποτ' ἐκτείσῃ δίκην, *Hcld.* 852–3 (~ 882) ... κἀποτείσασθαι δίκην / ἐχθρούς.

σὲ γὰρ δή: indignant, with δή perhaps stressing σέ (*GP* 207–8) rather than γάρ (*GP* 243) as usual in this combination: e.g. *Alc.* 1136–8 ὦ τοῦ μεγίστου Ζηνὸς εὐγενὲς τέκνον, / εὐδαιμονοίης ... / ... σὺ γὰρ δὴ τἄμ' ἀνώρθωσας μόνος, E. *El.* 82–3 Πυλάδη, σὲ γὰρ δὴ πρῶτον ἀνθρώπων ἐγώ / πιστὸν νομίζω, E. fr. 674a, Men. *Mis.* A1–2 Sandbach (p. 351), Pl. *Rep.* 337e7–338a 1.

814–15. The wording, if not so much the thought, resembles *Ai.* 454–5 κεῖνοι δ' ἐπεγγελῶσιν ἐκπεφευγότες, / ἐμοῦ μὲν οὐχ ἑκόντος (of the Atridae, having escaped Ajax' attack). Epic and even more, it seems, epic-style tragic heroes and heroines were acutely sensitive to the danger of falling victim to their enemies' gloats or mockery: *Il.* 4.172–82, 8.147–50, *Ai.* 79 οὔκουν γέλως ἥδιστος εἰς ἐχθροὺς γελᾶν; (with Garvie and Finglass), 303, 367, 382, 955–62, 1042–3, *Med.* 383 (with Mastronarde), 797 οὐ γὰρ γελᾶσθαι τλητὸν ἐξ ἐχθρῶν, φίλαι (B. M. W. Knox, *The Heroic Temper* ..., Berkeley *et al.* 1964, 30–1 and, on the limits of such exultation, M. W. Blundell, *Helping Friends and Harming Enemies* ..., Cambridge 1989, 55–6).

φροῦδοι: 662n.

ἄπληκτοι: 'uninjured'. So Hellenistic Posidipp. *Ep.* 93.3–4 Austin–Bastianini πόντου πάτερ, εἰ δὲ σὺ κεύθεις, / ἄπληκτον ψιλὴν ἔκθες ἐπ' ἠϊόνα and Chrysipp. Stoic. fr. 998 *SVF* ii (p. 292).35–8 ἄπληκτον (×2) of a boxer.

τῇ Φρυγῶν κακανδρίᾳ: In classical Greek κακανδρία is shared (in the same case and metrical position) only with A. fr. 132a 4 col. I.2 (*Myrmidons*?)]εγων κακανδρίᾳ and *Ai.* 1014–15 τὸν δειλίᾳ προδόντα καὶ κακανδρίᾳ / σέ, φίλτατ' Αἴας. Liapis (on 814–15) notes that this is the only passage in *Rhesus* where the proverbial cowardice of the 'Phrygians' (32n.) is alluded to.

816–19. 'Now be sure of this – Father Zeus is my witness – either the lash or death by decapitation awaits you for having done such a thing, or you may consider Hector to be a nobody and a coward.'

The passage bears a remarkable (if most likely coincidental) similarity to *Tr.* 1107–9 ἀλλ' εὖ γέ τοι τόδ' ἴστε, κἂν τὸ μηδὲν ὦ, / κἂν μηδὲν ἕρπω, τήν γε δράσασαν τάδε / χειρώσομαι κἀκ τῶνδε.

816. εὖ νυν τόδ' ἴστε: introduces a threat also in *Ai.* 1308–9 and, similarly, *Ant.* 304–12 ἀλλ' εἴπερ ἴσχει Ζεὺς ἔτ' ἐξ ἐμοῦ σέβας, / εὖ τοῦτ' ἐπίστασ', ὅρκιος δέ σοι λέγω, / εἰ μὴ τὸν αὐτόχειρα τοῦδε τοῦ τάφου / εὑρόντες ἐκφανεῖτ' ... / οὐχ ὑμῖν Ἅιδης μοῦνος ἀρκέσει (...), *Tr.* 1107–9 (816–19n.) and Men. *Epitr.* 375 εὖ ἴσθι, τηρήσω σε πάντα τὸν χρόνον (cf. Finglass on S. *El.* 605 and Collard, 'Supplement', 371, among doubtful examples of colloquial speech).

Ζεὺς ὀμώμοται πατήρ: passive ('Father Zeus has been sworn by'), as in Ar. *Nub.* 1241 καὶ Ζεὺς γέλοιος ὀμνύμενος τοῖς εἰδόσιν (KG I 296). The older, genuinely Attic ὀμώμοται is sanctioned by metre at *Ag.* 1290 ὀμώμοται γὰρ ὅρκος ἐκ θεῶν μέγας (susp. Schütz; cf. West's apparatus and Fraenkel on 1290) and Ar. *Lys.* 1007–8 τουτὶ τὸ πρᾶγμα πανταχόθεν ξυνομώμοται / ὑπὸ τῶν γυναικῶν and should therefore be restored here with Buttmann (*Ausführliche Griechische Sprachlehre* II[1], 198–9 ~ II[2], 255–6) and Matthiae (*GG* I[3], 624). For the sigmatic form entering our MSS see also Dem. 20.159 ἀλλ' ἀναμνησθέντες ... τῆς Δημοφάντου στήλης ... ἐν ᾗ γέγραπται καὶ ὀμώμοται (S: ὀμώμοσται AFY) and in general West, ed. *Aeschylus*, XLIII–IV.

817–18a. While previously, it seems, Hector did not want to hear of Rhesus' plan to impale Odysseus (467–526n.), he now threatens the chorus with a distinctly 'barbarian' form of capital punishment. Beheading was practised by the Persians (*Pers.* 369–71, Hdt. 7.35.3, 8.90.3, Xen. *An.* 2.6.1) and is ascribed to the Egyptian Herald in A. *Suppl.* 840. Our lines, like 513b–15 (n.), were almost certainly inspired by the collection of cruelties in *Eum.* 186–90 (below). The whip and decapitation also follow each other when the Scythian Archer loses his patience with 'Euripides' in Ar. *Thesm.* 1125–7.

ἤτοι ... γ' ἤ: For γε after disjunctive particles see *GP* 119 (cf. 622–3n.) and for ἤτοι ... ἤ *GP* 553.

μάραγνα: In extant literature the noun is paralleled only at *Cho.* 375 ἀλλὰ διπλῆς γὰρ τῆσδε μαράγνης δοῦπος ἱκνεῖται. Yet it may not have been so rare, given its metaphorical use there, the fact that Pollux (10.56) attests a most likely paratragic case (Fraenkel, *Rev.* 231) in Plato the Comedian (fr. 64 *PCG*) and the existence of σμάραγνα as a variant form (Hsch. σ 1226 Hansen). Herodian also employed it to illustrate the accentuation of nouns in -να: Σ[L] *Rh.* 817 (II 343.20–1 Schwartz = 112 a[1] Merro) οὕτως παροξύνει (προπαροξύνει Lentz) Ἡρωδιανὸς ἐν τῇ Καθόλου (I 256.24–5 Lentz).

καρανιστὴς μόρος: Cf. *Eum.* 186–7 καρανιστῆρες ... / δίκαι σφαγαί τε (above) and *Sept.* 199 λευστῆρα ... μόρον. Blaydes' καρανιστὴρ μόρος (*Adversaria critica*, 10) is rendered improbable by the observation that archaising *nomina agentis* in -τήρ tend to be found in tragic trimeters only when the paradigm in -της would not have given a metrically suitable form. Note e.g. *Sept.* 36 κατοπτῆρας – *Sept.* 41 κατόπτης, *Sept.* [1015] ἀναστατῆρα – *Ag.* 1227 ἀναστάτης, *Cho.* 280 ἐπαμβατῆρας – *Ba.* 1107–8 τὸν ἀμβάτην / θῆρ' (E. Fraenkel, *Nomina agentis* II, ch. 1, particularly pp. 8, 18, 23–4, 29, 43).

Despite the above reservations about the relative infrequency of μάραγνα, we have here yet another example of our poet's taste for combining choice words from different sources (Fraenkel, *Rev.* 231, 233, Introduction, 35–6).

819. τὸ μηδέν, 'a cipher, nobody' (with generalising μη-), has become fossilised and thus keeps the article even in predicative position (KG II 197–8 with n. 2; cf. KG I 61 n. 2 and Denniston on E. *El.* 370). Unlike simple οὐδέν / μηδέν (or their masculines), this form and ὁ οὐδέν / μηδέν are restricted to serious drama, including satyr-play,[290] and two elevated passages in Aristophanes and Herodotus (Ar. *Av.* 577, Hdt. 8.106.3).

820–32. The chorus defend themselves against Hector's charges and threats in a short piece of song, which technically forms the antistrophe to their enthusiastic praise of Rhesus at 454–66 (n.). The tone is one of reverent defiance, born out of despair. As previously Rhesus, they address Hector almost in terms of a tutelary deity (821–3, 827–8nn.), while denying any failure in their execution of duty. Given their general awareness of how the Achaeans penetrated the camp (cf. 722–7), this sounds like an attempt to protect themselves not only from the consequences of Hector's wrath, but also from the full realisation of the part they played in their hero's death.[291]

Structurally this antistrophe separates the Charioteer's lamentation and report from his ensuing quarrel with Hector, just as the strophe stands between the agonistic (388–453) and conversational (467–526) part of Hector's encounter with Rhesus. This reversed parallel position is further underlined by the fact that the badly injured Charioteer acts, as it were, as his master's representative at a time when all hopes in the Thracians are lost. Thus far from being isolated in their respective places, the stanzas look both ahead to and back on Rhesus' disaster, which is so closely linked with the sentries' behaviour. Similarly again in *Hippolytus* the corresponding laments of the chorus (362–72) and Phaedra (669–79) enclose the story of her tragedy by marking not two points of

---

[290] The only example of this idiom in Aeschylus would seem to be A. fr. 78a.67 (*Theoroi?*) ὡς οὐδέν εἰμι τὴν σιδηρῖτι[ν ‿ –].

[291] Here, if nowhere else, the audience may have noticed that not all the sentries should have abandoned their posts (cf. Introduction, 39–40). That the Thracians were extremely careless about their own safety (762–9n.) never becomes an issue.

opposing sentiment (as in our play), but a succession of fatal events in the revelation of her love and Hippolytus' violent rejection (cf. Ritchie 331).

Metre

454–66n.

821–3. 'O guardian power of our city, mighty, mighty in my eyes, they must have arrived at the time when I came to you with the message that fires were blazing around the ships.'

†μέγας ἐμοὶ μέγας ὦ† πολίοχον κράτος / τότ' ἄρ' ἔμολον ὅτε σοι / ἄγγελος ἦλθον ἀμφὶ ναῦς πῦρ' αἴθειν: If we regard 822 as sound (454–66 'Metre' 456/822n.), interpretation and conjecture must begin with ἔμολον, which despite e.g. Ritchie (309), Willink ('Cantica', 38 = *Collected Papers*, 566–7) and Liapis ('Notes', 95–6), can only be third person plural referring to the enemy spies at 809–15 (Σ^Q *Rh.* 822 [113 Merro] ἔμολον· ἐκεῖνοι; cf. Porter on 820–4, Feickert on 822). All of 821 then probably conceals an elevated address like that of the chorus to the deceased Astyanax in *Tro.* 1216–17 ἒ ἔ, φρενῶν / ἔθιγες ἔθιγες· ὦ μέγας ἐμοί ποτ' ὤν / ἀνάκτωρ πόλεως or, in terms of word-order, *Hel.* 1451–2 Φοίνισσα Σιδωνιὰς ὦ / ταχεῖα κώπα (with Kannicht) so that *exempli gratia* at least we may follow Porter, Dale (*MATC* I, 100) and Feickert among others in combining Nauck's easy μέγα σύ μοι μέγ' ὦ (II[1] [1854], XXIII) with Vater's certain πολίοχον (below).

†μέγας ἐμοὶ μέγας ὦ† πολίοχον κράτος: almost an invocation (cf. 827–8n.), for whereas κράτος, like μέγας (380–1n.), could be used of gods and mortal rulers alike (e.g. *Sept.* 128–30 σύ τ' ὦ Διογενὲς φιλόμαχον κράτος / ... Παλλάς, *Eum.* 27, *Ag.* 109 Ἀχαιῶν δίθρονον κράτος, 619; FJW on A. *Suppl.* 525–6), πολιοῦχος and its cognates were largely reserved for the tutelary god(s) or hero(es) of a city (LSJ s.vv. πολιοῦχος (A), πολισσοῦχος I; cf. LSJ s.v. ἔχω (A) A I 3, where add *SIG*[3] I 360.3–5, II 581.1–4, and 166n.).

Vater (on 808) restored πολίοχον (πολιοῦχον Ω) for metrical reasons. On this short form of the adjective see again 166n.

τότ' ἄρ': literally '*then* (they came ...)', with ἄρα expressing the realisation of a past event at the time of speaking, as in e.g. *Ant.* 1272–4 ἐν δ' ἐμῷ κάρᾳ / θεὸς τότ' ἄρα τότε με μέγα βάρος ἔχων / ἔπαισεν, *Andr.* 274–6 ἦ μεγάλων ἀχέων ἄρ' ὑπῆρξεν, ὅτ' Ἰδαίαν / ἐς νάπαν ἦλθ', ὁ Μαί- / ας τε καὶ Διὸς τόκος and Ar. *Av.* 513 ὃ δ' ἄρ' εἱστήκει τὸν Λυσικράτη τηρῶν ὅ τι δωροδοκοίη (*GP* 36).

ὅτε σοι / ἄγγελος ἦλθον ἀμφὶ ναῦς πῦρ' αἴθειν: Cf. the chorus at 41 πῦρ' αἴθει στρατὸς Ἀργόλας and 49–50 σοὶ δ' … / ἤλυθον ἄγγελος … (where no 'message' depends on the verbal phrase). In addition to Reiske's πῦρ' αἴθειν (41–2n.), Badham's ναῦς (*Philologus* 10 [1855], 338) for ναυσί (Ω) is required here to restore metre and responsion.

After 823 all MSS attest Ἀργείων στρατόν, which has no equivalent in the strophe and, since the text there is complete (455b–7n.), was rightly deleted by Badham (*Philologus* 10 [1855], 338) and Kirchhoff (I [1855], 561: στρατόν iam Tr¹).²⁹² As an intrusive gloss the phrase most probably arose from misguided recollection of 41 … στρατὸς Ἀργόλας and 78 … Ἀργείων στρατόν (cf. 57, 127, 146 and some fourteen times in other tragedy), although failure to understand the rare intransitive use of αἴθω probably also played a part (Feickert on 824, Liapis on 823). Cf. Pi. *Ol.* 7.48 αἰθοίσας … φλογός, *Ai.* 285–6 ἡνίχ' ἕσπεροι / λαμπτῆρες οὐκέτ' ᾖθον and perhaps *Cho.* 536–7 πολλοὶ δ' ἀνῆθον … / λαμπτῆρες (ἀνῆθον Valckenaer: ἀνῆλθον M, ἀνέλαμψαν Σ: ἀνήθοντ' Meineke), Ar. *Pax* 612 (N. G. Wilson, *Aristophanea*, Oxford 2007, 107).

824–6. 'For my eyes were wakeful in the night, I did not put them to rest, nor did I fall asleep, no, by the streams of Simoeis.'

ἄγρυπνον: In view of 2–3 (n.) τίς ὑπασπιστῶν ἄγρυπνος βασιλέως / ἢ τευχοφόρων; the adjective is best taken as proleptic. Alternatively, it could be generic as a defensive claim to universal wakefulness: e.g. *PV* 358 Ζηνὸς ἄγρυπνον βέλος (transferred from its owner), Theoc. 24.106 υἱὸς Ἀπόλλωνος μελεδωνεὺς ἄγρυπνος ἥρως (i.e. Heracles' tutor Linus).

ὄμμ' … **ἐκοίμισ':** similarly in connection with vigilance (desired or undesired) *Il.* 14.236 (Hera to Sleep) κοίμησόν μοι Ζηνὸς ὑπ' ὀφρύσιν ὄσσε φαεινώ, *Sept.* 2–3 ὅστις φυλάσσει πρᾶγος ἐν πρύμνῃ πόλεως / οἴακα νωμῶν, βλέφαρα μὴ κοιμῶν ὕπνῳ and, of death, *OT* 1221–2 ἀνέπνευσά τ' ἐκ σέθεν / καὶ κατεκοίμησα τοὐμὸν ὄμμα.

ἐν εὐφρόνᾳ: 91–2n. Diggle restored the 'Doric' α (εὐφρόνῃ Ω, *Chr. Pat.* 1840, 2331) in lyrics, as did Badham (*Philologus* 10 [1855], 338) with παγάς below. Cf. 546–50 (καὶ μάν) n.

οὔτ' ἔβριξ': ingressive aorist. βρίζω is a Homeric verb (*Il.* 4.223, *Od.* 9.151 = 12.7 and later e.g. Theoc. *Ep.* 19.4 Gow, Call. *Epigr.* 16.3 Pf.), taken over by Aeschylus alone of the tragedians: *Ag.* 275 οὐ δόξαν

---

292 Ritchie (50) follows H. L. Schrader (*De notatione critica a veteribus grammaticis in poeticis scaenicis adhibita*, diss. Bonn 1864, 28–9) in supposing that Σᵛ *Rh.* 41 (II 330.6–7 Schwartz = 82 Merro) τὸ χ̄ ὅτι συνθέτως ἀναγινώσκεται (*sc.* πυραίθει) καὶ ὅτι οὐκ ἔστιν Εὐριπίδειος ὁ στίχος was originally composed for 823 (cf. Introduction, 23 with n. 7).

ἂν λάβοιμι βριζούσης φρενός, *Cho.* 897 βρίζων (of the baby Orestes), *Eum.* 280 βρίζει γὰρ αἷμα καὶ μαραίνεται χερός.

The ancient definition of βρίζω as denoting drowsiness after eating (*LfgrE* s.v. B; cf. e.g. Σ^LQ *Rh.* 826 [II 343.22–3 Schwartz = 113 Merro] βρίξαι κυρίως τὸ μετὰ βορὰν ὀλίγον κοιμηθῆναι, Σ^AD *Il.* 4.223 [I 491.90–1 Erbse]) is not borne out by actual usage and, to judge by its first appearance in Orion *Et.* 10.1–2 Sturz (ἀποβρίξαι, ἀπὸ τοῦ τὴν βορὰν [ἀπὸ τοῦ βορὰ Sturz] καὶ τοῦ ἵζειν καὶ κατανεύειν· ὥστε κυρίως τὸ ἀποβορᾶς νυστάζειν), may have been inferred from the context of *Od.* 9.151 = 12.7 ἔνθα δ' ἀποβρίξαντες ἐμείναμεν Ἠῶ δῖαν.

οὐ τὰς Σιμοεντιάδας παγάς: For Greek and Near-Eastern oaths and treaties in the name of rivers see West on Hes. *Th.* 400 (Styx becoming the ὅρκος of the gods), *EFH* 20–1, *IEPM* 274–5 and Liapis on 824–6.

Hermann (*Opuscula* III, 309) corrected the transmitted οὐ μὰ τὰς Σιμοεντίδας πηγάς (παγάς Badham), which does not respond with 460. The interpolation of μά in negative oaths is paralleled in S. *El.* 1063, 1239 (with Finglass, Ll-J/W, *Second Thoughts*, 43), *OT* 660 and 1088, while the geographical feminine adjective in -ιάς would have been sufficiently unusual to get corrupted. Hermann inferred the same in the lyric *Tro.* 1116–17 καὶ Σιμοεντιάσιν / ... ῥοαῖσιν (Σιμοεντίσι(ν) VP) and *Pers.* 964–5 ἐπ' ἀκταῖς / Σαλαμινιάσι (σαλαμινῖσι(ν) vel -μινίσι Ω).

τὰς Σιμοεντιάδας παγάς: Plural πηγαί, 'streams', is a Homerism found in tragedy also at *Pers.* 311 πηγαῖς ... Νείλου, *PV* 89 ποταμῶν ... πηγαί, 434 and *HF* 1297 (~ *Il.* 20.9, *Od.* 6.124, *h.Ven.* 99 πηγὰς ποταμῶν). Aeschylus adds the singular in *Pers.* 201–2 and 613. Cf. Sideras, *Aeschylus Homericus*, 124, 136.

In contrast, adjectives derived from Σιμόεις are, with the exception of the personal name Σιμοείσιος (*Il.* 4.473–89), first attested in the lyrics of Euripides: *Andr.* 1019 ἐπ' ἀκταῖσιν Σιμοεντίσιν, 1183, *Hec.* 641 τᾷ Σιμουντίδι γᾷ, *El.* 441, *Tro.* 1116–17 (above), *Hel.* 250 παρὰ Σιμουντίοις ῥοαῖσι, *Or.* 809, *IA* 767 (in a doubtful passage). The uncontracted forms are even restricted to him.

827–8. μή μοι κότον ... θῇς: 'Do not be angry with me ...'. κότον τίθημι here functions as a simple periphrasis for κοτέω (LSJ s.v. τίθημι C 4), but the phrase also recalls the wrath Hera and Athena 'laid up (in their hearts)' at *Il.* 8.449 Τρῶας, τοῖσιν κότον αἰνὸν ἔθεσθε (cf. LSJ s.v. τίθημι A II 6). In *Hel.* 679 †τὰ δ' εἰς κρίσιν σοι τῶνδ' ἔθηχ' Ἥρα κακῶν;† Diggle combined conjectures of Reiske (τί δ') and Kayser (κότον) to the similar expression τί δ' ἐς κρίσιν σοι τόνδ' ἔθηχ' Ἥρα κότον; (*Euripidea*, 180–3; cf. his apparatus and Allan's note).

The epic κότος, found once in Pindar (*Pyth.* 8.9), is a favourite of Aeschylus (cf. Sideras, *Aeschylus Homericus*, 32), but was more or less avoided by the other tragedians. Apart from Kayser's conjecture at *Hel.* 679 (above), it occurs only in derivatives: *PV* 163, 601 ἐπικότως (-οισι), *Phil.* 1191 ἀλλόκοτος, S. fr. 1042 ἐνεκότουν, E. fr. 572.2 παλιγκότως (Hutchinson on *Sept.* 485).

ὦ ἄνα: This old vocative of ἄναξ is elsewhere exclusively used in approaching gods (LSJ s.v. ἄνα (A) with Suppl. [1996], Jouan 49 n. 247, Liapis on 826–8)[293] and therefore in line with the chorus' earlier extravagant addresses to Hector (821–3n.) and Rhesus (355–6, 357–9, 370–2a, 380–1, 385–7nn.). Cf. 820–32n.

ἀναίτιος γάρ / †ἔγωγε πάντων†: While sense and syntax are unexceptionable, the metre shows that something has fallen out in 828. Of the various *exempli gratia* remedies listed in Wecklein's apparatus and appendix on 829, Nauck's πάντων πάντῃ (-ᾳ Diggle) ἔγωγε (II[1] [1854], XXIII) has the double advantage of implying a simple process of corruption and keeping the ambiguity between pherecratean and contracted $D - \|$.

829–32. 'But if in time you find out that I have done or said anything inopportune, send me under the earth (i.e. bury me) alive; I do not protest.'

εἰ δὲ ... πύθῃ: In occasionally combining εἰ with a pure subjunctive the tragedians (except Euripides) followed the still more liberal practice of Homer (KG II 474 n. 1, SD 684–5, Jebb on *OT* 198, FJW on A. *Suppl.* 91–2 and J. Willmott, *The Moods of Homeric Greek*, Cambridge 2007, 199–204 for a possible explanation of the phenomenon).

παρὰ καιρόν: On prepositional phrases depending on nouns without article see 567–8a n. But Vater's παράκαιρον (on 817), for which cf. Isoc. 1.9 οὐδὲ τὸν πλοῦτον παρακαίρως ἠγάπα, Thphr. *CP* 2.2.2, 3.7.6 and [Epich.] fr. 243 *PCG*, is very attractive, particularly since, as Feickert (on 830) points out, forms of that adjective tended to be corrupted into παρὰ καιρόν: e.g. Luc. *Nigr.* 31, [Men.] *Mon.* 302 Jäkel, Hsch. π 1040 Hansen πάρωρον· παράκαιρον (Guyet: παρὰ καιρόν H). Sansone's χρόνῳ ποτ' ἄκαιρον (*BMCR* 2013.03.15, on 829–30) is less close to the MSS text, although ἄκαιρος has the advantage of being attested in tragedy (especially *PV* 1036–7 ἡμῖν ... οὐκ ἄκαιρα φαίνεται / λέγειν).

From the Cyril / Hesychius-gloss cited above Headlam (*CR* 15 [1901], 103) conjectured πάρωρον (e.g. Thphr. *CP* 3.23.3, 4.13.4, 5.1.2, Strato *AP* 12.199.6), which allows him to retain the paradosis in 464 εἰ γὰρ ἐγὼ τόδ' ἦμαρ (cf. 464–6n.). Metrically, however, this aristophanean (with a further period-end after ἦμαρ ~ πάρωρον) would look out of place in the

---

[293] Call. *Aet.* fr. 24.3 Harder and *Epigr.* 34.1 Pf. (ὦνα for Heracles) violate the rule no more than the mock invocation of Cleonymus at Ar. *Eq.* 1298.

present context, and so does the isolated dochmiac 465 ὅτῳ πολυφόνου ~ 830 πύθῃ, κατά με γᾶς, which Willink introduced by dividing after ... τόδ' ἦμαρ εἰσίδοιμ', ἄναξ and ... πάρωρον ἔργον ἢ λόγον ('Cantica', 33–5, 38 = *Collected Papers*, 572–3, 577).

ἔργον ἢ λόγον: a typical case of 'polar expression', where the second member may have been added by pure association (Kemmer, *Polare Ausdrucksweise*, 216–17).

κατά με γᾶς / ζῶντα πόρευσον· οὐ παραιτοῦμαι: The chorus acknowledge Hector's threat of capital punishment in 816–18 in a fashion resembling *Hcld*. 1026 (Eurystheus to Alcmena) κτεῖν', οὐ παραιτοῦμαί σε. For πορεύω in connection with killing and journeys to and from Hades note also e.g. Pi. *Pyth*. 11.19–22 ὁπότε ... / Κασσάνδραν πολιῷ χαλκῷ σὺν Ἀγαμεμνονίᾳ / ψυχᾷ πόρευ' Ἀχέροντος ἀκτὰν παρ' εὔσκιον / νηλὴς γυνά, *HF* 838–9, 1277–8 Ἀίδου πυλωρὸν κύνα τρίκρανον ἐς φάος / ὅπως πορεύσαιμ', *Alc*. 442–4, 1072–4 (G. A. Longman, *CQ* n.s. 12 [1962], 65 with n. 2).

833–81. With his predictable (776–7, 802b–3nn.), yet surprisingly elaborate, attack on Hector's integrity the Charioteer prevents any potential answer to the chorus' lyric defence. Like a forensic speech, it falls into a brief introduction (833–4), the accusations proper (835–42) and two supporting arguments κατὰ τὸ εἰκός (843–55) to the effect that the Greeks had neither the opportunity nor, short of supernatural assistance (852–4a n.), the knowledge to commit the crime in question (cf. Feickert on 833–55, 852–5, 856–65). Of these parts, however, especially the second one seems unduly circular and repetitious, a sign perhaps of the Thracian's delirious fury (Ritchie 131), which becomes even more prominent in his apparently unrelenting obstinacy towards the end (875–6n.).

Regarding the 'evidence', there is some irony in that the Charioteer draws his objectively wrong conclusion from irrefutable observations, whereas the chorus (805; cf. 692–721) and Hector (809, 861–5; cf. 498–509), on far less cogent grounds, both rightly suspect an enemy attack and identify Odysseus as one perpetrator of Rhesus' as well as Dolon's[294] death (Rosivach 69 with n. 45, 70 with n. 48). Still his charges again do not fail to leave their mark, for ἵππων ἐρασθείς (839) recalls Hector's earlier self-confessed desire for Achilles' horses (184n.), and although he vehemently denies such a quality (859b–60n.) to his desire, we are for a moment led to believe that under different circumstances he might

---

[294] Mentioned last in 863–5. Retrospectively, we will understand that for the Trojans his disappearance is never solved.

have been capable of betraying his allies (cf. G. Paduano, *Maia* n.s. 25 [1973], 24).

833–4. 'Why do you threaten these men and as a barbarian undermine my, a barbarian's, opinion by weaving words?'

βάρβαρός τε βαρβάρου: 404–5n. It is noteworthy that, while previously the phrase was used by Hector against Rhesus, it is now the Charioteer who accuses Hector of betraying the 'barbarian' unity (Liapis on 833–4).

γνώμην ὑφαιρῇ τὴν ἐμήν echoes the language of law-courts, where ὑφαιρέω / -έομαι, literally 'to steal (away)', is a contemptuous metaphor for weakening one's opponent's arguments in advance. Cf. Hyp. *Lyc.* 11 καὶ τοῦτο πῶς καλῶς ἔχει ... ὑφαιρεῖσθαί μου τὴν ἀπολογίαν; *Eux.* 10, Dem. 23.90 ὃ δὲ δεινότατον πάντων ἐστίν, τὸ μηδεμίαν κρίσιν ἐν παντὶ ποιῆσαι τῷ ψηφίσματι τοιαύτης αἰτίας, τοῦθ' ὑφαιρεῖσθαι πειράσεται (Feickert on 833).

πλέκων λόγους: here negative ('devising a deceitful speech'), as often with πλέκω (e.g. *Cho.* 220 ἀλλ' ἢ δόλον τιν' ὦ ξέν' ἀμφί μοι πλέκεις; A. fr. 373, *Andr.* 66, 995, *Ion* 826–7; Diggle, *Studies*, 115) and other words of 'weaving' and 'stitching' from Homer on: e.g. *Il.* 6.187 πυκινὸν δόλον ἄλλον ὕφαινεν, 18.367 κακὰ ῥάψαι (LSJ s. vv. ὑφαίνω II, ῥάπτω II 1), *Cho.* 221 αὐτὸς κατ' αὐτοῦ τἄρα μηχανορραφῶ (with Garvie). Similarly *Phoen.* 494–5 περιπλοκάς / λόγων (~ Antiph. fr. 75.1–2 *PCG*, Strato Com. fr. 1.35 *PCG*) connotes an over-intricate and potentially misleading way of arguing / speaking, which is also the sense in Pl. *Hp.Mi.* 369b8 Ὦ Σώκρατες, ἀεὶ σύ τινας τοιούτους πλέκεις λόγους. Conversely, the same metaphors could be applied to the artistic composition of poets: Pi. *Ol.* 6.86–7 ἀνδράσιν αἰχματαῖσι πλέκων / ποικίλον ὕμνον, *Nem.* 4.94, *Pae.* 3.12 (fr. 52c Sn.–M. = D3 Rutherford) ἀοιδαῖς ἐν εὐπλε[κέσσι], fr. 179 Sn.–M. ὑφαίνω δ' Ἀμυθαονίδαισιν ποικίλον / ἄνδημα, Bacch. 5.9–10. Cf. Mastronarde on *Phoen.* 494–6, H. Fränkel, *Glotta* 14 (1925), 3–6, West, *IEPM* 36–8.

835–7a. οὐδέν' ἂν δεξαίμεθα ... ἄλλον: expressing a fixed resolve (201–2n.): 'We shall not accept anyone else ...'

οὔθ' οἱ θανόντες οὔτ' ... οἱ τετρωμένοι could simply stand in periphrasis for all Thracian victims (Jouan 49 n. 250); cf. 847–8, 849–50. We therefore need not think with Feickert (on 835) of unavenged dead seeking to know the guilty party.

837b–40. μακροῦ γε δεῖ σε καὶ σοφοῦ λόγου: Impersonal δεῖ with an accusative (rather than dative) of the person and genitive of the thing is a favourite of Euripides (KG I 297 n. 5, Ritchie 249) and attested in other drama only at *PV* 86 αὐτὸν γάρ σε δεῖ προμηθίας and fr. com. adesp. 257 *PCG* εὐρυχωρίας σε δεῖ. For the formulation here Ritchie especially refers to *Hipp*. 490–1 οὐ λόγων εὐσχημόνων / δεῖ σ' ἀλλὰ τἀνδρός and 688 ἀλλὰ δεῖ με δὴ καινῶν λόγων ('thoughts, plan'), but see also *PV* 870 μακροῦ λόγου δεῖ ταῦτ' ἐπεξελθεῖν τορῶς and 875–6 ὅπως δὲ χὤπῃ, ταῦτα δεῖ μακροῦ λόγου / εἰπεῖν.

γε is exclamatory with perhaps a slightly sarcastic undertone, as in *Hipp*. 480–1 ἦ τἄρ' ἂν ὀψέ γ' ἄνδρες ἐξεύροιεν ἄν, / εἰ μὴ γυναῖκες μηχανὰς εὑρήσομεν (*GP* 129) and far more pointedly e.g. Ar. *Av*. 1401 χαριέντα γ', ὦ πρεσβῦτ', ἐσοφίσω καὶ σοφά (*GP* 128 and, for examples from the orators, 129–30).

ὅτῳ με πείσεις μὴ φίλους κατακτανεῖν: In the sense 'persuade (that)' πείθω (cf. 65–6n.) usually governs a substantival clause introduced by ὡς, but note e.g. *Phoen*. 30–1 ἣ δὲ τὸν ἐμὸν ὠδίνων πόνον / μαστοῖς ὑφεῖτο καὶ πόσιν πείθει τεκεῖν, Hdt. 3.155.4, 4.154.2 and Xen. *Mem*. 1.2.49 (KG II 9 n. 7, 32, Mastronarde on *Phoen*. 31).

ἵππων ἐρασθείς: 833–81n.

φονεύεις: 'present for perfect', as in e.g. *Ant*. 1173–4 (Αγ.) τεθνᾶσιν· οἱ δὲ ζῶντες αἴτιοι θανεῖν. / (Χο.) καὶ τίς φονεύει; (KG I 137 d, SD 275 and 926–8a n.).

φονεύω and φονεύς, although occasionally used by Aeschylus (*Sept*. 340–1, *Ag*. 1231, 1648, *Eum*. 122, 425) and Sophocles (also *Ai*. 409 and eight times in *OT*) are more typical of Euripides.

πόλλ' ἐπισκήπτων μολεῖν: 399–403, 401–3nn. The present participle here expresses a repeated (πολλά) action prior to that of the main verb (KG I 200 nn. 9, 10)

841b–2. 'More seemly did Paris dishonour the bonds of hospitality than you by killing your allies.'

The remark is even more strongly reminiscent of *Ag*. 399–402 οἷος καὶ Πάρις ἐλθών / εἰς δόμον τὸν Ἀτρειδᾶν / ἤσχυνε ξενίαν τράπε- / ζαν κλοπαῖσι γυναικός than *Rh*. 336–7 (n.) ὃ δ' οὖν ... σύμμαχος μὲν οὔ, / ξένος δὲ πρὸς τράπεζαν ἡκέτω ξένων and, given the usual attitude to violations of hospitality (and especially the case of Paris), a very serious insult. With the charge of having killed one's guest-friend out of greed Feickert (on 842–3) well compares Heracles' murder of Iphitus at *Od*. 21.27–30 ὅς μιν ξεῖνον ἐόντα κατέκτανεν ᾧ ἐνὶ οἴκῳ, / σχέτλιος, οὐδὲ θεῶν ὄπιν αἰδέσατ' οὐδὲ τράπεζαν, / τὴν ἥν οἱ παρέθηκεν· ἔπειτα δὲ πέφνε καὶ αὐτόν, / ἵππους δ' αὐτὸς ἔχε κρατερώνυχας ἐν μεγάροισι.

843. ὥς τις Ἀργείων μολών: 291b–3n.

844b–5. 'Who could have got past the Trojan companies and reached us without even being noticed?'

τίς ἂν ... ἦλθεν: Nauck (II¹ [1854], XXIII; cf. *Euripideische Studien*, 182–3) for τίς δ'... ἦλθεν (Ω). As in 852–3 τίς δ' ἂν (v.l. αὖ) χαμεύνας πολεμίων ... / Ῥήσου ... ἐξηῦρεν (...); we can hardly dispense with ἄν here, since passionate questions showing the pure 'modal' indicative are usually found in dialogue and almost exclusively introduced by πῶς (KG I 203, SD 307–8; in drama e.g. *Ag.* 1211, *OT* 1327–8, *Phil.* 250, Ar. *Ran.* 1186). Moreover, δ' after γάρ would again disrupt the nearly unbroken line of asyndeta in this first part of the Charioteer's speech (833–46), a minor objection which is not met by Beck's τίς δ' ... ἦλθ' ἄν (*Exercitatio critica*, 12 n. 3 = *Diatribe critica*, 451 n. 3).[295]

ὑπερβαλὼν λόχους / Τρώων: like a material, indeed often geographical, obstacle or boundary. Cf. 989–90 (989b–92n.) ὡς ὑπερβαλὼν τάφρον / τείχη τ' Ἀχαιῶν and e.g. *Ag.* 306–8, *PV* 721–2 ἀστρογείτονας ... / κορυφὰς ὑπερβαλοῦσαν, *Alc.* 829, *Or.* 443 (~ 1644) ... γῆς ὑπερβάλλων ὅρους. Unlike middle ὑπερβάλλομαι, 'overcome' (LSJ s.v. ὑπερβάλλω B I 1), the active does not imply any interaction.

For λόχους, 'troops, companies', see 26n.

ὥστε καὶ λαθεῖν: literally 'so as actually to escape notice', with καί denoting the addition of a limitative qualification to the main clause. So likewise in questions *Ai.* 1325 τί γάρ σ' ἔδρασεν, ὥστε καὶ βλάβην ἔχειν; *Hel.* 841 πῶς οὖν θανούμεθ' ὥστε καὶ δόξαν λαβεῖν; and Pl. *Tht.* 182d4–5 (*GP* 299).

846. The Charioteer's statement corroborates the relative positions of the Thracian and Trojan bivouacs ('Scene and Setting', 114, 613–15n.).

σύ was changed to οὐ in Π³ (cf. Introduction, 54), which would make sense only if the scribe or corrector understood the line as a question.

ἦσο: 613n.

Φρυγῶν στρατός: 32n.

847–8. †συμμάχων† / τῶν σῶν, if sound, must mean not just Hector's long-standing allies as opposed to the Thracians (e.g. Porter on 848, Jouan 50 n. 252, Feickert on 847), but, since we should expect another reference to the Trojans here, 'all [except us] who fight on your side' (L. Battezzato, *CQ* n.s. 50 [2000], 368 n. 9; cf. Liapis on 847–8, 'Notes', 98). Yet this sense seems difficult to extract from the Greek (Bothe II [1826], 124, on 806: '... sed Troiani et Phryges non possunt dici Hectoris σύμμαχοι'), especially in view of 839–40 συμμάχους / τοὺς σοὺς φονεύεις and 842 ἦ σὺ συμμάχους κτανών. Murray, therefore, was probably right in suspecting the phrase. Of his two conjectures, συγγενῶν / τῶν σῶν is superior to ἐν λόχῳ / τῷ σῷ, not so much for being palaeographically nearer (συμμάχων could, after all, have intruded on the analogy of 839–40 and then attracted the pronoun), but because Hector's unit, unless singled out as a personal taunt, would be too restric-

---

[295] On the elision of third-person-singular -ε before ἄν see Diggle, *Studies*, 100, 120 and *Euripidea*, 109 n. 61, 197.

tive a 'subject' after 844–5 λόχους / Τρώων and 846 σὺ ... καὶ Φρυγῶν στρατός.

ὧν: Bothe (3 [1824], 366, on 820) by *attractio relativi*. The transmitted ὡς (an easy slip, particularly with σὺ ... λέγεις) would give an impossibly convoluted word-order (cf. Bothe II [1826], 124, on 807).

849–50. ἡμεῖς δὲ καὶ τετρώμεθ': 'But we *have* been wounded ...' καί stresses τετρώμεθ' in a way that it contrasts its reality for the Thracians with their allies' alleged escape from that fate (847–8). Similarly *Ai*. 1393–6 σὲ δ' ... / τάφου μὲν ὀκνῶ τοῦδ' ἐπιψαύειν ἐᾶν / ... / τὰ δ' ἄλλα καὶ ξύμπρασσε (*GP* 321–3).

It is another sign of our poet's metrical conservatism (208–9, 804–5nn.) that we have here the only iambic trimeter, where the hephthemimeral caesura coincides with elision (Ritchie 285).

μειζόνως is not uncommon in Attic prose (especially Plato), but elsewhere in verse found only at *Hec*. 1121. The same applies to other such primarily Ionic (Schwyzer 621 n. 8) comparative adverbs in -όνως and -τέρως (*OC* 104 μειόνως, Ar. fr. 353 *PCG* ἀμεινόνως, *Hcld*. 543 ἐνδικωτέρως, *IT* 1375, *IA* 379, Ar. *Lys*. 419; KB I 577 n. 1, FJW on A. *Suppl*. 596 [II, p. 483]), whence Elmsley[1] (on *Hcld*. 544 [543]) here proposed μείζονα. But see his partial recantations in the 1821 and 1828 editions.

οὐχ ὁρῶσιν ἡλίου φάος: Together with *Hipp*. 4 φῶς ὁρῶντες ἡλίου and *Phil*. 663–4 ὅς γ' ἡλίου τόδ' εἰσορᾶν ἐμοὶ φάος / μόνος ἔδωκας this version of the common poetic metaphor for '(not) being alive' comes closest to the epic ... ὁρᾷ (-ᾶν) φάος ἠελίοιο (967–9n.). See also 970–1n. (βλέπων φάος).

851. ἁπλῶς δ': 'in a word'. Cf. e.g. Thuc. 3.82.5 ἁπλῶς δὲ ὁ φθάσας τὸν μέλλοντα κακόν τι δρᾶν ἐπηνεῖτο, καὶ ὁ ἐπικελεύσας τὸν μὴ διανοούμενον and Isoc. 4.154, Dem. 20.124 ὡς δ' ἁπλῶς εἰπεῖν.

852–4a. 'For which of our enemies could have come by night and found the resting-place of Rhesus, unless one of the gods had shown the murderers the way?'

With archetypal tragic irony the Charioteer hits upon the truth about Athena's initiative (cf. 611–21) in a sarcastic question designed to undermine Hector's theory of an Achaean night-raid. The difficulty of finding one's way round an enemy camp alone in the dark was pointed out by Odysseus in 587–8.

δ': 132n.
χαμεύνας: 9n.
κατ' εὐφρόνην: 91–2n.
εἰ μή ... / ἔφραζε: With the indicative εἰ μή is often ironic: *nisi forte* (KG II 486, SD 684). For φράζω in the epic sense 'point out, show the way to' see 658b–9n.

854b–5. 'They did not even know he had arrived at all. No, this is a plot.'

Pierson (*Verisimilium* I, 82–3) compared D. Chr. 55.14 (of Dolon) καὶ γὰρ τοὺς ἵππους ἐμήνυσε τοὺς Θρᾳκικοὺς καὶ τὸν Ῥῆσον, ὃν οὐδεὶς ᾔδει ἀφιγμένον, although in this case the verbal similarity may be fortuitous (cf. Introduction, 45).

οὐδ': 'with [a] sense of climax' (*GP* 196).

τὸ πάμπαν, which in other drama is found only at E. fr. 196.2 (*Antiope*) and without the article *Med.* 1091, Achae. *TrGF* 20 F 17.3 and Ar. *Pax* 121, should for lack of exhaustive evidence perhaps not be pressed into Ritchie's list of 'minor resemblances of phrase to Euripides' (211–12). Yet while πάμπαν alone is exceedingly common in epic (especially with negatives) and not rare in the early lyric poets, the articular form remains a prose expression from Plato and the Hippocratic corpus on.

ἀλλά: completive after a rhetorical question (852–4a), as in e.g. S. *El.* 804–7, *Med.* 309–11 σὺ γὰρ τί μ' ἠδίκηκας; ἐξέδου κόρην / ὅτῳ σε θυμὸς ἦγεν. ἀλλ' ἐμὸν πόσιν / μισῶ ('No, it is my *husband* I hate') and *Hcld.* 466–7 (*GP* 5).

μηχαναί: Musgrave's conjecture (*Exercitationes*, 95 ~ II [1778], 411) is confirmed by *Et. Gen.* cod. B (10th century) = Orus B 77 Alpers ... καὶ ἦσαν ἀντὶ τοῦ ᾔδεσαν (...) Εὐριπίδης Ῥήσῳ (854 sq.) οὐδ' ... ἦσαν· ἀλλὰ μηχαναὶ τάδε and, despite Feickert (on 855), also lends a more poignant conclusion to the impersonal second part of the speech (849–55). The MSS' μηχανᾷ (cf. *Ba.* 805 οἴμοι· τόδ' ἤδη δόλιον ἐς ἐμὲ μηχανᾷ) was an easy error by misinterpretation of ΑΙ or αι as α with iota subscript.

856–8. 'We have now had dealings with allies for all the time that the Achaean army has been in this land, and I am sure that I have never heard any harsh word from them.'

χρόνον ... / ὅσονπερ: See 865n.

Ἀχαιικὸς λεώς: 622–3n. The phrase also appears in *Ag.* 189 (lyric) and *Hec.* 510 ... λεὼς Ἀχαιικός, by analogy with the epic λαὸς Ἀχαιικός (*Il.* 9.521, 13.349, 15.218).

πλημμελές: literally 'out of tune, unrhythmical' (< πλήν + μέλος: Pl. *Lg.* 816a7, Arist. *Pr.* 919a31–2 [πλημμελέω], Plut. *De Pyth. or.* 5.396d [πλημμέλεια], *Quaest. Conv.* 8.9.2.732e), but like its verb and noun mostly used metaphorically with various nuances of 'deviation from the ideal'. Here, as often in classical Greek, the stem refers to injustice inflicted or suffered in word or action: e.g. *Med.* 306 ... μὴ τί πλημμελὲς πάθῃς, *Hel.* 1085 ... ἢν γὰρ καί τι πλημμελές σε δρᾷ, *Phoen.* [1655] τί πλημμελήσας (the only other certain poetic examples),[296] Aeschin.

---

[296] Blass conjectured π[λημμελου]μένων in fr. com. adesp. 1006.8 *PCG* and Kannicht [πλημ]μελῆ in E. fr. 953m.37–8.

1.167 (S. Daniel, *Recherches sur le vocabulaire du culte dans la Septante*, Paris 1966, 341–61, especially 341–2, 351–4).

κλυών: 109–10a, 286, 572–3nn.

859a. ἐν σοὶ δ' ἂν ἀρχοίμεσθα: 'But we seem to be making a start with you'. For ἐν = 'with, in the case of' cf. *Il.* 9.97 ἐν σοὶ μὲν λήξω, σέο δ' ἄρξομαι, *Ai.* 1091–2 μὴ ... ἐν θανοῦσιν ὑβριστὴς γένῃ and 1314–15 βουλήσῃ ποτέ / καὶ δειλὸς εἶναι μᾶλλον ἢ 'ν ἐμοὶ θρασύς (LSJ s.v. A I 7, SD 458).

From the Iliadic perspective, Rhesus and his Charioteer were by no means the first allies to come into conflict with Hector (251b–2, 319–26nn.).

859b–60. μή μ' ἔρως ἕλοι / τοιοῦτος ἵππων: By drawing a qualitative, not just quantitative, line between Hector's longing (184) and murderous passion for the horses (833–81n.), Ω's τοιοῦτος effects a more powerful defence than Wecklein's tentative τοσοῦτος (Feickert on 859). For the overall phrasing cf. E. fr. 331.1–2 καί μ' ἔρως ἕλοι ποτέ / οὐκ εἰς τὸ μῶρον οὐδέ μ' εἰς Κύπριν τρέπων.

861. καὶ ταῦτ' Ὀδυσσεύς: 'That is Odysseus again', with omission of ἐστίν, not ἔδρασεν (Σ^V *Rh.* 861 [II 343.17–18 Schwartz = 114 Merro]), which could not easily be understood retrospectively from 862 (contrast e.g. Xen. *Cyr.* 4.4.13 ὅπως ὑμεῖς ἐκείνων, μὴ ἐκεῖνοι ὑμῶν ἄρχωσιν, quoted by Liapis on 861–2). The idiom is paralleled in Theoc. 15.8 ταῦθ' ὁ πάραρος τῆνος, *Tr.* 1278 κοὐδὲν τούτων ὅ τι μὴ Ζεύς (where Σ$^{vet.}$ also adds ἔπραξεν), *Cyc.* 63–7 οὐ τάδε Βρόμιος, οὐ τάδε χοροί / Βάκχαι τε θυρσοφόροι (...), 204–5 and, less harshly, *Tro.* 99–100 οὐκέτι Τροία / τάδε καὶ βασιλῆς ἐσμεν Τροίας. In full see *Andr.* 168–9 οὐ γάρ ἐσθ' Ἕκτωρ τάδε, / οὐ Πρίαμος οὐδὲ χρυσός, ἀλλ' Ἑλλὰς πόλις and Thuc. 6.77.1 οὐ ... βουλόμεθα προθυμότερον δεῖξαι αὐτοῖς ὅτι οὐκ Ἴωνες τάδε εἰσὶν οὐδ' Ἑλλησπόντιοι καὶ νησιῶται (Gow on Theoc. 15.8).

There is thus no need for Fix's καὶ ταῦτ' Ὀδυσσέως (p. XXXI), which is in any case more difficult than the ellipsis in 722 εἴτ' οὖν Ὀδυσσέως (*sc.* τοὔργον ἐστὶν) εἴτε μή, φόβος μ' ἔχει (~ 704). Dawe's ἦ for καί (*apud* Diggle), by contrast, could remove the slightly obscure allusion to Odysseus' earlier Trojan exploits (498b–509, 705, 710–21nn.). On the frequent confusion of ἢ / ἦ and καί (abbreviated) see Diggle, *Studies*, 27 and *Euripidea*, 198 (with earlier literature).

863–4. 'But I fear, and something troubles my heart, that he has also run into Dolon and killed him.'

The sentiment and phrasing may have been inspired by *Il.* 10.538–9 (Nestor) ἀλλ' αἰνῶς δείδοικα κατὰ φρένα, μή τι πάθωσιν / Ἀργείων οἱ ἄριστοι ὑπὸ Τρώων ὀρυμαγδοῦ (Porter on 864; cf. Ritchie 181–2), but see below on the mood of κατέκτανεν.

αὐτόν: proleptic, as in *Med.* 37 δέδοικα δ' αὐτὴν μή τι βουλεύσῃ νέον and similarly *OT* 767–8 δέδοικ' ἐμαυτόν ... μὴ πόλλ' ἄγαν / εἰρημέν' ᾖ μοι (KG II 577–9). καί τί μου θράσσει φρένας then becomes a parenthetic variation on δέδοικ'.

καί τί μου θράσσει φρένας: Cf. *PV* 628 ... σὰς δ' ὀκνῶ θρᾶξαι φρένας, where the notable correspondence of word-ends and metrical position may be significant. Otherwise it is true that φρένα and φρένας form 'natural object[s]' (Ritchie 200) for θράσσω / ταράσσω (*Ant.* 1095, *Hipp.* 969, *Ion* 1538, E. fr. 1079.4).

μὴ ... κατέκτανεν (Matthiae, VIII [1824], 38) restores the standard construction in a statement of fear relating to a past event (KG II 394–5, SD 354, Kannicht on *Hel.* 119). The transmitted μὴ ... κατακτάνῃ is often defended with the few Homeric instances of the aorist subjunctive in the same application: *Il.* 1.555–6 νῦν δ' αἰνῶς δείδοικα κατὰ φρένα, μή σε παρείπῃ / ἀργυρόπεζα Θέτις, 10.97–9 ὄφρα ἴδωμεν, / μή τοι μὲν ... / κοιμήσωνται, ἀτὰρ φυλακῆς ἐπὶ πάγχυ λάθωνται, 538–9 (SD 675, Chantraine, *GH* II, 299).[297] But one may doubt whether that would have been recognised as a conscious epicism.

865. χρόνον alone as an adverb is found only here in tragedy and was classed as a Homerism by Pearson (*CR* 35 [1921], 56), who compared *Od.* 6.295 (to which add *Od.* 4.599 and 9.138). Yet it is also very rare in later Ionic and Attic literature (Hdt. 1.175, 7.223.1, Thuc. 4.73.4), perhaps because its lack of semantic precision ('time' in the expressive sense 'a considerable time') militated against the demands of standard speech. The more specific χρόνον ... ὅσον(περ) or ὅσον χρόνον (*Hec.* 436, *Hel.* 400–2, 612, *Rh.* 856–7) never underwent such apparent restriction.

φροῦδος: 662n.

οὐ φαίνεται: Unlike the aorist and perfect (e.g. *Tr.* 227–8 τὸν κήρυκα ... χρόνῳ / πολλῷ φανέντα, *OC* 77, 328 τέκνον, πέφηνας; *Andr.* 891), 'the forms of the present stem are not used frequently of characters appearing 'on stage' in tragedy' (Bond on *HF* 705 [704–5] παῖδας καὶ δάμαρθ' Ἡρακλέους / ἔξω κέλευε τῶνδε φαίνεσθαι δόμων). See also *Hec.* 666 ἐς δὲ καιρὸν σοῖσι φαίνεται λόγοις and *Ba.* 645–6 πῶς προνώπιος / φαίνῃ πρὸς οἴκοις τοῖς ἐμοῖς. The idiom need not be 'colloquial' (Wilamowitz on *HF* 705; cf. Ar. *Vesp.* 273, *Eccl.* 312, Pl. *Prot.* 309a1), but its restriction to later Euripides is noteworthy.

866–7. 'I don't know these Odysseuses of yours that you speak of. We haven't been struck by anyone of the enemies.'

---

[297] Liapis (on 863–5) questions this usage by reference to the wrong grammatical category (i.e. subordinate clauses dependent on a main verb in the past).

The closest parallel for this couplet with scornful *epanalepsis* of something mentioned by the previous speaker (KG I 559 n. 10, SD 203) is presumably S. fr. 165 οὐκ οἶδα τὴν σὴν πεῖραν· ἓν δ' ἐπίσταμαι· / τοῦ παιδὸς ὄντος τοῦδ' ἐγὼ διόλλυμαι (where lack of context precludes absolute certainty); then S. *El.* 1110 οὐκ οἶδα τὴν σὴν κληδόν' (taking up φήμης in 1109), *Hcld.* 284 φθείρου· τὸ σὸν γὰρ Ἄργος οὐ δέδοικ' ἐγώ (after 283 ἐν Ἄργει) and *Phil.* 1251 (with Hermann's στρατόν and Jackson's positioning of the lacuna, accepted by Lloyd-Jones and Wilson).[298] In our lines the notion of contempt is reinforced by the plural Ὀδυσσέας, for which cf. *Ag.* 1439 Χρυσηΐδων μείλιγμα τῶν ὑπ' Ἰλίῳ (with Fraenkel on 1438) and, in a comparable usage, *Rh.* 438 (438–9n.) τὰς ἐμὰς ἀμύστιδας. Moreover, οὓς λέγεις conveys the impression that, analogous to the Phrygian at *Or.* 1521 τὸ Γοργοῦς δ' οὐ κάτοιδ' ἐγὼ κάρα (with Willink on 1520–1), the Charioteer has never heard of or does not care about the Greek hero.

868. The Argive Herald begins his reply to Theseus with similar words in E. *Suppl.* 465–6 λέγοιμ' ἂν ἤδη. τῶν μὲν ἠγωνισμένων / σοὶ μὲν δοκείτω ταῦτ', ἐμοὶ δὲ τἀντία. His tone, however, is coldly polite rather than condescending.

δ' οὖν: 336–7n.

869. ὦ γαῖα πατρίς: Cf. E. fr. 696.1 Ὦ γαῖα πατρίς, ἣν Πέλοψ ὁρίζεται.

πῶς ἂν ἐνθάνοιμί σοι; For this kind of formulaic question expressing a wish in tragedy (KG I 235, SD 327–8) cf. e.g. *Rh.* 751b (n.) πῶς ἂν ὀλοίμην; *Ai.* 388–91 ὦ Ζεῦ προγόνων πάτερ, / πῶς ἂν ... τέλος θάνοιμι καὐτός; and particularly *Phil.* 1212–14 ὦ πόλις πόλις πατρία, / πῶς ἂν εἰσίδοιμ' / ἄθλιός σ' ἀνήρ;

The pathetic motif of dying 'far away' from one's homeland, where the tomb could not be tended by one's family (Liapis on 869), is especially common in the *Iliad* (e.g. 11.814–18, 16.538–40, 20.389–92; J. Griffin, *Homer on Life and Death*, Oxford 1980, 106–12). In addition, Patin (*Etudes sur les tragiques grecs. Euripide*, II, Paris ²1858, 165), followed by Porter and Feickert (on 869), compared Verg. *Aen.* 10.782 *et dulcis moriens reminiscitur Argos*.

870. 'Don't die! For the number of those who have died is already large enough.'

---

[298] *Ai.* 792 οὐκ οἶδα τὴν σὴν πρᾶξιν (of Tecmessa) is different in that it does not pick up Αἴαντος ... πρᾶξιν at 790, and *Hipp.* 113 τὴν σὴν δὲ Κύπριν πόλλ' ἐγὼ χαίρειν λέγω, though falling into the same category, rather means 'Cypris whom you worship as I do not' (Dawe, *STS* III, 107). At A. fr. 14 κἄγωγε τὰς σὰς βακκάρεις τε καὶ μύρα (cited with all the other examples by Wilkins on *Hcld.* 284) the context is again unclear.

The line seems to have been modelled on *Hec.* 278 μηδὲ κτάνητε· τῶν τεθνηκότων ἅλις (i.e. Hecuba pleading for Polyxena's life), and despite Meschini's attempts to assess it in context (*AFLPad* 1 [1976], 183), it is still worth quoting Valckenaer's verdict (*Diatribe*, 115; cf. Fraenkel, *Rev.* 238): '*Sithonia nive frigidior est versus*'.

μὴ θνῇσχ': Cf. *Alc.* 690 μὴ θνῇσχ' ὑπὲρ τοῦδ' ἀνδρός, οὐδ' ἐγὼ πρὸ σοῦ and *IA* 1418–19 σὺ δ', ὦ ξένε, / μὴ θνῇσκε δι' ἐμὲ μηδ' ἀποκτείνῃς τινά, where the qualifying prepositional phrases make all the difference between a contextually appropriate pleading and an absurd prohibition – even if it is taken *de conatu* ('Don't talk / think of dying!') with Morwood and Feickert (on 870).

ἅλις γὰρ τῶν τεθνηκότων ὄχλος: In addition to *Hec.* 278 (above), note *Hec.* 394 ἅλις κόρης σῆς θάνατος, *IT* 1008 (∼ *Or.* 1039) ἅλις τὸ κείνης αἷμα and for the structure of the whole verse *Alc.* 673 παύσασθ', ἅλις γὰρ ἡ παροῦσα συμφορά. The predicative or, with a dependent genitive, substantival use of ἅλις in such expressions may have been colloquial (Collard, 'Supplement', 367).

In contrast to E. *Suppl.* 756 πῶς φῄς; ὁ δ' ἄλλος ποῦ κεκμηκότων ὄχλος; where ὄχλος is neutral (cf. e.g. *PV* 827 ὄχλον ... τὸν πλεῖστον ... λόγων, *IA* 191 ἵππων τ' ὄχλον, Critias? *TrGF* 43 F 4.4–5 ἄκριτός τ' ἄστρων / ὄχλος), the noun sounds again rather crude here.

871. While the wording is reminiscent of *Ba.* 1366 ποῖ γὰρ τράπωμαι πατρίδος ἐκβεβλημένη; and *Alc.* 380 οἴμοι, τί δράσω δῆτα σοῦ μονούμενος; the Charioteer's concern for himself after Rhesus' death (cf. 733, 752–3nn.) first recalls the chorus' laments at *Ai.* 900–2 ὤμοι ἐμῶν νόστων· / ὤμοι, κατέπεφνες, ἄναξ, / τόνδε συνναύταν, τάλας and 1211–22.

δή: Porson (*Adversaria*, 227) for δὲ (VΛ: ν[ῦν Af') to restore metre and idiom.

872. κεύθων: 'shelter', as in *Od.* 6.303 ἀλλ' ὁπότ' ἄν σε δόμοι κεκύθωσι καὶ αὐλή, *Hel.* 573 ἦν ἄντρα κεύθει κἀκ Φρυγῶν κομίζομαι and, with perhaps a slightly sinister undertone, *Hec.* 880 στέγαι κεκεύθασ' αἵδε Τρῳάδων ὄχλον.

ἐξιάσεται: a technical term, it seems, which in other poetry occurs only metaphorically at E. *El.* 1024 κεἰ μὲν πόλεως ἅλωσιν ἐξιώμενος (... ἔκτεινε πολλῶν μίαν ὕπερ).

873. αὐθεντῶν: here more freely for members of a murderer's family or household, as in *Andr.* 172–3 καὶ τέκν' αὐθεντῶν (Heiland: αὐθέντου codd.) πάρα / τίκτειν (of Andromache in relation to Neoptolemus, whose father killed her husband) and *Tro.* 660 δουλεύσω δ' ἐν αὐθεντῶν δόμοις. On the specific meaning 'murderer of somebody's (or one's own) kin' see Parker, *Miasma*, 122 with nn. 68, 69. The likeliest derivation is from αὐτός + *ἕντης (< ἀνύω), i.e. 'one who accomplishes (something) himself' (E. Fraenkel, *Nomina agentis* I, 237–41, *GEW*, *DELG* s.v. αὐθέντης).

874. Diggle's punctuation as an impatient (αὖ) question is preferable. Cf. *Andr.* 240 οὐκ αὖ σιωπῇ Κύπριδος ἀλγήσεις πέρι; which Stevens, after Hermann (on 240), paraphrases with 'you're at it again! keep quiet, can't you?' and compares to Pl. *Euthd.* 296a8 οὐκ αὖ, ἔφη, παύσῃ παραφθεγγόμενος; Collard ('Supplement', 372–3) tentatively adds *Il.* 1.540 τίς δὴ αὖ τοι, δολομῆτα, θεῶν συμφράσσατο βούλας; which is different, however, for not being a veiled command (KG I 176–7, SD 292–3).

875–6. 'A curse on the perpetrator! For my tongue †is not aimed at you†, as you claim so loudly. But Justice knows.'

οὐ γὰρ †εἰς σὲ τείνεται† / γλῶσσ': At first sight this looks like a variation of the common metaphor that equates the tongue with a bow, shooting words for arrows: e.g. Pi. *Isthm.* 5.46–8 πολλὰ μὲν ἀρτιεπής / γλῶσσά μοι τοξεύματ' ἔχει περὶ κείνων / κελαδέσαι, A. *Suppl.* 446 καὶ γλῶσσα τοξεύσασα μὴ τὰ καίρια (with FJW), E. fr. 494.1–2, Pl. *Phd.* 63a7–8 καί μοι δοκεῖ Κέβης εἰς σὲ τείνειν τὸν λόγον (LSJ s.v. τείνω A I 1, 4). Yet the paradosis can hardly be correct, for (a) there is no reason why the Charioteer should suddenly phrase his accusations in more general or cautious terms, and (b) neither all nor part of that clause, modified by ὡς σὺ κομπεῖς (below), takes up anything Hector said after 855.[299] Thus rather than Diggle's '*numquam cohibebitur*' (apparatus 875), which could only indirectly refer to 874, we require a sense of '… does not utter lies' or, keeping the metaphor, '… is not aimed at you in vain', but this is difficult to reconcile with our text, unless (the equivalent of) a whole line were lost before or after γλῶσσ' (West). At the other end of the scale, *Chr. Pat.* 276 ὄλοιθ' ὁ δράσας· ἡ Δίκη δ' ἐπίσταται probably testifies not so much to interpolation of οὐ γὰρ … κομπεῖς (cf. Diggle, apparatus 875–6, Liapis, 'Notes', 99) than to the compiler's selection of what suited him best (Introduction, 53).

ὡς σὺ κομπεῖς: a rhetorical formula (Ritchie 244–5), intended to invalidate an opponent's argument. To the examples quoted in 438–9n. (*Med.* 555–7, *Or.* 570–1) add *Ba.* 686–8 οὐχ ὡς σὺ φῄς / ᾠνωμένας κρατῆρι καὶ λωτοῦ ψόφῳ / θηρᾶν καθ' ὕλην Κύπριν ἠρημωμένας (~ 221–5), a case of the poet's omniscience ascribed to a character (Dodds on 686–8).

---

[299] G. Norwood (Appendix to Porter's *Rhesus*, 91–2), followed by Kovacs, already saw these problems, but his interpretation, '… For 'tis no *tongue*, as thy taunts aver, that points at thee' (upon which the Charioteer would draw his sword and attack Hector), reads too much stagecraft into a few words and does not properly address the second objection. Moreover, it is hard to picture the severely wounded Thracian engaged in such vigorous action, and it would appear from 792–3 that he never carried an offensive weapon.

877–8. 'Seize him! And bring him to my house and look after him in such a way that he will find no reason to complain.'

This and the following command (779–81 ὑμᾶς δ' ...) are addressed to two different groups of Hector's silent attendants.

λάζυσθ'· ἄγοντες <δ'> αὐτὸν ἐς δόμους ἐμούς: similarly *Phoen.* [1660] λάζυσθε τήνδε κἀς δόμους κομίζετε. The epic-Ionic λάζυμαι with its compounds (LSJ s.v. λάζομαι II) is a Euripidean favourite and found elsewhere in drama only at Ar. *Lys.* 209. Apart from *HF* 943, moreover, the simplex always stands in the second person imperative plural and at the beginning of an iambic trimeter: *Med.* 956, *Ion* 1266, 1402, *Ba.* 503, *IA* 622, E. fr. 472e.46, maybe E. fr. 223.71 (suppl. Page).

ὅπως ἄν: retaining part of its original relative force ('as') after οὕτως (KG II 374–5 n. 3, SD 670, 672). For a parallel development in Latin see H.–Sz. II 631–2, 643 and cf. Pl. *Ps.* 579–83 *nam ego ... ita paravi copias / ... 583 facile ut vincam, facile ut spoliem meis perduellis, meis perfidiis.*

πορσύνετε: here, uniquely in tragedy, 'tend, look after' (LSJ s.v. πορσύνω III). Cf. A. R. 1.908–9 ἵν' ... / σφοῖσιν πορσύνωνται ἐφέστιοι ἐν μεγάροισιν (i.e. Jason's parents) and πορσαίνω in e.g. 'Hes.' frr. 43a.69, 70.8, 217.5 M.–W. and Pi. *Ol.* 6.32–3.

879–81. 'But you must go and tell those within the wall, Priam and the elders, to bury the dead where people may turn from (i.e. alongside) the public roadway.'

τοῖσιν ἐν τείχει ... / Πριάμῳ τε καὶ γέρουσι: The formulation can hardly fail to evoke the ambience of the τειχοσκοπία in *Il.* 3.146–53 οἳ δ' ... 149 εἴατο δημογέροντες ἐπὶ Σκαιῇσι πύλῃσι, / γήραϊ δὴ πολέμοιο πεπαυμένοι, ἀλλ' ἀγορηταί / ἐσθλοί ... 153 τοῖοι ἄρα Τρώων ἡγήτορες ἧντ' ἐπὶ πύργῳ (Vater on 866; cf. e.g. Paley and Porter on 879), although both the nocturnal setting of *Rhesus* and Homeric usage here compel us to place Priam and his contemporaries 'within the wall' (*Il.* 13.764 οἳ δ' ἐν τείχει ἔσαν βεβλημένοι οὐτάμενοί τε, 22.299 ἀλλ' ὃ μὲν ἐν τείχει, ἐμὲ δ' ἐξαπάτησεν Ἀθήνη). Contrast Andromache in *Il.* 22.463 ἔστη παπτήνασ' ἐπὶ τείχεϊ, and see Feickert on 879, Jouan 75 n. 262.

θάπτειν ... πρὸς ἐκτροπάς: implying motion, as in Hdt. 2.41.6 ἀνορύξαντες δὲ τὰ ὀστέα ἀπάγουσι καὶ θάπτουσι ἐς ἕνα χῶρον πάντες, Dem. 57.70 τὴν δὲ μητέρ' ἱκετεύω ὑμᾶς ... ἀπόδοτέ μοι θάψαι εἰς τὰ πατρῷα μνήματα and Is. 8.21 ἧκον γὰρ ἐγὼ κομιούμενος αὐτὸν ὡς θάψων ἐκ τῆς οἰκίας τῆς ἐμαυτοῦ ('... so as to conduct the funeral from my house').

In accordance with Greek practice, the main road leading out of Troy is thought to be lined with the tombs of important citizens, among whom Rhesus and his people would receive honourable burials in allied soil. Cf. *Alc.* 835–6 ὀρθὴν παρ' οἶμον ἣ 'πὶ Λάρισαν φέρει / τύμβον κατόψῃ ξεστὸν ἐκ προαστίου (with Dale and Parker), Jouan 75 n. 262 and Liapis on 879–81 (with further literature).

κελεύθου λεωφόρου: so also e.g. *Il.* 15.680–2 ὅς τ' ... / σεύας ἐκ πεδίοιο μέγα προτὶ ἄστυ δίηται / λαοφόρον καθ' ὁδόν, Theoc. (?) 25.155 λαοφόρου ... κελεύθου and Nic. *Alex.* 218 λαοφόροισιν ... κελεύθοις. For κελεύθου (Dobree, *Adversaria* II [1833], 102 = IV [1874], 100) the MSS have the redundant infinitive κελεύειν, an obvious error by assimilation to θάπτειν, which could have been assisted by the presence of σημῆναι (cf. *Hcld.* 488–90 χρησμῶν γὰρ ᾠδούς φησι σημαίνειν ὅδε / ... παρθένον / σφάξαι κόρῃ Δήμητρος [Pierson: κελεύειν μητρὸς L] ...)³⁰⁰ and the fact that λεωφόρου could theoretically stand on its own (LSJ s.v. λαοφόρος I 2).

The Ionic-Attic λεωφόρου (Af^uv, Σ^V), also conjectured by Vater (on 868), is required by metre. For the synizesis cf. Anacr. 346 fr. 1.13 *PMG* [λεῶφ]όρε λεῶφόρ' Ἡρο[τ]ίμη (a prostitute) and the examples in Diggle, *Studies*, 93, 120; for the epicising corruption into λαοφόρου (Λ: -ους V) e.g. *IT* 357 Μενέλεῶν θ' (Barnes: -λαόν L) ~ *Hel.* 131 (Björck, *Alpha Impurum*, 106).

ἐκτροπάς: 'turnings, side roads': Ar. *Ran.* 113, Xen. *HG* 7.1.29 ὡς δὲ ἐγένοντο ἐν τῇ ἐπ' Εὐτρησίους ἐκτροπῇ, Aen. Tact. 15.6 (LSJ s.v. II 2 a).

882–9. Like the far more elaborate lament of the Charioteer (728–55n.), this brief set of recitative choral anapaests functions as a link between the ultimately inconclusive 'messenger' scene and a divine finale which in the omniscient, but deeply afflicted Muse presents us with yet another unparalleled example of a character operating in two directions (Ritchie 134–5; cf. 890–914n.).

Dei ex machina seldom get entrance announcements. Extant exceptions are *Andr.* 1226–30, E. *El.* 1233–7 (both anapaestic), *HF* 815–21 (iambo-dochmiac) and *Ion* 1549–52 (3ia, spoken by Ion), with which our lines share first and foremost a situation that does not ask for a sharp conceptual contrast as in *Hippolytus* (Barrett on 1268–82, 1283) or a 'stopping-action' in the face of some human mistake: *Phil.* 1409–71, E. *Suppl.* 1183–1234, *IT* 1435–96, *Hel.* 1642–87, *Or.* 1625–90, E. frr. 223.96–132 (*Antiope*), 370.55–117 (*Erechtheus*).³⁰¹ Common features of language and content include an astonished exclamation (885n.), fear

---

300 Contrast Xen. *An.* 2.3.2 εἶπε τοῖς προφύλαξι κελεύειν τοὺς κήρυκας περιμένειν (wrongly cited by Feickert in support of the paradosis at 881), where κελεύειν is essential to both sense and syntax.
301 Similarly *Med.* 1317–22. The beginning of Dionysus' epiphany in *Bacchae* is lost in the lacuna at 1329–30, and the same applies to *IA* fr. (i) Diggle.

and exhortations to flee from the epiphany (889n.) and particularly the failure to identify the deities (886–8n.), until they introduce themselves (Denniston on E. *El.* 1233–7, J. D. Mikalson, *Honor Thy Gods. Popular Religion in Greek Tragedy*, Chapel Hill – London, 1991, 65).

As indicated by ὑπὲρ κεφαλῆς (886–8n.), the Muse arrives by means of the *mechane*,[302] from which she probably alights on top of the *skene*.[303] The loving presentation of Rhesus' dead body is generally thought to have been inspired by the end of A. *Psychostasia* (Poll. 4.130 ἡ δὲ γέρανος μηχάνημά ἐστιν ἐκ μετεώρου καταφερόμενον ἐφ' ἁρπαγῇ σώματος· ᾧ κέχρηται Ἡὼς ἁρπάζουσα τὸ σῶμα τὸ Μέμνονος), although one should doubt this piece of evidence at least for the original production (cf. Taplin, *Stagecraft*, 432–3, *TrGF* III, 375–6). If any connection existed then, our poet may have been influenced by a less spectacular realisation of Eos' 'rescue operation' or a later revival – as Pollux' source (?). Yet parental grief was just as essential to the stories of Sarpedon (*Il.* 16.431–61), Achilles (908–9, 915–49, 962–82, 962–6, 974–7nn.) and Eurypylus (S. frr. 210.30–48 and, if the lines belong to Astyoche, 211.1–6, 10–14), and the first two especially would have provided excellent models for the Muse's intervention: *Il.* 16.666–75 (Sarpedon), *Aethiopis* Arg. p. 112 (4) *GEF* καὶ ... ἐκ τῆς πυρᾶς ἡ Θέτις ἀναρπάσασα τὸν παῖδα εἰς τὴν Λευκὴν νῆσον διακομίζει[304] (cf. Ritchie 80–1, Introduction, 13–14). One also thinks of Medea's appearance *ex machina* standing in a flying chariot with the corpses of her sons (*Med.* 1317).

882–4. 'Why does some other deity lead Troy back to grief again from its great success? What is it initiating?'

Rhesus' death marks the end of the recent period of good fortune for the Trojans (317–18n.). But the chorus here also seem to forebode a more far-reaching reversal of the city's fate, an impression that is confirmed by their cautious departing words (995–6 τάχα δ' ἂν νίκην / δοίη δαίμων

---

[302] Actual allusions to flight are made only in *Andr.* 1228–9, E. *El.* 1233–6 and almost certainly *HF* 872 στεῖχ' ἐς Οὔλυμπον πεδαίρουσ', Ἴρι, γενναῖον πόδα (cf. D. J. Mastronarde, *Cl. Ant.* 9 [1990], 268–9 with n. 63). The last verse suffices to refute sceptics like Barrett (on *Hipp.* 1283 [p. 396 n. 1]) and Taplin (*Stagecraft*, 445), who out of undue desire to ban the crane from fifth-century tragedy are tempted to regard *Andr.* 1226–30 and E. *El.* 1233–7, or even all announcements except *Rh.* 885–9, as interpolations.

[303] That this was the usual procedure is primarily shown by *Andr.* 1229–30 τῶν ἱπποβοτῶν / Φθίας πεδίων ἐπιβαίνει. Still actors could deliver a considerable amount of spoken lines from the *mechane* (e.g. Trygaeus in Ar. *Pax* 82–179, perhaps Iris in Ar. *Av.* 1202–59). Cf. D. J. Mastronarde, *Cl. Ant.* 9 (1990), 263, 269 (on alighting), 278 n. 95. We do not know how the parodos of *Prometheus Bound* was staged (Introduction, 41–2 with n. 78).

[304] In accordance with this, West (*CQ* n.s. 50 [2000], 343 = *Hellenica* II, 234–5) thinks that at the end of A. *Nereids* (which he puts third in the Achilles-trilogy) Achilles was left in Thetis' care to be transported to the Island of the Blessed.

ὁ μεθ' ἡμῶν) in contrast to Hector's unperturbed optimism (989–92). Cf. 983–96, 993–6nn.

εὐτυχίας ἐκ τῆς μεγάλης: 52–84, 665–7nn.

ἀνάγει: so rightly Af and Heath (*Notae sive lectiones*, 97) instead of, by haplography, ἄγει (VL: ἄγοι Q). With πάλιν following, there is some similarity in expression, though not in semantics and imagery, to *Ai*. 131–2 ὡς ἡμέρα κλίνει τε κἀνάγει πάλιν / ἅπαντα τἀνθρώπεια ('causes to sink and brings up again', like weighing-scales). For metaphorical ἀνάγω, 'bring back' (LSJ s.v. A II 1), cf. *Hel.* 932 πάλιν μ' ἀνάξουσ' ἐπὶ τὸ σῶφρον αὖθις αὖ and for the words and sentiment also *Rh.* 332 πόλλ' ἀναστρέφει θεός (with the passages quoted there) and E. fr. 554 πολλάς γ' ὁ δαίμων τοῦ βίου μεταστάσεις / ἔδωκεν ἡμῖν μεταβολάς τε τῆς τύχης.

δαίμων ἄλλος, τί φυτεύων: Tyrwhitt (*apud* Beck, *Euripides* III, 480) for ... ἄλλό τι ... (Λ: ἄλλοτε V:]τι Af), which does not scan. The nearest parallels for δαίμων ἄλλος meaning 'an adverse deity (or fortune)' are Pi. *Pyth.* 3.34–5 δαίμων δ' ἕτερος / ἐς κακὸν τρέψαις ἐδαμάσσατο νιν (i.e. Coronis) and Call. fr. 191.63 Pf. ἀλλ' οὓς εἶχεν ἕτερος δαίμων. On the euphemism in general see West on Hes. *Op.* 344 (+ Addenda, p. 383).

φυτεύω, 'cause, bring about (evil)', is familiar from Homer on (LSJ s.v. I 3), but in other tragedy found only at *Ai.* 952–3 τοιόνδε μέντοι Ζηνὸς ἡ δεινὴ θεός / Παλλὰς φυτεύει πῆμ' Ὀδυσσέως χάριν and, with emphasis on the planning, *OT* 346–7 ἴσθι γὰρ δοκῶν ἐμοί / καὶ ξυμφυτεῦσαι τοὔργον.

885. ἔα ἔα: 574, 675–82 'Metre' 675nn. The exclamation here calls attention to the epiphany, as in *Hipp.* 1391, *HF* 815 and *Ion* 1549. Cf. 882–9n.

Dindorf's reduction (III.2 [1840], 623) of the transmitted ἔα ἔα ὦ ὦ (fere VQ et Tr³: om. L) is supported by the fact that, except for *Cho.* 870 ἔα ἔα μάλα, *PV* 114 ἆ ἆ ἔα ἔα, 687, *OC* 1477–8 and S. fr. 314.100 (?), 117 (*Ichneutae*), ἔα (ἔα) always stands on its own. The addition here may have been intended to 'complete' the verse (Feickert on 885), although MSS are generally unreliable with interjections.

886–8. 'What goddess overhead, o my king, is carrying in her arms the newly slain corpse?'

For the anxious question as to the arriving god's identity cf. *Andr.* 1226–7 τί κεκίνηται, τίνος αἰσθάνομαι / θείου; and *Ion* 1549–50 τίς οἴκων θυοδόκων ὑπερτελής / ἀντήλιον πρόσωπον ἐκφαίνει θεῶν; Similarly also *HF* 816–17 ἆρ' ἐς τὸν αὐτὸν πίτυλον ἥκομεν φόβου, / γέροντες, οἷον φάσμ' ὑπὲρ δόμων ὁρῶ; and E. *El.* 1233–5 ἀλλ' οἵδε δόμων ὕπερ ἀκροτάτων / βαίνουσί τινες δαίμονες ἢ θεῶν / τῶν οὐρανίων (882–9n.).

ὑπὲρ κεφαλῆς: 882–9n. Cf. E. *El.* 1233, *HF* 817 and *Ion* 1549 (above).

ὦ βασιλεῦ: 2–3, 388–9nn.

τὸν νεόκμητον νεκρόν: a common, epic-style tautology (e.g. *Il.* 6.71, 18.540 νεκροὺς ... (κατα)τεθνηῶτας, *Il.* 7.409, *Od.* 10.530 ... νεκύων κατατεθνηώτων). Tragic cases include *Ant.* 26 τὸν δ' ἀθλίως θανόντα Πολυνείκους νέκυν (with Jebb), 515 ὁ κατθανὼν νέκυς, E. *Suppl.* 16 νεκροὺς ... τοὺς ὀλωλότας δορί, 44 φθιμένων νεκύων, *Hel.* 1252 τοὺς θανόντας ... ἐν πόντῳ νεκρούς (Collard on E. *Suppl.* 16b–17, Liapis on 886–8 ~ 'Notes', 100).

νεόκμητος, a *hapax* (LSJ s.v. with Suppl. [1996]), is unproblematic given the regular use of καμόντες or κεκμηκότες for the dead (e.g. *Il.* 3.278, *Od.* 11.476, A. *Suppl.* 158, 231, S. fr. 284.2, E. *Suppl.* 756, Thuc. 3.59.2) and such athematic formations as δουρικμής, 'slain by the spear' (*Cho.* 365), σιδηροκμής, 'slain by the sword' (*Ai.* 325) and ἀνδροκμής, 'man-slaying' or, like the other two, intransitive after its verb (E. Fraenkel, *Nomina agentis* I, 81–2) 'where(by) men are slain' (A. *Suppl.* 678–9, *Cho.* 889, *Eum.* 248, 956, E. *Suppl.* 525). Those who with e.g. Wecklein, Zanetto and Feickert (on 887) wish to read νεόδμητον (Va, *Chr. Pat.* 1456; cf. Lyc. 65 πρὸς νεόδμητον νέκυν), will have to assume a rare example in Attic drama of synizesis in νέος and its derivatives (*Sept.* 327 νε͡ας, *IA* 615 νεα͡νιδές, Ar. *Vesp.* 1067, 1069; cf. *Phil.* 4, 241, *Andr.* 14, *Tro.* 1126 Νε͡οπτόλεμος, Archil. fr. 118 *IEG* Νε͡οβούλης). On the restrictive influence of lost intervocalic digamma see L. Battezzato, *BICS* 44 (2000), 64–5 with n. 116.[305]

φοράδην: 'borne along', as on a bier: *Andr.* 1166–7 καὶ μὴν ὅδ' ἄναξ ἤδη φοράδην / Δελφίδος ἐκ γῆς δῶμα πελάζει (followed by strophic lament; cf. 890–914n. with n. 306) and, of a wounded man in a litter, Dem. 54.20 καὶ ὑγιὴς ἐξελθὼν φοράδην ἦλθον οἴκαδε.

889. 'I am frightened at the sight of this calamity.'

ταρβῶ is intransitive with a supplementary participle, as in e.g. *Pers.* 684–5 λεύσσων δ' ἄκοιτιν τὴν ἐμὴν τάφου πέλας / ταρβῶ, *Eum.* 406–7 καινὴν δ' ὁρῶσα τήνδ' ὁμιλίαν χθονός / ταρβῶ μὲν οὐδέν, θαῦμα δ' ὄμμασιν πάρα and *PV* 898–9 ταρβῶ γὰρ ἀστεργάνορα παρθενίαν / εἰσορῶσ' Ἰοῦς (A. Meschini, *AFLPad* 1 [1976], 183–4). In support of Verrall's unnatural punctuation ταρβῶ, λεύσσων τόδε, πῆμα (*apud* Murray; cf. Porter and Zanetto), Jouan (76 n. 264) cites *Ion* 1551–2 φεύγωμεν, ὦ τεκοῦσα, μὴ τὰ δαιμόνων / ὁρῶμεν, εἰ μὴ καιρός ἐσθ' ἡμᾶς ὁρᾶν and *HF* 822–4 θαρσεῖτε Νυκτὸς τήνδ' ὁρῶντες ἔκγονον / Λύσσαν, γέροντες, κἀμὲ ... / Ἶριν (cf. 815–21, especially 820–1 ὦναξ

---

305 There may be a similar corruption in *Cho.* 616–18 Κρητικοῖς / χρυσεοδμήτοισιν ὅρ- / μοις πιθήσασα (M: χρυσεοκμήτοισιν Musgrave), but see Garvie on 615–18.

Παιάν, / ἀπότροπος γένοιό μοι πημάτων). But there is no reason why the normal sense and syntax could not also convey the typical human fear at the sight of undisguised divinity (F. Pfister, *RE* Suppl. IV s.v. Epiphanie, coll. 317–18; cf. 882–9n.), especially when they are viewed in such an intimate situation.

890–914. After a brief reassurance the Muse identifies herself not only to Hector and the chorus, but also the audience, who are likely to have been unfamiliar with this version of the myth (Introduction, 13). Yet the conventional nature of her opening words (cf. 890–2a n.) is proved deceptive when subsequently she shifts to a personal plane (892b–4) and, in a manner unprecedented for *dei ex machina*, conforms to her nature by giving lyric expression to her grief and anger (895–903 ~ 906–14).

As the first part of the exodos, the introduction and song confirm the Trojans' suspicion that at the human level Odysseus (and Diomedes) are responsible for Rhesus' death: 893b–4 (n.), 906–9. In addition, we gain some background information on his expedition, which he undertook against his parents' will (900–1). Already reminiscent of Achilles and related tales (899–901n.), this foreshadows the Muse's premonition of her son's fate at 934–5a (n.), which is followed by a recollection of the embassies Hector had sent to Thrace (935b–7n.). We may assume, therefore, that Rhesus made a conscious choice against a life without honour and glory, although the knowledge does little to mitigate our earlier impression of him (cf. H. D. F. Kitto, *YCS* 25 [1977], 342, Liapis on 895–903 = 906–14 [p. 307]).

Structurally, the brief strophic monody with two choral trimeters interposed corresponds to Euripides' earliest solo laments in *Alc.* 393–403 ~ 406–15 (Alcestis' son for his mother), *Hipp.* 817–33 ~ 836–51 (Theseus for Phaedra), *Andr.* 1173–83 ~ 1186–96 (the first part of Peleus' and the chorus' κομμός for Neoptolemus),[306] and to Euadne's wild epirrhematic 'wedding song' before she leaps to her death onto Capaneus' pyre: E. *Suppl.* 990–1008 ~ 1012–30 (cf. Collard on 990–1033).[307] Unlike any other monodist, however, the Muse not only passes straight from spoken verse into lyrics,[308] but also back again (Ritchie 340, H. Popp –

---

306 As this is followed by an anapaestic entrance announcement for Thetis (cf. 882–9, 886–8nn.), we get in a way the reverse pattern to that displayed in *Rhesus*.
307 Polymestor's astrophon (*Hec.* 1056–84, 1088–1106), the second surviving one after *Andr.* 103–16, is also still divided and concluded by iambics from the coryphaeus (Ritchie 339–40, who also refers to Io's more complex song in *PV* 561–612; cf. Griffith, *Authenticity of PV*, 119–20).
308 Cf. *Andr.* 103–116 (prepared for in 91–5), *IA* 1475–99 and in comedy Ar. *Ach.* 263–79, *Lys.* 1279–90, *Ran.* 1331–63, *Eccl.* 893–9 (all 'announced').

W. Barner, in W. Jens [ed.], *Die Bauformen der griechischen Tragödie*, Munich 1971, 274, 303–4), as if to underline the continuity of her thoughts in this extraordinary blend of mourning- and divine revelation-scene (882–9, 915–49, 962–82nn.).

890–2a. ὁρᾶν πάρεστι, Τρῶες: a declaration of favour analogous to *HF* 822–4 (quoted in 889n.) and *Ion* 1553–4 (Athena speaking) μὴ φεύγετ'· οὐ γὰρ πολεμίαν με φεύγετε / ἀλλ' ἔν τ' Ἀθήναις κἀνθάδ' οὖσαν εὐμενῆ. The notion implied here, that one should not look upon gods without prior permission (and at the risk of incurring their retribution) is another feature often associated with epiphanies (F. Pfister, *RE* Suppl. IV s.v. Epiphanie, coll. 320–1). Cf. *Ion* 1551–2 (889n.), *Od.* 16.178–9 θάμβησε δέ μιν (i.e. Odysseus) φίλος υἱός, / ταρβήσας δ' ἑτέρωσε βάλ' ὄμματα, μὴ θεὸς εἴη, A. R. 2.681–3 οὐδέ τις ἔτλη / ἀντίον αὐγάσσασθαι ἐς ὄμματα καλὰ θεοῖο, / στὰν δὲ κάτω νεύσαντες ἐπὶ χθονός and in general Call. *Lav. Pall.* 100–2 Κρόνιοι δ' ὧδε λέγοντι νόμοι· / ὅς κε τιν' ἀθανάτων, ὅκα μὴ θεὸς αὐτὸς ἕληται, / ἀθρήσῃ, μισθῷ τοῦτον ἰδεῖν μεγάλῳ.

ἡ γὰρ ... Μοῦσα ... / πάρειμι: For the third-person subject with a first-person verb in divine self-introductions see 646n.

ἐν σοφοῖς: 'poet-musicians'. Cf. Pi. *Ol.* 1.8–9 ὅθεν ὁ πολύφατος ὕμνος ἀμφιβάλλεται / σοφῶν μητίεσσι, *Pyth.* 1.113, *IT* 1238 (of Apollo) ἐν κιθάρᾳ σοφόν (LSJ s.v. σοφός I 1, 923–4a, 945b–7, 948–9nn.).

συγγόνων μία: 393–4a n. Here 'a *definite* individual [the Muse] is classified as a member of a group' (Dodds on *Ba.* 917). Substantival σύγγονος is extremely frequent in Euripides (Ritchie 172, Liapis on 890–2).

892b–3a. παῖδα τόνδ' ... οἰκτρῶς ... / θανόνθ': similarly S. *El.* 101–2 σοῦ, πάτερ, οὕτως / ἀκῶς οἰκτρῶς τε θανόντος (with Finglass on 102).

893b–4. While it was Diomedes who killed Rhesus (622–6), the Muse begins by singling out Odysseus as the arch-villain and leader of the expedition. It is tempting to see in her threat an anticipation of his future wanderings.

δόλιος Ὀδυσσεὺς ἀξίαν τείσει δίκην: The line may have been composed from *Phil.* 606–8 Ἕλενος, ὃν οὗτος ... / ... / δόλιος Ὀδυσσεὺς εἷλε and S. *El.* 298 (Clytaemestra to Electra) ἀλλ' ἴσθι τοι τείσουσά γ' ἀξίαν δίκην.[309] As a derogatory epithet of Odysseus δόλιος also occurs

---

309 If this is correct, it is an argument against adopting Housman's δόλοις in *Phil.* 608, with Pearson, Lloyd-Jones & Wilson and Diggle (in P. J. Finglass *et al.* [eds.], *Hesperos: Studies ... Presented to M. L. West ...*, Oxford 2007, 157–8), unless the corruption is very early or happened in our poet's mind.

in tragedy at *Tro*. 282–3 and, indirectly, *Or*. 1403–4 ὁ δὲ παῖς Στροφίου, κακόμητις ἀνήρ, / οἷος Ὀδυσσεύς, σιγᾷ δόλιος. The Charioteer had recounted how Rhesus fell δολίῳ πληγῇ (747–9).

For ἀξίαν τείσει δίκην see further 812b–13n. Murray again restored τείσει (τίσει Ω).

Metre

A 'variation on the hemiepes', which differs from true dactylo-epitrite in the absence of × *e* ×, the preference for short 'link-syllables' and the introduction of the here indivisible colon ⏑ ⏑ – ⏑ ⏑ – ⏑ – ⏑ – – (900–1/911–12n.). For a similar strophic pattern (with all except the second feature recurring) both Dale (*LM*¹163–4, ²173) and Ritchie (318) compare *Alc*. 435–44 ~ 445–54, and one can also find affinities with *Rh*. 224–32 + 233–41 ~ 242–52 + 253–63 (224b–5 ~ 233b–4 *D* | *ith* |, 243 ~ 255 *D*² |, 249 ~ 260 ⏑ ⏑ – ⏑ ⏑ – ⏑ – ⏑ – –, a prolonged version of 900–1 ~ 911–12).

895	906	⏑ – ⏑ ⏑ | – ⏑ ⏑ – |	⏑ *D* |
896	907	⏑ – ⏑ ⏑ – ⏑ ⏑ –	⏑ *D*
897	908	– ⏑ – ⏑ | – – |	*ith* |
898	909	⏑ – ⏑ | ⏑ – ⏑ ⏑ – – ||	⏑ *D* – ||
899	910	– ⏓ – ⏑ ⏑ – ⏑ ⏑ – |	*D*² (contr.) |
900	911	⏑ ⏑ – ⏑ ⏑ – | ⏑ – ⏑ – –	'enopl.'
901		⏑ ⏑ – ⏑ ⏑ – | ⏑ – ⏑ – – |	'enopl.' |
	912	†⏑ – ⏑ ⏑ – ⏑ ⏑† – | ⏑ – ⏑ – – |	
902	913	– ⏑ ⏑ – ⏑ ⏑ – ⏑ ⏑ – |	*D*² |
903	914	⏗ – | ⏑ ⏑ – | ⏑ ⏑ – – |||	⏗ *D* – |||

Notes

900–1/911–12 Synartesis is permitted in sets of identical pendent cola (catalectic or not), where their clausular effect may have been blurred by the lack of rhythmical contrast (L. P. E. Parker, *CQ* n.s. 26 [1976], 20, 22–5). Cf. A. *Suppl*. 631/2 ~ 644/5, 815/6 ~ 823/4, *Cho*. 387–90 ~ 411–14, *Ba*. 105–6 ~ 120–1 (all *ar*), *Ai*. 631–2 ~ 643–4 (*ph* + *ph*), Ar. *Vesp*. 318b–19 (*reiz* + *reiz*), *Thesm*. 1034–5 (2*ia*∧ + 2*ia*∧).

This 'enoplian' is a favourite of Euripides, found in various contexts from 'free dactylo-epitrite' (*Alc*. 437 ~ 447, 442 ~ 452) to iambodochmiac (*HF* 1080, *IT* 884, *Ion* 1458), aeolic (*Med*. 650 ~ 659) and 'mixed' (*Alc*. 460 ~ 470, *Hec*. 926 ~ 936, *IT* 1251 ~ 1275 and perhaps

Phoen. 1581).³¹⁰ See K. Itsumi, *BICS* 38 (1991–1993), 243–61, especially 246–7, 252, 255 with n. 39.

903/914 Genuine and 'free' dactylo-epitrite strophes rarely end with a dactylic colon, but see Ar. *Nub.* 474/5 ἄξια σῇ φρενὶ συμβουλευσομένους μετὰ σοῦ (West, *GM* 133). For the opening 'link-biceps' cf. *Rh.* 527/8 ~ 546/7 ⏒⏒ $D \asymp e \mid - - \parallel$.

895–8. 'In an unpremeditated dirge I lament you, my son, your mother's grief, for the voyage you made to Troy.'

ἰαλέμῳ αὐθιγενεῖ: Despite the Muse's foreknowledge of her son's fate (900–1, 934–5), αὐθιγενής, literally 'born on the spot', is here best understood with Σ^V *Rh.* 895 (II 343.19 Schwartz = 116 a² Merro) τῷ εὐθὺς γενομένῳ θρήνῳ, Porter (on 895) and others to denote a 'spontaneous', not 'genuine, sincere' (Paley on 894, LSJ s.v. 2), composition at the place of Rhesus' death (cf. 892 πάρειμι), similar to the hint at extempore performance in Bacch. 2.11–12 καλεῖ δὲ Μοῦσ' αὐθιγενής / γλυκεῖαν αὐλῶν καναχάν (Maehler [1982] on 2.11 [cf. p. 10], Th. Gelzer, *MH* 42 [1985], 95–120, particularly 104, 109, A. Bagordo, *Glotta* 73 [1995/6], 137–41). Kovacs' 'of native strain' (cf. Jouan 52 n. 266 and e.g. E. fr. 472.5–8 αὐθιγενὴς ... κυπάρισσος, Anaxandr. fr. 42.71 *PCG*, Hdt. 4.180.2) appears less significant in itself, although, as in Bacchylides, an allusion to the singer's homeland may be felt (cf. Liapis on 895–8, who notes the common tragic association of non-Greek characters with violent mourning).³¹¹

Bagordo (above), followed by Fantuzzi (*Eikasmos* 18 [2007], 190), finds in the Muse's choice of words an allusion to Calliope's grief at the premature death of her son Ialemos, the eponym of the dirge: Pi. fr. 128c Sn.–M. = Σ^V *Rh.* 895 (II 343.13–345.11 Schwartz = 114–15 a¹ Merro). Linguistically, ἰάλεμος (Ionic ἰήλεμος) is an expressive noun from the interjection ἰή (*GEW*, *DELG* s.v.).

τέκνον σ' ... ὦ / ματρὸς ἄλγος: Of a person ἄλγος occurs three times in Euripides (*Hipp.* 844–6 ὤμοι μοι < > σέθεν, / μέλεος, οἷον εἶδον ἄλγος δόμων, / οὐ τλητὸν οὐδὲ ῥητόν [i.e. the dead Phaedra], *Hec.* 663, *Ba.* 1282), but not in Aeschylus or Sophocles (Hutchinson on *Sept.* [865]).

---

310 With Willink's division (cf. Diggle, *Euripidea*, 361, Mastronarde on 1581 [p. 561]). The only other cases are *Tr.* 648 ~ 656, following a 'cyrenaic', and parodically Ar. *Av.* 1411, 1415 (after a 'greater asclepiad', *gl²ᶜ*), where, as in *Alc.* 460 ~ 470 and *Med.* 650 ~ 659, analysis as ⌣$tl_\wedge ia$ is also possible.

311 The sense 'innate' seems to be late and very rare: [Longin.] *De Subl.* 8.1 ἀλλ' αἱ μὲν δύο αὗται τοῦ ὕψους κατὰ τὸ πλέον αὐθιγενεῖς συστάσεις, αἱ λοιπαὶ δ' ἤδη καὶ διὰ τέχνης and presumably Philo Iud. *De Cherub.* 50. But it remains tempting also to see the Muse's inherent gift for song evoked in ἰαλέμῳ αὐθιγενεῖ.

L. Castiglioni (*RIL* 70 [1937], 60 = *Decisa Forficibus*, Milan 1954, 7–8) observed the similarity between our phrase and Ov. *Her.* 11.111 *nate, dolor matris, rabidarum praeda ferarum*, which need not, however, echo *Rhesus* so much as a related sentiment in Ovid's assumed tragic source for that poem, E. *Aeolus* (H. Jacobson, *Ovid's Heroides*, Princeton 1974, 162 n. 13).

οἵαν / ἔκελσας ὁδὸν ποτὶ Τροίαν: causal-exclamatory after ὀλοφύρομαι as an expression of feeling (cf. 309–10n.). Similarly e.g. *Hipp.* 844–6 (above), 878–80 ἀπὸ γὰρ ὀλόμενος οἴχομαι, / οἷον οἷον εἶδον γραφαῖς μέλος / φθεγγόμενον τλάμων and Xen. *Cyr.* 7.3.14 ὃ μὲν δὴ ... ἀπῄει, κατοικτίρων τήν τε γυναῖκα οἵου ἀνδρὸς στέροιτο καὶ τὸν ἄνδρα οἵαν γυναῖκα καταλιπὼν οὐκέτ' ὄψοιτο.

On κέλλω see 752–3n. The internal accusative here is paralleled in A. *Suppl.* 330–1 ἐπεὶ τίς ηὔχει τήνδ' ἀνέλπιστον φυγήν / κέλσειν ἐς Ἄργος κῆδος ἐγγενὲς τὸ πρίν (with FJW on 330–2 [II, pp. 265–7], West, *Studies*, 142–3), Nic. *Ther.* 295 ... βαιὸν πλόον αἰὲν ὀκέλλει and 321 ... ἀτὰρ στίβον ἀντί' ὀκέλλει.

899–901. 'An ill-starred and miserable voyage indeed it was, on which you went, although I said no and your father entreated you forcefully.'

The Muse's reluctance to let Rhesus go to Troy is explained in 934–5a (n.) with her foreknowledge of his fate. As a theme this is particularly familiar from the story of Achilles, whom Peleus (later Thetis: 'Apollod.' 3.13.8 [3.174], Hyg. *Fab.* 96.1) tried to conceal among Lycomedes' daughters: Σ^D *Il.* 19.326 (p. 516 van Thiel) Πηλεὺς δὲ προγινώσκων ὅτι μοιρίδιον ἦν ἐν Τροίᾳ θανεῖν Ἀχιλλέα, παραγενόμενος εἰς Σκῦρον πρὸς Λυκομήδην τὸν βασιλέα παρέθετο τὸν Ἀχιλλέα.[312] In the case of Eurypylus Astyoche had to be bribed by Priam to let her son help Troy: *Od.* 11.519–22, with Σ 520 (II 517.14–21 Dindorf) = Acusil. fr. 40a Fowler, *Il. Parv.* fr. 6 GEF, S. fr. 211 (*Eurypylus*). Cf. 935b–7n.[313]

Parthenius in *Erot. Path.* 36.4 transferred the anxiety to Rhesus' wife Arganthone (cf. Introduction, 17, 44–5).

ἦ δυσδαίμονα καὶ μελέαν: *sc.* ὁδὸν ἔκελσας, with ἦ underlining the epexegetic value of the clause (*GP* 281).

---

[312] The episode has falsely been attributed to the *Cypria* (West, *Epic Cycle*, 103–4, 184–5). It is first attested in a fifth-century painting by Polygnotus (Paus. 1.22.6) and was dramatised in Euripides' *Skyrioi*.

[313] *Il.* 11.328–34 recounts the fall of Amphius and Adrestus, whose prophet father Merops had foreseen their death at Troy and tried to retain them. The motif is varied at *Il.* 5.148–51 (a dream-interpreter, Eurydamas, fails to predict his sons' fate) and *Il.* 13.663–72 (Euchenor, son of the Corinthian seer Polyïdus, is given the choice between dying of a disease at home or falling in the Trojan war, and chooses the latter).

ἀπὸ μὲν φαμένας: Dindorf's correction (*PSG*¹, XXII = III.2 [1840], 623–4) of the MSS text (ἀπομεμφομένας V: -μεμψαμένας L: -πεμψαμένας Q et Tr^ls) provides the best sense and phraseological correspondence with 901 ἀπὸ δ' ἀντομένου πατρὸς βιαίως. The two tmeses here are of the easiest type (Barrett on *Hipp*. 256–7) and in drama most often found in Euripidean lyrics (KG I 533–5, L. Bergson, *RhM* N.F. 102 [1959], 33–5). Cf. *Andr*. 1022–3 ἀπὸ δὲ φθίμενοι βεβᾶσιν / Ἰλιάδαι βασιλῆες, *Hec*. 910–12 (both in similar metres), 928, *Tro*. 522.

ἀπὸ δ' ἀντομένου: a unique compound of ἄντομαι (+ accusative), 'entreat' (LSJ s.v. II), which 'undoubtedly stems from a desire to balance ἀπὸ μὲν φαμένας' (Liapis on 899–901 [p. 310]).

βιαίως in its final position is better taken with ἀπὸ δ' ἀντομένου πατρός than πορευθείς ('in defiance of us'), as Paley (on 900), Feickert (95) and others do.

902–3. ὤμοι ἐγὼ σέθεν: For the causal-ablatival genitive after interjections, indicating the 'source' of the feeling, see KG I 388 and SD 134. As here, *Hipp*. 844 ὤμοι μοι < > σέθεν (895–8n.).

ὦ φιλία / φιλία κεφαλά: an affectionate, epic-style form of address: *Il*. 8.281 Τεῦκρε, φίλη κεφαλή, Τελαμώνιε, κοίρανε λαῶν, 23.94 (Achilles to Patroclus' ghost) τίπτε μοι, ἠθείη κεφαλή, δεῦρ' εἰλήλουθας (*LfgrE* s.v. κεφάλη L, B 11); also, respectfully to Apollo, *Rh*. 226a (n.) Θυμβραῖε ... Ἄπολλον, ὦ Δία κεφαλά. In other tragedy only κάρα is found in such emotionally coloured periphrases (Barrett on *Hipp*. 651–2, Fraenkel, *Rev*. 239), but cf. Ar. *Ach*. 285 σὲ μὲν οὖν καταλεύσομεν, ὦ μιαρὰ κεφαλή (with Olson) and e.g. Pl. *Phdr*. 264a7–8, *Grg*. 513c 2 φίλη κεφαλή.

The use of φίλιος (properly 'of a friend, friendly') as a metrical synonym for φίλος is all but confined to tragic, particularly Euripidean, anapaests and lyric: A. *Suppl*. 533 φιλίας προγόνου γυναικός (with FJW), *Cho*. 719 εἶέν, φίλιαι δμωΐδες οἴκων, S. *El*. 226, *Alc*. 473 (playing on the literal sense), 876, 917, *Med*. 1262, 1399, *Andr*. 1181, *HF* 752, *Or*. 1246 Μυκηνίδες ὦ φίλιαι (Hermann: φίλαι codd.), *Phaeth*. 85 Diggle = E. fr. 773.41, E. fr. 953m.46. Cf. Arist. fr. 842.15 *PMG*.

904–5. 'As far as one who is no blood relation may, I pity your son for his painful death.'

A parallel in thought is offered by the (possibly interpolated) choral couplet *IA* 469–70 κἀγὼ κατῴκτιρ', ὡς γυναῖκα δεῖ ξένην / ὑπὲρ τυράννων συμφορᾶς καταστένειν. Fantuzzi (*Eikasmos* 18 [2007], 192–4, *JHS* 127 [2007], 161) refers to the Solonian ban on mourning by strangers (Plut. *Sol*. 21.4 ... καὶ τὸ κωκύειν ἄλλον ἐν ταφαῖς ἑτέρων ἀφεῖλεν; cf. the law quoted in [Dem.] 43.62), but the response remains somewhat lukewarm.

λύπης: i.e. the 'grievous fate' inflicted upon Rhesus, as by implication in 758–9 θανεῖν γὰρ εὐκλεῶς μέν ... / λυπρὸν μὲν οἶμαι τῷ θανόντι. Kirchhoff's causal genitive (I [1855], 562), for which cf. *Ag*. 1321 ὦ τλῆμον, οἰκτίρω σε θεσφάτου μόρου, Xen. *Smp*. 4.37 τούτους ... οἰκτίρω τῆς ἄγαν χαλεπῆς νόσου and perhaps A. *Suppl*. 209 ὦ Ζεῦ, κόπων (σκοπῶν Johansen) οἴκτιρε μὴ ἀπολωλότας (with FJW [II, pp. 167–9]), neatly disposes of the slightly tautological dative λύπῃ (-η L: -ην VQ), printed by most editors. Alternatively, one may follow Kovacs in adopting Wecklein's ὅσῃ ... λύπῃ ('With as much grief as befits ...'), where the relative would have been liable to alteration into the much more frequent (adverbial) accusative (e.g. Isoc. 20.16, Pl. *Smp*. 222a5 ὅσον προσήκει, Strabo 8.3.3 ἐφ' ὅσον προσήκει προσσκοπεῖν).

Liapis' rewriting of the couplet as ὅσον προσήκει μὴ γένει κοινωνίαν / ἔχοντα λύπης, τὸν σὸν οἰκτίρω γόνον ('Notes', 101) does not convince. For κοινωνίαν ... λύπης ('share in your grief') he may have compared Pl. *Rep*. 462b4 οὐκοῦν ἡ μὲν ἡδονῆς τε καὶ λύπης κοινωνία συνδεῖ (*sc*. τὴν πόλιν) ...; but γένει applied to a momentary rather than inherent state or quality (e.g. Dem. 23.24 ἡμῖν τοῖς γένει πολίταις) seems peculiar.

906–7. Curses, especially on the person(s) or circumstances held responsible for the victim's disaster, belong to the standard repertoire of Greek dirges ancient, medieval and modern: e.g. *Cho*. 367–71, S. *El*. 126–7, *OT* 1349–55, *Tro*. 766–72, *Phoen*. 350–4 (M. Alexiou, *The Ritual Lament in Greek Tradition*, Cambridge ¹1974 ~ Lanham ²2002, 178–9 and Index II s.v. 'curse', ¹272, ²290). Here the motif is further stressed by the kind of (near-)isometric parison that has again always been typical of, though by no means exclusive to, cultic-magical formulae and laments: *Pers*. 550–2 ~ 560–2, 694–5 σέβομαι μὲν προσιδέσθαι, / σέβομαι δ' ἀντία λέξαι ~ 700–1 δίομαι μὲν χαρίσασθαι, / δίομαι δ' ἀντία φάσθαι, *Sept*. 911–12, *Cho*. 327–8, *Tr*. 947–8 ~ 950–1, E. *Suppl*. 73–4, *Phoen*. 1033–4, 1036–7 and, in joy, *Phaeth*. 99 Diggle = E. fr. 773.56 θεὸς ἔδωκε, χρόνος ἔκρανε (with Diggle). Generally see E. Fraenkel, *Plautinisches im Plautus*, Berlin 1922, 365 = Oxford 2007, 246–7 with nn. 102–4, p. 380 (English), Kranz, *Stasimon*, 127–37, 188–90, Diggle, *Studies*, 55, West, *IEPM* 326–9.

Οἰνεΐδας: uniquely παππωνυμικόν, as perhaps Κρόνιος in 36 (36–7a n.).

908–9. '... who has deprived me of my most high-born son.'

ἄπαιδα γέννας / ... ἀριστοτόκοιο: Euripides was exceedingly fond of ἄπαις and ἀπαιδία to describe both absolute childlessness (e.g. *Med*. 490, *Andr*. 360, *Phoen*. 13, E. fr. 571.3; cf. *Rh*. 982) and, as here, the state of having lost all one's offspring (e.g. *Cyc*. 306, *Alc*. 621, *Med*. 1326, *Hel*. 849). For the separative genitive cf. *Andr*. 612 παίδων τ' ἄπαιδας γραῦς ἔθηκας ἐν δόμοις, 714, E. *Suppl*. 35, 810, *Ba*. 1305, Hdt. 1.109.3 καὶ ὅτι Ἀστυάγης μέν ἐστι γέρων καὶ ἄπαις ἔρσενος γόνου, 3.66.2.

ἀριστοτόκοιο, a *hapax*,[314] echoes the first line of Thetis' premature lament for Achilles, *Il*. 18.54 ᾧ μοι ἐγὼ δειλή, ᾧ μοι δυσαριστοτόκεια (see Edwards), as does perhaps Stes. fr. S 13.2–3 *PMGF = SLG* . . . .] ἐγὼν [μελέ]α καὶ ἀλασ- / [τοτόκος κ]αὶ ἄλ[ασ]τα παθοῖσα (3 init. suppl. Barrett, ἄλαστα iam Lobel). The epic genitive ending -οιο (Aldina: -τοτόκου VL: -τόκου Q) has good MSS authority in Aeschylean (*Pers*. 108) and Euripidean lyrics (e.g. *Hipp*. 560, *El*. 465, *HF* 123, E. fr. 727c.25 [Page on *Med*. 135]),[315] but is still easily corrupted into more regular forms. Cf. *Pers*. 568–9 πρωτομόροιο / ... ἀνάγκας (Blomfield: πρωτόμοροι ... ἀνάγκαν fere ΣΩ), 866–7, *Hipp*. 850, *Ba*. 875–6, E. *Suppl*. 1030 ἀλόχοιο (Wilamowitz: ψυχὰς ἀλόχῳ L), *Tro*. 538 λίνοιο (Bothe e Σ (λίνου): λίνοισι VPQ).

910–14. 'And (a curse) on her who left her Greek home and sailed away going to a Phrygian bed; †she who has killed you beneath Ilium† for the sake of Troy, my dearest son, and emptied countless cities of brave men.'

Such unmitigated hostility towards Helen as being the cause of Troy's fall or, from either side's perspective, the death of many good men had been traditional at least since Alc. fr. 42.15–16 Voigt οἳ δ' ἀπώλοντ' ἀμφ' Ἐ[λένᾳ ⏑ – ⏓] / καὶ πόλις αὐτῶν[316] and in surviving tragedy goes back to *Agamemnon* (404–15, 445–9, 681–716, 738–49, 1455–61, 1462–7).

910–11. **Ἕλλανα:** Badham (*Philologus* 10 [1855], 338) for the MSS' ἑλένα, which may be due to mental association or a marginal gloss.

Φρυγίων λεχέων: 32n.

ἔπλευσε πλαθεῖσ': As demonstrated above ('Metre' 900–1/911–12n.), the elision need not be emended away by writing πλέουσ' ἐπλάθη with Kovacs (*Euripidea Tertia*, 149–50) and, more tentatively, Willink ('Cantica', 42 = *Collected Papers*, 581). Regarding syntax, it is true that

---

314 Except for an undated Romano-Syrian verse-inscription: *EG* 896 (= *IGRom* III 1124, *GE* 26).1–2 Ἄμφω, ἀριστότοκος καὶ ἀγλαόπαις ἐστιν / Τιβέριος, ὃς Μαρκελλῖνον τέκετ' ἔξοχ<ον> ἀνδρῶν. The latest edition (*SGO* IV 22/22/01) reads ἀριστότοκος, 'father of a splendid son' (cf. Opp. *Cyn*. 3.62), which entails taking ἀγλαόπαις in the unnatural sense 'excellent son' and puts the relative clause rather out of sequence.

315 E. fr. 228.3–4 (*Archelaus*) ἐκ μελαμβρότοιο ... / Αἰθιοπίδος γῆς (3ia) is suspect. See A. Harder, *Euripides' Kresphontes and Archelaos. Introduction, Text and Commentary*, Leiden 1985, 182, 185–6 and J. S. Scullion, in D. Cairns – V. J. Liapis (eds.), *Dionysalexandros. Essays ... in Honour of Alexander F. Garvie*, Swansea 2006, 190–1 (with full references).

316 Contrast *Od*. 11.435–9 (with Heubeck on 435–43) and 14.68–71 in the light of her more sympathetic portrayals in 4.120–305 (though see S. R. West on 120 ff., 242 ff.), 15.56–181 and e.g. *Il*. 3.121–244, 383–447.

πλαθεῖσ' bears a superficial relationship to λιποῦσα as well as ἔπλευσε, although taking it as a coincident aorist participle (Kovacs; cf. KG I 197–9 with n. 8, SD 300–1) goes a long way to mitigating the incongruity. Mastronarde's suggestion that Φρυγίων λεχέων 'refers to a bed already shared with Paris ... not to a bed in Phrygia [Helen] has yet to reach' (*ElectronAnt* 8 [2004], 22) leaves ἔπλευσε entirely unqualified.

Intransitive πελάζω and πελάζομαι (passive) are common in sexual contexts and either govern a genitive as here (cf. *OT* 1098–1101, *Tr*. 17) or, more frequently, a dative: e.g. *Rh*. 920 (919–20n.) λέκτροις ἐπλάθην Στρυμόνος φυταλμίοις, Bacch. 9.55–6 (as supplemented by Wilamowitz), *Dith*. 3.33–6, *PV* 897, *Andr*. 25 (FJW on A. *Suppl*. 300).

912–14. †ὑπ' Ἰλίῳ ὤλεσε† μὲν σ' ἕκατι Τροίας: It is difficult, if not impossible, to weigh up the relative merits of three emendations that have been advanced for the unmetrical and redundant ὑπ' Ἰλίῳ. Wilamowitz' ὅπου ὤλεσε (*apud* Murray), accepted by Porter, Zanetto (cf. Feickert on 912) and Kovacs (*Euripidea Tertia*, 149), is most straightforward on the likely hypothesis that we have here an intrusive gloss, inspired by a standard phrase (e.g. *Cho*. 345–7 εἰ γὰρ ὑπ' Ἰλίῳ / ... πάτερ / ... κατηναρίσθης, *Andr*. 1182, *Hec*. 764, *Or*. 58–9, 102; also *Ag*. 1455–7 ἰώ, <ἰὼ> παράνους Ἑλένα, / μία τὰς πολλάς, τὰς πάνυ πολλὰς / ψυχὰς ὀλέσασ' ὑπὸ Τροίᾳ) and intended to clarify the link between Φρυγίων λεχέων and the relative. Henning's ἀπὸ δ' ὤλεσε (*teste* Wecklein, *Appendix*, 55: ἀπό τ' Wecklein), on the other hand, would create an elegant response to the tmesis in 901 (Willink, 'Cantica', 42–3 = *Collected Papers*, 581, Jouan 53 n. 270), while Jackson's ἃ διώλεσε (*Marginalia Scaenica*, 66–7) to go with Φρυγίων λεχέων subtly varies the syntactical pattern of 906–9.[317] In any case we require σ' ἕκατι Τροίας (E. Bruhn, *RhM* N.F. 48 [1893], 630) for the transmitted σε κατὰ Τροίας (Ω).

Believing (with Paley on 912) that κατὰ Τροίας rather than ὑπ' Ἰλίῳ is the gloss, Liapis ('Notes', 103) proposes ὑπό τ' Ἴλιον ὤλεσέν σε βάντα. But there is no parallel for such an annotation, and one fails to see the need for it here.[318] Moreover, Liapis does not mention that his conjecture entails period end after *brevis in longo*.

μυριάδας τε πόλεις / ἀνδρῶν ἀγαθῶν ἐκένωσεν: Cf. A. *Suppl*. 659–60 (... εὐχά) μήποτε λοιμὸς ἀνδρῶν / τάνδε πόλιν κενῶσαι, and

---

[317] This last solution is favoured by Diggle (apparatus) and Willink (above), who still prefers to explain ὑπ' Ἰλίῳ as a gloss. Jackson suggested the more complicated process of misreading and faulty augmentation of [.]ΔΙ(Ω)ΩΛΕΣΕ.

[318] For ὑπ(ὸ) Ἴλιον cf. *Il*. 2.216, 249, 492, 673, 23.297, 'Hes.' fr. 136.8 M.–W., *Ag*. 986, *Or*. 648. In fact both Paley and Liapis state that κατὰ Τροίας explained the MSS' ὑπ' Ἰλίῳ, although in that case the preposition with genitive ('against') would make no sense.

of war e.g. *Pers.* 548–9 νῦν γὰρ δὴ πρόπασα μὲν στένει / γαῖ' Ἀσὶς ἐκκενουμένα, 718, 730 ὡς Σούσων μὲν ἄστυ πᾶν κενανδρίᾳ στένει, 761, *Sept.* 329–30 βοᾷ δ' / ἐκκενουμένα πόλις.

In view of Hdt. 7.184.3 ἄνδρες ... τέσσερες μυριάδες καὶ εἴκοσι and the all but certain restoration of Corinn. fr. 654 col. i.32–4 *PMG* ὑκτρῶς / [.....]ων οὐψ[ό]θεν εἴρι- / [σέ νιν ἐ]μ μου[ρι]άδεσσι λᾶυς (cf. D. L. Page [ed.], *Corinna*, London 1953, 58 [x]),[319] there seems no reason to suspect the adjectival use of μυριάδας here and emend to either πόλεων (Reiske, *Animadversiones*, 92) or, less satisfactorily for leaving the object unqualified, μυριάδων (-ος) to go directly with ἐκένωσεν (Ritchie 177).

915–49. The Muse's 'spontaneous dirge' (895–8n.) is followed by an extended speech, which combines (and develops) the same elements of lamentation, blame and disclosure of the guilty party. The Trojans will learn that Athena was the driving force behind the Achaean raiders (938–40n.), whereas the audience gains further interesting and potentially moving information about the dead hero.

Fenik (*Iliad X*, 29) and Bond (*AJPh* 117 [1996], 263–4) have pointed out the structural similarities between *Rh.* 895–935 and Thetis' lament for Achilles in *Il.* 18.52–64 (cf. 974–7n.), where, differences in length discounted, an 'outcry of pain' (*Il.* 18.52–4 ~ *Rh.* 895–914, especially *Il.* 18.54 ~ *Rh.* 908 [908–9n.]) is succeeded in each case by the tale of the son's birth and rearing (*Il.* 18.55–7 ~ *Rh.* 915–33) and a (retrospective) anticipation of his death at Troy: *Il.* 18.58–60 ~ *Rh.* 934–5a (n.).[320] With regard to the latter, the Muse extends her accusations in a wide circle of responsibility (Rosivach 70–2), which includes not only Odysseus (893–4, 907–9), Diomedes (906) and Helen (910–14), but also Thamyris, whose insolence led to Rhesus' conception (915–25), Hector (935–7) and eventually Athena (938–40, 944–5; cf. 978). This last turn recalls the grudge Artemis expresses against Aphrodite in *Hipp.* 1325–8 and 1416–22 (cf. 938–40, 978–9nn.), although an even clearer precedent may exist in A. fr. 350.7–9 (Thetis of Apollo) ὁ δ' αὐτὸς ὑμνῶν, αὐτὸς ἐν θοίνῃ παρών, / αὐτὸς τάδ' εἰπών, αὐτός ἐστιν ὁ κτανών / τὸν παῖδα τὸν ἐμόν (Ritchie 80), especially if, with West (*CQ* n.s. 50 [2000], 342 = *Hellenica* II, 233–4) and others (cf. *TrGF* III, 417), we could assume that *Nereids* covered Achilles' death and the fragment belonged to its final lament (882–9, 978–9nn.).

---

[319] At *Pers.* 925–7 ἀγδαβάται γὰρ πολλοὶ φῶτες, / ... / πάνυ ταρφύς τις μυριὰς ἀνδρῶν, ἐξέφθινται, Franz' ταρφύς τις for the meaningless γὰρ φύστις (fere ΣΩ [φύσις HD]) is palmary.

[320] My division of parts differs slightly from that of Fenik and Bond.

The jointless transition from song to speech (890–914n.) is thus internally justified in what is essentially yet another example of the same topic being treated first in lyrics and then in more 'restrained' iambic trimeters (756–803n.). Similarly, at *Ai.* 430–80 the hero reviews his lot and prospects in a well-tempered speech, with only a choral couplet (428–9) intervening after his almost monodic pair of strophes (394–409 ~ 412–27) at the end of the preceding *amoibaion*.

915–25. The story of the Thracian singer Thamyris, who challenged the Muses to his doom, was already familiar to Homer (*Il.* 2.594–600) and 'Hesiod' (frr. 59, 65 M.–W.) and in the fifth and fourth centuries dramatised by Sophocles (frr. 236a–245) and Antiphanes (fr. 104 *PCG*). Yet it is difficult to see why it gets so much room here, other than as an interesting tale with a Thracian connection (919–25n.), which may lend colour to the probably largely invented background of Rhesus (Introduction, 13–14). Liapis' theory (on 915–16) that the Muses' punishment of Thamyris anticipates the threatened one of Athena and her city for killing Rhesus depends on our interpretation of 948–9 (n.).

915–16. εἰς Ἅιδου μολών: a common, inflectable 'verse-end formula': *OT* 1372, *PV* 236, *Tr.* 4, *Phil.* 1349 ... εἰς Ἅιδου μολεῖν, *HF* 1331 ... εὖτ' ἂν εἰς Ἅιδου μόλῃς.

Φιλάμμονος παῖ: i.e. Thamyris (919–25n.). On the apostrophe see 930–1n.

τῆς ἐμῆς ἥψω φρενός: The same phrase is given to Athena addressing Poseidon as *dea ex machina* at E. fr. 370.59–60 (*Erechtheus*) οὐ κατὰ χθονός / κρύψας Ἐρεχθέα τῆς ἐμῆς ἥψω φρενός; For the metaphor cf. also Ar. *Eq.* 1237 πῶς εἶπας; ὥς μού χρησμὸς ἅπτεται φρενῶν (paratragic), Pl. *Ion* 535a3–4 ἅπτει γάρ πώς μου τοῖς λόγοις τῆς ψυχῆς, *Med.* 55 ... καὶ φρενῶν ἀνθάπτεται, 1360, *Hel.* 960.

917–18. ὕβρις ... καὶ Μουσῶν ἔρις comes close to a hendiadys: 'the insolence of challenging the Muses'. ἔρις with an object genitive of the person is paralleled in e.g. Hdt. 5.88.3 κατ' ἔριν τὴν Ἀθηναίων and Corinn. fr. 664 (a) *PMG* μέμφομη δὲ κὴ λιγουρὰν / Μουρτίδ' ἰώνγ' ὅτι βανὰ φοῦ- / σ' ἔβα Πινδάροι πὸτ ἔριν.

τεκεῖν μ' ἔθηκε τόνδε δύστηνον γόνον: For τίθημί τινα ποιεῖν τι, 'make someone do something', see LSJ s.v. τίθημι Β Ι 4, A. E. Housman, *CR* 2 (1888), 243 = *The Classical Papers of A. E. Housman* I (edd. J. Diggle – F. R. D. Goodyear), Cambridge 1972, 25 and Diggle, *Studies*, 48. In particular *Med.* 717–18 παίδων γονάς / σπείραί σε θήσω.

919–25. The epic tradition disagreed as to whether Thamyris' encounter with the Muses took place in Messenian Dorion (*Il.* 2.594–600; cf. ΣΣ^V *Rh.* 916, 922 [420.24–7, 421.3–4 Rabe = 117.21–3, 2–3 Merro]) or on the Dotion plain in western Thessaly ('Hes.' frr. 65 + 59.2–3 M.–

W.). Unless therefore Asclep. Tragil. *FGrHist* 12 F 10.12–13 = A. fr. 376a.5 (Σ^V *Rh.* 916 [420.16 Rabe = 117.14–15 Merro]) ἀφικομένων δὲ τῶν Μουσῶν εἰς Θρᾴκην ... follows Aeschylus, who is mentioned earlier in the note,[321] and/or S. fr. 237 Θρήϊσσα(ν) σκοπιὰ(ν) Ζηνὸς Ἀθῴου indicates a Thracian setting for Sophocles' *Thamyras* (cf. Radt, *TrGF* IV, 234), our poet may have been the first to set the contest in the singer's homeland so as to motivate the Muses' crossing of the Strymon (cf. J. Rempe, *De Rheso Thracum heroe*, diss. Münster 1927, 37–8).[322]

919–20. Rhesus' conception was described in 351b–4 (n.) Στρυμών, ὅς ποτε τᾶς μελῳ- / δοῦ Μούσας δι' ἀκηράτων / δινηθεὶς ὑδροειδὴς / κόλπων σὰν ἐφύτευσεν ἥβαν.

περῶσα ... ποταμίους διὰ ῥοάς: L. Dindorf (I [1825], 492 ~ W. Dindorf, III.2 [1840], 624), after *Tro.* 1151 Σκαμανδρίους γὰρ τάσδε διαπερῶν ῥοάς, to which one may add *Ai.* 418–19 ὦ Σκαμάνδριοι / ... ῥοαί and many examples of ῥοαί with the genitive of a river's name (LSJ s.v. ῥοή 1), especially also from Euripides (e.g. *Med.* 835, *Andr.* 650, *HF* 1163, *Hel.* 1, *Ba.* 749). Corruption into the rare διαρροάς (Ω) was probably aided by the frequency of transitive περάω, 'pass through, traverse' (LSJ s.v. (A) I 2; cf. Feickert on 919), and such Euripidean lines as *Hec.* 567 τέμνει σιδήρῳ πνεύματος διαρροάς (cf. fr. 983 οἶνος περάσας πλευμόνων διαρροάς).

On the lengthening of a syllable 'by position' before initial ῥ (going back to original *sr-* or *wr-*) see West, *GM* 15–16 and, specifically for tragic trimeters as against lyrics, Diggle, *Euripidea*, 456–8.

γὰρ δή here gets a connotation of 'arresting [the] attention at the opening of a narrative' (*GP* 243).

λέκτροις ἐπλάθην Στρυμόνος φυταλμίοις: 910–11n. In particular cf. *Tro.* 203 ἢ λέκτροις πλαθεῖσ' Ἑλλάνων.

φυταλμίοις: 'procreative' (Hsch. φ 1066 Hansen–Cunningham φυταλμίοις· φυτευτικοῖς, γονίμοις), as of (grand)fathers in *Ag.* 327–8 φυταλμίων ... γερόντων (with Fraenkel) and S. fr. 788 προσῆλθε μητρὶ καὶ φυταλμίῳ πατρί (with Pearson) and, metaphorically, one's native land in Lyc. 341 ... τῆς φυταλμίας χθονός.

Fertilising rivers are a commonplace in Greek folklore and myth. See Liapis on 351–4 with ample documentation.

921–5. '... when in Thrace we came to gold-soiled rocky Pangaeus, we Muses equipped with our instruments, for the high contest in music-

---

[321] Radt on A. fr. 376a (*TrGF* III, 430) suspects that 'Aeschylus' is the scholiast's error for 'Sophocles', and the story went according to the latter's *Thamyras*.

[322] Nothing can be ascertained from Antiph. fr. 104 *PCG* (*Thamyras*) καὶ σοῦ γ' ἐπώνυμός τις ἐν φήμαις βροτῶν / Θρῄκην κατάρδων ποταμὸς ὠνομασμένος, / Στρυμών, μεγίστας ἐγχέλεις κεκτημένος, which is in any case likely to postdate *Rhesus*.

making with the famous Thracian poet, and blinded Thamyris, who had frequently insulted our artistry.'

921–2a. Throughout antiquity Mt. Pangaeus was renowned for its gold- and silver-mines (e.g. Hdt. 6.46.2–3, 7.112, Xen. *HG* 5.2.17, Strabo 7 fr. 16b) and thus at the centre of Athenian foreign interests from the time of Peisistratos until Philip II captured Amphipolis in 357 BC (P. Perdrizet, *Klio* 10 [1910], 1–27, B. Isaac, *The Greek Settlements in Thrace until the Macedonian Conquest*, Leiden 1986, 13–51, Introduction, 14–15, 18).

γῆς looks like a verse-filler and is perhaps best explained with Ammendola (on 921) as a 'chorographic' genitive, indicating the wider geographical location (i.e. Thrace) of 'gold-soiled rocky Pangaeus' (KG I 338, SD 113–14; cf. Thuc. 8.101.3 ἀφικόμενοι τῆς ἠπείρου ἐς Ἁρματοῦντα and with place names, as usual, e.g. Hdt. 3.136.1 ἀπίκοντο τῆς Ἰταλίης ἐς Τάραντα and *Phoen*. 37–8). An 'epic' partitive genitive with ἤλθομεν (Feickert on 921), which has one tragic parallel at *OC* 688–91 ἀλλ' αἰὲν ἐπ' ἤματι / ... πεδίων ἐπινίσεται [ὁ Κηφισός] / ... / στερνούχου χθονός (cf. KG I 384–5, SD 112a), seems even less compatible with the relative vagueness of γῆ, and the same applies to Liapis' possessive genitive (on 921–5), by analogy with *Andr*. 849 καθ' ὕλαν ὀρέων and maybe *Hipp*. 1127 δρυμὸς ὄρεος (Diggle [cf. *Euripidea*, 200]: ὄρειος codd.).

χρυσόβωλον ἐς λέπας / Πάγγαιον: Cf. 972 Παγγαίου πέτραν, A. fr. 23a (*Bassarai*) Παγγαίου γὰρ ἀργυρήλατον / πρῶν' †ἐς τὸ τῆς ἀστραπῆς† πευκᾶεν σέλας (quoted in Σ^V *Rh*. 922 [421.9–10 Rabe = 118 Merro])[323] and, in phrasing, *Or*. 1382–3 καλλίβωλον Ἴ- / δας ὄρος ἱερόν (with Willink on 1381–3 and 982–4 for βῶλος referring to other than fertile ground).

Like καλλίβωλος (above) and πολύβωλος in E. fr. 229.1 (of Thrace), χρυσόβωλος is a *hapax*, formed after epic ἐρίβωλος.

922b. ὀργάνοισιν ἐξησκημέναι: 'furnished, equipped with ...' (e.g. *OC* 1602–3 λουτροῖς τέ νιν / ἐσθῆτί τ' ἐξήσκησαν, Lyc. 857–8 ὄρχατον τεύξει ... / ... φυτοῖσιν ἐξησκημένον; cf. *Pers*. 182–3, S. *El*. 452, *IA* 82–3), not 'practised in', which in classical Greek would require an accusative (LSJ s.vv. ἐξασκέω II 1, ἀσκέω II 1, 2).

923–4a. μεγίστην εἰς ἔριν μελῳδίας: Among the tragedians Euripides was particularly fond of using ἔρις with a genitive of respect: *Phoen*. 1460 ἀνῇξε δ' ὀρθὸς λαὸς εἰς ἔριν λόγων, *Ba*. 715, *Andr*. 277–9 τρίπωλον ἅρμα δαιμόνων / ... / ἔριδι στυγερᾷ κεκορυθμένον

---

[323] The second verse is irretrievably corrupt (cf. Radt's apparatus). πρῶν' is part of Mekler's solution. V gives πρῶνες, whence Rabe wrote ἀργυρήλατοι.

εὐμορφίας (~ *IA* 182–4, 1307–8). In Aeschylus cf. *Eum.* 975 νικᾷ δ' ἀγαθῶν ἔρις ἡμετέρα διὰ παντός (with Sommerstein on 973–5).

Ar. fr. 596.3 *PCG* applies μελῳδία to Euripidean lyrics. For the adjective and verb see 351b–4n.

κλεινῷ σοφιστῇ Θρῃκί: Both Dobree's κλεινῷ (*Adversaria* II [1833], 88 = IV [1874], 85) and Valckenaer's δεινῷ (on *Hipp.* 921) will make the statement of Thamyris' fame clearer than κείνῳ (Ω), which unlike ἐκείνῳ in Luc. *Tox.* 27 αὐτὸς μὲν τὴν ἄσκησιν τὴν Κυνικὴν ἀσκούμενος ὑπὸ τῷ Ῥοδίῳ ἐκείνῳ σοφιστῇ, where 'the name of the character is omitted completely' (M. Fantuzzi, *BMCR* 2006.02.18, on 924), would have to be taken as a reference back to 916–17. κλεινῷ is palaeographically closer to the paradosis, while δεινῷ σοφιστῇ has equivalents at the same verse-position in *Hipp.* 921 δεινὸν σοφιστὴν εἶπας, E. *Suppl.* [902–3]? ἐν ἀσπίδι / δεινὸς σοφιστὴς πολλά τ' ἐξευρεῖν σοφά and fr. tr. adesp. 323 δεινὸς σοφιστής, τῶν ἀγυμνάστων σφαγεύς[324] (for the reverse corruption in each case cf. Pi. *Pyth.* 1.61 πόλιν κείναν [F¹γ, Σ 118a: κλεινὰν CEF] and *Hel.* 676 κείνων λουτρῶν [Stinton: δεινῶν L]). But δεινός ('marvellous, skilful') may be too laudatory an epithet in the present context so that, despite Liapis ('Notes', 104–5),[325] κλεινῷ is to be preferred.

σοφιστής is used here in its old neutral sense 'master of one's craft, expert' (LSJ s.v. I 1) and more specifically 'poet, musician'. Cf. Pi. *Isthm.* 5.28–9 μελέταν δὲ σοφισταῖς / Διὸς ἕκατι πρόσβαλον σεβιζόμενοι, A. fr. 314, S. fr. 906, Cratin. fr. 2 *PCG*, Eup. fr. 483 *PCG*, Pl. Com. fr. 149 *PCG*. Also 890–2a, 945b–7, 948–9nn.

924b–5. Blinding by the Muses seems to have been part of Thamyris' legend at least since the Hesiodic *Catalogue of Women* ('Hes.' fr. 65 M.–W.),[326] but unlike Homer (*Il.* 2.594–600) and Sophocles in his *Thamyras* (frr. 241, 244), our poet does not also have him deprived of his citharoedic skills (cf. Pearson, *The Fragments of Sophocles* I, 176–7).

On the whole Thamyris' fate comes closest to that of Marsyas, who suffered death and abuse after losing to Apollo in a self-imposed musical contest (cf. I. Weiler, *Der Agon im Mythos. Zur Einstellung der Griechen zum Wettkampf*, Darmstadt 1974, 37–59). Yet as a punishment for impiety or hybris against the gods blinding alone has several other paral-

---

[324] This may be an alternative version of E. *Suppl.* 903 (Wilamowitz, *Hermes* 11 [1876], 303 = *KS* I, 199) or a parody of a Euripidean line (Kannicht–Snell, *TrGF* II, 97).

[325] His argument against the MSS text is wrong, since κεῖνος can precede its noun without article. In tragedy cf. S. *El.* 201, 862, *Ant.* 1025.

[326] *Il.* 2.599 αἵ δὲ χολωσάμεναι πηρὸν θέσαν need not refer to mutilation of the eyes (Σ^A *Il.* 2.599 [I 311.67–312.71 Erbse] ~ Eust. 299.25–7, comparing Demodocus; cf. Kirk on *Il.* 2.599–600). One may add that, had Homer wished to be more specific, τυφλὸν θέσαν (~ *Il.* 6.139 τυφλὸν ἔθηκε) would have scanned no less.

lels in Greek myth: e.g. *Il.* 6.130–40 (Lycurgus), A. R. 2.178–93, 220–1 (Phineus), *PMGF* pp. 177–9 (Stesichorus). See A. Esser, *Das Antlitz der Blindheit in der Antike*, Leiden ²1961, 98, 155–62, 164–68, R. G. A. Buxton, *JHS* 100 (1980), 22–37 (especially 30–5).

κάτυφλώσαμεν (Hn) is almost certainly correct. The unaugmented κἀκτυφλώσαμεν (Ω), retained by e.g. Jouan, Kovacs, Zanetto and Murray, wins little support from the epic-Ionic ἐξαπώσατε in 811 (810b–12a n.) or a possible δρᾶσαν in 805 (804–5n.) – both following a heavily epicising messenger speech (756–803n.). The corruption can easily be explained by dittography of the initial κ (Porter on 924).

Θάμυριν: only here in classical Attic, which prefers Θαμύρας to the Homeric form (*Il.* 2.595). Cf. the titles of Sophocles' and Antiphanes' plays (*TrGF* IV, 234–8, *PCG* II, 365–6), S. fr. 245.2, Pl. *Ion* 533b8, *Rep.* 620a6, *Lg.* 829d8–e1 and Cyr. *An. Par.* IV, 183.13–14 ~ 84 ΘΑΜ 33 Drachmann Θάμυριν: … Ἀττικοὶ δὲ ὁ Θαμυράς (*sic*).

ἐδέννασεν: 'revile, abuse'. The rare verb of perhaps Ionic origin (Thgn. 1211; cf. δέννος in Hdt. 9.107.1 and Herod. 7.104) occurs twice in earlier Sophocles (*Ai.* 243, *Ant.* 758–9) and is repeated by our poet in 950 (950–1n.).

The complexive aorist (KG I 162 n. 4, SD 281.1) need not be changed into the imperfect, as Wecklein (*Appendix*, 55) tentatively suggested.

926–31. Given the later emphasis on Eleusinian themes (943–5a, 945b–7, 962–6nn.), it may not be surprising that Rhesus' childhood story shares several traits with that of Eumolpus, son of Poseidon, who was saved by the god and entrusted to a sea-nymph after his embarrassed mother Chione had secretly cast him into the waters: E. fr. 349 (*Erechtheus*) Αἰθιοπίαν νιν ἐξέσωσ' ἐπὶ χθόνα (cf. Richardson on *h.Cer.* 154), 'Apollod.' 3.15.4 (3.201) Χιόνη δὲ Ποσειδῶνι μίγνυται. ἡ δὲ κρύφα τοῦ πατρὸς Εὔμολπον τεκοῦσα, ἵνα μὴ γένηται καταφανής, εἰς τὸν βυθὸν ῥίπτει τὸ παιδίον. Ποσειδῶν δὲ ἀνελόμενος εἰς Αἰθιοπίαν κομίζει καὶ δίδωσι Βενθεσικύμῃ τρέφειν, αὑτοῦ θυγατρὶ καὶ Ἀμφιτρίτης. Even more obviously, however, his upbringing by nymphs (928b–9, 930–1nn.) connects him again with such epic heroes as Achilles (Pi. *Nem.* 3.43, A. R. 4.812–13; cf. 899–901, 908–9, 915–49, 934–5a, 974–7, 978–9nn.) and Aeneas (*h.Ven.* 257, 273–5),[327] whether or not there was also meant to be a hint at the 'Three Nymphs of the Springs', who were worshipped in Thrace (Hoddinott, *Thracians*, 162–3, 171, Jouan 54 n. 274).

---

[327] These and similar myths (H. Herter, *RE* XVII.2 s.v. Nymphai, col. 1551) only reflect the common belief in nymphs as κουροτρόφοι. Cf. Hes. *Th.* 346–8 τίκτε δὲ Κουράων (West: θυγατέρων codd.) ἱερὸν γένος, αἳ κατὰ γαῖαν / ἄνδρας κουρίζουσι σὺν Ἀπόλλωνι ἄνακτι / καὶ ποταμοῖς (with West on 347), E. *El.* 625–6 (Nilsson, *GGR* I³, 258–9).

926–8a. 'And when I had given birth to you, I cast you into your watery father's eddies, as I felt shame before my sisters and at the loss of my virginity.'

τίκτω: 'present for perfect' to denote the continuing relevance of Rhesus' birth for the Muse. This use of the tense is naturally common with 'verbs expressing "life-events"' (A. Rijksbaron, *Grammatical Observations on Euripides' Bacchae*, Amsterdam 1991, 1–4). Cf. e.g. *Ba.* 1–3 Ἥκω ... / Διόνυσος, ὃν τίκτει ποθ' ἡ Κάδμου κόρη / Σεμέλη, and see 837b–40n.

συγγόνους αἰδουμένη / καὶ παρθενείαν: The above rendering, where παρθενείαν equals 'the loss of my virginity' according to the schema *res ponitur pro defectu rei* (KG II 569–70), seems preferable to taking the noun of the Muse's unwedded state (Kovacs, Liapis on 926–8), since proper marriage is never an issue for these goddesses. Moreover, the zeugma of the original inhibitory and, in the non-personal object, a more recent retrospective sense of αἰδέομαι is characteristic of Euripides: *Hcld.* 813–15 ὁ δ' οὔτε τοὺς κλύοντας αἰδεσθεὶς λόγων / οὔτ' αὐτὸς αὑτοῦ δειλίαν στρατηγὸς ὤν / ἐλθεῖν ἐτόλμησ' ἐγγὺς ἀλκίμου δορός, *HF* 1199–1201 αἰδόμενος τὸ σὸν ὄμμα / καὶ φιλίαν ὁμόφυλον / αἷμά τε παιδοφόνον (with Bond). Cf. Cairns, *Aidōs*, 295, 299–303 with nn. 124, 133.[328]

ἐς εὐύδρου πατρός / δίνας: a suitably personalised version of a poetic commonplace (e.g. *Il.* 5.479 Ξάνθῳ ἔπι δινήεντι, *Od.* 6. 89 ποταμὸν πάρα δινήεντα) in Euripidean guise: *Tro.* 210 δίναν ... Εὐρώτα, *IT* 6–7, *Ion* 174–5 δίνας / τὰς Ἀλφειοῦ, 1083–4, *Or.* 1310 ἀμφὶ τὰς Σκαμάνδρου δίνας (with Willink on 1307–10). Of a river or spring εὔυδρος, 'abounding in water, with beautiful water', also occurs in Bacch. 11.119, *IT* 399–400 and *Pae. Delph.* 5–6 (*CA* 141 = Furley–Bremer II 85).

928b–9. βρότειον ἐς χέρα: Elmsley (*Edinburgh Review* 19 [1811], 78), as βροτείαν (Ω, *Chr. Pat.* 1348) violates Porson's Law.

πηγαίαις κόραις: 926–31n. For κόραι, 'nymphs', cf. e.g. *Od.* 6.122–4 ὥς τέ με κουράων ἀμφήλυθε θῆλυς ἀϋτή, / Νυμφάων αἳ ἔχουσ' ὀρέων αἰπεινὰ κάρηνα / καὶ πηγὰς ποταμῶν καὶ πίσεα ποιήεντα, Pi. *Pyth.* 3.78, *HF* 785–8 (with Bond on 785, 788–9), and see West on Hes. *Th.* 346 (quoted in n. 327).

---

[328] Since the Muse's dilemma stems from a specific, however involuntary, act of her own, it matters little that our passage differs from the Euripidean examples in that παρθενείαν, which Jouan (54 n. 274) and Feickert (95) refer to the other Muses' virginity by *hendiadys*, denotes 'not the conduct of which the agent is or should be ashamed, but ... the status/role which is the focus of the agent's respect, disregard of which would be a source of disgrace' (Cairns, *Aidōs*, 299 n. 124).

930–3. These lines, together with 935b–7 (n.), recall 399–412 in the simple chronological order of events. Understandably, however, the Muse does not mention the apparently substantial, and therefore binding (957 ὀφείλων), military aid rendered by Hector, which in his version showed Rhesus as little more than a Trojan vassal (406–11a n.).

930–1. ἔνθ' could be either relative (as usual outside epic) or demonstrative. In favour of the latter see 430–1n.

παρθένων need not be capitalised here (Murray, Zanetto) as a collective title for all or one particular group of nymphs. Contrast Ibyc. fr. 286.1–4 *PMGF* ἦρι μὲν αἵ τε Κυδώνιαι / μηλίδες ἀρδόμεναι ῥοᾶν / ἐκ ποταμῶν, ἵνα Παρθένων / κῆπος ἀκήρατος (with U. v. Wilamowitz-Moellendorff, *Der Glaube der Hellenen* I, Berlin 1931, 185 and West on Hes. *Th.* 346).

τέκνον: The emphatic address (cf. 916, 938) to the dead son helps to lend the speech a more personal note.

932–3. 'And as long as you marshalled bloodthirsty battles within your native land, I had no fear for your death.'

On the question whether Rhesus' Thracian exploits already featured in earlier versions of the myth see 406–11a n. and Introduction, 12.

καί σ' ... οὐκ ἐδείμαινον θανεῖν: Verbs of fearing rarely take an accusative and infinitive construction (KG II 398 n. 6). In tragedy note also *Sept.* 720–6 πέφρικα τὰν ὠλεσίοικον / θεὸν ... τελέσαι τὰς περιθύμους / κατάρας Οἰδιπόδα βλα- / ψίφρονος, *Hec.* 768 πατήρ νιν ἐξέπεμψεν ὀρρωδῶν θανεῖν, E. *Suppl.* 554–5 and *Ion* 1564–5 (Ritchie 249–50).

ἀμφὶ γῆν ... πατρίαν: either local, 'around, somewhere in ...' (408–10a n.) or causal, 'for the sake of ... ', which is much less frequent for ἀμφί with accusative (LSJ s.v. C I 5, FJW on A. *Suppl.* 246), but has an almost exact parallel in Tyrt. fr. 5.4–6 *IEG* ἀμφ' αὐτὴν (sc. τὴν Μεσσήνην) δ' ἐμάχοντ' ἐννέα καὶ δέκ' ἔτη / νωλεμέως αἰεὶ ... / αἰχμηταὶ πατέρων ἡμετέρων πατέρες.

φιλαιμάτους / ἀλκὰς κορύσσοντ' echoes such epic(-style) expressions as *Il.* 2.273 πόλεμόν τε κορύσσων, 'Hes.' fr. 190.2 M.–W. ἐ]μφύλιον αἷμ' ἐκόρυσσ ον, [Hes.] *Sc.* 148 Ἔρις ... κορύσσουσα κλόνον ἀνδρῶν ('stirring up'), 197–8, Ibyc. fr. 311 (b) *PMGF* ἀντία δῆριν ἐμοὶ κορύσσοι and Pi. *Isthm.* 8.53–4 (of Achilles) μάχας ἐναριμβρότου / ἔργον ... κορύσσοντα. On κορύσσω / -ομαι, properly 'furnish (oneself) with a helmet', in general see *LfgrE* s.v. B, Leumann, *Homerische Wörter*, 210 and M. Trümpy, *Kriegerische Fachausdrücke im griechischen Epos* ..., Basel 1950, 48–9, 77, 88–9.

Badham's φιλαρμάτους (*Philologus* 10 [1855], 338), attested only as a stock-epithet for Thebes (Pi. *Isthm.* 8.19–20, *HF* 467 [with Bond]; cf. *Ant.* 149 τᾷ πολυαρμάτῳ ... Θήβᾳ, 844–5 Θή- / βας τ' εὐαρμάτου ἄλσος),³²⁹ is no improvement on Ω's grim φιλαιμάτους of Aeschylean ring (*Sept.* 45–6 Ἄρη τ' Ἐνυὼ καὶ φιλαίματον Φόβον / ὠρκωμότησαν, which may also have inspired 'Anacr.' *Ep.* 1.3 *FGE* ὁ φιλαίματος Ἄρης). Cf. Introduction, 30–1.

934–5a. See 899–901n. Regarding Achilles' analogous fate, Σ^bT *Il.* 18.59 (IV 446.66–8 Erbse) observes that Thetis suffered more than a mortal mother because she foresaw his death at Troy: προειδυῖα τὴν τελευτήν (Edwards on *Il.* 18.59–60).

Τροίας ... ἄστυ μὴ κέλσαι ποτέ: 752–3, 895–8nn. For the accusative of direction cf. A. *Suppl.* 15 κέλσαι δ' Ἄργους γαῖαν.

935b–7. Just as in 930–3 (n.) the Muse suppressed Hector's part in the ascent of her son, she here keeps quiet about the gifts which the 'countless' embassies brought along (399–403, 403nn.). It is thus easier to believe for the moment that Rhesus, like Achilles, heroically defied the prospect of an early death (890–914n.).

πρεσβεύμαθ' αἵ τε μυρίαι γερουσίαι: For γερουσία in the sense 'embassy (of elders)' see 401–3n. πρεσβεύματα, 'ambassadors' (abstract for concrete), is almost as rare and in the fifth century found only at E. *Suppl.* 173–4 πρεσβεύματ' οὐ Δήμητρος ἐς μυστήρια / ἀλλ' ὡς νεκροὺς θάψωσιν, which may have been our poet's source. The pair of closely related terms depicts even more clearly than 401–2 how the envoys were treading on each other's heels.

ἔπεισαν: 65–6n.

ἐλθεῖν κἀπικουρῆσαι φίλοις: is almost literally repeated at 956 ... ἐλθεῖν κἀπικουρῆσαι χθονί.

938–40. 'And you, Athena, cause of this whole disaster – for neither Odysseus nor Tydeus' son did anything – do not believe that your deed escaped my notice.'

True to the preceding action, the Muse identifies Athena as the mastermind behind her son's destruction (cf. 945, 978), whereas Odysseus and Diomedes just functioned as the goddess' agents (595–674, 670–1a nn.). In the same way Artemis partly exculpates Theseus at *Hipp.* 1325–8 δείν' ἔπραξας, ἀλλ' ὅμως / ἔτ' ἔστι καί σοι τῶνδε συγγνώμης τυχεῖν· / Κύπρις γὰρ ἤθελ' ὥστε γίγνεσθαι τάδε, / πληροῦσα θυμόν. Cf. 915–49, 962–82, 978–9nn.

The sense of the lines remains the same, no matter which reading we choose in 940. Liapis ('Notes', 105–6) most recently defended the MSS' ... ἔδρασε δράσας – ... ('neither Odysseus nor Tydeus' son did anything, although they *acted*'), with reference to many similar verbal paradoxes in Euripides and elsewhere (cf. J. Diggle, *CQ* n.s. 47 [1997],

---

329 And as a race-horse's name on a third-century AD curse-tablet from Roman Berytus (P. René Mouterde, SJ, *MUB* 15 [1930], 111, 121).

106 with n. 46, Olson on Ar. *Ach.* 395–6 and Parker on *Alc.* 521, who most appropriately to our case cites 'Thgn.' 953–4 πρήξας δ' οὐκ ἔπρηξα, καὶ οὐκ ἐτέλεσσα τελέσσας, / δρήσας δ' οὐκ ἔδρησ', ἤνυσα δ' οὐκ ἀνύσας). Yet Lenting's ... ἔδρασε – δρῶσα ... (*Animadversiones*, 77) has the double advantage of providing λεληθέναι with a participle (cf. [Men.] *Mon.* 347 Jäkel θεὸν ἐπιορκῶν μὴ δόκει λεληθέναι, 432 Jäkel ... μὴ δόκει πονηρὸς ὤν) and being *lectio difficilior*, since δρῶσα could easily have been assimilated to the subject(s) of the preceding verb. At the price of slightly convoluted syntax, Paley (on 938–40), followed by Kovacs, combines τοῦτ' for τοῦδ' in 938 with Heath's ... ἔδρασ' – ἔδρασας· μὴ δόκει ... (*Notae sive lectiones*, 98–9).[330] Both this and the paradosis might benefit from replacing καί (938) with Kirchhoff's σύ (I [1855], 562, on 931).

Ἀθάνα: For the vocative see 930–1n. and for the Doric name form 501–2n.

οὐδὲν δ' ... / ἔδρασε: With both Lenting's and the MSS text the explanatory parenthesis is of the type that becomes immediately obvious only in spoken delivery (219–22a n.).

μὴ δόκει λεληθέναι: similarly *HF* 985 ... ὡς λεληθέναι δοκῶν.

941–2. 'And yet we sister Muses honour your city above all others and frequently visit your land ...'

The idea that Athens, the cultural centre of its day, was blessed by the Muses is familiar from *Med.* 830–2 ἔνθα ποθ' ἁγνὰς / ἐννέα Πιερίδας Μούσας λέγουσι / ξανθὰν Ἁρμονίαν φυτεῦσαι (with Page on 831, Mastronarde on 832–4) and its likely counterpart *OC* 691–2 οὐδὲ Μου- / σᾶν χοροί νιν (*sc.* τήνδε τὴν χθόνα) ἀπεστύγησαν (E. Kienzle, *Der Lobpreis von Städten und Ländern in der älteren griechischen Dichtung*, Kallmünz 1936, 75–6). In addition, we are reminded of the cults they enjoyed in the city's public and, even more, educational life (W. F. Otto, *Die Musen und der göttliche Ursprung des Singens und Sagens*, Darmstadt ²1956, 36–8, 66, Parker, *Polytheism and Society*, 251–2 with n. 147).

πόλιν σὴν ... πρεσβεύομεν / ... μάλιστα: so especially *Cho.* 488 πάντων δὲ πρῶτον τόνδε πρεσβεύσω τάφον (with Garvie on 486–8).

κἀπιχρώμεθα χθονί: literally 'have (regular) dealings with ...' (LSJ s.v. ἐπιχράω (C) II 2). In other classical literature this rare verb is exclusively attested with regard to persons: Hdt. 3.99.2 ἣ δὲ ἂν γυνὴ κάμῃ, ὡσαύτως αἱ ἐπιχρεώμεναι μάλιστα γυναῖκες ταὐτὰ τοῖσι ἀνδράσι ποιεῦσι, Thuc. 1.41.1, Pl. *Lg.* 953a1–3.

---

[330] Cf. *Chr. Pat.* 1411–12 ἔδρας, ἔδρασας, μὴ δόκει λεληθέναι, / Πόντιε, δίκης ὄμμα πανδερκέστατον, unless the author independently redivided the letters of the paradosis (Introduction, 53).

943–5a. '... while Orpheus introduced the torch-light rituals of your secret mysteries, Orpheus, the very cousin of this dead man, the one you murdered.'

From the Athenian perspective, and in view of 965–6 (of Persephone) ὀφειλέτις δέ μοι / τοὺς Ὀρφέως τιμῶσα φαίνεσθαι φίλους (962–6, 965b–6nn.), it is hard to see Orpheus here as the founder of any but the Eleusinian Mysteries (C. Plichon, *Kernos* 14 [2001], 13–4), a notion which, although not explicitly attested before late antiquity (Orph. testt. 102–104 Kern), may already have been present at Ar. *Ran.* 1032 Ὀρφεὺς μὲν γὰρ τελετάς θ' ἡμῖν κατέδειξε φόνων τ' ἀπέχεσθαι (with Sommerstein) and, shortly after *Rhesus*, [Dem.] 25.11 ὁ τὰς ἁγιωτάτας ἡμῖν τελετὰς καταδείξας Ὀρφεύς (cf. Ephor. *FGrHist* 70 F 104 = D. S. 5.64.4 καθ' ὃν δὴ χρόνον καὶ τὸν Ὀρφέα ... μαθητὴν γενέσθαι τούτων [*sc.* τῶν Ἰδαίων Δακτύλων], καὶ πρῶτον εἰς τοὺς Ἕλληνας ἐξενεγκεῖν τελετὰς καὶ μυστήρια). See Graf, *Eleusis*, 2 with n. 7, 22–39 (more restrained G. Zuntz, *Gnomon* 50 [1978], 528) and West, *Orphic Poems*, 24.

μυστηρίων ... τῶν ἀπορρήτων φανάς: Since torches were essential to (the later stages of) the Eleusinian Iacchus-procession, the ensuing παννυχίς and probably the rites conducted in the Telesterion (A. Markantonatos, *Ariadne* 10 [2004], 21–2 with 22, 25, Liapis on 943–5),[331] μυστηρίων ... φανάς could be employed κατὰ συνεκδοχήν (I. M. Linforth, *The Arts of Orpheus*, Berkeley – Los Angeles 1941, 63, C. Plichon, *Kernos* 14 [2001], 12) in the same way as φανάς ... Βακχίου at *Ion* 550 designates the entire biennial winter festival of Dionysus in Delphi; cf. Aristonous *Pae. in Apoll.* 33–7 (*CA* 163 = Furley–Bremer II 46–7) δωροῦντ[αι] δέ σ' ἀθάνατοι ... τριετέσιν φαναῖς Βρόμιος (with Furley–Bremer on 37). The apparent borrowing of this Euripidean passage will seem all the more natural if we recall the common literary and iconographical identification of Iacchus and Dionysus: e.g. *Ant.* 1119–21, 1146–54, S. fr. 959, *Ion* 1074–86, *Ba.* 725–6, fr. mel. adesp. 1027 (d) *PMG*, Philod. Scarph. *Pae. in Bacch.* 27–36 (*CA* 166 = Furley–Bremer II 53–4). Cf. Richardson on *h.Cer.* 489 (p. 320), Graf, *Eleusis*, 51–66.

ἀπόρρητος and ἄρρητος encompass the very essence of mysticism (Richardson on *h.Cer.* 478–9, W. Burkert, *Ancient Mystery Cults*, Cambridge [Mass.] – London 1987, 9 n. 44 [p. 137]). Cf. e.g. Ar. *Eccl.* 442–3 τἀπόρρητ' ... / ἐκ Θεσμοφόροιν, [Lys.] 6.51, Arist. *EN* 1111a9, Luc. *Pisc.* 33, *SEG* 10.321.1 [ἀ]ρρήτο τελετῆς (~ 455 BC), Ar. *Nub.* 302, Xen. *HG* 6.3.6 (below), *Hel.* 1307, *Ba.* 470–2, E. fr. 63.

---

[331] Of the references they quote see especially Richardson, *Homeric Hymn to Demeter*, 26–8 and E. Parisinou, *The Light of the Gods. The Role of Light in Archaic and Classical Greek Cult*, London 2000, 67–71.

ἔδειξεν: here almost a technical term for the institution (literally 'revelation') of a cult. Cf. *h.Cer.* 473–6 ἣ δὲ (Demeter) κιοῦσα θεμιστοπόλοις βασιλεῦσι / δεῖξεν ... / ... / δρησμοσύνην ἱερῶν, Xen. *HG* 6.3.6 ... ἐπεὶ λέγεται μὲν Τριπτόλεμος ... τὰ Δήμητρος καὶ Κόρης ἄρρητα ἱερὰ πρώτοις ξένοις δεῖξαι and, with the more frequent καταδείκνυμι in this sense, e.g. Ar. *Ran.* 1032, [Dem.] 25.11 (above), D. S. 1.29.2, [Plut.] *De lib. ed.* 14.10f (J. Gonda, ΔΕΙΚΝΥΜΙ. *Semantische Studie over den Indo-Germaansche Wortel* ΔΕΙΚ-, Amsterdam 1929, 44–5, 111–12, Graf, *Eleusis*, 31–2, Richardson on *h.Cer.* 474–6).

αὐτανέψιος: As Calliope's son, Orpheus was 'first cousin' to Rhesus. So also A. *Suppl.* 933 γυναικῶν αὐτανέψιον στόλον, 983–4, *Hcld.* 211–12 αὐτανεψίων (Aethra and Alcmene) / πατὴρ ἂν εἴη σός τε χὼ τούτων γεγώς, 987, Pl. *Euthd.* 275a9–b1. On kinship terms formed with αὐτός see FJW on A. *Suppl.* 8 (II, p. 13).

ὃν κατέκτεινας σύ: 670–1a, 938–40nn. Cobet's conjecture (*VL*², 585) provides the best explanation for the meaningless paradosis (οὖν κατακτείνασα Va: οὕνεκα κτείνασα Λ) and should therefore, with Diggle and Kovacs, be preferred to Bothe's ὃν κατακτείνεις σύ (5 [1803], 301) or Seager's ὃν κατέκτανες σύ (*CJ* 20 [1819], 273), for which Paley (on 945), to whom it occurred independently, compared 978 ... Παλλάς, ἥ σ' ἀπέκτανεν.

945b–7. 'And Musaeus, your revered fellow citizen and a man who reached the highest level of his artistry, was educated by Phoebus and us sisters.'

The words might suggest that Musaeus is introduced here mainly as the second great poet after Orpheus, and predecessor to Hesiod and Homer, in the order that remained canonical from Hippias of Elis (86 B 6 DK) to the later fourth century BC: Ar. *Ran.* 1032–6, Pl. *Ap.* 41a6–7, Chrysipp. Stoic. fr. 1077.12–13 *SVF* II (West, *Theogony*, 40, 47). However, given his fame not only for oracles (Hdt. 7.6.3, 8.96.2, 9.43.2, Ar. *Ran.* 1033, Pl. *Prt.* 316d7–9), but also for hymns, theogonic and eschatological poetry (Graf, *Eleusis*, 8–22 [cf. G. Zuntz, *Gnomon* 50 (1978), 527–8], West, *Orphic Poems*, 21, 23–4, 40–4), the Athenians could not have failed to draw another connection with Eleusis, where (against the genealogy given in 926–31n.) Musaeus had recently become the father of the 'official' founder-hero and first hierophant Eumolpus. Cf. *LIMC* IV.1/2 s.v. Eumolpos A 1 = *ARV*² 1313.7 (*Pelike* by the Meidias Painter of ca. 410 BC showing Musaeus in Thracian costume with his wife Deiope and little Eumolpus), Andron *FGrHist* 10 F 13 = 2 A 3a DK, Marmor Parium *FGrHist* 239 A.15 = 2 A 8 DK, very probably Pl. *Rep.* 363c3–4 = 2 A 5 DK and perhaps already E. fr. 370.100–1 (*Erechtheus*) Εὔμολπος γὰρ Εὐμόλπου γεγώ[ς] / τοῦ κατθ[ανόντος (suppl. Parsons) τοῦδε πέμπτος ἔκγονος (e.g. West)] (with Kannicht's apparatus and Cropp on 100–1).

σόν / σεμνὸν πολίτην: Musaeus' roots at Athens (Paus. 10.12.11, D. L. *Prooem*. 1.3 = 2 A 4 DK) and Eleusis (Aristox. fr. 91 Wehrli = 2 A 1a DK, *Suda* μ 1294 Adler = 2 A 1 DK) superbly suit the Muse's purpose. Other sources, as early as the Meidias vase (above), make him a Thracian by analogy with Orpheus (Graf, *Eleusis*, 17–19).

κἀπὶ πλεῖστον ἄνδρ' ἕνα / ἐλθόντα: *sc.* τῆς σοφίας (890–2a, 923–4a, 948–9nn.). For εἷς (ἀνήρ) emphasising a superlative and especially, by antithesis, πλεῖστος cf. Hdt. 6.127.1 Σμινδυρίδης ... ὃς ἐπὶ πλεῖστον δὴ χλιδῆς εἷς ἀνὴρ ἀπίκετο, *Pers*. 326–8 (quoted in 498b–500n.), *Tr*. 459–60 (with Davies), *OC* 563–4, *Hcld*. 7–8 (with Wilkins on 8) and Thuc. 8.68.1 πλεῖστα εἷς ἀνὴρ ... δυνάμενος ὠφελεῖν (KG I 28, Fraenkel on *Ag*. 1455).

Φοῖβος σύγγονοί τ' ἠσκήσαμεν: Although several later fifth-century vase paintings grant Musaeus (note the descriptive name) the company of Apollo and/or at least one Muse (A. Kauffmann-Samaras, *LIMC* VI.1 s.v. Musaios, B 2 – C 11, with *Commentaire*, 687), this is our only hint at their role in his education, except for a red-figure amphora of ca. 440 BC from Vulci (*LIMC* VI.1/2 s.v. Musaios B 3 / Mousa, Mousai 79 = *ARV*[2] 1039.13), which in a rare 'instruction scene' (A. Queyrel, *LIMC* VI.1 s.v. Mousa, Mousai, 676 col. 2) shows the young poet, crowned, with a lyre and laurel branch, listening to Terpsichore's harp, while behind her a Muse ΜΕΛΕΛΟΣΑ is adjusting her aulos.

948–9. 'And as a recompense for that, I sing a dirge with my son in my arms. I will call in no other poet to help.'

It is difficult, perhaps impossible, to know what the concluding statement in 949 was meant to be. With the transmitted ἐπάξομαι the above interpretation recommends itself on linguistic grounds, since it does justice to both the earlier use of σοφός and σοφιστής (890–2a, 923–4a, 945b–7nn.; cf. Luc. *Luct*. 20 μεταστειλάμενοί τινα θρήνων σοφιστήν and Ach. Tat. 3.25.7 ἐπιτάφιος σοφιστής)[332] and the middle ἐπάγομαι, 'bring for oneself, call to assistance' (LSJ s.v. ἐπάγω II 2). One may object to the rather loose connection with the preceding argument, and that it would make little sense for the Muse to say that she needs no professional mourners; yet it is possible that we have here and in 952 (952–3n.) οὐδὲν μάντεων ἔδει φράσαι a double echo of *HF* 911–12 μάντιν οὐχ / ἕτερον ἄξομαι or a similar, most probably proverbial, phrase (Bond on 911–12, who cites *Ag*. 1098–9 καὶ μὴν κλέος σου μαντικὸν πεπυσμένοι / ἦμεν· προφήτας δ' οὕτινας μαστεύομεν, *Hipp*. 236 τάδε μαντείας ἄξια πολλῆς, Pl. *Smp*. 206b9 μαντείας ... δεῖται ὅτι ποτε λέγεις and Aeschin. 1.76 ἔτι ταῦτα μαντείας προσδεῖται; cf. Introduc-

---

332 Quoted by Musgrave (on 952) and Vater (*Vindiciae*, cxxvi) respectively.

tion, 32). A recollection of this kind would also have shaped the thought of the passage.

However, the MSS reading is not above suspicion. Liapis ('Notes', 106–9; cf. on 948–9), most recently, endorsed the vindictive 'I will not bring another poet (into Athens)', which in principle goes back to Hardion ('Dissertation sur la tragédie de Rhésus', *Mém. Acad. des Inscr.* 10 [1736], 334–6) and admirably suits the Muse's tirade in 938–47. This rendering is difficult with ἐπάξομαι, but perfectly possible with Paley's ἐπάξομεν (on 948) if taken not as a *pluralis maiestatis* (as Paley intended), but as a genuine plural referring to all the Muses: 'We will not bring ...' (D. Sansone, *BMCR* 2013.03.15, on 949, who points to the plural verbs describing the Muses' services in 941–2 and 947). In view of the preceding θρηνῶ, corruption of ἐπάξομεν (perhaps understood as plural for singular) into -ομαι was easy (cf. Diggle, *Euripidea*, 263), and only by chance do the meanings differ so widely.[333] The conjecture certainly deserves a place in the apparatus; putting it into the text perhaps entails the risk of improving on the poet.

950–61. With characteristic lack of insight, both the chorus (950–1) and, even more obviously, Hector (952–3) fail to grasp the full meaning of Athena's responsibility, whereupon the general just tries to free himself from the minor charge of having induced Rhesus to come to his aid (954–7 – with many verbal and syntactical echoes of 399–411 and 935–7). His rather terse expression of sympathy for the dead ally (958) and offer of honourable burial in the Troad (959–61; cf. 879–81) then occasion the Muse's unexpected cultic prophecy (962–82n.).

950–1. τροχηλάτης: Valckenaer (*Diatribe*, 97–8 with n. 3) for Ω's impossible στρατηλάτης. Portus' διφρηλάτης (*Breves notae*, 72) would give equally good sense (cf. 781 ἵππους ... ἃς ἔθρεψα κἀδιφρηλάτουν), but τροχηλάτης is significantly rarer, palaeographically nearer to the paradosis and was also corrupted into στρατηλάτης in one MS at *Phoen.* 39.[334]

The latter passage and its likely model *OT* 806–7 are the only attestations of τροχηλάτης. Likewise τροχηλατέω occurs only twice (E. *El.*

---

[333] Several other renderings of the paradosis have rightly been rejected by Liapis (above), among them, by implication (108 n. 281), 'I will call in no other poet as witness (for Athena's ingratitude)' (R. Goossens, *Euripide et Athènes*, Brussels 1962, 287; cf. Feickert on 949). This is grammatically possible (LSJ s.v. ἐπάγω II 3), but too matter-of fact after the Muse's renewed lament in 948–9a.

[334] The first two arguments would be irrelevant if the initial letters of the word had become illegible (Cobet *VL*², 585; cf. Liapis on 950–1). And different ways of corruption may be assumed for different MSS.

1253, *Or.* 36), while τροχήλατος is quite common in various applications (LSJ s.v.).

ἐδέννασ': 924b–5n. δεννάζω does not elsewhere take an infinitive like verbs of saying, but note the internal accusative at *Ai.* 239–43 τὸν δ' ... 242 παίει λιγυρᾷ μάστιγι διπλῇ, / κακὰ δεννάζων ῥήμαθ' and, by analogy, [Pl.] *Hipparch.* 232c 7–8 οὐκ ἄρα ὀρθῶς ὀνειδίζει, εἴ τίς τῳ ὀνειδίζει φιλοκερδεῖ εἶναι.

τῷδε βουλεῦσαι φόνον: Cf. *Ag.* 1613–14 (Coryphaeus to Aegisthus) σὺ δ' ἄνδρα τόνδε φῄς ἑκὼν κατακτανεῖν, / μόνος δ' ἔποικτον τόνδε βουλεῦσαι φόνον; ~ 1625–7 γύναι, σὺ ... ἀνδρὶ στρατηγῷ τόνδ' ἐβούλευσας μόρον; 1634 (with Fraenkel on 1614), *Hec.* 854–6 εἴ πως ... μὴ δόξαιμι ... / Θρῄκης ἄνακτι τόνδε βουλεῦσαι φόνον and *Ai.* 1055 ὅστις στρατῷ ξύμπαντι βουλεύσας φόνον.

952–3. This 'second part' of our possible twofold allusion to *HF* 911–12 μάντιν οὐχ / ἕτερον ἄξομαι (948–9n.), recalls Hector's contempt for seers at 65–9 (n.) and, by implication, that of his epic self for Polydamas' bird omen in *Il.* 12.231–50 (cf. 56–69n.). Greek literary scepticism towards prophets and divination is as old as *Il.* 1.106–8 (Allan on *Hel.* 744–54 and for tragedy also Cropp on E. *El.* 399–400).

φράσαι / ... τόνδ' ὀλωλότα: 575–6n.

Ὀδυσσέως τέχναισι τόνδ' ὀλωλότα: similarly *IT* 24–5 καί μ' Ὀδυσσέως τέχναις / μητρὸς παρείλοντ' ἐπὶ γάμοις Ἀχιλλέως and *Hel.* 930–1 τέχναις θεῶν / ὤλοντ'.

954–6. 'But seeing the Greeks' army encamped in this land, how was I not to send heralds to my friends, asking them to come and help our country?'

γῆς ἔφεδρον: 'sitting upon ...' (LSJ s.v. ἔφεδρος I 1) in the military sense of 'waiting for an opportunity to attack', as in Plb. 2.13.6–7 (ὑπολαμβάνοντες ...) οὐδ' ἀσφαλῶς οἰκῆσαι τὴν ἑαυτῶν πατρίδα τούτους ἔχοντες ἐφέδρους τοὺς ἄνδρας (i.e. the Celts), Thuc. 4.71.1, 8.92.8 and, with the verb, *Rh.* 768–9 (n.) κἀφεδρεύοντας νεῶν / πρύμναισι. At 119 (n.) the word is a metaphor from boxing or wrestling.

τί μήν, 'why in truth ...?', stresses 'the wholly natural character of the course of action' voiced in this rhetorical question (G. Wakker, in *NAGP*, 214–15 n. 13).

πέμψειν ... / κήρυκας: sc. e.g. αἰτήσοντας (ἐλθεῖν ...). For this type of brachylogy cf. *IA* 360–2, Xen. *HG* 3.1.7 (quoted in 26n.) and in Latin e.g. Sall. *Iug.* 97.1 *at Iugurtha ... ad Bocchum nuntios mittit quam primum in Numidiam copias adduceret.*

ἐλθεῖν κἀπικουρῆσαι χθονί: 935b–7n.

957. ἔπεμψ'· ὀφείλων δ' ἦλθε συμπονεῖν ἐμοί: 930–3, 935b–7nn. Rhesus' late arrival, which Hector castigated in all but the same words at 321–2, 325–6 and 396–7, is conveniently ignored.

958. 'But I do not rejoice in his death at all.'

οὐ μήν ... γ': slightly adversative in a statement that as a whole contradicts what the Muse might suppose (G. Wakker, in *NAGP*, 223–5; cf. *GP* 334–5).

συνήδομαι: here not of shared gladness, corresponding to συλλυπέομαι, συνάχθομαι or συναλγέω, but *Schadenfreude*, as in *Med.* 136–7 οὐδὲ συνήδομαι ... / ἄλγεσι δώματος, *Hipp.* 1286–7 Θησεῦ, τί τάλας τοῖσδε συνήδῃ, / παῖδ' οὐχ ὁσίως σὸν ἀποκτείνας (with Barrett), Antipho 3 β 8 and Isoc. 8.87 οὐ συμπενθήσοντες τοὺς τεθνεῶτας, ἀλλὰ συνησθησόμενοι ταῖς ἡμετέραις συμφοραῖς (LSJ s.v. II).

959–60. Hector's proposal to burn 'splendid robes without number' on Rhesus' pyre reflects a heroic (and occasionally real-life) way of honouring and/or providing for the dead: *Il.* 22.510–14 (Andromache speaking) ἀτάρ τοι εἵματ' ἐνὶ μεγάροισι κέονται / λεπτά τε καὶ χαρίεντα ... / ἀλλ' ἤτοι τά γε πάντα καταφλέξω πυρὶ κηλέῳ, / οὐδέν σοί γ' ὄφελος, / ἐπεὶ οὐκ ἐγκείσεαι αὐτοῖς, / ἀλλὰ πρὸς Τρώων καὶ Τρωϊάδων κλέος εἶναι (with Richardson), *Od.* 24.67, E. *Suppl.* 980–3 καὶ μὴν ... ἐσορῶ δὴ / ... / μελάθρων τ' ἐκτὸς / Θησέως ἀναθήματα νεκροῖς (Diggle, *Studies*, 27–8), *IT* 632, Hdt. 5.92η.2 (Periander's wife complaining she was cold and naked in Hades because he had not burnt her clothes with her). Cf. D. C. Kurtz – J. Boardman, *Greek Burial Customs*, London 1971, 200–17, especially 206–7.

ἕτοιμος: *sc.* εἰμί, as proportionally quite often with that adjective, even when a subject pronoun is also lacking: *Ai.* 813, *OT* 92, *Med.* 612–13, *Hcld.* 501–2, *Phoen.* 968–9, Men. *Dysc.* 370, Dem. 4.29, 9.4 (Denniston on E. *El.* 796 ἕτοιμοι [*sc.* ἐσμέν], J. E. Harry, *TAPA* 34 [1903], viii-x ~ *RPh* n.s. 28 [1904], 132–5). Generally, however, the ellipsis of the first and second person of εἰμί is far rarer than that of the third (KG I 40–1, Denniston on E. *El.* 37).

τεῦξαι τάφον: 'erect a tomb' (*Il.* 21.322–3 αὐτοῦ οἱ καὶ σῆμα τετεύξεται, οὐδέ τί μιν χρεώ / ἔσται τυμβοχοῆς, ὅτε μιν θάπτωσιν Ἀχαιοί, Lyc. 532–3 ᾧ πάλαι τεύχει τάφους / ἀκτὴ Δολόγκων εὐτρεπὴς κεκμηκότι) rather than 'conduct the funeral rites' (LSJ s.v. τεύχω II; cf. *Od.* 1.277, 2.196 οἳ δὲ γάμον τεύξουσι, *Tr.* 756 μέλλοντι δ' αὐτῷ πολυθύτους τεύχειν σφαγάς), which would subsume the cloth-burning in a less than parallel sequence with καὶ ... καί.

μυρίαν πέπλων χλιδήν: Apart from giving a more stylish impression, Wecklein's μυρίαν (*Appendix*, 56) instead of μυρίων (Ω, *Chr. Pat.* 1379) is supported by the fact that in other examples of this (typically Euripidean) turn of phrase the epithet is always transferred to the governing noun: *Andr.* 2 ἕδνων σὺν πολυχρύσῳ χλιδῇ, *Phoen.* 223–4 κόμας ἐμᾶς / ... παρθένιον χλιδάν, 1491 στολίδος κροκόεσσαν ἀνεῖσα τρυφάν (Porson: στολίδα ... τρυφᾶς codd.; cf. Mastronarde on 1491).

961. δυστυχῶς: most likely refers to the circumstances of Rhesus' death, as described by the Charioteer in 756–61 (756–7a, 761nn.). See Feickert on 960 (*sic*).

ἀπέρχεται encompasses all stages of the Thracian's demise; hence the present tense. For ἀπέρχομαι of the doomed or dead cf. e.g. *Ant.* 817–18 οὔκουν κλεινὴ ... / ἐς τόδ' ἀπέρχῃ κεῦθος νεκύων; *Alc.* 379 ὦ τέκν', ὅτε ζῆν χρῆν μ', ἀπέρχομαι κάτω, D. L. 3.6 (of Socrates) ἐκείνου δ' ἀπελθόντος (LSJ s.v. ἀπέρχομαι II). Its use here may have been determined by the preceding ἐλθών (Liapis, 'Notes', 109), although the 'antithesis' does not seem strong enough to preclude Vater's ἀποίχεται (on 946). The participle could even have caused the corruption of the commoner verb (e.g. Pi. *Pyth.* 1.92–3 ὀπιθόμβροτον αὔχημα δόξας / οἷον ἀποιχομένων ἀνδρῶν δίαιταν μανύει, 3.1–3 and Ar. *Ran.* 83 (Ηρ.) Ἀγάθων δὲ ποῦ 'στιν; (Δι.) ἀπολιπών μ' ἀποίχεται – i.e. to Macedon, where he is 'as good as dead' for the Athenian theatre [Sommerstein on 84]).

962–82. Harking back perhaps to the chorus' almost god-like praise for Rhesus in their 'cletic hymn' and entrance greeting (342–79, 380–7nn.), the Muse proceeds to reveal her son's posthumous fate in a Euripidean-style cult *aition*, designed to reconcile the notions of the Homeric warrior and indigenous Thracian hero by connecting him, either traditionally or by re-interpretation of some local cult (Introduction, 13, 15),[335] with the famous Bacchus-oracle on Mt. Pangaeus (972–3n.). For the Athenians, who despite the silence of *Iliad* 10 and apparently Hippon. fr. 72 *IEG*, seem to have believed that Rhesus was buried at Troy (Polyaen. *Strat.* 6.53; cf. [Arist.] fr. 641.57 Rose), this connection was helped by the implicit analogy with such semi-divine cave-dwellers as Amphiaraus, Trophonius and Zalmoxis (970–1n.) and, since Rhesus could not also be portrayed as having gone down below earth alive, by a quasi-mystic release from Hades by virtue of his mother's pleading (962–6, 963–5a, 965b–6nn.).

The second part of the Muse's speech returns to Homeric-Cyclic themes. Like Dionysus' additional prediction of Cassandra's and Agamemnon's death at *Hec.* 1275–81 (Polymestor speaking), her personalised view into Achilles' future (974–9) places Rhesus' demise in the wider Trojan context and, for the last time, enhances his status by association with the 'best of the Achaeans' (314–16, 899–901, 908–9, 915–49,

---

[335] A good case for the tragedians' freedom to invent not only aetiologies but also (versions of existing) cults was made by J. S. Scullion, in D. Sansone *et al.* (eds.), *Euripides and Tragic Theatre in the Fifth Century* (*ICS* 24–5), Champaign (Ill.) 1999–2000, 217–33. See also F. M. Dunn, *CB* 76 (2000), 3–27.

926–31nn.). On the divine plane we are again reminded of the fierce, but ineffectual, opposition of Artemis and Aphrodite in *Hippolytus* (915–49, 938–40, 978–9nn.; cf. C. W. Keyes, *CPh* 24 [1929], 207 ~ *TAPA* 59 [1928], xxviii), before the mourning mother departs with a sorrowful commonplace of Euripidean ring (980–2n.).

962–6. To our knowledge the Muse's intercession for her son has most likely been adapted from the legends of Memnon and Achilles, who were granted immortality at their mothers' request (*Aethiopis* Arg. p. 112 (2) *GEF* ἔπειτα Ἀχιλλεὺς Μέμνονα κτείνει· καὶ τούτῳ μὲν Ἠὼς παρὰ Διὸς αἰτησαμένη ἀθανασίαν δίδωσι) or, in the case of the latter, originally just transferred to the Island of the Blessed: *Aethiopis* Arg. p. 112 (4) *GEF* (882–9n. with n. 304), Pi. *Ol.* 2.79–80 Ἀχιλλέα τ' ἔνεικ', ἐπεὶ Ζηνὸς ἦτορ / λιταῖς ἔπεισε, μάτηρ (probably after *Il.* 1.495–533). In addition, there have been attempts to see here a more far-reaching allusion to 'Orphic'-Dionysiac eschatology as most recently exemplified by the gold leaves from Pelinna (A. Markantonatos, *Ariadne* 10 [2004], 18–19, 33).[336] But the roles envisaged for Persephone, judge of the departed souls, and Dionysus (Lysius) at $P^1 = P^2.2$ εἰπεῖν Φερσεφόνᾳ σ' ὅτι Βά<κ>χιος αὐτὸς ἔλυσε are hardly comparable (C. Plichon, *Kernos* 14 [2001], 15, 18–19), and all we can get perhaps from *Rh.* 965 (963–5a n.) ψυχὴν ἀνεῖναι τοῦδ' before a reference back to Orpheus at Eleusis (965b–6) is a fleeting sense of mystic liberation after death, soon to be disproved by Rhesus' extraordinary future as a Thracian cult-hero (970–1, 972–3nn.).

962. γαίας ἐς μελάγχιμον πέδον: For γαίας (...) πέδον (or *vice versa*) cf. *Sept.* 304–5, E. *El.* 534–5, and see 278n. μελάγχιμος, 'black', is an Aeschylean favourite (*Pers.* 301, A. *Suppl.* 719–20, 745, *Cho.* 11, A. fr. 116.1), also found in E. *El.* 513, *Phoen.* 372, A. R. 4.1508 and Xen. *Cyn.* 8.1, 7 (of dark spots in the snow). As with δύσχιμος (*Pers.* 567, *Sept.* 503, *Cho.* 186, A. fr. 342, E. *Suppl.* 962, *Ba.* 15), its suffix may belong to χεῖμα (*GEW*, *DELG* s.vv. μέλας, χεῖμα, FJW on A. *Suppl.* 719; more reserved e.g. Garvie on *Cho.* 11–12, 185–6), and both were

---

[336] On the text and interpretation of these virtually identical leaf-shaped tablets ($P^1 \sim P^2$), which formed part of a late-fourth-century female burial at Pelinna (Thessaly), see e.g. K. Tsantsanoglou – G. M. Parássoglou, *Hellenika* 38 (1987), 3–16 (*ed. princ.*) and F. Graf, in Ph. Borgeaud (ed.), *Orphisme et Orphée: en l'honneur de Jean Rudhardt*, Geneva 1991, 87–102 and in H. Carpenter – C. A. Faraone (eds.), *Masks of Dionysus*, Ithaca (NY) – London 1993, 239–58. The view of Rhesus as a prototypical μύστης goes back to Perdrizet (*Cultes et mythes du Pangée*, 16), refuted by Rempe, *De Rheso Thracum heroe*, 27–8. Cf. V. J. Liapis, *CQ* n.s. 57 (2007), 397 n. 83, who generally, however, seems sympathetic to such a reading (394–5, 397–8).

regularly so corrupted, as here in Λ (FJW on A. *Suppl.* 811 [II, p. 161], where add the Xenophon passages quoted above).

963–5a. 'So much I will request from the bride below, the daughter of the harvest-producing goddess Demeter, to send up his soul.'

The Muse's confidence here and at 965b–6 contrasts with the ordinary mortal Admetus, who can only dream of charming the underworld gods into returning his wife: *Alc.* 357–60 εἰ δ' Ὀρφέως μοι γλῶσσα καὶ μέλος παρῆν, / ὥστ' ἢ κόρην Δήμητρος ἢ κείνης πόσιν / ὕμνοισι κηλήσαντά σ' ἐξ Ἅιδου λαβεῖν, / κατῆλθον ἄν ...

νύμφην τὴν ἔνερθ': similarly *Alc.* 746 Ἅιδου νύμφῃ παρεδρεύοις and *OC* 1548 ἥ τε νερτέρα θεός.

τῆς καρποποιοῦ παῖδα Δήμητρος θεᾶς virtually repeats 651 (n.) τῆς ὑμνοποιοῦ παῖδα Θρῄκιον θεᾶς, which likewise stands in apposition to a periphrasis for a proper name (650 ἄνδρα σοι μέγαν φίλον). The unique καρποποιός could be a metrical *ad hoc* alternative to Demeter's regular (cult-)epithet καρποφόρος (Ar. *Ran.* 384–5, Paus. 8.53.7, *CIG* III 4082, *IG* 12.5.226, *SIG*³ II 820.5, *SEG* 30.1341).

ψυχὴν ἀνεῖναι τοῦδ': i.e. 'to release his soul' (962–6n.), as in the very different context of 'Orphic'-Pythagorean metempsychosis at Pi. fr. 133.1–3 Sn.–M. (cited in Pl. *Men.* 81b8–c4) οἷσι δὲ Φερσεφόνα ποινὰν παλαιοῦ πένθεος / δέξεται, ἐς τὸν ὕπερθεν ἅλιον κείνων ἐνάτῳ ἔτεϊ / ἀνδιδοῖ ψυχὰς πάλιν (C. Plichon, *Kernos* 14 [2001], 14). In other tragedy these words are characteristic of prayers to call up the spirits of the departed: *Pers.* 628–30 ἀλλὰ χθόνιοι δαίμονες ἁγνοί, / ... / πέμψατ' ἔνερθεν ψυχὴν εἰς φῶς, 650–1 Ἀϊδωνεὺς δ' ἀναπομπὸς ἀνείης, Ἀϊδωνεύς, / [Δαρεῖον] θεῖον ἀνάκτορα Δαριᾶνα, *Cho.* 489, A. fr. 273a.6–10 (*Psychagogoi*), E. fr. 912.9.

965b–6. 'For she is under obligation to me to show that she honours the relations of Orpheus.'

In the reasoning of the Muse, the gratitude Persephone owes to Orpheus for founding the Eleusinian Mysteries (943–5a) is to be extended to his family, in particular his 'first cousin' (αὐτανέψιος) Rhesus.

ὀφειλέτις ... μοι / ... φαίνεσθαι looks like a syntactical echo of *Ai.* 589–90 οὐ κάτοισθ' ἐγὼ θεοῖς / ὡς οὐδὲν ἀρκεῖν εἴμ' ὀφειλέτης ἔτι; which is the only other place in classical Greek where the very rare ὀφειλέτης (cf. Pl. *Lg.* 736d5, Plb. 38.11.10, Plut. *Crass.* 12.2, *Demetr.* 5.5) governs a dative and infinitive in periphrasis for ὀφείλω (A. C. Pearson, *CR* 35 [1921], 56, Fraenkel, *Rev.* 232). Feminine ὀφειλέτις is a *hapax*.

δέ: 132n.

967–9. 'And to me he will henceforth be as one who has died and does not look upon the light (of day). For he will never meet me again or see his mother's figure.'

These lines find a striking parallel in A. (?) fr. 99.13–14 (*Cares* = *Europa*) ἀλλ' οὐκ ἐν αὐγαῖς ταῖς ἐμαῖς ζόη σφ' ἔχει · / τὸ μὴ παρὸν δὲ τέρψιν οὐκ ἔχει φίλοις (cf. 736–7n.), about Europa's second son Rhadamanthys, who in this passage alone is called immortal (12) and probably imagined as 'living' either in Elysium (*Od.* 4.564) or on the Island of the Blessed (Pi. *Ol.* 2.75). Europa's speech continues with deep apprehensions for Sarpedon's fate at Troy: A. fr. 99.15–23 (cf. 882–9n.).

θανών τε κοὐ λεύσσων φάος inverts phrases like *Il.* 18.61, *Od.* 4.540 (*et al.*) ... ζώει(ν) καὶ ὁρᾷ (-ᾶν) φάος ἡελίοιο, *Pers.* 299 ... ζῇ τε καὶ φάος βλέπει and *Ag.* 677 καὶ ζῶντα καὶ βλέποντα (codd.).[337] λεύσσων φάος is Euripides' version of the common poetic metaphor 'see the light' = 'live' (849–50, 970–1nn.). So at line-end E. *El.* 349, *Phoen.* 1084, E. fr. 293.2 ... λεύσσει(ν) φάος, otherwise *Phoen.* 1547–8, *Alc.* 81–3.

οὐ γάρ ... / ἔτ' ... οὐδέ: Kirchhoff (I [1855], 563, on 962), since ἔτι is desired here, no matter that οὐ γὰρ ... / οὔτ' ... οὔτε (Ω) could be justified as a rare case of postponement, comparable to *Ant.* 203–4 τοῦτον πόλει τῇδ' ἐκκεκήρυκται τάφῳ / μήτε κτερίζειν μήτε κωκῦσαί τινα (with Jebb and *GP* 519–20). L. Dindorf's οὐ γὰρ ... / ἔτ' ... οὔτε (I [1825], 493) would result in a more unusual, but probably legitimate, negative sequence (*GP* 509–10, Finglass on S. *El.* 1197, 1412).

ἐς ταὐτόν ... / ... εἶσιν: 'come face to face, meet'. Similarly *Hec.* 965–6 ἤδη πόδ' ἔξω δωμάτων αἴροντί μοι / ἐς ταὐτὸν ἥδε συμπίτνει δμωὶς σέθεν, *Phoen.* 37–8 καὶ ξυνάπτετον πόδα / ἐς ταὐτὸν ἄμφω Φωκίδος σχιστῆς ὁδοῦ, 1405 ἐς ταὐτὸν ἧκον (with Mastronarde) and Ar. *Lys.* 1239–40 ἀλλ' οὑτοιὶ γὰρ αὖθις ἔρχονται πάλιν / εἰς ταὐτόν.

'Both tragedy and comedy much prefer' ταὐτόν to ταὐτό (Barrett on *Hipp.* 1178–9). As often, the former is here guaranteed by metre.

μητρὸς ὄψεται δέμας: If this is a reworking of E. *El.* 968 μῶν σ' οἶκτος εἷλε, μητρὸς ὡς εἶδες δέμας; (~ *Eum.* 84 καὶ γὰρ κτανεῖν σ' ἔπεισα μητρῷον δέμας), the difference between a mere periphrasis with δέμας (cf. 90n.) and the poignantly physical use of the noun (Bond on *HF* 1036, Breitenbach 198–9) could not be more obvious.

970–3. 'But he shall lie hidden in caves of the silver-veined land as a man-god, beholding the light, a prophet of Bacchus, who took Pangaeus' rock as his abode, a revered god to those who know.'

970–1. To judge from 971, where the remarkable ἀνθρωποδαίμων, 'man and deity', is taken up separately by κείσεται (like a dead man)

---

337 West and Sommerstein (most recently) read χλωρόν τε καὶ βλέποντα (Toup, after Hsch. χ 553 Hansen–Cunningham χλωρόν τε καὶ βλέπον<τα>· ἀντὶ τοῦ ζῶντα), which would be *lectio difficilior* if the lemma was certainly taken from that line (see Fraenkel on *Ag.* 677 for moderate doubts).

and – somewhat unfortunately for a *subterranean* hero – βλέπων φάος, our poet was at considerable pains to render comprehensible within the limits of tragic language his novel idea of Rhesus' immortality, similar to those northern cave-dwellers (962–82n.), who have rightly been described as belonging 'neither to the living nor to the dead nor to the gods' (Y. Ustinova, *Kernos* 15 [2002], 286 + *Caves and the Ancient Greek Mind* ..., Oxford 2009, 89–109; cf. V. J. Liapis, *CQ* n.s. 57 [2007], 394–5, 398–406, C. Plichon, *Kernos* 14 [2001], 20, Jouan 79–80 n. 288). Little or nothing, by contrast, bears out Plichon's (15–16) assumed reminiscence of Hesiod's Silver Generation (*Op.* 141–2 τοὶ μὲν ὑποχθόνιοι μάκαρες θνητοὶ καλέονται, / δεύτεροι), unless μάκαρες there be given its proper divine associations (West on 141, who in refuting this possibility cites the description of the Dioscuri at *Od.* 11.301–4 τοὺς ἄμφω ζωοὺς κατέχει φυσίζοος αἶα· / οἳ καὶ νέρθεν γῆς τιμὴν πρὸς Ζηνὸς ἔχοντες / ἄλλοτε μὲν ζώουσ' ἑτερήμεροι, ἄλλοτε δ' αὖτε / τεθνᾶσιν· τιμὴν δὲ λελόγχασιν ἶσα θεοῖσι as another example of 'theology' straining poetic *Kunstsprache*).

τῆς ὑπαργύρου χθονός: Cf. 921–2a n. (with A. fr. 23a Παγγαίου ... ἀργυρήλατον / πρῶν' †ες τὸ τῆς ἀστραπῆς† πευκάεν σέλας), and for ὑπάργυρος, 'containing silver, veined with silver' (LSJ s.v. I 1), Xen. *Vect.* 1.5 (of Attica), 4.2 and especially *Cyc.* 293–4 ἥ τε Σουνίου / δίας Ἀθάνας σῶς ὑπάργυρος πέτρα, which has arguably left its trace both here and in πέτραν two lines further down (Introduction, 32).

ἀνθρωποδαίμων: a virtual *hapax*,[338] which was presumably coined for the occasion to express the same sort of 'appositive' relation between its components as the Aeschylean ἰατρόμαντις (*Eum.* 62 of Apollo ἰατρὸς ... καὶ μάντις [Ar. *Pl.* 11], *Suppl.* 263 [Asclepius], *Ag.* 1621–3) and other such nominal compounds from the classical and later ages (e.g. μητρόπολις, ξιφομάχαιρα and the comic titles Διονυσαλέξανδρος [Cratinus], Αἰολοσίκων [Aristophanes], Ἀνθρωπορέστης [Strattis]; Schwyzer 453–4, Fraenkel on *Ag.* 1623 with further literature). Simultaneously, however, the second part of the word recalls the more conventional belief in outstanding mortals *becoming* δαίμονες after death: Hes. *Op.* 121–6 αὐτὰρ ἐπεὶ δὴ τοῦτο γένος κατὰ γαῖα κάλυψεν, / τοὶ μὲν δαίμονές εἰσι ... / ἐσθλοί, ἐπιχθόνιοι ... / [124–5] / πλουτοδόται (with West on 122–3 δαίμονες, 141), *Pers.* 620–1 τόν τε δαίμονα / Δαρεῖον ἀνακαλεῖσθε, 642–3, *Alc.* 1002–4 αὔτα ποτὲ προὔθαν' ἀνδρός, / νῦν δ' ἔστι μάκαιρα δαίμων· / χαῖρ', ὦ πότνι', εὖ δὲ δοίης. Cf. C. Plichon, *Kernos* 14 (2001), 15 and the attestation of νεκυδαίμων on two,

---

338 The word does not recur until Procop. *Arc.* 12.14 ('devils incarnate', of Justinian and Theodora); cf. *Suda* α 2530 Adler. Hsch. β 1198 Latte βροτοδαίμων· ἡμίθεος cannot be traced to any specific source or period.

admittedly third- and fifth-century AD, 'magical' lead tablets from Egypt (*Suppl. Mag.* 39.1, 57.1).

βλέπων φάος: 849–50, 967–9nn. For the wording cf. e.g. *Ag.* 1646 Ὀρέστης ἆρά που βλέπει φάος, *Eum.* 746, *Hec.* 668, *IT* 674, *Hel.* 60, E. fr. 370.20 (LSJ s.v. βλέπω III 2 with Suppl. [1996]).

972–3. Βάκχου προφήτης, ὅς γε ... / ᾤκησε: Matthiae's ὅς γε (VIII [1824], 42, on 969), with 'emphatic' (*GP* 123–4) instead of 'limitative-causal' γε (*GP* 141–2: *quippe qui*), is clearly preferable to ὅστε (QP^c), which even Aeschylus seems to have shunned in spoken verse (*Pers.* 297, *Sept.* 501, *Eum.* 1024 only; all other tragic examples are lyric).[339] The case for a relative as against a comparative clause (ὥστε VaL) has been decisively stated by Diggle (*SIFC* 5 [1987], 167–72 = *Euripidea*, 320–6), on the grounds that (a) the Homeric use of ὥστε with a finite verb finds only one certain parallel in tragic iambics (S. fr. 474.4–5 ἴσον μετρῶν ὀφθαλμόν, ὥστε τέκτονος / παρὰ στάθμην ἰόντος ὀρθοῦται κανών)[340] and, more important, (b) our construction would deviate from the epic-poetic norm that ὥστε (usually with a correlative in the main clause) stands at the beginning of its comparison, describing '*une notion permanente*' (Ruijgh, *Te épique*, 598) and not, as here, a single event (ᾤκησε, 'took as his abode'; cf. *Hel.* 928, E. frr. 228a.18, 558.4). The anonymous 'prophet of Bacchus', variously identified in the past as Lycurgus, Orpheus and Zalmoxis, will thus be Rhesus himself, the mythical ancestor of the Thracian Bessi, who served as oracular priests at the Satrae's shrine of Dionysus, located probably on Mt. Pangaeus (Hdt. 7.111–12; cf. *Hec.* 1267 ὁ Θρῃξὶ μάντις ... Διόνυσος, with Σ^MAB [I 89.12–13 Schwartz] οἳ μὲν περὶ τὸ Πάγγαιον εἶναι τὸ μαντεῖόν φασι τοῦ Διονύσου, *Ba.* 298 μάντις δ' ὁ δαίμων ὅδε [with Dodds on 298–301]; Introduction, 14–15).

The present passage may have been alluded to by Asclepiades of Tragilus in the middle of the fourth century BC (Introduction, 27).

---

[339] On E. fr. 228a.13–15 Ἀλκαῖον ἠδὲ Σθένελον ὅς τ' (Π: ὅς γ' Lloyd-Jones) Ἄργους πόλιν / ε[ἶ]χεν (ἔ[σ]χεν Siegmann) Μυκήνας, πατέρα δ' Ἀλκμήνης τρίτον / Ἠλεκτρύωνα see A. Harder, *Euripides' Kresphontes and Archelaos. Introduction, Text and Commentary*, Leiden 1985, 197–9 and Diggle, *Euripidea*, 325 n. 17.

[340] A. fr. 39 εἷλκον <δ'> ἄνω λυκηδόν, ὥστε διπλόοι / λύκοι νεβρὸν φέρουσιν ἀμφὶ μασχάλαις, which seems to imitate a Homeric simile (*Il.* 13.198–202), may with due caution be added to the list (but note Mette's ὥς τε, with Ruijgh, *Te épique*, 571, 993). At *Tr.* 699–700 μορφῇ μάλιστ' εἰκαστὸν ὥστε πρίονος / ἐκβρώματ' ἂν βλέψειας ἐν τομῇ ξύλου read ἐκβρώμαθ' ἂν (Tyrrell; cf. Dawe, *STS* III, 91) or ὥστ' εἰ ... / ἐκβρώματα βλέψειας (Dawe³: ὡς εἰ iam Meineke), whereas *Ba.* 1066–7 κυκλοῦτο δ' ὥστε τόξον ἢ κυρτὸς τροχός / τόρνῳ γραφόμενος †περιφορὰν ἕλκει δρόμον† is best emended by combining περιφορὰν (*ed. Hervag.*²) with Reiske's ἑλικοδρόμον (cf. J. Diggle, *Eikasmos* 9 [1998], 48–9). S. fr. 840 μολυβδὶς ὥστε δίκτυον κατέσπασεν cannot be adequately judged in terms of syntax.

Βάκχου προφήτης: similarly *Or.* 363–4 ὁ ναυτίλοισι μάντις ... / Νηρέως προφήτης Γλαῦκος (who also began his existence as a mortal) and *Eum.* 19 Διὸς προφήτης δ' ἐστὶ Λοξίας πατρός.

Παγγαίου πέτραν: 921–2a, 970–1 (τῆς ὑπαργύρου χθονός) nn.

σεμνὸς τοῖσιν εἰδόσιν θεός: i.e. '... to *initiates*', as in *Ba.* 72–4 ὦ μάκαρ, ὅστις εὐδαί- / μων τελετὰς θεῶν εἰ- / δὼς βιοτὰν ἁγιστεύει, 472 (ὄργια) ἄρρητ' ἀβακχεύτοισιν εἰδέναι βροτῶν (Diggle, *Euripidea*, 325) and less obviously e.g. Orph. fr. 1 F a *PEG* II.1 = fr. 334 Kern ἀείσω (v.l. ἀείδω) ξυνετοῖσι (cf. Plut. *Quaest. Conv.* 2.3.2.636d τὸ δ' ἐπὶ τούτοις, ἔφη γελάσας, 'ἀείσω ξυνετοῖσι' τὸν Ὀρφικὸν καὶ ἱερὸν λόγον) and Pi. *Ol.* 2.85 (βέλη ...) φωνάεντα συνετοῖσιν (West, *Orphic Poems*, 83–4, 110 with n. 82; cf. C. M. Bowra, *CPh* 32 [1937], 109–10).

974–7. The Nereids' and Muses' funeral lament for Achilles is memorably described in *Od.* 24.58–64 ἀμφὶ δέ σ' ἔστησαν κοῦραι ἁλίοιο γέροντος / οἴκτρ' ὀλοφυρόμεναι ... / Μοῦσαι δ' ἐννέα πᾶσαι ἀμειβόμεναι ὀπὶ καλῇ / θρήνεον· ἔνθα κεν οὔ τιν' ἀδάκρυτόν γ' ἐνόησας / Ἀργείων· τοῖον γὰρ ὑπώρορε Μοῦσα λίγεια. / ἑπτὰ δὲ καὶ δέκα μέν σε ὁμῶς νύκτας τε καὶ ἦμαρ / κλαίομεν ἀθάνατοί τε θεοὶ θνητοί τ' ἄνθρωποι (with Heubeck on 60, 62) and also Pi. *Isthm.* 8.56a–60. But the motif perhaps goes back to a pre-Homeric source (cf. *Aethiopis* Arg. p. 112 (4) *GEF* καὶ Θέτις ἀφικομένη σὺν Μούσαις καὶ ταῖς ἀδελφαῖς θρηνεῖ τὸν παῖδα), which may also lie behind the dirge scenes in *Il.* 18.35–8 + 50–64 (cf. 908–9, 934–5a nn.) and 24.83–6. See further West, *Epic Cycle*, 153–4.

974–5. 'More lightly now will I bear the grief of the sea-goddess. For her son, too, is fated to die'.

ῥᾷον: Valckenaer (MS *Observationes in Aeschylum et Euripidem* [Leiden BPL 352]; cf. P. J. Finglass, *GRBS* 49 [2009], 201) and Musgrave (*Exercitationes*, 96 = II [1778], 412). In contrast to the transmitted βαιόν, 'small, light' or adverbial 'for a short time' (Paley on 974), this forms with οἴσω a well-attested Greek, and particularly Euripidean, idiom: *Hipp.* 205–6 ῥᾷον δὲ νόσον μετά θ' ἡσυχίας / καὶ γενναίου λήματος οἴσεις, E. *El.* 71–3, E. fr. 297.5, *Andr.* 744 τοὺς σοὺς δὲ μύθους ῥᾳδίως ἐγὼ φέρω, *Ba.* 640, E. fr. 62a.13, *PV* 103–4 τὴν πεπρωμένην δὲ χρή / αἶσαν φέρειν ὡς ῥᾷστα.

τῆς θαλασσίας θεοῦ: In view of 977 Θέτιδος ἐν πένθει and the fact that the Muse does not really seem to find consolation in Rhesus' semi-divine afterlife (967–9, 980–2), this is better taken as a possessive genitive, not a comparative one, with e.g. Kovacs, Jouan and Liapis (on 974–5, 'Notes', 110). In that way we also get a more immediate allusion to the famous epic mourning scene (974–7n.).

The phrase comes from E. fr. 885 ἄληθες, ὦ παῖ τῆς θαλασσίας θεοῦ; (parodied in Ar. *Ran.* 840). Similarly also *Andr.* 17–18 ἡ θαλασσία / ...

Θέτις, fr. tr. adesp. 69 (~ Ar. *Vesp.* 1518/19) ἄγ' ὦ μεγαλώνυμα τέκνα / τοῦ θαλασσίου <θεοῦ> (suppl. Bergk: θαλασσίοιο Burges), Pl. Com. fr. 143 *PCG* Ξενοκλῆς ... / ὁ Καρκίνου παῖς τοῦ θαλαττίου ‿ – (θεοῦ suppl. Cobet), *Cyc.* 21–2, *Phoen.* 1156–7.

977. Θέτιδος ἐν πένθει: 'in Thetis' (time of) grief'. By the addition of the genitive, ἐν πένθει here comes to describe not simply a person's inward state (S. *El.* 290 ἄλλος δ' οὔτις ἐν πένθει βροτῶν; 847, *Hel.* 1325–6 ῥίπτει τ' ἐν πένθει / πέτρινα κατὰ δρία πολυνιφέα, Hdt. 1.46.1, Pl. *Rep.* 395e1–2, 605d1 [LSJ s.v. ἐν A II 2, KG I 463, SD 458]), but – with a slightly temporal force to ἐν – the whole situation, in which the action takes place: e.g. *Ag.* 1287–8 οἳ δ' εἷλον πόλιν / οὕτως ἀπαλλάσσουσιν ἐν θεῶν κρίσει (with Fraenkel on 1288), A. fr. 258 (*Phineus*) καὶ ψευδόδειπνα πολλὰ μαργώσης γνάθου / ἐρρυσίαζον στόματος ἐν πρώτῃ χαρᾷ (i.e. the Harpies).

978–9. Like a shadowy equivalent of Artemis in *Hippolytus*, who will avenge her protégé on a favourite of Aphrodite (1416–22 [with Barrett]), the Muse expresses her satisfaction at the thought that Athena will be just as unable to save Achilles from falling victim to the gods' conflict before Troy. In order to emphasise that latter notion, our poet has (against the implication of 634–7) chosen to suppress Paris' role in the fight, as Aeschylus did for the angry Thetis in fr. 350.7–9 (915–49n.). Neither there nor at e.g. *Il.* 21.277–8 (φίλη μήτηρ ...) ἥ μ' ἔφατο Τρώων ὑπὸ τείχεϊ θωρηκτάων / λαιψηροῖς ὀλέεσθαι Ἀπόλλωνος βελέεσσιν (~ Q. S. 3.61–2 + 78–82), 'Apollod.' *Epit.* 3.26 (cf. *Cypria* Arg. pp. 74–6 (9) *GEF*), *Phil.* 334–5 τέθνηκεν, ἀνδρὸς οὐδενός, θεοῦ δ' ὕπο, / τοξευτός, ὡς λέγουσιν, ἐκ Φοίβου δαμείς and *Andr.* 53, 1002–3, 1107–8 does one have to presuppose an earlier story which left Apollo alone responsible for the hero's death.[341]

Παλλάς, ἥ σ' ἀπέκτανεν: 670–1a, 938–40nn. The words are all but repeated from 944–5 (943–5a n.).

980–2. 'O misfortunes of childbearing, distress of mortals! For whoever takes good account of you, will go through life childless rather than bear children and bury them.'

The Muse's speech ends, a little abruptly and without much regard for her divine status (980n.), with one of Euripides' favourite sentiments about marriage and parenthood: e.g. *Alc.* 880–8, *Med.* 1090–1115 (especially 1105–15), *Suppl.* 786–93, frr. 571, 908, 908a. Cf. Democr. 68 A 170, B 275, 276 DK, and see R. Kassel, *Quomodo quibus locis apud veteres scriptores Graecos infantes atque parvuli pueri inducantur describantur*

---

[341] Pindar's version that the god shot Achilles in Paris' guise (*Pae.* 6.79–86 [fr. 52f Sn.–M. = D6 Rutherford]; cf. Hyg. *Fab.* 107.1, 113.1) may have been invented for the occasion (Radt on Pi. *Pae.* 6.79).

commemorentur diss. Mainz 1951 (Meisenheim am Glan 1954), 49–50 = *KS*, 45–6.

The pathetic apostrophe of abstractions is likewise Euripidean in character: *Hcld*. 433–4, *Andr*. 319–20, 1081–2, *Suppl*. 1108 ὦ δυσπάλαιστον γῆρας, ὡς μισῶ σ' ἔχων, *Ion* 1502–4, *Or*. 126, E. frr. 792a, 805. But see also *OT* 380–2 ὦ πλοῦτε καὶ τυραννὶ καὶ τέχνη τέχνης / ὑπερφέρουσα τῷ πολυζήλῳ βίῳ, / ὅσος παρ' ὑμῖν ὁ φθόνος φυλάσσεται (Schadewaldt, *Monolog und Selbstgespräch*, 122–5, Liapis on 980–2).

980. ὦ παιδοποιοὶ συμφοραί: conversely *Phoen*. 338 παιδοποιὸν ἀδονάν. For παιδοποιός and its verb in poetry cf. further *Andr*. 4 δάμαρ ... παιδοποιός, S. *El*. 587–9 ἥτις ξυνεύδεις τῷ παλαμναίῳ ... / ... / καὶ παιδοποιεῖς, *Hcld*. 524, *Or*. 1080, Ar. *Eccl*. 615 and Men. fr. 298.2 *PCG*. Euripides, especially in his lyrics, was fond of replacing an abstract genitive attribute with a related compound adjective: e.g. *HF* 385 χαρμοναῖσιν ἀνδροβρῶσι ~ E. fr. 537 ἀνδροβρῶτας ἡδονάς (in 3ia), *Phoen*. 1300–1 μονομάχον / ἐπὶ φρέν' ἠλθέτην, *Ba*. 139 ὠμοφάγον χάριν (Breitenbach 207, Mastronarde on *Phoen*. 338).

πόνοι βροτῶν (~ *Ant*. 1276 ... ἰὼ πόνοι βροτῶν δύσπονοι) could mean that the Muse sees herself as subject to the same distress as any mortal woman. But a slight incongruity (980–2n.) remains, and one may wonder if, with 982 θάψει τέκνα following, our passage also echoes the words of Amphiaraus' well-known consolation at *Hyps*. fr. 60 ii.90–1 Bond = E. fr. 757.921–2 ἔφυ μὲν οὐδεὶς ὅστις οὐ πονεῖ βροτῶν· / θάπτει τε τέκνα ...

981–2. ὡς supplies the reason for the previous utterance, as in e.g. *Phil*. 914 τί ποτε λέγεις, ὦ τέκνον; ὡς οὐ μανθάνω, *Phoen*. 841–4.

ὅστις ὑμᾶς μὴ κακῶς λογίζεται comes closest to E. fr. 575.1–2 ὅστις δὲ θνητῶν βούλεται δυσώνυμον / εἰς γῆρας ἐλθεῖν οὐ λογίζεται καλῶς and Ar. *Eq*. 1275 ... ὅστις εὖ λογίζεται. Not surprisingly perhaps, λογίζομαι, properly 'to employ rational calculation' (Willink on *Or*. 555), looms large in Euripides compared with only three Sophoclean cases (*Ai*. 816, *OT* 461, *Tr*. 944) for all other tragedy. The pronominal address (ὑμᾶς) has parallels in *OT* 382 and E. *Suppl*. 1108 (980–2n.).

ἄπαις: 908–9n.

διοίσει: absolute (*sc*. τὸν βίον), as in the middle at *Ai*. 510–12 οἴκτιρε δ', ὦναξ, παῖδα τὸν σόν, εἰ ... / ... σοῦ διοίσεται μόνος / ὑπ' ὀρφανιστῶν μὴ φίλων (cf. Hsch. δ 1871 Latte διοίσεται· ... ἢ διάξει, καὶ βιώσεται ~ Σ *Ai*. 511, Suda δ 1281 Adler), Hp. *Art*. 56 ἢν οὖν μὴ τοιοῦτόν τι γένηται, ἱκανῶς ὑγιηροὶ τἆλλα διαφέρονται (~ 400 BC) and perhaps Xen. *Mem*. 2.1.24 ἀλλὰ σκοπούμενος †διέσῃ† τί ἂν κεχαρισμένον ... εὕροις (διέσῃ codd. pler.: δεήσει A: διοίσει Dindorf). Note the regular use of the active in 600 (n.) ὃς εἰ διοίσει νύκτα τήνδ' ἐς αὔριον.

983–96. With the Muse's departure (882) the focus returns to the Homeric account for a brief conclusion that roughly corresponds to the Trojan arming in *Il.* 11.56–66 and cannot have failed to leave the audience with dire apprehensions for what lies beyond that dawning day of battle (983–5, 993–6nn.). Like *Rh.* 52–75 (52–84n.), Hector's confident speech here harks back to *Il.* 8.497–541 (530–41), and many other verbal and thematic echoes of the parodos and first epeisodion (986–7, 988–9a, 989b–92nn.) convey the impression that he has not learned anything from the past night's experience. In this respect our lines indeed resemble *Hec.* 1284–95, where Agamemnon's contempt for Polymestor's prophecy about Clytaemestra leads him to display undue optimism at the long-awaited favourable winds (W. Buchwald, *Studien zur Chronologie der attischen Tragödie. 455 bis 431*, diss. Königsberg 1939, 53–4, Ritchie 78). The chorus, by contrast, faithfully obey the orders of their general (993–5a), though not without another ominous glimpse of scepticism in 995b–6 (n.). Cf. 882–4n. and Rosivach 7 2–3.

983–5. The coryphaeus' sharp, exhortatory turn to the present has a startling parallel in *Ant.* 1334–5 μέλλοντα ταῦτα (Creon's death). τῶν προκειμένων τι χρὴ / πράσσειν. μέλει γὰρ τῶνδ' ὅτοισι χρὴ μέλειν (with Griffith on the ambiguity of τῶνδ', which can resume either ταῦτα or τῶν προκειμένων). For πρόκειμαι in this sense see also *IT* 1433–4 νῦν δὲ τὴν προκειμένην / σπουδὴν ἔχοντες οὐ μενοῦμεν ἥσυχοι.

οὗτος ... μητρὶ κηδεύειν μέλει: a unique instance of personal (LSJ s.v. μέλω A I 1 'to be an object of care / thought') instead of impersonal μέλει(ν) with dative and infinitive (LSJ s.v. A I 2). κηδεύω, 'attend to a corpse' (LSJ s.v. I 2), covers all due funeral rites: S. *El.* 1138–42 κοὔτ' ἐν φίλαισι χερσὶν ἡ τάλαιν' ἐγώ / λουτροῖς σ' ἐκόσμησ' οὔτε παμφλέκτου πυρός / ἀνειλόμην ... ἄθλιον βάρος, / ἀλλ' ἐν ξένησι χερσὶ κηδευθεὶς τάλας / σμικρὸς προσήκεις ὄγκος ἐν σμικρῷ κύτει.

τῶν προκειμένων: i.e. Hector's long-standing plan to attack the Greek camp (59–64, 70–5, 100–4, 110–22, 143–6, 989–92).

φῶς γὰρ ἡμέρας τόδε heralds the end of the play and, like *Il.* 11.1–2 Ἠὼς δ' ἐκ λεχέων παρ' ἀγαυοῦ Τιθωνοῖο / ὤρνυθ', ἵν' ἀθανάτοισι φόως φέροι ἠδὲ βροτοῖσιν, the long third Iliadic day of battle.

986–7. χωρεῖτε, συμμάχους δ' ὁπλίζεσθαι τάχος / ἄνωχθε recalls the sentries 'advice' at 23–5 ὁπλίζου χέρα, συμμάχων, / Ἕκτορ, βᾶθι πρὸς εὐνάς, / ὄτρυνον ἔγχος αἴρειν, which was so eagerly adopted by Hector once he had concluded that the Greeks were fleeing (70–1, 84, 90, 99).

ἄνωχθε: Cf. *Od.* 22.437 ἄρχετε νῦν νέκυας φορέειν καὶ ἄνωχθε γυναῖκας, *HF* 241–2 τέμνειν ἄνωχθ' ἐλθόντες ὑλουργοὺς δρυός /

κορμούς. Like ἀνώχθω (Il. 11.189), this athematic second person plural imperative of ἄνωγα probably got its aspiration (for *-κτ-) from the singular ἄνωχθι (KB II 238–9, 370–1, 465, Schwyzer 800 n. 8, where, however, Ar. Ach. 335 κέκραχθ' need not be plural).

For the medial caesura with elision in 986 see 208–9n. Other indications of conservative trimeter versification are discussed in 804–5 and 849–50nn.

πληροῦν τ' αὐχένας ξυνωρίδων: '... and to fill the necks of the (two) yoke-horses', i.e. with the straps or collars that attached them to the yoke (303–4n.). No precise equivalent to this 'somewhat pretentious' (Ritchie 217) variation on 27 ἁρμόσατε ψαλίοις ἵππους exists, but Hel. 1570 πλήσασα κλιμακτῆρας εὐσφύρῳ ποδί (with Kannicht on 1569–71), HF 372–3 πεύκαισιν ... χέρας / πληροῦντες and, for what it is worth, Poll. 1.164 πληρωσάμενοι τὰ τόξα, ἐνθέμενοι τοὺς οἰστούς (where the first part amounts to a hagesichorean) seem much closer than the different expressions for 'manning' a ship or breastwork (LSJ s.v. πληρόω III 1) which commentators compare.

988–9a. πανοὺς δ' ἔχοντας: 'bearing torches' – for the purpose of setting the Greek ships on fire (990). πανούς is Reiske's correction (Animadversiones, 93) of the transmitted πόνους. The rare word of unclear origin, which apparently describes a torch bound together from several pieces of wood (Ath. 15.700d) tends to be corrupted: Ag. 284 πανόν (Ath., Phot. α 95 Theodoridis: φανόν Σ^ΛΩ), Ion 195 πανόν (Pierson: πτ- L), 1294, E. fr. 90 (Poll. 10.117) πανόν (CL: φανόν FS). It is correctly preserved in Diph. fr. 6 PCG, Men. fr. 59.2 PCG (both from Ath. 15.700e) and S. fr. 184 (Phot. π 152 Theodoridis).

χρὴ μένειν Τυρσηνικῆς / σάλπιγγος αὐδήν: similarly 144 (143–5a n.) σάλπιγγος αὐδὴν προσδοκῶν καραδόκει and, also at the same verse-position, Phoen. 1377–8 ἐπεὶ δ' ἀνήφθη πυρσὸς ὣς Τυρσηνικῆς / σάλπιγγος ἠχή, σῆμα φοινίου μάχης (with Mastronarde on 1377–8, 1377), Hcld. 830–1 ἐπεὶ δ' ἐσήμην' ὄρθιον Τυρσηνικῇ / σάλπιγγι, Eum. 567–8 ἥ τ' †τοῦν† διάτορος Τυρσηνικὴ / σάλπιγξ βροτείου πνεύματος πληρουμένη (our earliest witness to the belief that the trumpet was of Etruscan origin) and Ai. 16–17 φώνημ' ἀκούω ... / χαλκοστόμου κώδωνος ὣς Τυρσηνικῆς (with Finglass on 15–17).

989b–92. 'For once I have crossed the Achaeans' trench and walls, I am confident that I will set fire to their ships and that the coming sun-rays bring the Trojans the day of freedom.'

Hector's final statement hinges all on πέποιθα (991), which is pronounced with the same delusive confidence as at 331 (330–1n.). Cf. also Il. 8.538–41 εἰ γὰρ ἐγὼν ὣς / εἴην ἀθάνατος καὶ ἀγήρως ἤματα πάντα / ... / ὡς νῦν ἡμέρη ἥδε κακὸν φέρει Ἀργείοισιν (the end of Hector's speech in the temporary Trojan camp).

ὡς ὑπερβαλὼν τάφρον / τείχη τ' Ἀχαιῶν: Lenting's ὑπερβαλών (*Animadversiones*, 79) for the MSS' -βάλλων is uncontroversial, and so should be Jacobs' τάφρον (*Exercitationes criticae* I, 135) for στρατόν (Ω: [Af]), in the light of 110b–11 (n.) καὶ στρατὸν μέλλεις ἄγειν / τάφρους ὑπερβὰς νυκτὸς ἐν καταστάσει and the fact that, in contrast to 844b–5 (n.) τίς ἂν ὑπερβαλὼν λόχους / Τρώων ἐφ' ἡμᾶς ἦλθεν (...), the active ὑπερβάλλω, 'pass over, cross' a geographical obstacle (LSJ s.v. A III 1 a), cannot well be used of a fighting army, however disdainfully Hector may look at them (Feickert on 989). Moreover, the 'Achaean trench and wall' are often and naturally mentioned together (e.g. *Il*. 7.449–50, 8.177–9, 9.67, 12.4–6, 14.66, *Rh*. 213).

From Aeneas' admonition in 110–22 (cf. 105–30n.) the audience, if not Hector, will recall the dangers of taking the Greek fortifications.

ναυσὶν αἶθον ἐμβαλεῖν: Cf. *Rh*. 120 ὅς σ' οὐκ ἐάσει ναυσὶν ἐμβαλεῖν φλόγα (with aorist infinitive), *Il*. 15.596–8 Ἕκτορι γὰρ οἱ θυμὸς ἐβούλετο κῦδος ὀρέξαι / Πριαμίδῃ, ἵνα νηυσὶ κορωνίσι θεσπιδαὲς πῦρ / ἐμβάλοι ἀκάματον and, at the height of Hector's *aristeia*, *Il*. 16.122–4 τοὶ δ' ἔμβαλον ἀκάματον πῦρ / νηΐ θοῇ· τῆς δ' αἶψα κατ' ἀσβέστη κέχυτο φλόξ. / ὡς τὴν μὲν πρυμνὴν πῦρ' ἄμφεπεν (391b–2n.). Masculine αἶθος occurs elsewhere only in E. *Suppl*. 207–8, and the more recent neuter remains equally rare: A. R. 3.1304 τὸν δ' ἄμφεπε δήιον αἶθος, perhaps 'Orph.' *Lith*. 174 αἴθεϊ (Hermann: αἰθέρι codd.).

ἡμέραν ἐλευθέραν echoes the Homeric ἐλεύθερον ἦμαρ: *Il*. 6.455, 16.831, 20.193 and e.g. *Hcld*. 867–8 νῦν ἐμοὶ δεινοῦ φόβου / ἐλεύθερον πάρεστιν ἦμαρ εἰσιδεῖν, Hdt. 8.77.2 (oracle).

ἀκτῖνα τὴν στείχουσαν ἡλίου: like *Rh*. 331 (330–1n.) ... τοὐπιὸν σέλας θεοῦ, *Med*. 352 ἡ 'πιοῦσα λαμπὰς ... θεοῦ and E. fr. 816.7 τὴν ἐπιστείχουσαν ἡμέραν, but with full emphasis on the verb ('the *dawning* day') to increase the solemnity of the expression. Praxagora's daybreak oath at Ar. *Eccl*. 105 νὴ τὴν ἐπιοῦσαν ἡμέραν (with Sommerstein) is probably similar in emphasis.

φέρειν here signifies aspect, not the absolute tense (KG I 195–7 n. 7, SD 294–5, 296). By the same token, ἐμβαλεῖν could with Feickert (on 991) be interpreted as an aorist, were not true future infinitives so much more common with πέποιθα.

993–6. 'Obey our king. Let us put on our arms and go to carry this order to our allies. Perhaps the god who is on our side will grant us victory.'

In contrast to several Euripidean and Sophoclean plays, there can here be no question about the authenticity of the concluding choral anapaests.[342] Like *Hec*. 1293–5 ἴτε πρὸς λιμένας σκηνάς τε, φίλαι, / τῶν

---

342 See particularly Barrett on *Hipp*. 1462–6, Kannicht on *Hel*. 1688–92, Willink on *Or*. [1691–3] and, for a more sympathetic approach to these 'codas', D. H. Roberts, *CQ* n.s.

δεσποσύνων πειρασόμεναι / μόχθων· στερρὰ γὰρ ἀνάγκη (~ 1288–9 δεσποτῶν δ' ὑμᾶς χρεών / σκηναῖς πελάζειν, Τρῳάδες) and E. *Suppl.* 1232–4 στείχωμεν, Ἄδρασθ', ὅρκια δῶμεν / τῷδ' ἀνδρὶ πόλει τ'· ἄξια δ' ἡμῖν / προμεμοχθήκασι σέβεσθαι (~ 1187–95), they answer a preceding command and, together also with *Hcld.* 1053–5 and *HF* 1427–8 (~ 1425–6), form the fixed type of departure to a new, most often unpromising, end (Kannicht on *Hel.* 1688–92, D. H. Roberts, *CQ* n.s. 37 [1987], 60, Dunn, *Tragedy's End*, 18–19). The ensuing appeal to victory is likewise thoroughly grounded in the plot (983–96n.), although a metatheatrical allusion analogous to those in Old and New Comedy (e.g. Ar. *Ach.* 1224–34, *Lys.* 1291–4, *Thesm.* 1227–31, *Eccl.* 1180–3, Men. *Dysc.* 968–9 = *Mis.* 465–6 = *Sic.* 422–3, *Sam.* 736–7) has already been suspected by Beck (*Exercitatio critica*, 14; cf. e.g. Paley on 995, Jouan 57 n. 295) and may not have been out of place in a fourth-century tragedy (Mastronarde on *Phoen.* [1764–6] ὦ μέγα σέμνη Νίκη τὸν ἐμὸν / βίοτον κατέχοις / καὶ μὴ λήγοις στεφανοῦσα, the same suspicious tail-piece that is appended to *Iphigenia in Tauris*, *Orestes* and, in two MSS, *Hippolytus*).

993–5a. For the formulation of this choral self-exhortation (1n.) cf. *Phil.* 1469–71 χωρῶμεν δὴ πάντες ἀολλεῖς, / Νύμφαις ἁλίαισιν ἐπευξάμενοι / νόστου σωτῆρας ἱκέσθαι and *Hec.* 1293–5 (quoted in 993–6n.).

πείθου βασιλεῖ: 65–6, 388–9nn. Despite Kannicht (on *Hel.* 1392–4 n. 9), the present imperative here seems to be further proof against the strict applicability of Hermann's dictum (on S. *El.* 1003 [1015]) 'Πιθοῦ est obedi, *quod est statim mutari sententiam et fieri, quod iubeat, volentis:* πείθου *autem, sine tibi persuaderi*', which was refuted by Fraenkel (on *Ag.* 1054).

στείχωμεν: See 993–6n. At the end of a play also *Med.* 1394–5 (Μη.) στεῖχε πρὸς οἴκους καὶ θάπτ' ἄλοχον. / (Ια.) στείχω, δισσῶν γ' ἄμορος τέκνων, *Ion* 1616 (Κρ.) ὦ τέκνον, στείχωμεν οἴκους. (Αθ.) στείχεθ', ἕψομαι δ' ἐγώ and *IA* [1624] στείχειν πρὸς οἴκους.

ὅπλοις / κοσμησάμενοι: in periphrasis for ὁπλισάμενοι, as (by analogy) in *Phoen.* 861 βασιλεὺς μὲν οὖν βέβηκε κοσμηθεὶς ὅπλοις and 1359 ἐπεὶ δὲ χαλκέοις σῶμ' ἐκοσμήσανθ' ὅπλοις (with Mastronarde on 861). The aorist participle, for which cf. *Phil.* 1470 (above),

---

37 (1987), 51–56, F. M. Dunn, *Tragedy's End: Closure and Innovation in Euripidean Drama*, New York – Oxford 1996, 14–25. In Sophocles at least *El.* 1508–10 (after [1505–7], an independent problem) and *OT* 1524–30 (4tr$_\wedge$) should go for linguistic reasons (Finglass on S. *El.* [1508–10], [1508], [1509], [1510] and, for the latter, Dawe, *STS* I, 266–73 and P. J. Finglass, *Philologus* 153 [2009], 55–9, especially 59 n. 50, who traces the deletion to a lecture by the French scholar J. Boivin, delivered in 1718 and published posthumously in 1729).

is appropriate here if we take στείχωμεν not so much of the immediate 'stage movement' (Collard on E. *Suppl.* 940), but closely with φράζωμεν ('let us go and ...'). Feickert's κοσμησόμενοι (on 995), moreover, would restrict τάδε to Hector's arming order in 886.

ξυμμαχίᾳ: 'body of allies'. So in other poetry Pi. *Ol.* 10.72–3 καὶ συμμαχία θόρυβον / παραίθυξε μέγαν and fr. 169a.44–6 Sn.–M. Σθενέλο[ι]ό μιν / υἱὸς κέ[λ]ευσε<ν> μόνον / ἄνευ συ[μμ]αχίας ἴμεν.

995b–6. νίκην: Dindorf (III.2 [1840], 628) for νίκαν (fere Ω) in marching anapaests. Cf. 1, 20–2, 557–8nn.

δαίμων ὁ μεθ' ἡμῶν once again evokes Zeus and his deceptive support for Troy, which was clearest at 319–20 (n.) πολλούς, ἐπειδὴ τοὐμὸν εὐτυχεῖ δόρυ / καὶ Ζεὺς πρὸς ἡμῶν ἐστιν, εὑρήσω φίλους.

Select Bibliography

I. Notable Editions, Commentaries and Translations of *Rhesus*[1]

(T = Text, Tr = Translation, N = Notes, C = Commentary)

Aldine (Venice 1503)   T
Oporinus, J. (*apud* J. Hervagium, Basel [1]1537, [2]1544, [3]1551)   T
Brubachius, P. (Frankfurt [1]ca. 1558, [2]ca. 1560)   T
Stiblinus, G. (Basel 1562)   T (*ed. Hervag.*[2]) Tr C
Canter, W. (Antwerp 1571)   T N
Portus, M. Aem. (*apud* H. Commelinium, Heidelberg 1597)   T (Canter) Tr N
Stephanus, P. (Geneva 1602)   T Tr (Portus) N
Barnes, J. (Cambridge 1694)   T Tr N
Carmeli, M. (Padova 1743–54)   T Tr C
Musgrave, S. (Oxford [1]1778, Glasgow [2]1797)   T Tr C
Beck, C. D. (Leipzig [1]1778–88, [2]1792)   T Tr (Barnes) C
Bothe, F. H., *Euripides' Werke verdeutscht*, 5 vols. (Berlin – Stettin 1800–3)   Tr N
Schaefer, G. H. (Leipzig 1810)   T
Matthiae, A. H. (Leipzig 1810–37, Glasgow 1821)   T N
Bothe, F. H., *Euripides' Werke verdeutscht*, 3 vols. (Mannheim 1823–4, repr. 1837)   Tr N
Dindorf, L. (Leipzig 1825)   T N
Bothe, F. H. (Leipzig 1825–6)   T C
Boissonade, J. F. (Paris 1825–6)   T N
Pflugk, A. J. E. – Klotz, R. (Gotha-Erfurt [1]1829–60, I.1 – II.3 [2/3]1857–77)   T C
Dindorf, W. (Oxford [1]1832–40, [2]1851)[2]   T N
Vater, F. (+ *Vindiciae*, Berlin 1837)   T C
Fix, Th. (Paris 1843)   T Tr N
Hartung, J. H. (Leipzig 1848–53)   T Tr C
Nauck, A. (Leipzig [1]1854, [2]1857, [3]1869–71)   T
Kirchhoff, A. (Berlin 1855 *ed. maior*)   T
Paley, F. A. (London [1]1857–60, [2]1872–80)   T C

---

[1] In chronological order. For the history of the Euripides text after the first printed edition see Kannicht, *Helena* I, 109–29 (until 1969 and with special emphasis on *Helen*).
[2] Some conjectures are first or only found in the successive editions of his *Poetae Scenici Graeci* (*PSG*), beginning 1830. See my list of abbreviations for details.

Wecklein, N. (+ *Appendix coniecturas minus probabiles continens*, Leipzig 1902)   T
Murray, G. (Oxford ¹1902–9, vol. 3 ²1913)   T
— *The Rhesus of Euripides*, Oxford 1913   Tr N
Porter, W. H. (Cambridge ¹1916, ²1929)   T C
Ammendola, G. (Milan – Rome – Naples 1922)   T C
Ebener, D. (Berlin 1966)   T Tr N
Paduano, G. (Milan 1991)   T (Murray) Tr N
Zanetto, G. (Stuttgart – Leipzig 1993) T
— *Euripide. Ciclope, Reso* (Milan 1998)   T Tr N
Diggle, J. (Oxford 1981–94)   T
Klyve, G. E. (diss. Oxford 1995)   C (1–526)
Morwood, J., *Euripides. Bacchae and other Plays*, Oxford 1999   Tr N
Kovacs, D. (Cambridge [Mass.] – London 2002)   T Tr
Jouan, J. (Paris 2004)   T Tr N
Feickert, A. (Frankfurt am Main 2004)   Tr C
Liapis, V. (Oxford 2012)   T (Diggle) C

II. Scholia

Schwartz, E. (ed.), *Scholia in Euripidem*, 2 vols., Berlin 1887–91
Rabe, H., 'Euripideum', *RhM* N.F. 63 (1908), 419–22 ($\Sigma\Sigma^V$ *Rh*. 899–940)
Merro, G. (ed.), *Gli scoli al Reso euripideo*, Messina 2008

III. Secondary Literature

1. Commentaries, Editions and Translations generally referred to by Author's Name only

Allan, W., *Euripides. Helen*, Cambridge 2008
Arnott, W. G., *Alexis. The Fragments*, Cambridge 1996
Barrett, W. S., *Euripides. Hippolytos*, Oxford 1964
Bond, G. W., *Euripides. Hypsipyle*, Oxford 1963
— *Euripides. Heracles*, Oxford 1981
Braswell, B. K., *A Commentary on the Fourth Pythian Ode of Pindar*, Berlin – New York 1988
Collard, C., *Euripides. Supplices*, 2 vols., Groningen 1975
— *Euripides. Hecuba*, Warminster 1991
Collard, C. – Cropp, M. J. – Lee, K. H., *Euripides. Selected Fragmentary Plays* I, Oxford 1995 (repr. with corr. and add. 2009)
Collard, C. – Cropp, M. J. – Gibert, J., *Euripides. Selected Fragmentary Plays* II, Oxford 2004

Cropp, M. J., *Euripides. Electra*, Warminster 1988
Dale, A. M., *Euripides. Alcestis*, Oxford 1954
— *Euripides. Helen*, Oxford 1967
Davies, M., *Sophocles. Trachiniae*, Oxford 1991
Dawe, R. D., S*ophocles. Oedipus Rex*, Cambridge ¹1982, ²2006
Denniston, J. D., *Euripides. Electra*, Oxford 1939
Denniston, J. D. – Page, D. L., *Aeschylus. Agamemnon*, Oxford 1957
Di Benedetto, V., *Euripidis Orestes*, Florence 1965
Diggle, J., *Euripides. Phaethon*, Cambridge 1970
Dodds, E. R., *Euripides. Bacchae*, Oxford ²1966
Dover, K. J., *Aristophanes. Clouds*, Oxford 1968
Dunbar, N., *Aristophanes. Birds*, Oxford, 1995
Edwards, M. W., *The Iliad: A Commentary* V. *Books 17–20*, Cambridge 1991
Elmsley, P., *Euripidis Heraclidae*, Oxford ¹1813, ²1821, ³1828
— *Euripidis Bacchae*, Oxford 1821
Faulkner, A., *The Homeric Hymn to Aphrodite*, Oxford 2008
Finglass, P. J., *Sophocles. Electra*, Cambridge 2007
— *Sophocles. Ajax*, Cambridge 2011
Fraenkel, E., *Aeschylus. Agamemnon*, 3 vols., Oxford 1950
Furley, W. D. – Bremer, J. M. (eds.), *Greek Hymns. Selected Cult Songs from the Archaic to the Hellenistic Period*, 2 vols., Tübingen 2001
Garvie, A. F., *Aeschylus. Choephori*, Oxford 1986
— *Sophocles. Ajax*, Oxford 1998
— *Aeschylus. Persae*, Oxford 2009
Gomme, A. W. – Sandbach, F. H., *Menander. A Commentary*, Oxford 1973
Gow, A. S. F., *Theocritus*, 2 vols., Cambridge ²1952
Gow, A. S. F. – Scholfield, A. F., *Nicander. The Poems and Poetical Fragments*, Cambridge 1953
Griffith, M., *Aeschylus. Prometheus Bound*, Cambridge 1983
— *Sophocles. Antigone*, Cambridge 1999
Hainsworth, J. B., *The Iliad: A Commentary* III. *Books 9–12*, Cambridge 1993
Headlam, W. G., *Herodas. The Mimes and Fragments* (ed. A. D. Knox), Cambridge 1922
Hermann, J. G. J., *Sophoclis Electra* (rev. C. G. A. Erfurdt), Leipzig 1825 (repr. London 1827, Leipzig 1864)
— *Euripidis tragoediae*, 3 vols. (unfinished), Leipzig 1831–4
Heubeck, A. – West, S. R. – Hainsworth, J. B. – Hoekstra, A. – Russo, J. – Fernández-Galiano, M., *A Commentary on Homer's Odyssey*, 3 vols., Oxford 1989–98
Hornblower, S., *A Commentary on Thucydides*, 3 vols., Oxford 1991–2008
Horsfall, N., *Virgil*, Aeneid 2. *A Commentary*, Leiden – Boston 2008
Hutchinson, G. O., *Aeschylus. Seven against Thebes*, Oxford 1985
Janko, R., *The Iliad: A Commentary* IV. *Books 13–16*, Cambridge 1992
Jebb, R. C. (ed.), *Sophocles. The Plays and Fragments*, 7 vols., Cambridge 1883–96
— *Bacchylides. The Poems and Fragments*, Cambridge 1905

Jouanna, J., *Hippocrate* V. *Des Vents, De l'Art*, Paris 1988
Kamerbeek, J. C., *The Plays of Sophocles. Commentaries*, 7 vols., Leiden 1963–84
Kannicht, R., *Euripides. Helena*, 2 vols., Heidelberg 1969
Kidd, D. A., *Aratus. Phaenomena*, Cambridge 1997
Kirk, G. S., *The Iliad: A Commentary* I. *Books 1–4*, Cambridge 1985
— *The Iliad: A Commentary* II. *Books 5–8*, Cambridge 1990
Maehler, H., *Die Lieder des Bakchylides*, 2 vols., Leiden – New York – Cologne 1982–1997
— *Bacchylides. A Selection*, Cambridge 2004
Mastronarde, D. J., *Euripides. Phoenissae*, Cambridge 1994
— *Euripides. Medea*, Cambridge 2002
Morwood, J., *Euripides. Suppliant Women*, Oxford 2007
Norden, E., *P. Vergilius Maro. Aeneis Buch VI*, Leipzig ^{1}1903, Stuttgart ^{4}1957
Noussia-Fantuzzi, M., *Solon the Athenian, the Poetic Fragments*, Leiden – Boston 2010
Olson, S. D., *Aristophanes. Acharnians*, Oxford 2002
Page, D. L., *Euripides. Medea*, Oxford 1938
Paley, F. A., *The Tragedies of Aeschylus*, London ^{4}1879
Parker, L. P. E., *Euripides. Alcestis*, Oxford 2007
Pearson, A. C., *Euripides. The Phoenissae*, Cambridge 1909
— *The Fragments of Sophocles*, 3 vols., Cambridge 1917
Porson, R., *Euripidis Phoenissae*, London 1799
— *Euripidis Medea*, Cambridge 1801, London 1817
Radt, S. L., *Pindars zweiter und sechster Paian*, Amsterdam 1958
Richardson, N. J., *The Homeric Hymn to Demeter*, Oxford 1974
— *The Iliad: A Commentary* VI. *Books 21–24*, Cambridge 1993
— *Three Homeric Hymns. To Apollo, Hermes and Aphrodite*, Cambridge 2010
Seaford, R., *Euripides. Cyclops*, Oxford 1984
Sommerstein, A. H., *The Comedies of Aristophanes*, 11 vols. (+ Index), Warminster 1980–2002
— *Aeschylus. Eumenides*, Cambridge 1989
Stevens, P. T., *Euripides. Andromache*, Oxford 1971
Stockert, W. (ed.), *Euripides. Iphigenie in Aulis*, 2 vols., Vienna 1992
Valckenaer, L. C., *Euripidis Tragoedia Hippolytus*, Leiden 1768
West, M. L., *Hesiod. Theogony*, Oxford 1966
— *Hesiod. Works and Days*, Oxford 1978
— *Euripides. Orestes*, Warminster 1987
Whitehead, D. (tr.), *Aeneas the Tactician. How to Survive under Siege*, Oxford 1990
Wilamowitz-Moellendorff, U. von, *Euripides. Herakles*, 2 vols., Berlin ^{1}1889, ^{2}1895
Wilkins, J., *Euripides. Heraclidae*, Oxford 1993
Willink, C. W., *Euripides. Orestes*, Oxford 1986

2. Other Works

Alexiou, M., *The Ritual Lament in Greek Tradition*, Cambridge ¹1974, Lanham ²2002

Anderson, J. K., *Ancient Greek Horsemanship*, Berkeley – Los Angeles 1961

Badham, C., 'Miscellanea critica', *Philologus* 10 (1855), 336–40

Barrett, J., *Staged Narrative. Poetics and the Messenger in Greek Tragedy*, Berkeley – London 2002

Barrett, W. S., *Greek Lyric, Tragedy, and Textual Criticism. Collected Papers* (ed. M. L. West), Oxford 2007

Battezzato, L., 'The Thracian Camp and the Fourth Actor at *Rhesus* 565–691', *CQ* n.s. 50 (2000), 367–73

— 'Parola d'ordine e distribuzione delle battute in [Euripide], *Reso* 682–89, *Lexis* 22 (2004), 277–88

Beck, C. D., *Exercitatio critica de Rheso supposititio Euripidis dramate*, Leipzig 1780 = *Diatribe critica de Rheso supposititio Euripidis dramate*, in C. D. Beck, *Euripidis tragoediae, fragmenta, epistolae ...* III, Leipzig 1788, 444–67

Best, J. G. P., *Thracian Peltasts and their Influence on Greek Warfare*, Groningen 1969

Björck, G., *Das Alpha Impurum und die tragische Kunstsprache: Attische Wort- und Stilstudien*, Uppsala 1950

— 'Rhesos', *Arctos* 1 (1954), 16–18

— 'The Authenticity of *Rhesus*', *Eranos* 55 (1957), 7–17

Blaydes, F. H. M., *Adversaria critica in Euripidem*, Halle 1901

— *Analecta tragica Graeca*, Halle 1906

Bond, R. S., 'Homeric Echoes in *Rhesus*', *AJPh* 117 (1996), 255–73

Bruhn, E., 'Euripidea', *RhM* N.F. 48 (1893), 628–31

— *Sophokles*. Erklärt von F. W. Schneidewin und A. Nauck, 8. Bändchen: *Anhang*, Berlin 1899

Brunck, R. F. P. (ed.), *Euripidis tragoediae quatuor. Hecuba, Phoenissae, Hippolytus et Bacchae*, Strasbourg 1780

Bryce, T. R., 'Lycian Apollo and the Authorship of the *Rhesus*', *CJ* 86 (1990), 144–9

Burlando, A., *Reso: i problemi, la scena*, Genoa 1997

Buttmann, P. C., *Ausführliche Griechische Sprachlehre*, 2 vols., Berlin ¹1819–27, ²1830–9

Cairns, D. L., *Aidōs. The Psychology and Ethics of Honour and Shame in Ancient Greek Literature*, Oxford 1993

Carrara, P., 'Dicearco e l'hypothesis del *Reso*', *ZPE* 90 (1992), 35–44

Cobet, C. G., 'Euripidea', *Mnemosyne* 11 (1862), 435–48

Collard, C., 'Scaliger's Euripidean Marginalia', *CQ* n.s. 24 (1974), 242–9

— *Tragedy, Euripides and Euripideans. Selected Papers*, Exeter 2007

Collard, C. – Cropp, M. J. (eds.), *Euripides* VII. *Fragments*, Cambridge (Mass.) – London 2008

— *Euripides* VIII. *Fragments*, Cambridge (Mass.) – London 2008

Conomis, N. C., 'The Dochmiacs of Greek Drama', *Hermes* 92 (1964), 23–50
Dangel, M. (ed.), *Accius. Oeuvres (fragments)*, Paris 1995
Del Río (Delrius), M. A., *Syntagma tragoediae latinae in tres partes distinctum*, Antwerp 1593
Diggle, J., *Studies on the Text of Euripides*, Oxford 1981
— 'The Prophet of Bacchus: *Rhesus* 970–3', *SIFC* 5 (1987), 167–72
— *The Textual Tradition of Euripides'* Orestes, Oxford 1991
— *Euripidea. Collected Essays*, Oxford 1994
— 'Epilegomena Phaethontea', *AC* 65 (1996), 189–99
— 'Rhythmical Prose in the Euripidean Hypotheses', in G. Bastianini – A. Casanova (eds.), *Euripide e i papiri: atti del convegno internazionale di studi, Firenze, 10–11 giugno 2004*, Florence 2005, 27–67
Dobree, P. P., *Adversaria* (ed. J. Scholefield), 2 vols., Cambridge 1833–43 (= *P. P. Dobree Adversaria. Editio in Germania prima cum praefatione G. Wagneri*, 5 vols., Berlin 1874)
Družinina, J., 'A. Naucks nachgelassene Marginalien zu Euripides (nach der Vorlage V. K. Jernstedts)', *Hyperboreus* 5 (1999), 238–56
Duchemin, J., *L'ΑΓΩΝ dans la tragédie grecque*, Paris ²1968
Ebener, D., 'Textkritisches zum Rhesos', *WZRostock* 12 (1963), 205–7
Elmsley, P., Review: R. Porson, ΕΥΡΙΠΙΔΟΥ ΕΚΑΒΗ. *Euripidis Hecuba ... In Usum Studiosae Juventutis*, London 1808, *Edinburgh Review* 19 (1811), 64–95
Fantuzzi, M., 'Odisseo mendicante a Troia e a Itaca: su [Eur.] "Rh." 498–507, 710–719 e Hom. "Od." 4, 244–258', *MD* 36 (1996), 175–85 = *Arachnion* 2.1 (1996), 1–8
— 'Euripides (?) *Rhesus* 56–58 and Homer *Iliad* 8.498–501: Another Possible Clue to Zenodotus' Reliability', *CPh* 100 (2005), 268–73
— 'La Dolonia del *Reso* come luogo dell' errore e dell' incertezza', in M. Vetta – C. Catenacci (eds.), *I luoghi e la poesia nella Grecia antica. Atti del Convegno Università 'G. d'Annunzio' di Chieti-Pescara 20–22 aprile 2004*, Alessandria 2006, 241–62
— 'The Myths of Dolon and Rhesus from Homer to the 'Homeric/Cyclic' Tragedy *Rhesus*', in F. Montanari – A. Rengakos (eds.), *La poésie épique grecque: Métamorphoses d'un genre littéraire (Entretiens de la Fondation Hardt* LII), Geneva 2006, 135–76
— Review: F. Jouan (ed.), *Euripide. Tragédies VII.2. Rhésos*, *BMCR* 2006.02.18
— 'La *mousa* del lamento in Euripide, e il lamento della Musa nel *Reso* ascritto a Euripide', *Eikasmos* 18 (2007), 173–99
— Review: A. Feickert, *Euripidis Rhesus. Einleitung, Übersetzung, Kommentar*, Frankfurt am Main 2005, *JHS* 127 (2007), 161–2
— 'Scholarly Panic: πανικὸς φόβος, Homeric Philology and the Beginning of the *Rhesus*', in S. Matthaios – F. Montanari – A. Rengakos (eds.), *Ancient Scholarship and Grammar: Archetypes, Concepts and Contexts*, Berlin – New York 2011, 41–54

Fantuzzi, M. – Konstan, D., 'From Achilles' Horses to a Cheese-Seller's Shop. On the History of the Guessing Game in Greek Drama', in E. Bakola – L. Prauscello – M. Telò (eds.), *Greek Comedy and the Discourse of Genre*, Cambridge 2013, 256–74

Fenik, B., *The Influence of Euripides on Vergil's Aeneid*, diss. Princeton 1960

— *"Iliad X" and the "Rhesus". The Myth* (*Collection Latomus* LXXIII), Brussels 1964

— *Typical Battle Scenes in the Iliad. Studies in the Narrative Techniques of Homeric Battle Description*, Wiesbaden 1968

Finglass, P. J., 'Unpublished Conjectures at Leiden on the Greek Dramatists', *GRBS* 49 (2009), 187–221

Fraenkel, E., *Zu den Phoenissen des Euripides* (*SBAW* I 1963), Munich 1963

Fraenkel, E(rnst), *Geschichte der griechischen Nomina agentis auf* -τήρ, -τωρ, -της *(-τ-)*, 2 vols. Strasbourg 1910–12

Fries, A., 'The Poetic Technique of [Euripides]: The Case of *Rhesus* 118', *CQ* n.s. 60 (2010), 345–51

— Review: V. Liapis, *A Commentary on the* Rhesus *attributed to Euripides*, *Mnemosyne* IV 66 (2013), 814–21 + 'Corrigendum', *Mnemosyne* IV 67 (2014), 179

Gallavotti, C., 'Nuove hypotheseis di drammi euripidei', *RFIC* 61 (1933), 177–88

Giuliani, L., *Tragik, Trauer und Trost. Bildervasen für eine apulische Totenfeier*, Berlin 1995

— 'Rhesus between Dream and Death: On the Relation of Image to Literature in Apulian Vase-Painting', *BICS* 41 (1996), 71–86

Graf, F., *Eleusis und die orphische Dichtung Athens in vorhellenistischer Zeit*, Berlin –New York 1974

Griffith, M., *The Authenticity of 'Prometheus Bound'*, Cambridge 1977

Gygli-Wyss, B., *Das nominale Polyptoton im älteren Griechisch*, Göttingen 1966

Hagenbach, F., *De Rheso Tragoedia*, diss. Basel 1863

Hall, E., *Inventing the Barbarian. Greek Self-Definition through Tragedy*, Oxford 1989

Hanson, V. D., *The Western Way of War. Infantry Battle in Classical Greece*, Berkeley – London ²2000

Hardion, J., 'Dissertation sur la tragédie de Rhésus', *Mém. Acad. des Inscr.* 10 (1736), 323–37

Haslam, M. W., 'Euripides, *Phoenissae* 1–2 and Sophocles, *Electra* 1', *GRBS* 16 (1975), 149–74

Headlam, W., 'Notes on Euripides', *CR* 15 (1901), 98–108

Heath, B., *Notae sive lectiones ad tragicorum Graecorum veterum Aeschyli, Sophoclis, Euripidis quae supersunt dramata deperditorumque relliquias*, Oxford 1762

Heimsoeth, F., *De Madvigii Hauniensis adversariis criticis commentatio altera*, Bonn 1872

Hermann, J. G. J., 'De Rheso tragoedia dissertatio', in *Godofredi Hermanni Opuscula* III, Leipzig 1828, 262–310

— *De fragmentis poetarum in scholiis Vaticanis ad Euripidis Troades et Rhesum dissertatio*, Leipzig 1833 = in *Godofredi Hermanni Opuscula* V, Leipzig 1834, 182–206

Herwerden, H. van, *Exercitationes criticae in poeticis et prosaicis quibusdam Atticorum monumentis*, The Hague 1862

— 'Novae commentationes Euripideae (pars posterior)', *RPh* 18 (1894), 60–98

Hoddinott, R. F., *The Thracians*, London 1981

Hoffmann, W., 'Schedae criticae ad tragicos Graecos', *NJbbClPh* 8 (1862), 589–601

Isaac, B., *The Greek Settlements in Thrace until the Macedonian Conquest*, Leiden 1986

Itsumi, K., 'Enoplian in Tragedy', *BICS* 38 (1991–1993), 243–61

Jackson, J., 'Marginalia Scaenica I', *CQ* 35 (1941), 29–51

— *Marginalia Scaenica*, Oxford 1955

Jacobs, F. C. W., *Exercitationes criticae in scriptores veteres I. Curae secundae in Euripidis tragoedias*, Leipzig 1796

Jong, I. J. F. de, *Narrative in Drama. The Art of the Euripidean Messenger-Speech*, Leiden et al. 1991

Jouan, F., 'L'utilisation du *Rhésos* euripidéen par l'auteur du Christos Paschôn', in U. Criscuolo – R. Maisano (eds.), *Synodia. Studia humanitatis Antonio Garzya ... dicata*, Naples 1997, 495–509

Kaimio, M., *The Chorus of Greek Drama within the Light of the Person and Number Used*, Helsinki 1970

— *Physical Contact in Greek Tragedy. A Study of Stage Conventions*, Helsinki 1988

Kamptz, H. von, *Homerische Personennamen*, Göttingen 1982

Kannicht, R., 'Zum Corpus Euripideum', in C. Mueller-Goldingen – K. Sier (eds.), ΛHNAIKA. *Festschrift für Carl Werner Müller*, Stuttgart – Leipzig 1996, 21–31

Kassel, R., 'Hypothesis', in W. J. Aerts et al. (eds.) Σχόλια. *Studia ... D. Holwerda oblata*, Groningen 1985, 53–9

— *Kleine Schriften* (ed. H.-G. Nesselrath), Berlin – New York 1991

Kemmer, E., *Die polare Ausdrucksweise in der griechischen Literatur*, Würzburg 1903

Kessels, A. H. M., *Studies in the Dream in Greek Literature*, diss. Utrecht 1973

Keyes, C. W., 'Apollo and Athena in the *Rhesus*', *CPh* 24 (1929), 204–7 ~ *TAPA* 59 (1928), xxviii (abstract)

Kitto, H. D. F., 'The *Rhesus* and Related Matters', *YCS* 25 (1977), 317–50

König, A., *Die Aeneis und die griechische Tragödie – Studien zur* imitatio-*Technik Vergils*, diss. Berlin 1970

Kovacs, D., *Euripidea Tertia*, Leiden – Boston 2003

Kranz, W., *Stasimon. Untersuchungen zu Form und Gehalt der griechischen Tragödie*, Berlin 1933

Lachmann, K., *De choricis systematis tragicorum Graecorum libri IV*, Berlin 1819

— *De mensura tragoediarum liber singularis*, Berlin 1822
Lautensach, O., *Grammatische Studien zu den griechischen Tragikern und Komikern. Augment und Reduplikation*, Hanover – Leipzig 1899
Lazaridis, D., *Amphipolis*, Athens 1997
Leaf, W., 'Rhesus of Thrace', *JHS* 35 (1915), 1–11
Lenting, J., 'Animadversiones criticae in Euripidem', *Nova Acta Literaria Societatis Rheno-Trajectinae* I (1821), 1–120
Leumann, M., *Homerische Wörter*, Basel 1950
Liapis, V. (J.), 'An Ancient Hypothesis to *Rhesus*, and Dicaearchus' *Hypotheseis*', *GRBS* 42 (2001), 313–28
— 'Epicharmus, Asclepiades of Tragilus, and the *Rhesus*: Lessons from a Lexicographical Entry', *ZPE* 143 (2003), 19–22
— '*They Do it with Mirrors*: The Mystery of the Two *Rhesus* Plays', in D. I. Jacob – E. Papazoglou (eds.), Θυμέλη: Μελέτες χαρισμένες στον Καθηγητή Ν. Χ. Χουρμουζιάδη, Heraklion 2004, 159–88
— 'Zeus, Rhesus, and the Mysteries', *CQ* n.s. 57 (2007), 381–411
— '*Rhesus* Revisited: The Case for a Fourth-Century Macedonian Context', *JHS* 129 (2009), 71–88
— 'The Thracian Cult of Rhesus and the *Heros Equitans*', *Kernos* 24 (2011), 95–104
— 'Staging *Rhesus*', in G. M. W. Harrison – V. Liapis (eds.), *Performance in Greek and Roman Theatre*, Leiden – Boston 2013[3]
Lightfoot, J. L., *Parthenius of Nicaea. The Poetical Fragments and the* Ἐρωτικὰ Παθήματα, Oxford 1999
Lindemann, F., 'Emendationes ad *Rhesum*', *Ad annuam lustrationem Gymnasii Zittaviensis* (1834), 1–16
Lissarague, F., 'Iconographie de Dolon le Loup', *RA* n.s. fasc. 1 (1980), 3–30
Lloyd, M., *The* Agon *in Euripides*, Oxford 1999
Lloyd-Jones, P. H. J., *The Academic Papers of Sir Hugh Lloyd-Jones*, 2 vols., Oxford 1990
Longman, G. A., 'Gnomologium Vatopedianum: The Euripidean Section', *CQ* n.s. 9 (1959), 129–41
Lorimer, H. L., *Homer and the Monuments*, London 1950
Luppe, W., 'Die Hypothesis zum *Rhesos*. PSI 1286. Kolumne I', *Anagennesis* 2 (1982), 74–82
Macurdy, G. H., 'The Dawn Songs in *Rhesus* (527–556) and in the Parodos of *Phaethon*', *AJPh* 64 (1943), 408–16
Madvig, J. N., *Adversaria critica ad scriptores Graecos et Latinos* I, Copenhagen 1871
Magnani, M., '"Mozzi di parapetti'? (Suda α 2660 A. ~ [Eur.] *Rhes.* 118)', *Paideia* 56 (2001), 107–11
Magnelli, E., 'Miscellanea critica', *Eikasmos* 10 (1999), 101–17
Malkin, I., *Religion and Colonization in Ancient Greece*, Leiden 1987

---

3   This almost exclusively reprints material from Liapis' commentary. It seemed impractical to cross-refer to the relevant sections in each case.

Mantziou, M., 'Παρατηρήσεις στο κείμενο του Ευριπίδη', *Dodone* 14 (1985), 91–102
Markland, J. (ed.), *Euripidis dramata Iphigenia in Aulide et Iphigenia in Tauris*, London ¹1771, ²1783
Mastronarde, D. J., *Contact and Discontinuity: Some Conventions of Speech and Action on the Greek Stage*, Berkeley – Los Angeles 1979
— 'Actors on High: the Skene Roof, the Crane and the Gods in Attic Drama', *Cl. Ant.* 9 (1990), 247–94
— Review: D. Kovacs (ed.), *Euripides* VI. *Bacchae, Iphigenia in Aulis, Rhesus*, Cambridge (Mass.) – London 2002, *ElectronAnt* 8 (2004), 15–30
Mastronarde, D. J. – Bremer J. M., *The Textual Tradition of Euripides' Phoinissai*, Berkeley 1982
Matthiessen, K., 'Exzerpte aus sieben Tragödien des Euripides im Codex Vaticanus Barberini Graecus 4', *Hermes* 93 (1965), 148–58
— 'Ein weiteres Euripidesgnomologium (Escorialensis Graecus X. I. 13)', *Hermes* 94 (1966), 398–410
— *Studien zur Textüberlieferung der Hekabe des Euripides*, Heidelberg 1974
Menzer, O., *De Rheso Tragoedia*, diss. Berlin 1867
Meschini, A., 'Su alcuni luoghi del *Reso*', in *AFLPad: Scritti in onore di Carlo Diano*, Bologna 1975, 217–26
— 'Sugli gnomologi bizantini di Euripide', *Helikon* 13–14 (1973–74), 349–62
— 'Altre note al *Reso*', *AFLPad* 1 (1976), 177–84
Morstadt, R., *Beitrag zur Kritik der dem Euripides zugeschriebenen Tragödie Rhesos*, Heidelberg 1827
Musgrave, S., *Exercitationum in Euripidem libri duo*, Leiden 1762
Naber, S. A., 'Euripidea (I)', *Mnemosyne* n.s. 10 (1882), 1–26
Nauck, A. (ed.), *Aristophanis Byzantii Grammatici Alexandrini Fragmenta*, Halle 1848
— *Euripideische Studien* II (*Mémoires de l'Académie Impériale des Sciences de St. Petersbourg, VIIe Série*), St. Petersburg 1862
— 'Analecta critica', *Hermes* 24 (1889), 447–72
Nickau, K., *Untersuchungen zur textkritische Methode des Zenodotos von Ephesos*, Berlin – New York 1977
Nilsson, M. P., *Geschichte der griechischen Religion* I. *Die Religion Griechenlands bis auf die griechische Weltherrschaft*, Munich ³1967
Nock, A. D., 'The End of the *Rhesus*', *CR* 40 (1926), 184–6
— 'The *Rhesus*', *CR* 44 (1930), 173–4
Norden, E., *Agnostos Theos. Untersuchungen zur Formengeschichte religiöser Rede*, Leipzig – Berlin 1913
Norwood, G., 'Appendix on vv. 874–8', in W. H. Porter (ed.), *The* Rhesus *of Euripides*, Cambridge ¹1916, ²1929, 91–2
Pace, G., 'Nota metrica a [Eur.] *Rh.* 32–33 = 50–51', *QUCC* n.s. 60 (1998), 133–9
— '[Eur.] *Rh.* 454–466; 820–832', *QUCC* n.s. 65 (2000), 127–39
— *Euripide. Reso: I canti*, Rome 2001

— 'Note critico-testuali al *Reso*', in L. Torraca (ed.), *Scritti in onore di Italo Gallo*, Naples 2002, 453–61
— 'Congetture di Richard Porson al *Reso*', *Lexis* 27 (2009), 181–95
Paduano, G., 'Funzioni drammatiche nella struttura del *Reso* I: L'aristia mancata di Dolone e Reso', *Maia* n.s. 25 (1973), 3–29
— 'Funzioni drammatiche nella struttura del *Reso* II: Ettore e la frustrazione del piano eroico', *SCO* 23 (1974), 5–30
— 'In assenza del coro, l'azione', *Dioniso* 55 (1984–1985), 255–67
Palmer, C. E., 'Eur. *Rhesus* 59 60 [and other passages]', *CR* 4 (1890), 228–9
Parker, L. P. E., 'Some Observations on the Incidence of Word-end in Anapaestic Paroemiacs and its Application to Textual Questions', *CQ* n.s. 8 (1958), 82–9
— 'Porson's Law Extended', *CQ* n.s. 16 (1966), 1–26
— 'Split Resolution in Greek Dramatic Lyric, *CQ* n.s. 18 (1968), 241–69
— 'Catalexis', *CQ* n.s. 26 (1976), 14–28
— 'Trochee to Iamb, Iamb to Trochee', in E. M. Craik (ed.), *'Owls to Athens': Essays in Classical Subjects Presented to Sir Kenneth Dover*, Oxford 1990, 331–48
— *The Songs of Aristophanes*, Oxford 1997
Parker, R. C. T., *Miasma. Pollution and Purification in Early Greek Religion*, Oxford 1983
— *Athenian Religion. A History*, Oxford 1996
— *Polytheism and Society at Athens*, Oxford 2005
Parry, H., 'The Approach of Dawn in the *Rhesus*', *Phoenix* 18 (1964), 283–93
Parry, M., *The Making of Homeric Verse. The Collected Papers of Milman Parry* (ed. A. M. Parry), Oxford 1971, 266–324
Pattoni, M. P., 'La fastosa entrata del guerriero come modulo teatrale eschileo: il caso di Cicno, Memnone e Reso', *PapLup* 9 (2001), 313–31
— 'I pastoralia di Longo e la contaminazione dei generi: alcune proposte interpretative', *MD* 53 (2005), 83–123
Pavlock, B., 'Epic and Tragedy in Vergil's Nisus and Euryalus Episode', *TAPA* 115 (1985), 207–24
Pearson, A. C., 'Some Passages in Greek Tragedy', *CQ* 11 (1917), 57–68
— 'Notes on Euripides, *Rhesus* 252, 340', *CQ* 12 (1918), 79
— 'The *Rhesus*', *CR* 35 (1921), 52–61
Perdrizet, P., *Cultes et mythes du Pangée*, Paris 1910
— 'Scaptésylé', *Klio* 10 (1910), 1–27
Perris, S., 'Stagecraft and the Stage Building in *Rhesus*', *G&R* 59 (2012), 151–64
Pfeiffer, R., *History of Classical Scholarship: From the Beginnings to the End of the Hellenistic Age*, Oxford 1968
Pierson, J., *Verisimilium libri duo*, Leiden 1752
Platnauer, M., 'Prodelision in Greek Drama', *CQ* n.s. 10 (1960), 140–4
— '(?) Euripides, *Rhesus* 787–8', *Eranos* 62 (1964), 73
Plichon, C., 'Le *Rhésos* et l'orphisme', *Kernos* 14 (2001), 11–21
Poe, J. P., 'Unconventional Procedures in *Rhesus*', *Philologus* 148 (2004), 21–33

Porson, R., *Appendix* II, in J. Toup, *Emendationes in Suidam et Hesychium et alios lexicographos Graecos* IV, Oxford ²1790, 435–48
— *Adversaria* (edd. J. H. Monk – C. J. Blomfield), Cambridge 1812
Porter, W. H., 'The Euripidean *Rhesus* in the Light of Recent Criticism', *Hermathena* 17 (1913), 348–80 (= Preface to the First Edition of his *Rhesus*)
— 'On Some Passages in the *Rhesus*', *CQ* 11 (1917), 159–60
Portus, M. Aem., *Breves notae in omnes Euripidis tragoedias*, Heidelberg 1599
Rau, P., *Paratragodia: Untersuchung einer komischen Form des Aristophanes*, Munich 1967
Reiske, J. J., *Ad Euripidem et Aristophanem animadversiones*, Leipzig 1753
Rempe, J., *De Rheso Thracum heroe*, diss. Münster 1927
Renehan, R., Review: The New Oxford Sophocles, *CPh* 87 (1992), 335–75
Richards, G. C., 'The Problem of *Rhesus*', *CQ* 10 (1916), 192–7
Rossum-Steenbeek, M. van, *Greek Readers' Digests? Studies on a Selection of Subliterary Papyri*, Leiden – New York – Cologne 1998
Ruijgh, C. J., *Autour de „Te épique": Études sur la syntaxe grecque*, Amsterdam 1971
Rusten, J., 'Dicaearchus and the *Tales from Euripides*', *GRBS* 23 (1982), 357–67
Sallier, C., 'Correction d' un passage d'Euripides, et d'un autre de Longin', *Histoire de l'Académie royale des inscriptions et belles-lettres* 5 (1729), 125–6
Sansone, D., Review: V. Liapis, *A Commentary on the* Rhesus *attributed to Euripides*, *BMCR* 2013.03.15
Scaliger, J. J., *M. Manili Astronomicon ...*, Leiden 1600
Schadewaldt, W., *Monolog und Selbstgespräch*, Berlin 1926
Schmidt, F. W., *Kritische Studien zu den griechischen Dramatikern* II, Berlin 1886
Scullion, J. S., 'Tradition and Invention in Euripidean Aitiology', in D. Sansone et al. (eds.), *Euripides and Tragic Theatre in the Fifth Century* (*ICS* 24–5), Champaign (Ill.) 1999–2000, 217–33
Seager, J., 'In Euripidem commentarii', *CJ* 20 (1819), 78–87 + 271–85
Seidler, A., *De versibus dochmiacis tragicorum Graecorum*, Leipzig 1811–12
Sheppard, J. T., 'Note on Euripides, *Rhesus*, 287 ff.', *CR* 28 (1914), 87–8
Sicherl, M., 'Die Editio princeps Aldina des Euripides und ihre Vorlagen', *RhM* N.F. 118 (1975), 205–25
— *Griechische Erstausgaben des Aldus Manutius. Druckvorlagen, Stellenwert, kultureller Hintergrund*, Paderborn et al. 1997
Sideras, A., *Aeschylus Homericus. Untersuchungen zu den Homerismen der aischyleischen Sprache*, Göttingen 1971
Sneller, C. B., *De Rheso Tragoedia*, Amsterdam 1949
Snodgrass, A. M., *Arms and Armour of the Greeks*, London ¹1967, Baltimore – London ²1999
Sommerstein, A. H. (ed.), *Shards from Kolonos: Studies in Sophoclean Fragments*, Bari 2003
— (ed.), *Aeschylus*, 3 vols., Cambridge (Mass.) – London 2008

Sommerstein, A. H. – Fitzpatrick, D. – Talboy, Th. H. (eds.), *Sophocles. Selected Fragmentary Plays* I, Oxford 2006
Sommerstein, A. H. – Talboy, Th. H. (eds.), *Sophocles. Selected Fragmentary Plays* II, Oxford 2012
Steadman, S. H., 'A Note on the *Rhesus*', *CR* 59 (1945), 6–8
Stephanopoulos, Th. K., 'Tragica I', *ZPE* 73 (1988), 207–47
— 'Tragica II', *ZPE* 75 (1988), 3–38
Stephanus, H., *Annotationes in Sophoclem & Euripidem*, Geneva 1568
Stevens, P. T., Review: W. Ritchie, *The Authenticity of the Rhesus of Euripides*, *CR* n.s. 15 (1965), 268–71
Stinton, T. C. W., *Collected Papers on Greek Tragedy* (ed. P. H. J. Lloyd-Jones), Oxford 1990
Taplin, O. P., 'Aeschylean Silences and Silences in Aeschylus', *HSPh* 76 (1972), 57–97
— 'ΧΟΡΟΥ and the Structure of Post-Classical Tragedy', *LCM* 1 (1976), 47–50
— *The Stagecraft of Aeschylus. The Dramatic Use of Exits and Entrances in Greek Tragedy*, Oxford 1977
— *Pots & Plays. Interactions between Tragedy and Greek Vase-Painting of the Fourth Century B.C.*, Los Angeles 2007
Thomson, J. A. K., 'Dolon the Wolf', *CR* 25 (1911), 238–9
Thum, T., 'Der Rhesos und die Tragödie des 4. Jahrhunderts', *Philologus* 149 (2005), 209–32
Tuilier, A. (ed.), *La passion du Christ. Tragédie*, Paris 1969
— 'Nouvelles remarques sur le *Rhésos* d'Euripide', *Sileno* 9 (1983), 11–28
Turyn, A., *The Byzantine Manuscript Tradition of the Tragedies of Euripides*, Urbana (Ill.) 1957 (repr. Rome 1970)
Ustinova, Y., '"Either a Daimon, or a Hero, or perhaps a God:" Mythical Residents of Subterranean Chambers', *Kernos* 15 (2002), 267–88
— *Caves and the Ancient Greek Mind. Descending Underground in the Search for Ultimate Truth*, Oxford 2009
Valckenaer, L. C., MS *Observationes in Aeschylum et Euripidem* (Leiden BPL 352), 1749
— *Diatribe in Euripidis perditorum dramatum reliquias*, Leiden 1767
Wace, A. J. B. – Stubbings, F. H. (eds.), *A Companion to Homer*, London – New York 1962
Wackernagel, J., *Sprachliche Untersuchungen zu Homer*, Göttingen 1916
— *Vorlesungen über Syntax. Mit besonderer Berücksichtigung von Griechisch, Lateinisch und Deutsch*, 2 vols., Basel ¹1920–4, ²1926–8 ~ *Jacob Wackernagel. Lectures on Syntax. With Special Reference to Greek, Latin and Germanic* (tr. and ed. D. Langslow), Oxford 2009
— *Kleine Schriften*, 3 vols., Göttingen 1955–79
Wakker, G., 'Emphasis and Affirmation: Some Aspects of μήν in Tragedy', in A. Rijksbaron (ed.), *New Approaches to Greek Particles*, Amsterdam 1997, 209–31
Wathelet, P., *Dictionnaire des Troyens de l'Iliade*, 3 vols., Liège 1988–9

Wecklein, N., 'Studien zu Euripides. Mit einem Anhang zu Aeschylus, Sophokles und den Bruchstücken der griechischen Tragiker', *NJbbClPh* Suppl. n.s. 7 (1873–5), 305–448
— *Beiträge zur Kritik des Euripides* III (*SBAW* I 1897), Munich 1898, 445–96
— *Textkritische Studien zu den griechischen Tragikern* (*SBAW* V 1921), Munich 1922
West, M. L., 'The Prometheus Trilogy', *JHS* 99 (1979), 130–48 (~ *Hellenica* II, 249–86)
— *The Orphic Poems*, Oxford 1983
— 'Tragica VII', *BICS* 31 (1984), 171–92
— (ed.), *Aeschyli Tragoedia cum incerti poetae Prometheo*, Stuttgart – Leipzig ¹1990, ²1998
— *Studies in Aeschylus*, Stuttgart 1990
— *Ancient Greek Music*, Oxford 1992
— (ed.), *Homerus.Ilias*, 2 vols., Stuttgart – Leipzig – Munich 1998–2000
— 'Iliad and *Aethiopis* on the Stage: Aeschylus and Son', *CQ* n.s. 50 (2000), 338–52 (= *Hellenica* II, 227–49)
— (ed.), *Homeric Hymns, Homeric Apocrypha, Lives of Homer*, Cambridge (Mass.) – London 2003
— *The Making of the* Iliad. *Disquisition and Analytical Commentary*, Oxford 2011
— *Hellenica. Selected Papers on Greek Literature and Thought*, 3 vols., Oxford 2011–13
— *The Epic Cycle. A Commentary on the Lost Troy Epics*, Oxford 2013
Wilamowitz-Moellendorff, U. von, *Analecta Euripidea*, Berlin 1875
— *De Rhesi scholiis disputatiuncula*, Greifswald 1877 (= *KS* I, 1–16)
— *Einleitung in die attische Tragödie* (*Euripides. Herakles* I, ch. I–IV), Berlin 1889
— 'Lesefrüchte', *Hermes* 61 (1926), 277–303 (= *KS* IV, 404–30)
— *Kleine Schriften* (edd. P. Maas *et al.*), 6 vols., Berlin 1935–72
Willink, C. W., *Collected Papers on Greek Tragedy* (ed. W. B. Henry), Leiden 2010
Wilson, N. G., Review: G. Zuntz, *An Inquiry into the Transmission of the Plays of Euripides*, Cambridge 1965, *Gnomon* 38 (1966), 334–42
— 'A Mysterious Byzantine Scriptorium: Ioannikios and his Colleagues', *Scrittura e Civiltà* 7 (1983), 161–76
Xanthakis-Karamanos, G., *Studies in Fourth-Century Tragedy*, Athens 1980
Zuntz, G., *The Political Plays of Euripides*, Manchester ¹1955, ²1963
— *An Inquiry into the Transmission of the Plays of Euripides*, Cambridge 1965
— Review: F. Graf, *Eleusis und die orphische Dichtung Athens in vorhellenistischer Zeit*, Berlin – New York 1974, *Gnomon* 50 (1978), 526–31

Indexes

Figures in upright type refer to verse numbers (entry-headings) in the Commentary; those in italic type accompanied by '*p.*' or '*pp.*' refer to pages. In the case of longer notes page numbers are occasionally added in brackets.

I. General Index

Accius *p. 44*, 532–3 (*p. 325*)
Achilles *pp. 13–14*, 699–701,
    890–914, 899–901, 926–31,
    935b–7, 962–6
    horses of *p. 9*, 149–94, 184, 238,
        833–81
    see also Rhesus
Adrasteia 342–79, 342–3, 454–66
Aedon (Procne), *see* nightingale
Aeneas 926–31
    character modelled on
        Polydamas *pp. 9, 20, 28–9*,
        52–84, 85–148, 105–30,
        110b–18, 112–15, 112,
        119–24
Aeschylus
    Achilles trilogy *pp. 14, 40 (with
        n. 74), 43 n. 84*
    (?) *Cares* = *Europa* *pp. 13 n. 11,
        14*
    Memnon pp. 13 n. 11, 33 n. 48,
        342–79 (*p. 244*), 380–7,
        595–641 (n. 236)
    Myrmidons pp. 14, 32, 34–5,
        1–51 (*p. 116*)
    Nereids p. 14, 1–51 (*p. 116*)
    Niobe p. 114, 1–51 (*p. 116*)
    Persians p. 34, 35–6, 1–51
        (*p. 116*), 30

Phrygians p. 14
Psychostasia p. 13 n. 11,
    595–674, 882–9 (*p. 440*)
Seven against Thebes pp. 34,
    38–9, 19, 388–526 (*p. 264*)
Supplices 1–51 (*p. 116*)
[Aeschylus]
    Prometheus Bound pp. 41–2,
        1–51 (*p. 116*)
    Prometheus Unbound p. 114,
        1–51 (*p. 116*)
aetiology 962–82
agon *pp. 3, 5*, 264–341 (*p. 216*),
    319–26, 388–526, 388–453,
    467–526, 804–81
Ajax 461–3
    see also Rhesus
Aldine *p. 55*
Amphiaraus 962–82
Amphipolis *pp. 13, 14–15, 18*,
    921–2a
Apollo 224–63
    Lycian 224–5
    Φαναῖος 355–6
    (Phoebus) as watchword
        pp. 5–6, 521–2
    see also Lycians; Thymbra; Zeus
Ares 385–7
    see also Rhesus

Aristarchus *p. 23*, 715–16
Aristophanes, of Byzantium *pp. 26, 28, 112–13*
Asclepiades, of Myrlea *pp. 44–5*
Asclepiades, of Tragilus *pp. 24 n. 15, 27, 972–3*
astronomy 527–64
Athena
    epiphany of *pp. 5, 41*, 595–674
    impersonating Aphrodite *pp. 3, 41*, 595–674 (*p. 348*), 642–74, 647–8
    role in *Rhesus pp. 4, 9–10, 11–12*, 595–641, 661, 670–1a, 938–40
    see also Odysseus

Behaghel's Law 399–400, 752–3

Carcinus II *p. 38*
Catrares, Ioannes *pp. 51, 109 n. 1*
Charioteer *pp. 10, 30, 31, 41*, 728–55, 756–803, 762–3a, 776–7, 804–81, 833–81
chariot entry, *see* staging
chorus
    concluding anapaests 993–6
    division of 538–45, 557–64, 675–91, 683, 686, 687
    entering σποράδην *p. 40*, 1–10, 675–91
    exit in mid-play (μετάστασις χοροῦ) *pp. 337–8*
    role in *Rhesus pp. 39–40*
Christus Patiens pp. 48, 53
Cilicians 538–45, 540–2
comparatio compendiaria 219–22a
Coroebus 539
Crates, of Mallus *pp. 22–3*, 527–31, 538–45
Cycnus *pp. 13–14, 33*, 618
    see also Sophocles, *Poimenes*

decapitation 219–23, 257b–60, 605–6 (*p. 354*), 817–18a
    see also impalement

Dicaearchus *pp. 24 n. 15, 25–6, 27–8, 112*
Didymus *pp. 23, 111–12*
Diomedes 461–3, 497–8a, 498b–509, 565–94, 582–94, 589–90, 591–3, 675–91, 686 (n. 259)
Dionysodorus *p. 23*, 224–5, 507b–9a
Dolon *p. 4*, 149–94, 159b–60, 162b–3, 182–3, 219–23, 224–63, 523–6, 557–61, 562–4, 572–3, 833–81
    entry of *p. 39 n. 66*, 149–94 (*pp. 174–5*)
    see also staging, movements unclear
    etymology of his name 158–9a
    in vase paintings 201–23
    the Wolf *pp. 5, 9, 45*, 201–23, 211b–12, 591–3, 780–8
dream(s) 756–803 (*p. 399*), 780–8, 787–8

Eagle (constellation) 527–31, 527–30, 531
    see also Pleiades
eisodoi p. 114
Eleusinian Mysteries 943–5a, 945b–7, 962–6, 965b–6
    see also Orpheus; Musaeus
enjambement, between stanzas 242–4a, 348b–51a
entrance announcement
    anapaestic 380–7, 380–1
    for *deus ex machina* 882–9
    iambic 85–6
Epic Cycle
    influence on *Rhesus pp. 8, 13–14*
    see also Helenus, capture of; Palladion; 'Ptôcheia'
epiparodos *pp. 5, 10, 40*, 692–727
epiphany 889, 890–2a
    see also Athena; Muse
Eumolpus 926–31

I. General Index

Euripidean Selection
  formation of *p. 43*
  Rhesus in *pp. 3, 43–4, 46–7, 48, 54*
Euripides
  Iphigenia in Aulis p. 34, 1–51 (*p. 116*), 16–19
  Phaethon p. 33, 527–64
Eurypylus *pp. 13–14*, 399–403, 882–9 (*p. 440*), 899–901
Eustathius *p. 46*, 338

gnomologies *pp. 48, 52–3*
  gB (Vat. Barb. gr. 4) *p. 53*
  gE (Escorial. gr. X.1.13) *p. 53*
  gV (Athous Vatop. 36) *p. 52–3*
Gorgoneion 306b–8

Hector 56–69, 85–148, 105–30, 149–94 (*pp. 173–4*),
  character in *Rhesus* 131–6, 137–46, 137, 152–3, 184, 264–341, 319–26, 467–526, 483, 804–81, 808–19, 833–81, 859b–60
  delusion of 52–84, 56–8, 60b–2, 65–9, 102–4, 317–18, 319–20, 330–1, 882–4, 983–96, 989b–92
  see also staging, silence of Hector; Zeus
Helenus, capture of *p. 13*, 498b–509, 507b–9a
Hera Ἀργεία 375b–7
Hermes 199–200
Hesychius *pp. 46–7, 55*
Hippocoon *p. 10*, 728–55
hymn, cletic 224–63, 342–79
hymnic style 224–6a, 224–5 (*p. 205*), 226a, 229–30a, 231–2, 342–79, 346–8a, 351b–4, 355–6, 355–6 (*pp. 250, 251*), 370–2a, 380–7 (*p. 259*), 385–7
hypotheses *pp. 109–13*
  narrative *pp. 25 n. 19, 109, 112*

  see also *Tales from Euripides*
hysteron proteron 1–10, 23–51, 25–5a, 70–1, 93, 485–7 (*pp. 304–5*), 640–1

Iliad 10 *pp. 8–11*
imagery
  'Path of Words' 422–3
  'Ship of State' 246–9a, 322b–3
  'Wheel of Fortune' 332
impalement 257b–60, 467–526 (*p. 298*), 512–17, 513b–15
  see also decapitation
inconsistency 185, 355–6, 686
Ion, of Chios
  Phrouroi pp. 3–4 n. 3, 503–7a
isometric echo(es) 23–4, 131–6
  ~ 195–200 (*p. 167*), 224–63 (249/260), 454–66 (460–2/826–7 + *p. 293*), 722

language and style
  'Aeschylea' *pp. 29–30*
  colloquial expressions 87–9, 195, 273–4, 625, 680, 759, 816, 865, 870
  epicisms *p. 30*, 494–5, 513b–15, 523–5a, 627–9, 742b–4, 756–803 (*p. 399*), 810b–12a
  gnomic utterances *p. 46*, 69b, 206, 317–18, 325–6, 334–5, 482
  'mosaic composition' *pp. 32, 35–7, 38–9, 72–3*
  repetition *pp. 29–30, 37b–8a,* [652]
  'reverse composition' *p. 32*
Longus *p. 45*, 201–23 (*p. 192*)
LSJ, errors in 100–1, 113–14, 137, 145b–6, 557–8 (n. 216), 616–17 (with n. 241), 647–8, 784–6 (*p. 409*)
Lycians 224–5 (*p. 205*), 538–45, 543–5

manuscripts *pp. 48–54*
  errors in
    assimilation 601–2, 879–81
      (*p. 439*)
    'Attic' forms in lyrics
      546–50 (*p. 331*), 824–6
    columns read horizontally
      instead of vertically *p.
      113*
    confusion of letters: ΑΙ / αι /
      ᾳ 854b–5; αι / ε 560–1;
      β / δ 551–3; γ / χ 682;
      οι / α 362b–5a
    confusion of words or word-
      forms: ἀμπειρ- / ἐμπειρ-
      513b–15; ἀρ- / αἰρ- /
      αἱρ- 53–5, 451; Ἄρη /
      Ἄρην 445b–6; δεῖ /
      χρή 218; εἰδ- / ἰδ- /
      οἰδ- 658b–9; ἤ (ἦ) / καί
      861; ἦ / ἦν 63–4; -ομεν /
      -ομαι 948–9; πόρσω /
      πόρρω / πρόσω 482;
      ξυν(-) / συν(-) 440–2 (*p.
      286*); χρή / χρῆν 585–6;
      χρῆν / ἐχρῆν 63–4,
      642–3
    dittography 924b–5
    dochmiacs corrupted
      713b–14
    'Doric' α in recitative
      anapaests 1 (*p. 118*),
      20–2, 557–8
    epicisms 25, 554–6,
      879–81 (*p. 439*)
    epic -οιο corrupted
      908–9
    haplography 882–4
    interpolation 37b–8a, 279
      of μά in negative oaths
      824–6 (*p. 425*)
    intrusive gloss 560–1, [652],
      686, 821–3 (*p. 424*),
      912–14
    inversion of line
      beginnings 229–30a
    single for double consonant
      p. 50 n. 15, 461–3
    temporal augment / redupli-
      cation omitted 580–1,
      611–12
    *vitium Byzantinum p. 49 n.
      7*, 170, 635
  individual manuscripts
    Af (Ambr. F 205 inf.) *p. 52*
    Ao (Ambr. O 123 sup.) *p. 52*
    Hn (Haun. 417) *p. 50*
    L (Laur. plut. 32.2) *pp. 50–1*
    O (Laur. plut. 31.10)
      pp. 48–9
    P (Pal. gr. 287) *p. 51*
    Q (Harl. 5743) *pp. 51–2*
    V (Vat. gr. 909) *pp. 49–50*
    Va (Pal. gr. 98) *pp. 49–50*
    see also Aldine;
      gnomologies; papyri;
      scholia
Memnon *pp. 13–14, 33*, 399–403,
  962–6
Menander *p. 44*
messenger scene *pp. 3, 5, 42*, 1–51
  (*pp. 115–16*), 264–341, 333–41,
  804–81
messenger speech 264–341, 282–3,
  284–6, 285, 301b–2, 728–55,
  756–803, 756–61, 762–3a, 800–2a
metre and prosody
  aeolic 224–63, 342–79
  anapaests, recitative 23–51,
    527–64, 728–55
    inner-metric *antilabe* 16,
      560–1
    weak diaeresis between
      metra 16–19
  Archilochian dicolon 224–63
    (231–2/240–1), 527–64
    (530–1/549–50)
  aristophanean 342–79 (*p. 244*,
    350/359), 829–32
    (*pp. 426–7*)
  bacchiac(s) 23–51 (25–5a/
    43–3a), 527–64

I. General Index

(536–7/555–6), 692–727
(699–700/717–18)
corruption 342–79 (344/353)
cyrenaic 454–66 (458/824)
dactylic 527–64 (530–1/549–50)
dactylo-epitrite 23–51, 224–63,
   454–66, 527–63, 890–914
   (*pp. 445–6*)
dochmiac(s) 131–6 ~ 195–200,
   454–66 (*p. 291*, 456/822)
dochmius Kaibelianus p. 166 n.
   61, 454–66 (456/822),
   713b–14
enoplian 23–51 (27/45), 224–63
   (249/260), 454–66, 527–64
   (n. 201), 890–914
   (900–1/911–12)
   see also cyrenaic
hemiepes 890–914 (*p. 445*)
   contracted 454–66
      (463/828), 827–8
      (*p. 426*)
   pendant 342–79
      (363–5/373–5), 827–8
      (*p. 426*)
   prolonged (D^2) 23–51
      (27/45), 224–63
      (244/255)
   resolved 23–51 (33/51)
iambic trimeter 208–9, 286,
   804–5, 849–50, 986–7
   in lyrics 692–727
ionic 342–79
lecythion 131–6 ~ 195–200
   (136/200)
'palimbacchiac' 342–79 (n. 132)
paroemiac 557–64
pherecratean 827–8 (*p. 426*)
prodelision 804–5 (*p. 417*)
split resolution
   in dochmiacs 131–6 ~
      195–200 (131/195),
      675–91 (675b)
   in iambics 23–51 (33/51),
      131–6 ~ 195–200
      (135/199)
   in trochaics 675–91 (675b)
spondee 527–64 (527–8/546–7)
synartesis 131–6 ~ 195–200
   (136/200), 890–914
   (900–1/911–12)
telesillean 224–63 (249/260)
trochaic tetrameter catalectic
   675–91, 680–1, 683–91,
   687–8, 728–55
Musaeus 945b–7
   see also Eleusinian Mysteries;
      Orpheus
Muse (mother of Rhesus) *pp. 5, 10,*
   13, 348b–51a, 351b–4, 882–9,
   890–914
   sings from 'on high' *pp. 3, 41–2,*
      882–9, 890–914
Mysians 251b–2, 538–45, 540–2

Nemesis, *see* Adrasteia
night action *pp. 3–4 (with n. 3), 4–5,*
   29 n. 33
nightingale 546–50
night watches 538–45

Odysseus 498b–500, 565–94,
   699–701
   special bond with Athena
      595–674 (*p. 349*), 609b–10,
      637b–9, 642–74
   see also Helenus, capture of;
      Palladion; 'Ptôcheia'
'Oracle', version of Rhesus myth *p.*
   12, 595–641, 600–4
Orpheus 943–5a, 945b–7, 962–6,
   972–3
   see also Eleusinian Mysteries;
      Musaeus; Rhesus
Orus *pp. 46, 55*

Paeonians 408–10a, 538–45, 539,
   540–2
Palladion 501–2
   theft of *pp. 3–4 n. 3, 13,*
      498b–500, 501–2, 507b–9a,
      705, 709

Pan 36–7a
Pangaeus, Mt. 408–10a, 921–2a
  oracle of Bacchus *p. 14*, 962–82, 972–3
panic 15, 17–18 (with n. 15), 37b–8a, 138–9
  see also Pan
papyri *pp. 48, 54*
  P. Achmîm 4 (Π¹) *p. 54*
  PSI XII 1286 (Π²) *p. 54*
  P. Oxy. 4568 (Π³) *p. 54*, 846
parenthesis 11, 219–22a, 565–6, 938–40
Paris (Alexandros) *pp. 9–10*, 627–9, 640–1, 642–74, 656–60, 661
  played by fourth actor, *see* staging, fourth actor
Parmeniscus *pp. 22–3*, 527–31, 527–30
parodos *pp. 5, 40*, 1–51
Parthenius, of Nicaea *pp. 44–5*, 399–403, 426–42, 434–5, 899–901
peltasts 311–13, 311
pelte 305–6a, 372b–3a, 383–4
Penthesileia *pp. 13–14*
Phrygians 538–45, 539
  identified with Trojans 32
  language 294–7
  see also Thracians
Pindar 342–5, 348b–51a, 422–3 (n. 155), 978–9 (n. 341)
  version of Rhesus myth *pp. 9, 11–12, 13, 14 n. 13*, 447–53, 595–641, 600–4
Pleiades 527–31, 527–30, 531
  see also Eagle (constellation)
Polydamas 28–9, 65–9
  see also Aeneas
polyptoton 107b–8, 185, 336–7, 404–5, 445b–6
prologues, spurious iambic *pp. 12 n. 7, 25–6, 27–8, 38, 42*, 1–51 (*p. 116*), 595–641
'Ptôcheia' *p. 13*, 498b–509, 503–7a, 503–5 (*p. 311*), 507b–9a, 705, 710–21, 713b–14

responsion, separated *p. 5*, 131–6 ~ 195–200, 454–66, 820–32
Rhesus (hero)
  — and Arganthone *pp. 17, 44–5*
  character of 388–526 (*p. 264*), 467–526, 762–9
  associated with Achilles / Ajax *pp. 4, 5*, 314–16, 335, 454–66, 461–3, 491, 601–2, 962–82
    see also Achilles
  divine nature / appearance 224–64 (*p. 201*), 264–341, 301b–8, 301b–2, 306b–8, 600–4, 970–1, 972–3
  etymology of his name *pp. 15 n. 21, 17*
  horses of 303–4, 616–21, 670–1a, 756–803 (*p. 399*)
  identified with Zeus / Ares 342–79, 355–6, 357–9, 385–7
  indigenous Thracian hero *pp. 14–18*, 962–82
  prophet of Bacchus *pp. 14, 17, 27*, 355–6, 962–82, 972–3
  — and Orpheus 965b–6
  — and Thracian Horseman *pp. 16–17*
  — and Xerxes (in A. *Persians*) 264–341 (*pp. 215–16*), 375b–7, 388–526 (*p. 264*), 388–453, 436–7, 471–2
Rhesus (play)
  dramatic time-scale *p. 114*
  genuine play by Euripides *pp. 22, 27–8, 29*
  fourth-century revivals *pp. 26, 42*
  misattributed in Alexandria *pp. 22, 23–4*
  quoted by later scholars *p. 46*
  possible influence on vase paintings *pp. 26–7*
  reception in antiquity *pp. 44–5*
  school text *pp. 43, 46–7*

Sarpedon *pp. 13–14*, 28–9, 543–5,
    882–9 (*p. 440*), 967–9
schema
    καθ' ὅλον καὶ μέρος 266, 344–
        5, 513b–15, 781–3
    res ponitur pro defectu rei 59–
        60a, 534, 926–8a
scholia *pp. 22–3, 48, 54–5*
Scythians 426–42
skene, *see* staging
Sophocles
    Ajax p. 33, 595–674 (*pp. 348–9*)
    Lakainai pp. 3–4 n. 3, 501–2,
        503–7a
    Poimenes pp. 13 n. 11, 33,
        264–341 (*p. 216*), 342–79
        (*p. 244*), 388–526 (*p. 264*)
staging
    characters entering in
        conversation 565–94
    chariot entry *pp. 3, 41*, 380–7
    divine epiphany in midplay
        595–674
    fourth actor *p. 39 n. 66*, 595–641
        (*p. 350*)
    gestures 339, 595–674 (*p. 348*)
    movements unclear *p. 39 n. 66*,
        149–94 (*pp. 174–5*), 804–81
        (*p. 416*)
    'opening tableau' *p. 114*
    silence of Hector *p. 39 n. 66*,
        149–94 (*pp. 175–6*)
    skene ignored *pp. 40–1, 114*
    use of *mechane* 882–9 (*p. 440*)
Strymon
    bridge across 348b–51a
    river god (father of Rhesus)
        p. 13, 279, 348b–51a,
        351b–4 (*p. 250*)

*Tales from Euripides pp. 25, 54,
    109*
    see also hypotheses, narrative
τειχοσκοπία: 467–526 (*p. 297*),
    879–81
Thamyris 915–49, 915–25, 919–25,
    924b–5
Thessalians 699–700
Thracians
    dress 312–13
    drunkenness (stereotypical)
        404–5, 418b–19
    in *Rhesus* 123–4, 762–9,
        778–9
    language 294–7
    — and Phrygians 294–7, 404–5
Thymbra 224–5, 507b–9a
Triclinius, Demetrius *pp. 48, 50–2*,
    428b–9 (n. 159), 685
Triklines, Nikolaos *p. 50*
Trophonius 962–82

Virgil *p. 12*
    Nisus and Euryalus *pp. 3, 45*

Wackernagel's Law 65–6
watchword 12, 521–2
    see also Apollo (Phoebus)
wolves 201–23 (*p. 192*), 780–8
    see also Dolon, the Wolf

Zalmoxis 962–82, 972–3
Zeus 52–84, 56–8, 60b–2, 63–4,
    102–4, 995b–6
    Ἐλευθέριος 355–6, 357–9
    Φαναῖος 355–6
    Σωτήρ 355–6, 357–9
    Φίλιος 346–8a, 355–6
    see also Hector; Rhesus

II. Index of Passages

Bold print indicates passages which certainly or very probably were among the *Rhesus* poet's sources. To avoid repetition I have sometimes numbered inclusively, i.e. the index entry refers to both the entire passage indicated and parts of it.

Accius
   Ant. fr. III Dangel = IV *TRF*³: *p. 44*, 532–3 (*p. 325*)
Achaeus
   TrGF 20 F 35: 355–6
Aeneas Tacticus
   10.23: 434–5
   15.5: 296–7
Aeschylus
   ***Ag.* 22–4:** *p. 37*, 110b–11
   — 40: 342–3 (*p. 247*)
   — 87: 68–9a
   — 111: 368–9
   — **399–402:** 336–7, 841b–2
   — 563–6: 416–18a
   — **577–9:** 179–80, 180
   — 783–809: 380–7
   — 819–20: 790–1 (*p. 412*)
   — 903–4: 342–5
   — 1032–3: 742b–4 (*p. 396*)
   — 1273–4: 503–5
   — 1290: 816
   — **1316:** 724, 804–5 (n. 287)
   — **1343:** 750–1a
   — 1389–90: *p. 35*, 790–1
   — 1439: 866–7
   — 1502: 513b–15 (*p. 315*)
   ***Cho.* 288–90:** *p. 36 n. 56*, 303–4, 691
   — 375: *p. 36*, 817–18a
   — **659–60:** *p. 37*, 636–7a
   — 753–4: 759
   — 758: 759
   Eum. 34–8: 211b–12
   — 53: 784–6
   — 62: 970–1 (*p. 472*)
   — **90:** *p. 34 n. 49*, 158–9a
   — 117–20: 789 (*p. 411*)
   — **130:** 675b
   — **186–90:** *p. 36*, 512–17, 513b–15, 817–18a
   — [405]: 380–7 (n. 140)
   — 553–7: 322b–3
   — 913–14: 123–4
   ***Pers.* 1–154:** 1–51 (*p. 116*), 264–341 (*pp. 215–16*)
   — **25:** *p. 34 n. 50*, 30
   — **44:** *p. 34 n. 50*, 741
   — **47:** *p. 34 n. 50*, 16–19, 311
   — **53–4:** *p. 34 n. 50*, 56–8 (*p. 141*)
   — **87–9:** *p. 34 n. 50*, 290, 375b–7
   — **126–7:** *p. 34 n. 50*, 117
   — 155–8: 380–7
   — **177–8:** 471–2
   — **234:** 471–2
   — **357–60:** 72–3, 96–8
   — 401–7: 294–7
   — 412: 290
   — 429–30: 309–10
   — 444: 516–17 (with n. 192)
   — **480–514:** 388–453
   — **480–1:** 53–5
   — **500–1:** *pp. 35–6*, 440–2
   — 574: 790–1 (*p. 412*)
   — 589–90: 338
   — **816–17:** *pp. 35–6*, 430–1
   — 937: 551–3 (*p. 334*)
   — **974–6:** 734–5
   ***Sept.* 28–9:** *p. 34*, 19, 87–9
   — **36–8:** *p. 34*, 125–30, 557–8, 631–2
   — 41: *p. 34*, 631–2
   — **45–6:** 932–3 (*p. 460*)
   — **58 (~ 33–4):** *p. 34*, 513b–15

— **59–60:** *p. 34*, 20–2
— **79–80:** *p. 34 n. 49*, 290
— 169–70: 294–7
— **245:** *pp. 34 n. 49, 37*, 568b–9
— **249:** *pp. 34 n. 49, 37*, 568b–9
— **287–9:** *pp. 34 n. 49, 37*, 770–2
— **369:** *p. 34*, 631–2
— **385–6:** *p. 34 n. 49*, 306b–8, 383–4, 567–8a
— **447–8:** *p. 34 n. 49*, 122
— **593:** *p. 34 n. 49*, 795b–6
— 644: 380–1 (*p. 260*)
— **651–2:** *p. 34 n. 49*, 49–51
— **658:** *p. 34 n. 49*, 158–9a
— 734: 469–70
Suppl. 4–5: 226a
— 30–6: 430–1
— 182: 2–3
— 234: 380–7
— 263: 970–1 (*p. 472*)
— 350: 382
— 370–2: 287–9
— 806–7: 422–3
fr. 23a (*Bassarai*): 921–2a, 970–1
— 25b (*Glaucus Pontius* or *Potnieus*): 36–7a
— 46c.6 (*Diktyoulkoi*?): 333
— 57.8–11 (*Edoni*): *p. 37*, 255b–7a
— 74.7 (*Heraclidae*): 273–4 (*p. 219*)
— **99.13–14 (*Cares* = *Europa*):** *p. 32 n. 42*, 736–7, 967–9
— 99.15–23 (*Cares* = *Europa*): 28–9
— **131 (*Myrmidons*):** *p. 35*, 1–51 (*p. 116*), 404–5 (*p. 272*), 763b–4a
— **132 (*Myrmidons*):** *p. 35*, 557–8, 814–15
— **139 (*Myrmidons*):** 312–13 (with n. 126)
— 146b, 147 (*Neaniskoi*): 123–4
— 152 (*Nereids*): 373b–5a

— 158.2–3 (*Niobe*): 342–3
— 350.7–9 (inc. fab.): 915–49, 978–9
— **451c.33–4 (dub.):** 191–2
[Aeschylus]
PV 172: 16–19 (n. 14)
— 628: 863–4
— 742–3: 789 (*p. 411*)
— 792: 370–2a (n. 138)
— 925: 373b–5a
— 936: 342–3
fr. 192.4 (*Prometheus Unbound*): 16–19 (n. 14)
Alcaeus
fr. 34.1–4 Voigt: 370–2a
— 34.9–12 Voigt: 355–6
— 308 Voigt: 351b–4
Alcman
3 fr. 1.7 *PMGF*: 554–6
3 fr. 3.65–7 *PMGF*: 43–3a
Amphis
fr. 46 *PCG*: 642–74
Anacreon
fr. 346 fr. 1.13 *PMG*: 879–81 (*p. 439*)
— 356 (b) *PMG*: 418b–19
[Anacreon]
Ep. 1.3 *FGE*: 932–3 (*p. 460*)
Antigenes
Ep. 1.9 *FGE*: 527–64 (530–1/549–50)
Apollonius Rhodius
1.375: 145b–6
Appian
Mith. 1.1–2: *p. 16*
Archilochus
fr. 19.3 *IEG*: 166
— 42 *IEG*: 418b–19
— 114 *IEG*: 132
— 191.1 *IEG*: 527–64 (530–1/549–50)
— 196a.36 *IEG*: 394b–5
Aristides
Or. 1.106 Lenz–Behr: *p. 45*, 335
Aristophanes
Ach. 141: 418b–19

— **238–40:** *p. 32*, 680, 730
— **280–3:** *p. 32*, 675b, 685–6 (n. 256), 685
— 406: 646 (with n. 247)
— 435: 233–5a
— 470: 662
— 566–7: 370–2a
— 730: 346–8a
— 796: 513b–15
— **1190–1234:** 728–55
— 1192/3: 396–8
— 1229: 418b–19
Eccl. 1029: 762–3a
Lys. 1007–8: 816
Ran. 911–20: *pp. 35 n. 54, 114, 1–51 (p. 116)*
— 961–3: *pp. 33, 41*, 306b–8, 380–7, 383–4
— 1032: 943–5a
— 1289: 368–9
— 1331: 41–2
— 1337: 750–1a
— 1343: 662
Thesm. 889–90: 507b–9a (with n. 189)
— 904: 722
— 1020: 224–63 (n. 102)
— 1125–7: 817–18a
Vesp. 1065: 342–79 (344/353)
fr. 596.3 *PCG*: 923–4a
Aristotle
  Poet. 1453b7–11: *p. 42 n. 81*
  — 1456a25–7: *p. 40*
  — 1456a27–30: *p. 40*
  fr. 498 Rose: 305–6a
  — 626 Rose: *p. 22*
[Aristotle]
  fr. 159 Rose: 19 (n. 15), 138–9
  — 641.57 Rose: 962–82
Arrian
  FGrHist 156 F 59: *p. 18*
  — 156 F 83: *p. 18*
Asclepiades of Tragilus
  FGrHist 12 F 5: *p. 27*
Astydamas II
  TrGF 60 F 4: *pp. 6–7*

Bacchylides
  2.11–12: 895–8
  Pae. 4.61–80: 360–7, 554–6
Callimachus
  Aet. fr. 178.11–12 Harder: 418b–19
  Dian. 140–1: 118, 238
  Hec. fr. 260.67–8 Pf.: 532–3
Carcinus II
  TrGF 70 F 1d: 112
  — 70 F 5: *p. 38*
Cicero
  nat. deor. 3.45: *p. 18*
Demetrius of Scepsis
  frr. 20–8 Gaede: 224–5
[Demosthenes]
  25.37: 342–3
Dio Chrysostom
  Or. 55.14: *p. 45*, 854b–5
Diodorus Siculus
  11.72.2: 357–9
Epic Cycle
  Aethiopis Arg. p. 112 (2) *GEF*: 962–6
  — Arg. p. 112 (4) *GEF*: *p. 10*, 882–9 (*p. 440*), 962–6, 974–7
  Ilias Parva Arg. p. 120 (2) *GEF*: 507b–9a
  — Arg. p. 122 (4) *GEF*: 501–2, 503–7a, 710–21
  — fr. 5.2 *GEF*: 373b–5a
  — frr. 8–10 *GEF*: 503–7a, 715–16
  — fr. 11 *GEF*: 501–2
  Iliou Persis Arg. p. 146 (1) *GEF*: 175
Euripides
  Alc. 343–4: 759
  — 398: 382
  — **498:** 305–6a, 370–2a
  — **614–733:** 388–453
  — 690: *p. 37*, 870
  — **850–1:** *pp. 35–6*, 430–1
  Andr. 21: 430–1
  — 172–3: 873
  — 215–16: 408–10a

II. Index of Passages

— **399:** *pp. 36–7*, 605–6
— 602–4: 346–8a
— 1179–80: 736–7
— 1226–30: 882–9 (with nn. 302, 303), 886–8
— 1262: 428b–9 (with n. 159)
Ba. 224: 68–9a
— 298: 972–3
— 686–8: 875–6
— 781–5: 311–13
— **821–46:** 201–23
— **965:** 229–30a
— 1061: 781–3 (n. 281)
— 1267: 43–3a
Cyc. 63–7: 861
— 204–5: 861
— **293–4:** *p. 32*, 970–1
— **386–7:** 9
— 416–17: 418b–19
— **684–5:** 689
El. 135–9: 752–3
— **151–2:** *pp. 36–7*, 618
— 178–80: 375b–7
— 467–8: 527–30 (*p. 323*)
— 695–6: 273–4
— **747–8:** 565–6
— 787–9: 219–22a (*p. 200*)
— **842–3:** *p. 35*, 790–1
— 855–7: 219–22a (n. 99)
— 896–8: 512–17
— 988–97: 380–7
— 1233–7: 882–9 (with n. 302), 886–8
— 1238–9: 646 (with n. 247)
Hcld. **84:** *p. 36 n. 56*, 701
— 138: 312–13
— 216: 2–3
— 284: 866–7
— 337–8: 125–30
— **720–5:** 90
— **731:** 105
— 784–5: 264–5
Hec. 177–9: 291b–3
— **216–17:** *p. 37*, 85–6
— **239–41:** 503–5 (*p. 311*), 710–11

— **278:** 870
— 839: 312–13
— 962–3: 426–42 (n. 158), 467–8
— **1056–9:** *p. 37*, 211b–12, 255b–7a
— 1121: 849–50
— 1267: 972–3
Hel. **215:** *pp. 36–7*, 618
— 679: 827–8
— 1376: 383–4
HF **361–3:** 208–11a, 208–9
— 410: 428b–9
— 449: 16–19
— 465–6: 208–9
— 815–21: 882–9, 886–8
— 911–12: *p. 32*, 948–9, 952–3
— **1006–12:** 70–5, 770–2
Hipp. 113: 866–7 (n. 298)
— 362–72 ~ 669–79: 131–6 ~ 195–200, 454–66, 820–32
— 491–2: 422–3
— **519:** 80
— 585: 551–3 (*p. 334*)
— **1037:** 414b–15
— 1145–6: 494–5
— 1195: 312–13
— **1347–88:** 728–55
IA 1–48 + 115–62: 1–51 (*p. 116*)
— **2–3:** *p. 34*, 15, 16
— **6–8:** *p. 34*, 527–31 (*p. 322*), 527–30 (*p. 323*)
— 35–6: *p. 34*, 273–4
— 83: 301b–2 (*p. 229*)
— **171–7:** *pp. 32, 34, 36, 48*, 261–3
— 193: 175
— **220–2:** *p. 34*, 355–6 (*p. 251*)
— 263: 175
— 391–4: 219–22a (*p. 200*)
— 469–70: *p. 34*, 904–5
— 495: 261–3
— [590–606/634]: 380–7 (with n. 140)
— **651:** *p. 34*, 467–8
— **1172:** *p. 34*, 467–8

— 1305–6: *p. 34*, 717–19
— 1418–19: *p. 37*, 870
Ion 550: 943–5a
— 1549–52: 882–9, 886–8
***IT* 31:** *p. 35*, 404–5
— **67–122:** 565–94 (*p. 339*), 570–1, 574–9, 580–1, 582–94, 589–90, 594
— 124–5: 428b–9
— 395: 428b–9
— 438: 428b–9 (n. 159)
— 977–8: 43–3a
— 1111–12: 370–2a
— 1388–9: 428b–9
— 1429–30: 512–17
— 1437: 290
Med. 4–6: 479
— 196–7: 546–50 (*p. 332*)
— **446–622:** 388–453
— **686:** 625
— **759–60:** 201–23 (*p. 192*), 216–17
— 836–8: 385–7 (*p. 263*)
— 1266–7: 614–15
Or. 145–6: 551–3
— 268: 33
— 570–1: 438–9 (*p. 284*)
— **688–90:** *p. 37*, 276–7
— 1005–6: 527–30 (*p. 323*)
— 1125: *p. 35*, 382, 713b–14
— **1271–2:** *p. 35*, 713b–14
— 1315: 560–1 (with n. 218)
— 1353–65 ~ 1537–48: 131–6 ~ 195–200
— 1516: 219–22a (*p. 200*)
— 1521: 866–7
— 1541: 382
Phoen. [1–2]: 305–6a, 422–3 (n. 156)
— **45–6:** *pp. 35–6*, 440–2
— 86–7: 106–7a
— **92:** 296–7
— 163–7: 219–22a (*p. 200*)
— **261–73 (+ 361–4):** 565–94 (*p. 339*), 565–6, 575–6
— 376–8: 12

— **469–96:** 388–453
— 503: 388–453
— 657: 430–1
— **697–747:** 85–148, 105–30
— 784–92: 360–7
— 1126–7: 383–4
— 1130–1: 305–6a
— 1147: 31
— 1213: 2–3
— 1226: 646
— **1353–5:** 690
— 1356–1583: 149–94 (*pp. 175–6*)
— 1432–3: 333
— 1602–4: 5–6
Suppl. 173–4: 935b–7
— 599: 424–6 (with n. 157)
— 603–4: 123–4
— 638–9: 281 (n. 115)
— 651–3: 301b–2
Tro. 562–6: *pp. 36–7*, 605–6
— 568–76: 380–7
— 660: 873
— 1194–6: 383–4
— 1207–8: 403
fr. 78 (*Alcmeon*): 416–18a
— **124.2–5 (*Andromeda*):** 422–3, 527–30 (*p. 323*)
— 146.1 (*Andromeda*): 290
— 369 (*Erechtheus*): 360–7
— 370.100–1 (*Erechtheus*): 945b–7
— **397a (*Thyestes*):** 736–7
— 453 (*Cresphontes*): 360–7
— 472b.32 (*Cretans*): 214–15
— **473 (*Licymnius*):** 625
— **495.29–30 (*Captive Melanippe*):** *p. 37*, 603–4
— 530.1–2 (*Meleager*): 305–6a
— 741a (*Temenos*): 123–4
— 752h.31 (*Hypsipyle*): 43–3a
— **757.921–2 (*Hypsipyle*):** *p. 37*, 980
— **773.19–58 (*Phaethon*):** *p. 33*, 527–64

— 773.44–6 (*Phaethon*): 403
(with n. 150)
— 781.46 (*Phaethon*): 416–18a
— 815 (*Phoenix*): 43–3a
— **885 (inc. fab.):** 974–5
— 971.1–2 (inc. fab.): 43–3a
Euripides, scholia on
   Hec. 1267: 972–3
   Or. 57: 380–7 (n. 140)
Eustathius
   Comm. Il. 381.19–20: 440–2
    (*pp. 285–6*)
— 822.2–5: *p. 46 n. 96*, 338
— 909.27–8: 440–2 (*pp. 285–6*)
Hecataeus
   FGrHist 1 FF 18a, b: 428b–9
Heliodorus
   2.19.1: 503–5
   3.2.1: 385–7 (*p. 263*)
Hellanicus
   FGrHist 4 F 19b: 216–17
— 4 F 25a: 287–9
Herodotus
   1.85.2: 551–3 (*p. 334*)
   1.182.2: 224–5 (with n. 106)
   2.154.5: 145b–6
   2.159.1: 145b–6
   5.66.1: 703
   5.111: 2–3
   6.84: 418b–19
   7.111: 972–3
   9.97: 116
Hesiod
   Op. 515: 784–6
   Th. 260: 226a
[Hesiod]
   Sc. 64: 372b–3a
— 426–8: 784–6
   fr. 70.10 M.–W.: 226a
— 169.2 M.–W.: 226a
— 235.1 M.–W.: 175
Hesychius
   α 3775 Latte: 513b–15
— 5546 Latte: 118
— 7362 Latte: 464–6
   γ 850 Latte: 8

δ 2622 Latte: 804–5 (n. 287)
— 2671 Latte: 790–1 (*p. 412*)
ε 4304 Latte: 440–2 (*pp. 285–6*)
θ 626 Latte: 513b–15 (*p. 315*)
— 868 Latte: 224–5
κ 1840 Latte: 133–5a
π 1040 Hansen: 829–32
ρ 272 Hansen: *p. 27*
τ 1350 Hansen–Cunningham:
   373b–5a
χ 224 Hansen–Cunningham:
   208–9
Hipponax
   fr. 72 *IEG*: pp. 15–16, 20,
   616–17, 962–82
Homer
   Il. **1.1:** 494–5
— 2.23–5 (= 60–2): 642–3
   (with n. 245)
— 4.105–13: 33
— 5.728: 372b–3a
— 5.729–31: 303–4 (*p. 230*)
— **5.794:** 416–18a
— 6.526–9: 357–9
— **7.13 (= 17.140):** 28–9
— **8.130–58:** 565–94 (*p. 339*),
   582–94, 582–4, 589–90
— **8.497–541:** 52–84, 983–96
— 8.500–1: 56–8
— **8.512–15:** *p. 36*, 72–3, 93
— **9.115–61, 225–306,**
   308–429: 149–94
   (*pp. 173–4*), 388–453
— 9.312–14: 394b–5
— **10.2 (= 24.678):** 763b–4a
— **10.11–13:** 23–51
— **10.29–179:** 23–51
— **10.37–8:** 557–8
— **10.47–50:** 82–3
— **10.48 (289, 524):** 509b
— **10.80:** 7, 789
— **10.82–5:** 11–14, 587–8
— **10.83 (276, 386):** 41–2
— **10.100–1:** 56–69
— **10.141–2:** 587–8
— **10.182:** 523–5a

— **10.251–3:** *p. 114*, 527–64, 538–45 (with n. 212)
— **10.278–9:** 609b–10
— 10.281–2: *p. 338 n. 224*
— **10.299–337:** 149–94 (*pp. 173–4*), 149–53
— **10.333–5:** 201–23, 208–11a
— **10.378–9:** 170
— **10.416–20:** *pp. 39–40*, 570
— **10.420–2:** 149–94 (*p. 173*), 762–9
— **10.428–31:** 224–5, 538–45
— **10.433/436–41:** 264–341 (*p. 215*), 301b–8, 340–1, 595–641
— **10.434:** 519–20
— **10.449–51:** 233–5a
— **10.463–4:** 611–12
— 10.470: 311
— 10.471–3: 762–9, 763b–4a
— **10.474–5:** 616–17
— **10.479–81:** 622–3
— **10.482–501:** 624–6
— **10.483–4:** 789
— **10.484:** 790–1
— **10.489:** 793–5a
— 10.494–7: 780–8, 780
— 10.500–1: 762–9
— **10.509–11:** 668–74, 672–3a
— **10.518–22:** 728–55, 789
— **10.523–4:** 675–91
— **10.538–9:** 863–4
— **10.550:** 620b–1
— **10.561–3:** 233–6, 233–5a, 557–8
— **11.1–2:** 983–5
— **11.56–66:** 983–96
— 11.535 (= 20.500): 372b–3a
— **12.61–79:** 105–30, 110b–18, 112–15, 112, 115, 116–18
— **12.195–250:** 65–9, 84, 952–3
— **12.211–29:** 105–30, 112–15
— **13.131 (= 16.215):** 485–7
— **13.307–9:** 480, 485–7
— **13.315 (~ 19.423):** 480
— **13.397–403 (+ 429–38):** 710–21
— **13.726–47:** 105–30, 105–8, 105 (*p. 156*), 119–22, 120–1
— 14.80: 41–2
— 16.141–2: 373b–5a
— 16.278–83: 333–41, 335
— 16.367–71: 105–30, 116–18
— **17.36–40:** 257b–60
— **17.220–6:** 399–403, 403
— **18.54–64:** *p. 10*, 908–9, 915–49
— 18.197–238: 333–41, 335
— **18.249–83:** 105–30, 107b–8, 119–22, 122
— 20.216–18: 287–9
— **20.267–8 (~ 21.164–5):** 408–10a
— 21.37–8: 372b–3a
— 22.97: 485–7
— **22.118:** 171, 620b–1
— **22.488:** 712–13a
— 24.221: 68–9a
Od. **4.242–64:** *p. 37*, 503–7a, 710–21, 715–16
— 5.290: 480
— 11.241–4: 351b–4
— 13.397–403 (429–38): 710–21
— 20.49–50: 26 (n. 21)
— 21.27–30: 841b–2
— 21.145: 68–9a
— 21.393–5: 33
— 22.318 (321): 68–9a
— 24.58–64: *p. 10*, 974–7
Homer, scholia on
Il. 6.479–80: *p. 46 n. 93*
— 10.435: *pp. 11–13*, 406–11a, 595–641
Od. 22.9–12: 440–2 (*p. 285*)
Homeric Hymns
h.Ap. 14–18: 224–5 (*p. 205*)
h.Merc. 3–10: 351b–4
— 174–5: 216–17
— 292: 216–17
— 361: 736–7

h.Ven. 4: 43–3a
h.Hom. 33.4–6 (Dioscuri):
   351b–4
Horace
  Carm. 1.36.13–14: 418b–19
Inscriptions
  BCH 21.554/557.2: 523–5a
  CEG 2 488 (ii).3–4: 368–9
  EG 1108: 216–17
  Foed.Delph.Pell. I B 8: 216–17
  — II A 13: 216–17
  IG II² 4514.1–5: 226a
  — VII 1739.14: 523–5a
  — VII 2406.7: 523–5a
  Inscr. Cret. 4.171.14: 166
  SGO IV 22/22/01: 908–9
    (n. 314)
Ion
  fr. 745 PMG: 535–7
Isyllus
  Pae. Epid. 14–15: 193–4
  — 48–51: 351b–4
Josephus
  3.190–2: 201–23 (p. 192)
Leonidas of Tarent
  Ep. 92.4 Gow–Page HE: 312–13
Livy
  38.14.12: 484
Longus
  1.20.2: p. 45, 201–23 (p. 192),
    208–11a
Lycophron
  569: 309–10 (p. 233)
  949: 509b
  1150: 175
Lyrica Adespota
  fr. 947 (b) PMG: 546–50
    (p. 332)
Lysias
  6.49: 246–9a
Marsyas II
  FGrHist 136 F 7: pp. 13, 15
Menander
  Peric. 271–91: pp. 28 n. 27, 44,
    149–94 (n. 71)
  — 295–6: p. 44

— 304: 342–3
fr. 53 PCG: 346–8a
— 702 PCG: 338
Nonnus
  D. 40.469–70: 287–9
  Par. 1.64: 287–9
  — 19.224: 287–9
Oppian
  Hal. 2.464–6: 287–9
Orus
  B 77 Alpers: p. 46 n. 95,
    854b–5
Ovid
  Her. 11.111: p. 45, 895–8
    (p. 447)
Parthenius
  Erot. Path. 36: pp. 17–18, 44–5,
    399–403, 426–42, 434–5,
    899–901
Pherecrates
  fr. 102.4 PCG: 346–8a
Philostratus
  Her. 17.3–6: pp. 16–17
Phoronis
  fr. 2.1–4 GEF: 342–3
Photius
  ρ 103 Theodoridis: p. 27
Pindar
  Isthm. 8.49–50: p. 36, 72–3
  — 8.56a–60: 974–7
  Nem. 4.49–50: 428b–9
    (n. 159)
  — 9.34: 2–3
  Ol. 2.79–80: 962–3
  — 9.112: 175
  — 10.15–16: 762–3a
  — 12.1–2: 357–9
  — 13.24–6: 342–5, 455b–7
  Pyth. 1.28: p. 36, 72–3
  — 1.39: 224–6a
  — 4.15: 287–9
  — 4.203–4: 428b–9
  — 9.8: 287–9
  — 9.23–5: 554–6
  — 10.29–46: 360–7
  fr. 70d.38–9 Sn.–M.: 166

— 128c Sn.–M.: 895–8
— 262 Sn.–M.: *pp. 11–12*, 595–641
Pindar, scholia on
Nem. 6.50/85b: 373b–5a
Plato
Euthphr. 6b3–4: 346–8a
Leg. 637d2–e7: 418b–19
Phdr. 234e2: 346–8a
— 248c2–e5: 342–3 (*p. 247*)
Rep. 364b5–7: 503–5
— 451a4–5: 342–3
— 540a6–8: 736–7
Plutarch
De sera num. vind.
25.564e: 342–3 (*p. 247*)
Polyaenus
6.53: *pp. 14–15*, 962–82
Simonides
fr. 644 *PMG*: 538–45
Solon
fr. 4c.2 *IEG*: 480
— 33.4 *IEG*: 312–13
Sophocles
Ai. **1–133:** *p. 33*, 595–674 (*pp. 348–9*)
— **221/2:** 122
— **388–9:** *p. 35*, 498b–500
— 574–6: 383–4
— **589–90:** 965b–6
— **624–5:** *p. 37*, 388–9 (*p. 267*)
— 792: 866–7 (n. 298)
— **1030:** 567–8a
— **1088:** 122
— **1185–1222:** *p. 33*, 360–7
— **1204:** *p. 36*, 740
— **1275:** 82
— **1408:** *p. 36*, 740
Ant. 128–9: 290
— **162–3:** 246–9a
— 417–18: 25 (n. 20)
— 1238–9: 790–1
El. **298:** 892b–4
— **745–6:** *p. 37*, 118, 372b–3a
— 916–17: 106–7a
— 1110: 866–7

OC 188–9: 388–9
— 833–43 ~ 876–86: 131–6 ~ 195–200
— **1364:** 715–16
— 1463: 382
OT **22–4:** 246–9a
— 388–9: 503–5
— **911:** *p. 37*, 780
— 1219: 551–3 (*p. 334*)
Phil. **1–49:** 565–94 (*p. 339*), 570–1, 574–9, 574
— 88–91: 510–11
— 162: 16–19
— 290: 312–13
— 391–402 ~ 507–18: 131–6 ~ 195–200, 131–6
— **604–9:** *p. 36 n. 56*, 507b–9a, 893b–4
— 645–6: 428b–9 (n. 162)
— 1146–50: 13–14 (n. 12)
— 1251: 866–7
Tr. **216–17:** 25
— 222: 382
— 262–3: *p. 37*, 201–2
— 714: 312–13
— 1278: 861
fr. **61** (*Acrisius*): 565–6
— 136 (*Andromeda*): 36–7a
— 152 (*Achilleos Erastai*): 373b–5a
— 165 (*Danae*): 866–7
— **314.204** (*Ichneutae*): 565–6
— 314.243–50 ~ 290–7 (*Ichneutae*): 131–6 ~ 195–200 (n. 60)
— 314.329–37 ~ 371–9 (*Ichneutae*): 131–6 ~ 195–200 (n. 60)
— **384** (*Lemniai*): 426–8a
— 498 (*Poimenes*): 388–526 (n. 147)
— 502 (*Poimenes*): 770–2
— 513 (*Poimenes*): 551–3
— 515 (*Poimenes*): *p. 33 n. 45*, 380–1

— **859 (inc. fab.):** *p. 33 n. 45,*
  33, 383–4
— **913 (inc. fab.):** *p. 35,*
  498b–500
— 1131.7 (dub.): 382
Stephanus of Byzantium
  α 394 Billerbeck: *p. 18*
Stesichorus
  fr. S 13.2–3 *PMGF*: 908–9
  — 192.2 *PMGF*: 96–8
  — 226 *PMGF*: 175
  — 268 *PMGF*: 538–45
Stobaeus
  2.31.14: *p. 46 n. 91*, 206
  4.13.8: *p. 46 n. 91*, 105–8
Strabo
  7 fr. 16a: *p. 15*
  13.1.35: 224–5
  14.1.35: 355–6
Suda
  α 2660 Adler: 118
  ρ 143 Adler: *p. 27*
  — 146 Adler: *p. 16*
Theocritus
  15.8: 861
  16.44–5: 546–50 (*p. 332*)
  Ep. 3.1: 9
Theopompus
  fr. 26 *PCG*: 273–4
    (*p. 219*)

Thucydides
  2.71.2–4: 357–9
  3.15.1: 145b–6
  3.22.1: 41–2
  4.40.2: 312–13
Tragica Adespota
  fr. 692 col. II 14–16: 614–15
Tyrtaeus
  fr. 5.4–6 *IEG*: 932–3
  — 11.10 *IEG*: 480
  — 11.31 *IEG*: 485–7
  — 11.35–8 *IEG*: 31
Virgil
  Aen. 1.469–73: *p. 12*
  — 2.166: 501–2
  — 4.143–4: 224–5 (*p. 205*)
  — 9.176–458: *p. 45*
  — 9.247–50: *p. 45*, 245b–9a
  — 9.316–19: 762–9
  — 9.332–3: 789
  — 9.347–8: 793–5a
  — 9.354: 668–9
  — 9.376–7: 682
  — 9.377–8: 774b–5
Xenophon
  An. 4.2.20: 2–3
  — 5.2.5: 116
  — 5.2.29: 305–6a
  HG 4.5.14: 2–3
  — 4.8.39: 2–3

III. Index of Greek Words

ἃ 687, 747–9
ἀγρώ(σ)της 266
ἀγχιτέρμων 426–8a
ἀγύρτης *p. 37*, 503–5, 715–16
ἄδην (ἅδην) 480
αἴθω (intransitive) 821–3 (*p. 424*)
αἴθων 122
αἱμύλος *p. 35*, 498b–500
αἴρω / ἀείρω 25
ἁμαρτῇ 312–13
ἀμβλώψ *p. 31*, 736–7
ἄμυστις 418b–19
ἀναπείρω 513b–15
ἀνθρωποδαίμων *p. 31*, 970–1
ἀντίπρῳρος 135b–6
ἄντυξ 118, 238, 372b–3a
Ἄξενος (πόντος) 428b–9
ἄπλατος 309–10 (*p. 233*)
ἄποινα 177
ἀποινάομαι 177
ἀραγμός 568b–9
ἀρείφατος 123–4
ἀριστεύς 479
ἀριστεύω 193–4
ἀριστότοκος 908–9
ἀρτήριαι ('nostrils') *p. 31*, 784–6
ἄτρακτος 312–13
αὐγάζω (-ομαι) 793–5a
αὐγαί ('eyes') 736–7
αὐθέντης 873
αὐθιγενής 895–8
αὐλών 112
αὐτόρριζος *p. 31*, 287–9
αὐτός (+ genitive) 106–7a

βρίζω *p. 30 n. 37*, 824–6

γερουσία 401–3, 935b–7

δάπεδον 375b–7
δασμός 434–5
διαπρεπής 616–17
δίβαμος *p. 31*, 214–15

δίβολος 373b–5a
διιπετής / διειπετής 43–3a
δίοπος 741
διόπτης 233–5a
Δῖος / δῖος 226a
δόρη (accusative plural) 273–4
δυσθνῄσκων *p. 35*, 790–1
δυσοίζω (-ομαι) *p. 30*, 724, 804–5

ἔα (ἔα) 574, 675–91 (*p. 372*), 885
εἷς (+ partitive genitive) 393–4a
εἴσω (absolute) 750–1a
ἔνθα (demonstrative) 430–1
ἐξαπωθέω *p. 30*, 810b–12a
ἐξώστης *p. 31*, 322b–3
ἐπαινέω 647–8
ἐπεύχομαι 693–4, 703
ἐπιδέξιος 360–2a
ἐπιζαρέω *p. 31*, 440–2
εὐσπλαγχνία 191–2
εὐσταθέω 317–18
ἐφέστιος 201–2
ἐφίεμαι (+ accusative) 44–7a

ἢν ἄρα μή 118
ἡσσάομαι 497–8a

θάμβος 291b–3
θυμέλη 235b–7
θοινατήριον 513b–15
θυοσκόος 68–9a

ἰά 551–3
ἰάλεμος 895–8
ἰαύω 519–20, 740
ἰδέ 382
ἵημι (πόδα) 203
Ἰλεύς 175

καραδοκέω 143–5a
καρατόμος 605–6
κατάντης 317–18

III. Index of Greek Words

καταπνέω 385–7
κατασκάπτω 603–4
κατάστασις *p. 37*, 110b–11
κερόδετος 33
κεύθω 171, 620b–1, 872
κεφαλή (address) 226a, 902–3
κήρυξ 401–2
κλυεῖν 109–10a, 286, 572–3
κλωπικός 205
κομπέω 438–9
κομψός 625
κόσμος 403
κότος 827–8
Κρόνιος 36–7a
κρότημα *p. 35*, 498b–500
κρυσταλλόπηκτος 440–2

λάφυρα 179
λέπας 287–9
λόχος 17–18, 26, 507b–9a

μάραγνα *p. 36*, 817–18a
μελάγχιμος 962
μέρμερος 509b
μηνάς 534
μηνίω *p. 30*, 494–5
μῖμος *p. 37*, 255b–7a
μυχθισμός *p. 31*, 789

ναυκλήριον 233–5a
νεῖρα 793–5a
νεόκμητος 886–8
νυκτηγορέω *p. 34*, 19
νυκτηγορία *p. 34*, 19
νυκτίβρομος 551–3
νυχεύω 519–20

ξιφήρης 713b–14

οἰνοπλάνητος 360–2a
ὁλκός *p. 31*, 145b–6
ὁμηρεύω 434–5
ὀργάς 282–3
ὄρφνη 41–2
οὕνεκα 340–1

πανημερεύω 360–2a
πανός 988–9a
παράκαιρος 829–32
παρών (~ αὐτός) 141–2
πεδοστιβής 253–5a, 763b–4a
πλάστιγξ 303–4
πλέκω 833–4
πλημμελής 856–8
πόθι 251b–2
πολίοχος 166, 821–3
πολύχορδος 546–50 (*p. 332*)
πορπάματα 440–2
πόρπαξ 383–4
προπίνω 404–5
προσεικάζω 696–8
προταινί *pp. 23, 31*, 523–5a
προυξερευνητής *p. 31*, 296–7
πωλοδαμνέω 187–8

ρακόδυτος 712–13a
ρέγκω 784–6
ρύμη 63–4

σκόλοπες 116–18, 116
σκῦλα 179
σύρδην *p. 30*, 56–8

τετράμοιρος 5–6
τευχεσφόρος 267–8
τολυπεύω 742b–4
τορός 77

ὑπάρχω (+ participle) *p. 31*, 633
ὑπασπιστής *pp. 19, 20*, 2–3
ὕπαφρος *p. 31*, 710–11

φιλητής / φηλητής 216–17
φυλλόστρωτος *p. 40*, 9

χαράσσω 72–3
χάσμα 208–9
χρυσοκόλλητος 305–6a

ψάλιον 27
ψαλμός 360–2a
ψαφαρόχρους 715–16

www.ingramcontent.com/pod-product-compliance
Lightning Source LLC
Chambersburg PA
CBHW070255240426
43661CB00057B/2563